# Aspects of Hobbes

*Aspects of Hobbes*

Noel Malcolm, one of the world's leading Hobbes scholars, presents a set of extended essays on a wide variety of aspects of the life and work of this giant of early modern thought. The greater part of this volume is published here for the first time. Malcolm offers a succinct introduction to Hobbes's life and thought, as a foundation for his discussion of such topics as his political philosophy, his theory of international relations, the development of his mechanistic world-view, and his subversive biblical criticism. Several of the essays pay special attention to the European dimensions of Hobbes's life, his sources and his influence; the longest surveys the entire European reception of his work from the 1640s to the 1750s. All the essays are based on a deep knowledge of primary sources, and many present striking new discoveries about Hobbes's life, his manuscripts and the printing history of his works. *Aspects of Hobbes* will be essential reading not only for Hobbes specialists, but also for all those interested in seventeenth-century intellectual history more generally, both British and European.

# *Aspects of Hobbes*

NOEL MALCOLM

CLARENDON PRESS · OXFORD

# OXFORD
UNIVERSITY PRESS

Great Clarendon Street, Oxford OX2 6DP

Oxford University Press is a department of the University of Oxford.
It furthers the University's objective of excellence in research, scholarship,
and education by publishing worldwide in

Oxford New York

Auckland Bangkok Buenos Aires Cape Town Chennai
Dar es Salaam Delhi Hong Kong Istanbul Karachi Kolkata
Kuala Lumpur Madrid Melbourne Mexico City Mumbai Nairobi
São Paulo Shanghai Taipei Tokyo Toronto

Oxford is a registered trade mark of Oxford University Press
in the UK and in certain other countries

Published in the United States
by Oxford University Press Inc., New York

© in this volume Noel Malcolm 2002

The moral rights of the author have been asserted
Database right Oxford University Press (maker)

First published 2002

All rights reserved. No part of this publication may be reproduced,
stored in a retrieval system, or transmitted, in any form or by any means,
without the prior permission in writing of Oxford University Press,
or as expressly permitted by law, or under terms agreed with the appropriate
reprographics rights organization. Enquiries concerning reproduction
outside the scope of the above should be sent to the Rights Department,
Oxford University Press, at the address above

You must not circulate this book in any other binding or cover
and you must impose this same condition on any acquirer

British Library Cataloguing in Publication Data
Data available

Library of Congress Cataloging in Publication Data
Malcolm, Noel.
Aspects of Hobbes / Noel Malcolm.
p. cm.
Includes bibliographical references and index.
1. Hobbes, Thomas, 1588–1679. I. Title.
B1247 .M35 2002    192—dc21    2002074932

ISBN 0–19–924714–5

1 3 5 7 9 10 8 6 4 2

Typeset in AGaramond by Graphicraft Limited, Hong Kong
Printed in Great Britain
on acid-free paper by
Biddles Ltd, *www.biddles.co.uk*

For I. L. M.
in memory

# PREFACE

This book gathers together fourteen essays. Seven have previously been published as articles in journals or chapters of collective volumes, and seven—most of them much longer than the previously published items—are printed here for the first time. All of them relate more or less directly to the life and works of Thomas Hobbes, but some extend into other areas of subject-matter too, such as Virginian history, Comenianism, Spinoza, or the development of biblical criticism. (In just one case, that of the essay on Pierre de Cardonnel, the Hobbesian element in the essay plays a secondary role; I hope readers may share my feeling that the story of de Cardonnel himself is of sufficient interest to justify the attention given to it here.) Some of the studies are biographical, and some are bibliographical or textual; this is partly a reflection of the fact that several of these essays are 'parerga', preparatory or supplementary labours carried out while working on two larger projects—a biography of Hobbes, and a critical edition of *Leviathan*.

With the exception of the two introductory essays (on Hobbes's life and his political theory), this book does not try to provide any sort of general survey of Hobbes's life and works; the topics handled here are ones that happen to have caught my interest during many years of research on Hobbes, and on which I have thought I had something new to say. But I hope that the variety of subjects dealt with here will at least give a sense of the range of Hobbes's own interests and activities, from epistemology, optics and scientific method to biblical interpretation and international relations theory. While the flow of new books and articles on Hobbes grows larger year by year, the vast majority of them concentrate on just a small range of topics (in his political philosophy) and on an even smaller range of texts. His political theory is not, I hope, neglected in this book; but I also hope that these essays will help readers to see Hobbes not as an isolated political philosopher, but as someone connected in all sorts of different ways with the cultural and intellectual life of his age.

With the exception of the two introductory pieces, the essays in this book are arranged in a rather approximate chronological order of subject-matter. However, each essay is a self-contained piece of work: no cumulative knowledge is presumed in the reader, and the items may therefore be read in any order. (Those who do not already have some specialist knowledge of Hobbes may prefer, nevertheless, to read the two introductory essays first.) No changes have been made to the texts of the previously printed items, apart from typographical corrections and the standardizing of the references to sources. On a few points—the dating or attribution of some manuscripts, for example—I have revised my opinions since those items were first published. But I have felt that it would be unfair to readers, who may wish to refer equally to this printing or the original publication of these pieces, to oblige them to hunt for tiny textual differences between the two. Therefore, I have left the unrevised opinions in the text, and have merely added, at the end, an 'Additional Note' in which the revised judgement (or, in some cases, new information) is presented to the reader.

During more than two decades of research on Hobbes, I have accumulated very many debts of gratitude. I am particularly grateful to Peter Day, the Keeper of Collections at Chatsworth, for his unfailing help; I should also like to thank his Grace the Duke of Devonshire, and the Trustees of the Chatsworth Settlement, for permission to study and to cite the Hobbes manuscripts in their collection. I am grateful to the staff of all the other archives and libraries where I have conducted Hobbes-related research (including, but not only, the ones whose collections feature in the 'List of Manuscripts' at the end of this book); in particular, I should like to single out the staff of the rare books reading rooms in the British Library and Cambridge University Library. Several of these essays contain acknowledgements of help received from various individuals in connection with specific points; here I should just like to add a more general expression of thanks to Tim Raylor for much helpful information and criticism, and to Quentin Skinner and Sir Keith Thomas for advice and encouragement over many years. And I am especially grateful to Peter Momtchiloff, of the Oxford University Press, for taking such an interest in this book and not once flinching as its length just grew and grew.

N.M.

# ACKNOWLEDGEMENTS

The permission of the copyright-holders of the following items is gratefully acknowledged:

Chapter 1, 'A Summary Biography of Hobbes', first appeared in *The Cambridge Companion to Hobbes*, ed. T. Sorell (Cambridge, 1996), pp. 13–44: copyright Cambridge University Press.

Chapter 2, 'Hobbes and Spinoza', first appeared in *The Cambridge History of Political Thought, 1450–1700*, ed. J. H. Burns and M. Goldie (Cambridge, 1991), pp. 530–57: copyright Cambridge University Press.

Chapter 3, 'Hobbes, Sandys, and the Virginia Company', was first published in *The Historical Journal*, 24 (1981), pp. 297–321: copyright Cambridge University Press.

Chapter 5, 'Hobbes's Science of Politics and his Theory of Science', was first published in A. Napoli, ed., *Hobbes oggi* (Milan, 1990): copyright Franco Angeli Libri.

Chapter 7, 'The Title Page of *Leviathan*, Seen in a Curious Perspective', first appeared in *The Seventeenth Century*, 13 (1998), pp. 124–55: copyright the Centre for Seventeenth-Century Studies, University of Durham.

Chapter 8, 'Charles Cotton, Translator of Hobbes's *De cive*', first appeared in the *Huntington Library Quarterly*, 61, for 1998 (2000), pp. 259–87: copyright the Henry E. Huntington Library and Art Gallery.

# CONTENTS

*Abbreviations and references*     xi

1. A Summary Biography of Hobbes     1
2. Hobbes and Spinoza     27
3. Hobbes, Sandys, and the Virginia Company     53
4. Robert Payne, the Hobbes Manuscripts, and the 'Short Tract'     80
5. Hobbes's Science of Politics and his Theory of Science     146
6. Hobbes and Roberval     156
7. The Title Page of *Leviathan*, Seen in a Curious Perspective     200
8. Charles Cotton, Translator of Hobbes's *De cive*     234
9. Pierre de Cardonnel (1614–1667): Merchant, Printer, Poet, and Reader of Hobbes     259
10. Hobbes and the Royal Society     317
11. The Printing of the 'Bear': New Light on the Second Edition of Hobbes's *Leviathan*     336
12. Hobbes, Ezra, and the Bible: The History of a Subversive Idea     383
13. Hobbes's Theory of International Relations     432
14. Hobbes and the European Republic of Letters     457

*List of Manuscripts*     546
*Bibliography*     553
*Index*     607

# ABBREVIATIONS AND REFERENCES

The following abbreviations and short-title references are used throughout the book.

| | |
|---|---|
| BL | British Library, London. |
| BN | Bibliothèque Nationale, Paris. |
| Bodl. | Bodleian Library, Oxford. |
| *EW* | *The English Works of Thomas Hobbes of Malmesbury*, ed. W. Molesworth, 11 vols. (London, 1839–45). |
| Hartlib papers (electronic edition) | Sheffield University Library, Hartlib MSS: transcription edited by M. Greengrass and M. Leslie, published on CD ROM by University Microfilms International (Ann Arbor, Mich., 1995). |
| Hobbes, *Correspondence* | Hobbes, *The Correspondence*, ed. N. Malcolm, 2 vols., Clarendon Edition of the Works of Thomas Hobbes, VI, VII (Oxford, 1994). |
| Hobbes, *Elements of Law* | Hobbes, *The Elements of Law, Natural and Politic*, ed. F. Tönnies (London, 1889). (Quotations are from this edition; references are to chapter and article numbers.) |
| Hobbes, *Leviathan* | Hobbes, *Leviathan* (London, 1651). (All references are to the page numbers of this edition; these page numbers can be found also in the modern editions edited by W. G. Pogson-Smith, by C. B. McPherson, and by R. Tuck.) |
| Mersenne, *Correspondance* | M. Mersenne, *Correspondance*, ed. C. de Waard *et al.*, 17 vols. (Paris, 1933–88). |
| *OL* | *Thomae Hobbes malmesburiensis opera philosophica quae latine scripsit omnia*, ed. W. Molesworth, 5 vols. (London, 1839–45). |

Where appropriate, references to Hobbes's works are given in the form of the chapter and article number (e.g. '*De cive*, V.7', '*De corpore* XI.2'); these are equally valid for all editions. For *De cive*, the text cited is the edition by Warrender, and the translation that by Tuck and Silverthorne (except where otherwise stated). For other printed works by Hobbes, I normally cite from the first edition; where the work is not divided into chapters and articles, I also give a page-reference to *EW* or *OL*.

The following abbreviations are used not throughout the book, but only in the notes to specific essays, where they are also explained on their first occurrence. For the convenience of the reader, they are also listed here.

| | |
|---|---|
| AAS | Archives de l'Académie des Sciences, Paris. |
| ADC | Archives Départementales du Calvados, Caen. |
| BMC | Bibliothèque Municipale de Caen. |
| BMP | Bibliothèque Mazarine, Paris. |
| CAO | City Archives Office, Southampton. |
| FPCL | French Protestant Church of London, Soho Square. |
| HL | Huguenot Library, University College, London. |
| HLRO | House of Lords Record Office, London. |
| HRO | Hampshire Record Office, Winchester. |
| *HW* | Clarendon Edition of the Works of Thomas Hobbes (Oxford, 1983–). |
| PRO | Public Record Office, London. |
| RCHM | Royal Commission on Historical Manuscripts. |
| SC | Stationers' Company, Stationers' Hall, London. |
| UBA | Amsterdam University Library. |
| V.C.H. | Victoria County History. |

# – 1 –
# A Summary Biography of Hobbes

Both Hobbes and Locke came from families of West Country clothiers, and Bacon was the grandson of a sheep-reeve (a chief shepherd). All three family stories tell us something not only about the importance of wool in the English economy but also about the role of education in stimulating social mobility during the sixteenth and seventeenth centuries. Bacon's father, thanks to his studies at Cambridge, was able to become a prominent lawyer and marry into the aristocracy. Locke's father was also trained as a lawyer, although he remained a humble country attorney; thanks to his own education at Oxford, Locke was able to pursue a career that included diplomatic work, secretarial assistance to a rich politician, and, eventually, a well-paid government administrative post. Of the careers of these three philosophers, Hobbes's was certainly the least adventurous. But it too would not have been possible without his education at Oxford, which gave him his entrée to the Cavendish family, with whom he was to spend most of his life. The expense of educating a son up to university level may have been a threshold over which the poorest in society could not cross; yet the threshold was set relatively low, and once it had been passed a wide range of possible careers opened up.

One career that did not exist during this period was that of a professional philosopher. Not only was philosophy not defined or demarcated as a discipline in the way that it is today (the term was used to include the whole range of physical sciences as well), but there was no professionalization of the subject. Some of those who wrote about philosophical matters, such as Henry More or Ralph Cudworth, may have been employed as academics. By publishing philosophical works, however, they were not exhibiting academic 'research' so much as entering a republic of letters that was inhabited equally by churchmen, physicians, noblemen, officers of state, schoolmasters, and even, in the case of Hobbes's friend Sir Kenelm Digby, a one-time amateur pirate. With the proliferation of printing houses in seventeenth-century England, it was not difficult to get published. The modern system of royalties did not exist, but the code of patronage ensured that a well-chosen

---

This chapter first appeared in *The Cambridge Companion to Hobbes*, ed. T. Sorell (Cambridge, 1996), pp. 13–44.

dedication might be handsomely rewarded. Books were expensive to buy, however; for example, *Leviathan*, when it was first published, cost eight shillings, which was more than most ordinary labourers earned in a week. Any writer who wanted to keep up with what was being published on philosophical subjects needed one of four things: a private income, a well-paid job, membership of a circle of book-lending friends, or access to a well funded library. Hobbes's career as tutor and secretary to the Cavendish family gave him the last of these four in full; over the years he enjoyed the other three in smaller measure. He was content to remain the employee or retainer of a great noble household—a somewhat old-fashioned career pattern that gave him access to a higher social world without making him a member of it, and which kept him for months at a time in physical seclusion from the metropolitan intellectual scene. But it also gave him security, time to write a large quantity of works on a huge range of subjects, and powerful political protection against the public hostility to some of those works during the last three decades of his life.

# I

Hobbes was born on 5/15 April 1588, in Westport, a parish on the northwestern side of the small town of Malmesbury, in north Wiltshire. His father, an ill-educated country clergyman, was curate of the small neighbouring parish of Brokenborough, which was one of the poorest livings in the area.[1] Some members of the family had grown prosperous in the cloth-making business. These included Edmund Hobbes (probably Hobbes's great-uncle), who became alderman, i.e. mayor, of Malmesbury in 1600; an even richer cousin, William Hobbes, who was a 'great clothier'; and Francis, the elder brother of Hobbes's father, who was a prosperous glover and became alderman of Malmesbury in 1625.[2] Other Hobbeses in and around Malmesbury included some less prominent clothiers and two alehouse-keepers, Edmund and Robert Hobbes of Westport, whose exact relationship to

---

[1] John Aubrey mistakenly claims that Hobbes's father was vicar of Westport ('*Brief Lives*', *chiefly of contemporaries, set down by John Aubrey, between the years 1669 & 1696*, ed. A. Clark, 2 vols. (Oxford, 1898), I, p. 323). Ecclesiastical records for 1602–3 describe him as curate of Brokenborough (Wiltshire Record Office, Trowbridge: Archdeaconry of Wiltshire, Act Books [Office], vol. I [formerly vol. 40], fos. 107r, 132v, 177r). The church at Brokenborough had been one of the most poorly equipped in 1553: J. E. Nightingale, *The Church Plate of the County of Wiltshire* (Salisbury, 1891), p. 195), and in 1649 its tithes yielded an income of just £20 per annum: E. J. Bodington, 'The Church Survey of Wiltshire, 1649–50', *Wiltshire Archaeological and Natural History Magazine*, 41 (1920), p. 6.

[2] J. Aubrey, *Wiltshire: The Topographical Collections*, ed. J. E. Jackson (Devizes, 1862), p. 235 n. (where '1660' is a misprint for 1600); Aubrey, '*Brief Lives*', I, pp. 323–4, 387; R. Luce, 'An Old Malmesbury Minute Book', *Wiltshire Archaeological and Natural History Magazine*, 47 (1935–7), pp. 322, 325; G. D. Ramsay, ed., *Two Sixteenth Century Taxation Lists*, Wiltshire Archaeological and Natural History Society, Records Branch, 10 (Salisbury, 1954), p. 48.

A SUMMARY BIOGRAPHY

Thomas Hobbes cannot be established.[3] It seems likely that Hobbes's father spent more time in the Westport alehouse than he did in his church at Brokenborough; during the archdeacon's visitation of the deanery of Malmesbury in October 1602 he failed to appear before the visitors, and two months later he was hauled up before the archdeacon's court 'for want of quarter sermons and for not cathechisinge the younge'.[4]

Worse trouble was to follow. In October 1603 Hobbes's father was accused in the episcopal court of slandering Richard Jeane, the vicar of Foxley (a nearby parish), whom he had described as 'a knave and an arrant knave and a drunken knave'. Required to make a public act of penitence in Foxley church, Hobbes's father failed to turn up for the occasion; fined 33s. 3d., he failed to pay and was threatened (and eventually punished) with excommunication. In February 1604 he chanced on Jeane in the churchyard at Malmesbury, whereupon, in the words of a witness, he 'followed the said M$^r$ Jeaine revyling him and calling him knave and coming neare vnto him strooke him the saide M$^r$ Jeaine wth his fiste vnder the eare or about the head'.[5] Any act of violence in a church or churchyard was an excommunicable offence, but laying violent hands on a clergyman was an even more serious crime in ecclesiastical law, for which corporal punishment was possible; and any excommunicated person who failed to seek absolution from the Church could be arrested and imprisoned by the civil authorities after forty days.[6] Hobbes's father 'was forcd to fly for it' and died 'in obscurity beyound London'.[7]

By the time these dramatic events occurred, Hobbes was already at Oxford; whether he ever saw his father again is not known. It is possible that he had been sent to university because, like his father, he was a younger son who was expected to go into the Church. (His elder brother, Edmund, was to pursue the family trade as a clothier.) If so, we may suspect that these events strengthened whatever anticlerical tendencies were already present in Hobbes's character. Hobbes owed his Oxford education to two people: his uncle Francis, who paid for it, and a young clergyman, Robert Latimer, who had taught Hobbes Latin and Greek to a high standard at a little school in Westport. Latimer was evidently a keen classicist and

---

[3] Edmund received a licence to keep an alehouse in 1600 (Wiltshire Record Office, Trowbridge, Quarter Sessions, Criminal Business, 1598–1603, p. 20). Robert, possibly Edmund's son, is listed as an alehousekeeper in 1620: N. J. Williams, ed., *Tradesmen in Early-Stuart Wiltshire*, Wiltshire Archaeological and Natural History Society, Records Branch, 15 (Salisbury, 1959), p. 30.

[4] Wiltshire Record Office, Trowbridge: Archdeaconry of Wiltshire, Act Books (Office), vol. 1 (formerly vol. 40), fos. 107r, 132v.

[5] Wiltshire Record Office, Trowbridge, Episcopal Deposition Book (Instance), vol. 22b (1603–1603/4), fos. 19–20r (first quotation), 48v (second quotation); Episcopal Act Book (Instance), vol. 33a, fos. 56a (inserted loose sheet), 73r, 80v, 108v. See also A. Rogow, *Thomas Hobbes* (New York, 1986), pp. 25–9.

[6] H. C. Coote, *The Practice of Ecclesiastical Courts* (London, 1847), p. 111; R. Cosins, *An Apologie for Sundry Proceedings* (London, 1593), pp. 58–60; H. Consett, *The Practice of the Spiritual and Ecclesiastical Courts* (London, 1847), pp. 41–2.

[7] Aubrey, '*Brief Lives*', I, p. 387.

an inspiring teacher who may have become an intellectual and moral father-figure for Hobbes; as it happened, it was Latimer who replaced Hobbes's father as curate of Brokenborough.[8] Latimer had been an undergraduate at Magdalen Hall in Oxford, and it was there that Hobbes was sent to study at the age of 13 or 14.[9]

Magdalen Hall was one of the poorer foundations at Oxford, having developed out of a grammar school attached to Magdalen College. Both the College and the Hall had been regarded as centres of Puritanism since the 1560s and 1570s; Magdalen Hall's reputation for Puritanism was strengthened under a principal, John Wilkinson, who was appointed in 1605. The Hall, unlike the College, had no chapel, and since its daily services of morning and evening prayer were said in an unconsecrated building (the dining hall), it was possible to add Puritan 'exercises' to the forms of prayer contained in the Prayer Book.[10] The sympathy for some of Calvin's teachings that Hobbes displayed in later life may date from his time at Magdalen Hall. On the other hand, Calvinism was not the same as Puritanism, and his later hostility towards Presbyterians in particular and religious 'enthusiasts' in general is well known. In his autobiographical writings, Hobbes passes no comment on the religious climate of his undergraduate years. He tells us little about his studies either, except to dismiss the Aristotelian logic and physics that he was taught. Instead of such useless stuff, he says, he preferred to read about explorations of new-found lands and to study maps of the earth and the stars.[11] Astronomy thus emerges as his earliest scientific interest—an interest he evidently kept up, since we know that he observed the appearance of a comet in 1618.[12] In retrospect, Hobbes evidently regretted that he had not been taught the key to the exact sciences, mathematics. He complained in *Leviathan* that until very recently geometry had 'had no place at all' in the universities, and his advice on education was that a boy should be 'entered into geometry when he understands Latin [because] it is the best way of teaching logic'.[13]

It is hard to judge the fairness of Hobbes's criticisms of Oxford. The official curriculum laid down in the statutes of 1564–5 was indeed conservative and dominated

---

[8] Aubrey, '*Brief Lives*', I, pp. 35, 324, 328–9, 332, 393 (where Aubrey calls Latimer 'a good Graecian'); Wiltshire Record Office, Trowbridge: Bishops' Transcripts, Brokenborough, bundle 1, and Westport, bundle 1 (which includes elegant Latin tributes by Latimer to two dead parishioners).

[9] J. Foster, *Alumni oxonienses* (Oxford, 1891–2), entries in vols. II, III. The exact date of Hobbes's matriculation is not known; his autobiography states that it was during his fourteenth year (*Thomae Hobbes angli vita*, p. 1; *OL* I, p. xiii), i.e. between April 1601 and April 1602. He adds, however, that he stayed at Oxford for five years (ibid.), and we know that he was admitted BA in Feb. 1608. Aubrey says he entered Oxford 'at fourteen yeares of age', and dates his arrival there, plausibly, to the beginning of 1603 ('*Brief Lives*', I, pp. 328, 330).

[10] S. G. Hamilton, *Hertford College* (London, 1903), pp. 100–11; M. H. Curtis, *Oxford and Cambridge in Transition* (Oxford, 1959), pp. 191–2. On the general differences between a hall and a college, see N. Fitzherbert, *Oxoniensis academiae descriptio* (Rome, 1602), p. 28.

[11] Hobbes, *Thomae Hobbes angli vita*, p. 1 (*OL* I, xiii); *Thomae Hobbesii malmesburiensis vita*, p. 3 (*OL* I, lxxxvi–lxxxvii).

[12] Hobbes, *Critique du* De mundo *de Thomas White*, ed. J. Jacquot and H. W. Jones (Paris, 1973), p. 151.

[13] Hobbes, *Leviathan*, p. 370; J. Aubrey, *Aubrey on Education*, ed. J. E. Stephens (London, 1972), p. 61.

by the works of Aristotle (although it did include some standard astronomical and geometrical works, including Euclid, which Hobbes would have had to study if he had wanted to proceed MA). Hobbes's complaint that the philosophy taught at the universities was 'Aristotelity' had some truth to it. There had been a definite revival of Aristotelianism in England in the latter part of the sixteenth century, and extra decrees were issued in Oxford in 1586 to exclude the use of authors who disagreed with the 'ancient and true philosophy' of Aristotle.[14] But, on the other hand, there is a mass of evidence that academics in the early seventeenth century had intellectual interests, especially in the sciences, which went far beyond the official curriculum, and that these interests were often reflected in their teaching.[15] Nor should we assume that Hobbes's hostility to scholastic logic would have found no sympathetic echo in the Oxford of his day. The humanist criticism of scholasticism lingered on at the university. One fiercely anti-scholastic oration delivered in Magdalen Hall two or three years before Hobbes's arrival attacked the 'clumsy and barbarous words, "entities", "formal essences", and "quiddities",' and asked rhetorically: 'How are ethics improved by the knowledge of propositions or the manufacture of syllogisms?'[16]

## II

For someone who did not intend to pursue a career in the Church or the university, there was little point in staying on for the further degree of MA. Fortunately, Hobbes was offered employment immediately after completing his BA. On the recommendation of John Wilkinson he was taken on as a tutor by William Cavendish, a rich Derbyshire landowner who had been created a baron in 1605 and was to become first Earl of Devonshire in 1618. Hobbes's pupil, the future second Earl (also named William Cavendish), was only a few years younger than Hobbes himself. He had been entered briefly at St John's College, Cambridge; Hobbes joined him there in the summer of 1608 and accompanied him from Cambridge to Derbyshire in November.[17] Thereafter Hobbes's relation to his charge seems to have been less that of a tutor than that of a servant, a secretary, or a friend. In

---

[14] S. Gibson, ed., *Statuta universitatis oxoniensis* (Oxford, 1931), pp. 389–90 (1564–5), 437 (1586). On the Aristotelian revival, see H. Kearney, *Scholars and Gentlemen* (London, 1970), pp. 81–3; C. B. Schmitt, 'Philosophy and Science in Sixteenth-Century Universities', in E. Murdoch and D. Sylla, eds., *The Cultural Context of Medieval Learning* (Dordrecht, 1975), pp. 485–530; C. B. Schmitt, *John Case and Aristotelianism in Renaissance England* (Montreal, 1983), pp. 13–76.
[15] See M. Feingold, *The Mathematicians' Apprenticeship* (Cambridge, 1984).
[16] BL MS Harl. 6460, fols. 1v, 2r. This oration, an attack on logic, seems also implicitly anti-Ramist; but the Ramist movement (which divided logic from rhetoric and asserted the primacy of the former) was also hostile to scholastic logic.
[17] Cavendish proceeded MA (a privilege of nobility) in the summer of 1608, and Hobbes also incorporated at St John's (which he was entitled to do as an Oxford BA): Foster, *Alumni oxonienses*. Payment for the Nov. journey is recorded in Chatsworth, MS Hardwick 29, p. 38.

Aubrey's words, 'He was his lordship's page, and rode a hunting and hawking with him, and kept his privy purse.'[18]

The young William Cavendish was not without intellectual and literary interests. In 1611 he published (anonymously) a short but elegant work, *A Discourse against Flatterie*, the essayistic style of which suggests the influence of Bacon.[19] Three years later Hobbes and Cavendish went on a tour of France and Italy. During their stay in Venice in the winter of 1614–15 they both learned Italian, and Cavendish's exercises in the language included preparing a translation into Italian of Bacon's *Essayes*. Back in England, Cavendish was in personal contact with Bacon by 1616, and Bacon himself helped to revise the Italian translation of the *Essayes* before it was published in 1618.[20] We know from Aubrey and another source that Hobbes became acquainted with Bacon and did some secretarial work for him, taking down dictation 'in his delicate groves where he did meditate', and helping to translate some of his *Essayes* into Latin.[21] This contact has traditionally been assumed to have taken place during the final years before Bacon's death in 1626 (and it was from Hobbes that Aubrey learned the story of how Bacon died from a chill caught when experimentally stuffing a chicken with snow); however, Hobbes's personal acquaintance with Bacon probably dates from the work on the Italian translation of the *Essayes* in 1617–18. From the first Earl of Devonshire's account book, it is clear that Hobbes also visited the Lord Chancellor on his employer's legal business in May 1619, and another entry records the disbursement of the sum of two shillings 'to Mr Hobbs wch he gaue away at yᵉ Lo: Chanc.' in May 1620.[22]

Despite all these personal contacts, it is hard to find any evidence of a strong or direct Baconian influence on the substance of Hobbes's later philosophy. Some elements of Bacon's thinking may find an echo in Hobbes's works: the tendency towards naturalism or physicalism (as shown by Bacon's interest in ancient atomism or modern writers such as Telesio), for example, or the attack on false entities generated by language (the idols of the marketplace). The general project of replacing scholasticism with a new but equally all-encompassing system of knowledge was also common to both writers. But none of these tendencies or projects had been peculiar to Bacon. It is clear, on the other hand, that Hobbes rejected Bacon's obscure but largely traditional metaphysics of 'forms', and that the so-called inductive method propounded by Bacon had little influence on Hobbes compared with his later discovery of the Euclidean method of definition and deduction.

---

[18] *Brief Lives*, I, pp. 330–1.
[19] The work is dedicated to Cavendish's brother-in-law Lord Bruce and can be confidently attributed to Cavendish, both because of the wording of that dedication and in view of its later inclusion in *Horae subsecivae* (see below).
[20] N. Malcolm, *De Dominis (1560–1624)* (London, 1984), pp. 47–54.
[21] Aubrey, *Brief Lives*, I, pp. 70, 331; Hobbes, *Correspondence*, II, Letter 168.
[22] Chatsworth, MS Hardwick 29, pp. 605, 633.

A SUMMARY BIOGRAPHY

The influence of Bacon's *Essayes* on the young William Cavendish, however, was evidently powerful. In 1620 an original collection of essays was published anonymously under the title *Horae subsecivae*. It included a version of the *Discourse against Flatterie* and a group of other essays in the Baconian style that can definitely be attributed to Cavendish; a fair copy of these essays, in Hobbes's hand, survives at Chatsworth.[23] In addition to the *Discourse against Flatterie* and the essays in the Chatsworth MS, the published text of *Horae subsecivae* also included three new discourses. One was a description of Rome, obviously the fruit of Hobbes's and Cavendish's visit there in October 1614; the others were 'A Discourse upon the Beginning of Tacitus' and 'A Discourse of Lawes'. A recent statistical analysis of the prose characteristics of *Horae subsecivae* suggests that, while the rest of the work was not composed by Hobbes, these three discourses may have been.[24] This is a little surprising in the case of the description of Rome, since writing such accounts when on a tour of Europe was a traditional exercise performed by pupils, not their tutors.[25] But in the case of the other two discourses, it is possible to see resemblances between the arguments of these writings and Hobbes's later thinking. The discourse on Tacitus, for example, coolly assumes the importance of deception and self-interest in political affairs, and both discourses stress the unique evil of anarchy or civil war. On the other hand, the claims made in the 'Discourse of Lawes' about the relationship between law and reason and about the independent status of common law as something grounded in 'the Iudgement of the people' are in conflict with Hobbes's later position.[26] Even if these discourses were by Cavendish and not by Hobbes, they give us an important insight into the thinking of the man who was intellectually and personally closest to him at this time.

Hobbes's introduction to political life and contemporary political thinking came largely through Cavendish's activities. Cavendish was never a prominent politician, but he was a member of the 1614 and 1621 parliaments, and Hobbes would no doubt have followed those debates that Cavendish attended.[27] On his return

---

[23] From the nature of the corrections in this MS, which are in another hand, it can be demonstrated that Hobbes was not the author of these essays, as has sometimes been claimed: Hobbes was evidently transcribing from a rough draft that he sometimes misread. Although published anonymously, *Horae subsecivae* is attributed to Cavendish in an early (c.1657) library catalogue at Chatsworth, and the copy of the book in that library (pressmark 31 H) is inscribed 'written by Candysh' ('Candish' was the 17th-century pronunciation of 'Cavendish'). For other evidence confirming this attribution, see D. Bush, 'Hobbes, Cavendish and "Essayes"', *Notes and Queries*, n.s., 20 (1973), pp. 162–4.

[24] I am grateful to Noel Reynolds for allowing me to see details of a forthcoming study of this evidence by him and John Hilton.

[25] See e.g. M. G. Brennan, ed., *The Travel Diary (1611–12) of an English Catholic, Sir Charles Somerset*, Proceedings of the Leeds Philosophical and Literary Society, 23 (Leeds, 1993), p. 1.

[26] Cavendish, *Horae subsecivae*, pp. 239, 267, 516–17 (civil war); 531 (law and reason); 541–2 (common law).

[27] Richard Tuck, misled by the traditional but false belief that Hobbes and Cavendish began their European tour in 1610 (on which see Malcolm, *De Dominis*, p. 120, n. 280), has mistakenly identified the William Cavendish who was an MP for Derbyshire in 1614 as Cavendish's cousin, the future Earl of Newcastle (*Philosophy and Government 1572–1671* (Cambridge, 1993), p. 281). Both Cavendishes were elected to this parliament: see M. Jansson, ed., *Proceedings in Parliament, 1614*, Memoirs of the American

from Italy in 1615, Cavendish kept up a correspondence with the Venetian friar Fulgenzio Micanzio, who was the friend and personal assistant of Paolo Sarpi; Micanzio's letters were translated by Hobbes for further circulation.[28] In this way Hobbes must have gained a special interest in the writings and political actions of Sarpi, who had defended Venice against the papal interdict of 1606 and developed a strongly anti-papal theory of Church and State in which the temporal ruler alone 'is the source from whom all jurisdictions flow and to whom they all return'.[29] And through Cavendish and the connection with Micanzio, Hobbes must also have come into contact with the Croatian–Venetian churchman and writer Marc'Antonio de Dominis, who came to England in 1616, assisted in the project of translating Bacon into Italian, supervised the publication of Sarpi's *Historia del concilio tridentino*, and published a large and influential anti-papal treatise of his own, *De republica ecclesiastica*.[30] Also thanks to Cavendish, Hobbes became a member of two trading and colonizing companies in which Cavendish had an interest: the Virginia Company and the Somer Islands Company (which organized the settlement of the Bermudas). Hobbes was granted a share in the former by Cavendish in June 1622; the date of his formal involvement in the latter is not known, but his role as assistant to Cavendish would certainly have involved him in the affairs of both companies before he became a shareholder himself. At the thirty-seven separate meetings of the Virginia Company's governing body that Hobbes attended in 1622–4, he came into contact with prominent politicians and writers such as Sir Edwin Sandys (who criticized royal policy on taxation and foreign affairs in the parliament of 1621) and the lawyer John Selden (whose friend Hobbes later became).[31]

William Cavendish succeeded his father as second Earl of Devonshire in 1626, but he died only two years later, at the age of forty-three. At the time of his death, Hobbes was finishing work on a translation of Thucydides, which was published, with a dedication to Cavendish's elder son (the third Earl), in the following year. This was an important work of scholarship; it was the first translation of the work into English directly from the Greek, and it also included a detailed map of ancient Greece compiled from many sources and drawn by Hobbes himself. Although Thucydides' work is famous for its speech by Pericles in defence of Athenian democracy, its publication by Hobbes may nevertheless have been an implicitly pro-royalist political statement, since the main theme of the book is the gradual

---

Philosophical Society, 172 (Philadelphia, 1988), pp. 447, 451. For the 1621 parliament, see W. Notestein *et al.*, eds., *Commons Debates in 1621*, 7 vols. (New Haven, Conn., 1935), II, pp. 467, 482.

[28] V. Gabrieli, 'Bacone, la riforma e Roma nella versione Hobbesiana d'un carteggio di Fulgenzio Micanzio', *The English Miscellany*, 8 (1957), pp. 195–250.

[29] This quotation is from a *consulto* (statement of advice to the Venetian government) of 1609: see C. M. Francescon, *Chiesa e stato nei consulti di Sarpi* (Vicenza, 1942), p. 121 n. On Sarpi's theories of Church and State, see also B. Ulianich, 'Considerazioni per una ecclesiologia di Sarpi', in F. Iserloh and P. Mann, eds., *Festgabe Joseph Lortz*, 2 vols. (Baden-Baden, 1968), II, pp. 363–444.

[30] See Malcolm, *De Dominis*.

[31] See N. Malcolm, 'Hobbes, Sandys, and the Virginia Company', Ch. 3 below.

subversion of the Athenian state by ambitious demagogic politicians. In his verse autobiography Hobbes emphasizes this aspect of Thucydides' work, saying that Thucydides was Hobbes's favourite historian because 'he shows how incompetent democracy is'.[32]

After the death of the second Earl, Hobbes left the service of the Cavendishes for two years. He was again employed as a tutor for the son of a rich landowner, Sir Gervase Clifton, and in 1629–30 he travelled with the young Gervase Clifton to France and Switzerland.[33] From later accounts by Hobbes and Aubrey we learn that it was during his stay in Geneva in April–June 1630 that Hobbes began to read Euclid's *Elements* in 'a gentleman's library' and fell in love with its deductive method. It is unlikely, given his known earlier interest in astronomy, that this was Hobbes's first encounter with geometry; nor need we assume that he had never encountered Euclid's work before. What he stresses in his own account of the incident is that the work delighted him, 'not so much because of the theorems, as because of the method of reasoning'.[34] This strongly suggests that Hobbes's mind was already preoccupied with some philosophical problems to which Euclidean method seemed to supply the solution. Of the nature of those problems, however, there is no direct evidence from this period itself.

After his return to England, Hobbes was taken back into the service of the widowed Countess of Devonshire in early 1631 as a tutor to her son, the third Earl. Possibly Hobbes was already spending much of his time reading about mathematics and other scientific subjects; in a legal document written in 1639, he explained that he had accepted this tutorship 'amongst other causes chiefly for this, that y$^e$ same did not much diuert him from his studies'.[35] The boy was only 13, and Hobbes now had to teach at a more elementary level than he had done before. One of the methods he used was to go through a Latin translation of Aristotle's *Rhetoric*, making a 'digest' of it with his pupil. A version of this digest was later published in English by Hobbes. It is a largely faithful summary of Aristotle's analysis of how people can be swayed by appeals to their passions and interests.[36]

## III

The 1630s were crucial years in Hobbes's intellectual development. They saw not only the growth of his interest in science (especially optics) but also the formation of the main outlines of his political philosophy, which appeared as *The Elements of*

---

[32] *Thomae Hobbesii malmesburiensis vita*, p. 4 (*OL* I, p. lxxxviii). For a valuable discussion of Hobbes's translation of Thucydides, see M. Reik, *The Golden Lands of Thomas Hobbes* (Detroit, 1977), pp. 36–52.

[33] See Hobbes, *Correspondence*, I, Letters 3–8.

[34] Hobbes, *Thomae Hobbes angli vita*, p. 4 (*OL* I, p. xiv); Aubrey, *Brief Lives*, I, p. 332 (where Aubrey's manuscript gives the name of the city as '. . . . . a').

[35] Chatsworth, MS Hobbes D. 6, fo. 2r.

[36] See J. T. Harwood, ed., *The Rhetorics of Thomas Hobbes and Bernard Lamy* (Carbondale, Ill., 1986); L. Strauss, *The Political Philosophy of Hobbes*, tr. E. M. Sinclair (Chicago, 1952), pp. 35–42.

*Law* at the end of the decade. Although we know more about his intellectual and personal life in this decade than in the previous ones, there is much that remains obscure. Recent studies have tended to locate Hobbes in two particular intellectual groups during this period. One was the 'Welbeck academy' of scientists connected with the Earl of Newcastle (so called after one of his family seats, Welbeck Abbey in north Nottinghamshire). They included Newcastle's brother, Sir Charles Cavendish, a talented mathematician who corresponded with mathematicians and scientists on the Continent; Newcastle's chaplain, Robert Payne, who conducted chemical experiments with Newcastle; and Walter Warner, who had been one of a number of scientists and free-thinkers (including Thomas Hariot) patronized by the Earl of Northumberland in the 1590s and 1600s.[37] Hobbes was especially close to the Cavendish brothers in the late 1630s. He corresponded with Payne, who became one of his closest friends, and he also took an interest (although not an unsceptical one) in Warner's work on optics. We know that he was in contact with Warner, sending him suggestions of his own about the angle of refraction, as early as 1634.[38]

The other grouping was the so-called Great Tew circle that gathered round Lucius Cary, Viscount Falkland (whose house, Great Tew, was near Oxford). Its members included theologians such as William Chillingworth, Oxford divines such as George Morley and Gilbert Sheldon, London lawyers such as Edward Hyde (the future Earl of Clarendon), and poets such as Edmund Waller.[39] At the heart of the Great Tew circle lay the collaboration between Falkland and Chillingworth in an attempt to formulate a moderate and rational Anglicanism as a defence against Roman Catholicism. This defence of 'rational religion' was characterized as 'Socinianism' (an anti-Trinitarian heresy) by hostile critics, especially the more extreme Protestant ones; and the Great Tew writers' rejection of traditional ideas of spiritual authority in the Church, with their tendency to judge questions of church government in terms of mere convenience or conduciveness to temporal peace, set them apart from Laudians as well as Catholics. These characteristics would also be found in Hobbes's later writings, and attacked in even stronger terms. Hobbes certainly owed some of his ideas about religion to members of the Great Tew circle, even though his defence of rational religion was not based, as theirs generally was, on assumptions about the essential reasonableness of God.

[37] On Newcastle, Sir Charles Cavendish, and Robert Payne, see Hobbes, *Correspondence*, II, Biographical Register. On Warner, see ibid., I, Letter 16, n. 3. On the Welbeck circle and its connection with Warner and Hariot, see R. H. Kargon, *Atomism in England from Hariot to Newton* (Oxford, 1966), pp. 6–42.

[38] A proposition about the angle of refraction, in Hobbes's hand but entitled 'M͏ʳ Hobbes analogy' in Warner's hand, is in BL MS Add. 4395, fols. 131, 133.

[39] On Great Tew, see especially B. H. G. Wormald, *Clarendon*; H. R. Trevor-Roper, *Catholics, Anglicans and Puritans* (London, 1987), pp. 166–230; and J. C. Hayward, 'The *Mores* of Great Tew', Cambridge University Ph.D. dissertation, 1983.

A SUMMARY BIOGRAPHY

Although Hobbes's connections with various members of these two intellectual groupings are not in doubt, the idea of his belonging to two 'circles' located at Welbeck and Great Tew is misleadingly schematic. The phrase 'Welbeck academy' is just a metaphor for a group of people connected with the Cavendish brothers and does not refer to physical gatherings, either formal or informal; there is no evidence, for example, that Walter Warner ever set foot in Welbeck Abbey. As for Great Tew, while it is clear that there were physical gatherings there, it is unlikely that Hobbes was more than a very occasional visitor to Falkland's house. One possible opportunity for a visit came in 1634, when Hobbes may have stayed for a while in Oxford, using that town also as a base for a visit to his old friends in north Wiltshire.[40] Otherwise Hobbes is most likely to have encountered members of Falkland's circle in London. Outside its inner core of Oxford men, this circle had a more peripheral membership of London-based intellectuals, court wits, and poets, and it is among these that most of Hobbes's personal friendships with Great Tew writers are to be found—men such as the poet Edmund Waller and the lawyer Edward Hyde. Yet the intellectual and social world of early seventeenth-century England was so closely knit that one has only to begin pursuing possible connections to see any neat pattern of separate 'circles' break up before one's eyes. Thus, for example, Hobbes's intellectual contacts with the liberal Oxford theologians are likely to have come in the first place from Robert Payne, an Oxford man who was a friend of Sheldon, Morley, and Hammond; many of the poets and wits attached to Falkland's circle were also friends and admirers of Ben Jonson, whom Hobbes had known in 1628, before the Great Tew circle came into being; Jonson was himself a protégé of Newcastle and a friend of Payne; and Hyde was also connected with Walter Warner, whose patron during this period was Hyde's father-in-law, Sir Thomas Aylesbury.

In 1634 Hobbes embarked on another Continental tour with his pupil, the third Earl of Devonshire. They spent nearly a year in Paris, setting off for Italy at the end of August 1635; they were in Rome in December of that year, in Florence in April 1636, and back in Paris in early June, whence they returned to England four months later.[41] Even before he set out on this tour, Hobbes's mind had been filled, thanks partly to the stimulus of the Earl of Newcastle and his mathematician brother, Sir Charles Cavendish, with thoughts about optics, physics, and psychology. In early 1634 he had been commissioned by the Earl of Newcastle to find a copy of Galileo's *Dialogo*, and his earliest surviving letter sent from Paris during this tour answers a query from an unnamed correspondent about the functioning of vision and memory.[42] The two prolonged stays in Paris that this continental trip allowed him were clearly of great importance to Hobbes's intellectual life. From the Earl of Newcastle and Sir Charles he had introductions to French scientists and

[40] See Hobbes, *Correspondence*, I, Letter 11, n. 2.
[41] Ibid., I, Letters 12–21.   [42] Ibid., I, Letters 10, 12.

mathematicians such as Claude Mydorge, a writer on geometry and optics who was a close friend of Descartes.[43] It was probably through Sir Charles's good offices, either directly or indirectly, that he was introduced to the learned, pious, and charming friar Marin Mersenne, who was also a friend of Descartes, and who was already functioning as the centre of a huge network of scientific and philosophical correspondents. Hobbes later recorded in his autobiography that he had investigated 'the principles of natural science' in Paris at this time (principles that 'he knew ... were contained in the nature and variety of motions'), and that he had communicated his ideas on this subject to Mersenne on a daily basis.[44] We know that he observed experiments carried out by William Davisson, a famous Scottish chemist who taught at Paris, and during his final months in the French capital he was discussing philosophical matters with the maverick Catholic intellectual Sir Kenelm Digby.[45]

By the time Hobbes returned to England in October 1636, he was devoting as much of his time as possible to philosophical work: 'the extreame pleasure I take in study', he wrote, 'ouercomes in me all other appetites.'[46] His pupil came of age in the following year, and although Hobbes remained in his service his time was now largely his own; much of it was probably spent with the Earl of Newcastle and his brother at Welbeck. In a letter to the Earl from Paris in 1635, Hobbes had expressed an ambition to be the first person to give 'good reasons for y$^e$ facultyes & passions of y$^e$ soule, such as may be expressed in playne English'; and, from a later letter from Sir Kenelm Digby, it appears that Hobbes had been planning, during his final months in Paris, a work on 'Logike' that would begin, in Euclidean fashion, with the definitions of primary terms.[47] Whether these writings on logic and psychology or epistemology were conceived from the outset as a single, systematic project cannot be said with certainty, but all the evidence of Hobbes's later work indicates that the urge to systematize was located deep in his intellectual character. It is unfortunate that any manuscript drafts of this project that Hobbes may have written during this crucial period of his intellectual formation, 1636–9, have apparently not survived. One manuscript traditionally attributed to Hobbes (and dated by some authors to this period, although by others to the beginning of the 1630s), the so-called Short Tract, is in the handwriting of Robert Payne and can more plausibly be attributed to him.[48] Another manuscript on metaphysics

---

[43] See Hobbes, *Correspondence*, I, Letter 18.
[44] *Thomae Hobbes angli vita*, pp. 4–5 (*OL* I, p. xiv). For a brief reference to the contents of one such discussion, see Hobbes, *Correspondence*, I, Letter 34.
[45] Hobbes, *Correspondence*, I, Letter 19, n. 4: Letters 20, 25.
[46] Ibid., I, Letter 21.    [47] Ibid., I, Letters 16, 25.
[48] For a modern edition of this MS (BL MS Harl. 6796, fols. 297–308), see 'Hobbes', *Court Traité des premiers principes*. For the attribution to Payne, see R. Tuck, 'Hobbes and Descartes', in G. A. J. Rogers and A. Ryan, eds., *Perspectives on Thomas Hobbes* (Oxford, 1988), pp. 16–18, and Hobbes, *Correspondence*, II, Biographical Register, 'Payne'.

and epistemology, which definitely does contain material written by Hobbes and which has previously been dated to the period 1637–40, can more probably be dated to some time after July 1643.[49]

The earliest surviving scientific–philosophical work by Hobbes is a manuscript treatise on optics, the so-called 'Latin Optical MS', which must have been completed by 1640.[50] This important work evidently formed part of a larger body of writing; it refers back to a previous *sectio* (section) in which basic principles of physics had been discussed, such as the rule that 'all action is local motion in the thing which acts'.[51] Since Hobbes was later to use the term 'section' for each of the three works that made up his tripartite 'Elements of philosophy' (*De corpore, De homine*, and *De cive*), and since Hobbes put his main discussion of optics in *De homine*, it is possible that this optical treatise was a version of what later became *De homine*, and that the earlier 'section' to which it refers was a body of work corresponding to what was eventually published as *De corpore*.[52] How roughly the missing 'section' corresponded to that work can only be guessed at, but Hobbes's slow and hesitant drafting and redrafting of *De corpore* during the 1640s suggests that whatever existed before 1640 was probably more like a set of notes than a polished text. (This would fit the account of Hobbes's working methods given by Aubrey and by Hobbes himself.[53])

The striking thing about the Latin Optical MS, which probably set it apart from the previous 'section', was the fact that so much of it took the form of a running critique of Descartes's 'Dioptrique'. This was the short treatise on optics (in particular, refraction) that had been published as one of the essays accompanying Descartes's *Discours de la méthode* in 1637. (Hobbes had been sent a copy of the book by Sir Kenelm Digby soon after its publication.) Descartes's work had an unsettling effect on Hobbes, for two reasons. First, Descartes's mechanistic physics, and his assumption that perception is caused by physical motions or pressures that have no intrinsic similarity to the qualities (redness, heat, etc.) that are

---

[49] For a modern edn of this MS (National Library of Wales, MS 5297), see Hobbes, *Critique du De mundo*, pp. 449–60. For previous datings, see M. M. Rossi, *Alle fonti del deismo e del materialsmo moderno* (Florence, 1942), pp. 120–3, and A. Pacchi, *Convenzione e ipotesi nella formazione della filosofia naturale di Thomas Hobbes* (Florence, 1965), pp. 16–17. My reasons for dating it thus are given below.

[50] For a modern edition of this MS (BL MS Harl. 6796, fols. 193–266), though omitting the diagrams, see Hobbes, 'Tractatus opticus', ed. F. Alessio, *Rivista critica di storia della filosofia*, 18 (1963), pp. 147–228. For my reasons for this dating, see the section on 'missing letters' in Hobbes, *Correspondence*, VI, 'Textual Introduction'; and see also Tuck, 'Hobbes and Descartes'.

[51] Latin Optical MS, I. 3 (Hobbes, 'Tractatus opticus', p. 148).

[52] Tuck, 'Hobbes and Descartes', pp. 19–20. That the Latin Optical MS was part of a larger project, of at least two 'sections', is clear. But it is still unclear whether Hobbes was envisaging, from the outset, that this project would culminate in a treatise on politics. The account of the genesis of *The Elements of Law* given in the dedicatory epistle to that work (quoted below) makes it sound more of a *pièce d'occasion* than the neatly systematic retrospective explanation given in the preface to *De cive* (ed. Warrender, p. 82).

[53] Aubrey, '*Brief Lives*', I, pp. 334–5, 351; Hobbes, *Correspondence*, II, p. 82.

perceived, corresponded very closely to Hobbes's own theories. Although neither Descartes nor Hobbes was the first to have such ideas (they had been preceded by Isaac Beeckman and Galileo), this was still very much the frontier of modern thinking, and it must have been galling for Hobbes to see some of his own research pre-empted in print. In 1640–1 an exchange of letters between Hobbes and Descartes on optics and physics turned (at Descartes's prompting) into an acrimonious dispute about who had pre-empted—or even plagiarized—whom.[54]

The second reason for Hobbes's troubled reaction to Descartes was that the metaphysics of the French philosopher seemed to be radically out of step with the proper assumptions of his physics. That Hobbes had already possessed distinctive ideas of his own on metaphysics before he read Descartes's book is indicated by the shrewd comment Digby made when he originally sent the *Discours de la méthode* to Hobbes: 'I doubt not but you will say that if he were as accurate in his metaphysicall part as he is in his experience [i.e. his account of physical phenomena], he had carryed the palme from all men liuing.'[55] In the Latin Optical MS, Hobbes attacked the dualism at the heart of Descartes's theory, challenging the idea that the mind could be affected by the motion of objects without itself being a physical object. 'Since vision is formally and really nothing other than motion, it follows that that which sees is also formally and strictly speaking nothing other than that which is moved; for nothing other than a body . . . can be moved.'[56] And in a set of 'Objections' to Descartes's *Meditationes*, commissioned and published by Mersenne in 1641, Hobbes broadened his attack on Cartesian metaphysics, suggesting that Descartes had failed to extricate his thinking from the assumptions of scholastic philosophy, with its hypostatized qualities, its degrees of reality of being, and its blurring of the distinction between existent beings (*entia*) and essences.[57] In general, therefore, Descartes's philosophy was more an irritant than a stimulant to Hobbes. The idea that transcending Cartesian scepticism became a major aim of Hobbes's philosophical work cannot be supported by anything in Hobbes's writings; his belief in the causal dependence of all ideas (including qualities and 'essences') on the physical properties of existing objects was part of the primary assumptions of his metaphysics, by which radical scepticism was simply precluded.

Hobbes's work on science and metaphysics was interrupted at the end of the 1630s by politics. A number of issues were prompting discussion of the 'absoluteness' of sovereign power during the final years of King Charles I's personal rule. Of these, the most famous was the Ship Money case of 1637, which raised the question of whether any limits could be set to the power of the king, given that his normal powers could be exceeded in exceptional circumstances, and that the

---

[54] Hobbes, *Correspondence*, I, Letters 29, 31–4.   [55] Ibid., I, Letter 27.
[56] Latin Optical MS, IV. 14 (Hobbes, 'Tractatus opticus', ed. Alessio, p. 207).
[57] *OL* V, pp. 249–74.

king might judge which circumstances were exceptional.[58] The Short Parliament of April 1640 (to which the Earl of Devonshire unsuccessfully tried to get Hobbes elected as MP for Derby) voiced its concerns on these issues before it was abruptly dissolved. As one speaker put it, 'if the Kinge be judge of the necessitye, we have nothing and are but Tennants at will'.[59] Four days after the dissolution of that parliament, Hobbes signed the dedicatory epistle of a treatise, *The Elements of Law*, in which he aimed to settle all such questions by working out the nature and extent of sovereign power from first principles. The dedication was to his patron, the royalist Earl of Newcastle; the principles contained in the work, Hobbes explained, 'are those which I have heretofore acquainted your Lordship withal in private discourse, and which by your command I have here put into method'.[60]

That this was a polemically pro-royalist work was obvious; as Hobbes plainly stated in one of its final chapters, the idea that subjects could maintain rights of private property against the sovereign was a claim that he had 'confuted, by proving the absoluteness of the sovereignty'.[61] But *The Elements of Law* was no mere polemical pamphlet. In it Hobbes had attempted to base his political principles on an account of human psychology that was compatible with (although not necessarily dependent on) his mechanistic physics. The reduction of 'reason' to instrumental reasoning was an important part of this psychological picture. Reason, on this view of things, did not intuit values, but found the means to ends that were posited by desire; desires might be various, but reason could also discover general truths about how to achieve the conditions (above all, the absence of anarchic violence) in which desires were least liable to be frustrated. By defining that which is 'not against reason' as 'right', Hobbes also made the transition to a different type of general truth: definitional truths about rights and obligations, which would make the claims of the anti-royalist politicians as necessarily false as those of incompetent geometers. For sovereignty to exist at all, Hobbes argued, it was necessary for all the rights of the subjects to be yielded to it; what he tried to show was that the reasons that made sovereignty necessary also made it absolute. This was a work of extraordinary assurance, an almost fully fledged statement of Hobbes's entire political philosophy. His two later published versions of his theory, *De cive* and *Leviathan*, would develop further some of the points of detail, but the essential lineaments would remain the same.

---

[58] The best modern account is K. Sharpe, *The Personal Rule of Charles I* (New Haven, Conn., 1992), pp. 719–30.
[59] On Hobbes's candidature, see Hobbes, *Correspondence*, I, Letter 58 n. 2; for the speech in parliament by Sir John Strangways, see E. Cope and W. H. Coats, eds., *Proceedings of Short Parliament of 1640*, Camden Society, 4th ser., 19 (London, 1977), p. 159.
[60] Hobbes, *The Elements of Law*, ed. F. Tönnies (London, 1889), pp. xv–xvi.
[61] Ibid., II. 8. 8 (p. 174).

*The Elements of Law* circulated in many manuscript copies, which, Hobbes later recalled, 'occasioned much talk of the Author; and had not His Majesty dissolved the Parliament, it had brought him into danger of his life'.[62] Possibly Hobbes was already thinking, during the summer of 1640, about going to live in Paris, for reasons of political safety and intellectual stimulus. Apart from the scientists he had met through Mersenne, an old friend of the Cavendish family was there: the French courtier Charles du Bosc, whom Hobbes had known in the 1620s, and who may have extended a general invitation to Hobbes when he visited England in 1638.[63] In September 1640 Hobbes recovered £100 which he had asked the steward of Chatsworth to invest for him; he also had £400 banked with the Cavendish family (at 6 per cent interest), so if he withdrew all his money on deposit he must have felt financially independent enough to embark on a long period of residence abroad.[64] What finally prompted him to leave England was a debate on 7 November in the newly convened Long Parliament, in which John Pym and other anti-royalists attacked 'Preaching for absolute monarchy that the king may do what he list'.[65] Fearing that he might be called to account for *The Elements of Law*, Hobbes fled to Paris.

## IV

Thanks to his connection with Mersenne, Hobbes was quickly absorbed into the intellectual life of the capital. Mersenne had acted as intermediary for the correspondence between Hobbes and Descartes, and it was Mersenne who (as mentioned above) commissioned Hobbes's 'Objections' to the *Meditationes*, which were published, in 1641, with five other sets of objections and Descartes's replies. Mersenne also arranged the publication of *De cive* in 1642, over the initials 'T. H.' This book, a remodelled version of the arguments of *The Elements of Law*, was much admired for the cogency and concision of its arguments about the nature of the state, but the reductive treatment of Christian theology in the final section of the work caused many eyebrows to be raised.[66] It was *De cive* that really established Hobbes as a political writer of European repute when it was reissued (in two further editions, with additional explanatory notes by Hobbes) by the Dutch printer Elzevir in 1647. Meanwhile Mersenne had also published some small samples of Hobbes's work on physics and optics in two volumes of scientific compilations

---

[62] Hobbes, *Mr Hobbes Considered*, p. 5 (*EW* IV, p. 414).
[63] See Hobbes, *Correspondence*, II, Biographical Register, 'du Bosc'.
[64] Chatsworth, MS Hobbes D 8 (£100); MS Hardwick 30, half-yearly payments for midsummer 1638. In these accounts, which go up to Michaelmas 1639, Hobbes was also receiving wages of £50 per annum from the Countess of Devonshire.
[65] Hobbes, *Correspondence*, I, Letter 35 n. 5.
[66] For a typical reaction, see A. L. Schino, 'Tre lettere di Gabriel Naudé', *Rivista di storia della filosofia*, 4 (1987), pp. 697–708; p. 707.

that he edited in 1644, *Cogitata physico-mathematica* and *Universae geometriae synopsis*.[67] And through Mersenne Hobbes became acquainted, in the early 1640s, with a number of French philosophers and scientists, including the anti-Aristotelian Pierre Gassendi, the mathematician and anti-Cartesian Gilles Personne de Roberval, the Huguenot physician Abraham du Prat, and two other younger Huguenots with scientific interests, Samuel Sorbière and Thomas de Martel.[68]

For most of the 1640s Hobbes was preoccupied with physics, metaphysics, and theology rather than political philosophy. In 1642–3 he wrote (probably at Mersenne's request) a huge blow-by-blow refutation of a scientific and theological work by the Catholic Aristotelian philosopher Thomas White. Mersenne studied this refutation in manuscript and may well have encouraged Hobbes to have it printed, but it was to remain unpublished until 1973. The *Anti-White* (as it is now generally called) is a strange work, written obviously in a great outpouring of ideas but having recourse to a mass of earlier notes and drafts. It is not surprising that Hobbes, who had set himself the task of arranging all such material methodically in his tri-partite 'Elements of philosophy', should have been reluctant to publish it in this haphazard and repetitive form. And it is clear, within the text of the *Anti-White*, that one of the topics that was giving him the most difficulty was the nature of scientific method itself. Two different models of scientific knowledge jostle for position: the knowledge of causes, and the knowledge of definitional meanings.[69] Hobbes made some unsatisfactory attempts to reconcile or unite these two models; possibly his own dissatisfaction with this aspect of his work was one reason for the slowness with which he drafted and redrafted his major work on logic, metaphysics, and physics, *De corpore*, throughout the 1640s.

Several fragmentary early drafts of this work (which was not published until 1655) survive, the most puzzling of which is a rough copy in another hand of a text that mixes English and Latin phrases. The traditional assumption that this was a semi-translation of Hobbes's Latin text by somebody else is probably false, since one whole section of the English reappears in a later English work by Hobbes. This draft was probably written in the years 1643–4; the material it contains was later used in chapters 7, 8, 11, and 12 of *De corpore*, but in this draft the material forms the opening chapters of the entire work.[70] The exposition begins here with

---

[67] See Hobbes, *Correspondence*, II, Biographical Register, 'Mersenne'.
[68] On Roberval see L. Auger, *Gilles Personne de Roberval* (Paris, 1962); on Gassendi, Abraham du Prat, Sorbière, and de Martel, see Hobbes, *Correspondence*, II, Biographical Register.
[69] See 'Hobbes's Science of Politics and his Theory of Science' (Ch. 5 below).
[70] This MS was referred to above at n. 49. The English passage (from the introductory section of the MS: Hobbes, *Critique du* De mundo, p. 449) appears in Hobbes's 'Answer' to the Preface to *Gondibert*: see W. Davenant, *Gondibert*, ed. D. F. Gladish (Oxford, 1971), p. 49; *EW* IV, p. 449. As Rossi noted, the MS also borrows a phrase from Sir Thomas Browne's *Religio medici*, which was published in London in 1642. If we assume that the English in the MS was Hobbes's own, an easy explanation of this link with Browne suggests itself: Sir Kenelm Digby, who had read Browne's book and written a reply to it in London in Dec. 1642, returned to Paris in July 1643 and may well have brought a copy of *Religio medici* with him. That Hobbes

Hobbes's 'annihilatory hypothesis', which asks the reader to consider the nature of ideas after the annihilation of the world that those ideas described. This was not a sceptical device, but a way of severing the connection between real being and 'essences' (which in Hobbes's view were nothing other than descriptions of existing things, with no ontological status of their own). Later drafts (an undated manuscript by Hobbes, and a closely related set of notes taken by Sir Charles Cavendish in 1645–6) inserted, before this material, a more traditional account of logic, explaining the functioning of terms, propositions, and syllogisms.[71] Through Sir Charles's letters to the mathematician John Pell, we get a sense of the trouble Hobbes had with this work. 'Mr Hobbes puts me in hope of his philosophie which he writes he is nowe putting in order', wrote Sir Charles in December 1644, 'but I feare that will take a long time.' And again, in May 1645: 'I doubt [i.e., suspect] it will be long ere Mr Hobbes publish anything . . . he proceeds every day some what, but he hath a great deal to do.'[72]

There were many interruptions to Hobbes's progress, and the arrival in Paris of Sir Charles and his brother in April 1645 was the cause of several of them. In the summer of that year Hobbes was encouraged by the Marquess (formerly Earl) of Newcastle to engage in a disputation with an exiled Anglican cleric, John Bramhall, over the nature of free will. The short treatise that Hobbes wrote was eventually published (without his authorization) as *Of Libertie and Necessitie* in 1654, and caused a long-running controversy with Bramhall on a range of theological matters. In late 1645 Hobbes composed, at the Marquess's request, a treatise on optics in English, half of which would eventually form part of *De homine* (published in 1658).[73] And in the summer of 1646, just when Hobbes was planning to leave Paris to work intensively on *De corpore*, he was asked to be the mathematical tutor to the young Prince Charles, who had arrived in July. The Marquess of Newcastle, who had been in charge of the prince's education in 1638, probably had a hand in this offer of employment. Hobbes did not need the job for financial reasons (two years later he was actually lending money to Newcastle), but it was not an offer he could refuse.[74] It brought him into closer contact with the politicians, courtiers, and churchmen who gathered at the Louvre and St Germain: men such as John

---

should have begun drafting *De corpore* at about this time is also plausible, since he had been occupied with *De cive* in 1641 and with the *Anti-White* in late 1642 and early 1643. However, the planning of *De corpore* was clearly more advanced by the time Sir Charles Cavendish took his notes on Hobbes's latest draft in 1645 (see below). Hence my dating of the National Library of Wales MS to 1643–4.

[71] On these MSS, see Pacchi, *Convenzione e ipotesi*, pp. 18–26; for a composite printing of the two, see Hobbes, *Critique du* De mundo, pp. 463–513.

[72] J. Halliwell, ed., *A Collection of Letters Illustrative of the Progress of Science in England from the Reign of Queen Elizabeth to that of Charles the Second* (London, 1841), p. 87; H. Vaughan, *The Protectorate of Cromwell*, 2 vols. (London, 1838), II, p. 364.

[73] The MS, known as the English Optical MS, is BL MS Harl. 3360.

[74] See Hobbes, *Correspondence*, II, Biographical Register, 'William Cavendish, first Duke of Newcastle' and 'Charles II'.

## A SUMMARY BIOGRAPHY

Cosin, the future bishop of Durham, and Henry Bennet, the future secretary of state Lord Arlington.

Given such contacts with royalist exiles, Hobbes's thoughts would naturally have turned more often in the later 1640s to the political situation in England. He maintained his friendship with the poet Edmund Waller, who was in exile in France after 1644; he became well acquainted with the poet Sir William Davenant (for whom he wrote a long commendatory letter, published in 1650, on his poem *Gondibert*), and he also kept in contact with Edward Hyde. Hobbes kept up some correspondence with the Earl of Devonshire in England, and he also wrote regularly to his old friend Robert Payne, who was ejected from his Oxford college in 1648 but remained in England.[75] In May 1650 Robert Payne learned about *Leviathan* for the first time, when Hobbes told him that he had completed thirty-seven chapters out of a projected total of fifty.[76] Clearly, Hobbes's work on this new book had been rather secretive and very rapid; he probably did not begin it until the autumn of 1649 (he told Sorbière in June of that year that he was working on *De corpore*, which he hoped to finish by the end of the summer), and he seems not to have mentioned it to Hyde when the latter saw him in Paris in August and September of that year.[77] By the time Hyde returned to Paris in April 1651, Hobbes was able to inform him that 'his Book (which he would call *Leviathan*) was then Printing in England, and that he receiv'd every week a Sheet to correct . . . and thought it would be finished within little more than a moneth'.[78]

That Hobbes went to the trouble of arranging the printing of the work in London confirms the essential validity of the joking remark he made to Hyde when the latter asked why he wanted it published: 'The truth is, I have a mind to go home.'[79] As recently as May 1648, when Hobbes had discussed the possibility of returning to England in a letter to the Earl of Devonshire, he had written: 'When I consider how dangerous a time there is like to be for peaceable men, I am apter to wish you on this side, then my selfe on that side the sea.' But he had qualified this reluctance even then: 'I haue no inclinations to the place where there is so little security, but I haue such inclinations to your Lo[rdshi]ᵖ as I will come to any place (if I may haue a passe) where your Lo[rdshi]ᵖ shall be.'[80] Thereafter things had

---

[75] See Davenant, *Gondibert*; Hobbes, *Correspondence*, II, Biographical Register, 'Waller', 'William Cavendish, third Earl of Devonshire', 'Payne'; E. Hyde, *A Brief View and Survey of the Dangerous and Pernicious Errors to Church and State in Mr. Hobbes's Book, entitled Leviathan* (Oxford, 1676), pp. 6–8.

[76] Payne to Sheldon, 13 May 1650 (BL MS Harl. 6942, no. 128).

[77] Hobbes, *Correspondence*, I, Letter 61; Hyde, *Brief View and Survey*, p. 7. In late Sept. or early Oct. 1649, Sir Charles Cavendish (who was now in Antwerp) received a letter from Hobbes, in which Hobbes made no reference to *Leviathan*, but said he hoped his 'philosophie' (i.e. *De corpore*) would be printed in the following spring: BL MS Add. 4278, fol. 291v (Cavendish to Pell, 5 Oct. 1649).

[78] Hyde, *Brief View and Survey*, p. 7. It was in fact published in London in the following month. The printing had been rapid; the work was entered in the Stationers' Register on 20 Jan. 1651.

[79] Hyde, *Brief View and Survey*, p. 8.     [80] Hobbes, *Correspondence*, I, Letter 58.

changed in England, with the execution of King Charles I in January 1649. Things had changed too for Hobbes in Paris. The death of Mersenne in September 1648 and the departure soon afterwards of Gassendi to the south of France meant that he was deprived of his two dearest philosophical friends.

It would, however, be too limited an explanation to say that Hobbes wrote *Leviathan* merely to ease his passage to England. Certainly he was keen—and entitled—to point out that his theory of political authority based on necessary consent (and necessary consent based on a rational understanding of ultimate self-interest) was not inherently pro-royalist (as the trappings of the argument in *The Elements of Law* and *De cive* might have made it appear to be). His argument, as *Leviathan* makes clear, was about sovereignty *per se*, which might be exercised by a king or an assembly; the shift in a subject's obligation from one holder of sovereignty to another would occur 'when the means of his life is within the Guards and Garrisons of the Enemy'—it then being rational to consent to obey the conqueror.[81] Such calculations of interest had been a living issue for people such as the Earl of Devonshire, who had had to compound with the parliamentary authorities for his estates. Sir Charles Cavendish had done the same in absentia for his estates in 1649, and would be persuaded by his brother and by Sir Edward Hyde to return to England in 1651 to renegotiate for them. A decade later, Hobbes would explain that he had written *Leviathan* on behalf of 'those many and faithful Servants and Subjects of His Majesty' who had been forced to compound for their lands. 'They that had done their utmost endeavour to perform their obligation to the King, had done all that they could be obliged unto; and were consequently at liberty to seek the safety of their lives and livelihood wheresoever, and without Treachery.'[82]

It was reasonable of Hobbes to assume that this element of his argument would not cause intolerable offence among the courtiers of the young Charles II in Paris. Another aspect of the book that might reasonably be brought to the new king's attention was its attempt to analyse the nature of the false beliefs and harmful political practices—above all, those of organized religion—that Hobbes believed to have caused the destruction of Charles's father's kingdom. So it is not surprising that Hobbes actually presented a manuscript fair copy of the work to Charles II when the latter returned to Paris after his defeat at the Battle of Worcester in September 1651. Nor is it surprising that the theological arguments of the work, especially its ferocious attack on the Catholic Church, caused grave offence to some of the English courtiers in exile, notably those who were close to the Catholic Queen Mother, Henrietta Maria. Hobbes was barred from the court; and not long afterwards, according to the recollections of both Hobbes and Hyde, the French

---

[81] Hobbes, *Leviathan*, p. 390.   [82] *Mr Hobbes Considered*, p. 20 (*EW* IV, pp. 420–1).

Catholic clergy made an attempt to have him arrested.[83] He fled from Paris in mid-December 1651 and soon thereafter crossed the Channel to England.[84]

## V

Hobbes settled in London, where he was able to make contact again with Sir Charles Cavendish, who had arrived there a couple of months earlier.[85] Soon he was back in the employment of the Earl of Devonshire and had reverted to the old rhythm of life of a noble household, spending the summer months in Derbyshire and much of the rest of the year in London. His work for the Earl probably amounted to little more than some light secretarial duties and general intellectual companionship; otherwise his time was his own. He spent some of it in the stimulating company of the lawyers John Selden and John Vaughan, and the physicians William Harvey and Charles Scarborough. Scarborough, a mathematician as well as a medical man, held gatherings of scientists at his London house which Hobbes sometimes attended. Hobbes was also moving in the more unorthodox and free-thinking circles of Thomas White (the Catholic philosopher whose *De mundo* he had refuted), John Davies (who published Hobbes's *Of Libertie and Necessitie* in 1654 with a bitterly anti-clerical preface), and John Hall of Durham (the educational reformer and apologist for Cromwell).[86] It was probably in Davies's circle that Hobbes met Henry Stubbe, a young Oxford scholar and radical anti-clericalist who began work—which he never completed—on a Latin translation of *Leviathan*.[87]

The notoriety that *Leviathan* obtained for Hobbes was slow in coming. Early readers of the book were understandably startled by some of its theological contents, but there was no immediate outcry. A typical judgement was that of the moderate Anglican bishop of Salisbury, Brian Duppa, who wrote to a friend in July 1651: 'as in the man, so there are strange mixtures in the book; many things said so well that I could embrace him for it, and many things so wildly and unchristianly, that I can scarce have so much charity for him, as to think he was ever Christian.'[88] That some of the theological arguments in *Leviathan* were phrased in such a way as to make them sound highly unorthodox is undeniable; Hobbes himself seems to have recognized this when he pruned some of them (notably the passage in which

---

[83] Ibid., p. 8 (*EW* IV, p. 415); Hyde, *Brief View and Survey*, pp. 8–9. See also the comments in Hobbes, *Correspondence*, II, Biographical Register, 'James Butler, twelfth Earl and first Duke of Ormonde' and 'Charles II'.

[84] Hyde recalled that Hobbes had fled a 'few daies' before his own arrival in Paris, which was on 25 Dec. (*Brief View and Survey*, p. 8; R. Ollard, *Clarendon and his Friends* (London, 1987), p. 148).

[85] Hobbes, *Correspondence*, II, Biographical Register, 'Sir Charles Cavendish'.

[86] See 'Hobbes and the Royal Society', Ch. 10 below.

[87] Hobbes, *Correspondence*, II, Biographical Register.

[88] G. Isham, ed., *The Correspondence of Bishop Brian Duppa and Sir Justinian Isham, 1650–1660*, Publications of the Northamptonshire Record Society, 17 (Northampton, 1951), p. 41.

he appeared to make Moses a member of the Trinity) from his later Latin translation of the work. It is also true that his application of historical method—and caustic common sense—to biblical criticism had yielded some results, such as the denial of Moses' authorship of the Pentateuch, which were unacceptable to ordinary belief. But Hobbes was probably correct in thinking that his work would not have received the vast amount of subsequent denunciation had it not been seen as threatening by a number of special-interest groups. Of these the most important were 'ecclesiastics' of various sorts—Catholic, Anglican, and Presbyterian—who saw that the basis of priestly or ministerial authority was undermined by Hobbes's arguments.

One particular interest group that Hobbes managed to offend was the universities. His attack on these institutions in *Leviathan* became suddenly topical when a proposal was made in the Barebones Parliament in 1653 to abolish them altogether.[89] Two of the leading scientists at Oxford, Seth Ward and John Wilkins, published a defence of the universities in 1654 that included a frosty reply to Hobbes; Ward (who had previously been an admirer of Hobbes, regarding him as a fellow exponent of the mechanistic new science) also published a full-length attack on Hobbes's philosophy and theology.[90] The publication of Hobbes's *De corpore*, which contained a number of incompetent attempts at geometrical proofs, made Hobbes an easy target for another Oxford scientist, the mathematician John Wallis. Hobbes became embroiled in a sequence of polemical exchanges on mathematical subjects with Wallis that would last for nearly twenty years. The real animus behind this feud, however, was their disagreement over church politics, with Hobbes regarding Wallis as the chief representative of the Presbyterians.

Since Hobbes had, by the late 1650s, acquired the enmity of three leading scientists, it is not surprising that there was some reluctance to enlist him in the Royal Society (as it later became) when it first met in 1660. But the basic reason for his exclusion was probably not just personal animosities; he had more personal friends than enemies among its membership, and there was no provision for black-balling in its elections of new Fellows. Nor was he less of a scientist than many of the active members of that body. Although his mathematical work was sometimes incompetent, his major works on physics and optics, *De corpore* (1655) and *De homine* (1658), were comparable to similar work by other scientific writers who did become Fellows of the Royal Society, and he continued to publish works on the explanation of natural phenomena, such as his *Problemata physica* (1662) and *Decameron*

---

[89] For the motion, see B. Shapiro, *John Wilkins, 1614–72: An Intellectual Biography* (Berkeley, Calif., 1969), p. 97.

[90] J. Wilkins and S. Ward, *Vindiciae academiarum* (Oxford, 1654); S. Ward, *In Thomae Hobbii philosophiam exercitatio* (Oxford, 1656). Ward's attack was less extreme than some others, however; he explicitly conceded (p. 340) that Hobbes was probably a theist.

*physiologicum* (1678). The underlying problem seems to have been that the aura of religious notoriety clinging to Hobbes meant that any public association with him would be a source of embarrassment to the active members of the Royal Society, given that his basic assumptions about a mechanistic physical universe were quite similar to their own. Many traditionalists still regarded such a world-view as leading inevitably to atheism; several key members of the Royal Society were highly sensitive to such criticism, and reacted in a pre-emptive and diversionary way by directing fierce criticisms of their own against Hobbes.[91]

Throughout the 1660s and 1670s Hobbes was frequently attacked, in print and from the pulpit, for his supposed atheism, denial of objective moral values, promotion of debauchery, and so on.[92] At its crudest, this sort of criticism depended on a popular notion of 'Hobbism' that had little to do with Hobbes's philosophical arguments and instead constituted a veiled attack on the libertinism of the Restoration court. Occasionally, however, there were more serious threats to investigate Hobbes's writings. In the early 1660s there was rumour that some Anglican bishops were planning to have Hobbes tried for heresy, and in 1666 a House of Commons committee was empowered to 'receive Informacion toucheing such bookes as tend to Atheisme Blasphemy or Prophanenesse or against the Essence or Attributes of God. And in particular ... the booke of M[r] Hobbs called the Leuiathan'.[93] Hobbes responded to the first of these threats by composing a treatise on the law of heresy (demonstrating that people should not be burned for that offence); on one or other of these occasions he was sufficiently worried to consign many of his own manuscripts to the flames.[94] In a number of writings during these final decades, Hobbes publicly defended himself against the criticisms of his conduct and beliefs. These defences include a short autobiographical work, *Mr Hobbes Considered* (1662); the dedicatory epistle to *Problemata physica* (also 1662); an important appendix to the Latin translation of *Leviathan* (1668), in which he defended the work from charge of heresy; an angry public letter of complaint about libellous remarks inserted by the Oxford academic John Fell into a short biography of him published in 1674; an autobiography in Latin verse (1679); and, among his posthumously published works, a further defence of *Leviathan* against Bishop Bramhall (1682) and a polemical church history in Latin verse,

---

[91] See Ch. 10 below; for two important and rather different interpretations, see Q. Skinner, 'Thomas Hobbes and the Nature of the Early Royal Society', *The Historical Journal*, 12 (1969), pp. 217–39, and S. Shapin and S. Schaffer, *Leviathan and the Air-Pump* (Princeton, NJ, 1985).

[92] For a useful general survey, see S. Mintz, *The Hunting of Leviathan* (Cambridge, 1962).

[93] BL MS Harl. 7257, p. 220. For the earlier rumour, see Aubrey, '*Brief Lives*', I, p. 339.

[94] For the treatise on the law of heresy, see S. Mintz, 'Hobbes on the Law of Heresy', *Journal of the History of Ideas*, 29 (1968), pp. 409–14; for its dating, see R. Willman, 'Hobbes on the Law of Heresy', *Journal of the History of Ideas*, 31 (1970), pp. 607–13. For the burning of manuscripts, see Aubrey, '*Brief Lives*', I, p. 339, and the letter from James Wheldon to Adam Barker printed in *The Gentleman's Magazine*, vol. 54, pt 2, no. 4 (Oct. 1784), p. 729.

*Historia ecclesiastica* (1688), which ends with a Hobbesian credo in praise of simple Christian virtues.[95]

These various publications (plus a number of other works on mathematics and complete translations into workaday English verse of Homer's *Iliad* and *Odyssey*) testify to the extraordinary vigour of Hobbes's old age. He was, after all, 63 when *Leviathan* was published, and he continued writing until his final year (aged 91). This productivity is all the more impressive when one remembers that the 'shaking palsy' (probably Parkinson's disease) from which he suffered was so severe that he was forced to dictate his writings to an amanuensis from late 1656 onward.[96] Hobbes continued to live with the third Earl of Devonshire, alternating between his London residence and his country houses, Chatsworth and Hardwick. The earl's patronage gave him protection and security. He benefited too from a resumption of friendly personal relations with his old pupil, Charles II, to whom Aubrey cleverly arranged a re-introduction in London soon after the Restoration. The king gave him—for a while—a generous pension of more than £100 per annum and ordered that Hobbes should have 'free access to his majestie'. Hobbes was able to use this privilege in 1674 to get permission to print his public letter of complaint against John Fell, after approaching the King in person 'in the Pall-mall in S$^t$ James's parke'.[97] But there were limits to the King's indulgence of his old tutor. Hobbes's request for permission to print his dialogue-history of the Civil War, *Behemoth*, was turned down; attempts to reprint *Leviathan* in 1670 were abruptly suppressed by the Stationers' Company.[98]

While Hobbes was generally vilified in print, he retained some loyal personal friends and admirers, such as the lawyer John Vaughan and the scientist and antiquary John Aubrey. But he must have felt that he was a prophet without honour in his own country when he compared his reputation in England with the glowing praise of his philosophical achievements that came from his many foreign correspondents. The circle of French scientists and writers who, after Mersenne's death, had clustered round Gassendi in Paris in the early 1650s (men such as Samuel Sorbière, Thomas de Martel, and Abraham du Prat) regarded Hobbes, after Gassendi's death in 1655, as the greatest living philosopher, and told him in their letters that they eagerly read every new work of his that they could obtain.[99] Even more adulatory was François du Verdus in Bordeaux, who learned English in order to translate *Leviathan* into French (a project that never saw the light of day,

---

[95] For details of all these works, see H. Macdonald and M. Hargreaves, *Thomas Hobbes: A Bibliography* (London, 1952).

[96] See Hobbes, *Correspondence*, I, Letter 94, and my comments in the General Introduction to that volume.

[97] Ibid., II, Biographical Register, 'Charles II'.

[98] Ibid., II, Letter 208; Macdonald and Hargreaves, *Thomas Hobbes*, p. 29.

[99] See their letters in Hobbes, *Correspondence*, I, II, and the entries in the Biographical Register in ibid., II.

although Hobbes seems at first to have encouraged it[100]). Samuel Sorbière was not only a talented self-publicist but also an energetic publicizer of Hobbes's works; and it was through Sorbière's efforts that a collection of Hobbes's Latin writings, including a Latin translation of *Leviathan* made specially for it by Hobbes, was finally published by the Dutch printer Blaeu in 1668.[101] This edition, together with frequent reprinting of *De cive* on the Continent, helped to transmit Hobbes's ideas to a wide range of readers, including Spinoza and Leibniz. The latter, indeed, was influenced more by Hobbes than by any other writer during his period of philosophical awakening late in the 1660s and early in the 1670s, and wrote to Hobbes to say so: 'I shall, God willing, always publicly declare that I know of no other writer who has philosophized as precisely, as clearly, and as elegantly as you have—no, not excepting Descartes with his superhuman intellect.'[102]

Hobbes died on 4 December 1679. He had been seriously ill since October and apparently suffered a severe stroke one week before his death. As the Earl of Devonshire's secretary wrote to the Oxford historian Anthony Wood, this prevented Hobbes from taking holy communion: 'but as I am informed by my Lords Chaplaine (a worthy Gent) he has severall times lately received the Sacrament of him ... And I did once see him receive it and received it my selfe with him, and then he tooke it with seemeing devotion, and in humble, and reverent posture'.[103] Hobbes was buried at the parish church of Hault Hucknall, near Hardwick Hall, under a tombstone with a modest inscription, apparently written by Hobbes himself: 'He was a virtuous man, and for his reputation for learning he was well known at home and abroad.'[104] Rumour had it that he had also considered a different inscription, one that would have reminded those who knew him of one of his personal qualities which is too seldom mentioned, but which no reader of his works can fail to discover: his splendid sense of humour. The proposed inscription was 'This is the true philosopher's stone.'

### ADDITIONAL NOTES

The study by Noel Reynolds and John Hilton referred to in n. 24 was published as 'Thomas Hobbes and the Authorship of the *Horae Subsecivae*', *History of Political Thought*, 14 (1994), pp. 361–80. Noel Reynolds later co-edited the items in question: T. Hobbes (attrib.), *Three Discourses: A Critical Modern Edition of Newly Identified Work of the Young Hobbes*, ed. N. B. Reynolds and A. W. Saxonhouse (Chicago, 1995). That

---

[100] Ibid., I, Letters 67, 100, 108. Du Verdus also prepared a translation of *De corpore*, which was not published, and a partial one of *De cive*, which was: see ibid., II, Biographical Register, 'du Verdus'.
[101] Hobbes, *Correspondence*, II, Letters 154, 156, 166, 169.
[102] Ibid., II, Letter 189.
[103] A. Pritchard, 'The Last Days of Hobbes', *Bodleian Library Record*, 10 (1980), p. 184.
[104] Aubrey, '*Brief Lives*', I, p. 386.

these discourses derive, if not from Hobbes, then from someone (Cavendish) who was personally and intellectually very close to him, is more or less certain; that Hobbes may have contributed some ideas or arguments to them appears very probable; but that Hobbes himself was the author still seems to me quite doubtful.

The dating of the composition of the 'Latin Optical MS' given here (see n. 50) was based on an argument about the date at which the surviving manuscript was copied (presented in Hobbes, *Correspondence*, I, pp. liii–lv). Prompted by recent research by Dr Timothy Raylor, I have reconsidered the evidence, and now conclude that the manuscript was copied in Paris between December 1640 and, at the latest, April 1643 (or, more probably, August 1642). The composition of the work itself may perhaps be assigned to 1640 or 1641. See T. Raylor, 'The Date and Script of Hobbes's Latin Optical Manuscript', and my 'Hobbes, the Latin Optical Manuscript, and the Parisian Scribe', both in *English Manuscript Studies*, ed. P. Beal and J. Griffith, 13 (2003) (forthcoming).

The 'undated manuscript by Hobbes' referred to in n. 71 is in fact a set of notes by Robert Payne on a draft of part of *De corpore*: see Chapter 4 below on 'Robert Payne, the Hobbes Manuscripts, and the "Short Tract"', esp. pp. 99–103.

# – 2 –

# Hobbes and Spinoza

## 1. Hobbes

When the Parliament sat, that began in April 1640, and was dissolved in May following, and in which many points of the regal power, which were necessary for the peace of the kingdom, and the safety of his Majesty's person, were disputed and denied, Mr Hobbes wrote a little treatise in English, wherein he did set forth and demonstrate, that the said power and rights were inseparably annexed to the sovereignty; which sovereignty they did not then deny to be in the King; but it seems understood not, or would not understand that inseparability. Of this treatise, though not printed, many gentlemen had copies, which occasioned much talk of the author and had not his Majesty dissolved the Parliament, it had brought him into danger of his life.[1]

Such was Hobbes's own account, written twenty-one years later, of the origins of his first work of political theory, *The Elements of Law*. Hobbes had himself been an unsuccessful candidate for election to the Short Parliament,[2] so no doubt he followed its proceedings closely. The disputed 'points of the regal power' emerged most pointedly in John Pym's famous speech of 17 April, which asserted fundamental constitutional rights of Parliament against the Crown ('Parliament is as the soule of the common wealth', 'the intellectual parte which Governes all the rest') and attacked 'the Doctrine that what property the subject hath in any thinge may be lawfully taken away when the King requires it'. The latter point was taken up by Sir John Strangways on the following day: 'for if the Kinge be judge of the necessitye, we have nothing and are but Tennants at will'.[3]

The King dissolved this parliament on 5 May. Four days later Hobbes signed the dedicatory epistle of his treatise, which was addressed to his patron, the staunchly royalist Earl of Newcastle; he explained that the principles he was expounding were

---

This chapter first appeared in *The Cambridge History of Political Thought, 1450–1700*, ed. J. H. Burns and M. Goldie (Cambridge, 1991), pp. 530–57.

[1] T. Hobbes, *The English Works of Thomas Hobbes of Malmesbury*, ed. W. Molesworth, 11 vols. (London, 1839–45) (henceforth *EW*), IV, p. 414.

[2] L. Beats, 'Politics and Government in Derbyshire, 1640–1660', Sheffield University Ph.D. dissertation (1978), pp. 74–6.

[3] E. Cope and W. H. Coates, eds., *Proceedings of the Short Parliament of 1640*, Camden Society, 4th ser., 19 (London, 1977), pp. 149, 155, 159.

'those which I have heretofore acquainted your Lordship withal in private discourse, and which by your command I have here put into method'.[4] The polemical purpose of the work is evident, and is reflected in its circulation in numerous manuscript copies, at least nine of which survive. (Three of them were written by scribes and signed by Hobbes: this suggests a form of clandestine publication by a production-line of copyists.[5]) Hobbes's argument was designed to show first of all that government by a civil sovereign was necessary, and secondly that the reasons which made it necessary also made the sovereignty absolute. He attacked those who 'have imagined that a commonwealth may be constituted in such a manner, as the sovereign power may be so limited, and moderated, as they should think fit themselves'; he sought to overturn the claim that the sovereign power can be 'divided' or shared between king and people, and (in a transparent reference to the recent proceedings in parliament) he denounced those who 'when they are commanded to contribute their persons or money to the public service . . . think they have a propriety in the same distinct from the dominion of the sovereign power'.[6] It was Hobbes's argument on this last point above all which made him fear for his life when the next parliament assembled in November and began its impeachment of Strafford.[7] Within a few days Hobbes fled to Paris, where he was to remain for eleven years; and it was there that he wrote his two other major works of political theory (*De cive*, printed in 1642, and *Leviathan*, printed in 1651), each of which in turn developed and added to the arguments of *The Elements of Law*.

That Hobbes's career as a political writer should have begun with a polemically royalist work in 1640 is, in biographical terms, not very surprising. His entire adult life, since his graduation from Oxford in 1608, had been spent in the service of aristocratic families as a tutor, secretary, and companion. Employed at first by the Cavendish family at Hardwick and Chatsworth, he had gained some experience of quasi-public affairs cooperating with the second Earl of Devonshire as an active member of the Virginia Company.[8] In 1629 (prompted, it has been suggested, by the Petition of Right of the previous year),[9] he had published a translation of Thucydides, who appealed to him for his dispassionate analysis of the ways in which democratic governments could be corrupted and manipulated. For most of the 1630s Hobbes was a tutor to the young third Earl of Devonshire; wardship over

---

[4] T. Hobbes, *The Elements of Law*, ed. F. Tönnies (London, 1889), pp. xv–xvi.
[5] These three MSS are: BL Harl. MS 4235; Chatsworth, Hobbes MSS A2B and A2A (which now lacks the dedication, but cf. the description in W. Todd, 'An Early MS of Hobbes's *Leviathan*', *Notes and Queries*, 218 (1973), p. 181.
[6] Hobbes, *Elements of Law*, II.i.13; II, viii.4.
[7] J. Aubrey, *'Brief Lives', chiefly of Contemporaries, set down by John Aubrey, between the years 1669 & 1696*, ed. A. Clark, 2 vols. (Oxford, 1898), I, p. 334; P. Zagorin, 'Thomas Hobbes's Departure from England in 1640: An Unpublished Letter', *Historical Journal*, 21 (1978), pp. 157–60.
[8] N. Malcolm, 'Hobbes, Sandys, and the Virginia Company': see Ch. 3 below.
[9] M. Reik, *The Golden Lands of Thomas Hobbes* (Detroit, 1977), p. 37.

the young Earl was exercised by his cousin, the Earl of Newcastle, who helped to awaken Hobbes's philosophical interests and no doubt his royalist sympathies.

*The Elements of Law* is not, however, simply a piece of royalist propaganda. Its importance lies in the way that it derives its political conclusions from a set of philosophical assumptions. Hobbes's philosophical awakening had taken place, it seems, during the 1630s when he had become preoccupied with an area of overlapping fundamental problems in physics, metaphysics, and epistemology. He had adopted enthusiastically the Galilean principle of the subjectivity of secondary qualities; this meant that a secondary quality such as heat did not inhere in a 'hot' object, but was a feature of the experience of someone perceiving that object, and could be causally explained in terms of the primary qualities which belonged to the object itself (such as the shape and motion of its particles). For Hobbes, this principle was a lever which could be used to overturn scholastic physics and metaphysics. He attacked the notion that the ultimate reality of physical things consisted in their intelligible 'forms' or 'essences'; scholastic philosophy had used this explanation to account for the way in which our process of sense perception begins with the action of physical causes (light acting on the eye, for example) but ends with an immaterial mental object in the intellect. Most medieval philosophers, drawing on a mixture of Aristotelian and Neoplatonist thought, had distinguished between physical existence and non-physical intelligibility ('esse existentiae' and 'esse essentiae'), and had subordinated the former to the latter in the order of real being. A tree physically existed by virtue of being an expression of the essence of a tree, and so the mind could abstract this essence from its perceptions of a tree's physical properties.

This view of the world as constituted by intelligible essences had usually also assumed that these essences were systematically related to each other in an economy of perfection: they all participated in absolute Being, which was unitary and was derived from (or was perhaps identical with) God. The rational order of the whole system could be described in terms of the laws of reason or laws of nature which governed all its parts. This way of describing things gave rise to a way of valuing them: a thing became better the more it fulfilled its essential nature, and thereby fulfilled its place in the whole system of essences. The more arboreal a tree was, the more it expressed its essential nature. Human beings also had an innate teleology to fulfil, but as rational beings they were conscious of their own ends and were able to direct their actions towards them. In Richard Hooker's words, 'A law therefore generally taken, is a directive rule unto goodness of operation . . . The rule of natural agents that work by simple necessity, is the determination of the wisdom of God . . . The rule of voluntary agents on earth is the sentence that Reason giveth concerning the goodness of those things which they are to do'.[10]

---

[10] R. Hooker, *Laws of Ecclesiastical Polity*, in R. Hooker, *Works*, 7th edn, 3 vols., ed. J. Keble, R. W. Church, and F. Paget (Oxford, 1888), I, p. 228.

Hobbes rejected this notion of reason intuiting natural teleological values, because he rejected the metaphysics and theology from which those values were derived. His most thorough attack on the old metaphysics came in a monumental refutation of a work by a Catholic Aristotelian, Thomas White; this refutation, which remained unpublished till 1973, was written in 1642–3. The fundamental principle from which Hobbes argued in this work was that of God's freedom to create the world if, how, and when he pleased,[11] a principle which severed any intrinsic connection between the natures of created things and the nature of God, and reduced 'essences' to mere descriptions of existing things.[12] These metaphysical assumptions can already be seen at work in an earlier manuscript, probably written between 1637 and 1640, in which Hobbes had asserted that 'the original and summ of Knowledge stands thus: there is nothing that truly exists in the world but single and individuall Bodyes producing single and individuall acts or effects'.[13] And in another early manuscript, probably also written in the 1630s, he had begun to apply these principles to the construction of a system of psychology in which all change was to be accounted for in terms of mechanical causation (the 'Short Tract').[14]

Scholastic psychology had explained the operation of desire, for example, in terms of the mind's apprehension of the 'form' or essence of the desired thing; Hobbes explained it in terms of a strictly causal process leading from sense-perception to the setting in motion of the body's 'animal spirits' (conceived of as a fine fluid in the nervous system), causing the body's motion towards the desired thing. The 'thought' of the desired object was simply that part of the sequence of motion which took place in the brain, where it might also interact with memory's store of residual motions from previous sense-impressions. Hobbes denied that the *feeling* of desire was a special kind of thought, and analysed it as a combination of having the mental image of the desired object and beginning to move towards it.[15] This idea of the 'beginnings of motion' became a key feature of Hobbes's psychology and physics; later described by him as 'conatus' or 'endeavour', it enabled him to reduce intentions to infinitesimal actions.

For Hobbes, reason neither participated in the nature of desire nor supplied any substantive knowledge of values. 'For the Thoughts, are to the Desires, as Scouts, and Spies, to range abroad, and find the way to the things Desired'.[16] Reason could only calculate means to ends, applying the merely formal principles of ratiocination to the brute facts of sense-experience and desire. The ends themselves were supplied by the causal mechanism of desire and aversion. Such a view of human

---

[11] T. Hobbes, *Critique du* De mundo *de Thomas White*, ed. J. Jacquot and H. W. Jones (Paris, 1973), chs. 30–4.
[12] Ibid., p. 381.
[13] M. M. Rossi, *Alle fonti del deismo e del materialismo moderno* (Florence, 1942), p. 102.
[14] Printed in Hobbes, *Elements of Law*, pp. 193–210.
[15] *EW* V, p. 261.
[16] T. Hobbes, *Leviathan* (London, 1651), p. 35.

nature might suggest that, even if one tried to move from 'is' to 'ought' by assigning value to the fulfilment of desire, one would still not be able to form any universal value system: values would be individual rather than general, refracted and fragmented into a number of conflicting egoisms. These is, as we shall see, a deep sense in which Hobbes's values *are* individual rather than universal, but it is not simply a matter of having an 'egoistic' moral psychology. Motivation in Hobbes's account is necessarily egoistic only in a nugatory, definitional sense: each person strives to fulfil his own desires. This does not mean that the contents of those desires cannot be concerned with the good of others. The definitions of the passions which Hobbes supplies in chapter 16 of *Leviathan* include '*Desire* of good to another, BENEVOLENCE, GOOD WILL, CHARITY. If to men generally, GOOD NATURE'.[17] It is true that Hobbes did tend to explain the passions in terms of self-interest, as when he wrote that '*Griefe*, for the Calamity of another, is PITTY; and ariseth from the imagination that the like calamity may befall himselfe';[18] but it is often unclear in such cases whether 'ariseth from' explains the feeling in the sense of analysing its true content or in the sense of pointing to its causal predecessor. The origin of many of these definitions is found in Hobbes's early summary of Aristotle's *Rhetoric*; Aristotle is often as ambiguous as Hobbes and almost as reductive. And when Hobbes translated *Rhetoric* 1369b18 as 'In summe, every *Voluntary Action* tends either to *Profit*, or *Pleasure*',[19] we can see that draining away Aristotle's teleology from his psychology can leave us with a very Hobbesian residue.

Hobbes's contemporary critics denounced him for arguing that men were naturally selfish and hostile towards one another. His reply was commonsensical: first, that, although men were sometimes benevolent, a state could not be founded on benevolence alone, and secondly, that, 'though the wicked were fewer than the righteous, yet because we cannot distinguish them, there is a necessity of suspecting, heeding, anticipating'.[20] A third reason, more important but less commonsensical and less directly stated, also emerges: the primary state of conflict between individuals posited by Hobbes is not a contingent, factual conflict, which might not exist if people ceased to be irascible or competitive, but rather a necessary jural conflict between people whose *rights* overlap or conflict in some sense with one another until they have been renounced.

In order to show that men can all agree on the need to pass from a state of conflict to a state of peace, Hobbes argues that it is possible to abstract a set of universal rules of human action from the contingent facts of conflicting individual desires. Individual desires are various and are constantly in motion, so they can be neither

---

[17] Ibid., p. 26; cf. B. Gert, 'Hobbes, Mechanism and Egoism', *Philosophical Quarterly*, 15 (1965), pp. 341–9; and B. Gert, 'Hobbes and Psychological Egoism', *Journal of the History of Ideas*, 28 (1967), pp. 503–20.
[18] *Leviathan*, p. 27.
[19] J. T. Harwood, ed., *The Rhetorics of Thomas Hobbes and Bernard Lamy* (Carbondale, Ill., 1986).
[20] T. Hobbes, *De cive: The English Version*, ed. J. H. Warrender (Oxford, 1983), p. 33.

consummated in the achievement of a final, systematic goal (Hobbes rejects the notion of a 'summum bonum' in this life), nor dispensed with by means of Stoic withdrawal. (When Hobbes characterizes life as a 'restlesse desire of Power after power',[21] he is not making the empirical observation that men are power-hungry, but is merely conjoining his view of life as motion with his definition of power as the 'present means, to obtain some future apparent good'.[22]) Only one desire can have any sort of priority over all other desires, namely the desire to avoid death; being alive is a necessary condition, the present means to all future apparent goods. Having established this one general truth over and above the mass of individual desires, Hobbes proceeds to draw from it a system of means towards the avoidance of death, providing a set of rules of action which all men must find valid if they reason correctly. The most important means towards self-preservation is peace, the establishment of stable and trustable social relations. And the optimum means towards peace can be formulated as 'Laws of Nature' or moral principles which will be immutably and eternally true. In this way Hobbes has performed the transition from the subjective and relative vocabulary of 'good' and 'evil' ('good' meaning 'object of desire') to an objective system of virtues and vices which can apply universally.

And therefore so long a man is in the condition of meer Nature, (which is a condition of War,) as private Appetite is the measure of Good, and Evill: And consequently all men agree on this, that Peace is Good, and therefore also the way, or means of Peace, which (as I have shewed before) are *Justice, Gratitude, Modesty, Equity, Mercy*, & the rest of the Laws of Nature, are good; that is to say, *Morall Vertues*.[23]

Hobbes has thus cleverly passed from 'is' to 'ought' almost without appearing to take upon himself the responsibility for using normative language: given that men use such language in an unreliable way to express their own desires, Hobbes offers a reliable, systematic use of it in the form of 'Laws of Nature' with which they must all agree. The laws are 'Conclusions, or Theoremes concerning what conduceth to the conservation and defence of themselves';[24] although usually framed conveniently as imperatives, they would be more correctly spelt out as theorems of the form: 'given that you desire to do x y and z, if you reason correctly you will also desire to do the following'. The laws of nature specify an optimum set of actions designed to bring about peace, the optimum condition for self-preservation. But there will also be occasions when obeying those laws will endanger an individual's life rather than preserve it (e.g. when facing a man of violence); in such circumstances the need for self-preservation will dictate breaking the laws of nature and responding with violence in self-defence. This entitlement to go against the laws of nature in order to fulfil the purpose which they serve is called the 'right' of nature. In chapter 14 of *Leviathan* Hobbes shows that both laws and right flow from the

[21] *Leviathan*, p. 47.  [22] Ibid., p. 66.  [23] Ibid., p. 80.  [24] Ibid., pp. 122–3.

same source, which he calls the 'rule' of nature: 'That every man, ought to endeavour peace, as farre as he has hope of obtaining it; and when he cannot obtain it, that he may seek, and use, all helps, and advantages of Warre'.[25] While the laws put forward a determinate set of actions, the right covers an indeterminate range of possible actions contrary to natural law; hence Hobbes's statement in the same chapter that 'RIGHT, consisteth in liberty to do, or to forbeare; Whereas LAW, determineth nd bindeth to one of them'.[26] But in any particular set of circumstances, when the right needs to be used, using it will be no less necessary than obedience to the laws normally is when they can safely be obeyed. Calling the right a 'liberty' does not mean that at critical moments of self-defence it is a matter of indifference whether the right be used or not; it connotes rather the right's nature as an 'entitlement' to act against the usual requirements of natural law.[27]

This account has so far been concerned with what might be called an internal valuation of men's actions: each man has to consider his own need for preservation, and this need generates a particular set of laws and a general right. In the state of nature, when conditions are always potentially hostile and the scope for acting in accordance with the laws of nature is reduced almost to vanishing point, all sorts of actions may be justified by the right of nature. But some actions will still not be justified by it, if they do not meet the internal standard of conduciveness to self-preservation. In an important note added to the second edition of *De cive*, Hobbes explained that wanton cruelty or drunkenness in the state of nature would not be covered by the right of nature.[28] Yet elsewhere Hobbes clearly stated that in the state of nature 'Every man by nature hath right to all things, that is to say, to do whatsoever he listeth to whom he listeth, to possess, use, and enjoy all things he will and can'.[29] This suggests a different use of the term 'right'; we might call it Hobbes's account of men's external rights, that is, their rights *vis-à-vis* other men, as opposed to his internal account of rights overruling laws in the system of actions for self-preservation.

The old undifferentiated notion of a right or 'ius' as 'that which is right' was still in the process of being broken up during this period;[30] although Hobbes was one of its main attackers, his own arguments are sometimes ambiguous because he uses the term in more than one way. His internal account of the right of nature made a procedural and categorical distinction between it and the laws of nature, but still

---

[25] Ibid., p. 64.   [26] Ibid.

[27] Hence it is not necessary to accept the argument of J. H. Warrender (*The Political Philosophy of Hobbes*, (Oxford, 1957)) that the laws of nature cannot be based on self-preservation because self-preservation is a right, and rights involve 'liberty to do, or to forbeare'. It must also be stressed that Hobbes's argument in *Leviathan* is not that men have a right to preserve themselves, but that they have a right to attempt to preserve themselves. On this important distinction see F. Viola, *Behemoth o Leviathan?* (Milan, 1979), pp. 88–9.

[28] Hobbes, *De cive: English Version*, p. 73.

[29] Hobbes, *Elements of Law*, II.xiv.10; cf. *Leviathan*, p. 64: 'this naturall Right of every man to every thing'.

[30] See R. Tuck, *Natural Rights Theories* (Cambridge, 1979).

conceived of it as an 'objective' right of the traditional kind, a way of justifying actions because in their particular circumstances they were *right* to do. Externally, however (in the field of interpersonal relations), Hobbes put forward a strong version of the modern 'subjective' notion of a right, a freedom or liberty of action which, far from being generated by any normative requirements, consisted of an absence of obligations. Hobbes was presupposing a sort of moral vacuum so far as interpersonal moral duties were concerned. This was a condition of his argument that the only standard by which an action could be judged to be wrong in the state of nature was the internal standard of conduciveness to self-preservation: in the state of nature there is no requirement to 'respect' the rights of others, no duty towards other people. To illustrate: if in the state of nature A snatches B's food, this action can never be judged to be wrong on the grounds that A has some duties towards B which he is thereby breaking. A has no duties towards him or anyone else, and therefore his (external) rights of action are total and all-encompassing. So the only standard by which the action can be judged to be wrong is the (internal) standard of conduciveness to self-preservation: by this standard A will have the right to snatch the food if his preservation requires it, but he will not have that right if he does not need the food and is merely increasing his chances of suffering retaliatory hostility.

Separating external and internal rights in this way helps us to see that, although the natural laws and natural rights concerned with preservation are in some ways similar to a traditional corpus of 'objective' rights and duties, they are still fundamentally different from any normal set of universalizable moral rules. These laws and rights are universal only in the sense that they are duplicated in every individual. Their derivation is essentially egoistic: each person may assign a value to modesty, humility, generosity, etc., but his reason must ultimately be that each quality has an instrumental value *to him*. The altruism which flows from obedience to natural law is, for Hobbes, a form of enlightened self-interest, and it can only be expected of individuals once they have joined together in the common security of the State.

There is a danger, in following Hobbes's account of the state of nature and the formation of political society, that the reader will begin to treat it as a literal, historical narrative. Hobbes presented it in this way for the sake of exposition, but willingly admitted of the state of nature that 'I believe it was never generally so, over all the world'.[31] He concluded that families in the state of nature were to a limited extent miniature political societies, because children could be deemed to have consented to obey their parents.[32] His own favourite example of a state of nature was that of the relations between sovereign states;[33] in a letter to a friend he also suggested, rather unsatisfactorily, that soldiers or travelling masons, who passed through various states but owed settled allegiance to none of them, might also be

[31] *Leviathan*, p. 63.   [32] Ibid., pp. 102–6.   [33] Ibid., p. 63.

thought of in this way.³⁴ But in essence the state of nature is the product of a thought-experiment in which Hobbes considers what rights of action and reasons for action men would have if there were no common authority to which they could turn to settle their disputes, or on which they could rely to give stability to their expectations of how other men would act towards them.

Conversely, when Hobbes describes the formation of political authority through a covenant, he is not tying his argument to a putative historical event, but trying to characterize the kind of commitment which members of society must have towards the political arrangement that they accept. Contract theories of the State have often taken a quasi-historical form because of the element of contingency which is one possible reason for appealing to the notion of a contract. Instead of marshalling general principles to prove that the political arrangement in question is the only just and proper arrangement that could have been made, contract theorists can argue that it is one of a number of possible arrangements, and that men are bound to this one simply by the fact that they have agreed to it. In some cases, notably that of John Selden, the contract theory of the State did have a genuine, though complex, historical character; on the question of when resistance to the government becomes justified, his maxim was that 'we must look to the contract', and this required the services of legal and constitutional historians (such as himself). More frequently, however, contract theory became an excuse for ahistorical arguments about what people 'must have' rationally contracted to do; in other words, a way of presenting *conditions* which ought to be deemed to be incorporated in any grant of power from people to government. Hobbes followed this ahistorical tendency, but with a radical difference: he used the notion of necessary consent as a lever to overturn all claims about implicit conditions or limitations of the rights of government.

Hobbes was able to do this because of the unitary nature of his foundation for natural law: self-preservation. The main Ciceronian and Thomist traditions of natural law saw self-preservation as the ground floor, so to speak, of a whole structure of human needs and values, and it was out of those higher-order values that rational contractarians could construct the implicit conditions which they thought were involved in the grant of power from people to government. In Hobbes's argument, self-preservation is a sheer need which takes precedence over other needs; that a subject should be preserved by his government is the only essential condition of his allegiance to it. Since, in Hobbes's theory, self-preservation could *in extremis* justify doing anything, the subjects must have granted their government the power

---

[34] This letter does not survive, but the reply of its recipient does, objecting that these two instances are not proper examples of the state of nature 'because this is only a war of each against each successively and at different times': Peleau to Hobbes, Bordeaux, 4 Jan. 1657 (Chatsworth, Hobbes papers, letters from foreign correspondents, letter 34: printed in Hobbes, *Correspondence*, I, pp. 422–5). I am grateful to the trustees of the Chatsworth Settlement for permission to cite this letter.

to do anything for the sake of their preservation. Their consent to this eliminated all scope for further 'conditions' or constraints.

It may still be wondered, however, whether Hobbes's account needed to use a concept of contract at all: in any argument which hinges on the phrase 'must have contracted', it is surely the reasons for saying 'must have' which are doing the real work. Hobbes's reasons are laid down in his laws of nature, which enjoin people to enter society, submit to arbitration, and so on. Indeed, the third law of nature is 'that men perform their Covenants made'.[35] If the reasons for obeying covenants are to be found in a system of prudential rules, why has Hobbes not drawn up his whole theory of obedience in terms of long-term benefits and dispensed with the notion of contract altogether? The answer must be that contract was only a formal device in Hobbes's theory, but a device which served some important subsidiary purposes. First, it enabled him to insulate the language of justice from the rest of the moral vocabulary: a sovereign government might be iniquitous—that is, it might break the laws of nature—but it could not be unjust, because injustice consisted of breach of contract. (In Hobbes's theory, the sovereign is not a party to the contract: the contract is between the subjects, who agree to hand over their rights and power to the sovereign.[36]) In a classic example of his reductive technique of argument, Hobbes dispensed with the traditional claims of distributive and commutative justice, reducing the former to equity and the latter to contractual justice.[37] The claim that rulers cannot be convicted of injustice had not been without polemical point in the England of 1640.

Secondly, Hobbes's theory requires people to renounce not only rights of action but also rights of judgement. Only the sovereign can judge what will be necessary for the preservation of peace in the State: if subjects claimed the right to judge this, they would be undermining the sovereign's role as final arbiter and frustrating the purpose for which a sovereign was instituted. (This too had had a topical relevance in the late 1630s, following the Ship Money case.) The notion of a covenant is a kind of shorthand for the type of commitment to obedience this requires, in advance of any knowledge of the contingencies of particular decisions by the sovereign.

The State forces its subjects to keep their covenant by annexing punishments to its laws. 'Covenants, without the Sword, are but Words, and of no strength to secure a man at all'.[38] But Hobbes is not arguing here that the desire to avoid punishment is the only motivation for obeying the laws. The prospect of punishment is a short-term consideration, necessary to concentrate the minds of passionate men, and thereby to create secure surroundings for those who do wish to keep their covenant. And there is always an adequate long-term consideration prompting this wish, namely the conduciveness to self-preservation of peace and stable government. Hobbes is sometimes associated with modern 'positivist' or 'realist' theories

[35] *Leviathan*, p. 71.   [36] Ibid., p. 89.   [37] Ibid., p. 75.   [38] Ibid., p. 85.

of law which explain the obligation to obey laws in terms of the motivation to avoid the punishments which those laws predict; but in Hobbes's theory there is thus always a further motive to obedience. This point comes out strongly in his criticism of the doctrine of 'passive obedience' in *Behemoth*, his history of the Civil War. 'Every law is a command *to do*, or *to forbear*: neither of these is fulfilled by suffering'.[39] Laws do not propose value-free alternatives of action leading to punishment and action leading to non-punishment; there is always a value attached to obedience to laws, because there is always a duty towards the legislator, whose continuing authority ensures peace.

Hobbes does, however, raise an apparent exception to this principle when he writes about 'the Obligation a man may sometimes have, upon the Command of the Soveraign to execute any dangerous or dishonourable Office'. Here he concludes: 'When therefore our refusall to obey frustrates the End for which the Soveraignty was ordained, then there is no Liberty to refuse: otherwise there is'.[40] This seems to transgress Hobbes's rule that only the sovereign can decide whether an action is necessary for the safety of the State. But, leaving aside the mention of dishonour (which is not fully supported by the rest of Hobbes's theory), it is clear that Hobbes is concerned here with the uncertain, probabilistic borderline at which the need to obey gives way to the need for self-preservation; the 'danger' referred to here is danger to the subject's life, and it was an immovable sticking point in Hobbes's theory that no one could ever covenant to kill himself.[41] In cases of capital punishment, Hobbes argued, the convict had a right to resist his gaolers and executioners. But it was also an important feature of his argument that at the same time the sovereign (who could commit no injustice) had a right to execute the man. The sovereign acted with the rights of the people, on their behalf.

The most striking formulation of this point comes in *De cive*, where Hobbes writes that 'The *People* rules in all Governments, for even in *Monarchies* the *People* Commands'.[42] He contrasted 'the people', which was the corporate entity created by the political agreement of its members, with the 'multitude', which was any mere aggregate of individuals. His intention was to undermine those who claimed to speak on behalf of 'the people' against their ruler, by showing that individuals gained a corporate identity only by virtue of being united under a sovereign. But since 'the people' was also the term which Hobbes used for the sovereign itself in the case of a democratic constitution, this argument had the probably unintended consequence that the foundation of any type of state had required a primary phase of democracy. In the quasi-historical accounts of *The Elements of Law* and *De cive* this is what happened, and the democracy then dissolved itself if it handed over sovereignty to a monarchy or an aristocracy:[43] even if the handover occurred at the

---

[39] Hobbes, *Behemoth*, ed. F. Tönnies (London, 1889), p. 50.   [40] *Leviathan*, p. 112.
[41] Ibid., p. 69.   [42] Hobbes, *De cive: English Version*, p. 151.
[43] Hobbes, *Elements of Law*, p. 121; *De cive: English Version* (1983), pp. 109–11.

first gathering of the people, the fact that it did so by majority vote would imply the momentary existence of a democratic constitution. Hobbes was obviously troubled both by the quasi-populist appearance of his argument in these works (as if democracy were somehow more natural), and by the theoretical awkwardness of identifying the corporate will of the State with an entity, 'the people', which apparently continued to exist after it had disappeared, like the grin of the Cheshire cat. In *Leviathan* he streamlined his account by treating the original majority principle as a necessary procedural assumption (rather than as a mini-constitution), and worked out a new way of describing the continuing corporate entity as the 'person' of the State. Together with this concept of a 'person', which was drawn from the legal fiction that corporations could act as persons at law, he employed the related legal vocabulary of 'authorizing' and 'representing': the sovereign (whether an individual or an assembly) represents its subjects because it is authorized to act as the bearer of their 'person', and they have a unitary 'person' only by virtue of being represented by a unitary sovereign.[44] Throughout his account, Hobbes allows that the sovereign may be an aristocratic council or a democratic assembly; although he gives reasons for preferring a monarchy,[45] the nature of the sovereignty is the same in each case.

The notion of authorizing is taken up again when Hobbes considers the sovereign's legislative action and permissive inaction. 'All Lawes, written, and unwritten, have their Authority, and force, from the Will of the Common-wealth; that is to say, from the Will of the Representative'.[46] Customary law thus has its validity not from any intrinsic force of its own, but from being 'authorized' by the sovereign, who could cancel it if he wished. (This was the starting point for Hobbes's attack on the claims of common law jurists in his *Dialogue . . . of the Common Laws of England*.) In a wider sense, all activities within the State are authorized by the sovereign so long as they are not forbidden. The State authorizes geometry professors to teach geometry just as it authorizes people to walk through public parks; this does not mean that everyone is acting on instructions from the State, and it does not mean that the sovereign authority is making the professors' geometry true, or obliging people to believe it. Of course, the range of things which *might* be forbidden by the State is almost unlimited; but Hobbes's theory supplies no reason for the State to use this power except for the preservation of peace and prosperity. It is in the sovereign's interest to allow individuals to pursue their own interests, because this produces a more contented and prosperous population: 'where the publique and private interest are most closely united, there is the publique most advanced . . . The riches, power, and honour of a Monarch arise onely

---

[44] *Leviathan*, pp. 80–3; see also R. Polin, *Politique et philosophie chez Thomas Hobbes* (Paris, 1953), pp. 229–40; M. Forsyth, 'Thomas Hobbes and the Constituent Power of the People', *Political Studies*, 29 (1981), pp. 191–203.
[45] *Leviathan*, pp. 95–8.   [46] Ibid., p. 139.

from the riches, power, and honour of his Subjects'.[47] Hobbes summarized his argument at one point in the *Elements of Law* by saying that it was the sovereign's duty by the law of nature 'to leave man as much liberty as may be, without hurt of the public'.[48]

Hobbes's apparently unobjectionable claims about the authorization of geometry teachers shadowed forth his argument on a much more contentious subject: the status of the Church within the State. He regarded the Church as a society of men engaged in teaching the doctrine of the Bible. The sovereign might authorize this teaching in the strong sense of endorsing as laws the injunctions to action which the teaching contained; or the sovereign could authorize it in the looser sense of permitting the activity of teaching. The distinction between belief and action was an important one: 'For internall Faith is in its own nature invisible, and consequently exempted from all humane [i.e. 'human'] jurisdiction'.[49] If the Church claimed an independent authority to direct the actions of men within the State, this was contrary to the unitary and absolute nature of civil sovereignty. The Church's own actions must be subject to the civil power, and those actions must include not only acts of worship but also writing and speaking. But Hobbes distinguished carefully between forbidding teaching and forbidding men to believe what they were taught: 'such Forbidding is of no effect; because Beleef, and Unbeleef never follow mens Commands'.[50] Provided that the Church did not claim independent rights of action, and provided that the doctrine it taught was not subversive to the peace of the State, Hobbes's theory allowed for a great degree of religious toleration. Ideally, the sovereign should have no more reason to interfere with the Church than with geometry lessons. Hobbes is only loosely to be described as an Erastian; he did not think that any strong connection between State and Church was necessary, and his theory permitted Roman Catholicism in England, for example, provided that it was understood that the pope appointed teachers of doctrine in England only on sufferance from the English sovereign.[51] After the Restoration, Church of England bishops such as Edward Stillingfleet and Samuel Parker used Hobbesian arguments to justify government action against the Dissenters, on the grounds that they were a threat to civil peace; but in some ways it was the Dissenters who were wielding the most centrally Hobbesain arguments when they said that religious beliefs should not be subject to civil compulsion.

The difficulty, of course, was that some versions of religious belief would not fit into Hobbes's scheme, because they did involve belief in rights of action or jurisdiction independent of the sovereign. Most varieties of institutional Christianity

---

[47] Ibid., p. 96; cf. J. A. W. Gunn, *Politics and the Public Interest in the Seventeenth Century* (London, 1969), pp. 65–81.
[48] Hobbes, *Elements of Law*, p. 178. [49] *Leviathan*, p. 285.
[50] Ibid., p. 271. [51] Ibid., p. 296.

taught beliefs of this sort, and Hobbes's arguments on this point are thus fiercely anti-clerical and above all anti-Catholic. But even within the Roman Catholic Church there were traditions of Marsilian and Gallican argument on which Hobbes could draw in his attack on papal power.[52] Within the Anglican Church, Hobbes was in some ways following in the tradition of rationalist religion, of writers such as William Chillingworth and Falkland at Great Tew. Hobbes agreed with them that the essential doctrinal truths contained in the Bible were few and easily knowable.[53] And in the third part of *Leviathan* he subjected the Bible to a more thorough course of rational textual criticism than had been attempted by any previous English writer. His aim was to show that scripture, far from demanding beliefs or actions contrary to those of his own theory, actually matched and confirmed his account of men's duties at every point. It may be tempting to describe this as a rather cynical *arrière-pensée* on Hobbes's part; but, equally, it can be described as a necessary consequence of his own theological position. His theology, as we have seen, severed all essential links between the nature of God and the nature of the world. Natural theology might arrive at the knowledge that God existed, but it could supply no further knowledge of his nature. Evidence of God's will could exist in the form of something historically contingent, such as the text of scripture; but in order to interpret this evidence, principles of interpretation had to be applied, and they could not be derived from the evidence itself. It was inevitable, then, that in interpreting the Bible men would use their natural reason and interpret away any aspect of it which appeared to conflict with the dictates of natural reason—dictates already arrived at in the first two parts of *Leviathan*. Hobbes's similarity to rational theologians such as Falkland was therefore only skin-deep. They read rational beliefs into the Bible because they felt they had substantive knowledge of the rational nature of God; Hobbes did the same because of his *lack* of knowledge of God's nature, which forced him to interpret the Bible in the light of human nature and human reason. Denounced and dismissed as an 'atheist', Hobbes countered with a reply which it is hard to gainsay: 'Do you think I can be an atheist and not know it? Or, knowing it, durst have offered my atheism to the press?'[54]

## 2. Spinoza

Outside England, the Dutch republic was the country where Hobbes's writings exerted their greatest influence. The conditions of intellectual life there were favourable to 'free-thinking', with a flourishing book trade on which regulation and censorship were comparatively lightly enforced. The second edition of *De cive*

---

[52] N. Malcolm, *De Dominis (1560–1624): Venetian, Anglican, Ecumenist and Relapsed Heretic* (London, 1984), pp. 82–3.
[53] Hobbes, *Leviathan*, pp. 325–6.     [54] *EW* VII, p. 350.

was printed there in 1647; a Dutch translation of *Leviathan* appeared in 1667; and an important collection of Hobbes's Latin writings, including his new Latin version of *Leviathan*, was published in Amsterdam in 1668.

Given its recent birth and the continuing uncertainty of some of its constitutional arrangements, the Dutch republic was a country in which basic questions of political theory were often of pressingly topical concern. Hobbes's pupil, the second Earl of Devonshire, had written about 'such as professe to reade Theorie of Statisme; fellows that swarm in most places abroad, especially in *Germany*, or those places where the *Dutch* most usually frequent, that nation being easie and apt to be gulled by these Imposters'.[55] The word 'Statisme' has overtones of *étatisme* and *raison d'état*. Where the internal workings of the State were concerned, this meant a value-free, comparative study of constitutions as power structures; where their external actions were concerned, it meant a study of all the tricks and devices of diplomacy and warfare—a study which could be amply justified by the dependence of Dutch foreign policy, throughout the seventeenth century, on kaleidoscopically shifting patterns of uncertain alliances. The leading academic exponent of this sort of power analysis was M. Z. Boxhorn, who taught at Leiden University from 1633 to 1653; he published an edition of Tacitus in 1643, and in his own political writings he used examples from Tacitus to show that rulers would always be impelled by self-interest to encroach on the liberties of their subjects.[56]

The history of the Dutch republic had also fostered public interest in another area of political controversy: the relation between religion and the State. The main patterns of argument had been laid down in the second decade of the century, when the Remonstrants (liberal theologians who followed Jacobus Arminius) had appealed to the civil powers to protect them against the hard-line Calvinist Counter-Remonstrants. Pro-Remonstrant writers, such as Grotius in his *De imperio summarum potestatum circa sacra* (written c.1614 and printed posthumously in 1647), had developed a theory of jurisdiction in which all power over human actions—including teaching, preaching, and acts of worship—had to be vested ultimately in the civil authority. Churches, in this theory, were regarded as voluntary associations within the State. The Remonstrants defended a policy of religious toleration by arguing that the Calvinist Church had no jurisdictional power to persecute, and by claiming that religion was essentially a matter of beliefs, not actions, thus implying that a variety of religious beliefs should pose no threat to the State's activities. There was a natural congruence between this attitude and the Tacitean view of religion, which regarded public religious observances as part of

---

[55] W. Cavendish, *Horae subsecivae* (London, 1620), p. 40.
[56] E.g. M. Z. Boxhorn, *Varii tractatus politici* (Utrecht, 1663), pp. 18–22; E. H. Kossman, 'Politieke theorie in het zeventiende-eeuwse Nederland', *Verhandelingen der Koninklijke Nederlandse van Wetenschappen, afdeling letterkunde*, n.s., 67 (1960), p. 20; H. Wansink, *Politike wetenschappen aan de Leidse Universiteit, 1575–c.1650* (Utrecht, 1981), pp. 93–100, 149–53.

the trappings, the psychological theatre, of the State, and therefore as something which must be controlled by the civil power. In the abstract, of course, these arguments did not dictate whether the civil power should be monarchical or republican. The contingencies of political history ensured that the Remonstrants and tolerationists sided with republicanism, while the supporters of the princes of Orange upheld the powers of the Calvinist Church. But these alignments were not quite accidental. For it was the republican theorists who, in their attempt to work out from first principles what the nature and powers of the State should be, came closest to developing a rationalist–utilitarian type of political theory from which the traditional categories of sacerdotal and ecclesiastical power were most likely to be absent.

By the mid-century, the influence of Descartes's philosophy in the Dutch academic world was giving a powerful impetus to the desire to replace traditional bodies of theory with new systems of deductive science. Cartesianism flourished at the Universities of Utrecht and Leiden, where its influence was strongest in the areas of medicine and physics. The anti-scholastic nature of Descartes's views on human psychology was taken further by Dutch Cartesians such as Henricus Regius and Gerard Wassenaar at Utrecht, who developed a more mechanistic, materialist philosophy of mind which denied the existence of innate ideas and described the mind as a 'mode' of the body. This was a version of Cartesianism which was ideally suited to the reception of Hobbesian theories too. And Hobbes's work, for Cartesians, could usefully remedy the lack of any political theory in Descartes's own writings. Lambert van Velthuysen, for example, who had studied at Utrecht in the 1640s, published defences of Descartes, Copernicus, and Hobbes, and in the preface to his 'apologia' for *De cive* he defended Hobbes's work as if it were a straightforwardly Cartesian enterprise: all previous attempts at political philosophy were flawed, he wrote, because they had not used 'this device of doubting everything', and had failed to deduce their various principles from one single starting point.[57]

All these strands of argument—reason of State, Tacitism, religious toleration, the defence of unitary civil power, republicanism, Cartesianism, and Hobbesianism —came together in the work of the most influential Dutch political writers of the 1650s and 1660s, the brothers Johan and Pieter de la Court. After the death of William II in 1650, and during the childhood of William III (who was born a few days after his father's death), most of the Dutch provinces found themselves operating a truly republican constitution for the first time, holding in abeyance the office of 'stadtholder' which had previously been filled by the princes of Orange. Under John de Witt, the quasi-presidential 'grand pensionary' of Holland, a vigorous campaign of republican propaganda was waged to persuade Holland and the

[57] L. van Velthuysen, *Epistolica dissertatio de principiis iusti et decori, continens apologiam pro tractatu clarissimi Hobbaei, De cive* (Amsterdam, 1651), sig. *5r.

## HOBBES AND SPINOZA

other provinces to abolish the office of stadtholder altogether. The brothers de la Court and Spinoza were among the most prominent writers to support him.

Both brothers had studied at Leiden in the early 1640s, where they had become Tacitists and Cartesians, and Pieter had gone on in 1645 to study medicine under Regius at Utrecht.[58] Johan may have been responsible for the unauthorized printing of some lectures by Boxhorn, the *Commentariolus*, in 1649: the work bears a suspicious resemblance to Johan's own notes on the lectures, which he heard in 1643.[59] And a more spectacular example of literary piracy was Pieter's publication, over his own initials ('V.D.H.': 'van den Hove', the Dutch equivalent of 'de la Court') of a book, *Naeuwkeurige consideratie van staet* (*A Close Examination of the State*), which was in fact written by that other pupil of Regius, Wassenaar.[60] Wassenaar's book seems to have given the de la Courts the idea of combining Tacitus and Machiavelli with a Cartesian theory of the passions, so that the task of political philosophy was seen as that of constructing the State as a mechanism to regulate the passions of individuals and force both rulers and ruled to identify their individual interests with the common good. And it was with this task in mind that the brothers de la Court turned eagerly to the writings of Hobbes.

The writings of the de la Courts form a homogeneous group of works, in which the same arguments keep reappearing.[61] 'Self-love is the origin of all human actions', begins the *Consideratien*.[62] 'Self-preservation is the supreme law of all individuals'.[63] Men are governed by their passions, and most men are therefore evil by

---

[58] T. van Thijn, 'Pieter de la Court: zijn leven en zijn economische denkbeelden', *Tijdschrift voor geschiedenis*, 69 (1956), pp. 309–15.

[59] Wansink, *Politike wetenschappen*, pp. 150–1.

[60] E. O. G. Haitsma Mulier, 'De *Naeuwkeurige consideratie van staet* van de gebroeders De la Court: een nadere beschouwing', *Bijdragen en mededelingen betreffende de geschiedenis der Nederlanden*, 99 (1984), pp. 396–407.

[61] The corpus of their works, however, poses many problems of individual attribution. Most of the major works appeared over the initials 'V.H.', 'V.D.H.', or 'D.C.', but other works that have been attributed to them appeared anonymously. Johan died in 1660; he is thought to have been largely responsible for the *Consideratien* of that year, which was expanded in subsequent editions by Pieter, and Pieter may well have quarried material from Johan's papers in putting together the other works of the 1660s. The major works are: *'t Welvaren der stad Leiden* (The Prosperity of the City of Leiden), MS dated 1659, ed. F. Driessen (Leiden, 1911); *Consideratien en exempelen van staat* (Observations and Lessons on the State) (Amsterdam, 1660; 2nd (expanded) edn published 1661 under the title *Consideratien van Staat ofte Polityke Weeg-Schaal* (Observations on the State; or, the Political Balance); 3rd edn (also expanded) and 4th and 5th edns published under this title, 1662); *Politieke Discoursen* (Political Discourses) (Amsterdam, 1662); *Interest van Holland* (The Interest of Holland) (Amsterdam, 1662; 2nd edn expanded with two additional chapters, possibly by de Witt, published 1669 as *Aanwysing der heilsame politike Gronden en Maximen van de Republike van Holland en West-Vriesland* (An Indication of the Salutary Political Principles and Maxims of the Republic of Holland and West Friesland). On other works by the de la Courts, see P. Geyl, 'Het stadhouderschap in de partijliteratuur onder de Witt', *Mededeelingen der koninklijke Nederlandsche akademie van wetenschapen*, afd. Letterkunde, n.s., 10 (1947), pp. 17–84.

[62] J. de la Court and P. de la Court ['V.H.'], *Consideratien en exempelen van staat, omtrent de fundamenten van allerley regeringe* (Amsterdam, 1660), p. 1.

[63] P. de la Court ['D.C.'], *Politike discoursen handelde in ses onderscheide boeken, van steeden, landen, oorlogen, kerken, regeeringen, en zeeden* (Amsterdam, 1662), p. 91.

nature; without a political power to keep them in check they will lead a diffident and violent existence in a 'state of nature', each judging partially in his own cause.[64] People are equal by nature, and only the State, an artificial human construct, has introduced inequalities.[65] Once the State is established, the subjects owe it a debt of gratitude for their protection; and they are justified in rebelling only when their individual lives are threatened.[66]

Thus far, the Hobbesian overtones are obvious. The 1660 *Consideratien* shows a close familiarity with *De cive*, and the later editions suggest a reading of *Leviathan* as well. But this is a version of Hobbes from which all the jural categories—rights, covenants, authorization—have been stripped away. For Hobbes, the essential conflict in the state of nature is a conflict of *rights*. For the de la Courts, it is a conflict of passions; there is thus no qualitative distinction between men's relations in the state of nature and their relations in civil society. 'All obedience is caused by compulsion'.[67] Each individual wishes to live according to his own will:[68] this principle means that force is required to get any individual to live according to the will of another, and it also means that rulers will constantly be trying to extend their wills more fully over their subjects.

As a result of this line of argument, the problems of constitution-building assumed a central place in the work of the de la Courts. For Hobbes, the nature of an individual's covenantal commitment to obey the sovereign power would be the same, regardless of the constitutional form which that sovereign power assumed. The arguments in favour of monarchy in *De cive* and *Leviathan* thus have a purely secondary status in Hobbes's overall theory. But for the de la Courts the primary problem was to design a constitution which could keep the encroaching wills of both rulers and ruled in check. Monarchy was the least attractive solution, because any individual entrusted with power was likely to use it for his private benefit.[69] Government by a large assembly was better, because in such a gathering the divergent private passions would tend to cancel each other out;[70] and, since the basic urge of each individual was to live according to his own will, any more or less democratic system would enable individuals to obey the will of the government and at the same time obey their own will, which was a component of the government's will.[71] If this sounds like a version of consent theory, then it is a version quite unlike Hobbes's: this version does not explain the nature of sovereignty, but is confined to one type of constitution. It merely gives a democratic government a psychological advantage which may, in effect, increase the amount of power which the government can wield.

---

[64] de la Court and de la Court, *Consideratien*, pp. 1–8.   [65] Ibid., p. 346, mispaginated '246'.
[66] Ibid., p. 347, mispaginated '247'; de la Court, *Politike discoursen*, p. 27.
[67] de la Court, *Politike discoursen*, p. 29.   [68] de la Court ['D.C.'], *'t Welvaren der stad Leiden*, p. 10.
[69] de la Court and de la Court, *Consideratien*, pp. 13–74.   [70] Ibid., p. 203, mispaginated '103'.
[71] Ibid., p. 353, mispaginated '253'.

These considerations may prompt the conclusion that the de la Courts owed little to Hobbes beyond their starting point in mechanistic psychology. But there was one important area of their argument which did draw directly on Hobbes's political theories: their views on the unitary nature of sovereign power and the relation which this implied between Church and State. The State, they argued, must have power over all external acts, and therefore over all acts of religious worship. To further the interests of both rulers and ruled, it must exercise this power for purely secular ends, namely peace and prosperity. Hence the need to tolerate all religions which are not themselves subversive of the State.[72] And for the subject, mere outward conformity is sufficient.[73] The peculiarly Hobbesian twist to this argument is the insistence that 'the public determination of what is good and what is evil belongs only to the sovereign: otherwise the political state will change, through the conflict of many private judgements, into a state of nature'.[74] This argument struck at the moral jurisdiction of the Calvinist Church, and was accompanied by some thoroughly Hobbesian jibes against the deleterious effects of clerical power on intellectual life.[75]

The late 1650s and early 1660s saw numerous attempts by the Calvinists to reassert their moral and intellectual jurisdiction. Pressure was brought to bear on the university authorities at Leiden to curb the teaching of Cartesianism and 'the application of philosophy to the prejudice of theology';[76] the anti-clericalism of the de la Courts' writings provoked a storm of sermons and pamphlets;[77] and in Utrecht, where the Hobbesian philosopher van Velthuysen had penned similar attacks on clerical power in 1660 (*Ondersoeck* and *Het predick-ampt*), the leading anti-Cartesian, Gisbertus Voetius, wrote a major defence of the jurisdictional powers of the Calvinist Church (*Politia ecclesiastica*, 1663). In 1665 a brief but important treatise attacking the Calvinist arguments, *De jure ecclesiasticorum* (*The Right of the Clergy*), was published under the pseudonym 'Lucius Antistius Constans'. This work, which was once attributed to Spinoza himself, draws so heavily on the arguments of the de la Courts that it can quite plausibly be attributed to Pieter de la Court;[78] but it goes beyond the de la Courts' other published works in its attempt to assimilate the jural concepts of contract and 'jus' ('right'). It distinguishes between right and power, but observes that the former without the latter is worthless.[79] Differences of right within the State are created by the power of the State; and the State's power arises either through the conquest of the weak by the strong,

---

[72] de la Court, *Politike discoursen*, pp. 19–24.   [73] Ibid., pp. 69–74.
[74] Ibid., p. 24.   [75] Ibid., pp. 36–41.
[76] P. C. Molhuysen, ed., *Bronnen tot de geschiedenis der Leidsche Universiteit*, 7 vols. (The Hague, 1913–24), III, pp. 109–12.
[77] H. A. E. van Gelder, *Getemperde vrijheid* (Groningen, 1972), p. 253.
[78] E.g. by A. van der Linde, *Benedictus Spinoza: bibliografie* (The Hague, 1871; reprinted Nieukoop, 1961), p. 16.
[79] Ibid., pp. 54–5.

or through a social contract, whereby people transfer their 'right and power' to the ruler.[80] Just as the notion of 'right' is weakened, in the course of this argument, by its constant association with 'power', so too the notion of contractual obligation is absorbed into the pattern of factual power relations: the 'conventio' ('agreement') can be entirely implicit, something to be identified 'not in words but in deeds'.[81]

This is the background against which we must situate Spinoza's own writings on the nature of the State. It was in 1665 that Spinoza started work on what was to become his major political treatise, the *Tractatus theologico-politicus* (henceforth cited *TTP*), aiming, as he explained to one correspondent, to defend 'the freedom of philosophizing . . . for here it is always suppressed through the excessive authority and impudence of the preachers'.[82] And when the work was published in 1670, he explained that he had been prompted by the 'fierce controversies of the philosophers in church and state'.[83] His library contained copies of the de la Courts' *Polityke Weeg-Schaal* (the enlarged second edition of the *Consideratien*) and *Discoursen*,[84] and he described the former work as 'extremely shrewd'.[85] If Pieter de la Court was not the author of *De jure ecclesiasticorum*, then the most likely candidate is Lodowijk Meyer, a Cartesian doctor and theologian who was a close friend of Spinoza.[86]

The anti-clerical, tolerationist, republican writings of the 1660s form the main background to Spinoza's political works; but of course his own personal history had also given him cause to consider the relation between religion, State power, and individual freedom. Baruch (Benedictus in Latin) de Spinoza was the son of a Portuguese Jew; born in Amsterdam in 1632, he was educated at a Jewish school up to the age of thirteen, and probably attended a *yeshivah* (a society for the study of the Bible, the Talmud, and the Torah) for several years thereafter.[87] But in 1656 he was excommunicated from the synagogue for 'the horrible heresies which he taught and practised'; the exact nature of his offence is not known, but all the evidence suggests that he had propounded a rationalist, deist theology which demoted the status of the Bible as divine revelation, questioned its historical accuracy, and probably cast doubt on the immortality of the soul.[88] According to some early

---

[80] E.g. by A. van der Linde, *Benedictus Spinoza: bibliografie* (The Hague, 1871; reprinted Nieukoop, 1961), pp. 9–12.

[81] Ibid., p. 35.

[82] B. de Spinoza, *The Correspondence*, ed. and tr. A. Wolf (London, 1928), p. 206, letter 30.

[83] B. de Spinoza, *Tractatus theologico-politicus* (henceforth *TTP*), in *Opera*, ed. C. Gebhardt, 4 vols. (Heidelberg, 1924), III, p. 9.

[84] J. Freudenthal, *Die Lebensgeschichte Spinoza's in Quellenschriften, Urkunden und nichtamtlichen Nachrichten* (Leipzig, 1899), pp. 161–2.

[85] B. de Spinoza, *Tractatus politicus* (henceforth *TP*), VII. 31.

[86] Spinoza, *Correspondence*, p. 50; K. O. Meinsma, *Spinoza en zijn kring, over Hollandse vrijgeesten* (The Hague, 1896), pp. 146–50.

[87] Meinsma, *Spinoza*, pp. 58–65; A. M. Vaz Dias and W. G. van der Tak, *Spinoza mercator & autodidactus: oorkonden en andere authentike documenten betreffende des wijsgeers jeugd en diens betrekking* (The Hague, 1932), pp. 56–61.

[88] I. S. Revah, *Spinoza et le Dr Juan de Prado* (Paris, 1959).

sources, he wrote a thoroughly unapologetic 'Apology' after his excommunication, which contained an historical critique of the Bible and a wide-ranging attack on the Jewish religion.[89] If this is so, then it is reasonable to assume that some of this material was put to use in the *Tractatus theologico-politicus*. However, the main outlines of the political theory in that book are drawn not from debates within Judaism but from the Dutch Hobbesian–republican tradition. Even the lengthy discussions of the Old Testament in that treatise may also owe something directly to Hobbes: although Spinoza did not read English, he was a friend of the man who was translating *Leviathan* into Dutch in the period 1665–7, and he may also have had time to benefit from the Latin translation of *Leviathan* (1668) before finishing the *Tractatus theologico-politicus* in 1670.[90]

The main arguments of the treatise are succinctly summarized by Spinoza himself. He argues first that philopophy and theology are radically different in nature, 'and that the latter allows each person to philosophize freely';[91] then 'that rights over religion belong entirely to the sovereign, and that external acts of worship must be adapted to serve the peace of the state';[92] and finally that freedom of speech 'is not only compatible with civil peace, piety and the right of the sovereign, but in fact ought to be permitted in order to preserve all those things'.[93] The separation of philosophy and theology is carefully managed, in a way which preserves an apparent respect for the special nature of revelation while at the same time suggesting that it is ultimately unnecessary. Philosophy can teach both virtue and the knowledge of God (these two things being inseparable in Spinoza's theory); theology, on the other hand, which is based on revelation, aims only at teaching obedience to God.[94] For this purpose the teachings of the Old Testament were 'adapted' to the understandings of ordinary people of the time: the validity of a theological doctrine lies not in its truth but in its power to instil obedience.[95] Only gradually does Spinoza make it plain that obedience is an inferior substitute for understanding, that the principal contents of revelation—prophecy and miracles—are fictions adapted for weak minds which cannot understand that God works in nature by means of immutable laws, and that the peculiar injunctions given to the Jews in the Old Testament were essentially political devices, designed to further political obedience and social cohesion. Some of these arguments may have derived from Moses Maimonides' theory of divine law, which stressed that divine commands were adapted to historical conditions in the Old Testament, and suggested that the dietary and ceremonial laws were simply devices for instilling moral

---

[89] J. Préposiet, *Bibliographie spinoziste* (Paris, 1973), pp. 345, 417.
[90] C. W. Schoneveld, *Intertraffic of the Mind: Studies in Seventeenth-Century Anglo-Dutch Translation with a Checklist of Books Translated from English into Dutch, 1600–1700* (Leiden, 1983), pp. 8, 40.
[91] *TTP*, ch. 16; *Opera*, III, p. 189.   [92] Ibid., ch. 19; *Opera*, III, p. 228.
[93] Ibid., ch. 20; *Opera*, III, p. 247.   [94] Ibid., chs. 7, 14, 15.
[95] Ibid., ch. 14; *Opera*, III, pp. 176–7.

virtues—virtues which could in principle be arrived at philosophically, without the use of revelation.[96] But Spinoza's comments on the use of religion as an instrument of political power also reflect his careful reading of Tacitus and Machiavelli.

This is particularly apparent in his account of the Jewish state in chapter 17 of the treatise, where he implies that when the Jews made God their sovereign they were in fact being cleverly manipulated by Moses, who became their effective ruler as God's representative on earth. Since religion is such a powerful force in human psychology (combining love, fear, and admiration—the last two of which are the products of defective understanding), this pseudo-theocracy was a very successful form of covert monarchy; but Moses' system of government was flawed, Spinoza argues, because it allowed the Levite priests to retain a form of religious jurisdiction, and in later generations they were able to assume political power and reduce the Jewish nation to civil war.[97]

Spinoza's theory of the nature and purpose of political power is set out in the *Tractatus theologico-politicus* (especially chapter 16) and in the first six chapters of his later, unfinished work, the *Tractatus politicus*. Like the de la Courts, he starts with the assumption that men are passionate creatures, guided by short-term self-interest; as they become more rational they will be guided by longer term self-interest, but self-interest remains the key to all human actions.[98] Social cooperation is necessary for leading a secure and pleasant life. The more rational a man is, the more he will desire cooperation because he understands this; but political power, wielding coercive force, is needed to keep irrational men from pursuing their own short-term interest against the interests of society at large. And, since rulers as well as ruled will be subject to passions, constitutions must be designed to ensure that subjects and rulers will subordinate or assimilate their own interests to the interests of the whole state.[99] In the *Tractatus politicus* Spinoza intended to show how this could be achieved in each form of constitution (monarchy, aristocracy and democracy); unfortunately, he died before completing his section on democracy, which he held to be the natural and most rational of the three forms. Like the de la Courts, he argued in the *Tractatus theologico-politicus* that the subjects of a democracy would enjoy a greater sense of freedom, because in obeying the sovereign they were obeying themselves;[100] and he also followed the de la Courts in claiming that the process of decision-making in a large assembly would cancel out individual passions and ensure the prevalence of reason.[101]

Thus far, Spinoza's theory seems confined to the bare analysis of motivation and power structures. Much of the interest of his theory, however, lies in the way in

---

[96] M. Maimonides, *Ethical Writings*, ed. and tr. R. L. Weiss and C. Butterworth (New York, 1975), pp. 71–2; M. Maimonides, *The Guide for the Perplexed*, ed. and tr. M. Friedlander (London, 1904).
[97] *TTP*, ch. 18.   [98] Ibid., ch. 17; *Opera*, III, pp. 215–16.   [99] Ibid., ch. 17; *Opera*, III, p. 203.
[100] Ibid., ch. 16; *Opera*, III, p. 195.
[101] Ibid., ch. 16; *Opera*, III, p. 194; on his debt to the de la Courts in *TP*, see E. O. G. Haitsma Mulier, *The Myth of Venice and Dutch Republican Thought in the Seventeenth Century* (Assen, 1980), pp. 187–208.

which he assimilates the concepts of 'right' and 'contract' into his argument. He makes use of the concept of 'right', but identifies it completely with 'power'. This is not a piece of casual cynicism on his part: it flows from the heart of his philosophical theology, which attributes both infinite right and infinite power to God, and identifies the physical universe as an expression of God's nature. It follows from this that every event in the physical world is an expression both of God's power and of His right. 'Whatever man does, whether he is led to do it by reason or only by desire, he does it according to the laws and rules of nature, that is, by natural right'.[102] Where Hobbes argued both that natural rights were all-encompassing and that there were some actions (contrary to self-preservation) which people did *not* have the right to perform, Spinoza can argue both that men have the right to do whatever they can do, and that an order of preference can be established when considering alternative courses of action: actions which help ensure the agent's self-preservation will increase his right because they increase his power, so that in some sense he will have less right to perform those actions which diminish his power.

Just as Spinoza uses the term 'right' but reduces it to 'power', so too he uses the term 'contract' but reduces it to a relationship of power. In chapter 16 of the *Tractatus theologico-politicus* he describes, in terms reminiscent of *De cive*, how people must have transferred their natural right to the sovereign through a 'contract' ('pactum' or 'contractus'). In the later *Tractatus politicus*, this account of a contract is notably absent: the notion of 'agreement' ('consensus') is used instead, and men are said to 'come together' to form a state not because they are led by reason, but because they are driven by common passions.[103] This has led some commentators to suggest that Spinoza believed, in the earlier work, in an historical contract which the founders of society had entered into out of 'rational foresight', and that he later abandoned this belief.[104] Yet the real differences between the two accounts are not so great. A transfer of right, as the earlier work has already made clear, can only amount to a transfer of power, and this is something which can come about without 'rational foresight' playing any special role. Spinoza emphasizes in the *Tractatus theologico-politicus* that 'a contract is binding only by reason of its utility';[105] as soon as it becomes advantageous for someone to break his contract, he will have the right to do so. This means that men keep their contract of obedience only because the sovereign wields real power. Such a view is entirely compatible with the idea that the origins of the State go back not to a set of formal articles of agreement but to a gradual coalescence of human power relations. When Spinoza introduces the idea of a contract in chapter 16 of the *Tractatus*

---

[102] *TP*, II.5; *Opera*, III, p. 277.  [103] Ibid., VI.1; *Opera*, III, p. 295.
[104] A. G. Wernham, 'General Introduction' to B. de Spinoza, *Political Works*, ed. A. G. Wernham (Oxford, 1958), pp. 25–6.
[105] *TTP*, ch. 16; *Opera*, III, p. 192.

*theologico-politicus*, he says, in a revealing construction, that men 'must have' contracted;[106] the notion of a contract is nothing more than a device for describing a power relationship which is informed by an understanding of mutual benefit, and to describe such an arrangement as rational does not imply that it can only have been introduced through a conscious act of reason.

Spinoza seems to have adopted, at this point in the earlier treatise, a Hobbesian terminology of 'transferring' natural rights, because he wanted to make the Hobbesian anti-clerical point that *all* rights belonged to the sovereign. (This was the first stage of his tolerationist argument, aimed at removing the jurisdictional powers of the clergy which would otherwise be deployed against freedom of opinion). At one point he says that the subject must have 'completely yielded' his natural right.[107] But this is a misleading form of words for Spinoza to use, and it can only amount to saying that the subject is sufficiently motivated to act always in complete accordance with the will of the sovereign. For each person, in Spinoza's theory, retains natural right so long as he retains natural power: when asked by a friend to explain the difference between his theory and Hobbes's, he replied that it 'consists in this, that I ever preserve the natural right intact, so that the Supreme Power in a State has no more right over a subject than is proportionate to the power by which it is superior to the subject'.[108]

This is the essential argument which enables Spinoza to conclude that the toleration of religious and philosophical opinions is both compatible with the sovereign's power and beneficial to it. In Spinoza's State the power of the sovereign can rise or fall, according to how the subjects become more or less fully motivated to obey it. More power, and therefore more right, inheres in a policy which is popular: it is in the interests of the sovereign to avoid alienating his subjects. Laws forbidding beliefs are, as Hobbes pointed out, fatuous; but Spinoza adds that laws forbidding people to express their beliefs will render those people sullen and hostile, and thereby weaken the power of the State.[109] Only the preaching of seditious doctrines must be proscribed; all opinions which do not disturb the peace of the State are to be allowed.

Despite, or perhaps because of, his reductive style of power analysis, Spinoza seems possibly to have arrived at a liberal, pluralistic theory of the State which matches the liberal elements of Hobbes's theory. It is possible to argue that the role of the Spinozan State is simply to provide an external framework of peace and security within which individuals can continue to pursue their own interests.[110] Such an interpretation, however, ignores the implications of Spinoza's metaphysics and psychology. His major exposition of these subjects, the *Ethics*, was completed concurrently with the writing of the *Tractatus theologico-politicus* in the second half

---

[106] *TTP*, ch. 16; *Opera*, III, p. 191.    [107] Ibid., ch. 16; *Opera*, III, p. 195.
[108] Spinoza, *Correspondence*, p. 269.    [109] *TTP*, ch. 20.
[110] D. J. den Uyl, *Power, State and Freedom* (Assen, 1983), esp. pp. 111–28.

of the 1660s, and he referred to the *Ethics*, implying that it was part of the same systematic body of theory, in chapter 2 of the *Tractatus politicus*.[111] Only from the *Ethics* do we learn just how radically different Spinoza's metaphysics were from Hobbes's, and therefore how completely his theory of reason and his theory of human liberty differed from Hobbes's too.

In Spinoza's metaphysics, all reality is comprehended in God, who is the only substance, that is, the only absolutely self-subsistent being. God is knowable through an infinite number of 'attributes', of which only two are actually known to us: extension and thought. A human body is a 'mode' (i.e. a modification, a particular entity) of extension, and a human mind is a mode of thought. There is a strict parallelism between these modes of different attributes: neither can act causally on the other, but each is an expression (in a completely different dimension, so to speak) of the same component of the divine substance. Thus, a human mind is the 'idea of' a human body; the development of the mind and the development of the body will consist of the same development being manifested in different forms.

Physical bodies exist in an order of causes; thought exists in an order of reasons or implications. The human mind, being the idea of the human body, contains the ideas of the experiences which the body undergoes. If the mind fails to understand these ideas 'adequately' (that is, if it fails to recognize the way in which each is implicitly part of the whole system of the divine substance), then it experiences an impairment of power, a passive emotion, or 'passion' (e.g. fear). But if the cause or reason is understood adequately by the mind, then the mind is exercising and enlarging its power of action, and the passion is transformed into an active emotion (e.g. love). All active emotions are ultimately forms of the love of God, because they derive from acts of understanding which involve relating particular things to the totality of things, which is God. The more active the mind is—the more, in other words, it 'contains' the causes of its action within itself—the more free it is. Spinoza is a classic exponent of the rationalist theory of freedom,[112] and therefore lies at the opposite pole from Hobbes's view of freedom as the absence of impediment.

In Part IV of the *Ethics* Spinoza explains that, while passions are individual and particularizing, reason is universal and harmonizing. 'Men can be opposed to each other in so far as they are afflicted with emotions which are passions';[113] 'men necessarily agree with one another in so far as they live according to the dictates of reason'.[114] This 'agreement' is a real harmonizing and converging of minds, not just an attitude of liberal non-interference: as Spinoza wrote in his early *Short Treatise*, if I teach knowledge and the love of God to my neighbours, 'it brings forth the same desire in them that there is in me, so that their will and mine become

---

[111] *Opera*, III, p. 276.   [112] cf. *TP* II. 7.
[113] Prop. 34; *Opera*, II, p. 231.   [114] Ibid., prop. 35, dem.; *Opera*, II, p. 233.

one and the same, constituting one and the same nature, always agreeing about everything'.[115]

Although in his metaphysics he rejected teleology in the strict sense, Spinoza's account of reason as the defining feature of the 'human essence' gives rise to a quasi-teleological scale of values for mankind: man fulfils his nature more fully when he acts rationally. Such a theory could not be further removed from Hobbes's view, in which reason is simply the servant of the desires. Even the apparent agreement between the two writers on the primacy of self-preservation is removed by Spinoza's argument that a man's true self, his 'power of acting', is his reason.[116]

The aim of Spinoza's State is to make men rational and free. 'When I say that the best State is one in which men live harmoniously together, I mean a form of life ... which is defined above all by reason, the true virtue and life of the mind'.[117] Spinoza recognizes that the State must be constructed to contain those who are not predominantly rational and virtuous; but the State can aim gradually to mould its citizens into a more rational kind of existence by imposing rational laws on them. In very general terms, we might say that the history of republicanism in political philosophy presents two fundamentally different defences of republican government. There is a mechanistic type of theory, which sees the construction of a republic as the solution to the problem of organizing and balancing a mass of conflicting individual forces; and there is the rationalist–idealist type of theory, which believes that in a republic men are freed from the corrupting ties of dependence on or subjection to personal authority, and are enabled to participate most fully as rational beings in the rationality of the State and its laws. Spinoza manages to combine both types of theory in a single system: that is the distinction, and the ambiguity, of his achievement.

## ADDITIONAL NOTES

The manuscript published by M. M. Rossi (see n. 13) probably dates from a slightly later period than the one assigned to it here; some reasons for assigning it to 1643–4 are given in Chapter 1 above, 'A Summary Biography of Hobbes', n. 70.

The 'Short Tract', assigned here to Hobbes (see n. 14), is probably by Robert Payne: see 'Robert Payne, the Hobbes Manuscripts, and the "Short Tract"' (Chapter 4 below).

My description of the 'yeshivah' attended by Spinoza (at n. 87) was described by one reviewer as a 'howler'. In subsequent correspondence it became clear that this reviewer was quite unfamiliar with some of the standard works on Judaism in seventeenth-century Amsterdam—including the work I referred to in the note, by Vaz Diaz and van der Tak, which gives a detailed explanation (summarized by me here) of how the term 'yeshivah' was used in that particular time and place.

[115] XXVI.4; *Opera*, I, p. 112.
[116] *Ethics*, part 4, prop. 52, dem.; *Opera*, II, p. 248.  [117] *TP*, V.5; *Opera*, III, p. 296.

# – 3 –

# Hobbes, Sandys, and the Virginia Company

## I

The early years of Thomas Hobbes are almost entirely sunk in obscurity. Biographers from George Croom Robertson (1886) to Miriam Reik (1977) have added little, for the period before 1628, to the scant information provided by Aubrey and the Latin *Vitae*. If to this we add the handful of details which have been gleaned by modern scholarship, the picture remains a bare one, and one that can be briefly summarized.

On leaving Oxford in 1608, Hobbes was employed by William, Lord Cavendish, as a tutor for his son, who was Hobbes's junior by two years. Within a few years, Hobbes and his pupil (who, to prevent confusion, will henceforth be referred to simply as 'Cavendish') went on a grand tour of Europe, the chronology of which remains uncertain.[1] Between 1615 and 1628 Cavendish corresponded with Fulgenzio Micanzio, whose letters Hobbes appears to have translated from the Italian.[2] It has also been claimed, though on much more dubious grounds, that Hobbes was involved in the composition of the volume of essays entitled *Horae subsecivae*, which was published anonymously in 1620, and of which a prior version is preserved in manuscript with a dedication by 'W. Cavendisshe' to his father.[3] Little can be added to these facts up to 1629 (the year which saw the publication of Hobbes's translation of Thucydides, following the death of his pupil–patron), except Aubrey's account of the connexion with Bacon, and one letter written to Hobbes in 1622 by Robert Mason, who appears to have regarded him as a well-placed source of political gossip. At the start of his letter, Mason encouraged Hobbes to carry on 'communicating with your friend such occurrences of these active times,

---

This chapter was first published in *The Historical Journal*, 24 (1981), pp. 297–321.

[1] See the appendix to this chapter.
[2] Discussed by Vittorio Gabrieli in 'Bacone, la riforma e Roma nella versione Hobbesiana d'un carteggio di Fulgenzio Micanzio', *The English Miscellany*, 8 (1957), pp. 195–250.
[3] Friedrich Wolf, *Die neue Wissenschaft des Thomas Hobbes* (Stuttgart, 1969); see also the appendix below.

as your vacant hours from your most serious affairs shall permit you'.[4] What exactly these 'most serious affairs' were has not been determined.

Clearly, the nature of Hobbes's employment in the Cavendish household gradually changed from that of a tutor to that of a secretary, as his pupil developed a political career at court and in parliament. A legal document drawn up for Cavendish's widow in 1639 describes Hobbes as 'having been Secretary to her Husband, & served him 20 years . . .'.[5] Hobbes himself leaves the impression that their association was close and cordial.[6] So it is simply surprising that no one seems hitherto to have looked for traces of Hobbes's involvement in what was, for several years, the most important and time-consuming business interest of his pupil–patron, namely the Virginia Company. The extant records of the Company have been meticulously edited by Susan Kingsbury, and they include a copy of the Court Book which gives minutes of, and lists of attendance at, the meetings of the Court of the Company. In the account of the Court held on 19 June 1622, we find the following: 'It pleased the Right Hono$^{ble}$ the Lord Cauendish to passe ouer one of his shares of land in Virginia vnto M$^r$ Hobbs w$^{ch}$ beinge allowed of by the Auditors was also approued and ratified by the Court.'[7] And having thus gained membership of the Company, 'Mr Hobbs' (or 'Hobs' or 'Hobbes') is mentioned in the lists of attendance at no fewer than thirty-seven meetings in the following two years.[8] The Christian name is never specified (Miss Kingsbury leaves a blank for it in the index to her volumes), but every aspect of the evidence encourages one to identify this 'Mr Hobbes' with Cavendish's secretary, Thomas Hobbes.

The attendance of 'Mr Hobbes' never occurs in the absence of Cavendish, except during the period, from July 1623 to February 1624, when the latter was politically under a cloud after trying to circumvent the royal ban on duelling. Furthermore, on the one occasion when Hobbes's name appears in the list of those who voted for a particular issue, he is found to be voting with Cavendish.[9] Further evidence can be found in a document preserved among an important (and, it seems, hitherto unnoticed) group of Ferrar papers in Magdalene College, Cambridge. The document is a list of shareholders in the Somer Islands Company, which was

---

[4] F. Tönnies, 'Contributions à l'histoire de la pensée de Hobbes', *Archives de philosophie*, 12, cahier 2 (1936), p. 81.

[5] Quoted by Douglas Bush, 'Hobbes, William Cavendish and "Essayes"', *Notes and Queries*, n.s. 20 (1973), p. 163, n. 1; the document has not been published.

[6] Cf. the eulogy of Cavendish in the epistle dedicatory to the translation of Thucydides, and the description of this period in the verse autobiography: 'Huic ego servivi bis denos gnaviter annos; / Non Dominus tantum, verum et amicus erat./Pars erat illa meae multo dulcissima vitae, / Et nunc saepe mihi somnia grata facit.' *OL* I, pp. lxxxviii–viii.

[7] *Records of the Virginia Company of London*, ed. S. M. Kingsbury, 4 vols. (Washington, DC, 1906–35), II, p. 40.

[8] That is, including the separate notices of the Courts of the Somer Islands Company, which are only irregularly reported in the Court Book. Hobbes's name is also given in a separate report of an extraordinary meeting of the Court of that Company, printed by Kingsbury in *Records*, IV, pp. 43–8.

[9] Kingsbury, *Records*, II, p. 159.

an independent but largely subsidiary company responsible for the settlement of the Bermudas. The shareholders' names are divided principally into two numbered lists, representing the opposing factions in the company; a third group of names is headed 'thise men are doubtfull w^ch side'. In the column which begins with the Earl of Southampton, Cavendish is no. 3 and 'M^r Hobs' is no. 24.[10] The only other occurrence of Hobbes's name in the published records, apart from in the lists of attendance, is at a Court of the Somer Islands Company, following the reading of a list of grievances sent by some of the colonists. 'At length it was desired that the Co^rt would appoint some to drawe vp an answere, & that a coppy thereof might be sent to y^e Ilands. Wherevpon the Co^rt nominated Mr Deputy & M^r Hobbs who are desired to drawe it vp & present it to the Co^rt.'[11] Drafting documents is exactly the sort of work in which one would expect a tutor-turned-secretary to be engaged (and one might suspect him to have had a hand also in the document presented by Cavendish in April 1623, 'w^ch discourse his Lo^p said himselfe had drawne vp . . .').[12] The reply to the colonists' petition, presumably drawn up, as requested, by Hobbes and John Ferrar, has been preserved among the new group of Ferrar papers mentioned above. Unfortunately it is not signed, and the handwriting (which is certainly not John Ferrar's) does not resemble Hobbes's later hand. Nevertheless, this document may represent, in part at least, the earliest surviving work of Thomas Hobbes.

But the most compelling evidence for the purposes of identification is that of the original grant of land on 19 June 1622.[13] In the arguments that accompanied the dissolution of the Company two years later, there were frequent accusations of vote-packing by the grant of shares to friends, relatives and retainers. Sir Nathanael Rich, a major opponent of Cavendish in the Company, complained of filling the Court with 'a number of friends, allies and confidants ready to assist with their votes'.[14] His accusation was firmly based on fact; and although Hobbes was clearly more than just a vote in Cavendish's pocket, it was merely sensible, in the internal politics of the Company, to introduce members loyal to one's party by grants of single shares, given that the voting was by head-count only and not according to the size of each individual's stake in the Company.[15]

---

[10] This document, which is in the handwriting of John Ferrar, is endorsed 'Names of y^e Adventurors to y^e Summer Ilands Divided Feb: 1623'. I am most grateful to the Master and Fellows of Magdalene College for permission to consult these MSS, and to Dr Richard Luckett for having drawn my attention to them.

[11] Kingsbury, *Records*, IV, p. 48; Ferrar papers 1371. 'Mr Deputy' was John Ferrar.

[12] Kingsbury, *Records*, II, p. 351.

[13] The grant is also recorded in a document among the new group of Ferrar papers, listing transfers of shares; the entry for 'June 19' includes 'Lo. Cauendish to M^r Hobbs—1.'. Hobbes's name is given in two other lists of shareholders among these papers.

[14] Quoted by W. F. Craven, *The Dissolution of the Virginia Company* (Oxford, 1932), p. 275.

[15] In this connection one thinks, for example, of the innumerable relatives of Sir Edwin Sandys, and of Cavendish's own brother-in-law, who was made a member of the Company in May 1623. Alexander Brown prudently steers clear of this issue: 'I cannot here attempt to discuss . . . the motives which are said to have influenced the Sandys party in admitting so many new members': *The Genesis of the United States* (London, 1890), II, p. 983.

## II

The history of the Virginia Company up to its dissolution in 1624 has frequently been told; a brief sketch of its final years must suffice here.[16] Up to 1619, the office of Treasurer (that is, head of the Company) was held by the London merchant, Sir Thomas Smythe, but in April of that year he was unseated by Sir Edwin Sandys, who was supported, in his criticism of Smythe's management of the Company's finances, by a group which included his brother, Sir Samuel Sandys, John and Nicholas Ferrar, the Earl of Southampton, Sir Edward Sackville, Sir John Danvers, Sir Dudley Digges, and Cavendish. Royal intervention in the election of 1620 to prevent the re-election of Sandys led to the choice of Southampton in his place (while John Ferrar, who had become Sandys' deputy in 1619, remained in office); the policies of the new treasurer remained those of Sandys, who continued to play a leading role in the Company. But, despite considerable and to some extent misdirected efforts by the Sandys–Southampton administration to boost the economic growth of the colony, the Company found itself in increasingly great financial difficulties. These were exacerbated first when the Company's licence to raise funds from lotteries was terminated in March 1621, and secondly when the colony suffered the Great Massacre of 1622. In that year Sandys and Southampton became bogged down in negotiations with Cranfield for a 'tobacco contract', which was to be a mixture of import monopoly and tax farm, and it was as a result of the arguments which arose from this project that the privy council decided, at the end of 1623, to demand the surrender of the Company's patent. The final struggle of the Company against this demand lasted into 1624.

Prominent among Sandys's opponents in the Company were not only Sir Thomas Smythe and his son-in-law, Alderman Johnson (whose petition to the King in April 1623 first prompted the investigation of the Company by the privy council), but also the adherents of Robert Rich, Earl of Warwick, who had originally helped Sandys to oust Smythe, but who had soon aligned himself with the latter as a result of several quarrels and conflicts of interest with the Sandys group. So great was the hostility felt on each side that at one Court of the Somer Islands Company in July 1623, Warwick accused Cavendish of lying, whereupon Cavendish, who had been arguing heatedly in support of Sandys, challenged Warwick to a duel.[17] (They were both apprehended before they could meet, in Holland, to fight it out.) It is clear that Warwick and Smythe had more influence

---

[16] For general accounts see H. L. Osgood, *The American Colonies in the Seventeenth Century*, 3 vols. (New York, 1904–7), I, and C. M. Andrews, *The Colonial Period in American History*, 4 vols. (New Haven, Conn., 1934), I. The Company's finances are summed up in W. R. Scott, *The Constitution and Finance of English, Scottish and Irish Joint-stock Companies to 1720*, 2 vols. (Cambridge, 1910–12), II, and the best account of the final years is Craven, *Dissolution*.

[17] No minutes of this Court have survived. The evidence comes mainly from Chamberlain and other indirect sources: see Craven, *Dissolution*, pp. 308–10.

at the King's court than did Sir Edwin Sandys; but it would be wrong to attribute to the sinister intriguing of 'a court party' what was in fact the genuine concern no doubt felt by James and his council, and by Sandys' opponents, that the affairs of the Company should be taken in hand to save the colony from ruin.

Nevertheless, even when one has removed all the accretions of American patriotic historiography—when one has ceased to suppose that the dissolution of the Company was masterminded by Gondomar, or to regard James I as a proto-George III, and when one has attempted to reduce everything to conflicts of interest or to differing views of the economics of colonization—the fact remains that Sir Edwin Sandys *was* regarded with suspicion by the King and his council, and the Company under his direction was tarred with the brush of his own record of criticism and opposition in parliament. Three of Sandys's sons were later to become colonels in the parliamentary army; one of his close associates in the Company, Sir John Danvers, was actually to become a regicide. Such later facts as these may have no place in the story of the Virginia Company, but they do perhaps serve to explain why Hobbes, in Restoration England, remained silent about his own place in that story. In retrospect, the Virginia Company must have seemed, to Hobbes, tainted with anti-royalism. The bitter remarks about merchants in *Behemoth* thus take on a special significance: '. . . those great capital cities, when rebellion is upon pretence of grievances, must needs be of the rebel party: because the grievances are but taxes to which citizens, that is, merchants, whose profession is their private gain, are naturally mortal enemies; . . . most commonly they are the first encouragers of rebellion . . .'.[18]

Without attempting to judge the 1620s in terms of the Civil Wars, we may nevertheless be intrigued by the thought that Hobbes's introduction to the world of politics took place among politicians such as Sandys, Digges, and Danvers, whose sympathies lay, in general terms, with Country against Court, Common Law against Chancery, and parliamentary privilege against royal prerogative. One could falsely exaggerate the degree of Hobbes's later reaction against this milieu, if one supposed that the constitutional role of parliament, within which these men conducted their opposition and criticism, could not be accommodated within the Hobbesian idea of the 'sovereign': there is nothing in *Leviathan* to support such a supposition. But Hobbes surely did react against their political ideas, which were based, at times quite explicitly, on 'natural rights' which were thought to be both prior to and independent of political society, and derivable intuitively from natural law.

The leading member of this group, in parliament as in the Virginia Company, was Sir Edwin Sandys. No full-length study of his politics has ever been published, though there is at least one copious source of evidence in the records of the

[18] *EW* VI, pp. 320–1.

parliament of 1621.[19] Throughout this parliament we find Sandys working hand-in-hand with Coke; but, while Coke criticized actions on the grounds that they were unsupported by or contrary to precedent, Sandys framed his criticisms in terms of Natural Law. His views on the role of precedent were expressed on 5 May 1621, when he quoted the maxim, 'deficiente lege recurrendum est ad consuetudinem, deficiente consuetudine ad rationem naturalem'.[20] Three days later Sandys went further than this: 'For a President is nothing but an example of the like case before. To take away then this ground of Contention for presidents is the way to Compose this difference and to disavow all presidents. Where reason is new no man will dissent for that that is wise.'[21] The last sentence is obscure, but the general position is clear. In practice, there was no conflict with Coke's doctrine of Common Law (which anyway never involved a blind acceptance of precedents): the difference was rather one of emphasis in theory, and would have arisen on such matters as Coke's notion of a cumulative legal wisdom which was to be presumed to outweigh the powers of reasoning of any particular person. Sandys did think that individuals (and hence *a fortiori* the whole body of citizens) were competent to condemn actions of government as contrary to their natural rights.

How far this condemnation could go is not clear, since Sandys never articulated any theory of the justification of resistance. But that some such theory was implicit in his position was shown in the heated debate on impositions in 1614. In this debate Sandys defended the natural right to private property; on 6 June he exclaimed that 'if a subsedye be graunted nowe without layinge downe ymposition, no man coulde knowe his right and propertye in his owne goodes . . .'.[22] He had previously drawn heavily on arguments from precedent, concluding on 5 May that 'Never ymposition was layed in England till the rayne of Ed. 1 . . .'.[23] But the real basis of his opposition went far beyond this. On 21 May Sir Henry Wotton sought to counter the historical evidence, propounding 'some doubts that it could not be maintayned out of histories that Kinges cannot ympose. He made a division of elective and successive kinges affirminge that kinges elective coulde not ympose of their owne authoritye . . . but successive, their power is greater . . .'.[24] Sandys' reaction to this is recorded in the somewhat cryptic notes of the Commons Journal:

That the King of *Fraunce*, and the rest of the imposing Princes, do also make Laws:— That will, in short time, bring all to a tyrannical course, where confusion both to Prince and People—Death of the last great imposing Prince.—No successive King, but First

---

[19] *Commons Debates 1621*, ed. W. Notestein, F. H. Relf and H. Simpson, 7 vols. (New Haven, 1935). The first part of the Ph.D. dissertation of W. M. Wallace was published as *Sir Edwin Sandys and the First Parliament of James I* (Philadelphia, 1940); I have not been able to consult the rest of it. Wallace is qualified on several points by T. K. Rabb, 'Sir Edwin Sandys and the Parliament of 1604', *American Historical Review*, 69 (1964), pp. 646–70.
[20] *1621 Debates*, II, p. 348.   [21] Ibid. III, p. 205.   [22] Ibid. VII, p. 653.
[23] Ibid. VII, p. 633.   [24] Ibid. VII, p. 644.

elected.—Election double; of Person, and Care; but both come in by Consent of People, and with reciprocal Conditions between King and People.—That a King, by Conquest, may also (when Power) be expelled . . .[25]

This statement was certainly a bold one, and seemed so at the time; after parliament ended, Sandys was 'questioned for his speech of elective and successive kings', and was confined to London for several weeks by order of the privy council.[26] Yet it may have been less radical than it appears to us now. Sandys surely thought of 'consent' and 'reciprocal conditions' as expressions not of popular *will*, but of common ethical *judgement*. Common Law was, for Sandys, an historically formed index of this judgement, which was itself derivable directly from 'reason', or intuitions of Natural Law. This is the view taken by the 'Lawyer' in his defence of Coke in Hobbes's *Dialogue of the Common Laws of England*, and it becomes the main focus of Hobbes's attack:

*Philosopher:* It followeth then that which you call the Common-Law, Distinct from Statute-Law, is nothing else but the Law of God.
*Lawyer:* In some sense it is, but it is not Gospel, but Natural Reason, and Natural Equity.
*Philosopher:* Would you have every Man to every other Man alledge for Law his own particular Reason? . . .[27]

The question of how far Hobbes had, in his early contacts with Coke's political allies, been exposed to or even imbibed the principles against which his political theory was to react so strongly, must remain largely a matter for conjecture. These principles were, in any case, neither novel nor of limited currency. The parliamentary business of Sandys and other politicians in the Virginia Company may not have impinged directly on Hobbes, though we have no reason to suppose that he was ignorant of the debates which Cavendish often attended. But there were also related issues of principle which underlay the practical administrative business in which Hobbes did meet and talk with these men.

For a colonial company the most important theoretical issue was, of course, that of legitimizing the settlement and appropriation of land. The simplest argument was that the colonists held their territory by right of conquest. This appears to have been the official view of James I, as expressed in parliament by Secretary Calvert in 1621: '. . . if Regall Prerogative have power in any thinge it is in this. Newe Conquests are to be ordered by the Will of the Conquerour. Virginia is not anex't to the Crowne of England And therefore not subiect to the Lawes of this Howse'.[28] As we have already seen, Sandys was committed to a position in which he did not recognize that any right or title was to be gained by conquest alone. In parliament,

---

[25] *Journals of the House of Commons*, I (1547–1628), p. 493.
[26] Historical Manuscripts Commission, *Portland MSS*, IX, p. 138; S. R. Gardiner, *History of England from the Accession of James I to the Outbreak of the Civil War*, 10 vols. (London, 1883–4), III, p. 249.
[27] Ed. J. Cropsey (Chicago, 1971), p. 67/(26).     [28] *1621 Debates*, IV, p. 256.

in order to protect the administrative autonomy of the Company from the implications of Calvert's claims (and in order to pass a bill favourable to the colony's fishing rights), he insisted that 'Virginia is holden of East Greenwich and so may be bound by the parliament'.[29] But insistence on the ordinary tenurial status of the colony (socage) did not solve the problem of the justification of colonial settlement.

Although the Virginia Company emphasized, in all its public pronouncements, the importance of its work in the conversion of Indians, its members were reluctant to claim that this was sufficient to justify conquest. The closest anyone came to such a claim was in a sermon by John Donne, which he preached to the Company in November 1622 on the text: 'But yee shall receive power, after that the *Holy Ghost* is come upon you, and yee shall be witnesses unto me both in *Ierusalem*, and in all *Iudea*, and in *Samaria*, and unto the uttermost part of the Earth.'[30] (Hobbes's name appears, with that of Cavendish, in the list of those who met specifically to hear Donne preach, and he may be presumed to have also attended the supper which was provided after the sermon.[31]) Donne's sermon explores different meanings of the word 'power': 'There is a *Power* rooted in *Nature*, and a *Power* rooted in *Grace*; a power yssuing from the Law of *Nations*, and a power growing out of the *Gospell*...'[32] Needless to say, Donne attributes primacy to the '*Power* rooted in *Grace*'; but the question of the nature of its relation to '*Power* rooted in *Nature*' is rather unsatisfactorily passed by with a rhetorical flourish:

> ... *Accepistis potestatem*, you have your *Commission*, your *Patents*, your *Charters*, your *Seales* ... But then, *Accipietis potestatem, You shall receive power*, sayes the *text*; ... that is, when the instinct, the influence, the motions of the *Holy Ghost* enables your Conscience to say, that your principall ende is ... to gaine Soules to the glory of *GOD*, this Seales the great Seale, this iustifies Iustice itselfe, this authorizes Authoritie...[33]

These were inspiring words, but they can scarcely have supplied an adequate theory of legitimation to politicians, such as Sandys, whose language of natural rights functioned independently of the data of revealed religion. Nor did these men take the Sepulvedist line, which might be described as the Natural Law equivalent of the argument from paganism, which was that the Indians were semi-bestial 'natural slaves', incapable of the proper exercise of reason. Contemporary descriptions of the Indians (such as that compiled by Samuel Purchas, an active member of the Company) showed that they possessed rudimentary forms of government and religion. Purchas, following Thomas Harriot's account, attributes to the Virginian Indians a knowledge of the prime conclusion of natural theology,

---

[29] *1621 Debates*, II, p. 321.

[30] Donne, *A Sermon upon the VIII verse of the I chapter of the Acts of the Apostles preach'd to the Honourable Company of the Virginian Plantation. 13° Novemb. 1622* (London, 1622), p. 1.

[31] Kingsbury, *Records*, II, p. 122. The supper was held in Merchant Taylors' Hall, and tickets for it cost 3s.: E. D. Neill, *History of the Virginia Company*, p. 361, quoted in J. H. Lefroy, notes to *The Historye of the Bermudaes or Summer Islands* (London, 1882), p. 247 n. 3.

[32] Donne, *Sermon*, pp. 25–6. [33] Ibid., pp. 27–8.

namely that there is '... one only chiefe and great God, which hath beene from all eternitie'.[34] Indeed, since much of the process of conversion to Christianity was in practice dependent on argument, it would have been hard to maintain that the Indians were essentially deficient in a capacity for reasoning. Patrick Copland, for example, remarked in his sermon to the Company that the 'worthy over-seer of your Colledge Land [i.e. George Thorpe] ... found that the sayd *Opachankano* had more notions of religion in him, then could be imagined in so great a blindnesse, since he willingly acknowledged that theirs was not the right way, desiring to be instructed in ours...'.[35]

In the end, no extensive attempt at a solution to the problem of legitimation was ever offered by the Virginia Company; there was a tendency to regard the actual colonization as a *fait acompli* and to justify its continuation on the grounds of converting infidels. The problem seemed less important after the Great Massacre of 1622, when it became possible to regard any subsequent action against the Indians as self-defence or justifiable retaliation. (Even so, the Sandys–Southampton administration continued to exhort the colonists to deal equitably with them; a bitter comment on these exhortations is to be found in a letter from the Council in Jamestown: 'Whereas we are advised by you to observe rules of Justice w$^{th}$ these barbarous and pfidious enemys, wee hold nothinge iniuste, that may tend to their ruine...'[36]) If the administration had been pressed to provide a justification of colonization compatible with Natural Law, they might simply have given the prosaic solution put forward by Purchas:

This place hath hath [*sic*] yeelded many benefits, both opportunitie for lawfull purchase of a great part of the countrey from the Natiues, freely and willingly relinquishing and selling the same for Copper, or other commodities (a thing of no small consequence to the conscience, where the milde Law of Nature, not that violent Law of Armes, layes the foundation of their possession), and quiet enioying thereof...[37]

Or they might, more subtly, have followed Donne's derivation of the '*Power* rooted in *Nature*':

---

[34] Samuel Purchas, *Purchas his Pilgrimage, Or Relations of the World and the Religions Observed in Al Ages and Places Discovered, from the Creation unto this Present* (3rd edn, 'much enlarged', London, 1617), p. 948. Hobbes's attendance at Courts of the Company sometimes coincided with that of Purchas, e.g. 21 April 1624 (Kingsbury, *Records*, II, pp. 518–19). His familiarity with Purchas's work on Virginia may perhaps be assumed from the catalogue entry 'Imperfect treatise on Virginia (Purchas)' in the *Report on the Miscellaneous Deeds, Letters, Treatises etc. of the Earls and Dukes of Devonshire from the Muniment Room at Hardwick* (Royal Commission on Historical MSS, London, 1977), Drawer 146, item 3. It may also be of interest to note that Hobbes might thus, through Purchas, have had some virtually direct knowledge of the work of Harriot (one of Purchas's sections, for example, is entitled 'Of the Virginian Rites, related by Master Hariot'), knowledge which, much more indirectly and in a different connexions, is suggested by J. Jacquot in 'Harriot, Hill, Warner and the New Philosophy', in *Thomas Harriot, Renaissance Scientist*, ed. J. W. Shirley (Oxford, 1974), pp. 107–28.
[35] Patrick Copland, *Virginia's God Be Thanked* (London, 1622), p. 28.
[36] Kingsbury, *Records*, IV, p. 451.   [37] Purchas, *Pilgrimage*, p. 946.

In the Law of *Nature* and Nations, a Land never inhabited, by any, or vtterly derelicted and immemorially abandoned by the former Inhabitants, becomes theirs that will possesse it. So also is it, if the inhabitants doe not in some measure fill the Land, so as the Land may bring foorth her increase for the vse of men: for as a man does not become proprietory of the sea, because he hath two or three Boats, fishing in it . . .[38]

With this Grotian argument Donne touched on another question of justification, which was of more immediate practical interest to the Company. Fishing played an increasingly important role in the survival of the colony, both as a source of food and income, and as an incentive for the owners and captains of ships who were otherwise reluctant to undertake an Atlantic crossing.[39] The best fishing grounds were off the coast of New England, which was outside the jurisdiction of the Virginia Company. Rights over those territories had been granted to a second Virginia company, under Sir Fernando Gorges, which, without maintaining any settlement there, had claimed the fishing rights for itself. When Gorges and others revived this company as the Plymouth Company in 1620, their plans were partly based on the exercise of fishing and trading monopolies. The Virginia Company campaigned against these claims. The theoretical ground had already been thoroughly prepared by Grotius in his *Mare Liberum*, which, although directed mainly against restrictions on trade, had included a defence of free fishing as an implication of the denial of proprietary rights over the sea: 'Quae autem navigationis eadem piscatus habenda est ratio, ut communis maneat omnibus.'[40] Ironically it seems that Selden (whose *Mare Clausum*, written probably in 1618, or 1619, was commissioned by James I to attack Grotius' arguments with regard to fishing rights) was actively involved in the Virginia Company at this time. Henry Wilkinson, in his history of the Somer Islands Company, even claims that 'Selden was counsel for the [Virginia] Company' in its dispute with the Plymouth Company, but I have failed to find any evidence for this.[41]

---

[38] Donne, *Sermon*, p. 26.
[39] See Craven, *Dissolution*, p. 190. Scott (*Constitution and Finance*, p. 301) gives figures for fishing voyages from England, which rose from 4 ships in 1615 to 35 in 1622.
[40] *Mare Liberum sive de iure quod Batavis competit ad Indicana commercia dissertatio* (Leiden, 1609), p. 23.
[41] H. Wilkinson, *The Adventurers of Bermuda* (London, 1933), p. 177 n. 1. Wilkinson is not the only writer to have made claims about Selden's involvement without offering any proof. E. S. Sandys (presumably following the article on his ancestor in the *D.N.B.*) says that Selden helped Sandys to prepare the Company's revision of its patent in February 1621 (*History of the Family of Sandys* (Barrow-in-Furness, 1930), I, p. 98). Alexander Brown credits Selden (along with Sandys, Southampton, and others) with having drawn up 'plans for a reform government for our nation' (*English Politics in Early Virginia History* (London, 1901, reprinted New York, 1968), p. 28). Pollard, in his *D.N.B.* article on Sandys, also connects Selden's imprisonment in June 1621 with his involvement in the Virginia Company; but Gardiner (*History*, IV, p. 133) says that he had given offence by supporting the Commons jurisdiction over Floyd's case. Whatever the truth of these claims, we can be fairly certain that Selden was an active member of the Virginia Company. The name 'Mr Seldon' occurs frequently in the Court Book (sometimes in conjunction with that of Hobbes). The Christian name is never given, and the Court Book alone would not enable one to make the identification, though on one occasion 'Mr Seldon' is, significantly, appointed to a legal subcommittee (Kingsbury, *Records*, I, p. 395). The

According to Aubrey, Selden said he did not know Hobbes when the latter sent him a presentation copy of *Leviathan*; but on the other hand, Hobbes had been quick to read *Mare Clausum* after it was published in 1635.[42] (On June 13/23, 1636 he wrote from Paris to the Earl of Newcastle: 'All I study is a nights, and that for a little while is the reading of certayne new bookes, especially Mr Seldens *Mare Clausum*....')[43] So it is possible that he had earlier had the opportunity to be impressed by Selden's acumen and learning in the Virginia Company at first-hand. It must however be added that, even if there were firm evidence that Hobbes had heard Selden speak there, as there is, for example, that he heard Donne's sermon, we would of course still be unable to answer the most important question as to what he *thought* about these men's ideas—whether, and why, he agreed or disagreed. The evidence merely enables one to say that Hobbes did not have to wait till the period of his attendance at Great Tew in order to think about the theoretical issues of jurisdiction and dominion discussed by Grotius and Selden; a decade earlier he must have heard these issues discussed as a matter pertinent to the practical business in which he himself had an immediate concern.

## III

The Virginia Company was, after all, a practical affair. Theoretical claims were aired, but only in the service of practical business. It is of interest to us that these claims were in circulation at all; but if we are interested in the intentions of the men who circulated them, we must also look at the administrative policies which those men pursued.

Almost without exception, historians have declared that the policies of the Sandys–Southampton administration were dominated by the twin concerns of Puritanism and the promotion of democratic principles. The patrons of all such interpretations are E. D. Neill and Alexander Brown; even Pollard, in his life of Sandys in the *Dictionary of National Biography*, reports that he was 'suspected of harbouring designs to establish a republican and puritan state in America', and the article, though judicious in tone, does nothing to suggest that these suspicions were ill-founded.

This line of interpretation does not stand up well to examination. The evidence of 'democratizing' tendencies consists mainly in the ending of martial law in the colony, and the setting up of the House of Burgesses, which sat for the first time under Sandys' treasurership. But it is clear from the records that the plans for

---

only conclusive evidence is the inclusion of Selden in a list of 'Members of parliament in Virginia Company', prepared apparently by Nicholas Ferrar in 1624 and printed by Brown in *Genesis*, II, pp. 802–3.

[42] *Letters Written by Eminent Persons ... to which are added ... Lives of Eminent Men, by John Aubrey, Esq.* (London, 1813), II, 2 (= 3rd vol.), p. 628.

[43] H.M.C., *Welbeck Abbey MSS*, II, p. 128.

both of these measures were drawn up under the administration of Sir Thomas Smythe.[44] Furthermore, there were simple and essentially non-political motives at work in these decisions: martial law had been a disincentive to new settlers, and the Assembly was practically expedient as a court for the local settlement of disputes and hearing of petitions. (It need scarcely be added that martial law had been a measure of expediency in the first place, but it is of interest to note that the original instructions to Gates in 1609 on the administration of martial law have sometimes been attributed to Sandys himself.)[45] Professor Craven quotes the distinctly uncontroversial description of these reforms contained in a publication of the Company in 1620: '. . . the laudable forme of Justice and government used in this Realme [has been] established and followed as neere as may be'.[46] To this one can add that, if the setting up of an Assembly had been a politically radical measure, Sandys's party would not have later referred to it as they did in their *Discourse of the Old Company*, a document drawn up to persuade Charles I to reconstitute the company which his father had dissolved. In a list of the achievements of the Sandys regime, they included 'The libertie of a Generall Assembly being graunted them, whereby they find out, & execute those thinges, as might best tend to their good'.[47]

It is hard to assess the religious policy of the Sandys administration. To the difficulty of gaining an accurate picture of the complexion of the religious life of the colony must be added that of deciding to what extent it was determined by 'policy' at all. The evidence is fragmentary, and it may be unrepresentative as well, if there is any truth in the impression that the less Puritan ministers were sometimes also less active, or at least less apt to leave for the historian any evidence of their activity.

With these qualifications in mind, one can nevertheless still agree with the accepted description of religion in the colony as definitely low-church. Even more than in the question of 'democratizing', however, it is clear that the tendency predates the Sandys administration; Alexander Whitaker, for example (the Puritan 'Apostle of Virginia'), became rector of the parishes of Henrico and Charles City in 1611, exercising a double cure of souls because William Wickham, the other minister, had not been ordained an Anglican priest and so could not celebrate communion.[48] One of the charges made against the Smythe regime in the *Discourse of*

---

[44] Craven discusses the evidence in detail: *Dissolution*, pp. 47–68.

[45] E.g. Osgood, *American Colonies*, p. 64. Cf. also the 'Instructions to the Governor and council of state in Virginia' issued on 24 July 1621, over the signatures of Southampton, Sandys and others: para. 39 states that 'The Gouernor for the time being shall have absolute power and authoritie according to the implication of his particular commission to direct, determine and punish at his good discretion any emergent business . . .' (Kingsbury, *Records*, III, p. 469).

[46] Craven, *Dissolution*, p. 79, from the *Declaration of the State of the Colonie . . .* in *Tracts and Other Papers*, ed. Peter Force, 4 vols. (New York, 1947), III, no. 5, pp. 5–6.

[47] Kingsbury, *Records*, IV, p. 523.

[48] G. M. Brydon, *Religious Life of Virginia in the Seventeenth Century* (Williamsburg, Va., 1957), pp. 10–11.

*the Old Company* was that when Sandys took office he found 'Three Ministers in orders, & Two w^(th)out'.[49] But again, there were simple practical reasons for this. Presbyterian ministers were allowed to serve parishes in Virginia because of the sheer difficulty of providing enough priests of Anglican ordination. The primary obstacle of distance was responsible for the fact that there was no episcopal visitation of the colony, no ecclesiastical court in operation there, and indeed no diocesan organization of any sort.[50] And on the other hand, the instructions issued by the Company continued to emphasize (as admittedly they could hardly have failed to) 'the establishment of due order in administringe of all services according to the usuall forme and discipline of the Church of England and carefullie avoidinge all factions and needlesse novelties tending onlie to the disturbance of peace and unitie ....'.[51]

It is hard to find anything to support Professor Perry Miller's claim that 'Sandys inspired a sort of religious revival'.[52] He relies for evidence of this on the *Declaration* of 1620, which was issued after the termination of Sandys's treasurership as a mixture of apologia and advertisement, and on the thanksgiving sermon of Patrick Copland, which must surely be viewed in the same light. What can be said, without impugning the sincerity of Sandys's own professions of religious motives, is that the advancement of religion continued to play an invaluable part in the public rhetoric of the Company and that the Company did for this reason gain the attention of some religiously motivated benefactors (Copland among them). At a Court of the Company in November 1620, for example, 'a straunger stept in presentinge a Mapp of S^r Walter Rawlighes ... and w^th the same fower great books ... whereof one booke was a treatise of S^tt Augustine, of the Citty of God translated into English the other three greate Volumes wer the works of M^r Perkins newlie corrected ...', and in January 1622 the same donor presented 'a large Church Bible, the Comon prayer booke, Vrsinus Catichisme and a smale Bible richly imbroydered ...'.[53] The schemes in aid of which these benefactions were made (especially, as in these cases, the plans for a college to convert and

---

[49] Kingsbury, *Records*, IV, p. 521. This also suggests that the later charges of 'Puritanism' against Sandys should be seen in the context of an exchange of similar recriminations; cf. the 'Declaraĉon ...' of 1623, which accused Warwick of having patronized a minister 'who had preached in the Sum̃er Ilands that the Government of y^e Church of England by Bishops was Antichristian ...' (ibid. II, p. 406).

[50] As Brydon points out (*Religious Life*, pp. 11–12), in the absence of ecclesiastical courts no layman could be convicted as a dissenter. Brydon also quotes, as evidence of the Puritan complexion of the Virginian church, a letter from Alexander Whitaker: 'I marvaile much—that so few of our English ministers that were so hot against the surplis and subscription come hither where neither are spoken of' (ibid. pp. 10–11); but as evidence this quotation is, to say the least, double-edged.

[51] 'Instructions to the Governor ...', Kingsbury, *Records*, III, p. 468.

[52] 'The religious impulse in the founding of Virginia: religion and society in the early literature', *William and Mary Quarterly*, 3rd series, 5 (1948), p. 507.

[53] Kingsbury, *Records*, I, pp. 421, 589. Zacharias Ursinus was a pupil of Melanchthon and a friend of Calvin; the two catechisms published by him in 1563 aroused the opposition of Lutherans (*Realencyklopädie für protestantische Theologie und Kirche*, 3rd edn, 24 vols. (Leipzig, 1896–1913)).

educate Indians) had active supporters in the Company; but we have only to begin to list them to see the inappropriateness of the term 'Puritanism' as it is normally applied. They include Nicholas Ferrar (whose father left £300 to the College); his former mentor at Cambridge, George Ruggle, the author of the anti-Puritan play *Re Vera*; and John Donne, who was made a freeman of the Company in May 1622.[54]

## IV

It is of course much easier to agree that these men were not Puritans, than it is to agree on a definition of Puritanism (which it would in any case be beyond the scope of this article to elaborate or defend). It would surely be anachronistic to base such a definition on general tendencies to zeal, seriousness, ethical strictness or practical piety (unless, for example, we are willing to describe Laud as a Puritan). It seems equally wrong to make one's definition depend on Calvinism in theological doctrine, since one would then have to include many of the Elizabethan bishops in opposition to whom Puritanism first arose. Any attempt to define, or at least delineate, the nature of Puritanism must surely start with attitudes towards rites, observances, church government and the nature and sources of spiritual authority.

On these issues, the views of Sir Edwin Sandys are worthy of a special examination, not only because he seems to have been the most influential member of the group to which Hobbes was attached, but also because of the significant intermediate role which he played in the development of theories of Church and State between Hooker and members of the Great Tew circle. The principal source is Sandys's only book, which was written in 1599, and published first in 1605 as *A relation of the state of religion . . .*, and then posthumously in 1629 as *Europae speculum*. The book was suppressed, apparently with Sandys's connivance, within a few months of its first publication, but this probably does not indicate a change of mind about the arguments contained in it.[55] Sandys did not abandon interest in the work; two copies survive with annotations made by him with a view to later republication.[56] Nor was it forgotten by others. In 1609 William Bedell translated it into Italian for the benefit of (and apparently with some assistance from) Paolo Sarpi and Fulgenzio Micanzio, and a version of this translation, with notes reputedly by Sarpi, was published in 1625, to be followed by a French translation

---

[54] For Ferrar's bequest see Kingsbury, *Records*, I, p. 335; Ruggle left £100 for the same purpose (ibid. II, p. 136); Donne was made a freeman on 22 May 1622 (ibid. II, p. 18). Further details about Ruggle are given in A. L. Maycock, *Nicholas Ferrar of Little Gidding* (London, 1938), pp. 24–5.

[55] See T. K. Rabb, 'The editions of Sir Edwin Sandys' "Relation of the State of Religion" ', *Huntington Library Quarterly*, 26 (1963), pp. 323–36, and G. Cozzi, 'Sir Edwin Sandys e la "Relazione dello Stato della Religione" ', *Rivista storica italiana*, 79 (1967), esp. pp. 1110–11.

[56] E. S. Sandys, *Family of Sandys*, p. 93 and n.

by Jean Diodati.[57] The work was thus in print again within Sandys's lifetime, and in any case some copies of the 1605 edition had remained in circulation.

Little can be gleaned, from this book, about Sandys's doctrinal position. He appears not to have been especially sympathetic to Calvinism: he praised the Church of England for, among other things, having 'no LUTHER no CALVIN the square of theyr Faith . . .', and his frequent emphasis of the role of education in religious development does perhaps suggest a non-Calvinist continuum of the realms of Nature and Grace.[58] What does emerge clearly, both from this book and from his parliamentary speeches, is a strong vein of anti-catholicism. But this itself is based principally not on theological grounds, nor on the traditional rhetoric of protestant polemics (the pope as antichrist, and so on), but rather on arguments about the impropriety of the ecclesiastical exercise of temporal power. Thus, on matters of liturgy and religious practice Sandys steered closer to the wind than most Protestant writers: he was willing to praise the Roman church for its sermons, its desire for '*Adorning the Temples* of God', and its philanthropy.[59] In 1638 Chillingworth was to follow this line in his preface to *The Religion of Protestants*, introducing a long quotation from *Europae speculum* with the remarks:

Is this Devotion in the Church of England an argument that shee is comming over to the Church of Rome? Sir *Edwin Sands*, I presume every man will grant, had no inclination that way; yet he forty years since highly commended this part of devotion in Papists . . . His words . . . shew plainly, that what is now practis'd was approv'd by Zealous Protestants so long agoe . . .[60]

Of course, Sandys repudiated various Catholic doctrines; but he did not think that Catholics were incapable of being persuaded to renounce these beliefs, and he emphasized the common ground of 'the fundamentall Articles of Christian Faith'.[61] The real obstacle to religious unity, for Sandys, was the entrenchment of the Catholic Church's temporal power. So much of its organization and practice was so well developed for the purpose of maintaining this power (Sandys describes the use of confession, for example, as an instrument of surveillance and control), that it would be not only loth to give up this dominion but also extremely well equipped to defend it.[62]

Sandys regarded the religious exercise of temporal power as bad for religious unity; he also thought it bad for religion itself, leading to the corruption of doctrine. He gave an example of this in a Commons speech on 10 April 1621, during a discussion of the case of Sir John Bennett, who was accused of having corruptly

---

[57] Cozzi, 'Sandys e la "Relazione" ', pp. 1113–18.
[58] *Europae speculum* . . . (The Hague, 1629), p. 214. On education and the instillation of virtue: pp. 21, 80.
[59] Ibid., pp. 5, 6, 22.
[60] *The religion of protestants a safe way to salvation* (Oxford, 1638), the preface to the author of 'Charity maintain'd', sig. §§§3v.
[61] Sandys, *Europae speculum*, p. 183.   [62] On confession, ibid., p. 50; general assessment, ibid., p. 24.

suppressed wills in his capacity as judge of the Prerogative Court of the Archbishop of Canterbury:

> Noe course could be better for Testamentarie Matters then that which was established by the Civill Lawe till it was supplanted by the Cannonists, who wrested into the iurisdiction of the Clergie the twoe principall Acts of our Life and Death, Marriadge and Wills ... And that they might with more advantage be Maisters in this latter, from the Platonists was borrowed the device of Purgatorie And men browght to beleive that by disposeing of their goods they might purchase ease to their sowles.[63]

But beyond these considerations, Sandys thought that religious interference in the affairs of the State, besides being bad for religion, was bad for the State, and was to be checked by temporal punishments. Both recusants and separatists might be politically subversive, and against both of these Sandys encouraged political action; but the justification of such action was an almost intractable problem for someone in his position. His earliest extant work, the Notes which he wrote for Hooker on a draft of Book VI of the *Laws of Ecclesiastical Polity*, can be directly associated with his introduction of legislation against 'Brownists and Barrowists', and it was presumably with them in mind that he wrote: 'the Praecisians ... confound their ecclesiasticall jurisdiction and dominion; and so exclude the soveraine of the estate from bearing anie soveraigntie in the Church ...'.[64] The problem for Sandys was that he himself recognized no other ground for dominion than that supplied by ethical judgement. His Natural Law theory of sovereignty was in effect a hostage to hierocracy.

Two tendencies, however, can be detected in Sandys's attempts to solve this problem. The first tendency was to admit, in the interstices of his Natural Law theory, a slight element of legal positivism. The earliest sign of this occurs in another of the Notes on Hooker, during a discussion of the difficulty of separating the areas of civil and ecclesiastical jurisdiction:

> Some [cases] are meerely civill, as the tryall of title of land: some meerely ecclesiasticall, as crimes of heresie and schisme: other mixt, as matter of slaunder, incontinencie, testaments; wherein perhaps nature directing that the part praedominant in the mixture doe carrie the cause with it to that coort which this part praedominant belongs to, yet the declaration hereof is to be made by positive lawe of the whole state: which positive lawe itself is neither ecclesiasticall nor civill, but mixt of both ...[65]

This last phrase is anti-climactic, since Sandys has already indicated that neither component of the mixture is competent to determine the limits of its own compet-

---

[63] *1621 Debates*, IV, p. 218.
[64] Notes on the sixth book of the *Laws of Ecclesiastical Polity* in Hooker, *Works*, 7th edn, 3 vols. (Oxford, 1888), III, p. 133.
[65] Ibid., III, p. 132.

ence. It is politically understandable that he did not wish to develop a notion of 'positive lawe' as a *tertium quid*. But something similar did arise in his treatment of questions of religious controversies. The basis of positivism here was provided by adiaphorism and uncertainty: where it is either hard or comparatively unimportant to decide, within certain limits, what is best, it may be better simply to agree to abide by any particular decision.[66] The second tendency is suggested by the same passage from the Notes on Hooker. That passage obviously demands to be compared with the parliamentary speech on Bennett's case quoted above. The main difference is that testaments lose their status as 'mixt' and become merely civil affairs. The tendency was for religion to be considered increasingly in terms of beliefs only, so that any action, *qua* action, was seen as a temporal matter.

There is little point in trying to press parallels between these tendencies in Sandys's thinking and Hobbes's later views; the evidence for Sandys's ideas after the writing of *Europae speculum* is, for a start, too fragmentary and unspecific. But one can at least say that Sandys's views were symptomatic of serious tensions in the development of Hookerian Natural Law theory. Schematically, the problem is as follows. One starts with two parallel and similar forms of knowledge, namely ethical knowledge of what should be done because it is right, and religious knowledge of what should be done because it is holy. The noetic claims of both forms are similar and share, ultimately, the same source in God. The problem is to limit the scope or undermine the certainty of the second form of knowledge, without similarly weakening the first (which one is, on the contrary, attempting thereby to strengthen).

This problem was, in its practical aspects, so basic to the political and religious issues of the time that Sandys's thought about it seems significant largely as a symptom. But, so far as Hobbes is concerned, it may also have the significance of an influence, both directly and indirectly. The earliest milieu hitherto suggested for Hobbes's thinking on these subjects is that of Great Tew, and one might describe Sandys's role for that group as that of a posthumous patron: several members of his own family were connected with Great Tew, and we have already seen how Chillingworth quoted approvingly from *Europae speculum* in the preface to *The Religion of Protestants*.[67] To this we can add the possibility of some influence at first hand during the years of Hobbes's attendance at the Virginia Company.

Throughout his career, Sandys was consistent in his support for the Act of Supremacy. It was in order to strengthen the implications of the Act that he introduced the clauses against Brownists and Barrowists in 1593.[68] His sponsorship of

---

[66] *Europae speculum*, p. 198, advising Protestants to agree 'to abate the rigor of certain speculative opinions' for the sake of unity.
[67] The family connexions with Great Tew are discussed below.
[68] See D'Ewes, *Journal* (London, 1682), pp. 500 ff.

the publication of the *Laws of Ecclesiastical Polity* appears to have been part of the same campaign, in which he took a stronger line than Hooker, and received the quasi-official support of his father, the Archbishop of York.[69] Sandys's support for the established government of the Church seems never to have wavered: in 1614, for instance, he went out of his way to defend the episcopacy during an attack on some remarks made by the Bishop of Lincoln: 'Not to tax the reverent Degree of Bishops, by One Man's Error—Order of Angels, not of Men, where none of them without Error—'.[70]

It is only after considering in some detail Sandys's views on Church and State that one can fully appreciate the implausibility of the one major piece of evidence on which have been based the accusations that he harboured 'designs to establish a republican and puritan state in America'. This evidence consists of a manuscript written by Sir Nathanael Rich in May 1623 (that is, at the height of the hostility between the Rich and Sandys factions) and headed 'Note Which I Presently Took of Captain John Bargrave's Discourse to Me Concerning Sir Edwin Sandys'. Bargrave apparently claimed to have heard Sandys 'say that if eu$^r$ God from heauen did constitute and direct a forme of Gouermt it was that of Geneua' and 'that his intent was to erect a free state in Virginia . . .' 'And to that intent . . . he § S$^r$ E.S. § mooued my L. of Canterburye to giue leaue to the Brownistes and Separatists of Engt to goe thither . . . : those Brownistes by their Doctrine clayminge a libertie to disagreeing to the Gouerm$^t$ of Monarches . . .'.[71] Apparently Rich never attempted to use this, partly no doubt because Bargrave was not a witness who would inspire much credence.[72] Only three things could serve to make these charges seem remotely plausible. The first (which was the basis of most of the attacks on Sandys) was Sandys's parliamentary opposition and criticism; but this, as we have seen, certainly did not involve any admiration for the Genevan model of government. The second is the fact that he was in some way involved in the negotiations which led to the settlement of the Pilgrim Fathers in America. (His motives for this may, one suspects, have been less concerned with godliness than with the need to strengthen the colony's fishing claims by forming a new settlement at the northern edge of the Virginia Company's area of jurisdiction.) But if we look at the articles which Robinson and Brewster signed before receiving permission to sail to America, we find nothing to suggest that Sandys was acting as a sponsor of separatism. Article 1 states: 'To the confession of faith published in the

---

[69] On Sandys and Hooker see W. S. Hill. 'The evolution of Hooker's "Laws of ecclesiastical polity"', in *Studies in Richard Hooker*, ed. W. S. Hill (Cleveland, 1972), esp. pp. 132 ff.

[70] *Journals of H. of C.*, I, p. 498. Presumably the second sentence should read: 'where all of them . . .'.

[71] Kingsbury, *Records*, IV, p. 194.

[72] Bargrave appears to have changed sides several times in pursuit of his own interests, and was at the time of this conversation probably trying to gain Rich's support for his suit against Smythe. Three years earlier he had been currying favour with Sandys and Nicholas Ferrar, by granting shares to the latter's friends: ibid., I, p. 344.

name of the Church of England, and to every article thereof, we do, with the Reformed Churches where we live, and also elsewhere, assent wholly', and Article 4 reads as follows: 'We judge it lawful for his Majesty to appoint bishops, civil overseers or officers in authority under him . . . to oversee the churches, and govern them . . .'.[73]

Thirdly, it has been observed that in the latter part of Sandys's parliamentary career he virtually ceased his attacks on separatism, but continued to speak often and urgently against Catholics and in favour of a more actively Protestant foreign policy. This was, however, in response to James's policies towards recusants and the Palatinate respectively; there is no reason for supposing that it implied a change in Sandys's views on Church and State. Anti-catholicism supplies a significant common denominator of many of the members of the Virginia Company (including Sir Nathanael Rich): Spain was their major commercial rival, and it is not surprising that they shared the hopes, common among the English merchant community, that the King would undertake a tougher foreign policy against the Habsburgs and in favour of such potential allies as Savoy and Venice. In this latter connection Cavendish himself seems to have played an active part: it is probable that he circulated copies of the letters from Micanzio (translated by Hobbes), in which James's foreign policy was criticized in increasingly bitter terms.[74] One suggested reason for Southampton's confinement in 1621 is that he had been consulting with Members of Parliament in order to open direct negotiations with Frederick and Elizabeth.[75]

In the Commons debates on foreign policy at the end of that year, members of the Virginia Company were prominent in support of the Palatinate. On 26 November Sir Dudley Digges argued that 'The King hath done so much for peace, that he must now have a war' (later in the same debate observing that 'if the King of Spain's navy were intercepted from the West Indies, if he were kept from it two years, he would be bankrupt . . .').[76] The entry in Pym's diary for this debate tells us that 'SIR EDWARD SACKVILLE prest the same waye [sc. in favour of war]. Earnestly, after his manner, and elegantly.'[77] Sandys was not present, apparently for reasons of ill health, but his view had frequently been expressed earlier in the year: 'Religion rooted oute in Bohemia, in the Pallatinate, in France rootinge oute . . . I had rather speak now then betray my country with silence . . .'.[78] Cavendish most probably attended the November debates on foreign policy,

---

[73] E. D. Neill, *The English Colonization of America during the Seventeenth Century* (London, 1871), pp. 96–7.

[74] Gabrieli, 'Bacone, la riforma e Roma', p. 248. Cavendish also performed the introduction to court of the new Venetian ambassador, Alvise Valaressio, in June 1622 (ibid., p. 247, and *Calendar of State Papers (Venetian)*, XVII (1621–3), p. 356).

[75] Gardiner, *History*, IV, p. 133.   [76] 1621 *debates*, II, pp. 445, 451.   [77] Ibid. IV, p. 437.

[78] Ibid., III, p. 345. On 21 November Sandys 'by a letter to Mr Speaker excuses his absence by reson of sickness' (ibid., III, p. 412); he had been released from confinement by the King on 15 Nov. (ibid., V, p. 206).

which continued for a week. His presence was recorded on 29 November, and he is likely to have been present also on 1 December at the third reading of the bill for free fishing off the coast of North America, which had been piloted through the House by members of the Virginia Company.[79] On 3 December the King issued a letter to the Speaker, expressing his displeasure that the House was meddling in matters of foreign policy; it is perhaps significant that a copy of this letter is preserved among the Cavendish papers.[80]

These issues were just as pressing in November 1622, when Hobbes received the letter, mentioned earlier, from Robert Mason. This man can presumably be identified with the Robert Mason who was a fellow of St John's College, Cambridge; the letter is written from 'here among the Clerks in Cambr.', and it shows the keen interest in affairs of state which one might expect in the man who was to become, five years later, secretary to the Duke of Buckingham.[81] The letter expresses concern about the prospect of a Spanish marriage, and a sympathetic interest in the fate of the Palatinate: 'I am glad to hear Sir Horace Veere is past danger of intercepting, I hope he has likewise past the danger of his Majesty's displeasure.'[82] The criticism of royal policy is almost explicit; later in the letter Mason writes in a confidential tone: 'I pray hereafter be as free with me as you see I am with you, for you may with the same security impart your news to me, as, I hope, I have now writt my mind to you . . .'[83]

## V

If Hobbes was well placed in the Virginia Company for gaining information about political events, he was also in a good position to observe the nature of political action itself in the Company's internal conflicts. Perhaps this observation helped to stimulate his interest in Thucydides, whom he commends in the preface to his translation as 'the most politic historiographer that ever writ . . .'. He continues: 'Look how much a man of understanding might have added to his experience, if he had then lived a beholder of their proceedings, and familiar with the men and business of the time . . .'.[84] Hobbes may have started on the task of translation as

---

[79] *1621 debates*, II, pp. 469 (29 Nov.); 482 (1 Dec.); for discussions of the fishing bill see ibid., II, p. 321; III, p. 81; IV, p. 386; V, p. 378.

[80] RCHM, *Report on the Miscell. Deeds . . . of the Earls and Dukes of Devonshire*, Appendix, item 2. The letter is printed in G. W. Prothero, *Select Statutes and other Constitutional Documents . . . 1558–1625* (Oxford, 1913; 4th edn), pp. 310–11.

[81] Tönnies, 'Contributions', p. 84. Details of Mason's career are given in the *DNB* (in the entry on another Robert Mason) and in *Alumni cantabrigienses*, ed. Venn and Venn, part I, 4 vols. (Cambridge, 1922–4), III, p. 157. See also Cambridge University Library MS Mm. I. 38, which indicates that Mason was on public service abroad as early as May 1625 (pp. 270–1, 275).

[82] Tönnies, 'Contributions', p. 82.   [83] Ibid., p. 83.

[84] *EW* VIII, p. viii.

soon as the dissolution of the Company gave him the leisure for it: that it was completed several years before its publication in 1628 is suggested by the statement in the preface that 'After I had finished it, it lay long by me . . .'.[85]

There are almost no indications of how Hobbes was occupied after the dissolution of the Company. It is possible that, with Cavendish, he remained active in the Somer Islands Company, which was not dissolved. The only reason for dating his association with Bacon after 1621 is that the latter then became free to spend more time in his 'delicious walkes at Gorambery'. Cavendish had already been a friend of Bacon for several years; in 1616 it was through his good offices that Micanzio entered into a correspondence with the Chancellor.[86] Two of Cavendish's associates in the Virginia Company were also close friends of Bacon: Sackville, who, like Cavendish, received a special memento in Bacon's will, and Danvers.[87]

The social and intellectual world of Jacobean England was so closely-knit, however, that once one begins to follow lines of possible 'contacts' or acquaintances the speculation becomes endless. Danvers, for example, married the mother of Edward Herbert (whose acquaintance with Hobbes has never been properly dated), so it is possible that Hobbes met the son through Cavendish's acquaintance with the stepfather. One of the settlers in Bermuda, Captain Richard Herbert, has been tentatively identified as Herbert's brother; but the Edward Herbert who appears with Hobbes in the Court Book must have been Herbert's cousin, the lawyer, and not, as Neill supposes, the philosopher himself.[88]

A survey of the active membership of the Company raises further possibilities with regard to Hobbes's interests in science. (It must be stressed that it is the *active* membership that counts; nominal membership included several hundred people who never attended meetings of the Court of the Company.) It is at least possible that Hobbes was already interested in such matters; the account of his observation of a comet in 1618 given in the Criticism of Thomas White's *De mundo* does suggest that ignorance of Euclid had seemed no obstacle to some knowledge of astronomy.[89] One active member of the Company was the scapegrace courtier

---

[85] Ibid., p. ix.   [86] Gabrieli, 'Bacone, la riforma e Roma', p. 203.

[87] For the will, which left a gold vinaigrette to Cavendish and a ring to Sackville, see J. Spedding, *The Letters and Life of Francis Bacon*, 7 vols. (London, 1861–74), VII, pp. 228, 542; the will was drawn up in 1621. See also ibid. VII, p. 529 for a letter to Sackville. Danvers's intimacy with Bacon is recorded in Aubrey, *Brief Lives*, II, part I, p. 222. G. C. Robertson gives further evidence of Cavendish's friendship with the Chancellor: *Hobbes* (Edinburgh, 1886), p. 19 n. 2. One should of course add that Southampton was influential in bringing about Bacon's downfall: A. L. Rowse, *Shakespeare's Southampton, Patron of Virginia* (London, 1965), p. 270.

[88] For Richard Herbert see Wilkinson, *Adventurers of Bermuda*, p. 380. The Edward Herbert of the Virginia Company was attending its meetings during his namesake's residence in Paris. Neill's attribution is in *English Colonization*, p. 112.

[89] *Thomas White's* De mundo *Examined*, tr. H. W. Jones (London, 1976), p. 87. If it was at this time that Hobbes read all the works to which he goes on to refer in connection with this observation (ibid., pp. 88–91), then his interest must have been a considerable one.

Sir Robert Killigrew, who was one of the first English users of the telescope.[90] Nicholas Ferrar had studied 'every art and science' at Leipzig University, and had stayed at the University of Padua for a period of over two years, hiring tutors 'in those sciences in which he intended to be farther instructed'.[91] Ferrar's own friends in the Company included two professors at Gresham College. Dr Winston, who became professor of Physic there in 1615, had taken his MD at Padua and returned to that university for some time in 1617; Henry Briggs, professor of Geometry, is said to have recommended Ferrar as his successor when he moved to Oxford in 1620.[92] These men's active involvement in the Company appears to have ceased in 1621 and 1620 respectively (though a work by Briggs on the North West Passage appeared in 1622, and Winston was still corresponding with settlers in the Colony in 1623); but on the other hand, we do not know by how many years Hobbes's secretarial assistance to Cavendish in Company business preceded his actual membership in 1622, nor do we know when he became a member of the Somer Islands Company.[93] A more unorthodox scientific figure whose name does overlap with that of Hobbes in the Court Book was Dr Francis Anthony, the Paracelsian 'empiric' who quarrelled with the Royal College of Physicians.[94] And perhaps one should not omit the fact that it is Sir Dudley Digges's father, the astronomer Thomas Digges, who is credited with the introduction of Copernicanism to England.[95]

Whether Hobbes made use of any of these possible sources of ideas or information, or had any other contacts with these men, must remain a matter for speculation. One is on slightly firmer ground when considering another question of connections raised by the Court Books, namely that of the overlap between active members of the Company and associates of the Great Tew circle a decade later. George Sandys, Sir Edwin's brother, provides the main link.[96] He went to Jamestown as an officer of the Company in 1622, under the governorship of Sir Francis Wyatt, who had married Margaret Sandys, daughter of Sir Samuel. Her sister Anne married Sir Francis Wenman, another, though a less active, member of

---

[90] *Calendar of State Papers (Domestic)* (1619–23), p. 77, records a letter from Killigrew to Carleton (14 Sept. 1619): 'Sends him a perspective glass, after having forty broken in getting it ground.'

[91] P. Peckard, *Memoirs of the Life of Mr Nicholas Ferrar* (Cambridge, 1790), pp. 50, 57.

[92] On Winston, see Maycock, *Nicholas Ferrar*, pp. 23–4; on Briggs, see Peckard, *Memoirs*, p. 91 and n.

[93] Briggs's tract, *Of the Northwest Passage to the South Sea*, is printed in 'The English experience . . . in facsimile' no. 276 (Amsterdam, 1970). A letter from a colonist to Winston is given in Kingsbury, *Records*, IV, p. 37.

[94] See e.g. Court of 9 June 1624; Kingsbury, *Records*, II, p. 539. Anthony's chief claim to fame was his 'aurum potabile'. See A. G. Debus, *The English Paracelsians* (London, 1965), pp. 142–5. The entry on Anthony in *Alumni Cantabrigienses* corrects the chronology of the *D.N.B.* article; but it in turn must be mistaken in giving the date of his death as 26 May 1623, if my identification is correct. The Court Book records him as 'Dr Fr. Anthony' (Kingsbury, *Records*, I, p. 265), and I have been unable to trace any other doctor of that name.

[95] F. R. Johnson, 'Thomas Digges, the Copernican system and the idea of the infinity of the universe in 1576', *Huntington Library Bulletin*, 5 (1934), pp. 69–117.

[96] On George Sandys's career, and his connections with Great Tew, see R. B. Davis, *George Sandys, Poet–Adventurer* (London, 1955).

the Company, who became a close friend of Falkland and lived near Great Tew at Carswell.[97] Just over the border in Gloucestershire was the house of Sir Henry Rainsford, another friend and fellow-courtier, who was also a member of Falkland's circle; his father had held eight shares in the Company and had attended its meetings.[98] (Dr Walter Raleigh, another member of Falkland's circle, was also the son of a Virginia Company Adventurer.[99]) Some connection with the Great Tew group has also been claimed for Sir Dudley Digges, who remained a friend of George Sandys and was one of the contributors of commendatory verses to the latter's *Paraphrase upon the Divine Poems* in 1638, along with Falkland, Sidney Godolphin, Wyatt, Rainsford, Waller and others.[100] Selden's role in the Company has already been mentioned; Hyde had been a mere undergraduate when Hobbes was attending the Company's meetings, but his two distinguished uncles, Nicholas and Sir Lawrence, had been assiduous in their attendance there.

Whoever introduced Hobbes to Great Tew, he might, then, have found some familiar faces there. One later reminder of the Virginia Company occurs in Aubrey's life of Davenant, who, after fleeing to Paris during the Interregnum, 'layd an ingeniose designe to carry a considerable number of artificers (chiefly weavers) from hence to Virginia'.[101] Davenant was in the midst of writing *Gondibert*, and at the height of his friendship with Hobbes; it is surely probable that the latter was consulted about the plan, if he was not the originator of it. But beyond this episode, the striking thing is that Hobbes's involvement in the Virginia Company should have left, as it seems to have done, so few traces on his later life.

The problem of the American Indian in Hobbes's works, for example, is akin to the problem of the dog that did not bark in the night: why did Hobbes make so little use of his special knowledge? The answer must lie mainly in his distaste for anything that might tie his argument to empirical questions of fact. But it may also be suspected that the data raised more difficulties for Hobbes than they solved. Although he could write that 'the savage people in many places of America, except the government of small families, the concord whereof dependeth on natural lust, have no government at all . . .', he must have been aware, if he had read accounts such as that of Purchas, that some Indian tribes did conform to his model of a commonwealth.[102] This must have been embarrassing for his subsidiary theory that all the benefits of civilization sprang directly from the leisure provided by secure

---

[97] Family trees are provided in E. S. Sandys, *Family of Sandys*. Immediately after being given two shares in the Company by George Sandys, Wenman attended the Court at which Wyatt was chosen as governor: Kingsbury, *Records*, I, pp. 436–7, 440.

[98] Davis, *George Sandys*, p. 229; Kingsbury, *Records*, I, pp. 300, 304, 341, 365, 372.

[99] The presence of 'm<sup>r</sup> Carew Rawleigh' is recorded, with that of Hobbes, at a Court on 9 July 1623: ibid., II, p. 462.

[100] Davis, *George Sandys*, pp. 233 (n. 26), 238–40.

[101] Aubrey, *Letters*, II (2), p. 307. Davenant was captured *en route* and taken to England.

[102] *EW* III, p. 114.

government; if Indians could have a sovereign and remain savages, then the political explanation of civilization supplied at best a necessary, not a sufficient, cause.[103] This subsidiary argument was first introduced in *De cive*: it was needed to plug an important gap, namely the problem of whether considerations of the *quality* of life were so divorced from political factors that they could themselves be offered as grounds for resisting the sovereign power.

## VI

The four references to American Indians, the brief discussion of colonies in chapter 24 of *Leviathan*, and the single mention of the early administration of Virginia exhaust the direct echoes, in Hobbes's works, of his involvement in the Virginia Company.[104] There remain the murky questions of influences, connections and milieux. It is perhaps salutary to remember that, even if one did (or could) succeed in 'proving' an influence, one would still be left with the even more intractable problem of saying why the recipient was *apt* to be influenced in that particular way. Though the evidence of Hobbes's part in the Virginia Company makes it possible to illuminate in some detail a period of his life which was hitherto obscure, the light which this in turn casts on the development of his ideas remains necessarily oblique.

## APPENDIX

### *Chronology, 1610–1620*

In 1610 Hobbes and his pupil started their Grand Tour of Europe.[105] It has traditionally been assumed that this tour lasted three years. However, surviving documents make it clear that 'Sir William Cavendish' was in Venice in September 1614 and that he travelled with the merchant, Henry Parvis, and others to Naples via Rome in the following month. On his return to Venice, he appears to have stayed with Parvis till the end of April 1615.[106]

---

[103] A second necessary cause comes to light in part IV of *Leviathan*: 'Philosophy was not risen to the Grecians, and other people of the west, whose *commonwealths*... had never *peace*, but when their fears of one another were equal; nor the *leisure* to observe anything but one another.' (ibid., p. 666). But Hobbes is unable to give an adequate account of the changes in the external relations of states, when he has already stated that any two sovereign powers are *ipso facto* in a condition of war (ibid., p. 115).

[104] *EW* II, p. 12; III, p. 114; III, p. 665; *Elements of Law*, ed. Tönnies (London, 1889), p. 65; *EW* III, pp. 239–40 (the use of colonial land is mentioned also on p. 335); III, p. 216.

[105] The date is supplied by the second prose *Vita* (*OL* I, p. xxiv) which, like the first (ibid. I, p. xiii), says they visited France and Italy. The verse autobiography adds Germany: ibid. I, p. lxxxviii. None of these accounts specifies the date of their return.

[106] *C.S.P.* (*Venetian*), XVII, pp. 106, 127, 270 (Carleton to Chamberlain); Carleton's first letter, dated 6/16 Sept., is printed in *Dudley Carleton to John Chamberlain, 1603–1624*, ed. M. Lee (New Brunswick, NJ, 1972), pp. 167–9. For the sojourn with Parvis, see Gabrieli, 'Bacone, la riforma e Roma', p. 246; Gabrieli also offers further evidence that Cavendish was in Rome in Nov. 1614 (ibid., p. 200 n. 12). The issue was first raised by J. W. Stoye (*English Travellers Abroad, 1604–1667* (London, 1952)), who adds the possibility of a

The obvious conclusion to draw is that the tour lasted longer than has hitherto been supposed. But Cavendish was elected to the 1614 parliament, and the records of that session mention the contribution of 'Sir William Cavendish' to a debate on 23 May. The matter is further complicated by the fact that Cavendish's cousin, the future Duke of Newcastle, was also styled 'Sir William Cavendish' at this time, and was also a member of this parliament.[107] The speech on 23 May concerned the naturalization of two Scotsmen, Sir Francis Stewart and William Ramsey; 'Sir William Cavendish' spoke against limiting the rights of citizenship granted to them.[108] It might be possible to clinch the matter by discovering some particular connection between these two men and Cavendish, but I have been unable to find any link with, for example the latter's Scotch brother-in-law, Lord Bruce.[109]

However, the mere fact of election to this parliament is sufficient to determine that Cavendish did return to England for it. At the opening of the next parliament in 1621, the question was debated on several occasions of whether a member could be elected in his absence from the country; a great search for precedents was made, but even Sir Robert Cotton could not find any.[110] It is surely inconceivable that just such an election in absentia to the previous parliament could have then gone unnoticed.

The alternative to be considered is whether it is Cavendish's cousin who is referred to in the Venetian documents. This would involve a second tour for him too, since he had already travelled to Italy in 1612, in the retinue of Sir Henry Wotton.[111] But the references to Cavendish's recent stay in Venice in the correspondence from Micanzio, which began in October 1615, must be taken as conclusive, given the other details which show that the recipient of those letters was Hobbes's pupil, Cavendish.[112] We are left, then, with the conclusion that after the parliament of 1614 Cavendish went to Italy for a period of roughly eight months. I can think of no special reason for this extra trip; Cavendish was too young to be entrusted with any diplomatic business, and Carleton

---

meeting with Sir Edward Herbert in Rome (p. 129). One might also raise the possibility of a meeting with Nicholas Ferrar, who was based in Padua at this time; Peckard (*Memoirs*, p. 60) observes that 'Mr Ferrar thus passing his time between Venice and Padua . . . was much sought after, and visited by the English who were then also on their travels'.

[107] The list of MPs for 1614 in Kimbolton MS 143 is printed in *The Palatine Notebook*, III (1883), pp. 126–31.

[108] *Journals of the H. of C.* I, p. 494: 'Sir *Wm Cavendish*:—Not to have a particular tax upon these Gentlemen.' The account in *1621 Debates*, VII, pp. 628 ff. indicates that he was not an experienced speaker: 'SIR WILLIAM CANDISH spake in their behalf and red it out of his table booke, and was tolde by SIR JHON SAVIL that it was the order of the house not to reade but to speake' (p. 645). This debate was held, incidentally, only two days after Sandys's great speech on elective and successive monarchies.

[109] Details of Sir Francis Stewart, the second son of the second Earl of Moray, are given in *The Scots Peerage*, ed. Sir James Balfour Paul, 9 vols. (Edinburgh, 1904–14), VI, p. 318 and IX, p. 138; also in Aubrey, *Letters*, II, 2 (= 3rd vol.), p. 367 n.

[110] Hakewill's speech, *1621 Debates*, IV, p. 54; the MPs in question were Sir Dudley Digges, Maurice Abbott, and Sir Henry Pelham (ibid., V, pp. 11, 461; IV, p. 29).

[111] Margaret Cavendish also records that he then returned to England with Wotton: *The Life of the Duke of Newcastle* (London, 1915), p. 22. See also Logan Pearsall Smith, *The Life and Letters of Sir Henry Wotton*, 2 vols. (Oxford, 1907), I, pp. 120, 123.

[112] The first letter is dated 31 Oct. 1615 (Gabrieli, 'Bacone, la riforma e Roma', p. 246); the identification of the recipient of the letters is made by Gabrieli, ibid., pp. 244–6.

remarks merely that he 'doth . . . make good use of his travels'.[113] If the visit to Venice was just a second instalment of the earlier educational tour, then the biographer may assume that Hobbes accompanied him there as well. But this remains an uncertain assumption.

Stoye and Gabrieli both add further confirmation of Cavendish's stay in Italy: the trip to Rome mentioned by Carleton seems to have borne fruit in the 'Discourse on Rome' published in *Horae subsecivae* in 1620.[114] The 'Discourse on Rome' is, like the other three Discourses and the Essays 'A Country Life' and 'Religion', absent from the manuscript version preserved at Chatsworth; but it is also noticeable that in some of the other essays the published edition shows signs of having gained from the author's experience of travel. In the essay 'Of Affectation', for example, the published version adds a long satirical account of 'the levity of the *French*, and gravitie of the *Transalpine* Traueller', and goes on to describe 'such as professe to reade Theorie of Statisme; fellows that swarm in most places abroad, especially in *Germany*, or those places where the *Dutch* most usually frequent, that nation being easie and apt to be gulled by these Imposters . . .'.[115]

The evidence for the dating and attribution of the manuscript is complicated. Francis Thompson's summary of the main facts has been printed by Wolf; suffice it to add here that the dedication by 'Your Lordships mos observant and dutifull sonne W. Cavendishe' must be addressed to the first Earl by Hobbes's pupil, and that the apparently contradictory evidence of the coat of arms on the binding might be explained simply by supposing that it was added later by the third Earl.[116] On the basis of the additions concerning travel, I would suggest that the manuscript was written before 1610, and revised after Cavendish's return to England in 1615; the impulse towards publishing it may have come from Cavendish's friendship with Bacon, whose own *Essays* were gaining fame in England and abroad. The 'Discourse of Lawes' refers to the 'different Constitutions, & *Lawes*, in our two late Plantations, of *Virginia*, & the *Bermudas*'; the programme of settlement of the Bermudas was not started till 1612, and the Somer Islands Company became a distinct corporation only in 1615.[117]

Douglas Bush has summed up the serious doubts that must arise, so far as content and style are concerned, about Wolf's attribution of these essays to Hobbes.[118] To these one should add that, if it had been the work merely of an insignificant secretary, it seems impossible to imagine why it should not have been published under the name of its author. It is admittedly also difficult to see why Cavendish should have been chary of publishing the volume under his own name, but perhaps the claims made on behalf of Common Law in the 'Discourse of Lawes' might have earned him some displeasure at court.[119] Nevertheless, in the absence of further evidence, the attribution should rest

---

113 *Carleton to Chamberlain*, ed. Lee, p. 128.
114 Stoye, *English Travellers*, p. 128 (referring curiously to '*Horae Recidivae*'); Gabrieli, 'Bacone, la riforma e Roma, p. 200 n. 12.
115 *Horae subsecivae* (London, 1620), pp. 33–9, 40.
116 Wolf, *Neue Wissenschaft*, pp. 133–4; the dedication is on p. 136.    117 *Horae subsecivae*, p. 533.
118 Bush, 'Hobbes, Cavendish and "Essayes" '.
119 *Horae subsecivae*, pp. 541–2. I am assuming that the publisher's statement that 'The Author of this Booke I know not . . .' (ibid., sig. A2) is as disingenuous as it sounds.

with Cavendish, bearing in mind the curious deception that would have had to be performed originally if the pupil had presented to his father, with a false claim of authorship, a work which he had merely commissioned from his tutor.[120]

### ADDITIONAL NOTES

A major work of scholarship on Sir Edwin Sandys is now available: T. K. Rabb, *Jacobean Gentleman: Sir Edwin Sandys, 1561–1629* (Princeton, NJ, 1998). Also valuable is an edition (produced for the Roxburghe Club) of the manuscript at Chatsworth referred to in n. 34, which, as the editor has demonstrated, is not by Purchas but by Nicholas Ferrar: N. Ferrar, *Sir Thomas Smith's Misgovernment of the Virginia Company*, ed. D. R. Ransome (Cambridge, 1990).

The issues discussed in the appendix to this article have been clarified by subsequent research. The date '1610' for the start of Hobbes's Grand Tour of Europe with the future second Earl of Devonshire was simply an error (either factual or typographical) in the account of Hobbes's life published by Aubrey and Blackburne. As I pointed out in my *De Dominis (1560–1624): Venetian, Anglican, Ecumenist and Relapsed Heretic* (London, 1984), p. 120 (n. 280), the household accounts of the first Earl of Devonshire show that the tour took place only in 1614–15 (Chatsworth, MS Hardwick 29, pp. 371, 453: departure in June 1614, return by October 1615). This has subsequently been confirmed by Linda Levy Peck: see her 'Hobbes on the Grand Tour: Paris, Venice, or London?', *Journal of the History of Ideas*, 57 (1996), pp. 177–82. The attribution of the 'Essays' to Cavendish has also been strengthened by other evidence: see my comments in 'A Summary Biography of Hobbes' (Chapter 1 above), n. 23.

---

[120] Since this article was written, it has come to my notice that an earlier version of one of the Discourses in *Horae subsecivae* was published, also anonymously, in 1611 under the title *A Discourse against Flatterie*. This discourse is not included in the Chatsworth manuscript, and it is therefore not clear what conclusions can be drawn about the latter's dating. But it does provide further evidence for the attribution to Cavendish, since the dedication, which is written very much in the tone of a social equal, is to Cavendish's brother-in-law, Lord Bruce.

See also the letter by Douglas Bush in the *Times Literary Supplement*, 31 July 1943, p. 367, for evidence of contemporary attributions of *Horae subsecivae* to Cavendish.

I am most grateful to Peregrine Horden, of All Souls College, Oxford, for his help in furnishing information about these works.

# – 4 –

# Robert Payne, the Hobbes Manuscripts, and the 'Short Tract'

## I

Thomas Hobbes's manuscripts are scattered among several archives, but the most important concentration of them is, fittingly enough, at Chatsworth in Derbyshire. Hobbes spent nearly sixty years in the service of the Cavendish family; he lived at Chatsworth for the last four or five years of his life, and died not far away, at Hardwick Hall, the Cavendishes' other great Derbyshire house. What happened to Hobbes's papers after his death, however, is not known in any detail. His executor, James Wheldon (the Earl of Devonshire's baker at Chatsworth), tried to put some of them in order, writing endorsements, for example, on many of the letters from Hobbes's foreign correspondents. Those particular items are known to have been at Chatsworth in the early eighteenth century: when White Kennett was there in 1707 he was told that 'there was an old trunk of his [*sc.* Hobbes's] papers in the house, containing chiefly the correspondence between him and foreigners'.[1] Even that trunkful could not have been there continuously, though, as today's Chatsworth (the house White Kennett visited) is a completely different building from the Elizabethan Chatsworth where Hobbes had lived. Other items relating to Hobbes were moved sooner or later to Hardwick Hall; it was there that they were studied by that pioneering Hobbes scholar, Ferdinand Tönnies, in the 1870s.[2] Some manuscripts may have become detached from the collection, such as the group of letters to Hobbes now contained in British Library MS Add. 32553; on the other hand, some items were definitely added to it, such as the copy of Hobbes's poem 'De mirabilibus pecci' and the transcript of his translations of letters from Fulgenzio Micanzio to the second Earl, both of which were acquired in the nineteenth century. Only in the mid-twentieth century were the Hobbes papers systematically listed and given the catalogue numbers which they now bear. And, although this task was performed with considerable thoroughness, some items that

---

[1] A. Wood, *Athenae oxonienses*, ed. P. Bliss, 4 vols. (London, 1813–20), III, col. 1217.
[2] See F. Tönnies, *Thomas Hobbes: Leben und Lehre*, 3rd edn (Stuttgart, 1925), pp. 11, 286.

related directly to Hobbes among the Hardwick manuscripts were left out, while others unrelated to him (papers on the Exclusion crisis of 1679, and even a document dated 1682) were included, under the somewhat disarming heading 'MSS found among Hobbes's papers, but having no recognisable connection with him'.[3]

Altogether, the collection of 'Hobbes manuscripts' at Chatsworth comprises 98 items, of which the majority are listed as being in Hobbes's hand.[4] The cataloguers are known to have made some mistakes in their identification of Hobbes's handwriting: for example, one of the manuscripts of the *Elements of Law*, in a hand plainly very different from Hobbes's, is described by them as apparently 'in Hobbes's own hand'.[5] There are a few other obvious errors of the same sort, such as the description of an autograph letter by Christiaan Huygens as a document written by Hobbes. But the true extent of the misattributions goes far beyond those obvious cases. For what neither the cataloguers nor any Hobbes scholars until recently were aware of was the deceptive resemblance between Hobbes's hand and that of his old friend Robert Payne (1595/6–1651), the Oxford don, chaplain to the Earl of Newcastle and collaborator with the Earl and his brother (Sir Charles Cavendish) in their scientific and mathematical pursuits. A careful study of the 'Hobbes manuscripts' at Chatsworth yields the perhaps rather startling conclusion that the absolute majority of them are not Hobbes manuscripts (in the strict sense) at all. They are, rather, Payne manuscripts which had happened to come into Hobbes's possession. Of the 98 items, 58 are in Robert Payne's hand. Of the remaining 40 manuscripts, only five are Hobbes holographs; ten are items that include some writing by him (his annotations, corrections or signature); thirteen have some evident direct connection with Hobbes (three of the Payne manuscripts could, as it happens, also be put in this category, as they consist of Payne's notes on writings by Hobbes); and eleven have no discernible connection with Hobbes at all.[6]

To present these findings in terms of the number of manuscripts is, admittedly, to over-dramatize. Most of the Payne manuscripts are very minor items, in many

---

[3] Royal Commission on Historical Manuscripts, 'Report on the MSS and papers of Thomas Hobbes (1588–1679) Philosopher, c.1591–1684, in the Devonshire Collection, Chatsworth, Bakewell, Derbyshire' (typescript, 1977) [hereafter: RCHM, 'Report']. The numbering of the Hobbes MSS, followed in this catalogue, had been imposed some time in the 1950s. Hardwick MSS directly related to Hobbes that were omitted from the 'Hobbes MSS' include the short manuscript on heresy (MS Hardwick, drawer 145, item 18), and the medical treatise sent by Samuel Sorbière to Hobbes (MS Hardwick, drawer 145, item 21). For some reason the 'letters from foreign correspondents' to Hobbes were also excluded from the numbered 'Hobbes MSS'. The wrongly included items are MSS Hobbes G1, G2, G3 and G4; some of these may have come from the papers of James Wheldon. Throughout this essay, references given merely in the form 'MS A1' will refer to items from the Hobbes MSS at Chatsworth.

[4] I include in this total MS E1 A, a library catalogue written by Hobbes in the 1620s and 1630s, which was not part of the original listing of the Hobbes MSS, but was subsequently added to it. I also include two unnumbered items which were not included in the listing of the Hobbes MSS, but are now treated as part of the Hobbes collection: the letters from Fulgenzio Micanzio to the second Earl (translated by Hobbes), and the letters to Hobbes from his foreign correspondents.

[5] RCHM, 'Report', entry for MS A2 A.   [6] See the listing in the first appendix to this essay.

cases single scraps of paper, whereas the Hobbes-related and Hobbes-corrected manuscripts include entire treatises. Again, the majority of the Payne items consist self-evidently of notes taken while reading other authors, and would therefore be of only secondary interest even if they were to be attributed to Hobbes: this is one reason, perhaps, why they have been little consulted by Hobbes scholars. But on the other hand, they do include two items (a list of books, and a list of manuscripts) that have been published and commented on in the mistaken belief that they were written by Hobbes.[7] They also include a text of real importance for the study of Hobbes's philosophy, a set of notes on a draft of *De corpore*, which has been mistakenly treated as a draft in Hobbes's hand by all the scholars who have studied it.[8] Identifying these items as papers written by Payne has, in the first place, a negative or corrective value for the study of the manuscripts themselves: it enables us to dispense with some mistaken arguments that have been based on their attribution to Hobbes. But there is also a more positive use to be made of this large-scale re-attribution. It adds to our knowledge of Robert Payne; and, in doing so, it may prompt a reconsideration of the role played by Payne in the intellectual life of Thomas Hobbes.

## II

First, however, the evidence for the attribution. This is and must be primarily visual: it arises from a close comparison between the letter-shapes and other features of Payne's writing in known Payne holographs (such as his letters in British Library MS Harleian 6942) and those in these so-called Hobbes manuscripts. Some of these features are quite striking, such as Payne's frequent use of Greek 'e' (a form very rarely used by Hobbes except, curiously, in his signature), while others are more easy to recognize than to describe; fortunately, the task of describing them has recently been performed with great precision by Dr Timothy Raylor, whose analysis of various typical letter-forms in Payne's writing need not be repeated here.[9] To Dr Raylor's analysis (which is of English-language texts) it may

---

[7] A. Pacchi, 'Ruggero Bacone e Roberto Grossatesta in un inedito hobbesiano del 1634', *Rivista critica di storia della filosofia*, 20 (1965), pp. 499–502; 'Una "biblioteca ideale" di Thomas Hobbes: il MS E2 dell'archivio di Chatsworth', *Acme: annali della facoltà di lettere e filosofia dell'università degli studi di Milano*, 21 (1968), pp. 5–42.

[8] See e.g. C. von Brockdorff, *Die Urform der 'Computatio sive logica' des Hobbes*, Veröffentlichungen der Hobbes-Gesellschaft, Ortsgruppe Kiel, 2 (Kiel, 1934), which included the first printing of part of this MS, and the study by A. Pacchi, *Convenzione e ipotesi nella formazione della filosofia naturale di Thomas Hobbes* (Florence, 1965), esp. pp. 23–6. Unfortunately, when Pacchi tested his assumption that MS E2 was in Hobbes's hand, one of the tests he used was a comparison with MS A10 (see 'Una "biblioteca ideale di Thomas Hobbes", p. 6)—which is indeed in the same hand as MS E2, but not Hobbes's.

[9] T. Raylor, 'Hobbes, Payne, and *A Short Tract on First Principles*', *The Historical Journal*, 44 (2001), pp. 29–58; esp. pp. 33–42. As Dr Raylor notes, the identification of the 'Short Tract' as a manuscript in Payne's hand was first made by Dr Richard Tuck. I identified two of the 'Hobbes MSS' at Chatsworth (MSS

be added that Payne's writings in Latin make much more frequent use of contractions than any known example of a Latin text written by Hobbes: characteristic forms include 'p' with a line looping round to cut across its stem, for 'per-' or 'pro-'; 'ē' for 'est'; a superscript 'r' for the '-ur' ending of third-person passive verbs; and, for endings such as '-um' or '-am', a line which rises diagonally from the finish of the previous letter and then forms a superscript horizontal bar.[10] Payne also sometimes employs, in both Latin and English, a quasi-ampersand (in addition to both the standard ampersand and the Tyronian form) consisting simply of a stylized version of 'et', in which the main line of the 't' is a curving line continuing upwards from the finish of the 'e'. And in his notes he occasionally uses a characteristic marginal mark to draw the eye to passages of special interest, a little trefoil with a curving stalk.

In several cases, there are other kinds of evidence that support the attribution to Payne. The most striking example is MS C i 1, a set of notes on Athanasius Kircher's *Ars magna lucis et umbrae* (Rome, 1646). Payne is known to have read this book: he discussed it in his correspondence with Gilbert Sheldon in late 1650. In particular, he commented on an experiment Kircher presented, in which roasted worms were placed underwater to attract fish, thereby demonstrating 'That water is a fitt medium for y$^e$ conveyance of odors, as well as aer.'[11] The passage in question—which must have caught Payne's attention, not only because of his interest in the physics of transmission through a medium, but also because he was a keen fisherman—is Book 2, part 1, chapter 9, 'De radiatione osmetica siue odoratiua', which occupies pages 147–9 of Kircher's work. And in the notes on this large folio volume in the Chatsworth manuscript, while many long sections are passed over entirely, pages 147–8 are given detailed treatment, with the relevant sentences copied out verbatim.[12] Later on in his reading of the book, attending to a discussion by Kircher (on pp. 807–9) of the use of large physical features, such as hillsides, to form graphic designs, Payne inserted into his Latin notes the parenthesis '(white horse hill)'.[13] For most of the final period of his life, from 1648 to 1651, Payne was living in his native town of Abingdon—just a few miles from the Vale of the White Horse, with its famous hillside design.

---

E1 and E2), and another MS, formerly at Welbeck Abbey, as Payne MSS in my edition of Hobbes's correspondence, but failed at that time to make the systematic study of the script of the other Chatsworth MSS which is now presented here. In his article Dr Raylor also correctly identifies three Chatsworth items (MSS Hobbes B5, C i 9, and C i 10) as Payne manuscripts (p. 39).

[10] Early examples of this heavy use of contractions can be found in Payne's notes on Roger Bacon MSS, made when he was a student at Oxford: Bodl., MSS Univ. Coll. 47–49.

[11] BL, MS Lansdowne 841, fol. 33v (Payne to Sheldon, 16 Dec. 1650). Payne first mentioned Kircher's book in his letter to Sheldon of 11 Nov. 1650: BL, MS Harl. 6942, no. 69.

[12] MS C i 1, fol. 5v: 'Odor non est ipse fumus, sed in fumo est . . . Lumbricos terrestres tostos hamo infige, et in flumen dimitte . . .' ('The odour is not the smoke itself, but is in the smoke . . . Put roasted earthworms on a hook, and drop them into the river . . .').

[13] Ibid., fol. 7v.

That particular manuscript also has a physical characteristic shared by other items in Payne's hand among the so-called Hobbes manuscripts. It is in the form of a mini-notebook, with pages of roughly 9 × 15 cm (3½ × 6 inches). A standard folio sheet of writing-paper has been cut in half; each half-sheet has been folded over to make two leaves or four pages; and these little bifolia have been placed one inside another, to create a notebook. Several other manuscripts are in the form of such mini-notebooks, some of them sewn with thread, others loose: they include a set of notes on Torricelli (MS C i 4), notes on Luneschlos and various other mathematical writers (MS C i 12), a set of geometrical exercises (MS C iii 6), and the notes on a draft of *De corpore* (MS A10).[14] Many of the items that consist of single pieces of paper are also in this format. Exactly the same format was used by Payne in almost every one of his surviving letters to Gilbert Sheldon—an untypical paper size for personal correspondence during this period, and therefore one peculiarly characteristic of Payne.[15]

Finally, one other physical feature can also be matched, in a few cases, to a known Payne holograph. Several of the manuscripts at Chatsworth are on paper with a watermark in the form of a shield, bearing a crozier over a horn, above the name 'GILES DVRAND' (arranged in two cartouches, one over the other): this design is found in MSS C i 1 (the Kircher notes), C i 4 (the Torricelli notes), C i 12 (the notes on Luneschlos and other mathematical writers), C ii 7 (a brief text entitled 'De Paraboloide') and C vi 2 (notes on chronology). The same watermark is found in one of Payne's letters to Sheldon, written on 16 July 1650.[16]

Some of the details already presented can also be used for the dating of these manuscripts. The evidence of the watermark, combined with that of Payne's comments on Kircher's book in his letters to Sheldon in late 1650, suggests that the group of manuscripts just mentioned can all be dated to c.1650. Of course Payne may have possessed a stock of paper which he used over a longer period; but in any case the notes on Luneschlos cannot be earlier than 1646, the date of publication of Luneschlos's book.[17] Two of the manuscripts are themselves dated: MS E1 (a list of

---

[14] On Luneschlos see below, n. 17.

[15] BL, MS Harl. 6942, nos. 69, 104, 122, 128, 132, 134, 135, 173; MS Lansdowne 93, fol. 179; the only exception is MS Lansdowne 841, fols. 174–5, which uses the half-sheet format without folding it over.

[16] BL, MS Lansdowne 841, fols. 174–5. Another 'Giles Durand' watermark, with the same design but with the horn pointing the other way, is in his letter of 20 Jan. [1650], BL, MS Harl. 6942, fol. 135. Payne's notes on the draft of *De corpore* include some leaves with another related watermark, with a horn over the name 'DVRAND' only. Probably Payne had bought paper from a supplier who imported it from this French manufacturer; but the purchases, and/or the supplies, may have occurred at different times. Other watermarks with this manufacturer's name are noted in E. Heawood, *Watermarks mainly of the 17th and 18th Centuries* (Hilversum, 1950), nos. 677 (dated 1648), 1219 (dated 1634/5) and 1223 (dated c.1649).

[17] The notes are headed 'Ex Luneschlos Algebra'; this refers to the treatise by Johannes Luneschlos, *Thesaurus mathematum reseratus per algebram novam tam speciebus quam numeris declaratam et demonstratam* (Padua, 1646). The RCHM 'Report' gives the name mistakenly as 'Luneschles' and comments: 'This writer is untraced.' Surprisingly, Luneschlos is not mentioned in any reference work. The prefatory materials to the *Thesaurus* state only that he was from Solingen, and was 'counsellor' of the German 'nation' at Padua

– 84 –

manuscripts donated by Sir Kenelm Digby to the Bodleian in 1634) is dated '1634', and MS C vii 4 (notes on geometrical problems) is headed 'Septemb. 5. 1638. Welbeck'. Probable dates can be assigned to some other items: for example, MS E2 (a long list of books in the Bodleian) has been dated convincingly, on internal grounds, to 1631–2.[18] Two manuscripts (MSS C i 9 and C i 10) bear the heading 'Ad Nauticam Architecturam Problema', and discuss a design known as the 'mid-ship mould'; at the head of the first of them is the annotation 'per Walt. Warner'. These must relate to the papers on this subject which Walter Warner sent to Welbeck Abbey (the Earl of Newcastle's house in Nottinghamshire) in the summer of 1635: on 21 June of that year Payne wrote to Warner from Welbeck, 'I haue here returned you back your papers, conteining the probleme of the Mid-ship-mould. S$^r$ Charles, and my self haue perused them ...'[19] And in a few other cases of reading-notes, a definite *terminus a quo* is supplied by the date of publication of the book: Payne's note on a mathematical problem headed 'Math. Recr. p. 180' (MS C vii 3) refers to Claude Mydorge, *Examen du livre des recreations mathematiques* (Paris, 1630), his notes entitled 'E Torricellio' (MS C i 4) are taken from Torricelli's *Opera geometrica* (Florence, 1644), and his notes headed 'E Bonav. Cavalerij Exercit.' (MS C i 5) are from Cavalieri's *Exercitationes geometricae sex* (Bologna, 1647).

## III

This small archive of Payne manuscripts adds significantly to the little that was previously known about Robert Payne's intellectual life. Further details can be drawn from another source: books from his library, which later passed into the Savile collection in the Bodleian. A search through the Savile collection has yielded a total

---

University (sig. C2r). He matriculated there in 1646 and received his doctorate in 1648: see T. Weigle, 'Die deutschen Doktorpromotionen in Philosophie und Medizin an der Universität Padua von 1616–1663', *Quellen und Forschungen aus italienischen Archiven und Bibliotheken*, 45 (1965), pp. 325–84; p. 357. The only account of his life that I have been able to find is the short but detailed text (written, presumably, by him) accompanying the engraved portrait of Luneschlos in *Parnassus Heidelbergensis omnium illustrissimae huius academiae professorum icones exhibens* (Heidelberg, 1660), which states that he was born in Solingen in 1620. After Padua he spent some time in Scandinavia, before becoming Professor of Philosophy at Heidelberg in 1651. A brief account of him written in 1681 noted that he had once been 'a companion of Descartes in his travels' ('erat olim Cartesii Comes in suis itineribus': letter from I. E. Thomann to C. Sagittarius, from Heidelberg, 19 Nov. 1681, printed in B. G. Struve, *Acta litteraria ex manuscriptis eruta atque collecta*, vol. 1, fasc. 6 (Jena, 1709), pp. 87–92; here p. 90); this may perhaps refer to Descartes's voyage to Sweden in 1649, though Luneschlos's name has not been mentioned in that connection by any of Descartes's biographers. His treatise on natural philosophy is strongly Cartesian: J. 'à Leuneschlos', *Tractatus de corpore* (Heidelberg, 1659).

[18] Pacchi, 'Una "biblioteca ideale" di Thomas Hobbes', pp. 8–9.
[19] BL, MS Add. 4279, fol. 182r (printed with some inaccuracies in J. Halliwell, ed., *A Collection of Letters Illustrative of the Progress of Science in England from the Reign of Queen Elizabeth to that of Charles the Second* (London, 1841), pp. 65–6). I previously wrote, mistakenly, that this letter was addressed to John Pell (Hobbes, *Correspondence*, II, p. 873); the mistake is corrected in Raylor, 'Hobbes, Payne, and *A Short Tract*', p. 39, n. On the back of the letter (fol. 182v), which is heavily stained, the address in Payne's hand is in fact just discernible: 'For my worthy friend M$^r$ Walter Warner'.

of 33 items bearing inscriptions or annotations in Payne's handwriting. (These are listed below, in the second appendix to this essay.) Using the evidence from both of these sources, and from some others, it is possible to put together a slightly fuller picture of the life of Robert Payne—someone who, it seems, played an important role in the personal and intellectual life of Thomas Hobbes.[20]

Robert Payne was born in Abingdon in 1595 or 1596. His father (also Robert) was a woollen draper who served four times as mayor of the town.[21] His mother, Martha, was a daughter of William Branche (*c*.1522–1602), one of the most prominent citizens of Abingdon—woollen draper, maltster, mayor, and (briefly, in 1593) Member of Parliament. From him (indirectly, via her elder brother Thomas Branche, who died in 1603), Martha and her husband inherited a valuable property in the centre of Abingdon, the 'Bull' Inn.[22] The Payne family possessed various other properties: Robert Payne, who was one of three brothers, would eventually inherit various 'houses gardens orchards Mault howses and their appurtenances', which he generously passed on to his sister and one of his sisters-in-law 'to enioy during their naturall lives'.[23] In this small but prosperous Berkshire town, the Paynes were members of the *haute bourgeoisie*; and when Payne matriculated at Christ Church, Oxford, in 1611 he was described as the son of a 'gentleman'. (Another entrant to Christ Church in 1611, Sir William Backhouse, was a member of an old Berkshire gentry family; he and Payne would become life-long friends.) Robert Payne proceeded BA there in 1614, and MA in 1617.[24]

It was during this period that Payne's scientific interests were, apparently, first aroused: in 1617 he made transcriptions of several treatises by the medieval philosopher and scientist Roger Bacon, from manuscripts in the possession of Brian Twyne, John Prideaux, and Thomas Allen.[25] It is not surprising, therefore, that

---

[20] In the account of Payne's life which follows, I recapitulate some material presented in the entry on Payne in the 'Biographical Register' of my edition of Hobbes, *Correspondence*, II, pp. 872–7, with the addition of some details from the valuable study by Mordechai Feingold (unknown to me, unfortunately, when I compiled that entry), 'A Friend of Hobbes and an Early Translator of Galileo: Robert Payne of Oxford', in J. D. North and J. J. Roche, eds., *The Light of Nature: Essays in the History and Philosophy of Science Presented to A. C. Crombie* (Dordrecht, 1985), pp. 265–80, and from some other sources.

[21] B. D. Greenslade, 'The Falkland Circle: A Study in Tradition from Donne to Halifax' (University of London MA dissertation, 1955), p. 155.

[22] M. Cox, *The Story of Abingdon*, 4 vols. (n.p. [Abingdon], 1987–99), III, pp. 50–1.

[23] PRO, Prob. 11/219, fol. 157r (Payne's will, 16 May 1649: the properties, which he had previously passed on to his sister Martha Castle and the wife of his late brother, William, were bequeathed to William's children). For details of Payne's brothers see Cox, *Story of Abingdon*, III, p. 225.

[24] J. Foster, *Alumni oxonienses: The Members of the University of Oxford, 1500–1714*, 4 vols. (Oxford, 1891–2), ad loc.; Feingold, 'A Friend of Hobbes', pp. 266–8. Payne was described as 15 years old at his matriculation in July 1611; hence the '1595 or 1596' given above for his date of birth.

[25] Bodl., MSS Univ. Coll. 47–49. Altogether these MSS contain transcripts of nine treatises. Two are dated: 'Communia naturalium', MS Univ. Coll. 48, fols. 2–62r, 'Feb. 10. 1616 [*sc*. 1617]' (fol. 2r), and 'Opus tertium', MS Univ. Coll. 49, fols. 2r–105r, 'AD 1617' (fol. 2r). The former was first copied from an MS belonging to Thomas Allen, and then collated with a superior version of the text in an MS donated to the Bodleian by Lord Lumley: this gives some idea of the seriousness with which Payne studied Bacon's works at that time.

when Sir Kenelm Digby made his donation of manuscripts by Bacon, Grosseteste, and others to the Bodleian in 1634, Payne went to the trouble of compiling a list of them: most of the manuscripts had been bequeathed to Digby by Thomas Allen (who died in 1632), and they included items transcribed by Payne in 1617.[26] Some of Payne's later personal connections with English scientists may have been based on acquaintances made during his student days at Oxford. Allen, a famous alchemist and astrologer, had been a friend of Thomas Hariot and was a teacher of Thomas Aylesbury (who later became the patron of the last surviving member of the Hariot circle, Walter Warner); and another close associate of Hariot and friend of Warner, the mathematician Robert Hues, came to Oxford as tutor to Algernon Percy, who matriculated at Christ Church in 1617. Also influential, probably, was the mathematician Edmund Gunter (1581–1626), who was a Student (i.e. Fellow) of Christ Church throughout Payne's years of study there, leaving in 1619 to become Gresham Professor of Astronomy in London.[27] What appears to be one of the earliest items in Payne's hand among the 'Hobbes manuscripts' at Chatsworth is a transcript from a mathematical work by Gunter, headed 'Transcript. ex MS Autographo ipsius Authoris D[omini] Edm[und]i Gunter ex Aede Chr[ist]i Oxon' ('transcribed from the manuscript, which is in the hand of the author himself, Mr Edmund Gunter, from Christ Church'): the manuscript is in a rather neat and finicky version of Payne's hand, very similar to that of his Bacon transcripts, so it may well date from before Gunter's departure from Oxford, indicating personal contacts between him and Payne.[28] Gunter's own friends and colleagues in the mathematical world of early seventeenth-century England included Henry Briggs (1561–1630) and William Oughtred (1575–1660); among the Payne items at Chatsworth are a short text on binomials 'per Hen. Briggs' (MS C i 7), in Payne's hand, and a little treatise by Oughtred on the construction of sun-dials, in an unidentified hand (MS B2), annotated by Payne on the last page: 'By M$^r$ Will: Oughtred'. Payne may have had contacts with either or both of these mathematicians; and by 1624 he clearly thought of himself as serious practitioner of the mathematical sciences, not just a pupil, when he applied (unsuccessfully) to become Gresham Professor of Astronomy himself.[29]

---

[26] The list is MS E1 (printed in Pacchi, 'Ruggero Bacone'); for the bequest see BL, MS Add. 38175, fol. 61r.

[27] M. Feingold, *The Mathematicians' Apprenticeship: Science, Universities and Society in England 1560–1640* (Cambridge, 1984), p. 69.

[28] MS B3 (quotation: fol. 1r). This substantial manuscript (60 pp.) is a treatise explaining the use of 'Gunter's Rule'. The RCHM 'Report' asserts that 'The date of the transcript is probably between 1630 and 1640': no reason is given for this dating, which perhaps arises from the assumption that the MS is in the hand of Hobbes (who is thought to have become interested in geometry in 1630, and known to have left England in 1640). Payne possessed something described as 'Mr Gunter's brass instrument' ('Instrumentum aeneum M$^{ri}$ Gunteri': probably his 'rule'), which he donated to Christ Church in 1642 (Christ Church library, 'Donor's Book', p. 94).

[29] Feingold, *Mathematicians' Apprenticeship*, p. 75.

Also in that year Payne became a founding Fellow of Pembroke College, Oxford: the impetus to convert the old Broadgates Hall into a college came from Abingdon (where a large sixteenth-century benefaction had provided for scholars from that town to study at Oxford), and the Mayor and Burgesses played a major role in the inaugural ceremony on 5 August 1624, when Payne and the other Fellows were admitted.[30] Professor Feingold has suggested that Payne's reason for moving to Pembroke was that it had 'secular' fellowships, which did not require him to follow the normal course of an Oxford don's career—proceeding Bachelor of Divinity and taking holy orders.[31] But the Abingdon connection is a sufficient explanation (Payne was probably the most academically brilliant son of Abingdon at Oxford at the time); and, in any case, Payne must have taken holy orders within a few years, as by 1630 he was appointed chaplain to the Earl of Newcastle.

Much is uncertain about when and how Payne's connection with the Cavendishes first arose. The most likely explanation is that he had come to the notice of Sir Charles Cavendish through some mutual mathematical friend—perhaps William Oughtred (who was well acquainted with Sir Charles by 1631).[32] That Payne's employment as Newcastle's chaplain started as early as 1630 is indicated by the fact that he became rector of Tormarton, in Gloucestershire, in that year: Newcastle's rental book shows that he owned the manors of Tormarton, Littleton, and Acton Turville (which lie to the south and south-east of Chipping Sodbury, on either side of the modern M4), so this rectory was evidently a living in his gift.[33] (Payne was very much an absentee rector: in March 1632 he was obliged to travel there 'uppon summons from our Archdeacon, under peine of suspension, to appeare in person at his visitation'.[34])

The first definite evidence of Payne's sharing of his mathematical interests with Sir Charles is supplied by Payne's copy (now in the Savile collection in the Bodleian) of Thomas Hariot's *Artis analyticae praxis*, edited by Walter Warner (London, 1631), which bears the inscription in Payne's hand: 'Ex dono nobilissimi Equitis Caroli Cauendysshe Decemb. 18 1631'.[35] From at least as early as 1634, he was acting, together with Sir Charles, as a stimulus and sounding-board to Walter Warner, discussing principally Warner's optical researches. (He was engaged in a

---

[30] D. Macleane, *History of Pembroke College, Oxford* (Oxford, 1897), p. 200; Cox, *Story of Abingdon*, III, p. 65.

[31] Feingold, 'A Friend of Hobbes', pp. 268–9.

[32] See Oughtred's preface to his *Arithmeticae . . . institutio . . . quasi clavis* (London, 1631), in which he states that Sir Charles urged him to publish the work; further evidence of contacts between Cavendish and Oughtred is supplied by John Pell's notes taken from a copy of F. Vieta, *De aequationum resolutione* (Paris, 1615), which he described as corrected in Oughtred's hand and belonging to Cavendish ('Ex Di Cavendyshii libro, manu Oughtredi correcto . . .': BL, MS Add. 4423, fol. 146r). Other mutual contacts between Payne and Cavendish may have included Warner and Sir Thomas Aylesbury, though there is no datable evidence of Sir Charles's acquaintance with Warner before the mid-1630s.

[33] Nottingham University Library, MS Pl E 12/10/1/9/1 (rentals, 1634–42).

[34] BL, MS Add. 70499, fol. 68r.    [35] Bodl., pressmark Savile O 9.

special study of refraction, in relation to the physiology and epistemology of vision.[36]) Payne and/or Sir Charles also took notice of Warner's other interests: in addition to his notes on the 'mid-ship mould', Payne copied out a short geometrical treatise by Warner, 'De tactionibus' (MS B5), and made some notes on what was probably another Warner text, about the weights of coins in different metals (MS C vii 8).[37] In 1635 Payne translated the second half of a little book on hydromechanics by Benedetto Castelli, *Della misura dell'acque correnti*: the attribution of the translation to 'M<sup>r</sup> Robert Payen' is in Sir Charles's handwriting, and the manuscript itself ended up in a collection of Sir Charles's papers.[38] In the following year Payne also translated Galileo's short treatise *Della scienza mecanica*; this too ended up in Sir Charles's hands.[39]

Any or all of these intellectual pursuits (except, probably, the more technical studies in algebra and geometry) may also have involved the participation—or at least the encouragement and sympathetic attention—of the Earl of Newcastle, who was, after all, Payne's direct employer. In particular, the translations may have been for his benefit. Sir Charles read widely in Latin and wrote passable French (so may have been able to cope with Italian too), but his brother the Earl had a definite preference for English: it was at his specific request that Hobbes would write a treatise on optics in that language in the mid-1640s.[40] The Earl of Newcastle had active scientific interests, both practical and theoretical. He was particularly attracted to the theories of Galileo: he was eager to find a copy of the *Dialogo* in 1634, he commissioned a translation of the entire work from Joseph Webbe, and he was an enthusiastic proponent of Galileo's theory of the subjectivity of sensible qualities.[41]

---

[36] BL, MS Add. 4279, fols. 307 (Warner to Payne, 17 Oct. 1634), 182 (Payne to Warner, 21 June 1635); MS Add. 4407, fols. 186–7 (Cavendish to Warner, 2 May 1636); MS Add. 4444, fols. 93–4 (Cavendish to Warner, 2 Sept. [1636]); MS Add. 4458, fols. 26–7 (Payne to Warner, 3 Oct. 1636); MS Add. 4395, fols. 103r (undated note in Warner's hand, 'Three opticall problems in my letter to M.R.P. [*sc.* Mr Robert Payne]'), 116–17 (Warner, draft of letter to Cavendish, undated [Oct. 1636]).

[37] Warner's work on coinage, metals and alloys was prompted by the appointment of his patron, Sir Thomas Aylesbury, as Master of the Mint. His work on naval architecture was presumably also stimulated by Aylesbury's position as 'Surveyor of Ships' (see *Calendar of State Papers, Domestic, 1611–1618*, ed. M. A. E. Green (London, 1858), pp. 23, 246, 350). The treatise 'De tactionibus', relating to circles which touch one another externally or internally, seems to have been related to his work on the geometry of the 'mid-ship mould'; one other item in Payne's hand among the 'Hobbes manuscripts', MS C ii 2, is on this type of geometrical problem, and therefore may also be connected with Warner's work. Payne's transcript of 'De tactionibus' is undated, but the watermark of some of its pages (e.g. fol. 9, and final page: pot, surmounted by a crescent, with lettering on the body of the pot, 'G' above 'RO') is identical with that in Payne's holograph letter to Warner of 21 June 1635 (BL, MS Add. 4279, fol. 182).

[38] BL, MS Harl. 6796, fols. 309–16 (here fol. 309v).

[39] Ibid., fols. 317–30; the translation is dated 11 Nov. 1636.

[40] Sir Charles's reading, in Latin and French, is widely attested in his correspondence with John Pell (BL, MSS Add. 4278, 4280); for letters written by him in French see Mersenne, *Correspondance*, vols. IX, X, XIV–XVI. On Hobbes's English Optical MS (BL, MS Harl. 3360) see the comment by Sir Charles: 'It is in english at my brothers request' (BL, MS Add. 4278, fol. 223v: Cavendish to Pell, 1/11 Nov. 1645).

[41] Hobbes, *Correspondence*, I, p. 19 (hunt for *Dialogo*, 1634); Newcastle's adherence to the doctrine of the subjectivity of sensible qualities is implied in Hobbes's letter of August 1636, 'your Lo<sup>ps</sup> opinions . . . namely,

But he also took an interest in other theoretical writers: his reading of Campanella is reflected in the comments on pansensism by one of the characters in his play *Wit's Triumvirate*, written between October 1634 and March 1636.[42] Newcastle developed a practical interest in chemistry: he later recalled performing chemical experiments in the company of 'Dr *Payn*, a Divine, and my Chaplain, who had a very Witty Searching Brain of his own, being at my House at *Bolsover*, lock'd up with me in a Chamber, to make *Lapis Prunellae*, which is Salt-petre and Brimstone Inflamed'.[43] That Payne acquired some of his employer's interests in chemical theory is suggested by Payne's annotated copy of William Davisson's *Philosophia pyrotechnica . . . seu curriculus chymiatricus* (Paris, 1635), which contains both practical instructions and theoretical speculations along standard Paracelsian lines.[44] And a possible application of—or motivation for—some of Newcastle's chemical interests is indicated by Payne's copy of a treatise on military explosives and fireworks by François de Malthe, *Traité des feux artificiels pour la guerre, et pour la recreation* (Paris, 1632), where Payne's annotations include notes on other writers about artillery, and details of specific types of explosives: 'Composition for Granado's . . . 3 parts of Canon powder well [>dryed] poured & sifted'; 1/3 of Greek pitch . . .', and so on.[45] Another of Newcastle's special interests, dressage, must have prompted the composition of a little treatise, 'Considerations touching the facility or Difficulty of the Motions of a Horse', which is in Payne's hand and may reasonably be attributed to him.[46] In addition to these more or less scientific pursuits, Payne also performed a variety of secretarial functions: in 1633 or 1634 he transmitted a 'gratuity' from the Earl to Ben Jonson (who wrote in his thank-you letter to the Earl that 'I . . . doe ioy in the good friendship and fellowship of my

That the variety of thinges is but variety of locall motion in y$^e$ spirits or inuisible partes of bodies. And That such motion is heate' (ibid., I, p. 33; the emphasis on heat suggests a particular link with the arguments of G. Galilei, *Il saggiatore* (Rome, 1623), pp. 196–202, esp. pp. 201–2). Joseph Webbe is a somewhat neglected figure, better known as an innovatory language-teacher (see V. Salmon, 'Joseph Webbe: Some Seventeenth-Century Views on Language-Teaching and the Nature of Meaning', *Bibliothèque d'humanisme et de renaissance: travaux et documents*, 23 (1961), pp. 324–40) than as a scientist, though at least the outlines of his career as a physician are known (W. Munk *et al.*, *The Roll of the Royal College of Physicians of London* (London, 1861–), I, p. 159). He was a friend of Ben Jonson (see R. C. Evans, *Jonson and the Contexts of his Time* (London, 1994), pp. 132–47), and was employed by Newcastle in making telescopes, or 'glasses' of some sort, in 1631: see BL, MS Add. 70499, fol. 145r. His translation of Galileo's *Dialogo* is BL, MS Harl. 6320; its original binding (preserved inside a later cover) bears Newcastle's monogram, 'W.N.' A list of his mostly unpublished treatises, probably drawn up for Samuel Hartlib's benefit in the late 1620s, includes works on astronomy, mathematics, music and logic, as well as a concordance to the works of Paracelsus and a 'cabbalistical dictionary': BL, MS Sloane 1466, fol. 301r.

[42] See Raylor, 'Hobbes, Payne, and *A Short Tract*', p. 48.

[43] W. Cavendish, 'Opinion concerning the Ground of Natural Philosophy', in M. Cavendish, *Philosophical and Physical Opinions* (London, 1663), pp. 459–64; here p. 463.

[44] Bodl., pressmark Savile Aa. 12.

[45] Bodl., pressmark Savile Bb. 26 ('Malthus'), final leaf; the notes on the inside front cover include: 'H. Hexham. principles of Art military. Norton's. Gunner. Brissac. discours militaire fr.'

[46] S. A. Strong, *A Catalogue of Letters and Other Historical Documents Exhibited in the Library at Welbeck* (London, 1903), pp. 55, 237–40.

right learned friend M^r Payne, then whom your Lo^p: could not haue imployed a more diligent & iudicious Man'), and in the mid- and late-1630s he also acted—as Dr Raylor has recently demonstrated—as a sort of literary 'ghost', correcting and improving the drafts of Newcastle's poems and plays.[47]

Thomas Hobbes's contacts with the Earl of Newcastle must have pre-dated Payne's: the second Earl of Devonshire, whom Hobbes served first as tutor and then as secretary, had quite close relations with his cousin, and Hobbes was well acquainted with Ben Jonson, the star of Newcastle's literary world, by 1628.[48] In the period after the death of the second Earl of Devonshire in 1628, Newcastle sometimes visited Chatsworth, acting as an adviser and protector of the young widowed Countess; she would maintain affectionate relations with him and his wife throughout the 1630s.[49] Hobbes, who had been dismissed by the Countess after the death of the second Earl, returned to England from his European tour with Gervase Clifton in late October 1630 and was taken back into the Countess's service, as tutor to the young third Earl, within the following three months—'w^ch imployment' as he later explained, 'he neuertheless vndertooke amongst other causes cheifly for this, that y^e same did not much diuert him from his studyes'.[50] Throughout the 1630s, the interest and encouragement of the Earl of Newcastle and his brother were a major—perhaps the most important—stimulus to those 'studyes': Hobbes's period of closest intellectual involvement with the Newcastle Cavendishes thus coincided, more or less, with the years of Payne's chaplaincy. Whether Hobbes spent much time at Welbeck or Bolsover is not known; he would later mention discussing his philosophical theories at Welbeck in 1630 (which suggests that he may have spent some time there between his return to England and his re-appointment by the Countess of Devonshire), and as his continental tour of 1634–6 drew to a close he was telling himself to 'haue patience till I come to Welbecke'.[51] But in any

---

[47] BL, MS Harl. 4955, fol. 203r, printed in B. Jonson, *Works*, ed. C. H. Herford, P. Simpson, and E. Simpson, 11 vols. (Oxford, 1925–52), I, p. 212; T. Raylor, 'Newcastle's Ghosts: Robert Payne, Ben Jonson, and the "Cavendish Circle" ', in C. J. Summers and E.-L. Pebworth, eds., *Literary Circles and Cultural Communities in Renaissance England* (Columbia, Mo., 2000), pp. 92–114.

[48] In 1627 Newcastle (then styled Viscount Mansfield) came to Devonshire's financial rescue, lending him the huge sum of £3,666 13s. 4d.: the indenture is Nottinghamshire Archives, Nottingham, DD P6/1/6/5. On Hobbes and Jonson see J. Aubrey, *'Brief Lives', chiefly of Contemporaries, set down by John Aubrey, between the years 1669 & 1696*, ed. A. Clark, 2 vols. (Oxford, 1898), I, p. 365.

[49] See Newcastle's letter to his wife from Chatsworth, 28 July 1629: 'A great Change Inn Chatsworth since the death of my Lo: for priuaceye, I Coulde be wearye, but I will nott Inn my respectes to my La:' (BL, MS Add. 70499, fol. 128r); the Countess of Devonshire's letters to him and his wife are in ibid., fols. 182–3, 188–9, 192–5, and Nottingham University Library, MSS Pw 1/54–66.

[50] Chatsworth, MS Hobbes D6 (legal statement signed by Hobbes and the third Earl, 12 April 1639), fol. 2r: 'About y^e beginning of y^e yeare 1631. It hapned that y^e said Countesse dismissed y^e then Tutor of y^e Earle her sonne, & receaued into that place one Thomas Hobbes, who hauing been Secretary to her Husband, & serued him 20. yeares was vpon y^e death of his said Lord & Master discharged: w^ch imployment he neuerthelesse vndertooke [etc.].' Hobbes was at Hardwick Hall by 2 Nov. 1630: Hobbes, *Correspondence*, I, p. 17.

[51] BL, MS Harl. 3360 (Hobbes, English Optical MS (completed in 1646) ), dedicatory epistle, fol. 3r: 'that [>w^ch] about 16 yeares since I affirmed to your Lo^pp at Welbeck'; Hobbes, *Correspondence*, I, p. 32.

case it is not necessary to picture him closeted in a so-called 'Welbeck academy': Hobbes and Newcastle (and Payne) would often have overlapped in London, especially during the winter months.[52] And, while he was there, he might have met Payne in other contexts too: for example through Ben Jonson, or among London members of the 'Great Tew circle', a circle with which Payne was connected through his own Oxford friends such as Gilbert Sheldon and George Morley.[53] Some evidence that Payne did visit the residences of the Earl of Devonshire—probably Devonshire House in London, but perhaps, on occasion, the Derbyshire houses—is furnished by the fact that he later enjoyed close relations with that Earl too, being consulted by him on the tuition of his own son (in 1648) and staying for weeks on end as a guest at his house in Buckinghamshire.[54]

It is clear from Hobbes's comments in his letters of the 1630s that he developed a warm friendship with Payne: in 1635 he wrote from Paris to the Earl of Newcastle that 'my loue to you is iust of y$^e$ same nature that it is to m$^r$ Payne, bred out of priuate talke', and during this foreign trip he was corresponding directly with Payne on a regular basis.[55] His high opinion of Payne's scientific abilities also emerges in his comments to the Earl: although he was happy to describe Walter Warner as one of the most able practitioners of the optical sciences in the whole of Europe, his verdict on Warner's experimentation with lenses was that 'For my part I thinke m$^r$ Payne will do more that way then m$^r$ Warner.'[56] Nevertheless, modern readers—to whom Hobbes is self-evidently the major intellectual figure here, with Payne playing little more than a walk-on part—may still underestimate the degree of deference felt by Hobbes towards his friend. Payne may have been seven or eight years younger than Hobbes, but in most other respects he would have seemed his superior. This is true even of such comparatively unimportant matters as their social status. The family backgrounds of Payne and Hobbes were similar on paper (Payne's father, a woollen draper, was mayor of Abingdon; Hobbes's uncle, a glover, was 'Alderman', i.e. mayor, of Malmesbury); yet in reality Payne came from a prosperous home, while Hobbes—who was described as the son of a cleric at his matriculation, but otherwise would surely not have been called the son of a

---

[52] For the questionable description of Welbeck as an 'academy', see the otherwise valuable study by J. Jacquot, 'Sir Charles Cavendish and his Learned Friends', *Annals of Science*, 8 (1952), pp. 13–27, 175–91; here p. 19.

[53] Another possible connection would be George Aglionby, a member of the Tew circle and junior contemporary of Payne's at Christ Church, who appears to have replaced Hobbes as tutor to the third Earl in 1628–30 and corresponded on very friendly terms with Hobbes in 1629: see Hobbes, *Correspondence*, I, 7–8; II, 777–8.

[54] Ibid., I, p. 170 (2/12 May 1648); BL, MS Lansdowne 841, fol. 174r (Payne to Sheldon, 16 July [1650]): 'yours of Jun. 3. mett me at Abingdon y$^e$ beginning of July, after I had beene aboue a moneth at Latimers, & there entertaynd with very great kindness, by that Noble Lord . . . and though I am but newly returnd thence, yet I receiud letters since from thence, w$^{ch}$ invite me thither agayne.'

[55] Hobbes, *Correspondence*, I, pp. 28 (quotation), 32 (referring to letters to and from Payne).

[56] Ibid., pp. 29 (quotation), 33–4 (praise of Warner).

'gentleman'—came from a rather impoverished one. (And, by an odd quirk of fate, Payne's own income would be supplemented by the revenues from a valuable rectory, Tormarton, that was situated only ten miles from the parish of Brokenborough, where Hobbes's father had had his ill-paid curacy.) More importantly, Payne had much better academic credentials: unlike Hobbes, who left Oxford immediately after his BA, he had stayed on for his MA and become Fellow of a college. And, most importantly of all, Payne was much more experienced in the mathematical sciences, having been a candidate for a chair in astronomy in 1624 and having probably taught mathematics at Oxford.

While Hobbes's famous encounter with Euclid's *Elements* in 1630 was probably not his first introduction to geometry as such—twenty years earlier he had worked with the surveyor William Senior on his surveys of the Chatsworth estates, which may have involved the application at least of basic trigonometry—he is unlikely, at that stage, to have had anything like the familiarity with the subject enjoyed by Payne, whose collection of books included a carefully annotated edition of the Greek text of the *Elements* (Basel, 1533), another edition of it with the Latin translation by Commandinus (London, 1620), and Claude Hardy's edition of the Greek text of Euclid's *Data* (Paris, 1625).[57] One of the mysteries about Hobbes's intellectual development, indeed, is the question of how and when he acquired his own mathematical skills—skills that may have been mocked in the latter part of his life, but which, by the mid-1640s, were thought considerable enough to justify his appointment as mathematics tutor to the Prince of Wales, and to enable him to discuss, as an equal, issues such as the rectification of complex curves with leading practitioners such as Roberval. Hobbes must have engaged in an intensive study of mathematics—especially geometry—in the 1630s; and, of all his known acquaintances in that period, Payne stands out as the person most likely to have given him advice, encouragement, and, indeed, tuition. Something of the nature of the relationship between them on this account can be deduced from a comparison between two of the 'Hobbes manuscripts' at Chatsworth. MS D2 is a genuine Hobbes manuscript: it consists of a set of 30 geometrical problems in Latin, written out in a slightly juvenile-looking fair hand which is probably that of the young third Earl of Devonshire. Twelve of the problems are signed at the end 'T. H.'; and several have 'corollaries' added (usually in the margin) in Hobbes's hand. This looks like the product of Hobbes's tuition of the third Earl; it cannot be dated with any accuracy, but, as some of the problems are quite complex, it should probably be assigned to the last period of that tuition, which ended with the Earl's attainment of his majority in 1638. MS C iii 5 is a set of notes in Payne's hand on seven of

---

[57] Bodl., pressmarks Savile W. 7, Savile W. 3, Savile V. 15. Hobbes's work with Senior is recorded in Chatsworth, MS Hardwick 29 (first Earl of Devonshire, stewards' accounts), p. 128, entry for April 1610: 'Spent by m$^r$ Senior, and Tho: Hobbes in surveyinge of lettell Longston [Little Longstone] & mounsadalle [Monsal Dale] in xij daies . . . 21s'.

those problems, all of them annotated 'T. H.'[58] Payne's notes include the 'corollaries' added by Hobbes, so he had clearly been given MS D2 in its final version (or a copy of it) to look at. In several cases he simplifies Hobbes's setting-out of the problem, or suggests alternative ways of handling it. It looks very much as if Hobbes, proud of having produced some original work in this field, had submitted it to his friend and mathematical mentor, who had gone quickly through it, understanding immediately the natures of the problems and seeing better ways of presenting or solving them.

This does not mean, of course, that Hobbes's intellectual relationship with Payne was one of overall subservience or pupillage. Payne may have had technical mathematical skills which Hobbes took time to acquire, but the vigour of Hobbes's philosophical thinking must have made itself felt sooner or later. In the field of optics—a half-way house between mathematics and philosophy—they may have operated more as intellectual partners of roughly equal standing. In a letter of 26 October 1636, Payne mentioned 'my two former letters' in which he had shared his doubts about Walter Warner's optical theories with Hobbes; he also delicately ironized at the expense of Edward Herbert's *De veritate*, using a tone of mock-modesty ('I am content to think it my weaknesse of Vnderstanding that makes me uncapable of his sublime conceptions') that did not conceal his confidence that Hobbes would share his opinion of the work.[59] That he and Hobbes were engaged in a long-running interchange of ideas on optical matters is suggested also by Hobbes's letter of 21/31 October 1634 from Paris to an unnamed correspondent, in which Hobbes responded to the question, 'Why a Man remembers lesse his owne Face, which he sees often in a Glasse, then the Face of a Friend, that he has not seene of a great Time?' This was no stray query about everyday psychology; rather, it arose from a theory presented in the standard optical literature. John Pecham's *Perspectiva communis* included the proposition 'Things always appear more weakly in mirrors than in direct sight', and argued: 'that is why a man hardly remembers anything of his own face, which he has seen in a mirror, but always carries around in his mind that of another person whom he has seen directly.'[60] As the letter in which Hobbes replied to this query—and offered a very different explanation for the phenomenon—also gave thanks for news of 'Welbecke', Payne must

---

[58] The problems numbered 1 to 7 in Payne's notes are, respectively, problems 9, 10, 11, 13, 14, 30 and 7 in MS D2. All of these except problem 9 are signed 'T. H.' in MS D2; that problem is also annotated 'T. H.' in MS C iii 5.

[59] Hobbes, *Correspondence*, I, p. 40. Doubts have been expressed over whether this letter could have been addressed to Hobbes, on the grounds that it refers to him in the third person in the opening sentence. Such doubts must arise from an unfamiliarity with seventeenth-century English style. Hobbes's correspondence includes another example of this usage, in a letter from Henry Stubbe to Hobbes: 'I reuerenced yo$^u$ too much to distrust my owne abilityes, when M.$^r$ Hobbes cryed, On' (I, p. 271).

[60] J. Pecham, *Perspectiva communis*, ed. G. Hartmann (Nuremberg, 1542), bk. 2, prop. 11 (sig. h4r): 'Res in speculis apparere uniuersaliter debilius quàm directe . . . propter quod homo uix suae formae recordatur in speculo uisae, cum alterius quem directe uidit, ideam semper in animo se cum circumferat.'

be regarded as the most likely candidate for identification with this anonymous correspondent.[61]

Within a few years of Hobbes's return to England in the autumn of 1636, there were changes in the conditions of work of both Hobbes and Payne. The third Earl of Devonshire attained his majority in October 1638; thereafter Hobbes was no longer a tutor, but probably did secretarial work for him as he had done for his father. Hobbes's relations with the Earl of Newcastle seem to have grown closer during the next eighteen months: this was the period in which Hobbes composed, at Newcastle's request, his English-language treatise *The Elements of Law*. Payne, on the other hand, left Newcastle's service: in January 1639 he was appointed to a canonry at his old college, Christ Church, and he took up residence there.[62] The reason for his departure from Newcastle's household is not clear. His relations with the Welbeck Cavendishes remained good: he continued to correspond with Sir Charles (whose friendly letter to him of 6 December 1639 survives, tipped in to Payne's copy of the book Sir Charles sent him at that time, Mydorge's *Conicorum libri quatuor*), and a decade or so later Newcastle was also corresponding with him from the Continent, sending him one of Descartes's latest publications.[63] Professor Feingold has suggested that Payne left Welbeck when the Earl was appointed governor to Prince Charles in May 1638: 'with his host's departure for the Court, Robert Payne headed back to Oxford'. This cannot be correct in strict chronological terms, given that one of Payne's manuscripts, as mentioned above, is headed 'Septemb. 5. 1638. Welbeck'.[64] That Newcastle spent more time at Court did not mean, in any case, that he no longer had need of a chaplain; and in fact Payne was soon replaced in that office by another Christ Church man, Jasper Mayne, who was appointed by Newcastle in September 1639.[65] But life at Court may indeed have diverted the Earl's energies away from his intellectual pursuits, giving Payne a certain sense of redundancy; the impulse to leave may have come from Payne himself, who probably preferred to pursue his own wide-ranging interests in mathematics, philosophy, and the physical sciences among a larger community of like-minded

[61] I previously suggested three candidates: Payne, Mr Glen, and Robert Gale (Hobbes, *Corrrespondence*, I, p. 24). Of these, only Payne is known to have had a special interest in optical theory. Sir Charles Cavendish can be excluded, as he would not have been addressed merely as 'Worthy Sir'. Warner is also an implausible candidate, as Hobbes thanks his correspondent for news of Welbeck and Clifton: the Earl of Newcastle had contacts with Sir Gervase Clifton (which makes it likely that his chaplain did too), but there is no evidence to connect Clifton with Warner.

[62] *Calendar of State Papers, Domestic, 1638–9*, ed. J. Bruce and W. D. Hamilton (London, 1871), p. 323, entry for 17 Jan. 1639.

[63] Bodl., pressmark Savile Q. 9 (the letter is at p. 134); BL, MS Lansdowne 93, Payne to Sheldon, 8 April 1650: 'I had ye honour to receiue a remembrance lately from my Lord, w$^{th}$ a booke of Des Cartes of ye Passions.'

[64] MS C vii 4.

[65] Feingold, 'A Friend of Hobbes', p. 276; Nottingham University Library, MS Pw 1 181 (Mayne to Newcastle, from Oxford, 2 Sept. 1639). Mayne called this appointment 'one of my Lord of Chichesters fauours', referring to Brian Duppa, Bishop of Chichester; but one may suspect that Payne had also been consulted.

people. He had many friends at Oxford, including Robert Burton, the author of *The Anatomy of Melancholy*. (Possibly he had already introduced Burton to Hobbes, who presented him with copies of his published works.[66]) And Payne remained a point of contact between the world of Hobbes and the Cavendishes and his own university colleagues: at some time in the 1640s he was circulating a manuscript of Hobbes's *The Elements of Law* among his Oxford friends.[67]

Otherwise, however, little can be established about how Payne spent his time at Oxford, except that he was probably teaching mathematics again. This was a field in which he acquired a considerable reputation: the astronomer Seth Ward would later refer in the same breath to William Oughtred and Robert Payne as 'ornaments of the English nation'.[68] Among Payne's books are two copies of Oughtred's *Clavis*, each with the same annotations in Payne's hand: these include extracts from Pappus and Vieta on the basic procedures of 'resolution' and 'composition' used in mathematics, as well as instructions such as 'The following propositions must be committed to memory very carefully: chapter 6, propositions 2, 3, 9, 10, 11, 12.' Evidently this adapted version of Oughtred was used by Payne as a course-book for pupils. A note in it referring to Galileo's 'dialog: 1. de Motu'—meaning the first part of the *Discorsi e dimostrazioni* (1638)—dates it to the period of his return to Oxford, but it may be that these annotations preserve at least some elements of the tuition which he may have given to Hobbes in the early 1630s.[69] (Interestingly, this way of referring to Galileo's book was also used by Hobbes, who cited the first part of it as Galileo's 'first dialogue concerning local motions' in *The Elements of Law*, and had the work listed in the Hardwick library catalogue as 'Gallilei Dialogi de Motu 4$^{to}$ Ital.'[70]) Payne's copy of that book by Galileo also survives, bearing copious annotations; his admiration for Galileo is indicated by his gift to the

---

[66] A codicil to Burton's will was headed: 'An Appendix to this my Will if I die in Oxford or whilst I am of Christ Church and with good Mr Paynes': F. Madan, ed., 'Robert Burton and the *Anatomy of Melancholy*', *Proceedings and Papers of the Oxford Bibliographical Society*, 1 (1927), pp. 159–246; here p. 219. Burton owned copies of Hobbes's translation of Thucydides and his *De mirabilibus pecci*, both inscribed 'Ex dono authoris': N. K. Kiessling, *The Library of Robert Burton*, Oxford Bibliographical Society Publications, n.s., 22 (Oxford, 1988), pp. 154, 302–3.

[67] BL, MS Harl. 6942, no. 126 (Payne to Sheldon, 29 April 1650): 'M$^r$ H. booke of hum. nat. is but y$^e$ same first draught, w$^{ch}$ you saw heretofore in y$^e$ Originall MS. wch I lent you, in Oxf.'; MS Lansdowne 841, fol. 174r (Payne to Sheldon, 16 July 1650): 'y$^t$ entire M.S. dedicated to y$^e$ E. of Newcastle; y$^e$ originall whereof I shewd you long agoe, at Oxford'.

[68] S. Ward, *In Thomae Hobbii philosophiam exercitatio epistolica* (Oxford, 1656), p. 103. Ward refers to the patronage of mathematicians by the Cavendish family, and adds a comment on the source of his information: 'prout mihi saepiùs narrârunt Clarissimi viri D.D. *Painus*, & *Oughtredus*, gentis Anglicanae ornamenta'.

[69] Bodl., pressmarks Savile Z. 19 (sig. A4r: 'Diligentissimè memoriae mandandae s$^t$ propositiones 2, 3, 9, 10, 11, 12, capitis VI'; p. 80: 'Soluit$^r$ etiam hoc probl. ex Galilei dialog: 1. de Motu in hunc modum ... vide apud Galil: pag. 46'), Savile Z. 24.

[70] Hobbes, *Elements of Law*, p. 33 (VIII.2); Chatsworth, unnumbered Hardwick MS (library catalogue, late 1650s, drawn up by James Wheldon under Hobbes's direction). There was also a copy in the library at Welbeck: see N. Noel, *Bibliotheca nobilissimi principis Johannis Ducis de Novo-Castro* (London, 1719), p. 24. The full title of the book is *Discorsi e dimostrazioni matematiche, intorno à due nuove scienze attenenti alla mecanica & i movimenti locali* (Leiden, 1638).

college library in 1642 of a copy of *Systema cosmicum* (Strasbourg, 1635), the Latin translation of Galileo's other major publication, the *Dialogo . . . sopra i due massimi sistemi del mondo*.[71]

Payne stayed on in Oxford throughout the period 1642–6, when it was the royalist garrison town and seat of government.[72] At the start of that period, in November 1642, he was created Doctor of Divinity (along with several other royalist clerics, including Jeremy Taylor and George Morley).[73] He remained in residence after the fall of the city to the parliamentary forces in June 1646; in 1648 Payne was ejected, like other royalists, from his canonry at Christ Church (and from his fellowship at Pembroke, which he seems to have retained or renewed on his return to Oxford in 1639), and after a brief period of imprisonment in London he retired to Abingdon to live with his sister, Martha Castle.[74] Evidently he was able to salvage many of his books and manuscripts from his rooms in Christ Church, and he also had sufficient income to keep adding to his collection. Some of his books are annotated with a date of purchase: Descartes, *Principia*, bought in February 1647; Baldi, *In mechanica Aristotelica problemata exercitationes*, bought in May 1648; d'Espagnet, *Enchiridion physicae restitutae*, bought in May 1649; Gassendi, *Animadversiones*, bought in August 1650; and Descartes, *Specimina*, bought in September 1650. Other items acquired during this period include Vieta, *Opera mathematica* (published in 1646); Gassendi, *De proportione* (1646); Pell, *Controversiae de vera circuli mensura . . . pars prima* (1647); and Descartes, *Musicae compendium* (1650). Kircher's 'large volume in folio, w$^{th}$ many fine cutts & diagrams in it', the *Ars magna lucis et umbrae* studied by him in 1650, cost the exorbitant sum of £3.[75] Payne's purchases suggest a particular interest in Descartes; he also acquired a copy of the *Meditationes*, which he donated in 1649 to the library at Christ Church.[76] But in his letters the highest praise was given to Descartes's philosophical opponent Gassendi: commenting on his first reading of the *Animadversiones* in 1650, he wrote that 'His reason is so cleare & his modesty so great; y$^t$ he winnes belief & loue of all y$^t$ read him; & seemes to haue deservd the

---

[71] Bodl., pressmark Savile Bb. 13; Christ Church library, Donors' Book, p. 94 (entry for 1642): 'Galilaei Dialogum de Systemate Mundi'. Unfortunately this copy does not survive at Christ Church.

[72] He had a house with a garden on the eastern side of Christ Church; the garden was used to create a private access-route between the King's lodgings in Christ Church and those of Henrietta Maria (see A. Wood, *The Life and Times of Anthony Wood, Antiquary, of Oxford, 1632–1695, Described by Himself*, ed. A. Clark, 5 vols., Oxford Historical Society, 19, 21, 26, 30, 40, (Oxford, 1891–1900), vol. I (= 19), p. 93.

[73] Foster, *Alumni oxonienses*, ad loc.

[74] On the Pembroke fellowship see Feingold, 'A Friend of Hobbes', p. 276 n.

[75] BL, MS Lansdowne 841, fol. 33r.

[76] Christ Church library, Donors' Book, p. 96 (entry for 1649): 'Renati Des-Cartes Meditationes de primâ Philosophiâ, cum varijs obiect[ionibus], Et Sol[utionibus] Authoris'. This entry is mis-dated in M. Feingold, 'The Mathematical Sciences and New Philosophies', in N. Tyacke, ed., *The History of the University of Oxford*, vol. IV: *Seventeenth-Century Oxford* (Oxford, 1997), pp. 359–448 (here p. 409). Unfortunately this copy of the *Meditationes* does not survive at Christ Church, so it is not possible to see whether Payne had annotated the third set of objections, which was by Hobbes.

reputation he hath gotten, of the Best philosopher in France.'[77] Presumably it was not just the style or manner of Gassendi's writing that pleased him, but the whole nature of his philosophical enterprise—the development of a Christianized Epicureanism, in which the novelties of the mechanistic world-view were both anchored in a classical tradition and adjusted to Christian theological requirements.

During his final period of residence in Oxford, and thereafter when he stayed in Abingdon, Payne seems to have kept up, so far as was possible, his contacts with the Welbeck Cavendishes and with Hobbes. Evidence that he did not lose touch with Newcastle—the latter's gift of a copy of Descartes's treatise on the passions in 1650—has already been mentioned. Direct evidence of contacts with Sir Charles is lacking; no letters between him and Payne survive after 1639. The main source of information about Sir Charles's intellectual life thereafter, his correspondence with John Pell, makes no mention of Payne at all; but this is not surprising, as Cavendish had got to know Pell only after Payne's departure for Oxford in 1639, which means that Pell had probably never made Payne's acquaintance. However, one piece of evidence does strongly suggest that Cavendish had not forgotten his Oxford friend: Payne acquired not one but two copies of Pell's little mathematical publication of 1647, *Controversiae . . . pars prima*, which contained contributions by Cavendish and Hobbes. One of the copies has a price marked in Payne's hand ('pret. ij$^s$ ix$^d$'), while the other does not: this makes it seem likely that the second was sent to him as a gift, presumably by Cavendish, some time after he had bought a copy for himself.[78] Also suggestive is the fact that some of the books studied by Payne (such as the treatise by Luneschlos, which was little known in England) had also been previously discussed by Cavendish and Pell in their correspondence: perhaps Payne was prompted to seek out such works by queries or recommendations in letters from Sir Charles.[79] And near the end of Payne's life, in 1651, Cavendish was in direct contact with one of Payne's closest Oxford friends, George Morley (also an ejected Canon of Christ Church, now in exile on the Continent), who was himself in correspondence with Payne: Morley later wrote to Gilbert Sheldon that 'the last letter I had, from deere friend D. P[ayne *deleted*] was an excellent Censure of D$^r$ Harvyes last book [*Exercitationes de generatione animalium* (London, 1651)], w$^{th}$ y$^e$ Phylosophy whereof he was not satisfyed.'[80]

---

[77] BL, MS Lansdowne 93, fol. 179 (Payne to Sheldon, 8 April [1650]). This letter predated his purchase of the work; as his next letter (BL, MS Harl. 6942, no. 126) explained, he had seen a library copy.

[78] Bodl., pressmarks Savile Y 4 (inscription), Savile H 3. The former has various marginalia by Payne, who seems to have been summarizing the mathematical arguments as he read the work for the first time; the latter lacks such notes, bearing only two proofs of Pell's theorem, in Payne's hand, on the inside cover and the first blank leaf.

[79] See BL, MS Add. 4280, fol. 133r (Pell to Cavendish, 4 Nov. 1648).

[80] BL, MS Add. 4278, fol. 321 (Cavendish to Pell, 6 Oct. 1651): 'The worthye bearer heerof M$^r$: Doctor Morleie'; MS Harl. 6942, no. 151 (Morley to Sheldon, 9 March 1652). Morley had serious scientific interests of his own, as his library attests: see J. C. Hayward, 'New Directions in Studies of the Falkland Circle', *The Seventeenth Century*, 2 (1987), pp. 19–48, esp. p. 42.

Also corresponding with Payne from the Continent was his old friend Thomas Hobbes. Payne's letters to Sheldon from the period 1649–51 contain numerous references to 'my friend in Paris', or 'my friend M$^r$ H.' The frequency of this correspondence can be gauged from a comment which Payne made to Sheldon on 16 July 1650, 'Since I writt to you last, I received 3 from my friend at Paris'; the previous letter referred to here was probably the one sent on 13 May, which means that Payne was receiving letters from Hobbes at a rate of at least one every three weeks.[81] Payne informed Hobbes about the unauthorized publication of some of his works in England, and in return Hobbes told him about his otherwise rather secretive work on *Leviathan*.[82] A discussion of some of the arguments of Part 3 of that text then followed, with Payne defending episcopacy against his friend's criticisms. The gist of Payne's defence was preserved in his own comments on the matter to Sheldon; but, in addition, a copy of one of his letters to Hobbes on this subject has recently been discovered by Dr Jeffrey Collins, making a valuable addition to the corpus of Hobbes's known correspondence.[83] Payne would no doubt have preferred Hobbes to concentrate on the completion and publication of *De corpore* and *De homine*, which were on topics closer to his own heart: in his letter of 16 July 1650 he told Sheldon: 'As for y$^e$ other workes, not yet publishd, . . . I haue sollicited him to hasten their edition.'[84] His correspondence with Hobbes probably dealt mainly with such matters; in an earlier letter to Sheldon, on 29 April 1650, he wrote that he had received letters 'very lately' from Hobbes, and that 'y$^e$ discourse in them is all on some part of naturall philosophie, which I had proposed to him in some former letters'. And he added: 'He much desires my company with him there, for y$^e$ good Company he assures me he shall bring me acquainted w$^{th}$ there, & in particular w$^{th}$ Gassendi.'[85] Longing to have Payne's advice, criticism, and encouragement of his work on a more frequent and immediate basis, Hobbes had cleverly dangled in front of his friend the incentive of personal acquaintance with one of Payne's philosophical heroes. Sadly it was not to be: Payne did not visit France, and Hobbes's return to England, at the end of 1651, came just too late, less than two months after Payne's death.

Concrete evidence does survive, however, of the intellectual cooperation between Payne and Hobbes during the latter's stay in Paris: the two manuscripts at Chatsworth which consist of Payne's notes on chapters of Hobbes's *De corpore*. The longer of these (MS A10), a mini-notebook of 34 folios, has received much

---

[81] BL, MS Lansdowne 841, fol. 174r (quotation); MS Harl. 6942, no. 128.

[82] See the letters printed in W. Clarke, 'Illustrations of the State of the Church during the Great Rebellion', *The Theologian and Ecclesiastic*, 6 (1848), pp. 165–74, 217–24; 12 (1851), pp. 86–96 (esp. pp. 165–74).

[83] Ibid., pp. 167, 173; J. Collins, 'Christian Ecclesiology and the Composition of *Leviathan*: A Newly Discovered Letter to Thomas Hobbes', *The Historical Journal*, 43 (2000), pp. 217–31. The letter found by Dr Collins is BL MS Harl. 6942, no. 153; this is in Payne's hand, but not addressed to Hobbes, and is a copy sent by Payne to Sheldon.

[84] BL, MS Lansdowne 841, fol. 174r.      [85] BL, MS Harl. 6942, no. 126.

attention from Hobbes scholars. Part of it was published by Cay von Brockdorff in 1934; its contents were discussed by Arrigo Pacchi in 1965; the entire text was printed by Jean Jacquot and Harold Whitmore Jones in 1973; and most recently it has been discussed by Karl Schuhmann.[86] The other item (MS C iv 2) is much shorter, consisting of only one small bifolium, and has not been discussed in the modern Hobbes literature (though it has recently been included in a list of manuscripts related to *De corpore* by Professor Schuhmann).[87] A note added to the typescript catalogue of the Hobbes manuscripts at Chatsworth suggests that it was first identified as a 'draft' of a section of that work by the late Richard Talaska. It is in fact a set of notes on some of the same material (chapter 12, and part of an early version of chapter 13) that is covered by MS A10. Either these notes were the product of an initial sampling of the whole draft noted in MS A10, or one section of that draft had been sent to Payne first; these notes are no fuller than those in MS A10 (in places they omit details included in that manuscript), so there would have been no point in making them after MS A10 had been compiled.

All the scholars just mentioned assumed that MS A10 was in Hobbes's hand, and that it therefore constituted an early 'draft' of *De corpore*. (The material it contains corresponds to chapters 1–15 and 17 of a version of that text; the titles of chapters 16 and 18 are also listed, but their text is not noted. Up to the end of chapter 12 the correspondence with the final, published version of 1655 is, with the exception of chapter 6, very close; thereafter, in chapters dealing with mathematical subjects, there are some considerable divergences.) The assumption that this was a draft raised some puzzling questions, however, about Hobbes's working methods. As Jacquot and Jones noted, some of the 'articles' (sub-sections of the chapters, numbered in the 1655 edition) are entirely missing from this 'draft', but there are no inversions in the order in which material appears. Moreover,

> sometimes one finds the equivalent of the whole article as printed, sometimes one finds the same terms but in a condensed or fragmentary form, which may even be reduced to a simple definition . . . We may add that the writing is hasty, hard to read, and that there are many abbreviations . . . The most striking thing is the unequal way in which the articles are developed. This does not necessarily mean that some were simply sketched, while others had already attained their definitive state . . .

Their conclusion was that the manuscript probably represented not so much a single draft, as a compilation by Hobbes of notes on different topics written at different times.[88] Given the assumption that this was a 'Hobbes manuscript', that was

---

[86] Von Brockdorff, 'Die Urform'; Pacchi, *Convenzione e ipotesi*, pp. 23–5; Hobbes, *Critique du De mundo*, pp. 463–510 (with a discussion of the MS on pp. 78–80); T. Hobbes, *Elemente der Philosophie: erste Abteilung, Der Körper*, ed. and tr. K. Schuhmann (Hamburg, 1997), pp. xvi–xviii.

[87] T. Hobbes, *De corpore: elementorum philosophiae sectio prima*, ed. K. Schuhmann (Paris, 1999), p. civ.

[88] Hobbes, *Critique du De mundo*, p. 79 ('parfois c'est l'article entier du livre dont on trouve l'équivalent, parfois on retrouve les mêmes termes mais sous une forme condensée, ou fragmentaire, pouvant se réduire

perhaps the best explanation available. But with the knowledge that this is a set of notes by Robert Payne, all these difficulties fall away—as does the apparent oddity of the fact that the two sections of the manuscript are headed (in accordance with Payne's usual practice of recording the sources of his notes) 'Logica. Ex T. H.' and 'Philosophia prima. Ex T. H.' And one possible reason for the changes later made by Hobbes in several of the mathematical chapters immediately presents itself: he may have been prompted to make at least some of those changes by criticisms he received from Robert Payne.

On the question of the dating of MS C iv 2 and MS A10, recent scholarship has offered diverging views. Arrigo Pacchi dated MS A10 to the mid-1640s, because of its association with notes made by Sir Charles Cavendish, on a very similar draft of *De corpore*, soon after he had joined Hobbes in Paris in 1645. (These are discussed below.) However, Karl Schuhmann has assigned to it the surprisingly early date of 1639, and has proposed that MS C iv 2 was written in the year before that.[89] He has not explained why Sir Charles, who must have had plenty of opportunities to follow Hobbes's work in 1638–9, should have found the same material so interestingly novel in 1645. No definite clues as to dating are provided by the physical features of the manuscripts themselves. The watermarks offer no help. MS C iv 2 has an extremely faint 'paschal lamb' watermark. A similar (though much clearer) mark is found more in one other Payne manuscript (MS C iii 5), which may date from approximately 1637–8, but that mark has a countermark (a cross, with a trefoil at its head and '6' and 'V' on its arms) which is lacking in MS C iv 2.[90] MS A10 has two watermarks: a 'horn' design over the name 'DVRAND', and a 'pot' design with the letters 'N' over 'LM'. Neither of these corresponds precisely to the watermark in any other Payne manuscript. The physical format of MS A10 is reminiscent of other mini-notebooks which, as mentioned above, can be dated to 1650 or the late 1640s; but Payne also used this format for MS E2, which probably dates from the early 1630s. A slightly better guide is the handwriting, which is closer in style to that found in those later notebooks (for example the notes on Kircher and Luneschlos); but this is of no help for precise dating purposes.

Luckily, however, Sir Charles Cavendish's notes on the same draft of *De corpore* do survive, and they contain the dates 29 April 1645 and 6 August 1646. His jottings cover the same seventeen chapters as MS A10 (not omitting chapter 16), and

---

même à une simple définition . . . Ajoutons que l'écriture est hâtive, d'une lecture difficile, que les abréviations sont nombreuses . . . Ce qui frappe le plus c'est l'inégalité dans le développement des articles. Nous ne saurions en conclure que les uns étaient simplement ébauchés, que les autres avaient déjà atteint leur état définitif . . . Le manuscrit représenterait donc, plutôt qu'une rédaction ancienne du *De corpore*, une mise en ordre de notes éparses . . .').

[89] Schuhmann's comments are in Hobbes, *Elemente der Philosophie*, p. xvi; Hobbes, *De corpore*, ed. Schuhmann, p. civ. No clear reason is given for the assignment of MS A10 to 1639, and the dating of MS C iv 2 is presented without explanation.

[90] For the dating, see the comments on MSS C iii 5 and D2, above, at n. 58.

consist of three groups of notes. The earlier of those two dates is found in notes on some of the 'Logica' (i.e. chapters 1–6 of *De corpore*) and the first two chapters of the 'Philosophia prima' (chapters 7 and 8); the later date is in another set of rather cursory notes on the 'Logica'; but unfortunately the fullest set of notes, which runs through the material (including the later chapters) much more systematically, is undated.[91] As Cavendish had arrived in Paris some time in mid-April 1645, it seems that familiarizing himself with Hobbes's latest work was one of his first priorities.[92] The fact that he returned to Hobbes's work in August of the following year suggests that there was more material for him to study by then; this chimes with the evidence of his first letter to John Pell from Paris in May 1645, in which Cavendish described Hobbes as making steady incremental progress ('so far as I haue reade I like verie well; he proceeds euerie daie somewhat but he hath a greate deale to doe').[93] The simplest conclusion to draw from all this evidence would be that Hobbes had reached chapter 8 in April 1645 and chapter 17 in the summer of the following year; but, given that Cavendish's fullest set of notes is undated (and that Hobbes's progress may not have been simply unilinear), that conclusion cannot be drawn with any certainty. There are some grounds to suppose, however, that the material Cavendish saw did undergo a change in its formal presentation between his first study of it in April 1645 and whenever he took his fullest (undated) set of notes. When Cavendish wrote to Joachim Jungius in May 1645 he said that he had looked at Hobbes's 'schedulae' (literally, small leaves of paper), meaning probably a loose set of drafts; but in his fullest set of notes he was evidently drawing on a fair-copy manuscript presented in such a final form that it even included marginalia (found also in the edition of 1655), summarizing the argument in the text.[94] An example of this style of manuscript presentation, imitating so far as possible the format of a printed book, is the very formal copy of a chapter 19 of *De corpore* (not, in the end, included in the printed text) which also survives among the Hobbes manuscripts at Chatsworth (MS A4): this is in the hand of a scribe in Paris whom

---

[91] BL, MS Harl. 6083, fols. 71–4, 196–211; see the discussion in Pacchi, *Convenzione e ipotesi*, pp. 18–23.

[92] The approximate date is derived from Sir Charles Cavendish's correspondence with John Pell, who was in Amsterdam. In March 1645 Cavendish and his brother travelled from Hamburg via Amsterdam and Rotterdam to Antwerp; on 26 March [/5 April] he wrote from Antwerp, saying that 'wee are nowe goeing towards Bruxells'; on 1 /11 May he wrote from Paris that 'after our parting from you, wee made no haste hither, but went little iournies & made some staie by the waye'; and Pell's next letter recorded that he had received from Cavendish 'a greeting from Paris in Mr Hobbes his letter dated Aprill 22' (BL, MS Add. 4278, fols. 203r, 205r; MS Add. 4280, fol. 112r).

[93] BL, MS 4278, fol. 205r.

[94] Cavendish's letter to Jungius of [1/] 11 May 1645, referring to material in the draft version of chapter 8, is in Hamburg, Staats- und Universitätsbibliothek, MS Pe. 1a (= Sup. Ep. 97) ('Schedulas quasdam eius de Philosophia prima perlegi': no. 85, recto), printed in C. von Brockdorff, *Des Sir Charles Cavendish Bericht für Joachim Jungius über die Grundzüge der Hobbes'schen Naturphilosophie*, Veröffentlichungen der Hobbes-Gesellschaft, Ortsgruppe Kiel, 3 (Kiel, 1934), pp. 2–4 (here p. 2). For examples of the marginalia in Cavendish's notes see Hobbes, *Critique du* De mundo, p. 480 (ch. 8, arts. 19, 20, 21, 22).

Hobbes employed for several other such tasks during his stay in that city.[95] It is not clear, unfortunately, what sort of presentation of the material was scrutinized by Payne; his notes do not include the marginalia reproduced by Cavendish, but nothing can be concluded from that fact since, as it happens, Payne skipped those sections altogether. If Hobbes had sent a version of his material to Payne long before Cavendish saw it, one might expect Payne's criticisms to have prompted some revisions by Hobbes, with Cavendish's subsequent notes being taken from the revised version. Yet, wherever the notes taken by the two men overlap, it is clear that they were reading the same text. And this suggests in turn that Payne probably saw the material after Cavendish, not before: communications with the besieged royalist enclave of Oxford were difficult in the period 1645–6 (especially in the first half of 1646, when the siege intensified), and normal deliveries of letters can have been resumed only after the surrender of the city to the parliamentarian forces in June 1646. We may guess, therefore, that Payne received his copy of the draft chapters of *De corpore* some time after that date.

Robert Payne did not live to see the eventual publication of *De corpore* in 1655. He died in early November 1651: on 11 November Henry Hammond broke the news to Sheldon: 'Poor R. Payn is gone, Gods will bee done.'[96] Four months later George Morley paid his own tribute to Payne in another letter to Sheldon; and, in doing so, he added some vital information about the fate of Payne's manuscripts:

I conceiue no man hath a more particular losse in D. P. [*sc.* Dr Payne] then my self, haueing contracted & cherished a most Intimate freindship w$^{th}$ him for y$^e$ better part of 20 yeares together . . . His Moralls were as good as his Intellectualls & his Intellectualls such as I knew no man had better; & both accompanied w$^{th}$ a Modesty allmost to an excesse; I wish y$^e$ man you say hath his papers, had but half y$^t$ Modesty & honesty y$^t$ he had, it would haue bin much better legacy for him then any writeings, w$^{ch}$ he will but scorne, as he would haue done any though y$^e$ best Philosopher Devine y$^t$ ever was in y$^e$ world had bin y$^e$ author of them.[97]

Although Hobbes's name was not mentioned, there can be little doubt he was the person referred to; Morley's impression of his personal character might have been strengthened by recent encounters in Paris, but it is most likely that he had known Hobbes in England in the 1630s, where they may have met through common acquaintances of various sorts (the Great Tew circle, 'sons of Ben', Edmund Waller, and of course Payne himself ). The suggestion that Hobbes would 'scorne' Payne's papers derived, presumably, from a general sense of Hobbes's intellectual

---

[95] On this scribe see the path-breaking work by Timothy Raylor, 'The Date and Script of Hobbes's Latin Optical Manuscript', and my 'Hobbes, the Latin Optical Manuscript, and the Parisian Scribe', both forthcoming in *English Manuscript Studies*, ed. P. Beal and J. Griffith, 13 (2003). Possibly MS A4 has survived because it too was sent to Payne.

[96] BL, MS Lansdowne 841, fol. 9r.   [97] BL, MS Harl. 6942, no. 151 (9 March 1652).

self-confidence or arrogance, not from any particular evidence that he had scornful feelings towards Payne. Certainly the latter's executor (his sister Martha) cannot have had such an idea, and she may well have discussed the matter with Payne before his death.[98] Even if the bequest of his papers to Hobbes was not Payne's own suggestion (it does not feature in his will, drawn up in 1649), it must reflect in some sense the degree of intellectual intimacy between them: Martha Castle may have offered the papers to Hobbes because she had found so many of his own letters among them. Those letters, unfortunately, do not survive; possibly they were destroyed by Hobbes, along with other manuscripts by him, in the 1660s.[99] But the corpus of Payne manuscripts that does survive among the 'Hobbes manuscripts' at Chatsworth is still a significant body of material, which casts much light on Payne's own intellectual biography—and the occasional shaft of illumination on that of Hobbes himself.

## IV

One other issue remains to be discussed: the vexed question of the authorship of the so-called 'Short Tract on First Principles'. The Payne manuscripts at Chatsworth do not yield any evidence bearing directly on this question, but no re-assessment of Payne's role in Hobbes's intellectual biography would be complete if it failed to address it. The 'Short Tract' is an undated manuscript treatise, bearing neither a title nor the name of an author, contained in a group of Sir Charles Cavendish's papers in a volume of the Harleian papers in the British Library; it was first published (and given its modern title) by Ferdinand Tönnies in 1889.[100] Tönnies confidently identified this treatise as an early work by Hobbes, for two reasons: first, because he believed it to be in Hobbes's own hand, and secondly, because its contents—which develop some elements of a mechanistic physics and a deterministic psychology, in a quasi-Euclidean sequence of numbered principles and conclusions—seemed so close to Hobbes's theories. Although fitting this work into the known chronology of Hobbes's intellectual development raised problems which troubled some scholars, the attribution to Hobbes was not seriously challenged until 1988, when Richard Tuck pointed out that the 'Short Tract' was in the handwriting of Robert Payne, and constructed a different account of Hobbes's intellectual biography in which the treatise (which he ascribed to Payne's authorship) played no role.[101] This argument found no favour with the French Hobbes scholar Jean Bernhardt, who had just laboured to produce an edition of the 'Short Tract'

---

[98] The will was proved on 13 Nov., by the oath of Martha Castle, 'To whome Administration was committed of all and singuler the goods Chattells & Debts of the said deceased': PRO, Prob. 11/219, fol. 157r.
[99] See my comments in Hobbes, *Correspondence*, I, pp. xxv–xxvi.
[100] BL, MS Harl. 6796, fols. 297–308; Hobbes, *Elements of Law*, app. 1, pp. 193–210.
[101] R. Tuck, 'Hobbes and Descartes', in G. A. J. Rogers and A. Ryan, eds., *Perspectives on Thomas Hobbes* (Oxford, 1988), pp. 11–41 (here pp. 16–18).

accompanied by a lengthy analysis and commentary, in which it was claimed that this was not only a treatise by Hobbes, but a work of fundamental importance for the birth of the modern world-view.[102] Support for Bernhardt's opinion came in 1993 from Perez Zagorin, who reacted dismissively to Tuck's claims, but advanced arguments in favour of the traditional attribution that were either not very new or not very strong.[103] Two years later, however, Professor Karl Schuhmann published a masterly article analysing the contents of the 'Short Tract' and comparing them with passages contained in the later published writings of Thomas Hobbes: he noted a number of parallelisms in phrasing and argument, thus providing a substantial basis for his claim that the 'Short Tract' was indeed an early text by Hobbes himself.[104]

In the eyes of many Hobbes scholars, Schuhmann's article seemed to have settled the matter conclusively. But in 2001 Dr Timothy Raylor reopened the entire issue, using a combination of arguments (starting with the palaeographical evidence) to build up an imposing case for the identification of Payne as the author. Raylor pointed out that mechanics, not geometry, was the field from which the quasi-Euclidean method of presentation had been taken; in particular, he observed, the opening 'Principles' seemed to be closely modelled on those of the treatise by Benedetto Castelli, *Della misura dell'acque correnti*, which Payne translated in 1635. If the 'Short Tract' was written at the time of that translation, or thereafter, its attribution to Hobbes must be highly doubtful, as he was on the Continent in 1635 and returned to England in 1636 with a theory of the transmission of light radically different from the one set out in the 'Short Tract'. As for the parallelisms noted by Schuhmann, these might be accounted for by supposing that Payne was incorporating ideas and phrases derived directly or indirectly from Hobbes.[105]

The various arguments put forward by Raylor, set in the context of his nuanced account of the nature of intellectual life in the Earl of Newcastle's household, amount to a powerful—but not indisputable—case for the overall attribution of the 'Short Tract' to Payne. Of course, in the absence of any single piece of strong and direct evidence (a letter from Payne discussing his composition of the treatise,

---

[102] T. Hobbes (attrib.), *Court Traité des premiers principes: le Short Tract on First Principles de 1630–1631. La naissance de Thomas Hobbes à la pensée moderne*, ed. and tr. J. Bernhardt (Paris, 1988).

[103] P. Zagorin, 'Hobbes's Early Philosophical Development', *Journal of the History of Ideas*, 54 (1993), pp. 505–18. Zagorin advanced thoroughly traditional reasons for dating the work to 1630, and depended entirely on the opinions of others for his views on the handwriting. Arguments that cannot be called strong include one based on the 'geometric form' of the work ('Only Hobbes's previous exposure to Euclid's *Elements* . . . and the powerful intellectual effect it had upon him can explain this aspect of the work'), and one based on its style (claiming that the author 'speaks in the first person in a manner that bears the stamp of the philosopher', and quoting the very modestly-phrased example: 'Against this some Arguments are brought, which seeme not to me to conclude . . .') (pp. 509–11). Neither quasi-Euclidean form nor such use of the first person could be called distinctively Hobbesian.

[104] K. Schuhmann, 'Le *Short Tract*: première oeuvre philosophique de Hobbes', *Hobbes Studies*, 8 (1995), pp. 3–36.

[105] Raylor, 'Hobbes, Payne, and *A Short Tract*'.

for example—or one from Hobbes), any attribution must be based on putting together a pattern of less strong or less direct clues; and for each component of the pattern a possible alternative explanation might be found. It is possible, for example, to suppose that the work by Castelli was read by Hobbes years before it was translated by Payne, and that the 'Short Tract' was written by Hobbes under its influence before his departure for the Continent; or, conceivably, that the Castelli book had been encountered first of all by Hobbes on his continental tour, read by him in Paris, and sent to Payne together with a rough version of the 'Short Tract' which Payne then transcribed; and so on. (Of those two hypotheses the latter would seem slightly more plausible, as there is some evidence to show that Payne acquired the Castelli book only in 1635.)[106] All that a historian can do in such cases is to try to construct a pattern in which all the relevant evidence can be placed without strain, with as few unsupported assumptions as possible.

The primary evidence consists of the manuscript itself. Anyone who makes a careful study of the handwriting of Hobbes and Payne cannot fail to conclude that this manuscript is in Payne's hand. Obviously, this fact does not necessarily mean that Payne was the author of the text, though it does remove one of the prime reasons for the original attribution to Hobbes, made so unhesitatingly by Tönnies.[107] But while handwriting does not simply determine attribution, it is not irrelevant to it; sometimes information about handwriting can be combined with other aspects of the physical evidence to construct a more definite attributory argument. (Thus, for example, the fact that the early manuscript of 'Essays' at Chatsworth —MS D3—is in Hobbes's hand can be used to show that he was *not* the author of that text, as the presence of corrections in another hand indicates that he occasionally misread and misunderstood the text he was copying.) In the case of the 'Short Tract', it is clear that Payne was making a copy of a text that had already been

---

[106] The Castelli book used for the translation belonged to Payne: his closely annotated copy is Bodl., pressmark Savile Bb. 2, while no copy of it is mentioned in the later auction catalogue of the Welbeck library (Noel, *Bibliotheca*). The book was published in Rome in 1628. Payne's annotations do not include a date of acquisition, but one valuable piece of evidence has been presented by Dr Raylor, who notes that the blank leaf bound after the engraved title page in Payne's copy bears a 'pot' watermark with the letters 'G' above 'RO'; the same watermark appears in Payne's letter to Walter Warner, written at Welbeck on 21 June 1635 (BL, MS Add. 4279, fol. 182).

[107] In my brief biographical entry on Payne in the Hobbes *Correspondence*, I commented merely that 'The assumptions of this work are certainly very close to those of Hobbes's early philosophy; but since it is in Payne's own hand it can plausibly be attributed to him' (II, p. 874): a footnote to this sentence referred readers to the essay by Tuck, where that plausible attribution was developed. I did not claim, as Prof. Schuhmann suggests, that the fact that it was in Payne's hand 'proved' that he must be the author ('Le *Short Tract*', p. 25). Other writers have complained that I failed to engage in detail with the arguments of scholars such as Jacquot and Bernhardt in relation to the attribution of the manuscript (see e.g. R. Wokler, 'The Manuscript Authority of Political Thoughts', *History of Political Thought*, 20 (1999), pp. 107–23, esp. p. 113; P. Zagorin, 'Two Books on Thomas Hobbes', *Journal of the History of Ideas*, 60 (1999), pp. 361–71, esp. p. 371). These critics have perhaps lost sight of the nature of the work to which their criticisms apply, namely, an edition of Hobbes's correspondence; a detailed discussion of issues related to the 'Short Tract'—which is not referred to anywhere in the correspondence itself—would have been completely out of place in such a work, and I mentioned it in passing only because of its relevance to Payne's biography.

substantially composed: the arrangement on the page avoids breaking any sub-section over a page-turn, which must mean that he was able to see how long the sub-sections were before he copied them out. It is also a very fair copy, with minimal alterations—and there are certainly no corrections in any other hand. Just one very small correction is of the sort that might be explained as a result of Payne's copying a different author's text: in section 2, conclusion 8, referring to a diagram which presents the motion of a star, the phrase 'ascend aboue D' seems to have been written first as 'ascend about D' and then instantly corrected.[108] The evidence here is not crystal-clear, however, and such a mistake is not so grossly at variance with the meaning of the text that it could not have been made in a moment of inattention by the author himself.

On the other hand, there are several small changes in the text that do suggest that the copyist and the author were one and the same person. Some of the internal cross-references entered in the text seem to have been added by Payne at a slightly later stage: in section 1, conclusion 6, the phrase 'For seing Actiue & Passiue power are inherent accidents' is followed by a reference added as an interlineation: '(by y$^e$ 16. prin:)', and at the end of the first sentence of section 2, conclusion 8, the reference '(by Concl. 3. Sect. 2.)' has been squeezed in, in smaller script, in the space remaining at the end of the line.[109] A somewhat similar case is provided by section 3, conclusion 6, where Payne has written: 'but a Phantasma is the action of the brayne qualifyed [>on the Animal spirits]. (by Concl. 4. Sect. 3)'. (I use the symbol '>' for an interlineation, placing the interlineated material in square brackets.) Here the phrase 'an action of the brayne qualifyed' was, in context, sufficient to convey the meaning; the added interlineation seems to have been prompted by checking the cross-reference, and being reminded that section 3, conclusion 4, defined a Phantasma as 'an Action of the brayne on the Animal spirits'.[110] A copyist with the instincts of a methodical editor could have done this—but the necessity for it is hardly apparent. Again, some alterations involve clarifications of the sense or tightenings of the prose so tiny that one may doubt whether anyone other than an author polishing his work would have bothered to make them. Thus in section 1, conclusion 9, we find 'whensoeuer A toucheth B, it shall moue [it *altered to* B]'; in section 2, conclusion 6, 'but being fortifyed by other

---

[108] BL, MS Harl. 6976, fol. 302v. The transcription by Bernhardt gives 'about' (*Court Traité*, p. 36). Bernhardt's edition, though an improvement on Tönnies's, is far from perfect: for a valuable list of corrections see Raylor, 'Hobbes, Payne, and *A Short Tract*', pp. 56–8.

[109] BL, MS Harl. 6796, fols. 298v, 302r. In two such references on fol. 305r, Payne appears to have begun writing the reference in the wrong order: in '(by Concl. 8. Sect. 1)' and '(by Conc. 6. sect. 1)' the word 'Concl.' or 'Conc.' was apparently begun with a capital 'S' (for 'Sect.') and then altered. This might mean merely that he was trying to regularize the usage of an inconsistent text by someone else; but, combined with the evidence of interpolated references, it might rather suggest that many of these cross-references were lacking in the original draft, and entered by him as he wrote out the fair copy. This would seem more like the action of an author making final touches to his work—though of course the point is far from conclusive.

[110] Ibid., fols. 306v, 305v.

species added [to them *deleted*], proceed farther'; and in section 2, conclusion 8, 'moues the whole line [>AC] in Time' (where, in the context, no line other than AC could possibly have been meant).[111] More intriguing is the example of interlineation in the sentence 'Against this some Arguments are brought, w^ch seeme not [>to me] to conclude that for w^ch they are vrged.'[112] It is possible that Payne's eye had missed those words the first time round, jumping ahead to the second 'to', but one must wonder whether an author would have required a scribe to go back and make such an unimportant correction, or whether a scribe so keen to present a fair copy would have bothered to disfigure the text with it if he had noticed the omission later himself. This 'to me' looks more like an expression of Payne's habitual modesty, its insertion prompted by some authorial scruple—although, oddly, this very sentence has been cited by Professor Zagorin as evidence of a distinctively Hobbesian tone.

Two other alterations are possibly authorial. In section 2, conclusion 2, there is another explanatory interlineation: 'a [>solide] perspicuous medium (as Chrystall)'.[113] (The solidity of the medium is relevant to the argument here, though the point is sufficiently made by the contents of the rest of the sentence.) And in section 2, conclusion 8, the words summing up a possible objection were presented first as 'therefore they can not moue locally', and then changed it to 'therefore they are not moued locally'—no doubt to bring the objection into line with the wording of the 'conclusion' itself, 'Species are moued locally.'[114] This is unlikely to have happened as a result of Payne misreading, as a copyist, Hobbes's writing (where 'are' is easily distinguishable from 'can', and 'd' is clearly visible); if the alteration had been the other way round, one might explain it as the consequence of mental interference from the phrasing of the 'conclusion', but the nature of this change suggests authorial improvement instead.

Finally, one little pattern of alterations is of especial interest. In the corollary to section 3, conclusion 5, the text defines 'sense' as 'a passiue power of the Animal spirits'. The definitions of 'understanding' and 'appetite' in the corollaries to section 3, conclusions 6 and 8, are similar, but have undergone slight modifications: 'Understanding (as a power) is a passiue power [of *deleted*] in the Animal spirits', and 'Appetite, as a power, is a passiue power [of *deleted* >in] the Animal spirits.' The sentence following the one just quoted repeats the revised formulation, giving it correctly first time: 'a Motion, or passiue power in the Animal spirits'.[115] While the theoretical reason for this shift from 'of' to 'in' is a little obscure, the pattern of the changes is significant. It looks as if the original draft from which Payne copied had 'of' throughout, and that he thought of the change only while he was writing out

---

[111] BL, MS Harl. 6796, fols. 298v, 301v, 302r. The last example is preceded by a deletion made *currente calamo*, with the replacement following it on the line: 'because that [starre *deleted*] beame moues . . .'
[112] Ibid., fol. 302r.   [113] Ibid., fol. 300v.
[114] Ibid., fol. 302r.   [115] Ibid., fols. 306r, 306v, 307v.

the fair copy—in fact, between copying out conclusion 5 and conclusion 6. His first correction was made *currente calamo*, on the line; the second 'of the' was copied out automatically, and he only noticed it on looking back; but when he came to the next sentence he observed the 'of' in advance, and emended the text accordingly.

Other visual or physical features of the manuscript yield little evidence of value. The watermark is a 'pot' design with the letters 'PO' on the body of the pot.[116] 'Pot' designs were very common in paper of this period, and there are other examples in several other Payne manuscripts; but this particular lettering does not appear in any of them.[117] The collection in which the manuscript is preserved consists mainly (but not exclusively) of a group of Sir Charles Cavendish's papers; this group of papers passed to the Harley family in 1713, and entered the national collection—together with other materials, now bound with it—in 1753.[118] The items bound together in this volume (MS Harl. 6796) are numbered in red ink, with the 'Short Tract' as no. 26; but the numbering must be late, as the manuscript numbered '1' is a document dated 1724. Other items in the group of papers connected with Sir Charles Cavendish include undisputed manuscripts by both Payne (the translations of Castelli and Galileo) and Hobbes (a letter to Sir Charles, and the 'Latin Optical MS'), so the mere fact of inclusion here cannot tell us whether the 'Short Tract' was by one of them or the other. Evidence from the Cavendish–Pell correspondence indicates that this entire group of Cavendish-related manuscripts was left with Pell in London in the period 1642–3, brought by Pell's wife to Breda in 1648 and conveyed to Cavendish (in Antwerp) in 1649–50; it then returned to England, either with Cavendish himself in 1651 or after his death.[119] This provides a probable *terminus ad quem*, 1642–3, for the dating of the manuscript—but there are in any case other arguments that bring that limit further back by several years, as we shall see. The only other suggestive detail about the presentation of the manuscript is that it lacks any title or any mention of an author. As has been noticed, Payne's translations do bear such headings, and in all his transcripts or substantial sets of notes on other authors among the Chatsworth manuscripts he was scrupulous about recording such information. But, as usual, alternative explanations are

---

[116] Ibid., fols. 305, 307 and 308; on fol. 305 the line below the 'O' has suffered a slight deformation of the wire, with the result that the 'O' might be misread as a 'Q'. Dr Raylor has read the letters (mistakenly, I think) as 'RO'.

[117] Payne's translation of Castelli has a pot with 'RO', with a much thicker handle and a different design on the top part of the pot; two of his transcripts of Warner at Chatsworth (MSS B5, C i 9) and his letter to Warner of 21 June 1635 (BL, MS Add. 4279, fol. 182) have a pot with 'G' above 'RO'. As one leading authority has noted, the pot was 'perhaps the commonest mark in England in the seventeenth century' (E. Heawood, 'Papers used in England after 1600: I. The Seventeenth Century to *c*.1680', *The Library*, 2nd ser., 11 (1930), pp. 263–93, here p. 288.

[118] Raylor, 'Hobbes, Payne, and *A Short Tract*', p. 32.

[119] I have presented this evidence in detail in 'Hobbes, the Latin Optical Manuscript, and the Parisian Scribe'.

possible: it may be that this information was given on a separate title page, which has since been detached and lost.

The physical evidence thus provides some components of a case for Payne's authorship of the 'Short Tract', but is far from conclusive. Further arguments for or against this attribution must be sought in the contents of the work itself.

## V

The 'Short Tract' is in three sections. The first discusses action and causation: it includes the principles 'Agent is that w$^{ch}$ hath power to moue' and 'Patient is that w$^{ch}$ hath power to be moued', and the conclusion 'Euery Effect produc'd, hath had a Necessary Cause.'[120] The second deals with vision, beginning with the single principle 'Euery Agent, that worketh on a distant Patient, toucheth it, eyther by the Medium, or by somwhat issueing from it self. w$^{ch}$ thing so issueing lett be calld Species', and developing a theory in which these 'visible species', substantial physical things, are emitted by the object and travel to the eye.[121] And the third section is on the psychology of cognition and desire, containing the conclusions that 'Light, Colour, Heate, & other proper obiects of sense, when they are perceiu'd by sense, are nothing but the seuerall Actions of Externall things vpon the Animal spirits', and that 'The Act of Appetite is a Motion of the Animal spirits towards the obiect y$^t$ moueth them.'[122] The overall impression given by this work is of a very 'modern' physics and ontology, in which everything is reduced to causally determined events in a world of matter in motion. In the words of Frithiof Brandt (who made this text the foundation-stone of his major study of the development of Hobbes's scientific world-view), 'In this treatise we see how Hobbes emancipated himself from scholasticism through criticism; he rids himself of qualities, the free agent, the soul and the forms; there remains but the necessary causation and motion. In its broad features a tendency is consequently observed that if maintained and generalized must result in a mechanical conception of nature.'[123]

However, some qualifications need to be made to this judgement. To begin with, the 'mechanism' or mechanicism of the theory here is less absolute than at first appears. The author of the 'Short Tract' (who will be referred to hereafter just as 'the author') does not rule out non-mechanical causation at the level of ontology; he merely denies that it operates in the particular case of vision. And secondly,

---

[120] BL, MS Harl. 6796, fols. 297r, 299r.
[121] Ibid., fols. 300r, 300–303.   [122] Ibid., fols. 305v, 307v.
[123] F. Brandt, *Thomas Hobbes's Mechanical Conception of Nature*, tr. V. Maxwell and A. I. Fausbøll (Copenhagen, 1928), p. 85. Brandt's judgement is echoed by Bernhardt, who writes that the text reveals 'a strict mechanism of extended matter' ('un mécanisme strict de la matière étendue'): Hobbes, *Court Traité*, p. 126.

the nature of his theory of vision can be characterized more closely: various more or less mechanistic theories were possible in the early modern period, and this author's theory conforms to one particular type.

First, the question of mechanism. To the modern mind, the adjective in the phrase 'local motion' is redundant: motion cannot fail to be 'local', as to move is to move in relation to space. But in early modern terminology, derived from the scholastic tradition, 'motion' could include various sorts of change or transformation other than a change in location. At the start of the 'Short Tract' the author keeps his options open when he states that 'Agent is that w$^{ch}$ hath power to moue', and narrows the field when he writes that 'In Locall Motion, the Action of the Agent is the locall motion of the Patient'; he then widens the field considerably when he adds that 'An Agent produceth nothing in the Patient, but Motion, or some inherent forme.'[124] When he comes to discuss the transmission of light in the second section, he sets up two main theories as possible explanations: one depends on the movement of light as a substance travelling through space (the theory he supports), and the other involves what he calls 'successiue illumination of the aire'. This means that the light-source (in his example, the sun) conveys an inherent 'actiue power' to the adjacent part of the air, that part of the air conveys the same power to the next, and so on. His objection to this theory is not ontological but merely *a posteriori*, invoking observed facts: he points out that according to such a theory each successive part of the air would have the same power of radiating equally in all directions that the original light-source did, which means that, if a beam of light were shone horizontally across a horizontal surface, a deep cavity in that surface would be equally illuminated by the illuminated air just above it shining downwards. It is no part of his philosophical project to rule out the *possibility* of physical change happening by such successive inducing of forms. Hence the notably cautious phrasing of the 'conclusion' which summarizes his argument on this point, 'Agents at distance worke not all on the Patient, by successiue action on the parts of the Medium': there may be examples of such processes, though light is not one of them.[125] Later on he gives another example of a change being effected by one thing endowing another with 'active power': when the brain conjures up the image of something previously seen and thereby 'moves' the animal spirits, the explanation is that the species of the thing have somehow imparted their own active power to the brain. The brain can now be described as 'qualifyed by those species, with actiue power to produce the similitude of those obiects whence they issue': 'qualifyed' is a technical term, meaning that it has been endowed with a quality. And, in an attempt to illustrate the point which may strike readers as a classic case of *ignotum per ignotius*, the author adds: 'Though it may be doubted how the brayne can receiue such power from the externall obiect; yet it is no more,

---

[124] BL, MS Harl. 6796, fol. 297r.    [125] Ibid., fol. 300v.

nor otherwise, then when steele, touchd by the loadstone, receiueth from it a Magneticall virtue, to worke the same effects the loadstone it self doeth.'[126]

This theory of the 'successive illumination of the air' by the imparting of a 'quality', 'virtue' or 'active power' rests on scholastic metaphysics, but as an account of the transmission of light it is not typical of the late medieval optical tradition. It is, rather, a version of the distinctive theory of the 'multiplication of species' developed by two medieval writers, Robert Grosseteste and Roger Bacon. In Bacon's words, 'a species has active virtue by which it can produce its like along all diameters in the part of the medium immediately adjacent to it.'[127] This means that

a species is not a body . . . that species which is produced in the first part of the air is not separated from that part, since form cannot be separated from the matter in which it is . . . but it produces a likeness to itself in the second part [of the air], and so on. Thus there is no local motion, but a generation multiplied through the different parts of the medium.[128]

Although both these writers had a profound influence on the entire subsequent tradition of writing about optics, from Pecham to Kepler, the tendency of that tradition was to treat light increasingly in kinematic terms: light was described as something that travelled or 'flowed' with extreme (or infinite) velocity in rays or beams, and most writers used these quasi-metaphors even though—or perhaps because—they did not have a very definite theory about the underlying physical or metaphysical nature of light itself.[129] So, when the author of the 'Short Tract' put forward an account of the successive multiplication of species as the alternative to his own theory, he was not gesturing vaguely at the textbook tradition, but referring quite particularly to a doctrine found in the writings of Roger Bacon —writings in which, as we know, Payne had long had a special interest. Indeed, the passage from Bacon quoted above is taken from the 1614 edition of Bacon's *Perspectiva*, of which Payne's own carefully annotated copy survives.[130]

[126] BL, MS Harl. 6796, fols. 305r, 305v. This is an example of non-mechanical change being brought about by contact between agent and patient. Modern writers too easily assume that the emphasis in this text on contact implies purely mechanical causation: see e.g. F. Giudice, *Luce e visione: Thomas Hobbes e la scienza dell'ottica* (Florence, 1999), pp. 23–4, where it is claimed that the 'principle of exteriority' and the 'principle of direct contact' in the 'Short Tract', taken together, 'reduce every physical action to mechanical causation'.

[127] R. Bacon, *Roger Bacon's Philosophy of Nature: A Critical Edition . . . of* De multiplicatione specierum *and* De speculis comburentibus, ed. D. C. Lindberg (Oxford, 1983), p. 185.

[128] R. Bacon, *Perspectiva* (Frankfurt, 1614), p. 72: 'species non est corpus . . . sed illa quae in prima parte aeris fit non separatur ab illa, cum forma non potest separari à materia in qua est . . . sed facit sibi similem in secundam partem, et sic vltra, & ideo non est motus localis, sed est generatio multiplicata per diversas partes medii.' (This is from Bacon's *Opus maius*, part 5.1, dist. 9, ch. 4.)

[129] See D. C. Lindberg, *Theories of Vision from Al-Kindi to Kepler* (Chicago, 1976); A. E. Shapiro, 'Kinematic Optics: A Study of the Wave Theory of Light in the Seventeenth Century', *Archive for the History of the Exact Sciences*, 11 (1973), pp. 134–266, esp. pp. 140–2; and cf. J. Kepler, *Ad Vitellionem paralipomena*, in his *Gesammelte Werke*, II (Munich, 1939), pp. 20–1.

[130] Bodl., pressmark Savile Y 2. The secondary literature on the 'Short Tract' includes a curious debate in which Aldo Gargani maintained that its theory was influenced by Grosseteste (*Hobbes e la scienza* (Turin,

As for the author's own theory of 'visible species' produced by the object and travelling from it through the medium, this too can be characterized more precisely: it is a version of the Epicurean theory of εἴδωλα, fine films of material cast off by the surface of an object like the successive outer layers of an onion's skin.[131] (Lucretius called them 'membranae', and compared them to a skin sloughed off by a snake.) The 'Short Tract's' theory about how things are visible is not primarily a theory of light; rather, it is a theory of species emanating from objects, some of which—the ones that 'send out most species'—are light-sources. 'Suppose the poynt A be a particle of sand,' begins one demonstration, 'I say that A sendeth out species in infinitum.'[132] (Other types of species are sometimes mentioned in passing: the species of heat emanating from hot objects, the magnetic species flowing from magnets, and so on.) Although almost every commentator from Brandt to Bernhardt has supposed that the author's species consist of a flow of particles or corpuscles, this claim is made nowhere in the 'Short Tract'; the author says merely that species are 'substance', and implies that each individual object sends out an individual species.[133] Emanationist theories could take various different forms: for example, they might suppose that light is composed of a special type of light-particle proceeding from a luminous body, and that things become visible when these light-particles bounce off them. But the doctrine of the 'Short Tract' is not that sort of emanationist theory at all. It is, quite specifically, an Epicurean emanationist theory.

The sources for such a doctrine were easily available: the main ones were Epicurus' 'Letter to Herodotus' (contained in the life of Epicurus by Diogenes Laertius) and Lucretius' *De rerum natura*. Few writers on optics had made any use of the Epicurean theory, however, in their account of the nature of light; the obvious objection to all theories of physical emission—namely, the difficulty of explaining why the object was not physically diminished by the process—was apparently thought insuperable.[134] (The 'Short Tract' acknowledges this difficulty, admitting that 'This indeed is hard to determine', and suggesting that bodies draw 'fuell' from adjacent bodies.[135]) However, one early seventeenth-century writer,

---

1971), pp. 97–123), and Jean Bernhardt denied it ('Hobbes et le mouvement de la lumière', *Revue d'histoire des sciences*, 30 (1977), pp. 3–24, esp. pp. 11–12). Both were right and both were wrong: the influence of Grosseteste and Bacon is to be seen not on the theory the author defends (as Gargani thought) but on the one he criticizes.

[131] The only modern writer to have paid any attention to the Epicurean nature of the 'Short Tract's' theory was Arrigo Pacchi: see his 'Hobbes e l'epicureismo', *Rivista critica di storia della filosofia*, 33 (1978), pp. 54–71, esp. pp. 62–3.

[132] BL, MS Harl. 6796, fols. 302r, 301v.

[133] See e.g. Brandt, *Hobbes's Mechanical Conception*, p. 17; Gargani, *Hobbes e la scienza*, p. 101; Hobbes, *Court Traité*, p. 107. The statements that 'Species are substance' and 'those species must be substance' are made in section 2, conclusion 10; Bernhardt mistranscribes the word as 'substances' in both cases.

[134] See e.g. the treatise by François Aguilon ['Aguilonius'], *Opticorum libri sex* (Antwerp, 1613), pp. 49–50, which discusses the Epicurean theory (quoting Lucretius) and treats this objection to it as decisive.

[135] BL, MS Harl. 6796, fol. 302r.

Friedrich Reisner, did adopt this theory enthusiastically in at least the initial part of his treatise on optics, quoting Lucretius at length and declaring that the nature of the visible species had been 'splendidly' explained by him on the basis of the philosophy of Democritus and Epicurus; so it may be significant that the library at Welbeck included a copy of Reisner's book.[136] No other optical theorist seems to have attempted a serious defence of the Epicurean doctrine, however, until Pierre Gassendi published his *De apparente magnitudine solis* in 1642: that little book was studied carefully by Payne (whose annotated copy of it survives), and may well have been the work that first prompted what became his particularly strong interest in Gassendi.[137]

One other likely source also deserves mention: the account of the Epicurean theory of magnetic attraction presented in William Gilbert's *De magnete*, in which the iron and the magnet both send out an efflux of atoms, which 'agree together in their figures, so that they readily embrace mutually', drawing the two objects together. Gilbert cited this theory only to disagree with it; in his view magnets operated by means of an incorporeal 'form', not a physical effluvium (though he did accept that explanation for the phenomenon of static electricity).[138] But the account of magnetic attraction in the 'Short Tract' ('the species of the loadstone meeting with the species of the Steele in the medium, do so fortify their motion by Conveniency with them . . .') is so close to the Epicurean one presented and contested by Gilbert that it is hard to believe that the author had not been influenced by it.[139] Magnetism is discussed more than once in the 'Short Tract', and, as Dr Cees Leijenhorst has pointed out, it exerts an influence on the basic psychological vocabulary of the work's third section, where the words 'attract' and 'repel' (previously used in the discussions of magnetism) are applied to the actions of objects causing desire and aversion.[140] Clearly, the author had a special interest in this topic. The library at Welbeck had two copies of Gilbert's book; Hobbes seems to have gained an interest in magnetism (possibly from his friends at Welbeck) in the early 1630s, when the work was acquired for the Hardwick library; and Payne

---

[136] F. Reisner ['Risnerus'], *Opticae libri quatuor* (Kassel, 1606), pp. 3–26 (p. 4: 'Quid verò sit Optica species idem Lucretius è Democriti & Epicuri Philosophia luculenter exposuit'); later, however, Reisner denies that light is corporeal and shifts towards a kind of neoplatonized Aristotelianism (pp. 36–7). The Welbeck library had the 1615 edition: Noel, *Bibliotheca*, p. 25. On Reisner, a pupil of Ramus who was chosen as the first holder of the Ramus chair of mathematics at the Collège Royal and then dismissed for reasons of general inadequacy, see A. Lefranc, *Histoire du Collège de France depuis ses origines jusqu'à la fin du premier empire* (Paris, 1893), pp. 222–3.

[137] Bodl., pressmark Savile V 13(1). There was a copy of the book in the Welbeck library (Noel, *Bibliotheca*, p. 24). The Hardwick library catalogue compiled under Hobbes's direction in the 1650s also includes a copy (Chatsworth, MS Hardwick, unnumbered); this was presumably brought back by Hobbes from Paris in 1651. For the key passage (in which Gassendi refers to the transmission of 'membranulae', little membranes), see P. Gassendi, *Opera omnia*, 6 vols. (Lyon, 1658), III, pp. 425–6.

[138] W. Gilbert, *De magnete*, tr. P. Fleury Mottelay (London, 1893), pp. 87–109.

[139] BL, MS Harl. 6796, fol. 303r.

[140] C. Leijenhorst, 'Hobbes and Fracastoro', *Hobbes Studies*, 9 (1996), pp. 98–128; here p. 119.

evidently had a particular interest in magnetism, as his surviving books include his annotated copy of the *Magneticall Advertisements* (London, 1616) by Gilbert's epigone, William Barlow.[141]

The author of the 'Short Tract', then, was not just someone moving away from scholasticism towards mechanicism. He was someone moving away from the light-theory of Grosseteste and Roger Bacon (without fully rejecting its underlying ontology) towards Epicureanism. This fits quite precisely what we know about Payne; but how closely does it fit what we know about Hobbes? On the one hand, there is no evidence to connect Hobbes specifically with Grosseteste and Bacon— apart from the fact that he knew Payne, who may have talked to him about their theories. On the other hand, he did later develop a physical theory that was generically similar to Epicureanism (reducing the universe to matter in motion, and invoking, up until 1648, the idea of an interspersed vacuum), and he did develop friendly relations with Gassendi after he got to know him in Paris in the early 1640s. But by the time his overall position could be identified as similar to Epicureanism, he had definitely formed a theory of light that was quite different from the one defended by Epicurus, the author of the 'Short Tract' and Gassendi.

Hobbes's theory of light was mediumistic: the thing that moved through the medium was not a physical emission but a dynamic pulse. The first clear statement of Hobbes's mediumism came in a letter he wrote to the Earl of Newcastle on 16 October 1636, just after his return from the Continent: 'But whereas I vse the phrases, the light passes, or the coulor passes or diffuseth it selfe, my meaning is that the motion is onely in $y^e$ medium, and light and coulor are but the effects of that motion in $y^e$ brayne.'[142] Five years later he made the point even more clearly when discussing refraction in a letter to Sir Charles Cavendish: 'in the motion of a bullet, the bullet it selfe passeth through the seuerall media, whereas in the motion of light the body moued $w^{ch}$ is the medium, entreth not into the other medium but thrusteth it on, and so the parts of that medium thrust on one another . . .'[143] Although he later changed his views about the precise nature of the generative motion that started this process, the mediumistic theory which he held as early as October 1636 was never abandoned.[144] This evidence strongly suggests that, if Hobbes was the author of the 'Short Tract', he must have written it before October 1636.

When Ferdinand Tönnies first presented the 'Short Tract' to the world, he proposed a suitable date: 1630. His reason for this dating was that Hobbes had twice

---

[141] Noel, *Bibliotheca*, pp. 22 (London, 1600), 24 (Sedan, 1633); MS E1 A (the Hardwick library catalogue, compiled by Hobbes in the late 1620s, with a few additions made probably in the early 1630s: Gilbert's book is one of those); Bodl., pressmark Savile Cc 3(1).
[142] Hobbes, *Correspondence*, I, p. 38.   [143] Ibid., I, pp. 84–5, 29 Jan./ 8 Feb. 1641.
[144] There is one apparent exception: a passage in his letter to Mersenne of [28 Jan./] 7 Feb. 1641, in which he refers to the 'matter' of light rebounding from a surface. A later passage in the same letter makes it clear, however, that this matter is only the material medium: he explains that one medium can be driven back from

claimed to have propounded his theory of the subjectivity of sensible qualities in that year. In 1646, dedicating his English Optical Manuscript to the Earl of Newcastle, he declared that 'That which I haue written of it, is grounded especially upon that [>w$^{ch}$] about 16 yeares since I affirmed to your Lo$^{pp}$ at Welbeck, that Light is a fancy in the minde, caused by motion in the braine.'[145] Earlier, Hobbes had made the same point when responding to Mersenne's (or, originally, Descartes's) suggestion that he might have 'borrowed' his theories from Descartes's published work (i.e. the 'Dioptrique' of 1637). In his letter to Mersenne of [20/] 30 March 1641, he wrote:

Now, indeed, having received that warning [*sc.* the warning that Descartes was making such an accusation], I should go further and tell you this: that doctrine of the nature and production of light, sound, and all phantasms and ideas, which M. Descartes now rejects, was explained by me in the presence of those most excellent brothers William Earl of Newcastle and Sir Charles Cavendish (who is our mutual friend) in the year 1630.[146]

This evidence, first adduced by Tönnies, has been used by many writers—most recently, Professor Zagorin—to support a dating of the 'Short Tract' to the period when Hobbes stayed at Welbeck immediately after his return from the Continent in the late autumn of 1630. But other scholars, starting with Frithiof Brandt in 1921, have pointed out the weakness of this argument: the phrases used by Hobbes ('affirmed to' and 'explained by me in the presence of') clearly refer only to conversation. As Brandt put it, 'In neither of the passages does he mention a treatise wherein he has represented the case, indeed it decidedly appears that it is a question of verbal communication.'[147] Brandt therefore assumed that the 'Short Tract' was written a little later, between 1630 and Hobbes's departure from England in 1634. Recently Professor Schuhmann has made the same point about these two passages, and has proposed a date of 1632–3.[148] But, although the arguments used by Brandt and Schuhmann take some account of the passage in Hobbes's letter to Mersenne (quoted above), they miss its larger significance. Hobbes was desperate to prove that he had not 'borrowed' his fundamental ideas from Descartes. What he needed to produce or refer to, above all, was solid evidence that he had had those ideas

---

the surface of another but still propagate motion through it, as a hammer bounces back from a bell but sends vibrations through the bell's metal (Hobbes, *Correspondence*, I, pp. 67–8, 76–7). For a valuable summary of the changes in Hobbes's theories about the motion that generated light, see Giudice, *Luce e visione*, pp. 31–40.

[145] BL, MS Harl. 3360, fol. 3r.

[146] Hobbes, *Correspondence*, I, pp. 102–3, 108 ('Iam vero monitus, hoc dicere apud te amplius habeo, me doctrinam illam de naturâ et productione luminis, et soni, et omnium Phantasmatum siue idearum, quam Dominus deCartes nunc respuit, explicasse Coram Dominis fratribus excellentissimis Gulielmo Comite de Newcastell et Carolo Cauendish Equite aurato communi nostro amico, anno 1630').

[147] Brandt, *Hobbes's Mechanical Conception*, p. 50. The original Danish edition of Brandt's book was published in 1921 (see n. 172).

[148] Schuhmann, 'Le *Short Tract*', pp. 21–6. Bernhardt, who did not properly address this point, suggested that it was written at Welbeck in the first months of 1631: Hobbes, *Court traité*, p. 92.

some time before he read the 'Dioptrique' in 1637: the more solid the evidence, the better, so long as the date was before that year. In other words, if he had been able to say 'that doctrine was written down by me in a little treatise, which was read by the Earl of Newcastle and his brother in 1632', he would surely have done so: the testimony of members of the nobility was useful, but to combine it with reference to a written work would have been more useful still (*verba volant, scripta manent*), and the difference in time between 1630 and 1632 would have made no difference whatsoever to his argument.

One other potential problem arises from that passage in the letter to Mersenne. If it were literally true that the 'doctrine of the *nature and production* of light' held by Hobbes in 1641 had been propounded by him as early as 1630, this would mean that the 'Short Tract', which has a very different doctrine on that subject, could not have been written by him then (or, presumably, thereafter).[149] One way to overcome this problem might be to assume that Hobbes was using the term 'light' in that passage (as he sometimes did) to mean just the human experience of light, so that his comments really referred only to the doctrine of the subjectivity of sensible qualities. The difficulty with that explanation is that we know that Hobbes's theory of the physical nature and production of light (not just the mental perception of it) was actually at stake in his argument with Descartes: this whole dispute had arisen over Descartes's dismissive reaction to a text by Hobbes, part of which has been preserved in the form of Hobbes's little optical treatise published by Mersenne in 1644—and that treatise includes an explicit account of the physical production and mediumistic transmission of light.[150] An alternative explanation might be that Hobbes was expressing himself a little too categorically in his letter to Mersenne, glossing over some alterations in the details of his theories that had taken place after 1630. As we shall see, there is evidence to suggest that his thinking about the transmission of light did undergo some changes, or at least some significant elaboration of detail, in 1636; so this explanation has a certain plausibility.

Hobbes may not have had a properly worked-out mediumistic theory of light as early as 1630; but is there any evidence at all to show that he had ever believed in the transmission of physical species by local motion? Professor Schuhmann does offer such evidence: he quotes a passage from the appendix to the Latin version of *Leviathan* (published in 1668), in which 'A', one of the two speakers in the dialogue, says that the definition of 'body' which he now accepts is 'that of which it can truly be said that it exists really in itself, and also has some size'. The speaker continues:

---

[149] This point has been neglected by most writers, but was made in passing by Arrigo Pacchi: 'Hobbes e l'epicureismo', p. 63.

[150] M. Mersenne, *Universae geometriae synopsis* (Paris, 1644), pp. 567–89, 'Opticae liber septimus' (*OL* V, pp. 217–48).

I remember, however, that I once thought 'body' was merely that which presented itself to my touch or sight. Therefore the species of a body that appeared in a mirror, or in sleep, or in shadows, although I wondered at it, was nevertheless judged by me to be 'body' too. Later, though, considering that those species vanish away, as if their existence depended not on themselves but on animated nature, I no longer considered them to be real things, but phantasms.[151]

Professor Schuhmann calls this an 'autobiographical' statement by Hobbes, and argues that it 'confirms' that Hobbes once held the theory of the 'Short Tract'.[152] When he quotes this passage, however, he omits the words 'that appeared in a mirror, or in sleep, or in shadows', replacing them with three dots. The omission is unfortunate, as those words contain what is surely the clue as to the real meaning of 'species' in this passage—something quite different from the meaning of the term in the 'Short Tract'. The species of the 'Short Tract' are physical things that pass from an object to the viewer's eye, and then cause a motion or change in animal spirits or the brain. Such species can certainly pass via reflection from a mirror; but they are not present in dreams (which are caused by subsequent actions of the brain on the animal spirits), or in the appearances imagined by fearful people when they are awake. (That this is the significance of this reference to 'shadows' is indicated by other passages in Hobbes's works, such as his comment in *The Elements of Law*: 'proceeding from the ignorance of what those things are which are called spectra, images that appear in the dark to children, and such as have strong fears, and other strong imaginations . . .'[153]) In other words, the word 'species' here is used merely as a very general term for 'appearances'.[154] The speaker 'A' is just describing a pre-scientific mentality, using a first-person account as a pedagogical device; while there is little reason in any case to suppose that this is an autobiographical statement by Hobbes himself, there is no reason to think that it refers to the distinctive theory of 'species' propounded in the 'Short Tract'.

There is, however, one genuinely autobiographical passage in which Hobbes did use 'species' as a technical term in the theory of vision. In his verse autobiography,

---

[151] T. Hobbes, *Leviathan*, in his *Opera philosophica, quae latinè scripsit, omnia* (Amsterdam, 1668), sep. pag., p. 344 (*OL* III, p. 537): 'Ego per *Corpus* intelligo nunc id de quo verè dici potest, quod existit realiter in seipso, habetque etiam aliquam magnitudinem . . . Memini tamen quod *Corpus* putarem aliquando id solum esse, quod Tactui meo vel Visui obstaret. Itaque speciem quoque corporis in speculo, aut somno, aut tenebris apparentem, quanquam miratus, corpus tamen esse arbitrabar. Sed consideranti posteà Species illas evanescere, ut quarum existentia dependeret non à seipsis, sed à natura animata, non amplius mihi visae sunt reales, sed Phantasmata . . .'.

[152] Schuhmann, 'Le *Short Tract*', p. 20. The claim is supported by C. Leijenhorst, *Hobbes and the Aristotelians: The Aristotelian Setting of Thomas Hobbes's Natural Philosophy* (Utrecht, 1998), pp. 91–2.

[153] *Elements of Law*, XI.5 (p. 56).

[154] Cf. similar usage in *De corpore*, VII.1. Hobbes uses the terms 'fancy' and 'appearance' in a later discussion of the same examples of reflection, dream and hallucination: 'It is a fancy, such as is the appearance of your face in a Looking-glass; such as is a Dream; such as is a Ghost; such as is the spot before the Eye that hath stared upon the Son [*sic*] or Fire. For all these are of the Regiment of Fancy, without any body concealed under them' (*Seven Philosophical Problems* (London, 1682), pp. 28–9; *EW* VII, p. 27).

written in the 1670s, he criticized the scholastic physics and metaphysics which he was taught at Oxford: adopting a tone of open ridicule, he referred to 'species of things, which, by flying through the air, impart here the forms of things to the eyes, there sounds to the ears'.[155] If Hobbes's intellectual journey had been in three stages, starting with scholastic theories, then adopting the Epicurean species theory of the 'Short Tract', and finally shifting to a mediumistic explanation, one might expect him to have regarded (as the modern commentators do) the move from stage one to stage two as the really decisive one. Given that Hobbes himself clearly did think that his adoption of a theory of the subjectivity of sensible qualities in c.1630 was a watershed in his development, the theories of the 'Short Tract' would surely have been regarded by him—if he had written it after that watershed—as belonging to the 'modern' half of his intellectual biography, even if he had subsequently modified them on points of detail. But in this passage in his verse autobiography he wrote about the old, outmoded scholastic theory in a way that conflated it with the central doctrine of the 'Short Tract', as if there were no significant difference between them—though he must have been aware that this way of presenting the scholastic theory was a travesty. (And he added, for good measure, an attack on the doctrine of 'sympathy' and 'antipathy'—terms which are also used, with a non-scholastic theory attached to them, in the 'Short Tract'.[156]) It must be doubted whether he would have chosen, as a way of ridiculing the old theories, to dress them up in precisely the doctrine by means of which he had first emancipated himself from them.

In any investigation of these issues, the chief difficulty is that of finding out, in the virtual absence of direct evidence, what theories about the transmission of light Hobbes did hold before he wrote his 'mediumistic' letter in October 1636. The evidence is slight and somewhat indirect, but it is not lacking altogether. On 2 May 1636 Sir Charles Cavendish wrote to Walter Warner, saying that he had 'latelie' received a letter from Hobbes, and enclosing a 'paper' Hobbes had sent about a curious phenomenon observed in a cylindrical mirror, where the image of an object placed inside the mirror seemed to hang directly over the object itself. Cavendish added:

M[r] Hobbs coniectures that the approach of [>the] Image proceeds from the strength of action from the obiect, which is greater heere than in a plaine, by reason of the concauitie of the cylinder which gathers the beames, and by that meanes makes the motion or streame of the reflected beames stronger.[157]

---

[155] *OL* I, p. lxxxvii: 'Et species rerum, volitando per aera, formas / Donare hinc oculis, auribus inde sonos'.

[156] Ibid., I, p. lxxxvii, 'Multos effectus tribuit *syn et antipathiae*...'; BL, MS Harl. 6796, fol. 303r, 'in bodyes that work by Antipathy'. Hobbes's ridicule of the idea that the same species supplies both visual images and sounds would also apply to the doctrine of the 'Short Tract'.

[157] BL, MS Add. 4407, fol. 186r. This letter is printed in Halliwell, *Collection of Letters*, pp. 66–7, and in Mersenne, *Correspondance*, VI, p. 66; the latter misprints 'motion or streame' as 'motion of streame', and both printings give the reference incorrectly as MS Add. 4405, fol. 161.

This reference to the 'motion or streame' of the beams certainly seems, at first sight, to involve something much more like an emanationist transmission theory.

Hobbes had been discussing the reflection and refraction of light with Walter Warner before he left for the Continent in 1634. One likely fruit of those discussions is a short text and diagram by him, headed 'M$^r$. Hobbes analogy' in Warner's hand, which (though the identification is not entirely certain) Warner seems to have referred to in a letter he wrote to Payne on 17 October 1634.[158] The text offers a kinematic explanation of the sine-law of refraction, taking the example of a beam striking the surface of a second medium at an angle, and analysing the motion of the beam in terms of its vertical and lateral components. This too may suggest that Hobbes was operating with an emanationist theory, in which light was a physical thing actually travelling through space.

Are these two pieces of evidence sufficient, then, to show that Hobbes did hold the transmission theory of the 'Short Tract' in the period before October 1636? Unfortunately, they are not. If the doctrine summarized by Cavendish here was an emanationist theory, it was not the Epicurean theory of the 'Short Tract'. That text's account of the reason why images became weaker with distance was that the constant expansion of the species as it travelled outwards from the object made it more and more 'diffused' or attenuated: the significant factor was merely the quantity of species-substance in a given area.[159] So, although the author of the 'Short Tract' did talk about species becoming 'weaker' or 'stronger', his meaning was only that they were more or less diffused; dynamic explanation, taking into account the 'strength of action' of the object, played no part in his theory at all. As for the kinematic approach adopted in the 'analogy', it was merely the standard approach taken by all the optical textbooks: refraction had been treated on such a basis, distinguishing vertical and lateral components, by writers from Alhazen to Kepler.[160] As was mentioned above, the practice of talking about the action of light in terms of the 'motion' of rays or beams was extremely well established in the optical literature. Most writers referred to light as travelling outwards, in straight radial lines, as a 'flux' or 'efflux' from the luminous body.[161] This did not mean that they had

---

[158] BL, MS Add. 4395, fols. 131r, 133r (both thus headed in Warner's hand); MS Add. 4279, fol. 307 (Warner to Payne, 17 Oct. 1634: 'For the problem of refractions, w$^{ch}$ you write of, I pray you by any meanes, send it to M$^r$ Hobbes . . . For I haue found [>him] free with me, and I will not be reserued with him, yf it please god I may liue to see him again. That analogy w$^{ch}$ you haue, though it be but a particular passion of the subiect it concerns, yet it is very conducible to the theory and investigation of the cause of refraction').

[159] BL, MS Harl. 6796, fol. 301r.

[160] See A. I. Sabra, *Theories of Light from Descartes to Newton* (London, 1967), p. 98; Shapiro, 'Kinematic Optics', p. 170. It should be added that the term 'analogy' here does not refer to making an analogy between light and the motion of an object, as if that had been something new or remarkable (it was not); it is, rather, a mathematical term meaning 'proportion', and refers to the proportion here between the angle of incidence and the angle of refraction.

[161] See for example F. Maurolycus, *Photismi de lumine, & umbra* (Naples, 1611), p. 1: 'Omne lucidi punctum per rectam radiare lineam'; M. A. de Dominis, *De radiis visus et lucis* (Venice, 1611), p. 2: 'lumen quod effundit per medium diaphanum'; C. Scheiner, *Oculus, hoc est: fundamentum opticum* (Innsbruck, 1619),

adopted a particular theory about the underlying nature of light; it was, rather, just a more or less metaphorical way of handling their subject, at one remove from any physical or metaphysical theoretical commitments. As the Jesuit François Aguilon put it in his book,

> Let no one be worried by the fact that we talk about light being moved and conveyed, advancing and receding, or contracting and dilating. For although it is true that that which is moved is a body, and that any motion happens in time—whereas light is in fact incorporeal, and extends to the full in no time at all—nevertheless, this way of talking should not be condemned on those grounds, since we do not have a more adequate way of talking . . .[162]

Hobbes's kinematic approach to refraction in 1634, and his reference to the motion of beams in the letter he sent to Sir Charles in April 1636, do not indicate any particular commitment to an 'emanationist' transmission theory, still less to the peculiar theory of the 'Short Tract'; generally speaking, they show that he was just following standard practice. The only thing that is slightly distinctive about them is the hint of a dynamic conception of the action of light in the letter to Sir Charles. It is possible that this conception already depended on something like a mediumistic theory about how the 'strength of action from the object' was transmitted—though the phrasing there was still within the range of possibilities allowed by the loosely used kinematic metaphors of the mainstream optical tradition.

This impression—that Hobbes's thinking had been in line with traditional optical theory—is confirmed by the one other piece of significant evidence that survives from the period before Hobbes's 'mediumistic' letter to the Earl of Newcastle of October 1636: the letter he sent, also to the Earl, three months before that, on 29 July/8 August. This is perhaps the closest we can get to the turning-point in Hobbes's optical theories: for in this letter he dismisses, in a striking phrase, 'the old way by beames and reflection, and refraction'. That 'old way' (a reference, apparently, to the entire textbook tradition) was surely the way he himself had followed, only a few months earlier, in his letter to the Earl's brother about the reflection of beams in the cylindrical mirror.

The letter of 29 July/8 August deserves to be quoted at length. Hobbes begins by agreeing with Newcastle's opinion, expressed in his last letter to Hobbes, 'That the variety of thinges is but variety of locall motion in $y^e$ spirits or inuisible partes of bodies.' He continues:

---

p. 73: 'radiorum omnium & singulorum fluxus sit rectus'; J. Tarde, 'Telescopium, seu demonstrationes opticae', in his *Borbonia sidera* (Paris, 1620), p. 55: 'Radius est effluxus lucis à corpore lucido'.

[162] Aguilon ['Aguilonius'], *Opticorum libri sex*, p. 33 (bk 1, prop. 33): 'Neminem autem conturbet, quòd dicamus lucem moueri ac ferri, item accedere & recedere, contrahi ac dilatari: tametsi enim corpus sit quod moueatur, & in tempore quodlibet moueatur; lux verò incorporea sit, & simul tota; non potereà damnandus est hic loquendi modus, cùm potiorem non habeamus . . .'

For the optiques I know M$^r$ Warner and M$^r$ Mydorge are as able men as any in Europe, but they do not well to call their writings demonstrations, for the grounds and suppositions they vse, so many of them as [are of *deleted*] concerne light, are vncertayne and many of them not true. M$^r$ warner has sent a tract to S$^r$ Charles concerninge the place of the Image in conuexe and concaue glasses. I pray yo$^r$ Lo$^p$ let him see that peece of y$^e$ conuexe glasse wherein appeare the Images of the firre trees, and see if he can applye his reasons to it, and demonstrate why the Images of those trees w$^{ch}$ are long since perhaps burnt a thousand mile hence should be in that place where they are. If the experiment of y$^e$ mans image in y$^e$ glasse of bloud might be made againe, and shewed him I would haue him answer to that also. For my part my opinion of the firre trees is that the same [vertue *deleted*] motion by w$^{ch}$ the tree it selfe was able to produce the image of a tall tree in y$^e$ ey of a man that looked on it, remayning also in y$^e$ rosin and by it mouing in the glasse, workes that little image of a tree in the ey of him that lookes upon y$^e$ glasse, and therefore a little [>image of a] tree, because now a little or feynt motion. This reason is not cleare enough to make one see how nature workes it, but the old way by beames and reflection, and refraction leaues a man destitute of any thing to say to it.[163]

This passage has been largely ignored by modern writers on Hobbes's optical and physical theories, partly, no doubt, because they were unsure what the 'Images of the firre trees' and the 'image in y$^e$ glasse of bloud' referred to. Both were the products of experiments by chemists in Paris: in the former, a vessel in which pine resin had been distilled was found to be lined with little tree-like patterns, and in the latter, researchers distilling human blood saw a 'human image' in the glass retort.[164] The tree-like nature of the patterns in the former case was coincidental; the human-seeming image in the latter was probably the product of both coincidence and imagination. But (as often happens in the history of science) these 'unscientific' interpretations of chance phenomena may have played a role in stimulating real scientific progress—namely, the process by which Hobbes moved towards his mediumistic theory of light, which would in turn lead him to develop his more advanced and mathematizable concept of a moving wave-front.[165]

The explanation Hobbes puts forward here is that fir trees have a particular sort of 'motion' by which they produce the image of a tree in a person's eyes; the resin extracted from the trees still possesses that motion, and is somehow able to impart it to the glass (from where it is transmitted to the observer's eye). This is an application of the principle which Newcastle expressed in his letter, 'That the variety of thinges is but variety of locall motion in y$^e$ spirits or inuisible partes of bodies.'

---

[163] Hobbes, *Correspondence*, I, pp. 33–4.
[164] For a more detailed account, with references to sources, see Hobbes, *Correspondence*, I, p. 35.
[165] For a valuable discussion of the wave-front theory and Hobbes's pioneering role in its development, see Shapiro, 'Kinematic Optics', esp. pp. 137–8, 144–55. As a dynamic pulse was more susceptible to mathematical description than the path or course taken by a moving substance (however quasi-metaphorically that moving substance was conceived), this development actually gave new life to the 'old way' of beams, reflections and refractions.

Newcastle may have arrived at this view partly as a result of being influenced by Galileo's *Il saggiatore*; but we can assume that, when he stated this principle in his letter, he was repeating back to Hobbes a principle which Hobbes himself had been advocating for some time. As early as 1634, when Hobbes had taken part in a discussion with Mersenne and the mathematician Jean de Beaugrand about the rebound of a bow, he had argued that the peculiar characteristics of the bow's material (its ability to spring back into shape) must be due to the 'internal motion' of the subtle 'spirits' inside it.[166] The basic idea here, that the characteristics of things were determined by their internal motions at the microscopic (or, by seventeenth-century standards, sub-microscopic) level, seems to have been the dominant theme of Hobbes's approach to physics at this time. Sooner or later he would have tried to work out how he could apply it to light and vision; the little fir trees and the 'human image' may simply have been a catalyst that made him do so.

The problem was, as he put it in his letter, 'to see how nature workes it'—that is, to think of a way in which the tiny jiggling motions of the object could be transmitted to the viewer's eye. And in finding his mediumistic solution to this question he may have been helped by another catalyst: Mersenne's work on the propagation of sound, which was published in the first book of his *Harmonie universelle*.[167] Mersenne not only provided a model here, comparing the outwards movement of sound to the motion of ripples in a pond; he also made an explicit comparison between sound and light. 'If one considers the nature of light very carefully, one will perhaps find that it is nothing other than a movement of the air, which carries with it the image of the thing that first moved it, namely, the luminous body.'[168] The argument was not developed further by Mersenne, whose eclecticism (at least where theories about light were concerned) impelled him to offer a completely different explanation only two pages later.[169] But the hint may have been enough to prompt Hobbes to develop his own theory about how tiny vibratory image-creating motions could be transmitted through a medium.

Behind Hobbes's ideas about microscopic motions in the internal spirits of bodies there may have lain, finally, an even more fundamental idea. This is known to us only from his later writings; the clearest statement of it comes in his prose autobiography (though, unfortunately, in a passage separated from the main narrative, so that its precise place in the chronology of his life is not given).

---

[166] Hobbes, *Correspondence*, I, pp. 102, 108.
[167] This part of Mersenne's work was printed in 1636; Hobbes could have read it during his stay in Paris in the summer of that year.
[168] M. Mersenne, *Harmonie universelle* (Paris, 1636), bk 1, pp. 20, 45 ('si l'on considere bien attentiuement la nature de la lumiere, l'on trouuera peut-estre qu'elle n'est autre chose qu'vn mouuement de l'air, qui porte auec soy l'image de son premier moteur, à sçauoir du corps lumineux').
[169] Ibid., book 1, pp. 47–8 (suggesting that light is 'vne certaine liqueur semblable à de l'huile tres-subtile & tres-claire'); on this and other theories proffered by Mersenne, see A. Beaulieu, 'Lumière et matière chez Mersenne', *XVII*$^e$ *siècle*, 34 (1982), pp. 311–16.

By his nature, and from his earliest years, he was drawn to reading historians and poets
... But later, at a meeting of learned men, when mention was made of the cause of
sensation, somebody asked 'What is sense?', and he did not hear any reply ... From that
time on he thought frequently about the cause of sensation; and by good fortune it
occurred to him that if all physical things and their parts were at rest together, or were
always moved in a similar motion, the distinctions between all things would be removed,
and so, consequently, would all sensation. So that therefore *the cause of all things was to be
sought in the diversity of their motions*.[170]

The whole pattern of Hobbes's thinking on these matters is, however, rather hard
to unravel. It seems to involve an epistemological principle (that sense-perception
depends on the variety of motions) mutating into an ontological one (that the
variety in the nature of things depends on the variety of motions). In the process,
an argument that was based on variety in *perceived* motion has turned into one
that insists on a variety of *imperceptible* motions—what Newcastle called 'variety of
locall motion in yᵉ spirits or inuisible partes of bodies'. This latter version of
the argument is evidently connected to the doctrine of the subjectivity of sensible
qualities: it postulates the objective reality—different motions—that lies behind
the subjectively experienced qualities, and assumes that those motions must be
imperceptible as such (since, if we did perceive them as such, we would not be perceiving them as subjective qualities). Whether the subjectivity doctrine functions
as a cause or a consequence within this pattern of arguments is, however, much
less clear.

Still, whatever the internal structure of this cluster of assumptions about sense,
motion and subjectivity may have been, we can be fairly sure that its presence
in Hobbes's mind predated that of his mediumistic theory: that is implied by all
his relevant autobiographical statements, including his two references to the conversations he had in 1630. This means that, if Hobbes had written a little treatise
setting out his fundamental principles during this period of his philosophical
development, one might reasonably expect it to exhibit two features in particular: it would have an epistemologically based argument as its starting-point, and
it would take a particularly strong stand on the doctrine of the subjectivity of
sensible qualities. Something similar to this (though not quite the same) occurs
in the opening sections of *The Elements of Law*, where Hobbes begins with his
'annihilatory hypothesis' (an epistemological thought-experiment, separating our

[170] T. Hobbes, *Thomae Hobbes angli malmesburiensis philosophi vita* (London, 1681), pp. 18–19 (*OL* I, pp. xx–xxi): 'Naturâ suâ, & primis annis, ferebatur ad lectionem Historiarum & Poetarum ... Postea autem cum in congressu quodam virorum doctorum, mentione facta de causa sensionis, quaerentem unum quasi per contemptum *Quid esset sensus*, nec quemquam audisset respondentem ... Ex eo tempore de causa Sentiendi saepe cogitanti, forte fortunâ mentem subiit, quòd si res corporeae & earum partes omnes conquiescerent, aut motu simili semper moverentur, sublatum iri rerum omnium discrimen, & (per consequens) omnem Sensionem; & propterea *Causam omnium rerum quaerendam esse in diversitate Motuum*.'

conceptions of things from the things themselves) and then launches straight into an exposition of the subjectivity doctrine. These, Hobbes explains to the Earl of Newcastle in the dedicatory epistle to this work, are 'the principles . . . which I have heretofore acquainted your Lordship withal in private discourse'.[171]

The 'Short Tract' is organized very differently. It begins with general metaphysical statements about the nature of an agent, a patient, a cause, a substance, and an accident; the epistemological approach is entirely lacking here.[172] And although the 'Short Tract' does present the subjectivity doctrine, its presentation—and, indeed, its handling of the theoretical issues that surround this doctrine—is one of the weakest parts of the whole text. The statement of it (section 3, conclusion 3) is as follows:

Light, Colour, Heate, & other proper obiects of sense, when they are perceiu'd by sense, are Nothing but the seuerall Actions of Externall things vpon the Animal spirits, by seuerall Organs. & when they are not actually perceiu'd, then they be powers of the Agents to produce such actions.

For if Light & heate were qualityes actually inherent in the species, & not seuerall manners of action, seing the species enter, by all the organs, to the spirits, heat should be seene, & light felt. contrary to Experience.[173]

This conflicts with the claims made in section 2, conclusion 10, where the author stated that light and colour were 'accidents': what he called 'primitive' light and colour were accidents of the object itself, and 'derivative' light and colour were accidents of the species.[174] Indeed, his discussion of substance and accident in section 1 had been designed quite specifically to provide the basis of such an account of derivative light and colour as accidents inhering in a substantial 'species' that moved through space: 'Hence it followes, that No Accident can be locally moued, vnless his subiect be moued with it. & that all Accidents that inhere in the subiect, are moued with that subiect.'[175] The theory seems to have been that a hot, red object has the qualities of heat and redness inhering in it, and that the species that emerges from it has those qualities inhering in it too—indeed, the species is just a sort of sample of the object itself, differing from a piece carved off it with a knife only in so far as the species also represents the entire shape of the object. The reason why the text focuses in section 3, conclusion 3, on the 'seuerall manners of action' of the species is that the author has to explain how it is that, when this

---

[171] Hobbes, *Elements of Law*, p. xv (quotation), chs. I–II (pp. 2–7).
[172] Cf. Brandt's comment, in his comparison between Galileo and the 'Short Tract', that 'the epistemological motive is not to be found in Hobbes [sc. in the 'Short Tract'] at all': *Hobbes's Mechanical Conception*, p. 79. (This translation is misleading: the original has 'det erkendelsesteoretiske motiv', which means 'the epistemological *motif*': F. Brandt, *Den mekaniske naturopfattelse hos Thomas Hobbes* (Copenhagen, 1921), p. 74.)
[173] BL, MS Harl. 6796, fol. 305v.   [174] Ibid., fol. 303v.   [175] Ibid., fol. 298r.

single organic whole (the species, with all its inherent qualities) reaches the percipient person, its different qualities are perceived by different senses. Yet here too there is a conflict with what the text says elsewhere: in section 2, conclusion 2, the author suggests that there are different types of species, one for heat, one for light, one for other visible qualities, one for magnetism, one for astral influence, one for the lunar influence on humid bodies, and so on.[176]

The one basic proposition which we might expect a Hobbesian account of the subjectivity doctrine to include is that the real nature of the sensible qualities consists of different sorts of local motion ('motion', that is, conceived in opposition to 'rest'). Hobbes has a clear answer to the question about what light and sound really are 'out there': they are motions of matter. 'The things that really are in the world without us, are those motions by which these seemings are caused.'[177] The author of the 'Short Tract' side-steps the question: light, sound and such things 'out there', when we are not perceiving them, are merely the 'powers of the Agents to produce such actions' (i.e., actions on the animal spirits of perceivers). When light and heat are described by him as 'seuerall manners of action' on the animal spirits, no reason is given for thinking that those manners of action must be mechanical ones. He does write that 'The Act of Sense is a Motion of the Animal spirits'; but neither does he specify local motion here, nor, more importantly, does he set up a unified, mechanistic account connecting this motion with local motion in the world outside.[178] His species do travel through the air by local motion; but once they reach the organs of sense, different methods of action apply that are not part of a single mechanical or dynamic process. Apart from acting on the animal spirits in direct sensation, they also act on the brain, endowing it (as mentioned above) with a power or quality which enables it to produce its own 'similitude' of the species.[179]

Altogether, then, the 'Short Tract' seems out of alignment with some centrally Hobbesian doctrines—doctrines which, so far as one can tell, were part of his thinking even before he developed his special theory about mediumistic transmission. It also seems, in places, ill-at-ease with itself, making contradictory statements and exhibiting various other theoretical weaknesses.[180] Possibly the author was trying to produce a synthesis, combining elements of new thinking (his own or other people's) with some of the scholastic assumptions that had previously been part of his intellectual formation. Yet, for all its inadequacies, it is certainly an

---

[176] BL, MS Harl. 6796, fol. 300v.     [177] Hobbes, *Elements of Law*, II. 10 (p. 7).
[178] BL, MS Harl. 6796, fol. 306r.
[179] For a good discussion of the scholastic and non-mechanistic elements of the theories in the 'Short Tract', see D. L. Sepper, 'Imagination, Phantasms, and the Making of Hobbesian and Cartesian Science', *The Monist*, 71 (1988), pp. 526–42 (esp. pp. 527–30). Cf. also the comments of A. Minerbi Belgrado, *Linguaggio e mondo in Hobbes* (Rome, 1993), pp. 12–13.
[180] Bernhardt lists a number of other 'faiblesses' and 'imperfections formelles': Hobbes, *Court traité*, p. 122.

impressive piece of work, produced by a person who had thought long and hard about some of the most difficult problems in contemporary science and philosophy.

## VI

Is it likely that that person was Robert Payne? Professor Zagorin has dismissed Payne's candidature, for two reasons. 'Payne cannot, from the evidence, be connected specifically with the principles and conceptions set forth in the *Short Tract*; nor is there anything to indicate that he possessed the originality needed to produce this work.'[181] Reasons for doubting the first of these claims have been presented above in some detail, and supported by evidence to show that the 'principles and conceptions' of the 'Short Tract' cannot easily be connected with Hobbes. As for the second argument, it is, as Dr Raylor has pointed out, little more than a *petitio principii*: 'the premise that he was insufficiently original to have written it rests upon the conclusion that he did not.'[182] All those who knew Payne, including Hobbes, seem to have had a high opinion of his abilities. As we have seen, George Morley thought his intellectual powers were as great as those of anyone in England, Seth Ward placed him alongside the famous mathematician William Oughtred as an 'ornament' of the country, and the Earl of Newcastle not only described him as 'a Good Philosopher, and a Witty Man', but also emphasized his capacity for original thought: 'Dr. *Payn* . . . had a very Witty Searching Brain of his own.'[183] In addition, he would certainly have been familiar with much of the latest writing on the topics covered in the 'Short Tract': Payne's reading was both intensive (as the notes in some of his books show) and extensive. What survives in the Savile collection in the Bodleian Library is only a small selection from his library; but several of Payne's books do include, at the start or end, annotations listing other works on the same topic which he either had read or planned to read, and we also have the ambitious reading list he compiled in the early 1630s, MS E2 at Chatsworth.

It is possible that some of the apparent 'originality' of the 'Short Tract' might be diminished by a careful study of all the other works that Payne had read. One illustration of this point can be given here. The work on optics by Aguilon, which Payne included in his reading list in 1631–2, was read and studied carefully by him: one of his manuscripts at Chatsworth includes a reference to 'Fr. Aguilonij opt lib. 4. Lemm. 32 & 33'.[184] In book 5, proposition 12, of this work we find a discussion of the question whether each small part of a luminous body sends light to the full limits of the body's 'luminous sphere'. Aguilon declares that 'Those people stray

---

[181] Zagorin, 'Hobbes's Early Development', p. 511.
[182] Raylor, 'Hobbes, Payne, and *A Short Tract*', p. 46.
[183] Above, at nn. 68, 97; W. Cavendish, 'Opinion concerning Natural Philosophy', pp. 461, 463.
[184] MS C i 8; for the reading-list entry see Pacchi, 'Una "biblioteca ideale" ', p. 33.

very far from the truth who say that the larger parts of a luminous body terminate their action further away, and the smaller parts less far; they are misled by the argument which says that those larger parts must be stronger because they are larger.' Instead, he argues, they all contribute mutually, and have a combined effect, on the principle that an object can be moved more easily once it is already moving.[185] The 'Short Tract' contains a passage that appears to be both an adaptation of this argument and a refutation of it: in section 2, conclusion 6, the author states that each species, however small, proceeds infinitely, and offers the example of grains of sand in a heap. A grain on its own is visible only at a very small distance; a large heap of sand is visible much further away; but what causes perception of the heap is merely a large quantity of individual species (of individual grains), each of which must have travelled the whole distance. In rejecting the idea that small objects send their species less far than large ones, the author is making a claim similar to Aguilon's one about the small and large 'parts' of a luminous body. The author then puts forward, and refutes, a possible objection—namely that, although the species of a single grain can move only a short distance on its own, it is 'fortifyed by other species added' and thereby able to move further. That objection seems to be a version of Aguilon's own theory, as translated into the 'Short Tract's' species-terminology.[186] The whole passage in the 'Short Tract' is of particular interest because the same argument appears, in very similar terms (also involving grains of sand) in chapter XXII of Hobbes's *De corpore*: it is therefore presented by Professor Schuhmann as one of his strongest pieces of evidence to show that Hobbes must have been the author of the 'Short Tract'.[187] Seeing how the argument could have been adapted from Aguilon does not directly affect the case for or against the attribution of the 'Short Tract' to Hobbes; we happen to know that Payne had read Aguilon, but Hobbes could well have done so too, and might have gone through the same thought-process himself to arrive at this form of the argument. Nevertheless, understanding how close such an argument was to topics and debates in the available literature does at least permit us to resist the temptation to see it as something so distinctively Hobbesian that it could have been thought of only by Hobbes.

The parallelisms in thought and phrasing that exist between some sentences in the 'Short Tract' and passages in Hobbes's works, so meticulously identified by Professor Schuhmann, are of different degrees of evidential value. Some, as Schuhmann is the first to admit, are weak, perhaps nothing more than coincidental, but a small number are strong and striking. Any attribution of the 'Short Tract' to Payne must deal with this evidence. Four explanations, it seems, are

[185] Aguilon ['Aguilonius'], *Opticorum libri sex*, pp. 381–3 (quotation, p. 381: 'Procul à vero aberrant qui autumant maiores partes vnius luminosi corporis longiùs, minores verò propiùs actionem suam terminare: hoc delusi argumento, quòd illae vti maiores, ita valentiores sint').
[186] BL, MS Harl. 6796, fol. 301v. At one point the argument is put in terms of the heap and its 'parts', which brings the terminology closer to Aguilon's.
[187] Schuhmann, 'Le *Short Tract*', pp. 17–18.

possible. The first is that Payne and Hobbes had become so intellectually intimate, sharing so many of their thoughts on such matters in conversation or correspondence, that they were operating with a common stock of arguments and ideas. The second is that they were both drawing ideas (jointly or independently) from some other common source. The third is that Payne was directly influenced by Hobbes, basing some of his arguments in the 'Short Tract' on notes Hobbes had jotted down or theses he had expounded. And the fourth is that Hobbes was directly influenced by Payne—that he made a careful study of the 'Short Tract', stored away in his mind arguments that he found useful or compelling, and put them to good use in his later works.

It is difficult to think of any argument, *a priori* or *a posteriori*, that would enable one to exclude any one of these possibilities; the true and full explanation could well require all four. The second type of argument should not be undervalued: without exploring the entire range of possible reading by Payne and Hobbes, it will always be hard to know where any particular idea or formulation might have come from. Hobbes did like to project an image of himself as someone who did not depend on other people's writings, and whose arguments, conceived by first principles, sprang fully armed from his head; but in fact he made much use of the common stock of ideas. Occasionally a modern researcher may hit upon a 'source'; however, the source may also have its own source, *et sic deinceps*. To give just one instance: when Hobbes discusses in *De corpore* the process of 'ratiocination', in which we pass cumulatively from universal descriptions to more specific ones, he uses the example of someone watching a distant object gradually moving closer. At first the watcher has the idea 'body'; then the idea 'animate', then the idea 'man'.[188] Some past readers of Hobbes may have thought this a distinctively Hobbesian argument, as it so cleverly and reductively takes an abstract theme from traditional logic and brings it down to the level of concrete experience. Recently, Cees Leijenhorst has proposed a possible 'source' for it: a similar passage in Campanella's *De sensu rerum*, in which the approaching body is identified as 'man', then as 'monk', then as 'Peter'.[189] Three hundred years before Campanella, however, the same argument had been presented, in terms rather closer to Hobbes's, by William of Ockham (his sequence was 'being', 'animal', 'man' and 'Socrates').[190] No doubt others had copied the argument from Ockham in the intervening years. It is hardly possible to tell, in this case, from what source Hobbes had taken it. All we can be sure of is that he did—like any other author—borrow useful ideas from works he had read. And if he had found such ideas in a work written by Payne, he might just as well have borrowed them from there.

---

[188] Hobbes, *De corpore*, I.3 *(OL* I, p. 3).
[189] C. Leijenhorst, 'Motion, Monks and Golden Mountains: Campanella and Hobbes on Perception and Cognition', *Bruniana & Campanelliana*, 3 (1997), pp. 93–121, here pp. 114–15.
[190] William of Ockham, *Philosophical Writings*, ed. and tr. P. Boehner (New York, 1957), p. 30.

To use a combination of some or all of the four arguments just mentioned to account for the parallelisms between the 'Short Tract' and Hobbes's works may seem both complex and speculative; this type of explanation certainly lacks the streamlined simplicity of the theory that explains those parallels as the products of a single author's pen. But that simpler theory—simpler, at least, in relation to the limited field of verbal evidence—is not as unproblematic as it seems. A full account of the textual relationships between the 'Short Tract' and Hobbes's known writings should not only list the parallelisms, but also take notice of non-parallelisms or divergences. For example, the 'Short Tract' employs the term 'phantasma' in a specific sense, meaning the sort of mental image of an object that the brain is able to summon up when the object is not present; this is what later philosophical traditions would call an 'idea' or a 'concept' as opposed to a sense-perception, and would take to be the raw material of most mental activity and reasoning. But, although Hobbes uses the term in different ways in different writings, he never gives it the meaning it has in the 'Short Tract'. In *The Elements of Law* he offers a narrow sense: 'phantasms' (when writing in English he uses the English form, not the Graeco-Latin) are pseudo-sensations, illusory or hallucinatory images, created either by the after-effects of strong sensations or by the passion of fear. In his critique of Thomas White he uses the term 'phantasma' primarily for immediate sense-perception, and secondarily for that same 'effect' of motion from the perceived external object when it remains after the object has been removed. (This is quite different from the 'Short Tract', where the phantasm is not the same effect, but a new effect caused by a new action of the brain itself.) And in *De corpore* the term 'phantasma' seems to be used only for the immediate sense-perception —precisely the meaning from which it was excluded in the 'Short Tract'.[191] The 'Short Tract' also uses the term 'Understanding' in a peculiar sense, closely tied to its theory of the 'phantasma': 'We are sayd to vnderstand a thing, when we haue the Phantasma or Apparition of it.' In other words, merely to picture something to oneself in its absence is to 'understand' it. This has absolutely no counterpart in Hobbes's usage, where 'understanding' applies—understandably enough—to the realm of discourse, definitions, and propositions.[192] In explaining such divergences as these, the theory that attributes the 'Short Tract' to Payne does in turn enjoy its own advantage of simplicity.

---

[191] BL, MS Harl. 6796, fol. 305v; Hobbes, *Critique du* De mundo, esp. VII.1, XXX.3–4 (pp. 145–6, 349–51); *Elements of Law*, III.5; *De corpore*, XXV.2–3. The only overlap between the 'phantasma' of the 'Short Tract' and the 'phantasm' of the *Elements of Law* is that the former term is broad enough to include dreams (*op. cit.*, fol. 304r). But the criteria for the use of these terms are quite different: in the 'Short Tract' the essential condition is merely that the image should occur in the absence of the object, whereas in the *Elements of Law* it is that the image should be a delusion, i.e., one that carries with it the false belief that the object is actually present.

[192] BL, MS Harl. 6796, fol. 306v; Hobbes, *Elements of Law*, V.8. In his critique of White Hobbes argued explicitly against the type of theory presented in the 'Short Tract': *Critique du* De mundo, IV.1 (pp. 125–6).

If Payne was the author of this work, is there any evidence to suggest when and why he wrote it? The 'when?' can be approximately answered. A definite *terminus ad quem* is provided by the publication of Galileo's *Discorsi e dimostrazioni* in the early summer of 1638.[193] Given the passion for Galileo at Welbeck, and the fact that this publication, unlike the *Dialogo*, was issued by a Dutch publisher (Elzevier) who distributed widely in England, we may assume that a copy was quickly acquired—or, rather, copies, as we know that Payne had his own volume in addition to the one in the Welbeck library.[194] One of the topics treated in this book is the sympathetic vibration of strings: Galileo describes the simple mechanical causation involved (vibrations of the air) and explains why it is that the strings most affected are those in unison, at the octave, or at the fifth.[195] The 'Short Tract', on the other hand, presents the sympathetic vibration of strings as one of the various phenomena of 'sympathy' or 'antipathy' that can be explained, like magnetism, by an efflux of 'species': 'the species of $y^t$ string ... meeting with the species of another stringe ($y^t$ is eyther an vnison or an eyghth with it) by conveniency moueth the species of that other string', and so on.[196] It is scarcely conceivable that Payne could have written that after he had studied Galileo's book.

As for the *terminus a quo*, Timothy Raylor has made a good case for 1635, the date at which Payne probably read, and certainly translated, the work by Castelli which seems to have influenced the 'Short Tract' so directly. The most likely date of composition of the 'Short Tract', therefore, is some time between 1635 and 1638. If Raylor's argument were not accepted, however, the *terminus* could conceivably be pushed back all the way to Payne's first employment by Newcastle in 1630. But there are two pieces of evidence that might suggest slightly later starting-points, in 1636 and 1637 respectively. The first is a possible borrowing in the 'Short Tract' from Mersenne's *Harmonicorum libri*. This book was, roughly speaking (but only very roughly), a Latin version of the *Harmonie universelle*; it was completed, as a sort of digest of Mersenne's work-in-progress, in October 1635.[197] The Latin version was printed by or soon after October 1635: the original issue bears that year's date on its title page. But at some time during the following year the publisher, the Parisian bookseller Guillaume Baudry, produced a new issue of the same sheets, with a title page dated '1636' and a dedicatory epistle addressed to Sir Charles Cavendish. (The epistle was not by Mersenne: there is no datable evidence of contacts between him and Cavendish before 1639. Instead it was by Baudry,

---

[193] It was published in May or June: Mersenne, *Correspondance*, VII, pp. 107–08.
[194] See above, at nn. 70, 71.   [195] Galilei, *Discorsi e dimostrazioni*, pp. 98–9.
[196] BL, MS Harl. 6796, fol. 303r. Bernhardt's edition incorrectly has 'working with' instead of 'meeting with' here.
[197] For the date see Mersenne's letter to Peiresc, 12 Oct. 1635: Mersenne, *Correspondance*, V, p. 423.
[198] On the lack of contacts before 1639 see Jacquot, 'Sir Charles Cavendish and his Friends', p. 16. On Mersenne's dealings with Baudry (who may have been allowed a quantity of sheets of the book to dispose of in this way as a form of payment), see Lesure, 'Introduction' to Mersenne, *Harmonie universelle*, I, pp. v–viii.

who may have heard of Cavendish's mathematical and scientific interests from someone such as Claude Mydorge in Paris, and no doubt hoped for a munificent response.[198]) When exactly copies arrived in England is not known; but it is known that Payne acquired a copy of this issue.[199] Book 1 of this work contains comments on the differences between the propagation of light and sound which match quite closely the arguments against mediumistic light transmission in the 'Short Tract'. Mersenne writes that sound, unlike light, is impeded both 'by motions of the air, and by winds' and by 'hard bodies, however transparent they may be, such as crystal'[200] The same points are made, with reference to exactly the same impeding factors, in the 'Short Tract', where it is argued that if the transmission of light were mediumistic it would be weakened or interrupted 'if a contrary Agent (as the winde) disturbe that motion of the parts; or if a [>solide] perspicuous medium (as Chrystall) w$^{ch}$ is not easily moued, be interposd'.[201]

There is, however, one difficulty with the theory that this passage influenced the writing of the 'Short Tract'. Later on in the *Harmonicorum libri*, Mersenne did also present a brief explanation of the sympathetic vibration of strings, attributing it to wave-motions of the air.[202] If we are to assume that Payne had read the comments on the transmission of light in Book 1 of Mersenne's work when he composed the 'Short Tract', then we must also explain his failure to change his views on sympathetic vibration in the light of Mersenne's comments. The most straightforward explanation would be that Payne simply had not read the account of sympathetic vibration that appears in that volume: instead of being included in the treatment of the physical transmission of sound in Book 1, it is buried in a discussion of the foundations of harmony in Book 4, and Payne is not known to have had any particular interests in musical theory. Alternatively, it may be that he had read it, but remained unconvinced. The latter explanation is certainly possible; we can easily assume that Payne would have given more weight to Galileo's opinions than to Mersenne's. Nevertheless, it must be admitted that the exact nature of the relationship between the *Harmonicorum libri* and the 'Short Tract' is hard to determine.[203]

---

Sales of the book were evidently sluggish; the original sheets were also re-issued with new title pages in 1641 and 1648 (see Mersenne, *Correspondance*, V, p. 468).

[199] Payne's copy is Bodl., pressmark Savile Q 13.

[200] Mersenne, *Harmonicorum libri*, bk 1, prop. 6, p. 3 ('à motibus aëris, & à ventis . . . à corporibus duris quantumcumque diaphanis, vt à chrystallo').

[201] BL, MS Harl. 6796, fol. 300v (sect. 2, concl. 2).

[202] M. Mersenne, *Harmonicorum libri* (Paris, 1635), Book 4, 'De sonis consonis, seu consonantiis' (separate pagination), propositions 27–9 (pp. 65–7), 'aëris undationes' (p. 65).

[203] Mersenne's explanation of the sympathetic vibration of strings was also given in the first book of the 'Traitez des consonances, des dissonances . . .' in his *Harmonie universelle* (pp. 26, 52–3, 67); but, although that particular part of Mersenne's work was printed (minus its dedicatory epistle) by February 1635, and was apparently available for separate distribution in the late summer of that year, the book itself was not published in its final form until early 1637. (For the dating see Mersenne, *Correspondance*, V, pp. 40, 348; on the

The second piece of evidence relevant to the dating of the 'Short Tract' is contained in a little treatise on light, *De natura lucis*, published by Ismaël Boulliau in October 1637.[204] Boulliau was an anti-scholastic scientist who dismissed the Aristotelians (praising Patrizzi and Kepler instead) in the prefatory epistle to this work, and would later publish a famous defence of Copernican astronomy; nevertheless, the theory of light propounded here involved a somewhat hesitant compromise with scholastic metaphysics, a compromise in which light was described as a substance that 'participates' in both the corporeal and the incorporeal. This underlying theory is, it must be said, not at all similar to the Epicurean species-theory of the 'Short Tract'. On a few small points there are resemblances (light is said to proceed 'in infinitum' in a straight line, for example), but these are not of much significance.[205] What is specially interesting, however, is an argument Boulliau puts forward to demonstrate that the propagation of light is instantaneous. He gives the example of a solar eclipse, in which, he says, the sun's light as it reappears from behind the moon is seen at the very point of contact with the moon's edge, 'without any interruption'.[206] The reasoning is slightly obscure, but it seems to be the same reasoning (with the same degree of obscurity) as that presented in the 'Short Tract', section 2, conclusion 8, where the argument concerns a 'starre' moving round an 'opacous body' until the moment when it becomes visible to an observer on the far side of that body.[207] The author of the 'Short Tract' wrestles with this argument—which, if correct, would appear to disprove his claim that light travels by local motion at a finite velocity. Without an exhaustive search through the earlier optical and astronomical literature, one cannot be sure that this argument was original to Boulliau; and, even if it were, it is of course conceivable that Payne could have thought of it for himself. Boulliau's book is not listed in the Welbeck library catalogue, and if Payne owned a copy it has not survived.[208] Nevertheless, this evidence suggests at least the possibility that the 'Short Tract' was written after a reading of Boulliau's work—in which case the date of its composition could be narrowed to the time between October 1637 and the summer of 1638.

---

complex printing history of this entire book see the account by François Lesure in his 'Introduction' to a modern photo-reproduction of it (3 vols., Paris, 1963), I, esp. pp. v–vii, where he notes that the final 'tables' were printed in February 1637 and the first recorded delivery of a complete copy was in the following month.) The Welbeck library catalogue does not mention the *Harmonie universelle*, and it is not known when—or whether—Payne and the Cavendishes might have encountered it.

[204] I. Boulliau, *De natura lucis* (Paris, 1638). Despite the date on the title page, the 'achevé d'imprimer' is dated 8 October 1637 (sig. i2v), and copies had reached Holland by November: see H. J. M. Nellen, *Ismaël Boulliau (1605–1694): astronome, épistolier, nouvelliste et intermédiare scientifique* (Amsterdam, 1994), pp. 71–2.

[205] Boulliau, *De natura lucis*, sig. a4r (Patrizzi, Kepler, Aristotelians), pp. 39 ('Lux in infinitum rectà progreditur non occurrente opaco'), 62 ('Lux ergo substantia corporei, & incorporei particeps est').

[206] Ibid., pp. 34–5 (p. 35: 'sine aliqua interruptione'). [207] BL, MS Harl. 6796, fol. 302v.

[208] The copy of this book in the library of Christ Church, Oxford (pressmark OP. 6. 08) does not bear any annotations by Payne, and probably entered the library in the 18th century.

The main objection to such a dating is that, by that time, Hobbes was in more regular contact with Payne and the Welbeck Cavendishes; one might expect him to have argued against Payne on various points, thereby either converting him to the mediumistic theory or forcing him to make a more solid defence of his position against the new Hobbesian views. In fact, there is one brief passage in the 'Short Tract' (the passage just cited, drawing possibly on Mersenne's Latin text) which presents objections to the mediumistic theory of transmission—what it calls illumination 'by locall motion of the parts of the aire'.[209] Whether this is enough to indicate exposure to Hobbes (in his post-October 1636 mode) is not clear.

One possible sign that Payne was having difficulty defending his position may be the fact that the 'Short Tract' is unfinished. To be precise, the text is unfinished, although the manuscript is complete. The internal evidence clearly shows that the treatise was meant to be continued (many of the 'principles' set out at the beginning of the third and final section are put to no use in the ten extant 'conclusions' of that section, and the argument of all three sections contains elements that point beyond the subject-matter actually covered); but the manuscript ends on a recto, with a blank verso following it, which means that this fair copy contained all that there was to transcribe at the time. Given the fact that this is a fair copy, the fact that it is in English, and the nature of Payne's position, we can reasonably suppose that the work had been, in some sense, commissioned from him by the Earl of Newcastle and his brother. Having got as far as he could (or, conceivably, as far as time would permit—perhaps the Earl was about to leave for Court, to take up his appointment as governor to the Prince of Wales in May 1638, and asked Payne to summarize his work so far), he may have simply cut his losses and written out the manuscript copy that now survives.

How much further was the argument intended to go? Or, to put the question another way, what was the nature of the commission? The answer to these questions may once again involve interweaving the story of the 'Short Tract' with the intellectual biography of Hobbes. In August 1635 Hobbes wrote a letter to the Earl of Newcastle from Paris, in which he commented sceptically on Walter Warner's projects and capacities:

I vnderstand not how m$^r$ Warner will demonstrate those inuentions of the multiplyinge glasse and burning glasse so infinite in vertue as he pretends . . . For my part I thinke m$^r$ Payne will do more that way then m$^r$ Warner. I hope yo$^r$ Lo$^p$ will not bestow much vpon y$^e$ hopes . . . For y$^e$ soule I know he has nothinge to giue yo$^r$ Lo$^p$ any satisfaction. I would he could giue [a *deleted*] good reasons for y$^e$ facultyes & passions of y$^e$ soule, such as may be expressed in playne English. [I do *deleted*] if he can, he is the first (that I euer heard [>of] could] speake sense in that subiect. If he can not I hope to be y$^e$ first.[210]

---

[209] BL, MS Harl. 6796, fol. 300v; cf. the comments at nn. 201, 202, above.
[210] Hobbes, *Correspondence*, I, pp. 28–9 (15/ 25 Aug. 1635).

What this passage seems to imply is that the Earl had mentioned, in a previous letter, that he had asked, or was planning to ask, Walter Warner to write something explaining the basis of human psychology—a treatise, perhaps, 'in playne English', which would take the principles of the Galilean new science that interested Newcastle so strongly and apply them to this field too. If the Earl heeded Hobbes's words of caution about Warner, he may instead have asked his chaplain to turn his 'very Witty Searching Brain' to the exploration of this subject. For the whole aim and purpose of the argumentation of the 'Short Tract', as it passes from causation to the action of 'species' to sensation and imagination, is surely to lay out the groundwork of a theory of human psychology. That, after all, is what Hobbes referred to in his letter when he wrote of the 'facultyes & passions of y$^e$ soule'—a general phrase referring to all the ways in which the soul acts ('facultyes') and all the ways in which it is acted upon ('passions').[211]

As Hobbes's letter intimated, he had his own ambitions in this field. It would take him several years to develop his thoughts on psychology and systematize them in a treatise. Once again, it was the Earl of Newcastle who both stimulated the working-out of his ideas and obliged him to set them down on paper: the result was *The Elements of Law*, completed and scribally published in May 1640. The immediate purpose of that work was, evidently, to defend a particular position in a developing political crisis. But knowing what we do about Newcastle, we can be sure that, in his eyes, the physical and psychological theories with which the text begins were not just a makeweight to add a show of philosophical authority to a political pamphlet. Newcastle's keen intellectual appetite had previously made him long for an extension of the principles of the new science to psychology. He would have been no less interested to see how the principles could be carried forward in an extension of the same project: applying them, and the psychological theory derived from them, to the realms of ethics and political philosophy.

That entire, extended project may also have been the stimulus that prompted Payne to undertake the writing of the 'Short Tract'. This is not to suggest that the 'Short Tract' was simply commissioned as a political treatise (which would be a perverse suggestion, given the nature of the text that has survived), but rather to place it in what may have been its larger context. There is indeed almost no evidence that Payne had any interest in politics or political theory, apart from what we know of his general royalism and his attempt to defend the institution of episcopacy against Hobbes's arguments. But the evidence that we have is very

---

[211] Karl Schuhmann argues that this phrase cannot relate in any direct way to an intention to write the 'Short Tract', because that work does not discuss passions ('Le *Short Tract*', p. 23). He assumes that the subject-matter of the work is, more or less, its *intended* subject-matter—in other words, that it is more or less complete. Even on his own terms his argument is questionable, as the 'Short Tract' does discuss 'Love' and 'Desire' (and, though it is not named as such, aversion): BL, MS Harl. 6796, fols. 307v, 308r. But the term 'passion' had in any case a much broader sense: see *OED*, 'passion', subst., II.5.

incomplete, and the fact that Payne's surviving books are exclusively about science and mathematics reflects only the nature of the Savile collection in the Bodleian, in which they have been preserved. One tiny but intriguing piece of evidence can be put forward, however. Among those books is his heavily annotated copy of M. Varro's *De motu tractatus* (Geneva, 1584), an ambitious general treatise on the theory of motion. In the Preface, the author lists his as yet unpublished works on related subjects; Payne has paid careful attention to this listing, and has underlined items that caught his interest. One item in particular is not only underlined, but marked by his special trefoil mark in the margin: 'I have also written down some things about the motion, both internal and external, of republics, which I should like to set out in the same method: the attentive reader will find that the principles of all those things are set out here.'[212]

The suggestion that Payne's composition of the 'Short Tract' can be placed in the same overall context as Hobbes's work on *The Elements of Law* is, on the face of it, unconvincing, because the 'Short Tract'—what there is of it, anyway—offers almost nothing about ethics (only a naturalistic–descriptive definition of 'Goodness' and 'Badness'), and nothing at all about politics. But in order to understand the aim and purpose of the 'Short Tract', it is necessary to look at its general nature and tendency, and in particular at those elements of its argument that point beyond what survives of the work itself. The general nature of the work is to lay out the framework of a deterministic account of human psychology: the mechanicism of the theory is not absolute, but the causal determinism is. The first section culminates in a discussion of causation in which it is stated that all effects have necessary causes, and that 'Necessity hath no degrees'; the second section provides an explanation of what appears to be causation at a distance; and the third fits the essential features of human psychology—sense, 'understanding', and appetite—into this causal framework. Where might the argument have led to next? The clue is hidden in a rather unremarkable 'conclusion' at the end of section one, tacked on

---

[212] Bodl., pressmark Savile Y 11: M. Varro, *De motu tractatus* (Geneva, 1584), sig. A4r: 'Nonnulla etiam de *Rerumpublicarum motu tum interno tum externo notaui*, quae eodem *ordine tradere* optarem: *quorum omnium principia hic si quis diligenter animaduertat tradita sunt*' (italics here represent Payne's underlining). Payne's other annotations in this book include various definitions and axioms about the principles of mechanics. Some are drawn from the text (e.g. on p. 8: 'Aequales motus sunt, quorum tempora spatijs sunt proportionalia'); some, on four inserted blank leaves at the end, are headed 'Quaedam de Motu Naturali Axiomata Ex Jo: Bapt: Benedict. Disputat. Cap. 2 &c' (i.e. Giovanni Battista Benedetti, *Diversarum speculationum mathematicarum, & physicarum liber* (Turin, 1585), section 4, 'Disputationes de quibusdam placitis Aristotelis', pp. 168–97)—for example, 'Homogenea corpora apello, quorum aequales partes, sunt aeque graues, aut aeque leues' (first leaf, verso). These are in the mechanical tradition to which Castelli's work also belonged. However, the long list of authors on motion written by Payne on the reverse title page of this book mentions works published after 1635 (including Galileo's *Discorsi e dimostrazioni*); therefore, if we assume that this list was contemporaneous with the other annotations, Dr Raylor's argument about the importance of the Castelli text is not affected by this evidence. There was clearly a special interest in Varro's work at Welbeck: the library there included another copy of this work, 'with manuscript notes on the theory of weights' ('cum Notis MSS. de Doctrina Ponderum') (Noel, *Bibliotheca*, p. 26).

after the discussion of sufficient and necessary causes. This conclusion (no. 15) states: 'The Agent that hath actiue power inherent in it self, applyed to seuerall equall patients, shall worke on them equally.'[213] This is unremarkable because it is virtually redundant: it adds little to the argument presented so far, which has already included the principle 'Equall Agents, equally distant from the patient, moue it equally.'[214] Its significance lies not in what it adds to the theses of the work at that point, but in what it might contribute towards the framing of a problem at a later stage in the argument.

As that later stage was never actually reached, we must frame the problem in our own words. 'If human action is causally determined by external stimuli, why is it that human beings do not all act in the same way? Why do they react differently to the same stimuli?' These, surely, are the questions set up in advance by the observation that an agent applied to equal patients should work on them equally. And these might naturally lead to some further questions: 'Why is there human disagreement about values?' or even, 'Why is there human conflict?'

The 'Short Tract' also offers some clues as to how its author was preparing to answer these questions. The clues are to be found in a number of passages dealing with the theme of oneness or unity. Taken together, these passages amount to an important thematic element running through the whole text; but their connection with the rest of the work is not self-evident, which may explain why it is that almost every previous commentator on the text has passed over them in silence.[215] The first appearance of this theme is in section 2, conclusion 7: 'Species that come in one & the same straight line from seuerall obiects, are by the sense perceiu'd as one.'[216] The conclusion goes on to apply this principle to the phenomenon of colour: when a light passes through coloured glass to our eyes, we perceive the light and the colour as one thing. But this is just offered as an example; the general argument here has no need to digress into an explanation of the nature of colour, so it can be assumed that the example is there to serve the conclusion (not vice-versa), and that the conclusion has some further role to play. The next appearance of the 'unity' theme is in the principles at the start of section 3: it is in fact the subject of seven out of the ten principles stated there. Mostly, they list the different ways in which something can be 'one'. A thing can be 'One simply'—for example, a horse. Or it can be 'One by vnion of more Natures', as 'horse' and 'white' can be united in a white horse. Or it can be 'One by Comprehension of parts', as a man's head and body are 'one Man by Comprehension': this, however, is not true unity. Or it can

---

[213] BL, MS Harl. 6796, fol. 299v.   [214] Ibid., fol. 297r (sect. 1, princ. 6).
[215] The exception is Bernhardt (Hobbes, *Court Traité*, pp. 119–21); but he is an exception that proves the rule, as his interpretation offers no essential connection between these passages and the overall argument of the text, suggesting that the author's discussion of unity aimed at 'une exhaustivité purement formelle' and observing (correctly) that the principles about unity announced in the text are never really put to use in it.
[216] BL, MS Harl. 6796, fol. 301v.

be 'One, partly by Vnion, partly by Comprehension'. The final principle is that 'As Obiects are one, by Vnion, or Comprehension: soe are the Phantasmata that represent them; seing these are but their similitudes.'[217] Most of the rest of section 3 consists of an explication of sense, 'understanding', and appetite; the principles just discussed are not really put to use, but the theme of unity does make one more appearance. Conclusion 9 states that 'Whatsoeuer is perceiu'd by sense or Vnderstanding, is perceiu'd as one in number.' The reasoning which follows is curious. An object is presented to a person; one part of the object is 'good' and the other 'euill', and both parts are equidistant from the person. First, the author insists that the object will be 'perceiued as one' (on the grounds that in a case where the good and evil parts were of equal power, perceiving them 'as two' would lead to simultaneous motion towards and away from the object, which is impossible). Then he claims that if the good part possesses more power the person will move towards it, '& consequently C [the evil part] shall not be perceiu'd'. One important corollary is added to this conclusion: 'By the same reason it may be demonstrated, that whatsoeuer is desired, is desired as one.'[218]

These various passages dealing with how things are perceived as 'one' do not form a neat linear progression, but they do set up a range of possible ways of answering the question, why is it that one person will perceive something as good and another person will perceive it as bad? Or, indeed, why will the same person perceive it as good at one time and bad at another? The features of the thing that attract and repel are really in the object; the problem is to reconcile the apparent subjectivity of human value-judgements with the objective nature of attraction and repulsion in a deterministic universe. And the solution towards which the 'Short Tract' is pointing depends on examining and taking apart the apparent unity of the object of desire or aversion. Things can appear 'one' when they are not: for example, when different species are combined from several objects. Or a thing can be 'one by comprehension of parts'; but, although the sense and the appetite will perceive it as one, this is not true unity, as the parts are not 'one' with one another. Only things that exemplify a union of natures are truly one. Our aim must be, therefore, to subject the world around us to a more searching analysis, in which the good and bad 'parts' of apparent single goods or evils are separated; for the theory guarantees that, once we have isolated anything that is truly 'one' and truly good, all human beings will be equally drawn towards it. That, surely, was the eventual implication towards which section 1, conclusion 15, was directed: 'The Agent that hath actiue power inherent in it self, applyed to seuerall equall patients, shall worke on them equally.'[219]

If this interpretation of the aim and tendency of the 'Short Tract' is correct, then it allows us, once again, to see how close its author was to Hobbes's mental world,

[217] BL, MS Harl. 6796, fol. 304r.   [218] Ibid., fol. 308r.   [219] Ibid., fol. 299v.

and at the same time how different his arguments really were. The problem he was trying to tackle here was indeed the fundamental issue dealt with in Hobbes's *The Elements of Law* (and in each of his subsequent works of political theory): given the facts of human disagreement, disorder, and conflict, how are agreement and order possible? Hobbes shares some of the 'Short Tract's' assumptions, starting with a deterministic universe in which human beings are impelled by their desires and 'good' means merely 'object of desire'. But the argument which he goes on to develop is quite different from that intimated and prepared for by the 'Short Tract'. Instead of trying to make use of the realism of those assumptions about the objective world to initiate a search for what is 'really' good, Hobbes reconciles himself to the unavoidable subjectivity of goodness: 'insomuch that while every man differeth from other in constitution, they differ also one from another concerning the common distinction of good and evil. Nor is there any such thing as $\alpha\gamma\alpha\theta o\nu$ $\alpha\pi\lambda\omega s$, that is to say, simply good.'[220] Instead, he constructs a second-order system of values, based on the fact that the avoidance of death is a necessary condition for people's enjoyment of their subjective goods (whatever those may be), and on the argument that peace is the optimum condition for ensuring the avoidance of death. Analysis of the 'oneness' of apparent goods can play no part in this solution: what matters is not whether an apparent good is composed of good or bad parts, but how it measures when judged by the standard of conduciveness to peace.

It would be good to know more about the development of Hobbes's thinking on these subjects between 1635, when he expressed his ambition to write about human psychology, and 1640, when he produced his first philosophical work. Unfortunately, the evidence is lacking. It is very likely that discussions with Robert Payne, at Welbeck, in London, and perhaps elsewhere, played some part in that development. It also seems very likely that Payne, who possessed most of the requisite interests and abilities, was stimulated—both by his friend Thomas Hobbes and by his employer, the Earl of Newcastle—to work on the same set of issues himself. The 'Short Tract' is, most probably, the record of his attempt, and in the end his failure, to solve those problems; as such, it not only gives us a valuable insight into Hobbes's personal and philosophical milieu, but also helps us to measure, by contrast, the extent of Hobbes's success.

## APPENDIX I

### *The 'Hobbes Manuscripts' at Chatsworth*

This is a summary listing, the main purpose of which is to record which items are in Payne's hand. More information about many of these items can be found in the RCHM

---

[220] Hobbes, *Elements of Law*, VII.3.

'Report', and in the entry on Hobbes in Peter Beal's *Index of English Literary Manuscripts*. For discussions of the copyist referred to here as 'the Parisian scribe', see the articles referred to in n. 95. Entries of the form 'Payne, notes . . .' may mean extracts copied by him, or notes in his own words, or a combination of the two. Where material copied by him consists of an identifiable complete text, it is listed as such; it is possible that some of the minor notes (on geometry and proportions, for example) do consist of material by Hobbes, as yet unidentified. I am particularly grateful to Mr Peter Day, Keeper of Collections at Chatsworth, for his help during my visits there.

A1: Hobbes, *De mirabilibus pecci*: scribal copy, in two copyists' hands (previously owned by the 19th-century antiquary Bateman of Middleton Hall).
A2A: Hobbes, *Elements of Law*: scribal copy; lacks the epistle dedicatory (which may perhaps have been signed by Hobbes, and removed as an autograph).
A2B: Hobbes, *Elements of Law*: scribal copy, with epistle dedicatory in Hobbes's hand, and some corrections in the text in his hand.
A2C: Hobbes, *Elements of Law*: scribal copy; lacks the last page of the epistle dedicatory (which may perhaps have been signed by Hobbes, and removed as an autograph).
A3: Hobbes, *De cive*: copy on vellum (by the Parisian scribe), with epistle dedicatory signed by Hobbes.
A4: Hobbes, 'Philosophia Prima Capvt 19': copy (by the Parisian scribe) of an intended chapter of *De corpore*, with corrections by Hobbes.
A5: Hobbes, *De homine*, fragment (part of ch. 2; ch. 3): copy (by the Parisian scribe).
A6: Hobbes, *Vita carmine expressa*: copy (by James Wheldon), with corrections by Hobbes.
A7: List of geometrical terms and definitions: scribal copy.
A8: Latin digests of Scaliger, *De subtilitate*; Aristotle, *Rhetorica*; Aristotle, *Parva moralia*: in various scribal hands; the Scaliger digest has Hobbes's signature on the first page.
A9: Hobbes, 'Cyclometria': copy (by James Wheldon), with corrections by Hobbes.
A10: Payne, notes on Hobbes, draft of *De corpore*: in Payne's hand.
B1: 'G. F.', 'Glossopaedeia: that is The Ready way of teaching and learning The Languages': in an unknown hand (possibly that of 'G. F.'); dedicated to 'Ladie A.' (possibly Lady Arabella Stuart, in which case this work has no connection with Hobbes).
B2: William Oughtred, Treatise on sundials: scribal copy, with annotation in Payne's hand.
B3: Edmund Gunter, Treatise on the use of 'Gunter's Rule': copy in Payne's hand.
B4: Pierre de Fermat, 'De contactibus sphaericis' (fragment): copy (by the Parisian scribe).
B5: Walter Warner, 'De tactionibus': copy, in Payne's hand.
B6: Jean de Beaugrand, *Geostatice*: copy (by the Parisian scribe), from the printed edition (Paris, 1636).
C i 1: Payne, notes on Athanasius Kircher, *Ars magna lucis et umbrae* (Rome, 1646): in Payne's hand.
C i 2: William Oughtred ['W. O.'], two geometrical problems: one in an unidentified hand (perhaps Oughtred's), the other in Payne's hand.

C i 3: Payne, notes on geometrical problems by Thomas Hariot and Claude Mydorge: in Payne's hand.
C i 4: Payne, notes on problems of mechanics by Evangelista Torricelli: in Payne's hand.
C i 5: Payne, notes on Bonaventura Cavalieri, *Exercitationes geometricae sex* (Bologna, 1647): in Payne's hand.
C i 6(i) and (ii): René Descartes, parts of two letters to Mersenne (these copies are dated '1640', so were presumably transmitted by Mersenne in that year, but the original letters are from 23 August 1638 and 13 July 1638: printed in R. Descartes, *Oeuvres*, ed. C. Adam and P. Tannery, rev. edn., 11 vols. (Paris, 1974), II, pp. 307–38 and 222–52 respectively): scribal copies.
C i 7: Payne, notes on Henry Briggs, text relating to binomial equations: in Payne's hand.
C i 8: Payne, notes on Pappus of Alexandria, with reference also to François Aguilon, *Opticorum libri sex* (Antwerp, 1613): in Payne's hand.
C i 9: Walter Warner, 'Ad Architecturam Nauticam Problema' (fragment; text in Latin): copy, in Payne's hand.
C i 10: Walter Warner, 'Ad Architecturam Nauticam Problema' (fragment; different text, in English): copy, in Payne's hand.
C i 11: Henry Bond, geometrical demonstration: copy, in Payne's hand.
C i 12: Payne, notes on various writers (Luneschlos, Kepler, Cavalieri, Galileo, Archimedes, Renaldini, Stevinus): in Payne's hand.
C i 13: Payne, notes on an unidentified work on geometry ('lib. 1. In Parabolâ'): in Payne's hand.
C ii 1: Hobbes, geometrical problem (fragment): in Hobbes's hand (shaky, and probably late); identified by Professor Douglas Jesseph as related to his duplication of the cube of 1661–2.
C ii 2: Payne, notes on four geometrical problems, possibly related to Warner's 'Ad Architecturam Nauticam Problema': in Payne's hand.
C ii 3: Payne, note on a geometrical problem: in Payne's hand.
C ii 4: Payne, note on a geometrical problem: in Payne's hand.
C ii 5: Payne, notes on a geometrical problem (identified by Prof. Jesseph as a duplication of the cube): in Payne's hand.
C ii 6: Payne, notes on a geometrical problem: in Payne's hand.
C ii 7: Payne, notes on paraboloids (text in English): in Payne's hand.
C iii 1: Payne, notes on a problem of proportions: in Payne's hand.
C iii 2: Payne, notes on a problem of proportions: in Payne's hand.
C iii 3: Payne, notes on a problem of proportions: in Payne's hand.
C iii 4: Payne, notes on a problem of proportions: in Payne's hand.
C iii 5: Payne, notes on MS D2 (Hobbes, geometrical problems): in Payne's hand.
C iii 6: Payne, notes on 37 problems of proportions: in Payne's hand.
C iii 7: Payne, note on a geometrical problem: in Payne's hand.
C iii 8: Payne, notes on problems of proportions: in Payne's hand.
C iii 9: Payne, notes on problems of proportions: in Payne's hand.
C iii 10: Payne, notes on problems of proportions: in Payne's hand.
C iii 11: Payne, notes on geometrical problems: in Payne's hand.

C iv 1: Payne, notes on Galileo's theory of gravitational motion: in Payne's hand.

C iv 2: Payne, notes on Hobbes, draft of *De corpore* (chs. 12, 13): in Payne's hand.

C iv 3: Payne, notes on weight of bodies in vacuum: in Payne's hand.

C iv 4: Payne, note on astronomy: in Payne's hand.

C iv 5: Payne, note on astronomy: in Payne's hand.

C iv 6: Payne, notes on astronomy: in Payne's hand.

C iv 7: Payne, notes on an unidentified work on geometry, concerning parabolas (as in C i 13): in Payne's hand.

C v 1: Payne, note on refraction: in Payne's hand.

C v 2: Payne, note on refraction: in Payne's hand.

C v 3: Payne, note on optics: in Payne's hand.

C v 4: Payne, note on optics: in Payne's hand.

C vi 1: Chronological table: in an unidentified hand.

C vi 2: Payne, 'Problema Chronologicum, Helvico Adjectum' (relating to the work of Christopher Helvicus): in Payne's hand.

C vii 1: Payne, notes on arithmetical problem, with tables: in Payne's hand.

C vii 2: Payne, notes on arithmetical problem: in Payne's hand.

C vii 3: Payne, notes on Claude Mydorge, *Examen du livre des recreations mathematiques* (Paris, 1630), pp. 179–80 (the problem 'Des Escoliers de Pythagore'): in Payne's hand.

C vii 4: Payne, notes on geometrical problem, dated 'Septemb. 5. 1638. Welbeck': in Payne's hand.

C vii 5: Payne, notes on geometry and arithmetic: in Payne's hand.

C vii 6: Payne, notes on arithmetical problems: in Payne's hand.

C vii 7: Payne, note on sound, headed 'Monochordum ordinatum & perfectum': in Payne's hand.

C vii 8: Payne, notes on weights and metals of coins (probably from writings by Walter Warner): in Payne's hand.

C vii 9: Payne, notes on weighing: in Payne's hand.

C vii 10: Hobbes, notes on fortification (in English, but using much French terminology; possibly from a text in French): in Hobbes's hand.

C vii 11: Designs (described as 'sketch-plans of fortresses' in the RCHM 'Report', though this may be doubted); without any writing.

C vii 12: Payne, table of numbers, unfinished: Payne's hand.

D1: Hobbes, Latin 'Digest' of Aristotle's *Rhetoric*: a so-called 'dictation book', mainly in a juvenile hand (probably that of William Cavendish, third Earl of Devonshire), with corrections and insertions in Hobbes's hand.

D2: Hobbes, problems in geometry: copy, in a juvenile hand (probably that of William Cavendish, third Earl of Devonshire), with additions in Hobbes's hand.

D3: William Cavendish, second Earl of Devonshire, 'Essayes': copy, in Hobbes's hand, with some corrections in another hand (probably the second Earl's).

D4: Text on virtue and religion, asserting their interdependence: in an unidentified hand.

D5: William Cavendish, fourth Earl of Devonshire (?) and Hobbes, questions and answers on political issues (fragment): on the subject of the right of kingship and the possibility of a king disqualifying his heir from succeeding: the questions are possibly in the fourth Earl's hand, the answer is in James Wheldon's hand.

D6: 'A Narration of y$^e$ Proceedings . . . concerning y$^e$ Inheritance of . . . William Earl of Devonshire': legal statement about relations between the Earl and his mother, during and after his minority, and about Hobbes's conduct in relation to the dispute: in an unidentified hand (possibly that of Christopher Hallely), signed by the Earl and Hobbes.

D7: William Cavendish, third Earl of Devonshire, note, probably in his hand, and draft of letter, in James Wheldon's hand (1679); neither item by or relating to Hobbes (see Hobbes, *Correspondence*, I, pp. xlviii–xlix).

D8: Hobbes, note of return of £100 (previously invested on his behalf), 15 September 1640: in Hobbes's hand.

E1: Payne, list of manuscripts donated by Sir Kenelm Digby to the Bodleian in 1634: in Payne's hand.

E1 A: Hobbes, catalogue of Hardwick library, mainly compiled in late 1620s, with some additions in early 1630s: in Hobbes's hand.

E2: Payne, list of nearly 900 books in Bodleian (*c.*1631–2), by subject: in Payne's hand.

E3: 'A Note of y$^e$ Prospectiue Glasses bought of m$^r$. Hobbes y$^e$ 13$^{th}$ day of Aprill. 1659': in an unidentified hand (the telescopes were bought by the third Earl of Devonshire; this is probably in the hand of one of his servants).

E4: Christiaan Huygens, letter to Andrew Crooke for Hobbes, August 1662 (Hobbes, *Correspondence*, II, pp. 530–1): in Huygens's hand.

E5: Payne, notes listing authors cited in Bonaventura Cavalieri, *Lo specchio ustorio* (Bologna, 1632): in Payne's hand.

E6: Poem in praise of Hobbes (referring to 'the Picture I have drawn', so probably by a portraitist): in an unknown hand.

F1: Poems in imitation of Martial (in English), with an acrostic dedicatory poem to 'Maister William Cavendish' (which suggests a date before the knighting of William Cavendish, the future second Earl of Devonshire, in March 1609): in an unidentified hand.

F2: De la Moulinière, defence of Hobbes's views on ecclesiastical authority, sent in a letter of [21/] 31 December 1659 (now lost) by Samuel Sorbière to Hobbes (see Hobbes, *Correspondence*, I, pp. 507–11, II, 513–14): in the hand of (probably) de la Moulinière.

F3: French text beginning 'Mais depuis l'erection de tous les parlements', concerning the municipal constitutions of French cities and the system of appointments to benefices (fragment): in an unidentified hand; currently missing. The connection with Hobbes seems doubtful.

G1: 'Articles of Impeachm$^t$ . . . against William Earle of Powys' (1678–9): in an unidentified hand, endorsed 'For M$^r$ Halleley'.

G2: 'The Lord Shaftesburys Speech in the House of Lords March. 25. 1679': in an unidentified hand (with an endorsement in James Wheldon's hand).

G3: The Exclusion Act (5 May 1679): copy, in an unidentified hand (with a heading in James Wheldon's hand).

G4: Notes of books taken from, or returned to, the library (at Chatsworth or Hardwick), dated 1682 and 1683: in an unknown hand.

Unnumbered: Fulgenzio Micanzio, letters to William Cavendish, second Earl of Devonshire, translated by Hobbes: scribal copy (in two copyists' hands), with annotation in Hobbes's hand on the first page. This MS was acquired in the 19th century, having previously been owned by G. Dyer of Exeter (whose letter about it, dated 15 July 1813, is bound in at the start of the volume).

Unnumbered: 'Letters from foreign correspondents', a collection consisting mainly of letters to Hobbes from his correspondents in France (all originals), but also including a letter from Henry Stubbe to Andrew Crooke, a letter from John Wallis to Viscount Brouncker, and a copy of Hobbes's printed 'Duplication du cube'.

## APPENDIX 2

*Books from Payne's library, now in the Savile collection in the Bodleian*

Payne's annotated copy of Hariot's *Artis analyticae praxis* (listed below) also contains a note by John Wallis, which comments on Payne's annotations and adds: 'There were divers other Mathematicall Books, at y$^e$ same time, brought out of D$^r$ Pains study, [>and now put into y$^e$ Savilian Mathematick Study as well as this] most of which have divers notes of his own hand writing in them.' Payne did not write his name in his books; these items have been identified by his handwriting. He sometimes recorded the date of purchase, and/or the price: both are noted in these entries. His 'divers notes' could include marginal comments, extensive notes on endpapers (often listing authors cited in the work), or even extra pages tipped in or loosely inserted in the text. The books are listed here in alphabetical order of authors; the pressmark is given after the date of publication (in the form 'A.1'—meaning, 'Savile A.1'). I am very grateful to Dr Clive Hurst and Dunja Sharif, of the Bodleian Library Rare Books department, for their assistance and patience while I conducted this search.

Bacon, R., *Perspectiva* (Frankfurt, 1614), Y. 2.
Baldi, B., *In mechanica Aristotelis problemata exercitationes* (Mainz, 1621), Dd. 4 (bought 8 May 1648; price: 2s 4d).
Barlow, W., *Magneticall Advertisements* (London, 1616), Cc. 3(1).
Castelli, B., *Della misura dell'acque correnti* (Rome, 1628), Bb. 2.
Davison ['d'Avisson'], W., *Philosophia pyrotechnica . . . seu curriculus chymiatricus* (Paris, 1635), Aa. 12.
Descartes, R., *Principia philosophiae* (Amsterdam, 1644), T. 22 (bought 3 February 1646, price: 8*s*. 6*d*.).
Descartes, R., *Musicae compendium* (Utrecht, 1650), Y. 7 (price: 1*s*.).
Descartes, R., *Specimina philosophiae* (Amsterdam, 1650), T. 23 (bought 30 September 1650, price: 8*s*. 6*d*.).
Deusingius, A., *De vero systemate mundi dissertatio mathematica* (Amsterdam, 1643), Bb. 17 (price: 3*s*.).

D'Espagnet, J., *Enchiridion physicae restitutae* (Paris, 1647), Cc. 28 (bought 25 May 1649, price: 2s.).
Euclid, Στοιχεῖα [*Elementa*] (Basel, 1533), W. 7.
Euclid, Στοιχεῖα, [*Elementa*] ed. and tr. F. Commandino (London, 1620), W. 3.
Euclid, Δεδομένα [*Data*], and Marinus, Ὑπόμνημα [*Commentarius*], ed. C. Hardy (Paris, 1625), V. 15.
Galilei, G., *Discorsi e dimostrazioni matematiche* (Leiden, 1638), Bb. 13.
Gassendi, P., *De apparente magnitudine solis* (Paris, 1642), V. 13(1).
Gassendi, P., *De motu impresso a motore translato* (Paris, 1642), V. 13(2).
Gassendi, P., *De proportione* (Paris, 1646), T. 8.
Gassendi, P., *Animadversiones in decimum librum Diogenis Laertis*, 3 vols. (Lyon, 1649), N. 9–11 (bought August 1650, price: £2 10s.).
Hariot, T., *Artis analyticae praxis* (London, 1631), O. 9.
de Malthe ['Malthus'], F., *Traité des feux artificiels pour la guerre, et pour la recreation* (Paris, 1632), Bb. 26.
Mersenne, M., *Harmonicorum libri IV* (Paris, 1636), Q. 13.
Mydorge, C., *Prodromi catoptricorum et dioptricorum: sive conicorum operis... libri primus et secundus* (Paris, 1631), bound with books 3 and 4, published in the enlarged 2nd edition, *Conicorum operis... libri quatuor* (Paris, 1639), Q. 9.
Oughtred, W., *Arithmeticae... institutio... quasi clavis* (London, 1631), Z. 19.
Oughtred, W., *Arithmeticae... institutio... quasi clavis* (London, 1631), Z. 24.
Pell, J., *Controversiae de verâ circuli mensurâ... pars prima* (Amsterdam, 1647), Y. 4 (price: 2s. 6d.).
Pell, J., *Controversiae de verâ circuli mensurâ... pars prima* (Amsterdam, 1647), H. 3.
della Porta, G. B., *De refractione* (Naples, 1593), Y. 10.
van Schooten, F., *De organica conicarum sectionum in plano descriptione* (Leiden, 1646), Bb. 10.
Sirturus, H., *Telescopium: sive ars perficiendi novum illud Galilaei visorium instrumentum ad sydera* (Frankfurt, 1618), Cc. 3(9).
Stevin, S., *Les Oeuvres mathématiques*, ed. A. Girard (Leiden, 1634), Q. 10.
Torricelli, E., *Opera geometrica* (Florence, 1644), Y. 1.
Varro, M., *De motu tractatus* (Geneva, 1584), Y. 11.
Vieta, F., *Opera mathematica*, ed. F. van Schooten (Leiden, 1646), N. 6 (price: £1 8s.)

# – 5 –
# Hobbes's Science of Politics and his Theory of Science

Hobbes thought of his theory of politics as a 'science'. At the end of his English Optical Treatise he expressed the hope that 'I shall deserve the reputation of having been y$^e$ first to lay the grounds of two sciences; this of Optiques, y$^e$ most curious, and y$^t$ other of Natural Justice, which I have done in my booke De Cive'.[1] The parallel, or distinction, between natural science and civil science recurs again and again in Hobbes's writings; and the difficulty for Hobbes's commentators lies in deciding what the relationship is between these two different types of science. Most critics have assumed that the two types are closely related, and that we therefore have to understand how Hobbes conducts his physical science in order to be able to understand his science of politics. But a few writers, most notably Tom Sorell in his important recent study of Hobbes's philosophy, have argued in favour of a so-called 'autonomy thesis', according to which Hobbes's political science is independent, *qua* science, of his science of nature.[2]

Among interpretations which argue that Hobbes's two sciences were closely related, we can distinguish two versions of the argument: a strong version and a weak one. The strong version claims that Hobbes envisaged a single, continuous chain of derivation leading from physics, via psychology, to politics: this interpretation makes him a would-be 'social scientist' of a very literal kind, and an intellectual ancestor certainly of Comte, and possibly of Mill. The weak version, on the other hand, claims only that Hobbes applied the *method* of physical science to the science of politics, so that the political theory resembles or parallels the physics without necessarily being derived from it.

A classic example of the strong version of this argument can be found in Alan Ryan's book, *The Philosophy of the Social Sciences*:

Hobbes believed as firmly as one could that all behaviour, whether of animate or inanimate matter, was ultimately to be explained in terms of particulate motion: the laws

---

This chapter was first published in A. Napoli, ed., *Hobbes oggi* (Milan, 1990).

[1] *EW* VII, p. 471.   [2] T. Sorell, *Hobbes* (London, 1986).

governing the motions of discrete material particles were the ultimate laws of nature, and in this sense psychology must be rooted in physiology and physiology in physics, while the social sciences, especially the technology of statecraft, must be rooted in psychology.[3]

The phrase 'rooted in' is perhaps a little less confident than 'derived from' or 'entailed by' would be; but the general picture is clear. This interpretation is certainly faithful to Hobbes's ontology, in which matter in motion is the only knowable reality; and it is also faithful to the overall scheme of human knowledge which Hobbes adhered to in planning his tripartite system of the 'Elements of Philosophy': *De corpore, De homine, De cive*.

As is well known, however, the history of Hobbes's writing and publishing of his tripartite system belies any strict interpretation of its cumulative structure. 'What was last in order', he writes in the Preface to the second edition of *De cive*, 'is yet come forth first in time, and the rather, because I saw that grounded on its owne principles sufficiently knowne by experience it would not stand in need of the former Sections.'[4] There is a similar disclaimer in the first chapter of *Leviathan*, where Hobbes remarks that 'To know the natural cause of Sense, is not very necessary to the business now in hand . . . Nevertheless, to fill each part of my present method, I will briefly deliver the same in this place.'[5] This may suggest that Hobbes's 'present method' is more a system of organization than a system of deduction.

When Hobbes says that his political theory is 'grounded on its owne principles sufficiently knowne by experience', it is open to critics such as Ryan to argue that this indicates only a short-cut in the order of knowledge, not a break in the order of truth or logical deduction. But the resort to 'experience', i.e. introspection, which Hobbes makes use of when setting out the bases of his political theory, surely produces a quite different kind of truth from the truths which might be derived from the physiology of the brain and the nervous system. And this objection is not merely a special point about the peculiarity of introspection. If we attempted to follow Hobbes's 'method' through, ascending from one level of knowledge to the next, we would find that each new level required the introduction of concepts which were simply not contained in the subject-matter of the previous level. Physics will give us the concepts of 'motion towards' or 'motion away from'; but only psychology will provide the concepts of 'desire' or 'fear'. Hobbes seems to recognize this when, in the Introduction to *Leviathan*, he invokes the maxim 'Nosce Teipsum' and asks each reader to consider 'what he doth, when he does *think, opine, reason, hope, feare*, &c, and upon what grounds'.[6]

Alan Ryan's strong version of the argument seems unable to cope with Hobbes's actual practice. The weak version, as put forward by writers such as John Watkins

---

[3] A. Ryan, *The Philosophy of the Social Sciences* (London, 1970), pp. 102–3. I am grateful to Dr Sorell for this reference.

[4] *De cive* (English version), ed. H. Warrender (Oxford, 1983), p. 36.

[5] *Leviathan*, p. 3.   [6] Ibid., p. 2.

and Maurice Goldsmith, is better equipped to take on board Hobbes's frequent comments emphasizing the difference in subject-matter between physics and politics.[7] The diagram of the sciences in chapter 9 of *Leviathan*, for example, begins by dividing all philosophical knowledge into two: 'Consequences from the Accidents of Bodies Naturall', and 'Consequences from the Accidents of *Politique* Bodies'.[8] (This diagram is, admittedly, a puzzle for most theories of Hobbes's method, since it also places both ethics and the science of justice in the human subsection of the science of 'bodies natural'; but the diagram is, in any case, a system of classification of the sciences rather than a programme of deductive method.) The picture of physics and politics as two radically different areas of subject-matter, existing more or less in parallel and both qualifying as sciences, is confirmed by the first chapter of *De corpore*, which explains that there are 'two parts of philosophy, called *natural* and *civil*', concerned with 'two chief kinds of bodies', which are 'very different from one another'.[9] The principal thing which these two sciences have in common, it seems, is that they are sciences: in other words, they employ essentially the same method in searching after the 'generation' and 'properties' of their respective 'bodies'.

The classic text for this line of interpretation is the passage in the Preface to the second edition of *De cive*, where Hobbes argues that 'every thing is best understood by its constitutive causes', and compares the analysis of the body politic to the taking apart of a watch. In the English translation of *De cive* the passage appears as follows:

Concerning my Method. I though it not sufficient to use a plain and evident style in what I had to deliver, except I took my beginning from the very matter of civill government, and thence proceeded to its generation, and form, and the first beginning of justice; for every thing is best understood by its constitutive causes; for as in a watch, or some such small engine, the matter, figure, and motion of the wheels, cannot be well known, except it be taken in sunder, and viewed in parts; so to make a more curious search into the rights of States, and duties of Subjects, it is necessary, (I say not to take them in sunder, but yet that) they be so considered, as if they were dissolved....[10]

In his recent book, Tom Sorell argues ingeniously that the real significance of this comparison is not the similarity which it suggests between physical and political investigation, but the dissimilarity. The comparison here, he notes, is not between a watch and a body politic but between a watch and a set of rights and duties—the difference being that the 'parts' of a body politic are individual people, but the 'parts' of rights and duties are jural entities. He also notes that, while the watch is to be disassembled, the rights and duties are to be entirely 'dissolved' in thought:

---

[7] J. W. N. Watkins, *Hobbes's System of Ideas* (London, 1965); M. M. Goldsmith, *Hobbes's Science of Politics* (London, 1966).
[8] *Leviathan*, ch. 9, table.   [9] *De corpore* I.9; *EW* I, p. 11.   [10] *De cive* (English version), p. 32.

this means that, while the physical scientist merely puts the real watch back together again, the political scientist can construct an ideal political entity of rights and duties as they should be.[11]

Much of the reasoning with which Dr Sorell supports this argument is, I think, convincing. But as an analysis of the passage in *De cive* the argument fails, because it relies (as all previous commentators seem to have done) on the English translation. As I have indicated elsewhere, this translation was certainly not by Hobbes.[12] It is generally faithful, but often, as here, it blurs the details of Hobbes's argument. In the original Latin, Hobbes does in fact keep up a very close parallelism. The comparison is between the watch and the 'civitas'. In the one case we wish to investigate the function ('officium') of the cogs, wheels, etc.; in the other case we wish to investigate the function or office or duty ('officium' again—this is a sort of conceptual pun) of the citizens and the right ('jus') of the state. In the one case we take apart ('dissolvere') the watch; in the other case we do not actually take apart the state, but consider it as if taken apart ('ut dissoluta'). In the one case, in order to understand the function of the parts, we have to examine the material, shape, and motion of each of them; in the other case, we have to consider human nature, the ways in which it makes men draw together into a state and the exact way in which people must align themselves with one another if they are going to draw together.

By emphasizing the similarity between the two cases, I am contradicting Dr Sorell's textual analysis; but I think that emphasizing the similarity helps in the long run to confirm his general argument. Note first of all that Hobbes has not compared the state to a natural object such as a crystal or a sand-dune, which would be proper objects for investigation by the methods of physical science: he has compared it to an artefact, the nature of which can only be understood by understanding the intentions of the person who makes it or uses it. If you take a watch apart, you will find that one of its components is something called a governor, which turns the uneven motion of the unwinding of a spring into the even motion of the hands on the face of the watch. We could not understand the nature of the watch's arrangement of physical parts unless we understood what the governor was doing; and we could not have the concept of a governor unless we knew what watches were *for*. Of course, if a governor is to do its job it has to have certain physical properties: physics will describe the strength of the metal, the forces applied to it, the friction involved, and so on. The governor consists, after all, of nothing other than a piece of metal: there is no ghost in the machine. But a full physical description of it would not in itself give us the concept of a governor, any more than the physical description of a hemispherical metal object will give us the concept of a helmet or a cauldron.

---

[11] Sorell, *Hobbes*, pp. 20–1.
[12] N. Malcolm, 'Citizen Hobbes', *London Review of Books* (Oct. 1984), p. 22.

What I am trying to suggest here is the simultaneous truth and inadequacy of saying that the watch consists of nothing other than metal and is therefore entirely reducible to a physical explanation of its nature. And the point which I am making is not the same as the point which is usually made about 'emergent properties' in the case of physical phenomena which are not artefacts. A ripple in a lake, for example, is an emergent property of water under certain conditions: we know that there is nothing there except water molecules, and we also know that to talk of ripples is to use a level of description which is simply not appropriate to the molecular level of reality. But the nature of a watch *qua* watch or of a helmet *qua* helmet is not an emergent property. It didn't just emerge—it was put there. And to describe it we need not just a different level of description but a different kind of description: description in terms of intentions. The same applies, I believe, to the nature of the state in Hobbes's theory.

A brief comparison may be permitted here with Mill, whose notion of a social science is in fact so reductivist that it hardly allows emergent properties, let alone intentional ones. In book six of the *System of Logic*, he announces:

> The laws of the phenomena of society are, and can be, nothing but the laws of the actions and passions of human beings united together in the social state. Men, however, in a state of society, are still men ... [They] are not, when brought together, converted into another kind of substance, with different properties; as hydrogen and oxygen are different from water ... Human beings in society have no properties but those which are derived from, and may be resolved into, the laws of the nature of individual man.[13]

But we should be clear that Mill is talking here only about social science, not about politics or policy. At the end of the book he brings in a different level of knowledge, 'teleology' or the doctrine of values, and explains (although in fact he explains very little here) that it is on a completely different footing from the science of society which he has outlined. It makes use of the science of society just as an architect makes use of physics: the aesthetic values which shape the architect's design cannot themselves be derived from physical science. Although he leaves a great deal unsaid here, Mill does at least attempt a clean separation between fact and value—something which is sadly missing in the end from Hobbes's argument.

Returning to Hobbes's watch-analogy, it is worth noting, finally, that this passage from *De cive* resurfaces in the 'introduction' to *Leviathan*, where it is expanded into Hobbes's famous comparison between the state and an 'automaton or artificiall man'. Hobbes defines automata here as 'Engines that move themselves by springs and wheels as doth a watch'.[14] Seeing the derivation of this passage from the watch-comparison in *De cive* helps us to see that the essential point about the 'artificiall man' here is that it is artificial, not that it resembles a man—that

[13] J. S. Mill, *System of Logic* (London, 1893), VI, 7, 1, p. 573.   [14] *Leviathan*, p. 1.

resemblance is an extra layer of analogy, added in *Leviathan* because of the increased importance in that work of the theory of the 'person' of the commonwealth.

In the 'Introduction' to *Leviathan*, Hobbes indulges in a fanciful and elaborate enumeration of the 'parts' of this automaton which he proposes to investigate: the wealth of the population is the artificial man's strength; the counsellors are its memory; reward and punishment are its nerves; and so on. Both qualities and physical parts are mingled promiscuously here: they are on a par with one another not in terms of a physical description of the automaton but in terms of the nature of the automaton as an artificial object, an object constituted by the intentions of the people who make it and use it.

In the passage in *De cive*, Hobbes said that he would investigate human nature and the ways in which it was apt to join together. Here in *Leviathan* he says the following:

To describe the Nature of this Artificiall man, I will consider
First, the *Matter* thereof, and the *Artificer* . . .
Secondly, *How*, and by what *Covenants* it is made; what are the *Rights* and just *Power* or *Authority* of a Soveraigne; and what it is that *preserveth* and *dissolveth* it.
Thirdly, what is a *Christian Common-wealth*.
Lastly, what is the *Kingdome of Darkness*.[15]

And there, in other words, is the four-fold plan of *Leviathan*. If we look at his summary of Part I of the work, we can see that it contains, quite compendiously, both sides of the critical debate about Hobbes's 'science' of politics: 'I will consider', Hobbes writes, 'First the *Matter* thereof, and the *Artificer*; both which is *Man*.' Hobbes's politics must therefore include both a science of human nature as the material of the state, and a science of human meanings, the ways in which men define and create the nature of the state as they fashion it out of that material.

Behind all this talk of material and workmanship, there hovers, quite naturally, an Aristotelian argument about the relation between 'matter' and 'form'. There is nothing covert or shameful about the presence of this conceptual model: in the original passage in *De cive* Hobbes actually uses the terms 'materia' and 'forma', when he says that he has proceeded from the matter of the state to its generation and form.[16] Does this mean that Hobbes was betraying his allegiance to the 'new science' of mechanistic physics? Not at all. One way of putting the new scientists' objection to Aristotle's theory of formal causes would be to say that they felt that this theory involved imputing some sort of purposivity or intentionality to physical processes—an imputation which they believed to be superfluous or spurious. Hobbes, similarly, found the category of formal causation irrelevant to physical science. Yet there was no reason why he should abandon its use where the description of intentional actions was concerned: for this purpose it was ideally suited. The

---

[15] Ibid., p. 2.  [16] *De cive* (Latin version), p. 79.

methods of physical science could be used to describe the 'matter' of the commonwealth. But physical science itself would not supply a concept of the relation between matter and form; and in order to analyse the form of the commonwealth in terms of the intentions of the people who made it, a rather different type of science was also necessary.

Hobbes found the model for this type of science in the science of geometry. The essential similarity was striking. Both sciences yielded universal truths by expressing the connections between conceptual entities: lines, circles, and squares, or rights, duties, and laws. To express the relationship between the sovereign and the citizens was to expound an analytic truth, similar to that which states the relationship between a circle and its radii. Unfortunately, however, beyond this type of immediate similarity there lay a very shadowy terrain of uncertain resemblances and shifting implications. The difficulties arose partly because Hobbes's views on the nature of geometry changed, and partly because he always tended to play down the peculiar status of the objects of geometry as conceptual entities, preferring to absorb geometry into a general theory about the nature of universal truths.

Hobbes's theory of universal truths was a product of his nominalism; and his nominalism was a good deal less extreme than is popularly supposed. He was a nominalist, not an arbitrarist. Hobbes believed that all blue objects, for example, are really similar: our use of the same word to describe them is not a mere freak of human will or fancy. Indeed, his mechanistic theory of sense-perception ensures this, since the nature of the conception in our brains which we connote with the word 'blue' is *caused* directly by the motion of the object which we see. We experience objects as similar because they really do cause similar motions.

Hobbes defines a true proposition as follows: 'that, whose predicate contains, or comprehends its subjects, or whose predicate is the name of every thing, of which the subject is the name'.[17] This definition is not directed simply at analytical truths of the sort, 'a bachelor is an unmarried man'. When I hold a blueberry and say 'this berry is blue', I satisfy Hobbes's requirements for a true statement: 'this berry' and 'blue' are both names of the thing I hold in my hand.

Apart from this sort of particular contingent truth, Hobbes also distinguishes between what might be called general contingent truths and universal necessary truths. 'All crows are black' is a general contingent truth. It is true because 'black' happens to be a name of the thing of which 'all crows' is the name. But if we found a white crow we would still call it a crow; so this is not a universal necessary truth. 'All crows are birds' *is* a universal necessary truth, because we could never find a crow which was not a bird.[18] Hobbes is being something of a traditionalist here, setting up a hierarchy of levels of description. We might put it as follows. The real similarity connoted by the term 'bird' is a component of the more complex real

---

[17] *De corpore*, III. 7, *EW* I, p. 35.   [18] Ibid., III. 10, p. 38.

similarity connoted by the term 'crow'. We cannot identify something as a crow without (early on in the process) identifying it as a bird. In *De corpore* Hobbes gives an example of this sort of cumulative recognition of similarities: as we approach an object from a distance, we see first that it is a body (i.e. corporeal), then that it is animate, then that it is rational: we 'compound' these concepts and arrive at the true judgement that it is a man.[19]

This sort of conceptual 'compounding', and its converse, conceptual resolution, provided the primary model for Hobbes's theory of resolutive–compositive method—a method which, I believe, owed almost nothing to Galileo and very little to the Paduan tradition of commentary on Aristotle. The use of the terms 'resolutio' and 'compositio' was immensely widespread, across a whole range of disciplines: they were simply the Latin equivalents of the Greek terms 'analysis' and 'synthesis', terms used in the Galenist tradition of diagnosis and prognosis, and in the Euclidean tradition of the methodology of mathematical problems.[20] Galileo's use of resolution and composition was concerned with the investigation of the causes of phenomena. Hobbes's conceptual resolution was concerned with causes only indirectly or equivocally. Indirectly in the sense that, when an observer perceives an object to be first corporeal, then animate, then rational, these perceptions are the causes of his knowing that it is a man. Equivocally in the sense that having those properties is the 'cause' of the object's *being* a man—this is a use of the word 'cause' which was outlawed, strictly speaking, by Hobbes's ontology.

Conceptual resolution of this kind involved little more than a progression through different levels of description; as such, it offered a much less fruitful model for a theory of scientific method than, for example, the use of 'resolution' to solve mathematical problems in the Euclidean tradition. Yet what appealed to Hobbes about geometry was its ability to yield new knowledge from an initial store of definitions and axioms. Ethics might resemble this form of science, since it was possible to resolve terms such as 'justice' into terms such as 'contract', and then to compound again in ways which might reveal hitherto unknown truths about what could or could not count as justice. But it was difficult to see how resolving and compounding the concept of a crow could tell you anything you did not already know about crows. Hobbes would have benefited, perhaps, from Locke's distinction between natural objects, whose nominal essences differ from their real essences, and conceptual objects (such as mixed modes and relations), where the nominal essence *is* the real essence.

---

[19] Ibid., I.1, p. 4; cf. William of Ockham, *Quodlibeta* I, qu. 13, in *Philosophical Writings*, ed. P. Boehner (New York, 1957), p. 30.

[20] See W. F. Edwards, 'Randall on the Development of Scientific Method in the School of Padua: a Continuing Reappraisal', in J. Anton, ed., *Naturalism and Historical Understanding: Essays on the Philosophy of John Herman Randall Jr* (Buffalo, NY, 1967), pp. 53–68; H. Schüling, *Die Geschichte der Axiomatische Methode im 16. und beginnenden 17. Jahrhundert* (Hildersheim, 1969) (esp. pp. 67–73); J. Klein, *Greek Mathematical Thought and the Origin of Algebra* (Cambridge, Mass., 1968) (esp. pp. 154–60).

Hobbes's early works gave the special status of 'science' only to those disciplines, such as geometry, which yielded universal truths. The knowledge of physical causes, on the other hand, belonged to the realm of experience, conjecture and hypothesis. After a few years in Paris in the 1640s, however, Hobbes began to include the knowledge of causes in his definitions of science. He may have been prompted to explore this direction of argument partly by the Mersenne circle's preoccupation with physical science, and more generally by the feeling that the physical causation of one event by another was the only category of fundamental explanation suitable for a universe consisting entirely of matter in motion. But one further reason for importing physical causes into the realm of true science may have been, paradoxically, Hobbes's desire to explain the special power of geometry to yield new knowledge.

The first signs of this new line of thinking come in the notes on Hobbes's philosophy made by Sir Charles Cavendish in 1645, and in the undated manuscript at Chatsworth, the 'Logica ex T.H.', which closely resembles Cavendish's notes and represents a draft of the early chapters of *De corpore*.[21] In these accounts the description of philosophy or science is no longer concerned with attaining universal propositions through the use of settled definitions: 'Philosophy', Hobbes writes, 'is the knowledge of the properties of bodies, acquired by correct reasoning from the notions of their generations; and conversely the knowledge of possible generations, acquired by correct reasoning from known properties.'[22] The distinction between natural science and other sorts of philosophy is maintained only in so far as the former is hypothetical: both are concerned with 'generation'. Now, the use of this word, instead of the word 'cause', gives a clue as to how this transition was effected in Hobbes's mind. For it is a word which, in his subsequent works, is characteristically used for geometrical figures when they are conceived of as products of the motion of a point. This way of conceiving of lines was being developed by geometers such as Roberval, who used it to solve problems involving complex curves such as spirals and trochoids. And it was precisely in this period (1643–5) that Hobbes became a friend of Roberval and developed an interest in this method: a discussion between the two of them on the comparison between a spiral and a parabola bore fruit in a demonstration which Mersenne published in his *Hydraulica* in 1644.[23]

---

[21] For details of these MSS see A. Pacchi, *Convenzione e ipotesi nella formazione della filosofia naturale di Thomas Hobbes* (Florence, 1965), pp. 29–30, 147–9; and J. Jacquot and H. W. Jones, 'Introduction' to Hobbes's *Critique du* de Mundo *de Thomas White* (Paris, 1973), pp. 83–7. Jacquot and Jones print a composite text of the MSS on pp. 461–513.

[22] Ibid., p. 463: 'Philosophia est corporum proprietatum ex conceptis eorum generationibus, et rursus generationum, quae esse possunt, ex cognitis proprietatibus, per rectam ratiocinationem cognitio'.

[23] M. Mersenne, *Cogitata Physicomathematica* (Paris, 1644), p. 129; see Hobbes's account of this discussion in *Six Lessons to the Professor of the Mathematics*, EW VII, p. 343.

In this way, Hobbes gained the heady satisfaction of arriving at unified theory of science, uniting the knowledge of universal necessary truths with the knowledge of causes: to know the *meaning* of the word 'circle' was to know what sort of motion of a point was the *cause* of a circle. But here Hobbes was sliding, as I have already suggested, into an equivocal use of the word 'cause'. The motion of a pair of compasses certainly causes a mark on a page; but what 'causes' that mark to be a circle is the equidistance of the resulting line from the central point, and this was a sort of causation which Hobbes had already denied to involve causes properly speaking. The idea of uniting the knowledge of necessary truths with the knowledge of causes was in the end a snare and a delusion, and this accounts for much of the floundering in Hobbes's later writings on the subject—writings which include not only the chapter on method in *De corpore*, but also *Leviathan*, where the definition of 'science' compromises awkwardly between knowledge of the consequences of names and knowledge of the consequences of facts.[24]

According to this unsatisfactory unified theory, the only difference between the uncertain propositions of physics and the certain propositions of geometry and politics was that in the case of physics we hypothesize about how something might have been caused, whereas in politics or geometry we have certain knowledge because we have caused the object ourselves. This is not, however, an adequate distinction. It applies, for example, to the difference between finding a footprint in the sand, in which case one conjectures its cause, and making a footprint oneself, in which case one knows its cause. But the objects of geometry or politics have not just been 'made' by us in this contingent physical sense: they are intentional objects, constituted by the way in which we think of them.

To conclude: the distinction between two different types of science is reflected in Hobbes's actual practice, and in some of the methodological comments in his political writings—notably the distinction between the 'matter' and the 'form' of the commonwealth. But his own theoretical writings on the nature of scientific knowledge became more and more misleading as guides to his actual practice, because of his obsession with providing a unified theory of science. Hobbes's confusions have been (understandably) reflected in the confusions of his commentators, who have tried either to confine his theory of science to one of the two varieties, or to show that both varieties were based on a single underlying pattern of scientific method. Hobbes's formal science of rights and obligations assumes the existence of a human nature which can be described by a mechanistic science of causes; but it is not itself a product of that science.

---

[24] *Leviathan*, p. 21: 'till we come to a knowledge of all the Consequences of names appertaining to the subject in hand; and that it is, men call Science. And whereas Sense and Memory are but knowledge of Fact . . . *Science* is the knowledge of Consequences, and dependance of one fact upon another . . .'.

# – 6 –

# Hobbes and Roberval

## I

All accounts of Hobbes's life are agreed that the years he spent in Paris, from late 1640 to the end of 1651, were of enormous importance to his philosophical development. They are also agreed that two people played particularly significant roles, as friends and intellectual influences: Marin Mersenne and Pierre Gassendi. Both were philosophers in their own right, and it is understandable that modern students of Hobbes should try to relate his ideas to the arguments set out in their published works. There is a danger, however, that this approach to Hobbes and his Parisian milieu may lead us to underestimate the importance of a third figure, merely on the grounds that he published almost no philosophical work: the mathematician Gilles Personne de Roberval. Enough evidence has survived to suggest that his personal and intellectual relations with Hobbes were almost as close as those enjoyed by Mersenne, and perhaps even closer than those of Gassendi. Regardless of how one might choose to rank the three in precise degrees of friendship with Hobbes or influence on him, the fact remains that Mersenne, Gassendi, and Roberval constituted a triumvirate of friends, the third of whom has been strangely neglected hitherto in all accounts of Hobbes's life.

Gilles Personne was born in the village of Roberval, near Senlis, in 1602. Nothing is known about his early education; his father was a poor farmer or farm-worker, and the young mathematician (who would later add 'de Roberval' to his surname) seems to have led the peripatetic life of an impoverished student, passing through several universities and alternately studying and teaching. In 1628 he settled in Paris; there he got to know Mersenne, who recognized his talents and encouraged him to work on the problem of the curve known as the 'trochoid', 'roulette', or 'cycloid'. In 1632 Roberval was given a teaching post at the Collège de Maître Gervais; two years later he obtained a more eminent position, the Ramus chair of mathematics at the Collège Royal.[1] He would remain in this professorship

---

[1] On Roberval's early life and first appointments see L. Auger, *Gilles Personne de Roberval (1602–1675): son activité intellectuelle dans les domaines mathématique, physique, mécanique et philosophique* (Paris, 1962), pp. 7–10; P. Costabel, 'Gilles Personne de Roberval', *Cahiers d'histoire et de philosophie des sciences*, n.s.,

for forty-one years—a permanent fixture, as it were, of Parisian intellectual life—until his death in 1675. But the peculiar terms on which holders of this Ramus chair were appointed had a very negative influence on both his work and his later reputation. The chair was tenable for a period of three years; at the end of that time it was opened to a public competition, in which anyone (including the incumbent) could apply for it. Candidates were required not only to lecture, but also to demonstrate theorems and solve problems put to them by all comers; as a result, the practice grew up of the incumbent trying to ensure his re-appointment by proposing problems which only he could solve.[2] Whatever were the most advanced discoveries Roberval was making at any time, therefore, he had an incentive to keep them secret, so that he could use them to confound his competitors on these triennial occasions. One consequence was that most of his important work in his special field—geometry—remained unpublished in his lifetime. And another consequence was that Roberval would more than once become embroiled in disputes about precedence, insisting that he had made key discoveries long before they were published by others; in 1646, for example, he would make bitter accusations against Torricelli, alleging that his analysis of the cycloid had been derived in an underhand way from Roberval's own unpublished work.[3] Even when he did allow some of his work to circulate, he favoured a method of publication that was both limited and carefully monitored: as the English mathematician John Pell would later recall, 'many yeares agoe, some pieces of Mr Roberval were published after the old fashion. That is, they were not given to a Printer; but any man that would pay for the transcribing might have had a coppy of them.'[4]

Roberval was, by all accounts, a prickly character, quick to take offence, and with a high opinion of his own worth.[5] As those were also the most prominent characteristics of René Descartes, it is hardly surprising that a fierce enmity quickly sprang up between them. Roberval was almost ostentatiously unimpressed by Descartes's 'Géométrie' (one of the essays published with his *Discours de la méthode*

---

no. 14 (1986), pp. 21–31, esp. pp. 21–2; and D. J. Sturdy, *Science and Social Status: The Members of the Académie des Sciences, 1666–1750* (Woodbridge, 1995), pp. 101–3.

[2] A. Lefranc, *Histoire du Collège de France depuis ses origines jusqu' à la fin du premier empire* (Paris, 1893), pp. 221–2.

[3] Roberval had some justification for his claim against Torricelli: see E. Walker, *A Study of the Traité des indivisibles of Gilles Persone de Roberval* (New York, 1932), pp. 20–4. Another, less justified, example of Roberval's tendency to claim precedence concerned Huygens's theories about Saturn: see A. Gabbey, 'Huygens et Roberval', in R. Taton, ed., *Huygens et la France* (Paris, 1982), pp. 68–83, esp. p. 78. In the latter part of his life Roberval became convinced that his former pupil Edme Mariotte had plagiarized his work: for this there is solid evidence—see A. Gabbey, 'Mariotte et Roberval, son collaborateur involontaire', in P. Costabel, ed., *Mariotte, savant et philosophe († 1684): analyse d'une renommée* (Paris, 1986), pp. 205–44.

[4] Hartlib Papers, electronic edition, 31/12/14A, 'Mr Pels Quaeres' (undated, but datable on internal grounds to the period 1655–62).

[5] Auger, *Roberval*, p. 161; Walker, *Study of the Traité des indivisibles*, p. 7: 'There can be no doubt that Roberval was of a hasty temper, irascible and impatient in argument. There are too many references to this deplorable characteristic to leave it in any doubt.'

in 1637); his cool and critical comments, transmitted to the author by their mutual friend Mersenne, elicited an angry reaction. Relations between them were further soured by Descartes's quarrel with Fermat about the construction of tangents in 1638, in which Roberval became one of Fermat's leading defenders; not long afterwards, Descartes accused Roberval of purloining his own ideas about the cycloid.[6] Meanwhile Mersenne himself remained on the best of terms with both of these disputants. Indeed, he seems to have had not only a deep admiration of Roberval's mathematical talents—he described him as 'scarcely inferior to Archimedes'—but also a real personal fondness for him.[7] Mersenne made a special effort to promote the writings of this far from prolific author: he added Roberval's brief treatise on mechanics at the end of book 3 of his own *Harmonie universelle* (Paris, 1636); he included material from the Latin version of that treatise in his compilation of 1644, *Cogitata physico-mathematica*; he encouraged and assisted the publication of Roberval's astronomical work, *Aristarchi Samii de mundi systemate libellus*, in 1644; he also reprinted that entire work in his own later compilation of 1647, *Novarum observationum . . . tomus III*.[8] And throughout his own writings, Mersenne referred to Roberval in terms both laudatory and affectionate, calling him simply 'our geometer'—'Geometra noster'.[9]

For Hobbes, newly arrived in Paris and finding his way in French scientific and philosophical circles, Roberval thus had two prime qualifications for intellectual amity: he was a friend of Mersenne, and he was an enemy of Descartes. (Hobbes's feelings towards the latter may have involved nothing more than critical disagreement and intellectual rivalry at the time of his arrival in Paris; but within a few months, his bruising epistolary exchange with the French philosopher, conducted via Mersenne, gave him strong grounds for personal hostility as well.) From Roberval's point of view Hobbes must have been a welcome ally: he could challenge Descartes in areas where Roberval had no special expertise (such as metaphysics), and at the same time he had enough of an interest in mathematics to

---

[6] For a very partisan account of these quarrels, see A. Baillet, *Vie de Monsieur Descartes* (Paris, 1946), pp. 111–14, 121; Roberval's dismissive comments about Descartes, as recorded by Leibniz, are quoted in Auger, *Roberval*, p. 163.

[7] M. Mersenne, *Cogitata physico-mathematica* (Paris, 1644), 'Tractatus mechanicus', p. 47: 'à nostro Geometra, quem vix Archimedi cedere putem'.

[8] The material in *Cogitata physico-mathematica* is in the 'Ballistica', pp. 12–17, and the 'Tractatus mechanicus', pp. 47–56. The *Traité de méchanique* was published separately in French (Paris, 1636). The dedicatory epistle of Roberval's *Aristarchi Samii de mundi systemate, partibus, & motibus eiusdem, libellus* (Paris, 1644), addressed to Pierre Brulart de Saint Martin, begins: 'Here is the little book which, if I am not mistaken, you and the Reverend Father Mersenne expected from me' ('Ecce . . . libellus . . . qualem, ni fallor, tu & R. P. Mersennus à nobis expectastis': sig. a2r); the work was issued under the 'Privilège' granted to Mersenne to print 'various mathematical treatises written or collected by him' ('varios tractatus Mathematicos ab ipso compositos, vel recuperatos': sig. a4r).

[9] See e.g. Mersenne, *Novarum observationum . . . tomus III* (Paris, 1647), p. 71: 'The most distinguished M. de Roberval, whom I refer to elsewhere as "our geometer" ' ('Clarissimus D. de Roberual, quem aliàs nostrum appello Geometram'); cf. n. 7, above.

count as an intelligent admirer of Roberval's work, but not so much as to count as a rival. An episode in late 1642 gives some idea of the nature of the relationship between the two, where mathematical questions were concerned. According to Hobbes's own later account,

> I was comparing in my thoughts those two Lines, Spirall and Parabolicall, by the Motions wherewith they were described; and considering those Motions as uniform, and the Lines from the Center to the Circumference, not to be little Parallelograms, but little Sectors, I saw that to compound the true Motion of that Point which described the Spirall, I must have one Line equall to half the Perimeter, the other equall to half the Diameter. But of all this I had not one word written. But being with *Mersennus* and Mr. *Robervall* in the Cloister of the Convent, I drew a Figure on the wall, and Mr. *Robervall* perceiving the deduction I made, told me that since the Motions which make the Parabolicall Line, are one uniform, the other accelerated, the Motions that make the Spirall must be so also; Which I presently acknowledged; and he the next day, from this very method brought to *Mersennus* the demonstration of their equality.[10]

Mersenne then played his own characteristic role: he sent letters to other mathematicians about Roberval's solution in early 1643, and in the following year he published it in his *Cogitata physico-mathematica*, explaining briefly that the idea had been first proposed by 'a learned man' (meaning Hobbes) and then worked out by 'our geometer' (meaning Roberval).[11]

Another piece of evidence, dating from the mid-1640s, confirms this picture of Hobbes as a sort of junior colleague of Roberval, playing an accepted but subsidiary role. In c.1643 Roberval's star pupil, François de Bonneau, sieur du Verdus, summarized what he had learned from his teacher in a treatise, 'Observations sur la composition des mouvements'; various copies of this were then made, and Roberval seems to have used it as a textbook for his courses. One copy, which contains a demonstration by Roberval dated 20 October 1645, also includes a section entitled 'Of the pteroid, or "wing"-curve, from Mr Hobbes', which begins: 'Here is the method Mr Hobbes uses to describe this line.'[12] Du Verdus would later become a close friend and fervent admirer of Hobbes; it is possible that he met Hobbes, through Roberval, in the early 1640s, but the inclusion of this Hobbes section in Roberval's treatise probably has nothing to do with him, as he was in

---

[10] Hobbes, *Six Lessons to the Professors of Mathematicks* (printed with *Elements of Philosophy, the First Section, Concerning Body*, London, 1656), p. 59 (*EW* VII, p. 343).

[11] M. Mersenne, *Correspondance* (Paris, 1933–88), XII, p. 53 (Fermat to Mersenne, 16 February 1643); *Cogitata physico-mathematica*, 'Hydraulica', prop. 25, coroll. 2, pp. 129–3, (p. 129: 'vir doctus . . . Geometra noster'). See also the discussions of this episode by D. Whiteside in I. Newton, *Mathematical Papers*, ed. D. Whiteside et al., 8 vols. (Cambridge, 1967–81), III, pp. 308–11, and K. Møller Pedersen, 'Roberval's Comparison of the Arclength of a Spiral and a Parabola', *Centaurus*, 15 (1970), pp. 26–43.

[12] BN, MS f.fr. 9119, fol. 451v: 'De la Teroide ou Aisle de Mons[r] hobs'; 'Voicy la façon dont Mons[r] hobs se sert pour descrire cette ligne'. On du Verdus's role see Roberval's own comment in G. P. de Roberval, *Ouvrages de mathématique* (The Hague, 1731), p. 370.

Italy when this particular version of the treatise was compiled.[13] It shows, more generally, that Hobbes was accepted as a contributor to Roberval's mathematical projects—a sort of *secundus inter pares*.

The best source of information about Hobbes's friendship with Roberval is the correspondence between John Pell (professor of mathematics first at Amsterdam and then at Breda) and his patron Sir Charles Cavendish, who arrived in Paris in April 1645. At Sir Charles's prompting, Hobbes sent a letter to Pell on 22 April; significantly, he included in it a 'paper from Monsieur Robervall'.[14] A few weeks later, in his own first letter from the French capital, Sir Charles wrote: 'M^r: Hobbes is so auers from a friendship with M^r: de Cartes that he would not see him when he was heere. M^r: Hobbes commends M^r: Roberual extreamelie.'[15] Within a few months Pell was asking his friends to solicit demonstrations by other geometers of the theorem which he was defending in his controversy with the Danish mathematician Christian Severinus Longomontanus. One was duly obtained from Roberval (by Hobbes, no doubt), and forwarded to Pell; when Pell required Roberval's full name and title, this information was supplied by Hobbes.[16] When Cavendish discussed Descartes's geometrical work with Hobbes in February 1646, Roberval's name came quickly to the fore: 'M^r: [>Hobbes] Confesses Des Cartes to be a goode geometrician, & saies if he had imployed his time whollie in it, he thinkes he would haue bin inferioure to none, but now he prefers Roberual, Caualiero, Fermat, & Tauricel before him.'[17] Even more strikingly, when Pell forwarded to Cavendish in early April 1646 a letter from Descartes, discussing the 'centre of agitation' or 'centre of vibration' of suspended bodies, Cavendish described Hobbes's reaction as follows: 'M^r: Hobbes praised it verie much at first, but after Mons^r: Roberuall douted of it, M^r: Hobbes seemeth to doute too. M^r Roberuall is confident that neither the proposition is true nor his argumentation good for the proofe of it.'[18]

That Hobbes was in frequent contact with Roberval is suggested by a comment made in passing by Sir Charles in another letter: when Pell asked Sir Charles to find

---

[13] See Hobbes, *Correspondence*, II, pp. 905–8. (My argument there that du Verdus probably did not know Hobbes in Paris in the period 1641–3 was based partly on the supposition that the earliest datable evidence of Hobbes's friendship with Roberval was from 1644; this is undermined by the dating of the discussion of the spiral and the parabola, given above. On the other hand, the fact that du Verdus did not in 1641–3 know several members of Mersenne's circle who were friends of Hobbes (see p. 908) may still be significant.)

[14] Neither the letter nor the 'paper' survives; this quotation is from Pell's letter to Cavendish of 9/19 May, in which he acknowledges the receipt of Hobbes's letter: BL, MS Add. 4280, fol. 112 (draft).

[15] BL, MS Add. 4278, fol. 205r (1/11 May 1645).

[16] BL, MS Add. 4280, fols. 113v (Pell to Cavendish, 2/12 Aug. 1645, draft); MS Add. 4278, fols. 223 (Cavendish to Pell, 1/11 Nov. 1645), 228r (paper in Hobbes's hand, giving Roberval's title). Roberval's demonstration was printed by Pell in his *Controversiae de vera circuli mensura . . . pars prima* (Amsterdam, 1647), pp. 47–8.

[17] BL, MS Add. 4278, fol. 241r (Cavendish to Pell, 6/16 Feb. 1646). Square brackets and the '>' sign are used to indicate an interlineation.

[18] Ibid., fol. 249r (Cavendish to Pell, 18/28 April 1646). The letter from Descartes is printed in Mersenne, *Correspondance*, XIV, pp. 168–75 (Descartes to Cavendish, [20/] 30 March 1646).

out the first name of the mathematician Le Pailleur, he replied: 'I spoke to daie to Mʳ: Hobbes & he to Mʳ: Roberuall concerning it.'[19] And by the time Cavendish left Paris in the summer of 1648, he had himself become sufficiently intimate with the French mathematician to be entrusted not only with one of his propositions on spherical triangles, but also with a copy of an unpublished geometrical treatise by him, entitled 'De locis'.[20]

Further intriguing evidence, suggesting that Hobbes performed a friendly service for Roberval in the mid-1640s, is supplied by a manuscript in the Bibliothèque Sainte-Geneviève in Paris. It is a compilation of short treatises in French, of a rather elementary, didactic nature, on geometry, the use of instruments such as the pair of compasses, the 'graphometer' and the marine compass, the measurement of distances, and the basic designs of fortresses and other fortifications. Bound in at the end of the manuscript is a printed broadsheet, giving tables of figures for the proportions of a type of fortress known as a 'fortification royale': these tables refer back to the discussion in the relevant section of the manuscript. The broadsheet is dedicated, by Roberval, to the Duke of Buckingham, and a note on the verso side records that it was printed for the author (i.e. Roberval) in Paris, in 1645.[21] It thus appears that the whole compilation had been specially prepared, under Roberval's supervision, for the young Duke's studies. The manuscript is a very fair copy, on fine paper, and was presumably made for presentation to Buckingham himself; significantly, it is in the hand of a Parisian scribe who was frequently employed by Hobbes during his years in France.[22] Hobbes is known to have given some tuition in geometry to the young Duke (who was 17 years old in 1645, and left Paris in the early summer of the following year); so it was probably thanks to him that the Duke was passed on to Roberval for further tuition—especially in the science of fortification, where Roberval had expertise which Hobbes lacked.[23] Possibly the

---

[19] BL, MS Add. 4278, fol. 257r (Cavendish to Pell, 28 May /7 June 1646).

[20] Ibid., fols. 275v (Cavendish to Pell, 9 /19 Aug. 1648); 300r (Cavendish to Pell, [15/] 25 May 1650); 304r (Cavendish to Pell, [27 Aug./] 6 Sept. 1650). Pell pointed out that Roberval's proposition on the spherical triangle had previously been put forward by Hariot (BL, MS Add. 4280, fol. 133r: Pell to Cavendish, [25 Oct./] 4 Nov. 1648). The proposition appears, attributed to both Hariot and Roberval, in Cavendish's notes: BL, MS Harl. 6002, fol. 32r. Another volume of Cavendish's papers includes extracts from Roberval's then unpublished work on trochoids and other curves: MS Harl. 6083, fols. 307–21, 329–30.

[21] Bibliothèque Sainte-Geneviève, Paris, MS 1060; the broadsheet is entitled 'Trois Tables de la Grandeur des Parties d'une Fortification Royale', dedicated 'A Monsieur le duc de Buckingham Vostre tres humble & tres-obeissant seruiteur Roberval', and dated 'A PARIS, 1645 Pour l'Autheur'; the printed tables are keyed to the hexagonal fortress-design shown on fol. 63v, and to the definitions given on fols. 64r–66v.

[22] See my 'Hobbes, the Latin Optical Manuscript, and the Parisian Scribe', forthcoming in *English Manuscript Studies*, ed. P. Beal and J. Griffith, 13 (2003).

[23] Aubrey recorded that 'Mr. Hobbes told me that G., Duke of Buckingham at Paris . . . desired him to read geometry . . . Mr. Hobbes read, and his Grace did not apprehend, which Mr. Hobbes wondered at. At length Mr. Hobbes observed that his Grace was at masturbation—his hand in his codpiece. That is a very improper age for that reason for learning' (J. Aubrey, *Aubrey on Education: A Hitherto Unpublished Manuscript by the Author of Brief Lives*, ed. J. E. Stephens (London, 1972), p. 160). For the date of Buckingham's departure from Paris (11 /21 May 1646) see the Historical Manuscripts Commission, *Report*

tuition was a joint enterprise; that might explain the employment here of Hobbes's favourite scribe. In any case, we can assume that Roberval undertook this work in the hope of some sign of ducal favour—and that Hobbes was thus doing his best to promote his French friend, socially and financially, when he recommended his services.

After Cavendish's departure from Paris in July 1648, evidence of Hobbes's friendship with Roberval becomes much harder to find. The death of Mersenne in September of that year brought to an end one regular point of contact between them; and it was followed soon afterwards by the departure of another mutual friend, Gassendi, for the south of France. Roberval's energies were mainly absorbed in teaching—Cavendish noted that 'M$^r$: Roberuall imploies himself so much in teaching that I doute it will [>be] long ere he publish anie thing'—and this may have made him a less frequent attender at the various Parisian gatherings of scientists that tried to take the place of Mersenne's regular meetings.[24] For much of 1650 (and, probably, part of 1649) Hobbes was absorbed in the writing of *Leviathan*, which must have meant that he devoted less time to those topics in which he and Roberval shared an interest. On the other hand, 1651 saw the return to Paris of Roberval's pupil du Verdus, and it was probably at this time that du Verdus's friendship with Hobbes really blossomed.[25] It is not known whether Hobbes kept up any direct correspondence with Roberval after his return to England at the end of 1651; but news and indirect contacts were supplied by others of his correspondents. In March 1656 du Verdus, writing from his native Bordeaux, did promise that on his next visit to Paris he would obtain Roberval's opinion on the geometrical sections of *De corpore*; and one month later the physician Abraham du Prat sent Hobbes an account of the inaugural lecture given by Roberval at the Collège Royal, where he just had acquired, in addition to his own Ramus chair, the chair of mathematics previously occupied by Gassendi.[26]

That promised visit to Paris by du Verdus seems not to have taken place. Instead, it was apparently from Hobbes's enemy John Wallis that Roberval first heard—directly or indirectly—about the contents of *De corpore*. Writing his scathing refutation of the mathematical parts of Hobbes's book in July and August 1655, Wallis

---

*on the Manuscripts of the Earl of Denbigh*, part V (London, 1911: modern ref. no. 68), p. 79. On Roberval's expertise in fortification see Costabel, 'Roberval', p. 28, n. 3.

[24] BL, MS Add. 4278, fol. 273r (Cavendish to Pell, [23 July/] 2 Aug. 1648). Costabel notes a report by Frans van Schooten in 1646, describing Roberval as an extremely successful teacher, with a hundred students attending his lectures ('Roberval', p. 22).

[25] Hobbes, *Correspondence*, II, p. 908.

[26] Hobbes, *Correspondence*, I, pp. 232, 245–6: 'His speech did not match up to what had been expected of him. Several people said that he is as bad at oratory as he is good at geometry' ('Sa harangue ne respondit pas à ce qu'on s'attendoit de lui. Plusieurs disoyent qu'il est aussi mauuais Orateur, qu'excellent Geometre'). Gassendi had died in Oct. 1655; Michel de Marolles recorded that on his deathbed he had recommended the appointment of Roberval to his chair: *Les Memoires de Michel de Marolles, Abbé de Villeloin* (Paris, 1656), p. 275.

accused Hobbes of plagiarism: the comparison of the arc-length of a spiral and a parabola in chapter 17 of Hobbes's work was taken without acknowledgement, he said, from Mersenne's *Cogitata physico-mathematica*. 'Whether it is true or false, it is at any rate not yours, but Roberval's, as is clear from the passage I have cited from Mersenne's book.'[27] When he wrote those words Wallis must still have been a little unsure of his facts; as mentioned above, Mersenne's account did indeed give credit for the working-out of the comparison to Roberval, but it also stated that the original idea had come from another person, a 'learned man'. A few days after the completion of his attack on Hobbes, Wallis sent a letter to Gassendi in Paris, asking him if he could identify that 'learned man'; unfortunately Gassendi was then in the final stages of the illness that would soon kill him, and never sent a reply.[28] Hobbes was thus able, when he published his own response to Wallis's book, to give a detailed account of the original episode (quoted above), providing what must have seemed to most readers an adequate self-vindication.

One person, however, was not to be satisfied: Roberval himself. Whether he had by now seen the original text of *De corpore* (of which he eventually acquired a copy for his own library), or depended only on Wallis's account is not clear.[29] But in October 1656 he sent Wallis a letter in which he accepted, and repeated, the charge of plagiarism made by Wallis against Hobbes.[30] Jubilantly, Wallis referred to this letter in his next attack on Hobbes: after repeating his charge that 'all or most of what was worth any thing in your Mathematicks, was manifestly stollen from

[27] J. Wallis, *Elenchus geometriae hobbianae* (Oxford, 1655), p. 132: 'sive vera sit sive falsa, saltem tua non est, sed Robervalli, ut ex Mersenni loco citato patet.'
[28] The letter (dated 31 Aug. 1655) is printed in P. Gassendi, *Opera omnia*, 6 vols. (Lyon, 1658), VI, p. 540. In a later account, intended to be transmitted to Roberval, Wallis wrote that his letter of Aug. 1655 had been meant 'indifferently' ('indifferenter') for Gassendi or Roberval, and that he explicitly asked in it whether Hobbes could justly claim any credit in the matter (Österreichische Nationalbibliothek, Vienna, MS 7050, fol. 309r, Wallis to Brouncker, 16 Oct. 1656); the evidence suggests that these later remarks were dishonest, as his letter made no mention of Hobbes and was addressed only to Gassendi.
[29] Among the 136 books listed in the inventory of Roberval's possessions at his death was 'Hobbes philosopia [*sic*]'. (I am very grateful to Prof. David Sturdy for this information.) This almost certainly refers to *De corpore*, of which the full title is *Elementorum philosophiae sectio prima de corpore*.
[30] Österreichische Nationalbibliothek, Vienna, MS 7050, fols. 309–12 (Wallis to Brouncker, 16 Oct. 1656, citing a paper ('charta') by Roberval which he had just received from Brouncker, who had received it from Thomas White): 'I do not think he criticizes me for *having found out that Hobbes had been a plagiarist* and having restored to Roberval things that were his own property; rather, he thinks it—or at least ought to think it—a friendly act, done by me with the hand of friendship, even though he was unknown to me' ('Quod *plagiarium fuisse Hobbium detexerim*, ipsique Robervallio quae sua fuerint asseruerim . . . non mihi, credo, vitio vertit; sed amicè potiùs, quod amicâ sibi manu factum est, utut ignoto mihi, ipse reputat, (reputare saltem debet)': italics here represent underlinings by Wallis in the MS, used to indicate quotation from Roberval's text.) Douglas Jesseph discusses this letter (referring to a copy in BN MS f.fr. n.a. 3252, fols. 148–52) and suggests that the 'charta' may have been a printed broadsheet: *Squaring the Circle: The War between Hobbes and Wallis* (Chicago, 1999), pp. 119–20, n. However, Henry Stubbe referred to it merely as 'a letter' (Hobbes, *Correspondence*, I, p. 339), and Hobbes later wrote that Roberval had sent to England 'copies of a certain manuscript paper' ('chartulae cujusdam manuscriptae exemplaria'): *Examinatio et emendatio mathematicae hodiernae* (London, 1660), p. 121 (*OL* IV, p. 188). It thus appears to have been an open letter, distributed in a number of scribal copies.

*Galilaeo, Robervall, Cartesius, Fermat, &c.*', he added that 'one of them, as I perceive by somewhat but now come to my hand from him, doth not stick to call you *Plagiarius* again and again, for so doing.'[31] Hobbes was now obliged to write to another Parisian mathematician, Claude Mylon, for confirmation of his story: Mylon declared that 'whatever he [*sc.* Roberval] does, he cannot deny that he discovered this proposition thanks to you, since you gave him the idea and the notion of finding it. I shall always testify to that.'[32] What Wallis did not mention, naturally enough, was that Roberval's letter also contained some stiff criticisms of Wallis himself: the French mathematician was deeply offended by the suggestion that his comparison between the spiral and the parabola might not be correct, and he thought that Wallis's recent publications also contained ideas plagiarized from him.[33] Some details of these accusations were later publicized by Hobbes, when he discussed the whole affair in his *Examinatio et emendatio* of 1660. As it happens, Hobbes was reluctant to accept Roberval's charge that Wallis had stolen from him the comparison between parabolas and conoidal sections presented in Wallis's *De arithmetica infinitorum*, because he thought that that comparison committed errors so crude that they could not be attributed to a geometer as skilled as Roberval; in this back-handed way, Hobbes preserved at least some of the honour that he felt was due to his old acquaintance.[34] But he ruefully added: 'Roberval has this peculiarity: whenever people publish any remarkable theorem they have discovered, he immediately announces, in papers which he distributes, that he

---

[31] J. Wallis, *Due Correction for Mr Hobbes: Or, Schoole Discipline, for not Saying his Lessons Right* (Oxford, 1656), p. 130. The dedicatory epistle of this work is dated 15 Oct.; Thomason's copy (BL, pressmark E 1577(1) ), puzzlingly, is dated '7$^{ber}$ 26'—presumably a slip for '8$^{ber}$'.

[32] Cited by Hobbes in his *Examinatio et emendatio*, p. 122 (*OL* IV, p. 190): 'quoy quil fasse il ne peut desnier que vous ne soyes cause quil ait trouvé cette proposition, puisque vous luy aues donné l'idee, & le suiet de la trouuer, Cest ce que ie tesmoigneray tous jours.' For the identification of Mylon here, see Hobbes, *Correspondence*, I, p. 316, n. 5. Hobbes had signalled in his reply to Wallis's *Due Correction* that he was making further enquiries about the accusation Wallis had cited: 'whether it be *Roberval* or not that writ that paper, I am not certain. But I think I shall be shortly . . .' (*ΣΤΙΓΜΑΙ . . . or Markes of the Absurd Geometry, Rural Language, Scottish Church-Politicks, and Barbarismes of John Wallis Professor of Geometry and Doctor of Divinity* (London, 1657), p. 1 (*EW* VII, p. 361).

[33] Roberval's accusations are the main subject of Wallis's two letters to Brouncker, of 16 and 20 Oct. 1656 (Österreichische Nationalbibliothek, Vienna, MS 7050, fols 309–12, 313–14): the latter begins by explaining that Roberval is angry 'because I did not immediately accept his proposition about the equality of the spiral and the parabola' ('quod propositionem de Spiralis Parabolicaeque aequalitate . . . non statim admiserim'). Henry Stubbe, Hobbes's eyes and ears in Oxford, reported a little inaccurately to Hobbes on 9 Nov. 1656 that 'Roberval hath sent a letter to London, wherein hee chargeth d$^r$ Wallis with plagiaryanisme, as haueing stolne his quadrature of y$^e$ circle from him' (Hobbes, *Correspondence*, I, p. 339).

[34] Hobbes, *Examinatio et emendatio*, p. 121 (*OL* IV, p. 188). An authoritative modern study, however, has no hesitation in saying that key parts of Wallis's work were in fact indebted (without acknowledgement) to Roberval: Walker, *Study of the Traité des indivisibles*, pp. 24–9. No doubt these accusations by Roberval helped to inspire the caustic comments about him which Wallis inserted in his *Tractatus duo: prior, de cycloide . . . ; posterior, . . . de cissoide* (Oxford, 1659), pp. 76–9, where he defended Torricelli against Roberval's charges of plagiarism and declared: '*to have found something* is a matter of intelligence; but *to have found it first* is a matter of luck' ('*Invenisse*, quidem Acuminis est; at, *primum invenisse*, Fortunae': p. 76).

discovered it first.'[35] In the following year Hobbes had one of his own geometrical demonstrations printed anonymously in Paris, under the title *La Duplication du cube par V.A.Q.R.*: he later explained that the initials stood for 'Vn Autre Que Roberval', somebody other than Roberval.[36] Whether this was a jocular reference to Roberval's accusations against Wallis, or to his accusations against Hobbes, is not entirely clear. What is all too clear, however, is that Wallis's polemical manoeuvrings had succeeded, in the end, in destroying what remained of the relationship —once so close—between Hobbes and his irascible but brilliant French friend.

## II

What was the nature of the intellectual relationship between Hobbes and Roberval during the period of their personal closeness in Paris? It is already evident that Roberval must have encouraged and influenced the development of Hobbes's mathematical work. Douglas Jesseph doubts whether Hobbes would have gained much from him, on the grounds that 'Roberval's well-known reticence makes it highly unlikely that he would have shared much with his English acquaintance'; this is to overstate the secretiveness of the French geometer who, as we have seen, shared propositions and even manuscript treatises with Hobbes's friend and patron Sir Charles Cavendish, and did not hesitate to impart his methods to trusted individuals such as du Verdus.[37] Whatever particular methods he may have shared with Hobbes, Roberval's greatest influence appears to have been on Hobbes's conception of the basic nature of geometrical analysis—what Hobbes would later call 'analysis by computation of motions'. Taking their hint from passages in Archimedes, various seventeenth-century mathematicians conceptualized geometrical lines as paths taken by the motion of a point, in order to analyse them in terms of their acceleration and the components of their direction. Roberval was the leading practitioner of this sort of kinematic analysis, which, combined with the use of 'indivisibles' (infinitesimals), enabled him to solve problems relating complex curves on a basis completely different from that of the algebraic geometry practised by Descartes.[38] For Hobbes, this method was important not just as a

---

[35] Hobbes, *Examinatio et emendatio*, p. 121 (*OL* IV, p. 188): 'Habet hoc peculiare *Robervallus*: cum egregium quis a se inventum Theorema in publicum emiserit, ut statim distributis chartulis dicat idem a se inventum esse prius.'

[36] A copy is preserved at Chatsworth: Hobbes MSS, 'Letters from foreign correspondents', no. 85; the text is discussed and translated in J. Wallis, *Hobbius heauton-timorumenos* (Oxford, 1662), pp. 128–32. The explanation of 'V.A.Q.R.' was given by Hobbes in his *Dialogus physicus de natura aeris* (London, 1661), p. 38 (*OL* IV, p. 295); cf. also his account in *Seven Philosophical Problems* (London, 1682), p. 71 (*EW* VII, p. 59): 'It was I that Writ it, and sent it thither to be Printed, on purpose to see what objections would be made to it by our Professors of Algebra here'. See the discussion of it in Jesseph, *Squaring the Circle*, pp. 257–8.

[37] Jesseph, *Squaring the Circle*, p. 121.

[38] See Walker, *Study of the Traité des indivisibles*, pp. 124–30; H. Breger, 'Der mechanistische Denkstil in der Mathematik des 17. Jahrhunderts', in H. Hecht, ed., *Gottfried Wilhelm Leibniz im philosophischen Diskurs über Geometrie und Erfahrung* (Berlin, 1991), pp. 15–46, esp. pp. 29–32; Jesseph, *Squaring the Circle*, pp. 235–7.

matter of geometrical practice, but as a model for scientific knowledge more generally. It enabled him (as he thought) to bring together the concepts of definitional and causal certainty: in so far as geometry was Euclidean, it was an example of knowledge derived from definitions, but in so far as it was kinematic, it was an example of knowedge of the effects of known causes (because we 'make' the lines ourselves, by the motion of our pencils). This idea seems to have given Hobbes the confidence—delusory, as it turned out—to believe that he had arrived at a unified theory of scientific method.[39]

But although geometry was Roberval's special field, it was not the only area in which he worked. As Ramus professor he was required to lecture on subjects in applied or 'mixed' mathematics, such as mechanics, astronomy, and optics; and he had his own interests in fundamental questions of scientific method.[40] Unfortunately, he published little on these topics (apart from the two treatises, on mechanics and astronomy, mentioned above). Two brief but important texts survive, setting out his views on the nature of knowledge and scientific explanation, but in both cases the nature and status of the text are in some doubt, clouded by problems of attribution and transmission. One is a manuscript, not in Roberval's hand but with some corrections by him, the substance of which was later printed by Edme Mariotte without any acknowledgement of its Robervalian origins; the other is a text which Roberval included in his edition of an optical treatise by Mersenne, and of which the status is, as we shall see, also curiously uncertain.[41] A few other surviving manuscripts also touch on these subjects; in addition, there is Roberval's treatise on the elements of geometry, recently published for the first time.[42]

Studying these writings alongside those of Hobbes, one is struck again and again by small points of similarity—many of them, no doubt, points shared by other thinkers in the same period and intellectual milieu, but some of them suggesting a closer meeting of minds, in which it is not always easy to tell who may have been influencing whom. For example, when Roberval writes in one of his manuscript fragments that 'It may be doubted whether the appearances of objects are anything other than the movements of the parts of substance', this expresses an idea which, although not peculiar to Hobbes, had certainly been the dominant assumption of Hobbes's whole approach to physics and epistemology since the early 1630s.[43] Other traces of possible Hobbesian influence on Roberval include the insistence in the same manuscript that human beings can experience only particulars, not

---

[39] See my comments in Chapter 5 above (pp. 154–5).
[40] For the terms of the Ramus chair, see A. Lefranc, *Historie du Collège de France* (Paris, 1893), p. 221.
[41] On the former see Gabbey, 'Mariotte et Roberval'; the latter is presented below.
[42] G. P. de Roberval, *Éléments de géométrie*, ed. V. Jullien (Paris, 1996).
[43] Archives de l'Académie des Sciences, Paris [hereafter: AAS], Fonds Roberval, carton 7, dossier 124 (formerly carton 9, chemise 15), 'Quelle Creance l'homme doit auoir à ses sens, et à son Entendement', fol. 1r: 'Il y a lieu de douter si les especes des objets sont autre chose que les mouuemens des parties de la substance.' For Hobbes's adherence to this principle see Ch. 4 above (pp. 122–4).

universals, and the special emphasis given to the 'imposition of names' in the Preface to the *Éléments de géométrie*.[44] Roberval's optical writings also contain occasional points of similarity with Hobbes. For example, at an early stage in his set of notes on optics, Roberval writes: 'There is a problem concerning the nature of sight: does it take place by the reception of visible forms within the eye, or rather by the emission of certain rays from the eye to the object? The first opinion, however, is more plausible ('verisimilior'), and therefore more generally accepted.'[45] The same point is made in the opening sections of Hobbes's Latin optical manuscript, where he notes that 'it is still a matter of dispute, whether vision takes place by the intromission or extramission of rays, and it is possible that it can take place by either . . . However, since the hypothesis that the object acts on the eye is more plausible ('verisimilior') . . . let us now assume it.'[46]

This surprisingly insouciant attitude towards physical explanation, accepting that various hypotheses are possible and offering only a rather secondary criterion (either 'verisimilitude' or, elsewhere, the economy or simplicity of the theory) to guide the choice between them, was a constant theme of Roberval's writings. In the preface to his astronomical treatise he declared that the three rival theories of Ptolemy, Aristarchus (a classical surrogate for Copernicus), and Tycho were all possible explanations; that none of them had been proved; that they might all be false; and that, in the meantime, he would take the Aristarchan theory as the one that was 'most simple, and most closely suited to the laws of nature'.[47] Similarly, when Hobbes argued in his Latin optical manuscript that vision could be explained by intromission, extramission, or a combination of the two, he made an explicit comparison with the astronomical theories of Ptolemy, Copernicus, and Tycho, suggesting that each of them offered a viable explanation of the observed phenomena.[48] This argument about astronomical systems, suggesting that they were all merely possible ways of 'saving the phenomena', had been current since it

---

[44] AAS, Fonds Roberval, carton 7, dossier 124, fol. IV ('My external senses only know particular things as individuals; they do not know universals at all'; 'Mes sens exterieurs ne connoissent que les choses particulieres dans leurs Indiuidus; et non point les vniuerselles'); Roberval, *Éléments de géométrie*, p. 65 ('What is meant by a mathematical definition is the explanation of a certain name, distinguishing, among various things, the thing to which it is applied, by the will of the person who imposed it; this name can be changed, and has no necessary connection with the thing itself'; 'Par une définition mathématique, on entend l'explication de quelque nom pour distinguer entre plusieurs choses, celle à laquelle il est attribué, à la volonté de celui qui l'a imposé; ce nom pouvant être changé et n'ayant aucune connection nécessaire avec la même chose'.)

[45] AAS, Fonds Roberval, carton 6, dossier 47, fol. 2r ('circa visus naturam difficultas est an fiat per receptionem formarum visibilium intra oculum, an vero per emissiones radiorum quorundam ab oculo ad obiectum: sed prior sententia verisimilior est atque idea magis recepta').

[46] BL, MS Harl. 6796, fol. 193v (Hobbes, Latin Optical MS, I.2): 'disputatur adhuc, an per radiorum intromissionem, extramissionem fiat visio, et potest fieri per utrumque . . . Quoniam autem verisimilior est hypothesis de actione obiecti in oculum . . . ipsam nunc sumamus' (printed in T. Hobbes, 'Tractatus opticus', ed. F. Alessio, *Rivista critica di storia della filosofia*, 18 (1963), pp. 147–228, here pp. 147–8).

[47] G. P. de Roberval, *Aristarchi Samii . . . libellus* (Paris, 1644), sig. a3v: 'simplissimum, & Naturae legibus apprimè conueniens'.

[48] BL, MS Harl. 6796, fol. 193v (Hobbes, Latin Optical MS, I.2).

was first applied to Copernicus by Andreas Osiander, and had become especially common among Catholic scientists, for obvious prudential reasons, after the condemnation of Galileo. But it also expressed a deeper problem inherent in the very nature of mechanistic physical theories—the problem that, in Hobbes's words, 'it is not impossible that similar phenomena may be produced by dissimilar motions.'[49] The fact that the same argument about rival astronomical or optical theories was presented by both Hobbes and Roberval need not imply that one had taken it from the other; but it does help to show to what an extent they were both inhabiting the same mental world.

The particular place occupied by Roberval in that mental world was a place in which several different themes and preoccupations overlapped in a not altogether systematic way. Four themes predominated. First, there was an engagement with, and firm rejection of, sceptical arguments about the actual sense-experiences which human beings have: Roberval was confident that sense-experience could provide certain knowledge of fact. Secondly, there was a belief in the certainty of mathematical knowledge—though whether, or how, this was connected with the knowledge supplied by sense-experience was not very clear. Thirdly, there was what might be called an attitude of scepticism towards theory, a willingness to use sceptical arguments (and sceptical terms of abuse, such as 'dogmatism') against any physical theory that smacked of apriorism, or appeared to be directly derived from doctrines of metaphysics. And fourthly, there was a peculiar adaptation of sceptical arguments about the senses, in which it was claimed that, although the senses we possess are adequate to their objects, there may be aspects of the world around us for which we have no suitable senses at all, and about which we must therefore remain forever deprived of certain knowledge; this fourth type of argument was sometimes combined with the third, even though the bases on which they stood were really quite different.

The fullest statement of Roberval's views on all these issues is to be found in a text printed in his edition of an optical treatise by Mersenne, 'La Catoptrique'. The nature of this text is, however, problematic. Although all previous scholars have accepted it as a straightforward statement of Roberval's position, there are some grounds for thinking that it is in fact an expansion by Roberval of a text by Mersenne which may originally have described the views not of Roberval, but of Hobbes. Both for that reason, and because of its intrinsic interest, it deserves close scrutiny. The entire text is as follows.

First, for the benefit of those who love only pure truth, I want to make a little observation, and summarize in a few words the thoughts of a man equally skilled in philosophy and mathematics about that itching, unhealthy urge that makes some people want to

---

[49] BL, MS Harl. 6796, fol. 193r (I.1): 'cumque dissimilibus motibus produci Phaenomena similia non sit impossibile'.

seem knowledgeable, at any cost—even about things of which they know themselves to be ignorant. The origins of this he used to attribute to a vain desire for glory; but he accused them of arrogance, in so far as they very often claim the right to impose on others belief in things which they do not themselves believe, or, at least, things they do not clearly comprehend themselves; and, what is worse, they think they have established one of their claimed truths well enough, once they think it cannot be proved false—rather as if a murderer thought he was innocent, because the murder he had committed could not be proved. So it is that, in the matter we are discussing, concerning the equality of the angle of incidence and the angle of reflection, some would have us believe that light is reflected by rebound; others, that it is reflected by a continuation of the actual motion of the corpuscles which are the cause of light; others, by the continuation of that same motion of those alleged corpuscles, not actually but only potentially (like the action of several balls, arranged in a straight line, touching one another, with the first of them touching a wall, and the last pushed by some force designed to make them all move simultaneously along that straight line, towards that wall). Others again make a comparison with a stick thrown forcibly downwards, or obliquely, against a surface; others have other even more implausible visions. But all explain this notable action of nature by some resemblance they think it has with something else, which they believe they know well.

At all events, it is certain that they know nothing except by means of the senses. Either the senses produce this knowledge immediately, as they produce immediately our first sensation of light, colours, heat, cold, sound, odours, tastes, and so on; or they produce it only in so far as they occasion it, prompting the understanding to reason about the appearances which have reached it by their means. For example, when the senses have brought the understanding this or that appearance of a triangle, they have prompted it to represent to itself a perfect triangle, and then to search out its properties; similarly, when the senses have brought it the sensible appearances of Peter, John, Paul, and other individual men, they have given it the opportunity to consider what those have in common, and to form the idea of a human nature, which it thinks of as a universal thing corresponding to all those particulars.

If we consider the understanding as being, and having always been, deprived of all the senses, it becomes inconceivable that it could have any ideas of the things outside it. One might even doubt whether it would have an idea of its own existence.

That being so, it follows that if there are in nature some things that cannot fall under any of our senses, either directly or indirectly, the understanding will not be able to form any ideas of those things. In the same way, if someone who was born blind never heard anyone talk about colours, he would never think about them, and when he did hear people talking about them, he would be unable to form any true idea of them; all he could do, perhaps, would be to represent to himself something based on the ideas he had acquired by means of the other senses. If he were given scarlet cloth to feel, and found that it was soft, and had a certain taste or smell, or made a certain sound when handled, he would perhaps put together a certain idea out of all those sensations, and thereby form an idea of scarlet according to his own fashion—an idea which would be far removed from the true idea of that colour. If this blind man, having often felt the heat of the sun at different times of year, tried to theorize about all the properties and actions of that star, without having acquired any knowledge about it from any other source, it is likely that he would give sighted astronomers much to laugh at, when they heard him expounding his theories—even if he were the most knowledgeable of all blind men, who might pass for an oracle among the blind. Nevertheless, he would not be ignorant of the fact that there is a sun: he would have perceived that, by his sense of touch. But in the absence of some other sense, one much more suitable for discovering the sun's most noticeable properties, his understanding would form only very imperfect ideas about it, all of them relating in some way to the ideas he was used to forming at the prompting of the sense of touch. Thus his reasoning about the sun would necessarily be very imperfect.

Now, what assurance do we have that we possess a sense suitable for discovering what the nature of light is; how it is transmitted by a light-source through transparent bodies; how it is stopped by opaque bodies; how it is reflected by mirrors; how it is refracted in transparent bodies of different densities; and a large number of other ways in which it is affected—ways which, perhaps, are no more suited to any of our five senses than smell is suited to the sense of hearing? It is true that we do have an appropriate sense for making us perceive that light exists, that it is transmitted, reflected, refracted, and so on. But its nature, and the cause of its existence, transmission, reflection, refraction, etc., are unknown to us, and it very much seems as if we do not have an appropriate sense for discovering what that cause might be, any more than we do for discovering several other causes which are features of the nature of the entire universe. That is why we represent it to ourselves only by means of very imperfect ideas—for example, the idea of certain corpuscles sent from the sun to the earth in a period of time so short that it seems only momentary; or that of a certain very subtle matter composed of an innumerable quantity of perfectly round balls, which touch one another continuously all the way from the sun to here, in such a way that the sun, making a spherical motion about its own centre, presses continually against those balls, pushing them outwards in all directions, which means that at the moment when it presses the balls which immediately touch it, they press their neighbours, and so on, all the way to the backs of our eyes, where this pressure makes the sensation on our nerves which we call the sensation of light, a sensation which the soul perceives, by means of those nerves, in the brain, which is where those nerves originate.

I could describe here other ideas which others have had about light. But all such ideas, including these, might perhaps seem as ridiculous to someone who knew its real nature, as those of our blind man would to a sighted person, in the following example. Suppose that the blind man tries his hardest to hide from the sighted person in terrain bereft of any cover: he goes a good distance away from him, he makes no noise and leaves no scent, and yet, each time, he finds himself discovered and captured straight away, without any difficulty. He may dream up the theory that the sighted person has an extremely fine sense of touch or smell, and that he can feel at a distance the resistance of the air that is situated between them; or that the blind man, without noticing it, is continually emitting little corpuscles from his entire body, and that the sighted person can smell them, and thereby tell where the blind man is. And perhaps this fine theory put forward by a blind philosopher would be no less admired by his blind colleagues, who would have laboured, like him, to find out the reason why the sighted person found them so easily and called out their names so unhesitatingly, at the moment when he touched them, or even before he did so, no matter how they tried to muddle him by moving around among themselves. This would be a source of considerable amusement for the sighted person, among blind people who had never heard about sight.

And yet, we see the same thing happening every day in our places of learning, since the thoughts which are usually admired there are founded on nothing but ignorance—on the part of the person who thinks up the theory, no less than of his admirers. They all torment themselves to open up areas of knowledge for which, in many cases, they have no appropriate senses; in this they let themselves be so carried away by the desire to appear knowledgeable, that the person who comes up with the most extravagant theories about the most doubtful things is the one they admire and imitate most of all.

There you have the gist of the argument of this great philosopher and mathematician on the subject of the dogmatists of our time, whom he called 'visionary' thinkers, in philosophy no less than in mathematics and other sciences. And his conclusion was that, where the human sciences are concerned, we should use pure reasoning as far as possible, so long as it is founded on principles that are clearly and distinctly true, and draw from those principles conclusions that cannot be doubted. That is what we do in geometry and arithmetic, for which all our senses are appropriate: they inform us that there is a space or extension everywhere and in all directions, which prompts understanding to establish pure geometry, and they also inform us that there are several things in that space, which prompts it to meditate on number, and establish arithmetic. In the absence of such principles, we must make use of regular experience [or 'experiment'], made under the requisite conditions, and draw plausible conclusions from it. And he called the knowledge which comes from the first type of conclusions, 'science'; as for the conclusions drawn from experience, he called the knowledge derived from them 'opinion'. Otherwise, in the same field of purely human knowledge, he said that all the other beliefs men have were so many visions, which did not deserve any credence; and in general he preferred known ignorance to an ill-founded conviction.

It is true that we use the term 'science' for several fields of knowledge which he calls 'opinion': for example, mechanics, optics, astronomy, and some others. They all borrow something from experience; but because they also borrow much from geometry and arithmetic, which are pure sciences, we usually call them sciences, taking their name from their nobler part. He, on the contrary, took their name from the weaker part, because of that maxim in logic which says that when a conclusion is drawn from premises that are not of the same rank, it always follows its weakest part, and has no more strength or rank than the weakest of its premises. But let us not argue about names; if we wish to call them opinions, we shall understand that they are very certain opinions, compared with various other opinions that are of very little weight. If we wish to call them sciences, we shall understand that they are mixed sciences, compared with geometry or arithmetic—or, even better, compared with logic taken in its purest form and purged of extraneous issues. For these are pure sciences, lacking any uncertainty: doubt, which could creep into the other sciences from their component of experience, is absolutely excluded from these.[50]

---

[50] Mersenne, *L'Optique et la catoptrique* (sep. pag.), in *La Perspective curieuse du R. P. Niceron . . . avec l'Optique et la Catoptrique du R. P. Mersenne*, ed. G. P. de Roberval (Paris, 1652), pp. 88–92 (see endnote for the original French text).

The origins of this text are a little mysterious. At the time of his death on 1 September 1648, Mersenne had been working on two projects: he had been preparing for publication a new edition of the *Perspective curieuse* of his younger friend and colleague Jean François Niceron (who had died in 1646), and he had been trying to finish two treatises of his own on optics and 'catoptrics' (the branch of optics that deals with reflection). Roberval was entrusted by Mersenne with the completion of both tasks. Just over three years later the works were published, with separate title pages but issued together as a single volume, under the general title, *La Perspective curieuse du R. P. Niceron, divisée en quatre livres, avec l'Optique et la Catoptrique du R. P. Mersenne*. (The 'Achevé d'imprimer' is dated 25 November 1651; the title page gives the date as '1652', following the common practice with works published in the final months of the year.) Quite what had happened to Mersenne's text in the intervening thirty-nine months is far from clear: a tantalizingly vague note added by the printer explains that Mersenne left his two treatises 'almost finished, and with the printing of them already begun, but for some reasons it could not be continued until now'.[51] No full manuscript of Mersenne's text survives, and in his own hand there is very little of it—merely the Dedication, and a related text of thirty leaves, just one leaf of which was marked by Roberval and used as copy by the printers for one short section of the book. The only substantial manuscript that relates directly to the printed text is a sheaf of twenty-three leaves, giving that part of the text of Mersenne's second treatise, the 'Catoptrique', that appears on pp. 88–131 of the book. This manuscript, which was also used by the printers (it bears their numbering, marking off the pages), is in Roberval's handwriting.[52] The entire passage quoted above (with the exception of its last few sentences) is contained in this manuscript material.

Given that we know so little about the original state of Mersenne's work, it is hard to tell what degree of editorial intervention—or invention—Roberval may have applied to it overall. In the case of the text by Niceron, we have not only the original edition of the *Perspective curieuse* (Paris, 1638), but also the incomplete Latin translation and revision published in the year of Niceron's death, *Thaumaturgus opticus* (Paris, 1646). What Roberval published in the 1652 edition was more than a revision of the former in the light of changes made by Niceron in the latter; it also included some brief passages that were entirely new, of which Roberval himself may have been the author.[53] As for the text by Mersenne, the latter part of the 'Catoptrique' does contain some material explicitly attributed to

---

[51] 'laissant ces deux petits traitez de l'Optique, et de la Catoptrique, à peu près acheuez, et leur impression commencée, mais qui pour quelques considerations n'a pû estre poursuiuie iusques à maintenant'.

[52] BN, MS f.fr. n.a. 5175, fols. 22–44. See the discussion in R. Lenoble, 'Roberval "éditeur" de Mersenne et du P. Niceron', *Revue d'histoire des sciences et de leurs applications*, 10 (1957), pp. 235–54. As the works by Niceron and Mersenne in this printing have separate paginations, references to the latter will be given as 'Mersenne, *L'Optique*', with page number.

[53] See Lenoble, 'Roberval "éditeur" de Mersenne', pp. 240–2.

Roberval. But it is likely that Mersenne had been planning anyway to include in this book a sample or summary of his friend's work (as he had done in previous publications), so the presence of this material need not indicate that Roberval was abusing his editorial privilege; indeed, it may explain why Mersenne had chosen him to supervise the completion and printing of the work. However, in the case of the text quoted above, there is clear evidence that Roberval was adding, quite freely, at least some material of his own composition. One passage, in which an attempt is made to ground geometry in our experience of three-dimensionality and arithmetic in our experience of the plurality of physical objects (from 'for which all our senses are appropriate . . .' to '. . . which prompts it to meditate on number, and establish arithmetic'), has been added by Roberval in the margin of the manuscript; and another passage, the last part of the text (from 'It is true that we use the term "science" . . .' to the end), is not present in the manuscript at all, and must have been added by him to the proofs.[54] Given this evidence, and the fact that the whole text quoted here presents ideas and attitudes highly characteristic of Roberval himself, all modern scholars have agreed that the entire text was simply composed and inserted by him, as a way of presenting his own views to the reader.[55]

The difficulty with this theory is that the thinker whose views are presented in this text is referred to in a way quite different from any of the references to Roberval elsewhere in the book—or in any other of Mersenne's works. Just a few pages later, it is announced that the rest of the book will present the opinions of Roberval, 'the person who is called simply "our geometer" in several places in our writings'.[56] That phrase was, so to speak, Roberval's trademark, one by which he was universally recognized; it emphasized both his closeness to Mersenne and the fact that he was above all a mathematician specializing in geometry.[57] The unnamed thinker whose views are presented in the long passage quoted above, however, is introduced as 'a man equally skilled in philosophy and mathematics'; and immediately after the passage quoted, the next section begins: 'So now let us return to our main subject, and follow the advice of that philosopher.'[58] Unlike so many other mathematicians of the period, Roberval did remarkably little work in any field

---

[54] BN, MS f.fr. n.a. 5175, fol. 23v (the marginal addition).

[55] R. Lenoble, 'Roberval "éditeur" de Mersenne'; B. Rochot, in Mersenne, *Correspondance*, X, pp. 302–3; Auger, *Roberval*, p. 134; Gabbey, 'Mariotte et Roberval', p. 217; K. Hara, 'Roberval', in *Dictionary of Scientific Biography*, 18 vols. (New York, 1970–90), XI, pp. 486–91 (here pp. 489–90); Costabel, 'Roberval', p. 24; A. Gargani, *Hobbes e la scienza* (Turin, 1971), p. 199.

[56] Mersenne, *L'Optique*, bk. 2, p. 98: 'celuy qui en plusieurs lieux de nos oeuures, est nommé absolument nostre Geometre'. This is also in Roberval's manuscript: BN, MS f.fr. n.a. 5175, fol. 26r.

[57] It is used elsewhere in the book: Mersenne, *L'Optique*, bk. 2, e.g. p. 96: 'nostre Geometre en considere'; 'nostre Geometre fait voir'. For examples of its recognition see BL, MS Add. 4280, fol. 107r (Pell to Cavendish, 7 /17 Sept. 1644): 'What noster geometra (so Mersennus allwayes calls *Robervall*) will doe I know not'; Wallis, *Elenchus*, p. 132: 'Roberval, whom Mersenne says he always means when he uses the term "our geometer" ' ('Robervallus . . . quem *Geometrae nostri* nomine se semper intelligere dicit Mersennus').

[58] Mersenne, *L'Optique*, book 2, p. 92: 'Maintenant donc, reuenons à nostre principal sujet; & suiuons le conseil de ce Philosophe'; this is also in Roberval's manuscript: BN, MS f.fr. n.a. 5175, fol. 23v.

of philosophy, except those areas of 'natural philosophy', such as astronomy, that could be described as 'mixed mathematics'; in his own writings he referred to himself simply as a 'mathematician'.[59] At one point within the quoted text, where it begins its summing-up with the words 'There you have the gist of the argument of this great philosopher and mathematician', what Roberval originally wrote in the manuscript was merely 'this great philosopher'; the words 'and mathematician' were added by him later, in the margin.[60] This last piece of evidence strongly suggests that he cannot have been composing the text as a piece of self-description: he would never have referred to himself just as a 'philosopher' and then added 'and mathematician' as an afterthought. And if he was, as seems likely, copying at least this part of it from a prior text by Mersenne, then Mersenne's failure to use his trademark description of Roberval throughout this entire passage must also be taken as significant.

The most likely explanation is that this whole passage was based on a shorter text, written by Mersenne, presenting the views of a third party. Roberval may have found it so congenial that he embroidered on it and expanded it, until he had turned it into a long text which mainly expressed his own opinions; it appears that he may also have taken it from some other place in Mersenne's notes, as it interrupts the original sequence of 'propositions' here. (Their numbering is changed in the manuscript to accommodate it.[61]) But he must have felt that his expanded text was still close enough to being a presentation of that third party's views to warrant retaining Mersenne's distinguishing description of that person as primarily a 'philosopher'. As for the identity of that third person, there cannot be many candidates. One possibility, a member of Mersenne's circle who could have been called both a 'great philosopher' and 'a man equally skilled in philosophy and mathematics', might be Pierre Gassendi: the passages here about the blind astronomer are certainly reminiscent of his treatment of that theme in his objections to Descartes.[62] But the privileged status given in this text to geometry

---

[59] Roberval, *Aristarchi Samii libellus*, sig. a3v: 'Mathematicum'. In one of his rare autobiographical statements, summarizing his career and achievements in a letter to the astronomer Hevelius in 1650, Roberval wrote that he had concentrated on the mathematical sciences for the last thirty years: C. Henry, *Huygens et Roberval: documents nouveaux* (Leiden, 1880), p. 36. The only partial exception would be his work on the development of the Torricellian experiment (described below); but this was at least partly an application of mechanics.

[60] BN, MS f.fr. n.a. 5175, fol. 23v: 'et Mathematicien'.

[61] See Lenoble, 'Roberval "éditeur" de Mersenne', pp. 252–3.

[62] E.g. 'you may be likened to a blind man, who, on feeling heat, and being told that it proceeds from the sun, should think that he has a clear and distinct idea of the sun, inasmuch as, if anyone ask him what the sun is, he can reply: it is something which produces heat' ('dici potes similis caeco, qui calorem sentiens, admonitusque eum esse a Sole, putet se habere claram et distinctam ideam Solis, quatenus, si ex eo quaeratur quid sit Sol, respondere potest, res est calefaciens': P. Gassendi, *Disquisitio metaphysica seu dubitationes et instantiae adversus Renati Cartesii metaphysicam et responsa*, ed. and tr. B. Rochot (Paris, 1962), pp. 585–7; P. Gassendi, *Opera omnia*, 6 vols. (Lyon, 1658), III, p. 399; tr. from R. Descartes, *The Philosophical Works*, by E. S. Haldane and G. R. T. Ross, 2 vols. (Cambridge, 1931), II, p. 197).

and arithmetic, as examples of disciplines that yield not mere 'opinion' but certain knowledge or 'science', runs clean contrary to Gassendi's well-known belief that mathematics was not a demonstrative science.[63] If Gassendi is excluded, just one obvious candidate remains: Thomas Hobbes.[64] It may be instructive, then, to run through the principal themes of this Mersenne/Roberval text, and to consider the extent to which they resemble the treatment of such topics in Hobbes's writings.

Let us take them briefly in their order of occurrence in this text. The unnamed philosopher says that the underlying reason for the proliferation of ill-grounded theories is 'a vain desire for glory' ('vn vain desir de gloire'): this seems to correspond to 'vain-glory', one of Hobbes's most constant moral and psychological bugbears. In *The Elements of Law* he gave, as a prime example of vain-glory, 'counterfeiting attention to things they understand not'; in *Leviathan* he defined it in one place as 'the feigning or supposing of abilities in our selves, which we know are not' and in another as 'a foolish over-rating of their own worth', singling out 'such as have a great, and false opinion of their own Wisedome'.[65] The accusation of 'arrogance' or hypocrisy, suggesting that these vainglorious philosophers require others to believe things which they themselves either disbelieve or fail to see clearly, has its analogues in Hobbes's attacks on scholastic philosophers. Admittedly, the ones criticized here are offering rival versions of the new science, not scholasticism; but the basic accusation, centring on a moral charge of hypocrisy or deception, is nevertheless very similar. Thus, in *Leviathan* Hobbes complains of the Aristotelians: 'in many occasions they put for cause of Naturall events, their own Ignorance; but disguised in other words'; and he notes that their 'Insignificancy of language ... hath a quality, not onely to hide the Truth, but also to make men think they have it, and desist from further search.'[66] As for the comparison with a murderer who believes himself innocent so long as no one has managed to prove his guilt, this

---

[63] See M. Messeri, *Causa e spiegazione: la fisica di Pierre Gassendi* (Milan, 1985), pp. 49–52; P. Mancosu, *Philosophy of Mathematics and Mathematical Practice in the Seventeenth Century* (New York, 1996), pp. 19–24. The key text is Gassendi, 'Exercitationes paradoxae adversus Aristoteleos', bk. 2, ch. VI.8 (in Gassendi, *Dissertations en forme de paradoxes contre les Aristotéliciens*, ed. and tr. B. Rochot (Paris, 1959), pp. 507–13; Gassendi, *Opera omnia*, III, pp. 207–09). On the background to Gassendi's arguments about the non-demonstrative or non-scientific nature of mathematics, see also P. Mancosu, 'Aristotelian Logic and Euclidean Mathematics: Seventeenth-Century Developments of the *Quaestio de certitudine mathematicarum*', *Studies in the History and Philosophy of Science*, 23 (1992), pp. 241–64.

[64] The fact that the thinker is unnamed in this text also fits an identification with Hobbes, rather than with Gassendi (or with Roberval, who is himself named a few pages later). The motive for obscuring Hobbes's identity would have been supplied by the notoriety which the commercial publication of *De cive* in 1647 had quickly attracted, and of which both Mersenne and Roberval would have been well aware. The emphasis in this text that its epistemological strictures apply only to 'the human sciences' shows that its author or authors must already have been nervous of criticism from theologians: such criticisms would have been greatly exacerbated by the knowledge that the work was presenting the views of a suspect Protestant free-thinker.

[65] Hobbes, *Elements of Law*, ed. F. Tönnies (London, 1889), IX.1; *Leviathan*, pp. 27, 154.

[66] Hobbes, *Leviathan*, pp. 375, 379.

is reminiscent of similar *exempla* of self-deception in Hobbes's work, such as his comment that 'those that deceive upon hope of not being observed, do commonly deceive themselves (the darknesse in which they believe they lye hidden, being nothing else but their owne blindnesse); and are no wiser than Children, that think all hid, by hiding their own eyes.'[67]

The argument that all knowledge is derived either directly or indirectly from the senses, emphasized in this Mersenne/Roberval text, was of course a common one, but it was given special emphasis in Hobbes's epistemology. Discussing 'the Thoughts of men' in the opening chapter of *Leviathan*, he wrote that 'The Originall of them all, is that which we call SENSE; (For there is no conception in a mans mind, which hath not at first, totally, or by parts, been begotten upon the organs of Sense.) The rest are derived from that originall.'[68] Roberval also emphasized the importance of the senses, insisting (against the Pyrrhonists) that the factual knowledge supplied by well functioning senses must be regarded as certain; but he did not claim—as Hobbes did—that knowledge came exclusively from the senses, arguing instead that our knowledge of the primary axioms of logic was autonomous.[69] The claim that the 'perfect triangle' considered by geometers was a mental construct derived from observing physical triangles was made explicitly in Hobbes's 'Objections' to Descartes: 'The triangle in the mind comes from the triangle we have seen, or from one imaginatively constructed out of triangles we have beheld.'[70] Roberval observed, likewise, that the understanding possessed 'a considerable power to perfect the ideas which the senses only supply to it imperfectly . . . For example, my eye only supplies my understanding with an imperfect idea of the circle; my understanding forms a perfect idea of it; and from that it then discovers its admirable properties.'[71] And the similar argument that the

---

[67] Hobbes, *Leviathan*, p. 154.   [68] Ibid., p. 3.

[69] Roberval, 'Les principes du debvoir et des connoissances humaines', printed in Gabbey, 'Mariotte et Roberval', pp. 229–44: here p. 237, 'The propositions which assert the existence of a substance are held to be certain by those who, having their senses in a proper state and unimpeded by any internal or external obstacle, recognize immediately and precisely all the signs of that substance' ('les propositions qui asseurent une substance sont tenues pour certaines par ceux qui ayant les sens bien disposez et non empeschez par aucune chose externe où interne recognoissent immediatement et précisament tous les signes de ceste substance'); 229, 'There are some propositions so certain and self-evident to the understanding that one has only to think them . . . to find their truth impossible to doubt; they are accepted immediately, without supposing any other knowledge' ('Il y a des propositions si certaines et evidentes d'elles-mesme a l'entendement que pourveu qu'on y pense seulement . . . on ne peut douter de leur vérité; mais elles sont receues d'abord sans supposer aucune autre cognoissance').

[70] 'Objectio XV' in 'Objectiones ad Cartesii meditationes', in *OL* V, pp. 249–74, here p. 271: 'Triangulum in mente oritur ex triangulo viso, vel ex visis ficto'; translation from Descartes, *Philosophical Works*, II, p. 76.

[71] AAS, Fonds Roberval, carton 7, dossier 124, fol. 2r: 'une puissance considerable de perfectionner les Idees que les sens ne luy fournissent qu'imparfaites . . . Pour Exemple, mon oeil ne fournit à mon Entendement qu'vne Idee Imparfaite du Cercle: mon entendement s'en forme vne parfaite; de laquelle, en suite, Il decouure des proprietez admirables.'

so-called 'universal thing', human nature, is constructed by the mind out of its sense-experience of individual men, occurs repeatedly in Hobbes's works.[72]

These arguments were fairly commonplace; but the suggestion that we should imagine a human mind deprived of all the senses, which might therefore have no idea of external things, or even of its own existence, is a little more distinctive.[73] One might call it the converse of Hobbes's 'annihilatory hypothesis', his thought-experiment in which the external world was removed, but the thoughts derived from sense-impressions of it remained. The argument from total sense-deprivation does not appear, as such, in Hobbes's writings, but something very similar occurs when he asks readers to consider a situation in which the senses continue to function, but there is no activity of any kind in the external world for them to perceive: 'if all things in the world were absolutely at rest, there could be no variety of Fancy; but living Creatures would be without sense of all Objects, which is little less than to be dead.'[74] As for the suspicion that the person deprived of all sense would not even have an idea of his own existence, this would seem to follow directly from two of Hobbes's arguments: his agreement with Descartes that 'It is quite certain that the knowledge of this proposition, *I exist*, depends on that other one, *I think*, as he has himself correctly shown us', and his principle, quoted above, that 'the Thoughts of men' are all derived directly or indirectly from sense-experience.[75] Certainly few contemporary readers of this particular section of the Mersenne/Roberval text could have failed to notice its essentially anti-Cartesian character—anti-Cartesianism being, as we have seen, one of the common passions of Roberval and Hobbes.

The argument about the blind man, developed at such length in this text, may well have been influenced by the passages that develop such a theme in Gassendi's objections to Descartes; but it also has its counterparts in several of Hobbes's

---

[72] Hobbes, *Elements of Law*, V.6 ('This universality of one name to many things, hath been the cause that men think that the things themselves are universal. And do seriously contend, that besides Peter and John, and all the rest of the men that are, have been, or shall be in the world, there is yet somewhat else that we call man . . .'); cf. *Critique du De mundo*, II.6; *De corpore*, II.9; *Leviathan*, p. 13.

[73] A version of this argument, stating that such a person would have no idea of things but not stating that he would have no idea of his own existence, appears in Gassendi's *Syntagma* (*Opera omnia*, I, p. 92); this was the text on which Gassendi was working at the time of his death, and which appeared in print for the first time in the collected edition of 1658.

[74] T. Hobbes, *Decameron physiologicum: Or, Ten Dialogues of Natural Philosophy* (London, 1678), p. 16 (*EW* VII, p. 83). The argument then progresses from absolute rest to absolutely constant motion, with the other speaker in the dialogue, 'A', asking: 'What if a Childe new taken from the Womb should with open eyes be exposed to the Azure-Sky, do not you think it would have some sense of the Light, but that all would seem unto him Darkness?' 'B' replies: 'Truly, if he had no memory of any thing formerly seen, or by any other sense perceived (which is my supposition) I think he would be in the dark. For Darkness is Darkness, whether it be black or blue, to him that cannot distinguish.'

[75] Hobbes, 'Objectio II', in 'Objectiones' (*OL* V, p. 253: 'Certissimum est notitiam hujus propositionis *ego existo*, pendere ab hac *ego cogito*, ut recte ipse nos docuit'); translation from Descartes, *Philosophical Works*, II, p. 62.

writings. The theme first surfaces in *The Elements of Law* (written before Hobbes's move to Paris), where it is used to illustrate the point that men can have some knowledge of God's existence without having any proper knowledge of his nature: 'even as a man though born blind, though it be not possible for him to have any imagination what kind of thing is fire; yet he cannot but know that something there is that men call fire, because it warmeth him.'[76] Hobbes develops the argument a little more fully in his critique of Descartes: the blind man brought near to the fire 'has no acquaintance with its shape or colour, and has no idea of fire nor image he can discover in his mind', but acknowledges its existence because there must be some cause of the effect (heat) which he is at least able to experience.[77] The point Hobbes seeks to make by means of that argument (both in those passages and in the equivalent one in *Leviathan*) is different from the one in the Mersenne/Roberval text: he uses it to illustrate the possibility of a virtually contentless natural theology. But there is quite a strong formal resemblance between Hobbes's argument there and the discussion of the blind astronomer in this text, which also distinguishes between deducing the fact of a thing's existence from our experience of it, and having the sort of experience that enables us to understand its nature: 'Nevertheless, he would not be ignorant of the fact that there is a sun: he would have perceived that, by his sense of touch. But in the absence of some other sense, one much more suitable for discovering the sun's most noticeable properties, his understanding would only form very imperfect ideas about it . . .' Hobbes seems to have been particularly interested in blindness from birth, as it offered a sort of real-life version of one of his subtractive thought-experiments: he referred to it more generally elsewhere in *Leviathan*, and in *The Elements of Law* he told an anecdote about a man who claimed to have been cured of lifelong blindness, and whose fraud was discovered when he showed that he could not only see a green object, but also correctly describe it, without instruction, as 'green'.[78]

The Mersenne/Roberval text draws a strong distinction between 'science' and 'opinion', and offers geometry and arithmetic as the best examples of the former. Hobbes's arguments on these topics, and his usage of terms, shifted in some ways over time, but an appeal to some basic difference between 'science' and 'opinion' was a fairly constant feature of them. In *The Elements of Law* 'science' was certain knowledge of the truth of propositions (derived from the consistent use of names), whereas 'opinion' was the belief that a proposition was true, founded on either

---

[76] Hobbes, *Elements of Law*, XI.2.
[77] Hobbes, 'Objectio V', in 'Objectiones' (*OL* V, p. 260: 'nec tamen qualis figurae aut coloris ignis sit cognoscit, vel ullam omnino ignis ideam vel imaginem animo observantem habet'); translation from Descartes, *Philosophical Works*, II, p. 67.
[78] Hobbes, *Leviathan*, p. 333 ('As men that are utterly deprived from their Nativity, of the light of the bodily Eye, have no Idea at all, of any such light . . . so also is it of the light of the Gospel, and of the light of the Understanding, that no man can conceive there is any greater degree of it, than that which he hath already attained unto'); *Elements of Law*, VI.1.

error or trust in other people. (There is one Roberval text that offers a roughly similar dichotomy, dividing all forms of belief between 'science', which is based on primary truths, and 'opinion', which covers all other sorts.[79]) Hobbes's handling in *The Elements of Law* of our belief in theories based on 'supposition'—for example, a theory which 'supposes' a certain physical mechanism in order to explain observed phenomena—was rather hesitant; this was not included in his strict definition of 'opinion', but he did place both it and opinion in the same general category, thereby suggesting that, if it were a third type of thing, it was nevertheless closer in nature to opinion than to science, because it could produce only probability, not certainty.[80] In *Leviathan* he presented a simplified version of this distinction, with 'science' as the type of discourse which begins with definitions and arrives, via correctly constructed syllogisms, at conclusions, and 'opinion' as belief grounded on discourse of all other types.[81] But in *De corpore* he hedged his bets; on the one hand he put knowledge of *possible* generations of effects (i.e., the supposition-based type of explanatory physical theory) together with knowledge of *actual* generations of effects in a single definition of 'philosophy', but on the other hand his definition of 'science' was confined to knowledge of the actual.[82] One might conclude that, according to *The Elements of Law*, arithmetic and geometry were sciences, but physics was something closer to opinion, and that in *De corpore* physics qualified as a form of philosophy but not as a science; in the case of *Leviathan*, however, it is hard to know what to conclude, as his streamlined version of the science/opinion dichotomy coexists with a 'table' of the sciences in which almost everything, including not only the physical sciences but even poetry, is defined as a science.[83]

In several of his works Hobbes did give a privileged status to arithmetic and geometry; his reasons for setting them apart from other would-be sciences were, however, oddly contingent. According to the dedicatory epistle to *The Elements of Law*, all learning is either mathematical or dogmatical, and the difference arises merely from the fact that the latter sort is corrupted by the passions.[84] According to his critique of Thomas White, the weakness of the non-mathematical 'sciences' is due to the incompetence, ignorance, and over-assertiveness of their practitioners; in this way, Hobbes explained why geometry and arithmetic were the only truly demonstrative sciences to have appeared so far, but left open the possibility

---

[79] Roberval, 'Les principes du debvoir', in Gabbey, 'Mariotte et Roberval', pp. 227–44, here p. 230. This might indicate that Roberval was influenced by Hobbes; or it might merely show that he was closer at this stage to the traditional distinction between ἐπιστήμη and πίστις.

[80] Hobbes, *Elements of Law*, VI.4–6; here art. 6: 'But if running through many conclusions, we come to none that are absurd, then we think the supposition probable; likewise we think probable whatever proposition we admit for truth by some error of reasoning, or from trusting to other men. And all such propositions as are admitted by trust or error, we are not said to know, but think them to be true: and the admittance of them is called OPINION.'

[81] Hobbes, *Leviathan*, pp. 30–1.    [82] Hobbes, *De corpore*, I.2, VI.1.

[83] Hobbes, *Leviathan*, ch. IX, table.    [84] Hobbes, *Elements of Law*, p. xv.

that other disciplines could acquire this fully scientific status too.[85] He did in fact believe that a truly scientific 'philosophia civilis' could be established—and that he had been the first to do so, when he wrote *De cive*.[86] Only later, in *De homine*, did he try to clear up some of these uncertainties. He now placed geometry and civil science on one side of the divide as demonstrations *a priori*, because in their cases we have actual knowledge of causes, 'making' the objects of the sciences ourselves (this was the argument he had arrived at by way of Roberval's kinematic geometrical method); and he left physics on the other side as an *a posteriori* science of possible causes—a science, that is, but one of lower status.[87]

On this whole tangle of issues, the original summary of Hobbes's views by Mersenne may have just mentioned two things: the science/opinion distinction, and the privileging of mathematics. Roberval's expansion of the latter point is noticeably un-Hobbesian: in the passage which he added in the margin of the manuscript, he tries to build a bridge between the primacy of sense-experience and the superior certainty of mathematics by suggesting that mathematics is reliable because it is grounded in the sort of experience for which our senses are fully adequate—namely, our physical experience of three-dimensionality and plurality. That particular argument was never made by Hobbes. On the distinction between science and opinion, Roberval also goes beyond Hobbes, turning his dichotomy into a trichotomy, and thus bringing it into line with the sort of scheme presented by Roberval elsewhere.[88] But in doing so he actually offers an improved way of handling Hobbes's problems about the status of physical theories based on possible causes: physics of that sort can now occupy the second category, 'opinion'; and a third category can be filled, like a dustbin, with all the other, ungrounded, beliefs—dismissively referred to as 'visions'—that people are prone to.

The use of the words 'vision' and 'visionary' here is characteristically Robervalian, being found in several of his other writings. (For example, in a manuscript fragment about physics, mathematics, and moral philosophy he contrasted the true

---

[85] Hobbes, *Critique du De mundo*, p. 106: 'And it is to the rashness and ignorance of the writers on physics and morals that geometry and arithmetic owe the fact that they are, as of now, the only mathematical sciences' ('Debentque Geometria et Arithmetica temeritati et ignorantiae Physicorum et moralium scriptorum quod solae nunc sint Mathematicae': Hobbes has just explained the derivation of the word 'mathematica' from μανθανεῖν, meaning, he says, to teach in such a way as to leave no doubt).

[86] See Hobbes, *De corpore*, dedicatory epistle: 'Civil Philosophy . . . being no older . . . then my own book *de Cive*' ('philosophia civilis . . . quae antiquior non sit . . . libro quem *De Cive* ipse scripsi').

[87] Hobbes, *De homine*, X.5 (*OL*, II, pp. 93–4).

[88] AAS, Fonds Roberval, carton 7, dossier 124, fol. 2v: 'where the proper objects of my understanding are concerned, namely, ideas rectified by it, when its reasonings are founded on clear and distinct principles, I give it total credence. But if it has used the senses as witnesses, either by themselves, or in hearing something described or reading about it, I accept that only as opinion. In every other case, I remain in a state of indifference' ('dans l'Objet propre de [>mon] Entendement, c'est à dire dans les Idees rectifiees par luy meme, ses raisonnemens estans fondez sur des principes clairs et distincts; Je luy donne vne creance entiere. Mais si les sens luy ont seruy de temoins, soit par eux-memes, ou par rapport, our par lecture; Je prens l'opinion. En toute autre occasion, Je demeure dans l'Indifference').

principles of physics with 'the old and new chimeras which the visionaries have invented, and are still inventing every day'.[89]) This has no direct counterpart in Hobbes's comments on science, opinion, and philosophy; but the word 'visionary' does ring a not-too-distant Hobbesian bell. Discussing in *Leviathan* the need to examine pretended 'prophets', he emphasizes that 'visions' can be natural as well as supernatural, and cites a verse from Jeremiah: 'Thus saith the Lord of Hosts, hearken not unto the words of the Prophets, that prophecy to you. They make you vain, they speak a Vision of their own heart, and not out of the mouth of the Lord.' Hobbes then goes on to refer to them as 'the Visionary Prophets'.[90] According to the *Oxford English Dictionary*, this is the first recorded use of the English word 'visionary' in this sense.[91] It seems very likely that Hobbes had borrowed the term from Roberval; if he had got into the habit of using the term 'visionnaire', in Roberval's sense, in his conversations with him and Mersenne, it might have seemed quite natural to either or both of those writers to attribute the term to Hobbes in print.

If the themes and arguments listed above are Hobbesian, are there any in this text that seem particularly un-Hobbesian? It might be thought that the entire argument about the inadequacy of modern philosophers' theories about the nature of light is something unlikely to have been propounded by Hobbes, given that he himself had put forward a theory of his own on that very subject. Yet it is a striking fact that when this text runs through the various possible theories about the transmission and reflection of light, holding them up to implicit or explicit ridicule, the only one that gets off almost scot-free is Hobbes's. Probably the first of the explanations of reflection in the list presented here, using the single word 'rebound' ('ressort'), is intended to cover Hobbes's theory. But it is noticeable that when the text turns to the rival explanations of the transmission of light from the sun to the eye, the 'very imperfect' theories it discusses are only two out of the three standard mechanistic theories of the time: the emission of light-particles, and the transmission of pressure through the medium (which was the Cartesian explanation). The third theory, the transmission of motion through the medium—Hobbes's explanation—is silently excluded from these critical comments.

That this text contains a strong element of anti-Cartesianism is obvious enough. But at the same time it includes the phrase 'clearly and distinctly true' ('clairement & distinctement vrais'), the use of which, to the modern eye, looks like a badge of allegiance to Cartesianism. Is this, then, something that could not have been

---

[89] BN, MS f.fr. n.a. 5175, fol. 47 (text entitled 'L'Euidence / le fait aueré / la Chymere'), here fol. 47v: 'ni des vieilles ni des nouuelles chymeres que les visionnaires ont fait, et font encores tous les jours'. Cf. also his unpublished 'Liure Troisiesme de la Dioptrique', a treatise on refraction which he once intended to add to Mersenne's two optical treatises, BN, MS f.fr. 12279, fol. 8r: 'not to imitate those visionary philosophers, in explaining their visions, which are often so different from one another' ('ne pas imiter Ces Philosophes Visionnaires, en expliquant leurs visions, qui sont souuent si différentes l'vne de l'autre').
[90] Hobbes, *Leviathan*, p. 231 (Jer. 23:16).   [91] *OED*, 'visionary', adj., 1.

attributed to Hobbes? Not necessarily. The phrase was in fact not unique to Descartes (it was just a rendering of a stock phrase in Greek, σαφής καὶ ὡρισμένος), and its use did not have to imply any sort of loyalty to Cartesian principles. Hobbes employed it in the short optical treatise printed by Mersenne in 1644 ('clare, distincteque concipi'), and Roberval, himself a fervent anti-Cartesian, used it in the preface to his own treatise on geometry ('clairement et distinctement').[92]

There is, finally, one major theme in this text which has no precise counterpart in Hobbes's writings: the argument that there may be some important aspects of the physical universe of which a human being will always have an inadequate understanding, because the human body lacks a proper sense with which to perceive them. Hobbes did have a belief that was very similar to this, but it was not quite the same. From the 1630s onwards he was convinced that the different appearances and natures of physical things were to be explained in terms of different internal motions, and that those motions were on such a small scale that the human senses were quite unable to perceive them. This was the starting-point for his argument that explanations in physics could be only hypothetical or suppositional, as they could do no more than posit possible mechanisms at the level of reality that lay below the threshold of observation. Writing to the Earl of Newcastle in 1636, he observed: 'In things that are not demonstrable, of w$^{ch}$ kind is y$^e$ greatest part of Naturall Philosophy, as dependinge vpon the motion of bodies so subtile as they are inuisible, such as are ayre and spirits, the most that can be atteyned vnto is to haue such opinions, as no certayne experience can confute, and from w$^{ch}$ can be deduced by lawfull argumentation, no absurdity.'[93] And more than twenty years later his account of the suppositional basis of physics in *De homine* made the same point: 'Because the causes of natural things are not in our power, but depend on the will of God; and because the greatest part of them, namely the ether [i.e. the fluid 'subtle matter' which filled all the interstices of Hobbes's plenist universe], is invisible; we are not able to deduce their properties from their causes, as we do not see them.'[94]

To the modern reader, familiar with subsequent technological developments, it seems obvious that the need identified by this argument is not for a new *kind* of sense, but merely for new means (such as powerful microscopes) to enable the existing senses to perceive what has been hitherto imperceptible. Possibly this obvious distinction was not so obvious to seventeenth-century thinkers, who, when they imagined the ability to see physical reality at the atomic level, felt that this

---

[92] Hobbes. 'Opticae liber septimus', Prop. III, monitum (*OL* V, p. 221); Roberval, *Éléments de géométrie*, p. 65.

[93] Hobbes, *Correspondence*, I, p. 33 (Hobbes to Newcastle, 29 July/8 Aug. 1636).

[94] Hobbes, *De homine* X.5 (*OL* II, p. 93). Cf. also his *Decameron physiologicum*, p. 10: 'For the alterations of the things we perceive by our five Senses are made by the motion of Bodies (for the most part) either for distance, smalness, or transparence, invisible' (*EW* VII, p. 78).

would be so different from ordinary vision as to count as a different kind of sense altogether. A significant ambiguity on this point can be found in the writings of Gassendi, who observed on the one hand that 'If we possessed senses which enabled us to perceive how the internal operations of animals, plants and all things are brought about, then nothing would be hidden from us ... Perhaps many things are hidden from us, which other beings might be able to perceive by means of other senses', but on the other hand expressed the hope that the microscope might one day be developed to such perfection that it would reveal those very things to us.[95] Hobbes was well aware of the potential of the microscope (he mentioned a magnification of 100,000 in *De corpore*, and suggested that this could be increased to 10,000,000,000); but it is possible that he might still have referred generally to things which the senses were incapable of perceiving, and that such comments might have been expanded or embroidered by Mersenne or Roberval in terms of the lack of a different kind of sense altogether.[96]

Although Hobbes never actually wrote that we should need a new type of sense to perceive the underlying mechanisms of the physical world, he did, interestingly, have an argument which suggested that no matter how we managed to assist or enhance our existing senses, we would still be unable to attain absolutely certain knowledge of the causes of phenomena. This argument was not based on the radical inadequacy of the senses as such; rather, it arose from the nature of mechanism and mechanistic explanation. His clearest statement of it was in the opening section of his Latin Optical Manuscript:

The treatment of natural things differs greatly from that of the other sciences ... In the explanation of natural causes, we must necessarily have recourse to a different kind of principle, called 'hypothesis' or 'supposition'. For when a question is raised about the efficient cause of any event which is perceptible by the senses (what is normally called a 'phenomenon'), the question consists principally in the designation or description of some motion, from which such a phenomenon necessarily follows. And since it is not impossible that dissimilar motions may produce similar phenomena, it may happen that

---

[95] Gassendi, 'Exercitationes', book 2, VI.5: 'si nobis Sensus inessent, quibus agnoscere liceret quemadmodum facultates illae internae Animalium, plantarum. Atque omnium adeo rerum operantur: nihil jam prorsus nos lateret ... nos forte multa latent, quae aliis propter alios sensus possent innotescere' (*Dissertations*, p. 485; *Opera omnia*, III, pp. 202–03); *Syntagma*, 'Physica', III, memb. post., bk. 12, ch. 2: in *Opera omnia*, II, p. 560.

[96] Hobbes, *De corpore*, XXVII.1. Hobbes had direct experience of microscopy: in 1648 he had lent money to the Earl of Newcastle, taking the Earl's collection of telescopes and microscopes as surety, and this transaction was later converted by mutual agreement into a purchase (see Nottingham University Library, MS Pw. 1. 406). Samuel Sorbière later recorded that Hobbes gave him one large microscope, which was one-and-a-half feet long ('Monsieur Hobbes m'en a donné depuis d'vn pied & demi': *Lettres et discours de M. de Sorbière sur diverses matieres curieuses* (Paris, 1660), p. 436). Hobbes had previously given a valuable microscope to William Petty, perhaps as a reward for writing out the fair copy of the English Optical Manuscript (Hartlib Papers, electronic edition, 42/1/1A–2B, 'Copy of Mr Worsleys Letters', 22 June 1648: 'Mr Petty did assure me severall times he had such a one, which he valewed as I take it as 3 lb sterling Mr Hobbs of Paris giving it to him').

the effect is correctly demonstrated from the supposed motion, and yet that that supposition is not true.[97]

It is possible, of course, that Hobbes himself had not developed the full force of this argument, continuing to assume for the most part that the question of which motion produced the phenomenon could in principle be answered if fully adequate observation at the sub-microscopic level were possible. But the argument does point further than that. The same observed effects, it says, can always be caused by different motions; and whatever it is that we actually observe, if and when we are able to observe those causative motions, will itself be an effect—the effect of some other motion. This seems to imply that the lack of certainty here is not just the consequence of a contingent lack of observational opportunities, but something intrinsic to the whole enterprise of starting with a knowledge of effects, and trying to proceed from there to a knowledge of causes. This, surely, is the fundamental reason for Hobbes's eventual division of the sciences into those which supply demonstration *a priori*, and are therefore certain (such as mathematics, politics, and ethics), and those which supply demonstration *a posteriori*, and are therefore hypothetical or suppositional (such as physics).[98]

## III

The purpose of this investigation of the Mersenne/Roberval text quoted above has not been to take its contents as a source of particular items of new information about Hobbes's views. If the explanation of its origins suggested here is correct, what we have is a substantially Robervalian account, constructed around a version of Hobbes as seen through Mersennian spectacles; in so far as its contents differ from Hobbes's known views on some points, those differences are easily explained by attributing them to Roberval and/or Mersenne—which means that we cannot look to it for evidence of any hitherto unknown opinions on Hobbes's part. Its significance as evidence lies, rather, in what it tells us about Hobbes's intellectual milieu, and about how it may have been possible for someone close to him to present his views, even if they were in several ways gingered up in the process. What is striking, above all, is the expression of what was described above as a sceptical attitude, using sceptical rhetoric, towards the claims of rival physical theories. That Roberval himself had such an attitude is well known; that he, who knew Hobbes

---

[97] BL, MS Harl. 6796, fol. 193r (Hobbes, 'Tractatus opticus', p. 147): 'Rerum naturalium tractatio a caeterarum scientiarum tractatione plurimum differt . . . in explicatione Causarum naturalium, aliud genus principiorum necessario adhibendum est, quod vocatur Hypothesis sive suppositio. Cum enim quaestio instituta sit, de alicuius eventus sensibus manifesti (quod Phaenomenon appellari solet) causa efficiente, quae consistit plerumque in designatione seu descriptione alicuius motus, quem tale Phaenomenon necessario consequuntur; cumque dissimilibus motibus produci Phaenomena similia non sit impossibile; potest fieri ut ex motu supposito, effectus recte demonstretur, ut tamen ipsa suppositio non sit vera.'

[98] Hobbes, *De homine*, X.5 (*OL* II, p. 93).

well, may have felt that this attitude was also shared by his English friend deserves our consideration. For it presents a rather different image of Hobbes from the traditional one—recently presented in an impressively sophisticated form by Simon Schaffer and Steven Shapin—of Hobbes the dogmatist, someone whose theories about the physical universe were determined *a priori* by his ideological requirements.

The issue of Hobbes's relationship to scepticism is somewhat murky. One leading modern interpretation of his thought (that of Richard Tuck) argues that his primary philosophical purpose was to deal with the challenge of scepticism: this seems to overstate the importance of sceptical arguments for Hobbes, whose voluminous works contain extraordinarily little by way of direct commentary on them.[99] Although he took a close interest in Descartes's writings, there is no sign of Hobbes seriously thinking through the implications of the radical doubt posited in the *Meditations*. His own 'annihilatory hypothesis' is misunderstood if it is interpreted as an engagement with sceptical arguments about whether or not the external world could be known to exist; it was designed to serve a different purpose, the nominalist project of separating concepts from 'being', essence from existence—demoting essences to the status of mere descriptions of things if and when they did exist. Hobbes seems to have been essentially untroubled by Pyrrhonism; that our mental experiences are physically caused by events in a universe of matter in motion was for him an unshaken and unshakeable axiom. Professor Tuck's interpretation fails to convince as an account of Hobbes's primary motives or purposes in the construction of his philosophical position. However, Hobbes's cheerful willingness to use sceptical arguments, from time to time, against the 'dogmatists' does not in itself count against Tuck's interpretation. For his view of Hobbes is not that he was simply an anti-sceptic; rather, it is that he tried to construct a 'post-sceptical' position, which meant framing an answer to scepticism in which some important elements of the sceptical case could be acknowledged as valid and accommodated.[100] As Tuck has pointed out, the only certainty in Hobbes's physics was the existence of a material universe: 'Everything else ... must remain conjectural or hypothetical, though some hypotheses are better than others.'[101] If other physicists claimed certainty for their conjectures, or failed to support their hypotheses with appropriate reasoning, Hobbes would feel entitled to lay against them all the charges traditionally laid by sceptics against 'dogmatists'.

Others who were close to Hobbes—Mersenne and Gassendi—had engaged much more directly with scepticism; and, although they had travelled by different

---

[99] See T. Sorell, 'Descartes, Hobbes and the Body of Natural Science', *The Monist*, 71 (1988), pp. 515–25, esp. pp. 521–2, and his 'Hobbes without Doubt', *History of Philosophy Quarterly*, 10 (1993), pp. 121–35.

[100] See R. Tuck, 'Optics and Sceptics: The Philosophical Foundations of Hobbes's Political Thought', in E. Leites, ed., *Conscience and Casuistry in Early Modern Europe* (Cambridge, 1988), pp. 235–63; R. Tuck, *Hobbes* (Oxford, 1989), esp. pp. 51, 114–15.

[101] Tuck, *Hobbes*, p. 45.

paths, they had arrived at quite similar accommodations with it. Hobbes, it seems, had no qualms about making use of elements of scepticism, because he was not deeply troubled by it; they felt a more pressing need to come to some accommodation with it, precisely because they were so impressed, or troubled, by the power of its arguments. Mersenne had confronted Pyrrhonism as the great enemy in his *La Verité des sciences* (1625), salvaging mathematics as a source of certain truth but leaving physics largely at the mercy of the sceptics.[102] Gassendi had used a battery of sceptical arguments in his attack on Aristotelianism, *Exercitationes paradoxicae adversus Aristoteleos* (partly published in 1624), and continued to deploy them against 'dogmatists' of all kinds throughout his philosophical career.[103] Both had accepted that, in Gassendi's words, 'we must conclude that we cannot know what any thing is in itself, or by its own nature, but only how it appears to this or that set of people'.[104] The conclusion was that human beings must content themselves with a science of appearances, describing the phenomena but never claiming to identify the real reasons for them. Indeed, as the inner nature of things was unknown (and apparently unknowable), it was not even clear what type of explanation would count as giving the real reasons for them. Sometimes Mersenne and Gassendi wrote as if scholastic metaphysics were correct: the real reasons for a thing being as it was were to be found in its essence, form, or entelechy, and it was merely the misfortune of humans that they could have no access to such things.[105] More generally, however, these thinkers seemed to doubt whether any such metaphysical scheme could be known to be correct. One senses here how far their positions diverged from Hobbes's. He seems never to have doubted what the form of a correct explanation of a phenomenon would be: it would be a causal explanation in

---

[102] M. Mersenne, *La Verité des sciences: contre les septiques ou Pyrrhoniens* (Paris, 1625), esp. pp. 270–6. For a general account of this work see R. H. Popkin, *The History of Scepticism from Erasmus to Spinoza* (Berkeley, Calif., 1979), pp. 131–7. On physics and mathematics, see also the discussion in M. Mersenne, *Questions inouyes, ou recreation des scavans* (Paris, 1634), pp. 69–74.

[103] See O. Bloch, *La Philosophie de Gassendi: nominalisme, matérialisme et métaphysique* (The Hague, 1971), esp. pp. 81–92; W. Detel, *Scientia rerum natura occultarum: methodologische Studien zur Physik Pierre Gassendis* (Berlin, 1978), pp. 64–6. Both writers emphasize that, although Gassendi's 'probabilism' took time to develop, this development was not the same thing as a simple progression away from scepticism: whenever he confronted 'dogmatists' (Aristotle, Fludd, Herbert, Descartes) he deployed sceptical arguments.

[104] Gassendi, *Dissertations*, bk. 2, diss. VI.6, p. 487 (*Opera omnia*, III, p. 203): 'concludamus sciri non posse cujusmodi res aliqua sit secundum se, vel suapte naturâ; sed dumtaxat cujusmodi his aut illis appareat'.

[105] Robert Lenoble goes so far as to write that Mersenne was an Aristotelian in philosophy, although an anti-Aristotelian in science: 'A propos du tricentenaire de la mort de Mersenne', *Archives internationales d'histoire des sciences*, no. 7 (April, 1949), pp. 583–97, here p. 588. Cf. Tullio Gregory's comment that Gassendi was 'still thinking of the theory of substantial forms, even while radically denying their knowability' ('pensa ancora alla teoria delle forme sostanziali pur negandone radicalmente la conoscibilità'): *Scetticismo ed empirismo: studio su Gassendi* (Bari, 1961), p. 85. There is some evidence that Roberval had a similar position: in one text he declared that 'That by virtue of which natural substances have the qualities which they have, and keep them, and are as they are rather than of a different kind, is what I call the soul, the form, the particular nature of those substances' ('Ce par quoy les substances naturelles ont les qualitez quelles ont et les conservent et sont comme elles sont plustost que d'une autre sorte, je l'appelle Lame, La forme, La nature particuliere de ces substances': 'Les principes du debvoir', in Gabbey, 'Mariotte et Roberval', p. 234).

terms of matter and motion. The doubt, for him, arose only over its contents—in other words, over whether this or that particular explanation was correct, given that others were always possible. For Mersenne and Gassendi, on the other hand, the mechanistic scheme was preferable precisely because it was not properly explanatory (by the standards of scholastic metaphysics) at all. Matter and motion were all that humans could know by experience, and therefore the best 'science of appearances' would confine itself merely to arrangements of motion and matter.[106]

However, although Hobbes's position was thus less deeply penetrated by scepticism than theirs, this does not mean that his physics could come any closer to the attainment of certainty: dissimilar motions might always produce similar phenomena. At the surface level of the theory, therefore, his diffidence about any particular physical explanation could match theirs in full. Again and again in his writings, he emphasized that explanatory theories in physics could only be hypothetical or suppositional. In *De corpore* he announced that physics involved 'finding out by the Appearances or Effects of Nature, which we know by Sense, some wayes and means by which they may be (I do not say they are) generated', and his discussion of the motion of the earth in that book ended with an insistence that physical theories could be adequate without being true: 'though the causes I have here supposed be not the true causes of these *Phaenomena*, yet I have demonstrated that they are sufficient to produce them'. Summarizing his position in the epistle dedicatory to *Seven Philosophical Problems*, he wrote: 'The doctrine of natural causes hath not infallible and evident principles. For there is no effect which the power of God cannot produce by many several ways.'[107] Most strikingly of all, he ended one of the sections of that work, in which he had presented (in dialogue form) his physical theories on a range of topics including reflection and refraction, as follows:

B. All this that I have hitherto said, though upon better ground than can be had for a discourse of *Ghosts*, you ought to take but for a Dream.
A. I do so. But there be some Dreams more like sense then others. And that which is like sense pleases me as well [in natural Philosophy] as if it were the very truth.[108]

In their influential study of Hobbes's attitude to the theory and practice of science, Steven Shapin and Simon Schaffer argue that there was a fundamental difference between his position on these matters and that of Robert Boyle. In Boyle's philosophy of science, they observe, 'one recognized that God might produce the

---

[106] I differ here from Arrigo Pacchi, who assimilates Hobbes almost completely to the position of Mersenne and Gassendi: *Convenzione e ipotesi nella formazione della filosofia naturale di Thomas Hobbes* (Florence, 1965), pp. 10–13.
[107] Hobbes, *De corpore*, XXV.1, XXVI.11; *Seven Philosophical Problems*, epistle dedicatory, sig. A1v (*EW* VII, p. 3). Cf. similar passages in *Examinatio et emendatio* (London, 1660), dialogue VI (*OL* IV, p. 228), and *Problemata physica* (London, 1662), epistle dedicatory (*OL* IV, p. 300).
[108] Hobbes, *Seven Philosophical Problems*, pp. 70–1 (*EW* VII, pp. 57–8).

same effect by a number of different causes, and one professed the appropriately nescient attitude towards the search for real causes ... Knowledge of causes was at best conjectural.'[109] This was, as we have just seen, exactly the position that Hobbes himself adopted. Shapin and Schaffer argue, however, that it was 'attacked as unphilosophical' by Hobbes. 'In Hobbes's view, in order to be counted as philosophy an intellectual practice could not affect nescience concerning the causes of things. Indeed, philosophy could proceed *from* correct knowledge of causes to knowledge of effects.'[110] Hobbes certainly thought that philosophy could proceed from causes to effects, but that was not the relevant issue here: natural science was concerned with proceeding from effects to possible causes. Where several possible explanations were available, Hobbes asked the scientist to seek the most probable: the criteria that would apply in such a search were never clearly worked out by him, but they do seem to have included theoretical economy or 'simplicity'.[111] Boyle shared this view too: in a manuscript note on the requirements of 'an excellent hypothesis' in physics, he wrote that it should be 'the Simplest of all the Good ones we are able to frame', and 'the only Hypothesis tht Can explicate the *Phaenomena*, or at least tht does explicate them so well'.[112]

Where, then, did the difference between Hobbes and Boyle lie? Having at first presented their positions as far apart, Shapin and Schaffer later concede that their views about the hypothetical nature of physical theories were 'apparently identical'. The only difference they detect is that, when Hobbes finds a scientist proposing a hypothetical cause for a phenomenon, he requires that scientist to show that the effect would *necessarily* follow from that proposed cause: by this means, they think, a doctrine of demonstrative necessity is smuggled back into Hobbes's philosophy of science. And on this foundation they build a whole structure of argument in which Hobbes's science depends on 'absolute compulsion', which in turn depends on the power of the state ('the delegated force of society'), while Boyle's science, in contrast, allows 'room to differ' and regards 'tolerance' as 'essential'.[113] A simpler interpretation, surely, is possible here. Hobbes wanted explanatory theories to explain things: and in his view, a theory which posited a cause for an effect and then said that the effect might or might not follow from that cause would fail to do its explanatory job. There is no reason to think that Boyle would have accepted such a theory as an adequate explanation either. And if Boyle had disagreed with Hobbes on this point, then the distinctive feature of his position

---

[109] S. Shapin and S. Schaffer, *Leviathan and the Air-Pump: Hobbes, Boyle, and the Experimental Life* (Princeton, NJ, 1985), pp. 139–40.

[110] Ibid., p. 140.

[111] Hobbes, *De corpore*, XXVI.7, 'I thought best therefore to retain this Hypothesis of Simple Motion' ('Hanc igitur motus simplicis hypothesin visum est retinere').

[112] 'MS Notes on an Excellent Hypothesis' in R. Boyle, *Selected Philosophical Papers*, ed. M. A. Stewart (Manchester, 1979), p. 119.

[113] Shapin and Schaffer, *Leviathan and the Air-Pump*, pp. 147–53.

would not have been that Boyle allowed physicists a freedom to agree or not to agree in their hypotheses (a freedom which, in fact, Hobbes also granted); rather, it would have been that Boyle allowed causes a freedom to produce effects or not to produce them.

Some nuances of difference, certainly, may have existed between the two thinkers: it seems likely that Boyle's underlying position was closer to Gassendi's, and that, although he was a doughty defender of the 'corpuscularian philosophy', the basic idea that all phenomena must be reduced to matter in motion was less axiomatic for him than it was for Hobbes. In the abstract, as we have seen, Hobbes was able to make an absolute distinction between what might be called the form and the contents of a physical theory: every such theory must take the form of an account of causation by the motion of matter, but the contents of any particular theory could consist of different supposed motions. He was thus equipped with certainty on the one hand, and with varying amounts of doubt or nescience on the other. (Hobbes's comments on the causes of magnetism make the point with delicious brevity: 'Magnetical Virtue is a thing altogether unknown; and whensoever it shall be known, it will be found to be a motion of Body.'[114]) In practice, however, it was not always so clear what should count as an adequate description of causation by matter in motion. The boundary between theoretical form and theoretical content was in fact quite blurred; disputes between Hobbes and other scientists (including Boyle) sometimes arose from a disagreement over where that boundary was located. This is true of Hobbes's objections to Boyle's account of the 'spring of the air'—an account which, Hobbes thought, failed to satisfy the formal requirements of a physical theory, as it depended on an analogy (the 'restitution' of compressed wool when pressure on it is relaxed) that was not explanatory at all.[115] And the neat distinction just suggested between the form and the content of a theory was sometimes eroded in another way too. Particular physical theories were not all of equal power or status; some were subordinate to other, more general theories, and their plausibility might be judged in terms of how they cohered with them.

Both of these problems came to the surface in Hobbes's arguments about the vexed issue of the possibility of a vacuum. Until the late 1640s, Hobbes had no difficulty in accepting the existence of a vacuum in nature—the 'disseminated' vacuum that existed in the interstices between matter in the universe. In his English Optical Manuscript, written in 1645–6, he clearly stated that his theory of the alternate dilation and contraction of the sun required the existence of such vacua in the medium: 'I . . . find no impossibility, nor absurdity, nor so much as an improbability in admitting vacuity, for no probable argument hath ever beene

---

[114] Hobbes, *De corpore*, XXVI.7 ('vis magnetica quae sit ignoratur, & quando erit cognita, invenietur esse motus corporis').
[115] Hobbes, *Dialogus physicus*, pp. 6–7 (*OL* IV, pp. 247–8).

produced to the contrarie, unlesse wee should take a space or extension for a body or thing extended... For who knowes not that Extension is one thing and the thing extended another.'[116] This was a hit at Descartes, whose anti-vacuist theory evidently did not count, in Hobbes's eyes, as a possible causal hypothesis within the framework of a mechanistic science: on the contrary, Hobbes thought it showed that Descartes's metaphysics prevented him from having a proper mechanistic science at all. Similarly, he criticized Thomas White for ruling out vacuum *a priori*: White's theory on this point was a sort of Aristotelian equivalent of Descartes's, arguing that wherever there was space there must be *ens*.[117] Another example of an assumption that precluded the framing of proper physical hypotheses was the teleology of the scholastic world-view, with its traditional notion that a *horror vacui* in the nature of things would prevent the formation of empty spaces. Hobbes had nothing but contempt for such explanations: 'they will tell you the center of the earth is a place of Rest, and Conservation for Heavy things; and therefore they endeavour to be there: As if Stones, and Metalls had a desire, or could discern the place they would bee at, as Man does; or loved Rest, as Man does not; or that a peece of Glass were lesse safe in the Window, than falling into the Street.'[118] Nevertheless, if a mechanistic plenist theory had been available, satisfying Hobbes's requirements for the basic form of an explanatory theory in physics, there is no reason to think that he would have treated it with contempt or ruled it out *a priori*.

By the time he published *De corpore* in 1655, Hobbes had actually adopted such a plenist theory, denying the existence of any empty spaces—even at the atomic level—in the universe. Why did he make this change? According to Shapin and Schaffer, the fundamental reasons were political. Hobbes settled on a materialist plenism in order to exclude 'incorporeal substances', such as spirits and the human soul (as described in scholastic ontology), because these were the props and devices used by priestcraft to harness people's fears and thereby gain power in the state, subverting lawful authority.[119] The difficulty with this explanation is that his attack on 'incorporeal substance' required only materialism; it did not require plenism too. As a materialist, Hobbes argued that 'incorporeal substance' was a self-contradiction. The only substances were corporeal: a vacuum, therefore, was not a place where incorporeal substances might be located: it was a place where no bodies, and therefore no substances at all, were located. Those people who were so silly, in his opinion, as to believe in incorporeal substances did not need vacuums to put them in.[120] Hobbes was attacking 'incorporeal substance' long before he

---

[116] BL, MS Harl. 3360, p. 7.   [117] Hobbes, *Critique du De mundo*, III.8–12 (pp. 121–5).
[118] Hobbes, *Leviathan*, p. 375.   [119] Shapin and Schaffer, *Leviathan and the Air-Pump*, pp. 96–9.
[120] Shapin and Schaffer cite one passage, from Hobbes's critique of Thomas White (written in 1642–3), in which Hobbes appears to associate the popular belief in 'spirits' with the popular belief in a vacuum: he suggests that primitive people mistook their hallucinations for real things and called them 'spirits' because they took as their criterion of physical existence visibility or opacity, rather than dimensionality, 'just as they

became a plenist; he was also putting forward his political theory at a time when he was happy to acknowledge the possibility or even the necessity of vacuum.

To strengthen their case, Shapin and Schaffer would need to show that Hobbes actually identified materialism with plenism; and they do produce one text in which he seems to do just that. In chapter 46 of *Leviathan*, Hobbes declares: 'The World . . . is Corporeall, that is to say, Body; and hath the dimensions of Magnitude . . . and consequently every part of the Universe, is Body; and that which is not Body, is no part of the Universe: And because the Universe is All, that which is no part of it, is *Nothing*; and consequently *no where*.'[121] This appears to imply that an empty space, 'which is not Body', must be '*no where*': in other words, that there can be no such thing. That implication can certainly be drawn from Hobbes's wording. But it must seem very odd that Hobbes, having criticized both Descartes and White for their *a priori*, definitional disproofs of vacuum, should now have adopted the same style of argument himself—especially since his discussion of 'space' in *De corpore* repeated some of those criticisms, and made it quite clear that an empty space was at least conceptually possible.[122] In fact, the context of this passage in *Leviathan* strongly suggests that he was not trying to make a case for the impossibility of vacuum at this point. His argument here was part of one of his tirades against scholastic ontology: the phrase 'that which is not Body' referred back quite clearly to the sort of entity described by the scholastics, who claimed that 'there be in the world certaine Essences separated from Bodies, which they call *Abstract Essences, and Substantiall Formes*'.[123] These, rather than empty spaces, were what he wished to dismiss as '*Nothing*; and consequently *no where*'. A similar argument was present in Hobbes's first political treatise, *The Elements of Law*, written in 1640: criticizing the idea of 'spirits incorporeal', he observed that spirits were described in the Bible as coming and going, 'all which words do consignify locality; and locality is dimension; and whatsoever hath dimension, is body, be it never so subtile'.[124] It might similarly be claimed that the phrase 'whatsoever hath dimension, is body' implied a plenist physics; yet we know that, when Hobbes wrote those words, he not only accepted the possibility of empty spaces in the universe, but positively required them for his own physical theories.

---

think that whatever the eyes can see through is empty ['vacuum']' ('scilicet vacuum putantes quicquid oculis pervium est': Hobbes, *Critique du De mundo*, IV.3 (p. 127)). This makes precisely the opposite point, however: it does not locate spirits in a vacuum, but contradistinguishes them from it.

[121] Hobbes, *Leviathan*, p. 371; cited by Shapin and Schaffer, *Leviathan and the Air-Pump*, pp. 98–9.
[122] *De corpore*, VII.2: 'For no man calls it Space for being already filled, but because it may be filled; nor does any man think Bodies carry their Places away with them, but that the same Space contains sometimes one, sometimes another Body . . . more cannot be put into a Place allready filled, so much is Empty Space fitter then that which is Full for the receiving of new Bodies' ('Nemo enim spatium ideo esse dicit, quod occupatum jam sit, sed quod occupari possit; aut corpora loca sua secum absportare putant, sed in eodem spatio modo unum, modo aliud contineri . . . ubi aliquid jam est, nihil amplius poni potest; tanto vacuum pleno ad nova corpora recipienda accommadatius est').
[123] *Leviathan*, p. 371.   [124] *Elements of Law*, XI.5.

The real reasons for Hobbes's shift from vacuist to plenist are to be found in experimental physics—experiments in which his friend Roberval was closely involved. Information about the Torricellian barometric experiment (in which a tube of mercury is inverted and the mercury descends to a constant level, leaving an apparent vacuum above it) had first been transmitted from Italy to France by du Verdus. He sent details to Niceron and Mersenne in 1644; further researches in France were at first inhibited by a lack of suitable supplies of glass tubes, but they were well under way by early 1647, culminating in Pascal's famous experiment on the Puy-de-Dôme in the following year.[125] The first sign of Hobbes's interest in these matters comes in his letter of 17 February 1648 to Mersenne, in which he commented on a little anti-vacuist treatise, by Étienne Noël, which Mersenne had given him. Hobbes had been severely ill for several months in 1647, so it may be that he was only now catching up with the latest developments in this field. The Jesuit Étienne Noël was a friend of Descartes, and his treatise argued that no vacuum could be created at the head of the tube, since the apparently empty space would be filled by purified air or 'ether'—the ultra-fine fluid which occupied the interstices of Descartes's plenist universe, and which was assumed to be fine enough to pass through the pores in the glass of the tube.[126] Hobbes was not convinced. No doubt his suspicions were aroused in the first place by Noël's known Cartesian sympathies: any anti-Cartesian would be predisposed to accept the idea that a vacuum could be created in nature, as this could then be treated as experimental disproof of Descartes's philosophy. In addition, Hobbes disliked the scholastic terminology to which Noël sometimes resorted. But in any case, he saw no need to construct a plenist physics: there was nothing wrong, *a priori*, with the idea of a vacuum. 'The supposition of a vacuum accounts for those experiments more simply and more elegantly', he wrote to Mersenne. 'So, to sum up my opinion about the vacuum, I still think what I told you before, that there are certain minimal spaces here and there, in which there is no body.'[127]

Two features of the experimental evidence raised problems in his mind, however. First was the constant height: 'I do not yet understand why the mercury always stays in the tube at the same distance from the mercury in the vessel. So I must think about this . . .' And secondly, there was the transmission of light

---

[125] See P. Mouy, *Le Développement de la physique cartésienne, 1646–1712* (Paris, 1934), pp. 36–42; C. de Waard, *L'Expérience barométrique: ses antécédents et ses explications* (Thouars, 1936), esp. pp. 115–16; A. Beaulieu, 'Torricelli et Mersenne', in F. de Gandt, ed., *L'Oeuvre de Torricelli: science galiléenne et nouvelle géométrie* (Nice, 1987), pp. 39–51. The difficulty in obtaining suitable tubes was mentioned by Roberval (see Mersenne, *Correspondance*, XV, p. 430; pp. 323–8 also provide a useful chronology of French activities in this field during 1647).

[126] See E. Noël, *Le Plein du vuide* (Paris, 1648), reprinted in B. Pascal, *Oeuvres*, ed. C. Bossut, 5 vols. ('The Hague' [Paris], 1779), pp. 108–46.

[127] Hobbes, *Correspondence*, I, pp. 165, 167 ('positio Vacui ijsdem experimentis satisfaciat facilius elegantiusque . . . Itaque de Vacuo censeo summatim idem quod antè censui, esse nimirum loca quaedam, nunc haec nunc illa in quibus corpus nullum inest').

through the so-called vacuum: 'It is said that one can see through the empty space ... from which it follows that the action of a light-producing body is being propagated through a vacuum (which I think is impossible).'[128] While the first of these was just an open-ended mystery, the second was a direct contradiction of one of the fundamental theories of Hobbes's physics, his mediumistic explanation of the transmission of light. He asked Mersenne to supply more experimental evidence, suggesting that the researchers might find the image to be distorted, which would show that it had in fact been transmitted via the sides of the glass, not through the space inside. Presumably he received from Mersenne a definite and negative reply. This must have forced Hobbes to face up to the fact that his physics, in its present state, was simply incompatible with the known facts. Only two adjustments were possible: either he must suppose that the space at the head of the tube was not in fact empty, and supply an explanation of how some matter had filled it; or he must jettison his existing hypothesis about the transmission of light, and find a new one.

While Hobbes wrestled with these difficulties in early 1648, his friend Roberval was also having problems with the interpretation of this experiment. Since the summer of 1647 he had been corresponding sporadically with a Frenchman in Warsaw, Pierre Desnoyers, who reported the experiments carried out by a Capuchin scientist there, Valerian Magni. Working independently, Magni had duplicated some of the findings of the Italian and French researchers. As an outspoken anti-Aristotelian, Magni was happy to conclude that a genuine vacuum had been created, since this would help to overturn scholastic physics and metaphysics. He also placed great emphasis on the fact that light was propagated through the empty space; this too served his purposes, as the general scholastic doctrine was that light was an accident which must inhere in a substance.[129] In a long letter to Magni, dated 20 September 1647, Roberval expressed his overall agreement with him, but added some more cautious provisos. He noted the transmission of light through the vacuum as a possible difficulty; but, as he was not committed to any particular theory about how light was transmitted, this was not such a problem for him. He discussed the two main hypotheses that could be used to deny the presence of a vacuum. One was the 'rarefaction' theory of the Aristotelians, who supposed that a tiny quantity of air did remain in the tube after the descent of the mercury, and that it was then rarefied to fill the whole space: Roberval presented several objections drawn from the experimental evidence, and emphasized that this theory completely failed to explain the fact that the mercury always fell to a constant level.

---

[128] Ibid., I, pp. 166, 168 ('plura de hac re hoc tempore non scribam, quia causam quare Argentum viuum semper subsistit in tubo ad certam vnamque ab argento viuo ... distantiam non percipio'; 'Quoniam dicitur ... fieri per illum locum visionem, ex quo sequatur actionem lucidi corporis propagari per vacuum, id quod mihi impossibile videtur').

[129] See Z. Mysłakowsi, 'O. Waleryan Magni i kontrowersya w sprawie odkrycia próżni (1638–1648)', *Rozprawy wydziału matematyczno-przyrodniczego akademii umiejętności*, ser. 3, vol. 11, sect. A (1911), pp. 325–77; here pp. 350–2.

The other was the 'subtle matter' theory of the Cartesians: here he felt that the problem was the failure of these theorists to adduce any evidence *for* such matter, either in this case or in any other. He concluded that a vacuum could be assumed to exist, and that, although the Cartesian 'subtle matter' could not be ruled out, a space filled with it seemed indistinguishable, in any case, from a space that was empty. Several aspects of the evidence continued to puzzle him, however, and he recommended carrying out further experiments to test whether air was still present in the apparently empty space.[130]

In the winter of 1647–8, therefore, Roberval and Hobbes were occupying fairly similar positions: both were willing to assume that a vacuum had been created, but both found aspects of the evidence problematic, and were seeking further information. During the first half of 1648 Roberval himself became one of the leading experimenters on this issue, devising ingenious new methods of testing the various hypotheses. One of his experiments involved taking a carp's bladder, pressing it flat to expel the air from it, tying its end and then placing it in the head of the tube —whereupon it suddenly swelled up inside the evacuated space. The obvious explanation for this was that a tiny quantity of air had remained in the bladder, and that this had now expanded under conditions of reduced pressure. Having previously dismissed arguments based on the rarefaction of air, Roberval was now obliged to agree that air could increase in volume enormously, and that the space at the head of the tube might itself be filled with greatly rarefied air. And, at the same time, the strength of atmospheric pressure would explain why the mercury always fell to a constant level. By the summer of 1648 (when he wrote another long letter to Desnoyers in Warsaw), Roberval had thus reluctantly concluded that the key to the whole issue was rarefaction, and that a vacuum had not in fact been created. Nevertheless, he kept up his previous critical stances: he attacked the Aristotelians for basing their arguments on dogma rather than empirical evidence; he attacked Descartes for his aprioristic confusion between 'space' and 'body'; and he continued to say that it might be possible to make a vacuum, even though he did not think one had been made in these experiments.[131]

We can assume with reasonable certainty that Hobbes had followed, and probably witnessed, Roberval's experiments in the spring of 1648—not only because of what we know about his interest in this issue and his friendship with Roberval, but also because of the evidence of a letter sent from Paris by Sir Charles Cavendish to William Petty on 7/17 April 1648, describing the carp bladder experiment. 'There is an Experiment, how to shew as they suppose that there is, or may be, vaccuum,'

---

[130] Roberval, 'De vacuo narratio', in B. Pascal, *Oeuvres*, ed. L. Brunschvicg and P. Boutroux, 14 vols. (Paris, 1908–23), II, pp. 21–35.

[131] Roberval, 'Seconde narration sur le vide', in ibid., II, pp. 310–40. On Roberval's experiments see also the discussion on pp. 287–300, and W. E. K. Middleton, *The History of the Barometer* (Baltimore, Md, 1964), pp. 49–50.

he wrote; 'but a bladder being hung in that Vacuum, was as perfectly seene as could bee, soe that there must bee some body there to convey the Action of sight to the eye as I suppose, and divers others heere.'[132] In putting such emphasis on the visibility of the bladder (which was not the point of the experiment), Cavendish was surely reflecting the concerns of Hobbes, who was no doubt one of the 'divers others heere' he referred to. This problem, the transmission of light through the 'vacuum', was perhaps the major sticking-point for Hobbes. But, as we have seen, he was also aware of the problem of explaining the descent of the mercury to a constant level, which seemed to require some sort of equilibrium theory relating to the atmosphere outside the tube. Roberval had solved this problem by assuming that air could become denser or rarer, according to the pressure exerted on it. Hobbes, however, associated rarefaction with false metaphysics: for him, to say that the same quantum of matter could occupy different volumes was not just an unconvincing hypothesis, but a conceptual absurdity—and a transgression of the basic rules of mechanistic, materialist physics.[133] The only acceptable model for the compression of matter was provided by the analogy of a sponge: when a wet sponge is squeezed, the total quantum and volume of matter remain the same, and all that happens is that some of it—the water that was contained in the sponge—moves elsewhere.

Hobbes thus had two strong reasons for objecting to the theory that a vacuum had been produced. One was his attachment to a physical hypothesis, his mediumistic theory of the transmission of light: this was something of a master-hypothesis, to which other theories had to be subordinated. And the second was his belief that a theory invoking rarefaction did not even have the basic form of an explanatory physical theory. In principle, the mediumistic transmission theory could have been swapped (if necessary) for some other hypothesis within the realm of possible physical theories; but it could never have been swapped for a theory based on rarefaction, which, in Hobbes's view, lay outside that realm altogether.

So, just as Roberval found himself, to his surprise, lining up with his despised Aristotelians to defend a rarefaction theory, Hobbes found that he had to align himself with his hated Descartes to defend a theory based on the concept of 'ether' or 'subtle matter'. By late May 1648 he had crossed this Rubicon in his physical theory: writing to Mersenne on the twenty-fifth of that month, he declared: 'All the experiments which you and others have made with mercury do not prove that a vacuum exists, because when the subtle matter which is in the air is pressed, it will pass through the mercury, and through any other fluid or molten body

---

[132] Hartlib Papers, electronic edn, 8/29/1A–1B; printed in C. Webster, 'The Discovery of Boyle's Law, and the Concept of the Elasticity of the Air in the Seventeenth Century', *Archive for History of Exact Sciences*, 2 (1965), pp. 441–502; here p. 456.
[133] See *De corpore*, XXX.1, and the scathing attack on the 'absurdity' of rarefaction and condensation in *Six Lessons*, p. 14 (*EW* VII, pp. 224–5).

whatsoever—just as smoke passes through water.'[134] As these remarks show, Hobbes's theory provided not just an explanation of the presence of matter in the head of the tube, but also an account of the mechanism which had put it there: the increased pressure of the external air (caused by the descent of the mercury). In his own way, he too had come up with an equilibrium theory. Whether, by this stage, he had also formulated the fully worked-out plenist principles that would be set out in *De corpore* is not clear. But he had certainly acquired the two basic constituents of his later plenism: the idea of a 'subtle matter' so fine and so fluid that it would penetrate all spaces, no matter how small, and the concept of the 'circularity' of physical action, meaning that any moving object would set off a chain of effects that would move some other object into the space it had previously occupied.

Roberval and Hobbes had thus taken different paths. One had plumped for rarefaction, regarding the 'subtle matter' hypothesis as not absurd but merely worthless, and continuing to assume that a vacuum might be physically as well as conceptually possible. The other had opted instead for 'subtle matter', regarding rarefaction theories as not just worthless but absurd, and moving towards the view (expressed in *De corpore*) that, although a vacuum was conceptually possible, it could never be shown to exist in the real world. Perhaps this divergence of opinion was one aspect—a cause, and/or an effect—of a gradual estrangement between the two thinkers, one that was to be turned into a complete rupture by Wallis's interfering machinations eight years later. But however far apart Hobbes and Roberval may have strayed at the end, it is important to recognize how close they had once been, both personally and intellectually, as they fought against their common enemies (scholastic and Cartesian metaphysics) and wrestled with their common project of developing a new type of hypothetical physical science.

## ENDNOTE

The original text, from M. Mersenne, *L'Optique et la catoptrique* (sep. pag.), in *La Perspective curieuse du R. P. Niceron ... avec l'Optique et la Catoptrique du R. P. Mersenne*, ed. G. P. de Roberval (Paris, 1652), pp. 88–92, is as follows:

---

[134] Hobbes, *Correspondence*, I, pp. 172–3 ('Toutes les experiences faites par vous et d'autres, auec l'argent vif, ne concluent pas qu'il y a du vuide, parceque la matiere subtile qui est dans l'air estant pressée passera a trauers l'argent vif et trauers tout autre cors fluide ou fondu, que ce soit. Comme la fumee passe à trauers l'eau'). Such theories of 'subtle matter' were not exclusively Cartesian, however. A very similar theory was advanced by Claude Bérigard, discussing some pre-Torricellian vacuum experiments in 1643: 'I can reply, on behalf of Anaximander, Anaxagoras and other ancient writers who did not accept a vacuum, that extremely fine substances, which are naturally capable of mixing with other bodies, are drawn through pores in the glass' ('respondere possum pro Anaximandro, Anaxagora, & alijs antiquis vacuum non admittentibus ... attrahi per vitri meatus substantias tenuissimas, quarum natura est alijs corporibus permisceri': C. Bérigard ['Berigardus'], *Circulus pisanus* (Udine, 1643), part I, pp. 60–1).

'auparauant, ie veux icy en faueur de ceux qui n'ayment que la pure verité, faire vne petite consideration (sans toutesfois sortir de mon suiet, en ce qui regarde le general) & rapporter en peu de paroles, les meditations d'vn homme également versé en la Philosophie, & en la Mathematique, sur ce prurit & cette demangaison de plusieurs, qui veulent à quelque prix que ce soit, paroistre sçauans, mesmes aux choses qu'ils connoissent bien qu'ils ignorent. Il en attribuoit donc le principe à vn vain desir de gloire: mais il les accusoit d'arrogance, en ce qu'ils pretendent le plus souuent, faire croire aux autres, ce qu'ils ne croyent, ou au moins, ce qu'ils ne voyent pas clairement eux mesmes: & ce qui est pis, ils pensent auoir assez bien establi une verité pretenduë, quand ils croyent qu'on ne la peut conuaincre de faux, comme si vn meurtrier croyoit estre innocent, pource qu'on ne pourroit prouuer son assassinat. Ainsi, au suiet dont nous traitons, touchant l'esgalité des angles d'incidence, & de reflexion, les vns veulent nous faire croire que la lumiere se reflechit par ressort; d'autres, par vne continuation du mouuement actuel des corpuscules qui la font; d'autres, par vne continuation du mesme mouuement de ces pretendus corpuscules, non pas actuel, mais seulement en pussance; telles que seroit l'action de plusieurs boules disposées en ligne droite contigument, dont la premiere toucheroit vne muraille & la derniere seroit poussée par quelque force qui voudroit les faire mouuoir toutes à la fois le long de la mesme ligne droite, vers la mesme muraille; d'autres encor se seruent de la comparaison d'vn baston ietté par force perpendiculairement, ou obliquement contre vn plan; d'autres ont d'autres visions encor moins vrai semblables: mais tous expliquent cette illustre action de la nature, par quelque ressemblance qu'ils croyent qu'elle a auec quelque autre chose qu'ils pensent bien connoistre.

Et toutefois, il est certain qu'ils ne cognoissent rien que par l'entremise des sens; soit que ces sens produisent immediatement cette cognoissance; comme ils produisent immediatement la premiere sensation de la lumiere, des couleurs, du chaud, du froid, du bruit, des odeurs, des saueurs, &c. Soit qu'ils la produisent seulement par occasion, donnant suiet à l'entendement de raisonner sur les especes qui luy sont venuës par leur moyen: comme quand ils luy ont rapporté vne telle qu'elle espece d'vn triangle; ce qui luy a donné occasion de se representer vn triangle parfait, & en suitte d'en rechercher les proprietez: de mesmes, les sens ayans rapporté à l'entendement les especes sensibles de Pierre, de Iean, de Paul, & autres indiuidus des hommes; ils luy ont donné l'occasion de considerer ce qu'ils ont de commun, & de se former l'idée d'vne nature humaine, qu'il considere comme vne chose vniuerselle qui conuient à tous les particuliers.

Que si nous considerons l'entendement comme estant & ayant tousiours esté denué de tous les sens; alors nous ne sçaurions comprendre qu'il peust auoir aucunes idées des choses exterieures; & il y auroit occasion de douter s'il en auroit vne de sa propre existence.

Cela estant, il s'ensuit que s'il y a dans la nature quelques choses qui ne puissent tomber sous aucun de nos sens, ny directement, ny indirectement, l'entendement ne pourra former aucunes idées de ces choses: comme vn aueugle né qui n'auroit iamais ouy parler des couleurs, n'y penseroit iamais; & quand il en auroit ouy parler, il ne s'en sçauroit former d'idée veritable; mais seulement, il pourroit, peut estre, se representer quelque chose reuenant aux idées qu'il auroit acquises par les autres sens: & si en luy donnant à taster de l'escarlate, il la trouuoit douce, auec vn certain goust, ou vne telle odeur, ou faisant vn tel bruit au maniment; il se composeroit peut estre vne idée de toutes ces sensations, & en feroit à sa mode, l'idée de l'escarlate, qui seroit bien esloignée de la veritable idée d'vne telle couleur. Que si ce mesme aueugle ayant senty par plusieurs fois la chaleur du Soleil, durant les diuerses saisons, vouloit entreprendre de raisonner sur toutes les proprietez & les actions de cét astre, n'en ayant iamais rien appris d'ailleurs; il y a apparence qu'il s'apresteroit bien à rire aux Astronomes clair-voyans qui l'entendroient discourir, quoy qu'il fust le plus sçauant des aueugles, & qu'entreux il passait pour vn oracle. Cependant, il n'ignoreroit pas qu'il y eut vn Soleil, s'en estant aperçeu par le sense du tact; mais faute d'vn autre sens bien plus propre pour en descouurir les plus considerables proprietez, son entendement ne s'en formeroit que des idées tres imparfaites, qui toutes auroient quelque rapport à celles qu'il auroit accoustumé de se former à l'occasion du sens du tact; & ainsi il n'en pourroit raisonner qu'auec beaucoup d'imperfections.

Or, quelle asseurance auons nous d'auoir vn sens propre pour descouurir la nature de la lumiere; comment elle est produite par le luminaire dans les corps diaphanes; comment elle est arrestée par les corps opaques; comment elle est reflechie par les miroirs; comment elle est rompuë dans les diaphanes de differente densité; & vne grande quantité d'autres accidens qui luy arriuent, qui ne s'accommodent, peu estre, non plus à aucun de nos cinq sens, que l'odeur s'accommode au sens de l'ouye: il est vray que nous auons vn sens propre pour nous apperceuoir qu'il y a de la lumiere; qu'elle est produite, reflechie, rompuë &c. Mais sa nature, la cause de son existence, de sa production, de sa reflexion, de sa fraction &c. nous est inconnuë: & il y a grande apparence que nous n'auons aucun sens propre pour descouurir vne telle cause, non plus que plusieurs autres qui appartiennent à la nature de tout l'vniuers: c'est pour quoy nous ne nous en representons que des idées tres imparfaites, qui ont rapport à ces cinq sens dont nous iouyssons: comme sont les idées de certains corpuscules enuoyez du Soleil en terre en si peu de temps qu'il passe pour vne moment: ou celles de certaine matiere tres-subtile composée d'vn nombre innombrable de boules parfaitement rondes, si petites qu'il y en a des millions en vn seul grain de sable, & qui se touchent sans discontinuation depuis le Soleil iusques icy; tellement que le mesme Soleil; par vn mouuement sphérique qu'il a à l'entour de son propre centre, fait vn effort continuel contre ces boules, les poussant en dehors de toutes parts, ce qui fait qu'au mesme temps qu'il presse celles qui le touchent immediatement, celles-là pressent leurs voisines, & ainsi de suitte iusques au fonds de nostre oeil, où ce pressement fait cette sensation sur nos nerfs, laquelle nous appellons la sensation de la lumiere, dont l'ame s'apperçoit par le moyen des mesmes nerfs, dans le ceruau, d'où ils tirent leur origine. Ie pourrois icy rapporter d'autres idées que d'autres ont eu de la lumiere: mais toutes aussi bien celles-cy, paroistroient peut estre aussi ridicules à vn clair-voyant; si cét aueugle ayant fait tous ses efforts en vne campagne toute raze, pour se cacher de luy, s'esloignant assez loin, sans faire bruit, apres auoir destourné de soy toutes les odeurs; & se sentant neantmoins à toutes les fois trouué & pris promptement & sans peine; se fantastiquoit que le clair-voyant auroit le tact, ou l'odorat tres-subtil, & qu'il se sentiroit de loin la resistance de l'air compris entre eux deux; ou que l'aueugle enuoyant continuellement & sans s'en apperceuoir, quelques petits corpuscules de toutes parts hors de soy, le clair-voyant en auroit le nez frapé, ce qui luy descouuriroit la part ou seroit l'aueugle. Peut estre aussi que cette belle pensée d'vn tel Philosophe sans yeux, ne seroit pas peu admirée par les autres aueugles ses confreres, qui auroient trauaillé comme luy à rechercher la cause pourquoy le clair-voyant les trouueroit si facilement, les nommans sans hesiter, en mesme temps qu'il les toucheroit, ou mesmes auparauant, quelque mélange qu'ils peussent faire entr'eux par leurs differens mouuemens: qui ne seroit pas vn petit diuertissement pour le clair-voyant, entre des aueugles qui n'auroient iamais ouy dire ce que c'est que de voir.

Et cependant, nous voyons tous les iours arriuer la mesme chose dans nos escholes; puis que les pensées qu'on y admire ordinairement, n'ont autre fondement que l'ignorance, tant de l'inuenteur, que des admirateurs; qui tous se tourmentent, pour descouurir des cognoissances, pour lesquelles souuent, ils n'ont pas de sens propres: en quoy ils se laissent tellement emporter par le desir de paroistre sçauans, que celuy-là est le plus admiré, & le plus imité, qui aux choses les plus douteuses, produit les plus hautes extrauagances.

Voila quel estoit en substance, le raisonnement de ce grand Philosophe, & Mathematicien, sur le suiet des dogmatistes de ce temps, qu'il nommoit les sçauans visionnaires, tant en Philosophie, que Mathematique, & autres sciences. Et sa conclusion estoit, qu'en ce qui regarde les sciences humaines, nous deuons, tant qu'il est possible, nous seruir du pur raisonnement; pourueu qu'il soit establi sur des principes clairement & distinctement vrais, pour en tirer des conclusions indubitables; comme nous faisons en la Geometrie, & en l'Arithmetique: pour lesquelles tous nos sens se trouuent propres; nous faisans descouurir qu'il y a vn espace ou vne estenduë en tout sens & de toutes parts; ce qui donne occasion à l'entendement d'establir la pure Geometrie: & que dans cét espace il y a plusieurs choses: ce qui luy donne occasion de mediter sur le nombre, & d'establir l'Arithmetique. Au deffaut de tels principes, nous deuons auoir recours à vne experience constante faite auec les conditions requises, pour en tirer des conclusions vrai-semblables. Et il appelloit Science, la cognoissance qui vient des conclusions de la premiere sorte: quant aux conclusions tirées des experiences; il appelloit Opinion la cognoissance qui nous en vient. Hors quoy, dans les mesmes cognoissances purement humaines; il appelloit toutes les autres persuasions des hommes, autant de visions, qui ne meritoient aucune croyance: & en general, il preferoit l'ignorance cognuë, à vne persuasion mal fondée. Il est vray que nous nommons Sciences plusieurs cognoissances de celles qu'il comprend sous le nom d'Opinion: comme la Mechanique, l'Optique, l'Astronomie, & quelques autres; qui toutes empruntent quelque chose de l'experience: mais pour ce qu'elles empruntent aussi beaucoup de la Geometrie, & de l'Arithmetique, qui sont des pures sciences; nous les nommons ordinairement sciences, empruntans leur nom, de leur plus noble partie. Luy au contraire, tiroit leur nom de la partie la plus foible, à cause de cét axiome de la Logique, que quand vne conclusion est tirée de premisses qui ne sont pas de mesme dignité, elle suit tousiours la plus foible partie, & n'a ny plus de force, ny plus de dignité que la premisse la plus foible. Mais, pour ne pas disputer des noms; si nous les voulons nommer Opinions; nous entendrons que ce sont des Opinions fort certaines, à comparaison de plusieurs autres qui sont fort legeres. Que si nous les voulons nommer Sciences; nous entendrons que ce sont des sciences meslées, à comparaison de la Geometrie, de l'Arithmetique, & encore de la Logique prise dans sa pureté, & purgée des questions estrangeres: car celles cy sont des pures sciences sans incertitude, & desquelles le doute, qui se pourroit glisser dans les autres de la part de l'experience, est absolument banni.'

– 7 –

# The Title Page of *Leviathan*, Seen in a Curious Perspective

I

The engraved title page of Thomas Hobbes's *Leviathan* furnishes what is perhaps the most famous visual image in the history of modern political philosophy. Above a series of compartments depicting symbolic objects (representing temporal power on one side and ecclesiastical power on the other) there is a landscape, containing a town with its houses, fortress and church; and above the landscape itself there rises up a gigantic figure, with the symbols of temporal and ecclesiastical rule in its hands and a crown upon its head. What makes the image so striking is that the body of this colossus is itself made up of a mass of small figures who stand, hatted and cloaked, with their backs to the viewer, gazing upwards towards the head of the body which they compose.

This engraving is, in most respects, a very close copy of the original drawing (probably by Wenceslaus Hollar) which stands at the beginning of the manuscript of *Leviathan* presented by Hobbes to Charles II in Paris.[1] There is, however, one major difference between the two designs. In the drawing, the body of the colossus consists not of small full-length figures seen from behind, but of much larger faces or heads, all of them facing outwards, towards the viewer. (The length or diameter of each of these heads is roughly one third of that of the head of the colossus itself.) Most modern discussions of the iconography of the *Leviathan* title page have been concerned exclusively with the engraved version. However, as Keith Brown has convincingly argued, the drawing in the manuscript must have preceded the engraving; it very probably brings us closer, therefore, to Hobbes's original iconographical intentions.[2] That the overall scheme of the drawing, and many of its

---

This chapter first appeared in *The Seventeenth Century*, 13 (1998), pp. 124–55.

[1] British Library, London (hereafter: BL), MS Egerton 1910, fol. 1r; for the attribution to Hollar see K. Brown, 'The artist of the *Leviathan* title-page', *British Library Journal*, 4 (1978), pp. 24–36.

[2] Ibid., 28–9. Discussions devoted to the engraving include M. Corbett and R. Lightbown, *The Comely Frontispiece: The Emblematic Title-Page in England, 1550–1660* (London, 1979), pp. 218–30 (with a brief mention of the drawing on p. 222); R. Brandt, 'Das Titelblatt des Leviathan und Goyas El Gigante', in U. Bermbach and K.-M. Kodalle, eds., *Furcht und Freiheit:* Leviathan-*Diskussion 300 Jahre nach Thomas*

details, derived from Hobbes himself cannot be doubted. It is well known that he took great care over such matters, as the engraved title pages of his Thucydides translation and of *De cive* (at least, of the first edition of the latter) amply show.[3] In the *Leviathan* drawing the ecclesiastical objects in the compartments on the right-hand side of the page, for example, must have been suggested to the artist by someone intimately familiar with the contents of the text, and the idea of a colossus composed of people is clearly an attempt to present in pictorial terms the central theoretical innovation of that book—Hobbes's idea that the sovereign bears the collective 'person' of his (or its) subjects.

Two related questions arise, therefore, about the different forms taken by the colossus's body in the two versions of this design. Why was the change made? And what was the significance of the earlier form? The answer to the first of these can only be guessed at: there is no external evidence that could indicate whether the change was made at Hobbes's request, or on someone else's initiative (either the engraver's, or Hollar's when preparing the copy sent to be engraved). Keith Brown inclines towards the view that this was 'an interesting instance of the draughtsman overruling the philosopher': the reason he gives for the change is that the multiple heads were uncomfortably reminiscent of 'depictions of that devil whose name is Legion'.[4] To this somewhat speculative claim it may be added that the visual effect of the heads in the drawing is awkward, because the degree of three-dimensionality given to them turns the whole body into a lumpy mass of protuberances. But if the answer to the first question is that the change was made by the artist or the engraver as a matter of aesthetic common sense, that can only make the second question more urgent: why, if this was such a visually awkward rendering of Hobbes's idea, did he fix on this particular way of expressing it in the first place?

The aim of this paper is to give a very specific answer to that question. Hobbes had the idea of faces making up a larger figure with a face rather than little people with their backs to the viewer making up such a figure, because he had in mind a particular visual effect, created by an elaborate optical device which had been invented in the late 1620s and had become a fashionable scientific-aesthetic toy by the 1640s. There are, as it happens, two descriptions of this device by English writers, penned in the four years immediately preceding the publication of

---

*Hobbes* (Opladen, 1982), pp. 201–31; C. Pye, 'The sovereign, the theater, and the Kingdome of Darknesse: Hobbes and the spectacle of power', in S. Greenblatt, ed., *Representing the English Renaissance* (Berkeley, Calif., 1988), pp. 279–301; and R. Prokhovnik, *Rhetoric and Philosophy in Hobbes's Leviathan* (New York, 1991), pp. 130–48. Some of Pye's key arguments, e.g. on the 'paradoxical movement of gazes' from subjects to sovereign and from sovereign to viewer (pp. 296–7), are applicable only to the engraving.

[3] See M. M. Goldsmith, 'Picturing Hobbes's Politics? The Illustrations to *Philosophicall Rudiments*', *Journal of the Warburg and Courtauld Institutes*, 44 (1981), pp. 232–7; C. W. Schoneveld, 'Some features of the seventeenth-century editions of Hobbes's De Cive printed in Holland and elsewhere', in J. G. van der Bend, ed., *Thomas Hobbes: His View of Man* (Amsterdam, 1982), pp. 125–42.

[4] Brown, 'The artist', p. 32.

*Leviathan*; and one of those writers was Hobbes himself. In the final paragraph of his 'Answer' to Sir William Davenant's 'Preface' to *Gondibert*, he wrote:

> I beleeve (Sir) you have seene a curious kind of perspective, where, he that lookes through a short hollow pipe, upon a picture conteyning diverse figures, sees none of those that are there paynted, but some one person made up of their partes, conveighed to the eye by the artificiall cutting of a glasse. I find in my imagination an effect not unlike it from your Poeme. The vertues you distribute there amongst so many noble Persons, represent (in the reading) the image but of one mans vertue to my fancy, which is your owne; and that so deeply imprinted, as to stay for ever there, and governe all the rest of my thoughts, and affections . . .[5]

This text by Hobbes, written in the form of a letter to Davenant, is dated 10 January 1650. By this time Hobbes was already absorbed in his work on *Leviathan*; by May 1650 he had completed thirty-seven chapters (out of a projected total of fifty).[6] So it may not be entirely fanciful to detect a subliminal echo of Hobbes's political theory in the language of this passage, in which the image is said to 'governe' Hobbes's thoughts and affections.

The other description of the 'curious kind of perspective' was written roughly three years earlier, and was also used for the construction of an ingenious comparison in the prefatory materials to a literary work. The author here was Richard Fanshawe, in the dedicatory epistle (addressed to Prince Charles) of his translation of Guarini's *Il pastor fido*:

> Your Highnesse may have seen at Paris a Picture (it is in the Cabinet of the *great Chancellor* there) so admirably design'd, that, presenting to the common beholders a multitude of little faces (the famous Ancestors of that Noble man); at the same time, to him that looks through a *Perspective* (kept there for that purpose) there appears onely a single portrait in great of the *Chancellor* himself; the Painter thereby intimating, that in him alone are contracted the Vertues of all his Progenitors; or perchance by a more subtile Philosophy demonstrating, how the *Body Politick* is composed of many *naturall ones*; and how each of these, intire in it self, and consisting of head, eyes, hands, and the like, is a head, an eye, or a hand in the other: as also, that mens *Privates* cannot be preserved, if the *Publick* be destroyed, no more then those little Pictures could remain in being, if the great one were defaced: which great one likewise was the first and chiefest in the Painters designe, and *that* for which all the rest were made.[7]

Fanshawe's book was entered in the Register of the Stationers' Company on 8 June 1647, and was printed shortly thereafter; the author–translator had returned to

---

[5] Sir William Davenant, *Gondibert*, ed. D. F. Gladish (Oxford, 1971), p. 55.

[6] BL MS Harl. 6942, no. 128 (Robert Payne to Gilbert Sheldon, 13 May 1650, giving information contained in a recent letter from Hobbes). *Leviathan* has 47 chapters.

[7] *A Critical Edition of Sir Richard Fanshawe's 1647 Translation of Giovanni Battista Guarini's Il pastor fido*, ed. W. F. Staton and W. E. Simeone (Oxford, 1964), pp. 3–4.

England from France at the beginning of the year, so it is clear that this passage was written at some time in the first half of 1647.[8]

Apart from these literary references to the device, these are also some detailed accounts of it in optical treatises of the period. The earliest and the fullest description was provided in 1638 by a French scientist who was almost certainly known personally to Hobbes: the Minim friar Jean-François Niceron. (Details drawn from his technical description will be presented below.) These optical devices were rarities, because they were complicated to construct; but at the same time they were, in their day, famous rarities, and have left quite a few traces of their existence. Curiously, however, although some modern scholars have noticed some of the connections between the *Leviathan* title page and the Hobbes and Fanshawe passages just quoted, or between those passages and the description of the device by Niceron, no account has yet joined all of these connections together.[9] This paper will attempt to do that, and to supply a more detailed account of the history of the device—of how it developed, who made it, when, why, and for whom, and in what cultural context such objects were displayed and admired.

## II

The origins of the optic device lie in the tradition of anamorphic art that had developed in Western Europe since the early sixteenth century. An anamorphic picture (or 'anamorphosis') uses an exaggerated perspective to produce an image which appears grossly distorted when seen from the normal viewing position in front of the picture, but which, looked at from an unusual viewpoint or with the

---

[8] Ibid., p. xxv; *A Calendar of the Proceedings of the Committee for Compounding, &c., 1643–1660*, ed. M. A. E. Green, 5 vols. (London, 1889–92), III, p. 1649. On his next visit to France, in August 1647, Fanshawe distributed several copies among his friends there: *The Poems and Translations of Sir Richard Fanshawe*, ed. P. Davidson, 2 vols. (Oxford, 1997–), I, p. 330.

[9] None of the modern editors of Fanshawe's *Il pastor fido*, or of Hobbes's 'Answer' to Davenant, has commented on the device. Alfred Harbage noticed the Fanshawe passage (but not the Hobbes one) and suggested that it gave Hobbes the idea for the engraved title page of *Leviathan* (letter to the *Times Literary Supplement*, no. 1587 (30 June 1932), p. 480); James Turner has connected the Fanshawe passage with Niceron's device, but without making the connection with Hobbes (*The Politics of Landscape: Rural Scenery and Society in English Poetry 1630–1660* (Oxford, 1979), pp. 80, 201); Ernest B. Gilman has described Niceron's device in detail and linked it to the Hobbes 'Answer', but without making the connection with *Leviathan* (*The Curious Perspective: Literary and Pictorial Wit in the Seventeenth Century* (New Haven, Conn., 1978), pp. 47–9); Judith Graham has argued that Hobbes's title page was inspired by Fanshawe (and/or the picture Fanshawe described), without noting Hobbes's own account in the 'Answer' ('Sir Richard Fanshawe's Work as Public Poetry', Ph.D. dissertation, University of Maryland, 1984, pp. 22–3, 32); Graham Parry has done likewise ('A troubled Arcadia', in T. Healy and J. Sawday, eds., *Literature and the English Civil War* (Cambridge, 1990), pp. 38–55; here pp. 54–5); and Quentin Skinner has connected the 'Answer' to the *Leviathan* title page, without making any explicit reference to Niceron (*Reason and Rhetoric in the Philosophy of Hobbes* (Cambridge, 1996), p. 388). (For the reference to Graham Parry's work, and for other helpful comments on this article, I am very grateful to Dr Kinch Hoekstra.)

help of a correcting device (such as a mirror), exhibits a 'normal' image.[10] The best known anamorphosis in Western art, the distorted skull in the foreground of Holbein's painting 'The Ambassadors' (1533), is also one of the earliest; the technique was first mentioned in a treatise written in the 1530s, and Holbein's work may be only one or two years later than the famous woodcuts by Erhard Schön (the earliest known anamorphoses), which show the hugely elongated heads of various monarchs, with tiny figures and landscape details inserted into the design to enhance the illusion.[11]

Until the early seventeenth century, this straightforward geometrical distortion of the image was the only form of anamorphosis practised. Later theorists would describe it as 'optic' anamorphosis, as opposed to 'catoptric' or 'dioptric', meaning that the correction could be achieved by direct vision from a special viewpoint, not requiring the use of mirrors or lenses. However, there is evidence that even at this stage some kinds of simple optical device were used to control or enhance the effect, such as a small eyehole or viewing-glass fixed at the precise place of the correct viewpoint, or a similarly placed eyehole in a box surrounding the painting. It has been suggested that the skull in Holbein's painting was designed to be seen from the normal viewpoint in front of the painting, through a glass tube (such as the stem of a drinking-glass) held at an angle.[12] And, of course, any direct anamorphosis could be corrected by standing in front of the picture and viewing it in an angled mirror held at the picture's side. These various simple techniques must have formed the starting-point for the more elaborate experiments with mirrors and lenses in the seventeenth century that culminated in Niceron's optic device.

The first significant advance in these techniques in the seventeenth century was the discovery of a method for cylindrical catoptric anamorphosis—that is, a type of anamorphosis where the correction of the image is achieved by viewing the picture's reflection in a cylindrical mirror. (The distorted picture is drawn in a semi-circle or circle, and is placed on a flat surface; the correcting mirror, usually a cylinder of highly polished metal, stands upright on the central point of the circle.) The earliest known example is portrayed in an engraving of a design by the French artist Simon Vouet, made during Vouet's stay in Italy between 1624 and 1627, which shows a group of satyrs staring in amazement at a cylindrical anamorphosis

[10] The best general studies of anamorphoses are J. Baltrušaitis, *Anamorphic Art*, translated by W. J. Strachan (Cambridge, 1977), and F. Leeman, *Anamorphosen: ein Spiel mit der Wahrnehmung, dem Schein und der Wirklichkeit* (Cologne, 1975). See also the exhibition catalogue *Anamorfosen: spel met perspectief*, ed. S. H. Levie and F. Mathey (Cologne, 1975).

[11] Baltrušaitis, *Anamorphic Art*, pp. 11–12; S. Foister, A. Roy and M. Wyld, *Making and Meaning in Holbein's Ambassadors* (London, 1997), p. 50.

[12] W. B. Rye, *England as Seen by Foreigners in the Days of Elizabeth & James the First* (London, 1865), p. 280, and Foister, Roy and Wyld, *Making and Meaning*, p. 50 (viewing devices); Baltrušaitis, *Anamorphic Art*, p. 30 (box with eyehole); E. R. Samuel, 'Death in the glass: a new view of Holbein's "Ambassadors"', *The Burlington Magazine*, 105 (1963), pp. 436–41 (cylindrical glass).

of an elephant.[13] He had probably learned the technique in Italy, but the source of his knowledge is not known: when the leading Italian expert at the time, the Tuscan civil servant Pietro Accolti, discussed anamorphosis in his treatise on perspective, *Lo inganno de gl'occhi* (1625), he confined himself to the traditional or 'optic' type of image. However, it is significant that Accolti recommended the use of a plane mirror to correct the type of anamorphosis he was describing.[14]

The significance of this lies not only in the fact that the use of plane mirrors helps to explain the progression to mirrors of other shapes, but also in that it shows what kind of psychological effect the makers of anamorphoses were now aiming to achieve. When a direct or 'optic' anamorphosis is seen without the help of a mirror, the viewer has to move physically from one position to another to experience the contrast between the distortion and its resolution; in other words, that contrast will then be composed of two physically distinct experiences. But the piquancy and pleasure of anamorphic art—what Accolti called an 'effect of perspective which is as strange as it is delightful and ingenious'—lay precisely in the conjunction of the two experiences, and would be enhanced by bringing them as close together as possible, so that they became interchangeable and virtually simultaneous. When a mirror is employed, only a tiny movement of the eye is required to pass from seeing the distortion to seeing the resolution, and back again; in some cases (such as cylindrical anamorphoses) it may even be possible to hold both in the field of vision at the same time. Such a simultaneous experience of the 'strange' and the 'delightful and ingenious' matches quite closely the requirements of the seventeenth-century aesthetic of metaphor worked out by theorists such as Emanuele Tesauro, in which an 'ingenious' conceit would both surprise by its novelty (its apparent inappropriateness) and delight by its meaning (its revealed appropriateness)—a similar pattern of quasi-simultaneous distortion and resolution.[16]

The first writer to describe the technique for making cylindrical (and conical) catoptric anamorphoses was Jean de Vaulezard, whose *Perspective cilindrique et conique* was published in 1630. Vaulezard was a serious mathematician (and the author of an important translation of Vieta on algebra); this treatise on anamorphoses was set out in a Euclidean sequence of definitions, axioms, scholia, and so on. In his general preface he explained that he had been persuaded by friends to compose a study of this type of perspective, not only because no other author had yet written about it, but also because 'many people who are moderately skilled in

---

[13] W. R. Crelly, *The Painting of Simon Vouet* (New Haven, 1962), p. 17 and fig. 192; on the dating see J. Baltrušaitis, 'L'Anamorphose à miroir à la lumière de documents nouveaux', *La Revue des arts*, 6 (1965), pp. 85–98, here p. 88.

[14] P. Accolti, *Lo inganno de gl'occhi, prospettiva pratica* (Florence, 1625), p. 48.

[15] Ibid., p. 48: 'effetto quanto strano, tanto dilettoso, & ingegnoso di Prospettiva'.

[16] See J. A. Mazzeo, *Renaissance and Seventeenth-Century Studies* (New York, 1964), pp. 29–43; K.-P. Lange, *Theoretiker des literarischen Manierismus: Tesauros und Pellegrinis Lehre von der 'Acutezza' oder von der Macht der Sprache* (Munich, 1968), esp. pp. 87–103.

mathematics, and who have up till now seen the effects of it in public, would not fail to be pleased to be told how they are caused'.[17] Vaulezard's approach to the subject thus represented a rather different attitude from an aesthetic of wonder and delight, even though he also appealed to a certain type of pleasure: for him, the value of the enterprise lay in the demonstration that apparently marvellous effects could be rationally and fully explained by the application of the ordinary laws of geometry.

These two different approaches, aiming at an affective state (wonder and delight) on the one hand, and at rational understanding (knowledge of the causes of the wonderful effect) on the other, might seem, to the modern mind, to be in direct conflict. (After all, the modern stage magician does not normally include in his act a demonstration of how his illusions are created.) But for most people concerned with anamorphic art in the seventeenth century—the producers and the consumers—the two approaches seemed entirely complementary. Serious mathematicians and writers on optics, such as Vaulezard and Niceron, would publish treatises of these optical marvels to demonstrate their own mastery and to attract a wider public to the science they practised. As for the people who purchased and displayed anamorphic pictures or other optical devices, their motives could include either the pursuit of aesthetic or psychological delight, or the desire to engage in a kind of scientific experimentation, or, quite commonly, both at once.[18]

The actor William Cartwright, for example, was mainly interested in aesthetic pleasure: in his large collection of pictures he included 'a paintin of y$^e$ king of france his head, Luege y$^e$ 13th, to be seeing in a Sellinder glass put in y$^e$ midst of y$^e$ bourd, & looke in y$^{ee}$ glasse, you may see him perffetly', as well as several other cylindrical anamorphoses and a more elaborate device involving '2 bords tyde together' and 'a brass playt with a Lickell hole in it'.[19] The traveller John Bargrave also possessed two cylindrical anamorphoses (one of them depicting 'an emperor on horseback'); but they were just part of a larger collection of devices designed to demonstrate optical effects, such as the projection of images by means of a *camera obscura*, or the generation of a rainbow through the use of a light-source, a prism, and a darkened room.[20]

---

[17] J. L. de Vaulezard, *Perspective cilindrique et conique: ou traicté des apparences veuës par le moyen des miroirs cilindriques & coniques, soient convexes ou concaves* (Paris, 1630), sig. a4r: 'mesme que beaucoup qui sont mediocrement versez és Mathematiques, qui en ont cy-devant veu les effects en public n'en recevroient qu'avec plaisir les causes'.

[18] See L. Dimier, 'La Perspective des peintres et les amusements d'optique dans l'ancienne école de peinture', *Bulletin de la société de l'histoire de l'art français* (1925), pp. 7–22; R. L. Colie, 'Some Paradoxes in the Language of Things', in J. A. Mazzeo, ed., *Reason and the Imagination: Studies in the History of Ideas, 1600–1800* (New York, 1962), pp. 93–128.

[19] G. Waterfield, ed., *Mr Cartwright's Pictures: A Seventeenth Century Collection* (London, 1988), pp. 21–2.

[20] J. Bargrave, *Pope Alexander the Seventh and the College of Cardinals, with a Catalogue of Dr Bargrave's Museum*, ed. J. C. Robertson (London, 1867), pp. 131–5.

The modern reader might be inclined to ask whether anamorphic art-objects belonged, during this period, with other paintings in an art collection, or with other devices in a collection of scientific instruments or inventions. But such a question would be anachronistic. As several studies of the origins of the modern museum have shown, the *Kunstkammer, Wunderkammer* or 'cabinet of curiosities' of the sixteenth and seventeenth centuries could display any or all of an entire continuum of objects of interest, stretching from natural phenomena to works of art and mechanical inventions.[21] The earliest and most influential princely *Kunstkammern*, those of Archduke Ferdinand at Ambras and Rudolf II at Prague, included optical instruments, automata and other 'artificialia' alongside their specimens of unusual 'naturalia'.[22] John Bargrave's collection, for example, covered the whole range, from quartz crystals to Virginian wampum beads, from Roman pottery to modern paintings, from optical lenses to a desiccated chameleon.[23] And when the catalogue of one of the great private collections of seventeenth-century Italy, the 'museum' of Manfredo Settala in Milan, was printed in 1664, it began with optical devices (including two cylindrical anamorphoses), before moving on to mathematical instruments, astrolabes, clocks, corals, crystals, amber, shells, ethnographical specimens, archaeological items, paintings, and medals.[24] The taxonomy of the ordinary natural world was not conceptually segregated from the study of extraordinary natural phenomena, freaks, and rarities; and the underlying rationale of the scientific devices was to show that apparently extraordinary effects in the natural world (such as the rainbow) could themselves be replicated by artificial means.

It was therefore appropriate that the most elaborate inventions, such as Niceron's optical device, should find their place in the 'cabinets' of the richest and

---

[21] See especially A. Lugli, *Naturalia et mirabilia: il collezionismo enciclopedico nelle Wunderkammern d'Europa* (Milan, 1983); O. Impey and A. MacGregor, eds., *The Origins of Museums: The Cabinet of Curiosities in Sixteenth- and Seventeenth-Century Europe* (Oxford, 1985); K. Pomian, *Collectors and Curiosities: Paris and Venice, 1500–1800*, tr. E. Wiles-Portier (London, 1990); E. Bergvelt and R. Kistemaker, eds., *De wereld binnen handbereik: nederlandse kunst- en rariteitenverzamelingen 1585–1735* (Zwolle, 1992); P. Findlen, *Possessing Nature: Museums, Collecting, and Scientific Culture in Early Modern Italy* (Berkeley, Calif., 1994); and, for a penetrating account of the continuum between nature and art implied by these collections, H. Bredekamp, *The Lure of Antiquity and the Cult of the Machine: The Kunstkammer and the Evolution of Nature, Art and Technology* (Princeton, NJ, 1995). The classic study by J. von Schlosser, *Die Kunst- und Wunderkammern der Spätrenaissance: ein Beitrag zur Geschichte des Sammelwesens* (Leipzig, 1908), is also still valuable.

[22] See von Schlosser, *Die Kunst- und Wunderkammern*, p. 55; J. Neumann, *Obrazárna pražského hradu* (Prague, 1964), p. 14.

[23] See the catalogue in Bargrave, *Pope Alexander the Seventh*; Stephen Bann discusses the collection in *Under the Sign: John Bargrave as Collector, Traveler, and Witness* (Ann Arbor, Mich., 1994), pp. 85–96, and provides photographs of various objects (plates between pp. 80 and 81).

[24] P. M. Terzago, *Musaeum septalanium Manfredi Septalae patritii mediolanensis industrioso labore constructum* (Tortona, 1664); see p. 5 for the anamorphoses. The museum was visited in 1664 by Philip Skippon, who noted that Settala had equipment for making his own lenses ('An account of a journey made thro' part of the Low-Countries, Germany, Italy, and France', in J. Churchill, ed., *A Collection of Voyages and Travels*, 8 vols. (London, 1704–52), VI, pp. 359–736; here p. 575).

most princely collectors, who wanted to display the rarest products of both art and nature. Their possession of these objects was in some sense a reflection of their own status as exceptional specimens of the human—exceptional in terms of intellectual scope as well as wealth and social status. And since the logic of their collections implied comparability between 'naturalia' and 'artificialia', it could almost be said that there was an implicit correspondence here between the great personage, the extraordinary natural phenomenon *and* the extraordinary artificial device.

If that sounds like importing too deliberately Hobbesian an implication too soon into the argument, it may be worth pausing to consider what a high proportion of the anamorphic pictures known to us from the sixteenth and seventeenth centuries consists of portraits of princes or rulers. Cartwright's picture of Louis XIII and Bargrave's of 'an emperor on horseback' have already been mentioned; so too have Schön's woodcuts of several European monarchs, to which, from the same period, must be added the famous anamorphic portrait of Edward VI painted in 1546.[25] Cartwright also had a cylindrical anamorphosis of 'our kinge a horseback'; another such anamorphosis, now in Stockholm, has Charles I on one side and Charles II on the other; the Danish collector Ole Worm had one of Richelieu; Accolti proudly recorded that his own anamorphic portrait (optic, not catoptric) of Cosimo II de' Medici was displayed in the 'gallery' of Cardinal Carlo de' Medici; and, as we shall see, a more elaborate anamorphic portrait of Cosimo II's son Ferdinando II was created in 1642.[26]

Sometimes the portraits were commissioned, or at least bought, by the monarchs themselves: King Frederick III of Denmark, for example, purchased a 'silinder-porspectif' from the German artist Gert Dittmers in 1656, showing himself, the Queen, and their children.[27] And no doubt the producers of such images often took kings or princes as their subjects in the hope that, by dedicating in this way the finest examples of their skills to those figures, they might thereby attract patronage or financial rewards. But at the same time it is fair to assume that many of these anamorphoses were produced for general consumption. One obvious psychological mechanism may have been at work. Where the effect aimed at is one of astonishment at seeing a coherent image arising miraculously out of a distorted one, it can only reinforce that effect if the image is itself one that produces a sense of recognition—as the iconic image of a monarch's face (or that of a well-known

---

[25] The portrait of Edward VI is in the National Portrait Gallery, London; for photographs (of the anamorphic image and its correction) see Foister *et al.*, *Making and Meaning*, p. 51.

[26] *Mr Cartwright's Pictures*, p. 27; *Anamorfosen*, p. 88 (Stockholm); H. D. Schepelern, *Museum Wormianum: dets forudsaetninger og tilblivelse* (Odense, 1971), p. 346 (Richelieu); Accolti, *Lo inganno*, p. 49.

[27] E. Marquard, ed., *Kongelige kammerregnskaber fra Frederik III.s og Christian V.s tid* (Copenhagen, 1918), p. 34; the painting, now displayed in the National Museum, Copenhagen, is described in P. Eller, *Kongelige portraetmalere i Danmark 1630–82: en undersøgelse af kilderne til Karel van Manders og Abraham Wuchters' virksomhed* (Copenhagen, 1971), p. 238.

figure such as Richelieu) was guaranteed to do. Yet this psychological effect is in no way incompatible with the operation of a deeper one, involving the implicit link between the marvellous operation of the device and the super-human nature or activity of the monarch. As the chronicler of Louis XIV's building projects put it in his description of Versailles:

> A machine, by its movements, surprises and charms the spectators, and surpasses the ordinary effects of nature. In the same way His Majesty, by his virtues and his heroic actions, astonishes and delights all those who witness them, and surpasses the natural energies and the ordinary range of action of mankind.[28]

Finally, before turning to Niceron and his dioptric anamorphoses, it is necessary to consider one other aspect of the cultural background to these optical curiosities: the role of the religious orders. While princes and rich amateurs collected elaborate optical devices, the production of those objects, and the researches into optical effects that were exploited in them or illustrated by them, were carried out to a significant extent by members of the orders—especially Jesuits and Minims. There are obvious reasons for this: the orders included some highly educated men, with access to large and up-to-date libraries in their own religious houses, a ready-made institutional network for the circulation of knowledge, and the collective equivalent of a private income to sustain long-term research. The Jesuits were particularly strong in the mathematical sciences, thanks to their role as a teaching order and to the influence of the late sixteenth-century mathematician Clavius on their curriculum.[29] But the Minims, who included influential scientists such as Marin Mersenne and Emmanuel Maignan, also played a very active role during this period, even though they were a smaller order and did not engage in formal teaching; a sense of rivalry between the two orders was sometimes unmistakable.[30]

Large religious houses would contain, within or alongside their libraries, their own collections of specimens, rarities, instruments and devices; some, such as the collection assembled by the Jesuit polymath Athanasius Kircher in Rome, became world-famous.[31] And the construction of optical devices seems to have become

---

[28] 'Une machine par ses mouvements surprend et charme les spectateurs, et surpasse les effets ordinaires de la nature. Ainsi Sa Majesté par ses vertus et ses actions héroïques étonne et ravit tous ceux qui en sont les témoins, et surpasse les forces naturelles et la portée ordinaire des hommes', quoted in J.-M. Apostolidès, *Le Roi-Machine: spectacle et politique au temps de Louis XIV* (Paris, 1981), p. 134.

[29] See G. Cosentino, 'Le matematiche nella "Ratio studiorum" della Compagnia di Gesù', *Miscellanea storica Ligure*, 2 (1970), pp. 207–12, and F. de Dainville, 'L'Enseignement des mathématiques dans les Collèges Jésuites de France du XVIᵉ au XVIIIᵉ siècle', *Revue d'histoire des sciences et de leurs applications*, 7 (1954), pp. 6–21, 109–23.

[30] See P. J. S. Whitmore, *The Order of Minims in Seventeenth-Century France* (The Hague, 1967).

[31] The collection is catalogued in G. de Sepi ['de Sepibus'], *Romani Collegii Societatis Jesu musaeum celeberrimum* (Amsterdam, 1678); see pp. 35–40 for the optical devices. Cf. also Philip Skippon's account of his visit in 1664 ('Account of a journey', pp. 672–4), when the objects shown to him by Kircher included 'This pope's picture seen in a glass that reflects it from the plaits or folds of another picture' (p. 673).

a regular pastime for some monastic scientists. At the Benedictine house at Fontevrault in 1660, for example, the traveller Charles Bertie met 'the bon père Lardier here, a great mathematician . . . He shewed us a box in the library where you are to look through a round glass and you see many things to the life, which indeed is but a very bauble, but this he made himself and therefore esteems it the more.'[32]

Apart from the institutional factors stimulating optical research and invention within the religious orders, two powerful intellectual currents were also at work. One was the belief, shared by religious scientists such as Mersenne, Gassendi and many of the Jesuits, that the principles of the new science could be used to overturn the claims of demonology, occultism, Rosicrucianism, and so on. Mersenne used his optical demonstrations to denounce those charlatans who tricked the public into thinking that they had supernatural powers.[33] Kircher and his pupil Gaspar Schott both used the term 'magic' to describe their inventions, but did so merely to emphasize that this was 'natural magic' of the most natural kind—the exploitation of natural forces and processes, not the invocation of demons. Descartes (not, of course, a member of a religious order, but an ex-pupil of the Jesuits at La Flèche and a close friend of Mersenne) adopted a similar title, *Thaumantis regia*, for a treatise—now lost—describing artificial optical marvels, on which he worked in the 1620s. As he wrote in a letter to Mersenne at the end of that decade, 'There is an area of mathematics which I call "the science of miracles", because it teaches one to use air and light so aptly, that by its means one can cause all the same illusions to appear that are said to be produced by magicians with the help of demons.'[34]

Of course, for an orthodox Catholic this approach had its limits where 'miracles' were concerned. One scientist who appears to have transgressed them was the Minim friar Emmanuel Maignan, who compared the human experience of transubstantiation (in which the mind continues to interpret the sense impressions it receives as those produced by bread and wine) to the deception of the senses by optical illusions. This brought him into a long-running dispute with the Lyonnais Jesuit scholar Théophile Raynaud, during which Maignan insisted that he was not

---

[32] 'Diary of Charles Bertie during a journey in France, 1660–.', in Historical Manuscripts Commission, Report 79, *Supplementary Report on the Manuscripts of the Late Montagu Bertie Twelfth Earl of Lindsey*, ed. C. G. O. Bridgeman and J. C. Walker (London, 1942), pp. 275–372; here p. 304.

[33] See R. Lenoble, 'Histoire et physique: à propos des conseils de Mersenne aux historiens et de l'intervention de Jean de Launoy dans la querelle gassendiste', *Revue d'histoire des sciences et de leurs applications*, 6 (1953), pp. 112–34; esp. p. 115.

[34] M. Mersenne, *Correspondance*, ed. C. de Waard *et al.*, 17 vols. (Paris, 1933–88), II, p. 254 (letter of early Aug. 1629): 'Il y a une partie dans les mathematiques que je nomme *la science des miracles*, parce qu'elle enseigne à se servir si à propos de l'air et de la lumière, qu'on peut faire voir par son moyen toutes les mesmes illusions qu'on dit que les magiciens font paroistre par l'aide des démons.' Because of this approach to optics, the Minim friary where Mersenne and Niceron worked is described by Baltrušaitis as a 'Cartesian centre' (*Anamorphic Art*, p. 60). But although Descartes shared this approach, there was nothing peculiarly 'Cartesian' about it.

accusing God of planting delusions in men's minds, but was attributing to him a special kind of operation by 'objective actions'.[35]

The other intellectual current which contributed to the fashion for optical–pictorial devices was the cult of enigmatic symbolic images, which was particularly strong among the Jesuits. It is not a coincidence that the two most important seventeenth-century authors of treatises on the art of visual symbolism were an ex-Jesuit and a Jesuit: Emanuele Tesauro in Turin, and Claude Ménestrier in Lyon.[36] The art of interpreting iconography formed part of the Jesuit teaching programme; a special type of image—the 'enigma', or visual riddle—was much cultivated by them, and painters were often commissioned to produce such enigmas for the Jesuits' students to solve.[37] So it is not surprising that the pictures used in the elaborate optical devices that were developed in such a cultural context frequently carried complex symbolic messages of their own. Taking these two intellectual currents together, one might say, in summary, that a dual process was at work: first the scientists emptied these mysterious visual phenomena of their traditional charge of meaning (demonic magic), and then they filled them with a new, artificial and ingenious symbolic meaning of their own.

## III

Niceron was born in Paris, and christened 'François' in 1613; an uncle, Jean Niceron, was a Minim friar, and by the age of eighteen Niceron had joined the order as a novice, taking the additional name Jean in honour of his uncle. He made his full vows as a Minim in 1632.[38] Living in the main Parisian convent on the Place Royale, he became a close friend of Marin Mersenne, whose interests in optics and mathematics he already shared.[39] The earliest clear evidence of Niceron's skills is

---

[35] See T. Raynaud, 'Exuviae panis et vini', in his *Opera omnia*, 20 vols. (Lyon and Cracow, 1665–9), VI, pp. 407–[470] (mispaginated '148'); E. Maignan, *Philosophia sacra*, 2 vols. (Toulouse and Lyon, 1661–72), II, pp. 383–525 (2nd pagination); and the discussion of the quarrel in R. Ceñal, 'Emmanuel Maignan: su vida, su obra, su influencia', *Revista de estudios politicos*, 46 (= year 12, no. 66) (1952), pp. 111–49; here pp. 128–9.

[36] See E. Tesauro, *Idea delle perfette imprese*, ed. M. L. Doglio (Florence, 1975), and *Il cannocchiale aristotelico*, facsimile of 1670 Turin edition, ed. A. Buck (Bad Homburg, 1968), esp. pp. 624–93; C. F. Ménestrier, *L'Art des emblèmes* (Lyon, 1662), and *La Philosophie des images énigmatiques* (Lyon, 1682).

[37] J. Montagu, 'The Painted Enigma and French Seventeenth-Century Art', *Journal of the Warburg and Courtauld Institutes*, 31 (1968), pp. 307–35.

[38] See R. Thuillier, *Diarium patrum, fratrum et sororum ordinis minimorum provinciae Franciae*, 2 vols. (Paris, 1709), I, pp. 41–2, and II, pp. 143–4; J.-P. Niceron, *Mémoires pour servir à l'histoire des hommes illustres dans la république des lettres*, 43 vols. (Paris, 1727–45), VII, pp. 153–7; and M. Mahoney, 'Niceron', in *The Dictionary of Scientific Biography*, 18 vols. (New York, 1970–90). Modern scholars are divided about whether 'Niceron' should be spelt 'Nicéron'; but neither Thuillier nor Jean-Pierre Niceron, who was Jean-François's great-nephew, used the accent.

[39] It is sometimes claimed that he had been taught by Mersenne at Nevers (e.g. in Mersenne, *Correspondance*, X, p. 811 (n.) ); but Mersenne had returned from Nevers to Paris in 1619, when Niceron was only six (see R. Lenoble, *Mersenne ou la naissance du mécanisme* (Paris, 1943), pp. 22–3). For a possible explanation of this confused reference to Nevers, see below, at n. 60.

his cylindrical catoptric–anamorphic portrait of the scholar Jacques d'Auzoles de Lapeyre, reproduced in one of Lapeyre's books published in 1636 and dated by him to 1631.[40] (It has also been suggested that Niceron was the designer of two pictures 'in foreshortening' of Henri IV and Louis XIII, which, according to an early description, had to be seen with the help of 'a little steel tube' to correct the distortion; but the attribution seems chronologically dubious, as the pictures cannot have been made later than 1627, when Niceron was only fourteen.)[41] For most of the 1630s there is no direct evidence of Niceron's activities. But the nature of his intensive studies of mathematics and optics during those years became fully apparent in 1638, when he published his master-work, *La Perspective curieuse*.

This was a treatise specifically devoted to 'curious'—in other words, anamorphic—perspective. In his preface Niceron was unapologetic about his decision to confine himself to such an apparently frivolous area of applied science; he declared that optics provided many very useful things, as well as 'some very pleasant amusements for the satisfaction of the noblest of our senses, the sight'. Such a science, he said, could properly be called 'artificial magic', because it 'produces the most beautiful and admirable effects that can be attained by human art and industry'.[42] The treatise discussed each category of anamorphosis in turn: optic, catoptric, and dioptric. As this progression suggests, the culmination of the whole book was the final section on dioptric anamorphoses (i.e. ones involving the use of refracting lenses); and the highest achievement of human art and industry in this field, therefore, was the elaborate device of which Niceron now gave the first published description.

---

[40] J. d'Auzoles de Lapeyre, *Le Mercure charitable, ou contre-touche et souverain remede pour des-empierrer le R. P. Petau jesuite d'Orleans* (Paris, 1638), p. 73. The inscription on the reverse of this portrait says that Niceron drew it, and had it painted, in 1636 (p. 74); but Lapeyre clearly states that the portrait was made when Niceron was a novice, aged eighteen (p. 72). Presumably the inscription relates to a second version, made for the engraver.

[41] The attribution is made by J. Bousquet, *Recherches sur le séjour des peintres français à Rome au XVIIème siècle* (Montpellier, 1980), p. 141, citing a Barberini inventory of 1631. Bousquet is unaware that this inventory is merely a copy of an earlier list, in which the entry for these paintings is dated Aug. 1627: see M. A. Lavin, *Seventeenth-Century Barberini Documents and Inventories of Art* (New York, 1975), pp. 87 ('in Scorcio', 'con un cannoncino d'acciaro': this probably refers to a cylindrical mirror, in the form of a tube of highly polished metal), 107. However, there is one suggestive detail: these paintings were given to Francesco Barberini by Cardinal Spada (who had been nuncio in France until early 1627). Spada had close connections with the Minims, and later became the protector of the order. I am very grateful to Dr Michael John Gorman for pointing out to me that four cylindrical anamorphoses are currently displayed in the Palazzo Barberini, Rome. These have been attributed to Niceron, and dated *c*. 1635, because two of them correspond to—or were perhaps simply copied from—illustrations in *La Perspective curieuse*. But they have no original connection with the Barberini family, having been acquired by the Italian Ministry of Education in 1937 (see L. Mochi Onori and R. Vodret Adamo, *La Galleria Nazionale d'Arte Antica: regesto delle didascalie* (Rome, 1989), pp. 112–14).

[42] J.-F. Niceron, *La Perspective curieuse* (Paris, 1638), sigs. e4r ('de tres-agreables divertissemens pour la satisfaction du plus noble de nos sens, qui est la veuë'), e6r ('nous pouvons à bon droict appeller Magie artificielle, celle qui nous produit les plus beaux & admirables effets, où l'art & l'industrie de l'homme puissent arriver').

The key to the whole device was the polygonal or faceted lens in the little optic tube through which the picture was viewed. With the tube held in a fixed position at a short distance from the painted panel, each facet of the lens transmitted to the eye the image contained in a precise portion of the picture—a small trapezoid, lozenge, or other segment, depending on the shape of the facet. These portions of the picture were not contiguous on the picture itself, although they joined up and filled the visual field of the person looking through the lens. The trick, then, was in principle quite simple, though it required precision and some artistic imagination to do it well. First, the contents of those scattered geometrical portions would be painted in, so that when viewed through the lens they composed a unified image of a face; and then each of these dispersed fragments of faces on the panel would be completed, so that the picture itself consisted of a number of separate and whole faces. A clever artist could make each of these faces as different as possible from the master-face whose fragments were dispersed among them; this would intensify the astonishment and delight of those who looked first at the picture as a whole, and then at the hidden image revealed by the lens.

The example described by Niceron, and illustrated by him in the plates at the end of the book, was a picture he himself had drawn 'two or three years ago', which was kept in the library of the Minim convent on the Place Royale. The picture was of fifteen (or, in the published illustration, twelve) Ottoman sultans in Turkish dress, each of them modelled on a specific portrait in a published collection of engravings; but, on looking through the tube, the viewer saw a portrait of Louis XIII, dressed 'à la Françoise'. In this way, as Niceron explained, 'most of the emperors in this picture pay him homage, in so far as they each contribute a part of themselves to form his image, as if they were despoiling themselves to honour his triumph'.[43]

Another design, also illustrated in the plates to the book, was of St Peter and thirteen historic Popes, with Christ in the centre of the picture. When the viewer looked through the lens, he saw a portrait of the present Pope, Urban VIII—and, as a nice extra touch, the keys which St Peter was holding in the picture were now transferred miraculously into Urban VIII's own hands. In addition to these actual examples of designs, Niceron's text contained several further suggestions. One could, he wrote, take all the figures of the Old Testament who bear the same (typological) signification, and represent through the lens the thing they all foreshadowed. Or one could portray all the prophets who spoke of the Virgin Mary and the Incarnation, with the Virgin herself as the image seen through the lens. Again, if the portions of the master-image on the picture were too close together to permit whole figures for each of them, one could use fragments of the body,

---

[43] Ibid., p. 115 ('que ie traçay & fis peindre il y a 2 ou 3 ans' . . . 'la plus part de ces Empereurs en ce tableau luy rendent hommage, en sorte qu'ils tribuent chacun quelque partie de soy pour former son image, comme s'ils se despoüilloient euxmesmes pour honorer son triomphe').

illustrating the story of the valley of the dry bones in Ezekiel or the legend of Medea chopping up and magically reconstituting her brother.[44]

As Niceron scrupulously pointed out, he was not himself the inventor of this device. Some people, he said, had made these images before him; the one he singled out was Father du Lieu, a Jesuit in Lyon, who was 'the first person, so far as I know, to have really succeeded at it'.[45] Possibly du Lieu was the person described by a later writer on this device, the Parisian Jesuit Jean du Breuil, who claimed that 'one of our Fathers [i.e. a Jesuit] had the idea for it, and presented the first example to the world', dating the invention to 1628.[46] Details of du Lieu's iconographical designs have (with one likely exception, discussed below) apparently not survived. Various images used with this device were described, however, by later writers. Du Breuil, whose account was first published in 1649, gave an example in which the master-image revealed by the lens was a portrait of the young Louis XIV, while the painting showed cherubs bearing the emblems of rule (crown, scales of justice, and so on), with Louis's parents in the centre.[47] In 1650 the mathematician Nicolas Forest Duchesne discussed one recent design, in which the picture showed six planets and the motto 'sole latente patent' ('when the sun is hidden, they appear'), while the image seen through the lens was of the sun (anthropomorphized as Apollo), with the motto 'sole patente latent' ('when the sun appears, they are hidden').[48] And eight years later Gaspar Schott mentioned another such device in the Jesuit college in Rome: the image revealed by the lens was of St Ignatius Loyola, but Schott omitted to describe the picture itself.[49] Surprisingly, in view of the credit given by Niceron to a Lyonnais Jesuit for his prior work on the device, the Jesuit scientific community seems to have been quite slow to take up the idea. While du Breuil stood out as the only Jesuit in France to publish anything (albeit belatedly) on the subject, the two leading Jesuit writers in this field in Italy during the 1640s,

[44] J.-F. Niceron, *La Perspective curieuse* (Paris, 1638), plate 50 (Popes), pp. 118–19 (other examples).
[45] Ibid., p. 101 ('qui y a le premier bien reüssi, que ie sçache').
[46] J. du Breuil, *La Perspective pratique*, 2nd edn, 3 vols. (Paris, 1663–9), III, sigs. Zz1v ('Un de nos Peres l'a conceuë, & mis au monde le premier'), Zz2r (1628).
[47] Ibid., III, pp. 161–2. Three other designs are mentioned by du Breuil. One has the Host surrounded by angels as the painting and the infant Jesus as the master-image; another has St Martin giving away half his cloak in the painting and Christ and angels returning the half-cloak to him on his deathbed as the master-image; the third has the heads of cherubs as the painting, and portraits of four Jesuit saints as the master-image (pp. 162, 165).
[48] N. Forest Duchesne, *Florilegium universale liberalium artium et scientiarum* (Paris, 1650), p. 226.
[49] G. Schott, *Magia universalis naturae et artis*, 4 vols. (Würzburg, 1657–9), I, p. 471. Three more pictures used with this device are shown in 17th-century engravings. Two were kept in the abbey of Sainte-Geneviève, Paris, and are shown in plate 7 of C. du Molinet, *Le Cabinet de la bibliothèque de Sainte Genevieve* (Paris, 1692): one of these has winged angels and other figures on clouds, while the other has figures in various positions, with what may be smoke rising in the background. The pictures thus probably depicted heaven and hell, though these engravings do not of course reveal the master-images they contained. The third, which may be fictional or may represent an existing device, appears in the famous engraving by Sébastien Leclerc of 1698, 'L'Académie des sciences et des beaux arts' (reproduced in Baltrušaitis, *Anamorphic Art*, p. 111, and on the cover of Bredekamp, *Lure of Antiquity*); it depicts a mass of *putti* swirling around a central portrait, possibly of Christ, but again the master-image is not shown.

Mario Bettini in Bologna and Athanasius Kircher in Rome, made no reference to the device, and treated polygonal lenses only as means for the projection of patterns of light.[50]

This is all the more surprising in view of Niceron's many Italian contacts during the years immediately following the publication of his book. In 1639 he moved to the Minim convent of Santa Trinità dei Monti in Rome, which was the order's other leading centre of intellectual life and scientific research. There he became a close friend of Emmanuel Maignan, who, among his other interests, was an enthusiast for anamorphic art. Maignan had recently painted a huge elongated anamorphic picture along the wall of the gallery above the cloister, representing the order's patron saint, Francis of Paola; Niceron matched it with a similar portrait of St John the Evangelist on the other side of the gallery.[51] Although Maignan was already embroiled in some bitter disputes over priority and plagiarism with Athanasius Kircher, Niceron appears to have had more friendly contact with the Jesuit scientist, contributing his own observations on the declination of the magnetic needle to Kircher's work on magnetism, published in 1641.[52] He also cultivated the acquaintance of Italian mathematicians and researchers such as Bonaventura Cavalieri and Giovanni Battista Doni, becoming an intermediary between them and mathematicians in France; and he was befriended in Rome by the sceptic, polymath, and bibliomane Gabriel Naudé.[53]

Niceron returned to Paris in the spring of 1640 and remained there for the rest of the year. It was probably during this period that he painted another huge anamorphic portrait of St John in the Place Royale convent, and sketched the outline (later completed by Maignan) of a matching wall-painting of St Mary Magdalene. (There are admiring descriptions of these in later accounts of the convent; but no trace of them survives, as the building was turned into a barracks in 1790 and later demolished.[54]) He also prepared an adapted translation of an Italian work on cryptography, which he published in 1641 with a dedicatory epistle

---

[50] M. Bettini, *Apiaria universae philosophiae mathematicae*, 2 vols. (Bologna, 1642), I, pp. 33–4; A. Kircher, *Ars magna lucis et umbrae* (Rome, 1646), p. 818.

[51] The fullest account, based on a manuscript history of the convent, is in Ceñal, 'Emmanuel Maignan: su vida', p. 116. For Maignan's diagram of how his painting was executed, see his *Perspectiva horaria sive de horographia gnomonica* (Rome, 1648), plate between pp. 438 and 439. Maignan's painting survives (but is not accessible to the public); for photographs see Baltrušaitis, *Anamorphic Art*, pp. 52–3.

[52] J. Saguens, *De vita, moribus, et scriptis R. P. Emanuelis Maignani tolosatis ordinis Minimorum* (n.p., 1703), p. 10 (Maignan's dispute); A. Kircher, *Magnes sive de arte magnetica libri tres* (Rome, 1641), pp. 453–4 (Niceron observations). One friendly but brief letter from Niceron to Kircher survives, sent from Lyon in May 1640: Pontificia Università Gregoriana, Rome, MS 557, fol. 383 (as cited by J. Fletcher, 'Athanasius Kircher and his correspondence', in J. Fletcher, ed., *Athanasius Kircher und seine Beziehungen zum gelehrten Europa seiner Zeit* (Wiesbaden, 1988), pp. 139–78; here pp. 144, 148).

[53] Mersenne, *Correspondance*, IX, pp. 116, 218; X, pp. 67, 162; P. Wolfe, ed., *Lettres de Gabriel Naudé à Jacques Dupuy (1632–1652)* (Edmonton, 1982), pp. 93, 95.

[54] See C. Le Maire, *Paris ancien et nouveau*, 3 vols. (Paris, 1685), II, pp. 173–4; A. N. Dézallier d'Argenville, *Voyage pittoresque de Paris*, 4th edn (Paris, 1765), p. 266.

## ASPECTS OF HOBBES

addressed to Louis Hesselin, the powerful courtier who would later become the French equivalent of 'Master of the Revels' to the young Louis XIV. Niceron thanked Hesselin for 'so many personal favours', and expressed the hope that the book would be placed in Hesselin's 'cabinet' along with all his other 'rare curiosities'.[55] Niceron had already praised Hesselin's collection of elaborate mirrors and other rarities in *La Perspective curieuse*. Hesselin would become famous for the extraordinary optical illusions used in entertainments at his own house; it seems very likely, therefore, that Niceron was involved in some of his early experiments in this field.[56]

In the spring of 1641 Niceron returned to Rome; he remained in Italy until the summer of 1642, making at least one prolonged visit (probably on his return journey to France) to the court of Ferdinando de' Medici in Florence and developing a friendship with the Florentine scientist Torricelli.[57] It was during his stay in Florence, apparently, that he constructed the one example of the dioptric–anamorphic device that survived intact until very recently: the painting can still be seen in the Museo di Storia della Scienza in Florence, but the optic tube was unfortunately washed away in the flood of 1966.[58] The picture was an adaptation of Niceron's famous 'Ottoman sultans' design, depicting five Ottoman heads and a large central trophy of captured arms and banners, with the motto 'spolia ampla reportat' ('he brings back great spoils'); and the master-image seen through the lens was a portrait of Ferdinando II. A longer inscription on the base of the device referred to Ferdinando's naval victories over the Turks in the Mediterranean, and appended Niceron's name and the date, 1642.[59]

[55] J.-F. Niceron ['F.I.F.N.P.M.'], *L'Interpretation des chiffres, ou reigle pour bien entendre & expliquer facilement toutes sortes de chiffres simples, tirée de l'italien du S<sup>r</sup> Ant. Maria Cospi* (Paris, 1641), sigs. a4v–a5r ('tant de caresses particulieres'), a5v ('rares curiositez'). The connection between cryptography and anamorphic art is not made here, but had already been explicitly drawn by Accolti, who wrote that he had used anamorphic techniques to encrypt diagrams of fortresses drawn while visiting foreign countries: *Lo inganno de gl'occhi*, pp. 48–9. One definite example (from the following century) of a portrait being 'encrypted' by anamorphosis is known to me: the cylindrical–catoptric anamorphosis of Charles Edward Stuart (Bonnie Prince Charlie) which belonged to a Jacobite family in Scotland and is now in the West Highland Museum, Fort William.

[56] For a dazzling account of the illusions created at Hesselin's entertainment of Queen Christina in 1656, see N. L'Escalopier, *Relation de ce qui s'est passé à l'arrivée de la Reine Christine de Suède, a Essaune en la Maison de Monsieur Hesselin* (Paris, 1656), pp. 4–5. On Hesselin's house and its collection see A. Schnapper, *Curieux du grand siècle: collections et collectionneurs dans la France du XVIIe siècle* (Paris, 1994), pp. 182–6.

[57] Mersenne, *Correspondance*, X, p. 519; P. Galluzzi and M. Torrini, eds., *Le opere dei discepoli di Galileo Galilei: carteggio 1642–1648*, I (Florence, 1975), pp. 50–1, 61, 72. The date of his return to Paris (24 June 1642) is supplied by a letter from Naudé to Cardinal Francesco Barberini, written three days later: Biblioteca Apostolica Vaticana, Vatican City, MS Cod. Barb. Lat. 6471, fol. 34r.

[58] The painting is on public display, but unfortunately the Museum does not possess any photographic record of the image seen through the lens. For a photograph of the complete device (in its ante-diluvian state), and the text of the inscription, see M. L. Bonelli, 'Una lettera di Evangelista Torricelli a Jean François Niceron', in *Convegno di studi Torricelliani in occasione del 350o anniversario della nascita di Evangelista Torricelli (19–20 ottobre 1958)* (Faenza, 1959), pp. 37–41; here p. 38.

[59] Baltrušaitis mis-dates the device to 1635, and constructs a false chronology of Niceron's visits to Italy on that basis: *Anamorphic Art*, pp. 37, 61–2, 174(n.). Tuscany maintained its own order of naval 'knights' to

– 216 –

Once back in Paris, Niceron was given little chance to pursue his scientific interests: first he was ordered to complete his studies in theology, then he was put in charge of the Minim convent at Nevers, and then, after less than a year, he was appointed assistant to the Visitor-General of the order, Mersenne's scholarly friend François de La Noue. This plunged him into an almost ceaseless round of travels through France and Catalonia; he was trying, all the while, to prepare a revised and enlarged Latin version of his *La Perspective curieuse*, but although he estimated that it needed only four or five months' work, he was able to complete only the revision of the first half of the book (excluding, therefore, the account of the dioptric device).[60] That part was published (under the title *Thaumaturgus opticus* and with a dedicatory epistle addressed to Cardinal Mazarin, the patron of Naudé) by the beginning of July 1646; but within three months Niceron died of a fever at Aix-en-Provence.[61] Whatever revisions he had planned to make to the second half of the book would never see the light of day. A second edition of the entire text of *La Perspective curieuse* was issued, together with a treatise on optics and catoptrics by Mersenne, in 1652: the changes made to Niceron's text here were mainly stylistic ones, and were the responsibility of the editor of this volume, the mathematician (and friend of Hobbes) Gilles Personne de Roberval.[62]

## IV

From these biographical details some conclusions can be drawn—and supplemented by further evidence—about the actual dioptric devices seen in Paris by Hobbes and Fanshawe. Although Hobbes does not describe the specific image conveyed by the device he and Davenant had seen, we can be sure that Hobbes himself must have been very familiar with Niceron's own device, depicting fifteen Ottoman sultans and Louis XIII. This was exhibited in the library of the Minim convent on the Place Royale, where Hobbes came frequently to visit his friend Marin Mersenne. It was not the only optical curiosity displayed there: Niceron himself mentioned that several of his cylindrical anamorphoses were kept in the

---

pursue Barbary corsairs and Ottoman ships; their most recent triumph was the capture of a large Ottoman fighting vessel in 1635 (G. G. Guarnieri, *Cavalieri di Santo Stefano: contributo alla storia della marina militare italiana (1562–1859)* (Pisa, 1928), p. 238). Possibly Niceron's device was inspired by Ferdinando's gift of a new galley to replace the lost flagship of the other leading naval order, the Knights of Malta, in the spring of 1642 (R. C. Anderson, *Naval Wars in the Levant 1559–1853* (Liverpool, 1952), p. 118).

[60] The foregoing biographical details are from Niceron's letter to Naudé of 15 May 1645, in F. Liceti, *De quaesitis per epistolas a claris viris responsa*, 7 vols. (Bologna and Udine, 1640–50), III, pp. 225–8. This important autobiographical source was apparently unknown to the editors of the Mersenne *Correspondance* (and to Michael Mahoney when preparing his *DSB* entry), who describe Niceron as auxiliary visitor from 1640. Several of the other details of Niceron's movements given in the notes to the Mersenne *Correspondance*, and by Mahoney, are incorrect.

[61] Mersenne, *Correspondance*, XIV, pp. 317, 560.

[62] See R. Lenoble, 'Roberval "éditeur" de Mersenne et du P. Niceron', *Revue d'histoire des sciences et de leurs applications*, 10 (1957), pp. 235–54.

library, and when the Tuscan envoy Rucellai visited the convent in 1643 he was duly taken to the library and shown 'some curiosities of perspective by Father Jean-François Niceron'.[63]

Hobbes's contacts with Mersenne were particularly intensive during the period 1641–4, when Mersenne encouraged him to write his *Objections* to Descartes (1641), organized the printing and distribution of his *De cive* (1642), made a careful study of his refutation of Thomas White (1642–3), and included materials by Hobbes in the two compilations he published in 1644. For one of these, *Cogitata physico-mathematica*, the General of the Minims stipulated that the whole work be read through by the Visitor, de La Noue, and his auxiliary, Niceron.[64] So, as it happens, we can be certain that Niceron had read at least some of Hobbes's writings. Hobbes, in turn, would refer to Niceron in one of his later works, mentioning the huge anamorphic wall-painting of St John at the Minim convent.[65] He may well have made Niceron's acquaintance soon after this was painted, before the friar's second trip to Italy in the spring of 1641. Of all the sciences, optics was the one that most strongly engaged Hobbes's attention, because of its implications for epistemology; we can be certain, therefore, that he would have taken an interest in Niceron's work, and that, whatever other examples he may have encountered, the dioptric–anamorphic device with which he was most familiar was the one Niceron himself had made.

Fanshawe, on the other hand, specifically describes an example belonging to the Chancellor of France, Pierre Séguier, which was kept in the Chancellor's 'cabinet'. Much of the evidence presented above must make it unlikely that Niceron was the creator of this particular device. His own leading patron was Hesselin, and by the end of his life he had set his sights on Mazarin; but Séguier does not feature anywhere in the surviving evidence of Niceron's activities. (The existence of a specially bound copy of the first edition of *La Perspective curieuse*, stamped with Séguier's arms, does not imply any personal contact between them: the Chancellor was the supervisory authority for all cultural activities, including bookselling, and Séguier's huge library received such works automatically from the printers.[66])

The creation of Séguier's device, which depicted a 'multitude' of his 'famous Ancestors', can be dated with reasonable certainty to the period 1642–6. Fanshawe must have seen it on the brief visit he made to Paris in the final months of

---

[63] Niceron, *La Perspective curieuse*, p. 87; G. Temple-Leader and G. Marcotti, eds., *Un' ambasciata: diario dell'abate G. Fr.º Rucellai* (Florence, 1884), p. 218 ('alcune curiosità di prospettiva').

[64] Mersenne, *Correspondance*, XIII, p. 45 (n.).

[65] T. Hobbes, *Opera philosophica quae latine scripsit omnia*, ed. W. Molesworth, 5 vols. (London, 1839–45), II, p. 39 (*De homine*, IV. 12).

[66] The copy is in the Bibliothèque Nationale, Paris (hereafter: BN), pressmark Rés. V. 171; it does not contain any inscription from the author. The 'Privilège du roy' printed at the end of the book (p. 122) specifically required the printers to deposit one copy at Séguier's library. On the Chancellor's powers over cultural life see R. Mousnier, ed., *Lettres et mémoires addressées au Chancelier Séguier (1633–1649)*, 2 vols. (Paris, 1964), I, p. 25.

1646.[67] As for the *terminus a quo*, the artist must surely have been drawing on information contained in a somewhat pompous genealogy of Séguier published in 1642.[68] (Séguier's origins were in fact quite humble: his grandfather was a prosecutor or magistrate, and an ancestor at the beginning of the sixteenth century had been a grocer. But he was a notoriously vain man, 'of all people in the world', as Tallemant des Réaux put it, 'the most avid for praise'.[69]) As we have seen, the years 1642–6 were precisely the period in which Niceron was kept so busy by the requirements of his superiors that he could not find the time to complete even the one task that mattered most to him, the translation and full revision of his book. It is possible, of course, that he might have had some indirect contact with Séguier through the painter Simon Vouet, whose own early picture of an anamorphosis has already been mentioned: Vouet carried out important commissions at both Séguier's house and the Minim convent, and designed the engraved title page of Niceron's *Thaumaturgus opticus*. But most of Vouet's work for Séguier seems to have been completed well before 1642, and more direct evidence of friendship between Vouet and Niceron is lacking.[70]

The device made for the Chancellor is not extant, and the inventories of Séguier's possessions, which sometimes attribute works to particular artists, do not make any specific mention of it either.[71] Yet enough evidence has survived to suggest a plausible candidate for the maker of this particular device: the Jesuit from Lyon, Father du Lieu, whom Niceron himself credited as the first person to have produced a truly successful version. Charles du Lieu (1609–78) had entered the Society of Jesus in 1622 and taught for several years at Vienna before returning to his home town, Lyon, where he lectured at the Jesuit College.[72] This was an

---

[67] See H. C. Fanshawe, *The History of the Fanshawe Family* (Newcastle-upon-Tyne, 1927), pp. 143–4; W. E. Simeone, 'Sir Richard Fanshawe: An Account of his Life and Writings', Ph.D. dissertation, University of Pennsylvania, 1950, p. 59.

[68] Mousnier refers to this work, published by the bookseller Rocolet (*Lettres et mémoires*, I, p. 26), but I have not been able to locate a copy of it.

[69] Ibid., I, p. 27 (grocer); G. Tallemant des Réaux, *Historiettes*, ed. A. Adam, 2 vols. (Paris, 1960), I, p. 611 (grandfather, quotation: 'l'homme du monde le plus avide pour de loüanges'). For telling descriptions of Séguier showing off his possessions and boasting about his income, see M. Chéruel (ed.), *Journal d'Olivier Lefèvre d'Ormesson et extraits des mémoires d'André Lefèvre d'Ormesson*, 2 vols. (Paris, 1860–1), I, pp. 172, 403.

[70] See Crelly, *The Painting of Vouet*, pp. 16–17(n.), 112–20. Crelly suggests that Vouet may also have designed the engraved title page of the first edition of Niceron's book in 1638 (p. 16(n.) ), but this is denied in a more recent study of Vouet engravings: M. Grivel, 'Excudit et privilèges: les éditeurs de Simon Vouet', in S. Loire (ed.), *Simon Vouet: actes du colloque international, Galeries nationales du Grand Palais, 5–6–7 février 1991* (Paris, 1992), pp. 307–29; here p. 322. Most of Vouet's work in the Hôtel Séguier was carried out in 1636: see R. Kerviler, *Le Chancelier Pierre Séguier* (Paris, 1874), p. 79.

[71] There are two probate inventories, one compiled after Séguier's death, the other after that of his widow: Archives Nationales, Paris, Minutier Central, ET/XLV/232 (1672); ET/LI/435 (22 Feb. 1683). Possibly the picture of Séguier's ancestors was included among the 'ninety-two paintings' ('Quatre Vingt douze tableaux') summarily referred to in the former (fol. 4v), or the 'two pictures representing twenty portraits in miniature' ('deux tableaux representant Vingt portraicts en mignatures') mentioned in the latter (fol. 47).

[72] C. Sommervogel (ed.), *Bibliothèque de la Compagnie de Jésus: première partie, Bibliographie*, 2nd edn, 10 vols. (Brussels, 1890–1909), IV, col. 1825.

important institution, with a well stocked library and an 'observatory' of which one later account tantalizingly states: 'The observatory is filled with a large number of mathematical instruments, and a considerable amount of rarities.'[73] Du Lieu published nothing, unfortunately, apart from a commendatory poem for his colleague Théophile Raynaud, and the nature of his scientific interests can be pieced together only from a few fragmentary references. Athanasius Kircher mentioned a recent visit to Rome by du Lieu in the third edition of his *Magnes* (1654), describing him as 'extremely learned in mathematics' and referring to a famously large magnet in du Lieu's possession.[74] Eleven years earlier, in October 1643, one of Mersenne's correspondents in Grenoble described a recent meeting with du Lieu at which the same giant magnet was discussed: du Lieu declared that he had demonstrated its powers in front of the Chancellor himself, and that he had 'carried out experiments in the presence of the Chancellor'. Significantly, he also added that du Lieu had 'a large number of propositions about catoptrics, not yet published, and that is the science in which he excels'.[75]

Chancellor Séguier had evidently gone out of his way to encourage du Lieu to pursue his optical researches. On 8 December 1643 the Jesuit wrote to Séguier from Lyon, apologizing for his long delay 'in carrying out your orders for the treatise on the modification of intentional species [i.e. visual images]'. He also referred to this work as a 'treatise on dioptrics', and explained that he had had to engage in a 'considerable number of experiments'.[76] Together with this letter came one from du Lieu's brother, Jean-Baptiste, enclosing some of Charles's writings on mathematics and begging for Séguier's patronage too.[77] Jean-Baptiste had inherited from their father the important position of 'Maître des Courriers' of Lyon and Montpellier, a lucrative job which covered not only the local posts but also all international mail between France and Italy.[78] The reason for the du Lieu brothers' assiduous cultivation of Séguier becomes clear in their subsequent letters to him in 1644 and 1645: the 'Général des Postes' was trying to oust Jean-Baptiste from his job, and he

---

[73] D. de Colonia, *Histoire littéraire de la ville de Lyon, avec une bibliothèque des auteurs lyonnais*, 2 vols. (Lyon, 1728–30), II, pp. 757–67 (library), 776 ('L'Observatoire est rempli d'un grand nombre d'instrumens de Mathématique, & de quantité de raretez').

[74] Raynaud, *Opera omnia*, V, sig. e2v; Kircher, *Magnes* (1654), p. 373 ('doctissimus in Mathematicis'). This magnet is also described in G. Fournier, *Hydrographie, contenant la théorie et la pratique de toutes les parties de la navigation*, 2nd edn (Paris, 1667), p. 407.

[75] Mersenne, *Correspondance*, XII, pp. 338–9 (Jacques de Valois to Mersenne, 11 Oct. 1643): 'Il a fait des experiences en la presence de M. le Chancellier . . . un grand nombre de propositions de la Catoptrique, et c'est en cette science là qu'il excelle.' Another of Mersenne's informants described du Lieu as a specialist in optics and mechanics: ibid., p. 372.

[76] BN MS f.fr. 17375, fols. 122r ('l'execution de ses Commandements po$^r$ le traitté de la modification des Especes intentionelles'), 122v ('raisonnement de Dioptrique . . . quantité d'experiences').

[77] Ibid., fols. 126–7. Jean-Baptiste du Lieu apparently had some intellectual interests of his own: he was a close friend of the Parisian scholar Jacques Dupuy (see J. A. H. Bots, ed., *Correspondance de Jacques Dupuy et de Nicolas Heinsius (1646–1656)* (The Hague, 1971), p. 91).

[78] E. Vaillé, *Histoire générale des postes françaises*, 6 vols. (Paris, 1947–53), III, pp. 299, 309.

desperately needed Séguier's protection. This was apparently granted; a letter from Charles du Lieu of 23 June 1645 gives the Chancellor heartfelt thanks for his intervention, and promises to pray for him constantly.[79] Jean-Baptiste had a more practical way of showing his gratitude: he offered to send Séguier regular summaries of the intelligence he gathered out of the mail he received from Italy. By 1647 he was sending these every week; some of the surviving summaries from the following year are in the hand of his brother, the Jesuit, which shows what a joint effort this determined cultivation of Séguier had been.[80]

Against this background, it is reasonable to assume that the dioptric device glorifying Séguier and his ancestors was made by Charles du Lieu, probably in 1644 or 1645, either as part of the campaign to get Séguier's protection for his brother, or as a thanks-offering once that had been granted. And if this device was not made by Niceron, then it must appear much less likely that Hobbes (who can be linked quite closely to Niceron, but had no known connection with du Lieu) had seen it. It is possible, of course, that some intermediary might have gained permission for Hobbes to look at it in Séguier's 'cabinet': Hobbes's old friend du Bosc, who was also supplying intelligence to Séguier, might have done this, or his newer acquaintance La Mothe le Vayer (a member of the Académie, which met in Séguier's house).[81] But such favours are less likely to have been arranged for Davenant too; and if Hobbes was perfectly familiar with the device in the Minim convent, another such device cannot have held any new or special interest for him.

The most reasonable conclusion, then, is that Hobbes and Fanshawe had seen two different devices, one by the Minim Niceron, the other by the Jesuit du Lieu. The one seen by Hobbes had an explicitly political iconography, involving the submission of the Ottoman Empire to the King of France. The one seen by Fanshawe was not in itself political; but no reader of Hobbes who turns to Fanshawe's dedicatory epistle to Prince Charles can fail to be struck by the passage in which Fanshawe himself draws a political allegory out of the picture, describing it in terms uncannily reminiscent of the iconography of the *Leviathan* title page. Prince Charles had himself been receiving mathematics lessons from Hobbes in 1646–7; if he read Fanshawe's epistle, he might well have discussed the optical phenomenon itself (as well as Fanshawe's description) with Hobbes, in whose particular field of expertise such matters were known to lie.[82] Hobbes, in any case, could have met

---

[79] BN MSS f.fr. 17378, fols. 126–7 (Charles, 20 June 1644); f.fr. 17384, fols. 93 (Jean-Baptiste, 13 June 1645), 118–19 (Jean-Baptiste, 23 June 1645), 120–1 (Charles, 23 June 1645).

[80] BN MSS f.fr. 17379, fols. 175–6 (Jean-Baptiste, 1 July 1644); f.fr. 17386, fols. 116–17 (Jean-Baptiste, 25 Feb. 1646); f.fr. 17387, fols. 142–3 (Jean-Baptiste, 25 Oct. 1647); f.fr. 17388, fols. 106, 129, 152, 249–50 (summaries unsigned but in Charles's hand, 22 June, 30 June, 6 July, 20 July 1648).

[81] On du Bosc see T. Hobbes, *Correspondence*, ed. N. Malcolm, 2 vols. (= The Clarendon Edition of the Works of Hobbes, vols. VI, VII) (Oxford, 1994), II, pp. 795–7. La Mothe le Vayer became a member of the Académie in 1639 (Kerviler, *Le Chancelier*, p. 515).

[82] On the tuition see Hobbes, *Correspondence*, I, pp. 136–7, 155–9.

Fanshawe through mutual friends such as John Evelyn.[83] Or, indeed, he may simply have read Fanshawe's translation of Guarini for his own pleasure: his intellectual interests were certainly not confined to politics, mathematics, and optics—as his discussion of the nature and function of poetry in his 'Answer' to Davenant shows. The introduction into that quasi-prefatory work by Hobbes of an elaborate comparison based on the dioptric device is itself strikingly reminiscent of the similar comparison in Fanshawe's dedicatory epistle; the most natural conclusion must surely be that Hobbes was prompted here, consciously or subliminally, by his own earlier reading of Fanshawe. In other words, Hobbes's ideas about this device probably arose in two ways: directly, from his own knowledge of the device by Niceron which he had seen, and indirectly, from the device by du Lieu which he may not have seen, but of which he had probably read Fanshawe's heavily allegorized description.

## V

What implications, then, can be drawn from the details of this device assembled above, for the interpretation of Hobbes's title page? The specific designs mentioned by Niceron and other writers give us some clue, to begin with, about how people understood the iconographical potential of the device. Of those various designs, only one (that of the sun and the planets) plays on the idea of alternation—of what is absent in one image being present in the other, and vice-versa. Most of the others make use of the concept of multiple objects in the painting contributing to, or culminating in, a single image in the lens. Thus, we have sultans contributing parts of themselves, and thereby indicating their submission, to the French king; ancestors combining their virtues in their glorious descendant; attributes of rule, and the virtues of the parents, coming together in the person of the young Louis XIV; an historical tradition of popes culminating in the present one; Old Testament prophets joining to form the common object of their prophecy; Old Testament ante-types combining in the 'type' they all foreshadow; or, more simply, dry bones or dismembered limbs being reunited in living bodies. The multiple objects are subordinate to the single image, and gain their real meaning by being subsumed under it ('which great one', as Fanshawe put it, '... was first and chiefest in the Painters designe, and *that* for which all the rest were made'). And yet at the same time there is a simple sense in which the multiple images are more real: they physically exist, as paint-marks on a panel or canvas, whereas the master-image itself is only an image, a visual construct. They, in other words, are natural bodies, while it is an artificial one.

[83] See J. Evelyn, *Diary*, ed. E. S. de Beer, 6 vols. (Oxford, 1955), III, pp. 19 (visit from Fanshawe, 24 Sept. 1650), 41 (visit to Hobbes, 7 Sept. 1651). Fanshawe was also a close acquaintance of Hobbes's old friend Edward Hyde.

It is not hard to see, therefore, why the iconographical and conceptual implications of this device should have struck Hobbes as so richly appropriate to the argument of *Leviathan*. The most important way in which that book went beyond the theories of its predecessors, *The Elements of Law* and *De cive*, was in its development of two related concepts: representation and the person. Persons are either natural or artificial; an artificial person represents—i.e. 'bears the person of'—someone or something other than itself. When the natural persons who are represented 'own' the actions of their representative, they are the authors of the representative's actions and he (or it) is the actor to whom (or to which) their authority is given. The key terms here are all explicitly linked by Hobbes to their more literal meanings in the theatre: 'So that a *Person*, is the same that an *Actor* is, both on the Stage and in common Conversation; and to *Personate*, is to *Act*, or *Represent* himselfe, or an other; and he that acteth another, is said to beare his Person, or act in his name.'[84]

In Hobbes's political theory, the actor is the individual or assembly that exercises sovereignty. The sovereign 'bears the person' of the people: he or it represents them, not as a mere aggregate of individuals, but as a corporate entity. The key point for Hobbes is that the people as a whole can become a corporate entity only in so far as they are represented by a sovereign; in other words, he is ruling out the idea of a two-phase process, in which the people first come together and form an entity, and then decide, as an entity, to transfer authority to something outside themselves (a sovereign). Rather, the only way in which they can become such a corporate entity in the first place is by being represented by a sovereign. 'A Multitude of men, are made *One* Person, when they are by one man, or one Person, Represented . . . For it is the *Unity* of the Representer, not the *Unity* of the Represented, that maketh the Person *One*.'[85] (If the objection is made that the two-phase process is not only conceivable but an everyday occurrence, because it is what happens whenever a group of people form an association and that association then appoints an attorney to act on its behalf, Hobbes's reply is that such things are possible within the framework of laws provided by the commonwealth, but he is talking about the formation of the commonwealth itself.) In forming an entity which exists by means of its being represented by an 'artificial person', all the individuals involved have become subordinate parts of something greater than themselves. But at the same time it exists only because they will it to do so; they are natural and real, while it is artificial.

To find an appropriate way of presenting this theory in visual terms would have been hard enough, even if there had been a wide repertoire of symbolic images of the relationship between subjects and states to choose from. But, while the

---

[84] T. Hobbes, *Leviathan* (London, 1651), p. 80. (The page-numbers of this edition, the first of the three '1651' editions, can be found also in the texts of *Leviathan* edited by W. G. Pogson Smith (Oxford, 1909), C. B. Macpherson (Harmondsworth, 1968) and R. Tuck (Cambridge, 1991).)

[85] Hobbes, *Leviathan*, p. 82.

iconography of rulers was quite plentifully endowed—they could be depicted as classical deities or heroes, emblematic objects such as suns, and so on—the iconography of the relationship between sovereign, state, and people was extremely meagre. Almost the only standard visual image in this category was the 'Hercules gallicus', which depicted a large figure (Hercules, signifying the ruler, or in some versions the orator) controlling a multitude of smaller ones (the subjects, or the audience) by a skein of fine chains proceeding from his mouth to each of the smaller figures' ears.[86] This image, called 'gallicus' because it came from a description by Lucian of a picture of Hercules at Marseilles, had been added to the French edition of Alciati's emblem-book in 1549 as a way of honouring François I, and had become particularly popular in France.[87] Hobbes may well have seen representations of it there; he himself uses it in *Leviathan* to describe the 'Artificiall Chains' of civil laws, which proceed from the sovereign's mouth to the ears of every subject.[88] But the symbolism here was both too mechanical and too unidirectional to convey Hobbes's more complex general theory about the way in which the sovereign not only controls the people, but 'bears the person' of their collective identity.

The common literary trope which compared the state to a body (the 'body politic'), and therefore compared subjects to the various limbs or organs of that body, had seldom been presented visually.[89] If such a presentation were to be attempted, the result would be something akin to Arcimboldo's composite figures; and some commentators have indeed made comparisons between the *Leviathan* title page and the works of Arcimboldo.[90] Such an interpretation can easily be buttressed by the many passages in Hobbes's text in which he keeps returning to a comparison between the commonwealth and a 'Body naturall', with the 'Systemes' (i.e. businesses and other associations) of the commonwealth being described as its muscles, unlawful associations as 'Wens, Biles, and Apostemes' and colonies as its 'Procreation, or Children'.[91] The most concentrated example of such functional analogy-mongering comes in the 'Introduction' to the book, where Hobbes enumerates the features of his 'Artificiall Man': 'The *Magistrates*, and other *Officers* of Judicature and Execution, artificiall *Joynts*; *Reward* and *Punishment*... are the *Nerves*... *Counsellors*... are the *Memory*', and so on.[92]

---

[86] For a valuable discussion, noting the use made of this image by Renaissance rhetoricians, see Skinner, *Reason and Rhetoric*, pp. 92–3.

[87] See F. Bardon, *Le Portrait mythologique à la cour de France sous Henri IV et Louis XIII: mythologie et politique* (Paris, 1974), p. 49.

[88] Hobbes, *Leviathan*, pp. 108–9.

[89] On the trope itself see E. Kantorowicz, *The King's Two Bodies: A Study in Mediaeval Political Theory* (Princeton, NJ, 1957), pp. 207–32, and P. Archambault, 'The analogy of the "body" in renaissance political literature', *Bibliothèque d'humanisme et renaissance*, 29 (1967), pp. 21–53. One classic English text was based entirely on this trope: E. Forset, *A Comparative Discourse of the Bodies Natural and Politique* (London, 1606).

[90] E.g. Brandt, 'Das Titelblatt', p. 204.   [91] Hobbes, *Leviathan*, pp. 115, 123, 131.

[92] Ibid., p. 1.

But it is important to note that this very traditional type of allegorical description of the body politic (a kind of allegorizing-by-function to which Hobbes's use of the 'Hercules gallicus' trope also belongs) is not what is represented in the *Leviathan* title page—above all, not in the original drawing. If such functional allegorizing were the basis of the design, then the image of the colossus in that picture would need to be more Arcimboldesque in both visual and allegorical terms: that is, it would consist of non-interchangeable component figures having different shapes and performing different functions according to their respective places in the body of the commonwealth (firm but flexible magistrates holding the body together at the joints, stout businessmen swelling out as its muscles, and so on). The interchangeable faces in the title page drawing, however, are not there for any such functional purposes. The only role they perform is the one which they all share: exhibiting a peculiar relationship between multiplicity and unity. This image, in other words, is illustrating not the old, traditional trope of the body politic, but the new and peculiarly Hobbesian theory of a collective unity which exists by virtue of having its 'person' borne by the sovereign.

Which brings us, finally, to a point that may have been at the back of the reader's mind ever since the central claim of this paper was advanced. Why, if the figure in the title page drawing was inspired by Niceron's optical–iconographical device, does it look so different from Niceron's own specimen images? Instead of a neat pattern of isolated portraits (sultans, for example, or popes) we have a jumble of faces packed closely together; and instead of faces combining to form a single face, we appear to have faces forming a face and a body. In practical terms, these differences are not very significant. The neatly separated heads shown by Niceron may have been chosen by him for the design's clarity in illustrating how the trick was done; as he said, the components of the image could be more tightly packed together (as in his Ezekiel and Medea examples), and in some ways the trick would be enhanced if the painting were filled up with what might be called 'decoy' components, not contributing to the master-image.[93] As for whether faces turned into an image of a face, or of something else, this was entirely up to the ingenuity of the designer.

But there is a larger theoretical point at issue here—perhaps the most important point of all. What Hobbes is trying to do with the figure in the title page is to perform an impossible task: to show simultaneously, in the same picture, both the painting *and* the master-image that arises out of it. This task, a physical impossibility in the case of the original optical device, is for Hobbes a theoretical necessity. Understanding why this is so important for Hobbes involves looking at his theory of 'representation' in the most general sense—a theory that extends to the

---

[93] Some of the designs depicted in the engravings mentioned above (n. 49) have a much more 'jumbled' appearance.

science of perspective and the art of metaphor as well as the science and practice of politics.

Hobbes's main discussion of perspective comes in part 2, chapter 3 of the English optical treatise which he wrote in Paris in 1645–6. Part 2 of this treatise was later published in a revised, augmented, and translated form as the first part of *De homine* in 1658. (It was in re-working this chapter on perspective that Hobbes added the brief discussion of anamorphoses which ends with a reference to Niceron's wall-painting.[94]) Hobbes distinguishes between two ways of looking at a picture drawn in perspective: either we see the actual shapes on the canvas (for example, a parallelogram), or we 'see' the things which are represented in the picture (for example, the surface of a rectangular table). In the former case the 'fancy' of the observer is caused by the act of vision; in the latter case it is caused by the observer's memory, which has stored away the appearances of table-tops seen in the past:

> I say y$^e$ Reason why those figures generally haue an apparence [different] from their figures made in y$^e$ playne of perspective is this. That when we haue in memory y$^e$ Originalls w$^{ch}$ they are made to represent, y$^e$ plaine it self is not (to speake properly) seene, butt y$^e$ Originall remembred, and y$^e$ memory thereof mayntained by the proportions of y$^e$ lines drawne . . . So that when wee behold a perspectiue and acknowledge nott anything it represents butt it Selfe, then is y$^e$ fancie of y$^e$ beholder, vision, namely y$^e$ vision of y$^e$ plaine, Butt when wee conceyve by it a Gallery, Landskip or other thing represented by it, then is y$^e$ fancy of the beholder to bee called memorie, though that memorie bee raised and confirmed by the lines drawne on y$^e$ plaine.[95]

The point is made a little more strongly in *De homine*, where Hobbes writes that the people who 'see' the things depicted in such perspectival pictures 'do not see or perceive, properly speaking, the pictures themselves'. To be a good judge of these pictures, therefore, it is necessary to possess not only a well-stocked memory of the appearances of objects (against which the appearances in the painting can be checked), but also an *imaginationem constantem* (this translates 'a steddy fancy' in the manuscript), 'to prevent the ideas of the things previously seen from slipping out of the mind while it contemplates the painted things'.[96] To experience an illusion of representation, therefore, is never to be an entirely passive victim of it: the

---

[94] Hobbes, *OL* II, pp. 29–39 (*De homine*, ch. 4); the discussion of anamorphoses is on p. 39. The manuscript is BL MS Harl. 3360; the revision of this text may have been completed several years before 1658.

[95] BL MS Harl. 3360, fols. 114v–115r. In the first sentence the scribe wrote 'apparente difference'; Hobbes corrected 'apparente' to 'apparence', but forgot, it seems, to correct 'difference' to 'different'.

[96] Hobbes, *OL* II, p. 39 (*De homine*, ch. 4, sect. 11): 'proprie loquendo, non ipsas tabulas vident aut sentiunt'; 'habeatque praeterea imaginationem constantem, ne ideae rerum visarum, dum fictas contemplatur, animo elabantur.' Cf. BL MS Harl. 3360, fol. 115r: 'And hence it is, That to judge of perspectiue, a man has need of Experience in y$^e$ originall appearance of objects and a steddy fancy. . . .'

illusion works by enlisting our cooperation, as we bring to the interpretation of the image the similar images that we already possess. But Hobbes requires us to look at the image in the picture in two different ways at once: as the thing illusorily depicted, and as a shape that needs to be matched against the similar shapes in our memories. In this way we can see the depicted table-top as a table-top, while at the same time knowing that it is only a shape in a picture.

Similar points are made in Hobbes's discussions of both literary metaphor and theatrical representation. Because of his severe warnings against the deceptions of metaphor, Hobbes has often been portrayed as an enemy of metaphor *tout court*. Invariably, the critics who depict him in this way are then quick to convict him of hypocrisy, seizing on the fact that his own prose in *Leviathan* is full of arresting metaphors, as well as other forms of comparison and imagery.[97] But Hobbes was not trying to ban metaphor as such: his warnings were chiefly against those metaphors which conceal the fact that they are metaphors, or which, in circumstances where dispassionate argument is called for (such as a counsellor's advice to a ruler), are used to conceal deficiencies of logic.[98] To employ a metaphor—that is, to represent one thing by another—can, in Hobbes's view, involve the exercise of real cognitive skills, '*Distinguishing*, and *Discerning*, and *Judging* between thing and thing'. And a 'good Fancy', governed by such 'good Judgement', is a 'Vertue', enabling its possessor to 'please, not onely by illustration of his discourse, and adorning it with new and apt metaphors; but also, by the rarity of their invention'.[99] The key point, once again, is that we need to operate at two levels simultaneously: entertaining the image which the metaphor presents, and understanding it as a representation of something else.

Similarly, Hobbes's reference to the story of the theatre at Abdera, where many of the spectators fell into a kind of madness (doing 'nothing but pronounce Iambiques, with the names of *Perseus* and *Andromeda*') as a consequence of the heat and 'the Passion imprinted by the Tragedy', suggests that theatrical representations also require a simultaneous two-level response.[100] If we see the actors only as actors reciting lines, we shall get little benefit, aesthetic or moral, from the play; but if we see them only as the characters they represent, we no longer see the play, *qua* play, at all.

What, then, does this pattern of argument suggest about the way in which we should approach that other 'representative', the sovereign 'actor' who bears the person of the commonwealth? On the one hand, Hobbes's whole theoretical enterprise is an exercise in demystification; like the optical scientists who show that illusions are created by the operation of natural laws, not demons, Hobbes shows

---

[97] For references to several such critics—and a definitive reply to them—see Skinner, *Reason and Rhetoric*, p. 363 (and the discussion on pp. 363–72).
[98] Hobbes, *Leviathan*, pp. 13, 34.   [99] Ibid., p. 33.   [100] Ibid., p. 37.

that the sovereign power exists not as a supernatural entity or sacral authority but as a consequence of the rational acts of will of the people. The opposite pole to 'natural', throughout his argument, is not 'supernatural', but 'artificial'. The science of such artificial political constructions which Hobbes sets out is aimed partly at teaching the bearer—actual or potential—of the sovereignty how the security of the state can be preserved or lost (as Hobbes's gift of the manuscript of *Leviathan* to Charles II clearly shows). But it is not aimed only at informing the ruler: Hobbes believes that the ruled will become better subjects if they too are taught the precepts of this science. Hence his famously modest suggestion that his doctrine be 'profitably printed, and more profitably taught in the Universities'.[101]

And yet, on the other hand, the science of Hobbes's politics itself suggests that the sovereign should not be demystified altogether: opinion of power is power, and the sovereign has to possess such power in order to fulfil his (or its) purpose. Hobbes would be the first to admit that it is utopian to imagine, let alone aim at creating, an entire population of rational political scientists; 'for the Passions of men, are commonly more potent than their Reason'.[102] The sovereign functions as a 'visible Power to keep them in awe', having sufficient 'Power and Strength conferred on him, that by terror thereof, he is inabled to conforme the wills of them all'.[103]

So, although Hobbes's theory instructs the people that the sovereign is merely an artificial person, representing the collective identity of which they are the real constituents, at the same time, it requires them to believe in the 'person' of the commonwealth as something outside them and greater than any of them. In the end, Hobbes's theory requires the simultaneous presence of two different kinds of obedience: rational obedience, by those who understand the logic of their situation as 'authors' of the sovereign authority, and passionate obedience, by those who are in 'awe' or 'terror' of the sovereign's power. These two forms of obedience are not just two different psychological conditions, found contingently in people of different degrees of passion or intelligence. Rather, as Hobbes's whole complex argument about the conditional covenant underlying the institution of sovereignty suggests, they are entirely interdependent: the logic of authorization will come into play only when it implies the existence of a power sufficient to bind the passions. It is a curious structure of argument that requires two different ways of seeing the relation between the individual and the state to be entertained at one and the same time. And it was a 'curious kind of perspective'—the phrase he borrowed from Niceron's *Perspective curieuse*—that gave Hobbes a way of presenting that very argument in a picture.

---

[101] Hobbes, *Leviathan*, p. 395.  [102] Ibid., p. 96.
[103] Ibid., pp. 85, 87–8: 'conforme' here is the corrected text (replacing 'performe') in the large-paper copies (see Richard Tuck's comments in his edn of *Leviathan*, pp. xxx–xxxi).

# THE TITLE PAGE OF *LEVIATHAN*

## ADDITIONAL NOTE

An entry in Samuel Hartlib's diary–notebook for late 1649 raises the intriguing possibility that an example of Niceron's device, used for surreptitious Royalist propagandist purposes, was present in England at that time: 'Dr Charleton showed Mr Haack a very curious Picture on the outside nothing but Charities and Vertues were seene. But looking vpon the said Picture through a little glasse King Charles face appeared' (Hartlib Papers, electronic edition, 'Ephemerides', 1649, part 3: 28/1/30B). This device could have been made in England, following the instructions contained in Niceron's book. But if, like most other known examples, it was made in France, then the possibility must be considered that Walter Charleton may have acquired it from his friend Pierre de Cardonnel, who moved between Paris, Normandy, and London and was zealous in the English Royalist cause (see Chapter 9 below, especially pp. 283–4.)

Fig. 1. *Leviathan*, 1st edition (1651), engraved title page (by permission of the Syndics of Cambridge University Library).

FIG. 2. *Leviathan*, fair-copy manuscript (BL MS Egerton 1910), title page (faint pencil drawing on vellum, attributed to Hollan).

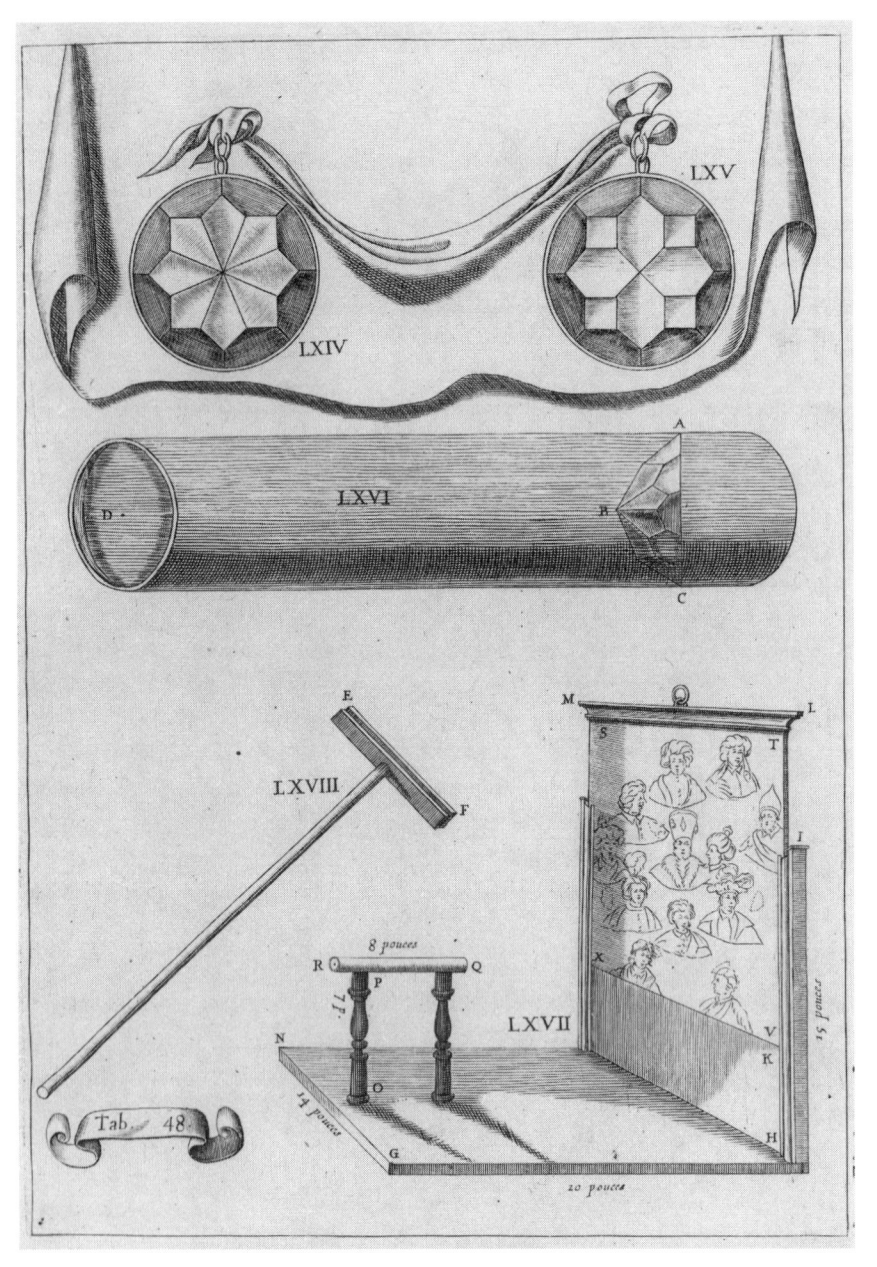

FIG. 3. Niceron, *La Perspective curieuse* (1638), table 48: the optical device, with polygonal lens (and drawing-stick for marking lines while viewing through the lens) (by permission of the Syndics of Cambridge University Library).

FIG. 4. Niceron, *La Perspective curieuse* (1638), table 49: the 'Ottoman sultans' design, showing the segments that form the portrait of Louis XIII when viewed through the lens (by permission of the Syndics of Cambridge University Library).

– 8 –

# Charles Cotton, Translator of Hobbes's *De cive*

I

The English translation of Hobbes's *De cive* was entered in the register of the Stationers' Company by the bookseller Richard Royston on 7 November 1650 under the title *The true citizen or, the Elements of philosophy &c.*[1] At some time during the following four months, the work was printed: Thomason's copy, in the British Library, is marked 'March 12 1650' (that is, 1651).[2] The printed title page bore a long title beginning *Philosophicall Rudiments concerning Government and Society*; it described the work simply as 'By THO: HOBBES'. And in most of the surviving copies of this edition (including Thomason's), the engraved title page bears an almost identical title, *Philosophicall Rudiments concerning Goverment and Civill Society*, and also describes the work as 'By Thomas Hobbes of Malmesbury'. These copies of the book do not contain any reference to a translator; largely by default, therefore, some writers on Hobbes in the past tended to assume that the translation was by Hobbes himself.[3]

Such an assumption was also encouraged by a reading of a passage in Aubrey's 'brief life' of Edmund Waller:

I have heard him [Waller] say, that he so much admired M$^r$ T. Hobbes booke *de Cive* when it came forth, that he was very desirous to haue it donne into English; and M$^r$ Hobbes was most willing it should be donne by M$^r$ Wallers hand, for that he was so great a Master of our English language; M$^r$ Waller freely promised him to doe it, but first he would desire M$^r$ Hobbes to make an essay, & he did the first booke: and did it so extremely well, that M$^r$ Waller would not meddle with it, for that no body els could doe

---

This chapter first appeared in the *Huntington Library Quarterly*, 61, for 1998 (2000), pp. 259–87.

[1] *A Transcript of the Registers of the Worshipful Company of Stationers: from 1640–1708 AD*, 3 vols. (London, 1913–14), I, p. 354. Throughout this paper, I use Old Style for dates but treat the year as beginning on 1 January.

[2] BL, pressmark E 1262.

[3] G. C. Robertson, for example, wrote that 'in 1651 . . . he issued a most vigorous translation of the "De Cive" itself': *Hobbes* (London, 1886), p. 67.

it so well, had he thought, he could have better performed it, he would haue himselfe beene the translator.[4]

All that can be deduced from Aubrey's account, however, is that Waller gave up his project; it does not imply that Hobbes completed the translation.

Clear evidence that Hobbes was not the translator was first presented by the bibliographer H. J. H. Drummond in 1974. He drew attention to the fact that a small number of copies of the translation have an extra gathering of six leaves, inserted into what was otherwise the first gathering of the book, between the signatures A2 (the printed title page) and A3 (the first page of Hobbes's 'Epistle Dedicatory' to the Earl of Devonshire). This inserted gathering contains a dedicatory letter by the translator, signed 'C. C', addressed 'To the honourable and truly virtuous, the Lady fane, Widdow to Sir george fane, Brother to the Earl of Westmerland of blessed memory', as well as a page of errata headed 'faults escaped'. The copies that have this extra gathering also have a slightly different version of the engraved title page (sig. A1v), in which the title is given as 'Philosophicall Elements . . .' (instead of 'Philosophicall Rudiments . . .') and the reference to Hobbes is presented as follows: 'Written in Latine by Tho: Hobbes of Malmesbury And now translated into English'. One copy of the book (in the Bodleian Library) has this version of the engraved title page, but does not have the extra gathering. As Drummond pointed out, the sequence of events revealed by this evidence was probably the following: first, the work was printed with the 'Elements' version of the engraved title page but without the extra gathering; then the new gathering was inserted, having been 'printed as an afterthought'; then, after a small proportion of copies had been issued in this format, the extra gathering was suppressed, after which the majority of copies were issued with a new version of the engraved title page.[5]

Drummond also noted that the earlier phrasing of the engraved title page, 'Written in Latine by Tho: Hobbes of Malmesbury And now translated into English', could be taken to imply that Hobbes was not himself the translator. This is not merely implied but openly proclaimed by the contents of C. C.'s letter to Lady Fane: in its first few lines it humbly remarks that 'except Master *Hobbs* (if he

---

[4] Bodl., MS Aubrey 6, fol. 113r; printed in J. Aubrey, '*Brief Lives*', *Chiefly of Contemporaries, set down . . . between the Years 1669 & 1696*, ed. A. Clark, 2 vols. (Oxford, 1898), II, p. 277. Robertson also used this passage to corroborate his claim; *Hobbes*, pp. 67–8 n. The term 'first booke' here means 'first chapter'; cf. the similar usage by 'C. C.' in the passage quoted in n. 21, below.

[5] H. J. H. Drummond, 'Hobbes's *Philosophicall Rudiments*, 1651', *The Library*, 5th ser., 28 (1973), pp. 54–6. The Bodleian's copy with the earlier engraved title page is pressmark Vet. A 3 f 1168. Closer inspection of the engraved title pages by Tito Magri later confirmed that the 'Rudiments' title page was printed from a partly retouched version of the 'Elements' plate; see T. Hobbes, *De Cive: The English Version*, ed. J. H. Warrender, The Clarendon Edition of the Works of Thomas Hobbes (Oxford, 1983–) [hereafter *HW*], II, p. 3 n.; and T. Hobbes, *De cive: elementi filosofici sul cittadino*, ed. and tr. T. Magri, 3d edn (Rome, 1992), p. 59 n. Confusingly, Drummond called the 'Elements' version of the engraved title page state 'b' and the 'Rudiments' version state 'a'; Warrender calls them state 'A' and state 'B' respectively, which correctly expresses their chronological order.

should chance to heare me nam'd) be a man as well practis'd in the Lawes of Nature, as he hath shewed himselfe eminent in their speculation, I see not how the injury my infirmity hath done his Booke will be reconcilable with the respect I beare to his Person.'[6] This also indicates that Hobbes was neither an instigator of the translation nor a collaborator in the project: he would not even know who the translator was, unless he chanced to hear him 'nam'd'.

Internal evidence also strongly supports the idea that the translation was not by Hobbes. In some passages the Latin has simply been misunderstood; and in the use of key terms, such as 'contract' and 'covenant', this translation ignores the conceptual distinctions so carefully set up by Hobbes and, in places, as one recent study puts it, 'goes haywire'.[7] The translator of *Philosophicall Rudiments* also has a deep and very un-Hobbesian affection for tortuously long sentences: in the opening of chapter 13, paragraph 7, for example, five of Hobbes's trenchantly brief Latin sentences are strung together into one lengthy and meandering sentence in English. (This tendency is given free rein in C. C.'s letter to Lady Fane, where the first three paragraphs contain one sentence each, consisting of 179, 430, and 114 words, respectively.)

One other point arising from textual evidence is also worth noting. From time to time, the Latin text of *De cive* gives biblical references that are slightly inaccurate; they are corrected in this English translation. If Hobbes himself had taken the trouble to correct them here, he would surely also have called for their correction when advising Blaeu about the reprinting of his Latin works in 1668; but the same errors recur in that edition's text of *De cive*.

Another argument against Hobbes's responsibility for this translation can be drawn from internal evidence—internal, that is, not to the text but to the printed book. A curious feature of *Philosophicall Rudiments* is the inclusion of three engravings, facing the first page of each of the three sections of the book. These were reproduced by Howard Warrender in his edition, but without any comment on their origin or iconographical significance; unfortunately, Warrender's work was completed just too soon for him to be able to take into account the separate but complementary researches of Maurice Goldsmith and Richard Pennington, which supplied the missing history of these plates. They were in fact selected by the printer of *Philosophicall Rudiments* from a previously published collection of allegorical engravings by Wenceslaus Hollar, entitled *Emblemata nova*; and Hollar had copied the designs from an earlier emblem book, Otto van Veen's *Q. Horatii Flacci emblemata* (Antwerp, 1607). These three emblems (each with a Latin text, drawn from one or more classical works, beneath it) were, in their original contexts, merely parts of larger sets of pictures designed to illustrate an amalgam of Senecan

---

[6] T. Hobbes, *Philosophicall Rudiments*, sigs. *1r–*1v (in the Aberdeen University Library copy); *HW* II, p. 269.

[7] P. Milton, 'Did Hobbes Translate *De cive*?' *History of Political Thought*, 11 (1990), pp. 627–38 at p. 634.

Stoicism and what might be called the quasi-Stoic moralism of Horace (his praise of simplicity and tranquillity, his warnings against ambition, and so on). The first—in the order of appearance in *Philosophicall Rudiments*—was on the theme 'despising wealth', and showed Minerva crowning with a halo-encircled crown a virtuous man who is free of ambition. The second was on the theme 'the sword of Damocles', depicting the legendary king-for-a-day presiding at a dining table in his court, with the sword suspended above him; its accompanying texts (from Horace and Seneca) were about the troubles and dangers of high temporal office or great wealth. And the third, on the theme of 'innocence', used the famous opening lines of Horace's ode 'Integer vitae scelerisque purus', and showed the virtuous man walking unharmed through a landscape teeming with wild beasts and weapons of war.[8]

Taken out of their original context and placed in a political treatise, however, these three engravings take on a very different significance. All three now seem to be on the special theme that appears to connect them, the theme of kingship— and, what is more, they give the impression of treating the holder of that office in an almost hagiographical way. The Latin texts accompanying the first two engravings both refer to kings and kingdoms; the halo-encircled crown in the first engraving now looks like a heavenly crown awarded to a virtuous king, and the king sitting under the sword of Damocles seems like a martyr to the cares of his office. (His pose is also curiously reminiscent of Christ at the Last Supper.) Most striking of all is the third engraving, which is in fact a modified version of Hollar's design— the modification being that the head of the allegorical man in the original has been replaced by a portrait of Charles I.[9]

This quasi-religious Royalist iconography is entirely in tune with what we know of the political sympathies of the bookseller Richard Royston, who had gone to extraordinary lengths to promote the royal cause ever since the outbreak of the Civil War. (One Royalist later recalled 'the Help of certain adventurous Women, hired for that purpose by Mr. *Royston* the Bookseller above-mentioned, to disperse every where ... his Books in Defence of the Royal Cause, whether printed at *London* or at *Oxford*'.[10]) Royston had been imprisoned for his activities in 1645 and was several times called before the Council of State for publishing 'scandalous'

---

[8] M. M. Goldsmith, 'Picturing Hobbes's Politics? The Illustrations to *Philosophicall Rudiments*', *Journal of the Warburg and Courtauld Institutes*, 44 (1981), pp. 232–7; and R. Pennington, *A Descriptive Catalogue of the Etched Work of Wenceslaus Hollar, 1607–1677* (Cambridge, 1982), pp. 66–7. The engravings are reproduced in *HW* II, plates 2–4, with translations of the texts on pp. xiii–xiv. While Pennington was apparently unaware of the earlier history of the images, Goldsmith was unaware of the Hollar engravings, and therefore assumed that these three plates had been specially adapted from van Veen for the translation of *De cive*. (He cited the 1612 edn of van Veen; I have used the 1st edn, of 1607.) His general argument about their iconographical significance remains, however, entirely convincing.

[9] See Pennington, *Descriptive Catalogue*, 67, no. 452 (describing this modified version as the third state of Hollar's engraving); and Goldsmith, 'Picturing Hobbes's Politics?' p. 236.

[10] P. Barwick, *The Life of the Reverend Dr. John Barwick, D.D.* (London, 1724), pp. 61–2.

(that is, polemically Royalist) books and pamphlets; he was also the publisher of the first edition of *Eikon basilike* (1649), the book attributed to Charles I that was to become a holy text for the cult of the King and Martyr.[11]

The inclusion of the three Hollar engravings must be seen, then, as part of a deliberate attempt to present Hobbes's book as a quasi-religiously Royalist work; and it is highly unlikely that Hobbes, had he had anything to do with the production of this volume, would have permitted such an ideological twist to be given to his text. It is true, of course, that Hobbes's first venture into political theory, *The Elements of Law*, had been made in defence of royal power; and it is also true that the text of *De cive* reflected the essentially Royalist position taken by Hobbes in the political quarrels of 1640–2. (That was why it appealed to Royston and, presumably, to C. C.) Hobbes's own 'Preface to the Reader' in *De cive* emphasized the relevance of his argument to the royal cause, asking rhetorically (in the words of C. C.'s translation): 'How many throats hath this false position cut, That a *Prince* for some causes may by certain men be deposed? And what blood-shed hath not this erroneous doctrine caused, That Kings are not superiours to, but administrators for the multitude?' Later in the preface, he did also state that he had tried 'not to seem of opinion, that there is a lesse proportion of obedience due to an *Aristocraty* or *Democraty*, then a Monarchy'; nevertheless, he devoted the whole of chapter 10 to a demonstration that 'the most absolute *Monarchy* is the best state of government'.[12]

By the end of the decade, however, Hobbes's views on the legitimacy of the parliamentary regime in England had obviously diverged from those of the diehard Royalists. His argument about the reciprocal relationship between protection and obedience, given special emphasis in the 'Review and Conclusion' to *Leviathan* (which, being evidently the last part of that book to be written, must have been composed within weeks of the publication of *Philosophicall Rudiments*), was plainly not acceptable to those Royalists who regarded the subject's personal allegiance to the king as a matter of literally religious obligation. This divergence did not go unnoticed. The first judgement recorded on *Leviathan* (in a letter of 6 May 1651 by Robert Payne, who was reporting what he had heard from those who had seen the book in Oxford) was that 'he seemes to favour y$^e$ present governmt'.[13] There may indeed have been an element of truth in the joking remark allegedly made by Hobbes when asked by Hyde why he was about to publish *Leviathan*:

---

[11] H. R. Plomer, *A Dictionary of the Booksellers and Printers Who Were at Work in England, Scotland, and Ireland from 1641 to 1667* (London, 1907), p. 159.

[12] *HW* II, pp. 30, 37, 139. Hobbes probably chose to make this point about democracies and aristocracies not for English readers, but for those citizens of non-monarchical European states who were potential readers of this Latin publication.

[13] BL, MS Harl. 6942, no. 132.

'The truth is, I have a mind to go home.'[14] His chances of a safe homecoming would certainly not have been improved by a version of *De cive* fitted out with the accoutrements of Royalist martyrology.

Finally, one piece of external evidence can also be used to support the claim that Hobbes was not involved in this translation of *De cive*. It comes from another letter from his old friend Robert Payne, who was in frequent correspondence with Hobbes during this period; none of the letters that passed between them is extant, but Payne's surviving letters to Gilbert Sheldon contain occasional comments on that lost correspondence. On 13 May 1650 Payne wrote to Sheldon:

I sent notice to M$^r$ Hobbes, y$^t$ his booke de Cive was translated into English, & desird him to prevent y$^t$ translation by one of his owne. but he sends me word he hath an other taske in hand, w$^{ch}$ is Politiques, in English. . . .[15]

It seems highly likely that the translation referred to by Payne was the manuscript of *Philosophicall Rudiments*: his suggestion that Hobbes 'prevent y$^t$ translation by one of his owne' indicates that he had been given the impression that this translation, already finished in manuscript, might be published quite soon. As we know, the text of *Philosophicall Rudiments* was in Royston's hands within the next six months. And Hobbes's response was exactly what one would have expected: he was far too busy writing *Leviathan* to be interested in preparing a translation of the very work that *Leviathan* was meant to supersede.

Almost every Hobbes scholar who has considered this question in recent times has been persuaded by some or all of the above arguments, and has concluded that *Philosophicall Rudiments* was translated by C. C., not by Hobbes.[16] Unfortunately, the one scholar to have persisted in attributing the translation to Hobbes was Warrender, who published it in the Clarendon edition. He was prepared to concede that Hobbes might have 'received assistance' from C. C.; but then, in a strange convolution of his argument, he used this concession to claim that the glaring differences in style between this text and Hobbes's other writings were proof of Hobbes's responsibility for the text, on the grounds that such differences amounted to 'a great deal more than Hobbes would have allowed without his own active participation and sanction'.[17] Accordingly, instead of printing C. C.'s epistle to Lady Fane in its proper place, he demoted it to an appendix; at the same time, however, he placed the list of 'Faults escaped' (which belongs to the same inserted

---

[14] E. Hyde, *A Brief View and Survey of the Dangerous and Pernicious Errors to Church and State in Mr. Hobbes's Book, entitled Leviathan* (Oxford, 1676), p. 8.
[15] BL, MS Harl. 6942, no. 128.
[16] See e.g. P. Milton, 'Did Hobbes Translate *De cive*?' and the reviews of Warrender's edition by R. Tuck (*Political Studies*, 33 (1985), pp. 308–15) and myself (*London Review of Books*, 6, no. 19, 18 Oct. 1984, p. 22).
[17] *HW* II, pp. 6–8.

gathering as the epistle) at the start of the text, annotating this list of errata with the bibliographically baffling statement that 'its authenticity is in some doubt'.[18]

Given his determination to minimize the responsibility of C. C., it is not surprising that Warrender made little attempt to identify the bearer of those initials. Drummond had already suggested four possible candidates: Sir Charles Cavendish, Christopher Cartwright, Sir Charles Cotterell, and Charles Cotton. As Warrender correctly noted, enough of the correspondence between Sir Charles Cavendish and John Pell survives to give us a fairly detailed picture of the former's intellectual life during the years preceding 1651, and there is no mention of any project to translate *De cive*.[19] It must also be said that, while Sir Charles Cavendish did not stand upon rank in his dealings with Hobbes, there was nevertheless an implicit and unavoidable sense of a master–servant relationship between Sir Charles (and his brother, the Marquess of Newcastle) on the one hand and Hobbes on the other; it would have been quite inappropriate for such a person to perform the almost secretarial task of translating one of Hobbes's works.[20]

Christopher Cartwright (who, unlike Cavendish, had no known connection with Hobbes) was an orthodox Protestant divine whose publications are exclusively on ecclesiological and scriptural questions. It is hard to believe that such a writer would have accepted without a murmur all the theological doctrines presented in the third section of *De cive*; and yet, when C. C. comments on the contents of the book in his epistle to Lady Fane, the only passage that prompts him to signal his personal disagreement is 'the eleventh Article of his thirteenth Booke'—which contains, of all things, Hobbes's argument that taxes on expenditure are preferable to taxes on wealth.[21]

Sir Charles Cotterell is, on the face of it, a more likely candidate than either of the above, since he is known to have published two translations from Spanish and

---

[18] *HW* II, p. 22. A translator's letter can be described as inauthentic if the claim it makes of responsibility for the translation is false; but it is hard to see how an errata list can be called inauthentic when it corresponds to errata in the text.

[19] Ibid., p. 5 n. From the period 1648–51 there are in fact 19 letters from Pell (BL, MS. Add. 4280, fols. 131v–138, 257) and 24 from Cavendish (BL, MS Add. 4278, fols. 271–321r). I have presented a brief account of Sir Charles's relationship with Hobbes in *HW* VII (= *Correspondence*, II), pp. 801–5. The identification of C. C. with Cavendish has recently been supported by E. Chaney, *The Grand Tour and the Great Rebellion: Richard Lassels and 'The Voyage of Italy' in the Seventeenth Century* (Geneva, 1985), p. 309.

[20] This is not meant to imply that translation in general was a socially inferior occupation. Translation of modern texts could of course be undertaken by members of the gentry or nobility (such as Sir Charles Cotterell, or Henry Carey, Earl of Monmouth), but in such cases the texts were usually well-known literary or historical works in Italian, Spanish, or French. My comment here concerns specifically the relationship between Hobbes and his Cavendish patrons. His 'English Optical Treatise' (BL, MS Harl. 3360), for example, was written in English (unlike his other works on optics) at Newcastle's request; had Newcastle or his brother wanted an English version of something Hobbes had written in Latin, they would most likely have asked him to produce it. Hobbes himself had previously undertaken two translations in a quasi-secretarial capacity: the English version of letters sent by Fulgenzio Micanzio to the second Earl of Devonshire (Chatsworth, Hobbes MSS, 'Translations of Italian letters'; BL, MS Add. 11309); and the Latin version of some of Bacon's essays; see Aubrey, '*Brief Lives*', I, p. 331.

[21] *HW* II, p. 271.

one from French; he also collaborated with Sir Edward Hyde's brother-in-law, William Aylesbury, on the latter's translation of the Italian historian Davila, published in 1647. But Cotterell had fled from England in 1649 and by 1650 was living in Antwerp. It was of course not impossible to organize publication in England from the Continent (as the case of *Leviathan* shows); but it must have taken more than usual commitment on the part of the organizer, and no special interest in, or connection with, Hobbes is attested to by any of the surviving evidence of Cotterell's life and works.[22] If no other more plausible candidate could be found, Cotterell's candidacy might still be allowed to stand. But there is in fact enough evidence to show that the translator of *De cive* was very probably the fourth person proposed by Drummond: the young poet Charles Cotton.[23]

## II

One of the most suggestive pieces of evidence has already been cited, though its real significance has been overlooked: it is the letter from Payne to Sheldon that refers to the translation of *De cive*. Anyone who reads this passage (quoted above) in the context of the rest of the letter must be struck by the curiously offhand way in which Payne introduces the subject of the translation. The previous sentence (at the end of the preceding paragraph) concludes: 'y$^e$ ArchB$^p$ of York is dead, suddainly, of an Apoplexy, about 2 monehts since.' And then Payne immediately goes on: 'I sent notice to M$^r$ Hobbes, y$^t$ his booke de Cive was translated.' This is the first mention of any such translation in Payne's letters to Sheldon, of which a fairly complete series has survived; and yet his way of alluding to the translation of *De cive* is so casual that it must seem unlikely that Payne is informing Sheldon about the existence of this translation for the first time. The most natural reading of this passage, surely, is to assume that Payne is referring to something Sheldon already knows—because it was Sheldon himself who told Payne of it in one of his previous letters.[24]

---

[22] See the account by Sidney Lee in the *DNB*, and the sources referred to there.

[23] A search through all the authors with the initials 'C. C.' listed in the *STC* who published any printed work between 1641 and 1660 does not reveal any other plausible candidates. Apart from Cartwright and Cotton, the list contains two writers of textbooks on English law (Sir Charles Calthrope, Charles George Cock); four writers of minor religious tracts (Charles Chauncy, Christopher Cheesman, Christopher Cob, and Clement Cotton—the first of these was an emigrant to New England); a poet–clockmaker (Christopher Clobery); and an author, later reprinted, who had died in 1629 (Sir Charles Cornwallis). None of them had anything published by Richard Royston.

[24] Payne was writing to Sheldon every two or three weeks; his previous surviving letters include those dated 7 March (BL, MS Harl. 6942, no. 127), 26 March (ibid., no. 129), 8 April (BL, MS Lansdowne 93, fol. 179), and 29 April (BL, MS Harl. 6942, no. 126). The letters from the Harleian MS (including the full text of the letter that refers to the translation of *De cive*) are printed, in modernized transcription, in W. Clarke, 'Illustrations of the State of the Church during the Great Rebellion', *The Theologian and Ecclesiastic*, 6 (1848), pp. 165–74, 217–24, and 12 (1851), pp. 86–96, here 6, pp. 169–73. Sheldon's letters to Payne, unfortunately, do not survive.

Once this more natural reading of Payne's words is adopted, the letter becomes an important piece of evidence for the identification of C. C. with Cotton, who was very probably in contact with Sheldon during precisely this period. For Sheldon, having been ejected from his fellowship at Oxford in 1648 and imprisoned for several months thereafter, had gone to live in Staffordshire, in the close vicinity of Beresford Hall, Cotton's family home.[25] It is easy to imagine that Sheldon, on occasional visits to Beresford Hall, took an interest in the intellectual activities of the young poet, who was aged nineteen in 1649; it is tempting also to suppose that they discovered their shared interest in angling.[26] That some real friendship was established between Sheldon and the young Cotton cannot be doubted. When Cotton published a translation of Girard's biography of the duc d'Épernon in 1670, he dedicated the work to Sheldon (who was by now archbishop of Canterbury), in order to show the world that he had 'sometime' been 'Favour'd' by such a distinguished man.[27]

Although frustratingly little biographical information about Charles Cotton has come down to us, such details as can be assembled about his early life and family background are entirely consonant with the idea that he was the translator of Hobbes's *De cive*. His father, also named Charles (who will be referred to throughout this article as Charles Cotton Sr), was a staunch Royalist, a man of wide literary interests, and a well-known figure in the world of the poets and court wits of pre-Civil War London. His friends had included Jonson, Donne, Lovelace, Davenant, and Sir Edward Hyde.[28] The last of these, indeed, numbered him among his 'chief acquaintance', and later wrote:

---

[25] Beresford Hall was located just on the Staffordshire side of the Staffordshire–Derbyshire border, roughly 8 miles north-west of Ashbourne, Derbys. Gilbert Sheldon's family was from Stanton, Staffords., a village 3 miles to the west of Ashbourne and only a couple of hours' walk from Beresford Hall. His brother Ralph still lived at Stanton, and may have been the first person he went to stay with after his release from prison at the end of 1648; but for most of the period 1649–53 he was the guest of a local gentry family, the Okeovers. Okeover Hall, the original family seat, was located 1 mile to the north-west of Ashbourne; the Okeover family also resided at East Bridgford, which lies just to the east of Nottingham, on the river Trent, roughly 35 miles away from Okeover Hall. See R. Thoroton, *The Antiquities of Nottinghamshire*, ed. J. Throsby, 3 vols. (Nottingham, 1790–96), I, p. 296; Clarke, 'Illustrations', 6, p. 166; V. D. Sutch, *Gilbert Sheldon, Architect of Anglican Survival, 1640–1675* (The Hague, 1973), pp. 33–5. Henry Hammond's letters to Sheldon during this period frequently include greetings to 'Mrs Ok:' (BL, MS Harl. 6942, e.g. nos. 7, 8, 16). The Okeovers also had property at Snelston, just south of Ashbourne; hence, perhaps, the statement in the *DNB* article on Sheldon that he resided at Snelston during this period.

[26] Payne's letters to Sheldon from this period make several references to fishing and to recipes for carp (BL, MS Harl. 6942, for example, nos. 126, 129, 130); and Izaak Walton's *The Complete Angler* (published in 1653, but apparently written about April 1650) contains a special tribute to Sheldon's skill as an angler (I. Walton and C. Cotton, *The Complete Angler*, ed. Sir Harris Nicolas (London, 1903), pp. xlvi–xlviii (dating), 169–70 (tribute)). Walton was an old friend of Sheldon's; Cotton was not involved in Walton's text at this stage, though it is likely that Walton had gone fishing at Beresford while preparing his book (E. M. Turner, 'The Life and Work of Charles Cotton (1630–1687), with a Bibliographical Account of Cotton's Writings' (B.Litt. diss., Oxford University, 1954), pp. 63–4).

[27] G. Girard, *The History of the Life of the Duke of Espernon, the Great Favourite of France*, tr. C. Cotton (London, 1670), sig. A2r. It has also been claimed that Sheldon was distantly related to the Cottons; see Turner, 'Life and Work of Cotton', p. 67 n.

[28] C. Cotton, *Poems*, ed. J. Beresford (London, 1923), p. 10.

Charles Cotton [Sr] was a gentleman born to a competent fortune, and so qualified in his person and education, that for many years he continued the greatest ornament of the town, in the esteem of those who had been best bred. His natural parts were very great, his wit flowing in all the parts of conversation. . . .[29]

Charles Cotton Sr had a very close friendship with his near relative, the poet Sir Aston Cokayne, whose family was from Ashbourne.[30] They shared their literary interests: together, they presided over gatherings of wits and minor poets at the Fleece Tavern, off Covent Garden in London.[31] Probably Sir Aston encouraged the younger Charles Cotton (his first cousin, once removed) in his earliest attempts at poetry. The first published work by Cotton was an elegy on Henry, Lord Hastings, the son of the Earl of Huntingdon, which appeared in the volume of tributes to Hastings, *Lachrymae musarum*, published in 1649. Other contributors to this volume included Sir Aston Cokayne, Lord Falkland, and Mildmay Fane, second Earl of Westmorland.[32]

The literary world in which Charles Cotton Sr moved would have provided various opportunities for him to become acquainted, indirectly or even directly, with Hobbes and his work. (One possible interpretation of the phrase quoted above from C. C.'s letter to Lady Fane, 'if he should chance to heare me nam'd', must be that, even though Hobbes did not know Cotton personally, he would recognize his name when he heard it because he did have some acquaintance with, or knowledge of, his father.) Hobbes too had had access to some circles of London poets and wits through his friend (and fellow-recipient of the Earl of Newcastle's patronage) Ben Jonson. Hobbes's acquaintance with William Davenant, which bore fruit in his 'Answer' to Davenant's Preface to *Gondibert* in 1650, probably dated back to the 1630s, when Davenant had been an assiduous member of the 'tribe of Ben'. The nature of Davenant's relations with the Cotton family is suggested by an inscribed copy of *Gondibert* that the poet sent from his cell in the Tower of London: the inscription reads, 'For the much Honoured Charles Cotton esquire from Sir your most faythfull thankefull and humble servant Will: Davenant. Tower: Decemb. 19th 1651.'[33] If Cotton had, as this seems to imply, sent money or some other form

---

[29] E. Hyde, *The Life of Edward Earl of Clarendon*, 3 vols. (Oxford, 1827), I, p. 36.

[30] Cokayne was a first cousin of Charles Cotton Sr's wife. See Walton and Cotton, *Complete Angler*, ccii–cciii; G. D. Squibb, ed., *The Visitation of Derbyshire, Begun in 1662 and Finished in 1664*, Harleian Society Publications, n.s., 8 (London, 1989), p. 47; and the life of Cokayne by G. E. Cokayne in the *DNB*.

[31] M. Weidhorn, *Richard Lovelace* (New York, 1970), p. 21. The dating of these gatherings is, however, uncertain.

[32] R. B. [probably Richard Brome], ed., *Lachrymae musarum* (London, 1649); Cotton's poem is on pp. 12–13.

[33] J. G. McManaway, 'The "Lost" Canto of *Gondibert*', *Modern Language Quarterly* 1 (1940), pp. 63–78 at p. 65 n. On the chronology of Davenant's later dealings with Charles Cotton, which prompted the latter's poem addressed to Davenant (written probably in 1659), McManaway's argument is corrected by A. I. Dust, 'The *Seventh and Last Canto of Gondibert* and Two Dedicatory Poems', *Journal of English and Germanic Philology*, 60 (1961), pp. 282–5. However, both McManaway and Dust identify the 'Charles Cotton esquire' of the 1651 inscription as Cotton Sr; this form of address was used for the son during the father's lifetime (see n. 77, below).

of assistance to the imprisoned Davenant, it is likely that his action arose from a friendship between Davenant and his father that went back to the literary world of pre-Civil War London.

The other literary figure through whom Charles Cotton Sr might have either met Hobbes, or come to know of Hobbes's work, was his close friend Edward Hyde. Hobbes and Hyde were well acquainted before the Civil War: Hyde would later begin his critique of *Leviathan* (written in 1673) by declaring that 'Mr. *Hobbes* is one of the most ancient acquaintance I have in the World, and of whom I have alwaies had a great esteem . . . it may be there are few Men now alive, who have bin longer known to him then I have bin.'[34] (Hyde was also well acquainted with Davenant, having shared lodgings with him in 1628.[35]) Both Hyde and Hobbes had been connected with what is loosely called the Great Tew circle, a network centring on Lord Falkland and consisting, roughly speaking, of two overlapping clusters of people: Oxford-based theologians and London-based literary men.[36] When Hobbes wrote *The Elements of Law* in 1640 and produced a number of manuscript copies for circulation, members of these two overlapping groups may have been among the first to read it: there is clear evidence that Hyde had read the work in manuscript at an early stage, and at least two copies had also circulated at Oxford.[37] One had been loaned in Oxford by Robert Payne to Gilbert Sheldon (who was also connected with Great Tew), and another, in the possession of Thomas Lockey (Student, that is, Fellow, of Christ Church and later Bodley's Librarian), was used for the unauthorized printing of the first half of the text in early 1650.[38]

Finally, Charles Cotton Sr might also have heard of Hobbes, or met him, through the network of Derbyshire and Nottinghamshire gentry families with which he was connected. Cotton Sr was a friend of Sir Gervase Clifton, who had employed Hobbes as a tutor for his son, Gervase, in 1629–30.[39] Evidence of

---

[34] Hyde, *Survey*, p. 3.   [35] M. Edmond, *Rare Sir William Davenant* (Manchester, 1987), p. 36.

[36] On Hyde, Hobbes, and Great Tew, see B. H. G. Wormald, *Clarendon: Politics, History, and Religion 1640–1660* (Cambridge, 1951), esp. pp. 240–325; R. Ollard, *Clarendon and His Friends* (London, 1987), pp. 29–41; and J. C. Hayward, 'The *Mores* of Great Tew: Literary, Philosophical, and Political Idealism in Falkland's Circle' (Ph.D. diss., Cambridge University, 1983).

[37] Hyde's autograph notes on *The Elements of Law* (which follow the pagination of one of the surviving MSS of the work, BL, MS Harl. 4236) are in Bodl., MS Clar. 126, fols. 129–30; Martin Dzelzainis has convincingly argued that they were made in the autumn of 1640 ('Edward Hyde and Thomas Hobbes's *The Elements of Law, Natural and Politic*', *The Historical Journal*, 32 (1989), pp. 303–17).

[38] BL, MS. Harl. 6942, no. 126 (Payne to Sheldon, 29 April 1650: 'yᵉ Originall MS. wch I lent you, in Oxf.'), and BL, MS Lansdowne 841, fol. 174r (Payne to Sheldon, 16 July 1650: 'yᵉ originall whereof I shewd you, long agoe, at Oxford'); BL, MS Harl. 6942, no. 129 (Payne to Sheldon, 26 March 1650: 'printed lately by Fr. Bowman out of an MS copy of Mr Lockeys, who persuaded Bowman to publish it').

[39] A letter from Cotton Sr to Sir Gervase survives from 1639, thanking him for the loan of several poetical manuscripts (Nottingham University Library, MS Clifton C 138); the younger Cotton would later begin a poem addressed to Sir Clifford Clifton (Sir Gervase's second son and heir) with the lines: 'When from thy kind hand, my dearest, dear brother, / Whom I love as th'adst been the son of my Mother' (Cotton, *Poems*, 265). The Clifton estate, at Clifton, south of Nottingham, was close to that of the Okeover family at East Bridgford, with whom Sheldon stayed.

personal connections between Cotton Sr and Hobbes's main employers, the Cavendishes of Chatsworth and Hardwick, is lacking, but it is reasonable to suppose that he would have had contact at some level with the Cavendishes, who were the leading landowners in Derbyshire. Later, Cotton was clearly acquainted with them, dedicating his poem about the Derbyshire Peak District (which contains a description of Chatsworth) to Elizabeth, Countess of Devonshire, who had married the third Earl in 1640.[40] It is also possible that the Cottons were acquainted with the Newcastle Cavendishes, who were also Hobbes's patrons: in 1651 both Charles Cotton and a close relative of the Marquess of Newcastle contributed prefatory poems to a translation of Seneca by the minor poet Edmund Prestwich.[41]

Charles Cotton was born in 1630 and was educated, so far as is known, only in his father's home. He acquired a good knowledge of languages and cultivated the art of translation; in a poem addressed 'To my most honoured Cousin Mr *Charles Cotton* the younger', Sir Aston Cokayne declared:

> The Greek and Latine Language he commands,
> So all that then was writ in both those Lands:
> The French and the Italian he hath gain'd,
> And all the wit that in them is contain'd:
> So, if he pleases to translate a piece
> From France, or Italy, Old Rome, or Greece,
> The understanding Reader soon will find
> It is the best of any of that kind . . .

And in another poem addressed to Cotton, he wrote:

> D'Avila, Bentivoglio, Guicciardine,
> And Machiavil the subtile Florentine,
> (In their Originals) I have read through,
> Thanks to your Library, and unto you . . .[42]

Given the conventions of such eulogistic poetry, Sir Aston's hyperbolic praise of Cotton's linguistic skills is understandable; the discrepancy between his judgement and the cooler verdicts of modern scholars on the accuracy of *Philosophicall Rudiments* need not be any bar to the identification of Cotton as the translator. Indeed, the picture of C. C. put together by one modern writer on the basis of the evidence of that book would make a very plausible portrait of the nineteen-year-old Charles

---

[40] C. Cotton, *The Wonders of the Peake* (London, 1681).

[41] E. Prestwich, *Hippolitus Translated out of Seneca* (London, 1651); the relative was Richard Rogers, the father-in-law of Charles Cavendish, Viscount Mansfield (son of the Marquess of Newcastle).

[42] Sir Aston Cokayne ['Cokain'], *Poems. With the Obstinate Lady, and Trapolin a suppos'd Prince* (London, 1662), pp. 114, 231 [mispaginated p. '131']. It is noteworthy (in view of the translation of Hobbes) that all four Italian authors wrote about politics and modern political history; Cardinal Bentivoglio's *Relatione* (Cologne, 1629) contained the texts of his reports from Flanders, where he was nuncio from 1607 to 1617.

Cotton: 'He would appear, if his letter to Lady Fane is anything to go by, to be a young man out to impress, and he had slightly shaky Latin and no legal training.'[43]

At some time soon after the expulsion of Royalist Fellows from Oxford in 1648, a young Oxford don, Ralph Rawson, appears to have come to stay at Beresford Hall and to have acted as a tutor to Cotton. This somewhat obscure figure supplies another important link, not only with Sheldon but also, potentially, with Hobbes's writings, one manuscript of which may have been brought by him into the Cotton household. Rawson, who was nine years older than his pupil, had become a Fellow of Brasenose College in 1642; strongly Royalist in his sympathies, he was to be implicated in Sir George Booth's plot in 1659, when, according to one account, he narrowly escaped punishment.[44] Rawson and Cotton evidently became firm friends; Cotton's 'Eclogue', a dialogue between Damon and Thyrsis, is headed 'Damon C.C. Thyrsis R.R.' The most important surviving manuscript of Cotton's poetry, the so-called Derby manuscript, begins with a poem by Rawson headed 'To my dear, and honour'd Patron M$^r$ Charles Cotton Ode Occasion'd by his Translation of an Ode of Joh: Secundus directed to mee, and inserted among his other Poems'.[45]

Cotton's biographers have not been able to fix the dates of Rawson's stay at Beresford Hall, noting only that it must have taken place at some time between his ejection from Oxford in the summer of 1648 and his move to Cambridge in early 1655. (It is clear that Cotton kept in touch with Rawson in later years; even if the poem by Rawson mentioned above were datable by its reference to an insertion among Cotton's 'other poems', therefore, this would not necessarily provide the date of Rawson's stay in Staffordshire.[46]) If Rawson was Cotton's tutor, however, it would surely be more reasonable to place his employment at the beginning of the period 1648–55 than at the end, given that Cotton was already eighteen years old in 1648. Cotton's acquaintance with Edmund Prestwich, to which his prefatory poem to Prestwich's Seneca translation of 1651 bears witness, may well have come about

---

[43] Milton, 'Did Hobbes Translate *De cive*?' p. 636.

[44] C. B. Heberden, ed., *Brasenose College Register, 1509–1909*, 2 vols. (Oxford, 1909), I, p. 168; M. Burrows, ed., *The Register of the Visitors of the University of Oxford, from AD 1647 to AD 1658* (London, 1881), pp. 98, 138; and A. Wood, *Athenae oxonienses*, ed. P. Bliss, 4 vols. (London, 1813–20), vol. 4, col. 635, note.

[45] Derby Central Library, MS 8470, p. 1 (where the bare form of address 'Mr Charles Cotton' suggests that this was written after the death of Charles Cotton Sr in 1658). Another item in this collection, by the Derbyshire poet Thomas Bancroft (who also contributed to *Lachrymae musarum* in 1649), is headed 'to CC: and RR:' (ibid., p. 99). For discussions of this manuscript, see A. J. Chapple, 'A Critical Bibliography of the Works of Charles Cotton' (M.A. diss., University of London, 1955), pp. 201–2 (with a listing of its contents, pp. 204–29); Turner, 'Life and Work of Cotton', pp. 381–24; S. Parks, 'Charles Cotton and the Derby Manuscript', in S. Parks and P. J. Croft, *Literary Autographs*, William Andrews Clark Memorial Library Seminar Papers (Los Angeles, 1983), pp. 1–35; and P. Beal, 'Charles Cotton', in his *Index of English Literary Manuscripts*, 5 vols. (London, 1980–), II, pt 1, pp. 209–33.

[46] Turner suggests that Rawson was at Beresford for the whole period from 1648 to early 1655: 'Life and Works of Cotton', 38, 44. For the evidence of later contacts, see J. Buxton, *A Tradition of Poetry* (London, 1967), p. 142; cf. also my comment on the form of address used by Rawson, in n. 45 above.

through Rawson: Prestwich had been admitted to Brasenose College in September 1642, two months after Rawson had become a Fellow there.[47] More significantly, two letters from Henry Hammond to Gilbert Sheldon from March 1651 show that Rawson was then seeking new employment; so the period of his stay with the Cotton family was most probably before that date.[48]

It can thus be assumed that Rawson was at Beresford Hall during precisely the period when—if the argument of this paper is correct—Cotton prepared his translation of *De cive*. At this point, a speculative suggestion may be added, based on a fact that has apparently gone unnoticed by Hobbes scholars: the fact that Cotton was almost certainly the owner of one of the surviving manuscripts (now in the British Library) of Hobbes's *The Elements of Law*. An explanatory note added to this manuscript by W. Ford states:

From the Library at Islam the ancient Residence of the Portes. Islam is near Ashbourne, and situated on the beautiful banks of the Dove . . . The Library was purchased by me in 1807 & among the Books was the Poems of Cotton in MS, unpublished, in the original binding, with silver clasps.[49]

The Port family of Ilam were close neighbors of the Cottons (Ilam is roughly four miles south of Beresford) and were related to them through Charles Cotton's mother's family. Cotton's poems include an epitaph on Robert Port of Ilam, and one of Cotton's few extant autographs is a leaf, probably extracted from a book, inscribed 'Present this to my honour'd Cosen Port from his humble servant Charles Cotton.'[50] The Derby manuscript of Cotton's poems must surely be identified with the 'Poems of Cotton in MS' referred to here by Ford, which it matches in every respect: it is in a late-seventeenth-century binding, it did have two clasps (one of which is now missing), and it does include several poems that were 'unpublished'. Among the various jottings on the final page of the manuscript are the inscriptions 'I. Port his Booke' and 'C. Port'.[51] It remains a little unclear, however, when the manuscript entered the possession of the Port family; it appears to have

---

[47] Heberden, *Brasenose College Register*, I, p. 179.

[48] BL, MS Harl. 6942, nos. 92 (2 March 1651): 'I had a letter this week from M<sup>r</sup> Rawson of Brasennose, whose health permits not his stay with Lady Ormond. I think you know him better than I, tell me I pray whither he be fit for S<sup>r</sup> G. S.:', and 93 (20 March 1651): 'I wish you had sayd a litle more to me of M<sup>r</sup> Rawson to make me discern his unfitness for S<sup>r</sup> G. [ . . . ] he desires me to recommend him to some place.' 'S<sup>r</sup> G. S.:' was Sir George Savile, later first Marquess of Halifax, political author and dedicatee of Cotton's translation of Montaigne. Savile was living at his family house of Rufford, 17 miles north of Nottingham. He was three years younger than Cotton, which makes it seem fitting that Rawson should have been proposed as a possible tutor for him two or three years after he had embarked on similar work for the Cotton family.

[49] BL, MS Egerton 2005, fol. 1r.

[50] Cotton, *Poems*, p. 282 (epitaph); Parks, 'Cotton and the Derby Manuscript', p. 13 (autograph, now in the Osborn Collection at Yale University).

[51] Derby Central Library, MS 8470, p. 258. This manuscript is known to have been in the possession of Richard Heber in 1832, but its history before that date has not hitherto been established: Stephen Parks merely speculates that it 'could have been at Beresford . . . until 1825' ('Cotton and the Derby Manuscript', p. 8).

belonged previously, during the final years of Cotton's life, to the family of William Fitzherbert (of Tissington, Derbyshire), a friend and neighbour of Cotton.[52]

What is important, however, is the fact that a manuscript of Cotton's poems, originating from either Cotton's own household or his close friends and relatives, should have been passed down in tandem with a manuscript of Hobbes's *The Elements of Law*. This raises the very strong possibility that the Hobbes manuscript had itself been owned by Cotton. And this in turn provides further intriguing evidence of Cotton's involvement in the preparation of the translation of *De cive*, since the first page of this manuscript of *The Elements of Law* has pasted on to it the engraved title page of *Philosophicall Rudiments* (in the second state), neatly cut down and framed with a border of inked ruled lines.[53]

The speculative suggestion that may be built on Cotton's possession of this manuscript of *The Elements of Law* is that it was Rawson who had brought the manuscript from Oxford to Staffordshire. This can only be a speculation; there is no evidence of any direct connection between Rawson and Hobbes, and, as we have seen, Charles Cotton Sr had indirect Hobbesian connections of his own through which such a manuscript might have been obtained. But of the very few things that are known about Rawson, one is the fact that he was a close acquaintance of Sheldon at Oxford; we know that Sheldon had been loaned by Payne a copy of *The Elements of Law*, and that at least one other copy (or a copy of that copy) was circulating in Oxford in the 1640s. The manuscript associated with Cotton is not one of the copies apparently produced by scribes under Hobbes's supervision and with the dedicatory epistle signed by him; but it does belong, textually speaking, among the earliest group of manuscripts, together with Chatsworth MS. Hobbes A. 2B (referred to by Ferdinand Tönnies as the 'Hardwick' manuscript, and described by him as the one retained by Hobbes) and the manuscript, no longer extant, that Lockey supplied to the printer of *Humane Nature*.[54] Payne was one of Hobbes's closest friends and a former chaplain to the Earl of Newcastle, for whom the work was written. It is not unreasonable to assume that he was one of the first people to obtain a copy of *The Elements of Law*, and that the version of the text in his possession would therefore have represented its earliest stage; the manuscript that Rawson may have brought to Beresford Hall could

---

[52] See Beal, 'Charles Cotton', p. 210, pointing out that William Fitzherbert's daughter Mary married into the Port family in 1684. Above the 'Port' inscriptions already mentioned, the last page of the manuscript also has the inscriptions 'Frances Fitz:Herbert may ij: 23 (81)' (that is, presumably, aged 23 in 1681), and 'Mercia Fitzherbert March ye 3ᵈ 1687'. Cotton's own library, according to a tradition recorded in 1860, was 'dispersed in the neighbourhood of Hartington' (a village one mile north of Beresford Hall, roughly six miles from Tissington and the same distance from Ilam); see T. Bateman, 'Notes on a Few of the Old Libraries of Derbyshire, and their Existing Remains', *The Reliquary*, 1 (1860–1), pp. 167–74 at p. 169.

[53] BL, MS Egerton 2005, fol. 2r. The engraving was added in the space below the written title of the manuscript, 'The Elements of Law Naturall and Politique'.

[54] See Hobbes, *The Elements of Law*, ed. F. Tönnies (London, 1889), p. ix.

derive either from the copy Payne circulated at Oxford, or from Lockey's copy, which may itself have been a copy of Payne's.

Speculation, too, is all that is possible about the process by which Cotton's translation of *De cive* came to be printed, first with, and then without, his dedicatory epistle. Cotton is known to have had a rather negligent attitude to the publication of his works: Peter Beal has commented on his pattern of 'literary activity coupled with relative carelessness about his manuscripts'.[55] His translation of du Vair, *The Morall Philosophy of the Stoicks*, for example, was printed in 1667 but bears a dedicatory epistle dated 27 February 1663/4; and in that epistle he stated that he had made the translation seven years earlier, 'by my Fathers command'. (Intriguingly, he added: 'so that what you see, was an effect of my obedience, and no part of my choice; my little studies (especially at that time) lying another way'.[56] From the letter from Payne to Sheldon of May 1650 in which the translation of *De cive* was first mentioned, it can be deduced that Sheldon had given him the impression that the translation had already been finished for some time—enough time, in fact, for the work to have been published by then. Later in the same letter Payne remarked: 'And now I am come hither [that is, to Oxford], I meet wth yᵉ 2 first parts of yt de Cive, printed in English. but yᵉ last, (viz Religio) left out.'[57] (In a subsequent letter Payne explained his mistake: 'The other Tract, de Corpore politico, printed at London, is not yᵉ Translation of yᵉ booke de Cive, but the other part of yᵗ entire M.S. dedicated to the E. of Newcastle.'[58]) As we know, the translation was not in fact entered in the Stationers' Company Register until November; possibly the manuscript had been circulating in some form, or been on offer to booksellers by an intermediary, for most of that year. Cotton may not have been dealing directly with Royston at first, and this might explain the comparatively tardy insertion of his dedicatory epistle, after he had been informed, at a late stage, of the work's imminent publication.

As for the removal of the inserted gathering, the most plausible explanation of this is surely the simplest one: that Royston decided on reflection, that the book would enjoy better sales if he concealed the fact that it was merely a translation of a previously published work. That would explain why he not only removed the translator's epistle but also went to the much greater trouble of having the plate of the engraved title page recut. (Of the two textual changes he had made to that engraving, the abandonment of 'Written in Latine . . . and now translated into

---

[55] Beal, 'Charles Cotton', pp. 209–10.
[56] G. du Vair, *The Morall Philosophy of the Stoicks*, tr. C. Cotton (London, 1667), sigs. A3v (quotation), A4v, and A2v (date).
[57] BL, MS Harl. 6942, no. 128.
[58] BL, MS Lansdowne 841, fol. 174r (16 July 1650); in other words, he had seen *De corpore politico* (London, 1650 (dated 4 May by Thomason)), the unauthorized printing of the second half of *The Elements of Law*.

English' was the more significant; he probably decided that, while he was having that change made, he might as well also change 'Elements' into 'Rudiments' to bring the engraved title page into line with the printed one. No doubt the engraving had been commissioned at an earlier stage, before he had hit upon the title 'Philosophicall Rudiments'.) Cotton, whose use of his bare initials shows that he was uninterested in gaining any personal fame by his translation, may have been quite content to have the inserted gathering removed, so long as a few copies were printed with it for his personal use—especially, one imagines, for presentation to Lady Fane herself. And, to complete this train of speculation, it may be that the second-state engraved title page that is now found pasted on to the *Elements of Law* manuscript was a copy sent by Royston to Cotton for his approval (or, at least, for his information) when these changes were being made.

As for the three engravings, it is impossible to tell whether Cotton was in any way involved in their selection. The emphasis on Senecan and Horatian Stoicism in these engravings does appear to chime rather closely with the translation of Seneca by Edmund Prestwich in 1651, Cotton's own versions of Horace in the Derby manuscript, and—if we take his disclaimer, quoted above, with a grain of salt—Cotton's interest in the neo-Stoicism of du Vair; but Stoicism was, naturally, a common enough doctrine among Royalists in defeat. There can at least be no doubt that the quasi-religious Royalist message conveyed by the use of these three engravings would have reflected Cotton's views: when the Earl of Derby was captured after the battle of Worcester and executed in October 1651, Cotton wrote a passionate expostulation on his death, expressing also deep feelings of grief and anger at the execution of Charles I.[59]

Before we turn to Cotton's possible contacts with Lady Fane, one other piece of evidence for Cotton's authorship of the English translation of *De cive* can also be mentioned. Arguments for attribution based on stylistic grounds are always problematic where translations are concerned, as the style of the translator may be influenced or contaminated in various ways by the style of the original: whatever the method of comparison used (whether traditional and 'subjective' or stylometric and computerized), it would be unsafe to assume that Cotton's translation of, say, Montaigne or du Vair could be used as a 'control' to test his authorship of a translation of Hobbes. The only element of Cotton's translations that does permit

[59] To what a formidable greatness grown
Is this prodigious beast Rebellion,
When Sovereignty, and its so sacred law,
Thus lies subjected to his Tyrant awe!
. . .
And first, the justest, and the best of Kings,
Rob'd in the glory of his sufferings,
By his too violent Fate informed us all,
What tragic ends attended his great fall.
(Cotton, *Poems*, pp. 241–2)

direct comparison, in fact, is the dedicatory epistles or prefaces—where the translator speaks *in propria persona* and works within the conventions of what is more or less a single genre. Anyone who reads in succession the dedicatory epistles of *Philosophicall Rudiments*, *The Morall Philosophy of the Stoicks*, and *The History of the Life of the Duke of Espernon* will be struck by their strong stylistic similarities— above all, by their involuted subordinate clauses, their recourse to parentheses, and their use of semicolons to join together what might otherwise stand as separate sentences. The extremely long sentence constructions of the dedicatory epistle to Lady Fane have already been mentioned; the entire epistle prefaced to Cotton's translation of du Vair consists of only two sentences, one of 210 words, the other of 111; and the preface to his translation of Girard's life of Épernon has twelve sentences taking up three folio pages, with one sentence of thirty lines of print (369 words), one of twenty-five lines, and one of nineteen.

## III

The final problem to be addressed is that of the connection with Lady Fane. Given that so little is known of Cotton's biography, and much less of the obscure Lady Fane's, it might seem unlikely that any link could be established between them. But, although evidence of direct contacts cannot be found (excepting, of course, the evidence of the dedicatory epistle itself), it is nevertheless possible to demonstrate that the Cotton family enjoyed friendships with two individuals who were connected with Lady Fane's immediate family circle.

Some contacts can be posited, of course, between Cotton and the Fane family more generally; but these are of doubtful value. For example, Cotton was a fellow-contributor with Mildmay Fane (Lady Fane's nephew), to the memorial volume for Henry, Lord Hastings, in 1649. But the mere appearance of their poems in this volume need not imply any real personal link between them: Fane contributed to the book because he was, as the subtitle to his poem put it, a 'Kinsman' of Hastings, while Cotton probably knew the Hastings family through their ownership of the estate of Osmaston, just to the south of Ashbourne.[60]

The Lady Fane who was the dedicatee of the translation of *De cive* was the daughter of Sir Oliver Boteler, of Teston (just to the west of Maidstone) in Kent. Sir Oliver's original family estate was at Sharnbrook, in Bedfordshire; but he had married the daughter of a Kentish landowner, Thomas Barham, and had inherited the Barham estate at Teston, which became his principal residence. The Barhams were already significant landowners in the area, and during the 1610s and 1620s Sir

---

[60] R. B., ed., *Lachrymae musarum*, p. 1 (Westmorland); J. T., *The Old Halls, Manors, and Families of Derbyshire*, 4 vols. (London, Buxton, Derby, 1892–1902), IV, p. 56.

Oliver Boteler built up his holdings of land in Kent, buying at least five more manors within a ten-mile radius of Maidstone.[61] He died in 1632, leaving two sons, John and William, and one daughter, Anne.[62] John, the elder son, inherited the principal family estates, in both Kent and Bedfordshire; his mother bought back the Sharnbrook estate and gave it to her younger son. William Boteler also owned Saltwood castle, near Hythe, which was his own main residence while his brother lived at Teston. But John died childless in 1634, whereupon William succeeded to all the other estates.[63]

William Boteler was now head of the family, and thus probably the most important male figure in Anne Fane's life apart from her own husband. Born in 1612 or 1613, William had studied at Jesus College, Cambridge, and had been admitted to Gray's Inn in 1622. He had married in 1631; his wife, Joan, was a daughter of Sir Henry Fanshawe of Ware Park (in Hertfordshire), and sister of the poet Richard Fanshawe.[64] Through his wife, William Boteler would become closely involved in the Fanshawe family's financial affairs: in the summer of 1642 he helped to bail out her spendthrift elder brother, Sir Thomas Fanshawe, agreeing to pay his debts in return for the rights to all the 'Rents and profitts' of the Ware Park estate.[65] Like the Fanshawes, William Boteler was a staunch Royalist. He was MP for Bedford in the Long Parliament, and was made a baronet in 1641; by 1642 he was a 'Gentleman Pensioner' at court, and in the spring of that year he was in attendance on the King at York. He earned his place in history when, immediately after his return from York, he was chosen, together with the poet Richard Lovelace, to deliver Sir Edmund Dering's Royalist 'Kentish Petition' to the House of Commons. When these two representatives of the Kentish gentry presented the petition on 30 April, they claimed to be unaware that on 7 April the House had ordered it to be burned by the common hangman. Boteler and Lovelace were imprisoned for

---

[61] E. Hasted, *The History and Topographical Survey of the County of Kent*, 13 vols. (Canterbury, 1797–1801), II, pp. 358, 447; IV, pp. 207, 388, 459; V, pp. 130–2. To prevent confusion, it should be pointed out that this Boteler family was quite separate from the Botelers of Woodhall, Watton Woodhall, and Tewin in Hertfordshire: the Francis Boteler who married Sir Aston Cokayne's sister, and whose daughter, Isabella Boteler, married Cotton's brother-in-law Charles Hutchinson, was from that family and unrelated to Lady Fane; see J. E. Cussans, *History of Hertfordshire*, 3 vols. (London, 1870–81), vol. II, *Hundred of Broadwater*, pp. 169–70; W. C. Metcalfe, ed., *The Visitations of Hertfordshire*, Harleian Society Publications, no. 22 (London, 1886), pp. 29–30, 111–12; Victoria County History (hereafter V.C.H.), *Hertfordshire*, no. 3 (London, 1912), pp. 107, 162, 484; Squibb, *Visitation of Derbyshire*, p. 47; J. T. Godfrey, *Notes on the Churches of Nottinghamshire: Hundred of Bingham* (London, 1907), p. 362.

[62] Hasted, *History of Kent*, V, p. 132 (date of death); G. E. Cokayne, *Complete Baronetage*, 5 vols. (Exeter, 1900–6), II, p. 96 (referring also to a third son, who presumably died young); V.C.H., *Northamptonshire: Genealogical Volume, 'Northamptonshire Families'* (London, 1906), p. 96 (describing Anne as the only daughter).

[63] V.C.H., *Bedfordshire*, III (London, 1912), p. 89 (Sharnbrook); Hasted, *History of Kent*, VIII, p. 224 (Saltwood). G. E. Cokayne seems unaware of John's existence, and makes William succeed his father in 1632; see *Complete Baronetage*, II, p. 96.

[64] *The Memoirs of Ann Lady Fanshawe* [ed. H. C. Fanshawe] (London, 1907), p. 373.

[65] BL, MS Add. 27,979 (abstract of evidences, Ware, 1570–1668), fol. 5r.

several weeks, and were released only on finding security for £40,000 between them.[66]

After the outbreak of the Civil War, Sir William was imprisoned again, and his property sequestrated; he escaped from prison in March 1643 and went to join the King in Oxford. Before long he had raised a regiment at his own expense for the King. Both Sir William and his wife were at Oxford, the Royalist garrison town and seat of government, in the first half of 1644; but he was killed at the battle of Cropredy Bridge, near Banbury, on 29 June 1644.[67] His son, Oliver, aged only six, succeeded to his baronetcy and estates, but remained in Oxford until the surrender of that city in 1646.[68]

William Boteler's sister, Anne, had presumably remained in close touch with him for much of the period after 1634, when he mainly resided at Teston; she herself had married into the Fane family, whose lands lay just to the south and south-west of the Teston estate. Sir Francis Fane, who became the first Earl of Westmorland, held the principal estate at Tudely, east of Tonbridge (roughly seven miles from Teston); his brother Sir George had the manor of Buston or Burston (near Hunton), which lies less than two miles to the south of Teston. Sir George was born in 1581; he served as MP for Dover (1601), Sandwich (1604), Dover again (1614), Kent (1621), and Maidstone (1624, 1626, 1628, 1640), and died in June 1640. Anne and Sir George were married in 1620 (his first wife, Elizabeth Spencer, having died in 1618); she bore him six children, of whom the eldest, Spencer, was born in 1622 or 1623.[69] With so many children to look after, all under the age of eighteen at the time of her husband's death, she would very probably have become even more dependent on the advice and assistance of her brother and close neighbour.

After the death of Sir William Boteler in 1644, his widow, Joan, Anne Fane's sister-in-law, took over responsibility for his estate, applying to compound for it in 1646. While she was negotiating with the authorities in London between August and October of that year she rented rooms in Fleet Street; she was joined there by her own brother's wife, Ann Fanshawe, in September.[70] Richard and

---

[66] *Memoires of Ann Fanshawe*, p. 373; A. Everitt, *The Community of Kent and the Great Rebellion, 1640–60* (Leicester, 1966), 95–104; R. Lovelace, *Lucasta*, ed. W. C. Hazlitt (London, 1864), pp. xv–xxix; R. Lovelace, *Poems*, ed. C. H. Wilkinson, 2d edn (Oxford, 1930), pp. xxiv–xl; Weidhorn, *Lovelace*, pp. 19–20.

[67] *Memoirs of Ann Fanshawe*, p. 373; H. C. Fanshawe, *The History of the Fanshawe Family* (Newcastle-upon-Tyne, 1927), pp. 83–4; Sir Philip Warwick, *Memoires of the Reigne of King Charles I, with a Continuation to the Happy Restauration of King Charles II* (London, 1701), p. 272 (describing him as 'a Gentleman of extraordinary zeal to his Majestie's service').

[68] G. E. Cokayne, *Complete Baronetage*, II, p. 96; M. A. E. Green, ed., *Calendar of the Proceedings of the Committee for Compounding, &c, 1643–1660*, 5 vols. (London, 1889–92), II, p. 1462 (giving Sir Oliver's age as 10 in Aug. 1646).

[69] V.C.H., *Northamptonshire, Genealogical*, pp. 95–96; G. E. Cokayne, *The Complete Peerage*, ed. V. Gibbs, G. H. White, and R. S. Lea, 12 vols. (London, 1912–59), III, p. 294 (incorrectly making Thomas the eldest son); P. W. Hasler, ed., *The House of Commons, 1558–1603*, 3 vols. (London, 1981), III, p. 102; PRO microfilm Prob. 11/183, fols. 391v–394v (Sir George Fane's will).

[70] Green, *Calendar of the Committee for Compounding*, II, p. 1462; *Memoirs of Ann Fanshawe*, p. 44.

Ann Fanshawe had evidently enjoyed very close relations with the Botelers. Describing her own marriage (at Wolvercote, just north of Oxford, on 18 May 1644) in her autobiography, Ann Fanshawe listed the small group of close friends and relations who attended the ceremony, among whom were 'my brother and sister Boteler'; and of the six executors named in Sir William Boteler's will, his own wife was the first, and her brother, Richard Fanshawe, was the second. (Also present at the Fanshawes' wedding was Sir Edward Hyde, who was an old friend of Ann Fanshawe's family, the Harrisons. Given that Hyde was also a close friend of Charles Cotton Sr, it is conceivable that he was the link between the Cotton and Boteler families; this possibility may be left open, but at the same time it must be said that there are no surviving traces of any later connection or friendship between Hyde and Cotton.[71])

Ann and Richard Fanshawe spent the period from the autumn of 1646 to late 1649 partly in London and partly on the Continent, sometimes together and sometimes apart. Richard's sister, Lady Boteler, remarried in 1647; her new husband was Sir Philip Warwick, the Royalist politician who acted as secretary to Charles I in some of his negotiations in 1647 and 1648. The Fanshawes and Warwicks evidently stayed in close contact: when Ann Fanshawe's third child was born in London in May 1647 Sir Philip Warwick was his godfather, and when her seventh child was born in London in 1651 the godfather was Lady Warwick's son, Sir Oliver Boteler.[72]

The movements of the widowed Lady Fane, meanwhile, are less easy to trace. She probably stayed mainly on the estate near Hunton, but would have had to make some visits to London on legal and other business. Presumably she was at Hunton when her son Francis was buried there in December 1651.[73] But at some time in the following year she went to join the Royalist émigrés on the Continent. In September 1652 the County Committee for Kent informed against her as an 'excepted person' (excepted, that is, from the general amnesty arrangements for Royalists), and reported to the authorities in London that she had 'been beyond seas and married Sir John Culpepper' (or Colepeper: one of the leading advisers to, and diplomatic agents on behalf of, Charles II in exile). Two months later, however, the lawyers representing her in London produced an affidavit from the Burgomaster and town council of Bruges, stating that she had solemnly sworn before them that she had not remarried. Her later movements are not recorded. Evidently she remained abroad for some time: during 1653 and 1654 further negotiations over her estates had to be conducted on her behalf by a close family friend,

---

[71] *Memoirs of Ann Fanshawe*, pp. 373 (wedding), 601 (will). For advice on Hyde's biography, I am very grateful to Dr Paul Seaward.

[72] Ibid., pp. 215–16. Part of Ware Park, the Fanshawe family estate, was sold by Sir Oliver Boteler to Sir Philip Warwick in 1649: BL, MS Add. 27,979, fol. 6r.

[73] Cokayne, *Complete Peerage*, III, p. 294.

Henry Lucas.[74] At some stage she returned to England; she died in March 1664 and was buried at Hunton.[75]

From what little is known of the life of this Royalist lady, it might seem strange that she should have been the dedicatee of such a dauntingly theoretical work as the translation of *De cive*. Yet the evidence of her will shows that two of her particular friends during the final period of her life were men with unusually strong intellectual interests. One was 'my very worthy friend Sir Roger Twysden', the immensely learned antiquary and historian, and the other was 'my deare cousin Henry Lucas', who founded the Lucasian Chair of Mathematics at Cambridge and left a significant collection of 'bookes of divers subiects' to the University library.[76]

The picture sketched above of the family connections of Lady Fane suggests a fairly close-knit world of Fanes, Botelers, and Fanshawes, who may have been particularly thrown on one another's company (especially when some or all of them converged in London) during the difficult years 1646–50. During that period the young Cotton is thought to have made some visits to London; and it was probably then that he made the acquaintance of Lady Fane. So it is of particular interest to note that Charles Cotton Sr was a personal friend of Richard Fanshawe. The evidence for this is a copy of Fanshawe's translation of Camoens, *The Lusiad* (1655), inscribed 'For my noble Friend M$^r$ Cotton Richard Fanshawe'.[77] The poet Charles Cotton also had a copy, which he signed, of the 1648 edition of Fanshawe's translation of Guarini's *Pastor fido*.[78]

Fanshawe's friendship with Charles Cotton Sr may have begun in the 1630s, as a consequence of his own close connection with the Aston family of Tixall in Staffordshire, who were related (through Cotton's mother's family) to both the Cottons and the Cokaynes. Fanshawe had served under the diplomat Lord Aston in Madrid; he visited the family in Staffordshire in 1636 and appears to have contemplated marriage to Aston's daughter Constantia at that time. That there was

---

[74] Green, *Calendar of Committee for Compounding*, IV, p. 3044.
[75] V. C. H., *Northamptonshire, Genealogical*, p. 96.
[76] PRO microfilm Prob. 11/313, fols. 281r–283v (Anne Fane's will); here fols. 281r, 282v. Henry Lucas's will is PRO microfilm Prob. 11/311, fols. 354v–356r (see fol. 355r for the Cambridge benefactions). Lucas, a distant cousin of the Botelers, left a total of £3,000 in personal bequests to Lady Fane's family, 'in a heartie and thankefull acknowledgement of the many Charities I receaved from them both [*sc.* Sir George and Lady Fane] during the distresses of my life' (fol. 355r). His collection of more than 3,000 books included four works by Hobbes: *The Questions concerning Liberty, Necessity, and Chance*; *De corpore*; *De cive*; and *De corpore politico* (Cambridge University Library, MS Mm. 4. 27, fols. 18r, 32v, 39r, 43r).
[77] The copy was sold by Parke Bernet Galleries, New York, on 15 Nov. 1977. I am grateful to Dr Peter Davidson for confirming that the inscription is in Fanshawe's hand. Peter Beal incorrectly identifies the addressee as the poet, rather than his father ('Charles Cotton', 216); during the latter's lifetime the poet was addressed as 'Charles Cotton Esq.' while his father was 'Mr Charles Cotton' (cf. the forms of address used by Lovelace in the headings of the poems cited below at nn. 83, 85).
[78] J. H. Shorthouse, 'Charles Cotton the Angler, and Sir Richard Fanshawe', *Notes and Queries*, 4th ser., 1 (1868), p. 146.

some active sharing of literary interests between Lord Aston and Charles Cotton Sr is suggested by the fact that they were both patrons of John Fletcher.[79] So it seems possible that Cotton could have been put in touch with the Fanshawes by his father on a visit to London in 1647; and, if he knew either or both of them, he probably knew the Boteler family too.

The second person who represents a possible point of contact between the Cottons and the immediate family circle of Lady Fane is the other Royalist poet already mentioned, Richard Lovelace. The biography of Lovelace is also, unfortunately, full of lacunae; but it is unlikely that his presentation of the Kentish Petition with Sir William Boteler in 1642 was the only connection between these two devoted Royalists. (One contemporary account of that episode suggests that the two men planned the event with some care, sending agents to Blackheath to prepare for the mass meeting of petitioners that elected them as their two chief representatives.[80]) The Lovelaces were an old Kentish family; the poet's estates centred on Bethersden and Chart, west of Ashford, less than twenty miles from Teston. Another branch of the Lovelace family with which Richard's own branch was still in contact in the seventeenth century had estates at Kingsdown, ten miles northwest of Teston, and adjoining the manor of Fawkham, which belonged to the Boteler family.[81]

Richard Lovelace, having been a courtier and an army officer in the late 1630s, was forbidden to join the army as a condition of his release from prison in June 1642; he sold most of his lands in 1643 and may have gone abroad for most of the next three years. But in 1647 he was back in England and probably living in London. He was imprisoned again in the following year, and released in April 1649; his modern editor writes that 'nothing is known of his movements during the next few years'. The final period of his life was apparently spent in poverty (though the lurid picture of his destitution given by Anthony Wood has been rejected by his more recent biographers), and he died some time before October 1657.[82]

It is evident from Lovelace's own poems that he had a particularly close friendship with Charles Cotton Sr. One of his finest odes, 'The Grasse-hopper', is addressed to 'my noble Friend, Mr. Charles Cotton'; it includes the lines

> Thou best of *Men* and *Friends*! we will create
> A Genuine Summer in each others breast

---

[79] See R. Fanshawe, *The Poems and Translations*, ed. P. Davidson, 2 vols. (Oxford, 1997–), I, pp. xii, 375–7, 379; A. Clifford, ed., *Tixall Poetry; With Notes and Illustrations* (Edinburgh, 1813), esp. xxviii; Walton and Cotton, *Complete Angler*, p. clxiv. I am indebted to Dr Peter Davidson for pointing out the possible significance of Fanshawe's Aston connections.

[80] Everitt, *Community of Kent*, p. 103.

[81] See A. J. Pearman, 'The Kentish Family of Lovelace', *Archaeologia cantiana*, 10 (1876), pp. 184–220, which corrects Hasted's identification of the poet's branch with the Hever or Kingsdown Lovelaces. On Fawkham, see Hasted, *History of Kent*, II, p. 447.

[82] See Lovelace, *Poems*, pp. xlix–lvii; Weidhorn, *Lovelace*, pp. 20–4.

and presents, at one point, a Stoic trope reminiscent of the iconography of the first of the three engravings in *Philosophicall Rudiments*:

> Thus richer then untempted Kings are we,
> That asking nothing, nothing need . . .[83]

Lovelace also wrote an elegy for Cassandra Cotton, the only sister of Charles Cotton Sr, who died before 1649.[84] Another, more ambitious poem, 'The Triumphs of Philamore and Amoret', was written for the marriage of Charles Cotton in the summer of 1656. Addressed to 'the Noblest of our Youth and Best of Friends, Charles Cotton Esquire', it includes a passage that has generally been taken to refer to some sort of assistance given by Cotton to Lovelace when the latter was in prison:

> What Fate was mine, when in mine obscure Cave
> (Shut up almost close Prisoner in a Grave)
> Your Beams could reach me through this Vault of Night,
> And Canton the dark Dungeon with Light!
> Whence me (as gen'rous Spahy's) you unbound,
> Whilst I now know my self both Free and Crown'd.[85]

It is, admittedly, not clear to what extent this reference to a 'Dungeon' is meant to be interpreted metaphorically; the popular tradition that takes the 'obscure Cave' to refer to one of the caves overlooking the river Dove at Beresford does seem ludicrously overliteral. But it is quite possible that Cotton was, as his modern editor puts it, 'in some way instrumental in procuring Lovelace's release after his second imprisonment'.[86] Aubrey recorded a story that Cotton and another benefactor were at one stage sending one pound a week to Lovelace; but the dating of this episode is uncertain.[87] All we can tell from Cotton's own tribute to Lovelace, the elegy he wrote on the latter's death, is that the feelings he wished to express towards his 'worthy Friend' were those not of a benefactor to a recipient, but of a younger poet filled with 'gratitude' towards a model he admired.[88]

With these two personal connections with people linked to the family circle of Lady Fane, the case for his authorship of the translation of *De cive* is more or less complete. Little can be added to the story of that book itself: we have no information, for example, about what Lady Fane thought about Hobbes's text, if she ever read it. But it can be noted that her sister-in-law's second husband, Sir Philip Warwick, did take a strong interest in Hobbes's theories. He owned one of the special large-paper copies of *Leviathan*; and his own treatise on sovereignty, written in 1678, devoted five pages to a discussion of Hobbes. Like almost every writer at that time, he adopted a critical stance; and yet his tone was less shrill and denunciatory

---

[83] Lovelace, *Poems*, p. 39.  [84] Ibid., pp. 87–9.  [85] Ibid., p. 169.  [86] Ibid., p. lvii.
[87] Aubrey, *Brief Lives*, II, p. 38.  [88] Cotton, *Poems*, pp. 240–1.

than that of many other contemporary critics of Hobbes. 'By all this,' he soberly observed at the end of his discussion of *Leviathan*, 'we see how fatal it is for men of strong natural parts and good literature, to entertain false principles.'[89]

One person who in no way joined the hue and cry against Hobbes, however, was Cotton. Quite the contrary: his long travelogue poem about Derbyshire, *The Wonders of the Peake* (published in 1681 but evidently written before Hobbes's death in 1679), was consciously modelled on Hobbes's own *De mirabilibus pecci*, and it contained an explicit tribute to the elderly philosopher. Discussing the famous 'ebbing spring' at Tideswell (for which Hobbes had offered a physical explanation in his poem), he referred openly to Hobbes, giving his name in a note at the foot of the page:

> And *He who is in Nature the best read,
> Who the best hand has to the wisest head,
> Who best can think, and best his thoughts express,
> Does but, perhaps, more rationally guess,
> When he his sense delivers of these things,
> And Fancy sends to search these unknown Springs . . .
> *Mr Hobbs[90]

Other details in Cotton's poem, such as his borrowing of Hobbes's rather risqué comparison of a rock formation to female pudenda, confirm that he had made a careful reading of Hobbes's text.[91]

It is not known, unfortunately, whether Cotton ever met Hobbes at Chatsworth. But one rather touching memento does exist of his special interest in the philosopher: a copy of the 1681 *Thomae Hobbes angli malmesburiensis philosophi vita*, bearing Cotton's signature and his inscription 'Ex dono Comitis Devoniae' ('Gift of the Earl of Devonshire') on the title page, and signed again by him, as was his habit, on the final printed page.[92]

---

[89] Sir Philip Warwick, *A Discourse of Government, as examined by Reason, Scripture, and Law of the Land* (London, 1694), p. 59. His large-paper copy of *Leviathan* (which would probably have been produced at the end of the print-run, incorporating all in-press corrections), was sold at Sotheby's, New York, on 19 Nov. 1974.

[90] Cotton, *Wonders of the Peake*, p. 27.

[91] Ibid., p. 1; cf. Hobbes, *De mirabilibus pecci* (London, 1678), p. 42. There is, however, no evidence for the claim, frequently encountered in libraries' or booksellers' catalogues, that Cotton wrote the English translation of Hobbes's poem that was printed in parallel with it in the 1678 edn: this idea must arise simply from a confusion of that translation with Cotton's own text.

[92] This copy is now in the library at Chatsworth (pressmark 114 F), having probably been re-acquired by the Devonshires in the 19th cent.; I am very grateful to the Keeper of Collections, Mr Peter Day, for showing it to me, and to the trustees of the Chatsworth Settlement for permission to cite the inscription. It is not included in the listings of books with Cotton's ownership inscriptions given in A. I. Dust, 'Charles Cotton: His Books and Autographs', *Notes and Queries*, 217 (1972), pp. 20–3; Parks, 'Cotton and the Derby Manuscript'; and Beal, 'Charles Cotton'. Possibly the book was given to Cotton on the occasion of his own presentation of his *Wonders of the Peake* to its dedicatee, the Countess of Devonshire.

# – 9 –

# Pierre de Cardonnel (1614–1667), Merchant, Printer, Poet, and Reader of Hobbes

## I

Among the many treasures of the Pforzheimer Library is an annotated copy of the first edition of Hobbes's *Leviathan* (London, 1651) with an unusually interesting provenance. The engraved title page is inscribed: 'Ex Bibl. P. de Cardonnel. MDCLII. ex dono nobiliss. Com. Deu'.[1] This is of interest not only for the date—which would make the marginal comments in the book, if written at that time, the earliest such annotations to have come down to us—but also for the donor, William Cavendish, the third Earl of Devonshire ('Com. Deu.'), who was Hobbes's patron and employer. That there were personal connections between Cavendish and de Cardonnel is confirmed by an entry in the Earl's Privy Purse accounts for 29 December 1653, recording a gift of £20 'to Mr Cardennele' for his child's christening, as well as by other evidence, which will be cited below, recording visits by de Cardonnel to the Devonshire household.[2] The possibility—likelihood, even— thus arises that this attentive reader of *Leviathan* had the opportunity to discuss the arguments of that book with Hobbes himself.

One of the few readily obtainable pieces of information about de Cardonnel also confirms this Cavendish connection, and adds the possibility of a further indirect link with Hobbes. In 1662 de Cardonnel published a slim volume of poetry celebrating the recent marriage of Charles II and his coronation in the previous year. It included a Latin poem written extempore on the occasion of an encounter with the King on the Thames one day in July 1661; the poem was dedicated to the Earl of Devonshire, and the wording of the dedication suggested

---

[1] Harry Ransom Humanities Research Center, University of Texas at Austin, pressmark Pforz. 491. The printed catalogue, Anon., *The Carl H. Pforzheimer Library: English Literature, 1475–1700*, 3 vols. (New York, 1940), II, pp. 492–3, mistakenly gives the last word of the inscription as 'Dese'.
[2] Chatsworth, Derbyshire, MS Hardwick 14, p. 12.

(albeit ambiguously) that de Cardonnel had been in the company of the Earl when that encounter had taken place.[3] De Cardonnel also included his own French translations of poems by Waller and Dryden; the former, whom he addressed as a 'very dear friend', was himself a friend of both the Earl of Devonshire and Hobbes.[4]

As the author of the first known French translations of works by Dryden and Waller, de Cardonnel must deserve at least a small place in Anglo-French literary history. However, all modern writers on those two poets have passed him by in silence, and he receives no mention in either of the two early twentieth-century works that are still the only general surveys of Anglo-French literary relations in the seventeenth century.[5] A recent biographical study of another of his friends, the physician and philosopher Walter Charleton, notes that Pierre de Cardonnel wrote a poem in praise of Charleton in 1649, but is unable to add any information about him, commenting only that 'no trace of Cardonnel can be found in the current biographical dictionaries'.[6] In fact, the *Dictionary of National Biography* does include a brief reference to Pierre de Cardonnel's published poetical works (in the entry on his nephew, Adam de Cardonnel); but it adds no other details about his life, and mis-identifies him as 'Philip' instead.

The evidence that has survived of de Cardonnel's activities is fragmentary, and lies scattered among various archives in France and England. Nevertheless, by piecing together information derived from a range of sources, it is possible to construct a fairly detailed account of his life. The peculiar combination of interests and activities engaged in by de Cardonnel may mean that he is scarcely to be described as a 'typical' figure. But the story of his career does illustrate one characteristic feature of seventeenth-century intellectual life—the ease and fluidity with which (long before the Huguenot exodus of 1685) many individuals were able to cross the linguistic and cultural frontiers between France and England.

---

[3] P. de Cardonnel, *Complementum fortunatarum insularum* . . . (for the full title see below, at n. 163) (London, 1662), pp. 78–80: 'Occvrsus Regis in Tamesi. Julio obeunte A. 1661. Carmine extemporaneo conscriptus hortatu Magnatis Anglici meritissimi. Et illustrissimo Gvillelmo C. Devoniae, Poëseos omnisque politioris literaturae dignissimo Maecenati optimóque judici, In observantiae & gratitudinis testimonium Dicatus. A Nunquam dignè satis. amica in se collata officia & beneficia persoluturo. P.D.C.'

[4] 'Anglorum Poetarum cultissimo, Sibique Amicissimo Dom. Edm. Wallero' (ibid., p. 48). For evidence of Waller's friendship with Devonshire, see his letter to Devonshire of c.1657 (V. Klinkenborg, ed., *British Literary Manuscripts*, series I (New York, 1981), item 40). On his friendship with Hobbes, see Hobbes, *Correspondence*, I, pp. 294–7; II, pp. 913–15.

[5] C. Bastide, *The Anglo-French Entente in the Seventeenth Century* (London, 1914); G. Ascoli, *La Grande-Bretagne devant l'opinion française au XVII<sup>e</sup> siècle*, 2 vols. (Paris, 1930), II. For the second half of the century, some useful information is contained in L. Petit, *La Fontaine et Saint-Evremond, ou la tentation de l'Angleterre* (Toulouse, 1953); but this somewhat belletristic work also makes no mention of de Cardonnel. A thorough survey of Anglo-French literary relations during this period is one of the desiderata of modern scholarship.

[6] S. Fleitmann, *Walter Charleton (1620–1707), 'Virtuoso': Leben und Werk* (Frankfurt am Main, 1986), p. 293, n. 69: 'Zu Cardonnel findet sich kein Eintrag in den gängigen biographischen Lexika.'

PIERRE DE CARDONNEL (1614–1667)

## II

Pierre de Cardonnel was born in Normandy, in the town of Caen, in 1614. Most of the records of the Protestant community in Caen, to which his parents belonged, were unfortunately destroyed in the Second World War; but enough details have been preserved in the notes of nineteenth-century scholars to supply the basic facts about his family. His parents, Pierre de Cardonnel and Marguerite Lecoq, had married in 1608; he was the second of ten children, being preceded by a sister and followed by one other sister and seven brothers.[7] His father was described as a *bourgeois* of Caen, and apparently belonged to one of the town's established Protestant merchant families; his own father had married there in 1571, and they were probably related to the lawyer Vincent de Cardonnel, whose name appeared in the 1560s in the earliest registers of the Protestant church in Caen.[8] In the eighteenth century a 'family tradition' was noted, apparently from de Cardonnel's great-niece, according to which his father had been 'stiled the Marquis de Cardonnel, Seigneur du Château de Cardonnel . . . [and] that a small town belonging to him, bore his name'.[9] Family tradition exaggerated, as such traditions do: there was no marquessate in the family, nor was the appellation 'Sieur de', borne by Pierre in later life, a title of nobility.[10]

Caen was a flourishing town in the early seventeenth century, its prosperity flowing from trade (mainly with England) and manufacture (especially of textiles and paper). Protestants played a major role in both activities; the Protestant community in Caen was one of the most important in France, and by the second half of the century it would consist of more than 4,000 people, served by no fewer than four ministers. It was also unusually well integrated, thanks to the presence of a significant number of Protestant families among the magistrates, the upper bourgeoisie, and the local nobility. Protestants were able to participate fully in the cultural life of the town, which, with its university (where Protestants were admitted from 1612) and its four colleges, produced so many scholars and writers that it has been described as the 'Athens of Normandy'.[11]

---

[7] The main sources are the notes made by Pierre Carel (Archives Départementales du Calvados, Caen [hereafter: ADC], F 5377, fols. 64–5), and the information assembled by Henry Wagner (Huguenot Library, University College, London [hereafter: HL], MS T 8/1, no. 115). These yield the following dates of baptism: Marie, 1613; Pierre, 1614; Philippe, 1616; Jean, 1617; Jacques, 1618; Loys, 1620; Adam, 1621; Collasse, 1623; Daniel, 1625; Ozias, 1626. A copy of the parents' marriage contract survives, stating that the union was blessed in the Protestant church at Caen on 3 February 1608: ADC, 1 B 880, fol. 96v.

[8] ADC, F 5377, fol. 64r ('bourgeois'); HL, MS T 8/1, no. 115, draft pedigree (father, grandfather); C. E. Lart, ed., *The Registers of the Protestant Church at Caen (Normandy)* (Vannes, 1907), pp. 117, 265 (Vincent).

[9] A. Collins, *The Peerage of England*, 5th edn, 8 vols. (London, 1779), V, 405. (This is in the entry on William, Earl Talbot, who had married Mary de Cardonnel.)

[10] See the valuable comments in C. E. Lart, 'French Noblesse and Arms', *Proceedings of the Huguenot Society of London*, 15 (1933–7), pp. 476–88.

[11] See S. Beaujour, *Essai sur l'histoire de l'église réformée de Caen* (Caen, 1877), p. 293; A. Galland, *Essai sur l'histoire du protestantisme à Caen et en Basse-Normandie de l'Édit de Nantes à la Révolution (1598–1791)* (Paris, 1898), pp. 61, 103–5; G. Vanel, *Une Grande Ville aux XVII<sup>e</sup> et XVIII<sup>e</sup> siècles*, 2 vols. (Caen, 1910–12), II, pp. 31, 223 ('Athènes normande').

No information has survived about Pierre de Cardonnel's education; given his later proficiency not only in Latin and Greek, but also in Hebrew, it must have been a thorough one. In a petition of 1644 he would describe himself as follows: 'The sieur Cardonnel . . . having been educated in the humanities, has always preserved an affection for those who appreciate and cultivate them.'[12] His knowledge of Hebrew may perhaps have been acquired at one of the Protestant academies (the most important being those of Saumur, Sedan, Montauban, and Nîmes), but their registers for this period have not survived.[13] If his education took place only in Caen, on the other hand, then one possible clue may be provided by his association with the poet Jean-François Sarasin, whom he would later describe as 'joined to me by an old bond of friendship'.[14] As Sarasin (who was born in Caen in the same year as de Cardonnel) was probably educated at the town's Collège du Bois, it may well be that de Cardonnel also studied there.[15] If so, he would have come under the influence of two distinguished classical scholars: Antoine Gosselin, the translator of Apuleius, and Antoine Halley, who was described by a contemporary as 'one of the best Latin poets of this century'.[16]

Given his later devotion to book-collecting, scholarly publishing, and poetic composition, one senses that Pierre de Cardonnel would have liked to prolong the process of being 'educated in the humanities'. But adult responsibilities fell quickly on his shoulders. His father had died before April 1627, when he was only twelve or thirteen.[17] Under Norman customary law the age of majority was twenty: then, if not before, he must have felt the need to embark on a career that would restore the family's fortunes.[18] At some time in the 1630s he moved to Southampton, and started work as a merchant.

[12] BN, MS f.fr. 18600, fol. 726r: 'Le Sieur Cardonnel . . . ayant esté Institué és bonnes lettres a tousiours conserué de l'affection pour ceux qui les ayment et Cultiuent.'

[13] Lists are available only of students of theology at Montauban (Bibliothèque de la Société de l'Histoire du Protestantisme Français, Paris, MS 397/2) and of those students who presented theses at Saumur (L. Desgraves, 'Les Thèses soutenues à l'Académie protestante de Saumur au XVIIᵉ siècle', *Bulletin de la Société de l'Histoire du Protestantisme Français*, 125 (1979), pp. 76–97): de Cardonnel appears in neither of these. Generally, the Norman Protestants did not send their sons to the academies in the south of France, preferring Saumur (or Sedan, which was outside France).

[14] Bibliothèque Municipale de Caen [hereafter: BMC], pressmark Rés. C 162/1 (see below, n. 66), sig. 3¶1r: 'veterique amicitiae vincvlo sibi conivncto'.

[15] Paul Festugière writes that Sarasin was educated 'sans doute' at either the Collège du Bois or the Collège du Mont: J.-F. Sarasin, *Oeuvres*, ed. P. Festugière, 2 vols. (Paris, 1926), I, p. 10; Pierre Gouhier notes that he was a pupil of Antoine Halley, who taught at the former: 'La Société intellectuelle à Caen aux XVIᵉ et XVIIᵉ siècles', in R. Lebegue, ed., *La Basse-Normandie et ses poètes à l'époque classique* (Caen, 1977), 179–94; here p. 191(n.).

[16] On Gosselin see Gouhier, 'La Société intellectuelle', p. 181 n.; the auction catalogue of de Cardonnel's library (see below, n. 207) shows that he owned a copy of Gosselin's *Historia Gallorum veterum* (Caen, 1636). On Halley see Vanel, *Une Grande Ville*, II, p. 281 n. ('un des premiers poètes latins de ce siècle'), and the comments by his pupil Pierre Daniel Huet, *Commentarius de rebus ad eum pertinentibus* (Amsterdam, 1718), p. 26.

[17] ADC, F 6181 (a legal document dated April 1627, referring to 'Margueritte Le Coq Veufue de feu Pierre de Cardonnel').

[18] See D. Hoüard, *Dictionnaire analytique, historique, étymologique, critique et interpretatif de la coutume normande*, 4 vols. (Rouen, 1780–2), I, pp. 47–9; III, pp. 197–200.

## PIERRE DE CARDONNEL (1614–1667)

## III

The first trace of de Cardonnel's activities in England is to be found in the Port Book of Southampton for 1637. An entry for 6 April of that year records duties paid for goods imported in the 'Margery' of Southampton, a small ship (of 16 tons) arriving from Caen: 'Peter Cardinall . . . for three packetts cont. neate iiij.$^c$ lx ells of Normandy Canvas browne val xviii.$^{li}$ three halfe packetts Cont. lxxx Reames of ordinarie writting pap. val. x.$^{li}$.'[19] The lion's share of goods in the same vessel belonged to another merchant, Nicholas Pescod (who imported the same commodities, plus a large quantity of vinegar and 'feathers for bedd').[20] Pescod, who would soon become de Cardonnel's father-in-law, clearly played the dominant role in his life during his early years in England. Originally a grocer, he had become one of Southampton's leading traders; he was admitted as a burgess in 1614, became sheriff in 1622 and served as mayor in 1625 and 1640.[21] His trading activities, as detailed in the Port Books, were extensive: he imported cloth and vinegar from northern France, wine and prunes from Bordeaux, raisins, wine, and oil from Malaga, wet fish and train oil from Newfoundland, butter and tallow from Ireland, and deal boards from Norway. Pescod's main export from England was 'perpetuanas', a type of woollen cloth, but most of his outwards cargoes consisted of goods imported from elsewhere; thus, a typical shipment to Caen in March 1637 contained Malaga oil, 'reysons of the sonne', wet fish from Newfoundland, three pipes of Malaga wine, and a large quantity of North Sea cod.[22]

The particular reasons for de Cardonnel's move to Southampton, and the precise nature of his attachment to Pescod, are not known. The English port contained a significant community of French Protestants (a mixture of Normans, Walloons, and Channel Islanders), with its own church, but no de Cardonnels are noted in its early records.[23] Several of these Francophones were already well-established

---

[19] PRO, E 190 824/2 (Port Book, Southampton, Christmas 1636–Christmas 1637), 2nd quarter, entry 33.

[20] Ibid., 2nd quarter, entry 32. The relative value of their shares in the ship's cargo is given by the total of 'imposts' payable: 26s. for de Cardonnel, and 76s. 4d. for Pescod.

[21] On Pescod see B. B. Woodward, T. C. Wilks and C. Lockhart, *A General History of Hampshire, or the County of Southampton*, 3 vols. (London, 1863), II, p. 312; S. D. Thomson, ed., *Southampton in 1620 and the 'Mayflower': An Exhibition of Documents by the Southampton City Record Office* (Southampton, 1970), pp. 44–5; S. D. Thomson, ed., *The Book of Examinations and Depositions before the Mayor and Justices of Southampton 1648–1663*, Southampton Records Series, 37, (Southampton, 1994), p. 225; and the genealogy of Pescod in HL, MS T 8/1, no. 115. He was born in 1576 or 1577, and died on 23 Sept. 1643: City Archives Office, Southampton [hereafter: CAO], D/LY38/144.

[22] PRO, E 190 824/2 (exports to Caen: final section, retrograde, inverted, item 30, 15 March 1636/7); E 190 824/7 (Port Book, Southampton, imported wines, Christmas 1637–Christmas 1638); E 190 824/8 (Port Book, Southampton, Christmas 1637–Christmas 1638); E 190 824/10 (Port Book, Southampton, Easter–Michaelmas 1638).

[23] On the history of this community see A. Spicer, *The French-Speaking Reformed Community and their Church in Southampton, 1567–c.1620*, Huguenot Society, n.s., 3 (London, 1997). The register of marriages and baptisms at the Walloon church, Southampton, 1567–1779 (PRO, RG 4/4600), mentions no de Cardonnels before the baptism of Pierre's nephew Adam in November 1663.

among the merchants of the city; one of the most prominent of them, Daniel Hersent, had married Pescod's sister.[24] Pescod was clearly keen to extend his own contacts with trading families in France, as a striking entry (dated 11 September 1638) in the Southampton 'Examination Book' shows:

The voluntary deposicion of Peter Rocques aged xix yeares or thereabout sonne of Anthoney Rocques late of Bourdeaux in France merchant deceased. I Peter Rocques doe ... declare ... that I am indebted and doe iustly owe to M$^r$: Nicholas Pescod of the Towne and County of Southampton merchant One hundred pounds sterling for money, diet, apparrell lodginge and educacion received by mee of him the said M$^r$: Pescod at his owne charge by the space of three yeares and an half or neare thereabouts, For w$^{ch}$ I have beene kept in prison during the space of Nyne monethes last past . . .[25]

The pattern here so closely matches the case of Pierre de Cardonnel (also the son of a deceased father) that one may wonder whether the last phase of his education had taken place not in Caen but in Southampton. If so, it probably would have involved tuition by the minister and former schoolmaster Alexander Ross, who was vicar of Holy Rood Church (Pescod's parish church, situated just on the other side of the High Street from his house): as we shall see, de Cardonnel was on very friendly terms with Ross by the mid–1640s.[26] But only speculation is possible here; the 'educacion' referred to in Rocques's case may have been little more than tuition in English. All that can be said with reasonable certainty is that, if de Cardonnel's attachment to Pescod was on the same basis as that of the unfortunate Pierre Rocques, de Cardonnel did at least pay his fees and earn the approval of his host and master, whose eldest daughter he would shortly marry.

The records of de Cardonnel's own activities in these early years are sparse. The Port Book for 1637 has eighteen entries for Pescod, but only one (quoted above) for de Cardonnel. In the Port Books for the following year there are entries for one shipment by 'Peter Cardonel and Companey', a cargo of wine and vinegar arriving from Bordeaux in December.[27] As this level of activity is clearly too low to have supported him financially, it seems likely that he was either working for Pescod, or spending much of his time elsewhere. The most valuable piece of evidence that has come down to us about de Cardonnel's later career as a merchant is a small

---

[24] Hampshire Record Office, Winchester (hereafter: HRO), 46 M 48/41 (copy of Nicholas Pescod's will), codicil: bequest of a ring 'to my sister Hersent the wife of M$^r$ Daniell Hersent'. On the Hersent family see Thomson, *Southampton in 1620*, pp. 22, 58, and R. D. Gwynn, ed., *A Calendar of the Letter Books of the French Church of London from the Civil War to the Restoration, 1643–1659*, Huguenot Society of London, Quarto series, 54 (London, 1979), p. 103.

[25] CAO, SC 9/3/11 (Examination Book, 1622–44), fol. 439r.

[26] See below, at n. 109. On Ross's earlier career (master of Southampton School, 1616–20; appointed vicar of Holy Rood, 1628), see C. F. Russell, *A History of King Edward VI School Southampton* (Cambridge, 1940), pp. 156–7.

[27] PRO, E 190 824/7, fourth quarter, item 56 (10 Dec. 1638: 'lxij tonnes & two hogshedes of frenche wynes'); E 190 824/8, fourth quarter, item 80 (10 Dec. 1638: iii Tonnes & halfe of Vinegar'); both were from Bordeaux, in the 'Blessing'.

notebook he compiled in the mid-1650s, in which he listed all his contacts and correspondents, arranging their names under the places (listed in alphabetical order) from which they traded. In most cases the names are annotated with dates, recording when he had contact with them. The earliest year mentioned is 1638: an entry for Augsburg specifies 'Christoph van Steten: travelled from London with me in 1638', and there are other names annotated with that date under Dover, Antwerp, Cologne, Bremen and Hamburg.[28] This suggests that de Cardonnel had travelled to northern Germany, via Antwerp, perhaps in the company of van Steten, during that year.

That de Cardonnel began his journey in 1638 in London is also significant; within a couple of years he would make that city his main place of residence. London too had its French Protestant community: another entry in his notebook shows that he was in contact with two of the leading merchants there, Abraham and Jacob de la Forterie, in 1638.[29] Pierre de Cardonnel also had a family connection with that community: his father's sister Jeanne had married a merchant from Caen, François Fontaine, and after his death she had gone to live in London with one of her children, the merchant Pierre Fontaine.[30] His own transfer to London took place just too late for him to be recorded in the 'Returns of Strangers' for 1639, but by the spring of 1640 he was established as a trader in the Port of London: an entry in the Port Book for 23 April records 'P[ete]r Cardonell . . . lxi cwt mader' (i.e. madder, the dye-plant).[31] An agreement made between de Cardonnel and Pescod in March 1641 referred to 'the now dwelling house of the said Peeter de Cardonell situate in St Lawrence Pountneys lane in London'.[32] Laurence Pountney Lane, which lies just to the west of London Bridge, is only a few hundred yards from Threadneedle Street, where the French Protestant community had its church; de Cardonnel thus probably became a member of that congregation, though, as we shall see, he would not remain in it for long.[33]

---

[28] BL, MS Sloane 1731B, fols. 10v, 11r ('Christoph van Steten. passé de Londres auec moy en 1638'), 14v, 17r, 19v, 24r. The catalogue of the Sloane MSS identifies the author of this MS only as 'Jean de Cardonnel' (Pierre's brother); a few pages (fols. 2–4r, 5–6, 46–8) are in his hand, but all the rest of the MS is by Pierre.

[29] Ibid., fol. 14r.

[30] HL, MS T 8/1, no. 115 (draft pedigree of de Cardonnel: marriage, 8 Nov. 1598); W. J. C. Moens, ed., *The Registers of the French Church, Threadneedle Street, London*, Publications of the Huguenot Society of London, 20 (Lymington, 1896), p. 176 (25 March 1632: 'Jeane de Cardonnel, veufue de Francois Fontaine', witness to the baptism of the daughter of Pierre Fontaine and Marie Papillon). François Fontaine had died before 1632 (information from Pasteur Denis Vatinel, to whom I am especially grateful).

[31] PRO, E 190 44/3 (Port Book, London, aliens, Christmas 1639–Christmas 1640), entry for that date. The 'Returns' are printed in I. Scouloudi, *Returns of Strangers in the Metropolis, 1593, 1627, 1635, 1639: A Study of an Active Minority*, Publications of the Huguenot Society of London, Quarto series, LVII (London, 1985).

[32] HRO, 46 M 48/38a (indenture of 11 June 1641, recapitulating the March agreement).

[33] De Cardonnel's name appears nowhere in the records of the church, but very few of these survive for this period. His friend or business contact Jacob de la Forterie was a prominent member of the church, serving as deacon in 1639, 1641, and 1643: French Protestant Church of London, Soho Square (hereafter: FPCL), MS 5 (Consistory Acts, 1615–1680), fols. 126v, 131r, 141r. See also Gwynn, *Calendar*, p. 92.

The agreement made between de Cardonnel and Pescod in March 1641 concerned the impending marriage of de Cardonnel and Katherine, Pescod's eldest daughter. She was the only child of his first marriage; a second wife, who died in 1630, had given him three more daughters and a son.[34] The financial arrangements made by Pescod were quite lavish, compared with those he would make for his other daughters: under his will (made just before his death in September 1643) they were to receive £400, £500, and £650 respectively when they married or reached the age of 21, whereas de Cardonnel was promised a dowry of £1,500. Unfortunately, the arrangement was complex and partly conditional, and subsequent changes, made by Pescod shortly before his death, would create a legal tangle against which de Cardonnel would struggle for the rest of his life. The original condition of the dowry was that within seven years of the marriage de Cardonnel would settle on Katherine 'lands . . . in the kingdome of France' worth 300 livres tournois per annum; he would then receive £1,000, and the other £500 would be paid within a year of Pescod's death. Until that condition was fulfilled, he would be given only the interest on the £1,000 (£75 per annum for three years, thereafter £65). In 'part performance' of this pledge, Pescod gave him a ninety-nine-year lease of the estate he owned near Fawley (to the west of Southampton), consisting of the manors of Cadlands, Holbury, and South Langley, at a peppercorn rent. On his deathbed in September 1643, however, he reassigned the manors to his executors, instructing them to hold the estate in trust for his son William, until William reached the age of thirty. Only three years later William died, and the estate was divided into four portions, one for each of the surviving children. De Cardonnel and his wife then sold their portion to his younger brother, Adam. The dowry originally promised to de Cardonnel was never paid; in the legal dispute that followed, the executors would claim that, while they had paid him the interest for seven years, he had failed to settle the requisite lands on his wife during that time—a surprising omission, if true, as 300 livres tournois came to only £22 5s. 6d. in English money.[35]

The stipulation that the jointure settled on Katherine by de Cardonnel should consist of 'lands . . . in the kingdome of France' suggests that de Cardonnel was not planning to settle permanently in England. The marriage itself took place in Caen, in April 1641; whether it was also solemnized in Southampton is not known.[36]

---

[34] HL, MS T 8/1, no. 115 (Pescod pedigree).

[35] The relevant documents are HRO, 46 M 48/38a (indenture of the 99-year lease, recapitulating the earlier agreement); 46 M 48/40 (indenture between Pescod and executors, 7 Sept. 1643); 46 M 48/41 (copy of Pescod's will, 9 Sept. 1643); 4 M 60/126 (indenture between de Cardonnel, Katherine, and executors, 9 March 1647, for the transfer to Adam, noting the death of William 'about eight monthes since'); 15 M 55/8 (judgment of Court of Exchequer, 1672, summarizing the subsequent dispute). The rate of exchange in 1641 was 52d. to one *écu de change*; one *écu de change* equalled three *livres tournois*; see J. J. McCusker, *Money and Exchange in Europe and America, 1600–1775* (Chapel Hill, NC, 1978), pp. 88–9.

[36] HL, MS T 8/1, no. 115, draft pedigree of de Cardonnel (marriage in Caen). The records of the Walloon church in Southampton (PRO, RG 4/4600) are defective for this period, with no entries for marriages between 1632 and 1660; those of Holy Rood church (of which a copy is in CAO) begin only in 1653.

PIERRE DE CARDONNEL (1614–1667)

Both Pierre de Cardonnel and his brother Adam obtained letters of denization in August 1641; unlike Adam, however, Pierre would never take the further (and much more important) step of applying for naturalization in England.[37] Between the marriage in April 1641 and the death of Nicholas Pescod in September 1643, there is no clear evidence that de Cardonnel set foot in Southampton again: he continued to import some goods there, but his affairs were handled by his father-in-law.[38] His brother Adam, on the other hand, did spend some time in Southampton, and the legal documents drawn up by Pescod at the end of his life bear the signature of Adam as a witness.[39]

Two of Pierre's other brothers had also begun their careers as merchants: Philippe had been on a trading journey in 1638, and Jean and Philippe were apparently trading as partners in England at the time of Pescod's death.[40] With such a network already in place, Pierre may in any case have planned to return to Caen, to take up residence in his widowed mother's house and direct the family's trading operations from there. The outbreak of the Civil War, in which both London and Southampton became parliamentary strongholds, can only have strengthened such a decision; for de Cardonnel, as we shall see, was a fervent Royalist.[41] By the spring of 1644 he and his wife were living in the family home in the centre of Caen. But his energies were concentrated on a project which, in view of his entire personal history up to this point, must come as something of a surprise to the reader: he was now setting up as a printer, with the intention of producing major works of Hebrew and Arabic scholarship.

## IV

On the afternoon of Monday, 13 March 1644, two senior officials of the 'présidial' court of Caen, accompanied by the town bailiff, went to the residence of 'the honorable Pierre de Cardonnel, merchant and *bourgeois*', in the rue de Saint-Pierre.

[37] W. A. Shaw, ed., *Letters of Denization and Acts of Naturalization for Aliens in England and Ireland, 1603–1700*, Publications of the Huguenot Society of London, 18 (Lymington, 1911), pp. 64 (denization), 70 (naturalization of Adam, 1657).
[38] CAO, SC 5/4/89 (Petty Customs Book, Southampton, 1637–44), second pagination, p. 6, 15 July 1642: 'M[r] Pescod oweth . . . out of the Margery 3 tunes of vineger 8[d] more for m[r] Cardinall 1 packett 7 dozen of Buckrums 3[d]'; cf. similar entries for 22 Sept. 1642 (p. 6) and 14 Jan. 1643 (p. 42). That this 'm[r] Cardinall' was Pierre and not Adam is confirmed by an entry dated 18 March 1642 in the Examination Book (CAO, SC 9/3/11, fol. 521r), a deposition relating to goods 'for the accompt of m[r]. Nicholas Pescod & m[r] Peter Cardonnell merchants', laden at Malaga and lost in a shipwreck off Dublin.
[39] HRO, 46 M 48/39 (indenture of 6 Sept. 1643); 46 M 48/40.
[40] BL, MS Sloane 1731B, fol. 24r (Philippe); HRO, 15 M 55/8 (referring to 'goods of Pescods remayning in the hands of John de Cardonnell partner of the said Philip de Cardonnell').
[41] On the parliamentary takeover of Southampton in Dec. 1642 (despite the mainly royalist sympathies of the city's elite), and the subsequent rule by the 'coarse despot' Governor Murford, see J. S. Davies, *A History of Southampton, partly from the MS of Dr Speed, in the Southampton Archives* (Southampton, 1883), pp. 485–9 (quotation: p. 489(n.) ), and G. N. Godwin, *The Civil War in Hampshire (1642–45) and the Story of Basing House* (Southampton, 1904), pp. 96–8.

Their purpose was to enforce a recent decree of the Parlement of Rouen, which had called for the investigation and suppression of unauthorized printing-houses in Caen. Clearly, they were acting on information received: they immediately entered 'a small building in the courtyard at the side of the large building of the said sieur de Cardonnel's house' and climbed upstairs to 'a small room which, we were told, was called the printing-place'. There they found a type-setter at work, and a master-printer, Jean Jannon, who said he was the type-setter's employer. All the boxes of equipment (except the trays of type, which contained an estimated 25,000 characters) were sealed and placed in a cupboard, which was then locked and sealed; the keys were entrusted to 'madame Catherine Pescod, wife of the said sieur de Cardonnel', who gave her word that the cupboard would not be opened without permission.[42]

De Cardonnel appealed to higher authority, sending a petition to the Chancellor, Pierre Séguier, who bore ultimate responsibility for the regulation of printing and publishing throughout France. His petition, which provides essential information about the background to the project, deserves to be quoted at length:

The sieur Cardonnel, merchant of the town of Caen and resident there, having been educated in the humanities, has always preserved an affection for those who appreciate and cultivate them. And, wishing to contribute his efforts, such as they are, for the public good, he has bought a large quantity of characters of all sorts, even for oriental languages, on the advice of the sieur Sergius, a relation of the sieur Gabriel Sionita, professor of oriental languages. He has taken on as his employee the sieur Jannon, who is very skilled in the art of printing and has practised that art for a long time in the printing-house of the Estiennes in Paris: Jannon has with him recommendations and references from people of honour, which serve as guarantees and assurances of his competence and probity. He [de Cardonnel] has collected the texts of Arabic proverbs and moral writings translated into Latin, with very fine annotations, as well as treatises on the animals, plants, precious stones, stars, and other things of peculiar interest mentioned in the Bible. He will not have anything printed without having first presented an accurate copy of it to the lord Chancellor, who will assign such persons as he wishes to look at it and examine it, so that he may then give him the privilege to print it, in the usual form and manner.[43]

---

[42] BN, MS 18600, fols. 728–729r (procès-verbal, 14 March 1644): 'honorable homme Pierre de Cardonnel, marchand bourgeois' . . . 'un petit corps de logis estant dans la cour d'à costé du grand logis des maisons dud[it] sieur de Cardonnel' . . .'une petite chambre que l'on nous a dit se nommer le lieu de l'imprimerie' . . .'damoiselle Catherine Pescod, femme dud[it] sieur de Cardonnel'; 730r (decree, 4 March 1644); printed in G. Lepreux, *Gallia typographica, ou répertoire biographique et chronologique de tous les imprimeurs de France*, Série départementale, 4 vols. (Paris, 1909–13), III(ii), pp. 180–3.

[43] BN, MS 18600, fol. 726r (petition signed by de Cardonnel but not dated): 'Le Sieur Cardonnel Marchand de la ville de Caen et y demeurant ayant esté Institué és bonnes lettres a tousiours conserué de l'affection pour ceux qui les ayment et Cultiuent, Et désirant contribuer ce qui est de son Industrie pour le bien publicq Il a achapté vn grand nombre de characteres de toutes sortes, mesmes pour les langues orientalles par l'aduis du sieur Sergius parent du sieur gabriel sionita, professeur és langues Orientalles. Il a pris a ses gaiges le sieur Jannon fort entendu en l'art d'Imprimerie et qui en a faict longuement la profession dans l'imprimerie des estiennes a paris et est porteur des tesmoignages et attestations des personnes d'honneur qui

## PIERRE DE CARDONNEL (1614–1667)

Of the three individuals mentioned by de Cardonnel here, two are easily identifiable. The printer Jean Jannon (1580–1658) was a Protestant from Paris, who had been apprenticed to Robert Estienne (III) and then had moved to Sedan, where he became official printer to the Protestant Academy. In 1621 he published samples of new type-sets he had designed, including one set of Hebrew characters, and announced his intention to make 'Hebrew, Chaldaean, Syriac and Arabic characters'. In 1640 he left his son Pierre in charge of the press at Sedan and moved to Paris to look after the press of another son, who had recently died. Jannon was hired by de Cardonnel some time in the autumn of 1643, and took his printing equipment to Caen in the last week of October. He would return to Sedan in late 1645 or 1646, having sold all the equipment (apparently, to de Cardonnel).[44] Gabriel Sionita (Jibrail as-Sahyuni: 1577–1648), a Maronite from the Lebanon, was one of the leading Arabic scholars in Europe; in 1614 he had moved from Rome to Paris, where he taught Arabic and Syriac at the Collège Royal and worked on the preparation of the Paris Polyglot Bible.[45] The third person mentioned by de Cardonnel, the 'sieur Sergius', a relative of Gabriel Sionita, is probably to be identified as Sarkis el-Jamari (d. 1668), another Maronite (from the same village as Sionita), who was ordained priest in 1635, became one of the interpreters of the Palais Royal and a professor of oriental languages in Paris, and later (in 1658) returned to the Lebanon, where he became bishop of Tripoli.[46]

However, the most important person to feature in de Cardonnel's project—the one, indeed, who had occasioned this unusual conjuncture of oriental linguistics and typography in the provincial town of Caen—was not mentioned by him anywhere in his petition. This was the Protestant minister Samuel Bochart (1599–1667), who, thanks to de Cardonnel's efforts, would eventually become

seruent de cauxtion et d'asseurance de sa suffisance et probité. Il a recouuré des escriptes de proverbes et moralitez Arabes traduits en latin, auec des nottes exquises[,] des traittées des animaux, plantes, pierres precieuses Astres et autres choses Curieuses dont est faict mention dans la Bible, Il mettra rien soubz la presse qu'il n'en ayt présenté vne coppie fidelle a monseigneur le chancelier qui commettra telles personnes qu'il luy plaira pour la veoir et examiner afin puis apres d'en donner le priuillege en la forme et maniere accoustumee': printed (with minor inaccuracies) in Lepreux, *Gallia typographica*, III(i), p. 436.

[44] On Jannon's career see J.-B. Brincourt, *Jean Jannon, ses fils, leurs oeuvres* (Sedan, 1902) ('caractères Hebrieux, Chaldaïques, Syriaques, Arabiques': pp. 34–5; date of return 1646: p. 70); Lepreux, *Gallia typographica*, II, pp. 18–25 (date of return 5 Nov. 1645: p. 22). For the move to Caen see H. Bots and P. Leroy, eds., *Correspondance intégrale d'André Rivet et de Claude Sarrau*, 3 vols. (Amsterdam, 1978–82), II, p. 122 (Sarrau to Rivet, from Paris, 29 Oct. 1643): 'son imprimeur est parti d'ici cette semaine avec tout l'appareil oriental qui lui estoit necessaire'.

[45] See J. de la Roque, *Voyage de Syrie et du Mont-Liban*, 2 vols. (Paris, 1722), II, pp. 123–4; G. Graf, *Geschichte der christlichen arabischen Literatur*, 5 vols. (Vatican City, 1944–53), III, pp. 351–3; P. Raphael, *Le Rôle du Collège Maronite romain dans l'orientalisme aux XVIIe et XVIIIe siècles* (Beirut, 1950), pp. 73–85.

[46] Raphael, *Le Rôle du Collège Maronite*, p. 118. 'Sarkis' is the Arabic form of 'Sergius'. Raphael does not comment on the relationship to Sionita, but records that both came from the village of Ehden. Gérald Duverdier describes him as Sionita's nephew, and notes that he held the chair of Arabic at the Collège Royal from 1647 to 1658. He also suggests that he had had type made from the matrices of Arabic type belonging to Sionita ('Les Impressions orientales en Europe et le Liban', in C. Aboussouan, ed., *Le Livre et le Liban jusqu'à 1900* (Paris, 1982), pp. 157–279; here pp. 268–9).

known as one of the greatest orientalists in France. Bochart had spent two years (1621–3) studying at Leiden under the doyen of Arabic scholarship in the West, Thomas Erpenius; in 1624 he returned to Caen, his native town, to become a minister. While actively fulfilling his pastoral duties there he also devoted himself intensively to oriental studies, compiling (by 1630) an Arabic dictionary of more than 30,000 words.[47] Possibly he was the teacher with whom de Cardonnel had first studied Hebrew; he may now have been giving him further tuition, as de Cardonnel seems to have acquired both an interest in Arabic (several Arabic texts would later feature in his library) and some knowledge of Syriac (de Cardonnel's marginalia in his copy of *Leviathan* include the name 'Cephas' in the Syriac script).[48]

The major work that Bochart had now completed—and which de Cardonnel would finally succeed in publishing, after many delays, in 1646—was his *Geographia sacra*, better known as *Phaleg*, a colossal survey of biblical geography and history, based on Hebrew, Arabic, and classical sources, which argued that all the peoples and cultures of the ancient world (including key elements of the pagan religions) could be traced back to Hebrew origins.[49] The 'texts of Arabic proverbs and moral writings translated into Latin, with very fine annotations' mentioned in de Cardonnel's petition can also be identified, thanks to the survival of items from Bochart's library in the Bibliothèque Municipale de Caen, as another of Bochart's projects. He had prepared a special copy of the collection of Arabic proverbs attributed to Ali (the Prophet Mohammed's son-in-law) published in 1629 by Erpenius's favourite pupil, Golius (Jacob Gool); Bochart's copy was interleaved with blank pages, on which he had written Latin translations of the proverbs.[50] Evidently he hoped to add his own annotations and publish a work that might rival in popularity the famous edition of another set of proverbs produced by Scaliger and Erpenius, *Proverbiorum arabicorum centuriae duae*.[51] And the other items referred to in de Cardonnel's petition, the 'treatises on the animals, plants, precious

[47] On Bochart see E.-H. Smith, *Samuel Bochart: recherches sur la vie et les ouvrages de cet auteur illustre* (Caen, 1833); Beaujour, *Essai sur l'histoire de l'église de Caen*, pp. 295–9; E. Haag, ed., *La France protestante, ou vies des protestants français*, 2nd edn, 6 vols. (Paris, 1877–88), II, pp. 647–66.

[48] For the library see the appendix to this essay; the marginal note is in his *Leviathan* (see above, n. 1) p. 302.

[49] The work is in two parts, with continuous pagination: the first is entitled *Geographiae sacrae pars prior Phaleg*, and the second, *Geographiae sacrae pars altera Chanaan*. The whole work is commonly referred to as *Phaleg*. This word, the name of a patriarch ('Peleg' in the Authorized Version of the Bible: see Gen. 10: 25), is derived from a Hebrew verb meaning to divide or share; Phaleg lived at the time when the world was shared between the grandchildren of Noah, and that sharing-out forms the basic theme of the book. The second part is devoted mainly to the ancient Phoenicians, arguing also for Hebrew origins.

[50] BMC, pressmark in-8° 26: *Proverbia quaedam Alis, imperatoris muslimici, et carmen Togra'i, poëtae doctis, nec non dissertatio quaedam Aben Sinae* (Leiden, 1629). On Golius see W. M. C. Juynboll, *Zeventiende-eeuwsche beoefenaars van het Arabisch in Nederland* (Utrecht, 1931), pp. 119–83 (on this publication: pp. 147–8).

[51] Bochart's copy of the 2nd edn of this work (Leiden, 1623) is bound with the *Proverbia quaedam Alis* (above, n. 50).

– 270 –

stones, stars, and other things of peculiar interest mentioned in the Bible', were also parts of Bochart's work-in-progress: one of these treatises, his voluminous study of the animals that feature in the Bible, *Hierozoicon*, would eventually be published in 1663.

The omission of Bochart's name from the petition, and the difficulties experienced by de Cardonnel over the publication of his book, have a simple explanation. Although relations between Catholics and Protestants at the personal level were generally cordial in mid-seventeenth-century Caen, the same could not be said of the attitude of the ecclesiastical authorities, either there or (still less) in Paris. Bochart had already had one unpleasant encounter with the Catholic establishment of the town: in 1630–1 a former Jesuit, François Véron (with whom he had conducted a public disputation in 1628), had had Bochart taken to court, on the charge that his negative comments about the Catholic Church made him guilty of *lèse-majesté*.[52] Protestant biblical scholarship was suspected, naturally enough, of surreptitious anti-Catholicism: when the young Caennais student Pierre Daniel Huet heard about Bochart's forthcoming book and sought him out for private tuition, their meetings were held 'cautiously and secretly, almost at night, without witnesses'.[53] And the authorities in Paris were particularly keen that French oriental scholarship should remain a Catholic preserve: after the death of Savary de Brèves (the former French ambassador to Istanbul, and chief patron of oriental studies in early seventeenth-century France), the King's printer was compelled by royal order in 1632 to buy his famous Arabic press, the 'Typographia Savariana', so that his rare type-faces 'should not be sold to foreigners ... as much because they could use them to do great harm to religion, as because they are one of the splendid ornaments of his kingdom'.[54] If de Cardonnel was in possession of Arabic type when his house was raided in March 1644, those characters were confiscated and never returned to him: the volume he eventually printed adopts the common convention of setting Arabic words, *faute de mieux*, in the Hebrew alphabet.

The story of the difficulties encountered by de Cardonnel can be followed in the correspondence between Bochart's closest friend in Paris, the scholar Claude

---

[52] See Galland, *Essai sur l'histoire du protestantisme à Caen*, pp. 42–4.

[53] Huet, *Commentarius*, p. 43 ('cautè & occultè, ac ferè noctu & sine testibus'). Huet, a future bishop, was the son of a convert from Protestantism to Catholicism. Bochart was a major influence on his life and thinking, and the arguments of Huet's most famous work, *Demonstratio evangelica* (Paris, 1679), tracing classical mythology to biblical sources, have their origins in Bochart's *Phaleg* (of which Huet's annotated copy survives: BMC, pressmark FN Rés. C 445).

[54] Quotation from a later memoir by the royal printer, Vitray or Vitré, in A. Bernard, *Antoine Vitré et les caractères orientaux de la Bible polyglotte de Paris* (Paris, 1857), p. 9: 'ne fussent point vendues à des estrangers ... tant par ce qu'ils en pourroient faire beaucoup de mal à la religion, qu'à cause que c'est un des beaux ornements de son royaume'; cf. the comments in Duverdier, 'Les Impressions orientales', p. 269, and G. J. Toomer, *Eastern Wisedome and Learning: The Study of Arabic in Seventeenth-Century England* (Oxford, 1996), pp. 30–2. The Imprimerie royale and the Bibliothèque du Roi did preserve their monopoly on Arabic type in France, with the result that the type remained entirely unused between 1645 and 1774.

Sarrau, and Bochart's uncle at The Hague, the theologian André Rivet. On 7 May 1644 Sarrau wrote: 'the plan to set up a printing-house in Caen is very much in jeopardy, as the Chancellor is strongly opposed to it, and will not listen to reason.'[55] De Cardonnel's petition had evidently been rebuffed. But he was, as we shall see, an unusually well-connected person; only a few days after Sarrau wrote this letter, de Cardonnel did obtain a 'Privilège' from the King (dated 10 May 1644), granting him exclusive rights of publication for Bochart's *Phaleg* for a period of ten years.[56] It seems that the Chancellor, and/or the local authorities in Normandy, continued to obstruct the publication none the less: they may well have argued that, although de Cardonnel's 'Privilège' entitled him to have the work printed (by others), he was still not an authorized printer himself. In September Sarrau wrote again to Rivet about his nephew in Caen: 'It's pitiful, all the trouble and misery we have had for the last six months, trying to get his printing-house set up again for him.'[57]

Relations between Bochart and de Cardonnel had obviously been close and cordial up until this time; Sarrau's letters also reveal that during the spring and summer of 1644 de Cardonnel had performed another valuable service for Bochart, paying a copyist to transcribe one of the latest and most important works of biblical scholarship, Louis Cappel's *Critica sacra*, which was then circulating in manuscript.[58] Some of de Cardonnel's book purchases at this time (listed in the appendix) seem to have been made with a view to providing Bochart with hard-to-obtain research materials for his other projects. But the long delay was taking its toll. In October Rivet received a letter from Bochart, in which the author despaired of seeing his work printed in Caen and offered to send the original manuscript to Holland instead, if Rivet could find a suitable printer there.[59] In early December Sarrau wrote acerbically, summarizing perhaps Bochart's most recent comments to him: 'He is footling around with Mr Cardonnel, who is wasting a lot of his time, and will achieve nothing in the end.'[60] And from the middle of December there is evidence that Bochart was circulating at least a substantial sample of his text in

---

[55] Bots and Leroy, *Correspondance*, II, p. 264: 'le dessein de l'Imprimerie de Caën court grand risque, M' le Chancelier s'y rendant fort contraire sans vouloir escouter raison.'

[56] Printed in S. Bochart, *Phaleg* (Caen, 1646) (see above, n. 49), 2nd part, final page.

[57] Bots and Leroy, *Correspondance*, II, p. 367: 'C'est pitié que la pene et misere en laquelle nous sommes depuis six mois pour tacher de lui restablir son imprimerie.'

[58] Ibid., II, pp. 301, 347, 354, 367.

[59] BN, MS f. lat. 10353, p. 574 (Rivet to Samuel Sorbière, from The Hague, 11 Oct. 1644): 'Typographo strenuo & fido opus erit, qui correctorem habeat in talibus exercitatum. Si talem reperiam promittit se αὐτόγραφον ad me missurum; Decolavit enim spes Typographiae linguarum Orientalium Cadomi erigendae postquam Cancellarius nonnullorum delationibus eo adductus est ut id prohiberet, & comparatos characteres sigillo muniri curaret.' Rivet did enter into negotiations with the Leiden printer Jean Le Maire (Bots and Leroy, eds., *Correspondance*, II, p. 418: Rivet to Sarrau, 24 Oct. 1644). He was presumably also responsible for obtaining a privilege for the book for Bochart from the Estates-General of the United Provinces, with exclusive rights of publication for 11 years, on 7 Sept. 1646: Bochart, *Phaleg*, 2nd part, final page.

[60] Bots and Leroy, *Correspondance*, II, p. 457 (10 Dec. 1644): 'Il s'amuse a M' Cardonnel qui lui fait perdre beaucoup de temps pour ne rien faire a la fin.'

Parisian learned circles, perhaps in the hope of attracting a sponsor for a printing of it there.[61]

Two long years would pass before the book was finally published in Caen (with a title page proudly proclaiming 'Typis Petri Cardonnelli'): the epistle dedicatory was dated 31 October 1646. Bochart was evidently dissatisfied with the printing: he included a special note apologizing for the quantity of misprints and complaining that the engraver of the map was ignorant of Hebrew.[62] A few years later, when he was preparing to publish his *Hierozoicon*, he was keen to find a publisher in Holland instead.[63] It seems that the distribution of *Phaleg* was also problematic: unsold copies were issued under a new title page, bearing the name of a bookseller in Rouen, in 1651.[64] Nevertheless, the fact remains that the publication of *Phaleg* did earn Bochart a Europe-wide reputation as a scholar (and an invitation from Queen Christina of Sweden, which he accepted, to study her fabled collection of oriental manuscripts in Stockholm).

For de Cardonnel too the experience must have been a bruising one. He would never print another book. Nevertheless, he was able to glean some personal benefit from the publication. In the prefatory material to the second part of the book he appeared in print for the first time as a poet, with two Latin verses in praise of Bochart.[65] More importantly, after the main print-run was finished, at the end of December 1646, he was able to produce a small number of large-paper copies with an extra ten leaves of dedicatory material (by him, in Latin prose and verse) inserted before the title page, for presentation to the most illustrious of his friends and patrons.[66] One of the individuals so honoured was, admittedly, neither a patron nor a friend: the poem in praise of Chancellor Séguier was no doubt composed with much grinding of the teeth. Otherwise, however, the list of dedicatees provides a valuable survey of the upper reaches of de Cardonnel's social world, both

---

[61] M. Mersenne, *Correspondance*, ed. C. de Waard *et al.*, 17 vols. (Paris: 1933–88), XIII, p. 272, Isaac Boulliau to Mersenne, from Paris (16 Dec. 1644).

[62] Bochart, *Phaleg*, sig. o1r (the engraver was a Caennais artist, R. Hubert).

[63] See P. Colomiès, *Gallia orientalis, sive Gallorum qui linguam hebraeam vel alios orientales excoluerunt vitae* (The Hague, 1665), p. 242. The work was eventually printed in England: *Hierozoicon, sive bipertitum opus de animalibus Sacrae Scripturae* (London, 1663) (with a note by Bochart thanking the publisher, James Allestry, for the care with which it was produced: sig. u2r).

[64] 'Typis Petri Cardonelli. Et vaeneunt Rothomagi, Apud Ioannem Berthelin, in area Palatij'. Copies of this issue are much rarer than those of the original edition. Another issue has also been recorded, dated 1647, with the wording 'Typis Petri Cardonnelli. Et prostant Parisiis Apvd Gervasivm Alliot in area Palatij .. et apvd vidvam Mathvrini Dv Puits' (see F. Martin, *Athenae Normannorum*, ed. V. Bourrienne and T. Genty, 2 vols. (Caen, 1904–5), I, p. 390; and cf. Smith, *Samuel Bochart*, p. 42 n.); but I have not seen any copy of this, and the issues of 1646 and 1651 are the only ones recorded in L. Desgraves *et al.*, *Répertoire bibliographique des livres imprimés en France au XVII*e *siècle*, XIII, *Normandie II*, ed. A. R. Girard (Baden-Baden, 1985) (see pp. 45, 49).

[65] Bochart, *Phaleg*, 2nd part, sig. 2†4v.

[66] Only one has survived, the copy intended for the Comte de Fiesque (with MS material inscribed to him in Latin and French verse, in de Cardonnel's hand, dated 1648), which passed instead to Bochart, and is now in the BMC (pressmark Rés. C 162/1–2). The paper is not only larger, but of much higher quality—nearly twice the thickness of that in the ordinary edition.

French and English; and it must also help to explain how it was that he had finally succeeded in wearing down the Chancellor's opposition.

On the French side, the first name after Séguier's is that of Charles d'Angennes, marquis du Fargis. A courtier and diplomat who had been Ambassador to Spain in the 1620s, he had spent the early 1630s in exile in the Spanish Netherlands as a supporter of Gaston's rebellion.[67] Two things, perhaps, made him particularly attractive to de Cardonnel: his closeness to his first cousin, Charles d'Angennes, marquis de Rambouillet (whose wife had the most famous literary salon in Paris), and the fact that another of his cousins, Jacques d'Angennes (the next name on de Cardonnel's list) was Bishop of Bayeux, with jurisdiction over Caen.[68] Another important dedicatee was Bernard Potier, marquis de Blérancourt, who served as 'Bailli' (governor) of Caen in 1646: an author *manqué*, he was a friend of the marquise de Rambouillet, and his wife was a patroness of poets (including Sarasin).[69] Also honoured were Dreux d'Aubray, who was responsible for the policing of the whole of Paris, and Charles-Léon, comte de Fiesque, another one-time political exile (he had fled to Sedan after joining a plot to assassinate Richelieu in 1637) who was known as a patron of writers—including Chapelain, Ménage, Rotrou, and the Caennais poets Sarasin and Segrais.[70] Sarasin himself also received a dedicatory poem.

The one name that is conspicuous by its absence from this list is that of the duc de Longueville, the most powerful nobleman in Normandy (and, it was said, the richest in France), whose wife, the royal princess Anne-Geneviève de Bourbon, was a leading patroness in the Parisian literary world.[71] Longueville was certainly well known to de Cardonnel: when he visited Caen in January 1645 he even took up residence in de Cardonnel's house.[72] The list of personal contacts in de Cardonnel's notebook would later include the duchesse de Longueville's chief 'valet de chambre' in Paris, and in 1654 he recorded an encounter with the duchesse on the road

---

[67] See G. Tallemant des Réaux, *Les Historiettes*, ed. A. Adam, 2 vols. (Paris, 1960), I, pp. 291–4, 961–4, 1157.

[68] On Jacques d'Angennes, Bishop of Bayeux 1606–47, see the *Dictionnaire de biographie française*, ed. J. Balteau *et al.* (Paris, 1933–), II, col. 1095.

[69] See P. Carel, *Histoire de la ville de Caen depuis Philippe-Auguste jusqu'à Charles IX* (Paris, n.d.), p. 260; Tallemant des Réaux, *Historiettes*, I, p. 499; II, pp. 650–2, 1424; A. Mennung, *Jean-François Sarasin's Leben und Werke, seine Zeit und Gesellschaft*, 2 vols. (Halle, 1902–4), I, p. 51.

[70] On Dreux d'Aubray, see *Dictionnaire de biographie française*, IV, cols. 224–6 (noting his strong cultural interests in the 1620s, when he corresponded about art and literature with Peiresc, de Thou, and the Dupuys); on the Comte de Fiesque, see Mennung, *Sarasin's Leben*, I, pp. 238 n., 266–9, II, p. 322, and *Dictionnaire de biographie française*, XIII, cols. 1305–7. For an official responsible for law and order, d'Aubray came to a sad end: he was poisoned by his daughter, the marquise de Brinvilliers, who used the same means to kill her brother and two of her sisters.

[71] See J. Debû-Bridel, *Anne-Geneviève de Bourbon, duchesse de Longueville* (Paris, 1938).

[72] Archives Municipales de Caen: Gustave Dupont, 'Registres de l'Hôtel de Ville de Caen: inventaire sommaire' (a bound photocopy of MS notes by Dupont on the registers, which were later destroyed), IV, p. 239: 'M.M. les échevins . . . sont allés attendre M.gneur le duc de Longueville en la maison des Srs Cardonney, Marchands, en la paroisse St Pierre, Neuve-rue, où M.gneur a pris son logement.'

## PIERRE DE CARDONNEL (1614-1667)

from Paris to Normandy.[73] Possibly the absence of Longueville's name from de Cardonnel's dedicatory materials was due only to the fact that he and his wife were out of the country at the time: he was minister plenipotentiary at Münster, involved in the negotiations that would lead to the Treaty of Westphalia in 1648. Soon thereafter, the duchesse would become a leading *frondeuse*; indeed, it is a striking fact that most of these prominent patrons of de Cardonnel were involved at some stage in rebellions against Louis XIII or the ministers of Louis XIV. This presents something of a contrast with de Cardonnel's own ardent royalism in the English Civil War. The explanation may be that his position was based not on political philosophy (*à la* Hobbes), but on loyalty to a social order—to the web of obligations and benefits that bound him to his noble patrons. And the nature of that web, in the case of his French connections, was clearly not only social, but cultural too: each of the leading patrons on his list was closely connected with the literary circles that centred on the Hôtel de Rambouillet—circles of which his friend Sarasin was a key member, and to which, we may guess, Sarasin had personally introduced him on his visits to Paris.[74]

That de Cardonnel's English dedicatees were almost all Royalists is, on the other hand, not surprising, as in nearly every case it was the parliamentary victories of the Civil War that had driven them across the Channel, thereby enabling de Cardonnel to make their acquaintance. The most prominent of them was Charles, Prince of Wales, who moved from Jersey to Paris in July 1646; the title page of the specially printed prefatory materials dedicated the whole work to him, presenting it as a New Year's gift for 1647. The long dedicatory epistle that followed was signed 'your most humble and devoted client P. de Cardonnel': the use of the term 'client' ('cliens') suggests that some relationship of patronage and service had already been established between them.[75] Evidently de Cardonnel had had contacts with the court of Henrietta Maria in Paris: another of his dedicatees was Henry Jermyn, her chief courtier, who had accompanied the Queen to France in the summer of 1644. He also addressed a poem to all the Anglican chaplains—Richard Stewart, John Earles, Edward Wolley, and others—who attended the Prince in Paris. (De Cardonnel would later take special care to cultivate the English court-in-exile: in 1654 he entered in his notebook systematic lists of the members of both Charles's household and that of Prince Rupert, and in the following year he proudly recorded in his copy of *Les Memoires du feu roy de la Grand' Bretagne Charles premier*—the French translation of *Eikon basilike*—that it was given to him by the Duke of York in Paris.[76])

---

[73] BL, MS Sloane 1731B, fols. 34r, 51v.

[74] Sarasin was both a favourite of the marquise de Rambouillet and a protégé of (and ghost-writer for) the duchesse de Longueville: see C. Hippeau, 'Jean-François Sarasin', in *Littérateurs normands* (composite volume, n.p., n.d.: BN, pressmark 8-LN9-261), and Sarasin, *Oeuvres*, I, pp. 366–9, 397; II, pp. 284–308, 434–41.

[75] BMC, pressmark Rés. C 162/1, sig. ¶4r: 'Humillimi ac devotissimi Clientis tui P. De Cardonnel'.

[76] BL, MS Sloane 1731B, fol. 64 (cf. also notes on fol. 56r, listing members of the Duke of York's household in Paris); *Les Memoires*, Cambridge University Library, pressmark Syn. 5. 64. 3.

Some contacts with Royalists in France may even have pre-dated the arrival of the Queen. George Goring, Earl of Norwich, had probably got to know de Cardonnel when he stayed in Paris in the winter of 1643–4, on a mission to obtain support for the King from Mazarin. De Cardonnel's dedicatory poem addressed to Goring was especially affectionate in tone, indicating a real personal friendship, and in March 1647 Goring would write from Brussels to Sir Edward Nicholas in Paris: 'I beseeche you, Sir, make my apology in this pressure to my trew friend Mons\.̄ Cardonell and my good goshipp.'[77] Also probably encountered in Paris, but in 1645 or 1646, was another recipient of a dedicatory poem, William Cavendish, Marquess of Newcastle, who stayed in the French capital between April 1645 and July 1648.

Other contacts with Royalists were probably made in Normandy—either in Caen or in Rouen, where de Cardonnel also did business. Some of the English exiles settled in these Norman towns for long periods. According to Hyde, it was because they found the dominance of Henry Jermyn over the Queen and the Prince in Paris so offputting that 'most persons of honour . . . [chose] rather to make their residence in any other place, as Caen, Rouen, and the like, than in Paris'.[78] The poem addressed to William Cavendish, Earl of Devonshire, is the first sign of de Cardonnel's acquaintance with him: Devonshire was in Rouen in the summer of 1645, and probably remained in Normandy until his return to England in late December.[79] John Digby, Earl of Bristol and another dedicatee, had actually taken up residence in Caen: just a few months after these dedicatory materials were printed, he published his own book there, a political apologia, with a preface signed 'Caen in Normandy, April 8. 1647'.[80] Another exile whose acquaintance de Cardonnel presumably made in Normandy was Edmund Waller (though he does not appear in the dedicatory materials to the Bochart volume): Waller spent the period from January 1646 to September 1647 in Rouen.[81] And de Cardonnel would later make contact with Thomas Butler, Earl of Ossory, the son of the Earl (later Duke) of Ormonde: in late August 1648 Ormonde visited Caen and made arrangements for Thomas and his younger brother, Richard, to stay in the house of

---

[77] G. F. Warner, ed., *The Nicholas Papers: Correspondence of Sir Edward Nicholas, Secretary of State*, 4 vols., Camden Society, n.s., 40, 50, 57; 3rd series, 31 (London, 1886–1920), I, p. 83 (9 March 1647). The poem: BMC, pressmark Rés. C 162/1, sig. 2¶2v.

[78] Edward Hyde, Earl of Clarendon, *The History of the Rebellion and Civil Wars in England*, 3 vols. (Oxford, 1807), III(i), p. 176.

[79] See T. Hobbes, The *Correspondence*, ed. N. Malcolm, 2 vols. (Oxford, 1994), I, p. 124, Hobbes to Waller, from Rouen, (29 July/8 Aug. 1645); *Calendar of State Papers, Domestic, 1645–1647*, ed. W. D. Hamilton (London, 1891), p. 280 (order for transportation, 27 Dec.).

[80] See the later reprint, *An Apologie of John Earl of Bristol Consisting of Two Tracts*, 'Caen, Printed in the Year 1647. And reprinted in 1656'. The reprint was possibly produced in London; I have not seen the 1647 edition. Neither appears in Girard's listing of Caen imprints in Desgraves et al., *Répertoire bibliographique*.

[81] BL, Evelyn Papers, JE A16, items 1340–8, letters from Waller to Evelyn (with a visit to Dieppe in Oct. 1646: item 1345). By Oct. 1647 Waller had moved to Saint Valéry, near Dieppe: J. Evelyn, *Diary*, ed. E. S. de Beer, 6 vols. (Oxford, 1955), II, pp. 536–7.

a French Protestant minister there, where they received tuition for more than a year.[82]

## V

The prefatory materials to de Cardonnel's edition of Bochart illustrate one aspect of his activities in the period from 1644 to the Restoration: his assiduous cultivation of noble English patrons. Other aspects of his life, however, are more obscure. His dedicatory epistle to the Prince of Wales contained the first statement of what was to become a constant theme in his later writings: the damage to his finances brought on by the Civil War in England. He hinted darkly at 'the various overthrows' his fortune had suffered amidst 'those abominable disorders'.[83] After the Restoration he would address a petition to Charles, in which he claimed that his financial losses related directly to his royalism: 'your Pet[itione]r having suffered much ... both in his person and fortune, for his duty and loyaltie, both to your Maj.[ty] and yo[r] Royal Father'; the claim was accepted by the King, who issued a patent referring to 'the faithfull services to vs and our said late Royall Father by the said Peter de Cardonell done and performed and ... his greate Suffering on that Account'.[84] What those 'services' may have been is largely unclear. Only one definite—indeed, striking—piece of evidence has survived of action by de Cardonnel on behalf of Charles I: in February 1645 a report was sent to Chancellor Séguier from Rouen, stating that 'Pierre Cardonne [sic], a famous merchant, who has offices in Paris, Rouen, Caen and London, has obtained from the King [sc. Charles I] letters of reprisals to take vengeance on those Parliamentarians', and that he had seized the goods of merchants in the port of Rouen who traded with the Parliamentarians in England.[85] The background to this episode is obscure (the issuing of such letters of reprisals is not recorded in the registers of the Privy Council), but the harm it may have done to de Cardonnel's commercial prospects,

---

[82] Huntington Library, San Marino: Hastings Collection, Irish papers, box 8, MS HA 14117 (Ormonde to John Bramhall, from Caen, 24 Aug. 1648); T. Carte, *The Life of James, Duke of Ormond*, 6 vols. (Oxford, 1851), III, p. 596 (noting that Ossory left Caen in Oct. 1649, but returned there with his mother in Dec. 1650 and stayed until the summer of 1652). The identity of the minister is not known; it was probably not Bochart, who made no reference to Ossory in his London publication (*Hierozoicon*, 1663: dedicated to Charles II). The other ministers in Caen in 1648 were Pierre du Bosc (whose biographer never refers to Ossory: P. Le Gendre, *La Vie de Pierre du Bosc* (Rotterdam, 1694) ) and Jean de Baillehache. Another possible candidate would be the young Jean Durel (see below, n. 133), though he was not actually a minister in 1648–9.

[83] BMC, pressmark Rés. C 162/1, sig. ¶2r: 'inter nefandos illos tumultus ... varios perpessa est casus fortuna nostra'.

[84] PRO, SP 29/77/32 (petition, July 1663), and C 66/3038 (Patents, 15 Charles II, part 7), membrane 20. De Cardonnel's copy of the patent, dated 17 Nov. 1663, is HRO, 16 M 55/2.

[85] R. Mousnier, ed., *Lettres et mémoires adressés au Chancelier Séguier (1633–1649)*, 2 vols. (Paris, 1964), II, p. 754: 'Pierre Cardonne, célèbre marchand, qui a des bureaux à Paris, à Rouen, à Caen, et à Londres, a obtenu du Roy des lettres de représailles pour se venger sur lesdits parlementaires' (report by the Sieur de Lafosse, 9 Feb. 1645: a group of Protestant merchants had complained to the *Procureur du Roi*, demanding the return of their goods).

both in Rouen and in England, can be imagined.[86] However, there is no sign of subsequent official action against de Cardonnel by the parliamentary authorities: his brother Adam (evidently identified as a Royalist) had been assessed for £150 by the Committee for the Advance of Money in 1644, but Pierre was apparently left unmolested.[87]

As for Pierre's other 'faithfull services' to Charles I and his son, these can only be guessed at. The family tradition recorded in the eighteenth century claimed that the de Cardonnel family 'lent King Charles II considerable sums of money, which were never repaid'; if there is any truth at all in this, it must refer to the 1650s, not the 1640s, as de Cardonnel's dedicatory epistle to Prince Charles, far from offering financial help to the Prince, actually requested it from him.[88] His services to the royal family are much more likely to have consisted of using his commercial contacts (above all, his own brothers) to organize courier services and deliveries between France and England. In February 1647 Nicolas Oudart, a secretary to Sir Edward Nicholas who had remained in England and would soon start doing secretarial work for the King, sent a message from London to his master in Paris; the message was written in invisible ink (probably lemon-juice) on the inside of a sheet of paper, the outside of which bore a fictitious letter referring to a shipment of serge. The secret letter began by explaining that Oudart had not written by the last post, 'having given a letter for you to Mr. Cardonel with divers of the portablest bookes of those you desire. He went not then nevertheles, but sayes to morrow he shall without faile. Yesternight I hoped to have seen him, but he was not at hoam . . .' At the end of the letter he mentioned items of Nicholas's property ('the 24 bottles of sack, bookes, &c.') still held by a friend in London, and noted: 'Mr. Adam Cardonel sayes that Mr. Fontaine will send anything carefully (and he sends often) to his brother at Caen. If you like that way, I will use it; for I thinck he is honest, though seemingly round.'[89] This may have been the start of more extensive secret dealings conducted on behalf of leading Royalists by these two contrasting brothers: 'round' Adam (the term means 'plain-spoken, not mincing matters,

---

[86] See the Indexes to the Privy Council Registers, 1637–45: PRO, Map Room, pressmark 12/82.

[87] M. A. E. Green, ed., *Calendar of the Proceedings of the Committee for the Advance of Money, 1642–1656*, 3 vols. (London, 1888), I, p. 328: entry for 23 Jan. 1644, referring to 'Adam Cardonella', and noting that he had already paid £45.

[88] Collins, *Peerage*, V, p. 405 (quotation). A version of this claim derived from a pedigree in the College of Arms specifies the sum lent as £40,000 (HL, MS T 8/1, no. 115, pedigree of de Cardonnel): this is wildly implausible, and would still seem dubious even if those 'pounds' were *livres tournois*. The credibility of this tradition is not improved by its claim that the money was lent by Adam, his brothers and their father—who had died before 1627. De Cardonnel's oblique but unmistakable request for money is in BMC, pressmark Rés. C 162/1, sig. ¶2r: 'Sed quid ab innatâ Tibi Humanitate . . . non iuuat sperare?'

[89] Warner, *Nicholas Papers*, I, pp. 73–4, 78 (18 Feb. 1647). 'Mr. Fontaine' was no doubt a relative of the François Fontaine who had married Jeanne de Cardonnel, the aunt of Adam and Pierre: see above, n. 30. Oudart was a Walloon Protestant (from Mechlin), and would have been familiar with the French Protestant community in London. The 'brother at Caen' may have been either Pierre or Philippe.

uncompromising'), and courtly Pierre, the composer of elegant complimentary poems.[90]

In March 1647 Pierre de Cardonnel was back in England, where he resolved his immediate financial problems by selling his wife's quarter-share in the Pescod estate in Hampshire to his brother Adam for a 'valueable consideracion'—perhaps as much as £800.[91] Not long afterwards (between October 1647 and September 1648) Adam married Mary Pescod, one of Katherine's younger half-sisters, thus acquiring a second quarter-share.[92] They lived in Pierre's London house, in Laurence Pountney Lane, and had a child baptized at St Lawrence Pountney in September 1649.[93] In 1651, when the other two Pescod daughters had married and were able to claim their portions, an agreement was drawn up by the four children, calling on the executors to submit accounts for the property, and specifying that 'y$^e$ some of one Thousand pounds, & y$^e$ interest thereof secured by y$^e$ s[ai]d mannors ... to y$^e$ s[ai]d Peeter de Cardonell & Katherine his wife ... shall be provided for either out of y$^e$ s[ai]d mannor Lands ... or otherwise'.[94] This would form the basis of Pierre de Cardonnel's future legal claims. The two other daughters then sold their quarter-shares to one of the executors, the Southampton merchant William Stanley, who would thus become not only the holder of a half-share of the manors, but also the principal object of Pierre's litigation.[95]

The pattern of Pierre de Cardonnel's activities suggests that he had made London his main base again by the end of the 1640s—though possibly not until the spring or summer of 1649, as his daughter Judith was baptized in Caen in February of that year.[96] At that time, and well into the 1650s, he was still very active as a merchant. The contact-list in his notebook, with dates mainly ranging from 1641 to 1654, covers a wide range of trading centres, including Amsterdam, Alicante, Cadiz, Danzig, Dublin, The Hague, Lisbon, Livorno, Lübeck, Marseille, Pernambuco, Seville, Venice and Vienna.[97] The dates do not always imply personal contact, still less that he visited those places himself: in some cases he noted

---

[90] See *OED*, 'round', adj., 13a.

[91] HRO, 4 M 60/126 (the indenture between Pierre and the executors, 9 March 1647); 15 M 55/8 (quotation); 4 M 60/165 (valuing another quarter-share at £800).

[92] HRO, 4 M 60/165.

[93] Guildhall Library, London, MS 7670 (registers of St Lawrence, 1538–1740), baptismal entry for 14 Sept. 1649: 'Adam the sonne of Adam Cardinall and mary his wife'. This child evidently did not survive; another son was baptized Adam in 1663 (PRO, RG 4/4600 (Walloon Church, Southampton), baptismal entry for 1 Nov. 1663).

[94] HRO, 46 M 48/42.

[95] HRO, 15 M 55/8. The *Victoria County History, Hampshire*, III (London, 1973), gives a very misleading account, describing Pierre as Adam's father and merely commenting: 'In the hands of these Cardonells the manor fell into two moieties' (p. 293, referring to the manor of Cadlands).

[96] ADC, F 5377, fol. 66r (7 Feb. 1649).

[97] BL MS Sloane 1731B, fols. 9–39r. The range, though certainly impressive, was not untypical of a trader at this time: cf. H. Roseveare, *Markets and Merchants of the Late Seventeenth Century: The Marescoe–David Letters, 1668–1680* (Oxford, 1987), pp. 17–112.

that the contacts were made by his brothers Philippe and Daniel.[98] But in addition to his frequent stays in Normandy and Paris, he did sometimes travel further afield. A prefatory poem composed by him for a book by Walter Charleton was dated 28 August 1649, and bore the explanatory note: 'written when I was about to leave for the Netherlands'.[99] Again, in March 1651 he received a pass from the Council of State, permitting him to travel to Holland; his notebook would record the names of people 'seen' or 'seen by me' in that year in Amsterdam, The Hague, and Antwerp.[100] A later section of the notebook contains a brief 'Journal of my trip to France in 1654', covering a period away from London (in Caen, Paris, Rouen, and Dieppe) that lasted from May of that year to April 1655.[101]

As his notes show, de Cardonnel was always on the look-out for commercial opportunities: near Vernon he had a long discussion about viticulture with a farmer, who promised to send him 'vine-stocks to England, from the best plants, next season'; and at Tancarville he noted that 'there are people here who could be taken to Cadlands, who know about making linen, etc.'[102] This last idea, which would have involved persuading his brother Adam to set up as a linen manufacturer, was to have a surprising after-echo. In 1685, soon after the Revocation of the Edict of Nantes (and long after Pierre's death), Adam de Cardonnel and a group of mainly Huguenot colleagues, including Nicolas Dupin, obtained a royal patent to manufacture paper in England, having 'lately brought excellent workmen from France'.[103] And five years later, Nicolas Dupin obtained not only a similar grant of letters patent to manufacture paper in Ireland, but also, with 'Henry Million and others', exclusive rights to manufacture linen in both England and Ireland.[104] Possibly Adam de Cardonnel had looked into the idea, raised by Pierre, of bringing linen-makers to Cadlands; if so, Pierre may have played a remote part in the process that led eventually to the creation of one of Ireland's major industries.

[98] E.g. against the entry for merchants in Alicante: 'de la cogn.$^{ce}$ de mon fr. Dan. 1650'; or against the name of a trader in Coutances: 'veu par mon fr. ph. en may 1653' (ibid., fols. 13r, 17v).
[99] W. Charleton, *A Ternary of Paradoxes: The Magnetick Cure of Wounds, The Nativity of Tartar in Wine, The Image of God in Man* (London, 1650), sig. g1v ('apud Belgas discessurus').
[100] *Calendar of State Papers, Domestic, 1651*, ed. M. A. E. Green (London, 1877), p. 524 (28 March 1651); BL MS Sloane 1731B, fols. 9r, 10v, 24r: 'veus', 'veus par moy'.
[101] BL, MS Sloane 1731B: the 'Journal de mon voyage de Fran. 1654' is fols. 50r–53v.
[102] These quotations are from a further section, 'Memoires de voyage en 1654' (ibid., fols. 56r–61r): fols. 57v: 'des seps de vigne en Engleterre du meilleur plant dans la saison prochaine'; 57r: 'on peut trouuer du Monde pour transporter a Cadland, qui entendent le labeur du lin &c.' Vernon is on the Seine, between Paris and Rouen; Tancarville is further downstream, between Rouen and Le Havre.
[103] *Calendar of State Papers, Domestic, February—December 1685*, ed. F. Bickley (London, 1960), p. 407 (warrant, 9 Dec.). See G. H. Overend, 'Notes upon the Earlier History of the Manufacture of Paper in England', *Proceedings of the Huguenot Society of London*, 8, for 1905–8 (1909), pp. 177–220, esp. p. 201; H. Hauser, 'La Révocation de l'édit de Nantes et la papeterie en Angleterre', *Bulletin de la Société de l'Histoire du Protestantisme Français*, 80 (1931), pp. 230–2; D. C. Coleman, 'The Early British Paper Industry and the Huguenots', *Proceedings of the Huguenot Society of London*, 19 (1956), pp. 210–25 (esp. pp. 218–21).
[104] *Calendar of State Papers, Domestic, 1690–1691*, ed. W. J. Hardy (London, 1898), p. 187 (warrant of 13 Dec. 1690).

## PIERRE DE CARDONNEL (1614–1667)

Pierre de Cardonnel's intellectual life, in the period between the mid-1640s and the Restoration, is traceable no less patchily than his physical movements. Some useful clues about the development of his interests are provided by books from his library, in which his ownership inscription is usually dated. Most of the surviving volumes with such inscriptions are dated 1645 or later. (They are listed at the end of this chapter.) It seems that his period of close association with Bochart in Caen led to a real flowering of intellectual activity, not only in Hebrew and Oriental studies, but in other areas associated with Bochart's interests, such as the history of the early Church. One of the books acquired in 1645, Drusius's *Annotationes in Coheleth* (Amsterdam, 1635), even has a few marginal notes in Bochart's hand.[105] At the same time, a strong interest in classical and neo-Latin poetry (natural enough in such a keen writer of Latin poems) is apparent. In the late 1640s and early 1650s de Cardonnel was also buying works relating to medicine, medical botany, and chemistry: these may reflect the concerns of some of his acquaintances in London (as we shall see), but his medical interests may also have been stimulated by contacts in Caen, where leading experts (such as Jacques and Étienne de Cahaignes) taught at the Faculté de Médecine. Caen was known for classical scholarship as well as elegant French poetry (Jean Chapelain would write in 1661 that Caen equalled Paris 'in respect of its exquisite urbanity and profound knowledge'): its luminaries included the classicist Jean Paulmier de Grentemesnil (widely regarded as the best Greek scholar in France) and the classicists and Hebraists Étienne Morin and Étienne Lemoine.[106] In 1652 the intellectual elite of Caen set up an 'académie' with a mixed Catholic–Protestant membership. Had de Cardonnel been resident there, presumably he would have joined it; he must have known many of its members (including Lemoine, whose Greek verse in praise of Bochart was given pride of place in the opening pages of *Phaleg*).[107]

The intellectual circles in which he moved in London, on the other hand, are less easy to map. One key contact was the schoolmaster, classicist, and prolific writer Alexander Ross, who was mentioned above in connection with de Cardonnel's earliest years in Southampton. At some time in the early 1640s Ross had left Southampton; after a brief stay on the Isle of Wight he moved to London, where he was well established as a private schoolmaster in Covent Garden

---

[105] Trinity College, Cambridge, pressmark A. 27. 30. This posthumous work by Drusius consisted of a new translation of the book of Ecclesiastes, with commentary.

[106] N. Hepp, 'Moisant de Brieux devant l'antiquité classique', in R. Lebegue, ed., *La Basse-Normandie et ses poètes à l'époque classique* (Caen, 1977), pp. 211–22 (p. 211: 'du costé de l'exquise politesse et du profond sçavoir'); on the three writers, see Huet, *Commentarius*, pp. 47, 52, 180–1; Galland, *Essai sur l'histoire du protestantisme à Caen*, pp. 133–7. On Lemoine see also Colomiès, *Gallia orientalis*, pp. 262–3.

[107] On the academy, see Galland, *Essai sur l'histoire du protestantisme à Caen*, pp. 117–21. For a list of members (1652–75), see A.-R. de Formigny de La Londe, ed., *Documents inédits pour servir à l'histoire de l'ancienne Académie Royale des Belles Lettres de Caen* (Caen, 1854), pp. 13–14. (The 'Jean de Carbonnel' listed there was a member of a different family, unconnected with the de Cardonnels.) The poem by Lemoine (signed Στέφανος Μοναχός) is on the reverse title page of Bochart, *Phaleg*.

by 1645.[108] Ross was the only person never to have left England to whom de Cardonnel addressed one of his dedicatory poems in the special printing of *Phaleg*: he called him his 'dearest and extremely revered friend', and described the poem addressed to him as an extemporaneous epigram, written while ill in bed—a piece of excuse-making which, whether truthful or not, perhaps betrays the nervousness of a former pupil submitting work to his mentor.[109] De Cardonnel's library would later contain at least two of Ross's books: *Mel heliconicum* (London, 1643), and *Arcana microcosmi* (London, 1658).[110] It must also be suspected that the most untypical item in the list of Ross's publications, his English version (1649) of du Ryer's French translation (1647) of the Koran, may have been produced at the prompting of—and/or using a copy supplied by—de Cardonnel, whose interest in Arabic had been stirred by his own recent contacts with Bochart.

Two other writers in London were the recipients of poems by both Ross and de Cardonnel in the period 1649–50. When Payne Fisher published his short Latin epic about the siege of York and the battle of Marston Moor in the spring of 1650, it included not only a prefatory poem by de Cardonnel (again, written 'on the eve of my departure to Holland'), but also a long final poem by him in French, with its own separate title page, a funeral ode in memory of Payne's brother Ferdinand, who had died in a shipwreck in 1646.[111] Presumably his acquaintance with the brother had come first; it may have led not only to his own friendship with Payne Fisher, but also to the introduction to Fisher (by de Cardonnel) of Alexander Ross, who contributed another prefatory poem. Other contributors included the poets Edward Benlowes and Thomas Philipot.[112] In the light of de Cardonnel's ardent royalism (and his recent cultivation of the Marquess of Newcastle), it may seem

---

[108] D. Allan, ' "An Ancient Sage Philosopher": Alexander Ross and the Defence of Philosophy', *The Seventeenth Century*, 16 (2001), pp. 68–94, gives a valuable account of Ross's intellectual position, but an erroneous one of his life in the 1640s. Ross was not under pressure to leave Southampton after a 'hostile deposition' had called him an 'extortioner' in 1641 (p. 72); the deposition (on 12 March 1642) was a denunciation for slander of the person who had made that remark (CAO, SC 9/3/11, fol. 520v). Nor did he spend the 1640s in the seclusion of Carisbrooke and Bramshill (Allan, 'Alexander Ross', p. 73); Henry Oxenden's correspondence with Ross and with Ross's pupil Thomas Denne shows that he was keeping a very profitable private school in London between 1645 and 1648 (BL, MS Add. 28001, fols. 34, 287–8, 309–10, 315–16). Cf. Sir John Oglander's note, in W. H. Long, ed., *The Oglander Memoirs* (London, 1888), p. 118: 'Mr. Rosse . . . sometimes Minister of Carisbrook, nowe in Covent Garden, London'.

[109] BMC, pressmark Rés. C 162/1, sig. 3¶2r: 'Amicissimo, sibique plvrimvm colendo viro Alexandro Rossaeo . . . Hoc extemporaneum Epigramma P. De Cardonnel, Rheumatismate in lecto detentus Salutis prorsem loco raptim exscripserit.'

[110] W. Cooper, *Catalogus* (see below, n. 207, for the full title), pp. 32–3.

[111] P. Fisher ['Paganus Piscator'], *Marston-Moor: sive de obsidione praelioque eboracensi carmen; cum quibusdam miscellaneis* (London, 1650) (Thomason's copy dated 11 April: BL, pressmark E 535), sigs. a1r ('Hoc Amicitiae juxta & condigni meriti testimonium, ad *Batavos* prope diem discessurus, reliquit P. de *Cardonnel*); final section, sigs. N4-P1r, entitled 'Parentatio generosis manibus Ferdinandi Fisheri, juxta Monam Insulam, A$^{no}$ M.DC.XLVI naufragio absorpti. Ode gallica Pagano Fishero . . .'.

[112] Ibid., sigs. a2v, a4. Whether de Cardonnel had any direct contact with Benlowes is not known, but his library did contain a copy of Benlowes's major work, *Theophila* (London, 1652): Cooper, *Catalogus*, p. 3.

strange that he contributed to a work that celebrated such a crucial parliamentary victory. But Fisher's poem is not—as it is sometimes painted—just the cynical production of a turncoat; it presents both sides in the conflict as highly principled, delineating a world of military virtue, honour, and mutual respect to which many (especially in retrospect) could subscribe.

The third recipient of a poem by de Cardonnel has already been mentioned: the physician and philosopher Walter Charleton. The poem was dated 28 August 1649, and appeared in a book printed later that year; Alexander Ross contributed a poem to the same volume.[113] Possibly Charleton and Ross had met as near neighbours: Charleton had moved to Covent Garden some time in 1649, when he set up his medical practice in Russell Street. But in this case too it is quite likely that de Cardonnel had performed the introduction: Charleton may have become known to de Cardonnel because he had been working for some time as an assistant to the most prominent member of the French Protestant community in England, the physician Theodore Turquet de Mayerne.[114] Alternatively, the connection may have been made earlier by de Cardonnel's brother Jean, who resided in Covent Garden and was undergoing 'a course of medicine under Dr Charleton' when he died there in August 1650.[115] Other mutual acquaintances probably included Thomas Philipot, a friend and admirer of Charleton, and the senior physician Francis Prujean (dedicatee of books by both Charleton and Philipot), some of whose medieval medical manuscripts were later acquired by de Cardonnel.[116]

But of all these conjunctures, that between Charleton and Ross is the most intriguing, especially in view of de Cardonnel's later interest in Hobbes. For nowhere was the gulf dividing Ross (an intellectually conservative Aristotelian) from Charleton (who rode each successive wave of the intellectual avant-garde, from Helmontianism to Cartesianism to Gassendian atomism) more clearly

---

[113] Charleton, *Ternary of Paradoxes* (Thomason's copy dated 20 Nov. 1649: BL, pressmark E 582 (1) ), sigs. g1v-g2r (de Cardonnel), g2v (Ross).

[114] See L. Sharp, 'Walter Charleton's Early Life, 1620–1659, and Relationship to Natural Philosophy in mid-Seventeenth Century England', *Annals of Science*, 30 (1973), pp. 311–40, esp. pp. 318–20; Fleitmann, *Walter Charleton*, p. 22.

[115] BL MS Sloane 1731B, fol. 48v: the last entry in Jean's hand in this notebook is dated 29 Aug. 1650: 'lodged in Covent Garden . . . at Mr Norton's house' ('logé en couent garden . . . chez Mʳ Norton'); Pierre has added: 'where, the same day, it pleased God to withdraw him from this world. He was undergoing a course of medicine under Dr Charleton . . . by whose care he was buried in the church of Covent Garden' ('ou le ditto il a pleu à Dieu le retirer de ce monde. Estant en un Cours de Medicine sous le Dʳ. Charleton . . . par les soins duquel il a esté inhumé dans l'eglise du Convengarden.')

[116] On Philipot's connection with Charleton see Fleitmann, *Walter Charleton*, p. 24; his *Historical Discourse of the First Invention of Navigation* (London, 1661) was dedicated to Prujean, as was Charleton's *The Darknes of Atheism Dispelled by the Light of Nature: A Physico-Theological Treatise* (London, 1652). The manuscripts are described in Cooper, *Catalogus*, p. 3: 'Collectio variorum Scriptorum de Re medica Latinè simul & Anglicè bene Pergamenta scripta circa An. D. 1280. in 2 Vol. & pertinebant ad D. Doctorem Fr. Prujean diebus suis ut manus ejus testat'.

displayed than in their contrasting attitudes to Hobbes.[117] In his *Leviathan drawn out with a Hook*, Ross portrayed Hobbes's work as a pullulating mass of heresies, concluding that it was 'a piece dangerous both to Government and Religion'.[118] Walter Charleton, on the other hand, went out of his way to compliment Hobbes in several of his works, praising 'that Noble *Enquirer* into *Truth, Mr. Hobbs*' and quoting from 'his inestimable manual of *Human Nature*' in 1650, and referring to 'our eminent M$^r$. *Hobbs*' in 1652.[119] Charleton not only admired Hobbes; he may well have met him in London in the 1650s, as he is known to have discussed scientific matters then with many of Hobbes's own acquaintances, including the Marchioness of Newcastle, John Evelyn, and Henry Pierrepont, Marquis of Dorchester.[120] The strength of de Cardonnel's interest in Charleton's work is indicated by the number of his publications in de Cardonnel's library: he owned the *Darknes of Atheism* (London, 1652), *Physiologia Epicuro-Gassendo-Charltoniana* (London, 1654), *The Immortality of the Human Soul* (London, 1657), *The Natural History of Nutrition* (London, 1659), and *Chorea gigantum* (London, 1663).[121] This apparently long-lasting friendship, therefore, provides another possible means by which de Cardonnel may have had direct contacts with Hobbes.

Before turning to his reading of *Leviathan* in 1652, it is necessary to fill in one other part of Pierre de Cardonnel's intellectual history: his attitude to the French Protestant Church in London. The evidence here is only circumstantial, but it all points in the same direction, indicating that he was probably a member of a group that broke away from the main French Protestant congregation in Threadneedle Street, eventually submitting, under special conditions, to the Church of England instead. The origins of the split were innocuous enough. In the words of the eventual leader of the breakaway congregation, Jean Durel, writing in 1662: 'About twenty years since the *Duke of Soubize* [a Huguenot exile in England], living near the Court, and finding it troublesome ... by reason of his infirmities, to go to Church as far as *Threadneedle-street*, ... he had commonly a French sermon preached before him in his own House every Sunday. Thither the French who live

---

[117] N. R. Gelbart, 'The Intellectual Development of Walter Charleton', *Ambix*, 18 (1971), 149–68, gives a valuable account of Charleton's early shift from Helmontianism to Epicurean atomism, but underplays the Cartesianism of his *Darknes of Atheism* (on which see A. Pacchi, *Cartesio in Inghilterra da More a Boyle* (Rome, 1973), pp. 77–8).

[118] A. Ross, *Leviathan drawn out with a Hook: or, Animadversions upon Mr Hobbs his Leviathan* (London, 1653), sigs. A9v–10r (list of heresies), A16r (quotation). The closest Ross comes to a conciliatory stance is at the start of the Preface: 'I finde him a man of excellent parts, and in this book much gold, and withal much dross' (sig. A12r).

[119] W. Charleton, *Deliramenta catarrhi: or, the Incongruities, Impossibilities and Absurdities couched under the Vulgar Opinion of Defluxions* (London, 1650), sig. a1v; *Darknes of Atheism*, sig. b3r.

[120] See Fleitmann, *Walter Charleton*, pp. 26, 70, 314 (n. 31). The scientist and physician Henry Pierrepont was the dedicatee of Hobbes's ΣΤΙΓΜΑΙ ... *or, Markes of the Absurd Geometry, Rural Language, Scottish Church-Politicks, and Barbarismes of John Wallis* (London, 1657).

[121] Cooper, *Catalogus*, pp. 3, 31, 32. His copy of the *Natural History of Nutrition*, bearing his annotations, is Glasgow University Library, pressmark Hunterian Ac. 4. 17.

## PIERRE DE CARDONNEL (1614–1667)

in those parts did usually resort . . .'[122] The minister who conducted these services, Jean d'Espagne, was an admired preacher who acquired a number of aristocratic English patrons, including the Earls of Pembroke and Clare. However, when the three ministers of the Threadneedle Street church died in rapid succession in 1641–2, his candidature for an appointment there was rejected by the Consistory.[123] One of the new ministers they did choose, Jean de la Marche, was a firebrand anti-royalist; even before the appointment was made, the Consistory felt obliged to ask him 'to abstain, henceforth, from speaking about matters of state in his sermons, and to pray for the King of England'.[124] For a while he was counterbalanced by another minister with royalist sympathies; but that minister soon left, and de la Marche (who became a member of the Westminster Assembly) grew more extreme, preaching an apocalyptic theology that encompassed the downfall of kings. In these circumstances, d'Espagne's congregation became an alternative London church, increasingly separated from its mother congregation, both ideologically and doctrinally.[125] In an outspoken attack on the Threadneedle Street church in 1657, d'Espagne would write: 'Can you deny that . . . from mid-1643 to mid-1651 various blasphemies were publicly taught in your church? . . . Is it not true that the opinions of the Millenarians about their glorious kingdom were flaunted there? . . . Is it not true that sermons were loudly preached there, saying that all kings who are opposed to reformation must be hanged?'[126]

It is not hard to see where Pierre de Cardonnel's sympathies would have lain. Even his brother Adam, when living only a few hundred yards from the Threadneedle Street church, seems to have withdrawn from it by 1649, having his child baptized in St Lawrence Pountney church instead.[127] When Pierre had a child baptized in December 1653, the ceremony was probably performed by d'Espagne: no such baptism is recorded in the registers of either Threadneedle

---

[122] J. Durel, *A View of the Government and Publick Worship of God in the Reformed Churches beyond the Seas* (London, 1662), p. 73. Benjamin de Rohan, duc de Soubise, died in 1642.

[123] See F. de Schickler, *Les Églises du refuge en Angleterre*, 3 vols. (Paris, 1892), II, pp. 77–82; Gwynn, *Calendar*, pp. 7–8; FPCL, MS 5, fol. 131v (decision of 17 Aug. 1642 that 'pour diuers raisons le consistoire ne peut pas accepter M<sup>r</sup> despagne pour pasteur de ceste eglise'; these 'diuers raisons' were not explained, but may have been connected with an old sexual scandal, which was raked up against him later).

[124] FPCL, MS 5, fol. 134v (7 March 1643): 'de sabstenir doresnauant de parler d'affair d'estat en ses sermons & quil aye a prier dieu pour le Roy D'Angleterre'.

[125] See de Schickler, *Les Églises*, pp. 93–111; Gwynn, *Calendar*, pp. 9–12; B. Cottret, *The Huguenots in England: Immigration and Settlement c.1550–1700*, tr. P. Stevenson and A. Stevenson (Cambridge, 1991), pp. 123–7.

[126] J. d'Espagne, *Examen de XVII. maximes judaiques* (London, 1657), pp. 47–8: 'Pouvez-vous nier que . . . depuis le milieu de l'an 1643, jusques au milieu de 1651 on ait publiquement enseigné divers blasphemes en votre Eglise? . . . Y-a-on pas estallé des opinions touchant le Regne glorieux des Millénaires? . . . Y-a-on pas presché à haute voix . . . qu'il faut pendre tous les Roix qui s'opposent à la Reformation?'

[127] See above, n. 93. Admittedly, it was not uncommon for Huguenots to make such use of Anglican churches: for burials it was a necessity, as they had no burial grounds of their own. But, given Adam's physical proximity to Threadneedle St on the one hand and his known Royalist connections on the other, the move seems significant. Living in Southampton after the Restoration, he would have all his children baptized at the Walloon church, of which he was an 'ancien' (elder) for many years.

Street or St Lawrence, and as the registers of d'Espagne's congregation have not survived, the only record of the event is the note of a christening present from the Earl of Devonshire (cited above).[128]

Pierre's sympathies and connections with the d'Espagne congregation would have been social and intellectual as well as political. For d'Espagne attracted not only Royalists and those moderate Parliamentarians who wanted a new constitutional arrangement with the king, but also the social and intellectual elite of London French Protestant society. This included Armand de Caumont, marquis de Montpouillan; the family of Turquet de Mayerne; two other leading physicians, Jean Colladon (who married de Mayerne's niece) and the convert from Catholicism Théophile de Garencières; the mathematician Isaac de Caus; and the coin-engraver Nicolas Briot.[129] D'Espagne was himself a man of considerable intellectual stature, publishing works on theology and biblical criticism; he had studied a wide range of rabbinical writings, and even had a debate with Menasseh ben Israel—concerns which must have attracted the interest of de Cardonnel, whose library was well stocked with Hebrew scholarship and included thirteen books printed in Hebrew by the Bomberg press in Venice.[130] De Cardonnel also owned copies of d'Espagne's *Popular Errors . . . concerning the Knowledge of Religion* (London, 1648), *Nouvelles observations sur le decalogue* (London, 1649), and *An Essay of the Wonders of God* (London, 1662), the translation of his *Essay des merveilles de Dieu* (London, 1657).[131]

When d'Espagne died in 1659, the authorities at Threadneedle Street made some tentative suggestions about reunion—while, at the same time, writing to colleagues in Paris in an attempt to block the appointment of a successor.[132] Soon after the Restoration they petitioned the King to force the breakaway congregation

---

[128] See above, at n. 2.

[129] See J. d'Espagne, *Essay des merveilles de Dieu en l'harmonie des temps* (London, 1657), sigs. A6r–7r (ode to d'Espagne by de Garencières), and *The Joyfull Convert: Represented in a Short, but Elegant Sermon, Preached at the Baptizing of a Turke* (London, 1658) (godparents: the marquis de Montpouillan and Lady de Mayerne); FPCL, MS 5, fol. 145r (listing several members, including 'de Caux' and 'Briot'), and MS 6 (Consistory Acts, 1658–1679), fols. 20v–21r (proposals sent to d'Espagne and Colladon); cf. the comments in de Schickler, *Les Églises*, II, p. 95, and Gwynn, *Calendar*, pp. 12–14. On de Garencières (who had graduated MD from Caen) and Colladon, see W. Munk et al., *The Roll of the Royal College of Physicians of London*, (London, 1861– ), I, pp. 257–8, 302–3. See also T. de Garencières's prefatory epistle to de Mayerne in his *Angliae flagellum seu tabes anglica* (n.p., 1647).

[130] In addition to the works cited above, see J. d'Espagne, *Popular Errors in Generall Poynts concerning the Knowledge of Religion* (London, 1648), and *Shibboleth, ou reformation de quelques passages és versions françoise & angloise de la Bible* (London, 1653). His rabbinical reading (albeit unremittingly hostile) was displayed in his *Examen de XVII. maximes judaiques*: in the preface to that work he referred to 'a little discussion I conducted recently with one of the most famous rabbis of our age' ('un petit Conference verbale que j'eus dernierement avec un des plus fameux Rabbins de ce temps'), and in the text he opposed arguments taken from Menasseh ben Israel's *Conciliador* (Frankfurt, Amsterdam, 1632–51) and *Vindiciae Judaeorum* (London, 1656). For de Cardonnel's Hebrew books, see Cooper, *Catalogus*, pp. 3–6.

[131] Cooper, *Catalogus*, pp. 28–9.

[132] FPCL, MS 5, fols. 219v–220r; MS 6, fols. 20v–21r; MS 45 (copies of letters, 1652–1695), fols. 39–40r (letters to Paris).

## PIERRE DE CARDONNEL (1614-1667)

to reunite with them. However, the minister who now led d'Espagne's congregation, Jean Durel, had a better idea. Durel was a member of the French Protestant Church in Jersey; he had been expelled from Oxford as a Royalist in 1643 and had moved to Caen, where he had studied philosophy at the Collège du Bois. During Bochart's absence in Sweden he served as pastor in his place. But he had also taken the unusual step of receiving Anglican orders in the chapel of Sir Richard Browne in Paris.[133] His idea now was that his entire French congregation in London should submit to the Church of England, retaining its special corporate identity but using a French translation (to be made by him) of the Book of Common Prayer. It would thus come under the authority of the bishop of London, escaping altogether from the jurisdiction of the Threadneedle Street Consistory. This scheme met with royal and episcopal approval, and Durel's congregation was granted the use of the 'Little Chapel of the Savoy'.[134] On 14 July 1661 the inaugural service for this new branch of the Anglican Church was held there, in the presence of a glittering roll-call of the English aristocracy. Prominent in the congregation were the Duke and Duchess of Ormonde, the Countess of Ossory, the Marquess of Newcastle, and the Earl of Devonshire. Given such company, it seems highly likely that Pierre de Cardonnel was also present: he appears to have had close contacts with the Earl of Devonshire at this time, as his poem written while with him on the Thames was probably composed only a couple of weeks later.[135]

This establishment of a 'conformist' French congregation did not involve a great shift in either practice or doctrine. The regular use by French Protestants of Anglican churches for burials has already been noted; in subsequent years some other congregations seem to have 'drifted' between non-conformity and conformity, and a generation later the prominent Huguenot merchant Thomas Papillon would remark that, 'though generally I and my Children do Receiue the Sacrament at y$^e$ french Church in London, Yet it hath beene our practice often at London and allwais when in the Country to attend on y$^e$ publick worship of G$^d$ and to Receiue the sacrament according to the Liturgy and discipline of the Church of England.'[136] In 1650 Samuel Bochart had had a public dispute with George Morley

---

[133] See the *DNB* entry on Jean Durel; de Schickler, *Les Églises*, II, p. 205(n.); J. Durel, *Theoremata philosophiae rationalis, moralis, naturalis et supernaturalis* [by] *Ioannes Durel, Caesaro-Britannus, in collegio Sylvano Academiae Cadomensis* (Caen, n.d. [1644]), and his *A View of the Government and Publick Worship of God*, p. 94.

[134] See de Schickler, II, pp. 218–21; *La Liturgie, c'est a dire, le formulaire des prieres publiques . . . selon l'usage de l'Eglise Anglicane*, tr. J. Durel (Geneva, 1665); G. Beeman, 'Notes on the Sites and History of the French Churches in London', *Proceedings of the Huguenot Society of London*, 8, for 1905–8 (1909), pp. 13–59 (p. 19); Cottret, *Huguenots in England*, p. 178.

[135] See de Schickler, *Les Églises*, II, p. 224 (roll-call); J. Durel, *The Liturgy of the Church of England Asserted in a Sermon Preached at the Chappel of the Savoy* (London, 1662) (with epistle dedicatory to Ormonde). For de Cardonnel's poem (written 'at the end of July' ('Julio obeunte')), see above, n. 3.

[136] See above, n. 127 (burials); Beeman, 'Notes on the Sites of the French Churches', p. 17 ('drifted'); Centre for Kentish Studies, Maidstone, Papillon papers, MS C 13 (4) (copy of letter to Sir Joseph Ashe, 11 June 1684).

over the refusal of some Anglicans in Paris to communicate with the French Reformed Church: he rejected Morley's claim that the French Protestants condemned episcopacy, commenting mildly that 'we do not think it matters greatly whether the Church be governed by bishops or by Presbyterian pastors, so long as those who govern it carry out their duties properly and well'. And in 1661 both he and his colleague in Caen, Pierre du Bosc, expressed their approval for Durel's actions.[137] Royalism (reinforced by the horror felt by most leading French Protestants at the killing of Charles I) was an important part of the background to these attitudes, but a political theory of Erastian conformism was not necessarily involved—though Durel's choice of Clarendon as the dedicatee of his book in 1662 was a canny one.[138] If anything, Durel's stance seems to have been conditioned more by the tradition of Protestant ecumenism represented by John Dury in the 1630s and 1640s: the work dedicated to Clarendon was a survey of the practices of various Lutheran and Calvinist churches on the Continent, arguing for their essential compatibility with Anglicanism; and in his inaugural sermon Durel paid special attention to what he called 'the remainders of the Church of the Brethren of *Bohemia*'—the church of Dury's friend and mentor, Jan Amos Comenius.[139] His views may have been shared by de Cardonnel, whose library included Samuel Hartlib's *A Briefe Relation of that which hath beene lately attempted to procure Ecclesiastical Peace amongst Protestants* (London, 1641), two works by Dury, and four by Comenius.[140]

## VI

It will be apparent that the nature of Pierre de Cardonnel's experiences and interests brought him in some ways quite close to Hobbes. The closest connections were personal—above all, his links with the Earl of Devonshire. As we have seen, de Cardonnel had probably got to know the Earl in Normandy in 1645, and in December 1653 he received a handsome christening present from the Earl in London (so handsome, indeed, that it may indicate that the Earl was a

---

[137] S. Bochart, *Lettre de Monsieur Bochart à Monsieur Morley Chapelain du Roy d'Angleterre* (Paris, 1650), p. 4: 'nous ne tenons pas, qu'il importe beaucoup si l'Eglise est gouuernée par des Euesques ou par des Pasteurs Presbyteriens, pourueu que ceux qui la gouuernent s'acquitent bien & deuëment de leurs charges'; Durel, *A View of the Government*, pp. 90–1 (du Bosc), and *The Liturgy of the Church of England*, sig. a1v (Bochart). Similarly, at the Restoration du Bosc had written to Daniel Brevint (another Channel Islander who had also taken Anglican orders, and who also preached at the inaugural service in the Savoy chapel), saying that he had no objection to episcopacy 'when it is administered well and legitimately' ('quand il est bien & legitimement administré'): Le Gendre, *Vie de Pierre du Bosc*, p. 21.

[138] Durel, *A View of the Government*, epistle dedicatory. Like Saumaise and du Moulin, Bochart fiercely rejected the idea that there was some connection between Presbyterianism and the regicide: *Lettre de Monsieur Bochart*, pp. 104–5.

[139] Durel, *The Liturgy of the Church of England*, p. 19. On Dury's long-running ecumenist campaign see J. M. Batten, *John Dury, Advocate of Christian Reunion* (Chicago, 1944).

[140] Cooper, *Catalogus*, pp. 22–3, 26–8, 34.

godfather).[141] One section of de Cardonnel's notebook records letters he sent in 1655–6: on 3 May 1655, soon after his return to London from France, he wrote 'a mons. le C. de Deuonshire', and again on 13 June and 10 August. On 30 June 1656 he was staying at Latimers, the Earl's country house in Buckinghamshire, from where he sent letters to his brothers in France.[142] He crops up again in the account book of the Earl's steward, in an entry for 9 July 1659, which states: 'To Mr Cardonell—£30'.[143] One later trace of de Cardonnel in the records at Chatsworth is the reference in a catalogue of the Earl's library to 'Cardonnell Eng 8o'— meaning presumably his *Complementum fortunatarum insularum*, which contains the text of his English poem 'The Fortunate Islands' as well as his Latin poem dedicated to the Earl of Devonshire.[144] Otherwise, however, the records fail to give any indication of the nature of the services de Cardonnel performed for the Earl. They may have involved arranging the importation of goods (works of art or other luxury goods, perhaps) from the Continent; or they may have concerned transactions of a politically more delicate nature. (The authorities might, after all, have had some grounds for their sudden but brief arrest of the Earl in late June 1655.[145])

Clearly, therefore, de Cardonnel had had plenty of opportunities for personal contacts with Hobbes, beginning with Hobbes's visit to the Earl of Devonshire in Rouen in August 1645—or, indeed, with Hobbes's presence in Paris throughout the 1640s and his many links with the Royalists in exile. Hobbes had apparently started working again for the Earl soon after his return to London at the end of December 1651; he is known to have been performing some duties by the spring of 1652—though these were probably very light, and he retained his own lodgings in London in the mid-1650s.[146] Other mutual friends or possible intermediaries have also been mentioned, the most important being Walter Charleton and Edmund Waller. De Cardonnel's library catalogue shows that he had a continuing interest in Hobbes's works: he owned *De homine* (London, 1658), *Mr Hobbes Considered* (London, 1662), and several works by critics of Hobbes, including Moranus's

---

[141] See above, nn. 2, 79.

[142] BL, MS Sloane 1731B, fols. 53v, 54r, 55r.

[143] Chatsworth, MS Hardwick 33, p. 42.

[144] Chatsworth, Hardwick MS, unnumbered ('Catalogue of Books' written by James Wheldon, late 1650s, with later items added: referred to as 'Catalogue B' in J. J. Hamilton, 'Hobbes's Study and the Hardwick Library', *Journal of the History of Philosophy*, 16 (1978), pp. 445–53). The book is in fact a quarto, but the terms were generally used in this period only as rough indicators of physical size.

[145] See Warner, *Nicholas Papers*, III, p. 9. The suggestion about works of art or luxury goods is made in the light of an entry in de Cardonnel's notebook for April 1656: 'escrit au P. le Buteux [at Middelburg] pour Anthony Lawes pour enuoyer les pacquets de soyerie . . . Item le cabinet & coffre lacq. . . . & à paul Biscop à flessingen pour 2 cassettes de toiles peintes receues de Rotterdam' (fol. 55r).

[146] Evidence of Hobbes's work for the Earl appears in the memoirs of Sir Stephen Fox: 'the Earle of Deuonshire sent his Gouernor the famous mr Hobbs to enuite mee to be Keeper of his priuey purse' (BL, MS Add. 51324, fols. 34v–35r). Fox took this job for 10 months, and left it in early 1653: see C. Clay, *Public Finance and Private Wealth: The Career of Sir Stephen Fox, 1627–1716* (Oxford, 1978), p. 9. For Hobbes's London residence, in Fetter Lane, see Hobbes, *Correspondence*, I, p. 294.

*Animadversiones in elementorum philosophiae sectionem I de corpore* (Brussels, 1655), Lucy's *Observations, Censures and Confutations of Divers Errors in the 12, 13 and 14 Chap. of Mr Hobs his Leviathan* (London, 1657), and Lawson's *Examination of the Political Part of Mr Hobbs's Leviathan* (London, 1657).

Ideologically, too, de Cardonnel shared some common ground with Hobbes. He was a Royalist; he accepted (in 1661) the authority of the civil sovereign in the government of his church; and he was a Protestant, with some experience of the misuse of power by Catholic authorities (in the matter of his printing venture), who could therefore be expected to sympathize with Hobbes's attitude towards Roman Catholicism. On the other hand, his opposition to rebellion was probably not as principled as Hobbes's (as his attachment to several rebellious French noblemen suggests); his church politics may have been more aligned to Protestant ecumenism than to the application of a theory of civil sovereignty; and his intellectual formation—in which the diehard Aristotelian Alexander Ross may have played an important role—was probably more conservative. De Cardonnel's library catalogue lists large quantities of mainstream Protestant theology (Calvin, Zwingli, du Moulin, Daillé), biblical scholarship, and works of erudition by standard authors such as Vives, Scaliger, Lipsius, Puteanus, and Salmasius. His holdings in contemporary philosophy were much less extensive (though it is possible that a section of his library, containing such works, was not included in this catalogue, which omits his known copies of *Leviathan*, Descartes's *Principia* and *Specimina*, and Naudé's *History of Magick*).[147] He did possess a range of modern logic textbooks, and a handful of items by Bacon; he also had works by Cusanus, Bruno, della Porta, Dee, Fludd, and Sendivogius, which suggests that, while he was not as committed to the defence of Aristotelianism as his friend Alexander Ross, his own divergence from it was in a very different direction from Hobbes's.[148]

Pierre de Cardonnel's copy of *Leviathan* bears the marks of a very close reading. There are underlinings, marginal marks (double lines, 'N.' for 'Nota' or 'Note', and the sign of a pointing hand) and marginal comments in most parts of the book; the only exception is the bulk of part 2 of the work (chapters 21–31, presenting the application of Hobbes's theory in the areas of government and law), which was left almost completely untouched. De Cardonnel's reading also involved re-reading and cross-checking: where, for example, Hobbes wrote at the end of chapter 2 'And of this kinde of Understanding I shall speak hereafter', de Cardonnel annotated: 'Vid. cap. 5. p. 20. infrà.' Sometimes these cross-references were used to point out apparent inconsistencies in Hobbes's argument: thus, against the discussion of a

---

[147] R. Descartes, *Principia philosophiae* (Amsterdam, 1650), bound with *Specimina philosophiae, seu dissertatio de methodo* (Amsterdam, 1650), in the author's collection; G. Naudé, *The History of Magick, by way of Apology for all the Wise Men who have Unjustly been Reputed Magicians*, tr. J. Davies (London, 1657), Cambridge University Library, pressmark N. 5. 17.

[148] For all these items see Cooper, *Catalogus*.

## PIERRE DE CARDONNEL (1614–1667)

Christian pastor honouring an idol on p. 362, de Cardonnel wrote: 'compare supra p. 272 touching Martyrs'.[149] Many of the marginal comments do nothing more than repeat or summarize Hobbes's arguments: 'Definition of the will by y$^e$ Schooles, reiected by y$^e$ auth.' (p. 28), and so on. But the marginal marks, especially the sign of a pointing hand, seem to indicate passages that had earned de Cardonnel's interest and approval—at least in the earlier part of the book. For the general impression given by his marginalia is that most of them were added in sequence, when he worked through the book for the first time; only gradually, as he engaged with the arguments of the third and fourth parts of the book, were his more critical reactions aroused.

Thus, for example, the passage on p. 36, 'Though the effect of folly . . . be not visible always in one man . . . yet when many of them conspire together, the Rage of the whole multitude is visible enough' receives the accolade of a pointing hand; so too does the comment on the 'Foole' (p. 72), 'From such reasoning as this, Successfull wickednesse hath obtained the name of Vertue . . .' (where the words 'Successfull wickednesse' are also underlined); and so do the principles of sovereign immunity set out on p. 90: 'whatsoever he [the sovereign] doth, it can be no injury to any of his Subjects', and 'no man that hath Soveraigne power can iustly be put to death.' Occasionally, passages of moral observation also receive this mark, such as that on p. 49: 'Eloquence, with flattery, disposeth men to confide in them that have it; because the former is seeming Wisdome, the latter seeming Kindnesse.' Some of the marginal annotations, while summarizing the contents, seem also to express an implicit approval—such as the note written on p. 73, 'The attempt of gaining Soverainty by Rebellion proved against reason.' And in one case de Cardonnel made explicit the anti-Catholicism that was only implicit in Hobbes's argument, when he wrote at the top of p. 74, 'The Jesuitical tenent y$^t$ Faith is not to be kept to Hereticks, refuted.'

The overall impression given by de Cardonnel's annotations in the first half of the book is that he happily went along with the main conclusions of Hobbes's political argument, in so far as it was Royalist, absolutist and anti-Catholic. Whether he was equally at ease with the philosophical premises of that argument is less clear; his annotations on the early chapters, where Hobbes sets out his epistemological and psychological theories, are confined, in almost every case, to summarizing their contents. The only exceptions are a flicker of interest in Hobbes's analysis of reasoning at the beginning of chapter 5 (p. 18), where, against Hobbes's words 'The Logicians teach the same in *Consequences of words*; adding together *two Names*, to make an *Affirmation*', de Cardonnel writes 'hint of mathematical

---

[149] All quotations of the marginalia are from the Harry Ransom Humanities Research Center, University of Texas, pressmark Pforz. 491. The page numbers of this edition can also be found in several modern editions of *Leviathan* (edited by Pogson Smith, Macpherson, and Tuck).

Philosophy', and a more critical comment added against the opening section of the Introduction (sig. A4r). Where Hobbes writes 'For seeing life is but a motion of Limbs . . . why may we not say, that all *Automata* . . . have an artificiall life?' de Cardonnel's note puts forward the query: 'is this not to narrow a definition since Regiomontanus eagle & fly might be reckoned amongst the Living creatures, by it; nay all automata as the text itselfe doth imply; w<sup>ch</sup> no strict & true philosophy will allow of.'[150] This is the only direct criticism expressed anywhere in de Cardonnel's comments on the first two parts of the book—unless one counts as critical his concise summary of a passage on p. 85, where Hobbes observes that 'in all places, where men have lived by small Families, to robbe and spoyle one another, has been a Trade, and so farre from being reputed against the Law of Nature, that the greater spoyles they gained, the greater was their honour', and de Cardonnel simply writes: 'robbing is not against y<sup>e</sup> Lawes of Nature'.

Soon after the opening of part 3 of the book, however, de Cardonnel begins to register his disagreements. Not surprisingly, his first clash with Hobbes is on a point of Hebrew exegesis. On p. 201 Hobbes deploys one of his standard arguments for showing that the early books of the Bible were not written by the people whose names they bear: he notes the reference in the Book of Joshua (4: 9) to the twelve stones set up by Joshua in the Jordan, 'of which the Writer saith thus, *They are there unto this day*; for *unto this day*, is a phrase that signifieth a time past, beyond the memory of man.' De Cardonnel writes in the margin: 'the original hath עד עולם in this place, w<sup>ch</sup> voydes y<sup>e</sup> argument'. He then adds: '& as for the other passag[es] & other like here under cited they are relations of things past w<sup>ch</sup> give wa[y] to the phrase of Scripture עד היום הזה si vertas usque ad hunc diem. sed & de re praesenta [*sic*] potest intelligi, dico, praesenti, si interprete[ris] secundum hunc diem ab hac die in posterum' ['if you translate it as "unto this day"; but it can also be understood as referring to the present—the present, I say, if you interpret it as "after this day", "from this day onwards" '].[151] Elsewhere (pp. 217, 244) de Cardonnel writes in the margin the Hebrew text of biblical verses cited by Hobbes; and on p. 340, against Hobbes's discussion of the account given in the Book of Genesis of the creation of souls in men and beasts, he comments: 'the text in the first chap. of Genesis speaking first of y<sup>e</sup> creation of man seemeth to import

---

[150] The mathematician and astronomer Johannes Müller (1436–76), from Königsberg (hence 'Regiomontanus'), was said to have made a wooden eagle, which flew from his fist to greet the Holy Roman Emperor, and an iron fly, which flew round the room and returned to his hand: the anecdote was popularized by du Bartas: see G. de Saluste du Bartas, *La Sepmaine (texte de 1581)*, ed. Y. Bellenger (Paris, 1981), pp. 290–1 (week 1, day 6, ll. 839–54).

[151] The first phrase means 'for ever'; de Cardonnel is wrong in saying that this appears in 'the original'. What appears there is the second phrase, which does indeed mean 'unto this day' (not 'after this day'), although this was sometimes glossed by commentators, such as the eighteenth-century David Altschuler, as meaning 'forever', in the sense of 'for each new generation of readers'. I am very grateful to Dr John London for his transcription, translation, and elucidation of de Cardonnel's Hebrew.

something more & deliver a greater mystery then in the other creatures. For it sayes ויברא אלוהים את האדם בצלמו בצלם אלוהים ברא אתו זכר ונקבה ברא אתם whereas in the other creatures the word יעש is but used.'[152]

De Cardonnel also reacted against Hobbes's dismissal of Job's authorship of the book that bears his name. When Hobbes commented on p. 202 that 'Verse is no usuall stile of such, as . . . are themselves in great pain', de Cardonnel observed: 'when Socrates was neere his death he tels Simias (to relate it to Euenus a poët) that although he neuer before had medled w.[th] verses he was advertised often in a dreame, to giue himself to Poetry, & did it. &c.' And when Hobbes later announced (on p. 334) a much more general principle concerning the inadequacy of human claims to theological knowledge ('so also is it of the light of the Gospel, and of the light of the Understanding, that no man can conceive there is any greater degree of it, than that which he hath already attained to'), de Cardonnel retorted: 'this position is crossed by the Axioma, quanto plus ad scientiae gradum supremum pervenimus, tantò magis inscitiae propriae nobis conscij sumus, nobisque plura ad scientiae perfectionem adipiscendam deficere intellegimus [the closer we come to the highest level of knowledge, the more aware we become of our own ignorance, and the more lacking we understand ourselves to be in those things that are needed for obtaining the perfection of knowledge]. We know that Spiritual intelligences are capable of a greater portion of knowledge then ourselves, ergo &c.' In two other places de Cardonnel's response to Hobbes's theological arguments was more brusque. Against the passage on p. 345, where Hobbes set out his idiosyncratic interpretation of the phrase 'eternal torments' (in which the wicked who are tormented will have finite lives, and it is only the succession of such torments, for them and their descendants, that will be eternal), he wrote: 'This is hard to be understood.' And against Hobbes's suggestion on p. 348 that 'perhaps there may be place left after the Resurrection for the Repentance of some sinners': 'Bold conjecture'.

On the other hand, there are many passages in the third and fourth parts of *Leviathan* that bear the marks of de Cardonnel's approbation. The relationship asserted by Hobbes between civil sovereignty and religion is never challenged; indeed, several marginalia seem to give it positive assent. Thus, we have the annotations 'The Popes Supremacy & Power of Excommunication ill grounded' (p. 279); 'Christianity doth not incroach upon civil or kingly power' (p. 295); and

---

[152] The verse quoted (with the addition of the letter 'vav', which is not part of the text) is Gen. 1: 27 ('So God created man in his own image, in the image of God created he him; male and female created he them'). The other word quoted means 'made', as in Gen. 1: 25 ('And God made the beast of the earth . . .'). De Cardonnel's distinction between the two verbs meaning 'make' and 'create' is undermined, however, by the fact that Gen. 1: 26 also uses the former when referring to the creation of man ('And God said, Let us make man in our image . . .'). Once again, I am very grateful to Dr John London for his explanation of these points.

'Evident Examples of Kings Soverainty in Matters of Religion' (p. 254). Where Hobbes observes that 'Soveraigns are supreme Teachers (in generall) by their Office; and therefore oblige themselves (by their Baptisme) to teach the Doctrine of Christ: And when they suffer others to teach their people, they doe it at the perill of their own souls' (p. 305), de Cardonnel writes in the margin: 'a heavy burthen on Soveraigns shoulders'. The simplified version of Christianity propounded by Hobbes also seems to have appealed to de Cardonnel. Against the passage where Hobbes announced that 'The (*Vnum Necessarium*) Onely Article of Faith, which the Scripture maketh simply Necessary to Salvation, is this, that JESUS IS THE CHRIST' (p. 324), de Cardonnel added his sign of a pointing hand. When Hobbes advised that ecclesiastics should cultivate the virtues of 'Wisdome, Humility, Clearnesse of Doctrine, and sincerity of Conversation' (p. 385), de Cardonnel wrote: 'seasonable & good admonition to the Christian Clergy'. Hobbes's principle that 'it is not the bare Words, but the Scope of the writer that giveth the true light, by which any writing is to bee interpreted' (p. 331) earned the comment: 'A good key to open the Texts of Scripture & bring them to their true sense'. And when Hobbes broke off from his attack on scholastic metaphysics to exclaim, 'these are but a small part of the Incongruities they are forced to, from their disputing Philosophically, in stead of admiring, and adoring of the Divine and Incomprehensible Nature . . .' (p. 374), de Cardonnel noted approvingly: 'Gods incomprehensible Nature not subject to y$^e$ termes or apprehension of Philosophy'.

Altogether, de Cardonnel's marginalia seem to represent a broadly sympathetic reading of *Leviathan*; his sharpest disagreements relate only to a few points of biblical exegesis, and to one or two of Hobbes's more risky theological innovations. He appears content to take at face value Hobbes's advocacy of a Christianity that would consist of adherence to a minimum of doctrine (one common to all denominations) plus the practice of the virtues. The fact that it was possible to read Hobbes in this way does not mean that Hobbes cannot have intended more than met such a contemporary reader's eye. But when the reader concerned may have known Hobbes—and certainly did know others who knew him well—the testimony of such a reading does have some value. It suggests, at the least, that, if Hobbes's arguments had more radical implications than that (as almost any modern reader will strongly suspect), the relationship between the acceptable surface features and the radical contents was not simply one of camouflage to reality, or hypocritical outward piety to sheer inner cynicism, but something more complex and organic.

However, these comments are prompted only by de Cardonnel's marginalia. Some time after he had read *Leviathan*, he filled the blank verso side of the engraved title page in his copy with admonitory quotations, presenting a much more negative judgement on the work. First came a verse (in Greek) from the apocryphal book of Ecclesiasticus, 'the ear of a listener is the desire of a wise man'

## PIERRE DE CARDONNEL (1614–1667)

(3: 28); this was from a chapter that also contained the advice, 'Seek not out things that are too hard for thee, and search not out things that are above thy strength.'[153] Then came three quotations from Heinrich Cornelius Agrippa's *De incertitudine et vanitate scientiarum et artium*:

Each sect tries to overturn all the others, to establish itself and its own principles; nor does any one sect allow that another one is wise, for fear of admitting that it is foolish. And when philosophy disputes about particular things, and offers its opinions, it is certain about nothing. So I am quite unsure whether I should count philosophers among brute animals or among human beings. It does seem that in some ways they are better than brutes, in so far as they have reason and understanding; but how can they deserve to be counted as humans, whose reason cannot establish any fixed principle and is always sliding around in a slippery mass of opinions, and whose understanding, unsure about everything, has nothing to hold onto or to follow?[154]

I think I have sufficiently shown what a total lack of agreement there is among philosophers about the truth: the more closely a person adheres to them, the greater the distance between him and the truth itself, and the further he strays from the catholic religion . . . All the heresy that ever existed flowed in its entirety out of the springs of philosophy.[155]

No people are less fit to receive Christian doctrine than those whose minds are already imbued with the opinions of the sciences. Such people are so stubborn and obstinate in their opinions that they leave no place for the Holy Spirit.[156]

Below these, de Cardonnel copied out two extracts from Lactantius. The first was a passage from his *Epitome institutionum divinarum*, in which Lactantius uses the arguments of Carneades to show that, without true religion, justice can only seem ill-grounded and absurd.[157] The second is a section of the *Divinae institutiones*,

---

[153] Similarly, on the blank leaf before the title page of Descartes, *Principia*, he copied out (in Latin) a verse from Ecclesiastes (3: 11), 'He hath made every thing beautiful in his time: also he hath set the world in their heart, so that no man can find out the work that God maketh from the beginning to the end.'

[154] 'Unaquaeque secta omnes alias evertit, ut se suaque confirmet: nec ulla alteri sapere concedit, ne se desipere fateatur. Quumque de singulis Philosophia disputat, & opinatur, de nullis certa est. unde Philosophos an inter bruta an inter homines numerem, planè nescio: brutis siquidem praestare videntur, eò quod rationem habeant & intelligentiam: homines autem quomodo esse merentur, quorum ratio nihil constans persuadere potest, sed semper in opinionum lubrico opinionibus vacillat, quorum intellectus ad omnia incertus, non habet quod teneat aut sequatur.' This wording varies in minor ways from that printed in H. C. Agrippa, *De vanitate scientiarum* (Leiden, 1644), ch. 49, pp. 104–5.

[155] 'Satis indicasse me arbitror quàm nihil inter Philosophos de veritate conveniat, quibus quo quis propinquior redditur, eo magis a vero ipso longiusque abest, & à Catholica Religione aberrat . . . & Quicquid haeresium vnquam fuit totum hoc & omne ex Philosophiae fontibus ceu primo seminario scaturiit' (ch. 53). The 17th-cent. English translation gave 'Catholica Religione' as 'the Truth it self': H. C. Agrippa, *The Vanity of Arts and Sciences*, tr. anon. (London, 1676), p. 144.

[156] 'Nullum est hominum genus suscipiendae Christianae Doctrinae minus idoneum, quàm qui scientiarum Opinionibus mentem iàm imbibitam habent. Hi enim tam pertinaces & obstinati in suis opinionibus sunt ut S. sancto nullum locum reliquant'. Again, there are minor divergences between this and the text in Agrippa, *De vanitate*, ch. 101, p. 304.

[157] The section from which he quotes states: 'If justice is the worship of the true God . . . then philosophers have not known justice . . . For that reason they might have been refuted by Carneades, whose

where he warns against the dangers of being led by those who have a reputation of superior wisdom.[158] As a final damning epigraph to the book, de Cardonnel added at the foot of the printed title page a quotation from Pliny the Elder: 'credulity is never more easily let down than when a false statement is attested by an authority of weight'.[159]

These comments appear to dismiss the whole of Hobbes's philosophical endeavour. The second of the quotations from Agrippa, with its reference to heresy, brings de Cardonnel close to the standard line of denunciation formulated by writers such as Ross; and the third goes far beyond any of the marginalia, suggesting that Hobbes—whose simplified Christianity those marginal notes had actually praised—had no room in his mind for 'Christian doctrine'.

Two possible explanations suggest themselves for this contrast in de Cardonnel's approaches. Either his judgement became more negative because he had the benefit—if that is the right word—of reading the criticisms penned by Alexander Ross and others; or his impression of Hobbes changed as a result of having more personal contact with him, perhaps discussing with him some of the arguments of *Leviathan*, and finding him frustratingly obdurate. Yet, even if the second is the correct explanation, it is still noteworthy that the passages de Cardonnel quoted from Agrippa might apply equally to other philosophers and their 'Sects', including ones that argued against Hobbes (dogmatic Aristotelians, for example). His attitude seems to have been not that Hobbes had set out deliberately to destroy

---

argument was this: "There is no natural right or justice, and so all living creatures, at the bidding of Nature herself, defend their own interests; and, as a result, if justice consults the interests of others, but neglects its own, it ought to be called folly . . ."' ('Nam si justitia est veri Dei cultus . . . nescierunt ergo justitiam philosophi . . . et ideo refelli potuerint a Carneade, cujus haec fuit disputatio: 'nullum esse just naturale; itaque omnes animantes, ipsa ducente natura, commoda sua defendere; et ideo justitiam, si alienis utilitatibus consulit, suas negligit, stultitiam esse dicendam . . .'): Lactantius, *Epitome institutionum divinarum*, ed. and tr. E. H. Blakeney (London, 1950), ch. 56, pp. 40, 103–4. De Cardonnel's quotation from this passage begins with the words attributed to Carneades.

[158] 'God gave to all people an equal amount of wisdom, so that they might investigate unheard-of things and consider carefully what they were told. The fact that some people long preceded us in time does not mean that they were superior to us in wisdom . . . Since to be wise, in other words, to seek the truth, is innate to all people, those who give their uncritical approval to the assertions of their superiors are just depriving themselves of their own wisdom, and being led by others like cattle' ('Dedit omnibus Deus pro virili portione sapientiam, ut & inaudita investigare possent, & audita perpendere; nec quia nos illi temporibus antecesserunt, sapientia quoque antecesserunt . . . Quare, cùm sapere, id est veritatem quaerere omnibus sit innatum, Sapientiam sibi adimunt, qui sine ullo Iudicio inventa majorum probant, & ab alijs pecudum more ducuntur . . .') De Cardonnel's version of the Latin does not differ significantly from that in J.-P. Migne, ed., *Patrologia latina*, VI, cols. 287–8 (bk. 2, ch. 8). The argument of this passage seems almost to conflict with that of the extracts from Agrippa: Lactantius is, after all, defending the use of human reason (in a chapter entitled 'Of the use of reason in religion' ('De rationis usu in religione') ). De Cardonnel's overall argument would seem to be that it is the professional philosophers who lead people astray, not reason as such.

[159] 'Non alius pronior fidei lapsus, quàm ubi res falsae gravis Author extitit' (translation from *Natural History*, ed. and tr. H. Rackham, W. H. S. Jones, and D. E. Eichholz, 10 vols. (London, 1967), II, pp. 226–7 (5.1.12), where the text is given as: 'haut alio fidei proniore lapsu quam ubi falsae rei gravis auctor existit'. The word 'fidei' here might be translated as 'trust' or 'faith' rather than 'credulity'.

religion, but that his head was so full of philosophical theories that he had, unfortunately, disqualified himself from receiving the truths of the Spirit. And of course, the main line of argument de Cardonnel picked up from Agrippa was one from which Hobbes himself had sometimes borrowed: only a few sentences after the end of his second quoted passage, Agrippa continues with a denunciation of 'adulterated' divinity that would not have been out of place in part 4 of *Leviathan*: 'By this Philosophy is all Divinity almost Adulterated, so that instead of Evangelical Doctors and Teachers, false Prophets and Heretical Philosophers have appear'd in the World [and] . . . have Transform'd true and simple Divinity . . . into swelling and Sophistical Loquacity.'[160] We should not forget that the reader who so sternly quoted Agrippa against Hobbes was also the reader whose approving summary of Hobbes's argument at one point had simply stated: 'Gods incomprehensible Nature not subject to y$^e$ termes or apprehension of Philosophy.'

## VII

The last period of Pierre de Cardonnel's life, from the mid-1650s to his death in 1667, is not well documented. He continued to live, apparently, in the metropolis, though at some time before his death he had moved from the City of London to Westminster. The entries in his notebook peter out in 1656; only in his geographical list of trading contacts did he add a few later dates, '1662' under Dover, and '1661' and '1662' under Cadiz.[161] The Restoration was no doubt a source of enormous satisfaction to him; but it was above all a source of hope, as he looked to the restored fortune of his royal and royalist patrons to raise up his own. In April 1661 he published a slim volume, consisting of a celebratory French ode in 59 stanzas, under the title *The Fortunate Islands: Presented to the Majesty of Charles II, for the Day of his Coronation*. The printed 'Preface to the King' referred plaintively to 'my solitude and retired life, since the frowns of Fortune, and the overthrow of my Estate, swallowed up in the tempest rais'd by the late unhappy Wars, in my endeavours to serve Your Majesties Royal Father'; hinting as broadly as he could, de Cardonnel explained that 'my present fortune . . . waits still for a change on your *Royal* Pleasure and Bounty, the only support, with your several gracious promises, whereon my hopes have relied for these many years'.[162] The copy he presented to the King (now in the Bodleian) contained an extra insertion of two leaves, with a manuscript epistle to Charles, in French, signed 'De cardonnel', which played on the same note: 'Sire, Fortune long ago deprived me of all the goods that were

---

[160] Agrippa, *Vanity*, pp. 144–5.
[161] BL MS Sloane 1731B, fols. 18v, 19v.
[162] P. de Cardonnel ['P.D.C.'], *The Fortunate Islands* (London, 1661), sigs. *2r, *2v. The coronation was on 23 April 1661.

under her jurisdiction, and I am left only with those things that she could not take away . . .'[163]

The following year brought an opportunity for producing further works in this special genre of patronage-seeking publication, when Charles II married Catherine of Braganza. The marriage itself took place in Portsmouth on 21 May; the royal couple then travelled to Hampton Court, from where they made their state entry to London on 23 August. De Cardonnel's first celebration of the marriage took the form of another French poem, published with a Latin translation: *Tagus, sive epithalamium Caroli II. Magnae Britanniae regis, et Catharinae Infantis Portogalliae* (London, 1662). This time the dedicatory epistle was addressed to Edward Hyde; the author signed himself 'your humble client P. D. Cardonnel', but no further details of his relations with Clarendon have survived.[164]

The second publication of that year was a more ambitious work, containing materials in French, Latin, and English. Its full title conveys both the nature of its contents, and something of the pomp of its style: *Complementum fortunatarum insularum, p. II. sive Galathea vaticinans. Being part of an Epithalamium upon the Auspicious Match of the most puissant and most serene Charles II. and the most Illustrious Catharina Infanta of Portugal. With a description of the Fortunate Islands. Written originally in French by P. D. C. Gent and since translated by him in Latin and English. With the translations also of The Description of S. James's Park, and the late Fight at S. Lucar, by Mr. Ed. Waller. The Panegyrick of Charles II. by Mr. Dreyden. And other pieces relating to the present times.* A special engraving was also made for insertion before the title page: spread over two pages, it contains portraits of the King and Queen, each with a quatrain in French signed 'P. D. C.'[165] The dedicatory epistle, addressed to the Earl of Ossory, referred to 'the love and esteem I have observ'd (having the honour to be sometimes in your Lordships company)'; unfortunately the printer gave the Earl's name as 'James' Boteler, and in several copies this has been altered in ink (by, one suspects, a mortified de Cardonnel) to 'Thomas'.[166] As the title indicated, de Cardonnel's rolling programme of self-republication had now reached the stage of including an English translation of his *Fortunate Islands*. This version, though marking the nadir of his poetic achievements, is not entirely charmless; and occasionally it conveys a sense of his more

---

[163] Bodleian Library, Oxford, pressmark Arch. A. e. 62, leaves between title page and sig. *2 (first leaf, recto: 'Sire, La Fortune m'ayant depuis longtemps depouillé de tous les biens qui étoient sous sa jurisdiction, & ne m'étant demeuré de reste que ce qu'elle ne me pouuoit oster . . .').

[164] P. de Cardonnel, *Tagus* (London, 1662), sig. A4r: 'Humilis Tui Clientis P. D. Cardonnel'. This is one of the works attributed to 'Philip' de Cardonnel in the entry on Adam de Cardonnel in the *DNB*. The copy of this book in the Bodleian (pressmark Vet. A3 e. 1549(1) ) is inscribed: 'Judeth Harcourt Har book—made by her father Mr Peter De Cardonnel'. (For Judith de Cardonnel see ascription in n. 96 above.)

[165] This is not present in most copies; an example is in BL, pressmark 11505.

[166] P. de Cardonnel, *Complementum fortunatarum insularum* (London, 1662), sigs. A2v-A3r (quotation), A2r (misprint). Corrected examples are: BL, pressmark 11504; Bodleian Library, pressmark Vet. A3 f. 885 and Vet. A3 e. 1549(2).

## PIERRE DE CARDONNEL (1614–1667)

personal concerns, as in the final stanza, which is addressed to the new commander of the British navy, Prince Rupert:

> Under thy Conduct and victorious armes
> Matcht to the *British* colours, Right shall aw
> The yielding Ocean, and restore that Law
> Which ships does free from greedy Pyrats harms . . .[167]

The other items included in this volume were the poem addressed to the Earl of Devonshire, the epigram addressed to Waller, and the works by Dryden and Waller, both of which had originally been published, like *The Fortunate Islands*, to celebrate the coronation. Dryden's *To His Sacred Majesty, a Panegyrick on his Coronation* was presented in a French translation (together with the original English, which thus forms the second edition of that text). Waller's *A Poem on St James's Park as lately improved by his Majesty* had also been published in the spring of 1661, with, appended to it, 'Of our late war with Spaine and first victory at sea near St Lugar'; de Cardonnel reprinted both of these, supplying French and Latin translations of the former and a French translation of the latter. De Cardonnel's epigram to Waller advertised his personal closeness to him, calling the English poet his 'dearest friend'. No such address was made to Dryden; but it is quite possible that de Cardonnel had at least had some personal contact with him, as it was in precisely this period that Dryden was most closely associated with Walter Charleton. Dryden's nomination for membership of the Royal Society was put forward by Charleton in November 1662, and in the following year Dryden contributed a prefatory poem to Charleton's *Chorae gigantum*, praising him fulsomely (and dismissing Aristotelianism in terms curiously reminiscent of Cowley's ode 'To Mr. Hobs').[168]

It is not known whether any of de Cardonnel's publications reaped the financial rewards they so evidently sought. One curious piece of evidence suggests that he had already been favoured by royal patronage: the minutes of a meeting of the Lords Commissioners of the Treasury in July 1660, held in the presence of the King, recorded: 'Ordered that the office and place of Customer outwards in the Port of Southampton void by the death of Thomas Wulfris be granted vnto Peter de Cardonell gent. during his Ma^ties pleasure.' However, two months later the records of the same body stated: 'Whereas his Ma^ty by his Letters Patents vnder the Great Seale of England hath appointed Adam de Cardonell Gent Customer in his Ma^ties Port of Southampton, These are therefore to will & require the said Adam de Cardonell to put in security . . . for the due Execucion of the said Office.'[169] The

---

[167] Ibid., p. 63.
[168] See the comments (and the text) in J. Dryden, *The Poems of John Dryden*, ed. P. Hammond (London, 1995–), I, p. 70; J. M. Osborn suggests that Dryden may have known Charleton since 1657, when he worked for the latter's publisher: *John Dryden: Some Biographical Facts and Problems* (New York, 1940), pp. 174–5.
[169] PRO, T 51/8, pp. 7 (3 July 1660), 56 (6 Sept. 1660).

office of customer at Southampton was an important one, which in the early years of the century had already been worth roughly £100 per annum: Pierre would not have been bemoaning his poor 'fortune' in his publication of 1661 if he had already been granted such a lucrative post.[170] And there is clear evidence that it was his brother Adam who took on the job: he moved to Southampton, became a burgess in 1662, and duly appears as 'Customer outwards' in the Port Books of the 1660s.[171] Two explanations are possible: either the earlier reference to 'Peter' in the Treasury minutes was a clerical error, or there was a change of mind—perhaps prompted by the fact that Peter (in contrast with Adam) was not a naturalized British subject.[172]

Pierre de Cardonnel's financial situation had apparently not improved by 1663; he was still locked in litigation with the executors of his father-in-law's estate. However, he now hit upon an ingenious legal device for undermining their position. His petition to the King in 1663 rehearsed the history of the manors of Cadlands, Holbury, and South Langley; it noted that Nicholas Pescod had left 'a plentifull estate both real and personal for all his Children, whereof yo$^r$ petitioner and his said wife haue hitherto had y$^e$ least share, and your Pet$^r$ is now in suite w$^{th}$ the said M$^r$. Pescods executo$^{rs}$ for recovery of such part of y$^e$ said personal estate, as is unjustly deteined from him'. It pointed out, however, that, when Pescod first conveyed the ninety-nine-year lease of the manors to de Cardonnel, 'y$^e$ said lease was so made to your Pet.$^r$ being an alien borne, and in time before he was created a Denizen of England, and is therefore by y$^e$ Law forfeited to yo$^r$ Maj.$^{ty}$'. At a stroke, this argument cut the ground from under the feet of the executors, annulling every legal transaction relating to those manors since 1641. And the petition concluded by asking the King to grant 'y$^e$ remainder of y$^e$ said lease in the premises so forfeited ... and y$^e$ meane profits thereof from the time of y$^e$ graunt of y$^e$ said lease to yo$^r$ Pet.$^r$ towards the better present subsistance of him and his family'.[173] The petition was referred to the Attorney General, who confirmed that the legal argument was sound; and on 3 August 1663 the King ordered a patent to be drawn up, granting de Cardonnel's request in full.[174] Nevertheless, even this knock-out blow

---

[170] Woodward, Wilks and Lockhart, *General History of Hampshire*, II, p. 315.

[171] W. W. Portal, *Some Account of the Settlement of Refugees (L'Eglise Wallonne) at Southampton, and of the Chapel of St Julian* (Winchester, 1902), p. 25 (Burgess); PRO, E 190/826/7 (Port Book for Portsmouth (administered from Southampton), Outwards, Christmas 1662–Christmas 1663, signed 'Adam de Cardonnel Collec$^r$ outwards'); E 190/826/10 (Port Book, Southampton, Christmas 1665–1666, signed 'Adam de Cardonnel Cust$^r$. outwards'). Cf. W. A. Shaw, ed., *Calendar of Treasury Books, 1667–1668* (London, 1905), pp. 223, 519, 626.

[172] David Agnew, the historian of Huguenot settlement in Britain, in a letter to Henry Wagner (6 Feb. 1884: HL, MS T 8/1, no. 115), argued that this was a 'clerical error'.

[173] PRO, SP 29/77/32.

[174] Ibid., annotation by Henry Bennet and (verso) memorandum of legal advice; PRO, SP 44/15 (Bennet, Warrant Book), pp. 138–9 (royal warrant, 3 Aug. 1663); PRO, C 66/3038, membrane 20, and HRO, 16 M 55/2 (copies of patent, latter dated 17 Nov. 1663). For a useful overview of the laws relating to the property-rights of denizens and non-denizens, see Scouloudi, *Returns of Strangers*, pp. 1, 7–8.

apparently failed to end the fight: the same issues would have to be argued over again by Pierre's wife, Katherine, after his death.[175]

One other piece of evidence of royal favour to de Cardonnel survives from this period, though its evidential status is not entirely certain. In 1664 an English translation was published of a work by the French physician Nicaise Lefèvre, *Traicté de la chymie* (Paris, 1660). According to the title page of the translation, the text had been 'Rendred into English by P. D. C. Esq. one of the Gentlemen of his Majesties Privy Chamber'; the author's dedicatory epistle to Charles II also referred, in passing, to the translator, calling him 'one of your Majesties Servants (a lover and great admirer of this noble Art)'.[176] Given de Cardonnel's use of 'P. D. C.' in his *Fortunate Islands* and *Complementum fortunatarum insularum*, and the lack of any other known authors with those initials, some modern bibliographers have identified him as the translator of this work.[177] On the face of it, this is a very plausible attribution. De Cardonnel was certainly interested in medicine and chemistry: one item in his library was a collection of medical and alchemical treatises, to which he added a detailed list of contents, using all the standard chemical symbols.[178] It is also very possible that he would have made Lefèvre's acquaintance. The French scientist, who was appointed 'professor of chemistry' to Charles II in November 1660 and 'apothecary in ordinary to the royal household' in December 1661, had previously taught at the Jardin royal des plantes in Paris, where he first worked as a 'demonstrator' under the professor of chemistry, the Scottish physician William Davidson or Davisson, and then succeeded him in that post in 1651: de Cardonnel's notebook includes an entry, in its list of contacts at Paris, 'D$^r$ Dauison. D$^r$ en medecine . . . 1648'.[179] But, on the other hand, the translation was originally entered in the registers of the Stationers' Company as 'translated by D. D. C.'; and a detailed list of the members of the royal household in late 1663 gives all the names of the gentlemen of the Privy Chamber, without mentioning de Cardonnel.[180] Perhaps the entry in the register was a slip of the pen; and the household list names only the gentlemen of the Privy Chamber 'in Ordinary' (in other words, in actual

---

[175] See HRO, 16 M 55/3 and 15 M 55/8 (discussed below).
[176] N. Lefèvre, *A Compendious Body of Chymistry* (London, 1664), sig. A2v.
[177] See e.g. P. Krivatsy, ed., *A Catalogue of Seventeenth Century Printed Books in the National Library of Medicine* (Bethesda, Md, 1989), p. 694, item 6792.
[178] See the appendix to this chapter, entry for 1648.
[179] BL. MS Sloane 1731B, fol. 34r. See the entry for 'Le Fevre' in the *DNB*, and J.-P. Contant, *L'Enseignement de la chimie au Jardin royal des plantes de Paris* (Cahors, 1952), pp. 39–43. For a valuable account of Lefèvre's book, placing his theories in the Paracelsian and Helmontian iatrochemical tradition, see H. Metzger, *Les Doctrines chimiques en France du début du XVII$^e$ à la fin du XVIII$^e$ siècle* (Paris, 1969), pp. 62–82.
[180] *A Transcript of the Registers of the Worshipful Company of Stationers*, 3 vols. (London, 1913–14), II, p. 290 (entry for 13 March 1661); 'Select Documents XXXIX: A List of the Department of the Lord Chamberlain of the Household, Autumn, 1663', *Bulletin of the Institute for Historical Research*, 19 (1942–3), pp. 13–24; here pp. 15–16.

attendance), whereas de Cardonnel may have enjoyed the title on a more honorary basis. So it does at least seem possible that de Cardonnel was responsible for this major translation; if so, it is a testimony to the seriousness of his scientific interests, as well as to his command of English and his grasp of some very recondite vocabulary.

Being a gentleman of the Privy Chamber was a position of honour, but not of profit. Nevertheless, de Cardonnel was clearly not poor in his final years; his library alone was an asset that must have been worth many hundreds of pounds, and the evidence of his book purchases (presented below) suggests that he enjoyed sufficient spending money to indulge his own tastes up to the end of his life. In 1665 the Corporation of Southampton recorded a list of 'Charitable Gifts for Relief of the Sick and Poor of Southampton during the Rageing of the Plague': one of the largest was the gift of £5 by 'Mr Peter de Cardonell, Merchant in Westminster'.[181] But that record is the last definite trace in the English archival evidence of de Cardonnel's life and activities. He was buried in the East Cloister of Westminster Abbey on 5 August 1667; ten days later letters of administration for the estate of 'Peter de Cardonell, late of St Margaret's, Westminster, Esq.' were granted to his widow and his brother Philippe.[182]

## VIII

The French archives yield one final surprise, however: a poem written by de Cardonnel during the last few months of his life, and addressed to Louis XIV, predicting a French triumph over the Ottoman Empire. It survives in a manuscript copy by an unnamed third party, whose comments also explain the origin of the work. In 1665 Comenius had published a book, *Lux e tenebris*, in which he presented the revelations of three 'prophets', the Silesian Christoph Kotter, the Moravian Mikuláš Drabík, and the Bohemian Kristina Poniatowska. All of them foretold the collapse of Habsburg power in central Europe, but one of them, Drabík, claimed in addition that the King of France would replace the Habsburgs, succeeding to the Holy Roman Empire.[183] 'These predictions,' wrote

---

[181] CAO, D/LY/38 (B. H. Greenfield, 'Extracts from Journals of the Corporation'), fol. 190. Adam de Cardonnel gave only £2 (fol. 192v).

[182] J. L. Chester, ed., *The Marriage, Baptismal, and Burial Registers of the Collegiate Church or Abbey of St Peter, Westminster*, Publications of the Harleian Society, 10, for 1875 (1876), p. 167: Chester's reference to 'Katherine, relict of Philip de Cardonell, brother of the deceased', mistakenly gives 'relict of' instead of 'relict, and'. De Cardonnel seems to have been a parishioner of St Margaret's only in the geographical sense: no de Cardonnel is mentioned in H. F. Westlake, L. E. Tanner and W. Ward, eds., *The Registers of St Margaret's Westminster*, 3 vols., Publications of the Harleian Society, 64, 88, 89 (1935, 1959, 1977).

[183] J. A. Comenius, *Lux e tenebris, novis radiis aucta* (Leiden, 1665). This was a revised and expanded version of his *Lux in tenebris* (Amsterdam, 1657); it was in turn expanded in a new edition in 1667, which combined sheets from the 1665 printing with new material printed (by Cunradus) in Comenius's printing-house in Amsterdam. The sections devoted to the three prophets are separately paginated; the key prophecy about

## PIERRE DE CARDONNEL (1614–1667)

the anonymous commentator, 'having touched the spirit of someone called Cardonnel, a Frenchman, who was full of zeal for the glory of his king, he wrote a poem in 1667 on this subject, which he addressed to the Archbishop of Paris, or indeed to the King himself. I copied it out, and delivered it to its intended recipient in 1668.'[184] What follows consists, in fact, of two poems. The first, which is shorter, is addressed to the Archbishop, praising him and asking him to pass on the second poem to the King. Each is described as 'Poeme du Sieur Cardonnel'. The main poem contains a great deal of pompous celebration of the King's virtues and military victories, beginning with the lines:

> Roy, la merueille de notre âge,
> Inuincible & sacré Loüis,
> Qui par ton eclat eblouis,
> Le Rhin, la Tamise & le Tage . . .
>
> (King, the marvel of our age,
> Invincible and holy Louis,
> Whose splendour dazzles
> The Rhine, the Thames and the Tagus . . .)

It continues with a little autobiographical reflection:

> J'ay trop souuent, Je le confesse,
> Mêlé par un prophane abus
> Les noms de Parnasse & Phoebus
> Aux premiers feux de ma jeunesse . . .
>
> Donc affranchissant mon genie
> De l'erreur de ces vains ecrits,
> Je veux occuper mes esprits
> Sur une plus noble harmonie.
> Loin de ces flateurs courtisans,
> Je veux du reste de mes ans
> Acheuer la paisible course,
> Employant pour mon Dieu ma plume & mon loisir . . .
>
> (I confess that too often
> I have mixed, profanely and wrongly
> The names of Parnassus and Phoebus
> With the first sparks of my youth . . .

---

the King of France is on pp. 351–2 of the Drabík section. On Drabík, see See M. Blekastad, *Comenius: Versuch eines Umrisses von Leben, Werk und Schicksal des Jan Amos Komenský* (Oslo, 1969), pp. 616–27.

[184] BN, MS f.fr. 12499, fols. 33–48, 'Predictions remarquables de l'etablissement de l'Empire françois par . . . Louis XIV'; here fol. 33v: 'Ces predictions ayant touché l'esprit d'vn nommé Cardonnel françois, zelé pour la gloire de son Roy, il fit en l'an 1667 vn poeme sur ce sujet qu'il addressa à l'Archevêque de Paris ou au Roy mesme. Je le coppiay, & le deliuray selon l'addresse en l'an 1668.'

> Therefore, freeing my genius
> From the error of those worthless writings,
> I wish to employ my spirits
> In a more noble harmony.
> Far away from those flattering courtiers,
> I want, during what remains of my life,
> To finish my peaceful career
> Using my pen and my leisure for my God . . .)

And it then develops the work's central theme, the future victory of French arms over the Ottoman Empire, leading to the conversion of all the Muslim territories to Christianity.[185]

There is more than one reason for attributing this strange production to de Cardonnel. To begin with, the title 'le Sieur Cardonnel' matches that used in de Cardonnel's earlier petition to Séguier. The style of the poetry, as it steers its unsteady course between bombast and doggerel, is also very reminiscent of his previous efforts. The reference to an earlier devotion to secular poetry fits de Cardonnel's case, as the works of modern poetry in his library help to show. And although this poem to Louis XIV professes to mark a turning-away from the past, it may have been motivated, if only in part, by the same thing as de Cardonnel's earlier poetic productions: a desire for patronage. Perhaps he had heard of the French King's generosity towards writers—a generosity which, it has been suggested, may even have been extended towards Hobbes, though direct evidence of a pension from Louis XIV has never been found.[186]

De Cardonnel had, as we have seen, a long-standing interest in the writings of Comenius. Works by that Protestant churchman (especially his more radical religious books, such as this one) were much less widely available in France than in England—a fact that weighs against the idea that the author of these two poems could have been one of Pierre's brothers in France. Admittedly, the work in question, *Lux e tenebris*, was not listed in the later auction catalogue of de Cardonnel's library; but that listing was not a complete record of the books he had owned. Also significant is the fact that his library, which was not otherwise well stocked with books about travel or foreign politics, did contain a number of publications about the Ottoman Empire, including several from the 1660s, which suggests that this may have been a special preoccupation of his final years. In particular, he owned *The New Survey of the Turkish Empire and Government* (London, 1663) and *The Conduct and Character of Count Nicholas Serini* (London, 1664), two related works (the latter, a glorification of the anti-Ottoman resistance of the

---

[185] BN, MS f.fr. 12499, fols. 36v–38r (first poem), 38r–47v (second poem): quotations from fols. 38r, 38v.
[186] See J. J. Jusserand, *A French Ambassador at the Court of Charles the Second: Le Comte de Cominges, from his Unpublished Correspondence* (London, 1892), pp. 60–1.

Hungarian–Croatian nobleman Miklós Zrínyi, borrows material from the former) which were produced by the same printer, and which, as recent research has indicated, were both linked to Comenian circles.[187]

A prima facie objection to identifying the author of this work with the Huguenot de Cardonnel might be that it is addressed to a Catholic archbishop and a Catholic king, and appears to celebrate the future imposition of their religion over a large part of Europe and Asia. However, the poem addressed to the Archbishop praises him not specifically as a Catholic, but only as a minister of the King; and the future conversion of the Turks is portrayed as a triumph of Christianity, not of Roman Catholicism as such. The idea of involving the French in such grand geopolitical designs was common to many people, Protestant as well as Catholic. Lutherans such as Hermann Conring saw a French conquest of the Ottomans as the best way of guarding against the expansion of Habsburg power in Central Europe; in 1671, for slightly different reasons, the Lutheran Gottfried Wilhelm Leibniz and the Catholic convert Johann Christian von Boineburg drew up a detailed set of proposals for the French conquest of Egypt.[188] And in any case, the enthusiasm for the French King expressed in these effusions by de Cardonnel goes no way beyond that of Comenius himself—a bishop of the Moravian Church who moved mainly in Calvinist and Lutheran circles. De Cardonnel probably possessed a copy of the augmented 1667 edition of *Lux e tenebris*, which included an impassioned address by Comenius to Louis XIV, calling on him to summon a general 'council of the Christian world' to settle all the controversies that divided Christianity, and declaring that he would become greater than Cyrus, Alexander or Augustus.[189]

Not only was de Cardonnel close in spirit to Comenius when he wrote his poems and sent them to Paris; the evidence even suggests that he was acting on the basis of knowledge supplied by someone close to Comenius himself. In 1664 one

---

[187] See A. Bukovszky, 'Londoni magyar vonatkozású kiadványok és az 1664. évi Zrínyi-életrajz', *Irodalomtörténeti közlemények*, 1987–8, nos. 1–2, pp. 207–11; and A. R. Várkonyi, *Europica* [sic] *varietas, Hungarica varietas* (Budapest, 2000), pp. 103–48. Cf. also Comenius's letter to a friend in England in 1664, commenting on Zrínyi: J. Kvačala, ed., *Korrespondence Jana Amosa Komenského*, 2 vols. (Prague, 1898–1902), I(ii), pp. 292–3.

[188] See H. Conring, *De bello contra Turcas prudenter gerendo* (Helmstedt, 1664); G. E. Guhrauer, *Kur-Mainz in der Epoche von 1672*, 2 vols. (Hamburg, 1839), I, pp. 207–36; II, pp. 140–9, 153–74 (Leibniz, 'Consilium Aegyptiacum'). The aim of Leibniz and von Boineburg was to divert France away from a direct war with the Habsburgs, because such a war would place unwelcome military and political obligations on minor German states to support the Habsburgs' war effort. Louis XIV did show some interest in presenting himself as a protector of Christianity in the Ottoman Empire (see E. Caron, 'Défense de la chrétienté ou gallicanisme dans la politique de la France à l'égard de l'empire ottoman à la fin du XVIIe siècle', *XVIIe siècle*, no. 199, 50 (1998), pp. 359–72). But his anti-Habsburg geopolitics made him follow the traditional French policy of cooperation with the Ottomans: for a dramatic example of this, see P. Roy, *Louis XIV et le second siège de Vienne* (Paris, 1999).

[189] Comenius, *Lux e tenebris* ('1665' [1667]), 'Cristianissime [sic] rex Ludovice XIV, Galliarum Imperator', pp. 19, 24.

of Comenius's most devoted disciples, the Swiss educationalist Johann Jakob Redinger, had been so inspired by copies of some of the prophecies of Drabík and the others, sent to him by Comenius, that he had travelled on his own initiative to France. On 2 June 1664 he visited Fontainebleau and left copies there for the King; four days later he called on the Archbishop of Paris, Hardouin de Beaumont de Péréfixe (Louis's confessor and former tutor), and gave him further copies. He then set off for Ottoman territory, reaching the campaign headquarters of the Ottoman army in Hungary in September: there he had two meetings with the Albanian Grand Vizier Ahmed Köprülü, whom he tried to convert to Christianity.[190] In early 1666 Redinger visited Comenius in Amsterdam, and was instructed by him to repeat his trip to France, this time with copies of the 1665 *Lux e tenebris*. He visited the Archbishop in his Paris residence on 9 April 1666; he then went to Saint Germain to give a copy of the book to the King, through the good offices of the comte de Cominges, the former French Ambassador to Charles II. The speed with which Redinger had fulfilled his task did not please Comenius, however, as he had told him to wait in Paris until he received some new material—new prophecies by Drabík, and formal letters to the King and the Archbishop from Comenius himself. A fragment of his draft letter to the Archbishop survives, in which he says that he prays to God to preserve his King, his Kingdom, and (even) his Church.[191]

It can hardly be a coincidence that de Cardonnel also directed his poem to the King via the Archbishop of Paris: he must surely have heard of Redinger's contacts with him. There is no evidence that de Cardonnel was in direct communication with Comenius, but there were several people in London who were. One possible candidate stands out: the young Czech scholar Christian Vladislav Nigrin, who was known personally to Comenius. After studying in Geneva, Nigrin moved to England and was given a job as a secretary in 1664 or 1665 by Philip Herbert, Earl of Pembroke. The Earl had taken a special interest in Drabík's prophecies; his main reason for employing Nigrin was that he wanted to be able to corrrespond directly with Drabík in Czech. But by 1667 or early 1668 his attitude had changed, and he refused to help transmit the Moravian seer's prophecies to Charles II. Nigrin left his service and moved to Paris, where before long he was employed by the Marquis de Ruvigny, another enthusiast for Drabík.[192] No evidence has survived of contact between de Cardonnel and either Pembroke or Nigrin, but connections with both

---

[190] See K. Schaller, 'Johann Jakob Redinger in seinem Verhältnis zu Johann Amos Comenius', in M. Bircher, W. Sparn and E. Weyrauch, eds., *Schweizerisch-deutsch Beziehungen im konfessionellen Zeitalter: Beiträge zur Kulturgeschichte 1580–1650* (Wiesbaden, 1984), pp. 139–66, here p. 148; and B. Schader, *Johann Jakob Redinger (1619–1688), Sprachwissenschaftler und Pädagoge im Gefolge des Comenius* (Zurich, 1985), pp. 21–3.

[191] See J. Kvačala ['Kvacsala'], *Johann Amos Comenius: sein Leben und seine Schriften* (Berlin, 1892), pp. 437–8; Schaller, 'Johann Jakob Redinger', pp. 153–6 (Comenius fragment, p. 153). Comenius's subsequent angry letters to Redinger are in Kvačala, *Korrespondence . . . Komenského*, I(ii), pp. 297–301.

[192] See Blekastad, *Comenius*, pp. 573, 619, 648, 658, 676.

would seem plausible: the Earl's father had been one of the main patrons of Jean d'Espagne in the 1640s (and had employed Isaac de Caus in his building projects at Wilton), so contacts between the Earl and the French Protestant community in London—especially with members of d'Espagne's breakaway congregation—can be assumed. As for Nigrin, his move to Paris, and his continued enthusiasm for the Drabician–Comenian cause, make him the ideal candidate for the unnamed third party who delivered de Cardonnel's poems to the Archbishop in 1668, and whose manuscript copy of them is now preserved in the Bibliothèque Nationale.[193]

This involvement of de Cardonnel in a Comenian religious–political campaign adds an unexpected twist to his final years; but it is not, after all, so out of keeping with his earlier concerns. In his mental and spiritual life, emotional Royalism had long co-existed with a Christian piety of a fairly non-denominational kind. His hymn to Louis XIV merely combines those motifs in a final coda:

> Alors la discorde etouffée
> Entre ceux que le nom chrétien
> Doit vnir d'vn mesme lien,
> Fera le pied de ton trophée.
> Lors cessant la rebellion
> L'Agneau paîtra pres du lion[194]
>
> (Then, the suppression of discord
> Among those whom the name 'Christian'
> Should unite with a single bond
> Will form the base of your trophy.
> Then, as rebellion ceases,
> The lamb will feed next to the lion.)

Most Huguenots did not see things in quite the same light. But perhaps de Cardonnel had explored a little further the possible implications of the passage he had marked in his copy of *Leviathan*: 'The (*Vnum Necessarium*) Onely Article of Faith, which the Scripture maketh simply Necessary to Salvation, is this, that JESUS IS THE CHRIST.'

## IX

Two postscripts can be added to the life of Pierre de Cardonnel—the second of them a melancholy one, but both of them providing further evidence of his closeness to the Earl of Devonshire. The first concerns the legal disputes that continued

---

[193] The notes added at the end of de Cardonnel's poem by the transcriber (BN, MS f.fr. 12499, fols. 47v–48r) include a reference to 'Broughton sur l'Apocalypse'—a natural enough reference for someone who, like Nigrin, had moved in Protestant circles in England, but an unlikely one for a Frenchman living in France.

[194] BN, MS f.fr. 12499, fol. 39v.

after his death. In September 1667 his executors, Katherine and Philippe, caused an official 'inquisicion' to be made to determine whether Pierre had been an alien when the three manors were granted to him in 1641; this confirmed the truth of that claim, and resulted in the manors being 'seized' for the King. Katherine and Philippe then arranged for the manors to be granted to the Earl of Devonshire, who agreed to hold them in trust for them—an arrangement of obvious benefit to them, as it brought the protection of a powerful magnate, and one that also indicates the degree of good will that the Earl must have felt towards the de Cardonnel family.[195] At the same time, they instituted a new set of proceedings against William Stanley and the other surviving executors for the other moneys which, they said, had never been paid. In 1668 the court ordered the executors to pay them £1,000, and in the following year it ordered the payment of another £500, plus interest. In 1672, pursuing their appeal against those judgements, the executors argued that 'goods & merchandizes of Pescods which came to the hands of the said Peter de Cardonnell since his death & . . . goods of Pescods remayning in the hands of John de Cardonnell partner of the said Philip de Cardonnell' had come to more than £1,000 anyway. Stanley himself was also seriously out of pocket, having paid (in 1651) for the two quarter-shares of the manors which had now been taken from him. This time the court reached a Solomonic judgement: it ordered that Stanley be permitted to retain his half-share of the manors for the rest of the ninety-nine-year lease, while decreeing that Katherine should keep the £1,000 she had been paid.[196] The Stanley family did enjoy the possession of that moiety until 1740, when it passed to Adam de Cardonel (the son of Pierre's brother Adam), who settled it on his daughter.[197]

Pierre's brother Adam lived into his ninetieth year; he died, a distinguished citizen of Southampton and pillar of its French Protestant Church, in 1711.[198] Two of his sons also had glittering careers. Adam served as MP for Southampton, and became the Duke of Marlborough's right-hand man; James worked as secretary to the Duke of Schomberg in Ireland, and married Mary Hicks, the illegitimate daughter of the Duke of Monmouth by Edmund Waller's daughter Elizabeth.[199]

---

[195] HRO, 16 M 55/3 (royal grant of the manors to the Earl of Devonshire, 17 Dec. 1669).

[196] HRO, 15 M 55/8 (Court of Exchequer judgement, 1672). The dispute did not stop there, however: another document (HRO, 46 M 48/73) relates to a case in Exchequer between Margaret Lovell, daughter of Katherine de Cardonell, and others on the one side, and George Stanley on the other, of c.1700. Nothing more is known of this daughter (or of the other daughter, Judith: see nn. 97, 162).

[197] See the Introduction to the 'Calendar of Sloane Stanley MSS' in the HRO.

[198] H. M. Godfray, ed., *Registre des Baptesmes, Mariages & Mortz . . . de l'eglise Wallonne . . . à Southampton*, Publications of the Huguenot Society of London, IV (Lymington, 1890), p. 121; E. Welch, ed., *The Minute-Book of the French Church at Southampton, 1702–1939* (Southampton, 1979), pp. 15–32.

[199] HL, MS T 8/1, no. 115, pedigree of de Cardonnel and notes by Hylton; on Adam see also the entry in the *DNB*. Possibly this marriage (in 1689, when the bride was 13 and the groom 22) indicates some continuing contacts between Waller and de Cardonnel's family.

## PIERRE DE CARDONNEL (1614-1667)

The fate of Pierre de Cardonnel's sons is, however, more sombre. Of the two sons known to have lived in England, the younger, Peter, entered Westminster School in 1673, matriculated at Christ Church, Oxford, in 1679 (aged eighteen), became a Student (i.e. Fellow) there, but died, at the age of only thirty-eight or thirty-nine, in 1699. His elder brother, William, also a King's scholar at Westminster, matriculated at Magdalen College, Oxford, in 1671 (aged 16), and became a Fellow of Merton five years later.[200] At first his academic career seems to have proceeded smoothly: he was praelector in Greek in 1676, had his fellowship confirmed as a life fellowship at the end of his probationary year, and was appointed one of the college's three Bursars in 1678.[201] But before long he had fallen out with the Warden, Sir Thomas Clayton. In the spring of 1681, when de Cardonnel was acting as second Bursar, the Warden sent a gardener to him with a request for payment for work he had done. De Cardonnel responded with the remark 'the warden be hang'd, he should have no money'. In the words of Anthony Wood, 'the warden took affidavit of it, drew up a recantation, which being shewn the fellows, Cardinall at a meeting read it, but this stuck so close to him, that bringing a melancholy fit on him, he could never shake it off.'[202] During the following year he apparently suffered also from pangs of conscience, having embezzled £3 or £4 during his time as bursar. In the summer of 1681 he 'threw himself into the water at Magd. walks to drowne himself but could not effect it'; finally, on 23 October, he 'hanged himself in his bedchamber on his dore'. The coroner's jury pronounced him *non compos mentis*.[203]

---

[200] G. F. Russell Barker and A. H. Stenning, eds., *The Record of Old Westminsters*, 2 vols. (London, 1928), I, p. 256; J. Foster, *Alumni oxonienses: The Members of the University of Oxford, 1500–1714*, 4 vols. (Oxford, 1891–2), I, p. 236. I am grateful to Pasteur Denis Vatinel for the information that another son, 'Jean, fils [de] Pierre, marchand de bois', was recorded in a list of the inhabitants of Caen in 1666, living in the parish of Saint-Pierre. The total number of Pierre's children is not known. The child christened in 1653 was not Judith, William, or Peter, but may have been Margaret (see above, n. 196). Jean, who appears to have inherited the family home, may have been the eldest son. The copy of Nicholas Pescod's will (HRO, 46 M 48/41) has a marginal note stating that Pierre and Katherine had two children between their marriage in 1641 and Pescod's death in Sept. 1643.

[201] Merton College Archive, MS Reg. 1.3, pp. 512, 514, 518, 528. (I am very grateful to Dr Michael Stansfield for all references to this document.)

[202] A. Wood, *The Life and Times of Anthony Wood, Antiquary, of Oxford, 1632–1695, described by himself*, ed. A. Clark, 5 vols. (Oxford, 1891–1900), II, p. 557. Wood's account is confirmed by an entry in the College Register for 27 April 1681: 'Comparuit coram Domino Custode et sex senioribus ad hoc convocatis M[agister] Cardonnel, quem Dominus Custos accusavit, quod de illo dixisset, Let ye Warden be hang'd; quod apparuit per iuramentum cuiusdam Fowler hortulani[;] censuere seniores quod chartae crimen suum fatenti nomen apponat, et veniam a Domino Custode petat' (Merton College Archive, MS Reg. 1.3, p. 542). On the tensions and divisions caused by Clayton, see G. H. Martin and J. R. L. Highfield, *A History of Merton College* (Oxford, 1997), pp. 214–15.

[203] Wood, *Life and Times*, II, p. 557. The College Register describes de Cardonnel as having been depressed for a long time ('diu animo afflictus') and records the jury's verdict: 'jurati re diligenter examinata, eum non mentis compotem sibi vim intulisse pronuntiarunt' (Merton College Archive, MS Reg. 1.3, p. 545).

Two days later, the Oxford don Humphrey Prideaux added a somewhat gloating comment on this affair in one of his letters to John Ellis: 'It seems he had lived with y$^e$ Earle of Devonshire as praeceptor to his grandson, where, having been poisened by Hobs, on his return hither blasphemy and atheisme was his most frequent talke; of the guilt of w$^{ch}$ beeing at last sensible, this, its supposed, precipitated him into despair.' Prideaux also noted that 'In his study . . . on the wals were stuck up in several papers verses of y$^e$ Penitential Psalms.'[204] As it happens, there is other evidence to confirm that William de Cardonnel had worked for the Devonshire family. On 5 December 1679 the Earl of Devonshire's secretary, Justinian Morse, had written to William de Cardonnel from Hardwick, giving the first news of Hobbes's death: 'We have noe alteration in our Family considerable since I saw you but this, yesterday about ten of clock Mr Hobbs calmly departed this life . . .'[205] The dates of de Cardonnel's work for the Cavendishes can be fixed with some accuracy: on 5 August 1678 he applied for permission to absent himself from Merton for one year, and his next appearance in the college was on 6 August 1679.[206] He thus had plenty of time in which to get to know the elderly philosopher. That William had some special regard for Hobbes's writings can also be surmised from one of the handful of items in the auction catalogue of Pierre de Cardonnel's library that postdate Pierre's death: 'Th. Hobbes Opera Philosophica omnia, 2 Vol. Dorsa deaurata ['with gilt covers']—Amst. 1668'.[207] Possibly the fact that this luxurious copy was consigned to the auctioneer in June 1681, four months before William's death, shows that he had indeed renounced Hobbes and (almost literally) all his works. Otherwise, however, Prideaux's version of events must raise some doubts in the reader's mind. His reference to William's Hobbist 'blasphemy and atheisme' has no echo whatsoever in the account given by Anthony Wood, who had much closer contacts with Merton. It is also noteworthy that de Cardonnel was appointed one of the three Deans of the college in August 1681: the Deans were responsible for the discipline and moral governance of the student body, and it is highly unlikely that a notorious atheist and blasphemer would have been promoted to such an office.[208] In any case, the image conjured up by Prideaux is an odd combination of the stereotype libertine, who is willing to commit suicide because he has no fear of an afterlife, and the stereotype penitent, obsessed with his sinfulness (who might, therefore, be thought unlikely to commit the even graver sin of self-murder). There is clear evidence that William de Cardonnel, like his father, had the opportunity to enjoy

---

[204] H. Prideaux, *Letters to John Ellis, 1674–1722*, ed. E. M. Thompson, Camden Society, n.s., 15 (1875), pp. 114, 116.

[205] Bodleian Library, Oxford, MS Wood F 46, fol. 81r; cited in A. Pritchard, 'The Last Days of Hobbes: The Evidence of the Wood Manuscripts', *Bodleian Library Record*, 10 (1980), pp. 178–87, here p. 182.

[206] Merton College Archive, MS Reg. 1.3, pp. 529, 535.

[207] Cooper, *Catalogus*, p. 35 (see n. 209).

[208] Merton College Archive, MS Reg. 1.3, p. 544.

PIERRE DE CARDONNEL (1614-1667)

friendly relations with Hobbes; but to the claim that that acquaintance was the cause of his spiritual downfall and death, the verdict can only be one of 'not proven'.

APPENDIX

*Pierre de Cardonnel's Library*

On 6 June 1681 the bookseller William Cooper began an auction of books from the library of Pierre de Cardonnel at his shop in Little Britain, near Smithfield, in the City of London. His printed catalogue nowhere mentioned de Cardonnel's name, describing the collection only as 'the library of a certain man of letters'; but in later years he published two dated lists of book auctions held in England—a method of sale he himself had pioneered in the 1670s—in which the name and date of the auction are clearly stated: 'Pet. Cardonnell, June 6. 1681'.[209] The identification cannot be in doubt, as several known items bearing de Cardonnel's signature are featured in the catalogue.

Some comments have already been made on the contents of this collection. The catalogue divides its material according to book size within two broad categories: 'Libri theologici' and 'Libri philologici'. In the former are many editions of Church Fathers; some works of medieval theology; a solid body of late sixteenth- and seventeenth-century English theology; and a significant number of works of Hebrew scholarship (by Reuchlin, Lévita, Génébrard, Drusius, Buxtorf, and others), as well as the Hebrew texts already mentioned. Works of Arabic scholarship include the proverbs edited by Golius, of which de Cardonnel had hoped to publish Bochart's improved edition, the Arabic translation of Bellarmine's *Doctrina christiana* (Rome, 1613), and Erpenius's edition of the Arabic Pentateuch (Leiden, 1622). Curiously, however, there is nothing by Bochart, not even a copy of *Phaleg*. In the second category, works of classical scholarship and general erudition are well represented, as well as classical texts, neo-Latin poetry and treatises about poetry, and works on medicine, astronomy, and some areas of modern philosophy, along the lines already described. (A few items in the fields of philosophy and theology stand out for their unorthodoxy: the works of Pomponazzi, for example, or a complete set of the Socinian *Bibliotheca fratrum polonorum*.) The collection is weak in several areas, such as law, medieval and modern history, and geography, though it has some items in each of those fields. Contemporary English printing is not well represented, except in the area of theology; but there are some works of modern poetry, including Waller's *Poems* (London, 1645) and items by Carew, Randolph, Benlowes, Fanshawe, and Davenant. The great strength of the collection, from a modern bibliographer's point of view, is that it contains so many sixteenth-century Continental printings—overall, roughly half of the entire list. This shows that de Cardonnel was a serious collector

---

[209] The full title of the catalogue is: *Catalogus librorum bibliothecae viri cujusdam literati. Quorum auctio habenda est Londini, ad insigne Pelicani in vico vulgò dicto Little-Britain sexto Junii, 1681* ([London, 1681)]. For the later lists see J. Lawler, *Book Auctions in England in the Seventeenth Century (1676–1700)* (London, 1898), pp. 21–2, 40–1.

of books, more interested in scholarly rarities than in the novelties of contemporary publishing. The nine incunabula on the list include the magnificent Aldine edition of Aristotle (10 volumes: Venice, 1497) and Caxton's *Cato's Book of Manners* (Westminster, 1483); there is also a rare breviary printed by Wynkyn de Worde in 1509. Three manuscripts are listed too: a verse treatise on virtues and vices in old French; a treatise on hunting; and a collection of English and Latin writings on medicine written on vellum. (The last of these, as the catalogue said, had previously belonged to Francis Prujean.[210])

Altogether, the list has 1,336 lots. Six items can be subtracted, as they have dates of publication later than de Cardonnel's death, and were presumably added to the collection by one of his sons. On the other hand, a small proportion of the lots contain multiple items, so the total number of works is in the region of 1,450. This in itself would make de Cardonnel's collection a large one for its time.[211] However, there is good reason to believe that the real total was much higher. Books from de Cardonnel's library survive in various modern collections: they are easily identifiable, as it was his habit to write an ownership inscription, in his neat, rounded script, at the bottom of the title page. Usually the formula included the date: 'Ex Bibl. P. de Cardonnel, 1645', and so on. A search for books and manuscripts with these inscriptions has yielded a total of 44 items; and of these, only 13 are included in the auction catalogue. Evidently a large part of the collection either was held back in 1681, or had been sold already. (The *Leviathan* had been sold soon after de Cardonnel's death: the second ownership inscription it bears, by Charles Crompton, is dated 1668.) If we apply the ratio established by the evidence of the dated books, we can conclude that the original collection numbered roughly 4,900 items—which would have made it one of the largest private libraries in the country during de Cardonnel's lifetime. The ratio is, of course, one established by only a slender body of evidence; but it is the best evidence available.[212]

The two modern collections with the largest quantities of these inscribed copies are the Cambridge University Library and the British Library. In each case, the line of transmission is fairly clear. All the de Cardonnel items in the Cambridge University Library came from the collection of John Moore, which was bought after his death (in 1714) and given to Cambridge by George I. Moore had been buying books intensively since the 1670s; some of his de Cardonnel items came from the 1681 auction, but others must have been

---

[210] Cooper, *Catalogus*, p. 3: 'Tractatus Antiquus Lingua Gallica scriptus Carmine de Virtutibus & Vitiis'; 'Le Liure de la Chace que fist le Comte de Foix'; and 'Collectio variorum Scriptorum de Re medica Latinè simul & Anglicè bene Pergamenta scripta circa An. D. 1280 in 2 Vol. & pertinebant ad D. Doctorem Fr. Prujean diebus suis ut manus ejus testat'.

[211] For useful comments on the size of private libraries during this period, see M. Hunter, G. Mandelbrote, R. Ovenden and N. Smith, eds, *A Radical's Books: The Library Catalogue of Samuel Jeake of Rye, 1623–90* (Cambridge, 1999), pp. xiv–xvi. Evelyn's 5,000 and Pepys's 3,500 were exceptional; Baxter had 1,500, John Webster 1,600, and Jeake a similar amount.

[212] A point of methodological explanation: the list of items with ownership inscriptions presented here is based almost entirely on the use of provenance indexes in the libraries concerned (plus notes on the provenance of CUL books compiled by Dr David McKitterick, to whom I am especially grateful). I have not taken the auction catalogue as the basis for further searches, looking for items mentioned therein, as that method would skew the results in favour of the catalogue's contents, thus depriving the findings of their value as a measure of the ratio between works included or not included in it.

bought on another occasion, as they are not in the auction list.[213] The items in the British Library came from another omnivorous collector, Hans Sloane; only one book and one manuscript, however, were in the 1681 auction, and Sloane probably did not purchase them then. The manuscript (the medical collection, on vellum, which had belonged to Prujean) was subsequently described in the first catalogue of the Sloane collection as having belonged first to Prujean and then to Francis Bernard—whose own library was auctioned in 1698.[214] Probably Bernard had been the purchaser at the de Cardonnel auction. And, while Sloane had been buying books intensively since his arrival in London in 1679, his first notebook recording his purchases, written in the mid-1680s, shows no signs of any acquisitions from de Cardonnel's library.[215] Finally, one other item listed below has an interesting provenance: the work by Lull, now in the library of Trinity College, Cambridge, was acquired, probably at the 1681 auction, by Isaac Newton.

Although the auction catalogue is by far the best guide we have to de Cardonnel's intellectual range, the volumes with his ownership inscriptions are also of real interest. Not only do they contribute items not included in the catalogue; they also add a chronological dimension to the story. For that reason they are listed here, in the order of the date of the inscription. (In a few cases, the inscriptions are undated: these are grouped at the end of the list.) An asterisk before the entry indicates that the work is not in the auction catalogue.

The library sigla used in this list are the following: BL: British Library. BLL: Brotherton Library, University of Leeds. BN: Bibliothèque Nationale, Paris. CUL: Cambridge University Library. DUL: Durham University Library. FSL: Folger Shakespeare Library, Washington. GUL: Glasgow University Library. HRC: Harry Ransom Humanities Research Center, University of Texas at Austin. NLS: National Library of Scotland, Edinburgh. NM: the author's collection. NYPL: New York Public Library. RCP: Royal College of Physicians, London. TCC: Trinity College, Cambridge. WLL: Wellcome Library, London

## 1641

N. de Hannappes, *The Ensamples of Vertue and Vice, gathered out of Holy Scripture* (London, 1561), NYPL.

## 1645

*F. S. Ambianates, *Griphi Ausoniani enodatio* (n.p., 1522), CUL.

T. Bell' Haver, *Dottrina facile, et breve per ridurre l'Hebreo al conoscimento del vero Messia* (Venice, 1608), BL.

---

[213] On Moore's book-buying, and the donation to Cambridge, see D. McKitterick, *Cambridge University Library: A History. The Eighteenth and Nineteenth Centuries* (Cambridge, 1986), pp. 47–69, 104.

[214] See *Catalogus librorum manuscriptorum Bibliothecae Sloanianae* (n.p., n.d.), pp. 32–3.

[215] On Sloane's book-buying see M. A. E. Nickson, 'Books and Manuscripts', in A. MacGregor, ed., *Sir Hans Sloane: Collector, Scientist, Antiquary, Founding Father of the British Museum* (London, 1994), pp. 263–77. The notebook is BL, MS Sloane 3995. One item in it does correspond to an inscribed de Cardonnel book among the Sloane items in the BL: Albucasis, *Methodus medendi*. But the notebook records (fol. 74r) that it was bought in a job lot with four other titles, for 2s. 6d., and the only one of those other titles now in the BL—Vesalius, *De radice* (Basel, 1546)—does not have a de Cardonnel inscription. There were many duplicates in Sloane's collection; it seems that this Albucasis item was, or became, one of them.

T. Beza, *Poemata* (Geneva, 1576), bound with S. Sammarthanus, *Poemata* (Paris, 1587), and S. Sammarthanus, *Hieracosophioy* [sic], *sive de re accipitraria* (Paris, 1587), and J. Dousa, *Epodon ex puris jambis* (Antwerp, 1584), CUL.

F. Christianus, ed. and tr., *Epigrammata ex libris graecae anthologiae* (Paris, 1608), CUL.

\*Caius Silius Italicus, *Punica* (Paris, 1512), NLS.

\**Conciliorum quatuor generalium Niceni, Constantinopolitani, Ephesini, & Calcedonensis* (Paris, 1535), CUL.

\*J. Drusius, *Annotationes in Coheleth* (Amsterdam, 1635), TCC.[216]

\*C. Durante, *Herbario novo* (Venice, 1617), BL.

\*H. Lhuyd, *Commentarioli Britannicae descriptionis fragmentum* (Cologne, 1572), CUL.

\*G. de Orta ['da l'Horto'], *Dell' historia de i semplici, aromati* (Venice, 1605), BL.

## 1646

\*J.-E. du Monin, *Nouvelles oeuvres* (Paris, n.d.), BN.

## 1647

\*A. B. de Boodt, *Gemmarum et lapidum historia*, ed. A. Tollius (Leiden, 1647), CUL.

\*J. Riolan, *Anthropographia et osteologia* (Paris, 1626), GUL.

\*G. B. Spagnuoli, 'Mantuanus', *Parthenice Catharinarea* (Caen, 1523), BN.

## 1648

\*Manuscript collection of alchemical and medical treatises, formerly owned by J. Grindley, alias Hammon: BL, MS Sloane 316.[217]

## 1649

R. Lull, *Ars magna generalis et ultima* (Frankfurt, 1596), TCC.

P. Melanchthon, M. Bucer et al., *The Actes of the Disputacion in the Cowncell of the Empyre holden at Regenspurg*, tr. M. Coverdale (Antwerp, 1542), DUL.

N. Monardes, *Joyfull Newes out of the New-Found World* (London, 1596), GUL.

\*J. Morhardus, *Tractatus de miraculis in creaturis elucentibus* (Strasburg, 1631), CUL.

\*J. Scaliger, *Publii Virgilii Maronis Appendix* (Lyon, 1572), CUL.

## 1650

\*P. de Crescentiis, *In commodum ruralium* (Speier, c.1495), CUL.

\*'G. M.' [Gervase Markham?], *Oedipus, or the Resolver . . . [of] the Chiefe Secrets . . . of Amorous, Naturall, Morall, and Politicall Problemes* (London, 1650), FSL.

\*Sophocles, $T\rho\alpha\gamma\omega\delta\acute{\iota}\alpha\iota$ (Frankfurt, 1544), GUL.

---

[216] This volume also bears the signature of Thomas Gale (c.1635–1702), High Master of St Paul's School and an active Fellow of the Royal Society, who made a donation of books and manuscripts to Trinity College in 1697.

[217] De Cardonnel's inscription (fol. 2r) reads: 'MSS. Quae Quondam fuerunt J: Grindley aliàs Hammon, Iatro-chymici Scotj: In Trinobantum Augustâ olim Med. Profitentis, Ibique è vivis A.° S. MDCXLVIII. Ereptj: nunc autem ex possessione & libris P. de Cardonnel'. At the end (fols. 273r–274v) de Cardonnel has added a detailed 'Index' (i.e., list of contents), using the standard chemical symbols.

## PIERRE DE CARDONNEL (1614–1667)

*Manuscript collection of treatises on precious stones, medicine, herbs, etc.: BL, MS Sloane 213.

Manuscript collection of medical treatises, on vellum, illuminated; previously owned by F. Prujean: BL, MS Sloane 282.

### 1651

J. Meggen ['a Megen'], *Peregrinatio Hierosolymitana* (Dillingen, 1580), BL.

### 1652

*T. Hobbes, *Leviathan* (London, 1651), HRC.

### 1654

*G. B. Marini, *La sampogna . . . divisa in idillij favolosi et pastorali* (Paris, 1620), FSL.[218]

### 1655

*[J. Gauden,] *Les Memoires du feu roy de la Grand' Bretagne Charles premier*, tr. D. Cailloué, revd. by J. B. Porrée (Paris, 1649), CUL.

*C. Guarinonius, *Commentarius in primum librum Aristotelis de historia animalium* (Frankfurt, 1601), RCP.

### 1658

*Albucasis, *Methodus medendi certa, clara et brevis* (Basel, 1541), BL.

### 1659

N. Leonicus Thomaeus, *De varia historia* (Basel, 1531), CUL.

### 1660

*S. Gentili, *Annotationi sopra la Gerusalemme liberata di Torquato Tasso* ('Leiden' [London], 1586), CUL.

*J. de Montemayor, *Parte primera y segunda de la Diana* (Barcelona, 1614), FSL.

### 1662

*C. Bartholinus, *Praecepta physicae generalis* (Strasburg, 1621), BL.

*R. Descartes, *Principia philosophiae* (Amsterdam, 1650), bound with Descartes, *Specimina philosophiae, seu dissertatio de methodo* (Amsterdam, 1650), NM.

### 1664

*D. Beckher, *Medicus microcosmus* (Leiden, 1633), WLL.

### 1667

*Il nuovo testamento tradotto . . . dal R. Padre Fra Zaccheria da Firenze* (Venice, 1542), BN.

---

[218] This volume is also annotated by de Cardonnel: 'Fu del fratello ozias de Cardonnel'. This is almost the only surviving trace of Pierre's brother Ozias, apart from his baptismal record (see above, n. 7); I am grateful to Pasteur Denis Vatinel for the information that he died, unmarried, in Rouen on 31 Aug. 1654.

*V. de Petrone, *Literarium duellum inter Salernitanos, et Neapolitanos medicos* (Venice, 1647), BL.

Ψαλτήριον (Venice, 1521), CUL.

## *Undated*

W. Charleton, *Natural History of Nutrition* (London, 1659), GUL.

P. Heylyn, *A Survey of the Estate of France* (London, 1656), BLL.

*G. Naudé, *The History of Magick*, tr. J. Davies (London, 1657), CUL.

## ACKNOWLEDGEMENTS

I am very grateful to the staff of all the archives and libraries mentioned in the notes for their help, and for permission to cite the materials in their collections. For other information, advice, and assistance I am particularly grateful to Dr Geoffrey Copus, Dr Brian Jenkins, Dr John London, Dr David McKitterick, Dr Giles Mandelbrote, Dr Timothy Raylor, Dr Michael Stansfield, and Pasteur Denis Vatinel.

# – 10 –

# Hobbes and the Royal Society

Why was Thomas Hobbes never elected a Fellow of the Royal Society? This is a question which has often been asked. I agree with many of the details of the answers which have been given to it; but I believe that, in putting those and other details together, it is possible to arrive at a rather different overall conclusion. In the process it may also be possible to add something to our knowledge of Hobbes—and perhaps even to our knowledge of the Royal Society.

Our first witness, as always, must be John Aubrey, FRS. As any biographer of Hobbes quickly comes to realize, Aubrey had an extraordinarily accurate memory for the details of Hobbes's life; this may be true in general of those subjects of *Brief Lives* who were personally known to Aubrey. But that does not mean that Aubrey had no concerns of his own to bring to bear on the interpretation and presentation of Hobbes's biography. His friendship and sympathy for Hobbes was itself one of the strongest of these moulding influences. He was keen to show that hostilities to his old friend were in the main personal, local, specific, and petty affairs. And in addition Aubrey was himself an active and enthusiastic member of the Royal Society—not a maggoty-headed antiquary but a thoroughly modern scientist, as Michael Hunter has amply shown—many of whose closest friends were also Fellows of the Society. So it is not surprising that his comments on this question in his 'Life of Hobbes' are, as Steven Shapin and Simon Schaffer have recently said, an act of posthumous reconciliation.[1]

In the middle of a list of Hobbes's friends and admirers, which includes eight Fellows of the Royal Society, Aubrey inserted the following passage:

To conclude, he had a high esteeme for the Royall Societie, having sayd (vide Behemoth pag. 242 . . . ) that 'Naturall Philosophy was removed from the Universities to Gresham Colledge', meaning the Royall Societie that meets there; and the Royall Societie (generally) had the like for him: and he would long since have been ascribed a member there, but for the sake of one or two persons, whom he tooke to be his enemies. In their

---

This chapter first appeared in G. A. J. Rogers and A. Ryan, eds., *Perspectives on Thomas Hobbes* (Oxford, 1988), pp. 43–66.

[1] S. Shapin and S. Schaffer, *Leviathan and the Air-Pump: Hobbes, Boyle and the Experimental Life* (Princeton, NJ, 1985), p. 132.

meeting at Gresham Colledge is his picture, drawen by the life . . . which they much esteeme . . .[2]

This account is reconciliatory to the point of being disingenuous. The picture was one commissioned by Aubrey himself, and presented by him to the Royal Society in 1670.[3] The passage quoted from *Behemoth* consisted, in its original context, not of praise for the Society but of vituperation against the universities, from which, Hobbes was claiming, science had fled. More difficult to judge is Aubrey's comment on Hobbes's relations with Henry Stubbe, 'whom he much esteemed for his great learning and parts, but at the latter end Mr. Hobbs differ'd with him for that he wrote against the lord chancellor Bacon and the Royall Societie'.[4] Here I suspect that what Hobbes objected to was not the fact that Stubbe wrote against the Royal Society, but rather the nature of the arguments on which he based those attacks: his defence of Aristotelian and Galenist medical theory, his qualified defence of scholastic philosophy, and his argument that the new philosophy was an engine to unhinge Protestant Christendom, by encouraging religious heterodoxy and allowing the scholastic weapons of controversial theology to rust away.

Aubrey's attempts at reconciliation had begun during Hobbes's lifetime. In 1675 he wrote to Hobbes, informing him of Robert Hooke's desire that, if Hobbes had any mathematical or scientific papers to be printed, he would send them to Hooke to have them published by the Royal Society.[5] Here again it is difficult to avoid the conclusion that this conciliatory gesture had been prompted by Aubrey himself. Hooke, so far as we know, met Hobbes only twice; his account of the impression Hobbes made on him is not favourable, and the only sporadic references to Hobbes in Hooke's private writings are not complimentary either.[6] But we do know that at this period Hooke was feeling increasingly resentful towards Hobbes's arch-enemy Wallis, whom he suspected of stealing his ideas, and it is likely that Aubrey wanted to make use of this common hostility to draw Hobbes and Hooke together. Hobbes's reply harped on this theme: 'does Mr. Hooke think it fit that any thing of mine should passe through the hands of Dr. Wallis . . . ?' The general tenor of Hobbes's answer was that he had no objections to the nature of the Society as such, but that he could not yet forgive them for having publicly sanctioned insulting attacks on him by some of their members—meaning, above all, Boyle and Wallis. If he had anything new to publish, Hobbes wrote,

I could be content it should be published by the society much rather then any other, provided that they that continually attend the businesse, and are of the society upon no other

[2] J. Aubrey, *'Brief Lives', chiefly of Contemporaries*, ed. A. Clark, 2 vols. (Oxford, 1898), I, pp. 371–2.
[3] Ibid., I, p. 354; Shapin and Schaffer, *Leviathan and the Air-Pump*, p. 132.
[4] Aubrey, *'Brief Lives'*, I, p. 371.
[5] Aubrey's letter does not survive, but its contents are made clear by Hobbes's reply: see n. 7, below.
[6] For a valuable summary of the evidence see Shapin and Schaffer, *Leviathan and the Air-Pump*, p. 133 n. For Hooke's account of his first encounter see n. 20, below.

account then of their Learning, either had forborn to do me injury or made me reparation afterwards... As for the members, I have amongst them for the most part sufficient reputation... but that is nothing to the body of the Society, by whose authority the evill words and disgraces put upon me by Dr. Wallis are still countenanced, without any publique Act of the Society to do me Right....[7]

This does at least furnish some solid evidence of Hobbes's view of the matter, and it is on such evidence as this that Quentin Skinner built his account of the whole affair in his important article of 1969. 'The truth', he wrote, 'seems to be simply that Hobbes first of all raised the enmity of three of the founding Fellows, who managed to keep him out, and that he eventually came to feel sufficiently slighted by this treatment to insist on holding aloof.'[8] The true explanation, in other words, should be in terms of the particular, the commonsensical, and the all-too-human, as opposed to large-scale explanation in terms of fundamental ideological or religious issues dividing Hobbes from the Society. I would want to agree very strongly on the importance of these human contingencies; but I shall try to argue that such an explanation still leaves something unaccounted for, and that we must have some recourse to the large-scale categories of what may be loosely called ideology. And I shall also try to argue that a proper understanding of those wider issues does not involve falling back into the old-fashioned, straightforward explanation in terms of Hobbes's unacceptable heterodoxy; nor does it involve falling forwards, so to speak, into the new-fashioned sociology of knowledge propounded by Shapin and Schaffer.

A good starting-point might be the letter just quoted, in which Hobbes complained that, although many individual members had a good opinion of him, 'the body of the Society', as a corporate person, seemed content for some reason to let itself be publicly associated with attacks on Hobbes by writers such as Wallis. When Professor Skinner writes that a handful of Fellows managed to keep Hobbes out, we want to know why this was such an apparently easy thing to do, given that Hobbes had more than a handful of friends and admirers in the Society. And quite properly, he supplies an answer to this question. The reason why the Society as a whole endorsed in this way the hostility of a few of its members was a very simple one: Hobbes was a club bore.

One reason for saying this is to point out that we should think of the Royal Society as a club, rather than as a modern professional institution operating strict criteria of admission. Some significant scientists in this period never became Fellows (particularly, as Michael Hunter's geographical analysis has shown, those living away from London); and conversely some Fellows—bishops and noblemen

[7] 24 Feb. 1674/5; F. Tönnies, 'Hobbes-Analekten I', *Archiv für Geschichte der Philosophie*, n.s. 17 (1904), pp. 291–317 (here pp. 313–14), from the copy of the letter in Bodleian MS Aubrey 12, fols. 166–7.

[8] Q. Skinner, 'Thomas Hobbes and the Nature of the Early Royal Society', *The Historical Journal*, 12 (1969), pp. 217–39 (here p. 220).

above all—were sleeping partners with little real interest in science.[9] This is a salutary point to make; but it may become misleading. The Royal Society was not just a club; although some of its members were appointed for largely honorific reasons, it was essentially intended as a club *of scientists*. Rather than say that they were not strictly applying the criteria of what counted as doing science, we should say that for the most part they were applying the criteria or standards of their day, standards which may seem very wide or vague in our eyes. And those criteria were certainly broad enough to include Hobbes. Hobbes was a scientist by anybody's standards; his major work on physics, *De corpore* (1655), is a description of the system of nature on a par with similar works by Descartes, Gassendi, or Digby; and if Walter Charleton could become a Fellow on the strength of similar, but derivative, exercises in system-building, it seems clear that Hobbes, *a fortiori*, could have been elected as a scientist.

Nor were Hobbes's scientific achievements confined to system-building. He had done intensive work on optics, analysing problems such as that of the place of the image in a parabolic reflector, and he had been the first person to give the correct dynamic explanation of the sine-law of refraction.[10] He was far from refusing to dirty his hands in practical science. When Descartes in his *Dioptrics* compared refracted light to a bullet fired at an angle into a solid surface, it was Hobbes who, as his Latin Optical Manuscript shows, performed experiments with an airgun to test the theory.[11] In Paris in the 1640s he took a course in chemistry in the Jardin des Plantes; he also studied Vesalius and performed dissections with William Petty.[12] It also seems likely that he had dissected deer with William Harvey.[13] He read widely in contemporary physics and astronomy; and in 1648 he bought the Marquess of Newcastle's collection of telescopes and microscopes, which included two telescopes by Torricelli and four by Eustachio Divino, of which the largest, 'Eustatio Divino, his Greate Glass', was 29 feet long.[14] This monster was probably left behind in France; of the two microscopes, Hobbes gave one to his friend Sorbière before he left the country, and the other he had already given to Petty, who proudly told Benjamin Worsley in 1648 that he valued it at '£3 sterling'.[15] When Hobbes rejoined his patron the Earl of Devonshire in England in the 1650s he

---

[9] See the 'Introduction' to M. Hunter, *The Royal Society and its Fellows 1660–1700*, BSHS Monographs, no. 4 (Chalfont St Giles, 1982), esp. pp. 7–8, 25–7.

[10] BL MS Harl. 3360, pp. 73–81; on Hobbes's optical work see A. E. Shapiro, 'Kinematic Optics: A Study of the Wave Theory of Light in the Seventeenth Century', *Archive for the History of the Exact Sciences*, 11 (1973), pp. 134–266 (esp. pp. 154–5), and J. Bernhardt, 'Hobbes et le mouvement de la lumière', *Revue d'histoire des sciences*, 30 (1977), pp. 3–24.

[11] Hobbes, 'Tractatus opticus', ed. F. Alessio, *Rivista critica di storia della filosofia*, 18 (1963), pp. 147–228 (here p. 164).

[12] Aubrey, '*Brief Lives*', I, pp. 336–7.

[13] G. Keynes, *The Life of William Harvey* (Oxford, 1978), p. 388.

[14] Portland MSS, Nottingham University Library, MS Pw. 1. 668.

[15] S. Sorbière, *Lettres et discours sur divers matières curieuses* (Paris, 1660), p. 436; Sheffield University Library, MS Hartlib 8/27, fol. 2r: 'copy of Mr Worsley's letter 22 June 1648'.

seems to have given him the taste for astronomy or optics: the Earl's accounts show that he bought a 'perspective glass' from the famous instrument-maker, Richard Reeve, in 1656.[16] (It was in Reeve's shop in 1663 that Hooke first encountered Hobbes, together with the Earl of Devonshire.[17]) In 1659 the Earl had bought Hobbes's entire collection of 'prospective glasses' for the huge sum of £80.[18]

Hobbes was, then, enough of a scientist to qualify for admission to any scientists' club. But was he a club bore? The evidence here is rather contradictory. Hostile sources suggest that he was generally overbearing and irascible. Walter Pope, for example, in the course of trying to show how opposed Seth Ward was to Hobbes (for reasons which will become clear later), wrote: 'if any one objected to his [sc. Hobbes's] Dictates, he would leave the Company in a passion, saying, his business was to Teach, not Dispute.' (Pope adds: 'He had entertained an aversion to Dr. *Ward*, for having written something against him . . . and before he would enter into the Assembly, he would enquire if Dr. *Ward* was there, and if he [were he] came not in . . .'.[19]) Robert Hooke's description of his first meeting paints a similar picture, though we should not forget that it occurs in a letter Hooke sent to Boyle shortly after the latter's public controversy with Hobbes: 'I found him to lard and seale every asseveration with a round othe, to undervalue all other men's opinions and judgments, to defend to the utmost what he asserted though never so absurd . . .'.[20] This was certainly a popular view of Hobbes. It was insinuated, for example, into the English translation of Sorbière's account of his visit to England in 1663. When Sorbière talked to Charles II, they both agreed that if Hobbes had been a little less dogmatic ('s'il eust esté un peu moins dogmatique'), he would have been very useful to the Royal Society. The English version subtly traduced Sorbière's meaning: 'it was agreed on all Hands, that if Mr. *Hobbs* were not so very Dogmatical, he would be very Useful and Necessary to the Royal-Society . . .'.[21]

Sorbière's own characterization of Hobbes, however, was rather different. In print he portrayed him as an amusing, thoughtful, and kindly man, and in a letter to Hobbes written after his return to France he exclaimed: 'you are a good friend, a good courtier, and of the best temperament in the world. I remember our walk together at Tilbourne, and the gaiety of all your conversations last year, which I shall always remember as one of the happiest times of my life.'[22] Aubrey, who

---

[16] Chatsworth, MS Hardwick 14, entries for Oct. 1656.
[17] See below, n. 20.
[18] Chatsworth, MS Hardwick 33, entries for Apr. 1659.
[19] W. Pope, *The Life of the Right Reverend Father in God Seth, Lord Bishop of Salisbury* (London, 1697), p. 118.
[20] BL, MS Add. 6193, fols. 68v–69r; printed in R. Boyle, *Works*, ed. T. Birch, 5 vols. (London, 1744), V, p. 533.
[21] S. Sorbière, *Relation d'un voyage en Angleterre* (Paris, 1664), p. 97; S. Sorbière, *A Voyage to England* (London, 1709), p. 40.
[22] Chatsworth, Hobbes MSS, Letters from foreign correspondents, letter no. 60 (1 July 1664). I am most grateful to the trustees of the Chatsworth Settlement for permission to cite this MS., and to the Keeper of Collections, Mr Peter Day, for his help.

was also Hobbes's familiar friend, wrote that '(though he was ready and happy in repartying in *drollery*) he did not care to give a present answer *to a question*, unless he had thoroughly considered it before: for he was against "too hasty concluding" . . . .'.[23] And Hobbes himself replied to his critics on this point in *Mr. Hobbes Considered*:

> Then for his morosity and peevishness, with which some asperse him, all that know him familiarly, know the contrary. 'Tis true that when vain and ignorant young scholars, unknowne to him before, come to him on purpose to argue with him, and fall into undiscreet and uncivill expressions, and he then appear not well contented, 'twas not his morosity, but their vanity, which should be blamed.[24]

This passage rings true, it may be said, precisely because it does carry the rather lofty tone of Hobbes's easily wounded pride. But we can appeal to Hobbes's deeds as well as to his words. As he pointed out parenthetically in his attacks on Boyle, one of the most important proto-scientific societies of the period had been the regular gathering of philosophers and scientists in Mersenne's rooms in the convent of Minim friars in Paris. Hobbes had attended these meetings frequently throughout the 1640s, and had formed a warm friendship with Mersenne, Gassendi, Roberval, and other leading figures with whom he disputed there. This is not the record of an unclubbable man.

The conflicting testimonies to Hobbes's character can after all be reconciled, if we assume that he was pleasant and tractable with those whom he regarded as his friends, and intolerant only in company which he felt was predisposed to hostility towards him. And Hobbes *did* feel that the Royal Society as a whole was hostile to him. Hooke's account of his first encounter with Hobbes begins by saying that he did not know who this old man was, and wondered why he was staring at him in a strange way without saying anything; but his surprise at this ceased when he learned that the old man was Hobbes, 'supposing', Hooke wrote, 'he had been inform'd to whom I belong'd'.[25] The fact that Hooke was an employee of the Society was sufficient to explain Hobbes's baleful glare. When in the following year the Danish scholar Ole Borch visited Sorbière in Paris, he noted in his journal what Sorbière had told him about his latest correspondence with Hobbes. Hobbes has tried to show, he wrote, 'that he has solved the problem of the duplication of the cube. There is however someone else who thinks his reasoning is faulty. But to him Hobbes has already replied that he is not a Fellow of the Royal Society, and that he (Hobbes) is arming himself against that society'.[26] ('Arming himself' here

---

[23] Aubrey, '*Brief Lives*', I, p. 356.
[24] Cited by Aubrey, ibid., I, p. 336; *EW* IV, p. 439.
[25] BL Additional MS 6193, fol. 69r.
[26] O. Borch, *Olai Borrichii Itinerarium 1660–1665*, ed. H. Scheperlern, 4 vols. (Copenhagen/London, 1983), III, p. 192. The term Borch uses for the Royal Society is 'Collegium Naturae': cf. III, p. 70. The 'someone else' was Slusius.

translates 'se armare', with its nicely balanced implication of defensive hostility.) And in the dedicatory epistle to the 1668 edition of the *Dialogus physicus* (the attack on Boyle), Hobbes wrote: 'Many political writers and clerics contend with me on the subject of the sovereign's right. A new sort of mathematicians contend with me about geometry . . . Those Fellows of the Royal Society who have most credit and are as it were the masters of the rest, contend with me about physics . . . All these people are inimical towards me.'[27] This passage was, admittedly, not present in the original edition of 1661. But the whole tone of the book, which gratuitously extended its criticism of Boyle's book into a criticism of the whole Society, had already expressed his feeling that the Society was influenced by what he openly referred to (in 1661) as 'hatred of Hobbes'.[28] He felt that he was, and would remain, an unwelcome outsider.

If the Society had been simply a club, it would be difficult to see why Hobbes's friends at least (who did not find him a bore) should not have made some attempt to elect him. Unlike most clubs, the Royal Society had a qualified majority-vote system of election, with no provision for blackballing. But the attempt was never made—this despite the fact that Hobbes was on good terms with the King, whose patronage the Fellows were keen to secure and strengthen, and despite the fact that Hobbes was perhaps the only living scientist (with the possible exception of the mathematician Richard White) who had direct personal relations with Bacon, the Society's patron saint and arch-bestower of intellectual respectability. Nor did Hobbes lack friends in the Society. Out of the 56 Fellows to join the Society before March 1661, no fewer than 15 are known to have been friends of Hobbes, or members of his circle of patrons, or admirers of his works.[29] And if we look back over the previous dozen years or so at the pattern of Hobbes's friendships and acquaintances, we find that he had belonged (and to some extent still did belong) to some of the main groupings of writers, philosophers, and practising scientists among whom the origins of the Royal Society are usually identified.

It is worth going back, then, to 1650 or before, to consider what patterns of acceptance and rejection Hobbes underwent in the intervening years. The striking thing that emerges, if we look at attitudes to Hobbes in the late 1640s, is that he was thought of by many people principally as a scientist, and that his reputation stood extremely high, on the basis of very little published work (a brief treatise on optics, and a few other pages on epistemology, physics, and in particular telescopes, in compilations published by Mersenne in 1644).[30] In England news and expectations

---

[27] *OL* IV, pp. 236–7.
[28] Ibid., IV, p. 273.
[29] Petty, Pell, Matthew Wren, Digby, Austen, the Earl of Devonshire, Ent, Brereton, Oldenburg, Lord Cavendish, Evelyn, Scarborough, Waller, the Marquess of Dorchester, Lord Bruce.
[30] M. Mersenne, *Cogitata physico-mathematica* (Paris, 1644), section of preface to 'Ballistica' and part of proposition 24 (pp. 74–82); M. Mersenne, *Universae geometriae synopsis* (Paris, 1644), 'Optica', bk 7 ('Tractatus Opticus') and a fragment on telescopes (pp. 473–5).

of his current work were spread by letter-writers, either corresponding directly with him like his old friend Robert Payne, or learning about his work from men such as Sir Charles Cavendish on the Continent. And in Europe there was the corresponding network of Mersenne himself, supplemented by the assiduous efforts of admirers such as Sorbière and Martel. Sorbière knew that Hobbes had written at least one more optical treatise in manuscript, and that he was preparing a major work on physics. And of course everyone who had seen one of the rare 1642 copies of *De cive* knew from its title (*Elementorum philosophiae, sectio tertia de cive*) that the two prior sections of Hobbes's complete system of philosophy were to be expected from the press. When Sorbière went to the trouble of arranging the printing of a second edition of *De cive* in Holland in 1646–7, his real motive was to stimulate Hobbes into producing the rest of his scientific works for Elzevier as well. (He wrote to Bartholin in 1647: 'I have organized the edition of *De cive* in order to elicit from that admirable man what he has promised to send on the subject of *nature*.'[31])

Others in England had the same appetite for Hobbes's scientific works. In February 1650 a book appeared which many readers thought was the long-awaited second section of Hobbes's system, *De homine*. The deception was probably deliberate: Robert Payne wrote in March to Sheldon that the book was 'printed lately by Fr. Bowman, out of a MS. Copy of Mr Lockey's, who persuaded Bowman to publish it as the second part of Mr Hobbes's intended Work'.[32] (Four months later Payne was telling Sheldon of his recent correspondence with Hobbes: 'As for ye other workes, not yet published . . . I have sollicited him to hasten their edition.'[33]) The publication of 1650 was in fact simply the first half of Hobbes's *Elements of Law*, which had been available in numerous manuscript copies in England since 1640. But the title given to it in 1650 was designed to appeal to all those who were eagerly awaiting Hobbes's scientific analysis of human psychology: *Humane Nature, Or, the fundamental Elements of Policie, Being a Discoverie Of the Faculties, Acts, and Passions of the Soul of Man, from their original causes; According to such Philosophical Principles as are not commonly known or asserted.* The prefatory material to this book included a letter to the reader which was almost certainly by Seth Ward, commending Hobbes's philosophy as constructed 'upon such principles and in such order as are used by men conversant in demonstration'.[34] In the eyes of Seth Ward, then, professor of astronomy and a leading figure in the Oxford experimental club, Hobbes was definitely 'one of us'.

To the same volume, Ward's friend and fellow-scientist Ralph Bathurst contributed an elegant and hyperbolic poem in praise of Hobbes, comparing him to

---

[31] F. Tönnies, 'Siebzehn Briefe des Thomas Hobbes an Samuel Sorbière, nebst Briefen Sorbière's, Mersenne's . . .', *Archiv für Geschichte der Philosophie*, 3 (1889–90), pp. 58–71, 192–232 (here p. 198), from a copy of Sorbière's letter in the Bibliothèque Nationale, Paris, MS fonds latin 10352, vol. I, fo. 112.
[32] BL, MS Birch 4162, fol. 112r (26 Mar. 1650).
[33] BL, MS Lansdowne 841, fol. 174r (16 July 1650).
[34] *EW* IV, *Human Nature*, 'To the Reader'.

Archimedes. Hobbes was touched by this and sent Bathurst two complimentary copies of *Leviathan* when it appeared a year later (one of which was perhaps intended for Ward); in reply Bathurst wrote to him that 'I hope your learned booke of Optickes, and that other *de corpore*, if it be yet finished, may no longer lie concealed: especially since now the best wits, as well here as in other countries, are so greedy to listen after workes of that nature, and to vindicate themselves from the superficiall doctrines of the schools . . .'.[35] Bathurst had probably heard about Hobbes's 'learned book of Optickes' from another active member of the Oxford experimental club; for the book in question was none other than the English Optical Treatise, of which William Petty had produced the fair copy for Hobbes in Paris in late 1645 and early 1646.[36] Petty was to remain a lifelong friend and admirer of Hobbes. So here we have three central figures in what is often presented as the main forerunner of the Royal Society, all with high opinions of Hobbes's importance as an exponent of the new philosophy. Most of the other members' attitudes to Hobbes at this stage are unknown. Aubrey lists Rooke as a friend of Hobbes, though on what evidence we do not know.[37] But even John Wilkins, when he came to criticize Hobbes in the *Vindiciae academiarum* four years later, described him as 'a person of good ability and solid parts', and in order to deflate Hobbes's claims of novelty emphasized that many of Hobbes's principles were already held by 'many men' who worked on science on Oxford.[38]

In these men's eyes Hobbes was a man of the present—and, where his works were concerned, of the future. But he was also a figure to be respected because he represented the older generation of English scientists and mathematicians, men such as Walter Warner or William Oughtred. Remnants of the intellectual world of Great Tew and Oxford in the 1630s lingered on in Oxford and elsewhere, and added depth to Hobbes's reputation: Hobbes's friend Payne (who was a friend of Bathurst) was one of them, the almost obscure Mr Lockey (later Bodley's Librarian) was another, and George Morley, whose scientific interests are strongly witnessed by his library catalogue, was a third.[39] History has turned Ward, Wilkins, and their colleagues into the impregnably central figures, beside whom even in this period Hobbes may seem like an upstart and an outsider. So it is worth remembering that in 1650 they looked up to Hobbes, both as a Grand Old Man and as an innovator of whom much was to be expected.

Hobbes's admirers had to wait a long time for the promised completion of his system. *De corpore* appeared in 1655, *De homine* (which incorporated part of the English Optical Treatise) in 1658. Perhaps it is true that the physical

---

[35] T. Warton, *The Life and Literary Remains of Ralph Bathurst* (London, 1761), p. 49 n.
[36] BL, MS Harl. 3360.
[37] Aubrey, '*Brief Lives*', I, p. 366.
[38] J. Wilkins and S. Ward, *Vindiciae academiarum* (Oxford, 1654), pp. 6–7.
[39] See J. C. Hayward, 'The *Mores* of Great Tew: Literary, Philosophical and Political Idealism in Falkland's Circle', Ph.D. dissertation, Cambridge University, 1983, p. 174.

explanations they offered disappointed some of their readers; that is certainly true of the mathematical excursions in *De corpore*; and perhaps some of the admirers already mentioned had developed a stronger taste for experimentalist science in the intervening years. But worse things than that had happened in the meanwhile. In 1654 Wilkins and Ward had attacked Hobbes in their *Vindiciae academiarum* because of his criticism of the universities in *Leviathan*. This was suddenly a serious issue, after a proposal had been made in the Barebones Parliament to abolish the universities altogether. It was precisely *because* Hobbes still appeared in 1654 as an authoritative speaker on behalf of the new science that Wilkins and Ward took such trouble to attack him. And having taken this step (which involved trying to marginalize Hobbes by making him appear dogmatic, magisterial, ignorant, unoriginal, and out of date), Ward went further in 1656 and attacked his theology in one of the first major theological critiques of *Leviathan*, entitled *In Thomae Hobbii Philosophia Exercitatio Epistolica*. Meanwhile Hobbes had foolishly taken up the challenge to demonstrate his superiority in geometry to the Oxford professors of mathematics, and was engaged in an increasingly bitter war of words with John Wallis. The real bitterness on Hobbes's side came from the fact that he regarded Wallis as a representative of the Presbyterian party. So with these two steps the argument had shifted into the realms of theology and church government.

What ideological significance should we accord to either or both of these steps? Ward's attack on Hobbes's theology sets a significant precedent. Hobbes's reputation for heterodoxy was growing gradually during this period. Ward could see which way the wind was blowing, and decided that attack was the best form of dissociation; and he needed to dissociate the new science from Hobbes precisely because Hobbes was such a major spokesman of it. Ward's attack on Hobbes was self-protective, diversionary, and pre-emptive.

In the case of church government, J. R. Jacob has suggested that this argument had a more profound significance at the level of metaphysics. The Oxford group, he argues, was deeply opposed to Hobbes's metaphysics because his attack on the notion of incorporeal spirits was an attack on their priestly powers to manipulate the world of spirits, and hence an attack on the claims of the clergy to exercise power over the people.[40] There is an argument of this sort in part 4 of *Leviathan*; but that argument was directed against scholastic Aristotelianism, and there is no reason why Wilkins or Ward should have felt affected by it—except in so far as it was generally anti-clerical in tone. The best disproof of Jacob's interpretation lies in Stubbe's letters to Hobbes during this period, in which the young Oxford scholar explained that Wallis was isolated on this issue: most of the other leading figures in Oxford were in fact quite close to Hobbes on the question of Church

---

[40] J. R. Jacob, *Henry Stubbe, Radical Protestantism and the Early Enlightenment* (Cambridge, 1983), pp. 16–17.

government, and Wallis was the odd man out in a ruling alliance consisting mainly of Independents and pragmatic Anglicans. 'Wilkins of Wadham', Stubbe told Hobbes in 1656, 'maintained in his colledge yt no forme of Church-gouernemt is *jure diuino*.'[41] There is a revealing comment in Bathurst's letter to Hobbes of 1651, a comment which Warton partly omitted from the printed version of the letter. After reading *Leviathan*, Bathurst begs Hobbes to publish his other works. 'And', he adds, 'thus much am I the rather bold to suggest to you, because if by your other workes already published, you have gained so high an esteeme, even when almost a whole order of men thought it concern'd them to cry downe your opinions, how much more shall those be received with honour, in whose argument no man's *Diana* will be call'd in question.'[42] The whole order of men here must surely be the priests or presbyters who claimed rights and powers over men's actions in the state.

Jacob's attempt to read a deep metaphysical significance into the division between Hobbes and men such as Wilkins on the issue of clericalism in the state fails, I believe, because there was in fact little division between them; compared with high Church sacerdotalists or doctrinaire Presbyterians, Wilkins and Hobbes were in the same camp. J. G. A. Pocock has written, in a very suggestive phrase, that 'it is tempting to define the politics of the Oxford scientists at this time as conservative and empirical, authoritarian and latitudinarian'.[43] The general nature of their position was one of pragmatic acceptance of the need for authority. Wilkins's interest in the maintenance of the Cromwellian regime became a more personal one when he married Cromwell's sister in 1656. Not surprisingly, he favoured a monarchist, authoritarian system of government—authoritarian in the sense that is should be based on the authority of an individual rather than on the inherent rationality of a republican constitution. In 1657 he commissioned Matthew Wren (another scientist and future FRS) to write a defence of monarchy in answer to Harrington's *Oceana*. Wren's arguments in this work (*Considerations on Mr. Harrington's Commonwealth of Oceana*) often take on an explicitly Hobbesian tone. When Harrington contrasts the Empire of Laws with the Empire of Men, Wren replies: 'I do not thinke my self bound to undertake all Challenges that are sent to Mr. *Hobs*: but the easinesse of the Defence in this Particular that Men Govern and not Laws, tempts me to be his second . . .'.[44] Wren was strongly influenced by Hobbes, and it was a singular piece of bad judgement that Sir Edward Hyde should have urged him in 1659 to write a refutation of *Leviathan*. (Wren toned down his

---

[41] BL, MS Add. 32,553, fol. 24r.

[42] The MS of this letter has not been found, but a copy of Warton's book (see n. 35 above) in the Old Library, Trinity College, Oxford, has annotations by someone (perhaps James Ingram) who was able to compare the original MS with Warton's partial transcription of it. I am most grateful to Dr Dennis Burden, the Librarian, for this information.

[43] J. Harrington, *The Political Works*, ed. J. G. A. Pocock (Cambridge, 1977); 'Introduction', p. 84.

[44] M. Wren, *Considerations on Mr. Harrington's Commonwealth of Oceana* (London, 1657), p. 8.

support for Hobbes in his next book, *Monarchy Asserted*, but he could not resist surreptitiously waving a Hobbist flag by quoting Thucydides on the state of nature in Hobbes's translation.[45])

When Harrington treated Wren as a representative of 'the Virtuosi' or 'the University Wits', this was not strictly accurate; but he was representative of some of the most prominent among them, whose views can be ascertained on the subject of government or church government. When Seth Ward preached a sermon *Against Resistance of Lawful Powers* to the King in 1661 he put in some obligatory jibes against the Hobbist doctrine. But some of his own arguments have a distinct congruence with Hobbes, and help to explain Ward's pragmatic acceptance of authority for the sake of peace during the Interregnum. For example, commenting on 'the Power of the Magistrate in Matters of Religion', he writes: 'If none have Power to order Matters of Religion, there must be Confusion; if any other beside the supream Magistrate, there will be Division.'[46]

Looking back on Hobbes's disputes with Ward, Wilkins, and Wallis in the 1650s, one is struck at first by the contingency of it all; if only the universities had not felt politically threatened in 1653–4, one feels, Hobbes would never have become embroiled in these disputes, and would never have suffered the running sore of his mathematical controversy with Wallis—which did in the end damage his reputation as a scientist. But, on the other hand, one is struck by the way that religious or political issues arose in which, the more disreputable Hobbes became, the more necessary it was for the other scientists to dissociate themselves from him by attacking him, precisely because he was in some ways embarrassingly close to their own position. The political issues did not greatly embarrass them till after the Restoration; the association between a mechanistic world-view and religious heterodoxy had begun to trouble them in the 1650s and would continue to do so after the formation of the Royal Society.

Before turning to some of those issues in the 1660s, it is necessary to look briefly at Hobbes's other contacts with future Fellows in the previous decade. Hobbes was based in London for much of each year from 1652 onwards; the evidence for his activities is fragmentary, but we do know that he was on good terms with a number of future Fellows—beginning with Brereton, who probably negotiated on his behalf with the Council of State to sanction his return to England.[47] We know that in the early 1650s Hobbes moved in the circles of Selden and Harvey; Selden's friend John Vaughan, lawyer, amateur mathematician, and future FRS, became a

---

[45] C. Wren, *Parentalia: Or, Memoirs of the Family of the Wrens* (London, 1750), pp. 53–4; M. Wren, *Monarchy Asserted* (Oxford, 1659), p. 35.

[46] S. Ward, *Against Resistance of Lawful Powers* (London, n.d.), pp. 12–13.

[47] On Brereton's friendship with Hobbes see his letter to Pell, 5 Mar. 1652, in R. Vaughan, ed., *The Protectorate of Oliver Cromwell*, 2 vols. (London, 1838), II, p. 384; and his letter to Huygens, 29 Mar. 1652, in C. Huygens, *Œuvres complètes*, 22 vols. (The Hague, 1888–1950), I, p. 176.

great admirer of Hobbes, and it was probably through Harvey that Hobbes met John Aubrey.[48] He already knew Edmund Waller and John Evelyn, and he gained some acquaintance with Henry Oldenburg through the latter's employment under the Earl of Devonshire.[49] We also know that he was moving in the rather more free-thinking circles of Thomas White, the Catholic philosopher, his brother Richard White (astronomer and future FRS), John Davies, the translator of Naudé on witchcraft and the man who published Hobbes's *On Liberty and Necessity* with a fiercely anti-clerical preface, and John Hall of Durham, the educational reformer, friend of Hartlib, and apologist for Cromwell.[50] Thomas White was an intermediary between Hobbes's old friend Kenelm Digby and the Oxford mathematicians.[51] But perhaps the most important friend of Hobbes for our purposes was the physician and mathematician Charles Scarborough, whose house Walter Pope described as 'the Rendezvous of most of the Learned Men about London'.[52] (This was the 'Assembly' which, according to Pope, Hobbes would not enter when Seth Ward was there.) Scarborough was an admirer of Hobbes (he had a picture of him hanging in his chamber), and a central figure in those gatherings of scientists in London at the end of the decade which led to the formation of the Royal Society.[53]

It is in this context that I should like to offer a very speculative interpretation of a very slender piece of evidence. On 1 February 1659 Sorbière wrote to Hobbes

[48] Selden and Vaughan: Aubrey, '*Brief Lives*', I, p. 369; on the 'triumvirate' of Selden, Harvey, and Hobbes, see Keynes, *Life of Harvey*, pp. 386–90. Aubrey's personal acquaintance with Hobbes seems to date from the early 1650s; Aubrey had become a friend of Harvey in 1651 (Keynes, *Life of Harvey*, p. 383).

[49] J. Evelyn: see his *Diary and Correspondence*, ed. W. Bray, 4 vols. (London, 1859), I, pp. 280, 327 (7 Sept. 1651, 14 Dec. 1655). Waller: see Aubrey, '*Brief Lives*', I, pp. 369, 372; P. Wikelund, ' "Thus I passe my time in this place": An Unpublished Letter of Thomas Hobbes', *English Language Notes*, 6 (1969), pp. 263–8; P. Hardacre, 'A Letter from Edmund Waller to Thomas Hobbes', *Huntington Library Quarterly*, 11 (1948), pp. 431–3, H. Oldenburg: see his *Correspondence*, ed. A. R. Hall and M. B. Hall, 13 vols. (Madison, Wis., and London, 1965–87), I, p. 74, letter 32.

[50] T. White: see Hobbes, *Critique du De mundo de Thomas White*, ed. J. Jacquot and H. W. Jones (Paris, 1973), 'Introduction', pp. 24–5. R. White: Aubrey, '*Brief Lives*', I, p. 369. Davies: see J. Tucker, 'John Davies of Kidwelly (1627?–1693), Translator from the French', *Papers of the Bibliographical Society of America*, 44 (1950), pp. 119–51; G. Naudé, *The History of Magick* (London, 1657). Hall: see the 'Account' of his life by Davies, prefixed to Hall's *Hierocles upon the Golden Verses of Pythagoras* (London, 1657), which mentions that he knew Thomas White and was known by Hobbes (sigs. b7r–A1r). Hall refers obliquely to Hobbes in his *Confusion Confounded* (London, 1654), sig. C1v.

[51] See the letters from Digby to Wallis (and Brouncker) in J. Wallis, *Commercium epistolicum de quaestionibus quibusdam mathematicis* (Oxford, 1658).

[52] Pope, *Life of Seth [Ward]*, p. 117.

[53] See Pope's account (cited above); J. Wallis, *A Defence of the Royal Society* (London, 1678), p. 7, includes Scarborough in his list of London scientists in the mid-1640s (but cf. M. Purver, *The Royal Society: Concept and Creation* (Cambridge, Mass., 1967), pp. 161–82); see also the letter from Anthony Thompson to Pell, 22 Nov. 1658, inviting him to a 'meeting . . . of some mathematicall friends' in London, which would be attended by Rooke, Wren, Brouncker, Neile, Goddard, and Scarborough: J. Halliwell, ed., *A Collection of Letters Illustrative of the Progress of Science* (London, 1841), pp. 95–6. It is clear, I think, that Sprat's claim that the Oxford club removed to London in 1658 implies too sudden and definite a transition; there was a gradual process of osmosis during the 1650s, in which established scientists in London, such as Scarborough, acted as important focuses of association. (On the portrait see Aubrey, '*Brief Lives*', I, p. 369.)

from Paris, giving him further news of Montmor's academy, the group of French scientists who gathered at Montmor's house and had recently adopted a formal constitution (drawn up by Sorbière and another friend of Hobbes, du Prat). In this letter Sorbière sent Hobbes the complete list of rules for the academy, with the comment: 'I send them to you because you ask for them; and I do not mind if they are seen by everybody' (*& ie seray bien aisé qu'ils soient veus de tout le monde*).[54] The phrasing of this suggests, perhaps, that Hobbes had asked for permission to show these rules to other people; and the most likely people to show them to would be men such as Scarborough, who had held similar meetings in his own house. It would be a rich irony if Hobbes had in this way contributed to the setting up of a formally constituted society at the end of the following year; and it would help to explain his deep resentment at being excluded from it.

The underlying reasons why that exclusion was bound to continue have already been hinted at. Hobbes was becoming an increasingly disreputable figure, both politically and theologically; and the people who felt that it was most in their interest to blacken his reputation further were the ones who were vulnerable to embarrassing comparisons between his position and their own. Most modern descriptions of the early years of the Royal Society still fail to give a sufficient sense of just how nervous of criticism the publicists of the Society were.[55] The whole of part III of T. Sprat's *History of the Royal Society*, for example, is taken up with arguing that the Society is not a danger to government, manners, education, or religion; Sprat's words are so convincingly soothing that we may tend to forget that there *was* a great mass of hostile opinion that needed to be soothed. Critics associated the new science with Epicureanism and atheism, and these were not just the hysterical fears of the ignorant outsiders: this problem deeply exercised the minds of Fellows such as More and Boyle. Critics attacked the Latitudinarianism of some of the principal publicists of the Royal Society, seeing a link between their claims on behalf of reason in natural knowledge, and the rationalism of their religious views, which demoted doctrinal differences and questions of divinely ordained Church government in favour of moral virtues, peace, and comprehension. And critics insinuated that just as their views implied an 'indifferency' in questions of Church government, so too they implied an 'indifferency' in politics.

On each of these overlapping issues there was a risk of being compared to Hobbes. As late as 1682 we can catch a revealing glimpse of this problem in Boyle's correspondence, which shows a sudden flurry of concern over the publication under the Society's aegis of John Houghton's *Collection of Letters for the Improvement of Husbandry and Trade*. At a late stage it was noticed that the work included a sort of proto-Mandevillian argument, which appeared to recommend

---

[54] Sorbière, *Lettres et Discours*, p. 632.
[55] For an important exception to this rule, see M. Hunter, 'The Debate over Science', in J. R. Jones, ed., *The Restored Monarchy 1660–1688* (London, 1979), pp. 176–95.

luxury and prodigality on economic grounds. Boyle's correspondent, John Beale, expressed fears of the criticisms this would unleash, and suggested that the Royal Society should reprint the public recantation of the penitent Hobbist Daniel Scargill.[56]

There is not space to discuss properly each of the areas of criticism and dissociation which have been briefly outlined. So the last part of this paper will concentrate on one of them, that of Latitudinarianism and rational religion, because, although the comparisons with Hobbes were dangerously close to the mark in this area, it was here that the publicists of the Royal Society found their most useful weapons of anti-Hobbesian rhetoric.

Histories of English religious thought in this period are still dominated by the feeling that the rational or liberal theologians were making claims which were just obviously right, true, and reasonable, and that they can only have been opposed by obscurantists, reactionaries, or fanatics. We have swallowed, in other words, the Latitude-men's own account of their role. It is, I believe, impossible to understand the true nature of the movement in the 1650s and 1660s unless we realize that they were a campaigning minority (though rapidly gaining power through the hierarchy of the Church in the 1660s), and that their views were widely and correctly regarded as going against what had been the orthodox theology of the Church. Their emphasis on the reasonableness of religion and the reasonableness of God involved subverting the central tenet of anti-Tridentine Protestantism, the belief that man was saved by imputed righteousness only, not by any growth in his own intrinsic righteousness as a moral agent. In Mark Pattison's words, 'They spoke not of sin, but of vice . . . They had adopted the language of the moralists.'[57] It would be unreasonable of God, they felt, to damn those who tried hard, or to require of them anything more than they were naturally capable of: moral virtue and rational belief. A great deal of dogmatic theology was thus cast aside as irrelevant; this is echoed in the complaints of Stubbe, Barlow, Casaubon, and others that the New Learning encouraged neglect of the weapons of Protestant controversial theology. In the Restoration period the rational theologians were criticized on both sides: by high Anglicans such as Beaumont, and by sectarian writers such as Bunyan. In each case the critics were trying to reassert the importance of getting one's doctrinal theology right. It is important to recognize, in other words, that, when the Latitude-men loftily declared that they were above or outside theoretical controversies, this declaration was itself a way of taking sides in one of the most fundamental controversies of contemporary theology.

---

[56] Boyle, *Works*, V, pp. 508–10.
[57] M. Pattison, *Essays*, ed. H. Nettleship, 2 vols. (Oxford, 1889), II, p. 64. For the theological background to this change, see C. F. Allison, *The Rise of Moralism: The Proclamation of the Gospel from Hooker to Baxter* (London, 1966).

One of the strongest arguments they were able to use in this controversy after the Restoration was the myth of religious fanaticism and anarchy in the 1640s and 1650s. (By calling it a myth I do not mean to suggest that there was no truth in it, but rather to indicate the way it functioned talismanically in argument.) They could use this to suggest that the old Protestant theology led unacceptably to Antinomianism, and to imply that their moralizing version of religion was a necessary protection against the forces of enthusiasm and social disruption. And they could also suggest that any uncompromising attachment to particular details of doctrinal theology was a sign of fanaticism and—to use the key word—dogmatizing. In the rhetoric of the Latitude-men, their liberal theology offered a safe *via media* between two opposite dangers: atheism on the one hand, and dogmatism or fanaticism on the other. Against atheism they offered rational belief; and against dogmatism they offered a programme of moral virtues which emphasized charitableness, moderation, and a devotion to peace.

It was, I think, Joseph Glanvill who realized just how neatly this structure of argument could be turned to the defence of the new science. He was able to present the Royal Society as pursuing a virtuous *via media*, which could be described in terms of two interlocking sets of polarities. There was the polarity of Pyrrhonist scepticism on the one hand and dogmatism on the other: here Hobbes was an archdogmatist. But it was the dogmatic, a priori metaphysical theories of mechanistic Nature which were popularly regarded as leading to atheism; so on the religious pole, Hobbes was associated with the polarity of atheism, and the Royal Society was presented as treading the middle path of calm, rational belief between the atheists on one side and the fanatics and enthusiasts on the other.

The fullest expression of this pattern of argument comes in J. Glanvill's *Philosophia pia; or, a Discourse of the Religious Temper, and Tendencies of the Experimental Philosophy, Which is profest By the Royal Society* (1671). 'It is the perverse opinion', Glanvill writes, 'of hasty, inconsiderate Men, that the study of Nature is prejudicial to the interests of *Religion*; And those that are *very* zealous, and *little* wise, endeavour to render the *Naturalist* suspected of holding secret correspondence with the *Atheist* . . .'[58] Not so, Glanvill explains—the study of Nature disproves the Atheist, and is a psychological corrective to fanaticism and 'the humour of disputing'. When Glanvill turns to attacking religious superstition, his arguments begin to seem uncomfortably close to those of Hobbes. But Hobbes is cleverly linked to enthusiasm through an anecdote about a madwoman in Warwickshire who made 'odde fetches of discourse . . . that look'd like scraps taken out of *Hobbes*, and *Epicurus*'; and then the display of hostility to Hobbes is taken further with an attack on 'men of the Epicurean sort' who 'have left *God*, and *Providence* out of their accounts . . .'. Here Glanvill hastens to explain that 'the late

[58] J. Glanvill, *Philosophia pia* (London, 1671), p. 1.

Restorers of the *Corpuscularian Hypothesis*, hate and despise that vile doctrine . . .'. Their version of mechanistic science, he insists, 'doth not in the least grate upon any *Principle* of *Religion*. Thus far I dare say I may undertake for most of the *Corpuscularian Philosophers* of our times, excepting *those* of Mr. *Hobb's* way.'[59]

Glanvill's favourite theme was 'the humour of disputing', which he had already turned into a key element of the debate with his *The Vanity of Dogmatizing* (published in 1661; rewritten as *Scepsis Scientifica* and published in 1665 with a dedication to the Royal Society). It was probably from him that Sprat had derived the idea of obliquely presenting Hobbes as a 'Modern dogmatist'.[60] And it is on this issue that the underlying or parallel argument in defence of rational religion comes most visibly to the surface. When Glanvill speaks about the value of empirical and practical knowledge, what I hear is not the voice of modified scepticism arising from a concern with problems of certainty in a Protestant–Catholic debate; nor is it a Puritan exaltation of practical activity. What I hear is the voice of the Latitude-man defending himself against the doctrinal theology of the old orthodoxy:

> The *Real* experimental Philosophy [teaches] that the most *valuable* knowledge is the *practical*; By which means they will find themselves disposed to more *indifferency* towards those *petty notions* in which they were before apt to place a great deal of Religion; and so to reckon, that *that* which will signifie lies in the *few, certain, operative* principles of the Gospel, and a *life* suitable to such a *Faith*.[61]

It was Sprat who announced that 'The universal Disposition of this *Age* is bent upon a *rational Religion*.'[62]

Hobbes too had offered a sort of rational religion in the second half of *Leviathan*; Sprat's version of the argument is significant because it shows just how far the rational theologians could go in resembling Hobbes while at the same time posing as defenders of true religion against the 'threat' of Hobbism. If anyone pointed out the similarities, the only response was to raise the stakes by expressing yet more disapproval of Hobbes, and presenting him as more of a danger in those terms (dogmatist, atheist, and so on), which enabled them to present their own position as a necessary defence and corrective. And the similarities could, as Meric Casaubon noticed, be striking indeed. 'Religion ought not to be the subject of *Disputations*,' Sprat wrote; 'it should in this be like the Temporal Laws of all Countries.'[63] The Church should 'derive its *Doctrine* from the plain and unquestion'd parts of the *Word of God*, and . . . keep itself in a due subjection to the Civil Magistrate'.[64] When Sprat wrote that 'most of our religious controversies, may be

---

[59] Ibid., pp. 16, 62–3, 106–9.
[60] T. Sprat, *The History of the Royal Society* (London, 1667), p. 33.
[61] Glanvill, *Philosophia pia*, p. 44.
[62] Sprat, *History*, p. 374.
[63] Ibid., pp. 354–5.
[64] Ibid., p. 370.

... decided by plain reason', Meric Casaubon exploded: 'this I do not understand. The sense is obvious enough; but a sense so amazing, that it is not credible'. He compared it to Herbert's *De veritate*, 'the end and drift whereof was, out of the Religions of mankind to extract a religion that should need no Christ'. Then, with a transparent reference to Hobbes, Casaubon added: 'Since him it is well known, that some body hath taken some pains to attemperate Christianity to the laws of every Countrey, and commands of Supreme Powers: and this he doth ground, or endeavour to ground, upon divers passages of Scripture. What can this import, in ordinary construction, but a new Religion?'[65]

There is not space here to enter into the complex question of just how far Hobbes's rational religion did resemble that of the Latitudinarian theologians—though it is a question worth investigating, now that some Hobbes scholars are beginning to treat him as a perfectly typical liberal Anglican from Great Tew.[66] Suffice it to say that there were some strong similarities on the surface, just as there were similarities in their attitudes to politics and church government, and similarities between Hobbes and many of the Fellows of the Royal Society in their assumptions about the mechanistic nature of the physical universe. Significant differences can also be found in most cases, but it is the similarities that mattered—forcing the Royal Society to dissociate itself from Hobbes, and in the process to fuel the fires of criticism against him. Individuals may have known and befriended him; but it was the public image of the Society that was at stake, an image the management of which had been taken over by the publicists of rational religion.

Finally, a short and rather negative methodological postscript. Nowhere in this paper has the claim been made that there *was* an intrinsic connection between being a proponent of rational religion and being a scientist of the sort found in the Royal Society. If one happened to be both of these, one might well want to make some connections between them, and use the same sorts of argument to defend them both—particularly if those arguments were such very successful ones. If there is some truth in the impression that the more significant members of this group of scientists did have this type of religious attitude, then it is reasonable enough to seek an explanation of that fact. But it is simply not necessary to suppose that when we find that explanation it will also be the 'explanation' of the scientific beliefs they held. A statistical prevalence of liberal Jews among psychiatrists would not necessarily mean that the principles of psychiatry are derived from the doctrines of liberal Judaism.

---

[65] M. Casaubon, *A Letter . . . to P. du Moulin . . . concerning Natural Experimental Philosophie, and some Books lately set out about it* (Cambridge, 1669), p. 17.

[66] For example, P. Johnson, 'Hobbes's Anglican Doctrine of Salvation', in R. Ross, H. Schneider, and T. Waldman, eds., *Thomas Hobbes in his Time* (Minneapolis, 1974), pp. 102–25. I put forward a rather different view of Hobbes's underlying theological position in my 'Thomas Hobbes and Voluntarist Theology', Ph.D. dissertation, Cambridge University, 1983.

The search for unifying explanations, located in different underlying categories of belief or action, may often be misleading. When a seventeenth-century scientist says that searching into nature is an inducement to greater piety towards God, the creator of nature, this does not necessarily mean that his fundamental reasons for doing science are deeply religious. When he says that useful applications can be derived from scientific research, this does not necessarily mean that his fundamental reasons for doing science are deeply social. Such statements might mean these things; but they might just mean that the speaker wanted to defend his activity and had a reasonable command of current platitudes. So I should like to offer just one possible reason for doing science in this period which is perhaps so obvious that one would not expect to find it mentioned by any modern historian of science: curiosity.

# – 11 –

# The Printing of the 'Bear': New Light on the Second Edition of Hobbes's *Leviathan*

## I

There are three early editions of Thomas Hobbes's *Leviathan*, all of them bearing the imprint 'Printed for Andrew Crooke at the Green Dragon in St. Paul's Churchyard, 1651'. The identity of the genuine first edition is not in doubt: known as the 'Head' edition (from the ornament on the printed title page), it was indeed produced by Hobbes's usual publisher, Andrew Crooke, in 1651. The other two editions, known by their title page ornaments as the 'Bear' and the 'Ornaments', are page-by-page reprintings of the 'Head'. The order in which these two further editions appeared is also beyond dispute: from the evidence of errata, and from the changes in the state of the famous engraved title page (worn in the Bear, heavily retouched in the Ornaments), it is clear that the Bear was the second edition, and the Ornaments the third.[1] However, nothing has yet been established with any certainty about the dating of these two editions. To Hobbes scholars the issue is, or should be, of more than antiquarian interest: the Bear contains a small number of significant textual changes, and it is therefore important to know whether this printing was, as it is sometimes called, a 'pirated' edition, or whether these material variants may have originated with Hobbes himself.[2] (The Ornaments edition reproduces these changes, being evidently copied from the Bear; but it makes no new material alterations, and is therefore of much less interest to editors of Hobbes.) Our knowledge of Hobbes's final intentions, where the English text of *Leviathan* is concerned, is incomplete so long as the key questions about the Bear edition—who printed it, where, when, and why?—remain unanswered.

---

[1] See H. Macdonald and M. Hargreaves, *Thomas Hobbes: A Bibliography* (London, 1952), p. 27.
[2] Variants are listed in T. Hobbes, *Leviathan*, ed. A. R. Waller (Cambridge, 1904), pp. 529–30: there are five significant changes relating to the work's eschatological theory (listed by Waller in the entries for pp. 335, 336, 464 (l. 2), 464 (ll. 4–9), and 465 of his edn), which might be explained as authorial interventions.

Fig. 1. 'Bear' ornament, *Leviathan*, 2nd edition, printed title page (from the copy in the author's collection).

Fig. 2. 'St. Christopher' ornament, *Leviathan*, 2nd edition, sig. A4r (from the copy in the author's collection).

A few clues have been presented by previous writers, and some tentative conclusions drawn from them. Discussing this issue in their bibliography of Hobbes, Hugh Macdonald and Mary Hargreaves noted that the 'bear' ornament was commonly found in Dutch books of the period 1617–71; they were also advised by a Dutch librarian that the 'St Christopher' ornament which appears at the head of the 'Introduction' in the Bear edition (and in which the figure of St Christopher stands between the letters 'C.C.') was probably—although 'as yet we cannot prove it'—a device of the Amsterdam printer Christoffel Cunradus. On this basis, they concluded: 'All the evidence seems to suggest that this edition was printed in Holland and probably not long after 1651.'[3]

They also noted that, according to documents among the State Papers in the Public Record Office, an attempt at a surreptitious printing of *Leviathan* was made in 1670 by the printer John Redmayne, but was halted when his press was raided by officials of the Stationers' Company. Redmayne testified that he was given the work by John Williams, 'who had it from Mr. Crook to print'. Macdonald and Hargreaves commented: 'It is possible that Andrew Crooke, who died in 1674, had given *Leviathan* to more than one printer, or that the Stationers' Company suppressed only a part of the edition. It is tempting to seek here the origin of the "ornaments" edition but this can be no more than conjecture.'[4] A later discussion of this evidence by William Williams came to the same conjectural conclusion: 'It does seem possible that Redmayne, in conjunction with whomever, could have produced some copies of *Leviathan* either before or after the Company's efforts to suppress the edition, and that these copies may constitute the "ornaments" edition.'[5]

Two other clues pointed to the year 1680. Anthony Wood, in the entry on Hobbes in his *Athenae oxonienses*, listed 'Leviathan . . . Lond. 1651. fol. Reprinted there again with its old date *an.* 1680 fol.'[6] And a catalogue of 'Books Printed for and sold by *Richard Chiswel*', appended to Gilbert Burnet's *Some Passages of the Life and Death . . . of Rochester* (London, 1680), included, in the category 'Folio', '*Hobbes's* Leviathan'.[7] These details, which were noted by Macdonald and Hargreaves, have also been associated with the Ornaments edition: it is commonly assumed that that edition went on sale for the first time in 1680, and was either a completion of the aborted London printing of 1670, or a new and more successful

---

[3] Macdonald and Hargreaves, *Bibliography*, p. 28.   [4] Ibid., p. 29.

[5] W. P. Williams, 'Was There a 1670 Edition of *Leviathan*?' *The Papers of the Bibliographical Society of America*, 69 (1975), pp. 81–4 (here p. 84).

[6] A. Wood, *Athenae oxonienses*, ed. P. Bliss, 4 vols. (London, 1813–20), III, p. 210. This information found its way into some reference works: thus R. Watt, *Bibliotheca Britannica*, 4 vols. (Edinburgh 1824), I, col. 501, lists *Leviathan* as 'Lond. 1651, 1680'.

[7] G. Burnet, *Some Passages of the Life and Death . . . of Rochester* (London, 1680), sig. N4ʳ. It has not apparently been noticed that *Leviathan* was also advertised in another such catalogue of books 'printed for, and sold by Richard Chiswell' two years later: G. Burnet, *The Abridgment of the History of the Reformation of the Church of England* (London, 1682), sig. CC2ʳ. (The catalogue is present in some copies of the first issue of the 1682 edition, e.g. the copy in the British Library (hereafter: BL), pressmark 1508. 829.)

venture by some of the people who had been involved in it. However, many variations on this theme are possible: Richard Tuck, while accepting that the Ornaments edition was produced in London, has suggested that Wood's '1680' may simply have been a mistake for '1670', while Arnold Rogow has proposed that the Ornaments, like the Bear, 'may also have been printed in Holland . . . perhaps even as late as 1680'.[8]

To this day the most widely accepted view—accepted, that is, by compilers of reference works, and of catalogues for libraries, auction houses, and book-dealers—is the one expressed by Macdonald and Hargreaves: that the Bear was printed in Holland in the 1650s, and the Ornaments in London in 1680.[9] Among Hobbes specialists, most of the same assumptions still apply.[10] In the half-century since Macdonald and Hargreaves's bibliography appeared, Hobbes scholarship has made only one significant alteration to their argument: several writers have suggested that the date of publication of the Bear should be shifted from the 1650s to the period soon after 1668. This proposal was first advanced by Maurice Goldsmith, who pointed out that the Latin version of *Leviathan* (printed by Johan Blaeu in Amsterdam as part of Hobbes's *Opera philosophica* in 1668) was based on the Head edition, not the Bear or the Ornaments: a phrase that appears in the Head as 'those have least Pitty' is printed as 'those hate Pitty' in the Bear and the Ornaments, but is translated as 'minus Misericordes sunt illi' in the Latin.[11] On these grounds C. B. Macpherson observed that it was possible that both the Bear and the Ornaments 'were published . . . after 1668'.[12] However, it must be said that this argument is intrinsically very weak: the phrase 'those hate Pitty' is obviously a misprint, and one would not expect Hobbes to have translated it even if he had had a copy of the Bear edition on his desk at the time. (On the other hand, the significant textual changes in the Bear do have their equivalents in alterations made in the Latin text; but from this fact no conclusion can be drawn about the chronological order in which the Bear and the Latin translation were produced.)

[8] T. Hobbes, *Leviathan*, ed. R. Tuck (Cambridge, 1991), p. xlvii; A. Rogow, *Thomas Hobbes: Radical in the Service of Reaction* (New York, 1986), p. 155.

[9] The revised edition of Wing supports this date for the Ornaments, which it lists as '1651 [1680]', but offers no opinion on the Bear, which it merely describes as '[Anr. Ed.] . . . 1651' (D. Wing, *Short-Title Catalogue . . . 1641–1700*, 2nd edn, rev., 3 vols. (New York, 1982–94), II, p. 245). The Bear is listed as '1651 [*i.e.* 1655?]' in M. S. G. McLeod *et al.*, *The Cathedral Libraries Catalogue: Books Printed before 1701 in the Libraries of the Anglican Cathedrals of England and Wales*, 3 vols. (London, 1984–98), I, p. 274.

[10] See e.g. the comments by the French Hobbes scholar and translator of *Leviathan*, François Tricaud: '2° l'édition à l'ours . . . imprimée sans doute en Hollande, et peut-être peu après 1651; 3° l'édition aux ornements . . . plus tardive, peut-être des environs de 1670, et peut-être londinienne' (T. Hobbes, *Léviathan*, tr. F. Tricaud (Paris, 1971), pp. xvi–xvii).

[11] Goldsmith's observation (which relates to p. 27 of the English edns) was reported by C. B. Macpherson in his edition of *Leviathan* (Harmondsworth, 1968), p. 67 (n.).

[12] Ibid., p. 68: 'It is just possible, though unlikely, if only in view of the inferior quality of the typesetting and proof-reading in the two later editions, that they were published with Hobbes's knowledge after 1668.' Macpherson's 'just' and 'unlikely' here applied apparently to the idea of Hobbes's involvement, not to the post-1668 dating, which he seemed to accept.

Similarly, Cornelis Schoneveld has argued that the Bear edition was probably produced after 1667, because the Dutch version of *Leviathan*, translated by Abraham van Berkel and published in that year in Amsterdam, was also based on the Head edition.[13] This, again, is not a strong argument. It rests on two assumptions: first, that the Bear was printed in Holland (which remains to be proved), and secondly, that copies of that edition would therefore have been more easily available in that country, if it had in fact been produced before van Berkel started work on his translation. Even if the first assumption is correct, the second does not follow: if the edition had been commissioned from a Dutch printer by an English bookseller, the entire printing might then have been shipped to England. (And, of course, if van Berkel had already possessed a copy of the Head, he would hardly have felt the need to buy an apparently identical reprint, even if Bears had been available in Holland at that time.) Nevertheless, Schoneveld has proposed on these grounds that the Bear was printed in Holland in or soon after 1670: he suggests that the failure of the attempted printing in London in that year 'may have been the immediate reason for seeking a foreign publisher'.[14]

More recently, a similar dating has been proposed by Horst Bredekamp, who writes that the Bear was printed in Amsterdam in or around 1670. However, one argument he uses to support this conclusion is rather different from Schoneveld's: he suggests the reason for this Dutch printing of the English text was that van Berkel's 1667 translation had stimulated interest in Hobbes's work in Holland. This would imply that the initiative came from a Dutch bookseller, and therefore that there was no necessary connection with the interrupted London printing of 1670.[15] Yet, at the same time, Bredekamp continues to use a date for the Bear— 1670—that has been introduced to the scholarly literature by writers such as Schoneveld only on the basis of what is known about the interrupted London printing. The idea that a Dutch bookseller would have printed a work in English to satisfy the interest of Dutch readers is, it must be said, highly implausible; although Dutch presses produced large quantities of English-language material, they did so only for the English market. While a few Dutch booksellers would keep small quantities of English-language works in their shops, there was only one who specialized in this material: Steven Swart. None of the English books sold by Swart (or, later, his widow) was printed in Holland specifically for Dutch readers; even

---

[13] C. W. Schoneveld, *Intertraffic of the Mind: Studies in Seventeenth-Century Anglo-Dutch Translation with a Checklist of Books Translated from English into Dutch, 1600–1700* (Leiden, 1983), p. 58.

[14] Ibid., p. 58. He also notes the suggestion by Macdonald and Hargreaves that the abortive 1670 printing was connected with the Ornaments edition, but argues that 'in the present argument it would fit better to connect that edition [*sc.* the Ornaments] to the references that exist to an edition in 1680' (p. 152, n. 91).

[15] H. Bredekamp, *Thomas Hobbes visuelle Strategien: Der Leviathan, Urbild des modernen Staates* (Berlin, 1999), p. 23: 'Möglicherweise hat die niederländische Ausgabe von 1667 das Interesse für das Original bestärkt, denn um 1670 wurde vermutlich in Amsterdam eine zweite Auflage der ersten, englischen Ausgabe publiziert.'

Willem Sewel's *A New Dictionary English and Dutch*, printed for the widow Swart, was aimed primarily at the English market (hence its English title).[16] Later in his argument, however, Bredekamp does also propose that the Dutch printer of the Bear must have been working hand in hand with Crooke: otherwise, he observes, the plate for the engraved title page would never have found its way to Holland. And he also alludes to what is perhaps the strongest argument in favour of assigning the Bear to the late 1660s or early 1670s, namely, the fact that (as Pepys recorded) copies of *Leviathan* had become so sought-after by 1668 that the price had risen to a dizzying thirty shillings.[17] This, clearly, was a level of demand that cried out for an increase in the supply.

## II

Thus far, the problem has resembled an equation with too many unknowns; it will never be possible to arrive at anything more than a range of possible but conjectural conclusions, unless new evidence is brought forward. One potentially valuable form of evidence, not considered by previous writers, is that provided by early ownership inscriptions, some of which record the date of acquisition. A search for dated inscriptions among a large number of recorded copies of *Leviathan* has yielded the following results.[18]

Head: 1652 (Rochester University, NY)[19]
Head: 1652 (Pforzheimer Library copy, University of Texas, Austin)
Head: 1653 (Christie's, London, 21 November 1961, lot 97)
Head: 1654 (State Library of Victoria, Australia)
Head: 1656 (Edinburgh University)[20]
Head: 1656 (Sotheby's, London, 15 December 1987, lot 294)
Head: 1656 (Berg Collection, New York Public Library)
Head: 1668 (Pepys Library, Magdalene College, Cambridge)
Head: 1669 (University of Southern California)

---

[16] See P. G. Hoftijzer, *Engelse boekverkopers bij de Beurs: de geschiedenis van de Amsterdamse boekhandels Bruyning en Swart, 1637–1724* (Amsterdam, 1987), and the comments in N. Hodgson and C. Blagden, *The Notebook of Thomas Bennet and Henry Clements (1686–1719) With Some Aspects of Book Trade Practice*, Oxford Bibliographical Society Publications, n.s., 6 (Oxford, 1953), p. 15. W. Sewel's *A New Dictionary English and Dutch* (Amsterdam, 1691) contains prefatory materials in Dutch as well as English, but the whole arrangement of the work gives priority to the needs of English users.

[17] Bredekamp, *Hobbes visuelle Strategien*, pp. 24–6 (referring to the Pforzheimer Library catalogue, which cites Pepys's diary entry for 3 Sept. 1668: see n. 29 below).

[18] This search has been conducted over a period of 16 years, by questionnaire and by personal inspection; I am very grateful to all the librarians and other individuals who have assisted me (including, of course, the great majority who had no such inscriptions to report), and regret that it is not practicable to thank them all individually here.

[19] The date in this copy is attached not to an ownership inscription but to a poem written on p. 331.

[20] The date in this copy is the date of presentation to the library.

Bear: 1678 (Trinity College, Cambridge)
Bear: 1681 (University of Colorado, Boulder)
Bear: 1681 (Bloomsbury Book Auctions, London, 16 July 1987, lot 222)
Bear: 1683 (House of Lords Library)

Ornaments: 1702 (Huntington Library, San Marino, Calif.)
Ornaments: 1709 (Aberdeen University)
Ornaments: 1717 (Trinity College, Cambridge)
Ornaments: 1731 (Juniata College, Penn.)
Ornaments: 1733 (Guildhall Library, London)

Two other copies, excluded from this list because they can be assumed to have been later second-hand purchases, may also be mentioned: a Head dated 1692 (Case Western Reserve) and a Bear dated 1717 (Temple University). Leaving aside those two copies, we can observe that the evidence presents a satisfyingly consistent pattern. The pattern, while of course not conclusive, is at least highly suggestive: the cluster of Bears in the period 1678–83 tallies quite closely with the evidence of Anthony Wood's remark and the entry in the Chiswell catalogue. And the dates of the copies of the Ornaments edition confirm the subjective impression which anyone who handles this edition is likely to have, namely, that the look and feel of the print and paper are those of an early eighteenth-century production.[21]

This chronological pattern is consistent too with the evidence of the watermarks in the Bear and Ornaments editions. In the Bear, the commonest watermarks are versions of the 'circles' design (three circles arranged vertically, topped by a crown): these are similar to (but not identical with) Heawood's no. 309 (London, 1683) and no. 314 (London, 1684).[22] Also found in the Bear edition is a 'pot' design, surmounted by a fleur-de-lis; this is similar to (but, again, not identical with) Heawood's nos. 3684–7 and 3689–93, which yield the following dates: London, 1673; England, 1677; London, 1662; London, 1657 or later; London, 1659; London, 1672; England, 1665–80. The paper of the Ornaments edition is not watermarked; but in the Bodleian's copy, which is in a contemporary binding, the endpaper before the engraved title page has a watermark of the arms of Amsterdam, similar to Churchill's nos. 32–40 (which are dated 1693–1703).[23] As is so often the case, the evidence of watermarks is too blunt an instrument to provide an answer to any precise question of chronology; but it can at least be said that it is in no way inconsistent here with the evidence of the dated inscriptions.

Since all the evidence now suggests that the Ornaments edition was not produced until the early eighteenth century, more than twenty years after Hobbes's

---

[21] I am grateful to Dr David McKitterick and Dr Giles Mandelbrote for giving me their personal confirmation of this point.

[22] E. Heawood, *Watermarks mainly in the 17th and 18th Centuries* (Hilversum, 1950).

[23] Bodl., pressmark Fol. *Δ* 753; W. A. Churchill, *Watermarks in Paper in Holland, England, France, etc., in the XVII and XVIII Centuries and their Interconnection* (Amsterdam, 1935).

death (in 1679), the relevance of that edition to the study of Hobbes's textual intentions must be assumed to be minimal. On the other hand, the firm evidence that the Bear was on sale during Hobbes's lifetime can only make the question of its origins more pressing: if this edition, available in 1678, was in any way related to the abortive printing of 1670 (carried out, apparently, at the behest of Hobbes's own publisher Andrew Crooke), then its textual changes might well have been derived from Hobbes himself. A closer examination of the story of that attempted printing is therefore needed.

Before leaving the dated inscriptions, however, it is useful to consider one other aspect of the evidence they provide: that of price. As was mentioned above, the most obvious reason for printing a second edition of *Leviathan* was to cash in on the notoriety of the book, which had pushed its price to unusually high levels. The evidence of the inscribed copies, combined with details drawn from other documents, is as follows:

Head: 1651, 8s. 6d. (Robert Payne, letter)[24]
Head: 1651, 8s. 6d. (Samuel Hartlib, bookseller's bill)[25]
Head: 1653, 8s. (William Cavendish, third Earl of Devonshire, account-book)[26]
Head: 1654, 9s. (State Library of Victoria, Australia)
Head: 1668, 24s. (Pforzheimer Library copy, University of Texas, Austin)
Head: 1668, 30s. (Pepys Library, Magdalene College, Cambridge)
Bear: 1678, 15s. (Trinity College Library, Cambridge)
Bear: 1681, 11s. (Bloomsbury Book Auctions, 16 July 1987, lot 222)
Bear: 1683, 17s. (House of Lords Library)
Head: 1692, 17s. (Case Western Reserve)
Ornaments: 1702, 21s. (Huntington Library, San Marino, Calif.)

The pattern here is a fairly consistent one, in which the Bear edition, although highly priced—at almost twice the sum charged for the Head on its first appearance—must have seemed like a bargain in comparison with the exorbitant price to which copies of the Head had risen.[27] The only anomaly here, the dip to 11s. in 1681, might be explained by supposing that this 1681 Bear was already a second-hand copy. The 1668 Head that sold for 24s. definitely was a second-hand copy; the

---

[24] BL, MS Harl. 6942, no. 132, Payne to Sheldon, 6 May 1651: 'I am advertisd from Oxf. y$^t$ M$^r$ Hobbes's booke is printed & come thither . . . It is in folio, at 8$^s$. 6$^d$. price.'

[25] Hartlib Papers, Sheffield University Library, electronic edn (Ann Arbor, Mich., 1993), 31/20/12A: 'Mr harlibs Bill 6th Iuly 1651 . . . hobs Leviathan 08—6.'

[26] Chatsworth, MS Hardwick 14, Privy Purse accounts, p. 6 (entry for Dec. 1653): 'By m$^r$ Halily for Bookes . . . Leuiathan 8s.'

[27] The prices recorded here may not, however, be strictly comparable, as in some cases they may not have included the cost of binding—which might have added a few shillings. (I am grateful to Dr Giles Mandelbrote for this point.)

previous owner, who had been given the book in 1652, had died in 1667.[28] But the 30s. recorded by Pepys was the price of a new copy, not a second-hand one—even though there must be some doubt over whether Pepys actually paid it. His diary entry for 3 September 1668 recorded 'calling on several businesses, and perticulary my bookseller's, among others, for Hobbs's *Leviathan*, which is now mightily called for; and what was heretofore sold for 8s I now give 24s at the second hand, and is sold for 30s, it being a book the Bishops will not let be printed again.'[29] Pepys's wording clearly implies that he had the choice between a second-hand copy and a new one; while the inscription in the copy he bought says 'Sept 1668—30s', the diary entry, together with other evidence, suggests that he did in fact take the cheaper option (afterwards, perhaps, entering the higher price in his copy in a spirit of self-aggrandizement).[30]

Clearly, the key development was the rise in price of the Head edition from 9s. in 1654 to 30s. in 1668. It is unfortunate that there appear to be no datable records of prices between those years. (Two undated inscriptions in seventeenth-century hands do exist in copies of the Head, giving the price as 18s. (University of Oklahoma) and 25s. (collection of the late Michael Gillingham, London): these may be conjecturally assigned to this period.)[31] It is possible that the price had risen steadily during the late 1650s and the 1660s, as Hobbes's notoriety grew.[32] However, two special factors may have boosted the price from 1666 onwards: the Fire of London, which destroyed many booksellers' stock, and the announcement in October of that year that the House of Commons committee considering the Bill against Atheism and Profaneness was investigating *Leviathan*.[33] This must

[28] The inscriptions are by P. de Cardonnel ('MDCLII ex dono nobiliss. Com. Deu.') and Charles Crompton: Harry Ransom Humanities Research Center, University of Texas at Austin, pressmark Pforzheimer 491. (The Pforzheimer catalogue (Anon., *The Carl H. Pforzheimer Library: English Literature 1475–1700*, 3 vols. (New York, 1940), II, p. 492) mistakenly gives the first inscription as '. . . Com. Dese'.) Pierre de Cardonnel received the volume from Hobbes's patron the Earl of Devonshire ('Com. Deu.'), and may well have known Hobbes personally. He died in Aug. 1667. See Ch. 9 above, pp. 259–316.

[29] S. Pepys, *Diary*, ed. R. Latham and W. Matthews, 11 vols. (London, 1970–83), IX, p. 298.

[30] Pepys Library, Magdalene College, Cambridge, pressmark 2037. On the same end-paper as this inscription there is a succession of inked pressmarks in Pepys's hand. These are preceded by two pressmarks in pencil (which Pepys never used for such purposes), one of which is crossed out in Pepys's ink; presumably those two were entered by a previous owner. Pepys recorded the price in a book only in very rare cases—all of them involving impressively high sums. Hence, no doubt, his recording of the higher price here. (I am very grateful to Dr Richard Luckett, Pepys Librarian, for his helpful comments on these matters, and for letting me inspect this copy.)

[31] One other undated copy is the Head edition in the Miami–Dade Public Library, Florida, inscribed with the price '5s'. This was presumably a second-hand purchase at an early stage, when new copies of the Head were still available for 8s. or 8s. 6d.

[32] As a rough index of Hobbes's notoriety, see the chronological 'Checklist of Anti-Hobbes Literature' in S. Mintz, *The Hunting of Leviathan: Seventeenth-Century Reactions to the Materialism and Moral Philosophy of Thomas Hobbes* (Cambridge, 1962), pp. 157–60.

[33] *The Journals . . . of the House of Commons* (London, 1742– ), VIII, p. 636; J. Milward, *Diary*, ed. C. Robbins (Cambridge, 1938), p. 25. I know of no evidence to justify the puzzling statement by George Kitchin that the Fire of London 'happened to coincide with the publication of . . . the *Leviathan*' (*Sir Roger L'Estrange: A Contribution to the History of the Press in the Seventeenth Century* (London, 1913), p. 165).

THE PRINTING OF THE 'BEAR'

have strengthened the impression that the ecclesiastical authorities would never allow the book to be reprinted. Presumably the new copies offered for sale in 1668 were the very last of the 1651 printing; when they were exhausted, perhaps later that year or in 1669, all the conditions would then be in place to encourage a surreptitious reprinting of the book.

## III

The first raid on John Redmayne's press took place on Wednesday, 28 September 1670. As he stated in his later affidavit: 'There came to my house M$^r$ Leak Master of the Company of Stationers with Warden Roper, accompanied with M$^r$ Norton and M$^r$ Mearne, who found at my house printing a book intituled Hobbes Leuiathan, and there seized on two sheets.'[34] On the following Monday (3 October) the Court of the Stationers' Company discussed Redmayne's case; the decisions made by the Court were recorded as follows:

Whereas this Co$^{rt}$ of Assistants were this Day given to vnderstand, that one Redmayne (a Printer, and member of this Company) has been lately discovered to Print a Book Called, Hobbs his Leviathan, w$^{ch}$ (as he affirmes) he was Imployed to doe, by one M$^r$ John Williams; It is Ord'red, That the Printing Presse, of the said Redmayne, be forthw$^{th}$ by the Wardens of this Company, taken downe and demolished And that the said Redmayne be suddenly indicted vppon the Act, for preventing vnlycensed Bookes, and Regulating the Presse.

Ordred that the foresaid Redmayne, be summoned to bring in all the heapes (now in his house) of the bookes called Hobbs his Leviathan, and Esopps Fabules, w$^{ch}$. he hath vnlawfully Printed &c.[35]

Redmayne's affidavit takes up the story.

The Thursday sennight following [sc. following Wednesday 28 September, i.e. Thursday 6 October] they came again and took away my Press, and demanded where the residue of the Sheets were, which I told them, were thirty eight more, & were also seized upon. They likewise demanded of me who I printed this book for, I told them for M$^r$ John Williams, who had it (he said) from M$^r$ Andrew Crook, with his order to print.[36]

The chronology of Redmayne's account is confirmed by an entry for 6 October 1670 in the Wardens' Accounts of the Stationers Company: 'Item paid at the

---

[34] PRO, SP 29/279/95(I). The date 'September 28$^{th}$ 1670' is written at the head of this page. All previous writers (e.g. Macdonald and Hargreaves, *Thomas Hobbes*, p. 29; Williams, 'Was There a 1670 *Leviathan*?' p. 82) have assumed that this is the date of the affidavit; but the sequence of events described in it, and confirmed by the other documents quoted here, plainly shows that this was the date of the first raid. The affidavit was written on 19 Oct., as the covering sheet by Samuel Mearne makes clear.

[35] Stationers' Company, London [hereafter: SC], Court Book D (Chadwyck Healey microfilm edn, reel 56), fol. 176r.

[36] PRO, SP 29/279/95(I).

taking downe of M̄ Redmaines Presses M̄ Tyler M̄ White M̄ Flesher M̄ Mearne at 3 severall places: 000 06 01.' And a further entry records an extra payment to a Company employee, Mr Cleaver: 'Item paid him more that hee had laid out vpon the taking downe M̄ Redmaines Presse and seizing of the sheetes of the Leviathan: 000 04 06.'[37]

As Redmayne's own account suggests, he was merely the small fry in this venture, the operative employed by not one but two more prominent booksellers. John Redmayne was a printer who had married the daughter of a well-known printer and bookseller, Roger Daniel, and had entered the Livery of the Stationers' Company, probably in 1658. (Even then there was a black mark on his record: as his petition to the Stationers' Company of December 1658 shows, he had been involved with his father-in-law in another unlicensed or irregular printing, for which both of them had been punished by the Company.[38]) From 1659 onwards Redmayne had a steady output as a printer: a survey in 1668 reported that his printing-house had four compositors, two pressmen, one apprentice, and two presses.[39] Although he did occasionally issue works under his own imprint, most of his printing was done for other booksellers: these included John Williams, among many others.[40]

During the 1640s and 1650s Williams had published a number of Anglican, royalist or anti-Cromwellian works, for which he frequently employed Redmayne's father-in-law, Roger Daniel, as his printer. Among them were as many as four editions of *Eikon Basilike*, an edition of Clement Walker's *The High Court of Justice: Or, Cromwells New Slaughter House in England* (the third part of his *History of Independency*), and several editions of works by Thomas Fuller. Given the evidence

---

[37] SC, Wardens' Accounts (reel 76), entry for that date.

[38] SC, Court Book D (reel 56), fol. 38v (6 December 1658): 'A peticion from M̄ John Redmayne was read setting forth that for his Father in law M̄ Daniells former miscarriages certaine Printing materialls were seized by the Wardens & by M̄ Field & M̄ Hills promising for himselfe all future Conformity to the Companies orders affirming that he accepted the Livery to testifie his respects to the Company & now desires to be admitted to the Livery or Yeomandry part in the Stocke & therefore praies restitucion or loane of the said Materialls to be returned if required which peticion was referred to the Wardens who are empowered to do therein as to them shall seem meete.' Redmayne's relationship with Daniel has not hitherto been noticed. On Daniel's career, see the valuable account in D. McKitterick, *A History of the Cambridge University Press*, 3 vols. (Cambridge, 1992– ), I, pp. 168–77, 296–306. After his dismissal from the post of university printer at Cambridge in 1650, Daniel had quickly established himself in London. The address he used in 1651 (Lovell's Court, Paternoster Row: see H. R. Plomer, *A Dictionary of the Booksellers and Printers who were at work in England, Scotland and Ireland from 1641 to 1667* (London, 1907), pp. 60–1) was the same as that later used by Redmayne (see below, n. 40).

[39] Plomer, *Dictionary 1641–1667*, p. 153. Redmayne was thus successful, but not exceptionally so: the same survey recorded, out of 26 printing-houses in total, one with six presses, two with five, and one with four (PRO, SP 29/243/181).

[40] Examples of Redmayne's solo productions include Anon., *Relation de l'entrée magnifique de Monsieur le Prince de Ligne* (1660: 'A Londres Par *Iean Redmayne*, & les vend au même lieu, en la ruë *Pater-Noster*, en la Maison *Lovellian*'); William Dugard, *The English Rudiments* (1665); J. A. Comenius, *Janua linguarum cum versione anglicana* (1670). Examples of his work for Williams include Thomas Fuller, *The Holy State* (1663) and J. A. Comenius, *Janua linguarum trilinguis* (1670).

of Redmayne's petition of 1658, it can be assumed that he had been working for Daniel up until that date—perhaps for several years. The connection between Daniel and Redmayne is also indicated by the ornaments they used: when Redmayne printed Fuller's *The Holy State* for Williams in 1663, he used precisely the same ornaments that Daniel had used in his earlier printings of that work in 1648 and 1652.[41]

One ornament used by Redmayne (and, probably, Daniel) deserves special attention. In 1655 Thomas Fuller's *The Church-History of Britain* was published in London, under the imprint 'printed for Iohn Williams'. On one page of this edition (sig. B3$^v$) there appears a version of the 'bear' ornament familiar to us from the second edition of *Leviathan*. At some time between 1655 and 1659 the bear ornament was used again on the title page of a work which was probably also published by Williams: another printing of Walker's *The High Court of Justice*. And in 1660 the bear reappears in the anonymous pamphlet which Redmayne printed on his own account, *Relation de l'entrée magnifique de Monsieur le Prince de Ligne* (p. 14, sig. B4$^v$).

This important evidence that a version of the bear ornament was being used in England in the 1650s and 1660s was first presented by K. A. Coleridge in 1984; unfortunately, her work seems not to have been noticed by Hobbes scholars.[42] Coleridge suggested, on the basis of the 1660 pamphlet, that Redmayne had also been the printer of the two earlier bear-ornamented works. Given what is known of Redmayne's relationship with Daniel, it seems more likely that Daniel was responsible for the two earlier publications, albeit with Redmayne working under him: the bear may then have passed from Daniel to Redmayne, by gift or loan. Coleridge also argued that the bear used in these three publications was 'identical' (apart from the displacement of a piece of foliage in the second and third of them) with the ornament used in the Bear *Leviathan*. As we shall see, the story is more complicated than that. Nevertheless, it is a striking fact that the only examples of a version of the bear ornament known to have been printed in England are all associated with either John Williams or John Redmayne—two of the three people involved in the attempted printing of *Leviathan* in 1670.[43]

As for the third of those printers and booksellers, Andrew Crooke, he seems not to have been penalized in any way as a result of the 1670 raid, despite being named

---

[41] All these details are presented in K. A. Coleridge, 'The Printing and Publishing of Clement Walker's *History of Independency 1647–1661*', *Bulletin of the Bibliographical Society of Australia and New Zealand*, 8 (1984), pp. 22–61 (except for the petition of 1658 and the relationship between Daniel and Redmayne, of which Coleridge was unaware).

[42] Ibid., esp. pp. 31, 51.

[43] One other English-language book contains a bear ornament: Anon. [Joseph Jane?], *EIKΩN AKΛAΣTOΣ: The Image Unbroken: A Perspective of the Impudence, Falshood, Vanitie, and Prophannes, Published in a Libell entitled EIKKONOKΛAΣTHΣ* (n.p., 1651), p. 267. However, it is likely that this work was printed abroad: see E. Almack, *A Bibliography of the King's book or Eikon Basilike* (London, 1896), p. 74.

in Redmayne's own affidavit. While Williams was eventually forced to pay the Stationers' Company £2 13s. 6d. in reimbursement of the expenses incurred in raiding Redmayne and obliterating the confiscated sheets, Crooke apparently escaped scot-free.[44] This may indicate that his slightly unusual procedure of commissioning another bookseller to commission a printer had served its essential purpose: deniability. And Crooke had good reason to wish to distance himself from any such surreptitious printing. On the one hand, he had his own reputation to consider, as one of the most senior and respected members of the Stationers' Company: he had served as Under Warden in 1660, Upper Warden in 1663, and Master of the Company in 1665 and 1666.[45] And, on the other hand, as Hobbes's regular publisher, he was well placed to know that the authorities (both civil and ecclesiastical) were strongly opposed to the printing or reprinting of any work by Hobbes on such a contentious subject.

Ever since the so-called Licensing Act came into force in June 1662 (requiring books on most subjects to be licensed by the Archbishop of Canterbury or the Bishop of London), a general ban seems to have been imposed on the publication of any works by Hobbes in the fields of politics, law, ecclesiology, or theology. His polemical defence of his own political record, *Mr Hobbes Considered*, just scraped through: it was probably already in the press in June 1662. Thereafter, the only books by Hobbes to be published in his lifetime (and the lifetime of the Licensing Act, which lapsed in the year of Hobbes's death, 1679) by Andrew Crooke or his cousin, William Crooke, were either mathematical and scientific treatises, or translations of Homer.[46] Works on more contentious subjects written in the 1660s such as *Behemoth* (a history of the Civil War) and the *Dialogue . . . of the Common Laws of England* were refused a licence—in the former case, even after Hobbes had personally asked for permission from the King. (As Aubrey later explained in a letter to Locke, the manuscript of *Behemoth* was a work which 'the King has read and likes extreamly, but tells him there is so much truth in it he dares not license for feare of displeasing the Bishops'.[47]) Hobbes managed to break through this barrier in only one rather minor case: after writing a brief response to the personal attack on him published by John Fell in 1674, he obtained the

---

[44] SC, Wardens' Accounts (reel 76), 12 Feb. 1675: 'Received of m\[r\] John Williams for soe much Expended in the seizure & Damasking part of Hobbs his Leviathan 002 13 6'. Admittedly, Crooke died in Sept. 1674, before this penalty was imposed on Williams; but there is no trace in the Stationers' Company records of any attempt either to penalize Crooke for this attempted printing in the period 1670–4, or to impose any charge for it on his widow thereafter.

[45] Plomer, *Dictionary 1641–1667*, pp. 56–7; D. F. McKenzie, 'Masters, Wardens and Liverymen of the Stationers' Company, 1605–1800' (typescript, 1974), s.v. 'Crooke'.

[46] See the entries in Macdonald and Hargreaves, *Bibliography*, and the valuable comments in P. Milton, 'Hobbes, Heresy and Lord Arlington', *History of Political Thought*, 14 (1993), pp. 501–46, esp. pp. 534–5.

[47] M. Cranston, 'John Locke and John Aubrey', *Notes and Queries*, 197 (1952), pp. 383–4; here p. 383. For Hobbes's own account of his approach to the King over *Behemoth*, and for a similar reference to the *Dialogue*, see Hobbes, *Correspondence*, II, pp. 771–2.

King's permission to publish it after approaching him in person 'in the Pall-mall in S<sup>t</sup> James's parke'.[48]

Otherwise, Hobbes seems to have professed a stoical acceptance of the ban, warning William Crooke not to publish *Behemoth* with the words, 'The King knows better, and is more concerned in publishing of Books than I am: Therefore I dare not venture to appear in the business, lest it should offend him . . . Rather than to be thought any way to further or countenance the printing, I would be content to lose twenty times the value of what you can expect to gain by it.'[49] Only the most suspicious reader of those sentences would wish to argue that the key phrases in them were 'to appear' and 'to be thought to'—meaning, in other words, that Hobbes's real objection was not to the fact of publication, but to the risk that his responsibility for it might be found out. And yet, where the 1670 printing of *Leviathan* is concerned, such suspicions may not be altogether far-fetched.

In the case of *Leviathan*, one extra factor may also have added to the apprehensions of both Andrew Crooke and Thomas Hobbes. The Bill against Atheism and Profaneness introduced in 1666 was given its final reading by the House of Commons in January 1667, and then passed to the House of Lords. In October of that year the Lords added to its provisions the creation of a further criminal offence: that of denying the immortality of souls, eternal rewards in Heaven, or eternal punishment in Hell. Progress on the Bill was halted by a legal opinion in 1668 (the judges consulted by the Lords said that such offences were not of temporal cognizance); but the Bill was never formally voted out, and would later be revived in both 1674 and 1675.[50] The significance of this further offence would not have been lost on Hobbes or his publisher: two of the themes of *Leviathan* most bitterly attacked by Hobbes's critics were his apparent 'mortalism', and his curious theory of the meaning of 'eternal punishment'. (He supposed that after the Last Judgement the wicked would live 'eternally' on earth, in the sense that there would be an unending succession of generations, but that each individual life would be finite.[51]) Indeed, the five significant changes made in the text of the Bear *Leviathan* all involved toning down this idiosyncratic eschatological theory.

Technically, of course, even if the Bill had been passed, Hobbes could not have been subjected to a retrospective prosecution for *Leviathan*: the Bill was not

---

[48] Bodl., MS Ballard 14, fol. 104r (Aubrey to Wood, 23 July 1674). For the background to this episode, and the text of Hobbes's response, see Hobbes, *Correspondence*, II, pp. 744–50, 918–19.

[49] Hobbes, *Correspondence*, II, p. 771.

[50] For all these details see Milton, 'Hobbes, Heresy and Arlington', pp. 517–20.

[51] On Hobbes's eschatology and 'mortalism' see J. G. A. Pocock, 'Time, History and Eschatology in the Thought of Thomas Hobbes', in his *Politics, Language and Time* (New York, 1971), pp. 148–201; N. T. Burns, *Christian Mortalism from Tyndale to Milton* (Cambridge, Mass., 1972), esp. pp. 183–91; J. M. Lewis, 'Hobbes and the Blackloists: A Study in the Eschatology of the English Revolution' (Harvard Ph.D. thesis, 1976), esp. pp. 137–50; D. Johnston, 'Hobbes's Mortalism', *History of Political Thought*, 10 (1989), pp. 647–63; P. D. Cooke, *Hobbes and Christianity: Reassessing the Bible in* Leviathan (Lanham, Md, 1996), pp. 214–19.

retroactive, and in any case a book published in 1651 was covered by the Act of Oblivion of 1660.[52] But there may well have been some doubt as to whether the action of producing a new edition of *Leviathan* would be covered by that indemnity, even if the text were the same as that produced in 1651. Such doubts would not only have strengthened the wish to produce the book as secretly as possible; they would also have suggested that the safest procedure was to print something which would look—to the casual observer—as if it were not a new edition at all. Hence, perhaps, the decision to produce a page-by-page reprint, with a repetition of the 1651 imprint on the title page. (That the title page contained, at the same time, an obviously different ornament is, however, one puzzle that remains to be solved: further comments on this point will be offered below.)

## IV

If the actions of Crooke, Williams, and Redmayne thus took place in a context of grave political risk, the same could be said for the actions of Samuel Mearne and the other officers of the Stationers' Company. For the long-running war of attrition between the Stationers and the 'Surveyor of the Press', Sir Roger L'Estrange, had just entered a new and much more critical phase. Since the mid-1660s there had been a rising tide of 'libels' (printed works offensive to Parliament, the Church or the Crown), and a new flood of such productions by disgruntled non-conformists had followed the passing of the Conventicle Act in 1670. As L'Estrange could see, merely to enforce the existing system of control was not sufficient, because that system had too many loopholes and overlapping jurisdictions—special warrants to the King's Printers, special licences from the Bishop of London which encroached on the rights of others, rights asserted by booksellers who were not Stationers but were free of some other company (especially the Haberdashers), and so on.[53] L'Estrange wished to reform the system itself; and a major part of his plan was that the Stationers should enact a completely new set of by-laws regulating their business. Discussions with the Company over this had been going on since the spring of 1670, but the Stationers, as always, dragged their feet. Then, on 19 August of that year, they received a notable shock. A *quo warranto* order was issued, requiring them to show by what authority they acted: the barely veiled threat was that their Charter would be revoked.[54]

L'Estrange now set out his terms. On the one hand, all booksellers would be forced to join the Stationers' Company, so that 'Private Presses will then fall of themselves: for yᵉ Greatest part of their Support is yᵉ Profit, they make of Stolen Coppies.' And on the other hand, 'When by this Course all Dealers in Bookes shall

---

[52] Milton, 'Hobbes, Heresy and Arlington', p. 519.   [53] See Kitchin, *Sir Roger L'Estrange*, pp. 184–7.
[54] Ibid., p. 190; C. Blagden, *The Stationers' Company: A History, 1403–1959* (London, 1960), pp. 154–5.

be subjected to yᵉ same Rule, it will be no hard matter to find out such Rules for yᵉ Company, as may secure yᵉ Press.'[55] The Company promised both to improve its conduct, and to draw up new by-laws, as requested; armed with these pledges, L'Estrange was then able to have the *quo warranto* proceedings halted on 20 September.[56]

It was thus a singular piece of ill-judgement that Crooke, Williams, and Redmayne should have chosen precisely this time to undertake a surreptitious printing of such a notorious book—or, if not ill-judgement, then at least bad luck, given that Redmayne had probably started work before 19 August.[57] Even after the *quo warranto* threat was withdrawn, the officers of the Stationers' Company must have felt unusually nervous about their future: one of the items of business at the meeting of the Court of the Company on 3 October (the same meeting at which the decision was taken to deal so severely with Redmayne) was the formation of a committee 'to treate wᵗʰ Mʳ L'estrange about Regulating the Presse'.[58] In such circumstances, a show of zeal in the suppression of unlicensed books was obviously a very desirable thing. And so it was that Mearne not only ordered the seizure of Redmayne's sheets and the dismantling of his presses, but also took the unusual step of obtaining a written account of these proceedings from Redmayne himself, and trying to deliver it in person to the Under-Secretary of State, Joseph Williamson, on 19 October.[59]

On the face of it, Samuel Mearne was a loyal servant of the Crown, and such zealous activity was no more than was to be expected of him. Originally the King's bookbinder, he had been promoted to partnership in the English Stock of the Stationers' Company at the special request of Secretary of State Nicholas in 1662; six years later, after his participation in a successful 'search' of an unlicensed printing, it was at the King's own request that he was admitted to the Court of the Company.[60] One modern writer has gone so far as to describe Mearne as one of 'Arlington's agents'—referring to Lord Arlington, the Secretary of State whose

---

[55] PRO, SP 29/278/167 (L'Estrange, memorandum dated 14 Sept. 1670).
[56] Kitchin, *Sir Roger L'Estrange*, p. 191; Blagden, *Stationers' Company*, p. 155.
[57] Redmayne's affidavit stated that 40 sheets had been printed by 6 October; normal production by one press-crew could be as high as six sheets per week, or as low as one or two (see D. F. McKenzie, 'Printers of the Mind: Some Notes on Bibliographical Theories and Printing-House Practices', *Studies in Bibliography*, 22 (1969), pp. 1–75; esp. pp. 14–15).
[58] SC, Court Book D (reel 56), fol. 176r.
[59] Mearne's covering note, addressed to Williamson and written at the 'Councell Chamber dore', states: 'If yᵉ Leviathan should be called for this Inclosed may serve for yᵉ Present. Yᵉ Printer is gon & I am in great hast & Just Leasure enough to Subscribe my selfe Sr your most humble Seruant Sam: Mearne' (PRO, SP 29/279/95).
[60] On Mearne see Plomer, *Dictionary 1641 1667*, p. 126, and the comments in J. S. T. Hetet, 'A Literary Underground in Restoration England: Printers and Dissenters in the Context of Constraints 1660–1689' (Cambridge University Ph.D. dissertation, 1987), pp. 83–4. On the 'English Stock' see Blagden, *Stationers' Company*, pp. 92–106.

deputy was Joseph Williamson, and under whose authority Sir Roger L'Estrange acted.[61]

But the truth was very different. Once the threat to the Company's Charter had been lifted, the officers of the Company, led by Mearne, resumed their procrastination. As a later denunciation of the Company, drawn up by John Seymour for a House of Lords enquiry in 1677, put it, 'The Danger (as they thought) being over, Notwithstanding divers express Commands from His Majesty under the Hand of a Secretary of State, requiring them to despatch their By-Laws; and continual Instances from Mr *L'Estrange* in His Majesties Name, by word of mouth, to the same purpose, they put off the Business above Six Years, without coming to a Conclusion.'[62] According to this writer, when L'Estrange addressed a Court of the Company on 14 July 1676 and demanded that they settle their new by-laws, 'a Leading Man at the Table [*sc.* Mearne] started up, and cry'd out, *This is Mr. L'Estranges humour, He has a mind to make the Company Slaves, Faith Ile be none of them.*'[63] It may be true that Mearne was very active during these years in closing down unauthorized presses; but the motivation for this was a desire to strengthen the monopoly of the Company, not a zeal to prevent the publication of so-called scandalous books.[64]

Indeed, where the interests of the Company—or, rather, the financial interests of Mearne and his friends—could be served by publishing such works, he seems to have had no scruples at all. The evidence assembled by John Seymour for the House of Lords inquiry in 1677 included the following statement, attested by two witnesses: 'M$^r$ Mearne and others of the Stationers having seized upon 1000: of Dyers Sermons an Vnlicensed Book M$^r$. Mearn sold the said Bookes to M$^r$: Royston, and M$^r$: Royston sold them to M$^r$. Write who sold them publickly in his shop.'[65] Another example of such behaviour concerned a notorious treatise against infant baptism by the dissenter Henry Danvers, printed by Francis Smith: when Samuel Mearne and Robert White had seized the entire print-run of 1,500 copies, and Lord Arlington ordered Mearne to deliver them to Whitehall, Mearne replied that he could not do so because he had already sent them to the Bishop of

---

[61] Milton, 'Hobbes, Heresy and Arlington', p. 536.

[62] House of Lords Record Office, London [hereafter: HLRO], House of Lords papers, 1676/7, item 338, fol. 121r, [John Seymour,] *The Case of Libels* (printed broadside, endorsed 'M$^r$ Seymours Paper Read 20° Martij 1676'). A useful summary of the papers of this House of Lords committee is printed in the Historical Manuscripts Commission, *Ninth Report*, App., pp. 69–79.

[63] HLRO, House of Lords papers, 1676/7, item 338, fol. 121r. The identification of Mearne is made in the Court's reply (fols. 125–6).

[64] SC, Box A, envelope II, item (ii) (reel 97): 'In Anno 1672 & 1673 M$^r$ Mearne being then one of the Wardens of the Company of Stacion:$^{ers}$ expended in Searches & disbursed in buying severall Printing Materialls of deceased Print:$^{ers}$ neer the summe of 1000$^{li}$ in hopes to reduce the number of printers according to the Act of Parliam$^t$.' (I am very grateful to Dr Robin Myers, Honorary Archivist of the Stationers' Company, for her help in tracing this document.)

[65] HLRO, House of Lords papers, 1676/7, item 338, fol. 127r. The summary of this document in the Historical Manuscripts Commission printing mistakenly gives 'White' for 'Write' (p. 77).

London, 'which thing was most apparently false'. Later, when Mearne and White discovered that the same book was being reprinted by another stationer, 'and understanding that it was printed for Thomas Sawbridge & Randal Taylor, two of Mearns great Favourits', they 'took no notice at all of it'.[66] Nor was such behaviour uncommon. An earlier witness statement acquired by L'Estrange, made by the wife of a well-known printer, said that Richard Royston had also sold copies of an unlicensed book which he had seized; in addition, Royston was said to have warned one of his friends about an impending search of his premises.[67] John Seymour's list of 'Particulars' against the Company began, therefore, with three serious charges: 'That several of the Chief men of the Company do both Sell, and Connive at many of those Libells, which they are Commanded to Search for, and Discover'; 'That they give Notice beforehand, of a Search to be made'; and 'That upon Information, they do sometimes put off Searching till things may be removed out of the way.'[68]

This is the background against which the episode of the 1670 printing of *Leviathan* must be considered. There are, after all, several aspects of that story— not only the story of the initial raid, but also of what later happened, or did not happen, to both the confiscated sheets and the printer—that arouse suspicion. It is odd, to begin with, that the officials of the Company on their first raid should only have made off with a sample of two sheets, not bothering at that stage to seize the rest of what had been printed. It is strange too that the decision to go ahead with a full-scale raid should have been made at a Court meeting on 3 October, but not carried out until three days later: the Court of the Company, which must have contained its fair share of friends of Crooke and Williams, was hardly the ideal vessel to contain such a secret. Then, when the second raid was carried out, the Company's officials seem to have depended on Redmayne to tell them how many other sheets he had printed, and where they were. This was a curiously gentlemanly affair, quite different from, for example, the raid on Nathaniel Thomson described in another submission to the House of Lords inquiry, at which 'the said Nathaniell Thomson making all the opposicion he could & cryed out Robbers, Theives Murderers Rogues, Notwithstanding the Wardens Constable and others were well Knowne to him and kept them out soe long that most of the Nights work was conveyed away'.[69]

---

[66] HLRO, House of Lords papers, 1676/7, item 338, fols. 127r, 127v: again, this story was confirmed by two witnesses.

[67] PRO, SP 29/187/172, 'The Fact concerning yᵉ Master & Wardens of yᵉ Company of Stationers'. For another striking example of such behaviour (by Royston) see Hetet, 'Literary Underground', p. 77.

[68] HLRO, House of Lords papers, 1676/7, item 338, fol. 121r. It is noteworthy that Mearne's response was not to attempt to disprove the allegations, but merely to make counter-charges of corruption against L'Estrange (fol. 129r). See also the valuable discussion of these issues in J. Hetet, 'The Wardens' Accounts of the Stationers' Company, 1663–79', in *Economics of the British Booktrade 1605–1939*, ed. R. Myers and M. Harris (Cambridge, 1985), pp. 32–59.

[69] HLRO, House of Lords papers, 1676/7, item 138, fol. 98r.

ASPECTS OF HOBBES

But the oddities do not stop there. The Court's decision to raid Redmayne's printing-house had referred not only to *Leviathan*, but also to an edition of Aesop (which infringed another printer's rights to that work). Yet within a few months, as John Hetet has noted, an edition of *Fabulae Aesopi* went on sale, with the imprint 'Ex officina Johannis Redmayne'.[70] Similarly, one of the entries in the Wardens' Accounts for 6 October (quoted above) clearly indicates that both of Redmayne's presses were dismantled; and yet Redmayne was able to produce five books in 1671, and four in 1672.[71]

No less puzzling is the subsequent history of the confiscated sheets of *Leviathan*. After the seizure in September and October 1670, a complete silence descended on this subject in the Stationers' Company records for more than three years. Then, on 11 December 1673, an order was sent to the Company by the Bishop of London: 'These are to Require You to Damask or obliterate whatsoever Sheets you have seized of a Book intitled, Leviathan: & for your so doing this shall be your Warrant.'[72] Despite this rather peremptory command, it took the Company roughly three months to comply: only on 24 March 1674 did the Wardens' Accounts record the payment of £1 13s. 'for damasking the Leviathan'.[73] On the following day the Company servant who had been entrusted with the task, William Bailey, wrote out a receipt for the payment he was given: 'Received of M$^r$ Samuell Mearne y$^e$ Summe of Thirty shillings for Damasking forty five Reames of the Leviathan and for carriage three shillings'.[74] The sheets made their next appearance in the records on 2 November 1674, when it was 'Ordred that the Damask sheetes of a Booke called Hobbes Leviathan bee delivered to Randall Taylor Beadle of this Company to be delivered to M$^r$ Jn$^o$. Williams and M$^r$. Tho: Sawbridge Members of this Company'.[75] And finally, on 12 February 1675, four years and four months after the original seizure, John Williams paid the Company £2 13s. 6d. 'for soe much Expended in the seizure & Damasking part of Hobbs his Leviathan'.[76] Taking these last two entries together, it becomes clear that Williams had not only reimbursed the Company for its expenses, but had also, in effect, bought back the sheets.

[70] Hetet, 'Wardens' Accounts', p. 45.
[71] Williams, 'Was There a 1670 *Leviathan*?' p. 83. Redmayne remained active as a printer until his death in c.1683: see M. Treadwell, 'London Printers and Printing Houses in 1705', *Publishing History*, 7 (1980), pp. 5–44, p. 36.
[72] SC Box A, envelope 3, item vi (reel 97). A later memorandum by the Company also referred somewhat casually to this order: under the heading 'In Michaelmas terme 1673' it stated, 'About this time came an order from the Bishopp of London to damask Hobbs his Leviathan which was accordingly done' (ibid., envelope 4, item vii). Damasking involved over-printing or stamping the sheets to render them illegible: see the discussion in C. C. Oman and J. Hamilton, *Wallpapers: A History and Catalogue of the Collection of the Victoria and Albert Museum* (London, 1982), p. 14, which also cites this example.
[73] SC, Wardens' Accounts (reel 76), entry for that date.
[74] SC, Box A, envelope 3, item vii (reel 97).   [75] SC, Court Book D (reel 56), fol. 240r.
[76] SC, Wardens' Accounts (reel 76), entry for that date.

## THE PRINTING OF THE 'BEAR'

There are, broadly speaking, three significant possibilities here. Redmayne may have yielded only some of his work (keeping either the entire print-run of some sheets, or a portion of the production of the forty sheets he handed over). Or, if all his work was handed over, some of the sheets may later have been siphoned off (before the damasking) and returned to him, or to Williams, or to Crooke. Or, again, the claim that the sheets were damasked may have been fictitious, with Williams bribing Bailey, the Company servant, to return some or all of the sheets to him in a usable condition. Combinations of these possibilities are also conceivable. There is no sure way of knowing what happened; but one intriguing aspect of the evidence does suggest that the first and second scenarios are more likely than the third. According to Redmayne's affidavit, forty sheets were taken; but according to William Bailey's receipt (quoted above), only forty-five reams were damasked. The discrepancy is striking. The normal print-run for such a work would most probably have been at least 1,000 copies, which would imply, therefore, that at least 40,000 sheets were seized. Yet forty-five reams of paper is only 21,600 sheets: if this was the genuine total, with nothing withheld or siphoned off before that stage, then the print-run would have had to be the surprisingly low figure of 540 copies. If William Bailey had been responsible for any deception (such as saving, on average, 460 copies of each sheet from the damasking process), he would surely have covered his tracks more convincingly, instead of leaving what, in the eyes of experienced printers, would have been such a glaring clue.

This suggests two things: that the record of damasking is probably genuine, and that a significant proportion of the printing had indeed been either withheld at the outset or subsequently siphoned off. Again, if the first and second scenarios are therefore to be preferred to the third, then on the same grounds one might suspect that the second is more plausible than the first: the officers who raided Redmayne's printing-house on 6 October were also experienced printers, and would have had some idea of the quantity of paper taken up by forty sheets in a normal print-run. But this is to assume that they were not already conniving with Redmayne at that stage, which is a rather uncertain assumption.

These various speculations all point, however, towards the same two overall conclusions. First, if the Bear *Leviathan* was indeed based on a salvaged rump of Redmayne's printing, then it would seem likely that the total number of copies of the Bear was, in the end, smaller than that of a normal print-run. While there is no sure way of testing this hypothesis, some evidence does at least support the idea that the quantity of Bears printed was much smaller than that of Heads. Anyone who has searched for early editions of *Leviathan* will be aware that there are simply many more Heads than Bears in existence today. A rough indication is given by the annual volumes of *Book-Auction Records*, which record the number of copies offered for sale between 1962 and 1997 as 101 Heads and 37 Bears.[77] (Before 1962 the records are less reliable, as many auction catalogues failed to differentiate between the editions; apparently it took ten years after the publication of Macdonald and Hargreaves's bibliography for the distinctions to become generally recognized. Many other earlier cataloguings are unreliable: a significant number of 'Bears' listed in the *National Union Catalog* are in fact Heads.[78]) In England the holdings of cathedral libraries and Oxford colleges are heavily weighted in favour of Heads; but there may be some special reasons for this.[79] (It was, for example, at Oxford that *Leviathan* was publicly burnt, together with other 'false, seditious, and impious books', by order of Convocation in 1683; many of the copies that fuelled those flames may have been of the newly available printing.[80]) On the other hand, the argument could be turned round by supposing that the print-run of the Head had been unusually large: the state of the title page engraving, which was seriously worn by the time it was used in the Bear, might be offered as evidence for this theory. Overall, therefore, this particular line of argument must be regarded as inconclusive.

The second implication of the scenarios sketched above is, however, more promising. For what they all suggest is that there should be two different types of sheet in any copy of the Bear—the salvaged sheets, and the subsequent completion—with, perhaps, some discernible differences between them. It cannot be assumed, however, that this distinction would apply simply to forty sheets (or thirty-eight, if Redmayne had reprinted by 6 October the two sheets seized on 28 September) versus the rest. The salvaging may have been a more haphazard process, in which varying amounts of different sheets were retained or recovered; if some sheets survived only in small quantities, these might then have been discarded, to be replaced by new sheets in the completion of the printing. Nevertheless, a closer examination of the internal make-up of the Bear is clearly called for.

Before leaving the records of the Stationers' Company, it is useful to consider the light they shed on one further aspect of the story: the possible line of transmission connecting Andrew Crooke, the organizer of the 1670 printing, with Richard

---

[77] *Book-Auction Records: A Priced and Annotated Annual Record*, 59 (1962, for 1961–2)–95 (1999, for 1997). The total for the Ornaments edition is even smaller, however: 23.

[78] So-called Bears that are in fact Heads include copies at the British Columbia Legislative Assembly Library, Case Western Reserve, Swarthmore College, the University of Michigan (W. L. Clements Library), and Wellesley College.

[79] The cathedral libraries of England and Wales have eight Heads and one Bear (*Cathedral Libraries Catalogue*, I, p. 274); the Oxford colleges have nine Heads and one Bear (see the annotated copy of Wing's *Short-Title Catalogue* in the catalogue room of the Bodleian Library, pressmark B1. 456*).

[80] For the decree see Mintz, *Hunting of Leviathan*, pp. 61–2; for the bonfire (at which 'the scholars of all degrees and qualities in the meane time surrounding the fier, gave severall hums whilst they were burning'), see A. Wood, *The Life and Times of Anthony Wood, Antiquary, of Oxford, 1632–1695, Described by Himself*, ed. A. Clark, 5 vols. (Oxford, 1891–1900), III, p. 63.

Chiswell, the advertiser of *Leviathan* in 1680. Andrew Crooke died in September 1674, leaving his widow, Elizabeth, substantial debts: he had, apparently, been badly affected by the Fire of London, from which his finances never fully recovered. So tangled were his affairs that the Court of the Company ordered a special investigation of 'M$^r$ Crookes Acc:$^{ts}$ w$^{th}$ this Company' at its meeting on 5 February 1675.[81] Elizabeth Crooke was doing her best to realize available assets, by, for example, selling the rights in some of her late husband's titles to other booksellers. But at a meeting of the Court of the Company on 22 February 1675, this process underwent a significant intervention: 'Vpon the reading of an Assignm$^t$ made by M$^{rs}$ Crook to M$^r$ Wright & alsoe of a Catalogue of severall bookes thereunto annexed it is ordered that Hobbes Leviathan be not entred.'[82]

John Wright was a well established bookseller (active since the 1630s) whose name has already featured briefly in this account: he was the 'M$^r$. Write' who obtained copies of a seized book from Richard Royston, and 'sold them publickly in his shop'.[83] Someone who had so openly flouted the law would not have allowed a mere resolution of the Company's Court to deter him from obtaining the rights to such a desirable title as *Leviathan*—especially if there was some prospect of putting a new printing of it on sale. And if John Wright did buy the rights to *Leviathan* from Mrs Crooke, then the connection with Richard Chiswell is easily made: Wright and Chiswell had been acting as business partners as early as 17 September 1673, when another list of titles was sold to them jointly by Samuel Mearne.[84] By the end of the decade, when Richard Chiswell was helping to pioneer the 'conger' system of joint publication, his name would be linked quite frequently to that of Wright: both men were in congers producing one book in 1678, two in 1679, and four in 1680.[85] And in 1681 Chiswell and Wright would appear jointly as defendants in an action for debt.[86] Richard Chiswell was one of the most active and enterprising booksellers of the period; he was also no stranger to under-the-counter dealing, as a later reference in John Strype's correspondence makes clear.[87]

---

[81] SC, Court Book D (reel 56), fol. 242r.

[82] Ibid., fol. 244r. Hetet incorrectly attributes the attempted assignment to Andrew Crooke: 'Wardens' Accounts', p. 45.

[83] See above, n. 65. On Wright see Plomer, *Dictionary 1641–1667*, p. 198, and his *A Dictionary of the Booksellers and Printers who were at work in England, Scotland and Ireland from 1668 to 1725*, ed. A. Esdaile (Oxford, 1922), p. 321.

[84] Anon., *A Transcript of the Registers of the Worshipful Company of Stationers from 1640–1708 A.D.*, 3 vols. (London, 1913–14), II, p. 469.

[85] Wing R2106 (1678); D192, P3170 (1679); R1084A, R2318, S2766, T2232 (1680).

[86] Plomer, *Dictionary 1668–1725*, p. 321.

[87] Cambridge University Library, MS Add. 1, no. 59, Strype to his cousin, 7 Dec. 1687 (referring to a 'dangerous' book); Strype has annotated his copy of the letter: 'This was y$^e$ Bp of Corks Discourse intitled Free thoughts, w$^{ch}$ I got printed by Rich. Chiswel: but soon after search was made for y$^m$ by H. Hills Master of Stationers company, & some hundreds seized.' On Chiswell see the entry in the *DNB*; Plomer, *Dictionary 1641–1667*, pp. 45–6; and M. Treadwell, 'London Trade Publishers 1675–1750', *The Library*, 6$^{th}$ ser., 4 (1982), pp. 99–134; esp. pp. 104, 115.

The evidence of the dated inscriptions, given above, shows that the Bear edition was on sale by 1678. At this stage, perhaps, the distribution of copies by Wright and/or Chiswell was still somewhat secretive; it was probably the lapsing of the Licensing Act in 1679 that emboldened Chiswell to advertise the book in his catalogue of the following year. He had, after all, a valuable finished product to sell, with a premium price (probably 15s.) attached to it. What remains to be determined is exactly how that product had been finished.

## V

The Bear edition of *Leviathan*, like the Head edition which it imitates, is a small folio, in fours. Thus, a gathering contains two sheets: the outer sheet has the signatures 1 and 4, and the inner sheet has 2 and 3. There are a hundred sheets, plus a folding table, plus the engraved title page. Some features of the Head have been quite carefully reproduced, such as the page numbering (which repeats 247–8, and omits 257–60) and the signature numbering (signed on 1 and 2 up until sig. Bb, then 1, 2, and 3 from Cc to the end).[88] In the Head edition, the change in the signature numbering halfway through the book is one of several indications that the work was divided between two printers at that point.[89] The fact that the Bear mimics this division in its signature numbering does not, of course, imply that its own printing was similarly divided into two neat halves.

However, a close inspection of the Bear does in fact reveal that its sheets were divided between two compositors or printers using different typefaces—though the division is far from neat. In most cases (but not all), the pages can be quickly identified by their running titles: one typeface is usually associated with a running-title in small capital letters, while the other sets its running-title in a larger type. As a rough guide, therefore, the two typefaces can be distinguished by reference to 'small-title' pages and 'large-title' pages. The most easily identifiable feature of the small-title pages is the use of a semi-colon in which the comma element makes an unusually full, billowing curve; the equivalent element in the large-title pages is modest and quite normal. In the small-title pages the top of the most commonly used long 's' also leans generously far over to the right; again, the large-title pages have a more normal version of this letter. Italic '*w*' in the text of the small-title pages has the form of two contiguous 'v's; the equivalent in the large-title pages is looped at the centre. The design of italic ampersand is also different—and, indeed, there are minute differences of design or proportion to be observed in almost every other letter-form. It must be said, nevertheless, that in overall character the two typefaces

---

[88] There are, however, a few discrepancies. While the final pages of the Head are correctly numbered up to 396, those in the Bear end with the sequence 393, 394, 397, 394. Also, the sheets in the gatherings Vv and Xx are signed in the Bear only on 1 and 2.

[89] See the comments in the Pforzheimer Library catalogue, Anon., *English Literature 1475–1700*, II, p. 493.

| Small-title typeface | Large-title typeface | Small-title typeface | Large-title typeface |
|---|---|---|---|
|  | A |  | Aa |
| B |  |  | Bb |
| C |  |  | Cc |
|  | D |  | Dd |
|  | E | Ee |  |
|  | F1, F4 | Ff |  |
| F2, F3 |  | Gg |  |
| G1, G4 |  | Hh |  |
|  | G2, G3 | Ii |  |
|  | H1, H4 |  | Kk1, Kk4 |
| H2, H3 |  | Kk2, Kk3 |  |
| I1, I4 |  |  | Ll |
|  | I2, I3 |  | Mm |
|  | K |  | Nn |
|  | L |  | Oo |
| M |  |  | Pp |
|  | N |  | Qq |
|  | O |  | Rr |
|  | P | Ss |  |
|  | Q1, Q4 | Tt |  |
| Q2, Q3 |  | Vv |  |
|  | R | Xx |  |
| S |  | Yy |  |
| T |  | Zz |  |
|  | U | Aaa |  |
|  | X | Bbb |  |
|  | Y | Ccc |  |
|  | Z | Ddd |  |

are a good match—so good, indeed, that the difference between them has apparently remained unnoticed to this day.

But the most striking aspect of this evidence is the pattern of distribution of the pages between the two typefaces. The first gathering, sig. A, is in the large-title typeface; sigs. B and C are in the typeface of the small-title pages; then sig. D reverts to large-title, and so on. In some gatherings each sheet is in a different typeface. The distribution through the whole volume can be tabulated as shown above. (The folding table also shares the typeface of the small-title pages.)

By any standards, this distribution of the material is quite bizarre—even allowing for the fact that, in this case, the book was being copied page by page from a previous printing. If two press-crews had been employed simultaneously in the same printing-house, they might well have started at opposite ends of the book, or could perhaps have worked out some slightly more elaborate division of labour; but they would surely not have shared individual gatherings between them in what seems here, in places, to be such an utterly randomized way. (They would also surely have used the same typeface.) *A fortiori*, no normal sharing-out of the work between two printing-houses would have adopted such a pattern. Only some very abnormal circumstances could explain this division—such as a raid on a printing-house, a somewhat haphazard salvaging of sheets, and a subsequent completion of the printing elsewhere. This typographical evidence constitutes, in other words, the strongest possible confirmation of the hypothesis that the Bear *Leviathan* is the completed rump of Redmayne's 1670 printing.

The same evidence, however, raises another question, to which the answer is not immediately apparent: which of those two sets of sheets was the original Redmayne printing, and which was the completion? In theory, it might be possible to match one or other of these typefaces—or the watermarks of the pages on which they appear—with known Redmayne printings of the same period. An examination of all Redmayne's recorded output has yielded some suggestive findings, but nothing absolutely conclusive. The small-title typeface appears to be identical with the type used in two books printed by him, Samuel Hinde's *England's Prospective-Glasse* (1663) and Peter du Moulin's *A Vindication of the Sincerity of the Protestant Religion* (1664)—with the exception, however, of that distinctive long 's'. As for watermarks, the ones already mentioned (the 'circles' design, and the 'pot') are found only in the small-title pages of the Bear, while the large-title pages have only one rather infrequent watermark, consisting of the initials 'A P'. (This correlation of watermarks and typefaces also counts strongly against the idea that the book could have been produced by two press-crews in the same printing-house.) A close match for the 'pot' design can be found in two Redmayne printings of just the right period, *Remains of Sir Walter Raleigh* (1669) and T. B. [Thomas Beverley,] *The General Inefficacy and Insincerity of a Late, or Death-bed Repentance* (1670); nevertheless, there are some small differences, for example in the lettering on the body of the pot.[90] On balance, this evidence suggests that the small-title pages are more likely to have been the ones printed by Redmayne; but it fails to prove the point. Firmer proof can be obtained, however, from an examination of

---

[90] The comparison here is between the following copies: Bear *Leviathan*: Houghton Library, Harvard, pressmark *fEC65 H6525 651bb, watermarks of sigs. M3 and Zz2; W. Raleigh, *Remains of Sir Walter Raleigh* (London, 1669): Houghton Library, Harvard, pressmark *EC R1384 657rd, watermarks of sigs. A7 and E12; T. Beverley, *The General Inefficacy and Insincerity of a Late, or Death-Bed Repentance* (London, 1670): BL, pressmark T. 995 (1), watermarks of sigs. b2, A2.

the two famous ornaments that decorate this volume: the St Christopher, and the bear.

## VI

As mentioned above, the existing state of knowledge about these two ornaments is based largely on a letter from an unnamed Dutch bibliographer (at the Royal Library in The Hague) sent in reply to a query from Macdonald and Hargreaves, and reproduced in their bibliography of Hobbes. On the St Christopher ornament, this writer observed: 'As yet we cannot prove it, but it seems highly probable that the vignette of Christophorus with the initials C. C. must be some device of the Amsterdam printer Christoffel Cunradus.' And on the bear, the only comment was: 'Although the bear is well known from Amsterdam books, we were not able to trace any Cunradus edition with it.'[91] Macdonald and Hargreaves let the matter rest there—not least, perhaps, because so few Cunradus imprints (the majority of them being in Dutch or German) have ever found their way into the major British research libraries.[92]

However, a search of Cunradus printings, conducted using the imprint catalogues in the Royal Library at The Hague and the Amsterdam University Library, has yielded a more definite result. In 1671 Cunradus printed, as a quarto pamphlet, a Dutch sermon preached at the inauguration of the second Lutheran church in Amsterdam: Volckard Visscher, *De waare tempel voorgesteld in een inwyings predicatie van de tweede en nieuwe kerck van de gemeente d'onveranderde Ausburgse* [sic] *belydenis toegedaan in Amsterdam*. Here, at the head of the first page of text, one finds the St Christopher ornament, exactly as in the Bear *Leviathan*.[93] This appears to be the only occurrence of this ornament in a work issued under Cunradus's own individual imprint, though a variety of other designs used by him as title page or

---

[91] Macdonald and Hargreaves, *Bibliography*, p. 28.
[92] One significant exception deserves mention: the composite volume in the BL (pressmark 855 i l), issued with the general title page *Collectio, of versamelinge, van eenige van de tractaten, boeken, en brieven, die geschreven sijn door verscheyde vrienden der waerheyt, die van de wereld, spots-gewijse, genoemt worden Quakers*, which contains 72 Dutch-language Quaker tracts, produced by various printers between 1657 and 1674 (many of them translations of English works, omitted from the checklist of Anglo-Dutch translations in Schoneveld, *Intertraffic of the Mind*). Eighteen items here were printed by Cunradus; none of them, however, contains the bear or the St Christopher ornament. (See also n. 156 below.)
[93] Amsterdam University Library [hereafter: UBA], pressmark 394 E 22(4); Royal Library, The Hague, pressmark 559 J 66 (11); the ornament is on p. 3 (sig. A2r). I am particularly grateful to the staff of the Fontaine Verwey reading room at the UBA for their patience in letting me order up such a large number of volumes in succession. After I had completed this research, I was enabled (by the kindness of Nicholas Smith) to consult the newly published reference work by P. van Huisstede and J. P. J. Brandhorst, *Dutch Printer's Devices 15th–17th Century: A Catalogue*, 3 vols. (Nieuwkoop, 1999). This is not a list of ornaments in general, only of those used as printer's devices; therefore it does not include the use of the St Christopher discussed here. (But it does list one example of its use as a device, in the work issued by Cunradus, van Meurs and van Someren in 1678: I, p. 362, no. 0714.)

colophon ornaments in many of his books did include either the image of St Christopher, or the initials 'C.C.', or both.[94]

But, just like John Redmayne, Christoffel Cunradus did not print only for himself: he was also frequently engaged as a printer for other booksellers. In 1678 the Amsterdam engraver and bookseller Jacob van Meurs (together with another bookseller, Johan van Someren) issued a German translation of a travel narrative by Johan Struys, *Joh. Jansz. Straussens sehr schwere, wiederwertige, und denckwürdige Reysen durch Italien, Griechenland, Lifland, Moscau*. This work also must have been printed by Cunradus: it contains a vignette with his monogram on the title page, another device with the same monogram on the final page, and, over the first page of the preface, the St Christopher ornament used in *Leviathan*.[95] There can be little doubt that Cunradus was regularly employed by van Meurs: significantly, the same St Christopher block can be found in at least five other books published by van Meurs (or, in the last case, his widow) in 1669, 1675, 1677, 1680, and 1681.[96]

The last two of these books were typical van Meurs publications: lavishly illustrated editions of a geographical compilation about Asia by Olfert Dapper, issued first in Dutch and then in German translation. And, together with the St Christopher ornament which marks them as Cunradus printings, they also contain one other significant piece of evidence: the 'bear' ornament, exactly as it appears in the second edition of *Leviathan*.[97] Cunradus did not apparently use this in any of the books he produced under his own imprint; but precisely the same bear can be found in two other Dapper compilations which he must have printed for van Meurs, in another geographical work printed for van Meurs's widow, and in one other book printed by him for some of van Meurs's known associates.[98]

---

[94] For example, *Jakob Böhmens erste Apologia wider Balthasar Tilken* (Amsterdam, 1677) has two St Christopher devices, one (oval) on the title page, the other (oblong) on the final page; the oval also contains a monogram which includes the letters 'C.C.' J. Colerus, *Des menschen roem, is maer een bloem* (Amsterdam, 1683), has a version of that monogram in the ornament on the final page, and a memento mori device on the title page with the initials 'C.C.' These ornaments are listed as devices used by Cunradus in van Huisstede and Brandhorst, *Dutch Printer's Devices*, I, pp. 360–2 (nos. 0191, 0144/1905, 1952, 1129).

[95] UBA, pressmark 1733 A 23: the St Christopher is on sig. *3r.

[96] J. Nieuhof ['Neuhof'], *Die Gesandtschaft der Ost-Indischen Gesellschaft in den Vereinigten Niederländern an den tartarischen Cham* (Amsterdam: van Meurs, 1669), sig. *3r; Anon., *Bedenkwürdige Berichtung der Niederländischen Ost-Indien Gesellschaft in dem Kaiserreich Taising oder Sina* (Amsterdam: van Meurs, 1675), sig. †3r; P. Valckenier ['Valkenier'], *Das verwirrte Europa*, vol. I (Amsterdam: van Meurs, van Someren, H. and D. Boom, 1677), sig. *1r; O. Dapper, *Naukeurige beschryving van Asie* (Amsterdam: van Meurs, 1680), sig. *3v; O. Dapper, *Asia, oder genaue und grundliche Beschreibung* (Amsterdam: widow van Meurs, 1681), 'Vorrede an den Leser'.

[97] Dapper, *Naukeurige beschryving van Asie*, title page; Dapper, *Asia, oder genaue und grundliche Beschreibung*, second section, separately paginated with the new title page *Genaue und grundliche Beschreibung des gantzen Palestins*, title page and final page of text (p. 456).

[98] O. Dapper, *Naukeurige beschrijvinge der Afrikaensche gewesten*, 2nd edn (Amsterdam: van Meurs, 1676), second section, separately paginated, p. 349; O. Dapper, *Naukeurige beschryving van gantsch Syrie, en Palestyn of Heilige Lant* (Amsterdam: van Meurs, 1677), title page; J. Nieuhof, *Zee en Lant-reize, door verscheide gewesten van Oostindien* (Amsterdam: widow van Meurs, 1682), p. 303; A. Müller ['Mullern'], *Des*

There can thus be little doubt that the completion of the printing of *Leviathan* was carried out by Christoffel Cunradus in Amsterdam. And, since the first gathering of that volume (sig. A), which includes both the St Christopher ornament and the title page bear, uses the typeface of the 'large-title' pages, this means that Redmayne must have printed the small-title pages—as other evidence, presented above, had already suggested. There is some more circumstantial evidence that also supports the attribution of the large-title pages to Cunradus. Those pages of *Leviathan* include three ornamental capitals: 'Y' on sig. A2r, 'N' on sig. A4r (p. 1), and 'I' on sig. Cc1r (p. 195). All are from the same alphabet of ornaments, with letters enhanced by strong shadowing and set against a background of foliage in a very distinctive style. Many Cunradus printings have ornamental capitals which appear to be from the same set, and in some cases the individual letters can be matched; thus, the *Leviathan* 'N' appears to be identical to one in Dapper, *Naukeurige beschryving van Asie* (sig. *3v), and the *Leviathan* 'I' matches one in a book issued under Cunradus's own imprint in 1668, an edition of J. A. Comenius, *Via lucis vestigata & vestiganda* (sig. *2r). However, similar sets of ornamental capitals appear to have been in wide circulation during this period, so this cannot be treated as more than a supporting argument.

One other kind of circumstantial evidence may also be mentioned: the fact that the large-title pages of the Bear *Leviathan* contain a much higher proportion of misprints. To give just one example: while p. 44 (sig. G1v, a small-title page) has no misprints at all, p. 45 (sig. G2r, a large-title page) contains 'opininon', 'rasnesse' (for 'rashnesse'), 'hat' (for 'hath'), 'Amonghst' and 'cotinually'. Even the title page has a glaring misprint, describing the work as 'Printed for ANDREW CKOOKE'. These blunders are easily explained on the assumption that the large-title pages were set by Dutch compositors. Although many English-language works were produced in Holland in the seventeenth century, it cannot be presumed that the average compositor there had any knowledge of the language. Even Willem Sewel's *A New Dictionary English and Dutch* (1691)—printed, as mentioned above, for the widow Swart, a specialist in English-language materials—included an apology to the readers for the number of misprints it contained, 'because the Workmen, not understanding the English, have not used that carefulness which was requisite in such a Work as this'.[99] At the same time, when the Dutch setters of the large-title pages were

---

*verwirrten Europae Continuation* (Amsterdam: widow van Someren, and H. and D. Boom, 1680), p. 300 and end of index (sig. h1r). This was the second volume of the work by Valckenier, also printed by Cunradus, listed above (n. 96).

[99] Sewel, *New Dictionary*, end of second section (p. 431). Curiously, Sewel's book also includes both the *Leviathan* bear (second section, end of Preface, sig. *2v), and one of Cunradus's 'C.C.' devices (third section, p. 72). Cunradus probably did work for Steven Swart, and there are 'C.C' ornaments in other Swart imprints (see Hoftijzer, *Engelse boekverkopers*, p. 70). But he was not responsible for this book: he had died in 1684, and his widow had sold off not only his press but also his type and ornaments ('alderhande curieuse houte gesnedene letteren en figuren') at an auction in 1690 (I. H. van Eeghen, *De Amsterdamse boekhandel 1680–1725*, 5 vols. (Amsterdam, 1963–78), IV, p. 272).

not introducing misprints, they followed the spelling of the original quite slavishly; whereas the small-title pages, set by English compositors, frequently modernized the old forms of the 1651 text, with 'war' for 'warre', 'do' for 'doe', and so on.

Having established which sheets were printed by Cunradus and which by Redmayne, one may now try to construct some sort of scenario to explain the distribution tabulated above. While much remains unclear about what exactly happened when, and after, Redmayne's printing-house was raided, one possible deduction might be that he had set two teams to work at the book from both ends, and that they had almost met in the middle, with one team getting at least as far as Kk3, and the other reaching Ss. Perhaps the sheets from the end of the book were retained by Redmayne, with a selection of sheets from the first half being handed over—some of which (though perhaps not the full print-run in the case of all the sheets) were later re-acquired. Presumably, too, the plate of the engraved title page was not handed over; the engraving, which is not part of the first gathering of the book, may have been printed in England when the book was finally assembled. Other scenarios might be devised; but at least the attribution of the small-title pages to Redmayne now seems secure.

One other point is worth looking at again in the light of this attribution: the fact that the significant textual changes in the Bear edition are all to be found on small-title pages, in the final part of the book. Of course, even if they were on large-title pages, they could still be attributed to Hobbes. Cunradus must have received a copy of the Head, marked with those pages that he was required to reproduce, and it would have been an easy matter to insert any Hobbes-derived textual changes in the margins of that copy. On balance, however, it does seem more in keeping with the idea of Hobbesian responsibility for these changes that they should be found in the pages of the initial printing: we know that Andrew Crooke, who was in direct contact with Hobbes, was involved at that stage, but we do not know what degree of involvement he had in the printing by Cunradus, which may have taken place after his death.

Bibliographically, the most important of these changes is the one affecting pp. 345–6 (sig. Xx3): here an entire passage has been omitted, and the printer, to compensate, has had to adjust the setting of the text over the entire gathering. Accordingly, this is the one place in the book where the page-by-page matching of the Head edition breaks down. (The disruption thus caused may also explain the fact, noted above, that Xx and Vv are the only gatherings that fail to copy the signature-numbering of the original.[100]) The omitted passage ran as follows: 'For the wicked being left in the estate they were in after Adams sin, may at the Resurrection live as they did, marry, and give in marriage, and have grosse and corruptible bodies, as all mankind now have; and consequently may engender

---

[100] See above, n. 88.

perpetually, after the Resurrection, as they did before: For there is no place of Scripture to the contrary.' Significantly, this passage was also omitted from Hobbes's Latin translation of *Leviathan*, published in 1668. There he modified his theory, conceding that the generations of the reprobate would not continue 'perpetually' on earth, but only until some far-off moment, the 'finis seculi', when the earth itself would cease to exist; and so in place of this passage he inserted a short excursus on the meaning of the word 'seculum'.[101]

Hobbes may have been seriously rattled by the provisions of the Bill against Atheism and Profaneness. He must also have been aware that this feature of his theory had become a favourite target for his critics. Bishop Bramhall, for example, had cited the offending passage in his *The Catching of the Leviathan* in 1658, adding the sarcastic comment: 'It is to be presumed, that in those their second lives, knowing certainly from T. H. that there is no hope of redemption for them from corporal death upon their well-doing, nor fear of any torments after death for their ill-doing, they will pass their times here as pleasantly as they can. This is all the damnation which T. H. fancieth.'[102] In his reply to Bramhall, not published until 1682 but written apparently in 1668, Hobbes tried somewhat disingenuously to extricate himself from his position: 'the whole paragraph was to prove, that for any text of Scripture to the contrary, men might, after the resurrection, live as Adam did on earth . . . But that they shall do so, is no assertion of mine.'[103] It thus seems highly likely that the excision of this passage from the Bear *Leviathan* was also made on Hobbes's own initiative. Where this and the handful of other related textual changes are concerned, the Bear edition thus probably represents the final expression of Hobbes's intentions.

## VII

The bear used by Christoffel Cunradus in the works he printed for Jacob van Meurs has been described above as 'exactly' and 'precisely' the same as the one in *Leviathan*. These adverbs are used advisedly; for there are many examples in seventeenth-century publications of bears that are roughly the same, but not identical. A little more needs to be said, therefore, about the history of this ornament.

The earliest known examples of the general design familiar to us from the *Leviathan* title page—a bear clasping long fronds of foliage, flanked by two coiled

---

[101] T. Hobbes, *Opera philosophica quae latinè scripsit, omnia* (Amsterdam, 1668); *Leviathan* (separate pagination), p. 300.

[102] J. Bramhall, *The Works of the Most Reverend Father in God, John Bramhall, D.D.*, 5 vols. (Oxford, 1842–5), IV, pp. 538–9. The issue was of real importance for Hobbes: if 'eternal punishment' (as threatened by churchmen in their interpretations of revelation) outweighed the maximum ill known to man by experience and reason (death), this would overturn the entire risk–benefit analysis on which his naturalistic version of natural law theory was based.

[103] *EW* IV, p. 359. See also the discussion of this point in Milton, 'Hobbes, Heresy and Arlington', p. 538.

snakes—are in books printed in the second decade of the seventeenth century.[104] These, however, probably do not represent the original version of the design. Its true origins can be found in a larger ornament, of which examples survive in several works printed in Leiden, by the Elzeviers and by Govert Basson, between 1618 and 1631.[105] This engraving is an extended oblong, sufficiently elongated to cover the full width of a folio page. In it, the foliage-clasping bear forms the central element; on each side of the bear there is a dog, with ears laid back and head pointing aggressively towards it; and behind each dog stands a huntsman holding a long staff. Other fronds of foliage fill out the rest of the design; the two coiled snakes are present, but they have an extra loop of tail (not present in the smaller, bear-only version), which emerges from another element of the design, just above the dogs. This design forms a coherent whole (albeit with some whimsical touches, such as the bells hanging from the snakes' necks): the frowning, scornful or defiant expression on the bear's face, found also in the *Leviathan* bear, makes sense when one sees that in this original design the bear is looking directly at the dog on its right-hand side.

At some time before 1615, apparently, the bear and its attendant snakes had been extracted from this design and turned into a free-standing ornament. That this became a much more popular design must be due partly to the fact that it was small enough (unlike the original) to be used in quarto printings. The discarded elements of the original design—huntsmen, dogs, and associated foliage—were also re-worked into a new, less elongated oblong ornament: after the extraction of the bear from the centre of the design, the outer parts were simply pushed together, so that the two dogs now faced each other nose to nose. This ornament (which will be called here the 'huntsmen') was sometimes used on its own, and sometimes in conjunction with the bear ornament—which, having the overall shape of a downward-pointing triangle, could be placed below it as a pendant.[106] Christoffel

[104] The earliest example known to me is in L. van Ceulen, *Fundamenta arithmetica et geometrica cum eorundem usu* (Leiden: van Colster, 1615), reverse title page and p. 31. Macdonald and Hargreaves refer to an example seen by them in a book (unspecified) printed in Holland in 1617 (*Thomas Hobbes*, p. 28); an extract from a catalogue, tipped in to the Bodleian's Bear *Leviathan* (pressmark Antiq. c. E. 1651/1), states that the bear is found in *Tractaet Plutarchi van de op-voedinghe der kinderen* (Middelburg, 1619).

[105] For the Elzevier printings see E. Rahir, *Catalogue d'une collection unique de volumes imprimé par les Elzevier et divers typographes hollandais du XVII<sup>e</sup> siècle* (Paris, 1896), pp. 429 (ornament no. 39), 15 (no. 120: S. Stevin, *La Castrametation* (Leiden: Elzevier, 1618); no. 121: S. Stevin, *La Castrametation*, 2<sup>nd</sup> edn (Leiden: Elzevier, 1618) ), 36 (no. 320: P. Cluverius, *Germaniae antiquae libri tres* (Leiden: Elzevier, 1631) ). The Basson printing is C. Barlaeus, *Send-Brief op de naam van Me-Vrouwe de Princesse Amalia* (Leiden: G. Basson, 1630). This ornament is reproduced (from the copy in the UBA) in T. S. J. G. Bögels, *Govert Basson: Printer, Bookseller, Publisher: Leiden 1612–1630* (Nieuwkoop, 1992), p. 311 (no. 3). A similar bear-with-huntsmen ornament was used by Pieter Rammazijn in Gouda in 1633: H. Briggs, *Trigonometria britannica, sive de doctrina triangulorum libri duo* (Gouda: Petrus Rammasenius, 1633). A rather crude imitation of this ornament was used by the printer François Langlois in J.-F. Niceron, *La Perspective curieuse . . . avec L'Optique et la catoptrique du R. P. Mersenne* (Paris, 1652), first pagination, p. 147 (sig. T2r); 2nd pagination, p. 75 (sig. K2r).

[106] The earliest example of this combination known to me is also in van Ceulen, *Fundamenta arithmetica*, pp. 79, 269. The 'huntsmen' design on its own was also used by the Leiden Elzeviers in several printings of 1622: see Rahir, *Catalogue*, pp. 428 (ornament no. 32), 20–1 (nos. 166, 172, 174).

Cunradus had a huntsmen ornament, which he used on its own (to decorate the head of a page) in books printed in 1657 and 1678.[107] He also had another version of this ornament which he used in conjunction with a bear ornament: this particular bear is not identical with the *Leviathan* bear which he used elsewhere, and signs of a crack running through both the bear and the huntsmen above it suggest that the combination of the two designs here may in fact have been a single block.[108]

As for the bear on its own, there are many versions of this to be found in Dutch printings of the seventeenth century. The 1630 Leiden publication mentioned above also has a bear ornament, which reproduces some of the details of the original full design: thus, the right-hand snake, for example, has an arrow-tongue, while the left-hand snake does not.[109] A similar bear, with one arrow-tongued snake, can be found in another publication of the 1630s (probably printed in Middelburg), and in two volumes of the famous Socinian series, *Bibliotheca fratrum polonorum*, printed by Frans Kuyper in Amsterdam in 1668.[110] Apart from the arrow-tongue, there are other small details in this ornament (the lines on the bear's chest, the curlicue of foliage beside the bear's right knee, and so on) which differentiate it from the *Leviathan* bear. Also different—both from the *Leviathan* bear, and from one another—are bears used by Johan Blaeu in Amsterdam in 1642, by Henrik Smidt in Middelburg in 1659, and by Cornelis Noenart in Utrecht in 1671.[111]

---

[107] J. A. Comenius, *Opera didactica omnia* (Amsterdam: printed by Cunradus and G. à Roy for L. de Geer, 1657), part 2, separate pagination, sig. A4r; J. Struys, *Joh. Jansz. Straussens sehr schwere . . . Reysen*, sig. *1r (Amsterdam, 1678); see above, at n. 95.

[108] O. Dapper, *Naukeurige beschrijvinge der Afrikaensche eylanden* (Amsterdam: van Meurs, 1676), sig. Q4r.

[109] Barlaeus, *Send-Brief*: this ornament is also reproduced in Bögels, *Govert Basson*, p. 312 (no. 5).

[110] P. Lansberg, astronomical tables printed in Holland and issued in England with prefatory material entitled *Ephemerides: The Celestiall Motions, for the yeeres . . . 1633. 1634. 1635. 1636* (London: W. Jones, 1635), final page (sig. N4v). (Lansberg's previous work, *Tabulae motuum coelestium perpetuae* (1632), was printed in Middelburg for a Leiden bookseller.) *Bibliotheca fratrum polonorum*, 6 vols. (Amsterdam, 1665–8), I, general title page, and title page of F. Socinus, *De coena Domini* (before p. 757); VI, sig. *1v. For the dating of these two volumes of the *Bibliotheca* see C. C. Sandius, *Bibliotheca anti-trinitariorum* ('Freistadt', 1684), p. 79. In these 1668 printings the ornament has been cut down at its top corners, losing some foliage. In this respect, and in many others, it closely matches the bear used on the title page of W. Caton, *Den matelijken ondersoeker voldaen* (n.p., 1659), a translation of a tract by one of the most active Quaker missionaries in the Netherlands (see the photo-reproduction of the title page in W. I. Hull, *The Rise of Quakerism in Amsterdam 1655–1665* (Philadelphia, 1938), plate facing p. 212). If this identification is correct, it suggests the hitherto unsuspected fact that Frans Kuyper—later famous as a fierce critic of the Quakers—was actually printing Quaker materials in the late 1650s.

[111] J. Volkelius, *De vera religione libri quinque* (n.p., n.d. [Amsterdam: J. Blaeu, 1642] ), sig. d4v (for the date and the attribution to Blaeu see Mersenne, *Correspondance*, XI, p. 126); L. de Bils, *Anatomische beschrijvinge van een wanschepsel* (Middelburg: H. Smidt, 1659), title page; J. Melchior ['J.M.V.D.M.'], *Epistola ad amicum, continens censuram libri, cui titulus: Tractatus theologico-politicus* (Utrecht: C. Noenart, 1671), final page. In this last case the ornament is similar to that in the *Bibliotheca fratrum polonorum*, but not identical to it; it also retains the foliage cut in the *Bibliotheca*, while omitting another frond of foliage just below it (which the *Bibliotheca* retains). Also probably to be added to this group is another bear already mentioned, that in Jane's polemical response to Milton (see above, n. 43), printed presumably in Holland in 1651: it too

– 367 –

## ASPECTS OF HOBBES

And there is also a rather severely reduced version of the bear design, omitting the snakes, the outer fronds of foliage, and even the bear's feet: one version of this was used in Leiden in 1615 and 1616, and another appears in works printed in Amsterdam in the 1660s.[112]

Some of these bears have been mistakenly identified with the *Leviathan* bear by previous writers.[113] But a close examination of such details as the outer corners of the foliage, the snakes' bells, the bear's feet, the curlicues on either side of the bear's knees, the trefoil under the bear's feet, and the lines on the bear's neck and chest shows that the only cases where the ornament is identical to that of *Leviathan* are in the six books, mentioned above, printed by Christoffel Cunradus between 1676 and 1682, plus the book printed in 1691 by someone who had bought Cunradus's ornaments after his death.[114] One distinctive feature of this particular ornament can be found in the curlicues by the bear's knees: on both sides, the final twist of the curlicue has been partly sliced off, leaving what is almost a straight edge. And even the smallest blemishes on the plate—such as a roughness in the outline of the bear's right knee, and a tiny smudge-mark in the space between the bear and the right-hand snake—can be found in every printing of this ornament.

The confusion of previous writers is, however, understandable, as the differences between this bear and most of the others are to be found only in matters of quite small detail. Some writers may have thought it unlikely that there could be several copies of the same ornament so similar to one another: after all, for a craftsman to copy such a design by eye on to a new block with such accuracy would have required an extraordinary investment of time and skill, to no obvious advantage. But this puzzle has a simple solution: the design was not copied by eye. There was in fact a standard technique for making a copy of an engraved block or plate. The pristine surface of the new plate was prepared with a special varnish, and a fresh print taken from the old plate was pressed on to it, leaving a design

---

differs from the *Leviathan* bear. In a separate category is the bear used in A. M. Schyrlaeus de Rheita, *Oculus Enoch et Eliae* (Antwerp: Hieronymus Verdussius, 1645), sigs. **2v, ***3r, which differs in several significant details from all the bears just mentioned.

[112] See van Ceulen, *Fundamenta arithmetica*, p. 184; C. Barlaeus, *Discours ofte vertoogh van Caspar Barleus, Onder-regent van 't Collegie der Godtheydt tot Leyden* (Leiden: G. Basson, 1616) (ornament reproduced in Bögels, *Govert Basson*, p. 312 (no. 6) ); P. de la Court ['V.D.H.'], *Interest van Holland, ofte Gronden van Hollands-Welvaren* (Amsterdam: J. Cyprianus van der Gracht, 1662), p. 267; G. Voetius, *Politiae ecclesiasticae partis primae libri duo posteriores* (Amsterdam: J. [Jansson] van Waesberghe, 1666), sig. 6g4r. A version of this ornament was used as a printer's device by Jan Evertsz [I] Cloppenburgh and Abraham van Herwijck in a book printed in Amsterdam in 1619 (van Huisstede and Brandhorst, *Dutch Printer's Devices*, I, p. 327); of the various bear ornaments discussed here, this is the only one to have been used for this purpose.

[113] The typescript catalogue of Keynes's Hobbes collection (A. N. L. M[unby], *A Catalogue of First and Early Editions of the Works of Thomas Hobbes, Forming Part of the Library Bequeathed by John Maynard, Baron Keynes of Tilton to King's College, Cambridge* (Cambridge, 1949), Cambridge University Library, pressmark B151.HOB2), for example, wrongly describes the Utrecht 1671 bear (see above, n. 111) as 'the same block' as the *Leviathan* bear (p. 17).

[114] See nn. 97–9. In these comparisons, allowance has of course been made for wear, and for the vagaries of inking.

## THE PRINTING OF THE 'BEAR'

which the engraver could then follow with his burin.[115] A popular ornament such as the bear could thus be produced in multiple copies, and widely distributed.

Where copies of the bear design were concerned, the distribution extended, as we have seen, as far as England. Not only was there a copy of the bear; there was also a version of the huntsmen ornament, which was used in the 1655 printing of Fuller's *Church-History*, once on its own, and once in conjunction with the bear.[116] As for the English bear itself, a close inspection establishes two things: that the three Williams/Daniel/Redmayne publications mentioned above did all employ the same bear ornament, and that that ornament was different from the one used in *Leviathan*.[117] (Areas of significant difference include the lines on the bear's chest, the lines on the bear's left knee, the claws of the bear's right foot, the foliage next to the bear's left elbow, the trefoil under the bear's feet, and the foliage in the top right-hand corner, as well as the curlicues, which are not cut down.)

This raises, however, an obvious question. The only known copy of the bear ornament in England was used by John Redmayne and John Williams, two of the three people involved in producing the first stage of the Bear *Leviathan*; and yet the bear that now graces the title page of that book was added only in the second stage, by a different printer in a different country. Can we really suppose that this was just a coincidence? Coincidences do happen, of course; but it would seem preferable to find another explanation.

Little more than guesswork, however, is possible here. One explanation could be that Redmayne himself had used his own bear on the title page of his printing, and that when Williams (or whoever) commissioned the completion of the work from Cunradus, a specific request was made for a 'bear' title page, to match some sheets of A1–A4 that had been preserved from the raid. (Such a theory would have to contend, however, with the fact that no copy of the Bear has yet been found with a title page differing from the one printed by Cunradus.[118]) This theory raises, in turn, the question of why something designed as a virtual facsimile of the Head should have had such an obviously different ornament placed on its title page. Perhaps Redmayne, Williams, and Crooke were hedging their bets: while they wanted an edition that could be palmed off on the general public as the original 1651 printing,

---

[115] See the account in the article 'Gravure', in D. Diderot *et al.*, eds., *Encyclopédie ou dictionnaire raisonné des sciences, des arts et des métiers*, 17 vols. (Paris, 1751–65), VII, pp. 877–903, esp. p. 898: the authority quoted for this technique is the 17th-century engraver Abraham Bosse. The technique also accounts for the changes between the original bear-and-huntsmen design and the subsequent bear-only and huntsmen-only ornaments: while blocks or plates cannot be simply cut up and rearranged, designs on paper can.

[116] T. Fuller, *The Church-History*, of Britain (London, 1655), bk. I, cent. 2, sigs. A1r, B3v. For another English example of the huntsmen ornament see A. Olearius, *The Voyages and Travells of the Ambassadors sent by Frederick Duke of Holstein, to the Great Duke of Muscovy, and the King of Persia*, tr. J. Davies, 2nd edn, 2 vols. (London: for John Starkey and Thomas Basset, 1669), I, sigs. A2r, B1r. This huntsmen ornament differs in some details from the one used by Cunradus.

[117] For these three works see above, at nn. 42–3.

[118] It should also be added here that I have not found any signs of resetting in any of the copies of the Bear edition that I have consulted.

they knew that the imitation would not withstand a moment's scrutiny by experts, such as the officers of the Stationers' Company. If they had used the original 'head' ornament, this would merely have made it easier for the authorities to trace them, via the owner of that ornament. Using, instead, an ornament hardly known to exist in England but widely recognized as Dutch might have enabled them to say that the whole edition was a Dutch counterfeit, for which they could not be blamed.[119] One possible piece of evidence in support of this theory can be found in the extraordinarily ugly ornamental capital, a crudely carved wood-block, which Redmayne used at the start of the fourth part of the book (p. 333, sig. Vv1r). Nothing so cheaply crude can be found in any other productions by Redmayne, or Williams, or Crooke. The explanation may be that it had been prepared as a one-off, to be used in this printing and then destroyed, in order to leave no clue by which the printer could be identified.[120]

Other explanations are also possible. Perhaps Redmayne did not use his own bear ornament when printing his sheets of *Leviathan*. The bear may have entered the story only at the commissioning of the subsequent completion by Cunradus, which may have been accompanied by a specific request (from Williams, perhaps, who knew that Redmayne possessed a 'bear' ornament) that Cunradus should use a version of the bear. The idea may have been that, if the Redmayne–Cunradus edition sold out quickly, the use of this particular ornament would then have allowed Redmayne to make another edition thereafter, which could similarly be passed off as just a further quantity of the same Dutch printing. Given the state of the evidence, however, the full explanation may never be known with any certainty.

## VIII

As these speculations suggest, it would be useful to have more information about when, how, and why the commissioning of the work from Cunradus took place. Unfortunately, there is no direct evidence available; all that can be done is to draw some inferences from the evidence already presented, and supplement it with further details about Anglo-Dutch printing practices, and about Cunradus's output and career.

So far as the dating of Cunradus's completion of *Leviathan* is concerned, the relevant facts have already been mentioned. The earliest recorded copy is dated '1678' (unfortunately, the ownership inscription does not give the month); this supplies the *terminus ad quem*. The earliest of the other 'bear' printings by Cunradus was produced in 1676; but this is not necessarily the date at which he acquired the

---

[119] The only use of the bear in a publication with Redmayne's name on it was, after all, in a French-language pamphlet, probably printed in small quantities and mainly distributed abroad; only one copy of this work (acquired by Thomason) is known in England (see above, at n. 42).

[120] I am very grateful to Nicholas Smith for this suggestion.

ornament. The *terminus a quo* could be said to be October 1670, when the second raid took place. However, the attempted assignment of *Leviathan* to John Wright by Elizabeth Crooke in February 1675 may be taken to imply that the printing, by that stage, had not yet been completed: if Mrs Crooke, who was in financial difficulties, had possessed finished copies of such a money-spinner at that time, she would surely have gone ahead and dealt in them, instead of passing away her rights. The 1680 advertisement by Chiswell also suggests, given the known links between Chiswell and Wright, that Wright did get involved after all in the production of the Bear; and February 1675 appears to be the *terminus a quo* for Wright's involvement. The Bear was thus probably completed in the years 1675–8.

As for the idea of commissioning a printing in Holland, there was nothing very unusual about it. Huge quantities of Dutch-printed books were imported into England in the seventeenth century. Broadly speaking, these can be divided into three categories. First, there were the 'libels' and other subversive or dangerous works, commissioned from Dutch printers by English authors or booksellers and smuggled into England: examples included Edward Sexby's sarcastically anti-Cromwellian pamphlet *Killing no Murder* (1657), and the large quantities of works by dissenters reported to be arriving at Newcastle and Hull in 1667–8.[121] Another category consisted of work undertaken at the initiative of Dutch booksellers, primarily for sale to the English market: this included large numbers of English Bibles, as well as pirated editions of books first printed in England.[122] And the third main category consisted merely of the Dutch printers' standard output of Latin texts of all kinds, which were distributed to all European countries, England included. (Occasionally a special issue would be made for an English bookseller, with a title page which stated that the work was printed for sale by him.[123]) English printers, indeed, found it increasingly hard to compete with the Dutch in the international market: thanks to a variety of factors (including the restrictive practices of the Stationers' Company on the one hand, and the control of the French paper industry by Dutch capital on the other), the Dutch product was both of higher quality, and saleable at a lower price. By the early 1680s the complaint could be heard in England that the Dutch printers were undercutting all others.[124]

---

[121] C. H. Firth, *The Last Years of the Protectorate 1656–1658*, 2 vols. (London, 1909), I, p. 229 (Sexby); Kitchin, *Sir Roger L'Estrange*, p. 169 (1667–8). See also the comments in Hoftijzer, *Engelse boekverkopers*, pp. 7–8.

[122] For examples see D. W. Davies, 'The Geographic Extent of the Dutch Book Trade in the Seventeenth Century', *Het Boek*, n.s., 31 (1952–4), pp. 10–21, esp. pp. 15–16; F. F. Madan, 'Milton, Salmasius, and Dugard', *The Library*, 4th ser., 4 (1923–4), pp. 119–45, esp. p. 123.

[123] On the 'Latin trade' in general, see Hoftijzer, *Engelse boekverkopers*, pp. 4–5. For examples of title pages naming English booksellers, see Davies, 'Geographic Extent', p. 17 (Grotius, *Opera theologica*, printed by the heirs of J. Blaeu for Moses Pitt, 1679), and Macdonald and Hargreaves, *Bibliography*, p. 78 (Hobbes, *Opera philosophica*, printed by J. Blaeu for Cornelius Bee, 1668).

[124] See G. C. Gibbs, 'The Role of the Dutch Republic as the intellectual entrepôt of Europe in the seventeenth and eighteenth centuries', *Bijdragen en mededelingen betreffende de geschiedenis der Nederlanden*, 86 (1971), pp. 323–49, esp. p. 324 (French paper and other advantages); Hodgson and Blagden, *Notebook of*

Clearly, the completion of the Bear *Leviathan* falls into the first of these categories—though it is worth noting that, despite the extra costs of transportation, the work may actually have been carried out more cheaply in Amsterdam. (In London, printers would also have charged an extra premium for unlicensed printing: this may not have applied in Cunradus's case.[125]) What is also important to note, however, is that activities in the first category took place not in isolation, but against the broad background of the second and third categories, with all the opportunities they created for contacts, interchanges, and business arrangements at many levels. Some English booksellers made business trips to Holland; many traded regularly with their Dutch counterparts; some engaged in joint publishing ventures; and some Dutch printers and booksellers did so much business with England that they were prepared to hire lawyers to enforce their rights, or recover their debts, in London.[126] There is no way of telling whether the approach to Cunradus was made by Wright, or Chiswell, or Williams (who may well have been involved, having probably ended up as the possessor of the salvaged sheets of Redmayne's printing). But it is likely that such contacts, in themselves, would not have aroused any particular suspicions in London.

On the other hand, what of Cunradus's own suspicions? The question of whether this Amsterdam printer had any idea of the nature of the book he was handling is one of the most intriguing problems raised by this whole story. For, on the face of it, it is hard to tell whether Cunradus—who enjoys the unique distinction of having printed both Hobbes's *Leviathan* (at least in part) and Spinoza's *Tractatus theologico-politicus*—was a mere *ingénu*, or one of the most adventurous printers of his age.

To Spinoza scholars, what little is known about the production of the *Tractatus* has generally seemed to support the '*ingénu*' hypothesis. The book was printed in late 1669 or early 1670, and issued with a fictitious imprint (reminiscent of Cunradus's own name), 'Hamburgi, Apud *Henricum Künrath*'.[127] Its attribution to Cunradus is confirmed by an unimpeachable source—none other than a Lutheran pastor, Johannes Colerus, who knew Cunradus personally and had two of his

---

*Bennet and Clements*, p. 16 (English books higher-priced); Hoftijzer, *Engelse boekverkopers*, p. 1 (complaint). For valuable comments on the economics of a late 17th-century Dutch printing house, see O. S. Lankhorst, *Reinier Leers (1654–1714), uitgever & boekverkoper te Rotterdam: een Europees 'Libraire' en zijn fonds* (Amsterdam, 1983), pp. 19–23.

[125] In the 1670s a printer would have charged 24s. or 25s. a sheet for licensed printing, but 30s. for unlicensed: see Historical Manuscripts Commission, *Ninth Report*, Appendix, p. 75.

[126] See Hodgson and Blagden, *Notebook of Bennet and Clements*, pp. 11, 25–6; Davies, 'Geographic Extent', p. 17; Hoftijzer, *Engelse boekverkopers*, pp. 1–14; M. M. Kleerkooper, 'Daniel Elseviers betrekkingen met Engeland', *Tijdschrift voor boek- en bibliotheekwezen* 8 (1910), pp. 115–25, esp. pp. 117–20; and the assignment of power of attorney by Johan Blaeu for the recovery of debts from the heirs of James Allestree, 11 Feb. 1671, in the Gemeentelijke Archiefdienst, Amsterdam, NA 3206, fols. 145v–146r.

[127] The entry in A. van der Linde, *Benedictus Spinoza: bibliografie* (The Hague, 1871), p. 2, is slightly inaccurate. For the dating see F. Bamberger, 'The Early Editions of Spinoza's *Tractatus Theologico-Politicus*: a Bibliohistorical Reexamination', *Studies in Bibliography and Booklore*, 5 (1961), pp. 9–33, esp. pp. 12, 29 (n.).

own books printed by him. Discussing the *Tractatus* in his biography of Spinoza (published long after Cunradus's death), Colerus observed: 'There is no doubt whatsoever that this book was printed in Amsterdam, at the house of the printer Christoffel Cunradus on the Egelantiersgracht. In 1679, when I was called to that city on some matters of business, Cunradus himself brought me some copies of this treatise, and made me a present of them, not knowing what a pernicious work it was.'[128] This personal testimony seems to imply an unusual degree of naiveté on Cunradus's part. There is other evidence, too, to suggest that the bookseller who organized the printing was Spinoza's close friend Jan Rieuwertsz. It can therefore be supposed that Cunradus was merely doing a job of work, and hardly knew what he had printed. On these grounds, Spinoza scholars have paid little further attention to him.[129]

The matter does, however, deserve further consideration. Generally speaking, when a printer produces such a controversial book, there are three possible ways of accounting for his action. He may be naively unaware of the contents of the work; he may be aware of the book's controversial nature, and sympathetic towards it; or he may be aware of it, and interested only in the fact that this makes it a better commercial proposition. Of these three explanations—*ingénu*, sympathizer, or profiteer—the third seems hardly compatible with the fact that Cunradus offered the book to a visiting Lutheran pastor. The first is somewhat undermined by the use of the fictitious imprint, which indicates some knowledge of the book's controversial nature (though, on the other hand, the puzzling similarity of 'Künrath' to Cunradus seems to suggest a certain nonchalance in the matter). But even if the *ingénu* hypothesis can explain Cunradus's original printing of the book in 1669–70, it hardly fits his later gift of copies to Colerus: it is very difficult to believe that a professional printer in Amsterdam can have remained in complete ignorance, up until 1679, of all the denunciations and official prohibitions directed against Spinoza's works during the previous nine years.[130] The possibility should not be

---

[128] J. Colerus, *La Vie de B. de Spinoza, tirée des ecrits de ce fameux philosophe* (The Hague, 1706), pp. 99–100: 'Il n'y a point de doute que ce Livre fut imprimé à Amsterdam chez Christophle Conrad Imprimeur sur le Canal de l'Eglantir. En 1679 étant appellé en cette Ville là pour quelques affaires, Conrad même m'apporta quelques Exemplaires de ce Traité, & m'en fit présent, ne sçachant pas combien c'étoit un Ouvrage pernicieux.' Colerus had been called in 1679 (from his previous employment at Weesp) to be German Preacher ('Hooghduytse Predicant') to the Lutherans of Amsterdam: see the account in Anon., *Historisch verhaal, van den beklaaglyken opstand 't sedert eenige Jaren in de gemeente, toegedaan de onveranderde Confessie van Augsburgh, binnen deser Stede, ontstaan* (Amsterdam, 1690), p. 13.

[129] See J. P. N. Land, 'Over de uitgaven en den text der Ethica van Spinoza', *Verslagen en mededeelingen der Koninklijke Akademie van Wetenschapen, afdeeling Letterkunde*, 2nd ser., 11 (1882), pp. 4–24, esp. p. 6. However, Land's notion that Rieuwertsz must have taken over ('overgenommen') Cunradus's printing-house between 1670 and 1677 rests on an elementary misunderstanding of the relationship between booksellers and printers during this period. On Rieuwertsz's role see K. O. Meinsma, *Spinoza en zijn kring, over Hollandse vrijgeesten* (The Hague, 1896), pp. 326–8.

[130] See Bamberger, 'Early Editions', pp. 13–14, 25–7 (noting the exceptional severity of the prohibitions of 1678).

excluded, therefore, that Cunradus was both aware of the contents of Spinoza's book, and keen to persuade Colerus that its evil reputation was undeserved. Perhaps Colerus was trying to do a favour to the memory of his long-dead printer (and, it may be, friend) when he wrote those words, drawing a veil over any positive expressions of interest in Spinoza's work that Cunradus had made. This explanation of his involvement in the production of Spinoza's book is, of course, only speculative; but the speculation can be strengthened by placing it in the context of Cunradus's career, and of what might be called the ideological pattern of his other publications.

Christoffel Cunradus was a German, from Saxony: he was born in 1614 or 1615, in the small town of Freiberg, to the west of Dresden. Some time before 1645 he had settled in Holland; his marriage (to a Dutch widow) was recorded that year in Amsterdam.[131] Five years later he set up his own printing-house, from which he issued a large quantity of publications until his death in 1684.[132] His normal imprint used the Dutch and Latin forms 'Christoffel Cunradus', but in his German-language publications he gave his name as 'Kristof Konrad', 'Kristof Konraden' or 'Christoff Cunraden'. Naturally enough, German-language books were one of his specialities: according to a description of Amsterdam by the German poet Philip von Zesen in 1664, Cunradus's shop was the best place in the city for 'all kinds of publications in High German'.[133] It is not surprising, therefore, that Jacob van Meurs engaged him to print the German translations of his geographical and historical compilations.

Cunradus was evidently a member of the German Lutheran community in Amsterdam; indeed, he appears to have functioned, to some extent, as that community's printer. One of his first productions was an edition of the Augsburg Confession; he also printed Luther's translation of the New Testament, together with a Lutheran catechism; and, in addition to the sermon by Visscher already mentioned, he issued seven works by three of the Lutheran pastors in Amsterdam.[134] If his output had consisted only of such books, plus the sprinkling of standard educational, historical, or literary works issued by him in Dutch, German, and Latin,

---

[131] M. M. Kleerkooper and W. P. van Stockum, *De boekhandel te Amsterdam voornamelijk in de 17ᵉ eeuw*, 2 vols. (The Hague, 1914–16), I, pp. 155–6. He was sometimes also described as from Meissen (e.g. by Philip ['Filips'] von Zesen, *Beschreybung der Stadt Amsterdam* (Amsterdam, 1664), p. 508: 'ein Meisner'); Freiberg is 18 miles south of Meissen.

[132] J. A. Guys and C. de Wolf, *Thesaurus 1473–1800: Nederlandse boekdrukkers en boekverkopers met plaatsen en jaren van werkzaamheid* (Nieuwkoop, 1989), p. 48. According to A. M. Ledeboer, *Alfabetische lijst der boekdrukkers, boekverkoopers en uitgevers in Noordnederland* (Utrecht, 1876), part 1, p. 42, he was active as a printer from 1649; but his own imprint begins in 1650.

[133] Von Zesen, *Beschreybung*, p. 508: 'alle ahrten der Hochdeutschen schriften'.

[134] *Confessie, ofte belijdenisse des geloofs* (1650); *Das Newe Testament* and *Cathechismus, oder kurze Unterricht* (1669); and works by P. Cordes (1660, 1673, 1673), J. E. Blum (1674, 1683), and J. Colerus (1683, 1684): see the card-index imprint catalogue in the UBA. Ledeboer also notes that he issued engraved portraits of Lutheran pastors: *Alfabetische lijst*, part 1, p. 42.

he would have gone down in printing history as a modest and unadventurous representative of his own particular community's intellectual and religious mainstream. However, from the late 1650s onwards his productions would range much more widely than that, taking him far beyond the bounds of Lutheran—or indeed any other—orthodoxy.

The turning-point seems to have come in 1657, when Cunradus was employed, together with another printer, in producing the monumental folio collection of Comenius's Latin educational works, *Opera didactica omnia* (1657), for the philanthropic Comenian patron Laurentius de Geer.[135] During his work on this edition Cunradus must have become personally acquainted with Comenius, who had settled in Amsterdam in the previous year: a friend of the Czech philosopher who visited the city in June 1657 records how he met Comenius on the Rozengracht, and was immediately taken by him to 'the printing-house' (evidently Cunradus's establishment on the Egelantiersgracht, which was only a couple of hundred yards away).[136] Soon thereafter, when Comenius helped one of his compatriots, Jan Teofil Kopydanský, to set up as a printer of Czech and Polish books in Amsterdam, he placed him first of all with Cunradus: one of their first productions was an edition of the Bible in Polish, issued over the imprint 'w drukární Chrysztoffá Cunráda' and distributed (thanks to the munificence of de Geer) free of charge among Polish exiles in Amsterdam.[137] Modern Czech scholars have suggested that Cunradus may already have had Czech connections, given the significant community of exiled Czechs in his home-town of Freiberg.[138] One writer has gone much further, claiming that Cunradus married Comenius's sister, Maria; but the leading modern expert on Comenius's life makes no reference to any such marriage, or, indeed, to any such woman.[139] Nevertheless, there can be little doubt that

---

[135] On de Geer's patronage and the preparation of this edition see W. Rood, *Comenius and the Low Countries* (Amsterdam, 1970), pp. 98–108. '1657' is the date on the title page, but Comenius's correspondence shows that the printing finished in early 1658 (G. H. Turnbull, *Hartlib, Dury and Comenius: Gleanings from Hartlib's Papers* (London, 1947), pp. 378–9).

[136] R. Prümer, ed., 'Tagebuch Adam Samuel Hartmanns über seine Kollektenreise im Jahre 1657–1659', *Zeitschrift der historischen Gesellschaft für die Provinz Posen*, 14 (1899), pp. 67–140, 241–308; 15 (1900), pp. 95–160, 203–46; here 14, p. 244 ('Ging damals fort in die drükerey').

[137] See *Unbekannte Briefe des Comenius und seiner Freunde 1641–1661*, ed. M. Blekastad (Kastellaun, 1976), p. 44, n. 13, and J. Bruckner, *A Bibliographical Catalogue of Seventeenth-Century German Books published in Holland* (The Hague, 1971), p. xviii.

[138] N. Moutová and J. Polišenský, *Komenský v Amsterodamu* (Prague, 1970), p. 105.

[139] The claim was made by R. J. Vonka, 'Een Cechische boekdrukkerij te Amsterdam in de XVIIe eeuw', in *Cechoslovakije en de internationale tentoonstelling voor oeconomische ontwikkeling te Amsterdam, 1929*, ed. B. Mendl and R. J. Vonka (Prague, n.d. [1929]), pp. 15–20, esp. p. 16. It is accepted by Rood (*Comenius and the Low Countries*, p. 150, n. 3) and by E. G. E. van der Wall (who even describes Cunradus himself as Czech: *De mystieke chiliast Petrus Serrarius (1600–1669) en zijn wereld* (Leiden, 1987), p. 303), but rejected by I. H. van Eeghen ('De "Uitgever" Henricus Cunrath of Künraht van de polygamist Lyserus en van de Philosoof Spinoza', *Amstelodamum: maandblad voor de kennis van Amsterdam*, 50 (April, 1953), pp. 73–80; here p. 79). According to the leading modern biographer, Milada Blekastad, the only sisters of Comenius to survive beyond infancy were Kateřina and Margeta, who both married Czechs and lived in Moravia (*Comenius:*

Cunradus did become well acquainted with the Czech philosopher: he also produced two other works by him under his own imprint: *Unum necessarium* (1668) and *Via lucis* (1668).

Comenius's circle during this period included many people who rejected the orthodoxies—Lutheran or Calvinist—of the day. He himself regarded most of the credal and ceremonial differences between the Protestant churches as unimportant; his Protestant irenicism was linked not only to geopolitics (he hoped for a grand anti-Habsburg alliance) but also to an apocalyptic theology, as he supposed that the removal of such differences would herald the Second Coming of Christ. This made him a natural ally of members of the 'Collegiant' movement, who stood apart from the organized Churches and also developed a strong interest in millenarian theories: one of Comenius's closest friends in Amsterdam was the Collegiant chiliast Petrus Serrarius.[140]

The Collegiants were drawn from a variety of backgrounds; Serrarius had been a Calvinist, but many were Remonstrants or Mennonites. Lutherans were less well represented (there were not many in Holland anyway), but the intellectual influence of a certain kind of Lutheranism—or perhaps one should say 'post-Lutheranism'—on Comenius and many of his Collegiant friends was profound. They were fascinated by a group of German preachers and religious writers (some of whom had been expelled from their Lutheran ministries) who taught a mystical, spiritualist, millenarian, non-confessional, or even anti-confessional type of Christianity: men such as Joachim Betke, Friedrich Breckling, and Christian Hoburg.[141] Comenius is known to have been in personal contact with all three; Breckling and Hoburg spent some time in the Netherlands, and the latter was for a while a member of the religious community established there by another non-confessional religious leader revered by Comenius, the 'prophetess' Antoinette Bourignon.[142]

The spiritual fountainhead from which all these German religious teachers drew was the theosophical writer Jakob Böhme. Comenius himself had not known Böhme personally (he died in 1624), but he had been profoundly influenced by

*Versuch eines Umrisses von Leben, Werk und Schicksal des Jan Amos Komenský* (Oslo, 1969), p. 11 n.). The best discussion of this issue is by Moutová and Polišenský, who firmly reject Vonka's theory: *Komenský v Amsterodamu*, pp. 104–5

[140] See A. C. Fix, *Prophecy and Reason: The Dutch Collegiants in the Early Enlightenment* (Princeton, NJ, 1991), esp. pp. 57–83, and van der Wall, *De mystieke chiliast*.

[141] On Betke see M. Bornemann, *Der mystische Spiritualist Joachim Betke (1601–1663) und seine Theologie* (Berlin, 1959); on Breckling and Hoburg see J. Moller, *Cimbria literata, sive scriptorum ducatus utriusque Slesvicensis et Holsatici . . . historia*, 3 vols. (Copenhagen, 1744), I, p. 67, II, pp. 337–47, and van der Wall, *De mystike chiliast*, pp. 306–8. For an early account of all three, see G. Arnold, *Unparteyische Kirchen- und Ketzer-Historie von Anfang des Neuen Testaments biss auff das Jahr Christi 1688*, 2 vols. (Frankfurt am Main, 1699–1700), II, part 3, pp. 125–33, 145–6.

[142] See Bruckner, *Bibliographical Catalogue*, pp. xvi–xviii; Blekastad, *Comenius*, pp. 570, 634; M. van der Does, *Antoinette Bourignon (1616–1680): la vie et l'oeuvre d'une mystique chrétienne* (Amsterdam, 1974), pp. 129, 136–7.

his writings; and he was an old friend of Böhme's follower and biographer, the Silesian nobleman Abraham von Franckenberg.[143] Another Silesian Behmenist, Johann Theodor von Tschesch, had spent four years in Amsterdam in the 1640s; he was befriended there by the poet Philip von Zesen, who also became a member of Comenius's circle soon after the latter's arrival in 1656.[144] Thanks to these and other contacts with the German lands, Amsterdam became the centre of a flourishing Behmenist tradition: at least forty editions of Böhme's works were published there during the seventeenth century.[145] And, while moderate Behmenists such as Comenius and Serrarius could be found at one end of the spectrum, at the far end there were radical visionaries such as Breckling's friend Quirinus Kuhlmann, who travelled to Istanbul to convert the Sultan, warned the Pope of the imminent end of the world, and was finally burnt as a heretic in Moscow.[146]

This, then, was the milieu into which Christoffel Cunradus was drawn from the late 1650s onwards. In addition to the works by Comenius already mentioned, he printed three books by Serrarius, the third of which included material by Comenius as well.[147] He seems to have had particularly close relations with von Zesen, publishing no fewer than seven of his books (starting in 1657); and it was probably thanks to Cunradus that von Zesen was employed by Jacob van Meurs as the translator into German of two of his geographical publications, in 1669 and 1670.[148] Between 1660 and 1667 Cunradus also printed one book by von Franckenberg, one by von Tschesch, three by Betke, four by Breckling, two by Hoburg, and one by Kuhlmann.[149] That he had personal contacts with the last three of these seems clear. Most of his Breckling publications were printed 'for the

---

[143] Blekastad, *Comenius*, p. 379. In his MS notebook from the 1660s, 'Clamores Eliae', Comenius cites Böhme, von Franckenberg, Breckling, and Hoburg: ibid., pp. 712–26.

[144] On von Tschesch see C. Sepp, *Geschiedkundige nasporingen*, 3 vols. (Leiden, 1872–5), II, pp. 146–7; K. Dissel, *Philipp von Zesen und die deutschgesinnte Genossenschaft* (Hamburg, 1890), pp. 23–4; van der Wall, *De mystieke chiliast*, pp. 114–15. On von Zesen and Comenius see Dissel, *Phillip von Zesen*, p. 42, and L. Forster, 'Philip von Zesen, Johann Heinrich Ott, John Dury, and Others', *Slavonic and East European Review*, 32 (1953–4), pp. 475–85, esp. p. 476.

[145] See Sepp, *Geschiedkundige nasporingen*, II, 137–228; L. Brummel, 'Jacob Boehme en het 17e-eeuwsche Amsterdam', in *Historische opstellen aangebeden aan J. Huizinga* (Haarlem, 1948), pp. 7–28; L. Kolakowski, *Świadomość religijna i więź kościelna* (Warsaw, 1965), pp. 458–63, 482; F. van Inghen, *Böhme und Böhmisten in den Niederlanden im 17. Jahrhundert* (Bonn, 1984); M. J. Petry, 'Behmenism and Spinozism in the Religious Culture of the Netherlands, 1660–1730', in *Spinoza in der Frühzeit seiner religiösen Wirkung*, ed. K. Gründer and W. Schmidt-Biggemann (Heidelberg, 1984); F. A. Janssen, ed., *Abraham Willemsz van Beyerland: Jacob Böhme en het Nederlandse hermetisme in de 17e eeuw* (Amsterdam, 1986); and the listings in W. Buddecke, *Die Jakob Böhme-Ausgaben: ein beschreibendes Verzeichnis*, 2 vols. (Göttingen, 1937–57).

[146] See W. Dietze, *Quirinus Kuhlmann, Ketzer und Poet: Versuch einer monographischen Darstellung von Leben und Werk* (Berlin, 1963).

[147] *Vox clamantis in Babylone* (1663); *De Judaeorum universali conversione* (1665); *Responsio ad exercitationem paradoxicam* (1667).

[148] Bruckner, *Bibliographical Catalogue*, nos. 243, 245, 356, 393, 492, 499, 512 (von Zesen); 389 (Montanus, tr. von Zesen), 395 (Dapper, tr. von Zesen).

[149] Ibid., nos. 427 (von Franckenberg); 446 (von Tschesch); 267, 359, 394 (Betke); 271–2, 308, 321 (Breckling); 329, 443 (Hoburg); 459 (Kuhlmann).

author'; he is mentioned in correspondence between Kuhlmann and Breckling; the first of his Hoburg publications was subsidized by de Geer, who knew Hoburg personally, and in the second there is a note to the reader explaining that Hoburg's works are available both from Cunradus and from Hoburg's son, a bookseller in Hamburg.[150]

Most of the books just mentioned were issued over Cunradus's own imprint; but in some cases—the works by Hoburg and von Franckenberg—he printed for a German bookseller in Amsterdam, Hendrick Beets. A personal friend of von Franckenberg, Breckling, Hoburg, Serrarius, and Paul Felgenhauer (another influential mystical and millenarian writer, one of whose books Cunradus issued in a Danish translation), Beets was one of the most active Behmenists in Amsterdam: between 1658 and 1678 he published twenty-eight editions of Böhme's works, no fewer than thirteen of which were printed for him by Cunradus. The imprint used by Beets on these books was 'Betkius' or 'Betke'—a distortion of his own name, made in honour of Joachim Betke, whom he revered.[151] This detail furnishes what must surely be the explanation of Cunradus's later use of the imprint 'Heinrich Künrath': in similar fashion, he was probably honouring the mystical alchemist and cabbalist Heinrich Kunraht (1560–1605), whose writings were highly praised by both Friedrich Breckling and Quirinus Kuhlmann.[152]

Cunradus's choice of unorthodox writers was not confined, however, to these Behmenist and Comenian circles. He also appears to have printed the controversial treatise *Discursus politicus de polygamia* by the German proselytizer for polygamy, Johannes Lyser, which was issued over the imprint 'Friburgi apud Henricum Cunrath' in 1674. The organizer of this printing was Dirk Boom, but the printer was probably Cunradus: the imprint adapts that of the Spinoza volume, with Hamburg replaced by a place-name which—perhaps coincidentally—resembles that of Cunradus's birthplace, Freiberg.[153] This was no libertine tract: its author was a former Lutheran pastor in Leipzig, whose scripturally based defence of

---

[150] Ibid., pp. xvii–xviii, 231–2; W. Heijting, 'Hendrick Beets (1625?–1708), Publisher to the German Adherents of Jacob Böhme in Amsterdam', *Quaerendo*, 3 (1973), pp. 250–80; p. 272.

[151] On Beets's imprint, friends and Böhme editions see Heijting, 'Hendrick Beets'. The Danish edition of Felgenhauer printed by Cunradus was *Probatorium theologicum, eller theologischer proberung* (1664). For the Cunradus printings of Böhme see Bruckner, *Bibliographical Catalogue*, nos. 306, 352–3, 432–3, 435–7, 450–3, 465.

[152] On Kunraht see Moller, *Cimbria literata*, II, pp. 440–1 (referring also to Breckling and Kuhlmann). Kuhlmann praises him at length in *Der neubegeisterte Böhme*, ed. J. Clark, 2 vols. (Stuttgart, 1995), I, pp. 110–12. The idea that Cunradus's fictive imprint alluded to Kunraht was first proposed by W. Meyer, 'De veris et fictis Tractatus theologico-politici editoribus', *Chronicon Spinozanum*, 1 (1921), 264–7; but Meyer was apparently not aware of the cult of Kunraht in Cunradus's circle, nor of the Beets–Betke precedent.

[153] On this whole story see van Eeghen, 'De "Uitgever"'. In confirmation of van Eeghen's attribution, it can be noted that Cunradus printed other works for Dirk Boom (in conjunction with van Meurs and others): see above, nn. 96, 98. However, his argument about 'Friburg'/Freiberg is more dubious: as Meyer pointed out, 'Freiburg' was just a German rendering of the fantasy place-name (often used for Amsterdam) 'Eleutheropolis' ('De veris et fictis editoribus', p. 266).

polygamy had caused his ejection from that post and had reduced him to the life of a mendicant preacher. In this way he fits the profile of a typical Cunradus author, an earnest seeker after truth who had fallen foul of the religious establishment.[154] The same description applies, naturally enough, to Spinoza himself. Even if Spinoza's dealings over the printing of the *Tractatus* were only with Rieuwertsz and not with Cunradus, it may still be significant that Rieuwertsz chose this particular printer for such a work: he must have been aware not only of Spinoza's friendship with Serrarius and long-standing connections with the Collegiant movement, but also of Cunradus's sympathy for such outcasts from organized religion. Other unorthodox writers printed by Cunradus included a Socinian theologian, Jeremias Felbinger: he published a Dutch translation of a treatise by him in 1660, as well as his annotated German New Testament.[155] And, last but not least, there is Cunradus's intensive involvement in the printing of Quaker materials: between 1665 and 1674 he issued eighteen Quaker pamphlets, including works by George Fox, William Caton, Steven Crisp, George Keith, Benjamin Furly, and Pieter Hendricksz.[156]

What emerges from this brief survey of Cunradus's output, therefore, is a figure very different from the foolish *ingénu* of traditional Spinoza scholarship. Here was a printer prepared to put his name to Quaker pamphlets at a time when Quakers were still being actively persecuted by the Dutch authorities, and whose fictitious imprint, used in the even more controversial works of Spinoza and Lyser, was hardly designed to conceal his name at all.[157] The authors he published do not form a homogeneous group—Serrarius, for example, having been attracted, like Spinoza, to the Quakers in the 1650s, later became an obdurate critic of them.[158] But they all have in common three things: their direct, personal engagement with Scripture, their estrangement from mainstream confessional religion, and their hostility to religious persecution.[159]

---

[154] See C. G. Jöcher, *Allgemeines Gelehrten-Lexicon*, 4 vols. (Leipzig, 1750–1), II, cols. 2629–30.

[155] J. Felbinger, *Een christelik bericht* (1660); Bruckner, *Bibliographical Catalogue*, no. 283.

[156] These are all contained in the compilation *Collectio, of versamelinge* (see above, n. 92): this volume is discussed, but misdescribed and misdated, by W. I. Hull, *Benjamin Furly and Quakerism in Rotterdam* (Philadelphia, 1941), pp. 42, 51.

[157] On the hostility to the Quakers see Hull, *Rise of Quakerism* and *Benjamin Furly*; for an account of their persecution, by a German visitor to Amsterdam in 1665–6, see F. Lucä, ed., *Der Chronist Friedrich Lucä: ein Zeit- und Sittenbild aus der zweiten Hälfte des siebenzehnten Jahrhunderts* (Frankfurt, 1854), p. 84.

[158] See J. van den Berg, 'Quaker and Chiliast: The "contrary thoughts" of William Ames and Petrus Serrarius', in *Reformation, Conformity and Dissent: Essays in Honour of Geoffrey Nuttall*, ed. R. Buick Knox (London, 1977), pp. 180–98, and van der Wall, *De mystieke chiliast*, pp. 214–30. On Spinoza's Quaker contacts see R. Popkin and M. A. Signer, *Spinoza's Earliest Publication? The Hebrew Translation of Margaret Fell's* A Loving Salutation to the Seed of Abraham among the Jews (Assen, 1987), pp. 2–14.

[159] See e.g. F. Breckling's *Religio libera persecutio relegata* ('Freystat' [Amsterdam], 1663), or von Zesen's two treatises, both printed by Cunradus, *Des weltlichen Standes Handlungen und Urteile wider den Gewissenszwang in Glaubenssachen* (1665) and *Des geistlichen Standes Urteile wider den Gewissenszwang in Glaubenssachen* (1665).

Is it conceivable that Cunradus, who may have had some acquaintance with the Dutch translation of *Leviathan*, could have seen Hobbes in a similar light? The answer must be 'yes'. Although the interpretation of Hobbes as a cynical anti-Christian eventually became the dominant one, it was not the only one available to early readers. Some, such as Hartlib's Amsterdam correspondent William Rand, regarded Hobbes as an original and *bona fide* interpreter of Scripture; others, such as the Dissenter Edward Bagshaw, saw him as a sincere defender of fundamental theological truths.[160] It was certainly possible to read Hobbes as satisfying all three criteria for a Cunradus author: he did engage in an original way with the Bible; he was evidently hostile to both Presbyterianism (which, to a Dutch reader, would mean the established Reformed Church) and Catholicism; and his ideas about religious toleration, although ambiguous where the role of the state was concerned, were set firmly against ecclesiastical jurisdiction and persecution. The approach to Cunradus by Redmayne, Williams, Wright, or Chiswell may have been made merely on the basis that he was known to be a printer willing to take on risky materials; only speculation is possible here, as the known details of Cunradus's links (direct or indirect) with England do not yield a connection with any of the English producers of the Bear edition.[161] Nevertheless, the fact that Cunradus agreed to take on the work may well tell us something about his own attitude towards Hobbes's religious theories.

That decision by Cunradus cannot have been taken lightly. It is impossible to believe that Hobbes's notoriety had entirely passed him by: ever since the appearance of the Dutch translation of *Leviathan* in 1667, the condemnations in the Netherlands had come thick and fast. And not only condemnations, but a legally binding prohibition too: the popular modern image of seventeenth-century Holland as a publisher's paradise, where censorship was so slight as to be virtually non-existent, is somewhat misconceived.[162] The sequence of public denunciations

---

[160] See Rand's letter to Benjamin Worsley, 11 Aug. 1651: 'Mr Hobbs in his ingenious booke [*Leviathan*] ... gives a smart interpretation of the trinity & a suitable reason why men were to be baptised in the name of father, Sonne & holy spirit' (Hartlib Papers, electronic edn, 62/21/1A); and Bagshaw's letter to Hobbes, 1/11 March 1658, in Hobbes, *Correspondence*, I, pp. 497–8.

[161] His direct links were with Quakers, though limited apparently to those who visited or resided in the Netherlands; none of the English printers and booksellers mentioned hitherto had any Quaker connection. (John Redmayne's son William Redmayne did print a book by George Keith, *An Account of the Quakers Politicks*, in 1700; but this fact will hardly suffice to endow the father with Quaker connections in the 1670s.) I have also failed to find any link via Quirinus Kuhlmann, who spent nearly two years in England (1676–8), and had two of his own works printed there (but by unidentified printers): see his *The General London Epistle* (London, 1679) and *Quinary of Slingstones* (London and Oxford, 1683).

[162] See the important essay by S. Groenveld, 'The Mecca of Authors? States Assemblies and Censorship in the Seventeenth-Century Dutch Republic', in *Too Mighty to be Free: Censorship and the Press in Britain and the Netherlands*, ed. A. Duke and C. A. Tamse (Zutphen, 1987), pp. 63–86. Cf. also the account of prohibitions and book-burnings in 17th-century Holland given in C. Sepp, *Het staatstoezicht op de godsdienstige letterkunde in de noordelijke Nederlanden* (Leiden, 1891), pp. 39–101. The fullest modern study of this issue is I. Weekhout, *Boekencensuur in de noordelijken Nederlanden: de vrijheid van drukpers in de zeventiende eeuw* (The Hague, 1998).

and exhortations issued against *Leviathan* included the following: decrees forbidding people to read it, issued by the Classis of Amsterdam in 1667; complaints about it in the Synod in 1668; a formal request to the States of Holland from the Deputies of the Synods of South and North Holland, asking for a ban on it in 1670; a repetition of that request in 1671; and, finally, a general decree (acceding to those requests) by the Court of Holland, issued over the name of the stadhouder in July 1674, forbidding the 'printing, distributing or selling' of *Leviathan*, as well as Spinoza's *Tractatus*.[163]

The ecclesiastical denunciations did not, admittedly, deter the publisher of the Dutch translation of *Leviathan* from reissuing the work in 1672.[164] But the civil decree was a more serious matter. Some sign of the fear it engendered is given by the fact that, when a Dutch translation of Hobbes's *De cive* was issued in 1675, the names of the translator, printer, and bookseller were all omitted from it.[165] Cunradus must have known that he was dabbling in dangerous matters when he agreed to print the completion of *Leviathan*. Yet at the same time he would have been reassured by the knowledge that the sheets he printed would all be shipped to England: they could not be distributed in Holland, even if there were enough English readers there to make a market for them, for the simple reason that they would not even constitute a book until they had been added to the other sheets already printed in London. And so it was that Cunradus (who seems to have been averse, on principle, to any strategy of complete self-concealment) felt confident enough to use an ornament bearing the initials 'C.C.' which, to many Amsterdam readers, would instantly have identified the printing as his own. Christoffel Cunradus would naturally have assumed that no one in England would be able to make the link with him—and, of course, so long as the link were made only in England, it would not have mattered if anyone had. Since his responsibility for the completion of this printing has remained unproven for

---

[163] See, respectively: Meinsma, *Spinoza en zijn kring*, p. 270; W. P. C. Knuttel, *Verboden boeken in de Republiek der Vereenigde Nederlanden*, Bijdragen tot de geschiedenis van den Nederlandschen boekhandel, 11 (The Hague, 1914), p. 57; Kleerkooper and van Stockum, *Boekhandel*, I, pp. 157–9; Meinsma, *Spinoza en zijn kring*, p. 386; C. Cau et al., *Groot placaet-boek, vervattende de placaten, ordonnantien ende edicten van de ... Staten Generael van de Vereenighde Nederlanden*, 7 vols. (The Hague, Amsterdam, 1658–1797), III, pp. 523–4 ('te Drucken, divulgeren ofte verkopen'). A later reference to a condemnation of *Leviathan* by the pastors of Utrecht (G. Cocq, *Hobbesianismi anatome, qua ... philosophi illius à religione christianâ apostasia demonstratur, & refutatur* (Utrecht, 1680), sig. *3v) probably alludes to the Synodal resolution of 1670.

[164] Macdonald and Hargreaves, *Bibliography*, p. xvi. For what little is known about the activities of Jacobus Wagenaar, the publisher of the 1667 and 1672 edns, see A.-J. Gelderblom, 'The Publisher of Hobbes's Dutch *Leviathan*', in *Across the Narrow Seas: Studies in the History and Bibliography of Britain and the Low Countries*, ed. S. Roach (London, 1991), pp. 162–6.

[165] T. Hobbes, *De eerste beginselen van een burger-staat* (Amsterdam, 1675). On this edition (omitted from Macdonald and Hargreaves's bibliography) see C. W. Schoneveld, 'Some Features of the Seventeenth-Century Editions of Hobbes's *De Cive* Printed in Holland and Elsewhere', in *Thomas Hobbes: His View of Man*, ed. J. G. van der Bend (Amsterdam, 1982), pp. 125–42, esp. pp. [135], 141.

more than 300 years, it must be admitted that his confidence was thoroughly justified.

## ACKNOWLEDGEMENT

I am especially grateful to Dr Nicholas Smith (Cambridge University Library) for his advice and help on matters relating to typefaces and ornaments, and to Dr David McKitterick (Trinity College, Cambridge) and Dr Giles Mandelbrote (the British Library) for guidance on printing-house practice. I am also particularly grateful to the staffs of the Houghton Library, Harvard, Cambridge University Library, and the University Library of Amsterdam, as well as to those of all the other libraries and archives mentioned in the notes.

# – 12 –

# Hobbes, Ezra, and the Bible: The History of a Subversive Idea

## I

On 23 December 1696 Thomas Aikenhead, a twenty-year-old student of Edinburgh University, was put on trial for blasphemy. Under a recently passed Scottish law, this offence could include not only 'railing upon' God and denying his existence, but also impugning 'the authority of the holy Scripture'. Aikenhead's opinions about the Bible featured prominently in his indictment:

Lykeas you scoffed at, and endeavoured to ridicule the holy scriptures, calling the Old Testament Ezra's fables, by a profane allusion to Esop's fables, and saying that Ezra was the inventor therof, and that being a cunning man he drew a number of Babylonian slaves to follow him, for whom he made up a feigned genealogie as if they had been descended of kings and princes in the land of Canaan, and therby imposed upon Cyrus who was a Persian and stranger, persuading him by the device of a pretendit prophecy concerning himself.[1]

In other words, the Pentateuch and the historic and prophetic books of the Bible were written not by Moses and the prophets, but by Ezra the Scribe—the person who, according to the books of Ezra and Nehemiah, was allowed by Cyrus to go to Jerusalem and teach the law to those Jews who had returned there from the Babylonian captivity. Even without the extra details of trickery and pretence embroidered, apparently, on to Ezra's story by Aikenhead, the mere suggestion that the Pentateuch was written not by Moses, but by someone who lived many centuries after that prophet's death, would have been shockingly offensive to orthodox faith. On 24 December Aikenhead was found guilty of blasphemy, and on 8 January 1697 he was hanged.

Thirteen years later a book was published anonymously in Holland, under the title *Les Voyages et avantures de Jaques Massé*; it would become a popular work

[1] W. Cobbett, T. B. Howell, *et al.*, eds., *A Complete Collection of State Trials*, 34 vols. (London, 1809–28), XIII, col. 919. The best modern account of the trial is M. Hunter, ' "Aikenhead the Atheist": The Context and Consequences of Articulate Irreligion in the Late Seventeenth Century', in M. Hunter and D. Wootton, eds., *Atheism from the Reformation to the Enlightenment* (Oxford, 1992), pp. 221–54.

among eighteenth-century free-thinkers, with three more editions in French, four in English, and two in German. Its author, Simon Tyssot de Patot, not only made use of the device of an imaginary voyage, but also took care to place his most radical ideas in the mouth of a fictional character, a Gascon atheist, whose views he professed to find extreme. One such opinion was about the authorship of the Pentateuch: 'I defy you, or anyone at all, ever to prove that any of those books existed before the time of Ezra, that is, more than a thousand years after Moses . . . Also, if one reads carefully these books allegedly written by Moses, one finds a very large number of passages which demonstrate that they were written long after him.'[2]

By now, this idea was beginning to circulate as part of the common stock of radical theories nurtured by the early Enlightenment. During the 1720s an obscure parish priest in the Ardennes, Jean Meslier, compiled one of the most thorough and outspoken attacks on Christianity ever written; known as his 'Mémoire' or 'Testament', it began to be distributed in manuscript a few years after his death (in 1729). In his discussion of the Old Testament, Meslier cited a passage from the apocryphal 'Second Book of Esdras', in which Ezra the Scribe is represented as miraculously rewriting the scriptures after they had perished in the destruction of Jerusalem. (Ezra says to God: 'For thy law is burnt, therefore no man knoweth the things that are done of thee . . . But if I have found grace before thee, send the Holy Ghost into me, and I shall write all that hath been done in the world since the beginning, which were written in thy law'; subsequently, filled with the inspiration of the Holy Ghost, Ezra dictates non-stop to five scribes for forty days.[3]) Meslier commented as follows: 'If those books were partly lost, and partly corrupted, as Ezra confirms . . . it follows that there is absolutely no certainty about their contents, and as for Ezra's claim to have corrected them and restored them in their entirety by the inspiration of God himself, nothing about that is certain, and there is no impostor in the world who could not say as much.'[4]

---

[2] [S. Tyssot de Patot,] *Les Voyages et avantures de Jaques Massé* ('Bordeaux', 1710), p. 461 ('je vous défie, ou qui que ce soit, de pouvoir jamais prouver qu'aucun de ces Livres ait existé avant le tems d'Esdras, c'est-à-dire plus de 1000. ans après Moïse . . . Aussi en lisant avec attention les Livres atribuez à Moïse, on trouve un très-grand nombre de passages, qui font voir qu'ils ont été écrits long-tems après lui'). On the author see D. R. McKee, *Simon Tyssot de Patot and the Seventeenth-Century Background of Critical Deism,* Johns Hopkins Studies in Romance Literatures and Languages, 40 (Baltimore, Maryland, 1941) (esp. p. 11 on the popularity of the work).

[3] 2 Esdras 14: 21–2, 37–45. This apocryphal book may be referred to as 2 Esdras or 4 Ezra; it will be referred to as '2 Esdras' or 'the Second Book of Esdras' in this essay. (The two canonical books entitled Ezra and Nehemiah in Protestant editions of the Bible are 1 Ezra and 2 Ezra in the Vulgate, having originally formed a single text; there is one other apocryphal book, derived from a compilation of those two canonical books but with some other inserted material, which may be referred to as 1 Esdras or 3 Ezra.)

[4] J. Meslier, *Oeuvres complètes,* ed. J. Deprun, R. Desné and A. Soboul, 3 vols. (Paris, 1970), I, pp. 123–4 ('Si ces livres ont été en partie perdus, et en partie corrompus, comme le temoigne le dit Esdras . . . il n'y a donc certainement pas de certitude sur ce qu'ils contiennent, et quant à ce que le même Esdras dit les avoir corrigé et remis en leur entier par l'inspiration de Dieu même, il n'y a point d'imposteur qui n'en pourroit dire autant'); see also I, pp. l–lviii for the MS history of this text.

Also composing a radical critique of Christianity in the 1720s, quite independently of Meslier, was the prominent scholar Nicolas Fréret, Secretary of the Académie des Inscriptions et Belles-Lettres in Paris. His 'Lettre de Thrasybule à Leucippe' (a survey of paganism, Judaism and Christianity, written as if by a learned Greek in the first century AD) raises some standard objections to the theory of the Mosaic authorship of the Pentateuch: those books of the Bible contain things that 'can only have been written a long time after the Law-giver', a fact which 'greatly diminishes their authority'. The prophetic books, too, may have been put together only after the events referred to in their so-called prophecies.[5] But Fréret goes further. Cleverly, he turns the tables on the traditional claim that divine revelation was authenticated by prophecies and miracles: he remarks that the Jews were more obedient to God after the return from the Babylonian captivity, despite the lack of miracles, whereas their worst disobedience to God had come in earlier times, when miracles were (allegedly) in plentiful supply. His conclusion is that the miracles had never happened, and that the significant new factor here was that after the captivity the Jewish people had, for the first time, come under the spell of a Scripture which claimed that they had. 'Those miracles . . . were inserted after the event into a history which, as they admit, was compiled by the person— Ezra—who led them back from Babylon, who established their new government, rebuilt their city with the temple of their God, and determined the form of their religion, which had been entirely abolished.'[6]

Fréret's text received its first (surreptitious) printing in the mid-1760s. A few years earlier, in 1762, an abridged version of Meslier's 'Mémoire' was published by Voltaire; the abridgement included the discussion of Ezra and the Bible.[7] Voltaire himself had touched on the question of the Mosaic authorship of the Pentateuch many times in his own writings: it was a topic for which he reserved his most mordant sarcasm. 'People ask me who wrote the Pentateuch. They might as well ask me who wrote 'The Four Sons of Aymon', 'Robert the Devil', or the tale of

---

[5] Bibliothèque Mazarine, Paris [hereafter: BMP], MS 1193, 4th item, pp. 86–7, ('qui ne peuvent avoir été ecrittes que long temps après le Legislateur' . . . 'ce qui donne une grande atteinte à leur autorité'), p. 88 ('Nous ne sommes point surs que leurs prédictions n'aient point été ajustées après coup avec les evenemens par ceux qui les ont mis en ordre'), printed in N. Fréret, *Lettre de Thrasybule à Leucippe*, ed. S. Landucci (Florence, 1986), pp. 309–10). Landucci dates this work to the early 1720s (p. 73), lists 16 known MS copies (pp. 186–95), and argues cogently for Fréret's authorship (pp. 15–64); Miguel Benítez adds four more MSS, and suggests that, while the work is substantially by Fréret, it may include additional material by another hand ('La Composition de la *Lettre de Thrasybule à Leucippe*: une conjecture raisonnable', in C. Grell and C. Volpilhac-Auger, eds., *Nicolas Fréret, légende et vérité* (Oxford, 1994), pp. 177–92; here pp. 177 (n.), pp. 191–2).

[6] BMP, MS 1193, 4th item, pp. 92–3 ('ces prodiges . . . ont été inserés après coup dans une histoire qui de leur propre aveu a été compilé par celui (Esdras) qui les ramena à [*sic*—for 'de'] Babylone, qui etablit leur nouveau gouvernement, qui rebâtit leur ville avec le temple de leur Dieu, et qui regla la forme de leur Religion entierement abolie'; printed in Fréret, *Lettre de Thrasybule*, pp. 310–11).

[7] *Extrait des sentimens de Jean Meslier*, in Voltaire, *Mélanges*, ed. J. van den Heuvel (Paris, 1965), pp. 455–501; here p. 466.

Merlin the sorcerer... My guess is that Ezra made up all those Tales of a Tub when he returned from the Babylonian captivity.'[8] By the mid-eighteenth century, therefore, the authorship of the Pentateuch had become an issue on which free-thinkers felt such confidence in their opinions that they could treat it with the utmost levity. Indeed, it was central to their whole enterprise of stripping Revelation not only of its epistemological status, but also of its claim to be treated with respect. As the anonymous author of one clandestine anti-theological treatise put it, if the Pentateuch was in fact written by Ezra, 'we need not believe Ezra any more than the poet Homer, or a hundred other authors whose stories we have'.[9] Among the faithless, Aikenhead's joke about 'Ezra's fables' had become, so to speak, an article of faith.

## II

When and how had this Ezran hypothesis first arisen? Many of the arguments used in eighteenth-century attacks on Christianity had long histories. The naturalistic rejection of miracles and prophecies went back to Vanini, Cardano, and Pomponazzi; the portrayal of religion as 'imposture', a device for the political control of the masses by ambitious individuals, could be traced at least as far as to Machiavelli. However, in the whole tradition of implicitly or explicitly anti-religious writing in Renaissance and early modern Europe, there is no sign of any such use of this Ezran theory before the middle of the seventeenth century. It is significant that 'Theophrastus redivivus', the monumental 'libertine' treatise which, written some time in the 1650s, functions more or less as a *summa* of the entire radical tradition up until that time, makes no mention of the Ezran theory, blithely referring instead to 'the Pentateuch, that is, the five books written by Moses himself'.[10]

In some ways, indeed, the traditional critique of religion had developed a position which was positively resistant to the Ezran theory: this critique's portrayal of Moses as one of the great practitioners of manipulation or imposture required,

---

[8] *Examen important de Milord Bolingbroke ou le Tombeau du Fanatisme*, in Voltaire, *Mélanges*, pp. 1019–1117; here pp. 1027–8 ('On me demande qui est l'auteur du *Pentateuque*: j'aimerais autant qu'on me demandât qui a écrit *les Quatre Fils Aymon*, *Robert le Diable*, et l'histoire de l'enchanteur Merlin... Je conjecture qu'Esdras forgea tous ces *Contes du Tonneau* au retour de la captivité'). The 'Quatre Fils d'Aymon' and 'Robert le Diable' were popular (and anonymous) verse-romances. For details of other comments by Voltaire on Moses, Ezra and the Bible see D. Levy, *Voltaire et son exégèse du Pentateuque: critique et polémique* (Banbury, 1975), esp. pp. 98–103, and F. Bessire, *La Bible dans la correspondance de Voltaire* (Oxford, 1999), pp. 64–6, 195–7.

[9] BMP, MS 1194, 1st item, 'Dissertation et preuves de l'éternité du monde', p. 75 ('on ne doit pas plus croire Esdras que le Poete Homere et cent autres auteurs dont nous avons les histoires'). On this text see I. O. Wade, *The Clandestine Organization and Diffusion of Philosophic Ideas in France from 1700 to 1750* (Princeton, NJ, 1938), pp. 244–6.

[10] G. Canziani and G. Paganini, eds., *Theophrastus redivivus*, 2 vols. (Florence, 1981), II, p. 451 ('in Pentateuco id est in quinque libris a Mose ipso scriptis').

after all, some basic acceptance of the authenticity of the Pentateuch. In its simplest form, the traditional argument regarded the writing of the 'Mosaic books' as a major element of the imposture practised by Moses. A more sophisticated version of the argument might allow some doubts about the way in which the Pentateuch was put together, but would still presuppose the essential historicity of the text—from which all the detailed evidence of Moses' manipulative actions had to be derived. Thus, a late exemplar of this tradition, the *Traité des trois imposteurs*—written at the turn of the seventeenth and eighteenth centuries—makes just a brief nod in the direction of the Ezran theory: discussing the political nature of Moses' actions against the rule of the Pharaohs, it mentions 'the history which he left of this revolution, or at least the one left to us by the author of those books which are attributed to Moses'. Elsewhere, however, it refers unconcernedly to the 'writings' of Moses; and its entire treatment of the story of Moses involves using those writings as historically reliable evidence.[11] All this would be put in jeopardy by the most extreme version of the Ezran theory, which reduced the Pentateuch to a mere 'fable'. It took some time, apparently, for writers in the radical tradition to recognize that with the Ezran theory they could have the best of both worlds: they could discredit the authority of Revelation all the more thoroughly, while still retaining the basic idea of politically motivated imposture, merely reassigning it from Moses to Ezra himself.

As the Ezran theory spread in the late seventeenth and eighteenth centuries, it drew a large number of responses from defenders of Christian orthodoxy, both Catholic and Protestant. Among these writers of apologetics and polemics, there was at least no doubt about the origins of this dangerous new idea. It came from an unholy trinity of writers: Spinoza, La Peyrère, and Hobbes. Sometimes a fourth heresiarch was added to the list: the French Oratorian and biblical scholar Richard Simon, whose *Histoire critique du Vieux Testament* (1678) propounded a much more sophisticated version of the theory, in which the biblical texts were compiled by a succession of 'public scribes' (of whom Ezra was merely one prominent example).

---

[11] F. Charles-Daubert, ed., *Le 'Traité des trois imposteurs' et 'L'Esprit de Spinosa': philosophie clandestine entre 1678 et 1768* (Oxford, 1999), text of the 1768 edn., pp. 730 ('l'histoire qu'il a laissée de cette révolution, ou du moins que nous a laissée l'auteur des Livres qu'on attribue à Moyse') and 743 ('Moyse, Jésus et Mahomet étant tels que nous venons de les peindre, il est évident que ce n'est point dans leur écrits qu'il faut chercher une véritable idée de la Divinité'). Another version of this text, the 'Fameux livre', includes a reference to 'the different compilations of histories which Ezra or the rabbis have stuck into the books of Moses' ('Les differentes compilations d'Histoires qu'Esdras ou les Rabbins ont fourrées dans les Livres de Moyse': p. 579). There is a large modern literature on the dating and authorship of this work (which was first printed in 1719). The best recent studies are S. Berti, '*L'Esprit de Spinosa*: ses origines et sa première édition dans leur contexte spinozien', in S. Berti, F. Charles-Daubert, and R. H. Popkin, eds., *Heterodoxy, Spinozism, and Free Thought in Early Eighteenth-Century Europe: Studies on the* Traité des Trois Imposteurs (Dordrecht, 1996), pp. 3–51, Winfried Schröder's Introduction to her edition (W. Schröder, ed., *Traktat über die drei Betrüger* (Hamburg, 1992), pp. xvi–xxviii), and Françoise Charles-Daubert's Introduction to hers (*Le 'Traité des trois imposteurs'*): for a summary of her findings see Ch. 14 below, pp. 491–2.

Simon's views were considered to be, in some ways, the most dangerous of all, both because they were backed up by his formidable scholarship, and because he wrote from within the Catholic tradition—professedly, as a critic of Spinoza.[12] The favourite tactic of Simon's own critics, therefore, was to insist that his writings constituted not a refutation of Spinoza, but a repetition of the claims of those three notorious atheists Spinoza, La Peyrère, and Hobbes. In this way, the defenders of orthodox belief not only fixed, so to speak, the canon of unorthodoxy; they also gave the claims of those three writers a much wider circulation than they would otherwise have received. While few could easily get their hands on a copy of Spinoza's *Tractatus theologico-politicus*, many thousands of readers throughout Europe could study a popular work of apologetics such as Jacques Abbadie's *Traité de la vérité de la religion chrétienne*, in which no fewer than sixty-five pages were devoted to the refutation (and, therefore, unavoidably, the exposition) of Spinoza's views on the authorship of the Bible.[13]

Not all defenders of orthodoxy gave such detailed attention to the arguments of their enemies; for some, a rhetorical flourish of denunciation was enough. Most, however, supplied at least the gist of their opponents' claims. Thus, the Catholic scholar Pierre Daniel Huet, writing in 1679, accurately summarized Spinoza's arguments against the Mosaic authorship, before remarking that they were borrowed partly from Hobbes, and partly from La Peyrère.[14] Five years later the Lutheran theologian Johann Benedict Carpzov, giving his inaugural lecture as professor of Hebrew and Theology at Leipzig University, discussed the 'new hypothesis' that Moses had little or nothing to do with writing the Pentateuch, dismissed Richard Simon as no better than Spinoza, and noted that Spinoza had taken the idea mainly from the writings of La Peyrère and 'that propagator of atheism in England, Thomas Hobbes'.[15] The Professor of Divinity at Paris, Louis Ellies du Pin, writing in 1688, noted that 'Hobbes, La Peyrère and Spinoza wrote that the Pentateuch

---

[12] Simon criticized Spinoza in general terms in the Preface to his *Histoire critique du Vieux Testament*, and in more detail in his *Lettre à Monsieur l'Abbé P., D. & P. en T., touchant l'inspiration des livres sacrés* (Rotterdam, 1687), pp. 43–8. (The first edition of the former (Paris, 1678), was almost entirely suppressed; I shall cite from the second edition (Rotterdam, 1685).) On the nature and extent of Spinoza's influence on Simon, see the important study by J. D. Woodbridge, 'Richard Simon's Reaction to Spinoza's "Tractatus Theologico-Politicus" ', in K. Gründer and K. W. Schmidt-Biggemann, eds., *Spinoza in der Frühzeit seiner religiösen Wirkung* (Heidelberg, 1984), pp. 201–26.

[13] J. Abbadie, *Traité de la vérité de la religion chrétienne*, 2 vols. (Rotterdam, 1684), I, pp. 264–329. Abbadie also refers to Hobbes (I, p. 31) and La Peyrère (I, p. 81).

[14] P. D. Huet, *Demonstratio evangelica ad serenissimum Delphinum* (Paris, 1679), pp. 140–4, 145 ('rationes . . . quarum partem aliquam è Leviathane Thomae Hobbesii Angli mutuatus est; partem è Praeadamitico Systemate').

[15] J. B. Carpzovius, *Historia critica Veteri Testamenti autore Ricardo Simone . . . edita, oratione inaugurali discussa* (Leipzig, 1684), pp. 12 ('nihilo melior Benedicto Spinosa') and 31 ('Nova etiam hypothesis de Mose Pentateuchi minimè autore conferre huc debebat plurimum, cujus bonam partem à Prae-Adamitarum architecto Isaaco Peyrerio, & illo Atheismi per Angliam propagatore Thomâ Hobbesio post maledictum Spinosam didicerat').

was not by Moses' (while observing that 'To these authors one should add M. Simon ... his theory is no less rash and dangerous than that of Spinoza').[16] In 1692 the hard-line Lutheran theologian Johann Friedrich Mayer presented a public refutation of the biblical theories of La Peyrère, Hobbes, and Spinoza in Hamburg.[17] Calvinist theologians also entered the fray. Friedrich Spanheim, professor at Leiden University, inveighed against 'the hypotheses of Simon, Hobbes, Spinoza and some others of our day, who have not blushed to launch their petulant attacks against the writings of Moses'.[18] His co-religionist Hermann Witsius, professor at Utrecht, observed in 1692 that the Mosaic authorship of the Pentateuch had been universally accepted until the appearance of Hobbes's *Leviathan*, La Peyrère's *Prae-adamitae*, and Spinoza's *Tractatus theologico-politicus*, and bitterly complained that these modern writers treated the Mosaic books with less respect than they would the works of Xenophon, Thucydides, Polybius, and Livy.[19] In Zurich, a few years later, the Calvinist theologian Johann Heinrich Heidegger likewise defended the Pentateuch against 'those critical innovators, La Peyrère, Hobbes, Spinoza, Simon and others'. He dismissed Simon as the 'ape' of Hobbes and Spinoza, and gave priority, among these modern writers, to La Peyrère. As for Hobbes: 'He has copied several arguments from La Peyrère. He has none of his own.'[20]

While agreement about the authors responsible for this modern 'hypothesis' was virtually universal, there was some room for disagreement over which one of them had said it first. On the face of it, the chronology is straightforward: Hobbes's *Leviathan* came out in 1651, La Peyrère's works putting forward his 'pre-Adamite'

[16] L. Ellies du Pin, *Nouvelle bibliothèque des auteurs ecclésiastiques*, 3 vols. (Paris, 1688–9), I, pp. 68–9 ('Hobbés Peretirere [*sic*] & Spinoza ... ont ecrit que le Pentatheuque n'étoit point de Moïse. Il faut ajoûter à ces Auteurs Mr. Simon ... son Systeme ... n'est pas moins temeraire ni moins dangereux que celuy de Spinoza').

[17] J. F. Mayer, ed., *Dissertationes selectae kilonienses & hamburgenses* (Frankfurt-am-Main, 1693), diss. xix, pp. 545–72 ('Utrum autographa biblica hodie extent?'). On Mayer, an influential adviser to Charles XII of Sweden and a zealous suppressor of the Pietists, see M. Faak, 'Die Verbreitung der Handschriften des Buches "De impostoribus religionum" im 18. Jahrhundert unter Beteiligung von G. W. Leibniz', *Deutsche Zeitschrift für Philosophie*, 18 (1970), pp. 212–28, esp. pp. 215–18; and S. Åkerman, 'Johan Adler Salvius' Questions to Baruch de Castro concerning *De tribus impostoribus*', in S. Berti, F. Charles-Daubert, and R. Popkin, eds., *Heterodoxy, Spinozism, and Free Thought* (Dordrecht, 1996), pp. 397–423, esp. pp. 414–15.

[18] F. Spanheim, *Historia ecclesiastica a condito Adamo ad aeram christianam*, in his *Opera*, 3 vols. (Leiden, 1701–3), I, cols. 257–480; here col. 260 ('hypotheses Simonii, Hobesii, Spinosae, & qui alii, nostro tempore in Mosis scripta, petulanter insurgere non erubuerunt'). Spanheim's main target in his discussion of these theories (cols. 260–70) is Simon, whom he frequently links to Hobbes, Spinoza, and La Peyrère.

[19] H. Witsius, *Miscellaneorum sacrorum libri IV* (Utrecht, 1692), I.14, 'An Moses Auctor Pentateuchi?' (pp. 102–30), esp. pp. 104–5, 119.

[20] J. H. Heidegger, *Exercitationes Biblicae, Capelli, Simonis, Spinosae & aliorum sive aberrationibus, sive fraudibus oppositae* (Zurich, 1700), diss. IX, 'De Pentateuchi scriptore' (pp. 244–75), pp. 246–7 ('Novatores Critici, Peyrerius, Hobbesius, Spinoza, Simon, aliique'), 268 ('praecedentium, Hobbesii inprimis & Spinozae simia'), and 265–6 ('Argumenta nonnulla ex Peyrerio excerpsit. Propria nulla habet'). This work was written before 1698, and may have been influenced by that of Witsius: see J. D. Woodbridge, 'German Responses to the biblical Critic Richard Simon: From Leibniz to J. S. Semler', in H. Reventlow, W. Sparn, and J. Woodbridge, eds., *Historische Kritik und biblischer Kanon in der deutschen Aufklärung*, Wolfenbütteler Forschungen, XLI (Wiesbaden, 1988), pp. 65–87; esp. p. 73.

theory were published in 1655, and Spinoza's *Tractatus theologico-politicus* in 1670. But many continental writers knew Hobbes's work only in its Latin version, printed in Amsterdam first as part of his *Opera philosophica omnia* (1668) and then as a separate book (1670); hence the common assumption that La Peyrère's work had preceded it.[21] The issues of priority and transmission are, however, more complicated than they may seem. Modern scholarship, noting that La Peyrère's text was available in manuscript long before its publication, has reopened the question of the direction in which ideas were transmitted between La Peyrère and Hobbes. Some modern writers on Spinoza, meanwhile, have doubted whether his arguments owed anything to *Leviathan*.[22] And while the title of 'founder of modern biblical criticism' is nowadays given sometimes to La Peyrère, sometimes to Spinoza, and sometimes to Simon, it is hardly ever awarded to Hobbes, despite his prima facie claim to priority.

Not all of these uncertainties can be entirely dispelled; but, taking the three writers in the reverse order of their publications, it is possible to clarify some of the issues concerning influence and transmission. When Spinoza wrote his *Tractatus* he had almost certainly read La Peyrère's book: the evidence for this consists not only in the duplication of some arguments between the two, but also in the fact that he had a copy of the *Prae-adamitae* in his library.[23] The same library catalogue, however, includes only one work by Hobbes, a duodecimo entitled 'Elementa Philosophica'—that is, one of the Elzevier editions of *De cive*.[24] While Spinoza's overall debt to Hobbes's political theories is not in doubt, it is possible to argue that his knowledge of those theories came only from that text, not from *Leviathan*. In any case, Spinoza did not read English; so he would have had to wait until a translation of *Leviathan* was available. From a remark in one of his letters, it is known that he was working on the text of the *Tractatus* in the autumn of 1665.[25] It is on the basis of this remark, the only datable reference to the writing of the work, that some modern scholars have concluded that the whole work was written without any

---

[21] This assumption was surprisingly long-lived: the 19th-century scholar Carl Siegfried knew *Leviathan* only in its 1670 edn, and therefore supposed that Hobbes's arguments were 'mainly borrowed from La Peyrère' (*Spinoza als kritiker und Ausleger des Alten Testaments: ein Beitrag zur Geschichte der alttestamentlichen Kritik und Exegese* (Berlin, 1867), p. 8).

[22] For a discussion of this issue see W. Sacksteder, 'How Much of Hobbes might Spinoza have Read?', *Southwestern Journal of Philosophy*, 11 (1980), pp. 23–39.

[23] For examples of shared arguments see L. Strauss, *Spinoza's Critique of Religion*, tr. E. M. Sinclair (Chicago, 1997), p. 327. For the library catalogue see J. Freudenthal, *Die Lebensgeschichte Spinoza's in Quellenschriften, Urkunden und nichtamtlichen Nachrichten* (Leipzig, 1899), p. 161 (item 54). Richard Popkin suggests that La Peyrère may also have influenced Juan de Prado, who, like Spinoza and apparently for similar reasons, was expelled from the Amsterdam synagogue in 1656: 'Spinoza and La Peyrère', in R. W. Shahan and J. I. Biro, eds., *Spinoza, New Perspectives* (Norman, Okla., 1978), pp. 177–95; esp. p. 189.

[24] Freudenthal, *Lebensgeschichte*, p. 163 (item 129).

[25] B. Spinoza, *Opera*, ed. C. Gebhardt, 4 vols. (Heidelberg, 1924), IV, p. 166, letter 30 ('Compono jam tractatum de meo circa scripturam sensu'); A. Wolf, ed. and tr., *The Correspondence of Spinoza* (London, 1928), p. 206 (dated Sept.–Oct. 1665).

knowledge of *Leviathan*—an unwarrantable conclusion, given that we have no information about when Spinoza finished writing the *Tractatus*, which was not printed until late 1669 or early 1670. Spinoza could have read *Leviathan* in Latin; or, indeed, he may have read it first in the Dutch translation which appeared in 1667, and which had been prepared by a member of one of the heterodox groups with which he was in contact, Abraham van Berkel.[26] There is clear evidence that another member of Spinoza's circle, Adriaen Koerbagh, was in close contact with van Berkel and had read his translation of *Leviathan* with great care: several of the entries in Koerbagh's philosophical dictionary, *Een bloemhof van allerley lieflijkheyd* (1668), including the one for the word 'leviathan', show the direct influence of Hobbes's work.[27] In the summer of 1668, Koerbagh was denounced by a printer to whom he had consigned another book, *Een ligt schijnende in duystere plaatsen*, and was put on trial: one of the key claims made in this work, and held against Koerbagh at his trial, was that the Pentateuch was not by Moses but by some other author, possibly Ezra.[28] Whether Koerbagh had discussed this issue with Spinoza is not known; but it can be assumed with reasonable certainty that he had studied Hobbes's presentation of the question in chapter 33 of *Leviathan*.

Internal evidence also strongly suggests that Spinoza had read Hobbes's work before he completed his final version of the *Tractatus*. Particularly striking is the similarity in method between the two writers when they discuss the interpretation of biblical terms such as 'spirit' or 'the word of God'. In chapter 34 of *Leviathan* Hobbes lists the various meanings of 'spirit' in the Bible, starting with the literal sense of 'a Wind, or Breath' and then including 'extraordinary gifts of the Understanding', 'extraordinary Affections' (in particular, 'an extraordinary Zeal, and Courage'), 'the gift of Prediction', 'Life', 'a subordination to authority', and 'Aeriall Bodies'.[29] Spinoza produces a similar listing in chapter 1 of the *Tractatus*, with 'wind' given first as the literal meaning, followed by 'life, or breathing', 'courage and strength', 'virtue and aptitude', 'habit of mind', 'will', 'passions and faculties', 'mind or life' and the directions of the wind; ten of the biblical references given by Spinoza are the same as those used by Hobbes.[30]

[26] See C. W. Schoneveld, *Intertraffic of the Mind: Studies in Seventeenth-Century Anglo-Dutch Translation with a Checklist of Books Translated from English into Dutch, 1600–1700* (Leiden, 1983), pp. 8, 40.

[27] For a list of Hobbes-influenced entries see J. Lagrée and P.-F. Moreau, 'La Lecture de la Bible dans le cercle de Spinoza', in J.-R. Armogathe, ed., *Le Grand Siècle et la Bible* (Paris, 1989), pp. 97–115; p. 106 (n.). On Koerbagh see Ch. 14 below.

[28] A. Koerbagh, *Een ligt schijnende in duystere plaatsen*, ed. H. Vandenbossche (Brussels, 1974), p. 343. Margaret Gullan-Whurr notes that, according to the records of the trial in the Gemeente Archiefdienst, Amsterdam, this was one of the points on which Koerbagh was questioned: *Within Reason: A Life of Spinoza* (London, 1998), p. 352.

[29] T. Hobbes, *Leviathan* (London, 1651), pp. 208–10.

[30] Spinoza, *Opera*, III, pp. 21–3; cf. the comments in Strauss, *Spinoza's Critique*, p. 326, and A. Pacchi, '*Leviathan* and Spinoza's *Tractatus* on Revelation: Some Elements for a Comparison', in his *Scritti hobbesiani (1978–1990)*, ed. A. Lupoli (Milan, 1998), pp. 123–44; esp. pp. 138–9.

As for the two writers' discussions of the authorship of the Bible (*Leviathan* chapter 33; *Tractatus* chapters 8–10), there is certainly a strong generic similarity between their projects, as both run through all the major books of the Old Testament using textual criticism and historical reasoning to determine the period at which they were written. In many of these cases, however, the arguments adduced by Spinoza are quite different from those used by Hobbes. Where the Pentateuch is concerned, the three pieces of textual evidence presented by Hobbes are all offered by Spinoza too; but as proof of direct transmission this overlap is not very compelling, given that Spinoza has used a much longer list of examples, among which the three cited by Hobbes are merely some of the most obvious. (These arguments will be discussed in more detail below.) In any case, the first six pieces of textual evidence for non-Mosaic authorship cited by Spinoza—one of which features also on Hobbes's list—are drawn explicitly from a discussion of this issue in the work of a medieval Jewish commentator, Abraham Ibn Ezra. We know that profound disagreements over the interpretation of Scripture, and indeed over its very status as revelation, were among the reasons for Spinoza's expulsion from the synagogue in 1656; an early tradition also records that he wrote an 'Apology', a defence of his position at that time, some of which may later have been incorporated in the *Tractatus*. That Spinoza should have searched through the works of a respected rabbinical scholar such as Ibn Ezra for confirmation of his views makes particularly good sense in the context of such a dispute within the Jewish community: quite possibly, therefore, this element of Spinoza's argument dates back at least as far as 1656.

If Spinoza's doubts about the Mosaic authorship of the Pentateuch were first expressed at the time of his dispute with the elders of the synagogue in the mid-1650s, they may have received some stimulus from the publication of La Peyrère's work, but they cannot have been derived in any direct way from Hobbes. On the other hand, it is possible that the eventual formulation of those doubts published in the *Tractatus* was influenced to some extent by Hobbes: while the negative arguments against Mosaic authorship are found in Ibn Ezra (embryonically) and in La Peyrère, Hobbes, and Spinoza (explicitly), the positive argument for Ezra's responsibility is found only in Hobbes (ambiguously) and Spinoza (emphatically). Only the discovery of that Holy Grail of Spinoza scholarship, the manuscript of his early 'Apology', could answer the question of how fully formed Spinoza's views on these issues were before he had read Hobbes. In the absence of such evidence, it seems reasonable to suppose that he had probably arrived at his position independently, but that his arguments may have received some reinforcement from *Leviathan* during the later stages of composition of the *Tractatus*.

In the case of the maverick Huguenot writer Isaac La Peyrère, there is also much uncertainty about the precise date at which he formulated his theory. What is frequently referred to as a single work by him, under the title *Prae-adamitae*, consists in fact of two separate texts, issued together in one volume. The first, a short treatise based on Romans 5: 12–14, is entitled *Prae-adamitae, sive exercitatio super versibus duodecimo, decimotertio, & decimoquarto, capitis quinti Epistolae D. Pauli ad Romanos, quibus inducuntur primi homines ante Adamum conditi*; it states La Peyrère's theory that Adam was not the first man, but otherwise consists almost entirely of a reinterpretation of the doctrine of original sin. The second, *Systema theologicum ex praeadamitarum hypothesi pars prima*, a much longer text, is more wide-ranging, developing (among other things) the argument that many episodes in biblical history, such as the Flood, concerned not mankind in general but only the Jews in their particular territory. As part of his project of downgrading the significance of Adam, La Peyrère also tries to diminish the authority of the Book of Genesis (from which all knowledge of Adam is derived). So it is that in book 4 of this work he presents his argument that the Pentateuch, far from being an inspired text set down word for word by Moses, is a muddled and much later compilation of various materials, which at most might include some information ultimately derived from Moses' 'diaries' or journals.[31]

When did La Peyrère set down these theories in writing? The first reference to some such work dates from March 1642, when Gabriel Naudé told one of his friends in Paris that 'La Peyrère has written a book, which is not yet printed, in which he proves that Adam was not the first man.'[32] Three months later Naudé mentioned, in a letter to his patron Francesco Barberini, that 'a few months ago' a manuscript had been presented to Cardinal Richelieu in which the author sought to show, mainly by means of texts from the New Testament, that the world had been populated long before Adam; Richelieu had been so scandalized that he had promptly forbidden the author to print it.[33] La Peyrère was not altogether cowed

---

[31] I. La Peyrère, *Prae-adamitae, Systema theologicum* (n.p., 1655), IV.1, p. 153 ('Crediderim certe, diurnos commentarios Mosem confecisse'). There are at least two different printings (in several different issues) of this book, all dated 1655. The one I use is the volume probably printed by Janssonius in Amsterdam, containing the *Prae-adamitae, sive exercitatio* and the *Systema theologicum*; it can be distinguished by the number of pages (52 for the former and 260 for the latter). I have not made a detailed comparison of these editions; however, given that the publication was sponsored by Queen Christina of Sweden, who had previously made Janssonius her 'royal typographer', I think it likely that his was the first of the 1655 printings.

[32] Österreichische Nationalbibliothek, Vienna, MS 7071, 'Naudéana', fol. 29r ('la Pereire a fait vn liure qui n'est pas encore imprimé dans lequel il prouue qu'Adam n'a pas esté le premier homme'). This statement appears in a part of the MS consisting, according to a note on fol. 2r, of comments made by Naudé to the anonymous compiler at a meeting on 19 March 1642; it has apparently not been noticed by previous writers on La Peyrère. One earlier alleged reference to La Peyrère's writings appears in a letter from Mersenne to Rivet, dated 16 Jan. 1642: 'Un des professeurs de philosophie de cette ville vient de faire imprimer un gros volume dans lequel il prouve que toutes les ames des hommes viennent de celle d'Adam'; this is glossed by the editors of the letter as a reference to La Peyrère's published work, *Du Rappel des Juifs* (M. Mersenne, *Correspondance* ed. C. de Waard *et al.*, 17 vols. (Paris, 1933–88), XI, p. 3 and n.). However, the identification is surely incorrect: that work did not appear until 1643; it was not a 'gros volume'; its author was never a professor of philosophy in Paris; and the argument summarized here by Mersenne is virtually the opposite of La Peyrère's.

[33] Biblioteca Apostolica Vaticana, Vatican City, MS Cod. Barb. Lat. 6471, fols. 22–3; here fol. 22v ('Fu presentato un Manoscritto alcuni mesi fa a detta sua E.za il cui Autore pretende haver demonstrato con testi

by this reverse, however: in November 1643 he informed Claude Sarrau that he was thinking of having the text printed, and during the same month Mersenne told André Rivet that he had a manuscript copy of the work, in which La Peyrère tried to prove, by means of St Paul's Epistle to the Romans, that there had been men before Adam.[34] These comments (especially the references to St Paul's Epistle and the New Testament) strongly suggest that the work in question was the *Prae-adamitae sive exercitatio*—which, though it presents the essence of La Peyrère's pre-Adamite theory, says nothing whatsoever about the authorship of the Pentateuch. There is simply no evidence to show that the *Systema theologicum* was already written at that stage. Indeed, it could not then have been written in its present, final form—containing, as it does, references to later works such as Samuel Bochart's *Phaleg*, which was published only in 1646.[35] In February 1647 Mersenne reported to Rivet that the version of La Peyrère's *Prae-adamitae* that he had recently seen was 'enlarged'; but the comparison with an earlier version, together with Mersenne's comments on its contents (concentrating exclusively on the issue of original sin), once again implies that this was the *Prae-adamitae sive exercitatio*, not the *Systema theologicum*.[36]

The existing evidence suggests that it was only after the stimulus of a publication by Claude Saumaise in early 1648 (*De annis climactericis*, which noted that Chaldaean and Egyptian chronologies went back much further than the biblical account of creation) that La Peyrère started a new phase of writing on this topic; Saumaise's findings would be incorporated in book 3 of the *Systema theologicum*.[37] At some time before the end of that year, La Peyrère circulated a copy of his work among members of the 'Cabinet' of Pierre and Jacques Dupuy—two rich and scholarly brothers whose patronage extended to some of the leading historians, literary men, philologists and philosophers of Paris. He received a storm of objections and criticisms in response.[38] From the fact of this new distribution, and from

---

espressi della Sacra Scrittura e massimamente del Nuovo Testamento, che il Mondo non era solamente creato, ma anche habbitato da moltissimi Huomini avanti Adamo'.) This letter is mistakenly dated '1641' in R. Popkin, *Isaac La Peyrère (1596–1676): His Life, Work and Influence* (Leiden, 1987), p. 6.

[34] C. Sarrau, *Claudii Sarravii senatoris parisiensis epistolae, opus posthumum* (Orange, 1654), p. 74 (Sarrau to Saumaise, 12 Nov. 1643); Mersenne, *Correspondance*, xii, p. 364. For some other early references to La Peyrère's work see D. R. McKee, 'Isaac de la Peyrère, a Precursor of Eighteenth-Century Critical Deists', *Publications of the Modern Language Association of America*, 59 (1944), pp. 456–65 (esp. pp. 456–7), and H. J. Schoeps, *Philosemitismus im Barock* (Tübingen, 1957), p. 9 (n.).

[35] La Peyrère, *Prae-adamitae, Systema theologicum*, IV.2, p. 160.

[36] Mersenne, *Correspondance*, XV, p. 98 (Mersenne to Rivet, 15 Feb. 1647).

[37] Popkin, *Isaac La Peyrère*, p. 12 (noting that he received a copy of Saumaise's book early in 1648 and 'worked feverishly on his manuscript' during the rest of that year); La Peyrère, *Systema theologicum*, III.5, p. 118, III.6, p. 125, and III.10, pp. 140–1. La Peyrère also thanks Ismaël Boulliau for supplying a passage from a manuscript in the Bibliothèque Royale: III.4, p. 112. Boulliau was absent from Paris for most of 1645–7, and this service was presumably performed after his return.

[38] H. J. M. Nellen, *Ismaël Boulliau (1605–1694): astronome, épistolier, nouvelliste et intermédiaire scientifique* (Amsterdam, 1994), p. 427.

the nature of the reaction it caused (among a circle of people some of whom had probably seen the earlier work in manuscript), it is reasonable to conclude that La Peyrère was now presenting a substantially new text to his friends: the *Systema theologicum*, with its argument against the Mosaic authorship of the Pentateuch. Some version of this work, we may presume, was therefore in existence by late 1648.

Did the friends who read La Peyrère's controversial text in manuscript include Thomas Hobbes? The leading modern authority on La Peyrère, Richard Popkin, has described him as 'close . . . to Hobbes' and 'probably an acquaintance of Hobbes'; he has also stated that Hobbes was 'probably' a member of the circle of philosophers, scientists, and writers who were being 'sponsored' by the Prince de Condé—whom La Peyrère served as secretary for part of the 1640s and the early 1650s.[39] There is, unfortunately, no firm evidence to support either of these claims. Other modern writers have described Hobbes as having attended meetings of the group patronized by the brothers Dupuy; but again, evidence for this is lacking.[40] Hobbes certainly counted four members of the Dupuy's circle among his friends— Mersenne, Gassendi, Sorbière, and La Mothe le Vayer—and had some personal acquaintance with a fifth, Jean-Baptiste Lantin.[41] But the key question here is how close his contacts were with members of that circle in the period between the circulation of the manuscript of the *Systema theologicum* in late 1648 and the composition of chapter 33 of *Leviathan*—which was completed some time before May 1650.[42] Mersenne had died in September 1648; Gassendi had left Paris for the south of France soon thereafter, and would not return until 1653; and Sorbière was entirely absent from Paris between 1645 and 1654. That leaves only La Mothe le Vayer and Lantin. Unfortunately, nothing is known of the closeness of the former's relationship with Hobbes, beyond the fact that a mutual acquaintance described him as one of Hobbes's 'good frends' in a letter of 1659, and the evidence of the latter's friendship consists of one mention in the same letter, plus a few jottings in

---

[39] R. H. Popkin, *The History of Scepticism from Erasmus to Spinoza* (Berkeley, Calif., 1979), p. 215; 'Spinoza and Bible Scholarship', in J. E. Force and R. Popkin, eds., *The Books of Nature and Scripture: Recent Essays on Natural Philosophy, Theology and Biblical Criticism in the Netherlands of Spinoza's Time and the British Isles of Newton's Time* (Dordrecht, 1994), pp. 1–20 (at p. 6); *Isaac La Peyrère*, p. 5. In the first of these works Popkin comes close to implying that Hobbes's theory about the Pentateuch was derived from La Peyrère: 'Hobbes in the *Leviathan* is usually credited with being the first to deny the Mosaic authorship. The date of Hobbes's text is 1651, ten years after La Peyrère had written his manuscript' (p. 217; for this mis-dating—of a text that was not, in any case, the *Systema theologicum*—see above, n. 33). In his monograph on La Peyrère, however, he merely observes: 'Whether Hobbes got this from La Peyrère or vice-versa, we do not know' (p. 49).

[40] R. Pintard, *Le Libertinage érudit dans la première moitié du XVIIe siècle*, 2nd edn. (Geneva, 1983), p. 94; Nellen, *Ismaël Boulliau*, p. 84.

[41] See Hobbes, *Correspondence*, II, pp. 862–5 (Mersenne), pp. 834–6 (Gassendi), pp. 893–9 (Sorbière), and I, pp. 438 (n. 2), p. 504 (La Mothe le Vayer), 505 (n. 5) (Lantin). For these people's membership of the 'Cabinet Dupuy' see Pintard, *Libertinage*, p. 94 (also listing more than 40 other people with whom Hobbes had no known connection). On the 'Cabinet Dupuy' see also I. Uri, *Un Cercle savant au XVIIe siècle: François Guyet d'après des documents inédits* (Paris, 1886), pp. 8–63.

[42] BL, MS Harl. 6942, no. 128, Robert Payne to Gilbert Sheldon, 13 May 1650: 'he [*sc.* Hobbes] sends me word he hath an other taske in hand, w$^{ch}$ is Politiques, in English, of w$^{ch}$ he hath finishd 37 chapters.'

a notebook recording some comments made by Hobbes in conversation.[43] Of course Hobbes may have enjoyed other friendships with members of the Dupuy circle, evidence of which happens not to have survived. But all that can be concluded from the existing evidence of his personal contacts during these years is that, while he may have known some people who knew about La Peyrère's work, there is no strong reason to suppose that he would have received a copy of the manuscript itself.

As for the internal evidence of the texts, it does not offer any clear support for the idea that Hobbes had derived his arguments from a reading of La Peyrère. Of the three pieces of textual evidence used by Hobbes to disprove the Mosaic authorship of the Pentateuch, two are given by La Peyrère but the third is not; on the other hand, La Peyrère gives four other textual arguments, not used by Hobbes. (Details of these arguments will be presented below.) If Hobbes had been working directly from La Peyrère's text, he might well have included some or all of those other arguments too. On the other hand, the two arguments that these writers did both employ were available (as we shall see) from other sources. And, while negative proofs are of course never conclusive, it is worth noting that the most striking claims about other biblical topics in La Peyrère's work, such as his propositions on the Flood or indeed on the non-priority of Adam, are all absent from Hobbes's account.

Still, the fact remains that during the writing of *Leviathan*, in 1649 or early 1650, Hobbes did adopt a position on the authorship of the Pentateuch which broadly resembled that of La Peyrère, and which went significantly beyond the more cautious argument set out in *De cive* in 1642. In that earlier work Hobbes concentrated on the question of canonicity—that is, he was concerned with the date at which the books of the Bible were given canonical status, not the date at which they were written. Even with this limitation, however, his argument was distinctly modern in style, treating the evidence in the same way that one would treat any non-sacred historical texts:

The Jews accepted the book of the whole law (which is called *Deuteronomy*) as the written Word of God. And that was the only book they accepted down to the time of the captivity, so far as can be inferred from the sacred history . . . But it is not clear when the rest of the books of the old Testament were first received into the canon. As for the Prophets . . . since they predicted things which were to happen only during the captivity or after it, their writings could not be taken as Prophetic right away, by the condition cited above from Deut. 18.21–2, by which the Israelites were bidden only to take as a Prophet someone whose predictions were confirmed by events.[44]

[43] Hobbes, *Correspondence*, I, p. 504; BN, MS f.fr. 23253 ('Lantiniana'). One other token of La Mothe le Vayer's friendship with Hobbes may also be mentioned: the copy of Jouvin's *Solution et esclaircissement de quelques propositions de mathematiques* (Paris, 1658) at Chatsworth, Derbyshire (pressmark 128 C), inscribed on the cover: 'for M[r] Hobbes from M[r] de la mote le vayer [*signed*:] Du Bosc'.
[44] T. Hobbes, *De cive*, XVI.12 (translation quoted here: *On the Citizen*, ed. and tr. R. Tuck and M. Silverthorne (Cambridge, 1999), pp. 194–5).

One key element of the argument of *Leviathan* is already present here: the idea that the crucial period for the formation of most of the Old Testament in its present form was during, or just after, the Babylonian captivity. But in *De cive* Hobbes has left the question of the date of writing entirely open: readers are allowed to assume, if they wish, that the other four books of the Pentateuch (and the various prophetic books) had been in existence all along, even if they had not enjoyed the authority of the canon. This is what changes in *Leviathan*, where Hobbes produces his three textual arguments against Mosaic authorship and confidently declares: 'It is therefore sufficiently evident, that the five Books of *Moses* were written after his time, though how long after it be not so manifest.'[45] (He accepts, however, that the law-code set out in the central part of Deuteronomy—chapters 11–26—did consist of Moses' own words.) Even if Hobbes had never had a copy of La Peyrère's manuscript in his hands, he might perhaps have heard about La Peyrère's arguments on this point: this possibility cannot be excluded. On the other hand, the logic of his position may simply have pushed his argument in this direction anyway. After all, if the Israelites had actually possessed four other books which they believed, from the outset, to consist of Moses' own words, they would surely have accepted them as canonical too, instead of waiting many centuries for such status to be granted: the natural implication of the argument in *De cive* was that they had not actually possessed those books to begin with, and therefore the obvious next step for Hobbes would have been to look for evidence that those books were put together at a later stage.

The conclusions to be drawn from this brief examination of the relationship between the arguments of Hobbes, La Peyrère, and Spinoza are, at first sight, frustratingly inconclusive. Spinoza may have been influenced by La Peyrère on the question of Mosaic authorship, and he may later have been influenced by Hobbes on the issue of Ezran responsibility; but it seems quite likely that his anti-Mosaic thesis had developed independently, partly as a result of his reading of medieval Jewish sources. Hobbes may have been influenced by La Peyrère, at least indirectly, through hearing about his work; or he may have developed his own argument independently. As for La Peyrère himself, his adoption of the anti-Mosaic thesis remains unexplained; none of the modern specialists on La Peyrère has put forward any suggestions for the sources of his ideas on this issue. (Some of the seventeenth-century writers mentioned above assumed that La Peyrère, like Spinoza, had derived his theory from Ibn Ezra; but Ibn Ezra's work was available only in Hebrew, and there is no evidence that La Peyrère had any knowledge of that language.[46])

[45] Hobbes, *Leviathan*, p. 200.
[46] See e.g. Ellies du Pin, *Nouvelle bibliothèque*, p. 68: 'Et c'est principalement sur l'autorité & sur les raisons de ce Rabin que se sont fondez Hobbés Peretirere [sic] & Spinosa.' Some modern writers have attributed a Marrano origin to La Peyrère; but no solid evidence for it has ever been produced. Even if his family had in fact been originally Marrano, that would hardly suffice to show that he himself had received tuition in Hebrew. Richard Simon, who conversed and corresponded with him in his final years, confidently stated that he knew neither Hebrew nor Greek: Simon, *Lettres choisies*, 4 vols. (Amsterdam, 1730), II, p. 30.

However, the very open-endedness of this pattern of evidence may in fact be the most significant thing about it. What it suggests is the possibility that at almost the same time—in the short period between 1648 and 1656—three people had arrived, more or less independently, at the same position on the non-Mosaicity of the Pentateuch. In addition at least one of them, Thomas Hobbes, had identified Ezra the Scribe as the person who was probably responsible for issuing the Old Testament in its present form; this idea dovetailed so neatly with the anti-Mosaic theory that it would become an inseparable part of it for most subsequent writers on this topic. If three people could reach such similar conclusions more or less independently, this should encourage us to search not for a single chain of transmission, but for the availability more generally of related ideas at the time—ideas which may not in themselves have had such radical force, but which may have supplied some of the components for these new theories, or at least prompted some of the questions to which these three theorists supplied such radical answers.

Such related ideas were indeed available. But in order to understand how and why they had arisen, it is necessary to look at the more long-term development of both Jewish and Christian arguments about Ezra and the authorship of the Pentateuch.

## III

Jewish tradition venerated Moses as the writer of the Pentateuch; but it also gave special honour to Ezra, who helped to re-establish the Mosaic Law after his return to Jerusalem in c.458 BC.[47] According to the book of Nehemiah (also known as the second book of Ezra), 8: 1–3, 'all the people gathered themselves together . . . and they spake unto Ezra the scribe to bring the book of the law of Moses . . . And Ezra the priest brought the law before the congregation . . . And he read therein . . . from morning until mid-day.' Particular attention was paid by Jewish exegetes to Nehemiah 8: 8, which described the method used on that occasion by Ezra and his fellow teachers of the law: 'So they read in the book in the law of God distinctly, and gave the sense, and caused them [*sc.* the people] to understand the reading.' Jewish tradition used this passage to attribute to Ezra several features of the Hebrew text (and its related traditions) which were in fact the products of a much later period.

The early Hebrew text was only consonantal; the vowel-points were added to it in the latter part of the first millennium AD—a process that involved significant interpretative decisions, since the choice of a different vowel could often produce a completely different meaning.[48] The scholars who thus fixed the vocalization of

[47] For a summary of modern scholarship on Ezra and his historical context see D. W. Rooke, *Zadok's Heirs: The Role and Development of the High Priesthood in Ancient Israel* (Oxford, 1999), pp. 152–74.

[48] For a valuable illustration of the nature of the problem, see E. Breuer, *The Limits of Enlightenment: Jews, Germans, and the Eighteenth-Century Study of Scripture* (Cambridge, Mass., 1996), pp. 36–40.

the text also surrounded it with a protective layer of annotations, known as the 'Masorah', which in some cases distinguished between how the text was to be written and how it was to be read. By the tenth century AD this standardized version of the Hebrew scriptures, known as the Masoretic Bible, had achieved general acceptance among the Jews, and it would in turn be taken as the authoritative text by Christian scholars.[49] Before long, however, these features of the text were being confidently attributed to Ezra, on the basis of Nehemiah 8: 8. Thus the phrase 'they read . . . distinctly' was taken to refer to the vocalization (and the system of accents or cantilation); 'and gave the sense' was assumed to mean that Ezra and his colleagues supplied the Masoretic annotations; and, in addition, the phrase 'and caused them to understand the reading' was taken to imply that they also produced the Targum, the Aramaic paraphrase of the Hebrew Bible which had considerable authority as an aid to its interpretation. The colleagues of Ezra were identified in rabbinical tradition as members of the 'Great Synagogue' (not a synagogue in the normal sense of the term, but an assembly or convention), a gathering of 120 men including famous prophets such as Zachariah and Malachi: the tradition recorded that these were the people who, acting under divine guidance, completed the collection of twenty-two sacred books that made up the Hebrew Bible, and made some small corrections to the text, known as the 'tiqqune soferim' or 'corrections of the scribes'.[50] By presiding over this enterprise, Ezra had thus played a role second only to Moses in the transmission of God's word to his chosen people. In the words of a Talmudic saying, 'If Moses had not anticipated him, Ezra would have received the Torah.'[51]

The most extreme claim made on behalf of Ezra the Scribe, however, had developed long before these rabbinical traditions. It was probably in the last decade of the first century AD that an unknown Jewish writer composed the main part of the text known to us as 2 Esdras (or 4 Ezra), in which, as cited above, Ezra was credited with having miraculously rewritten the whole of the Hebrew Bible. This text was never regarded as canonical by the Jews, and indeed no Hebrew version of it has survived (though scholars presume that it was originally written in that language); but its author was certainly Jewish, and the purpose of this particular claim about Ezra may have been to console the Jews in the period after the second destruction of the Temple (in AD 70) by emphasizing the miraculously restorative powers of God. Other parts of what is now the text of 2 Esdras were added by Christian writers,

---

[49] See M. J. Mulder, 'The Transmission of the Biblical Text', in M. J. Mulder and H. Sysling, eds., *Mikra: Text, Translation, Reading and Interpretation of the Bible in Ancient Judaism and Early Christianity* (Assen, 1988), pp. 87–135, esp. pp. 104–15; I. Yeivin, *Introduction to the Tiberian Masorah*, tr. E. J. Revell (Missoula, Mont., 1980), esp. pp. 34–6, 52–61, 137.

[50] See G. F. Moore, *Judaism in the First Centuries of the Christian Era: The Age of the Tannaim*, 3 vols. (Cambridge, 1927–30), I, pp. 29–36; G. E. Weil, *Élie Lévita: humaniste et massorète (1469–1549)* (Leiden, 1963), pp. 297–8, 307; Yeivin, *Introduction*, pp. 49–50. For a useful survey of rabbinical tradition on the Men of the Great Synagogue see J. Buxtorf, *Tiberias sive commentarius masorethicus* (Basel, 1620, quarto edition), pp. 95–8; cf. also G. Bartolocci, *Bibliotheca magna rabbinica*, 4 vols. (Rome, 1675–93), IV, p. 4.

[51] L. Ginzburg, *The Legends of the Jews*, tr. H. Szold, 7 vols. (Philadelphia, 1913–38), IV, p. 355.

probably in the second and third centuries.[52] The result was a strange hybrid, containing an explicit reference to Jesus but regarded by Christians as part of the apocrypha of the Old Testament. Many of the Church Fathers cited it with respect, and its claim about Ezra's miraculous re-constituting of the Scriptures found some echoes in their writings. In a few cases they seem to have accepted the story without reserve (Basil, writing in the fourth century, declared that 'by God's command, Ezra spewed forth all the holy books'); more commonly, they described Ezra's role in somewhat more guarded terms. (Isidore of Seville, writing in the seventh century, noted that Ezra had 'restored' the Scriptures.[53]) Jerome, commenting on the words 'unto this day' in Genesis and Deuteronomy (which seem to imply that the text was written a long time after the events it describes), suggested that that phrase was either written by Moses or added by Ezra, the 'restorer' of the work.[54] Thanks to the apocryphal 2 Esdras, therefore, some notion of the peculiar role of Ezra in relation to the Bible had entered the Christian tradition.

It also entered the anti-Christian tradition. When the Greek philosopher Porphyry was assembling the arguments of his *Against the Christians* in the latter part of the third century, he included a radical objection to the Old Testament which seems to have been derived directly from a reading of 2 Esdras 14 ('For thy law is burnt, therefore no man knoweth the things that are done of thee . . .'). Porphyry wrote: 'nothing has been preserved of Moses, as all his writings are said to have been burnt together with the Temple. And all those which were written under his name afterwards were composed inaccurately one thousand one hundred and eighty years after Moses' death by Ezra and his followers.'[55] If this text had remained in circulation, it would be tempting to assume that the radical deniers of the Mosaicity of the Pentateuch, from Hobbes to Voltaire, had simply borrowed their argument from it. But Porphyry's treatise did not survive; this particular fragment of it is known only because it was quoted by one of his Christian opponents, in a text discovered in Athens in 1867 and printed for the first time in 1876.[56] Nevertheless, Porphyry's work—or at least the argument he used here, which

---

[52] On the composition of the book see the extremely valuable study by A. Hamilton, *The Apocryphal Apocalypse: The Reception of the Second Book of Esdras (4 Ezra) from the Renaissance to the Enlightenment* (Oxford, 1999), pp. 14–16.

[53] See R. Bellarmine, *De verbo Dei* II.1, in his *Opera omnia*, 8 vols. (Naples, 1872), I, p. 61 (Basil; also Irenaeus, Tertullian, and Clement of Alexandria); T. Denter, *Die Stellung der Bücher Esdras im Kanon des Alten Testaments: eine kanongeschichtliche Untersuchung* (Freiburg, 1962), p. 64 (Isidore). John Chrysostom also wrote that the books of the Bible had been burned, and that Ezra restored them with divine assistance: J.-P. Migne, ed., *Patrologia graeca*, 161 vols. (Paris: 1857–66), LXIII, col. 74.

[54] J.-P. Migne, ed., *Patrologia latina*, 221 vols. (Paris, 1844–55), XXIII, col. 190. See also the comments in F. Stummer, *Die Bedeutung Richard Simons für die Pentateuchkritik*, Alttestamentliche Abhandlungen, 3, Heft 4 (Münster in Wuppertal, 1912), pp. 8–9.

[55] M. Stern, ed. and tr., *Greek and Latin Authors on Jews and Judaism*, 3 vols. (Jerusalem, 1974–84), II, p. 480.

[56] Ibid., I, p. 425 (n.): the work is the *Apocritus* of Macarius Magnes. In the 17th century scholars were aware (via early secondary sources) of the general nature of Porphyry's work: Lucas Holstenius noted that book 1 of *Against the Christians* tried to demonstrate that the Holy Scriptures were written 'not by God, but

may have been available in other no longer extant anti-Christian writings of the period—does seem to have had some influence, albeit through a much more roundabout process of transmission.

It was, apparently, the early Islamic writers against Christianity and Judaism who picked up this Ezran theory and ensured its continued development. (In this they were helped by the fact that 2 Esdras was available, probably from an early period, in Arabic translations taken from the Greek, Syriac or Coptic.) One text from the eighth century, in the form of correspondence supposedly conducted between the Caliph Umar II and the Byzantine Emperor Leo III, presents the argument that the Christian scriptures—unlike the Koran—were composed by men, that they were lost several times, and that Ezra wrote their 'second version'.[57] Whether Islamic writers had derived this idea only from 2 Esdras and the use made of it by anti-Christian texts of late Antiquity, or in addition from Christian–Jewish or intra-Jewish polemics, is not known; it is striking that an anti-rabbinical treatise written in Arabic by a Karaite Jew in AD c.900 contains a strong statement of this argument, accusing the Rabbanites of believing 'that the Torah which is in the hands of the people [of Israel] is not the one brought down by Moses, but is a new one composed by Ezra, for, according to them, the one brought down by Moses perished and was lost and forgotten.'[58] But the most thorough expositions of this argument were by Muslim polemicists—above all, the Spanish scholar Ibn Hazm (d. 1065), whose detailed study of the Bible, alert to internal contradictions and errors in chronology and geography, strikingly prefigures early modern biblical criticism. Central to Ibn Hazm's case was the claim that the transmission of the Bible was unreliable: it had been intentionally corrupted and falsified by Ezra, whom Ibn Hazm did not hesitate to describe as a liar and a crook.[59] Thanks to Ibn

---

by men' ('non à Deo sed ab hominibus') and that book 4 was about the Pentateuch: Holstenius, 'De vita & scriptis Porphyrii philosophi dissertatio', appended to Porphyrius, *De abstinentia ab animalibus necandis libri quatuor*, ed. L. Holstenius (Cambridge, 1655), pp. 59–60. In the 1640s a rumour circulated that a complete manuscript copy of Porphyry's work was in the Bibliotheca Laurentiana in Florence: both Holstenius and Isaac Vossius searched for it there, without success (see F. F. Blok, *Isaac Vossius and His Circle: His Life until his Farewell to Queen Christina of Sweden, 1618–1655* (Groningen, 2000), pp. 128–9).

[57] H. Lazarus-Yafeh, *Intertwined Worlds: Medieval Islam and Bible Criticism* (Princeton, NJ, 1992), pp. 56 (Arabic versions of 2 Esdras), 64 (Umar and Leo). The earliest surviving Arabic version, a fragment containing part of ch. 14, is from the 9th century; two other versions of the whole book are found in 14th-century manuscripts (see J. M. Myers, ed., *The Anchor Bible: I and II Esdras* (New York, 1974), p. 114).

[58] L. Nemoy, 'Al-Qirqisani's Account of the Jewish Sects and Christianity', *Hebrew Union College Annual*, 7 (1930), pp. 317–97; here p. 331. (Al-Qirqisani adds: 'If the Moslems only knew about this assertion of theirs, they would not need any other thing to reproach us with and use as an argument against us.') The accusation was quite unfair: rabbinical writers insisted that any writing-out of the Pentateuch performed by Ezra was done by copying from an existing scroll (see Ginzburg, *Legends*, vi, p. 446).

[59] See Lazarus-Yafeh, *Intertwined Worlds*, pp. 26–35, 39–41 (method), 43–5, 66–8 (Ezra). On Ibn Hazm's fiercely polemical style, see M. Asín Palacios, *Abenházam de Córdoba y su historia crítica de las ideas religiosas* (Madrid, 1927), pp. 192–3 (quoting also his comment that the author of the Pentateuch was so imbecilic that, compared with him, 'an ox has more discretion, a donkey more wisdom'). Lazarus-Yafeh nevertheless says of Ibn Hazm: 'his level of argumentation and systematic critical approach to the text often equals the standard of modern Bible criticism' (p. 66).

Hazm, this became a standard theme in the writings of anti-Judaic Muslim polemicists. Thus, the treatise *Silencing the Jews*, written in Iraq in the 1160s by a Jewish convert to Islam, Samau'al al-Maghribi, confidently declared: 'When Ezra saw that the Temple of the people was destroyed by fire, that their state had disappeared ... and their book vanished, he collected some of his own remembrances and some still retained by the priests, and from those he concocted the Torah that the Jews now possess ... Now this Torah that they have is in truth a book by Ezra, and not a book of God.'[60]

Both Jewish and Christian writers were aware of this brand of Muslim polemics. Peter the Venerable (d. 1156), who commissioned a translation of the Koran into Latin, responded at some length to the claim that the Old Testament had been falsified by Ezra. So too, more briefly, did the rabbi Abraham ben David (Ibn Da'ud) of Toledo (d. 1180).[61] But perhaps the most important effect of these Muslim arguments on Jewish and Christian thinking was not the transmission of the Ezran theory itself, but the impact of a whole new method of biblical criticism, with its emphasis on the detection of contradictions, anachronisms, and other apparent human errors. One of the first Jewish scholars to apply a textual–critical approach to the Bible was the Spanish rabbi Abraham Ibn Ezra (1089–1164); he knew Arabic, had travelled in the Islamic East, and had a son who belonged to the same circle of Jewish intellectuals in Iraq as Samau'al al-Maghribi (in the years before the latter's conversion to Islam). As Hava Lazarus-Yafeh has suggested, 'it was perhaps his ties with the Islamic world and its polemic against the Torah that gave particular impetus to Ibn Ezra's approach'.[62]

In his commentary on Deuteronomy 1: 1, Ibn Ezra drew attention to a number of passages in the Pentateuch which appeared to be incompatible, on logical or chronological grounds, with its Mosaic authorship. His way of hinting at the significance of these passages was, however, somewhat guarded and mysterious; it may have been this display of caution that later attracted the attention of the young Spinoza, making him suspect that an explosively unorthodox theory was concealed within his words. Commenting on the phrase 'beyond Jordan' in Deut. 1: 1, Ibn Ezra wrote: ' "Beyond Jordan in the wilderness, in the plain"; and if you know the secret of the twelve, further "And Moses wrote", "And the Canaanite was then in

---

[60] Samau'al al-Maghribi, 'Ifham al-Yahud: Silencing the Jews', ed. M. Perlmann, *Proceedings of the American Academy for Jewish Research*, 32 (1964), pp. 1–104; here p. 55. For similar criticisms by other Islamic writers see E. Fritsch, *Islam und Christentum im Mittelalter: Beiträge zur Geschichte der muslimischen Polemik gegen das Christentum in arabischer Sprache* (Breslau, 1930), pp. 59–60.

[61] See J. Kritzeck, *Peter the Venerable and Islam* (Princeton, NJ, 1964), pp. 177–80; M. Schreiner, 'Zur Geschichte der Polemik zwischen Juden und Muhammedanern', *Zeitschrift der deutschen morgenländischen Gesellschaft*, 42 (1888), pp. 628–30; Lazarus-Yafeh, *Intertwined Worlds*, pp. 71–2.

[62] *Intertwined Worlds*, p. 73. She also states that Ibn Ezra 'could easily have read some of Ibn Hazm's or Samau'al's writings': this seems likely in the former's case but not in the latter's, as Samau'al's anti-Jewish treatise was written in Iraq during the years 1163–7, and Ibn Ezra died (in his native Spain) in 1167.

the land", "In the mount of the Lord it shall be seen", and further, "Behold, his bedstead was a bedstead of iron", then you will know the truth.'[63] As Spinoza correctly observed, each one of these allusions was to a phrase that could be offered as evidence for non-Mosaic authorship. Thus 'beyond Jordan', used to describe the wilderness, implied that the person writing those words was situated inside the promised land—which, of course, Moses never reached. The phrase 'Moses wrote' (Exod. 24: 4; Deut. 31: 22) was one of many references to Moses in the third person —also an unnatural manner of expression for Moses himself.[64] The statement that the Canaanite was 'then' in the land (Gen. 12: 6) seemed to have been written at a time when the Canaanite was no longer in the land—that is, subsequent to the seizure of the promised land by the people of Israel, which took place after Moses' death. The reference to Mount Moriah as 'the mount of the Lord' (Gen. 22: 14) also seemed anachronistic, as it gained that appellation only after the building of the Temple. The iron bedstead was mentioned in Deut. 3: 11 as a proof of the physical stature of the giant Og: 'For only Og king of Bashan remained of the remnant of giants; behold, his bedstead was a bedstead of iron; is it not in Rabbath of the children of Ammon?' This method of proving Og's height seemed appropriate to a writer who lived long after his time, not to Moses, his contemporary and enemy in battle.

As for Ibn Ezra's tantalizing phrase about the 'secret of the twelve', this was a reference to the last chapter of the Pentateuch, Deuteronomy 34, which describes the death of Moses, and which contains just twelve verses. Ibn Ezra subscribed to the theory that this chapter was written not by Moses but by his follower Joshua— a theory already familiar to Jewish scholars, as a version of it (concerning the chapter's last eight verses) was stated in the Babylonian Talmud.[65] Hitherto this theory had been the only exception allowed by Jewish tradition to the otherwise inviolable principle that Moses was the author of the Pentateuch; Ibn Ezra's remark about 'the

---

[63] A slightly abbreviated version of the original Hebrew, with Spinoza's Latin translation, is given in Spinoza, *Opera*, III, p. 118. The full Hebrew text is printed in J. Buxtorf, ed., *Biblia rabbinica*, 2 vols. (Basel, 1618–19), I, fol. 191r, and translated in Stummer, *Die Bedeutung Simons*, p. 11. My translation is derived from Stummer's, using the Authorized Version's phrasing of the relevant texts (except for the first, where the AV 'corrects' the text by reversing the meaning).

[64] The two references given here are the ones intended by Ibn Ezra; Spinoza incorrectly identified the phrase as a reference to Deut. 31. 9 (see W. Maier, 'Aben-Ezra's Meinung über den Verfasser des Pentateuchs', *Theologische Studien und Kritiken*, 5 (1832), pp. 634–44; here p. 638).

[65] *Baba Bathra*, tr. M. Simon and I. W. Slotki, 2 vols. (London, 1935) (= vols. V and VI of *Seder Nezikin*, ed. I. Epstein, 6 vols. (London, 1935)), I, p. 71 [14b]: 'Joshua wrote the book which bears his name and [the last] eight verses of the Pentateuch.' Spinoza gave the reference to Deut. 34 as one possible interpretation of Ibn Ezra's phrase, but offered two other possibilities: the altar (consisting, according to rabbinical tradition, of 12 stones) referred to in Deut. 27. 1, and the 12 curses uttered in Deut. 27. 15–26 (*Opera*, iii, p. 119). Maier has shown that the reference must be to the last chapter of Deuteronomy; in his commentary, Ibn Ezra gives a different account of the altar, passes over the 12 curses without comment, but specifically says that the last chapter was written by Joshua ('Aben-Ezra's Meinung', pp. 636–7). For a valuable discussion of rabbinical views about Deut. 34 (among which Ibn Ezra's re-assignment of the entire chapter was the most advanced) see Simon, *Lettres choisies*, III, pp. 209–15.

secret of the twelve' suggested that he had a more general theory that might be applicable to other passages too. However, his use of the word 'secret' did not mean, as Spinoza apparently thought, that he was in possession of a truth so upsetting or extreme that it could never be uttered—namely, that the entire Pentateuch was written by someone who lived long after Moses.[66] It was Ibn Ezra's common practice to half-conceal his thinking on some points, using the phrase 'it is a secret' and inserting some clues as to where the secret might be found. As one of his modern interpreters observes, these 'secrets' were not unspeakable mysteries: 'They are usually related to a rational, philosophical explanation, that for various reasons, Ibn-Ezra does not want to reveal in its entirety in one place.'[67] The rational theory in this case seems to have been that just a few phrases interpolated here and there in the Pentateuch were also the work of a later writer. As some of Spinoza's contemporaries were quick to point out, and as modern scholarship confirms, Ibn Ezra never suggested that the whole of the Pentateuch was non-Mosaic.[68] He may have had a reputation among some later writers as a 'scoffer'—not least because of his caustic treatment of other commentators with whom he disagreed.[69] But he neither denied the essential Mosaicity of the Pentateuch, nor attributed any part of it to Ezra the Scribe.

Nevertheless, in subsequent centuries Ibn Ezra's commentaries would exert a strong influence on Christian biblical scholars, who were thereby alerted to the possibility that at least some parts of the Pentateuch were non-Mosaic; and, thanks to their study of the Church Fathers and the text of 2 Esdras, these writers were much more likely to identify Ezra as the person responsible for any such additions or interpolations.[70] Of such writers, by far the most important and influential was the Spanish theologian and Hebraic scholar Alfonso Tostado Ribera de Madrigal (1400–55), known as 'Tostatus' (or, from his diocesan title, as 'Abulensis': he was bishop of Avila from 1449 until his death).[71] Although Tostatus's name is hardly known today, his writings were studied attentively by theologians throughout

---

[66] Spinoza, *Opera*, III, p. 120: 'clarissime indicat horum librorum Scriptorem longe vixisse post Mosen.'

[67] S. Regev, ' "Ta'amei ha-mitzvot" in R. Avraham Ibn-Ezra's Commentary: Secrets', in F. Díaz Esteban, ed., *Abraham Ibn Ezra y su tiempo: actas del simposio internacional Madrid, Tudela, Toledo 1–8 febrero 1989* (Madrid, 1990), pp. 233–40; here p. 233.

[68] Simon, *Lettre à Monsieur l'Abbé P.*, p. 35; Heidegger, *Exercitationes biblicae*, pp. 256–60; Spanheim, *Historia ecclesiastica*, in *Opera*, i, col. 263; Maier, 'Aben-Ezra's Meinung', p. 639; Siegfried, *Spinoza als Kritiker*, pp. 10–11; Stummer, *Die Bedeutung Simons*, p. 11.

[69] L. Rabinowitz, 'Abravanel as Exegete', in J. B. Trend and H. Loewe, eds., *Isaac Abravanel: Six Lectures* (Cambridge, 1937), pp. 75–92, esp. p. 80; M. Orfali, 'Abraham Ibn Ezra, crítico de los exégetas de la Biblia', in F. Díaz Esteban, ed., *Abraham Ibn Ezra y su tiempo: actas del simposio internacional Madrid, Tudela, Toledo 1–8 febrero 1989* (Madrid, 1990), pp. 225–32.

[70] See e.g. the comments of the influential 14th-century biblical scholar Nicholas de Lyra on Ezra 7. 3, describing Ezra as having restored 'the law which was burnt by the Chaldaeans' (an implicit acceptance of 2 Esdras): *Bibliarum sacrarum cum glossa ordinaria, primum quidem a Strabo Fuldensi collecta*, 6 vols. (Lyon, Paris, 1589–90), II, p. 1316.

[71] See P. L. Suarez, *Noematica biblico-mesianica de Alfonso Tostado de Madrigal, Obispo de Avila (1400–1455)* (Madrid, 1956), esp. pp. 11–12 (biographical details), 144 (knowledge of rabbinical writers and Nicholas de Lyra).

Europe for three centuries or more: multi-volume editions of his collected works appeared three times in the sixteenth century, twice in the seventeenth, and once in the eighteenth (a 27-volume folio publication, in 1728). George Hakewill, writing in 1627, described him as one of the greatest scholars of the modern age: 'For beside *Phylosophy* & *Divinity*, the *Canon* & the *Civill* Lawes, *history* & the *Mathematiques*, he was well skilled in the *Greeke* & *Hebrew* tongues: so as it was written of him, *Hic stupor est mundi, qui scibile discutit omne.*'[72] And it is this now forgotten Spanish theologian who, more than any other Christian writer, was responsible for the eventual development of modern critical thinking about the authorship of the Pentateuch.

Tostatus had made a careful study of Ibn Ezra's writings on the Bible, and referred to them throughout his own voluminous commentaries. He had also read many other rabbinical texts; commenting on the last chapter of Deuteronomy, for example, he noted that 'the Jews' attributed the last eight verses to Joshua.[73] On this particular point, Tostatus was in agreement with Ibn Ezra and the Talmudic tradition: while he accepted that, in principle, it was quite possible that Moses could have described prophetically his own death (Deut. 34: 5), he thought that to attribute the phrase 'no man knoweth his sepulchre to this day' (Deut. 34: 6) to Moses would involve imputing to him a kind of falsehood, in relation to the time at which he wrote. As for the author of that entire additional passage (Deut. 34: 5–12), 'though some people say that it was written by Ezra, it is more probable, nevertheless, that it was written by Joshua'.[74]

On one other point raised by Ibn Ezra, Tostatus was also in full agreement: the reference to the iron bed of the giant Og (Deut. 3: 11) must have been written long after the death of Moses. To this Tostatus added a comment on Deut. 3: 14, which says that Jair took some of the lands seized from Og 'and called them after his own name, Bashan-havoth-jair, unto this day': the conquest itself took place only three months before the death of Moses, but the phrase 'unto this day' implied, Tostatus noted, a much greater lapse of time. He concluded: 'Those are not the words of Moses, but of Ezra.' And he further explained: 'I do not therefore deny that Moses wrote that book ... but after the destruction and burning of the books of the Law by the Babylonians, Ezra the prophet, Scribe of the Law, re-wrote the Law while filled with the inspiration of the Holy Spirit, and added those and other similar things.'[75]

---

[72] G. Hakewill, *An Apologie of the Power and Providence of God in the Government of the World* (Oxford, 1627), p. 213 ('here is the wonder of the world, who discusses everything that can be known'). More than 50 years later Richard Simon also quoted this Latin tag, and praised Tostatus's insight into 'le style de la Bible': *Histoire critique du Vieux Testament*, p. 423.

[73] A. Tostatus, *Opera omnia*, 23 vols. (Venice, 1596), V, fol. 184r ('Hebraei'). Cf. n. 65, above.

[74] Ibid., V, fol. 183r ('licet aliqui dicant eam scriptam fuisse ab Esdra, verisimilius tamen est eam scriptam fuisse a Iosue').

[75] Ibid., V, fol. 15v ('Ista non sunt verba Moysis sed Esdrae'; 'non nego propter hoc Moysen scripsisse librum istum ... sed post destructionem & combustionem librorum legis per Babylonios Esdras scriba legis, & propheta spiritu divino afflatus legem rescripsit, & ista & similia addidit').

The 'other similar things' were, however, never clearly identified. Tostatus did discuss other apparent additions and interpolations, including some of the ones referred to by Ibn Ezra, but returned a negative verdict in each case. Thus, he dismissed the argument from the references to Moses in the third person, and insisted that the phrase 'beyond Jordan' ('trans Jordanem' in the Vulgate) was unproblematic, as the Hebrew preposition could mean either 'ultra' or 'cis'. (His view would later prevail with the translators of the Authorized Version, who gave the phrase as 'on this side Jordan'.) Also, commenting on the opening phrase of Deuteronomy, 'These be the words which Moses spake . . .', he noted that 'some people' claimed that Moses only uttered the words orally, and that Joshua then edited them in writing: this argument, he said, was 'frivolous'.[76] Several other possible arguments were raised by him only to be dismissed. He observed, for example, that some commentators regarded the reference to 'Bethlehem' in Gen. 48: 7 as anachronistic, as the place had gained that name only in the time of Ruth. 'But this is false, because if that name "Bethlehem" had been imposed in the time of Ruth and Naomi, given that those people lived a long time after Moses, it would follow that that part of the text was written not by Moses but by Ezra, or by somebody else'; he insisted, accordingly, that the name had also been in use in Moses' day.[77] Another such case concerned Deut. 2: 12, in which God said to Moses that the children of Esau had driven out another tribe from the territory of Seir, 'and dwelt in their stead; as Israel did unto the land of his possession': as Tostatus noted, 'On the basis of that phrase "as Israel did", some people argue that Ezra wrote that book, on the grounds that during Moses' lifetime Israel had not yet acquired its promised land.'[78] This argument too he dismissed as unwarranted. Another apparent anachronism in the book of Genesis (36: 31), a reference to kings reigning in the land of Edom 'before there reigned any king over the children of Israel', was also swiftly dealt with: 'And if you say, "How then did Moses describe this [*sc.* a king reigning over Israel] when it had not yet happened?", the answer is that he spoke prophetically.'[79] Most striking was the argument Tostatus invoked when rejecting the idea that the description of Moses in Numbers 12: 3 ('Now the man Moses was very meek, above all the men which were upon the face of the earth') was by someone other than Moses himself. 'Some people think that those words were not written by Moses,' he noted, 'but that other writers and copyists, such as Ezra, inserted them.' Nevertheless, 'this is

---

[76] A. Tostatus, *Opera omnia*, 23 vols. (Venice, 1596), V, fol. 2r (third person; ultra, cis; 'Aliqui volunt quod Moysen solum verba ista protulerit, post autem Iosue id scriptum redegit . . . sed hoc friuolum est').

[77] Ibid., I, fols. 397r ('Hoc autem falsum est, quia istud nomen Bethlehem impositum fuisset tempore Ruth, & Noemi, cum istae multo tempore post Moysen fuerint, sequeretur, quod ista litera non fuisset scripta per Moysen, sed per Esdram, vel per aliquem alium'); 342ᵛ (name in Moses' day).

[78] Ibid., V, fol. 10r ('Aliqui volunt quòd Esdras scripserit librum istum propter istam clausulam *Sicut fecit Israel*, quia viuente Moyse nondum acquisierat Israel terram promissionis suae').

[79] Ibid., I, fol. 346v ('Et si dicas, quomodo ergo Moyses hoc descripsit cum nondum contigisset? Respondetur, quòd Prophéticè dicebat').

wrong, because no one, however great his authority might be, would presume to add or subtract anything to the holy Scripture, given that that was forbidden, as Deut. 4 shows'.[80]

On the face of it, this statement flatly contradicted Tostatus's comments on the iron bed of Og (Deut. 3: 11) and 'unto this day' (Deut. 3: 14); when discussing those cases he noted the apparent contradiction, and said that they were cases of a different kind. The sort of difference he seems to have had in mind was perhaps between substantive additions and merely explanatory ones; but no clear criterion was ever set out in his writings. So far as his subsequent influence is concerned, however, this is not very important. What matters is not so much the answers he gave, as the potential questions he raised—not his particular verdict on each or any of these cases, but the way in which he alerted readers to the possibility of constructing such textual arguments for post-Mosaic additions and alterations. Indeed, his first thematic discussion at the beginning of his commentary on Deuteronomy was the 'quaestio' 'Who wrote the book of Deuteronomy: Moses or Ezra, or Joshua?' which began: 'Doubts are raised by many people over who might have written this book.'[81] Who those 'many people' were, he never said; perhaps this was nothing more than a rhetorical device. But by countering so explicitly these 'many' unnamed opponents, and by explaining so openly the logic of their argument, Tostatus ensured that the number of people considering—or even sharing—such doubts would indeed be many in the end.

After Tostatus, the next significant writer to admit the presence of non-Mosaic material in the Pentateuch was the early Reformation theologian Andreas Bodenstein (known also, from his place of birth, as Karlstadt); however, Bodenstein's little book on the scriptural canon seems to have had little or no influence, and is not mentioned in any of the mainstream literature on this subject in the following two centuries.[82] Much more important was the work of a Flemish Catholic, Andreas Masius, who was recognized as one of the most brilliant Hebrew scholars of his day.[83] In his posthumously published book about Joshua (issued in 1574, one year

---

[80] A. Tostatus, *Opera omnia*, 23 vols. (Venice, 1596), IV, part 1, fol. 161r ('aliquibus videtur ista non fuisse scripta a Moyse . . . sed quòd alii scriptores, & translatores, sicut Esdras interposuerint . . . Sed hoc non stat, quia nemo quantaecunque auctoritatis esset sacrae Scripturae aliquid addere, vel detrahere praesumeret, quia hoc vetitum erat, vt patet Deute. c. 4').

[81] Ibid., V, fol. 2r ('Quis scripsit librum Deuteronomij, Moyses an Esdras, vel Iosue'. . .'Quis hunc librum scripserit apud multos in dubium vertit').

[82] A. Bodenstein, *De canonicis scripturis libellus* (Wittenberg, 1520), sigs. C3–H1. See H.-J. Kraus, *Geschichte der historisch-kritischen Erforschung des Alten Testaments*, 2nd edn (Neukirchen, 1969), pp. 28–31 (quoting the key passage on pp. 29–30).

[83] On Masius, who published a Syriac grammar and helped to correct the Antwerp Polyglot Bible, see C. G. Jöcher, *Allgemeines Gelehrten-Lexicon*, 4 vols. (Leipzig, 1750–1), III, cols. 259–60; the comments in L. Diestel, *Geschichte des Alten Testaments in der christlichen Kirche* (Jena, 1869), pp. 311–12; and the biographical sketch by H. de Vocht, 'Andreas Masius (1514–1573)', in *Miscellanea Giovanni Mercati*, 6 vols. (Vatican City, 1946), IV, pp. 425–41. One leading modern biblical scholar, Moshe Goshen-Gottstein, reserves special praise for Masius: see his 'The Textual Criticism of the Old Testament: Rise, Decline, Rebirth', *Journal of Biblical Literature*, 102 (1983), pp. 365–99 (at p. 372 (n.)).

after his death) he presented a new version of the role of Ezra in the preparation of the Bible—one that was to have far-reaching consequences. According to Masius, Ezra the Scribe had not miraculously rewritten the whole of Scripture, nor had he merely 'restored' it in the sense of tidying up the text and removing minor corruptions: rather, he had taken a group of materials which were 'dispersed, scattered and mixed together in annals' and had 'collected, arranged and united them in, as it were, a single volume'.[84] In this way, Ezra (with, possibly, the assistance of other pious and learned men from the Great Synagogue) had 'compiled' the books of Joshua, Judges, Kings, and 'others', from 'various annals kept in the House of God'.[85]

Masius did not explicitly include the Pentateuch in this list of Ezran compilations; with regard to the Mosaic books, he commented only that Ezra had inserted a few words and sentences 'here and there'. One example he gave was the use of the place-name 'Hebron' in the book of Genesis—a name which, as was explained in Judges 1: 10, was given long after the Mosaic period to a place originally known as Kirjath-Arba.[86] However, in a later discussion of another such example (the use of the place-name 'Dan'), he remarked more ambiguously: 'The Mosaic books, in their present form, were not composed by Moses, but by Ezra, or by some other godly man.'[87] Also, in presenting his theory about the use of 'diaries and annals' in the compilation of the historical books, Masius gave the example of the 'Book of the wars of the Lord' mentioned in the Pentateuch (Numb. 21: 14). At the very least, this seemed to be another example of an Ezran interpolation (given that that book had contained descriptions of the actions of Moses, and presumably was written not by him but by a later chronicler). But if, as Masius said, the Jews had kept such diaries and annals 'in ancient times', and if Ezra had had access to such materials going back almost to the time of Moses, the possibility might reasonably have occurred to some readers of Masius that the story of Moses himself had been compiled out of similar materials.[88] Masius's account thus formed a starting-point for the textual theories of Richard Simon (who saw the Old Testament as the product of a long accumulation of material written by 'public scribes') and, ultimately, for the *Quellenforschung* of scholars such as Jean Astruc in the eighteenth century.[89]

---

[84] A. Masius, *Iosuae imperatoris historia illustrata atque explicata* (Antwerp, 1574), 1st pagination, p. 119 ('dispersa, dissoluta, confusa in annalibus'; 'ab Ezdra collecta, dispositaque, & tamquam in uno codice compacta').

[85] Ibid., 2nd pagination, p. 2 ('non solùm hunc Iosuae, verùm etiam Iudicum, Regum, alios, quos in sacris, vt vocant, Bibliis legimus libros, ex diversis annalibus apud Ecclesiam Dei conservatis compilasse').

[86] Ibid., 2nd pagination, p. 2 ('interjectis, saltem, hîc, illic, verborum, & sententiarum clausulis'; discussion of 'Cariath-Arbe').

[87] Ibid., 2nd pagination, p. 301 ('Neque Mosis libros sic, vt nunc habentur, ab illo esse compositos: sed ab Ezdra, aut alio quopiam divino viro').

[88] Ibid., 2nd pagination, p. 2 ('priscis temporibus apud Ecclesiam fuisse diaria, & annales'; 'liber bellorum Domini'). 'Ecclesia' here, as above (n. 85), is Masius's term for the religious institutions of the Jews.

[89] See J. Astruc, *Conjectures sur les mémoires originaux dont il paroit que Moyse s'est servi pour composer le livre de la Genèse* (Brussels, 1753).

While Masius's arguments may have pointed in radical new directions, their orthodoxy was apparently never in question; indeed, they were taken up by some of the most respected Catholic commentators of the next two generations. Thus, the Spanish Jesuit Benedictus Pererius (Bento Pereira), who lectured at the Collegium Romanum from the 1580s until his death in 1610, wrote that it was 'very likely' that in ancient times 'diaries and annals' had been kept in the synagogue. He supposed that most of the Pentateuch was Mosaic, but that various passages had been inserted into it 'long after the time of Moses'.[90] Another Jesuit, the Flemish biblical scholar Cornelis van den Steen (universally known by the Latin version of his name, Cornelius à Lapide), who taught at Louvain before moving to the Collegium Romanum in 1616, was strongly influenced by Masius's theories. At one point in his commentary on the Pentateuch, à Lapide even made explicit the suggestion about the Mosaic writings that had been merely implicit in Masius's account: 'Note that Moses wrote the Pentateuch in a simple way, in the form of a diary or annals; Joshua, however (or someone like him) set those Mosaic annals in order and divided them into books, adding and interpolating quite a few sentences.'[91] As this statement shows, à Lapide's prime candidate for the role of editor was not Ezra, who lived long after Moses, but Joshua, Moses' immediate successor. The last chapter of Deuteronomy, he suggested, was 'by Ezra, or rather, by Joshua'; and, when discussing Tostatus's attribution to Ezra of two phrases in Deuteronomy 3 (about the iron bed, and the place-name 'Bashan-havoth-Jair'), he wrote: 'if these things were added by someone, they were added not by Ezra, but by the person who edited these Mosaic diaries soon afterwards.'[92] Nevertheless, in his later commentary on the Book of Ezra he maintained the standard view that Ezra had ordered and corrected the whole of the Hebrew Bible, and accepted that he was probably responsible for the phrase 'unto this day' wherever it occurred.[93]

Although à Lapide thus had two different theories at his disposal to account for apparently anachronistic passages in the text, he was not over-eager to identify the anachronisms and subject them to such explanation: several of the points raised by

---

[90] B. Pererius, *Commentariorum et disputationum in Genesim, tomi quatuor* (Cologne, 1622), p. 3 ('Placet mihi eorum sententia, qui existimant hoc Pentateuchum longo post Mosen tempore interiectis . . . verborum & sententiarum clausulis . . . esse dispositum. Illud quoque simillimum vero est, fuisse in Synagoga priscis illis temporibus Diaria & Annales'); cf. another echoing of Masius's phrasing on p. 510. This commentary on Genesis was first published in 4 vols. in Rome, 1589–98. For a very positive assessment of Pererius's work, see A. Williams, *The Common Expositor: An Account of the Commentaries on Genesis 1527–1633* (Chapel Hill, NC, 1948), pp. 16–17.

[91] C. à Lapide, *In Pentateuchum Mosis commentaria* (Paris, 1630), p. 23 ('Aduerte, Mosen Pentateuchum simpliciter conscripsisse, per modum diarij vel annalium; Iosue tamen, vel quem similem, eosdem hos Mosis annales in ordinem digessisse, distinxisse, & sententias nonnullas addidisse, & intexuisse'). This commentary was first published in Antwerp in 1616.

[92] Ibid., pp. 899 ('ab Esdra, vel potiùs a Iosue'), 907 ('si haec addita sunt ab alio quopiam, non ab Esdra, sed ab eo, qui diaria haec Mosis paulò post digessit, esse addita').

[93] C. à Lapide, *Commentarius in Esdram, Nehemiam, Tobiam, Judith, Esther, et Machabaeos* (Antwerp, 1734), p. 4. This commentary was first published posthumously at Antwerp in 1645; à Lapide died in 1637.

Ibn Ezra, Tostatus and Masius were passed over by him in silence, and he also covered his position by stating, as a general principle, that 'Moses often uses prolepsis or anticipation: that is, he calls towns and places by the names which they were given long afterwards.'[94] Once again, what matters here is not so much the judgements à Lapide gave on particular passages, as his endorsement of the general possibility that passages in the Pentateuch might be later interpolations. His commentary on the Pentateuch was enormously popular (it was reprinted ten times between 1617 and 1661), not only with Catholics, but with Protestant scholars too, who appreciated his concentration on the literal meaning of the text.[95] Thanks to à Lapide, the idea that there were post-Mosaic materials in the Pentateuch became widely diffused in early seventeenth-century Europe. Even those who disagreed with this theory were forced to argue against it (and/or to admit that it might be correct in at least a few cases), thus giving it an even wider circulation. Thus, for example, when Jacques Bonfrère (Bonfrerius), a Walloon Jesuit who taught Hebrew and theology at Douai, discussed many of the apparently anachronistic passages in his commentary on the Pentateuch (1625), he defended their Mosaic authorship whenever he could, but noted as he did so that other scholars had attributed them to Joshua or Ezra; and in the end he too was obliged to admit that the praise of Moses in Numbers 12: 3, the use of the place-names 'Hebron' and 'Dan', and indeed the whole of the last chapter of Deuteronomy were later interpolations.[96]

Set against the background of this tradition of textual explanation, from Ibn Ezra and Tostatus to Masius, Pererius, à Lapide, and Bonfrerius, the theories of La Peyrère, Hobbes, and Spinoza begin to look much less innovatory. True, the radical conclusion drawn by those three writers—that the anachronisms in the Pentateuch prove not merely that some passages were added, but that the entire text was non-Mosaic—had not been put forward by any of the earlier commentators (though the Masius–à Lapide thesis about a subsequent editor forming the text from an assortment of Mosaic raw materials might be taken to point in that direction). But La Peyrère's basic idea—that there lay behind the biblical text a collection of disparate source materials—had already been adumbrated in this, the scholarly mainstream tradition. Indeed, the very phrase he used for Moses' original materials, 'diurni commentarii' (daily commentaries), seems little more than a paraphrase of the term 'diaria' (diaries), which had already been used by Masius,

---

[94] à Lapide, *In Pentateuchum commentaria*, p. 24 ('Moses saepe vtitur prolepsi sive anticipatione: vocat enim vrbes & loca eo nomine, quod longè posteriùs eis esse inditum').

[95] For a list of editions (all at Antwerp or Paris) see Williams, *Common Expositor*, p. 276; Williams also notes that the next most popular commentary was that of Pererius (p. 8).

[96] J. Bonfrerius, *Pentateuchus Moysis commentario illustratus* (Antwerp, 1625), pp. 94 (praise, Hebron, Dan), 1062 (Deut. 34). For examples of his rejection of the thesis in other instances, see pp. 280–1, 906, 914, 917 (misprinted '719'). Perhaps because of his overall intellectual conservatism in these matters, Bonfrerius was specially cited by Richard Simon as a supporter of the theory of post-Mosaic interpolations: *Histoire critique*, p. 32.

Pererius, and à Lapide.[97] It is not necessary, therefore, to suppose that La Peyrère's approach was either that of a revolutionary genius, or that of an autodidactic trouble-maker who had just applied to the Bible his iconoclastic but home-made common-sense.[98] What La Peyrère, Hobbes, and Spinoza were doing was to take some theories that were already widely available and set them off in a new direction; as so often seems to be the case in the history of ideas, the advance of radical heterodoxy came about not by means of a frontal assault on the orthodox tradition, but through a more complicated and opportunistic judo-like manoeuvre, in which the impetus set up by the orthodox thinkers played its own essential role.[99]

In order to see the extent of these three writers' indebtedness to the earlier tradition, it may be helpful to tabulate the arguments that were used (or at least discussed) by these three and their major predecessors. (In the case of Tostatus, à Lapide, and Bonfrerius, what matters here is the fact that the argument for non-Mosaicity was raised by them in connection with a particular biblical passage, even if their final judgement was that the passage was Mosaic after all.)

What emerges most strikingly here is that virtually all the arguments used by La Peyrère had previously been discussed by à Lapide and Bonfrerius (the only exception being the treatment of Deuteronomy 2: 12, where La Peyrère cited the same passage but argued a different point—perhaps he had simply misunderstood Bonfrerius's discussion of this verse).[100] Spinoza's arguments, with one minor exception, were also all to be found in the standard commentaries. In the case of Hobbes—who offered only three pieces of evidence before peremptorily concluding that 'It is therefore sufficiently evident, that the five Books of *Moses* were written after his time'—two out of his three arguments could have been drawn from à Lapide or Bonfrerius; he did not need to have seen La Peyrère's work in manuscript in order to be alerted to the significance of these passages. During his

---

[97] La Peyrère, *Prae-adamitae, Systema theologicum*, IV.1, p. 153 ('Crediderim certe, diurnos commentarios Mosem confecisse . . .'). Klaus Scholder exemplifies a common overestimation of La Peyrère's originality when he writes that he was one of the first to develop a 'literary history' of the Pentateuch with his innovatory 'Fragmenten-Hypothese' (*Ursprünge und Probleme der Bibelkritik im 17. Jahrhundert: ein Beitrag zur Entstehung der historisch-kritischen Theologie* (Munich, 1966), pp. 102–3).

[98] The first interpretation is that of Richard Popkin, who portrays La Peyrère as a 'revolutionary' thinker and the founder of modern Bible criticism (*Isaac La Peyrère*, pp. 1–2, 48–50; on p. 50 he comments that 'Only the wildest radical enthusiasts of the Puritan Revolution and La Peyrère were willing to conclude that Moses was not the author of it all [*sc.* all the Pentateuch]'). The second is that of Anthony Grafton, who, while agreeing that 'no one did more' to make the 'exegetical revolution' happen than La Peyrère, assumes that his response to the Bible was largely unmediated: 'Two centuries later, La Peyrère might have stood at the back of a revival meeting, shouting "Hey, mister, where *did* Cain's wife come from?' (*Defenders of the Text: The Traditions of Scholarship in an Age of Science, 1450–1800* (Cambridge, Mass., 1991), pp. 205, 211–12).

[99] While this background to the theories of Hobbes, La Peyrère, and Spinoza on the Pentateuch has been largely ignored by writers on those three thinkers, it has been briefly acknowledged by some historians of biblical interpretation: see Diestel, *Geschichte des Alten Testaments*, p. 357; Stummer, *Die Bedeutung Richard Simons*, p. 28; Kraus, *Geschichte der historisch-kritischen Erforschung*, p. 57.

[100] La Peyrère, *Prae-adamitae, Systema theologicum*, IV.1, p. 154.

|  | Ibn Ezra | Tostatus | Masius | à Lapide | Bonfrerius | La Peyrère | Hobbes | Spinoza |
|---|---|---|---|---|---|---|---|---|
| Moses in 3rd person, Deut. 31: 9 | X |  |  |  |  |  |  | X |
| 'trans Jordanem', Deut. 1: 1 | X |  |  | X |  | X |  | X |
| death of Moses, Deut. 34 | X |  |  | X | X | X |  | X |
| iron bed, Deut. 3: 11 | X |  |  | X | X | X |  | X |
| Canaanite 'then' in the land, Gen. 12: 6 | X |  |  |  |  |  | X | X |
| Mt Moriah 'of God', Gen. 22: 14 | X |  |  |  |  |  |  | X |
| 'unto this day', esp. Deut. 34: 6 |  | X |  | X | X | X | X |  |
| 'spoke', not 'wrote', Deut. 1: 1 |  | X |  |  |  |  |  |  |
| praise of Moses, Num. 12: 3 |  | X |  | X | X |  |  | X |
| Bethlehem, Gen. 48: 7 |  | X |  |  |  |  |  |  |
| 'as Israel did', Deut. 2: 12 |  | X |  |  | X | (X) |  | X |
| before king of Israel, Gen. 36: 31 |  | X |  | X |  |  |  | X |
| Hebron, e.g. Gen. 13: 18 |  |  | X |  | X |  |  |  |
| 'book of wars of Lord', Num. 21: 14 |  |  | X | X | X | X | X | X |
| Dan, e.g. Gen. 14: 14 |  |  |  | X | X |  |  | X |
| post-Moses narrative, Ex. 16: 34– |  |  | X | X | X |  |  | X |

years in Paris, the one major library to which Hobbes can be presumed to have had easy access was that of the Minim convent on the place Royale, where he went regularly to visit his friend Mersenne. One of the surviving volumes of that library's catalogue (compiled in 1730) lists its holdings in theology: it includes the commentaries of Tostatus (in the 1613 Cologne edition), Pererius (Mainz, 1612), à Lapide (Paris, 1617), and Bonfrerius (Antwerp, 1625).[101] Mersenne, who had himself written a large though untypical commentary on Genesis, might well have directed Hobbes's attention to these standard works.[102] As for the third of Hobbes's arguments, concerning the statement that the Canaanite was 'then' in the land, no modern source for it is apparent; Hobbes cannot have derived it directly from Ibn Ezra, as it is quite certain that he did not know Hebrew.[103] Possibly Mersenne (who did) had discussed it with him; or perhaps Hobbes, having grasped the well established textual–critical principles on which these anachronisms were identified, had merely gone looking for further examples and found this one for himself.

## IV

This brief survey of earlier theories about the text of the Pentateuch has answered one question—from where might Hobbes, La Peyrère and Spinoza have derived the material for their arguments?—only to raise another. If these ideas had been current for such a long time (at least since the publication of Masius's work in the 1570s), why did the radical use of them, denying Mosaic authorship and attributing the Pentateuch to Ezra instead, spring up only in the middle of the seventeenth century? Surely the same arguments could have occurred to anyone at any time in the previous seventy-five years or so?

In fact, there is one recorded example of an individual free-thinker of the late sixteenth century reaching similar conclusions about Moses—though without making any reference to Ezra. In 1582 a schoolteacher from the Ardennes, Noël Journet, was burnt as a heretic in Metz; details of his errors were supplied in a subsequently published refutation. His main claims about the Pentateuch were, first, that Moses could not have written it, because it described his death; secondly, the argument

---

[101] Bibliothèque de l'Arsenal, Paris, MS 6203, pp. 153–4, 159.

[102] M. Mersenne's *Quaestiones celeberrimae in Genesim* (Paris, 1623) takes Genesis as the basis or pretext for a mass of excursuses on other (mainly scientific and musical) subjects; it displays a wide knowledge of the works of other commentators, but does not deal with the textual issues discussed here.

[103] Proof of Hobbes's ignorance of Hebrew can be found in *Leviathan*, ch. 46, where, commenting on 'the verbe *Is*', he remarks: 'Whether all other Nations of the world have in their severall languages a word that answereth to it, or not, I cannot tell' (p. 372). At some stage in the next 17 years Hobbes did at least acquire some elementary knowledge of the Hebrew language: in his *Answer to Bishop Bramhall* (written probably in 1668) he mentioned 'the Hebrew language, which has no word answerable to the copulative *est*' (*EW* IV, p. 304; cf. a similar reference in *Decameron physiologicum*, *EW* VII, p. 81).

from 'beyond Jordan'; and thirdly, the argument from the place-name 'Hebron'.[104] As we have seen, the first two points could have been derived from Tostatus, and the third might have been taken (directly or indirectly) from Masius; to this extent, Journet can properly be described as a forerunner of the mid-seventeenth-century writers, a radical adaptor of the mainstream textual–critical tradition.

Nevertheless, there was a considerable difference in style and purpose between Journet's approach and that of Hobbes, La Peyrère, and Spinoza. His aim was simply to portray the Bible as an absurd tissue of lies (in the words of his indictment, 'saying that the holy Scripture is full of fables, and of all sorts of fantasies and falsehoods').[105] Theirs, on the other hand, was to treat it as a normal document, a human artefact which had a history of its own, and which could thus be subjected to historical analysis. In the accounts of Hobbes and Spinoza, the role of Ezra was therefore not some contingent extra detail; it was an essential part of their human, historical, and indeed political explanation of the nature and function of the text. These two writers in particular were drawing not only on a tradition of argument about textual interpolations in the Pentateuch, but also on other debates that had developed during the late sixteenth and early seventeenth centuries—not only about the role of Ezra, but also about the whole nature of the biblical text. Their position cannot be properly understood unless it is also set against this broader background.

The general idea of applying the methods of classical textual scholarship to sacred texts had been current since the writings of Valla in the fifteenth century and Erasmus in the early sixteenth. But its strongest stimulus came from the doctrinal warfare of Protestants and Catholics in the latter part of the sixteenth century. Although the early Reformers had shown some flexibility in their approach to the Old Testament (occasionally suggesting emendations of the Hebrew), the standard Protestant position that emerged in the second half of the century was that the Hebrew text—which meant, in practice, the Masoretic vowel-pointed text printed in Venice in 1525—was the inspired and inerrant Word of God.[106] At the fourth session of the Council of Trent, however, the Roman Catholic Church attributed a primacy of authority not to the Hebrew (or the Greek of the New Testament), but to the Vulgate. This was, on the face of it, a paradoxical position to adopt, as

---

[104] R. Peter, 'Noel Journet, détracteur de l'Ecriture sainte (1582)', in M. Lienhard, ed., *Croyants et sceptiques au XVI* siècle: le dossier des 'Épicuriens'* (Strasbourg, 1981), pp. 147–56; here pp. 148–50. Journet's other arguments concerned petty inconsistencies (for example, if Moses had just turned 'all the waters' into blood (Exod. 7: 20), what did the magicians of Egypt work on when they did the same?). See also F. Berriot, 'Hétérodoxie religieuse et utopie dans les "erreurs estranges" de Noël Journet (1582)', *Bulletin de la Société de l'Histoire du Protestantisme Français*, 124 (1978), pp. 236–48 (with further examples of petty inconsistencies, p. 242). The refutation was by Jean Chassanion, *La Refutation des erreurs estranges & blasphemes horribles contre Dieu & l'Escripture saincte* (Strasbourg, 1583).

[105] Peter, 'Noel Journet', p. 147 ('disant que l'Ecriture sainte est pleine de fables, de toute rêveries et mensonges').

[106] See the comments in Goshen-Gottstein, 'Textual Criticism of the Old Testament', pp. 370–1.

no one denied that the Vulgate's version of the Old Testament was itself a translation from the Hebrew. But the post-Tridentine Catholic polemicists argued that the version of the Hebrew which was used by Jerome (and which was now lost, its substance surviving only in the form of his translation) was actually superior to the present-day Masoretic text: in the centuries after Jerome, the Hebrew had been progressively corrupted by the Jews. In the words of one of the most outspoken Catholic writers on this subject, James Gordon Huntley, 'the *Hebrew text* which is now in vse, is in many places corrupted and depraued, in which the vulgar Edition is entire and vncorrupted'.[107]

The Catholics' strategy was thus to undermine confidence in the Masoretic Bible, by demonstrating that it was, to some extent at least, the product of an historical process of human interventions. In this they were greatly helped by the researches of a Jewish scholar, Elias Levita, who had argued in 1538 that the vowel-points in the Masoretic text must have been added at a late stage, hundreds of years after Christ: he had thus undermined the traditional theory that the whole text had been fixed, in its present form, by Ezra and the men of the Great Synagogue.[108] Among the Catholics who took up Levita's argument was the leading English controversialist Thomas Stapleton (who taught at Douai until 1590, and thereafter was professor of Scripture at Louvain until his death in 1598). 'There is today nothing certain', he wrote, 'about the Hebrew text, as it appears now in our Bibles—first of all because the points in the text, which function as vowels, were added 400 years or more after Christ by the Masoretes, Rabbis of the Jews, and not by Christians.'[109]

This whole approach promoted the application of textual–critical methods to the Hebrew Bible. Among some of the Catholic hard-liners it also encouraged, or fed upon, an element of anti-Jewish feeling: Melchior Cano, for example, attacked the Protestant elevation of the Hebrew text on the grounds that it would reduce Christian exegesis to the indignity of dependence on Jewish learning, and complained

---

[107] J. Gordon Huntley, *A Summary of Controversies, wherein are briefly treated the cheefe Questions of Divinity, now a dayes in dispute betweene Catholickes & Protestants*, tr. by 'I.L.', 2nd edn (n. p., 1618), Controv. 1, ch. 6, art. 3, p. 20. The author, a Jesuit, was a son of the Earl of Huntley; this was a translation of his *Controversiarum epitomes* (1612) (see P. Milward, *Religious Controversies of the Jacobean Age: A Survey of Printed Sources* (London, 1978), pp. 178–80).

[108] On Levita's work see Weil, *Élie Lévita*, esp pp. 297–313; on the use made of it by Catholic polemicists see S. G. Burnett, *From Christian Hebraism to Jewish Studies: Johannes Buxtorf (1564–1629) and Hebrew Learning in the Seventeenth Century* (Leiden, 1996), pp. 205–9.

[109] T. Stapleton, *Principiorum fidei doctrinalium relectio scholastica & compendiaria* (Antwerp, 1596), Controv. 5, qu. 3, art. 1, p. 516 ('Hebraici contextus, vt simpliciter nunc in Biblijs habetur, nulla hodie certitudo est: primùm, quia puncta contextus, quae vocalium vice sunt, & 400. post Christum annis & ampliùs à Masoretis Rabbinis Iudaeorum, non à Christianis, adiecta sunt'). Cf. the complaint of the Protestant Hebrew scholar John Weemes that 'The Church of *Rome*, that they may advance the authority of the vulgar Latine translation, which they have made canonicall; doe labour to disgrace the originall Text, the Hebrew and Greeke, holding that they are corrupt in many things' (J. 'Weemse', *Exercitations Divine: Containing diverse Questions and Solutions for the Right Understanding of the Scripture* (London, 1632), p. 109).

that 'the teachers of the Jews, who are our enemies, have taken great pains to corrupt the Hebrew text'.[110] However, there were other Catholic writers, more sympathetic to Hebraic scholarship, who argued that, precisely because the text was corrupted, it was necessary to use rabbinical writings in order to get at its true meaning. One such was the early sixteenth-century Italian friar (of Albanian origin) Petrus Galatinus; another, writing towards the end of that century, was the French Benedictine Hebraist Gilbert Génébrard.[111] Both were enthusiastic defenders of the apocryphal Second Book of Esdras; both therefore reaffirmed the importance of Ezra as the 'restorer' of the text after the Babylonian captivity. Galatinus accepted that Ezra had rewritten the entire Hebrew Bible; he thought the vowel-points had been added a little later, and argued that the corruptions to the text had crept in during the centuries between the death of Ezra and the birth of Christ.[112] Génébrard, writing with the benefit of Levita's findings, also denied that Ezra added the vowel-points, but accepted all the other activities traditionally ascribed to him (re-transcribing the text, correcting it, ordering the books, and dividing them into verses).[113] This, the maximal version of the story of Ezra's restitution of the Bible, appealed to such Catholic writers because it could also function as a weapon of anti-Protestant polemics. It suggested that, just as the authentication and interpretation of the Scriptures now depended on the authority and tradition of the Catholic Church, so too the priestly authority of Ezra, together with the 'tradition' embodied in the Great Synagogue, had been essential to the survival and re-establishment of the Hebrew Bible. As the leading Huguenot theologian André Rivet put it in 1627, Catholic writers, 'who leave no stone unturned to diminish the authority of the Scriptures', were using the apocryphal story of Ezra to insinuate that 'the Church had been preserved only by means of tradition, during the entire period of the Babylonian captivity'.[114]

The current of argument identified here by Rivet certainly existed on the Catholic side, but it was an extreme view, and a minority one. The mainstream Catholic position was set out by Robert Bellarmine (Roberto Bellarmino) in his lectures to the Collegium Romanum during the 1580s—which, in their published form, rapidly became one of the classic works of Catholic controversial theology.

---

[110] M. Cano, *De locis theologicis libri duodecim* (Louvain, 1564), bk 2, ch. 13, p. 111 ('Hebraeorum doctores, nostri videlicet inimici, multo studio contenderunt textum Hebraicum corrumpere'); cf. p. 113, 'Indignum autem est, vt nunc denuo ab Hebraeis nostrae fidei oracula petantur.'

[111] See Hamilton, *Apocryphal Apocalypse*, pp. 49–53, 63–5.

[112] P. Galatinus, *Opus de arcanis catholicae veritatis* (Basel, 1550), pp. 3, 27, 32. This work was first published in 1518.

[113] G. Génébrard, *Chronographia in duos libros distincta*, 2nd edn (Louvain, 1572), fols. 27v–28r.

[114] A. Rivet, *Isagoge seu introductio generalis, ad Scripturam Sacram Veteris & Novi Testamenti*, in his *Opera theologica*, 3 vols. (Rotterdam, 1651–60), II, pp. 841–1040; here ch. 6, art. 18, p. 877 ('qui nullum non movent lapidem ut sacris literis derogent . . . absque scripturis conservatam fuisse Eccles. solâ traditionis ope, toto tempore captivitatis Babylonicae').

Bellarmine rejected the idea that Ezra had miraculously rewritten the entire Bible; rather, he had merely collected and corrected the text, from copies that had survived throughout the captivity. Also dismissed was the claim that the Hebrew had been maliciously and systematically corrupted by the Jews: Bellarmine noted the extreme reverence of the Jews for the text of Scripture, and he added that, if they had made any alterations to it for anti-Christian purposes, they would surely have removed all the Old Testament prophecies of the coming of Christ, which are still to be found in the Masoretic text.[115] Instead, he concluded that 'the Hebrew Scriptures have not been generally corrupted by the efforts or malice of the Jews; nor, however, are they absolutely intact and pristine. Rather, they do contain some errors, which crept in partly through the negligence or ignorance of the copyists, and partly through the ignorance of the Rabbis who added the vowel-points.'[116]

In this way Bellarmine satisfied all the essential post-Tridentine requirements: he confirmed that the Vulgate represented a more authentic version of the text (because some corruptions had entered the Hebrew at a later stage, during the process of vocalization); he attributed just enough unreliability to the existing Hebrew to undermine the Protestant position, but not so much as to imply that the Hebrew could not be relied on at all; and he emphasized that, amid such uncertainties, Christians needed a source of authoritative judgement on the text.[117] This last argument—from the need for authority and certainty—would remain the most distinctive feature of the Catholic position, and the favourite vantage-point from which to attack the Protestants. In the words of the Scottish Jesuit James Gordon Huntley, 'according to the doctrine of our Adversaries, nothing either solide or certayne is contayned in the holy Scripture: for wheras all dependeth of the true sense of the Letter, and with them there is no certayne or sure meanes by which to finde out this sense; it followeth, that they call all into doubt.'[118]

In response, the commonest strategy of Protestant writers was to attack the extreme Catholic claim that Ezra, acting as an embodiment of ecclesiastical authority, had rewritten the Hebrew Scripture, which had otherwise entirely perished. The influential Calvinist theologian Daniel Chamier dismissed this as a 'fable'; his co-religionist André Rivet called it 'an extremely inept fable'; and the chief theologian of the Remonstrants, Simon Episcopius, said it was 'obviously

---

[115] Bellarmine, *Disputationes de controversiis Christianae fidei, adversos hujus temporis haereticos*, Controv. I, *De verbo Dei*, in his *Opera omnia*, I, pp. 23–141, here pp. 61–3.

[116] Ibid., I, p. 65 ('Scripturas hebraicas non esse in universum depravatas, opere vel malitia Judaeorum; nec tamen esse omnino integras et puras, sed habere suos quosdam errores, qui partim irrepserint negligentia, vel ignorantia librariorum . . . et partim ignorantia Rabbinorum qui addiderunt puncta').

[117] For a valuable discussion of Bellarmine's position *vis-à-vis* Protestant controversialists on these issues, see J. C. H. Lebram, 'Ein Streit um die hebräische Bibel und die Septuaginta', in T. H. Lunsingh Scheurleer and G. H. M. Posthumus Meyjes, eds., *Leiden University in the Seventeenth Century: An Exchange of Learning* (Leiden, 1975), pp. 21–63; esp. pp. 35–8.

[118] Gordon Huntley, *Summary of Controversies*, Controv. I, ch. 4, art. 3, p. 11.

untrue'.[119] Often the Protestant writers would cite, in support of this aspect of their argument, the writings of Bellarmine, as if to show that the Catholic position was self-contradictory.[120] All they really demonstrated thereby, however, was that there was little disagreement between most Catholics and most Protestants on the nature of the tasks actually performed by Ezra: he had not miraculously rewritten the Hebrew scriptures, but he had collected, edited, corrected, ordered, and subdivided them. Those activities were considered to be of great importance, and one of the consequences of this whole debate was thus to give new prominence, in scholarly circles and more generally, to the role played by Ezra in the formation of the Bible.

Rashly, a few Protestants did also include among those activities the imposition of the vowel-points: the leading representative of this hard-line Protestant position was Johannes Buxtorf the elder, whose influential work *Tiberias* (1620) extolled Ezra and the men of the Great Synagogue as the people who, acting under divine instruction, had fixed the Hebrew Scripture in its present form.[121] But such an argument was all too vulnerable to the advances of biblical scholarship. In the second quarter of the seventeenth century Catholic writers launched a new wave of attacks on the Masoretic Hebrew text: they not only developed the existing arguments about the lateness of the vowel-points, but also made use of a new weapon, the Samaritan Pentateuch (i.e. the Hebrew Pentateuch as preserved in the archaic script of the Samaritans, who had separated from the Jews), copies of which had just been obtained from the Levant.[122] One Catholic scholar, the Oratorian Jean Morin, used this version of the Pentateuch to argue that the Septuagint (the Greek translation, made by Hellenistic Jews in the third century BC) was a better version of the text than the Masoretic Hebrew. According to Morin, the original Hebrew text, as represented by the Samaritan version, had been without vowel-points or even word-divisions, and was thus profoundly enigmatic and ambiguous; only with the divinely ordained guidance of the Church was it possible to establish its true meaning.[123]

Morin's publications—which included an edition of the Samaritan text (1632), issued as part of the Paris Polyglot Bible, and several treatises denigrating the Hebrew

---

[119] D. Chamier, *Panstratiae catholicae, sive controversiarum de religione adversus Pontificios corpus*, 4 vols. (Geneva, 1626), I, p. 427 ('At ea fabula est'); Rivet, *Isagoge*, ch. 6, art. 18, in *Opera theologica*, II, p. 877 ('fabula ineptissima'); S. Episcopius, *Institutiones theologicae*, bk. 3, sect. 5, ch. 3, in his *Opera theologica*, 2 vols. (Amsterdam-Rotterdam, 1650–65), I, p. 221 ('sed id plane absimile est à vero'). John Weemes also called it 'that fable of *Esdras*' (*Exercitations*, p. 119). The frequent use of the word 'fabula' or 'fable' for this theory suggests a subliminal origin for Aikenhead's phrase 'Ezra's fables', in which, conversely, the theory is accepted as genuine and it is the biblical text that is dismissed as fabulous (see above, at n. 1).

[120] See e.g. Buxtorf, *Tiberias*, p. 105; Rivet, *Opera theologica*, II, p. 878.

[121] Buxtorf, *Tiberias*, pp. 93–105; cf. the discussion in Burnett, *From Christian Hebraism*, pp. 219–25.

[122] See J.-P. Rothschild, 'Autour du Pentateuque samaritain: voyageurs, enthousiastes et savants', in J.-R. Armogathe, ed., *Le Grand Siècle et la Bible* (Paris, 1989), pp. 61–74.

[123] See P. Auvray, 'Jean Morin (1591–1659)', *Revue Biblique*, 66 (1959), pp. 397–414 (esp. p. 401 on his theory of the Septuagint), and Lebram, 'Ein Streit', esp. pp. 30–2, 39.

as a product of rabbinical corruption—caused outrage not only among his Protestant opponents, but also among Catholic Hebrew scholars in the French capital. Bitter quarrels on this subject raged throughout the 1630s and 1640s. One of Morin's supporters, a Maronite scholar from the Lebanon, Abraham Ecchellensis (Ibrahim al-Hakilani), who had come to Paris in 1640 to assist with the preparation of the Paris Polyglot, so offended one of the professors of Hebrew at the Collège Royal with his disparagement of the Hebrew Bible that the professor, Valérian de Flavigny, tried to take him to court.[124] According to a later memoir written by Ecchelensis, the main argument he deployed against de Flavigny was as follows: 'Although the Vulgate is indeed a translation, we must hold it to be as authentic as the original; for it has been declared such by the Pope, and by his general Council, in just the same way that the Hebrew text was restored and declared authentic by Ezra and his Great Synagogue after the Babylonian captivity.'[125]

While divisions thus opened up among the Catholics, they also emerged on the Protestant side: the Huguenot scholar Louis Cappel, who had been one of the first to reject Buxtorf's claims about the antiquity of the vowel-points, composed a major work admitting—to the dismay of Protestant hard-liners—that the Masoretic Hebrew text was unreliable. Cappel dismissed as a rabbinical fantasy the idea that the present text did not differ from 'the originals written by Moses or Ezra'.[126] He was building, to some extent, on Morin's work; but unlike Morin, he believed that a reliable meaning could be extracted from the consonantal Hebrew by a careful application of the methods of textual criticism, without dependence on the authority of the Church.[127] Protestant scholars blocked the publication of Cappel's major treatise, *Critica sacra*, in both Holland and Switzerland; it was eventually published in Paris, thanks to the help of the Oratorian Jean Morin, the Jesuit Denis Petau, and Hobbes's close friend the Minim friar Marin Mersenne.[128]

It seems likely that Mersenne had followed these controversies over the nature and transmission of the Hebrew text very closely; he was also a personal friend of

---

[124] See P. J. A. N. Rietbergen, 'A Maronite Mediator between Seventeenth-Century Mediterranean Cultures: Ibrahim al-Hakilani, or Abraham Ecchellense [sic] (1605–1664) between Christendom and Islam', *Lias: Sources and Documents relating to the Early Modern History of Ideas*, 16 (1989), pp. 13–41; esp. pp. 26–7. See also Ecchellensis's polemical reply to de Flavigny, *Epistola apologetica prima* (n.p. [Paris], 1647), esp. pp. 45–6, 54–5.

[125] Archivio di Stato, Rome, Fondo Cartari-Febei, vol. 64, fols. 70–84, 'Vita d'Abramo Ecchellense Maronita. Ab ipsomet die 16 Feb. 1657', here fols. 78v–79r ('se bene la Vulgata è versione, si deue hauere, e tenere per authentica come il suo proprio originale, essendo per tale dichiarata dal sommo Pontefice, et dal suo generale Concilio, nell' istesso modo appunto, che fù restaurato, e dichiarato per authentico il testo Hebraico da Ezra, e dalla sua gran Congregatione doppo la Cattiuità di Babilonia'). Seen through Hobbesian eyes (with the authority of both the Pope and Ezra viewed as purely human), this formulation would bear a striking similarity to Hobbes's own position.

[126] L. Cappel, *Critica sacra* (Paris, 1650), p. 5 ('Mosis vel Esdrae autographis'). On his dispute with Buxtorf see Burnett, *From Christian Hebraism*, pp. 229–39.

[127] For a valuable account of Cappel's theories see F. Laplanche, *L'Écriture, le sacré et l'histoire: érudits et politiques protestants devant la Bible en France au XVIIᵉ siècle* (Amsterdam, 1986), pp. 229–43.

[128] Ibid., pp. 226–8.

Abraham Ecchellensis, and it is probably significant that the library of his Minim convent acquired copies of all the works issued in the polemical exchange between Morin and his chief critic among the Parisian Hebraists, Siméon de Muys.[129] No one played a greater role in Hobbes's intellectual life in Paris in the 1640s than Marin Mersenne. So, although (or, indeed, because) Hobbes was not himself a Hebrew scholar, it is reasonable to suppose that he would have discussed these matters with his learned friend, and therefore would have been made aware of some of the latest developments in the theory of biblical interpretation—a theory which, with the transition from Morin to Cappel, had just entered a peculiarly critical phase.

The key problem was how to reconcile the text's authority, which was divine, with its history, which was more and more evidently human. Catholics depended on the authority of the Church to vouch for the divine authority of the text—an argument which could take surprisingly hyperbolic forms. One sixteenth-century Catholic writer, Wolfgang Hermann, observed that the Scripture, 'if deprived of the authority of the Church', would have no more validity than Aesop's fables; a catechism published by Cardinal Sourdis included the question and answer, 'To whom does it belong to define the canonical books?' 'To the Church, without whose authority I would grant no more credence to St Matthew than I do to Livy.'[130] This authority to declare the status of the text had traditionally been regarded as bound up with the authority to interpret it. Writers such as Bellarmine had thus been able to accept the idea that the text had been rendered uncertain (to some extent, at least) by a human process of transmission and corruption, because they thought this could only strengthen the need for an authoritative interpreter. But if modern research was making the Bible seem more and more similar to a human artefact such as the text of Livy, then it was also suggesting that the way to establish its meaning was simply to engage in more research and textual criticism: that, after all, is how editors of Livy resolve their textual problems, not by seeking out some superior authority.

The Protestants too had a theory of the authority of the Bible that was becoming increasingly dislocated from the practice of its textual study and interpretation. The standard Protestant view was that the Scripture was self-authenticating: as Calvin put it, 'As to the question, how shall we be persuaded that it came from God without recurring to a decree of the Church? It is just the same as if it were asked,

---

[129] For the friendship with Ecchellensis see Mersenne, *Correspondance*, XIII, p. 479; XIV, pp. 283, 391. The convent library held de Muys, *Assertatio hebraicae veritatis* (1631), Morin, *Exercitationes biblicae* (1633), de Muys, *Censura* (1634), Morin, *Exercitationes ecclesiasticae* (1635), de Muys, *Castigatio Morini* (1639) and Morin, *Diatribe . . . contra . . . de Muys* (1639): Bibliothèque de l'Arsenal, Paris, MS 6203, pp. 45–7.

[130] J. Brentius [Brentz], *Apologiae confessionis . . . Christophoris Ducis Wirtenbergensis* (Frankfurt, 1559), p. 1377 ('si destituatur autoritate ecclesiae'); Chamier, *Panstratiae catholicae*, I, p. 148 ('Ad quemnam pertinet definire libros Canonicos?' 'Ad Ecclesiam: cuius absque authoritate non maiorem fidem adhibuerim Diuo Matthaeo: quam Tito Livio').

How shall we learn to distinguish light from darkness, white from black...? Scripture bears upon the face of it as clear evidence of its truth as white and black do of their colour.'[131] Every verse, every word of the Bible shared this self-evidencing divine quality; and this meant, in turn, that the only authority to be drawn on in interpreting any one passage of Scripture must be that of other passages. So, while Catholics used the description of Ezra and his colleagues teaching the people (Neh. 8: 5–11) to illustrate the authority of the Church, Protestants used it for exactly the opposite purpose: in the standard Protestant Latin translation, Nehemiah 8: 9 included the words 'dabant intelligentiam per scripturam ipsam', 'they gave the meaning, by means of the Scripture itself'.[132]

This approach to the Bible was especially vulnerable to the application of textual–historical methods. The problem was not merely that some words or verses might be shown to be corrupted and inauthentic—thus breaking the spell of the text's divine perfection. Rather, any internal differentiation of the text, distinguishing, for example, between primary materials and later editorial ones, or between directly inspired passages and merely historical narratives, might put at risk the belief in the Scripture's total uniformity of authority, suggesting that some parts of it were more human (and therefore less reliable) than others. This was the fundamental reason why a die-hard Calvinist such as David Pareus refused to accept the idea that some of the apparent anachronisms in the Pentateuch could be explained as later interpolations, insisting instead that they were all written prophetically by Moses:

How can Moses write about kings who lived long after him? You may as well ask: how did he know about the creation of the world, the flood, the lives of Noah and Abraham, etc., which happened long before him? If you say, he knew these things because he had heard about them, it is clear that no mere rumour could have supplied him with such a precise and infallible history. Rather, one should say that he wrote that history by means of prophetic inspiration... For stories which are accepted merely on the basis of rumour and hearsay often contain something unreliable or fictitious.[133]

---

[131] J. Calvin, *Institutes of the Christian Religion*, tr. H. Beveridge, 2 vols. (London, 1953), bk. 1, ch. 7, art. 2, I, p. 69.

[132] The standard Protestant translation was by Junius and Tremellius. In the Vulgate this is given as 'et intellexerunt cum legeretur'; in the AV (where this verse is Neh. 8: 8) the translation is closer to the Vulgate than to Junius–Tremellius, but different again ('and caused them to understand the reading'). For a typical expression of the Protestant argument see J. A. Comenius, *Unum necessarium, scire quid sibi sit necessarium, in vita & morte, & post mortem* (Amsterdam, 1668), p. 62: 'Explicatio Scripturarum per Scripturas esse debebat, qvalis Esdrae Sacerdotis fuit.' For Morin's use of the Catholic argument see Lebram, 'Ein Streit', p. 39. For a penetrating discussion of this passage, rejecting the Protestant view, see the work by Spinoza's friend Lodewijk Meyer, *Philosophia S. Scripturae interpres* ('Eleutheropolis' [Amsterdam], 1666), pp. 77–8.

[133] D. Pareus, *In Genesin Mosis commentarius* (Frankfurt, 1615), col. 1683 (on Gen. 36. 31) ('quomodo scribat Moses de ducibus, qui multo post eum fuerunt?... Pariter quaeras, vnde creationem rerum, diluuium, Noachum, Abrahamum, &c Moses nouerit, qui multo ante eum fuerunt? Si dicas, auditione eum haec habuisse, certe fama nulla tam exactam tamque infallibilem historiam ei suppeditare potuit. Potius prophetica inspiratione illam scripsisse dicendus est... Quae enim fama & relatione tantum accipiuntur, non raro lubricum vel fabulosum quid admixtum habent'). This work was first published in 1609.

Pareus was resisting an incoming tide of textual–historical interpretation, which was flowing through both Protestant and Catholic channels. As we have seen, the commentators on the Pentateuch may have maintained the theoretical possibility that the anachronistic passages had been written by Moses prophetically; but in many cases they thought they were actually strengthening the reliability of the text by providing a more natural and human explanation. Similarly, it was increasingly assumed that the veracity of the historical parts of the text could be defended (not weakened) by treating them as eye-witness reports, on the same basis as any other direct account of human experience. As Cornelius à Lapide put it, 'Moses received and disseminated these things partly from tradition, partly from divine revelation, and partly from knowledge as an eye-witness: for the events he narrates in Exodus, Leviticus, Numbers and Deuteronomy are events at which he himself was present, as participant or witness.'[134] In this way the miraculous uniformity of the Scriptures was subtly undone, as they were transformed into a complex artefact containing elements of different kinds and different derivations. Similarly Hugo Grotius, replying to criticism directed at him by André Rivet, explained: 'It is true that I said that not all the books in the Hebrew canon were dictated by the Holy Spirit. I do not deny that they were written with a pious intention ... But there was no need for the Holy Spirit to dictate histories: it was sufficient for the writer to have a good enough memory of the things he had seen, or enough diligence in setting out the commentaries of the Ancients.'[135]

What this line of argument seemed to imply was that divine revelation, instead of being the condition or constitutive quality of the entire Bible, was something contained in just some of its parts: the words spoken by God or by angels, or the specifically prophetic utterances of the prophets. These might now be seen as isolated fragments of divinity, floating in a sea of human text. Admittedly, few orthodox theologians were willing to look at the Bible in that way, as they continued to believe that the human text too was written under divine guidance of a more general and providential kind. But one person who did not hesitate to push the argument to this conclusion—and, indeed, a little further—was Thomas Hobbes. He distinguished carefully between two senses of the phrase 'the Word of

---

[134] à Lapide, *In Pentateuchum commentaria*, p. 23 ('Moses haec partim traditione, partim diuina reuelatione, partim oculari inspectione didicit & accepit: nam quae in Exodo, Leuitico, Numeris & Deuteronomio narrat, ea praesens ipse vidit & gessit').

[135] H. Grotius, *Votum pro pace ecclesiastica*, in his *Opera theologica*, 4 vols. (Basel, 1732), IV, pp. 653–76; here p. 672 ('Verè dixi non omnes libros qui sunt in Hebraeo Canone, dictatos à Spiritu Sancto. Scriptos esse cum pio animi motu, non nego ... Sed à Spiritu Sancto dictari historias nihil fuit opus: satis fuit scriptorem memoriâ valere circa res spectatas, aut diligentiâ in describendis Veterum commentariis'). This work was first published in 1642. Grotius was accused (by Rivet, among others) of following Socinus in these matters: see J.-P. Heering, *Hugo de Groot als apologeet van de christelijke godsdienst* (The Hague, 1992), pp. 117–20. The similarity of their views on the nature of historical materials in the Pentateuch (which Socinus compared to the accounts of earlier periods in Livy and Plutarch: *De sacrae Scripturae auctoritate* ('Seville' [Amsterdam?], 1588), p. 29) was genuine; but this position was not peculiar to Socinus.

God': in the narrow sense it meant words spoken by God, and in the broad sense it signified merely words *about* God, the 'Doctrine of Christian Religion'. In the second sense, he observed, the whole of the Bible was the Word of God, 'but in the former sense not so. For example, although these words, *I am the Lord thy God, &c.* to the end of the Ten Commandements, were spoken by God to Moses; yet the Preface, *God spake these words and said*, is to be understood for the Words of him that wrote the holy History.'[136] The radical step taken by Hobbes (and avoided by all orthodox writers) was to point out that, where a fragment of divine revelation is conveyed to us by a merely human narrative, its reliability can be no greater than that of the narrator himself—in other words, merely human. 'If *Livy* say the Gods made once a Cow speak, and we believe it not; wee distrust not God therein, but *Livy*. So that it is evident, that whatsoever we believe, upon no other reason, then what is drawn from authority of men onely, and their writings; whether they be sent from God or not, is Faith in men onely.'[137]

Hobbes thus adopted a position precisely opposite to the old Protestant theory about the self-evidencing, self-authenticating nature of Scripture as divine revelation. For Hobbes, no revelation, once imparted to one human being, could be transmitted to any other human being in a self-authenticating way, as the means of transmission would be necessarily (and merely) human. 'How God speaketh to a man immediately, may be understood by those well enough, to whom he hath so spoken; but how the same should be understood by another, is hard, if not impossible to know. For if a man pretend to me, that God hath spoken to him supernaturally, and I make doubt of it, I cannot easily perceive what argument he can produce, to oblige me to beleeve it.'[138] Traditionally it had been claimed that revelation could also be verified by the fact that it was accompanied by miracles and/or prophecies; these had been used as supporting arguments, by both Catholics and Protestants, for belief in the divine authority of the Bible. But Hobbes was able to dismiss this whole line of thought, using a devastating combination of Scriptural arguments (about the ability of sorcerers to replicate miracles, and about the need to examine even successful prophets for their conformity with true doctrine) and ontological assumptions about the existence of natural causes for all such phenomena.[139]

Having thus placed the special authority of divine revelation out of human reach, and having reduced the status of the Bible to that of a human document, Hobbes might have left it there, on a par with the works of Livy, Plutarch, Thucydides, and the rest. Instead, he insisted that its composition was defined, and its interpretation regulated, by special authority—the authority of the Church, acting under that of the sovereign. Not having any direct instructions about the

---

[136] Hobbes, *Leviathan*, pp. 222, 223 (quotation). [137] Ibid., p. 32.
[138] Ibid., p. 196. [139] Ibid., esp. chs. 12, 36, 37.

Scriptures from God, ordinary citizens must be guided by 'the authority of their severall Common-wealths; that is to say, of their lawfull Soveraigns. According to this obligation, I can acknowledge no other Books of the Old Testament, to be Holy Scripture, but those which have been commanded to be acknowledged for such, by the Authority of the Church of *England*'.[140] On the face of it, Hobbes was thus adopting a version of the Catholic position—albeit one in which the authority of the Church was strictly subordinated to that of the political ruler. As some commentators on Hobbes have noted, there was a general congruence between his political theory and the Catholic theory of scriptural and doctrinal interpretation: in both, the need for an ultimate authority was paramount.[141] Occasionally the similarity could be quite striking. Thus, Bellarmine, deriding the reliance of radical Reformation theologians on 'private inspiration' ('internus afflatus'), had exclaimed: 'How much confusion and universal chaos would ensue if, in any human republic, the laws and decrees of the higher powers were taken away, and each person were allowed to do whatever seemed to him fair and just according to his own natural prudence? What, then, would happen if private inspiration were the only thing to be looked for, and acted on, in that republic which is not human but divine [*sc.* the Church]?'[142] But, in the writings of Catholic theologians such as Bellarmine, this human, political analogy was only an analogy. The real argument was theological: Catholics claimed that the only sure place in which the gifts of the Holy Spirit (requisite for the correct interpretation of Scripture) were located throughout the ages was the Roman Catholic Church. The resemblance between Hobbes's argument and that of the Catholics was thus quite contingent; what for them was merely an illustrative analogy was for him the only real argument, because the only real authority on earth was human and political.

Hence the importance of Ezra. Hobbes's prime aim in setting out his Ezran hypothesis was not to ridicule the Scriptures, not to portray them as 'Ezra's fables', not to show that the whole Mosaic story was fictitious: rather, it was to substantiate historically his view that the only 'authority' the Scriptures could have was a

---

[140] Ibid., p. 199. Hobbes's views on the relation between the authority of the Church and that of the sovereign in this context do seem to have undergone a significant development between *De cive* and *Leviathan*: in the earlier work, the former type of authority had a different derivation from the latter, even though the exercise of it was entirely subordinate to the sovereign's authority (see L. Strauss, *The Political Philosophy of Hobbes: Its Basis and Genesis*, tr. E. M. Sinclair (Chicago, 1952), p. 72; H. Reventlow, *The Authority of the Bible and the Rise of the Modern World*, tr. J. Bowden (London, 1984), p. 213; J. P. Sommerville, *Thomas Hobbes: Political Ideas in Historical Context* (London, 1992), pp. 119–27).

[141] Robert Orr, for example, has commented on the 'somewhat bizarre agreement' between Hobbes and the Roman Catholic Church on the need for a sovereign interpreter: *Reason and Authority: The Thought of William Chillingworth* (Oxford, 1967), p. 86.

[142] Bellarmine, *Opera omnia*, I, p. 25 ('si in quavis humana republica, sublatis legibus institutisque majorum, id unicuique liceret, quod naturali sua prudentia aequum ac justum censeret; quanta perturbatio rerum omnium? Quanta confusio sequeretur? . . . Quid igitur fieret, si in ea republica, quae divina potius quam humana est . . . solus internus afflatus expectandus et sequendus esset?').

human and political one. This, indeed, was what distinguished them from the works of Livy and the rest. 'By the Books of Holy Scripture, are understood those, which ought to be the *Canon*, that is to say, the Rules of Christian life. And because all Rules of life, which men are in conscience bound to observe, are Laws; the question of the Scripture, is the question of what is Law throughout all Chistendome.'[143] When people asked '*From whence the Scriptures derive their Authority*', he observed, they misunderstood the issue if they thought this was a question about why people believed those texts to be divine; different people had different criteria of belief (or, one might say, degrees of credulity), and there could be no general answer to such a question. Instead, 'The question truly stated is, *By what Authority they are made Law.*'[144]

Hobbes did not deny that parts of the Pentateuch (such as the 'Book of the Law' contained in Deuteronomy) were derived from Moses himself; Moses had been the legislator and civil sovereign of his people, and Hobbes had no difficulty in supposing that such utterances had had a genuine legal and historical status in the 'commonwealth' that Moses founded. What he objected to, however, was the idea that any text could have operated, through the centuries after Moses, as an independent locus of authority—independent, that is, of the political rulers of the day. Equally, therefore, he rejected the idea that when other texts were written (for example, the prophetic books) they immediately became authoritative by virtue of their own nature as divine revelation.

Accordingly, his history of the authority of the Bible was a chronicle of discontinuities, punctuated by political acts. Under Moses, and for many generations thereafter, the only canonical scripture had been the 'Book of the Law'; then, for a long time, this book had been lost, and the rulers of Israel had 'had no written Word of God, but ruled according to their own discretion'; then the Book of the Law was 'found again in the Temple in the time of Josiah, and by his authority received for the Law of God'. But, Hobbes emphasized, 'Moses at the writing, and Josiah at the recovery thereof, had both of them the Civill Soveraignty. Hitherto therefore the Power of making Scripture Canonicall, was in the Civill Soveraign.'[145] What Ezra did was in some ways just a repetition of what had happened under Josiah: a previously canonical text was reaffirmed as canonical (with, in this case, a large quantity of other texts being added to it). The key point, once again, was political:

From hence we may inferre, that the Scriptures of the Old Testament, which we have at this day, were not Canonicall, nor a Law unto the Jews, till the renovation of their Covenant with God at their return from the Captivity, and restauration of their Common-wealth under *Esdras* . . . Now seeing Esdras was the High Priest, and the High Priest was their Civill Soveraigne, it is manifest, that the Scriptures were never made Lawes, but by the Soveraign Civill Power.[146]

---

[143] Hobbes, *Leviathan*, p. 199.   [144] Ibid., p. 205.
[145] Ibid., pp. 283–4.   [146] Ibid., p. 284.

For Hobbes, then, the story told in the apocryphal Second Book of Esdras was simply too convenient to be disregarded: here was a ready-made foundation for the claim that the whole body of the Old Testament had been issued, at a particular time, by someone exercising sovereign power. He quoted at length, approvingly, from the passage in 2 Esdras 14 which begins with Ezra's address to God, 'Thy law is burnt . . .', and goes on to describe his miraculous non-stop dictation for forty days. Of course, Hobbes's own comments elsewhere on inspiration and the gifts of the Holy Spirit implied that any such story should be given a more naturalistic explanation. What exactly he thought Ezra had done, however, is not clear. One of the phrases Hobbes used, describing the Scripture as 'set forth in the form wee have it in, by *Esdras*', could have meant either that Ezra edited it (which was the orthodox view) or that he actually composed it; but he also referred to '*Esdras*, who by the direction of Gods Spirit retrived them [*sc.* 'the Bookes of the Old Testament'], when they were lost', which implies that they had previously existed in some form or other.[147] In his comments on particular books, Hobbes did argue in some cases (Kings and Chronicles, for instance) that they must have been written during or after the captivity; in other cases (the Pentateuch, Joshua, Judges, Samuel) he commented merely that they were composed 'long after' the time they described, without trying to identify the precise time of composition or the author. In several cases he accepted the traditional attributions: the Song of Songs was by Solomon, for example, and the prophet Amos did write the book that bears his name. And his general conclusion was that 'these Books were written by divers men'.[148] One might say that Hobbes was combining, in a somewhat nonchalant way, the orthodox view of Ezra as an editor of pre-existent materials with the more radical idea that he composed some of these books (including, possibly, the Pentateuch) himself. Nowhere in Hobbes's account does one find the sort of argumentation deployed by Spinoza, who insisted that all the historical books of the Bible must be the work of a single writer, and tried to demonstrate that that writer must be Ezra.[149] Hobbes could afford to be nonchalant, even agnostic, about such matters. Questions of authorship were, for him, of secondary importance; the primary question concerned not authorship, but authority.

What Hobbes and Spinoza had in common, nevertheless, was that they were both trying to explain the development of the Bible in essentially historical and political terms.[150] Commenting on Spinoza's theory, the nineteenth-century scholar Ludwig Diestel observed that, in presenting the Old Testament as something both natural and national (that is, to be understood as part of the political history of the Jews), Spinoza had broken out of the old dilemma, in which the

---

[147] Ibid., p. 203.   [148] Ibid., pp. 200-02, 204.
[149] Spinoza, *Tractatus theologico-politicus*, ch. 8, in *Opera*, III, pp. 126–7.
[150] See the valuable comments in J. P. Osier, 'L'Herméneutique de Hobbes et de Spinoza', *Studia Spinozana*, 3 (1987), pp. 319–47, esp. pp. 334–41.

Bible was to be viewed either as pure revelation, or as the work of impostors.[151] The same can also be said of Hobbes (with the qualification that the dilemma had not been entirely unbroken before he wrote). Unlike the radical anti-Christians who came after him, such as Aikenhead, Meslier, and Fréret, he did not portray the Old Testament as a piece of outright imposture, cooked up by Ezra the Scribe. His account of its political history—of its establishment, in particular circumstances, as an authoritative text—gained more sense and solidity from supposing that the text itself had a previous history up to that point (albeit a various and uncertain one), that its narrative could be used as historical evidence, and that one component of it, the 'Book of the Law' in Deuteronomy, had been preserved from a much earlier political context, the government of the Israelites by Moses. In comparison with the orthodox tradition of biblical interpretation from which Hobbes had drawn many of his materials, his argument was, undoubtedly, heterodox and innovatory. But in comparison with the later arguments of the radical anti-Christians, it seems positively old-fashioned in its assumptions about the historical development (and therefore, in a sense, the historicity) of the text. Why, then, was Hobbes's Ezran theory so quickly and automatically assimilated to the radical tradition, by foes and friends alike?

Some commentators have felt that Hobbes's other remarks in *Leviathan* about the nature and reliability of the Scriptures, and his style of exegesis itself, were sufficient proof of a desire to ridicule and discredit the Bible entirely.[152] But the evidence here is ambiguous, at best. For example, when Hobbes states that, 'although these Books were written by divers men, yet it is manifest the Writers were all indued with one and the same Spirit, in that they conspire to one and the same end, which is the setting forth of the Rights of the Kingdome of *God*', it may be tempting to argue that his choice of the word 'conspire' is a heavy-handed hint at deception and malevolence.[153] The word could have those overtones in early modern English, but it could also refer quite neutrally to the sharing of a common purpose: one sixteenth-century text declared that 'The cyvyle lyfe ys a polytyke ordur of men conspyryng togyddur in vertue and honesty.'[154] Hobbes's formulation was in fact strikingly similar to that of Robert Bellarmine, which he had

---

[151] Diestel, *Geschichte des Alten Testaments*, p. 359 (n.).
[152] For a strongly stated expression of this view see T. L. Pangle, 'A Critique of Hobbes's Critique of biblical and Natural Religion in *Leviathan*', *Jewish Political Studies Review*, 4, no. 2 (1992), pp. 25–57, esp. p. 31.
[153] Hobbes, *Leviathan*, p. 204; cf. Q. Skinner, *Reason and Rhetoric in the Philosophy of Hobbes* (Cambridge, 1996), p. 412: 'There is thus a considerable *frisson* attaching to Hobbes's use of the term to describe the books of the Bible.' Professor Skinner does not argue that 'conspire' could only have had a negative sense; he cites it as an example of the rhetorical figure 'aestismus', which depended on inherent ambiguity between an acceptable meaning and a negative or satirical one. However, in most of the examples he gives (pp. 409–12), there could be little doubt that it was the negative meaning that was really intended; that, indeed, is why aestismus functioned as a 'mocking trope' (p. 409). My point is that in this case, given the direct precedent of Bellarmine's wording, there is a real possibility that the acceptable meaning was the one intended.
[154] Thomas Starkey, *Dialogue between Cardinal Pole and Thomas Lupset*, I, i, 19; cited in *OED*, 'conspire' (3).

almost certainly read: Bellarmine gave, as one of the proofs of the authenticity of Scripture, 'the incredible and obviously divine conspiring ['conspiratio'] and harmony of so many men, who together wrote the sacred books in different places, times, languages and circumstances'.[155] Similarly, it might be thought that one key argument presented by Hobbes in defence of the reliability of the Scriptures was surreptitiously and destructively ironic: noting that the Scriptures had been preserved for centuries by the 'Doctors of the Church', who had an interest in promoting their own claims to power, he declared that 'yet I am perswaded they did not therefore falsifie the Scriptures . . . because if they had had an intention so to doe, they would surely have made them more favorable to their power over Christian Princes, and Civill Soveraignty, than they are'.[156] But this argument too had a formal counterpart in Bellarmine's work, where (as noted above), a similar point was made about the alleged corruption of the text by the rabbis: 'If the Jews had wished to falsify the holy Scriptures out of hostility to the Christians, they would doubtless have removed the main prophecies [of the Messiah].'[157]

The point is not that these congruences with orthodox argumentation prove that Hobbes's overall purpose and meaning must have been equally orthodox. It is, rather, that the reasons why his treatment of the Bible was thought to be radically hostile to orthodox belief are to be found not in any of his particular arguments about the biblical text itself, but in the whole surrounding structure of argument—above all, in his naturalistic treatment of miracles and prophecy, and his epistemological blocking of any transmission of divine revelation from one human being to another. These surrounding arguments, after all, were the reason why his presentation of biblical texts as historically developed documents differed from the approach of those orthodox scholars who were also engaging in historical–textual analysis. Orthodox theologians such as Cornelius à Lapide or Hugo Grotius could treat the Scriptures as composite, human documents because they retained the assurance that one could know that God had been at work through those human channels. But Hobbes removed the basis for that assurance, making it unattainable and unknowable, and thus causing the Scriptures to be essentially indistinguishable from any other human writings. The fact that he regarded them as partly historical, while later radicals saw them as works of fiction, was therefore a secondary issue; the radicals were correct in supposing that, where the fundamental issues were concerned, Hobbes was on the radical, heterodox side.

[155] Bellarmine, *Opera omnia*, I, p. 24 ('incredibilis quaedam et plane divina conspiratio atque concordia tot virorum, qui diversis locis, temporibus, linguis, occasionibus sacra volumina conscripserunt'). This is from Bellarmine's *De verbo Dei*, the first part of his *Disputationes de controversiis*. Hobbes wrote at length against the third part of that work (*Leviathan*, pp. 300–20), and also commented on the sixth (pp. 346–7); so it seems reasonable to assume that he had read the whole work with some care.

[156] Hobbes, *Leviathan*, p. 204.

[157] Bellarmine, *Opera omnia*, I, p. 63 ('Si Judaei falsare voluissent divinas Scripturas in odium Christianorum, sine dubio praecipua vaticinia sustulissent').

Leo Strauss made a similar point in his study of Spinoza's biblical criticism, when he observed that philological–historical arguments in themselves could not destroy belief in the authenticity of revelation; for that purpose, more fundamental arguments of a theological or metaphysical kind were needed.[158] But his presentation of this point risked giving the impression that anyone who was deploying philological–historical arguments was at least trying to undermine revelation—even if the attempt, in the absence of those more fundamental arguments, was bound to be unsuccessful. As we have seen, there was a long tradition of applying philological–historical analysis to Scripture within orthodox Christianity; there was nothing implicitly or necessarily anti-Christian about it. While some of the claims made by Hobbes and Spinoza went far beyond what orthodox writers had hitherto allowed, their philological–historical arguments were, *qua* philological–historical arguments, products of that tradition. Which prompts the question: can it really be true to say that Hobbes and Spinoza (and/or La Peyrère) were the 'founders' of modern biblical criticism?

That these writers had a great impact is clear: the numerous denunciations of them, some of which were cited above, are testimony to that. To some extent they polarized opinion, pushing many people to extremes of acceptance or rejection. Thus, on the one hand, Hobbes's and Spinoza's theories about the Pentateuch were taken up enthusiastically by free-thinkers such as Charles Blount in England and Antonie van Dale in Holland; on the other hand, there were critics who insisted on the Pentateuch's Mosaicity, dismissing even the commonly accepted proofs of interpolations as a threat to true faith.[159] In some cases the defence of the biblical text took on an extraordinarily reactionary character: the Independent divine John Owen, for example, published a treatise in 1658 defending the idea that the Hebrew text was uncorrupted and unchanged—vowel-points and all—from the version edited by Ezra and the men of the Great Synagogue.[160] (Owen was subsequently attacked by a Quaker Hebraist, Samuel Fisher, who ridiculed his outdated views on the vowel-points, and used a few standard pieces of evidence, such as the description of the death of Moses, to argue that there had been some changes in the text:

---

[158] Strauss, *Spinoza's Critique*, pp. 141–4.
[159] C. Blount, *The Oracles of Reason* (London, 1693), pp. 16–17 (summarizing Hobbes); A. van Dale, *Dissertationes de origine ac progressu idololatriae et superstitionum* (Amsterdam, 1696), pp. 686–7 (asserting Ezran authorship); A. Ross, *Leviathan Drawn out with a Hook: Or, Animadversions upon Mr Hobbs his Leviathan* (London, 1653), p. 35 (claiming that Moses 'writes of his death and sepulcher by anticipation'); J. Templer, *Idea theologiae Leviathanis* (London, 1673), pp. 123–4 (insisting on Mosaic authorship of the whole text, with the sole exception of Deut. 34: 6–12).
[160] J. Owen, *Of the Divine Originall, Authority, Self-evidencing Light, and Power of the Scriptures* (Oxford, '1659'). (The date in Thomason's copy, BL pressmark E 1866(1), is corrected to November 1658.) This work was directed primarily against Brian Walton's Polyglot Bible, and hence at the theorics of Morin and Cappel on which Walton drew. But Owen had made a careful study of *Leviathan* (see Hobbes, *Correspondence*, I, p. 459), and some of his arguments seem to have been framed in response to Hobbes (e.g. on how revelation is known to be authentic, pp. 66–7).

because of this, Fisher is sometimes hailed, quite unjustifiably, as an innovatory biblical scholar.[161])

Yet the most significant developments in biblical-critical thinking took place not at these extremes but, so to speak, in the middle. Most of the mainstream critics whose denunciations of Hobbes, La Peyrère, and Spinoza were cited in the second section of this essay took it for granted that there were interpolations and editorial changes in the biblical text. Jacques Abbadie even put forward a theological argument *for* textual corruptions: the books of the Bible had undergone the vicissitudes normally suffered by all human texts, he suggested, so that wrestling with the resulting difficulties would provide good spiritual exercise for the faithful.[162] Richard Simon, while he was certainly innovatory in the contents of his philological–historical arguments, and although he was therefore denounced by many of these writers, belongs essentially to this middle ground: he defended the Mosaicity of the Pentateuch in broad terms by arguing that it was compiled mainly by 'public scribes' working under Moses' direction.[163] Simon was able to pursue his philological–historical arguments to their novel conclusions because he had worked out, at the theological level, a more subtle and advanced theory of revelation, in which divine inspiration was thought of as inhering in a whole collective process of human writing, not merely in the supernatural experiences of individual authors.[164]

After Simon, other writers were able to advance innovatory theories of their own, relying on the increasingly common assumption that the divine authority of the Scripture was not incompatible with a human textual history; thus, for example, the Remonstrant theologian Jean Le Clerc proposed that the Pentateuch was compiled neither by Ezra nor by public scribes, but by the priest sent to Samaria by the King of Assyria, and the Catholic Hebraist Étienne Fourmont suggested that it was written in the reign of David.[165] Fourmont's style of reasoning gives an especially good indication of how philological–historical arguments could be used

---

[161] S. Fisher, *Rusticus ad academicos in exercitationibus explostulatoriis, apologeticis quatuor: The Rustick's Alarm to the Rabbies: Or, the Country Correcting the University, and Clergy* (London, 1660), sigs. c4v–d1v (points); Second Exercitation, p. 71 (death of Moses). For exaggerated claims about Fisher see C. Hill, *The World Turned Upside Down* (London, 1972), pp. 213–15.

[162] Abbadie, *Traité de la vérité*, pp. 267–8 ('il a esté nécessaire aussi que la révélation des Juifs parût sugette aux accidens qui arrivent aux autres livres, pour exercer la foi encore à cet égard').

[163] Simon, *Histoire critique*, p. 3 ('Ainsi l'on pourra dire en ce sens-là, que tout le Pentateuque est veritablement de Moïse, parce que ceux qui en ont fait le Recueil, vivoient de son tems, & qu'ils ne l'ont fait que par son ordre').

[164] See Simon, *Lettre à Monsieur L'Abbé P.*, pp. 13–27, and the comments in J. Steinmann, *Richard Simon et les origines de l'exégèse biblique* (Paris, 1960), p. 209.

[165] J. Le Clerc, *Sentimens de quelques théologiens de Hollande sur l'Histoire Critique du Vieux Testament* (Amsterdam, 1685), esp. pp. 125–9 (referring to 2 Kings 17); E. Fourmont, *Lettres à Monsieur ** sur le commentaire du Père Calmet sur la Genèse*, (Paris, 1709–10: two parts, continuously paginated), pp. 24, 35. Both arguments were based on the idea that the Samaritan Pentateuch must have existed before Ezra (who was traditionally credited with replacing the Samaritan script with the 'square' Hebrew alphabet); the presumed interpolations, which were also in the Samaritan text, therefore could not have been made by Ezra.

within the theological mainstream. Responding to Calmet's reactionary defence of the Mosaicity of the Pentateuch, he noted that Calmet used the apparent anachronisms to disprove the claim that the Pentateuch was a work of imposture, on the grounds that no impostor would have left such obvious contradictions in his work. This was indeed a good argument against outright forgery, Fourmont observed, but it did not remove all doubts about when the text was written. 'If one supposed that an honest man had written the Pentateuch, basing his work on the writings of Moses, and that he had done so at the behest of an enlightened prince such as David, or of the whole nation, one could follow the rules of proper textual criticism, without fearing any ill consequence, and perhaps one might even bring oneself to do so for reasons of piety.'[166]

It was this principle—following the rules of textual criticism, for reasons of piety—that would lie behind the work of later scholars such as Jean Astruc; it had previously been applied by a whole series of writers, from Masius and à Lapide to Grotius, Cappel, and Simon. Modern biblical criticism grew out of this tradition; it was not 'founded' by Hobbes or Spinoza, even though it may have been stimulated in some ways by their writings. It would also be an exaggeration to say that the anti-Christian tradition of the radical Enlightenment was 'founded' by those authors: it too had many other, and deeper, roots. But it can at least be said that the influence of their theories on that radical tradition was long-lasting and profound; and, of all their theories relating to the Bible, none proved more congenial to radical minds, or more effective in radical hands, than the attribution of the Pentateuch to Ezra.

---

[166] Fourmont, *Lettres*, p. 24 ('mais il reste toûjours un doute sur l'antiquité du livre; parce qu'il semble qu'en supposant un honnête homme qui auroit composé le Pentateuque, sur les écrits même du Législateur, & cela par l'ordre de quelque Prince éclairé comme David, ou de toute la nation, on pourroit suivre les regles de la veritable critique, sans craindre aucune mauvaise consequence, on se porteroit peut-être même à le faire par un principe de piété').

– 13 –

# Hobbes's Theory of International Relations

## I

A strange asymmetry prevails in modern writings on Hobbes's theory of the relations between states. For specialists in international relations theory, Hobbes is a canonical figure, a key representative of one of the major traditions. He stands alongside Machiavelli (and, in many accounts, Thucydides) as an archetypal proponent of 'Realism'. E. H. Carr portrayed Hobbes as the second great Realist, after Machiavelli; Martin Wight, whose system of classification influenced a generation of modern theorists, called Hobbes an 'extreme Realist'; Michael Walzer located Realism 'at its source and in its most compelling form' in the works of Thucydides and Hobbes. One influential modern text, Charles Beitz's *Political Theory and International Relations*, takes what it calls 'the Hobbesian conception of international relations' as the basis of 'skeptical' or 'Realist' theory, and devotes twenty-three pages of detailed argument to refuting it.[1] No student of international relations theory, it seems, can afford to disregard Hobbes's contribution to that field.

And yet, if one turns from the international relations specialists to the Hobbes specialists, one finds that such disregard is perfectly normal. Writers who have devoted years of their lives to the examination of Hobbes's political philosophy seem content to pass over his theory of international relations in a few paragraphs or sentences: it is rare to find any full-length study of Hobbes giving more than a couple of pages to this topic.[2] Consequently, the insights or advances achieved by

---

[1] E. H. Carr, *The Twenty Years' Crisis 1919–1939: An Introduction to the Study of International Relations* (London, 1939), pp. 81, 83; M. Wight, *International Theory: The Three Traditions*, ed. G. Wight and B. Porter (Leicester, 1991), p. 36; M. Walzer, *Just and Unjust Wars: A Moral Argument with Historical Illustrations* (Harmondsworth, 1980), p. 4; C. Beitz, *Political Theory and International Relations* (Princeton, NJ, 1979), pp. 14, 27–59.

[2] Howard Warrender devotes just over two pages to what he calls a 'speculation' about how Hobbes's theory might be applied to modern international relations (*The Political Philosophy of Hobbes: His Theory of Obligation* (Oxford, 1957), pp. 118–20); David Gauthier has a 6-page appendix to his book, in which he also speculates about the applicability of Hobbesian principles to international relations in the nuclear age (*The Logic of Leviathan: The Moral and Political Theory of Thomas Hobbes* (Oxford, 1969), pp. 207–12). Raymond Polin has a few pages on Hobbes's theory of the justifiability of wars of conquest (*Hobbes, Dieu et les hommes*

Hobbes scholars in their work on other areas of his thought have (with a handful of exceptions) hardly begun to impinge on the study of this aspect of his political theory.³ And the interpretation of Hobbes put forward by modern international relations theorists, meanwhile, has become fixed and ossified, functioning at best as an 'ideal type' and at worst as a caricature.

That fixed view of Hobbes goes roughly as follows. The basic Hobbesian assumption is that there are no objective principles of morality. In the state of nature, before the existence of the civil state, there are (as Hedley Bull puts it) 'no legal or moral rules'; moral terms, at this stage, are merely the expressions of personal preferences, with (in the words of Thomas Johnson) 'every person defining truth relative only to their own needs or desires'.⁴ Morality is determined only by the sovereign, once the state is formed; according to Hans Morgenthau, it is 'Hobbes's extreme dictum' that 'the state creates morality as well as law and that there is neither morality nor law outside the state'.⁵ Hence 'the realist view that no ethical standards are applicable to relations between states' (E. H. Carr): for Hobbes, 'there can be no effective moral principles in the state of nature' (Charles Beitz), and relationships between sovereign states can only be a matter of 'simple amorality' (Stanley Hoffmann).⁶ This leads in turn to a celebration of power-politics; Hobbes shares Machiavelli's conception of politics as 'the practical art of obtaining and preserving state power as an end in itself'.⁷ Where Hobbes goes beyond Machiavelli, however, is in his explicit account of the role played by the urge for power in human psychology: according to Morgenthau, Hobbes posits 'an urge toward expansion which knows no rational limits, feeds on its own successes and, if not stopped by a superior force, will go on to the confines of the political world'.⁸ E. H. Carr reached a similar conclusion: 'Nationalism . . . develops almost automatically into imperialism. International politics amply confirms the

---

(Paris, 1981), pp. 197–200). Hobbes specialists have contributed to two volumes of essays dealing with his theory of war and peace (P. Caws, ed., *The Causes of Quarrel: Essays on Peace, War, and Thomas Hobbes* (Boston, 1989); T. Airaksinen and M. A. Bertman, eds., *Hobbes: War among Nations* (Aldershot, 1989) ), but their findings are largely inconclusive or negative. The negativity of the latter volume is intensified by the fact that its contributors were invited to answer the question, 'Is it possible to justify world government on Hobbesian principles?' Not surprisingly, the unanimous answer was 'No'.

³ Two notable exceptions are M. Forsyth, 'Thomas Hobbes and the External Relations of States,' *British Journal of International Studies*, 5 (1979), pp. 196–209, and L. M. Johnson, *Thucydides, Hobbes, and the Interpretation of Realism* (DeKalb, Ill., 1993), esp. pp. 85–98.

⁴ H. Bull, *The Anarchical Society: A Study of Order in World Politics* (London, 1977), p. 47; T. J. Johnson, 'The Idea of Power Politics: The Sophistic Foundations of Realism,' in B. Frankel, ed., *Roots of Realism* (London, 1996), pp. 194–247; here p. 224.

⁵ H. J. Morgenthau, *American Foreign Policy: A Critical Examination* (London, 1952), p. 34. Cf. Walzer, *Just and Unjust Wars*, p. 10: 'the sovereign . . . fixes the meaning of the moral vocabulary.'

⁶ Carr, *Twenty Years' Crisis*, p. 194; Beitz, *Political Theory*, p. 28; S. Hoffmann, *The State of War: Essays on the Theory and Practice of International Politics* (London, 1965), p. 65.

⁷ Wight, *International Theory*, p. 103.

⁸ H. J. Morgenthau, *Politics among Nations: The Struggle for Power and Peace*, 2nd edn (New York, 1955), p. 52.

aphorism . . . of Hobbes that man "cannot assure the power and means to live well which he hath present, without the acquisition of more". Wars, begun for motives of security, quickly become wars of aggression and self-seeking.'[9] Hannah Arendt, similarly, described Hobbes as a forerunner of imperialism.[10]

The Hobbesian state, on this standard view, is little more than Hobbesian man writ large. Indeed, according to Hobbes's modern critics, the great weakness of his theory lies in its assumption of a complete equivalence between individual human beings in the state of nature and sovereign states in international relations. Hobbes's description of the predicament of individuals in the state of nature assumes that they are all equal, and that assumption is based on the fact that 'the weakest has strength enough to kill the strongest'.[11] As Hedley Bull emphasizes, states are not vulnerable in the way that individuals are, and there is no real equality between states great and small.[12] Charles Beitz agrees, and points out a further weakness in the analogy. Hobbes implies that there is a national right of self-preservation analogous to the individual one, but 'it is not clear what such a right involves or how it can be justified'; the 'death' of a state need not involve the death of its citizens, since individual citizens often survive changes in national boundaries.[13]

Beitz also questions Hobbes's assumption that, just as atomic individuals are the only agents in the state of nature, so sovereign states are the only actors in international relations: Hobbes's account of the interpersonal state of nature is plausible only because it denies the existence of any other actors, such as 'secondary associations, functional groups, economic institutions, or extended families', and it is equally arbitrary of Hobbes to exclude 'coalitions, alliances, and secondary associations' at the international level. Doubling back for a moment on his argument, Beitz admits that Hobbes does allow for the possibility of coalitions and alliances in the interpersonal state of nature: but he observes that, according to Hobbes, 'they would, if anything, increase the chances of violence among coalitions'. At the international level, accordingly, Hobbes believes that alliances 'have made no significant contribution to peace and cooperation'. Also at that level of argument, Hobbes 'denies the possibility' that there might be 'transnational associations of persons' whose 'common interests' could 'transcend national boundaries'. Instead, he sees a simplified world in which the units—sovereign states—are able to order their internal affairs in complete independence of one another: this rules out the possibility that 'the pursuit of self-interest by any one unit might require

---

[9] Carr, *Twenty Years' Crisis*, p. 144.

[10] H. Arendt, *The Origins of Totalitarianism*, 2nd edn (London, 1958), p. 143.

[11] T. Hobbes, *Leviathan*, p. 60.

[12] Bull, *Anarchical Society*, pp. 49–50; cf. also his article 'Hobbes and the International Anarchy,' *Social Research: An International Quarterly of the Social Sciences*, 48 (1981), pp. 717–38, esp. pp. 733–4.

[13] Beitz, *Political Theory*, pp. 40–2, 52. Robinson A. Grover similarly argues that Hobbes's theory breaks down on the implications of the individual/state analogy: 'Hobbes and the Concept of International Law,' in T. Airaksinen and M. A. Bertman, eds., *Hobbes: War among Nations* (Aldershot, 1989), pp. 79–90.

cooperation with other units in the system'. It follows that, in the absence of either any superior authority or any structural incentives or constraints built into the international system, there can be 'no reliable expectations of reciprocal compliance' in inter-state conduct. Nor are these conditions ever likely to change, given that, on Beitz's view of Hobbes, 'no state has an obligation to improve the system'.[14] The state of affairs Hobbes describes is thus little more than an arena for inherently unstable interactions of mutual fears and ambitions. In modern terminology, this is barely an 'international system', and certainly not an 'international society'. And even those writers whose interpretation of Hobbes goes a little further, allowing for the operation of a few procedural rules and principles at the international level (such as mutual recognition, and an acknowledgement of the desirability of honouring agreements), are willing to describe Hobbes's view only as 'a minimalist conception of international society'.[15]

## II

How accurate is this portrayal of Hobbes's theory of international relations? It appears to be based, for the most part, on a handful of passages in one or two of his works (ignoring many comments on international affairs elsewhere in his writings); and even those few passages have been misunderstood. The most commonly cited texts are those in which Hobbes sets up his parallelism between the interpersonal state of nature and the international one. In chapter 13 of *Leviathan*, Hobbes first describes the interpersonal state of nature as a state of war, using the latter phrase in a carefully defined and analytical sense: 'So the nature of War, consisteth not in actuall fighting; but in the known disposition thereto, during all the time there is no assurance to the contrary.' Then he suggests that the most realistic (and perhaps the only universal) example of such a state of war is the one that prevails at the international level:

But though there had never been any time, wherein particular men were in a condition of warre one against another; yet in all times, Kings, and Persons of Soveraigne authority, because of their Independency, are in continuall jealousies, and in the state and posture of Gladiators; having their weapons pointing, and their eyes fixed on one another; that is, their Forts, Garrisons, and Guns upon the Frontiers of their Kingdomes; and continuall Spyes upon their neighbours; which is a posture of War.[16]

Within this international state of nature, Hobbes goes on to argue, the only rules of behaviour that can apply are those he describes as the Laws of Nature:

---

[14] Beitz, *Political Theory*, pp. 37–8, 42, 46, 48.
[15] A. Hurrell, 'Society and Anarchy in the 1990s', in B. A. Roberson, ed., *International Society and the Development of International Relations Theory* (London, 1998), pp. 17–42; here p. 25 (contrasting it with the 'pluralist' and the 'Grotian, or solidarist' conceptions).
[16] Hobbes, *Leviathan*, pp. 62, 63.

Concerning the Offices of one Sovereign to another, which are comprehended in that Law, which is commonly called the *Law of Nations*, I need not say any thing in this place; because the Law of Nations, and the Law of Nature, is the same thing. And every Sovereign hath the same Right, in procuring the safety of his People, that any particular man can have, in procuring his own safety. And the same Law, that dictateth to men that have no Civil Government, what they ought to do, and what to avoyd in regard of one another, dictateth the same to Common-wealths, that is, to the Consciences of Sovereign Princes, and Sovereign Assemblies; there being no Court of Naturall Justice, but in the Conscience onely; where not Man, but God raigneth; whose Lawes, (such of them as oblige all Mankind,) in respect of God, as he is the Author of Nature, are *Natural* . . .[17]

These passages, the ones most commonly referred to in support of the standard view of Hobbes's theory, indicate both the basis of the comparison he makes between persons and states, and the limitations of the parallelism between those two levels. The basis is jural, and negative: the rulers of sovereign states resemble individuals in the state of nature 'because of their Independency'—in other words, because they are not under any common authority. And the parallelism, such as it is, does not go all the way. Hobbes does not argue that there is one law of nature based on the preservation of individuals on the one hand, and an equivalent law of nature, based in parallel fashion on the preservation of states, on the other. Rather, he claims that there is a single Law of Nature, 'the same Law', applying to actions undertaken at both levels. This is a key point, the significance of which will be explored below.

The few words already cited on the subject of natural law—which obliges 'all Mankind'—are enough to suggest, also, that the standard view of Hobbes seriously misrepresents his theory when it portrays him as a proponent of moral subjectivism (in the state of nature) or arbitrarism (in the civil state, if morality is whatever the sovereign says it is) or sheer amorality (in international relations). Hobbes's account of morality and law is more complex, and more resourceful, than that. He deals differently with three different levels of evaluation: these might be called the psychological, the moral, and the jural. Psychological evaluative terms, such as 'pleasant' and 'unpleasant' (or, in primitive usage, 'good' and 'bad'), are indeed subjective: 'good', in this pre-moral sense, means 'object of desire', and is therefore always relative to the desirer. Moral terms, on the other hand, relate to a system of values that applies to all human beings: pride, humility, equity, iniquity, and other terms for virtuous or vicious actions and dispositions are of universal application, and can be neither subjective nor arbitrary. Jural terms, such as 'right', 'wrong', 'just', and 'unjust', have meanings that are both universal and analytic: 'unjust', for example, means 'in breach of covenant', the covenant being a transfer of rights.[18]

---

[17] Hobbes, *Leviathan*, pp. 185–6.    [18] Ibid., pp. 24, 71, 79.

Hobbes carefully manages the transition in his argument from the psychological level to the moral, and again from the moral to the jural. While the contents of people's desires differ, he suggests, the basic conditions for the fulfilment of those desires are the same for all human beings: the most basic condition is being alive, the situation in which that condition can best be fulfilled is peace, and a set of universally valid rules can be drawn up for 'endeavouring' peace and ensuring its continuance. Those rules are the laws of nature, the rules of morality: they remain the same both inside and outside the civil state, being neither subjective nor determined by the sovereign's will. 'The Lawes of Nature are Immutable and Eternall; For Injustice, Ingratitude, Arrogance, Pride, Iniquity, Acception of persons, and the rest, can never be made lawfull. For it can never be that Warre shall preserve life, and Peace destroy it . . . And the Science of them [*sc* the laws of nature], is the true and onely Moral Philosophy.'[19]

The transition from the moral level to the jural comes about because one of the dictates of the laws of nature is that people should transfer rights to a sovereign: the laws of nature also demand that people keep the covenants through which such transfers are made. (Hence the inclusion of 'Injustice' in the list of violations of morality above.) A special kind of open-ended transfer of rights creates a common authority endowed with sovereignty over a group of people who can then be described as a single jural community. A sovereign power has the right to legislate for its subjects; its laws can never be described as 'unjust', because the sovereign has been authorized to make whatever laws it wants, but they can be called 'iniquitous' (in other words, immoral) if they go against the laws of nature. 'It is true that they that have Soveraigne power, may commit Iniquity; but not Injustice, or Injury in the proper signification.'[20] This shows that morality remains an objective standard, by which the laws or actions of the sovereign can still be judged: it is simply not true that the Hobbesian sovereign 'creates morality as well as law'.[21] Such a misinterpretation of Hobbes's argument arises only because he says that the civil law promulgated by the sovereign 'contains' the law of nature: the sovereign is the only authorized interpreter of the law of nature, and it is the framework of civil laws and punishments set up by the sovereign that makes obedience to the law of nature generally obligatory in act as well as in intention.[22] Although there may be some uncertainty here about the latitude of 'interpretation' allowed to the sovereign, Hobbes clearly does not mean that the law of nature is whatever the sovereign wills it to be. When he turns to the category of 'divine positive laws' (i.e. ones conveyed to mankind by revelation, not by reason), he remarks: 'in all things not contrary to the Morall Law, (that is to say, to the Law of Nature,) all Subjects

---

[19] Hobbes, *Leviathan*, p. 79. Hobbes recapitulates the transition from the psychological level to the moral on pp. 79–80.
[20] Ibid., p. 90.   [21] Morgenthau, *American Foreign Policy*, p. 34.
[22] Hobbes, *Leviathan*, p. 138.

are bound to obey that for divine Law, which is declared to be so, by the Lawes of the Common-wealth ... for whatsoever is not against the Law of Nature, may be made Law in the name of them that have the Sovereign power.'[23]

In the state of nature, whether interpersonal or international, the laws of nature therefore exist as an objective standard, available to all human beings who reason correctly. The problematic thing about them is not their existence or their knowability, but their applicability. They always oblige in the internal court of conscience ('in foro interno'), that is, 'to a desire, and endeavour' to follow them; however, since they are rules for maximizing one's chances of self-preservation, a person cannot be obliged to act upon them in circumstances where doing so would endanger the actor's life.[24] According to the popular view of Hobbes, the laws of nature are permanently in abeyance in the state of nature, because under such conditions it can never be rational to act in accordance with them: as Beitz puts it, 'Hobbes holds that there can be no effective moral principles in the state of nature.'[25] But Hobbes does not say that. On the contrary, he presents specific examples of cases in which the laws of nature do oblige, in act as well as intention, in the state of nature. The laws of nature forbid self-regarding acts, such as drinking to excess, that weaken or destroy the ability to reason; they also forbid acts of cruelty to others—cruelty being the commission of gratuitous harm, which will only reduce the actor's chances of self-preservation by unnecessarily increasing the enmity of the victim. In a note added to the second edition of *De cive*, Hobbes insisted that these particular laws of nature must still oblige, in act, in the state of nature. 'However, there are some natural laws whose observance does not cease even in war. For I cannot see what drunkenness or cruelty (which is vengeance without regard to future good) contribute to any man's peace or preservation.'[26]

It is true that Hobbes writes, in *Leviathan*, that 'The Lawes of Nature oblige ... in Effect then onely when there is Security'; but 'Security' here means not the general condition of the civil state, but the particular circumstances surrounding an individual action.[27] The key example he gives of a case where the actor does have sufficient security, even outside the civil state, concerns a pact or agreement between two individuals: if one of them shows his good will by performing his side of the bargain first, then it is rational (and a dictate of the laws of nature) that the other should also fulfil his promise. 'For the question is not of promises mutuall, where there is no security of performance on either side ... But either where one of the parties has performed already; or where there is a Power to make him performe; there is the question whether it be against reason, that is, against the benefit of the other to performe, or not. And I say it is not against reason.'[28] Similarly, Hobbes argues that, once an international agreement is in force between two states, it remains binding unless the relevant security situation changes in a way

---

[23] Ibid., pp. 149–50.    [24] Ibid., p. 79.    [25] Beitz, *Political Theory*, p. 28.
[26] Hobbes, *De cive*, III.27(n).    [27] Hobbes, *Leviathan*, p. 79, marginal note.    [28] Ibid., p. 73.

that may justify its breach: 'if a weaker Prince, make a disadvantageous peace with a stronger, for feare; he is bound to keep it; unlesse . . . there ariseth some new, and just cause of feare, to renew the war.'[29]

If the laws of nature can apply, in act as well as intention, in the state of nature, then it cannot be true that Hobbes's international state of nature is *ipso facto* a state of 'simple amorality'. Their application may be patchy and sporadic, but they cannot be excluded on principle from the international arena. Indeed, there is something very implausible about the claim that Hobbes's laws of nature cannot apply at the international level, given that one of them relates directly to diplomatic practice: his fifteenth law is 'That all men that mediate Peace, be allowed safe Conduct.'[30] Naturally this rule would also apply to someone mediating between two individuals in the interpersonal state of nature; but, in the context of seventeenth-century debates on the structure and basis of international law, the point of the inclusion of this rule in Hobbes's list was evidently to settle the long-standing dispute about the status of 'ius feciale', the special area of international law relating to envoys and mediators, by showing how the basic principle of such law could be located within the natural law.[31]

The fundamental division, among seventeenth-century writers in this field, was between those who thought that some or all areas of international law were 'positive law', based on human will and human agreement, and those who thought that international law was directly derived from (or identical with) natural law. What in retrospect seems the mainstream tradition, represented by Vitoria, Suárez, and Grotius, adopted the former position, while Gentili, Hobbes, and Pufendorf adopted the latter. The debate was a real one, and even those contemporary writers who strongly rejected Hobbes's viewpoint treated it as a serious argument about how to classify international law, not as a rejection of international law as such.[32] Modern writers do not do Hobbes justice when they describe him either as completely 'silent' on the subject of international law, or as expressing 'the ever recurrent feeling that international law is no more than an inane phrase'.[33] And the fact that, on this fundamental issue, Hobbes was clearly identified as a 'naturalist'

---

[29] Hobbes, *Leviathan*, p. 69. For a useful survey of Hobbes's arguments for the validity of laws of nature in the state of nature, see D. Boonin-Vail, *Thomas Hobbes and the Science of Moral Virtue* (Cambridge, 1994), pp. 72–81.

[30] Hobbes, *Leviathan*, p. 78.

[31] See e.g. F. Suárez, *De legibus*, ed. L. Pereña *et al.*, 8 vols. (Madrid, 1971–81), IV, p. 133 (II.xix.7); H. Grotius, *De jure belli et* [sic] *pacis libri tres*, ed. & tr. W. Whewell, 3 vols. (Cambridge, n.d. [1854]), II, pp. 200–7 (II.xviii.1–2); R. Zouch ['Zouche'], *Juris et judicii fecialis, sive, juris inter gentes, et quaestionum de eodem explicatio* (Oxford, 1650), pp. 1–3, 16–22.

[32] For a useful short summary of the debate see P. E. Corbett, *Law and Society in the Relations of States* (New York, 1951), pp. 21–6. For a contemporary reply to Hobbes, taking his argument seriously as a 'naturalist' theory of international law, see S. Rachelius, *De jure naturae et gentium dissertationes* (Kiel, 1676), pp. 306–10.

[33] S. Goyard-Fabre, 'Les Silences de Hobbes et de Rousseau devant le droit international,' *Archives de philosophie du droit*, 32 (1987), pp. 59–69; A. Nussbaum, *A Concise History of the Law of Nations*, rev. edn (New York, 1954), p. 146.

arguing against the 'positivists', should give pause to those modern commentators who, classifying Hobbes's theory of international relations as 'realist', automatically align him with the positivist tradition.[34]

If the Hobbesian international state of nature is not a realm of sheer amorality but, rather, one in which the actors must examine the circumstances of each decision to see whether or not the dictates of natural law are applicable, then perhaps Hobbes's international agents are not such 'Machiavellian' figures after all. In fact, readers will search Hobbes's works in vain for anything like a depiction of the Machiavellian prince. It is true that Hobbes states that 'Force, and Fraud, are in warre the two Cardinall vertues'; but this observation flows from his argument that the state of war is the worst possible state for mankind.[35] The Machiavellian analysis of political success, which picks out key qualities of alertness, decisiveness, and forcefulness in the ruler and identifies the operation of those qualities in all forms of political action—internal to the state and external, within the bounds of morality and outside them—finds no echo in Hobbes's account of the sovereign.[36] Nor does Hobbes conceive of anything similar to Machiavelli's republican citizenry exhibiting its own 'virtù'; citizen-soldiers have no special political significance in his theory, which happily allows people to hire substitutes to perform their ordinary military duties.[37] In the words of one modern study of Machiavelli's theory of international relations, 'civil life allows citizens to redirect the satisfaction of their passions from each other toward foreigners. Consequently, Machiavellian republics are warlike and rapacious, for they are constrained to make war abroad to maintain peace at home.'[38] The Hobbesian state performs no such role: it merely

---

[34] Martin Wight, for example, having described Hobbes as an 'extreme Realist', continues: 'There is also a general or conventional Realist position, which can be illustrated from the positivists of international law. It is the basic proposition of legal positivists that international law emanates from the free will of sovereign independent states' (*International Theory*, p. 36). On this classification, Grotius would be to a large extent a Realist and Hobbes an anti-Realist.

[35] Hobbes, *Leviathan*, p. 63. Hedley Bull, although generally a purveyor of the standard view of Hobbes, does comment perceptively on this point: 'There is no sense in Hobbes of the glorification of war, nor of relish for the game of power politics as an end in itself' ('Hobbes and the International Anarchy,' pp. 728–9).

[36] For a powerful elaboration of this contrast, see C. Navari, 'Hobbes and the "Hobbesian Tradition" in International Thought', *Millennium: Journal of International Studies*, 11 (1982), pp. 203–22, esp. pp. 207–12. Friedrich Meinecke, similarly, commented on the profound difference in approach between Machiavelli and Hobbes, characterizing the latter's argument as a mechanistic-utilitarian version of natural law theory: *Die Idee der Staatsräson in der neueren Geschichte*, 3rd edn (Munich, 1929), pp. 263–70. Cf., more generally, P. A. Clark, 'Hobbes and the Enlightenment Rejection of Military Virtue', Catholic University of America Ph. D. dissertation, 1996, pp. 6–9, 106–16, for the contrast between Hobbes's position and classical theories of military 'virtus'.

[37] Hobbes, *Leviathan*, p. 112. The best recent discussion of the significance of this point in Hobbes's overall theory is in B. Dix, *Lebensgefährdung und Verpflichtung bei Hobbes* (Würzburg, 1994), pp. 134–45.

[38] M. Fischer, 'Machiavelli's Theory of Foreign Politics', in B. Frankel, ed., *Roots of Realism* (London, 1996), pp. 248–79; here p. 255. Quentin Skinner similarly concludes that 'The pursuit of dominion abroad is thus held to be a precondition of liberty at home': *Machiavelli* (Oxford, 1981), p. 73. Cf. Machiavelli's formulation: 'Ambition uses against foreigners that violence which neither the law nor the king allows her to use internally; as a result, internal trouble almost always ceases' ('l'ambizion contra l'esterna gente / usa il furor ch' usarlo infra se stessa / né la legge né il re gliene consente; / onde il mal proprio quasi sempre cessa'): *Opere letterarie*, ed. A. Borlenghi (Naples, 1969), p. 154.

provides a framework within which people can seek the satisfaction of their desires, whatever those desires may be.

For a Machiavellian, evaluating a state's engagement in wars of aggression or conquest is partly a matter of appreciating the qualities (of vigour, fortitude, and so on) which those actions exhibit. For Hobbes, such considerations are irrelevant; the only point to be considered is whether the action is justified on objective criteria—for example as a necessary act of pre-emptive self-defence. Some wars may be justifiable on that basis; but the general presumption in Hobbes's theory is strongly against wars of aggression or aggrandizement. 'For such commonwealths, or such monarchs, as affect war for itself, that is to say, out of ambition, or of vainglory, or that make account to revenge every little injury, or disgrace done by their neighbours, if they ruin not themselves, their fortune must be better than they have reason to expect.'[39] Noting that Athens and Rome sometimes grew rich from foreign conquests, he comments: 'But we should not take enrichment by these means into our calculations. For as a means of gain, military activity is like gambling ['sicut alea': like throwing dice]; in most cases it reduces a person's property; very few succeed.'[40] Both these passages suggest that Hobbes thinks there is an inbuilt balance of probabilities that weighs against success in such cases; the reason for this is not spelt out here, though one possible mechanism (involving the need for 'confederates', and the dangers of acquiring a reputation for aggression) is presented elsewhere in his writings, and will be discussed below. But even if he does not regard this adverse probability as a necessary truth, he certainly believes it to be a valid generalization from historical experience. In his *Dialogue . . . of the Common Laws*, he writes: 'The subjects of those Kings who affect the Glory, and imitate the Actions of *Alexander* the Great, have not always the most comfortable lives, nor do such Kings usually very long enjoy their Conquests.'[41] And in *Leviathan* he includes in his list of the 'diseases' of a commonwealth 'the insatiable appetite, or *Bulimia*, of enlarging Dominion; with the incurable *Wounds* thereby many times received from the enemy; And the *Wens*, of ununited conquests, which are many times a burthen, and with lesse danger lost, than kept'.[42]

The comments just quoted should also suffice to show that Hobbes was not an enthusiastic proto-imperialist. Having direct experience of colonial policy (he was an active participant in the Virginia Company), he had good reason to consider the question of how colonization could be justified. The most convenient justification available was the neo-Aristotelian argument, which portrayed the native people of the Americas as 'natural slaves'; but Hobbes responded to Aristotle's original

---

[39] Hobbes, *Elements of Law*, II.ix.9 (p. 184).
[40] Hobbes, *De cive*, XIII.14 (tr. p. 150).
[41] T. Hobbes, *A Dialogue between a Philosopher and a Student of the Common Laws of England*, ed. J. Cropsey (Chicago, 1971), p. 60.
[42] Hobbes, *Leviathan*, p. 174.

version of this argument with withering scorn.[43] In his view, colonization was a permissible way of employing people who could not otherwise be supported by the economy of the mother-country; however, the colonists were under a moral duty to treat the native people humanely, and to encourage them to use greater productivity to compensate for the loss of territory. As he explains in *Leviathan*, the colonists 'are to be transported into Countries not sufficiently inhabited: where neverthelesse, they are not to exterminate those they find there; but constrain them to inhabit closer together, and not range a great deal of ground, to snatch what they find; but to court each little Plot with art and labour.'[44]

For commentators such as Carr and Morgenthau, Hobbes's alleged endorsement of wars of expansion flows directly from his account of individual psychology, in which the urge to acquire more and more power is the driving force of human life. One of the most commonly cited Hobbesian texts is the statement: 'I put for a generall inclination of all mankind, a perpetuall and restlesse desire of Power after power, that ceaseth only in Death.'[45] It is true that restlessness, in the most literal sense, is a basic condition of human life in Hobbes's view: he sees all activity in the universe as describable in terms of matter in motion, and rejects any teleological metaphysic that would posit a 'summum bonum' of static fulfilment. But his argument is not based on any claim about a universal desire for power in the political sense. Nor does he operate with the concept of a 'will to power', if such a phrase implies that power itself is a primary good, something intrinsically motivating for the human will. On the contrary, power in Hobbes's argument has a purely instrumental character: he defines it as the 'present means, to obtain some future apparent Good'.[46] His concept of power, in other words, is analytic, not psychological; even if all human beings were extremely placid and benevolent, they would still require, at any given moment, the present means to obtain what they saw as a future good—for example, the means to give help to other less fortunate people. Of course, Hobbes's empirical judgement of human nature is much more negative than that: he believes that many people (and many rulers) are indeed willing to attack others in order to acquire the riches or fame that they value. 'Kings,

---

[43] Ibid., p. 77. On the argument (put forward by Sepúlveda and contested by Las Casas), see L. Hanke, *Aristotle and the American Indians: A Study in Race Prejudice in the Modern World* (London, 1959); on English knowledge of this debate see H. C. Porter, *The Inconstant Savage: England and the North American Indian 1500–1660* (London, 1979), pp. 171–80. For details of Hobbes's involvement in the Virginia Company see Ch. 3 above. Hannah Arendt's attempt to identify Hobbes as a forerunner of racism (*Origins of Totalitarianism*, p. 157) is particularly ill-conceived: no writer of the early modern period argued more robustly against the idea that any group of human beings was naturally superior to any other group.

[44] Hobbes, *Leviathan*, p. 181. [45] Ibid., p. 47.

[46] Ibid., p. 41. For a classic modern account of the analytic or formal nature of Hobbes's concept of power, see F. S. McNeilly, *The Anatomy of Leviathan* (London, 1968), pp. 144–7, 152. For a valuable account of the implications for Hobbes's international theory, contrasting him with those 'realists' who assume a universal 'animus dominandi', see R. Malnes, *The Hobbesian Theory of International Conflict* (Oslo, 1993), pp. 122–9.

whose power is greatest, turn their endeavours to the assuring it at home by Lawes, or abroad by Wars: and when that is done, there succeedeth a new desire; in some, of Fame from new Conquest; in others, of ease and sensuall pleasure.'[47] But because Hobbes's account is not based on universalizing or essentializing a psychological drive, it does not imply that such wars of aggression are inevitable—still less that they are desirable. Rather, he regards them as the products of mistaken judgement about what will really serve the long-term interests of those rulers, and he aims to supply a true science of politics from which the correct judgements may be derived.

It should also be observed that, in the passage just quoted, Hobbes referred to the desires and actions of 'Kings', not of states. Much modern commentary on his theory of international relations is fixated on the idea that Hobbes set up a complete parallelism between individuals and states, so that anything he said about the psychology and the predicament of the former in the state of nature must equally apply to the latter. Once this parallelism is assumed, critics find it easy to argue that it cannot properly work; such arguments are then taken to prove the inadequacy of Hobbes's theory in general. A closer analysis of his comparison between states and individuals will show, however, that the parallelism is only partial: it operates at the jural level, but not at the moral one.

As the famous engraved title page of *Leviathan* reminds us, Hobbes does indeed have a theory of the collective person-hood of the commonwealth. But his use of the concept of a 'person' here is not a matter of some generalized psychological comparison between individual and collective behaviour. A group of people can act in a coordinated way, with shared fears and desires—for example the members of a mutual defence association in the state of nature—without being, in Hobbes's special sense, a person.[48] What transforms a 'multitude' of cooperating individuals into a 'person' is something that happens at the jural level. A sovereign authority is created when people transfer their rights to it: by the fact of such a transfer, it becomes their 'sovereign representative', which means that it 'bears the person' of the people, and such a 'person' can exist only by virtue of being 'borne' in this way.[49] What matters is not just that one will is substituted for many wills: the key point is that it is an *authorized* will. It is endowed with a special kind of open-ended authority: sovereignty, the power to legislate, potentially on any aspect of life, for the whole community. For those who live within the realm of this authority, a new jural situation has been created. Inside the commonwealth, individuals now have claims on one another's behaviour: they enjoy legally protected rights to property and other forms of 'meum and tuum', which means that their fellow-citizens have

---

[47] Hobbes, *Leviathan*, p. 47.   [48] Hobbes, *De cive*, V.4 (tr. p. 70); *Leviathan*, pp. 85–6.
[49] Hobbes, *De cive*, V.8–9 (tr. p. 73); *Leviathan*, pp. 87–8. Although the concept of a 'person' is much more developed in the latter text, it is not absent from *De cive*, where Hobbes writes: 'A Union so made is called a *commonwealth*, or *civil society* and also a *civil person* [*persona civilis*]' (V.9; tr. p. 73).

a duty of non-interference in those matters, and they have a claim not be interfered with. People practise justice, Hobbes says, when they learn 'not to deprive their Neighbours, by violence, or fraud, of any thing which by the Sovereign Authority is theirs': justice consists in 'taking from no man what is his'.[50] They are now linked in a network of mutual rights and duties: these are direct correlatives, the former being, in Hohfeld's famous classification, 'claim'-rights. Citizen A has a claim on citizen B's behaviour, and citizen B has a duty *to* citizen A.[51]

That is the essential difference between conditions inside the commonwealth and conditions outside it. In the absence of a common authority, there is no overall pattern of jural duties or claims—no duties *to* or claims *on* others in general. (At best, there are particular bilateral jural duties generated by covenants or treaties; these are, however, limited in scope, and liable to be annulled by the advent of any new 'just cause' of fear.) There are moral duties, the duties of the laws of nature; but these are fundamentally self-regarding, in the sense that, according to Hobbes's derivation of morality, they are grounded in each individual's own need for self-preservation. A law of nature is defined as 'a Precept, or generall Rule, found out by Reason, by which a man is forbidden to do, that, which is destructive of his life, or taketh away the means of preserving the same; and to omit, that, by which he thinketh it may be best preserved'.[52] Such laws of nature are indeed universal, but only in so far as they are duplicated in every individual. They do not require a person to respect the good of any other human beings, still less of humanity in general, as a primary good; although they dictate that each individual should act in a way that will benefit others too, they do so only because such behaviour is instrumental to that individual's own good. One might call them 'duties *of behaviour towards*', but they could not be described as 'duties *to*'. (In the same way, one might say that the natural-law duty to refrain from eating poisonous berries is a duty to behave in a certain way towards the berries, but not a duty to them.) Thanks to the peculiar nature of Hobbes's derivation of morality, there is thus an important formal difference between moral and jural duties in his theory. Of course, his argument implies that the jural duties of people as citizens are backed up by their moral duties as human beings: the transition from the moral level to the jural in his argument comes about precisely because people are required by the laws of nature to make the necessary transfer of rights, and thereafter to honour that commitment. In normal circumstances, people always have a moral duty to perform a jural duty. But the conceptual distinction between the two types remains—indeed, the whole Hobbesian theory of the state of nature would be unintelligible without it.

[50] Hobbes, *Leviathan*, p. 179 (adapting the standard Ciceronian and scholastic definition of justice, 'suum cuique tribuere').
[51] See W. N. Hohfeld, *Fundamental Legal Conceptions*, ed. W. W. Cook (New Haven, Conn., 1946), pp. 36–9.
[52] Hobbes, *Leviathan*, p. 64.

Outside the commonwealth, the general absence of duties (at the jural level) means that there is a universal right in the other basic sense of that term—not a claim, but a jural freedom. (In Hohfeldian analysis, just as a claim-right correlates with a duty on the part of others, so this sort of freedom-right correlates with a 'no-claim' on the part of others; it might therefore be called a 'no-duty'.[53]) In the state of nature, therefore, we have on the one hand a universal right or freedom at the jural level, and on the other hand a specific set of moral duties. The picture is complicated, however, by the fact that Hobbes's system of morality also generates its own variety of rights. While the laws of nature prescribe the optimum long-term means to self-preservation, it may be necessary in the short term to break those laws in order to preserve one's life. And when breaking the laws of nature is necessary on such grounds, a person has the right to do so: this is the 'Right of Nature', a moral right based on the same justificatory principle (self-preservation) as the laws themselves. Hobbes combines both the right and the laws in a single 'Rule of Nature': '*That every man, ought to endeavour Peace, as farre as he has hope of obtaining it; and when he cannot obtain it, that he may seek, and use, all helps, and advantages of Warre.* The first branch of which Rule, containeth the first, and Fundamentall Law of Nature; which is, *to seek Peace, and follow it.* The Second, the summe of the Right of Nature; which is, *By all means we can, to defend our selves.*'[54]

Much of the obscurity in Hobbes's account of the state of nature arises because he apparently thought that this moral right of nature could be used to explain the universal jural freedom-right. Since almost any conceivable action could be justified as an exercise of the right of nature in some conceivable set of circumstances, he summarized the right itself as 'this naturall Right of every man to every thing'.[55] Such a description ignored the fact that in any particular set of circumstances the individual would not be entitled under the right of nature to do anything and everything: he would be entitled to do only the specific thing that was necessary to preserve his life. Another of Hobbes's formulations went even further beyond what his account of the right of nature would allow: describing the situation of a man in the state of nature, he referred to 'this Right, of doing any thing he liketh'.[56] Evidently, Hobbes was running together two conceptually distinct things: the (moral) right of nature, and the (jural) universal freedom-right. The distinction between the two comes out most clearly if one considers the case of an unjustified breach of the laws of nature in the state of nature—for example, a gratuitous act of cruelty. The reason for saying that the individual does not have the right to inflict cruel harm on other people is drawn from the internal system of natural rights and duties arising from that individual's need for self-preservation.

---

[53] Hohfeld, *Fundamental Legal Conceptions*, p. 36. Hohfeld calls it a 'privilege', because he is concerned with the functioning of such rights within a legal system; but the term 'freedom' seems more appropriate for the universal right in the Hobbesian state of nature.
[54] Hobbes, *Leviathan*, p. 64.   [55] Ibid.   [56] Ibid., p. 65.

It is not drawn from any external set of duties *to* other people in general; such duties come into being only when people are united in a jural entity under the authority of a sovereign.[57]

Having made these distinctions, we are now in a better position to see what happens when people come together to form a commonwealth. When they authorize a sovereign to 'bear their person' and to legislate for them, their jural situation undergoes a radical change *vis-à-vis* their fellow-citizens; but their basic lack of jural duties to anyone outside the commonwealth remains the same. The only difference, where external relations are concerned, is that their relationship with outsiders is now managed for them by the sovereign: the sovereign decides when to go to war and when to make peace. The various commonwealths that exist in the world are in the same jural vacuum as individuals in the state of nature. At the jural level, therefore, the parallel between states and individuals holds precisely: each commonwealth is indeed like a giant person, acting with a universal freedom-right *vis-à-vis* other such persons in the state of nature.

However, because the jural universal right is not identical with the moral 'right of nature' derived from the principle of self-preservation, it is simply not necessary to continue the parallelism all the way, in an attempt to ground the international jural situation on some putative principle of self-preservation for states *qua* states. That would be to attribute to Hobbes two justificatory systems (one for individuals, the other for states) so perfectly parallel that they would never actually meet. Critics would be entitled to object to such a structure of argument, pointing out that, if the demands of individual-preservation and state-preservation came into conflict, it would offer no way of adjudicating between them. But in fact Hobbes operates with only one concept of the law of nature, and it is based, as the definition quoted above makes clear, on each individual's need to preserve his or her own life.

How and why does the law of nature guide the actions of the sovereign? Where the citizens or subjects are concerned, the argument is very straightforward: each is obliged by the laws of nature, for the sake of self-preservation, to enter into a commonwealth and to do whatever is necessary to maintain its existence. But the case of the sovereign (at least, in a 'commonwealth by institution') is different. Hobbes insists that the sovereign is not a party to a contract with the people: rather, he—or she, or it—is a third-party beneficiary of their mutual covenanting. Strictly speaking, an instituted monarch in Hobbes's theory remains in a state of nature *vis-à-vis* his own subjects: he is jurally entitled to treat them just as he would treat his enemies. And yet, Hobbes's entire political theory depends on the presumption that living under a sovereign is better than remaining in the state of nature.

Accordingly, Hobbes takes special care to point out that it is in the sovereign's own interests to protect and promote the interests of his subjects. The connection

---

[57] I develop here an analysis first presented in my 'Hobbes and Spinoza', Ch. 2 above, esp. pp. 32–4.

is made very directly: 'The riches, power, and honour of a Monarch arise onely from the riches, strength and reputation of his Subjects. For no King can be rich, nor glorious, nor secure; whose Subjects are either poore, or contemptible, or too weak through want, or dissention, to maintain a war against their enemies.'[58] The use of the word 'secure' in that second sentence indicates the way in which this argument is directly linked to the laws of nature, as they apply to the sovereign. But there is also a more indirect connection. In *De cive*, discussing the duties of instituted sovereigns, Hobbes writes: 'Those who have taken it upon themselves to exercise power in this kind of commonwealth, would be acting contrary to the law of nature (because in contravention of the trust of those who put the sovereign power into their hands) if they did not do whatever can be done by laws to ensure that the citizens are abundantly provided with all the good things necessary not just for life but for the enjoyment of life.'[59] This reference to a 'trust' ['fiducia'] is at first sight somewhat puzzling; it cannot imply a contractual relationship, in other words a conditional sovereignty of the Lockean variety, as that is strictly excluded by Hobbes's overall theory. It must refer to something more like a free gift, made in expectation of an equally voluntary return of benefit. This too is covered by the laws of nature; indeed, Hobbes regards the relevant principle as one of the most important laws, placing it third on his list of them in *De cive*: '*If someone has conferred a benefit on you, relying on your good faith* ['fiducia tua'], *do not let him lose on it.*' (He follows up the statement of this law with the comment: 'Without this precept . . . there would be no mutual assistance nor any initiative to win gratitude. As a result, the state of war will inevitably persist.'[60]) This supplies a more long-term reason for thinking that it is in the interests of the sovereign to requite the trust of his subjects by promoting their well-being.

There is thus a two-fold basis in natural law for Hobbes's claim, repeated insistently in every one of his political treatises, that the sovereign has a duty to look after the interests of his people. As he puts it in *Leviathan*,

The Office of the Soveraign, (be it a Monarch, or an Assembly,) consisteth in the end, for which he was trusted with the Soveraign Power, namely the procuration of *the safety of the people*; to which he is obliged by the Law of Nature, and to render an account thereof to God, the Author of that Law, and to none but him. But by Safety here, is not meant a bare Preservation, but also all other Contentments of life, which every man by lawfull Industry, without danger, or hurt to the Common-wealth, shall acquire to himselfe.[61]

It is important to note that the sovereign's concerns thus go beyond the 'bare Preservation' of his people. Hobbes takes care to emphasize that the Latin phrase

---

[58] Hobbes, *Leviathan*, p. 96.  [59] Hobbes, *De cive*, XIII.4 (tr. p. 144).
[60] Ibid., III.8 (tr. p. 47). In *Leviathan* this is the fourth law of nature (p. 75).
[61] Hobbes, *Leviathan*, p. 175. For similar statements about the principle of 'salus populi' see *Elements of Law*, II.ix.1 (p. 179); *De cive*, XIII.2 (tr. p. 143).

'salus populi' implies more than just safety or security: in *Behemoth* he translates it as 'the safety and well-being' of the people.[62] The most general term he uses in this context is 'benefit': discussing the liberty of sovereigns in *Leviathan*, he observes that 'in States, and Common-wealths not dependent on one another, every Common-wealth, (not every man) has an absolute Libertie, to doe what it shall judge (that is to say, what that Man, or Assemblie that representeth it, shall judge) most conducing to their benefit.'[63] Natural law, as it relates to individuals, does not make any direct use of the criterion of 'benefit', because concepts of benefit will vary from person to person. Instead, it starts from one absolute requirement which all humans must share (self-preservation), and draws from it one general condition to be aimed at: the condition of peace—peace being the bare minimum framework within which people are preserved. If Hobbes were positing a state-based natural law, parallel to the individual-based one, he would be obliged to construct an exactly equivalent argument: the absolute requirement would be the preservation of the state, and the aim would be international peace. (This would require states to join together in a super-state, the only guarantor of genuine peace between them, just as individuals unite in a state.) However, because Hobbes's argument here consists not of making some new, parallel, state-based natural law, but of making an *application* of the existing natural law to the particular situation of sovereigns *vis-à-vis* their subjects, he is not obliged to argue for a super-state, and he is enabled to invoke the much more wide-ranging criterion of 'benefit'. In Hobbes's theory 'salus populi', the safety and benefit of the people, is the aim of the sovereign's foreign (as well as domestic) policy. Unlike the caricature version of the Hobbesian position, such a theory can give a prominent place to the pursuit of prosperity through international trade, and of other advantages that may flow from international cooperation. And it might even allow, in special circumstances, the extinction of the state itself—for example, by voting to become part of another state, on terms that would benefit both the people and the sovereign.

Naturally, while promoting the 'Contentments of life' of the people is a genuine policy aim, it must take second place to the requirement of their preservation. The primary role of the sovereign is 'the preserving of Peace and Security, by prevention of Discord at home, and Hostility from abroad'.[64] In Hobbes's discussions of the military role of the state, the emphasis is usually on the protection of the people from external attack. His general presumption, as we have already seen, is that wars of conquest do not conduce to the benefit of the people. However, offensive

---

[62] Hobbes, *Behemoth: Or, the Long Parliament*, ed. F. Tönnies (London, 1889), p. 68.

[63] Hobbes, *Leviathan*, p. 110. 'Their' benefit here should clearly be 'its'. The manuscript of *Leviathan* (British Library, MS Egerton 1910) shows that such mis-matching of single and plural forms in general or impersonal constructions was a common fault in Hobbes's writing, corrected in many cases—but not this one—by the printers.

[64] Hobbes, *Leviathan*, pp. 90–1.

warfare may be justified, according to his theory, in some circumstances. Hobbes's fullest discussion of this issue is in the *Dialogue of the Common Laws*, where the 'Lawyer' asks the 'Philosopher' whether it is lawful for a sovereign to make war on another and 'dispossess him of his Lands'. The Philosopher (who speaks for Hobbes) replies: 'The intention may be Lawful in divers Cases by the right of nature; one of those Cases is, when he is constrained to it by the necessity of subsisting.' If the sovereign's subjects cannot otherwise preserve their lives, they are entitled, by the moral right of nature, to invade the more fertile lands of their neighbours: the example given here is that of the Children of Israel seizing the territory of the Caananites. One type of justification for offensive warfare, therefore, is 'Necessity'. The other, according to the Philosopher here, is 'Security': in cases where a state has 'just cause' to fear its neighbour, it is entitled to engage in a pre-emptive attack.[65]

According to the standard view of Hobbes, there is always 'just cause' for every state to fear every other one, and the international state of nature is therefore a situation of permanent anarchic violence. That is not, however, the implication of Hobbes's argument. Indeed, his specifying of cases where the state has just cause to fear its neighbour sets up an implicit contrast with other cases where it does not. A just fear is an assessment of danger that must, presumably, be based on some empirical judgement about matters of fact. For example, a large and powerful state would not have just cause to fear that a small, weak, and solitary neighbouring state was about to attack it. Hobbes clearly thought that it was important for states to form well grounded empirical judgements about such matters: in *De cive* he included a long section on the state's need for intelligence operations, to gather information about 'the plans and movements of all those who have the capacity to do it harm'.[66] And, of course, even when a state does have just cause to fear the intentions of a neighbour, it must still weigh the possible advantage of a pre-emptive strike against the possible dis-benefit to its citizens of involvement in war. Since the ultimate aim is inherently defensive, the optimum strategy is not belligerence but deterrence. And there are two ways in which a state can raise its level of deterrence: by building up its own defensive military strength, and by entering into alliances with other states.

Alliances or 'confederacies' do in fact play a major role in Hobbes's account of the state of nature. As we have seen, he allows that valid pacts or contracts are possible in the state of nature: where one side has performed first, the other does not have just cause to fear it and therefore is obliged to keep its own side of the bargain. Hobbes sets out his reasoning in *Leviathan*, arguing that a man in the state of nature will damage his long-term prospects of self-preservation if he acquires a reputation as a wilful breaker of covenants:

[65] Hobbes, *Dialogue of the Common Laws*, p. 159.   [66] Hobbes, *De cive*, XIII.7 (tr. p. 145).

Secondly, that in a condition of Warre, wherein every man to every man, for want of a common Power to keep them all in awe, is an Enemy, there is no man can hope by his own strength, or wit, to defend himself from destruction, without the help of Confederates; where every one expects the same defence by the Confederation, that any one else does: and therefore he which declares he thinks it reason to deceive those that help him, can in reason expect no other means of safety, than what can be had from his own single Power. He therefore that breaketh his Covenant, and consequently declareth that he thinks he may with reason do so, cannot be received into any Society, that unite themselves for Peace and Defence, but by error of them that receive him . . .[67]

Most aspects of this argument are also directly applicable to the case of a commonwealth in the international state of nature: it too can join an alliance, 'confederation', or 'society' for mutual defence, and its natural-law obligation to keep its agreement with its confederates can be explained in the same way. (The same type of argument, about the long-term consequences of acquiring a reputation for untrustworthiness, could also be used to explain why states are bound to suffer in the long term if they get into the habit of waging aggressive war, or of making preemptive attacks with insufficient 'just cause'.) Admittedly, what Hobbes claims in the first sentence here about the utter necessity of 'Confederates' is not so compelling in the case of commonwealths: states, unlike human beings, do not go to sleep at night, and an exceptionally powerful state may conceivably be able to defend itself, on its own, against all those that are likely to attack it. Yet most other states will have a clear incentive to form defensive alliances, if only because they might otherwise be vulnerable to offensive ones. (A common criticism of Hobbes's theory of international relations is that it assumes 'that the units that make up the state of nature must be of relatively equal power in the sense that the weakest can defeat the strongest'—an assumption that is manifestly wrong in simple terms.[68] But when Hobbes makes his claim about the parity of individuals in the state of nature, he makes explicit reference to alliances: 'the weakest has strength enough to kill the strongest, either by secret machination, or by confederacy with others.'[69] This makes the theory much less implausible at the international level: it will be generally true that a weak country can defeat a powerful one, if it joins in an alliance with other sufficiently powerful countries.)

One of the strangest modern misunderstandings of Hobbes is the claim made by Charles Beitz when he refers to 'Hobbes's hypothesis that forming alliances increases the chances of war'. (A few sentences later, he attributes to Hobbes the similar and equally strange belief 'that they [*sc.* alliances] have made no significant contribution to peace and cooperation'.[70]) The passage in *Leviathan* to which

---

[67] Hobbes, *Leviathan*, p. 73.  [68] Beitz, *Political Theory*, pp. 40–1.
[69] Hobbes, *Leviathan*, p. 60.  [70] Beitz, *Political Theory*, p. 37.

Beitz alludes says no such thing. In it, Hobbes observes first of all that disunited individuals in the state of nature 'make warre upon each other, for their particular interests', and therefore cannot defend themselves against a common enemy; then he says that if they unite for a limited time in an alliance they may indeed 'obtain a Victory by their unanimous endeavour'; and finally, he points out that, after such a temporary alliance has broken up, the individuals may find themselves back in a state of mutual hostility: 'afterwards . . . they must needs by the difference of their interests dissolve, and fall again into a Warre amongst themselves'.[71] The one positive feature of this account is the period of cooperation and successful mutual defence while the alliance lasts; the return to war here is a consequence of the *ceasing* of the alliance, and to present it as a consequence of the alliance's existence is to commit the fallacy of *post hoc, ergo propter hoc*.

Generally speaking, Hobbes does not argue that alliances as such must either increase or decrease the quantity of fighting (though they must, by definition, increase the quantity of cooperation); he notes that alliances may be either offensive or defensive. The 'Conquests of the ancient Germans', for example, were achieved by a 'Confederacy' of 'many absolute Lords joyning together to conquer other Nations'.[72] Such an alliance may indeed increase the chances of war. Equally, however, a defensive alliance may deter aggression. The primary function of 'mutual aid' associations in the state of nature is deterrence: 'the mutual aid of two or three men is of very little security; for the odds on the other side, of a man or two, giveth sufficient encouragement to an assault. And therefore before men have sufficient security in the help of one another, their number must be so great, that the odds of a few which the enemy may have, be no certain and sensible advantage.'[73]

While Hobbes's account of international relations gives special prominence to security alliances or 'Leagues between Common-wealths' (which, he says, are 'not onely lawfull, but also profitable for the time they last'), those are not the only forms of international agreement or cooperation to be considered.[74] One unusual international (or transnational) agreement which caught his eye was that practised by the ancient Amazons, who 'Contracted with the Men of the neighbouring Countries, to whom they had recourse for issue, that the issue Male should be sent back, but the Female remain with themselves'.[75] Other international agreements are more usual, underpinning as they do the ordinary transnational activities of human beings. Thus, 'he that is sent on a message, or hath leave to travell, is still Subject [*sc.* to his own sovereign]; but it is, by Contract between Soveraigns . . . For whosoever entreth into anothers dominion, is Subject to all the Laws thereof; unlesse he have a privilege by the amity of the Soveraigns, or by speciall licence.'[76]

---

[71] Hobbes, *Leviathan*, p. 86.   [72] Ibid., p. 184.
[73] Hobbes, *Elements of Law*, I.xix.3 (p. 101); cf. *De cive* V.3 (tr. p. 70).
[74] Hobbes, *Leviathan*, p. 122.   [75] Ibid., p. 103; cf. *Elements of Law*, II.iv.5 (p. 133).
[76] Hobbes, *Leviathan*, p. 114.

International trade, in Hobbes's view, was essential for the well-being of a commonwealth, because 'there is no Territory under the Dominion of one Commonwealth, (except it be of very vast extent,) that produceth all things needfull for the maintenance, and motion of the whole Body'.[77] In the *Elements of Law* he included in his list of the laws of nature the rule '*That men allow commerce and traffic indifferently to one another*'.[78] He recognized that trade required a system of commercial law in which subjects of different states could litigate and seek redress: in his *Dialogue of the Common Laws* he noted that the Court of Admiralty fulfilled such a function, and observed that this court operated on Roman law principles because 'the causes that arise at Sea are very often between us, and People of other Nations, such as are Governed for the most part by the self same Laws Imperial'.[79] And at sovereign-to-sovereign level, Hobbes also recognized the existence of commonly agreed procedures for such matters as the payment of reparations.[80]

The general picture that emerges here is of cooperation and interaction between states, and between the subjects of states, taking place at many levels. Hobbes's comments on trade, for example, are sufficient to refute the claim made by Charles Beitz that he ignores the interdependence of states in non-security matters and has no idea of the economic advantages of cooperation between them.[81] Overall, Hobbes's account contains many of the ingredients of what modern theorists describe as an 'international society': shared practices, institutions, and values. The widely held belief that no society of any kind can exist in a Hobbesian state of nature is drawn from a few places in his writings (such as the famous 'nasty, brutish, and short' passage in chapter 13 of *Leviathan*) where he sets out the ultimate or worst-case implications of a state of war; however, many other passages go to show that social formations of various kinds can exist in his state of nature, and the extreme case he describes should probably be understood by analogy with an asymptotic limit, a theoretical absolute which may be approached but never reached.[82]

---

[77] Ibid., p. 127.   [78] Hobbes, *Elements of Law*, I.xvi.12 (p. 87).

[79] *Dialogue of the Common Laws*, pp. 89–90. On the nature of this court, which dealt with actions for freight and maritime contracts made on foreign soil, see D. E. C. Yale, 'A View of the Admiralty Jurisdiction: Sir Matthew Hale and the Civilians', in D. Jenkins, ed., *Legal History Studies 1972: Papers Presented to the Legal History Conference, Aberystwyth, 18–21 July 1972* (Cardiff, 1972), pp. 87–109.

[80] Hobbes, *Dialogue of the Common Laws*, p. 159: 'Injuries receiv'd justifie a War defensive; but for reparable injuries, if Reparation be tendred, all invasion upon that Title is Iniquity.'

[81] Beitz, *Political Theory*, p. 42. For a proper appreciation of the positive role of international trade in Hobbes's theory, see D. Boucher, *Political Theories of International Relations: From Thucydides to the Present* (Oxford, 1998), pp. 160–1.

[82] See e.g. G. Schochet, *Patriarchalism in Political Thought* (Oxford, 1975), pp. 225–43; C. D. Tarlton, 'The Creation and Maintenance of Government: A Neglected Dimension of Hobbes's Leviathan,' *Political Studies*, 26 (1978), pp. 307–27; R. Ashcraft, 'Political Theory and Practical Action: A Reconsideration of Hobbes's State of Nature', *Hobbes Studies*, 1 (1988), pp. 63–88. For the most penetrating and wide-ranging recent study of social formations and interactions in Hobbes's state of nature, see K. Hoekstra, 'The Savage, the Citizen, and the Foole: The Compulsion for Civil Society in the Philosophy of Thomas Hobbes', Oxford University D.Phil. dissertation (1998), pp. 8–97; this also includes a valuable discussion of the international state of nature (pp. 70–6).

It has often been noted that one of Hobbes's basic causes of conflict in the state of nature, the desire for 'glory', presupposes some sort of social context of shared values. Such a context exists also at the international level: commenting in *Behemoth* on the ill-will of the Scots towards the English in the late 1630s, Hobbes puts forward as a possible explanation 'that from the emulation of glory between the nations, they might be willing to see this nation afflicted by civil war'.[83] Later in the same work he presents a carefully nuanced account of the factors behind the outbreak of the Anglo-Dutch war of 1652. While the main Dutch motive was 'the greediness to engross all traffic', the ostensible *casus belli* was a dispute over the English claim to 'dominion of the narrow seas': 'the Dutch knowing the dominion of the narrow seas to be a gallant title, and envied by all the nations that reach the shore, and consequently that they were likely to oppose it, did wisely enough in making this point the state of the quarrel.'[84] Shared values, relating to a code of honour, can thus play a significant role (though not, in this case, a primary one) in international relations.

The basis of shared values is a common culture. Hobbes had a particular reason for paying serious attention to the common cultural heritage of Europe, or 'Christendom'. He was convinced that the amalgam of Graeco-Roman philosophy and biblical doctrine, developed over the centuries by the Roman Church and taught in all European universities, was the biggest single threat to the stability of states: it undermined them at the most vulnerable point of all, in the minds of the subjects. As 'the Actions of men proceed from their Opinions', the essential rights of sovereignty could be maintained only if the people held correct beliefs about them; and such beliefs had been systematically corrupted and subverted by Papal teachings.[85] In Hobbes's view, the Roman Church was an international conspiracy, a '*Confederacy of Deceivers . . . to obtain dominion over men in this present world*'; he put it in the category of 'Corporations of men, that by Authority from any forraign Person, unite themselves in anothers Dominion, for the easier propagation of Doctrines, and for making a party, against the Power of the Common-wealth'.[86] It was responsible for fomenting rebellions within states, and wars between them: the false doctrine propagated by it was the prime cause of the fact 'that in Christendome there has been, almost from the time of the Apostles, such justling of one another out of their places, both by forraign, and Civill war'.[87] While it was true that the Pope also happened to be a sovereign, ruling the inhabitants of an area

---

[83] Hobbes, *Behemoth*, p. 30. This passage must cast some doubt both on Jean Hampton's claim that 'Hobbes does not consider the way in which a nation's longing for glory can provoke war with other nations' ('Hobbesian Reflections on Glory as a Cause of Conflict,' in P. Caws, ed., *The Causes of Quarrel: Essays on Peace, War, and Thomas Hobbes* (Boston, Mass., 1989), pp. 78–96; here p. 95), and on William Sacksteder's observation that 'nation' is 'a non-Hobbesian term' ('Mutually Acceptable Glory: Rating Among Nations in Hobbes', in Caws, *Causes of Quarrel*, pp. 97–113; here p. 106). Cf. also the passage quoted above at n. 72.
[84] Hobbes, *Behemoth*, pp. 174, 176.   [85] Hobbes, *Leviathan*, pp. 91 (quotation), 175–6.
[86] Ibid., pp. 333, 121.   [87] Ibid., p. 334.

of Italy, the way in which the Church functions in Hobbes's account is obviously very different from the normal operations of one state *vis-à-vis* another: even if the Papacy had lost its own territorial sovereignty, it could have continued to operate as a significant factor in international affairs through its far-flung confederacy of priests. Once again, it is necessary to reject Charles Beitz's assertion that, in Hobbes's theory, the only actors in international relations are sovereign states. And it is also necessary to point out that the Catholic Church, as described by Hobbes, is very much a 'transnational association of persons' with its own collective interest —the sort of association of which, according to Beitz, Hobbes simply 'denies the possibility'.[88]

As several recent studies of Hobbes have emphasized, a programme of political re-education (or, on some accounts, 'cultural transformation') was thus central to his entire political and philosophical project.[89] The aim was to clear out of people's minds the false metaphysical assumptions, bogus religious doctrines, and pernicious political principles that had accumulated there as the products of centuries of priestcraft. Once this cultural lumber had been removed, people could easily be taught the true principles of political science—Hobbes's principles—and would then clearly understand their duties as citizens and subjects. His main concern here was with the internal conditions of states; but he did also suggest that this process of political education could have international ramifications. Describing his project in the dedicatory epistle to *De cive*, he wrote: 'For if the patterns of human action were known with the same certainty as the relations of magnitude in figures, ambition and greed, whose power rests on the false opinions of the common people about right and wrong, would be disarmed, and the human race would enjoy such secure peace that (apart from conflicts over space as the population grew) it seems unlikely that it would ever have to fight again.'[90]

This may have been a maximal claim about what was possible; but it should not be dismissed as a mere rhetorical flourish. Elsewhere Hobbes gave some quite specific indications of how an improved understanding of political principles could lead to a change in international conduct. Commenting in *Behemoth* on the failure of 'the Kings and States of Christendom' to deal with the papal threat to their own power, he wrote: 'if they would have freed themselves from his tyranny, they should have agreed together, and made themselves every one, as Henry VIII did, head of the Church within their own respective dominions. But not agreeing,

---

[88] Beitz, *Political Theory*, pp. 36–8.

[89] See especially D. Johnston, *The Rhetoric of Leviathan: Thomas Hobbes and the Politics of Cultural Transformation* (Princeton, NJ, 1986); R. P. Kraynak, *History and Modernity in the Thought of Thomas Hobbes* (Ithaca, NY, 1990); and M. G. Dietz, 'Hobbes's Subject as Citizen', in M. G. Dietz, ed., *Thomas Hobbes and Political Theory* (Lawrence, Kan., 1990), pp. 91–119.

[90] Hobbes, *De cive*, 'Epistle dedicatory', para. 6 (tr. p. 5). For some perceptive comments on the international implications of Hobbes's educative project, see D. W. Hanson, 'Thomas Hobbes's "Highway to Peace"', *International Organization*, 38 (1984), pp. 329–54.

they let his power continue, every one hoping to make use of it, when there should be cause, against his neighbour.'[91] This is a clear example of how a better-grounded political understanding would lead to a more cooperative policy at the international level. Later in the same work, the other speaker in the dialogue remarks: 'It is methinks no great polity in neighbouring princes to favour, so often as they do, one another's rebels, especially when they rebel against monarchy itself. They should rather, first, make a league against rebellion and afterwards, (if there be no remedy) fight against one another.'[92] While the last part of that remark shows that such an appreciation of common interests would not suffice to eliminate all other causes of war, this suggestion of a 'league against rebellion' is nevertheless a positive example of how international conflict can be reduced by the application of sound political science. And if sovereigns have a joint interest in taking such political action, they must also have a joint interest in reforming the common culture that nurtures and propagates false political principles—a European culture of writings and teachings that crosses national boundaries.

## III

To conclude: although Hobbes has a famously low opinion of human nature in general, he does believe that human behaviour can be improved; and he implies that international cooperation may be both a means towards such improvement and a consequence of it. In this respect, Hobbes is much closer to the ameliorism of the rationalist tradition than to the changeless pessimism of the Realists. However, his utter rejection of teleological metaphysics, and his strict derivation of the natural laws from the principle of individual self-preservation, set him far apart from the mainstream of rationalist natural law theories. Unlike the Stoic, scholastic, or Lockean versions of natural law, Hobbes's theory takes no cognizance of the good of mankind as such. There can therefore be no equivalent in it to Locke's concept of the 'executive power of the law of nature', by virtue of which a third party can intervene in other people's affairs to enforce that which is objectively right.

As has been suggested above, it is this peculiar quality of Hobbes's natural laws—their derivation from purely individual long-term self-interest—that makes it possible to open a conceptual gap in his theory between the nature of 'moral' rights and duties on the one hand, and of jural ones on the other. In the Lockean scheme of things no such gap exists, because the laws of nature set out a single, interpersonal scheme of values: if, in the state of nature, A is justly attacking B, then C cannot be justified in assisting B against A. But in Hobbes's theory, where people are acting in the state of nature in accordance with their 'natural' rights and duties, such clashes are perfectly possible. In his *Dialogue of the Common Laws*, the

[91] Hobbes, *Behemoth*, p. 21.   [92] Ibid., p. 144.

'Philosopher' remarks that a king will be justified in going to war in support of 'Neighbours . . . born down with the Current of a Conquering Enemy' if he judges that his own state may be next in line for conquest. The 'Lawyer' objects: 'If the War upon our Neighbour be Just, it may be question'd whether it be Equity or no to Assist them against the Right.' But the 'Philosopher' (representing Hobbes) dismisses all such objections as irrelevant: 'For my part I make no Question of that at all . . .'[93]

This is a crucial passage, illustrating the peculiar nature of the Hobbesian international state of nature: moral rights and duties do exist in it, but they are not fixed by nature in any pattern of mutual harmony or reciprocity.[94] Outside the commonwealth, rights and duties may be in direct conflict; only inside the commonwealth can they be presumed to be in harmony. While the rationalist tradition of thought about international relations strives to overcome the distinction between those two realms, Hobbes emphasizes it and makes it central to his theory. That, in the end, is why he has so often been described as a 'Realist', despite all the other features of his thinking that such a description so signally fails to capture.

[93] Hobbes, *Dialogue of the Common Laws*, p. 65.
[94] On this point it is necessary to disagree with Murray Forsyth, whose important study 'Thomas Hobbes and External Relations' is flawed by its assumption that Hobbesian natural law is based on 'reason as by definition the taking into account of the *other* person's rights as well as one's own' (p. 197).

# – 14 –

# Hobbes and the European Republic of Letters

## I

'So racy as they were of the soil, it is in England that we are to look for the proper effect or development of Hobbes's ideas.'[1] The phrasing used by George Croom Robertson when he penned this judgement in 1886 may have dated quite rapidly (the *Oxford English Dictionary* defines 'racy of the soil' as 'characteristic of a certain country or people', giving examples only from 1870 and 1889), but the sentiment has not altogether disappeared. Anglophone scholars still tend to discuss not only the intellectual context of Hobbes's work, but also its influence and the responses it aroused, in a largely Anglocentric way. The fact that *Leviathan* is in English—a masterpiece, indeed, of seventeenth-century discursive and polemical prose—must be partly responsible for this; Hobbes's philosophy speaks the vernacular with such ease and such force that it may seem natural for any reader to assume that there is something peculiarly English about it. And from that assumption it is only a short step to supposing that continental readers must have found Hobbes's works somehow alien (even if they read them in Latin, or some other European language), and that they cannot have felt the impress of his arguments quite so deeply as those readers who were rooted in the same 'soil'. Samuel Mintz, in what is still the only general study of the early reaction to Hobbes's philosophy, commented especially on the power of Hobbes's English prose style; to the continental critics, who would presumably have been impervious to its attractions, he devoted just under three of the 156 pages of his text.[2]

Yet it has long been known to Hobbes scholars that this English philosopher had a thoroughly European intellectual formation: he read widely in the universal language of European culture (Latin), he acquired a high level of competence in

---

[1] G. C. Robertson, *Hobbes* (London, 1886), p. 224.
[2] S. Mintz, *The Hunting of Leviathan: Seventeenth-Century Reactions to the Materialism and Moral Philosophy of Thomas Hobbes* (Cambridge, 1962), pp. 37, 57–9. The valuable essay by Mark Goldie, 'The Reception of Hobbes', in J. H. Burns and M. Goldie, eds, *The Cambridge History of Political Thought, 1450–1700* (Cambridge, 1991), pp. 589–615, similarly concentrates almost entirely on English reactions.

Italian (high enough to translate Fulgenzio Micanzio's letters to the second Earl of Devonshire for circulation in England), and evidently became fluent in French. The evidence of the earliest Hardwick library catalogue—compiled by Hobbes—suggests that his reading in the 1620s and 1630s included Machiavelli, Bodin, Botero, Boccalini, Huarte, Montaigne, Sarpi, de Dominis, and Grotius.[3] Much of Hobbes's philosophical development took place on foreign soil: in a period of just over twenty-two years, from October 1629 to December 1651, Hobbes spent only eight years in his native land. By the time he finally settled again in England, he must have struck his fellow countrymen as a positively Frenchified figure; Lodewijk Huygens, who visited him in London in February 1652, noted that 'He was still dressed in the French manner, however, in trousers with points and boots with white buttons and fashionable tops.'[4] No doubt he changed his dress sooner or later; but his intellectual attachments to France remained strong, and he would always look back on his time there with a certain wistfulness. For, while he had friends and admirers in England, he could never recreate in London the experience he had enjoyed for much of his time in Paris—that of being an accepted member of an intellectual group (the Mersenne circle) which was active, innovatory, and at the same time thoroughly respectable. For many years after his return to England, he was the recipient of adulatory letters from members of that circle, such as Samuel Sorbière, Thomas de Martel, and François de Bonneau, sieur du Verdus; the praise he received from France must have contrasted painfully with the mounting barrage of hostile criticism he encountered in England, making him feel more and more like a prophet without honour in his own country.[5] Responding to his English critics, he made a point of referring to his reception on the Continent: in *Six Lessons* he proudly mentioned Sorbière's translation of *De cive* ('The Book it self translated into French hath not only a great Testimony from the Translator *Serberius* [sic], but also from *Gassendus*, and *Mersennus*'); in *Mr. Hobbes Considered* he wrote, 'as for his reputation beyond the Seas, it fades not yet', and quoted a letter from Sorbière in which he was compared to Galileo, Bacon, Descartes, and Gassendi; and in his public letter of complaint to Anthony Wood he loftily declared, 'my reputation, such as it is, took wing a long time ago and has soared so far that it cannot be called back'—using a metaphor of distance that was, one may suspect, not only metaphorical.[6]

[3] Chatsworth, Derbyshire, MS Hobbes E1 A. See the edition and study of this catalogue by R. Talaska, *The Hardwick Library and Hobbes's Early Philosophical Development* (forthcoming).
[4] L. Huygens, *The English Journal, 1651–1652*, ed. and tr. A. G. H. Bachrach and R. G. Collmer (Leiden, 1982), pp. 74, 218 ('Hij . . . was evenwel noch op sijn Fransh gekleet, met een broeck met nestelingen en leersen met witte kanons aen, en een rabat vande mode').
[5] See the comments on this contrast in Q. Skinner, 'Thomas Hobbes and his Disciples in France and England', *Comparative Studies in Society and History*, 8 (1965–6), pp. 153–67, esp. p. 163.
[6] *Six Lessons*, p. 56 (*EW* VII, p. 333); *Mr. Hobbes Considered*, p. 51 (*EW* IV, p. 435); Hobbes, *Correspondence*, II, pp. 744–5, 746 ('fama enim mea qualiscunq; est jamdudum pennata evolavit irrevocabilis').

To explore this European dimension in full—investigating Europe's influence on Hobbes as well as Hobbes's influence on Europe—would be a huge labour, and a hugely difficult one, given his constant reluctance to refer to his sources. This essay will attempt two much more modest tasks. First, it will sketch a rough outline or overview of the ways in which Hobbes's work was received by the European literary world during his lifetime and for one or two generations thereafter. And secondly, it will try to assess Hobbes's own relationship to the international 'Republic of Letters', asking to what extent he was not only a participant in that literary and social world, but also a subscriber to the ideology that was implicit in its practices.

## II

In any account of the continental reception of Hobbes, the 'how' must be preceded by the 'what': what writings by him were available, and in which languages? Without doubt, the work that dominated the European understanding of Hobbes was *De cive*—a book of which, significantly, the entire printing history took place on the Continent. The printing of the first edition was organized by Mersenne in Paris in 1642; only a small number of copies were produced then, for private distribution. Five years later Samuel Sorbière arranged the publication of an enlarged edition, with a new preface and explanatory notes, by Elzevier in Amsterdam, one of the best known and most widely distributed publishers in Europe. The work sold out and was re-set within the year; thereafter it was frequently reprinted, with editions appearing in 1657 (Amsterdam), 1669 (Amsterdam), 1696 (Amsterdam), c.1704 (Halle?), 1742 (Amsterdam?), 1760 (Lausanne) and 1782 (Basel).[7] Several translations into modern languages also appeared (these are described below). Consequently, this was the one work by Hobbes most likely to be cited by any continental writer discussing his ideas in the late seventeenth and eighteenth centuries.

The next most important publication was the collection of his Latin works, *Opera philosophica*, arranged by Johan Blaeu (with some help from Sorbière as an intermediary) and issued by him in Amsterdam in 1668: this included yet another printing of *De cive*, but it also contained the Latin version—undertaken by Hobbes especially for this publication—of *Leviathan*. In addition, it offered to European readers several of Hobbes's works on metaphysics, physics, and optics (*De corpore, Dialogus physicus, Problemata physica, De homine*), plus a few of his mathematical works, all of which had previously been available only in London

---

[7] See H. Macdonald and M. Hargreaves, *Thomas Hobbes: A Bibliography* (London, 1952), pp. 16–20; C. H. Hinnant, *Thomas Hobbes: A Reference Guide* (Boston, Mass., 1980), pp. 20, 30, 37, 41. On the Halle printing see below, at n. 286. The 1742 edition is commonly listed as having been printed in Amsterdam, but its title page states only that it was printed 'according to' ('juxta') the Amsterdam edition of 1696; it may have been a German production.

editions. A small number of copies of this edition's printing of *Leviathan* appear also to have been issued separately. A new edition of that text was produced by Blaeu in 1670, but its distribution seems to have been quite limited, suffering perhaps from the fire that destroyed Blaeu's printing-house in 1672 as well as from the official prohibition of the book by the Court of Holland in 1674.[8]

A few other Latin texts by Hobbes—minor works, or fragments—were also printed on the Continent: the objections to Descartes; the extracts from Hobbes's writings included by Mersenne in his compilations of 1644; the mathematical demonstration published by John Pell; letters to Sorbière and Gassendi; a reprinting of Aubrey and Blackburne's 'Vitae auctarium' (which included Hobbes's letter of protest to Anthony Wood); and some substantial extracts from the *Historia ecclesiastica*.[9] A small number of copies of the London printings of Hobbes's major Latin works—particularly *De corpore* and *De homine*—also found their way to the Continent; but these texts were, in any case, included in the 1668 *Opera philosophica* produced by Blaeu.[10] Some evidence from France can give an approximate guide to the relative scale of distribution there of the English and continental printings. Yves Glaziou's analysis of thirty-eight catalogues of French eighteenth-century private libraries yields the following results: ten had *De cive* in Latin and fourteen had it in French, thirteen possessed the *Opera philosophica*, three had the Latin *Leviathan*, one had *De corpore*, and one *De homine*.[11] A fairly similar pattern emerges from the 'Catalogue collectif de la France', which lists the holdings of fifty-five major public libraries: thirty-six copies of *De cive* in Latin and thirty-seven in French, fourteen copies of the *Opera philosophica*, five of the Latin *Leviathan*, five of *De corpore*, and five of *De homine*.[12]

---

[8] See Macdonald and Hargreaves, *Bibliography*, p. 45 (1670 edn); H. de la Fontaine Verwey, 'Het werk van Blaeu's', in H. de la Fontaine Verwey and W. G. Hellinga, *In officina Ioannis Blaev* (Amsterdam, 1961), pp. 1–12 (here p. 10: fire); on the prohibition see my 'The Printing of the Bear', (Ch. 11 above), n. 163.

[9] Objections to Descartes: R. Descartes, *Meditationes de prima philosophia* (Paris, 1641), pp. 233–71. Mersenne compilations: a useful but incomplete listing of these is given in K. Schuhmann, 'Hobbes dans les publications de Mersenne en 1644', *Archives de philosophie*, 58 (1995), no. 2, 'Bulletin hobbesien' (separate pagination), pp. 2–7 (omitting the presentation of Hobbes's theory of percussion and *conatus* in *Cogitata physico-mathematica* (Paris, 1644), 'Tractatus mechanicus theoricus et practicus', pp. 87–9). Pell: *Controversiae de vera circuli mensura . . . pars prima* (Amsterdam, 1647), pp. 49–51. Letters to Sorbière: *Illustrium et eruditorum epistolae* (n.p., n.d. [Paris, 1669]) (a book privately printed by Sorbière). Letter to Gassendi: in P. Gassendi, *Opera omnia*, 6 vols. (Lyon, 1658), VI, p. 522A. 'Vitae auctarium': reprinted in F. C. Hagen, ed., *Memoriae philosophorum, oratorum, poetarum, historicorum et philologorum nostrae aetatis clarissimorum* (Frankfurt, 1710), pp. 69–125. *Historia ecclesiastica*: S. J. Baumgarten, *Nachrichten von merkwürdigen Bücher*, 12 vols. (Halle, 1752–8), X (1756), pp. 222–35.

[10] For examples of continental writers studying a Latin work by Hobbes in its London edn, see the comments on Mauritius and Leibniz below (pp. 520, 528).

[11] Y. Glaziou, *Hobbes en France au XVIII$^e$ siècle* (Paris, 1993), pp. 19–20.

[12] The Latin *Leviathan*s comprise one separate issue of the 1668 printing, two of 1670, and two of the 1676 'Thomson' reissue of sheets from the 1670 edn. One copy of *De corpore* listed (that of the Bibliothèque municipale de Versailles) is not extant, having been lost in the early 19th century; its variant wording of the title page is probably a scribal error, having been copied by an early cataloguer from the title page of *De homine*.

So long as copies of the *Opera philosophica* were available, European readers had access to most of the major statements of Hobbes's theories (the main exceptions being *Behemoth*, the *Dialogue of the Common Laws*, the writings on 'liberty and necessity', and the *Historia ecclesiastica*). However, by the end of the seventeenth century demand must have been growing for a new collection of his works. One enterprising German publisher, Thomas Fritsch, saw this gap in the market. Fritsch (1666–1726) came from a well established family of booksellers in Leipzig, where he had inherited the family business in 1693.[13] His brother, Caspar, started a business in Amsterdam and Rotterdam (taking over the famous firm of Reinier Leers in 1709), and developed a special interest in the works of philosophical radicals and Spinozists; in 1712 Caspar Fritsch took on Prosper Marchand, an *érudit* connoisseur of such writings, as an editor and adviser.[14] Possibly it was from Caspar and his free-thinking friends in Amsterdam and The Hague that the impetus to plan a new edition of Hobbes first came. In 1711 the Elector of Saxony, Friedrich Augustus, wrote to the book-licensing authorities in Leipzig, commenting with some alarm on the news that Fritsch was preparing a new edition of the works of Hobbes, and asking them to halt the printing of the edition, if it was in progress, or to suppress the sale of the books, if they were already printed. Intriguingly, his letter mentioned that Fritsch was planning to include 'several manuscripts which have not previously been printed'.[15] A letter from Leibniz to

---

[13] See A. Bauer, 'Johann Ludwig Gleditsch: Leichenpredigt mit Lebenslauf 1741', *Archiv für Geschichte des Buchwesens*, 9 (1969), cols. 1597–1612, here col. 1598. (Gleditsch married Fritsch's widowed mother, and passed the Fritsch business on to Thomas in 1693.) Fritsch printed both Pietist and Catholic books: for details of his brushes with the authorities in Leipzig over such printings, see A. Kobuch, *Zensur und Aufklärung in Kursachsen: ideologische Strömungen und politische Meinungen zur Zeit der sächsisch-polnischen Union (1697–1763)* (Weimar, 1988), pp. 117–18, 179–80.

[14] See A. M. Ledeboer, *De boekdrukkers, boekverkoopers en uitgevers in Noord-Nederland* (Deventer, 1872), p. 326; M. C. Jacob, *The Radical Enlightenment: Pantheists, Freemasons and Republicans* (London, 1981), pp. 144, 159–60 (describing the businesses of the Fritsch brothers as 'two of the largest publishing firms in northern Europe'). On Marchand, see C. Berkvens-Stevelinck and J. Vercruysse, *Le Métier de journaliste au dix-huitième siècle: correspondance entre Prosper Marchand, Jean Rousset de Missy et Lambert Ignace Douxfils* (Oxford, 1993), esp. pp. 5–8. On Caspar's later correspondence with Marchand, see also S. Berti, '*L'Esprit de Spinosa*: ses origines et sa première édition dans leur contexte spinozien', in S. Berti, F. Charles-Daubert, and R. Popkin, eds., *Heterodoxy, Spinozism, and Free Thought in Early Eighteenth Century Europe. Studies on the Traité des trois imposteurs* (Dordrecht, 1996), pp. 3–51, esp. p. 21.

[15] Sächsisches Hauptstaatsarchiv, Dresden, MS 10753 (Oberkonsistorium, Büchersachen, vol. II (1711–13)), fo. 18, copy of letter from the Elector to the 'Büchercommissarien', 11 October 1711: here fols. 18r ('Nachdem Wir in erfahrung kommen, ob sollte Thomas Frizsche, buchhändler in Leipzig [>Thomae] Hobbesii schrifften, worzu itzo noch etliche Manuscripta, so vorhero nicht in druck gewesen, kommen wären, wiederumb auslegen und drucken zulassen . . .'), 18v ('. . . Immittelst aber den Verkauff derselben, auch, da selbige in Leipzig gedrücket würden, das fortdrucken inhibiren'). See also Kobuch, *Zensur und Aufklärung*, p. 235. The identity of these works in manuscript remains a mystery: the only Hobbes MS associated with Leipzig is a short fragment of Hobbes's critique of Thomas White, with notes by Claude Guiraud, formerly in the city library and now in the Leipzig University Library, MS Stadtbibliothek Rep. IV. 47, fols. 5–7r. This in itself is too insignificant to have warranted mention, but perhaps it was once accompanied by some other, more substantial, texts. Alternatively, the manuscripts may have been translations of published works that had not previously appeared in Latin, French, or German. One possible candidate might be the manuscript Latin version of *Behemoth*, 'De rebus gestis Olivarij Cromvelli Protectoris

Laurentius Hertelius, written in July of that year, refers to this project and gives some indication of the seriousness with which Fritsch was preparing for it: 'Mr Fritsch has had people chivvying me for Hobbes's book about liberty, as he wants to print his works, and finds that something is missing from the copy which he has of that book; so I have entrusted my copy to a friend, who will supply Mr Fritsch with the passages missing from his own one.'[16] Thirteen years later Gottlieb Stolle wrote, somewhat wistfully, that 'Thomas Fritsch in Leipzig promised us a new edition of the collected works of this Englishman several years ago'; but two years after that Fritsch was dead, and so too—if it had not already perished by then—was the project.[17] Quite what Fritsch had had in mind is not clear: the work referred to by Leibniz was in English (either *Of Libertie and Necessitie* or, more probably, *The Questions concerning Liberty, Necessity, and Chance*), so perhaps the Leipzig publisher had planned to commission a translation into German, French, or Latin.[18] Evidently, he intended to produce a more complete collection of Hobbes's writings than the 1668 *Opera philosophica*; whether other English-language items would have been included, and in what form, remains uncertain.

One thing is clear, however: the overwhelming majority of continental readers, no matter how well educated and scholarly, would not have been able to read Hobbes in English. As an accomplished English-reader, Leibniz was a remarkable exception to the general rule; so too, later, was Voltaire, and the *anglomanie* he inspired would lead a few intellectuals to make some attempt on the language. But even such a voracious bookworm as Pierre Bayle, living in a city (Rotterdam) where English lessons would not have been hard to arrange, could only make the shoulder-shrugging remark: 'it is a great misfortune that I do not understand English, as there are many books in that language that would be very useful for me.'[19] Translations of Hobbes into modern languages from the English were,

sive historia bellorum civilium Angliae', made in 1708 by Adam Ebert (1653–1735), Professor of Law at the University of Frankfurt an der Oder, and presented by him to King Friedrich I of Prussia (the presentation copy is in the Staatsbibliothek, Berlin, MS Lat. 2° 129). It may be that Fritsch had obtained a copy of this recently completed translation.

[16] J. Burckhard, *Historia bibliothecae Augustae quae Wolffenbutteli est*, 2 vols. (Leipzig, 1744–6), II, p. 336 (Leibniz to Hertelius, 23 July 1711: 'M. Fritsch m'ayant fait presser pour *l'Ouurage de Hobbes sur la Liberté*, puisqu'il en veut imprimer les Oeuvres, et qu'il trouve quelque manquement dans l'exemplaire, qu'il a de cet Ouvrage: j'ay mis le mien entre les mains d'un ami, qui communiquera à *M. Fritsch* ce qui manque au sien)'.

[17] G. Stolle, *Anleitung zur Historie der Gelahrheit* (Jena, 1724), p. 413: 'Thomas Fritsch zu Leipzig hat uns schon seit einigen Jahren eine neue Edition der gesammelten Wercke dieses Engländers versprochen.'

[18] Leibniz was familiar with *The Questions concerning Liberty, Necessity, and Chance* (London, 1656), which he summarized and criticized in one of the appendices to his *Essais de théodicée* (see below, n. 274). On 27 Dec. 1698 he had written to Hertelius: 'I have read Hobbes's book about liberty and necessity; I even think I have a copy. But I do not recall ever having seen it translated from English into any other language' ('J'ay lû *le Livre de Hobbes de Libertate et Necessitate*: je croy même, de l'avoir. Mais je ne me souviens [*sic*] point, l'avoir vû traduit de *l'Anglois* dans une autre langue': Burckhard, *Historia bibliothecae*, II, p. 326).

[19] Quoted in G. Ascoli, *La Grande-Bretagne devant l'opinion française au XVIIe siècle*, 2 vols. (Paris, 1930), II, p. 4; cf. pp. 1–2 on the general French ignorance of English. In 1717 a journal, *La Bibliothèque angloise*, was started in Amsterdam with the specific purpose of informing European readers about English publications;

– 462 –

however, quite rare. The most influential version of Hobbes in the vernacular was the translation (already mentioned) of the Latin treatise *De cive* by Samuel Sorbière, *Elémens philosophiques du citoyen*. This was published by Blaeu in Amsterdam in 1649; another edition which appeared with the same details on the title page was probably a pirated edition produced in Paris; and sheets from that second edition were then re-issued under two different Parisian imprints in 1651.[20] Another translation of *De cive*, by Hobbes's friend and disciple François du Verdus, appeared in two editions in Paris in 1660, entitled *Les Elemens de la politique de M. Hobbes*, and a third in 1665, under the title *Maximes heroïques de la politique moderne au roy*; although—or perhaps because—du Verdus's translation omitted the third part of the book, dealing with religion, it seems to have circulated much less widely than Sorbière's.[21] The same text was also translated into Dutch in 1675 (by an anonymous translator who appears to have consulted the English version of *De cive*, *Philosophicall Rudiments*, as well as the original Latin).[22] And in 1776, improbably enough, a Russian translation of *De cive* appeared in St Petersburg, dedicated to Prince Potemkin.[23] Other major Latin works remained untranslated; du Verdus's

---

its editor noted that English books were 'scarcely known outside that island' ('guère connus hors de cette isle': quoted in J. I. Israel, *Radical Enlightenment: Philosophy and the Making of Modernity 1650–1750* (Oxford, 2001), p. 149).

[20] See A. Morize, 'Th. Hobbes et Samuel Sorbière: notes sur l'introduction de Hobbes en France', *Revue germanique*, 4 (1908), pp. 195–204, esp. pp. 202-03: Morize treats the second edn as a genuine 1649 Blaeu edn. He also notes that the first edn appeared in two states (the second of which added a translation of Hobbes's dedicatory epistle to the Earl of Devonshire), but incorrectly says that Sorbière's 'Avertissement du Traducteur' was added only in the second edn. (It was in fact added by Blaeu, to copies with or without Hobbes's dedicatory epistle, thus making four states of the first edn.) Macdonald and Hargreaves give descriptions of the two edns and one of the Paris issues (*Bibliography*, pp. 20–1), but they treat the second as a genuine Blaeu imprint, give an inadequate account of the states of the first edn, and wrongly present the Paris issue as a third edn. The suggestion that the second was a piracy was made by Édouard Rahir, *Catalogue d'une collection unique de volumes imprimés par les Elzeviers et divers typographes hollandais du XVII<sup>e</sup> siècle* (Paris, 1896), p. 221, no. 2015. Of the 1651 issues, Macdonald and Hargreaves list only the one by Pepingué and Maucroy (*Bibliography*, p. 21, no. 34); the other was by Jean Henault. (There are copies in the municipal libraries of Alençon and Toulouse, and in the BN, pressmark E* 1564.) For a modern edition of Sorbière's translation see T. Hobbes, *Le Citoyen, ou les fondements de la politique*, tr. S. Sorbière, ed. S. Goyard-Fabre (Paris, 1982).

[21] See G. Lacour-Gayet, 'Les Traductions françaises de Hobbes sous le règne de Louis XIV', *Archiv für Geschichte der Philosophie*, 12 (= n.s., vol. 5) (1899), pp. 202–7, esp. p. 204; Morize, 'Hobbes et Sorbière' p. 203. The first edn was a large quarto, its 'achevé d'imprimer' dated 30 April 1660; the second was an octavo, dated 4 May 1660; both were by Henri Le Gras (BN, pressmarks E* 256, E* 1566). Montesquieu had a copy of the first edn: Bibliothèque municipale de Bordeaux, pressmark LAB 989. The 1665 edn is not mentioned by Lacour-Gayet or Morize, and I have not found any copy of it in France; there is one in the Bayerische Staatsbibliothek, Munich, pressmark Ph. u. 256.

[22] Hobbes, *De eerste beginselen van een burger-staat* (Amsterdam, 1675): this is omitted from Macdonald and Hargreaves's *Bibliography*. On the translation see C. W. Schoneveld, *Intertraffic of the Mind: Studies in Seventeenth-Century Anglo-Dutch Translation* (Leiden, 1983), pp. 59–60. There are copies of this work in Leiden University Library; the Royal Library, The Hague; and Trinity College, Dublin.

[23] Hobbes, *Nachal'nya osnevaniia filosoficheskaia o grazhdaninie*, tr. S. Venitsieev (St Petersburg and Moscow, 1776): see the entry in Hinnant, *Thomas Hobbes*, p. 40, noting that a copy is in the Spencer Library of the University of Kansas. I have not seen this volume, but from Hinnant's statement that it contains only 188 pages I suspect that the translation is incomplete.

version of *De cive* carried a note by the printer stating that du Verdus had also prepared translations of *De corpore* and *De homine*, but these have not survived.[24] (Within months of the original publication of *De corpore*, no fewer than five separate plans to translate it into French were under way or subject to discussion; it seems that the others then gave way to du Verdus, whose work was completed but never published.[25]) A few shorter Latin works did become accessible, however, to German readers: in 1715 Christian Thomasius published first a German-language synthesis of the two *Vitae* and the Aubrey-Blackburne 'Vitae auctarium', and then a condensed translation of the *Historia ecclesiastica*.[26]

Just four works were translated from English into continental European languages: the two parts of *The Elements of Law*, *Leviathan*, and *Of Libertie and Necessitie*. From manuscript versions of *The Elements of Law* circulating in England, unauthorized printings had been made of its two parts: the first, under the title *Humane Nature*, appeared in two editions (Oxford and London, 1650; London, 1651), and the second, *De corpore politico*, also in two editions (London, 1650, 1652).[27] It was the second of these that appeared in a French translation, *Le Corps politique, ou les elemens de la loy morale et civile*, in 1652, issued by an unnamed printer at an unspecified place; another edition followed in 1653, with a title page that stated 'A Leide, chés Jean & Daniel Elsevier'. The first printing was probably made in Rouen; the second cannot have been produced by the Elzeviers, as it uses a system of signature-numbering different from theirs, and was probably made by another Leiden printer, Philippe de Croy.[28] Even more shadowy, however, is the identity of the translator, who is described on the title page as one of Hobbes's friends ('un de ses amis'). Modern scholars—including the compilers of the standard Hobbes bibliography and Louis Roux, who published a modern photo-reproduction of this translation—have simply assumed that this 'friend' was Samuel Sorbière; but there are strong reasons for doubting the attribution. Sorbière, an

---

[24] T. Hobbes, *Les Elemens de la politique*, 1st edn, tr. F. du Verdus (Paris, 1660), sig. i3v. The translation of *De corpore* was apparently completed by [February/] March 1656, but du Verdus's plans to publish it were then 'suspended' at Hobbes's request—probably because Hobbes was still considering changes to the contents of this work (see Hobbes, *Corrrespondence*, I, pp. 221, 229, 231, 237).

[25] See Hobbes, *Correspondence*, I, pp. 212, 214 (du Verdus; Abraham du Prat; an unnamed person; a plan by Paris booksellers to commission a translation by Jacques du Roure; and Sorbière).

[26] C. Thomasius, *Summarischer Nachrichten von auserlesenen, mehrentheils alten, in der Thomasischen Bibliotheque verhandenen Büchern*, 24 parts (Halle and Leipzig, 1715–18), part 2 (1715), pp. 166–83; part 4 (1715), pp. 314–57. On these summaries see below, at nn. 283–4. Hobbes's prose *Vita* was also reprinted in the prefatory materials of the 1742 (Amsterdam?) edition of *De cive* (sigs. †1r–2†3v).

[27] Macdonald and Hargreaves, *Bibliography*, pp. 10–13. The third edn of *De corpore politico* listed by Macdonald and Hargreaves would be more correctly described as a second state of the second edn.

[28] For basic descriptions see Macdonald and Hargreaves, *Bibliography*, pp. 13–14. Alphonse Willems noted that the former could not have been produced anywhere in Holland, but accepted the latter as an Elzevier (*Les Elzevier: histoire et annales typographiques* (Brussels, 1880), pp. 179–80); Gustav Berghman argued that the latter was by de Croy or Hackius (*Supplément à l'ouvrage sur les Elzeviers de M. Alphonse Willems* (Stockholm, 1897), p. 77); Rahir suggested Rouen for the former, and de Croy for the latter, noting that all the ornaments used were de Croy's (*Catalogue*, pp. 75, 401).

– 464 –

inveterate self-publicist, never claimed responsibility for the translation; it differs from his version of *De cive* in the wordings used for key Hobbesian concepts and phrases; there is no definite evidence that Sorbière could read English (and quite strong evidence, from his garblings of simple names in his account of his visit to England, that he could not); and the bookseller's notice to the reader specifically says that the translator was not a Frenchman.[29] There are not many non-French friends of Hobbes who could have done this job; the only likely candidate is John Davies, who lived for several years in France (until c.1652) and became a prolific translator from the French. Davies was the person who produced the unauthorized printing of *Of Libertie and Necessitie* in 1654; indeed, the reason why he possessed a manuscript copy of that work was that, as Hobbes later explained, he had borrowed it in order to translate it into French for the benefit of 'a French Gentleman of my acquaintance in *Paris*'.[30] So perhaps *Le Corps politique* had its origins, similarly, in some private commission to Davies by one of Hobbes's French admirers. The translation achieved a moderately wide distribution (it is found in six of the library catalogues analysed by Yves Glaziou); and in the late eighteenth century it was re-issued in a two-volume collection of *Oeuvres philosophiques et politiques de Thomas Hobbes* (Neuchâtel, 1787).[31] The other items included in that collection were Sorbière's translation of *De cive*, and a translation of *Humane Nature*—the first part of *The Elements of Law*—which had been produced by the Baron d'Holbach in 1772.[32]

The next English work to be translated into a European language was *Leviathan*, which appeared in Dutch in 1667; a second edition of this translation came out in 1672. The translator was Abraham van Berkel, a former schoolmaster who had studied medicine in Utrecht and settled in Leiden, where he produced a translation of Sir Thomas Browne's *Religio medici* in 1665. He was a close friend of the radical free-thinker Adriaen Koerbagh (who had connections with members of Spinoza's circle), and it was probably through Koerbagh that he obtained the services of the publisher Jacobus Wagenaar in Amsterdam, who produced both

---

[29] Macdonald and Hargreaves, *Bibliography*, p. 13; T. Hobbes, *Le Corps politique*, ed. L. Roux (Saint-Étienne, 1977).This attribution was propounded by Lacour-Gayet (who thought the work was simply an abridgement of the *De cive* translation: 'Les Traductions', p. 203) and Morize ('Hobbes et Sorbière', p. 204), but has been convincingly rejected by Ascoli (*La Grande-Bretagne*, II, p. 109) and Schoneveld (*Intertraffic of the Mind*, pp. 33–4). The bookseller's notice says: 'Even though the translator was not born on our soil . . .' ('Encore que le Traducteur ne soit pas né sous notre climat . . .': 1652 edn, sig. a3v).

[30] Hobbes, *The Questions concerning Liberty*, p. 19 (*EW* V, p. 25). From Hobbes's account, it is not clear whether this translation of *Of Libertie and Necessitie* was written, or merely delivered *viva voce*. On Davies see J. Tucker, 'John Davies of Kidwelly (1627?–1693), Translator from the French', *Papers of the Bibliographical Society of America*, 44 (1950), pp. 119–51; Hobbes, *Correspondence*, I, p. 459.

[31] Glaziou, *Hobbes en France*, pp. 19–20. On the significance of Neuchâtel (which lay just beyond the French borders) as a publishing centre for heterodox works, see R. Darnton, *The Literary Underground of the Old Regime* (Cambridge, Mass., 1982).

[32] Hobbes, *De la Nature humaine*, tr. P. H. Thiry, Baron d'Holbach ('London', 1772); a photo-reproduction of this edn was issued in Paris in 1971.

editions.³³ Dutch was quite widely read, not only in the Netherlands but also in parts of northern Germany and the Baltic region, and the fact that this edition was reprinted after the printings of the Latin version in 1668 and 1670 suggests that there was a significant demand to satisfy; even a scholarly writer such as Adriaen Houtuyn, composing a Latin treatise in 1681, would give references to this Dutch translation rather than to the Latin *Leviathan*.³⁴ In the library of Samuel Pufendorf (who, unusually, possessed at least a basic reading knowledge of English), the only edition of *Leviathan* was this Dutch translation.³⁵ But a French translation would of course have had a much broader appeal.

At least two attempts were made, and a third and fourth planned, before any French version of the text actually appeared in print. The first—and the most intriguing—was arranged by Hobbes himself. All that is known about it is contained in a letter from Robert Payne to Gilbert Sheldon of 13 [/23] May 1650, summarizing information he had received in a recent letter from Hobbes in Paris: 'he sends me word he hath an other taske in hand, w$^{ch}$ is Politiques, in English of w$^{ch}$ he hath finished 37 chapters. (intending about 50 in y$^e$ whole) w$^{ch}$ are translated into French, by a learned french man, of good quality, as fast as he finishes them.'³⁶ If steps were then taken to arrange the publication of this French version, we may presume that they must have been thwarted by the Parisian clergy; the licensing process would typically have involved sending it to be read by two theologians at the Sorbonne, who certainly would not have liked what they saw—even if we assume, as we surely must, that the fourth part of the book, containing Hobbes's ferociously sarcastic comments on Roman Catholicism, was not included.³⁷ As for the identity of the 'learned french man', there is only one obvious candidate from among Hobbes's known circle of French friends: Charles du Bosc, a courtier who had lived in England and acquired good command of the English language. However, in 1659 du Bosc would write, in a letter to Hobbes, that 'All y$^e$ learned men I know desire that Leuiathan were in french or Latine', without making any

---

³³ See Schoneveld, *Intertraffic*, pp. 4–9; A.-J. Gelderblom, 'The Publisher of Hobbes's Dutch *Leviathan*', in S. Roach, ed., *Across the Narrow Seas: Studies in the History and Bibliography of Britain and the Low Countries* (London, 1991), pp. 162–6; Israel, *Radical Enlightenment*, pp. 185–96. Both Schoneveld and Gelderblom are mistaken, however, in thinking that Schoneveld was the first to identify van Berkel as the translator: his responsibility for it was clearly stated in one of the most influential encyclopaedic works of the 18th century, J. Brucker's *Historia critica philosophiae*, 6 vols. (Leipzig, 1744–5), IV.2, p. 157 (n.). On Koerbagh see below, n. 103.

³⁴ On the wide area of Dutch readership see Israel, *Radical Enlightenment*, pp. 139–40; A. Houtuyn, *Politica contracta generalis, notis illustrata* (The Hague, 1681), where the final section (sigs. Z4–Z7r) lists 'Errores Hobbesiani' and refers to *De cive* and *'Leviat. edit. Belgica'*.

³⁵ F. Palladini, ed., *La biblioteca di Samuel Pufendorf: catalogo dell'asta di Berlin del settembre 1697* (Wiesbaden, 1999), pp. 195–6. Pufendorf's other Hobbes items were *De cive*, *Humane Nature*, *Le Corps politique* and the 1682 edn of the *Vita* (pp. 56, 195). Palladini notes that he had 11 books in English (p. xviii).

³⁶ BL, MS Harl. 6942, no. 128.

³⁷ In one of his later accounts, Hobbes blamed 'the French clergy' for forcing his departure from Paris: *Mr. Hobbes Considered*, p. 8 (*EW* IV, p. 415).

reference to a translation he himself had made; so this identification must remain quite uncertain.[38]

In the case of the second attempt, there is no doubt about the identity of the translator—François du Verdus—nor, unfortunately, about the inadequacy of his linguistic qualifications. As he proudly told Hobbes in the summer of 1654, he had started to learn English specifically in order to translate *Leviathan*. He began by preparing an 'interlinear translation' in his copy of the text; in December 1656 he sent Hobbes queries about the meanings of various words (including quite elementary ones) that he had been unable to understand; and on [22 December 1656/] 1 January 1657 he announced that he had completed his translation of the entire first part of the book, sending Hobbes a specimen chapter (the fourth, on language) for his approval.[39] Possibly Hobbes, realizing that his friend was not up to the task, now gently dissuaded him from it.

The next person to think of undertaking such a project was certainly better qualified: François du Prat, son of a French father and an English mother, who served as a travelling companion and tutor to the elder son of the third Earl of Devonshire in the late 1650s. He informed Hobbes of his plan to translate *Leviathan* in the autumn of 1661, and returned to the same theme in a letter from Paris in September 1663:

I have this very day spoken to a bookseller about y$^e$. printing of y$^e$. Leviathan here, who did open his eares to y$^t$. proposition. & answered y$^t$. y$^t$. de Cive in French is sold publickly & y$^t$. you were an author so well knowne, as he made no doubt but y.$^e$ booke would sell away. For my part, I have such a minde to y$^e$. worke, as y.$^t$ I shall never be satisfi'd till I come to an end of it.[40]

This plan, too, apparently came to nothing.

If other attempts or proposals were made during the next six decades, they would appear to have left no trace in the historical record. The fourth person to have thought seriously about translating *Leviathan* into French was Antoine de La Barre de Beaumarchais, in the late 1720s or early 1730s. A defrocked priest who had once been a canon of the Maison de Saint-Victor in Paris, he had fled to The Hague in 1723, where he worked as a teacher, a hack writer, and—having learned English there—a translator. He married in 1725 and converted, at some stage, to the Reformed Church. All that is known about his plan to translate Hobbes is contained in one sentence in a memoir by one of his contemporaries: 'He had the idea of translating Hobbes's *Leviathan*; but after he fell out with the bookseller

---

[38] Hobbes, *Correspondence*, I, p. 504 (5/15 Sept. 1659); on du Bosc see also II, pp. 795–7.
[39] See ibid., I, pp. 187–8, 190–1, 216–17, 223, 345–74, 398–419.
[40] Ibid., II, pp. 522–3 (21 Sept./1 Oct. 1661); 559 (quotation: 19/29 Sept. 1663); 881–5 (biography of du Prat).

Scheurleer, this plan remained unfulfilled.'[41] Both the bookseller and the would-be translator belonged to the same free-thinking circles as Caspar Fritsch and Prosper Marchand—circles that may thus be credited with originating two separate plans to publish works by Hobbes. Soon after his arrival in The Hague, de La Barre de Beaumarchais had found employment in a private school; its founder and director was another fugitive from France, Jean Rousset de Missy, who was also a prolific journalist, translator, and hack writer with a special interest in 'underground' literature.[42] In 1713 Rousset de Missy had helped to polish the style of a translation of Anthony Collins's *A Discourse of Free-Thinking* which had been prepared by the bookseller Hendrik Scheurleer; many of Rousset de Missy's own writings were Scheurleer publications.[43] Scheurleer himself evidently had a special interest in contemporary English philosophy; his shop in The Hague was unusual in holding a significant stock of English-language books, including works by Locke, Shaftesbury, Swift, Collins, and Toland.[44] These circumstances, together with the fact that de La Barre de Beaumarchais had learned English, suggest that it was the English *Leviathan* that they planned to translate. Whether Prosper Marchand was also involved is not known, but his sympathetic interest in the project can be assumed: Rousset de Missy was a close friend of Prosper Marchand; Scheurleer had frequent contacts with Marchand too, until he quarrelled with him in 1737; and de La Barre de Beaumarchais succeeded Marchand as one of the editors of the *Journal litéraire* in 1732. The date of this plan to translate *Leviathan* cannot be fixed with any certainty; it is known that de La Barre de Beaumarchais left the Netherlands for Germany in 1735, and the project may perhaps have predated 1729, when he entered the service of a rival bookseller, Jan van Duren.[45] If so, French readers had to wait more than thirty years before even a very truncated version of *Leviathan* became available to them: in 1760 the journal *Le Conservateur* included in its July–October issues an abbreviated and self-confessedly 'free' translation of chapters 1–10 and 17–20. As the anonymous translator recorded, the text used was the Latin

[41] F. Bruys, *Mémoires historiques, critiques, et littéraires*, 2 vols. (Paris, 1751), p. 160: 'Il se proposoit de traduire le *Leviathan* de Hobbes; mais s'étant brouillé avec le Libraire Scheurleer, ce dessein est demeuré sans exécution.' For de La Barre de Beaumarchais's biography see ibid., pp. 159–64, and the *Dictionnaire de biographie française* (Paris, 1933– ), XVIII, cols. 1305–6.

[42] Bruys, *Mémoires*, I, p. 160; on Rousset de Missy see Jacob, *Radical Enlightenment*, pp. 197–9, and Berkvens-Stevelinck and Vercruysse, *Le Métier de journaliste*, pp. 8–13, 269–75.

[43] A. Collins, *Discours sur la liberté de penser*, 2 vols. ('London', 1713–14); Bruys, *Mémoires*, I, p. 159; Jacob, *Radical Enlightenment*, p. 197.

[44] See the 'Catalogue des livres, qui se trouvent à la Haye dans la Boutique de Henri Scheurleer', appended to R. Aubert de Vertot d'Aubeuf, *Histoire des révolutions de Portugal*, 4th edn (The Hague, 1734), sigs. I7r–M10; here sigs. M9–10. On Scheurleer see Ledeboer, *De boekdrukkers*, pp. 173–4; E. F. Kossmann, *De boekhandel te 's-Gravenhage tot het einde van de 18e eeuw* (The Hague, 1937), p. 349. For summaries of, or comments on, Locke and Swift by de La Barre de Beaumarchais, see his *Lettres serieuses et badines sur les ouvrages des savans*, 8 vols. (The Hague, 1729–33), III, pp. 201–28; IV, pp. 112–20; VII, pp. 227–8; VIII, pp. 110–30.

[45] Berkvens-Stevelinck and Vercruysse, *Le Métier de journaliste*, p. 47 (n.) and *passim*; *Dictionnaire de biographie française*, XVIII, cols. 1305–06.

version (in one of the separate issues of the 1668 printing).[46] Similarly, when a German translation of *Leviathan* was eventually published at the end of the eighteenth century, it too was taken from the Latin.[47]

The fourth work to be translated from English into a modern European language was *Of Libertie and Necessitie* (London, 1654). A Dutch version of this book appeared in Rotterdam in 1698, under the title *Een tractaatje van vrijwilligheyd en noodsaakelijkheyd*. The translator introduced the text with a preface addressed 'To the reader who loves pleasure and learning'; he defended Hobbes as a writer 'who is considered unorthodox by some, but is regarded as a learned and worthy thinker by all those who know his writings', and declared that Hobbes's arguments were formed 'not in the common way, but out of the nature of things'.[48] Nevertheless, like several of Hobbes's other continental translators, he prudently omitted his own name.

## III

As several details from this brief summary of Hobbes's continental printing history may suggest, there was a delicate interaction at work here between popularity and condemnation. Publicly disapproved of, and sometimes actually banned, Hobbes's works gained the allure of forbidden fruit: appetites were whetted, prices rose, and publishers acquired a stronger incentive. (A classic mid-eighteenth-century guide to the second-hand book market described the 1668 *Opera philosophica* as follows: 'Highly sought-after collection, copies of which have become quite rare in the trade—which has raised their value.'[49]) Conversely, the official disapproval was itself a reflection, in some cases, of the degree of popular interest in Hobbes's works;

---

[46] *Le Conservateur*, Jul.–Oct. 1760; here July, pp. 33–4: '4°, s.d. s.l.'; 'une traduction libre'. I have consulted the copy in the Bibliothèque Nationale, Paris (pressmarks Z 27 516–517).

[47] *Des Engländers Thomas Hobbes Leviathan, oder der kirchliche und bürgerliche Staat*, 2 vols. (Halle, 1794–5). This is not properly complete, however: the anonymous translator explains that he has omitted the 'Appendix'. The reason he gives is that 'to some extent this does not belong to the work itself' ('dieser theils zum Werke selbst nicht gehöret': II, p. vi); but, given his defensive remarks about Hobbes's theology, which he admits to be unsuitable for the young or for those whose faith is not well grounded (II, pp. iv–v), it may be suspected that he wished to omit Hobbes's defence of his apparently materialist conception of God. I have consulted the copy in the Österreichische Nationalbibliothek, Vienna, pressmark 12.989-B.

[48] *Een tractaatje van vrijwilligheyd en noodsaakelijkheyd daar in alle verschillen aangaande prdistinatie* [sic], *verkiesinge, vrye wil, genade, verdienste, verwerpinge &c. ten volle besligt en verklaart wort* (Rotterdam, 1698), sig. A2r: 'Den Oversetter aan den Lust en Leer-lievende Leeser'; 'die door sommige niet voor Orthodox, maar by alle die syn Schriften kennen ... voor een geleert en deftig redenaar geagt werd'; 'niet na de gemeyne weg, maar uyt de Natuure der Saake'. Possibly it was some news of the appearance of this translation that prompted Leibniz's remark in his letter to Hertelius of 27 Dec. 1698 (quoted above, n. 17). This work is omitted from Macdonald and Hargreaves, *Bibliography*. I have consulted the copy in Leiden University Library, pressmark 1155 F 22.

[49] G.-F. de Bure, *Bibliographie instructive: ou traité de la connoissance des livres rares et singuliers*, 7 vols. (Paris, 1763–8), II, p. 181 ('Collection fort recherchée, & dont les exemplaires sont devenus assez rares dans le Commerce: ce qui en a fait augmenter la valeur'). De Bure also described Sorbière's translation of *De cive* as sought-after, and *Le Corps politique* as even more difficult to find (pp. 213–14).

had they been obscure and little read, much less trouble would have been taken to suppress them.

The formal bans came from several quarters. The Catholic Church first took official notice of Hobbes in 1654, when the Holy Office in Rome placed *De cive* on its index of prohibited books; half a century later, in 1703, *Leviathan* was added to the index, and in 1709 the condemnation was extended to all Hobbes's other works.[50] While such decrees made it harder for Catholics to read Hobbes, at the same time the fact that they were issued does indicate that Hobbes was being read: in Spain, a country hardly touched by knowledge of Hobbes until at least the mid-eighteenth century, the separate index maintained by the Spanish Holy Office never mentioned him at all.[51] Protestant countries also banned some of Hobbes's works: the Court of Holland imposed severe penalties for the printing or distribution of *Leviathan* in 1674, and in 1698 the Calvinist authorities in the Swiss canton of Bern added 'the atheistical and deistic writings of Hobbes'—together with those of Aretino, Machiavelli, Herbert, Spinoza, and Simon—to their own index of prohibited books.[52] Official condemnation could be a serious obstacle to publication: the opposition of the Elector of Saxony seems to have been the main reason why Thomas Fritsch's project foundered. But the obstacle was not entirely insuperable, and the steady succession of inexpensive editions of *De cive* shows that it was always possible for continental readers to obtain at least one significant section of Hobbes's philosophical system. Other works were also widely read; indeed, some of the strongest evidence of this consists in the constant stream of publications by academics, theologians, and lawyers attacking Hobbes's views, in which the fruits of a careful study of Hobbes's works are often on display. Of course, in some cases one may suspect that an author is merely copying his references or citations from the writings of some previous critic of Hobbes. But there is enough evidence of direct engagement with Hobbes's writings to show that in most parts of northern Europe anyone who wished to criticize him could easily get hold of the major Latin works.

Several of these critics argued that the task of opposing Hobbes was all the more important because his books were becoming such popular reading. Thus the

---

[50] *Index librorum prohibitorum Alexandri VII. Pontificis maximi iussu editus* (Rome, 1664), pp. 45, 367 (the full text of the decree of 10 June 1654); *Index librorum prohibitorum sanctissimi domini nostri Gregorii XVI. Pontificis maximi jussu editus* (Naples, 1853), p. 203 (decrees of 12 March 1703, 4 March 1709). The standard modern listing of the index has a misleading entry which appears to suggest that Hobbes's complete works were condemned first in 1649, then in 1701, and finally in 1703: *Index librorum prohibitorum* (Vatican City, 1938), p. 221.

[51] G. H. Putnam, *The Censorship of the Church of Rome and its Influence upon the Production and Distribution of Literature*, 2 vols. (New York, 1906), II, p. 128.

[52] 'Die atheistischen und deistischen Schriften von Nicolo Machiavelli, Bened. de Spinoza, Thomas Hobbes, Lord Edward Herbert, Père Richard Simon, Pietro Aretino': K. Müller, *Die Geschichte der Zensur im alten Bern* (Bern, 1904), p. 206. (I am very grateful to Béla Kapossy for this reference.) For the Dutch prohibition, see Ch. 11 above, n. 163.

Dutch Calvinist minister Gijsbert Cocq explained in 1668 that he had been moved to write his critique of Hobbes 'when I saw that copies of *De cive* were being worn out with use by many hands, and—what is more serious—that some people were commending it'; and six years later the Lutheran Adam Rechenberg, a lecturer at Leipzig University, felt obliged to combat the doctrines of *Leviathan* 'especially because those accursed books are nowadays being sold with impunity in Germany, and worn out with use even by the hands of students'.[53] As is always possible with such polemical works, these authors may have been exaggerating the popularity of their foe in order to magnify the importance of the task of confuting him; similarly, when the pious Lutheran court official Immanuel Weber complained in 1697 that Hobbes was commonly read at the princely courts of Protestant Germany, he may have been overstating the nature of the problem (fashionable atheism) that his own work was intended to tackle.[54] But the ambiguous nature of the relationship between popularity and condemnation enters also into the very contents of the works written by Hobbes's critics.

To some readers, the propagation of Hobbes's ideas may have come mainly via the writings of his enemies: the summaries they offered of his thought, though often highly prejudicial, were in some cases quite detailed, and tended always to focus on the most extreme and challenging of his doctrines. In this connection a revealing comment was made by Leibniz, when he wrote that he regretted that no one had done for Hobbes what the pioneering German Cartesian Johannes Clauberg had done for Descartes, namely, produced an ordered sequence of his key doctrines in condensed form: the best thing available, he added, was the list of Hobbesian 'theses' published by Samuel Andreas in 1672 for the purpose of refuting them.[55] Even more striking is the case of the little treatise published by the jurist Johann Friedrich Hombergk in 1722, which set out to disprove Hobbes's claims about the nature of society and government by means of principles taken from Hobbes's own writings. As Hombergk explained, this book arose from a successful course he had given at Marburg during the previous winter: for the sake of refuting Hobbes, he had thus been teaching a whole classroom of students to

---

[53] G. Cocq, *Hobbes ἐλεγκόμενος, sive vindiciae pro lege, imperio, & religione, contra tractatus Thomae Hobbesii, quibus tit. De cive & Leviathan* (Utrecht, 1668), sig. A3v: 'cum viderem libellum hunc [*De cive*] multorum manibus teri, & quod magis est, à nonnullis commendari'. A. Rechenberg, *Εὕρημα compendiarium in religione Christianâ novum* (Leipzig, 1674), p. 5: 'Praecipuè, cùm dicti libri sacerrimi impunè divendi in Germania & manibus etiam Studiosorum teri soleant'. (Rechenberg cites Cocq's book, and may have been influenced by his wording.) I have consulted the copy of Rechenberg's book in the Niedersächsische Landesbibliothek, Hanover, pressmark T-A 2917.

[54] I. Weber, *Beurtheilung der atheisterey* (Frankfurt, 1697), pp. 22–6, cited in Israel, *Radical Enlightenment*, p. 62.

[55] G. W. Leibniz, *Otium hanoveranum, sive miscellanea, ex ore & schedis illustris viri, piae memoriae, Godefr. Guilielmi Leibnitii*, ed. J. F. Feller (Leipzig, 1718), p. 181. The work by Andreas referred to here was a disputation at the University of Herborn; I have not been able to locate a copy of it.

engage in a close reading of Hobbes's works, hunting for positive principles that could be used to overturn his unacceptably negative conclusions.[56]

Given such inherent ambiguities, any bare division of the contemporary reactions to Hobbes into the categories of 'for' and 'against' will always be an unsatisfactory thing; even if the intentions of the writers could be so simply categorized, the effects of their writing could not. Nevertheless, some distinctions can and must be made. Three broad categories present themselves. First, there were writers—especially clerics and academics—who attacked Hobbes, because they regarded his views as objectionable and extreme. Secondly, there were radicals, who defended, propagated, or exploited his works precisely because they too regarded his views as extreme and anti-orthodox. And thirdly, there were others who made some positive use of Hobbesian ideas, not in order to shake the foundations of orthodox belief, but rather to develop arguments and positions that belonged within the intellectual mainstream. This third category is in some ways the most difficult to characterize, not only because it shades off on either side into the first and second categories, but also because it contains a variety of mutually conflicting interpretations of Hobbes's views. Yet it is perhaps the most interesting of the three. If the term 'Republic of Letters' is used in its most general sense, meaning simply the world of scholarly and literary publication, correspondence, and discussion, then all three types of reaction to Hobbes fall equally within the activities of that Republic. But the third type was of a more special significance: it involved treating Hobbes as intellectually respectable—neither denouncing him as an outsider nor hailing him as one, but regarding him, so to speak, as a fellow-citizen of the Republic, someone who participated in the debates of the scholarly world and might have something positive to contribute to them.

Let us briefly take these three categories in turn.

## IV

Hostile reactions to Hobbes's work began to appear soon after its first publication on the Continent. In late April or early May 1642, Mersenne distributed copies of the printing of *De cive* which he had organized. The first recorded response was from Grotius, on 7 May, who described its ideas as 'bold' and added, more guardedly, 'some are of a sort that I should not wish to defend'.[57] The nature of Grotius's objections was sketched by him in a letter to his brother in the following

---

[56] J. F. Hombergk zu Vach, *Pacem et societatem humani generis natura constitutam ex ipsis principiis T. Hobbii probatam* (Marburg, 1722), esp. pp. 1–2. This work is mainly concerned with *De cive*.

[57] M. Mersenne, *Correspondance*, ed. C. de Waard *et al.*, 17 vols. (Paris, 1933–88), XI, p. 144, Grotius to Mersenne, 7 May 1642 ('conceptions hardies . . . Il y en a de telles, que je ne voudrois pas entreprendre de soustenir'). The identification of the work referred to here with *De cive* is rendered likely by Mersenne's letter to André Rivet of 9 May 1642 (ibid., p. 151), which shows that Mersenne had just sent a copy to Huygens.

year: 'I like what he says in favour of kings, but I cannot approve of the foundation on which he builds his opinions. He thinks that all men are naturally at war with one another, and has some other principles which differ from my own. For example, he thinks it is the duty of each private individual to follow the official religion of his country—if not with internal assent, then at least with outward observance.'[58] In September 1642 a Catholic correspondent of Mersenne's put forward what were broadly the same objections, albeit expressed in more hostile tones: 'It is a rhapsody of heresies. Its basic principles are pernicious and absurd, namely, that society was founded on mutual fear and on the avoidance of violent death . . . He wants to unite sovereign priesthood with princely power, with the result that there will be as many heads of religion as there are princes . . . The only sort of correction this book deserves is that made by fire.'[59] And some time in the following year these strictures were echoed, at least in part, by Descartes, who gave his opinion of *De cive* to a Jesuit priest: 'I find him much more clever in moral philosophy than in metaphysics or physics, though I cannot approve at all of his principles and maxims, which are very bad and very pernicious, in so far as he supposes that all men are wicked, or gives them reason to be so.'[60]

Mersenne had of course been aware that Hobbes's work would meet with such reactions, from Catholics and Protestants alike. In October 1642 he wrote to one of his regular correspondents, the Calvinist theologian André Rivet in The Hague, asking for his opinion of *De cive* and commenting that 'it will doubtless be unfavourable, where many sections of the book are concerned'.[61] Rivet appears never to have seen that first edition of *De cive*; but when Samuel Sorbière sent him a copy of his French translation of it in 1649, he received what was evidently a stern condemnation in reply.[62]

---

[58] H. Grotius, *Epistolae quotquot reperiri potuerunt* (Amsterdam, 1687), pp. 951–2, 11 April 1643 ('placent quae pro Regibus dicit. Fundamenta tamen quibus suas sententias superstruit, probare non possum. Putat inter homines omnes à natura esse bellum & alia quaedam habet nostris non congruentia. Nam & privati cujusque officium putat sequi Religionem in patria sua probatam, si non assensu, at obsequio').

[59] Mersenne, *Correspondance*, XI, pp. 264–5, Baptiste Masoyer-Deshommeaux to Mersenne, 10 Sept. 1642 ('C'est une rhapsodie d'heresies. Les fondements sont pernicieux et absurdes, que la société est fondée sur la crainte l'un de l'autre, et pour eviter la mort violente . . . Il veut que le souverain sacerdoce soit joint à la principauté, et par consequent autant de princes, autant de chefs de religion . . . Cela ne merite correction que du feu').

[60] R. Descartes, *Oeuvres*, ed. C. Adam and P. Tannery, rev. edn, 11 vols. (Paris, 1974), IV, p. 67 (undated, assigned to 1643 by the editors) ('ie le trouue beaucoup plus habile en Morale qu'en Metaphysique ny en Physique; nonobstant que ie ne puisse aucunement approuuer ses principes ny ses maximes, qui sont tres-mauuaises & tres-dangereuses, en ce qu'il suppose tous les hommes méchans, ou qu'il leur donne suiet de l'estre').

[61] Mersenne, *Correspondance*, XI, p. 296, 12 Oct. 1642 ('qui sans doute ne sera pas favorable en beaucoup d'articles').

[62] Leiden University Library, MS BPL 302, fol. 293r (Sorbière to Rivet, 29 Nov. 1649: 'I could not fail to take your criticisms in good part, because I am sure that they come accompanied by affection and charity—especially those which concern the political treatise by my friend the English philosopher' ('Je ne scaurois prendre qu'en bonne part uos censures, parce que je suis asseuré que uous les accompagnés d'affection & de charité, & sur tout celles qui regardent la Politique de nostre Philosophe Anglois') ).

These early responses to *De cive* prefigured the two main lines of criticism of Hobbes's works that would develop during the following decades: political and theological. One of the most influential critics of Hobbes's political theory was the polymathic Lutheran scholar Hermann Conring, who taught at the University of Helmstedt. His first reaction to *De cive* (of which he possessed one of the 1647 editions) was given in a letter to his friend and former pupil Johann Christian von Boineburg in 1651: 'Hobbes's *Elementa . . . de cive* theorizes wickedly, when it argues that all right to rule depends on predominant power, and takes hatred or human animosities as the basis of civil government. Would any good man put up with such paradoxes? The author seems to deserve the hatreds that are directed at him by everyone.'[63] Twelve years later he set out this criticism in print, in his *De civili prudentia*, where he condemned 'that horrible principle, *that nature instituted discord rather than society among men*', and concluded: 'if that principle were granted as true, it would follow that all human society was instituted against nature. I do not know whether anything more absurd or wicked could be devised than that proposition.'[64]

Conring was one of the last great representatives of the old tradition of Protestant humanist Aristotelianism; it is not surprising, therefore, that he gave such weight to the idea of man's natural aptitude for social and political life, nor that he regarded Hobbes's theory more generally as symptomatic of the destructive innovatory forces at work in modern philosophy. (In another letter he described Hobbes as 'extremely eager to clutch at novelties, rash, over-confident and inept'.[65]) Similar reactions could be found elsewhere in the Protestant academic world. Thus, at the University of Tübingen a doctoral student, Heinrich Friedrich Forstner, presenting his dissertation in 1662, condemned the 'crass mistake' of supposing that the state of nature was a state of war, and declared that such a theory 'has a strong

---

[63] J. D. Gruber, ed., *Commercii epistolici Leibnitiani . . . tomus prodromus, qui totus est boineburgicus*, 2 vols. (Hanover, 1745), I, p. 20, 23 Jan. 1651 ('HOBBII elementa *de Cive* impie philosophantur, dum ius regendi omne ex potentia praeualente suspendunt, et odium seu simultates humanas pro fundamento habent ciuilis regiminis. Quis bonus ferat haec paradoxa? Auctor dignus videtur, quem odia omnium excipiant'). For Conring's ownership of a 1647 *De cive*, see M. Stolleis, 'Machiavellismus und Staatsräson: ein Beitrag zu Conrings politischem Denken', in M. Stolleis, ed., *Hermann Conring (1606–1681): Beiträge zu Leben und Werk* (Berlin, 1983), pp. 173–99; here p. 195. Conring's was not quite the first recorded reaction to Hobbes by a German writer. In the previous year the jurist Franz-Julius Chopius had made very similar criticisms of *De cive*, singling out the theory of the state of nature and the apparent derivation of right from power, in his *Philosophia juris vera* (Leipzig, 1650), 2nd pagination, pp. 14–20. (I have consulted the copy of this work in the Herzog August Bibliothek, Wolfenbüttel, pressmark A: 86. 48 Jur (4).).

[64] H. Conring, *Opera*, ed. J. W. Goebel, 7 vols. (Braunschweig, 1730), III, p. 421 ('ex illo horribili principio: *natura inter homines non societatem, sed discordiam institutam esse*. Et vero illo posito, omnis societas humana contra naturae fuerit institutum. Quo asserto, nescio, num quid excogitari possit absurdum magis aut improbum'). Cf. similar criticisms in his *Dissertatio de civitate nova*: ibid., III, p. 743.

[65] Ibid., VI, p. 575 (extract from letter, undated) ('*Hobbesii ingenium*, deprehendi novitatum studiosum maxime, temerarium, praefidens & ineptum'). On the tradition, see H. Dreitzel, *Protestantischer Aristotelismus und absoluter Staat: die Politica des H. Arnisaeus* (Wiesbaden, 1970); on Conring's relation to this tradition, see H. Dreitzel, 'Hermann Conring und die politische Wissenschaft seiner Zeit', in M. Stolleis, ed., *Hermann Conring (1606–1681): Beiträge zu Leben und Werk* (Berlin, 1983), pp. 135–72.

whiff of irreligion about it'; the modern writers on such topics, whose works he said 'should not be read without great caution', included not only Hobbes— he specified *De cive* and *Le Corps politique*—but also Grotius, Selden, Gassendi, and Pufendorf.[66] Such criticisms were also made at Leipzig, where the influential Lutheran philosopher Jakob Thomasius seems to have taken a special interest in the confutation of Hobbes.[67] One of his students, Christfried Wächtler, attacked Hobbes's 'war of all against all' in a dissertation of 1670, calling it 'a horrid doctrine, and a more or less blasphemous one'.[68] Another pupil, Johannes Justinus Mühlpfort, similarly observed in 1672 that this doctrine 'subtly prepares the way for atheism', on the grounds that its denial of traditional natural law was akin to blasphemy. Mühlpfort singled out two fundamental errors in *De cive*: the idea that there is no innate obligation on men not to harm others, and the claim that man's religious duties towards God arise from an opinion of God's power, rather than his goodness. He concluded: 'Hobbes's doctrine turns God into a devil, and man into a pitiless beast: we must shrink in horror from the former idea, and reject the latter with contempt.'[69]

As these examples show, objections to Hobbes's political theory had quickly become associated with criticisms of his theology. The earliest criticisms of Hobbes on religious grounds were concerned mainly with his theories about ministerial authority and the relationship between Church and State: these were, after all, prominent features of his treatment of religion in *De cive*, whereas many of his most radical arguments on points of doctrine appeared only later, in the second half of *Leviathan*. For the tireless Calvinist polemicist (and anti-Cartesian) Gijsbert Voetius, writing in the 1660s, Hobbes was objectionable above all because of his downgrading of ministerial authority: the implication of his argument, Voetius suggested, was that no religious ministers were necessary at all. In chapter XVIII of *De cive*, he observed, Hobbes 'seems to transform the church into the

[66] H. F. Forstner, *Antesignanus politicus, sive de studii politici ortu & progressu, dissertatio* (Tübingen, 1662), pp. 7 ('crasso errore'), 27 ('non abs magna cautione legendi'), 28 ('multam profanitatem sapit').

[67] According to Johann Gottlieb Krause, some of Thomasius's critical notes on Hobbes's writings were later published by Leibniz's assistant J. F. Feller: J. G. Krause, ed., *Neue Zeitungen von Gelehrten Sachen*, vol. 2, no. 16 (15 Apr. 1716), p. 135. I have not been able to locate a copy of Feller's publication. Among Thomasius's criticisms of Hobbes was the standard accusation that he described men as naturally bad: see the comment on this in N. H. Gundling, *Gundlingiana, darinnen allerhand zur Jurisprudenz, Philosophie, Historie, Critic, Litteratur, und übrigen Gelehrsamkeit gehörige Sachen abgehandelt werden*, 45 parts (Halle, 1715–32), part 14 (1717), p. 307. For details of Thomasius's comparison of Spinoza to Hobbes in 1670, see below, at n. 87. On Thomasius's Aristotelianism and general intellectual conservatism see T. J. Hochstrasser, *Natural Law Theories in the Early Enlightenment* (Cambridge, 2000), pp. 19–21.

[68] C. Wächtler, *De societatis civilis statu naturali ac legali, dissertatio politica* (Leipzig, 1670), sig. B2r ('Horrendum dogma, qvodque à blasphemiâ parùm abest'). Wächtler referred to *De cive*. This dissertation is attributed to Jakob Thomasius by Fiammetta Palladini: see her *Discussioni seicentesche su Samuel Pufendorf: scritti latini, 1663–1700* (n.p. [Bologna], 1978), p. 290.

[69] J. J. Mühlpfort, *Exercitatio politica de latrocinio gentis in gentem* (Leipzig, 1672), sigs. D3v ('subtilem viam atheismo sternit'), E4r ('Hobbesii dogma ex DEO Diabolum facit, ex homine bestiam immitem. Qvorum illud horrendum est, hoc despuendum').

commonwealth, and ministers into ministers of the commonwealth or state, that is, of kings or magistrates'.[70] In 1669 Voetius also refered to the Dutch *Leviathan* ('very recently translated into our language, lest this Africa of ours should fail to produce new monsters'). Even before the appearance of van Berkel's version, he had had some knowledge—probably at second hand—of the contents of the work, albeit relating mainly to the arguments he had already framed against *De cive*: thus, he referred in 1663 to 'Hobbes's fanatical and paradoxical idea, put forward in a certain English book entitled *Leviathan*, that princes and magistrates have the power to preach the Word publicly, and administer the sacraments'.[71]

What is most noticeable about Voetius's anti-Hobbesian polemics is his eagerness to link Hobbes's arguments to those of other enemies, both philosophical and religious. Thus, in one somewhat strained piece of argumentation he associated Hobbes with Descartes, on the grounds that both solved cases of conscience not by appealing to authoritative interpretations of Scripture, but either by referring to decrees of the magistrate (Hobbes) or by depending on their own imaginations (Descartes)—'according to those new principles, "Whatever my spirit suggests to me is true," and "Whatever I perceive clearly and distinctly is true." '[72] More generally, he associated Hobbes with Erastians and Remonstrants (and Grotius in particular), as advocates of what he called 'caesaro-papism', the merging of political and religious authority; and his list of those who denied the necessity of religious ministers included not only 'Hobbesians' but also 'Enthusiasts', Quakers and 'Libertines'.[73] Voetius thus furnishes an early example of what was to become a common syndrome among Hobbes's critics: the charges they laid against him usually served wider ideological purposes, and reflected the nature of other religious or political disputes in which they were already engaged.

Closely associated with Voetius was another Calvinist minister, Gijsbert Cocq, whose first book attacking Hobbes was published in 1668. It contained two dissertations directed against *De cive* which Cocq had previously defended at the University of Utrecht, as well as a short disputation by Voetius on kingship in the Old Testament; but the main part of the book was a 202-page treatise attacking the religious ideas of *Leviathan*, which Cocq had recently read in the Dutch

---

[70] G. Voetius, *Politia ecclesiastica*, 4 vols. (Amsterdam, 1663–76), II, p. 222 ('ecclesiam in civitatem, & ministros in ministros civitatis seu politiae, regum sc. & magistratuum transformare videtur').

[71] Ibid., II, p. 222 ('nuperrime in nostrum idioma translato: ne Africa nostra novorum monstrorum sterilis esset'); I, p. 895 ('*Hobbesii* fanaticum paradoxum de potestate Principum & Magistratuum in verbo publicè praedicando, & sacramentis administrandis (quod ostendat in libro quodam Anglico tit. *Leviathan*)'. When he referred to *Leviathan* in a lecture given in 1665, he cited it at second hand, via a Latin sermon by Henry Wilkinson: G. Voetius, *Selectae disputationes theologicae*, 5 vols. (Utrecht, Amsterdam, 1648–69), IV, p. 64 (citing H. Wilkinson, *Conciones sex ad academicos oxonienses latinè habitae* (Oxford, 1658), pp. 187–8, where Wilkinson attacks Hobbes's argument that subjects ordered by their sovereign to deny Christ may do so without sin).

[72] Voetius, *Selectae disputationes*, IV, p. 65 ('juxta nova principia, *Quod* spiritus meus mihi suggerit, hoc verum est; quod *clarè et distinctè percipio, hoc verum est*').

[73] Voetius, *Politia ecclesiastica*, I, p. 895; II, pp. 217–23.

translation. Throughout his criticisms of Hobbes, Cocq's strategy was to associate him with what had hitherto clearly been his main polemical preoccupation, the danger of Socinianism; but he also identified in Hobbes's teachings the related errors of Pelagianism, Sadducism, and Epicureanism.[74] As the first Continental polemicist to tackle some of the theological arguments of *Leviathan*, Cocq was able to produce an influential text, which would often be cited by later critics. Indeed, the years immediately following the publication of this book mark something of a turning-point in continental attitudes to Hobbes: it is from the 1670s onwards that the emphasis of the anti-Hobbesian writings shifts towards the denunciation of heresy, irreligion, or even outright atheism.

There seem to be three main reasons for this change in approach. The first is the availability of *Leviathan* in Dutch (1667) and, more importantly, Latin (1668). The second is the appearance during the 1670s of several major attacks on Hobbes's theology by English authors writing in Latin, by means of which the much better established English tradition of vilifying Hobbes was transmitted to continental Europe: works such as John Templer's *Idea theologiae Leviathanis* (1673) and Samuel Parker's *Disputationes de Deo et providentia divina* (1678) circulated widely on the Continent, exerting a much greater influence there than they ever did at home.[75] And the third is the publication in 1670 of Spinoza's *Tractatus theologico-politicus*, which quickly drew a barrage of hostile criticism from writers who were not slow to comment on the similarities between Spinoza and Hobbes. Thus, when Gijsbert Cocq, buoyed up by the success of his first anti-Hobbesian book, produced a second one in 1680, he began by explaining that there had been a double outbreak of heresies in recent times, the Cartesian and the Hobbesian, and that Spinoza represented a combination of the two—of which the Hobbesian variety was by far the more malignant.[76]

Eventually, the link with Spinoza would come to characterize the terms in which Hobbes was criticized and denounced: extreme naturalism (undermining faith in

---

[74] Cocq, *Hobbes ἐλεγκόμενος*, first pagination ('De lege in communi'), pp. 25–7, 37, 84; second pagination ('Vindiciae'), sigs. †1v, †2r, p. 19. On Cocq (1630–1708), who had studied at Utrecht and served as a preacher at Kockengen, see E. H. Kossmann, 'Politieke theorie in het zeventiende-eeuwse Nederland', *Verhandelingen der Koninklijke Nederlandse Akademie van Wetenschappen, afdeling letterkunde*, n.s., vol. 67, no. 2 (1960), pp. 24–5.

[75] For example, of 8 writers referred to below (Arnold, Diecmann, Grapius, Gundling, Pasch, Rechenberg, Seckendorff and Staalkopff), 6 cited Parker and 4, Templer. Also regularly cited were two other Latin anti-Hobbesian works, Richard Cumberland's *De legibus naturae* (London, 1672) and Robert Sharrock's Ὑπόθεσις ἠθική, *de officiis secundum naturae jus*, which, originally published at Oxford in 1660, was known on the Continent through a reprinting issued at Gotha in 1667. On the influence of both Cumberland and Sharrock on continental writers, see H.-P. Schneider, *Justitia universalis: Quellenstudien zur Geschichte des 'christlichen Naturrechts' bei Gottfried Wilhelm Leibniz* (Frankfurt am Main, 1967), esp. pp. 159–60, 175–81, 186–95.

[76] G. Cocq, *Hobbesianismi anatome, qua innumeris assertionibus ex tractatibus de homine, cive, Leviathan juxta seriem locorum theologiae christianae philosophi illius à religione christianâ apostasia demonstratur, & refutatur* (Utrecht, 1680), sigs. *2v–*3r.

miracles), radical biblical criticism (undermining faith in Revelation), and so on. But before the standard line on Hobbes had thus begun to incorporate him in to a tradition of philosophical atheism, a very different accusation had exercised the minds of many of his critics: 'indifferentism'. This was a general term used by defenders of confessional orthodoxy (especially Lutherans and Calvinists) to stigmatize a variety of thinkers—Erastian political theorists, rationalist philosophers, ecumenist and irenicist theologians—who down-played the differences between the denominations and suggested that practices or doctrines could legitimately vary from Church to Church or from state to state, so long as the few fundamentals of Christian belief were maintained by all. Among Lutherans in mid-seventeenth century Germany, this tendency was particularly associated with the liberal theologian Georg Calixtus, whose irenicism extended even to the Catholics.[77] The so-called doctrinal 'syncretism' of Calixtus was linked by his critics to dangerous rationalistic tendencies in contemporary religion and philosophy: a favourite tactic was to make the connection with Edward Herbert, whose few simple principles of natural religion seemed to obviate the need for any revelation whatsoever. This was the context into which Hobbes's views, too, were fitted.

One of the first people to interpret Hobbes in this way was Conring's former pupil Johann Christian von Boineburg. Writing to a friend in 1655 about the recently deceased scholar Caspar Barth, he asked what his religion had been, and suggested that Barth had adhered to no confession, preferring his own beliefs, like Hobbes, Vossius, Caspar Barlaeus, Marc'Antonio de Dominis, Georg Calixtus, Conrad Berg, Grotius, Thomas Browne, Acontius, Scioppius, Casaubon, and La Peyrère; a few months later, in a letter to Conring, he made the connection with Herbert, referring to 'Hobbes, Herbert, and other similar teachers of self-love, licence, and religious indifference'.[78] Von Boineburg's position—on indifferentism and on Hobbes—was in fact quite ambiguous; while the contemptuous tone of the second of those comments was evidently adapted to the prejudices of its recipient, the scatter-shot list in the first included one of von Boineburg's greatest intellectual heroes, Hugo Grotius. (Only five years earlier von Boineburg had written in praise of Marc'Antonio de Dominis and of the entire ecumenist tradition, exclaiming: 'If only the authority and advice of more moderate people might at last prevail—people such as Cassander, Grotius and Episcopius in the past, and Calixtus today.' But in the interim he had converted to Catholicism, and had

---

[77] See E. L. T. Henke, *Georg Calixtus und seine Zeit*, 2 vols. (Halle, 1853–60); H. Schüssler, *Georg Calixt: Theologie und Kirchenpolitik* (Mainz, 1961). A good account of the polemics waged by orthodox Lutherans in the 'syncretist controversy' is in S. Göransson, *Ortodoxi och synkretism i Sverige, 1647–1660* (Uppsala, 1950), pp. 99–135.

[78] B. G. Struve, *Acta litteraria ex manuscriptis eruta atque collecta*, 2 vols. (Jena, 1703–20), I, fasc. 3, p. 33, von Boineburg to Zacharias Prüschenk, 1655; Gruber, ed., *Commercii epistolici*, I, pp. 150–1, von Boineburg to Conring, 23 January 1656 ('cum Hobbio, Herberto, idque genus ceteris Philautiae, et licentiae ac religionum Adiaphorae magistris').

thereupon changed his tune, excoriating the Catholic heretic de Dominis as the source of all modern 'Indifferentismus'.[79]

Protestant writers of the 1660s and 1670s kept up the fight against 'syncretism' or indifferentism: Johann Conrad Dannhauer denounced it as 'Grotiano-Erasmo-Cassandrico-Antonio-Dominic', Anton Reiser linked it to 'Puccianism, Acontianism, the libertinism of the Arminians and the atheism of the Socinians', and Conrad Rango produced a list of characteristics of syncretism, of which the first two were 'An ambiguous, general and deceptive confession of faith' and 'A denial of fundamental disagreement'.[80] The connection between these tendencies and Hobbes's approach to religion was seized on by polemical writers, Calvinist as well as Lutheran: when the French Calvinist theologian Pierre Jurieu wanted to discredit the irenicist treatise by Isaac d'Huisseau, *La Reünion du christianisme* (1671), for example, he accused the author of borrowing 'indifferentist' arguments from Hobbes.[81] In 1674 a critique of Hobbes based on these assumptions was published by Jakob Thomasius's son-in-law and protégé at Leipzig, the orthodox Lutheran theologian Adam Rechenberg.[82] In the final section of his book, entitled 'Hobbes's syncretistic-atheistic purpose', he explained that atheism was the 'child' of syncretism, and that Hobbes intended 'to introduce a *universal syncretism*, in which all religions of the Christian world would be included. For however many sects or heresies there are among the Christians, according to Hobbes they all believe that

---

[79] J. C. von Boineburg, *Epistolae ad virum clarissimum Jo. Conradum Dietericum*, ed. R. M. Meelfuhrer (Nuremberg, 1703), p. 117, von Boineburg to Dieterich, 17 Oct. 1650 (praise of de Dominis); Struve, *Acta litteraria*, I, fasc. 3, pp. 14, von Boineburg to Prüschenk, 1650 ('Vtinam vero tandem valeret paulo magis auctoritas & consilium moderatorum hominum, quales fuere, *Cassander* . . . *Grotius, Episcopius,* & hodie *Calixtus*'), 22, von Boineburg to Prüschenk, 1653 or 1654 ('Indifferentismus'). On von Boineburg's conversion, see G. Denzler, *Die Propagandakongregation in Rom und die Kirche in Deutschland im ersten Jahrzehnt nach dem Westfälischen Frieden* (Paderborn, 1969), pp. 74–5. On de Dominis see my *De Dominis (1560–1624): Venetian, Anglican, Ecumenist and Relapsed Heretic* (London, 1984), and W. B. Patterson, *King James VI and I and the Reunion of Christendom* (Cambridge, 1997), pp. 220–59.

[80] J. C. Dannhauer, *Dissertatio historico-theologica . . . cui adjectus . . . dialogus apologeticus pro mysterio syncretismi* (Strasbourg, 1668), p. 246; A. Reiserus, *De origine, progressu et incremento antitheismi, seu atheismi* (Augsburg, 1669), p. 300 ('Puccianismus, Acontianismus, Arminianorum Libertinismus, Socinianorum Atheismus'); C. T. Rango, *Brevis de origine & progressu syncretismi à mundo condito historia, das ist, historische Beschreibung der Religions-Mengerey von Anfang der Welt* (Stettin, n. d. [1674]), sig. b9r ('1. Ambigua, Generalis, & dolosa Confessio. 2. Dissensus Fundamentalis Negatio').

[81] See H. Kretzer, *Calvinismus und französische Monarchie im 17. Jahrhundert* (Berlin, 1975), p. 369. D'Huisseau's *La Reünion du christianisme, ou la maniere de rejoindre tous les Chretiens sous une seule confession de foy* (Saumur, n.d. [1671]) does not in fact bear any special signs of Hobbesian influence; it merely calls for a return to the purity of primitive Christianity, and dismisses disputes about 'external and accidental matters' (p. 135: 'des choses exterieures & accidentelles').

[82] On Rechenberg, who taught history and classical languages at Leipzig for many years before becoming Professor of Theology there in 1699, see N. Hammerstein, *Jus und Historie: ein Beitrag zur Geschichte des historischen Denkens an deutschen Universitäten im späten 17. und im 18. Jahrhundert* (Göttingen, 1972), pp. 272–4. Ten years later Rechenberg published a more narrowly focussed criticism of Hobbes, responding to the account of ancient and medieval schools and universities in chapter 46 of *Leviathan: De origine et usu scholarum, contra Thomae Hobbesii Leviathanis cap. XLVI ex historia* (Leipzig, 1684). (I have consulted the copy of this work in the Staatsbibliothek, Berlin, pressmark Ah 8821 (no. 27).)

one article of faith [sc., that 'Jesus is the Christ'].'[83] Rechenberg produced a long list of syncretists: at the head of it were the usual suspects, Cassander, Pucci, and de Dominis, and also included were Edward Herbert, Sir Thomas Browne (on account of *Religio medici*), the Remonstrant theologian Étienne de Courcelles, the irenicist Daniel Zwicker, Spinoza, and even Thomas Sprat (on account of remarks in favour of rational Christianity in his *History of the Royal Society*).[84] For all the oddity of this line-up—to modern eyes, at least—one thing at least is clear: the charge of atheism-by-implication levelled here was different from a straightforward accusation of philosophical atheism, reflecting instead the concerns of contemporary inter-confessional politics.

This interpretation of Hobbes would remain current for several decades. In 1680 Christian Kortholt, a Lutheran professor at the University of Kiel, argued that Hobbes's theory of religion was derived from Herbert's: the purpose in each case was to produce a version of religion so malleable, and so independent of revelation, that its form could be entirely dictated by the civil ruler.[85] And in 1700 Georg Pasch, also from the University of Kiel, described Hobbes's position as follows: 'He sets his doctrine on such foundations that, even if they do not quite overturn true religion, they nevertheless render it ambiguous; they may not lead to a complete atheism, but they certainly lead to a sort of neutralism, which recognizes that some God should be worshipped, but thinks that the way of worshipping him need not be derived from Holy Scripture.'[86]

By this time, however, accusations of 'complete atheism' had come to predominate in the writings of Hobbes's critics. The scandal and horror provoked by the publication of Spinoza's major works in the 1670s had played a large part in this: critics had been quick to point out that some of the most objectionable features of Spinoza's theories could be linked to—and were perhaps derived

---

[83] Rechenberg, Εὕρημα *compendiarium*, ch. 3 ('De scopo Hobbesii Syncretisto-atheistico'), pp. 220 ('proles'), 202 ('*Syncretismum universalem* introducere, sub quô omnes in orbe Christiano Religiones complecteretur. Nam quotquot inter Christianos inveniuntur sectae vel haereses, sensu Hobbesiano, illum unum articulum credunt').

[84] Ibid., pp. 205–18.

[85] C. Kortholt, *De tribus impostoribus magnis*, 2nd [or 3rd?] edn (Hamburg, 1701) (previously published at Kiel, 1680), pp. 50–75. On Kortholt see J. Lagrée, 'Christian Kortholt et son *De tribus impostoribus magnis*', in P. Cristofolini, ed., *L'Hérésie spinoziste: la discussion sur le Tractatus Theologico-Politicus, 1670–1677, et la réception immédiate du spinozisme* (Amsterdam, 1995), pp. 169–83. According to Johannes Moller, Kortholt's book had originally been published at Jena in 1658, and was 'now reprinted in an enlarged version' ('nunc vero auctior recusa': *Cimbria literata*, 3 vols. (Copenhagen, 1744), III, p. 371). If so, the 1658 edn must have been a rather different work, without the material on Spinoza and therefore also without the play on the idea of the 'three impostors' (see below, at n. 125) in the title. But a date in the 1650s would anchor the work more firmly in the 'syncretist controversy', which was then raging.

[86] G. Pasch, *De novis inventis, quorum accuratiori cultui facem praetulit antiquitas, tractatus* (Leipzig, 1700), p. 191 ('talia doctrinae suae fundamenta ponat, quae si veram religionem non evertunt penitus, eam tamen ambiguam reddunt, sique non perfectum Atheismum, certe Neutralismum quendam inducunt, qui Deum quidem colendum agnoscit, sed derivare modum colendi ex Sacra Scriptura non necessarium arbitratur').

from—Hobbes. The similarities were, after all, unmistakable. The very first recorded reaction to the *Tractatus theologico-politicus*, a 'harangue' delivered at Leipzig by Jakob Thomasius on 8 May 1670, compared Spinoza to Herbert and Hobbes; four months later, when Leibniz penned his first comments on that book in a letter to Thomasius, he remarked that 'the author seems to adhere not only to Hobbes's politics, but also to his religion'.[87]

Linking Hobbes and Spinoza—and, frequently, Herbert—soon became a commonplace of polemical writing. Kortholt's book was about 'the three great impostors' Herbert, Hobbes and Spinoza; in 1692 Michael Berns (a Lutheran preacher at Dittmarschen, near Hamburg) produced a similar work about the same 'three arch-impostors'; in 1694 Friedrich Ernst Kettner published the dissertation he had presented at Leipzig on 'the two impostors', Spinoza and Balthasar Bekker, in which he noted that Hobbes had anticipated Bekker in his denial of the existence of spirits, and described Spinoza as 'Hobbes's lickspittle'; and in 1702 an anonymous writer published a tract denouncing Descartes, Spinoza, Bekker, and Hobbes.[88] What all these works were attempting, in slightly different ways, was not merely to kill more than one bird with one stone, but to construct a genealogy of modern atheism. This ran back, through Hobbes and Herbert (and, sometimes, Descartes) to the arch-atheist of the early seventeenth century, Vanini; the connection with Vanini was made explicitly, for example, by both Berns and the influential political writer and statesman Veit Ludwig von Seckendorff.[89] By the first decade of the eighteenth century, an entire canon of unorthodoxy had thus been established: according to writers such as Valentin Ernst Löscher in Dresden and Zacharias Grapius in Rostock, it ran from Pomponazzi, the early Socinians, and Vanini, via Herbert, Descartes, Hobbes, and Spinoza, to Bekker, Locke, and Toland.[90]

---

[87] See P. Vernière, *Spinoza et la pensée française avant la révolution*, 2 vols. (Paris, 1954), I, pp. 38, 99 ('Videtur auctor non tantum politicam sed et religionem Hobbianum sectari').

[88] Kortholt, *De tribus impostoribus*; M. Berns, *Altar der Atheisten, der Heyden und der Christen . . . wider die 3 Ertz-Betrieger Hobbert* [sic], *Hobbes und Spinosa* (Hamburg, 1692); F. E. Kettnerus, *De duobus impostoribus, Benedicto Spinosa et Balthasare Bekkero, dissertatio historica* (Leipzig, 1694), sigs. B3v, A2v ('sputum Hobbesii lambit'); Anon., *Fürstellung vier neuer Welt-Weisen, nahmentlich Renati des Cartes, Thomae Hobbes, Benedicti Spinosa, Balthasar Beckers, nach ihrem Leben und führnemsten Irrthümern* (n.p., 1702). According to Hinnant, *Thomas Hobbes*, p. 19, this last item was published as part of a compilation edited by J. F. Corvinus, *Anabaptisticum et enthusiasticum pantheon*. The copy I have consulted is a *separatum* in Amsterdam University Library, pressmark OG 73–62 (9).

[89] Berns, *Altar der Atheisten*, sig. χ5r-v; V. L. von Seckendorff, *Christen-Staat* (Leipzig, 1693), 'Additiones' (separate pagination), p. 28 (linking Hobbes, Vanini, and Descartes).

[90] Grapius associated Pomponazzi with Hobbes and Spinoza as deniers of miracles, and argued that Locke had spread '*Hobbesianismum & Socinismum* [sic]' by denying the existence of an innate idea of God: *Systema novissimarum controversiarum*, 4 vols. (Rostock, 1738) [first published 1709], II, p. 56; I, p. 3. Löscher referred to Hobbes throughout his book, also describing Locke and Toland as 'champions of Hobbesian theology', and paid special attention to Pomponazzi: *Praenotationes theologicae contra naturalistarum et fanaticorum omne penus atheos, deistas, indifferentistas, antiscripturarios &c.* (Wittenberg, 1708), esp. pp. 54, 58, 61, 68–71, 79–80, 115, 179, 181 ('Io. Lockius & Io. Tolandus . . . Hobbesianae Theologiae promachi'), 218 (associating Pomponazzi, Hobbes and Bekker). On Löscher's career as a passionate defender of orthodox

The 'atheistic' tradition addressed by such writers had three main components: rationalism, naturalism, and anti-scripturalism. The first was the most general, embracing Socinianism, Cartesianism, and any other school of thought that seemed to elevate the authority of human reason above revelation or spiritual knowledge. The second component, naturalism or materialism, was associated mainly with Hobbes and Spinoza—the former for his denial of 'incorporeal spirits' and his suggestion that God himself must be conceived of as corporeal, and the latter for his identification of God and nature. The mystical theologian Pierre Poiret, writing in Amsterdam in the early 1680s, identified 'naturalismus' as one of the species of atheism, and complained that Hobbes 'denied not only the knowledge, but even the existence, of spiritual things, declaring that all things, even God himself, are bodies'; he then devoted four pages to the refutation of Hobbes's pernicious idea, concluding that 'these things must be said, because many people share his false views'.[91] In 1683 Johannes Diecmann presented a dissertation on philosophical naturalism at the University of Kiel; he noted that extreme naturalists, such as Vanini, denied the existence of God, and added that 'some people argue that Hobbes too was a naturalist of this sort'.[92] Nine years later another Lutheran scholar, Nathanael Falck, presented a dissertation on demonology at the University of Wittenberg in which he condemned the 'Naturalistae' who attributed all effects in the world to natural causes. Hobbes had been, he said, 'a champion of the naturalists'; but Spinoza, 'following Hobbes's tracks', had proceeded even further, trying to eradicate all belief in God's existence.[93] This idea that Spinoza offered merely a more explicit version of Hobbes was widely held; as yet another young Lutheran, Jakob Staalkopff, put it in 1707, when he presented his anti-naturalist dissertation at the University of Greifswald, Spinoza taught openly what Hobbes had taught 'more covertly'.[94]

This view of Spinoza's role was confirmed, in the eyes of most commentators, by the third component of the atheistic tradition: the attack on the validity of

---

Lutheranism see F. Blanckmeister, *Der Prophet von Kursachsen Valentin Ernst Löscher und seine Zeit* (Dresden, 1920).

[91] P. Poiret, *Cogitationes rationales de Deo, anima et malo*, 2nd edn (Amsterdam, 1685), 2nd pagination, pp. 11 ('non tantum notitiam, sed & existentiam rerum spiritualium negavit, statuens omnia, etiam ipsum Deum, esse corpora'), 15 ('Haec... quia plurimi cum illo decipiuntur, ideo dicta sunto'). Poiret cites the Latin *Leviathan*, *De cive* and *De corpore*. On Poiret see G. A. Krieg, *Der mystische Kreis: Wesen und Werden der Theologie Pierre Poirets* (Göttingen, 1979); G. Mori, *Fra Descartes e Bayle: Poiret e la teodicea* (Bologna, 1990).

[92] J. Diecmann, *De naturalismo cum aliorum, tum maxime Io. Bodini, ex opere ejus MSCto, & usque adhuc ἀνέκδοτω, de abditis rerum sublimium arcanis* (Kiel, 1683), pp. 21–2 (Vanini), 23 ('Hujus ipsius Naturalismi Hobbesium quoque sunt qui arguant'). As his title made clear, Diecmann's main focus was on Bodin's 'Colloquium heptaplomeres': in his discussion of Bodin he managed to bring together both naturalism and religious syncretism.

[93] N. Falck, *Dissertationes quatuor, de daemonologia recentiorum autorum falsa* (n.p. [Stettin?], 1694), pp. 5 ('Naturalistarum Promachus'), 4 ('Hobbesii legisse vestigia').

[94] J. Staalkopff, *Ab impiis detorsionibus Thomae Hobbesii, & Benedicti de Spinoza, oraculum Paulinum Per ipsum vivimus, movemur, & sumus, Act. XVII, 28* (Greifswald, 1707), p. 16.

Scripture. The denial of Mosaic authorship of the Pentateuch was the central issue here; and on this issue it was clear that, while Spinoza did go further than Hobbes, the techniques of textual and historical analysis on which he depended were very similar to those set out in Hobbes's *Leviathan*.[95] Indeed, this was the one element of the atheist tradition that seemed, in the eyes of many critics, to have originated with Hobbes himself. Almost every polemical attack on Spinoza's biblical criticism —and, after 1678, on Richard Simon's too—made the connection with Hobbes. Increasingly, therefore, he was treated not as the advocate of some defective version of Christianity, but as an enemy of Christian religion *tout court*, someone determined to destroy all faith in the revelation on which Christianity was founded. The attacks came from all quarters: Lutherans such as Johann Benedict Carpzov at Leipzig (where he held the chair of theology later occupied by Rechenberg), Calvinists such as Hermann Witsius at Utrecht or Johann Heinrich Heidegger at Zurich, and Catholics such as Pierre Daniel Huet in Paris.[96]

It was in fact only now—in the late 1670s—that Catholic theologians began to take serious notice of Hobbes; and this issue appears to have played the key role in awakening their interest. Hitherto, theological attacks on Hobbes had come mainly from Protestants who associated him with their own more or less Protestant bugbears: Socinianism, Arminianism, 'syncretism', and so on. Catholics had felt little interest in those quarrels; if they knew the contents of the second half of *Leviathan* they may well have regarded it as so fervently anti-Catholic as to be beyond the pale of serious debate, whereas Protestant writers would have been all the more conscious of the dangers of heresies lurking behind such an exuberantly anti-Catholic façade. But with the publication of Richard Simon's work in 1678, Catholic writers—especially in Paris—were forced to confront the issue of Spinozan biblical criticism directly. Huet's attack on Spinoza in 1679, in which he argued that Spinoza's theories were derived partly from Hobbes, was followed three years later by a similar work from the pen of Claude Frassen, a professor of theology in Paris, identifying Hobbes as Spinoza's source; and another Parisian professor, Louis Ellies du Pin, echoed the claim five years after that.[97] Before long, Catholics too acquired the habit of referring to Hobbes and Spinoza as key figures in the genealogy—and, one might say, demonology—of modern atheism. Their notoriety became quite universal. Even in the Italian states, where Hobbes's works were not widely available, the denunciations were commonplace: in 1725 the Neapolitan priest and diplomat Francesco Antonio Spada published a book in

---

[95] See my 'Hobbes, Ezra and the Bible: The History of a Subversive Idea' (Ch. 12, above), esp. pp. 390–2.

[96] For details of their criticisms see ibid., pp. 388–9.

[97] P. D. Huet, *Demonstratio evangelica ad serenissimum Delphinum* (Paris, 1679), pp. 140, 145; C. Frassen, *Disquisitiones biblicae quatuor libris comprehensae* (Paris, 1682), p. 104 (and polemicizing against Simon, though not by name, on pp. 132–3); L. Ellies du Pin, *Nouvelle bibliothèque des auteurs ecclésiastiques*, 3 vols. (Paris, 1688–9), I, p. 68–9(n.) (attacking Simon, by name).

Venice in which he attacked Hobbes and Spinoza; in 1737 Bonaventura Lucchi's 'oration' at the University of Padua on the study of philosophy railed against Hobbes, Spinoza, and Toland; and in 1750 Tommaso Vincenzio Moniglia, professor of theology at Pisa, attacked the same unholy trinity of 'materialisti'.[98] Some of these Italian writers—and a few others, such as Vico and Giannone, discussed below—had actually studied Hobbes's works; but often the denunciations had a somewhat ritualistic quality. When Lucchi wrote that it was not necessary to describe the theories of Hobbes, Spinoza, and Toland as they were so well known, the modern reader's first reaction may be to take this as striking evidence of how widely read the works of Hobbes and the others must have been; but a more considered judgement would be that Lucchi was referring to sheer notoriety—their works were more *known of* than known directly.[99] By the early eighteenth century, the criticisms of Hobbes had achieved, so to speak, critical mass: they had reached a point where it was the anti-Hobbesian writings themselves that functioned as the main vehicle for the propagation of the most radical versions of Hobbes's teaching.

## V

The category of 'radical' Hobbesians—those who responded positively to his ideas precisely because they regarded them as anti-orthodox—is curiously hard to delineate. A writer such as Sorbière, for example, who used elements of Hobbes's political thought to mount a self-consciously paradoxical defence of oriental 'despotism', could easily be described as a radical; yet his general position was not far removed from that of other contemporary theorists of absolutism, and he may perhaps be better described as situated at the edge of the mainstream. He will therefore be placed here in the third category, that of the mainstream users and adaptors of Hobbes. Pierre Bayle (who expressed cautious approval of some elements of Hobbes's philosophy) might well be said to belong, in general terms, to the 'radical' tradition; his writings played a key role in transmitting the heritage of the seventeenth-century *libertinage érudit* to the eighteenth century, and thus were an essential source for much of the 'underground' literature of the Enlightenment. Nevertheless, his handling of Hobbes had the overall effect of emphasizing what was acceptable in his theories, while keeping the most heterodox elements at arm's length. He too seems to belong in the third category here. Even Spinoza's use of Hobbesian ideas cannot be described as radical without qualification. The one area

---

[98] On Spada's *Antelucanae vigiliae* (Venice, 1725) and Lucchi's *Oratio pro studiis primae philosophiae* (Padua, 1737), see G. Ricuperati, *L'Esperienza civile e religiosa di Pietro Giannone* (Milan, 1970), pp. 247–8, 511. T. V. Moniglia, *Dissertazione contra i materialisti, e altri increduli*, 2 vols. (Padua, 1750), I, p. 47.

[99] Lucchi's comment is cited in Ricuperati, *L'Esperienza civile*, p. 511. On the knowledge of Hobbes in 18th-century Italy, see also Ricuperati's comments on Capasso, Biscardi, Sanfelice, and Giannone (pp. 27–30, 113–14, 309–13, 574, 610–15), and E. Garin, 'Appunti per una storia della fortuna di Hobbes nel settecento italiano', *Rivista critica di storia della filosofia*, 17 (1962), pp. 514–27.

in which his debt to Hobbes is most clearly visible is his political theory; but if the *Tractatus politicus* were all that Spinoza had ever written, he would surely be regarded as little more than a developer of theories within the Hobbes-influenced Dutch republican tradition—a minor but distinct sub-mainstream in itself. Only in some other Hobbes-related aspects of his work, such as his biblical criticism (where he seems to have been directly influenced by *Leviathan*) and his socio-political analysis of religion (where his affinity with Hobbes is strong, but his debt more difficult to measure), does Spinoza clearly qualify as a radical underminer of orthodoxy.

In any case, it must be emphasized that the 'radical' tradition that received the most widespread propagation was—as mentioned above—the one constructed by the defenders of orthodoxy itself. An example of how Hobbes's radical status was enhanced and elevated in this way is furnished by the reaction to Balthasar Bekker's famous book *De betoverde weereld* (The World Bewitched) in the early 1690s. Bekker was a Cartesian rationalist as well as a Calvinist preacher, and his thesis— denying the existence of demons and satanic possession, and arguing that all references to such things in the Bible were merely figurative—was certainly radical in its opposition to the accepted beliefs of the time. But in his long, multi-volume work he made no reference to Hobbes, nor is there any sign of direct borrowing from Hobbes's writings.[100] Nevertheless, in the storm of hostile reaction that followed the publication of Bekker's first volume in 1691—Jonathan Israel has described it as 'assuredly the biggest intellectual controversy of Early Enlightenment Europe' —almost every critic claimed that Hobbes was one of the main sources of Bekker's ideas; one opponent, the Calvinist minister (and pupil of Voetius) Jacobus Koelman, listed thirteen heresies in Bekker's work and traced each one to its origin in Hobbes.[101] When Bekker addressed this point in a reply to his critics, he declared that he had never thought about Hobbes when writing his book; that the only work by Hobbes that he had previously read was *De cive*; and that he looked at *Leviathan* for the first time only when he read the accusations that he had borrowed his ideas from it.[102] Although it is possible that Hobbes had exerted

---

[100] B. Bekker, *De betoverde weereld, zijnde een grondig ondersoek van 't gemeen gevoelen aangaande de geesten*, 4 vols. (Leeuwarden, Amsterdam, 1691–4). On Bekker, see W. P. C. Knuttel, *Balthasar Bekker: de bestrijder van het bijgeloof* (The Hague, 1906); Israel, *Radical Enlightenment*, pp. 378–405, gives a valuable account of the work and its influence.

[101] Israel, *Radical Enlightenment*, p. 382; Knuttel, *Balthasar Bekker*, pp. 228, 235, 262; J. Koelman, *Wederlegging van B. Bekkers betoverde werelt* (Amsterdam, 1692), pp. 118–28.

[102] B. Bekker, *Kort bericht . . . aangaande alle de schriften, welke over sijn boek de Betoverde Wereld . . . verwisseld sijn* (Amsterdam, 1692), p. 66 (cited in Knuttel, *Balthasar Bekker*, p. 247). Cornelis Schoneveld writes that 'According to Koelman, Bekker knew Hobbes personally and "it seems out of sheer curiosity, purposely went to speak to him" ' (*Intertraffic of the Mind*, p. 153). I hesitate to correct a Dutch scholar on the interpretation of a passage in Dutch, but it seems to me that Dr Schoneveld has misread Koelman here. The comment comes in a discussion of Spinoza; Hobbes is mentioned as a source of Spinoza's ideas, but the comment which follows clearly refers to Spinoza rather than Hobbes: 'Bekker knew this man [sc. Spinoza, the subject of the entire passage], and, it seems, out of sheer curiosity, purposely went to speak to him; what he learne

some influence on Bekker in more indirect ways, there seems to be no reason to doubt the truth of Bekker's statement. Yet what matters most of all, so far as the public knowledge of Hobbes is concerned, is that dozens of anti-Bekkerian tracts were spreading the idea that anyone interested in radical anti-demonism or anti-spiritualism would find a classic statement of that position in Hobbes's writings.

Even if Balthasar Bekker was not consciously a Hobbesian, there were others in the Netherlands who were; indeed, the first signs of a positive European reception of Hobbes for radical purposes were to be found in that country. One of the key figures here was Adriaen Koerbagh, who studied medicine and law at Leiden in the late 1650s, where he got to know van Berkel (the future translator of *Leviathan*) as well as several other members of Spinoza's circle.[103] In 1668 Koerbagh published a philosophical dictionary, *Een bloemhof van allerley liflykheyd*, in which the influence of *Leviathan* was unmistakable: one modern study has identified borrowings from Hobbes in the entries for 'duivel' (devil), 'demoniaak', 'bisschop', 'consecratie', 'haeresie', 'metaphysica', 'representeerder des staats' (representative of the state), and 'leviathan' itself, among others.[104] No less striking than the Hobbesian content was the tone of the entries—for example, the debunking attitude expressed in the entries for 'demoniaak', 'necromantie', and 'visioen' (which may possibly have influenced Bekker, thus furnishing him with Hobbesian ideas at one remove). The entry for 'Bibel', for example, began by noting that the word 'bible' just means 'book', so that any book—for example *Reynard the Fox* or *Till Uylenspiegel*—might be called a bible. And it continued: 'Who the writers of the Jewish scriptures were cannot be known with certainty. Some of the best theologians think that a certain Ezra adapted them from other Jewish writings. So far as the first five books are concerned, people inform us that Moses must have written them, even though that cannot be established from the contents of the books themselves. But they can be called Moses' books, insofar as they are written about him.'[105]

---

from him we should be able to guess from a comparison between his book and Spinoza's, even though he has publicly declared that he is no Spinozist' ('*Bekker* heeft dezen mensche gekent en expres uit curieusheidt zo 't schijnt gaan aanspreken; wat hy 'er van geleert heeft zouden wy mogen gissen uit zijn boek met dat van *Spinosa* vergeleken; evenwel hy heeft openlijk verklaart dat hy geen *Spinosist* is') (J. Koelman, *Het vergift van de cartesiaansche philosophie grondig ontdekt* (Amsterdam, 1692), p. 487). He later refers again to Bekker's 'visit or discussion' ('visite of conferentie') with Spinoza when the latter was living in The Hague (p. 489).

[103] See K. O. Meinsma, *Spinoza en zijn kring, over Hollandse vrijgeesten* (The Hague, 1896), pp. 296–324; P. H. van Moerkerken, *Adriaan Koerbagh, 1633–1669: een strijder voor het vrije denken* (Amsterdam, 1948); H. Vandenbossche, *Adriaan Koerbagh en Spinoza* (Leiden, 1978); G. H. Jongeneelen, 'An Unknown Pamphlet of Adriaan Koerbagh', *Studia Spinozana*, 3 (1987), pp. 405–15; Gelderblom, 'Publisher of Dutch *Leviathan*'; Israel, *Radical Enlightenment*, pp. 185–96.

[104] Unpublished study by G. H. Jongeneelen, cited in J. Lagrée and P.-F. Moreau, 'La Lecture de la Bible dans le cercle de Spinoza', in J.-R. Armogathe, ed., *Le Grand Siècle et la Bible* (Paris, 1989), pp. 97–115, here p. 106(n.).

[105] Cited in van Moerkerken, *Adriaan Koerbagh*, p. 43 ('Wie de schrijvers van de Joodse geschriften zijn, kan men niet met zekerheid weten. Enigen van de beste godgeleerden menen dat en zekere Esdras ze uit

Despite this drily sceptical tone, it is probably not correct to assume that Koerbagh was a 'Hobbist' of the caricature variety, a scoffing unbeliever; he was a fierce enemy of clericalism and organized religion, but his own beliefs seem to have been closer to those of the more radical Collegiants, with Socinian or even Quaker affinities. (His entry for 'paradijs' attacked the idea of a celestial heaven and insisted: 'That is expressly contrary to Scripture, which says that the Kingdom of God is within us.'[106]) At all events, however, his views were utterly unacceptable to the authorities. Both Adriaen and his brother were arrested; in July 1668 he was sentenced to a heavy fine and ten years' imprisonment, and less than a year later he died, broken in body and spirit, in an Amsterdam workhouse.[107]

Even more radical than Koerbagh was the German writer Friedrich Wilhelm Stosch, who led a quiet life in Berlin, first as a court secretary, then as a private scholar, before falling foul of the authorities in the early 1690s. Stosch also had Socinian affinities, but his rationalist approach to Scripture was so far-going as to render Scripture itself superfluous: the message of revelation must be validated by its conformity with reason, which meant that it could not go beyond what was in any case rationally knowable. He denied the existence of spirits, demons, or any human soul separate or distinct from the body; and, above all, he absorbed Spinoza's philosophical theology, identifying God and nature. The treatise in which Stosch set out his ideas, *Concordia rationis et fidei*, was clandestinely distributed, having been printed in 1692 in an edition of only one hundred copies; but the Berlin authorities found it, burned it and banned it, arrested the author in late 1693, and forced him to make a public recantation. (The chief errors thus recanted were his denial that natural acts could be sinful, his dismissal of angels and devils, and his denial of the eternity of punishments in Hell.[108]) While Spinoza was

andere Joodse Schriften heeft overgenomen. Wat de vijf eerste boeken betreft, men tracht ons wijs te maken dat Mozes die zou hebben geschreven, hoewel dit niet uit de boeken zelf bewezen kan worden. Men zou se Mozes' boeken kunnen noemen, omdat er over hem in geschreven wordt'). Cf. T. Hobbes, *Leviathan* (London, 1651), p. 200 ('it is not argument enough that they were written by *Moses*, because they are called the five books of *Moses* . . . For in titles of Books, the subject is marked, as often as the writer'); and the discussion of the 'Ezran' theory in 'Hobbes, Ezra and the Bible', Ch. 12 above, pp. 383–431.

[106] Cited in van Moerkerken, *Adriaan Koerbagh*, pp. 45–6 ('Dit is uitdrukkelijk tegen de Schrift, die zegt dat het Koninkrijk Gods binnen in ons is'). Adriaen's brother Johannes (who also contributed to *Een bloemhof*) preached—as did Spinoza's friend Petrus Serrarius—at a meeting-house on the Rokin in Amsterdam which was frequented by Socinians and Collegiants (M. Gullan-Whur, *Within Reason: A Life of Spinoza* (London, 1998), pp. 215–16); Koerbagh himself had discussions with a Socinian Collegiant, Jan Knol (A. Fix, *Prophecy and Reason: The Dutch Collegiants in the Early Enlightenment* (Princeton, NJ, 1991), pp. 146–7). On the Socinian character of the central tenets of the Koerbagh brothers, see Israel, *Radical Enlightenment*, pp. 188–92. Koerbagh may thus furnish another example of the positive reception of Hobbes by radical religion, rather than radical irreligion: cf. my comments on Cunradus in 'The Printing of the Bear', Ch. 11 above, pp. 372–80.

[107] See van Moerkerken, *Adriaan Koerbagh*, pp. 63–72; Gullan-Whur, *Within Reason*, pp. 216–20; Israel, *Radical Enlightenment*, pp. 194–6.

[108] F. W. Stosch, *Concordia rationis et fidei*, ed. W. Schröder (Stuttgart, 1992), 'Einleitung', pp. 10–13; see also G. Stiehler, 'Friedrich Wilhelm Stosch', in G. Stiehler, ed., *Beiträge zur Geschichte des vormarxistischen Materialismus* (Berlin, 1961), pp. 139–63, esp. p. 158.

probably the most important influence on Stosch, his book also made repeated references to Hobbes, whose works he had evidently read with some care. He cited *De cive* and *De homine*; in support of his argument that angels and demons were imaginary he directed readers to *Leviathan*; he recommended Hobbes's analysis of the passions; and on the non-original nature of the biblical text he also referred his readers to Hobbes's arguments in *Leviathan*.[109]

Writers such as Koerbagh and Stosch may have had essentially theological motives and intentions, even though the nature of their theology placed them far beyond the bounds of contemporary orthodoxy. Other radical writers, however, were developing a much more straightforwardly anti-theological position. From the late seventeenth century onwards a clandestine literature began to develop of manuscript treatises—mostly anonymous—attacking the very basis of Christianity.[110] Often an element of theology was present, whether pantheist, deist, or Epicurean; but the main purpose of these treatises was not to preach a new faith but to undermine an old one. The most typical writers and readers of such materials seem to have been coffee-house intellectuals, disaffected priests, or sceptical aristocrats. Although a few distinguished scholars contributed to the genre (Nicolas Fréret, for instance), the intellectual level was generally quite low; many of the texts simply re-worked a common stock of ideas, derived from a very eclectic mixture of secondary works (such as Bayle's *Dictionnaire*), second-rank writers (such as Guillaume Lamy), and the occasional major philosopher (Spinoza being the leading example). Given the nature of such material, the task of identifying particular sources or influences is a peculiarly difficult one. A reference to *Leviathan* might indicate that the author had read that work, but it might well have been copied from some other clandestine text, or taken from the orthodox anti-Hobbesian literature; similarly, the appearance of a Hobbesian argument might be a sign of direct knowledge, or it might have come via knowledge (itself direct or indirect) of a writer influenced by Hobbes, such as Toland, or Collins, or indeed Spinoza himself.

According to some modern scholars, Hobbes's influence on this clandestine literature was very slight. John Spink, for example, has claimed that *Leviathan*'s approach to the Bible left almost no trace on French writings, whether clandestine or open; Aram Vartanian has observed that, because of his unacceptable absolutism, Hobbes was rarely invoked by the underground writers; likewise, Jonathan Israel has argued that Hobbes's well-known support for absolutism and established authority 'prevented' him from serving as a major stimulus to radical

---

[109] Stosch, *Concordia*, pp. 8, 21, 99–100, 117.
[110] See the classic study by Ira O. Wade, *The Clandestine Organization and Diffusion of Philosophic Ideas in France from 1700 to 1750* (Princeton, NJ, 1938); for a valuable listing of manuscripts and a survey of more recent research, see also M. Benítez, *La Face cachée des Lumières: recherches sur les manuscrits philosophiques clandestins de l'âge classique* (Oxford, 1996), pp. 20–124.

thought.[111] It is true that reliable signs of direct knowledge of Hobbes are infrequent in this underground literature, and that some of the best-known authors, such as the provincial priest Jean Meslier, had evidently never read anything by him (apart from one key passage about the identity of body and substance, which Meslier found discussed in a work by Louis La Forge, an anti-Hobbesian Cartesian).[112] It is also true that there does not seem to have been much 'underground' circulation of manuscript copies of Hobbes's own texts—though the simple explanation of this must be that the most important texts were widely available in print.[113] But Hobbes's notoriety as a radical critic of clerical power and as a subverter of Christian theology was just too great to be ignored. His works were read by the leading collectors and promoters of underground literature—men such as Prince Eugene of Savoy, who owned a copy of *Leviathan*, and his right-hand man and fellow bibliophile Baron Hohendorf, who had the 1670 *Leviathan* and the 1668 *Opera philosophica*.[114] In the circles of Grub Street journalists, hack-working scholars, and coffee-house debaters among whom much of this literature was produced and circulated, there were many with Hobbesian interests—the circle of Prosper Marchand, Caspar Fritsch, Rousset de Missy, and de La Barre de Beaumarchais (from which, as noted above, two separate Hobbesian publishing

---

[111] J. S. Spink, *French Free-Thought from Gassendi to Voltaire* (London, 1969), p. 289; A. Vartanian, 'Quelques réflexions sur le concept d'âme dans la littérature clandestine', in O. Bloch, ed., *Le Matérialisme du XVIII*ᵉ *siècle et la littérature clandestine* (Paris, 1982), pp. 149–63, here p. 162; Israel, *Radical Enlightenment*, p. 603 (on which claim, see my comment below, p. 536).

[112] On this indirect debt see O. Bloch, 'Hobbes et le matérialisme des Lumières', in A. Napoli and G. Canziani, eds., *Hobbes oggi* (Milan, 1990), pp. 553–76, here p. 558. (For the passage, discussed by La Forge, see below, at n. 155) On Meslier, see G. Mori, 'L'ateismo "malebranchiano" di Meslier: fisica e metafisica della materia', in G. Canziani, ed., *Filosofia e religione nella letteratura clandestina: secoli XVII e XVIII* (Milan, 1994), pp. 123–60, here p. 125 (noting that Hobbes was not mentioned by him, and that Meslier had never read Spinoza either).

[113] The one work that may have had some underground circulation was Hobbes's powerfully anticlerical *Historia ecclesiastica*, which, published in England in 1688, had never received a continental printing. Two continental manuscripts are known: the Royal Library, Copenhagen, MS Thott 213 4°, and the Stiftung Fürst Liechtenstein, Vienna, MS N-7-6 (where it is bound with a transcript of a popular 'underground' text, the anti-Trinitarian *De trinitatis erroribus* by Michael Servetus). The Copenhagen manuscript was transcribed from a manuscript in London in 1685 by Georg Grund, a German (from Stade: see W. Hillebrand, ed., *Die Matrikel der Universität Helmstedt, 1636–1685* (Hildesheim, 1981), p. 221), who later entered the service of the Danish crown, becoming Danish envoy to Peter the Great in 1705. (For details of his career see R. Aerebo, *Autobiografi (1685–1744)*, ed. G. L. Grove (Copenhagen, 1889), pp. 102–3, and G. L. Grove, ed., *Des Kgl. Dänischen Envoyé Georg Grund's Bericht über Russland in den Jahren 1705–1710*, Zapiski imperatorskoi akademii nauk, ser. 8, vol. 4, no. 7 (St Petersburg, 1900), p. v.) The manuscript may have passed directly from Grund's estate (he died in Denmark in 1729) to the voracious collector Otto Thott (1703–85); on Thott's death it was bequeathed to the Royal Library (see the entry on Thott in the *Dansk biografisk leksikon*, 3rd edn, 16 vols. (Copenhagen, 1979–84), XIV, pp. 558–60, and K. Bogh, *Det Kongelige Bibliothek gennem 300 år* (Copenhagen, 1980), pp. 7–8). The provenance of the Vienna manuscript is unknown; it is a copy of the 1688 London edn, reproducing even its title page. (I am very grateful to Dr Evelin Oberhammer, of the Stiftung Fürst Liechtenstein, for providing a copy of this manuscript.)

[114] G. Canziani and G. Paganini, eds., *Theophrastus redivivus*, 2 vols. (Florence, 1981), I, p. c (Eugene); *Bibliotheca hohendorfiana, ou catalogue de la bibliotheque de feu Monsieur George Guillaume Baron de Hohendorf*, 3 vols. (The Hague, 1720), II, p. 25.

projects may have arisen) being a striking example. Hobbes's support for monarchical absolutism was not, after all, such an insuperable problem: as Margaret Jacob has pointed out, 'The radicals simply stripped Hobbes of his royalism ... it was his materialism, and in particular its implications for established religion and churches that most delighted his radical readers.'[115] To some extent, Hobbes even became a totem-figure, a name to be invoked for the purpose of conjuring up both intellectual authority and sheer notoriety. Thus one clandestine treatise was entitled 'La Foi anéantie, ou Demonstration de la fausseté des faits principaux qui sont contenus dans les deux Testamens. Ouvrage traduit du latin de Hobbes' ('Faith annihilated, or a demonstration of the falsity of the main facts contained in the two Testaments: a work translated from Hobbes's Latin'); another treatise, apparently inspired by the second part of that work, was called 'Notes de Hobbes sur le Nouveau Testament' ('Hobbes's notes on the New Testament').[116] And in the case of another such tract, the 'Cymbalum mundi' or 'Symbolum sapientiae', the two copies owned by Prince Eugene were listed in his library catalogue as follows: 'A creed of wisdom, with a treatise on the origin of good and evil, from the teachings of Hobbes', and 'A creed of Hobbesian wisdom'.[117]

Such Hobbesian attributions or ascriptions were spurious, of course; but in some cases an element of Hobbesian argumentation was present. The main aim of the treatise entitled 'La Foi anéantie', for example, was to apply the principles of biblical criticism that Hobbes had set out in chapter 37 of *Leviathan*, using anachronisms and inconsistencies to demonstrate that the Scriptures were historical and human artefacts: the conclusion of the first part of that treatise announced that it had proved 'that the Old Testament is a purely human work'.[118] Traces of Hobbesian influence have been found in the 'Cymbalum mundi' too: a possible borrowing from *De cive*, and a passage asserting that men can have no idea of God, as all human 'ideas' are of corporeal things only.[119] Another such treatise, 'L'Âme matérielle', included Hobbes in its listing of distinguished thinkers who had denied the incorporeality and immortality of the soul; it also invoked, indirectly, both Hobbes's ridicule in *Leviathan* of the term 'incorporeal substance' and his argument in *De corpore* against the Cartesian separation of 'thought' and 'extension' (its source in each case being not Hobbes's text, but the discussion of it by

---

[115] Jacob, *Radical Enlightenment*, p. 76.
[116] Bibliothèque Mazarine, Paris, MS 1189; Bibliothèque Municipale de Rouen, MS M 74. See Wade, *Clandestine Organization*, pp. 181–2, 298, 309.
[117] G. Canziani, 'Critica della religione e fonti moderne nel *Cymbalum mundi* o *Symbolum sapientiae*: prime note di lettura', in G. Canziani, ed., *Filosofia e religione nella letteratura clandestina: secoli XVII e XVIII* (Milan, 1994), pp. 35–81, here p. 37(n.) ('Symbolum sapientiae, cui accedit tractatus de Boni et mali origine ex Hobbesii doctrina'; 'Symbolum sapientiae hobbesianae').
[118] Bibliothèque Mazarine, Paris, MS 1189, p. 171: 'que le vieux testament est un ouvrage purement humain'.
[119] See Canziani, 'Critica della religione', pp. 46, 77.

Cartesian Louis La Forge).[120] Another tract, 'Opinions des anciens sur la nature de l'âme', has nominalist elements which may have been drawn, at second hand, from Hobbes.[121] And the popular anti-Christian treatise by Nicolas Fréret, the 'Lettre de Thrasybule à Leucippe', contains several passages about the psychological origins of religion which must have been derived, directly or indirectly, from *Leviathan*.[122]

In two important cases, however, the debt to Hobbes is strong, direct, and of central importance to the works' arguments. The first is the treatise 'De tribus impostoribus' or 'De imposturis religionum', which became one of the most widely distributed works of the European literary underground during the eighteenth century, with more than seventy copies having been recorded in collections in Germany, Austria, Italy, France, England, Holland, Denmark, and Russia.[123] The treatise had a curious pre-history, being famous long before it was actually written; rumours of the existence of such a work—an exposure of Moses, Mohammed, and Jesus as 'impostors'—circulated widely in the sixteenth and seventeenth centuries, but recent research by Winfried Schröder has shown that the text we now have was written only in 1688, by Johann Joachim Müller, a somewhat obscure Hamburg intellectual. Müller's previous publications (a handful of minor academic dissertations) displayed an unusually detailed knowledge of Hobbes's writings, with references to *De cive*, *Leviathan*, and *De homine*. And in 'De tribus impostoribus', the analysis of religion in chapter 12 of *Leviathan*, attributing it to 'fear of invisible powers', is central to the entire argument: Hobbes's book is thus, as Schröder has noted, 'one of the most important sources of inspiration' of the work.[124]

The second case is that of the most famous and most widely distributed clandestine treatise of all, a work of which at least 169 manuscript copies have been recorded.[125] Its history is unusually complex; several different versions of the

---

[120] A. Niderst, ed., *L'Âme matérielle (ouvrage anonyme)* (Paris, 1973), pp. 42, 48, 150–1. For the La Forge passage, see below, at n. 155.

[121] Benítez, *La Face cachée des Lumières*, p. 340.

[122] N. Fréret, *Lettre de Thrasybule à Leucippe*, ed. S. Landucci (Florence, 1986), pp. 344–5, 346, 358; cf. Landucci's comments on p. 132.

[123] See W. Gericke, 'Die handschriftliche Überlieferung des Buches Von den Drei Betrügern (De Tribus Impostoribus)', *Studien zum Buch- und Bibliothekswesen*, 6 (1988), pp. 5–28; 9 (1995), pp. 37–45; Benítez, *La Face cachée des Lumières*, pp. 29–30. This work is unfortunately omitted from Jonathan Israel's listing of the 22 most popular clandestine manuscripts of the enlightenment (*Radical Enlightenment*, p. 690); the number of surviving copies should make it the third on his list, after the 'Traité des trois imposteurs' and Bodin's 'Colloquium heptaplomeres'.

[124] J. J. Müller, *De imposturis religionum (De tribus impostoribus); Von den Betrügereyen der Religionen*, ed. W. Schröder (Stuttgart, 1999), pp. 40–66, here p. 58 ('eine der wichtigsten Inspirationsquellen'). Müller cites Hobbes's phrase (p. 103: 'metu invisibilium potentium'; cf. references to 'invisibiles potentiae' on pp. 106, 109, 112); he also shows knowledge of *De cive* (p. 104) and makes use of other arguments drawn from *Leviathan*, ch. 12 (pp. 116–17).

[125] M. Benítez, 'Une Histoire interminable: origine et développement du *Traité des Trois Imposteurs*', in S. Berti, F. Charles-Daubert, and R. H. Popkin, eds., *Heterodoxy, Spinozism, and Free Thought in Early Eighteenth-Century Europe: Studies on the* Traité des Trois Imposteurs (Dordrecht, 1996), pp. 53–74; here p. 54.

text emerged at different times, under different titles. The earliest version, a short treatise on religion, was entitled 'L'Esprit de Monsieur de Spinosa', and was probably written in the 1680s. By 1704, or possibly as early as 1700, a slightly altered version of this text was being presented as the long sought-after treatise on the 'three impostors', with some copies bearing the title 'Traité des trois imposteurs'. In the second decade of the eighteenth century two main versions emerged: a short one, in six chapters, entitled 'Le Fameux Livre des trois imposteurs', and a long one, in twenty-one chapters, which was printed under the title *La Vie et l'esprit de M<sup>r</sup> Benoît de Spinosa*. And another edition, based on an early six-chapter version and entitled *Traité des trois imposteurs*, was printed in 1768.[126] As its earliest title indicated, this work was primarily Spinozist in its inspiration; its original author may have been the physician Jean Maximilien Lucas, who is credited with having written one of the earliest biographies of Spinoza. But it also borrowed directly and extensively from Hobbes. Once again, chapter 12 of *Leviathan*—Hobbes's discussion of the origins of religion in human psychology—was a major influence. Large parts of the third chapter of the original 'L'Esprit de Monsieur de Spinosa' consisted of passages translated from that chapter of the Latin *Leviathan*, discussing the origin of religion in human fear, the epistemological confusion that led primitive man to invent the concept of 'spirits', the absurdity of pagan religion, and the manipulation of popular psychology by priests. Also important was chapter 45 of Hobbes's work, on those pagan ideas about demons and spirits that were passed on to Christianity: again, the sixth chapter of the treatise consisted mainly of passages translated from that part of *Leviathan*, ridiculing traditional demonology.[127] Elsewhere, the anonymous author also drew on other parts of Hobbes's book. Defending the thoroughly non-Spinozan claim that God was corporeal, he copied from the third chapter of the 'Appendix' to the Latin *Leviathan*, in which Hobbes appealed to the authority of Tertullian to show the acceptability of talking about God in that way.[128] And in his opening chapter he copied a passage from *Leviathan*'s chapter 32, in which Hobbes presented one of his most important (and most destructive) arguments: his observation that, when one person claims to have received revelation direct from God, others cannot be under any

---

[126] See the masterly analysis by Françoise Charles-Daubert in the Introduction to her edition, *Le 'Traité des trois imposteurs' et 'L'Esprit de Spinosa': philosophie clandestine entre 1678 et 1768*, ed. F. Charles-Daubert (Oxford, 1999), pp. 1–455 (esp. pp. 5–7, 102-06, 449–55).

[127] See the detailed presentation of the evidence in ibid., pp. 283–7, 362–4.

[128] Ibid., pp. 493–4 ('L'Esprit', II.10: 'Et afin que l'on ne croie point que cette Opinion est nouvelle, Tertulien, l'un des premiers hommes que les Chretiens aient eus, a prononcé contre les Appellés [*sic*] que ce qui n'est point corps n'est rien; et contre Praxeas, que toute Substance est un Corps; sans que cette Doctrine ait été condamnée dans les quatre premiers Conciles Oecuméniques et Généraux'); cf. Hobbes, *Leviathan*, in his *Opera philosophica* (separate pagination), p. 360: 'Affirmat quidem Deum esse Corpus. Sed ante eum idem affirmavit Tertullianus. Disputans enim contra Apellem ... dictum hoc universale pronuntiavit, *Quicquid Corpus non est, non est Ens.* Item contra Praxeam, *Omnis Substantia est Corpus sui generis.* Neque in ullo ex quatuor Conciliis primis generalibus doctrina haec condamnata est.'

divine obligation to accept what he says, as their reasons for credence could only be human, not divine.[129]

The presence of Hobbesian material in this text is in fact more pervasive than any of its modern editors or commentators have realized.[130] Thanks to the enormous popularity of this treatise (in its various forms), some of Hobbes's most radical ideas about the nature of religion were thus propagated throughout Europe. Many readers, no doubt, were quite unaware that they were reading passages lifted from *Leviathan*; but the debt was evident enough to the anonymous preparer of the 1768 printed edition, who added several footnotes giving page references to Hobbes's text.[131]

Both directly and indirectly, therefore, knowledge of some of Hobbes's theories were available to the radical thinkers of the early- and mid-eighteenth century. Pietro Giannone, for example, who fled to Vienna in 1723 and was able to steep himself there in the rich collection of heterodox literature in Prince Eugene's library, acquired a good knowledge of *Leviathan*, as well as of other writings (such as Toland's) that were influenced by Hobbes's anti-clerical and more or less anti-theological views.[132] Hobbes's most important contribution, for the purposes of the radically inclined Enlightenment philosophers, was his epistemological and psychological account of the origins of religion, which he located in two closely related principles: ignorance of causes, and fear of unknown powers. This Hobbesian analysis (fortified, naturally, by arguments from other writers such as Naudé, La Mothe le Vayer, Spinoza, and Toland) played an important part in the radical theories about religion and priestcraft developed by d'Holbach and other members of his circle, such as the eccentric theorist of 'oriental despotism',

---

[129] *Le 'Traité des trois imposteurs'*, p. 485 ('L'Esprit', I.5: 'Supposez même que Dieu se fist entendre à quelqu'un par les Songes, par les Visions, ou par quelqu'autre voie; Personne neanmoins n'est obligé de croire un homme qui peut errer, et qui pis est, qui est sujet à mentir'); cf. Hobbes, *Leviathan*, in his *Opera philosophica* (separate pagination), p. 174: 'Quanquam autem in Somnio, in Visione, per Vocem, & per Inspirationem hominem alloqui potest Deus omnipotens, dicenti tamen Deum sibi ita loquutum esse, credere obligatur nemo, homini scilicet qui & errare, & (quod pejus est) mentiri potest.'

[130] Charles-Daubert, for example, ignores the two borrowings just mentioned, and suggests that the author's knowledge of *Leviathan* was confined to chs. 11, 12 and 45 (*Le 'Traité des trois imposteurs'*, pp. 293, 362). She also observes (pp. 250–1) that the author makes no use of Hobbes's political theory, concentrating only on his comments on religion; but the treatise the author was writing was, after all, about religion, not the theory of the state. Jonathan Israel, emphasizing the Spinozan character of the work, writes that 'the borrowings from Hobbes . . . are actually used only to illustrate Spinozistic arguments and do not substantially influence the systematically mechanistic, deterministic, materialist, and non-providential principles on which the work is uncompromisingly based' (*Radical Enlightenment*, pp. 697–8). Yet mechanism, determinism, materialism and non-providentialism were all principles associated with Hobbes too—indeed, materialism was a principle of Hobbes, of radical 'Hobbism', and of some forms of radical 'Spinozism', but it was not a principle of Spinoza's own philosophy.

[131] *Le 'Traité des trois imposteurs'*, pp. 726–8, 733.

[132] See Ricuperati, *L'esperienza civile*, pp. 574, 610–11 (noting Giannone's debt to Hobbes in his theory of natural law and the division of temporal from spiritual); L. Mannarino, 'Pietro Giannone e la letteratura "empia"', *Annali dell'istituto di filosofia dell'Università di Firenze, facoltà di lettere e filosofia*, 2 (1980), pp. 195–241, esp. p. 196.

Nicolas-Antoine Boulanger.[133] D'Holbach's enthusiasm for Hobbes even led him, as we have seen, to produce a translation of *Humane Nature* (the first part of *The Elements of Law*). And it was probably thanks to him that another radical thinker of the French Enlightenment, Claude-Adrien Helvétius, acquired much of his knowledge of Hobbes: Helvétius made a careful study of *Humane Nature*, and plagiarized an entire passage from its dedicatory epistle.[134] Otherwise, however, the *philosophes* were surprisingly slow to latch on to Hobbes's works—even those of them, such as La Mettrie, who were developing a materialistic and deterministic psychology with strong affinities to Hobbes's own position. Strangely, La Mettrie seems to have had no direct knowledge of Hobbes's works when he wrote his *Histoire naturelle de l'âme* (1745) and *L'Homme machine* (1747); he did refer to Hobbes in some of his later writings, but it was the moral and political theory that concerned him there. (The only Hobbes items in his library, it appears, were Sorbière's translation of *De cive* and *Le Corps politique*, the anonymous translation of the second half of *The Elements of Law*.[135]) Similarly, Voltaire's direct knowledge of Hobbes seems to have been confined to *De cive*, of which he had a copy of the 1696 edition; although he read English with ease, there is no sign of his reading anything by Hobbes in that language, and one can only speculate as to the intense pleasure he would have gained from the fourth part of *Leviathan*, with its scathing attack on superstition and clerical power. Accused by some of his own critics of Hobbesian atheism and 'Hobbism' more generally, he took a sympathetic interest in Hobbes, defending him from the charge of atheism; but his knowledge was largely second-hand, depending heavily on Diderot's article 'Hobbisme' in the *Encyclopédie*.[136]

---

[133] See A. Minerbi Belgrado, *Paura e ignoranza: studio sulla teoria della religione in d'Holbach* (Florence, 1983), esp. pp. 57, 73, 106–18, 183–6; on d'Holbach's interest in Hobbes more generally see P. Naville, *D'Holbach et la philosophie scientifique au XVIII<sup>e</sup> siècle*, 2nd edn (Paris, 1967), pp. 218–24. On Boulanger see also J. Hampton, *Nicolas-Antoine Boulanger et la science de son temps* (Geneva, 1958), and P. Sadrin, *Nicolas-Antoine Boulanger (1722–1759), ou avant nous le déluge* (Oxford, 1986).

[134] Glaziou, *Hobbes en France*, pp. 184–98 (p. 195: plagiarism). Even before d'Holbach obtained the text of *Humane Nature*, Helvétius had exhibited traces of Hobbesian influence in the psychological theory of his *De l'Esprit* (1758): the official condemnation of that book by the Sorbonne in 1759 named Hobbes as one of his sources (ibid., pp. 186–9, 196(n.) ), though his knowledge at that stage may well have been indirect only.

[135] See A. Vartanian, *La Mettrie's 'Homme machine': A Study in the Origins of an Idea* (Princeton, NJ, 1960), p. 65; A. Thomson, *Materialism and Society in the Mid-Eighteenth Century: La Mettrie's Discours Préliminaire* (Geneva, 1981), pp. 148–55. Similarly, Vartanian comments elsewhere on the 'secondary, even peripheral' role of Hobbes as an influence on the materialism of Diderot's circle: *Diderot and Descartes: A Study of Scientific Naturalism in the Enlightenment* (Princeton, NJ, 1953), p. 294.

[136] See L. J. Thielemann, 'Voltaire and Hobbism', *Studies on Voltaire and the Eighteenth Century*, 10 (1959), pp. 237–58; for accusations of Hobbism see ibid., p. 255, and R. R. Palmer, *Catholics and Unbelievers in Eighteenth-Century France* (Princeton, NJ, 1939), p. 219. On Voltaire's library, see the two articles by G. R. Havens and N. L. Torrey, 'The Private Library of Voltaire at Leningrad', *Publications of the Modern Language Association of America*, 43 (1928), pp. 990–1009, and 'Voltaire's Books: A Selected List', *Modern Philology*, 27 (1929), pp. 1–22 (p. 11: *De cive*). For a useful survey of Voltaire's comments on Hobbes, see Glaziou, *Hobbes en France*, pp. 106–18.

This article, published in 1765, also contained a great deal of second-hand material: most of Diderot's information was drawn from the long and detailed entry on Hobbes in Jakob Brucker's *Historia critica philosophiae*. Brucker defended Hobbes from the worst charges laid against him—above all, that of 'direct atheism'—but presented many of the standard criticisms, and gave some of them his endorsement; Diderot, though himself a critic of some aspects of Hobbes's political theory (especially in his articles 'Citoyen' and 'Droit naturel'), presented a more sympathetic account in his 'Hobbisme' article, omitting many of Brucker's criticisms and concluding that Hobbes was a 'penetrating and profound' thinker.[137] Only seven years later did Diderot engage directly and fully with a work by Hobbes, when he received a copy of d'Holbach's translation of the first part of *The Elements of Law*.[138] It made a strong impression on him: 'How vague and cowardly Locke seems, and how poor and petty La Bruyère and La Rochefoucauld, in comparison with this Thomas Hobbes!' he exclaimed. 'This is a book to read and comment on all one's life.'[139] Yet, as those comparisons suggest, what he admired in Hobbes was the style of psychological analysis and the way in which such analysis was used to construct a theory of natural law and social organization. This was not the 'radical' Hobbes of the anti-Christian underground, but a Hobbes contributing to a well established tradition of debate about the origins of society and government. Curiously, therefore, it seems that the radical philosophers of the French Enlightenment were interested mainly in the non-radical aspects of Hobbes. The underground literature may have continued to propagate elements of radical Hobbism (usually without his name attached); but in above-ground publications the idea that Hobbes was a rampant atheist, an anti-Christian, and a dangerous subverter of morality was kept alive much more by the campaigners for orthodoxy, who ritually denounced him, than by any of the 'radical' *philosophes*, who came to his defence.

One episode may suffice to illustrate this odd state of affairs. In November 1751 a young priest, Jean-Martin de Prades, defended a thesis before the Faculty of Theology at the Sorbonne. Drawing on the arguments of the famous 'Discours préliminaire' to the *Encyclopédie*, he began the opening section of his thesis with an account of man in a state of nature, and described how the need to escape from conflict would lead to the acceptance of natural law and the establishment of civil

---

[137] Brucker, *Historia critica*, IV, part 2, pp. 145–99 (p. 174: indirect, not direct, atheism); D. Diderot, 'Hobbisme', in T. Hobbes, *Le Citoyen, ou les fondements de la politique*, tr. S. Sorbière, ed. S. Goyard-Fabre (Paris, 1982), pp. 379–405; E. Vitale, 'La lettura diderotiana di Hobbes nell'*Encyclopédie*', *Il pensiero politico: rivista di storia delle idee politiche e sociali*, 28 (1995), pp. 384–406.

[138] Diderot appears to have read some parts of Sorbière's translation of *De cive* in 1747 (see J. Proust, *Diderot et l'Encyclopédie*, 3rd edn. (Paris, 1982), p. 343); but the impact made by d'Holbach's translation of *Humane Nature* in 1772 suggests that his earlier experience of Hobbes can only have been quite superficial.

[139] L. J. Thielemann, 'Diderot and Hobbes', in *Diderot Studies II*, ed. O. E. Fellows and N. L. Torrey (Syracuse, NY, 1952), pp. 221–78; here p. 230 ('Que Locke me paraît lache et diffus, La Bruyère et La Rochefoucauld pauvres et petits en comparaison avec ce Thomas Hobbes! . . . C'est un livre à lire et à commenter toute sa vie').

society.[140] The thesis was passed by the Faculty; but within three months it had been condemned by two bishops, the Parlement de Paris, the Archbishop of Paris, and the Pope. A storm of hostile publications was unleashed, many of which accused de Prades directly of 'Hobbism'. Charles-Gabriel de Caylus, bishop of Auxerre, wrote that de Prades's ideas came from England: 'These pernicious writings have been eagerly sought out, and avidly read; people have drunk from the poisoned cup, and the impiety they have breathed out has spread among us like gangrene.' Another writer, the Abbé Duhamel, declared that de Prades's ideas represented 'the opinions of Hobbes, that great leader of the impious'; the Abbé Brotier, likewise, noted that de Prades was a follower of 'that atrabilious Englishman'.[141] In the unapologetic 'Apologie' which he subsequently published, de Prades firmly rejected these accusations. 'I wanted to set up my arguments against Hobbes's system,' he explained; 'for that purpose I had to consider, as that author did, man in the state of nature.' While they both agreed that human selfishness would inevitably lead to conflict in that state, there was, according to de Prades, a fundamental difference between them: Hobbes accepted that victorious Might in such a conflict conferred Right, while de Prades did not.[142] Even though de Prades's interpretation of Hobbes was defective, his sincerity here can hardly be doubted; the rest of his thesis displayed, in places, a remarkable intellectual conservatism, defending the entire Mosaicity of the Pentateuch (against Hobbes, La Peyrère and Spinoza), for example, or criticizing Descartes, Clarke, and Malebranche for failing to offer sufficiently strong arguments against 'les Matérialistes'.[143]

The fact that a serious attempt to argue against Hobbes had to be based partly on the acceptance of some Hobbesian premisses is in itself noteworthy; but the most significant aspect of the 'de Prades affair' is the contrast between this critical engagement with Hobbes and the reflex hostility of de Prades's denouncers, who thought that any reference to a state of nature was Hobbist and therefore pernicious. The point was made with considerable glee by Diderot, who entered the fray in defence of de Prades: these ignorant clerics, he observed, were unaware that the field of argument traversed here by de Prades was one that had been occupied, without danger to Christian faith, by mainstream theorists for many years.[144] One could not wish for a neater vignette to illustrate the way in which Hobbesian radicalism might persist in the minds of the orthodox, while writers who had genuinely

---

[140] J.-M. de Prades, *Thèse soutenue en Sorbonne le 18 novembre 1751* (Amsterdam, n.d. [1753]), pp. 4–6.

[141] See Thielemann, 'Diderot and Hobbes', pp. 225 ('Ces pernicieux écrits ont été recherchés avec empressement, & lûs avec avidité: on a bû dans la coupe empoisonnée; & l'impiété qu'ils exhalent, a gagné parmi nous comme la gangrène'), 227 ('le sentiment de Hobbes, ce grand chef des impies'; 'cet Anglois atrabiliaire').

[142] J.-M. de Prades, *Apologie*, 2 vols. (Amsterdam, 1753), II, pp. 28 ('Je voulois m'élever contre le système de Hobbes: pour cela je devois considérer avec cet Auteur, l'Homme dans l'état de Nature'), 29.

[143] de Prades, *Thèse*, pp. 20–2, 10.

[144] See Thielemann, 'Diderot and Hobbes', esp. pp. 224–6.

radical sympathies, such as Diderot, were able to situate Hobbes—with some justification—in the mainstream. It is to the rich and varied tradition of mainstream discussions of Hobbes that we should now turn.

## VI

Hobbes was first presented to the European Republic of Letters not as a political theorist but as a metaphysician, when Mersenne published his 'Objections' to Descartes's *Meditations* in 1641. He also appeared as a writer on metaphysics, physics, and optics in other Mersenne publications of the 1640s, which had a much wider circulation than the privately distributed 1642 *De cive*; indeed, for most of his stay in Paris Hobbes was engrossed in those topics rather than political theory. The circles of French intellectuals in which he moved were interested primarily in those aspects of his work; Sorbière even told one correspondent that he had organized the 1647 publication of Hobbes's *De cive* merely 'to elicit from that admirable man what he has promised to send us on the subject of *nature*'.[145] Some European scholars would have thought of him primarily as a writer on natural philosophy: the German scientist Joachim Jungius, for example, first learned of Hobbes's work in 1645 from Sir Charles Cavendish, who sent him details of Hobbes's theory of motion.[146] After Hobbes's departure from Paris, the key members of his circle of admirers (Sorbière, Abraham du Prat, Charles du Bosc, Thomas de Martel, François de La Mothe le Vayer) clustered around Gassendi, who returned to the capital in 1653 and stayed with the wealthy patron Henri Louis Habert de Montmor until his death in 1655. Later, regular scientific gatherings were held in de Montmor's house: Hobbes's theories were the object of respectful discussion there, both directly and—given Sorbière's tendency to plagiarize from him—indirectly too.[147] Similar gatherings organized by Pierre Bourdelot (with a membership overlapping that of the de Montmor assemblies) also discussed Hobbes's work.[148]

---

[145] BN, MS f.l. 10352, part 1, fol. 112r, Sorbière to Thomas Bartholinus, 1 Feb. 1647: 'vt eliceremus quae Vir ille admirandus circa Naturam mittere pollicitus est'.

[146] Staats- und Universitätsbibliothek, Hamburg, MS Pe. 1a (= Sup. ep. 97), no. 85, Cavendish to Jungius, 11 May 1645 (printed in C. von Brockdorff, *Des Sir Charles Cavendish Bericht für Joachim Jungius über die Grundzüge der Hobbes'schen Naturphilosophie* (Kiel, 1934), pp. 2–4). Jungius did also make a careful study of *De cive*: his notes on chapters 16–18, entitled 'Hobbii theologia', are in MS Pe 47b, item 18, fols. 239–49, and on chs. 2–3, 6–8, 14, entitled 'Hobbii politica', are in ibid., item 19, fols. 250–65. But these notes contain only extracts and summaries, not comments or objections.

[147] See H. Brown, *Scientific Organizations in Seventeenth Century France (1620–1680)* (New York, 1934), pp. 64–90. Sorbière set out the rules of the de Montmor academy in a letter to Hobbes in 1658 (Hobbes, *Correspondence*, I, pp. 491–7; for his account of an earlier discussion of Hobbes's theories among this group, at a dinner in du Bosc's house, see also pp. 433–8). For an example of Sorbière's plagiarism from Hobbes see his *Lettres et discours . . . sur diverses matieres curieuses* (Paris, 1660), pp. 714–17.

[148] P. Le Gallois, *Conversations de l'académie de Monsieur l'abbé Bourdelot* (Paris, 1672), p. 62.

There was thus a solid basis for a positive reception of Hobbesian philosophy in French intellectual life—a basis consisting mainly of people associated with Gassendi, who had known Hobbes well and who, according to Sorbière, had received a copy of *De corpore* on his deathbed, greeting it with a kiss.[149] Despite the differences between the plenist physics of that book and the Epicurean atomism of Gassendi himself, the affinities between the two writers were clear—above all, in their hostility to Cartesianism, expressed in very similar terms in their 'Objections' to the *Meditations*. Gassendism (an important, though still somewhat neglected, influence on French intellectual life in the second half of the century) was thus a habitat in which Hobbesian sympathies could also flourish.[150] Indeed, it may have served to some extent as a substitute for Hobbesianism: while Hobbes was suspect as a Protestant free-thinker, Gassendi was a pious Catholic priest whose works (unlike those of Descartes, incidentally) were never placed on the Church's index of prohibited books.[151]

However, outside the immediate circle of Hobbes's friends and admirers, his reputation as a writer on non-political and non-theological matters was in something of a decline from the mid-1650s onwards. The publication of *De corpore* contributed to this, for more than one reason. The world-view it presented, which might have seemed adventurous and challenging had it appeared in 1640, was much less novel in the mid-1650s; and Hobbes's botched mathematical demonstrations helped to deflate his reputation among continental scientists. The critical book published by Moranus in Brussels before the end of 1655, which included disproofs of Hobbes's mathematics by André Tacquet, may have had some effect, as did the circulation of John Wallis's *Elenchus geometriae hobbianae*.[152] But competent mathematicians could, in any case, make up their own minds: Christiaan Huygens wrote in 1661 that 'Mr Hobbes lost all credit with me, in matters of geometry, a long time ago,' and René-François de Sluse was filled with dismay by the blundering demonstrations forwarded to him by Sorbière.[153] Referring to Hobbes's defective geometry became—as Wallis had intended from the start—a convenient device for discrediting Hobbes's philosophy more generally: the only explicit reference to Hobbes in the entire oeuvre of Nicolas Malebranche, for example, was a comment on the absurdity of Hobbes's claim (in his publication of 1666, *De*

---

[149] S. Sorbière, Preface to P. Gassendi, *Opera omnia*, 6 vols. (Lyon, 1658), I, sig. 5*2r.

[150] On Gassendism see S. Murr, ed., *Bernier et les Gassendistes*, 'Corpus', no. 20/21 (Paris, 1992); T. M. Lennon, *The Battle of the Gods and the Giants: The Legacies of Descartes and Gassendi, 1655–1715* (Princeton, NJ, 1993); S. Murr, ed., *Gassendi et l'Europe, 1592–1792* (Paris, 1997).

[151] Descartes's works were placed on the index in 1663, 'until they are corrected' ('donec corrigantur'): for the text of the decree see *Index librorum prohibitorum Alexandri VII*, p. 396.

[152] G. Moranus, *Animadversiones in elementorum philosophiae sectionem I. De corpore, editam a Thoma Hobbes Anglo Malmesburiensi Londini 1655* (Brussels, 1655); Tacquet's objections are on pp. 13–29.

[153] C. Huygens, *Oeuvres complètes*, 22 vols. (The Hague, 1888–1950), III, p. 384 ('il y a longtemps qu'en matiere de Geometrie M. Hobbes a perdu tout credit aupres de moy'); Bibliothèque Nationale, Paris, MS f.l. 10352, part 2, fol. 180v, de Sluse to Sorbière, 28 January 1664.

*principiis et ratiocinatione geometrarum*) that the existing science of geometry was full of errors.[154]

The steady advance of Cartesianism, from the 1650s onwards, also contributed to the marginalization of Hobbes in the area of metaphysics and natural philosophy. Descartes's low opinion of Hobbes was well known, not only from his curt replies to Hobbes's 'Objections', but also from the scathing remarks he made about him in his letters to Mersenne in 1641—letters published in 1667 in the third volume of Clerselier's *Lettres de Mr Descartes*. Even before the appearance of that volume, Hobbes was criticized by one leading Cartesian, Louis de La Forge, who treated him as the third in a triumvirate of anti-Cartesian materialists (the others—his principal targets—being Gassendi and Regius). Defending the fundamental Cartesian distinction between the two types of substance, thought and extension, La Forge cited a passage from *De corpore* (against 'separated essences') and offered a refutation of it; he also quoted (in French) a passage from *Leviathan*, though his source was probably Seth Ward's Latin refutation of Hobbes, rather than the original.[155] Nevertheless, despite his complete disagreement with Hobbes, La Forge did regard him as a serious opponent to be argued against; he did not see him as a heretic, atheist, or libertine to be merely exclaimed at and denounced. The same is broadly true of the Jesuit René Rapin, whose philosophical sympathies were primarily Cartesian. In his *Reflexions sur la philosophie ancienne et moderne* (1676) he offered a judgement on *De corpore* that had positive as well as negative elements: 'Thomas Hobbes has displayed great intellectual profundity in his physics; for he is one of the boldest Epicureans of modern times, and follows Epicurus' principles in all things, without compromise. His arguments are mistaken on everything that concerns the understanding and its principal operations.' Overall, he characterized Hobbes as 'obscure in a charmless way; peculiar in his ideas; learned, but not very solid; inconstant in his teaching', but still he included him in his select list of the most prominent modern philosophers (Galileo, Bacon, Hobbes, Boyle, Gassendi, Descartes and van Helmont).[156] Similarly, the Huguenot philosopher Pierre de

---

[154] *De la Recherche de la vérité* (1674), bk. 4, ch. 3, sect. 1, in N. Malebranche, *Oeuvres*, ed. G. Rodis-Lewis, 2 vols. (Paris, 1979–92), I, p. 405.

[155] L. de La Forge, *Traitté de l'esprit de l'homme, de ses facultez et fonctions, et de son union avec le corps, suivant les principes de René Descartes* (Paris, 1666), pp. 46–50 (p. 50: citing Ward's book). On La Forge see P. Mouy, *Le Développement de la physique cartésienne, 1646–1712* (Paris, 1934), pp. 106–8; D. Garber, *Descartes Embodied: Reading Cartesian Philosophy through Cartesian Science* (Cambridge, 2001), pp. 189–91. La Forge was in contact with Clerselier in 1660, and may well have known the anti-Hobbesian letters before they were published: see R. Descartes, *Lettres de Mr Descartes, où sont traittées les plus belles questions de la morale, de la physique, de la médecine, & des mathématiques*, 3 vols (Paris, 1657–67), III, pp. 640–6.

[156] [R. Rapin,] *Reflexions sur la philosophie ancienne et moderne, et sur l'usage qu'on en doit faire pour la religion* (Paris, 1676), pp. 54 (list), 55 ('obscur sans agrément, singulier en ses idées, sçavant, mais peu solide, inconstant dans sa doctrine'), 194 ('Thomas Hobbes a fait paroistre une grande profondeur d'esprit en sa Physique, comme il est un des plus hardis Epicuriens des derniers siecles & qu'il suit en tout les principes d'Epicure, sans rien ménager: il a mal raisonné en tout ce qui regarde l'entendement & ses operations principales'). Rapin was sometimes critical of Descartes too; but in this book he reserved his highest praise for him.

Villemandy, who made a gradual transition from Aristotelianism to Cartesianism, referred to the text of *De corpore*, categorized Hobbes as an 'Epicurean', and included him in a list of those leading modern thinkers (Ramus, Kepler, Galileo, Bacon, Campanella, Descartes, Hobbes) who were against submission to 'authority' in philosophical matters.[157]

So although Cartesians were aware of the differences between Hobbes and Descartes on questions of metaphysics and natural philosophy, they were able to regard those two thinkers as allies in the larger conflict of 'moderns' against 'ancients'. In the field of political philosophy the alliance could be drawn together more tightly still. Descartes had said extraordinarily little about political matters himself; to some Cartesians, looking for a political theory that would be non-Aristotelian, quasi-deductive, and based on a mechanistic world-view, it seemed that Hobbes provided a ready-made supplement or annexe to the main body of Cartesian philosophy.

One of the first publicists of Cartesianism was the Parisian philosophy teacher Jacques du Roure, who produced a three-volume general philosophical textbook in 1654. Most of the work consisted of a comparative presentation of scholastic and Cartesian theories, systematically favouring the latter. But the last part of the third volume, entitled 'La Morale démontrée' ('Morality demonstrated'), was a barely modified exposition of the political theory of *De cive*. After a brief nod in the direction of theological orthodoxy (a chapter on man's duties towards God, preceding the discussion of man's duties to other men), he began with an account of the state of nature ('a revolt in which all fight against all'), deduced from it the first law of nature ('to seek to make peace if one can; and, if one cannot, to prepare for war and seek the most advantageous means of defending oneself'), followed this with a listing of fifteen other laws of nature (all taken directly from *De cive*), and concluded that a political sovereign must be formed (by each person 'submitting his will to that of some man or assembly') and that such a sovereign must be absolute.[158] This whole section of du Roure's book—more than fifty pages—was a running summary, and in many places a direct translation, of Hobbes's work. Nor did he conceal his source: he explained at the outset that he had not tried to present his 'demonstration' of morality in a strictly geometrical method, 'because Hobbes and

---

[157] P. de Villemandy, *Manuductio ad philosophiam veterem-novam* (Saumur, 1674), pp. 15, 24–6. On de Villemandy see J. Prost, *La Philosophie protestante à l'Académie protestante de Saumur* (Paris, 1907), esp. pp. 120–6.

[158] J. du Roure, *La Philosophie divisée en toutes ses parties, établie sur des principes évidents*, 3 vols. (Paris, 1654), III, pp. 492 ('une sedition où tous combatent contre tous'), 493 ('tacher à faire la paix si on peut: sinon, de se preparer à la guerre & de rechercher les plus avantageux moyens de se deffendre'), 507 ('soumet sa volonté à celle de quelque homme ou de quelque assemblée'), 518. On du Roure see F. Bouillier, *Histoire de la philosophie cartésienne*, 3rd edn, 2 vols. (Paris, 1868), I, pp. 506–7; G. Canziani, 'Tra Descartes e Hobbes: la morale nel "Système" de Pierre-Sylvain Regis', in A. Napoli and G. Canziani, eds., *Hobbes oggi* (Milan, 1990), pp. 491–552, here pp. 493–5.

Descartes, whose inspiration will easily be recognized in this book, hardly made use of it themselves'.[159] Du Roure's enthusiasm for Hobbes seems to have incurred no criticism, even though *De cive* was placed on the Church's index in the very year of this book's publication. But his interest did not go unnoticed: one year later, Abraham du Prat wrote to Hobbes from Paris that 'The booksellers in this city wanted to pay M. du Roure, who teaches Descartes's philosophy here, to translate your book [sc. *De corpore*].'[160]

Even more remarkable than du Roure's adherence to Hobbes was that of one of the leading Cartesians of the next generation, Pierre-Sylvain Regis. He too wrote a general philosophical textbook in three volumes, the *Système de philosophie*, presenting a discussion of 'morality'—including politics—in its final part. (It was published in 1690 but written, apparently, ten years earlier.[161]) Here too the central arguments of *De cive* were reproduced, virtually unaltered. The starting-point was perpetual war in the state of nature, caused by 'the right to all things which nature has given to each person'. After the fundamental law of nature (to seek peace if it were possible, and to prepare for war if it were not), Regis listed eighteen further natural laws, which he copied, with very minor modifications, from Hobbes.[162] A short section on the passions and the virtues, drawn mainly from Descartes's *Les Passions de l'âme*, was spliced into his account; but it then resumed with a summary (much more detailed than that offered by du Roure) of Hobbes's chapters on the state and its powers, discussing sovereignty, forms of government, the duties of the sovereign, law, injury, and justice.[163] Later in this volume Regis even reproduced some of the arguments of the controversial third part of *De cive*, on religion, when he discussed God's covenant with Abraham, the history of spiritual and temporal power among the Israelites, and the role of Christ. 'It is enough to know that Jesus Christ is the Messiah,' he concluded, and he emphasized that the Kingdom of God 'will begin only at the second coming of Jesus Christ'.[164]

---

[159] du Roure, *La Philosophie*, III, p. 458 ('par ce qu'Hobbes, & Descartes, don't les lumieres se feront aizément remarquer en cét ouvrage, ne s'en sont presque pas servis').

[160] Hobbes, *Correspondence*, I, pp. 212 ('les libraires de cette ville ont voulu donner de l'argent a M⁻ Roure qui enseigne icy la Philosophie de M⁻ des Cartes [>pour traduire vostre liure]', 214. Cf above, n. 25.

[161] J.-P. Niceron, *Mémoires pour servir à l'histoire des hommes illustres dans la République des lettres*, 44 vols. (Paris, 1727–45), VI, p. 408. On Regis's general philosophical position see Bouillier, *Histoire de la philosophie*, I, pp. 517–27; Mouy, *Le Développement de la physique*, pp. 145–67. On his political theory and indebtedness to Hobbes see I. M. Wilson, *The Influence of Hobbes and Locke in the Shaping of the Concept of Sovereignty in Eighteenth Century France* (Banbury, 1973), pp. 58–60; B. Tocanne, *L'Idée de nature en France dans la seconde moitié du XVII⁻ siècle: contribution à l'histoire de la pensée classique* (Paris, 1978), pp. 194–6; and (the fullest study) Canziani, 'Tra Descartes e Hobbes'.

[162] P.-S. Regis, *Système de philosophie*, 3 vols. (Paris, 1690), III, pp. 412 ('le droit que la nature a donné à chacun sur toutes choses'; fundamental law of nature), 417–23 (natural laws). He also reproduces Hobbes's definitions of 'gift', 'contract' and 'pact', distinguishing carefully between renouncing and transferring a right (pp. 413–15).

[163] Ibid., III, pp. 435–46 (passions, virtues), 447–76 (sovereignty etc.).

[164] Ibid., III, pp. 494–6 (Abraham), 505–9 (Israelites), 513 ('Il suffit de sçavoir que JESUS-CHRIST est le Messie'; 'ne commencera qu'au second avenement de JESUS-CHRIST').

Elsewhere Regis produced a very Hobbesian list of man's duties towards God: the first was to attribute existence to him, the second to avoid attributing finite characteristics, and so on. The whole structure of natural laws was given a theological basis of a somewhat questionable kind: obeying those laws was a way of honouring the glory of God, he claimed, as it led to the preservation of his creatures. To the obvious question which then arose, whether men should therefore sacrifice themselves for other creatures, Regis replied with the assertion that each person is specially obliged to look after his own preservation.[165] Some element of 'amour-propre' was involved in every human desire and every human action, he observed; the important distinction was between 'amour-propre ignorant', which led to war, and 'amour-propre éclairé' (which might be translated as 'enlightened self-interest'), which led to peace and human fulfilment.[166]

Regis never referred directly to Hobbes, but the mere omission of his name can hardly suffice to explain the fact that Regis's critics never accused him of Hobbism. One opponent, the former professor of theology Jean du Hamel, who wrote an entire volume attacking his work, explained on his final page that he had not said anything about Regis's arguments on 'morality' (i.e. this whole section of his book), because those arguments contained nothing unusual.[167] By putting the underlying argument in terms of *amour-propre*, Regis was able to align himself with a range of more familiar contemporary views, from the political theory of the *libertinage érudit* and the reductive psychology of writers such as La Rochefoucauld to the strong tradition of Augustinianism in both Catholic and Protestant moral theology.

One writer who belonged to the *libertinage érudit*, and who was a devoted Gassendist as well as a Hobbesian, was Samuel Sorbière. His enthusiasm for Hobbes's philosophy emerges from his correspondence and from several of his published writings; his importance in the distribution of Hobbes's works (as organizer of the 1647 *De cive*, translator of it into French in 1649, and facilitator of Blaeu's edition of Hobbes's Latin works in the 1660s) has already been mentioned. He was, however, a somewhat inconstant Hobbesian where the political theory was concerned. When he issued his French translation of *De cive* he praised the work both publicly (in the dedicatory epistle) and privately: writing to Isaac Vossius, he explained that he had been urged to translate it by some French noblemen, and said he had done so willingly because Hobbes was a brilliant defender

---

[165] Ibid., III, pp. 424–6 (duties to God), 431–2 (preservation of creatures and self).
[166] Ibid., III, pp. 404–6 (*amour-propre*), 489, defining fulfilment or 'béatitude' as 'the internal contentment which arises in the soul from making good use of the things that contribute to its preservation' ('le contentement intérieur que l'ame reçoit du bon usage qu'elle fait des choses qui contribuent à la conserver').
[167] J. du Hamel, *Reflexions critiques sur le système cartésien de la philosophie de Mʳ Regis* (Paris, 1692), p. 344. Some other critics (Malebranche and Henri Lelevel) did object to his moral theory, but did not mention Hobbes: see Canziani, 'Tra Descartes e Hobbes', pp. 548–51.

of the rights of the Crown.[168] But he then quickly back-tracked, adding an 'Advertissement' to later states of the 1649 edition in which he remarked, with breath-taking disingenuousness: 'Those who speak ill of M. Hobbes's political theory would give me pleasure if they refuted it . . . Indeed, I translated this philosopher's arguments into French for no other reason than to stimulate learned men to undertake its refutation.'[169]

During the following decade, however, Sorbière spoke frequently in praise of Hobbes's theory; his comments were mainly made in 'discourses' addressed to gatherings of like-minded friends in Paris, but several of these were subsequently published.[170] The most extraordinary was his 'discours sceptique' in favour of oriental despotism, in which he contrasted the miseries of the inhabitants of European states, racked by dissension and sedition, with the peaceful life enjoyed by subjects of the Sultan. 'This total dependence of life and fortune does not make them more miserable. On the contrary . . . they thereby have less to fear from the injurious acts of private persons; they are all immediately under the protection of their sovereign.'[171] Although he did not mention Hobbes's name, the Hobbesian nature of his comments on sedition (and, in particular, of his denunciation of any claim by the 'Estates' to share in the sovereign power) was clear to many readers —such as Pierre Bayle, who remarked on it.[172] Admittedly, Sorbière's argument here was in one respect quite un-Hobbesian: he posited a peaceful 'state of nature', exemplified by the quiet life of savages in Canada and Brazil, and regarded it and the state of despotism as lying benignly at the two ends of a spectrum, with the evils of civil discord in between. Nevertheless, the main thrust of his argument was in keeping with the sceptical–authoritarian political theories of the *libertins érudits*, who feared the volatile passions of the common people as a source of violence and instability, and looked to human convention and human coercion as their best guarantees of protection. 'Men are incapable', Sorbière once remarked, 'of following right reason for its own sake, and of doing what is good, just and honest because

---

[168] T. Hobbes, *Elemens philosophiques du citoyen*, tr. S. Sorbière (Amsterdam, 1649), sigs. *6r–*7v (praise); Amsterdam University Library, MS III. E. 8[213], Sorbière to Vossius, 17 Sept. 1649 ('Nuper nos gallicè ejus librum de ciue reddidimus, efflangitantibus [sic] nobilibus Gallis, neque me, cùm otio abundarem, reluctante, Regiae enim Majestati asserendae magno ingenij acumine author laborat').

[169] Hobbes, *Elemens philosophiques du citoyen*, sig. Kk1r ('Ceux qui blasment la Politique de Monsieur Hobbes me feroient plaisir de la refuter . . . En effect, ie n'ay mis en nostre langue les raisonnemens de ce Philosophe à autre dessein que d'exciter les doctes à en entreprendre la refutation').

[170] Sorbière, *Lettres et discours*, esp. pp. 63, 614–15.

[171] S. Sorbière, 'II. Discours sceptique', in M. de Marolles, *Suitte des memoires de Michel de Marolles, abbé de Villeloin* (Paris, 1657), pp. 80–6, here pp. 84 ('cette entiere dependance de leur vie & de leur fortune ne les rend pas plus malheureux. Au contraire . . . ils en ont moins à craindre les insultes des personnes privées; ils sont tous immediatement sous la protection de leur Souuerain'), 84–5 (on disorders in European states, especially the Fronde). Sorbière does not use the word 'despotisme' (his phrase is 'Gouvernement absolu', p. 85), but the volume's list of contents (p. 2) entitles his discourse 'en faueur . . . du Gouuernement Despotique'.

[172] Ibid., p. 84 (on Estates); P. Bayle, *Réponse aux questions d'un provincial*, 5 vols. (Rotterdam, 1704–7), I, p. 590. Overall, however, Bayle was puzzled by Sorbière's 'discours', suspecting a large degree of irony (p. 588).

it is their duty; they must be made to do it by politics.'[173] Similar views were expressed by Richelieu's protégé Louis Machon, a fierce defender of royal absolutism who was strongly influenced by the Machiavellian elements in the political theories of the *libertinage érudit* (above all, in the writings of Gabriel Naudé). In his own 'Apologie pour Machiavelle', he argued that malice, brutality, and violence were so ingrained in human nature that both violence and fraud were needed in order to govern mankind—the fraud including the manipulation of religious sentiment for political purposes. Writing an expanded version of his 'Apologie' in or near Bordeaux in the 1660s—where he may well have had contacts with Hobbes's friend and admirer du Verdus—he cited Hobbes's *De cive* in confirmation of his arguments.[174]

The *libertins érudits* were not the only thinkers to make the connection between an authoritarian political theory (usually, absolutist monarchy) and a gloomy moral–psychological analysis of the common people. Ever since St Augustine, a powerful tradition in Western Christian thought had derived the justification for coercive rule from the corruption of man's fallen nature. In the seventeenth century many French Calvinist writers used this type of argument to justify absolutist monarchy. Their reasons for doing so were not merely theological, but also prudential: they wished to show that Protestantism was no bar to loyalty to the Crown, and they depended on the monarchy to protect their status against the claims and demands of intransigent Catholic churchmen.[175] One striking example of this was the treatise by the French Calvinist minister Élie Merlat, *Traité du pouvoir absolu des souverains*, written in 1681 or 1682 but published in the year of the Revocation of the Edict of Nantes, 1685.[176] Merlat's main aim in this work was to separate the

---

[173] [S. Sorbière,] *Sorberiana, ou bons mots, rencontres agreables, pensées judicieuses, et observations curieuses, de M. Sorbiere* (Paris, 1694), p. 14 ('Les hommes sont incapables de suivre la droite raison pour elle-même, de faire ce qui est bien, juste, honnête, parce qu'il est de son devoir: Il faut que la politique les porte à cela'). For a valuable study of Sorbière's political theory, in relation to that of the French sceptical–authoritarian tradition, see D. Taranto, *Pirronismo ed assolutismo nella Francia del '600: studi sul pensiero politico dello scetticismo da Montaigne a Bayle (1580–1697)* (Milan, 1994), pp. 131–56.

[174] See R. Céleste, *Louis Machon, apologiste de Machiavel et de la politique du Cardinal de Richelieu: nouvelles recherches sur sa vie et ses oeuvres (1600–1672)* (Bordeaux, 1883); K. T. Butler, 'Louis Machon's "Apologie pour Machiavelle"—1643 and 1668', *Journal of the Warburg and Courtauld Institutes*, 3 (1939–40), pp. 208–27; L. Rothkrug, *Opposition to Louis XIV: The Political and Social Origins of the French Enlightenment* (Princeton, NJ, 1965), pp. 62–3. For the citation of Hobbes, see G. Procacci, *Studi sulla fortuna del Machiavelli* (Rome, 1965), p. 197; for comments on the political advantages of religious imposture, see L. Machon, 'Apologie pour Machiavelle', in N. Machiavelli, *Oeuvres complètes*, ed. J. A. C. Buchon, 2 vols. (Paris, 1837), I, pp. xxiii–lxiv, here pp. xli–xlviii. In the late 1650s and early 1660s Machon catalogued the library of Arnaud de Pontac in Bordeaux (see L. Machon, 'Discours pour servir de regle ou d'avis aux bibliothecaires', ed. Daspit de Saint-Amand, *Tablettes des bibliophiles de Guienne*, 9 (1882), pp. 41–113); du Verdus was close to the Pontac family, and named Arnaud's son as his literary executor in his will of 1666 (Archives départementales de la Gironde, Bordeaux, MS 3 E 12995, fol. 903v).

[175] See Kretzer, *Calvinismus und französische Monarchie*.

[176] É. Merlat, *Traité du pouvoir absolu des souverains: pour servir d'instruction, de consolation & d'apologie aux Églises Réformées de France qui sont affligées* (Cologne, 1685), sig. A1v (saying it was written nearly four years earlier). I have consulted the copy in the Huguenot Library, University College, London, pressmark

essential nature of religion from the nature of secular life. The former was independent of human political power: this meant on the one hand that it could not legitimately be imposed or 'forced' by governments, and on the other hand that good Christians could and should submit to the absolute power of sovereigns in all secular matters.[177] Some elements of this argument chimed quite closely with Hobbes's views. Thus, Merlat contrasted coercive political power with ecclesiastical power, insisting that the latter amounted only to a power to 'persuade'; he also argued that, when making an 'external' profession of faith will lead to our deaths without serving the edification of the faithful, 'in that case, the *simple omission* of the external actions of religion does not in any way harm our salvation, and obedience to the princes of the world is compatible with a good conscience'.[178] His justification of political power was fully in the Augustinian tradition: coercive government is necessary after the Fall, because 'amour-propre' will always bring men into conflict—indeed, if there were only two men in the world, they would fight to the death.[179] Merlat offered a list of justifications for sovereign power: ninth on his list was '*fear of anarchy*', which, he noted, was 'the basis of all the political arguments of the famous Englishman Hobbes'.[180] He hastened to assure his readers that the 'excessive opinions' of Hobbes were not to his liking: Hobbes regarded submission to absolute power as 'just, reasonable and natural', whereas he thought it 'an extreme remedy for the extravagant licentiousness of wicked men'. Warming to his theme, he declared:

Indeed, it is quite false to say that man is not a sociable animal by nature; it is quite false that force is the law of actions, etc. But it is true that society is ruined by the malice of the majority of men; that most aim only at their own interest, and that many would commit whatever murders they could, were they not forced to restrain themselves by the more powerful. *De facto*, therefore, and in accordance with events, human sin does justify Hobbes's principles . . . *De jure*, however, in accordance with justice, those principles are no less abominable than the men who have rendered them true or necessary. True politics should use its strength and intelligence to make men gentle, sociable and united by

---

RBO 285. Merlat (1634–1705) had studied philosophy at Saumur and theology at Montauban, and had served as a pastor for more than 20 years before moving to Geneva in 1680 and Lausanne in 1682: Bibliothèque de la Société de l'Histoire du Protestantisme Français, Paris, MS 397/2, fol. 169r. On his work see also G. H. Dodge, *The Political Theory of the Huguenots of the Dispersion* (New York, 1947), pp. 7–10.

[177] Merlat, *Traité du pouvoir absolu*, p. 15.

[178] Ibid., pp. 118 ('en ce cas là, *la simple omission* des actes exterieurs de Religion ne nuit point au salut, & l'obéïssance aux Princes du monde compatit avec la bonne conscience'); 162 (political and ecclesiastical power).

[179] Ibid., pp. 26–7.

[180] Ibid., p. 220 ('*la crainte de l'anarchie*... celle qui fonde tous les raisonnemens Politiques du célebre Anglois Hobbes'). He directed readers to a work which he called '*les Principes de la Politique de Hobbes*'. This evidently referred to *De cive*; the wording is closer to du Verdus's version of the title (*Les Elemens de la Politique de Monsieur Hobbes*) than to Sorbière's, so this may count as a rare example of acquaintance with du Verdus's translation. If so, Merlat would not have known the third part of the book, unless he had also consulted the Latin.

their wills and their reason; it should not merely try to restrain them like wild beasts, through the bonds of *force majeure* or through the necessity of amour-propre.[181]

This remarkable passage, in which Merlat foreshadowed some of the Enlightenment's responses to Hobbes (such as that of de Prades, discussed above), was in essence an awkward attempt to yoke together the Augustinian and Hobbesian views on the one hand, and the Grotian or even Aristotelian ones on the other. Hobbes's views were criticized as inadequate; yet, to a significant extent, they were accepted as true.

Catholic theologians were also capable of making positive use of Hobbes; the Augustinian view of fallen man was a strong presence in seventeenth-century French Catholicism, and not only among the Jansenists. Jean-Bénigne Bossuet, who referred constantly to Augustine in his sermons, evidently read Hobbes with some care.[182] In one of his polemical responses to Pierre Jurieu, he based his whole criticism of the concept of popular sovereignty on a purely Hobbesian premiss: 'For if one looks at men as they are by nature, before any government has been established, one finds only anarchy, where each person may lay claim to everything and at the same time contest every other claim; where all are on guard, and consequently in a perpetual war against all.' The people thus described could not possess sovereign authority: sovereignty, Bossuet observed, is not 'a sort of pre-existing thing, which one must have in order to convey it; it is formed and comes about as a result of a yielding-up by individuals, when they have let themselves be persuaded to renounce that right which reduced everything to chaos'.[183] This showed a surer grasp of the peculiar significance of Hobbes's theory of sovereignty than that of almost any other seventeenth-century continental writer. Bossuet made the same

---

[181] Merlat, *Traité du pouvoir absolu*, p. 221 ('En effet, il est trés-faux que l'homme ne soit pas un animal sociable de sa nature; il est trés-faux qu'il n'aime que soi-même; il est trés-faux que la force soit la loy des actions, &c. mais il est vray pourtant, que la malice de la plûpart des hommes ruïne la Société; que la plûpart n'ont en vûë que leur interest; & que plusieurs ne borneroient leurs attentats, que par leur impuissance, si de plus puissans qu'eux ne les forçoient de se contenir. Ainsi, selon *le fait*, & quant aux événemens, le péché des hommes autorise les Principes d'Hobbes . . . Mais selon *le droit*, & quant à la justice, ces mêmes Principes sont aussi abominables, que ceux qui les ont rendus véritables, ou nécessaires; & la vraye Politique doit déployer sa force, & ses lumiéres à rendre les hommes doux, sociables, & unis par leur volontez, & par leur raison; & non pas à les retenir simplement comme des bêtes farouches, par les liens d'une force majeure, ou d'une nécessité d'amour-propre').

[182] On Bossuet's Augustinianism see A. J. Krailsheimer, *Studies in Self-Interest from Descartes to La Bruyère* (Oxford, 1962), pp. 178–82.

[183] J.-B. Bossuet, *Oeuvres complètes*, ed. F. Lachat, 31 vols. (Paris, 1862–6), XV, pp. 464 ('Car à regarder les hommes comme ils sont naturellement et avant tout gouvernement établi, on ne trouve que l'anarchie . . . où chacun peut tout prétendre et en même temps tout contester: où tous sont en garde, et par conséquent en guerre continuelle contre tous'); 465–6 ('une chose comme subsistante, qu'il faille avoir pour la donner; elle se forme et résulte de la cession des particuliers, lorsque . . . ils se sont laissés persuader de renoncer à ce droit qui met tout en confusion'). Before the Revocation, Jurieu had in fact been a supporter of absolutism, not popular sovereignty, with a general position not far removed from that of Merlat: see Kretzer, *Calvinismus und französische Monarchie*, pp. 369, 401, and R. J. Howells, *Pierre Jurieu: Antinomian Radical* (Durham, 1983).

point in his major political treatise, *Politique tirée des propres paroles de l'Escriture Sainte*: 'It is by the sole authority of government that union has been established among men.'[184] Elsewhere in that work he made use of Hobbes's concept of 'authorization': this suggests that his knowledge of Hobbes's theory came not only from *De cive* but also from *Leviathan*.[185] Hobbes's name was never mentioned; but the use made of his ideas by Bossuet in the construction of a Catholic absolutist political philosophy was entirely positive.

A more open—and more extensive—use of Hobbes was made in an important text published anonymously in Lyon in 1687 under the title *Essais de morale et de politique*. The origins of this text are quite mysterious. The second half of the book, which deals with politics, contains some of the same material as a manuscript treatise, the 'Abrégé de politique', which survives in several copies and has been dated on internal evidence to the period 1668–79. If the manuscript treatise was, as its title suggests, an abridgement of a longer work, then the printed text may have been derived independently from that longer original.[186] No clues are given about the author's identity or affiliations; but the first half of the printed text, dealing with human felicity and man's relation to God, has several of the hallmarks of the Jansenist movement: frequent reference to St Augustine, invocation of Cartesian arguments, an emphasis on divine grace as the precondition of true felicity, and a simple but strongly homiletic style. The second half of the book consists of an almost undiluted version of Hobbes's political theory, from the war of all against all to the rights and duties of the sovereign; the arguments are presented very faithfully, but in a lively paraphrase, which shows that the author has fully assimilated Hobbes's ideas. (These include not only the central argument about absolute sovereignty, but also such potentially 'liberal' points as the insistence that punishments must be justified by the principle of utility.[187]) In the short preface to

---

[184] J.-B. Bossuet, *Politique tirée des propres paroles de l'Escriture Sainte*, ed. J. Le Brun (Geneva, 1967), p. 18, bk 1, art. 3, prop. 3 ('C'est par la seule autorité du gouvernement que l'union est établie parmi les hommes').

[185] Ibid., p. 20, bk 1, art. 3, prop. 5: 'One gains thereby [sc. by transferring one's power to the sovereign], because in return one finds more power in the person of this supreme magistrat than one has abandoned in order to authorize him' ('On y gagne; car on retrouve en la personne de ce suprême magistrat plus de force qu'on n'en a quitté pour l'autoriser'). Raymond Schmittlein notes that Bossuet possessed several editions of *Leviathan*: *L'Aspect politique du différend Bossuet-Fénelon* (Mainz, 1954), p. 5. For discussions of Bossuet's borrowings from Hobbes see R. Gadave, *Thomas Hobbes et les théories du contrat et de la souveraineté* (Toulouse, 1907), pp. 243–4, and N. O. Keohane, *Philosophy and the State in France: The Renaissance and the Enlightenment* (Princeton, NJ, 1980), pp. 251–8.

[186] Bibliothèque Sainte-Geneviève, Paris, MSS 2215, 2997, 3082. For the dating see Rothkrug, *Opposition to Louis XIV*, p. 316.

[187] Anon., *Essais de morale et de politique, ou il est traité des devoirs de l'homme, considéré comme particulier, & comme vivant en societé* (Lyon, 1687), part 2, pp. 135–6: 'one must not inflict a punishment on another person merely to do him ill; so one must not regard the punishment as a punishment, but as something useful. Therefore punishments must be measured by their utility' ('on ne doit point faire souffrir de peine à un autre simplement pour luy faire de la peine: on ne doit donc pas regarder la peine comme peine, mais comme utile, c'est donc par l'utilité que se doivent mesurer les peines').

the volume (which referred to the author in the third person, but may have been written by him), readers were both forewarned and reassured about the nature of this political theory:

> It is true that the author raises the authority of sovereigns very high, and pushes their rights rather far . . . His work contains some maxims which may seem extraordinary, and of which readers may at first disapprove . . . It can be admitted without hesitation that these essays follow the principles of the English author Hobbes, in his book *De cive*; but that fact, far from harming these essays, should lead to their being esteemed more highly, because all clever people are convinced that would have been difficult to write with more solidity than that wise man did about things that are the concern of reason and good sense. One would not wish to say the same about what he has written on matters relating to religion; so in those matters he has not been followed here.[188]

That brief disclaimer about religion was, apparently, sufficient to render such an open acknowledgement of Hobbes's authority acceptable, even though the text referred to here, *De cive*, had been on the Church's index for more than thirty years when this book was granted its 'Privilège' in 1685. And a generation later, in 1715, this book's exposition of Hobbes's arguments would be thought sufficiently cogent and acceptable to gain another lease of life, when a minor lawyer, Louis Desbans, plagiarized it wholesale in his *Principes naturels du droit et de la politique*—a work subsequently reprinted three times in the eighteenth century.[189]

Roughly contemporaneous with the original text of those anonymous *Essais* were the similarly named *Essais de morale* by one of the Jansenist movement's leading intellectuals, Pierre Nicole, which were published in the 1670s. Nicole's debt to Hobbes was much less overt; but the presence of a Hobbesian influence in his writing is unmistakable. Once again, Augustinianism was the starting-point. Corrupted man was consumed by self-love; this made people 'violent, unjust, cruel, ambitious, deceptive, envious, insolent, quarrelsome'; in short, 'other men's amour-propre conflicts with all the desires of our own'.[190] He continued: 'So that is why all men are in conflict with one another; and if the person who said that

---

[188] Ibid., part 1, pp. 4–6 ('il est vray que l'Auteur y releve beaucoup l'autorité des Souverains, & qu'il pousse leurs droits un peu loin . . . L'on trouvera des maximes qui paraoîtront extraordinaires, & que peut-être l'on désaprouvera d'abord . . . L'on ne fait pas difficulté d'avoüer que l'on n'ait suivy dans ces *Essais* les principes d'Hobbez, Auteur Anglois, dans son livre *De Cive*: Mais bien loin de leur faire tort, cela les doit faire estimer davantage, puisque tous les habiles gens sont persuadez qu'il étoit difficile d'écrire plus solidement que fait ce sçavant Homme sur les choses qui sont du ressort de la raison & du bon sens, l'on n'en voudroit pas dire autant de ce qu'il a écrit sur les sujets qui regardent la Religion, aussi n'est-ce pas en cela qu'on l'a suivi').

[189] Ibid., part 2, pp. 237–40 (Privilège); G. Lacour-Gayet, *L'Éducation politique de Louis XIV* (Paris, 1898), pp. 383–4 (Desbans). The later editions of Desbans's book (not mentioned by Lacour-Gayet) were in 1716, 1765 and 1768.

[190] P. Nicole, *Essais de morale, contenus en divers traittez sur plusieurs devoirs importans*, 4 vols. (Paris, 1672–8), III, pp. 119–20 ('violents, injustes, cruels, ambitieux, flatteurs, envieux, insolens, querelleux . . . l'amour propre des autres hommes s'oppose à tous les desirs du nostre').

men are born in a state of war, and that each man is naturally an enemy of all other men, had thereby meant only to describe the feelings men have for one another in their hearts, without trying to make it seem legitimate and just, he would have said something consistent with truth and experience.'[191] Like Merlat, Nicole thought— or professed to think—that Hobbes approved of such conflict and that he rested political authority directly on it in a crude version of the 'might is right' argument. But the theory which he offered as an alternative to this caricature Hobbesianism was itself a sophisticated application of Hobbesian principles: for, unlike Merlat, Nicole did place his trust in 'the necessity of amour-propre'. (Indeed, Merlat may well have had Nicole in mind when he invoked such a theory in order to dismiss it.) As Nicole explained, 'the amour-propre which is the cause of this war will easily find out the way to make men live in peace. It loves domination, but even more strongly than it loves domination, it loves life and the advantages and comforts of life.'[192] The rules of behaviour evolved by this milder or more rational kind of *amour-propre* were not (as Hobbes thought they were) the very principles of morality itself: true morality depended on 'la charité', a theological virtue flowing directly from divine grace. But the principles of enlightened *amour-propre* led to a kind of simulacrum of true morality, so that in a society utterly devoid of grace—a non-Catholic one, for example—it would still be possible to live 'with as much peace, security and advantage as if one were living in a republic of saints'.[193]

This concept of 'enlightened self-interest' would be taken up by many later writers. As we have seen, it was used by the Cartesian Pierre-Sylvain Regis in 1690: he may well have borrowed it from Nicole, whose own touches of ostentatious Cartesianism (such as his comparison between human beings interacting in mutual mechanisms of self-interest and the pattern of interacting 'vortices' of Descartes's cosmology) would no doubt have appealed to him.[194] The Jansenist lawyer Jean Domat also quarried arguments from Nicole while developing his account of rational *amour-propre* as the basis of society in his *Les Loix civiles dans*

---

[191] P. Nicole, *Essais de morale, contenus en divers traittez sur plusieurs devoirs importans*, 4 vols. (Paris, 1672–8), III, pp. 120–1 ('Voilà donc par là tous les hommes aux mains les uns contre les autres; & si celuy qui a dit qu'ils naissent dans un estat de guerre, & que chaque homme est naturellement annemy de tous les autres hommes, eust voulu seulement representer par ces paroles la disposition du coeur des hommes les uns envers les autres, sans pretendre le faire passer pour legitime & pour juste, il auroit dit une chose ... conforme à la verité & à l'esperience').

[192] Ibid., III, p. 121 ('l'amour propre qui est la cause de cette guerre, sçaura bien le moyen de les faire vivre en paix. Il aime la domination ... mais il aime plus encore la vie & les commoditez, & les aises de la vie que la domination').

[193] Ibid., III, p. 123 ('avec autant de paix, de seureté, & de commodité, que si l'on estoit dans une Republique de Saints'). On Nicole's theory of *amour-propre*, see A. M. Battista, 'Psicologia e politica nella cultura eterodossa francese del Seicento', in T. Gregory *et al.*, *Ricerche su letteratura libertina e letteratura clandestina nel Seicento* (Florence, 1981), pp. 320–51, esp. pp. 340–5; on the Hobbesian (and Pascalian) background to Nicole's theory, see also H. Bouchilloux, 'La Pensée politique de Pierre Nicole', *Chroniques de Port-Royal*, 45 (1996), pp. 197–209.

[194] Nicole, *Essais de morale*, III, p. 125.

*leur ordre naturel* (1689–94).[195] But the most important writer to be influenced directly by Nicole was Pierre Bayle. His own theory reproduced quite closely the structure of Nicole's quasi-Hobbesian theory: he began with the corruption of human nature, noted that the initial tendency of the state of nature was to make physical domination the only source of rule and order, but then argued that several human passions (love of rest, desire for the pleasures of social life, and, above all, fear of violence and death) created the conditions for a new, consensually based system of society operating on a basis of mutual self-interest.[196] A kind of rationality was at work here, he observed, but it was merely instrumental reasoning working out a method for the satisfaction of the passions: his basic claim that men were not led by reason to establish society was not undermined thereby, as this instrumental reasoning was not 'the reason which precedes the passions' but merely 'the reason which follows in their wake'.[197] Bayle could not fail to be aware of the Hobbesian origins of this theory. Reviewing a book by an anonymous Dutch writer on the origins of society in 1685, he noted: 'He shows very clearly that it was nothing other than fear that led men to form societies . . . It was only their interest in protecting themselves against fear that led them to lay down their freedom, and renounce those rights to dominate others which each of them possessed by nature . . . He concludes with a comment by Hobbes, which shows that men love one another's society only because of the utility which they hope to gain from it.'[198]

In the entry 'Hobbes' in his *Dictionnaire*, Bayle expressed a cautiously positive view of Hobbes's political theory. Commenting on *De cive* (which he knew both in the original and in Sorbière's translation), he observed that 'Hobbes made many enemies with that work, but he made the most clear-sighted people declare that no one had analysed the foundations of political theory so well before him.' However, he continued: 'I do not doubt that he went too far in some matters.'[199]

---

[195] See Tocanne, *L'Idée de nature en France*, p. 190.

[196] P. Bayle, *Oeuvres diverses*, 4 vols. (The Hague, 1727–31), II, p. 280 (love of rest, fear); III, pp. 174 (fear, pleasures of social life), 199–200 (corruption, domination by the strong). On Bayle's indebtedness to Nicole, see Battista, 'Psicologia e politica', pp. 346–9; G. Cantelli, *Teologia e ateismo: saggio sul pensiero filosofico e religioso di Pierre Bayle* (Florence, 1969), esp. pp. 81–90.

[197] Bayle, *Oeuvres diverses*, II, p. 282 ('la Raison qui précède les passions . . . la Raison qui vient à leur suite').

[198] Ibid., I, p. 287, *Nouvelles de la république des lettres*, May 1685, art. 5 ('Il y fait voir très-clairement, que ce qui a porté les hommes à former des Societez, n'a été autre chose que la crainte . . . C'est donc le seul intérêt de se garantir de la peur, qui a fait consentir à ce dépôt de la liberté, & à cette renonciation aux droits de la Maîtrise, qui appartenoient naturellement à chaque homme . . . il conclut par une remarque de Hobbes qui fait voir, que les hommes n'aiment la Société les uns des autres, que par l'utilité qu'ils en esperent'). The book was *Dissertationes de origine juris naturalis & societatis civilis* (Utrecht, 1684), by 'G.V.M.' (possibly Gerard van der Meulen).

[199] P. Bayle, 'Hobbes', in T. Hobbes, *Le Citoyen, ou les fondemens de la politique*, tr. S. Sorbière, ed. S. Goyard-Fabre (Paris, 1982), pp. 367–78, here p. 371 ('Hobbes se fit beaucoup d'ennemis par cet ouvrage; mais il fit avouer aux plus clairvoyants qu'on n'avait jamais si bien pénétré aux fondemens de la politique. Je ne doute point qu'il n'ait outré plusieurs choses').

The two points he singled out for criticism were Hobbes's defence of unbounded royal authority, and his argument that the externals of religion must be subject to the sovereign's will. Given Bayle's commitment to religious toleration, one might have expected him to develop such criticism into a major assault on the Hobbesian state. Yet, far from doing so, he went on to suggest that the 'inconveniences' of Hobbes's system were no worse than those that might be encountered by any other theory when put into practice. He did refer the reader to one hostile judgement on Hobbes, a passage by Conrad Samuel Schurzfleisch (under the pseudonym 'Galeottus Galeatius Karlsbergius') quoted in a recent book by Johannes Deckherr. But even this may have been a deliberately ambiguous act: Schurzfleisch's strictures were preceded and followed by comments in defence of Hobbes by Deckherr, and as the most recent edition of Deckherr's book included a letter from Bayle himself, Bayle's readers might well have suspected that his sympathies were more with Deckherr than with Schurzfleisch.[200] Overall, the tone of Bayle's article was positive, but somewhat distant; and much of it was taken up not with the discussion of Hobbes's theories but with the use of Hobbes's personal biography as evidence for Bayle's theory (itself, as we have seen, of partly Hobbesian origins) that atheists could live virtuous lives as fully participating members of human society.

Although Bayle's variety of Hobbesianism takes its natural place in the late seventeenth-century French Hobbesian tradition, his coolness towards absolute monarchy does set him apart in some ways from the other French writers. For obvious reasons, most of the French Hobbesians (at least, those living in the French kingdom) did defend absolutism—that, indeed, was part of the attraction of Hobbes's theory for them. Conversely, most absolutist Hobbesians in continental Europe were French. An appeal to Hobbes's theory of the rights of monarchical sovereigns was also possible in Habsburg territory; thus, for example, the Neapolitan writer Serafino Biscardi referred approvingly to the 'most learned Englishman Thomas Hobbes' in 1703, when defending the claim that the rights of the sovereign must include the power to decide the rules of succession to the Crown.[201] (That more famous Neapolitan defender of absolute monarchy, Giambattista Vico, made no such use of Hobbes, though his political and historical theory more generally was certainly influenced by Hobbes's analysis of the state

---

[200] P. Bayle, 'Hobbes', in T. Hobbes, *Le Citoyen, ou les fondements de la politique*, tr. S. Sorbière, ed. S. Goyard-Fabre (Paris, 1982), p. 373; J. Deckherr ['Deckherrus'], *De scriptis adespotis, pseudepigraphis, et supposititiis conjecturae*, 3rd edn (Amsterdam, 1686), pp. 328–9 (Schurzfleisch criticism, e.g. 'he defines the law badly, and wickedly releases the prince from it' ('legem malè definit, & Principem impie solvit lege')). Deckherr disagrees with this, and recommends that Hobbes should be read and discussed with care: he notes (p. 327) that many have tried to expel Hobbes 'from the society of the philosophers' ('ex consortio Philosophorum'), but without success. Elsewhere he refers approvingly to *Leviathan* (pp. 31, 322). Bayle's letter (to Theodore Almeloveen, the dedicatee of the book) is on pp. 367–411. For the identification of 'Karlsbergius', see Palladini, *Discussioni seicentesche*, pp. 92–3, n. 3.

[201] S. Biscardi, *Epistola pro augusto Hispaniorum monarcha Philippo V* (Naples, 1703), cited in Ricuperati, *L'esperienza civile*, pp. 113–14.

of nature.²⁰² ) In Scandinavia, too, Hobbes's theories may have had some attraction to monarchist ideologues: it has been suggested, for example, that Peter Griffenfeld, one of the architects of the new absolutist constitutional settlement in Denmark under Frederick III and Christian V, had come under the influence of Hobbes's works when he studied at Oxford in the late 1650s.²⁰³ But in most of the German lands, where writers owed their primary allegiance to princes and Electors, the Hobbesian theory of sovereignty was not welcome: any claim of indivisible sovereign authority was contrary to the traditional constitutional theory of the Holy Roman Empire.²⁰⁴

There were, however, some exceptions. One intriguing case is that of Wilhelm von Schröder, or von Schröter, the son of a high official at the Saxon court. He studied at Jena before travelling first to Holland (where he published a poem in praise of the restoration of Charles II) and then to England. There he got to know both Boyle and Digby, and in late 1662, aged only 22, he was elected a Fellow of the Royal Society. It has also been suggested that he became acquainted with Hobbes in London; the claim is not implausible, although no direct evidence for it has ever been produced.²⁰⁵ On his return to Jena in 1663 von Schröder published a dissertation on political matters which, although it had apparently met with the approval of the Rector Magnificus of the university, was promptly denounced and banned by the State authorities. The most controversial part of this work was the first section, on reason of State, which identified the good of the State with the person of the ruler and argued that all actions were justified by it—declaring, for example, that 'Treaties and promises must be judged according to utility and advantage, and

---

²⁰² See F. Nicolini, 'Di alcuni rapporti ideali tra il Vico e il Hobbes con qualche riferimento al Machiavelli', *English Miscellany: A Symposium of History, Literature, and the Arts*, 1 (1950), pp. 43–70, esp. pp. 43–7. Vico's initial acquaintance with Hobbes's ideas may have come from the hostile account in Pasch's *De novis inventis* (see above, n. 86), and some of the dismissive references to Hobbes as an 'Epicurean' in Vico's work reflect this: see e.g. *Scienza nuova* § 179 (G. Vico, *Opere*, ed. F. Nicolini (Milan, 1953), pp. 447–8). But Vico was influenced by Hobbes's psychological theory (see ibid., § 211, p. 454, on the relationship between imagination and memory), and he may also have been influenced by Hobbes's comments in *De homine* when developing his 'verum-factum' theory of truths 'made' by human intention: on this see the discussion in R. Mondolfo, *Il 'verum-factum' prima di Vico* (Naples, 1969), pp. 58–61; F. Focher, *Vico e Hobbes* (Naples, 1977); J. Barnouw, 'Vico and the Continuity of Science: The Relation of his Epistemology to Bacon and Hobbes', *Isis*, 71 (1980), pp. 609–20.

²⁰³ See A. D. Jørgensen, *Peter Schumacher Griffenfeld*, 2 vols. (Copenhagen, 1893), I, pp. 46 (Oxford), 54 (influence of Hobbes).

²⁰⁴ See Dreitzel, 'Hermann Conring', p. 162; M. Stolleis, *Geschichte des öffentlichen Rechts in Deutschland*, vol. I: *Reichspublizistik und Policeywissenschaft, 1600–1800* (Munich, 1988), p. 281.

²⁰⁵ The best biographical account is H. von Srbik, 'Wilhelm von Schröder: ein Beitrag zur Geschichte der Staatswissenschaften', *Sitzungsberichte der kaiserlichen Akademie der Wissenschaften in Wien, philosophisch-historische Klasse*, 164, part 1 (1910), pp. 1–161; the claim of acquaintance is made in K. Zielenziger, *Die alten deutschen Kameralisten: ein Beitrag zur Geschichte der Nationalökonomie und zum Problem des Merkantilismus* (Jena, 1914), p. 296; E. Dittrich, *Die deutschen und österreichischen Kameralisten* (Darmstadt, 1974), p. 63; Stolleis, *Geschichte des öffentlichen Rechts*, p. 211. The poem is W. von Schröder ['Schroeter'], *Magni monarchae Caroli secundi . . . institutio felix* (Leiden, 1661), a magniloquent work in praise of monarchy as well as of Charles II.

must be broken if they cause harm.'[206] The final part also displayed absolutist attitudes, denouncing the institution of a 'ministrissimus' or all-powerful minister (such as Richelieu or Mazarin) as a dangerous encroachment on the powers of the monarch.[207] The young Leibniz, who was in Jena at the time, commented in a letter to Jakob Thomasius on the scandal this dissertation had produced, describing von Schröder as a 'Hobbianus'. 'Since he makes utility the mother of equity, it follows that every right may stand or fall, depending on whether the wind is filling utility's sails. Since he gives absolute rule to every prince, a prince will be able to put people to torture on mere suspicion. Finally, since he makes all justice spring from the civil law, all obligation and necessity to keep treaties between states will necessarily collapse. I have often heard you criticizing these things in Hobbes.'[208]

Ten years later von Schröder entered the service of the Habsburgs in Austria (having converted, conveniently, to Catholicism). After advising on various aspects of trade and economic policy, he published a book in 1686, *Fürstliche Schatz- und Rent-Kammer*, which became one of the classic works of 'Cameralist' theory on the economic management of the state. His aim in this book, he announced, was to show how to make the prince 'independent of his subjects, and absolute for himself'; however, his way of achieving this aim depended on grasping the central principle that the wealth and well-being of the ruler depended on the wealth and well-being of his subjects. 'I have observed throughout', he noted in the Preface, 'how interconnected are the interest of the prince and the interest of the subjects.'[209] The pattern of thought here was quite Hobbesian: in *Leviathan* Hobbes had insisted that 'the good of the Soveraign and People, cannot be separated. It is a weak Soveraign, that has weak Subjects; and a weak People, whose Soveraign wanteth power to rule them at his will.'[210] Other points of von Schröder's argument also chimed with Hobbes—his warnings against adventurous foreign wars, for example, or his comparison between the economic life of the state and the

---

[206] W. von Schröder ['Schröter'], *Dissertatio academica, cuius prima pars de ratione status, altera de nobilitate, tertia de ministrissimo* (Jena, 1663), sigs. A1v–A2v (here sig. A2r: 'Foedera et fides ex utilitate et commodo aestimanda, et propter damnum rumpenda'). I am very grateful to Mary Person, of the Harvard Law School, for supplying me with a copy of this rare work (catalogued there under the name of the Jena Rector, S. C. Olpe, who presided over the dissertation: pressmark, Rare Foreign Dissertations O).

[207] This part was later published separately: W. von Schröder ['Schröter'], *Dissertatio de ministrissimo* (n.p., 1671).

[208] Struve, *Acta litteraria*, vol. I, fasc. 7, p. 56, Leibniz to Thomasius, 2 Sept. 1663 ('Cum enim utilitatem aequi matrem habeat, igitur, prout ille velificabitur, ius omne stabit cadetque: cum cuilibet Principi absolutum det imperium, sola suspicio Principi ad supplicia ius dabit. Demum quia a ciuili Lege omnis iustitia propullulat, necessario obligatio omnis ac foederum seruandorum necessitas ruet inter ciuitates. Haec in Hobbesio saepe reprehendentem te audiui').

[209] W. von Schröder ['von Schrödern'], *Fürstliche Schatz- und Rent-Kammer* (Leipzig, 1744), sigs. 2π4r–2π4v ('Ich habe durchaus darauf gesehen, wie des Fürsten interesse mit dem Interesse der unterthanen zusammen verknüpffet werde'), p. 9 ('von seinen unterthanen independent und vor sich absolut').

[210] T. Hobbes, *Leviathan* (London, 1651), p. 182.

anatomic processes of the human body.[211] Von Schröder showed little interest, admittedly, in Hobbes's theory of the origins of sovereignty: for him, divine-right theory, on the warrant of Scripture, was sufficient. Nevertheless, by means of his widely read treatise (which went through nine editions between 1686 and 1752) some elements of Hobbesian theory did enter the mainstream Cameralist tradition, exerting an influence on the practice of the central European absolutist state.[212]

Otherwise, however, the main influence of Hobbes's theories on European political thought was not on absolutism or monarchism, but on two different areas of political philosophy: Dutch republicanism, and the development of natural law theory more generally in Germany and the Netherlands. That Hobbes should have exerted any influence at all on republican theorists is at first sight surprising, given the fact that in both *De cive* and *Leviathan* he went out of his way to argue for the superiority of monarchy over all other forms of government. But his theories did have a special appeal for writers who were trying to set republicanism on a new 'scientific' basis: they liked his analysis of the primary justification of the State (conflict in the state of nature, leading to the creation of political rule as a purely human mechanism of control), and saw that they could develop such an argument in a specifically republican direction.

The key figures here were Johan de la Court (1622–60) and his brother Pieter (1618–85), who produced a series of influential publications in the republican, anti-Orange cause.[213] Their starting-point was a naturalistic and egoistic psychology: 'Self-love is the origin of all human actions, whether good or evil.'[214] In a state of nature, people driven by such self-regarding passions would naturally come into conflict: in support of this point, the authors paraphrased Hobbes's comment in the Preface to the second edition of *De cive* on the fact that states set guards on their borders, men go armed when travelling, and so on.[215] Peace through adjudication in the state of nature would never be possible, as each would wish to be judge in his own cause: a sovereign authority must therefore be created, endowed not only with

---

[211] See Zielenziger, *Die alten deutschen Kameralisten*, p. 311; Dittrich, *Die deutschen und österreichischen Kameralisten*, p. 64. The key Hobbesian text here is ch. 24 of *Leviathan*, 'Of the Nutrition and Procreation of a Common-wealth'.

[212] On Hobbes's influence on von Schröder (and the contrast with the latter's divine-right theory) see von Srbik, 'Wilhelm von Schröder', pp. 95–7; Zielenziger, *Die alten deutschen Kameralisten*, p. 332; L. Sommer, *Die österreichischen Kameralisten in dogmengeschichtlicher Darstellung*, 2 vols. (Vienna, 1920–5), I, pp. 82–3.

[213] On the de la Courts see T. van Thijn, 'Pieter de la Court: zijn leven en zijn economische denkbeelden', *Tijdschrift voor geschiedenis*, 69 (1956), pp. 304–70; Kossmann, *Politieke theorie*, pp. 36–44; W. Röd, 'Van den Hoves "Politische Waage" und die Modifikation der hobbesschen Staatsphilosophie bei Spinoza', *Journal of the History of Philosophy*, 8 (1970), pp. 29–48; H. A. E. van Gelder, *Getemperde vrijheid* (Groningen, 1972), pp. 250–5; and my 'Hobbes and Spinoza' (Ch. 2 above, esp. pp. 42–5).

[214] J. de la Court and P. de la Court ['V.H.'], *Consideratien en exempelen van staat, omtrent de fundamenten van allerley regeringe* (Amsterdam, 1660), p. 1 ('Eige liefde is de oorsprong van alle menschelikke actien, 't zy goed, 't zy quaad').

[215] Ibid., p. 3. In the 2nd edn of this work, *Consideratien van staat, ofte politike wegen-schaal* (Amsterdam, 1661), a marginal reference to *De cive* was added at this point (p. 15).

the sword, but also with wide-ranging legislative and judicial power. 'And therefore the public determination of what is good and what is evil belongs only to the sovereign: otherwise the political state will change, through the conflict of many private judgements, into a state of nature, a natural state of war of all against all.'[216]

Thus far the account was quite a straightforward version of Hobbes's theory (albeit one omitting the jural level of his argument). But the de la Courts now added two republican twists to it. Given that all men acted out of self-love, it followed that a man entrusted with the sole exercise of sovereignty would use it to further his personal interest—indeed, he would be bound to misuse such power, since he would be the one person whose conduct was under no higher restraints. The second argument against monarchy, and in favour of government by a republican assembly, was that the different passions and interests of the assembly-men would tend to cancel one another out, making rational decisions more likely.[217] For the aim of politics was 'to form the state and all laws in such a way that the ill-natured rulers and subjects will always be forced to behave well'.[218] Thus was established that connection between mechanistic psychology and constitution-building which would preoccupy constitutional theorists for more than a century to come.

In one other area of their theory the de la Courts showed a Hobbesian cast of mind: the question of the relation between religion and the State. The authority of the sovereign government must extend over all external actions; religious disagreements should not be allowed to disrupt the peace, and the clergy should certainly not be granted any coercive powers of their own. The worst examples of disobedience were those of wicked preachers and interpreters of Scripture stirring up the people; only a 'particular revelation from God' to an individual could free that individual from his obligation to obey the sovereign.[219] At the same time, however, the de la Courts observed that religious persecution was harmful to the State: people would become better-motivated subjects if they were able to worship as they thought fit, so the secular sovereign power could and should tolerate all forms of worship that posed no threat to peace.[220] As a positive theory of religious toleration, this went a little further than Hobbes's explicit statements ever did; but it was a theory built on thoroughly Hobbesian foundations.

---

[216] P. de la Court ['D.C.'], *Politike discoursen handelde in ses onderscheide boeken, van steeden, landen, oorlogen, kerken, regeeringen, en zeeden* (Amsterdam, 1662), p. 24 ('En naademal *publijk ordeel wat goed, en quaad zy*, alleen de *Ooverheid* toe-komt, vermits andersints door deese meenigvuldige strydende particuliere oordeelen, de *politie* in een *status naturalis* naturelike Oorlogs stand aller menschen ander malkanderen soude veranderen').

[217] de la Court and de la Court, *Consideratien en exempelen*, pp. 8–11, 13–74, '102–7' (mispaginated for 202–7). Various other disadvantages of monarchy, some of them mentioned by Hobbes (influence of favourites, problems of succession), are also discussed at length.

[218] Ibid., pp. 75–6 ('om de Politie en alle Wetten zodanig te formeeren, dat de boosaardige Regeerders en Onderdanen altijd genootzaakt werden zich wel te dragen').

[219] de la Court, *Politike discoursen*, pp. 21–32 (p. 24: 'een *particuliere revelatie* van God').

[220] Ibid., pp. 24, 57.

Spinoza was a keen reader of the works of the de la Courts, and many features of their theory of the State were incorporated in his own political philosophy—the republican approach to constitution-building, for example, and the defence of religious toleration. The Hobbesian principles on which the de la Courts had based these arguments were absorbed into Spinoza's political thought; as he also read Hobbes's work in the original (certainly *De cive*, and very probably *Leviathan* too), he received, so to speak, a double dose of Hobbes, both indirect and direct. Unlike the de la Courts, Spinoza engaged with the jural concepts that Hobbes had used to frame his theory, taking the notion of a natural right and showing how it could be reduced to a synonym for natural power. His notion of the rationality of the state—of its capacity to work not merely as an efficient mechanism, but as a structure moulding human nature and enabling it to become more fully rational—also took his theory beyond that of the de la Courts, in a direction further away from Hobbes. Nevertheless, in any general classification of late seventeenth-century political theories, Spinoza's must be described as standing directly in the Hobbesian tradition: on this area of his thought, Hobbes clearly exercised a stronger influence than any other writer.[221]

While the de la Courts showed no interest in the concept of natural law, and Spinoza invoked it only to explain it away in other terms, most Dutch and German writers on political theory in the second half of the seventeenth century were concerned with the derivation of natural law and the ways in which it underlay and justified the authority of the State. This was one area in which modern thought seemed capable of making real advances, applying new methods (deductive, empirical or analytic) to produce, potentially, a 'science' of morality and of politics. To many readers of *De cive*, whether enthusiastic or critical, it was clear that Hobbes was one of the writers at the forefront of these new developments: his method could be admired even by those who disagreed with his conclusions.

The first book openly defending Hobbes was published in 1651: *Epistolica dissertatio de principiis iusti et decori, continens apologiam pro tractatu clarissimi Hobbaei, De cive*, by the Dutch physician Lambert van Velthuysen. Having studied at Utrecht and Leiden in the 1640s, van Velthuysen had become an enthusiastic Cartesian, hostile to traditional 'authorities' and convinced that the fundamental problems of philosophy could be solved by pure, unassisted reason.[222] He was attracted to *De*

---

[221] The nature of Spinoza's debt to, and development of, Hobbes's political theory is of course a huge subject; for a slightly fuller discussion see my 'Hobbes and Spinoza', Ch. 2 above, pp. 27–52, esp. pp. 44–51. The best study of his debt to the de la Courts is E. O. G. Haitsma Mulier, *The Myth of Venice and Dutch Republican Thought in the Seventeenth Century* (Assen, 1980), pp. 187–208.

[222] On van Velthuysen see A. C. Duker, *Gisbertus Voetius*, 4 vols. (Leiden, 1897–1915), III, pp. 264–90; the entry 'Lambertus van Veldhuyzen' in *Nieuw nederlandsch biografisch woordenboek*, 10 vols. (Leiden, 1911–37), IV, cols. 1368–70; H. J. Siebrand, *Spinoza and the Netherlanders: An Enquiry into the Early Reception*

*cive* above all by its method, which he saw as the equivalent, in political philosophy, to that of Descartes in metaphysics. As he put it in the preface to his book, answering the objection that the principles established by so many centuries of previous moral and political philosophy could not be wrong, 'since no one, until now, has used his industry in this art of doubting everything, many of those principles, which are uncertain if they are not supported by further proof, have never been brought back to a single principle; and in the absence of such a principle the certainty of the rest will be shaky and unstable.'[223] Hobbes dispensed with authorities, and made no appeal to the 'consensus gentium', the agreed common practice of nations, in order to establish his natural law theory; and he did propose a single fundamental principle (self-preservation) on which the whole structure of natural law could be built. Van Velthuysen was attempting, at the same time, to produce a less radical version of Hobbes's theory, one that could accommodate natural-law duties towards God (and towards fellow-men, on the grounds that their preservation was willed by God); his own argument developed a sort of twin-track theory, in which theological ethics furnished the formal justification of natural law and self-preservation provided a system of motivation to comply with it. He emphasized that self-preservation did not explain the 'formal reason' of virtue in the revised edition of his work which he published in 1680—from which, also, he removed almost all references to Hobbes.[224]

Curiously, the structure of argument thus developed by van Velthuysen was very close to that worked out by Pierre Nicole in the 1670s, in which *amour-propre* was able to produce an exact imitation or simulacrum of virtue, without being the true ground of its virtuousness. The difference was that, while Nicole was moving from orthodox Augustinian theology in a Hobbesian direction, van Velthuysen was, to some extent, drifting away from Hobbes. Other writings by van Velthuysen show that his debt to Hobbes did in fact extend further than an interest in the theoretical outlines (as he saw them) of the argument of *De cive*: his writings against the jurisdictional power of the Reformed Church (which included a defence

---

*of his Philosophy of Religion* (Assen, 1988), pp. 79–95; W. N. A. Klever, *Verba et sententiae Spinozae or Lambertus van Velthuysen (1622–1685) on Benedictus de Spinoza* (Amsterdam, 1991); and the Introduction to L. van Velthuysen, *Des Principes du juste et du convenable: une apologie du* De cive *de Hobbes (1651–1680)*, tr. C. Secretan (Caen, 1995), pp. 7–37.

[223] L. van Velthuysen, *Epistolica dissertatio de principiis iusti et decori, continens apologiam pro tractatu clarissimi Hobbaei, De cive* (Amsterdam, 1651), sig. *5r ('cum enim antehac nec ipsi suam . . . industriam exercuerint hoc dubitandi de omnibus artificio, etiam nunquam factum est, ut multa illa principia, incerta si ulteriori probatione non innitantur, ad unum aliquod principium deducta sint, sine quo principio reliquorum certitudo nutat & vacillat'). An English translation of this work by van Velthuysen was published anonymously: *A Dissertation, wherein the Fundamentals of Natural or Moral Justice and Decorum are Stated, according to the Principles of Mr. Hobbes. By a Learned Pen* (London, 1706). The only copies known to me are in Trinity College, Dublin, and the State Library, Melbourne.

[224] See van Velthuysen, *Des Principes du juste*, pp. 17, 93. It might be said that van Velthuysen was thus closer to Howard Warrender's version of Hobbes's theory than to Hobbes's version.

of a utilitarian theory of punishment, and a plea for religious toleration, to be extended even to the Jews) were heavily dependent on Hobbesian arguments.[225] But those writings were mostly in Dutch, and would be much less widely read than his defence of *De cive*—which some European readers seem to have attributed to Hobbes himself.

The idea of reducing natural law and/or politics to a new, unified system appealed to many other thinkers in Europe at this time. One was the statesman and polymath Johann Christian von Boineburg, whose ambiguous attitude towards Hobbes (in the context of arguments about 'indifferentism') has already been mentioned. Von Boineburg had long been interested in the works of Grotius, and in the early 1660s he circulated to several scholars a project for combining law and ethics in a single system of natural jurisprudence.[226] It is not surprising that he should also have taken an interest in Hobbes: he had read *De cive* by October 1650, and within the next three months asked his mentor, Hermann Conring, for his opinion of it (receiving, as we have seen, an entirely negative response).[227] A few years later von Boineburg seems to have been the first person in Germany to take notice of *Leviathan*: he wrote to Conring in December 1655 that 'Hobbes has published a book, which he has entitled *Leviathan*; in it, he claims to demonstrate that the authority of the sovereign depends on the opinion of the common people.' A month later he added: 'Hobbes's *Leviathan* has come out only in English. A certain Englishman, who is staying in Cologne, will deliver it to me shortly.'[228] Corresponding with Conring in the 1650s, von Boineburg was content to echo his anti-Hobbesian judgements; but as time went by, his own sympathetic interest in Hobbes became more apparent. In 1661 he quoted to Conring the damning comments made by him ten years earlier, and enquired: 'I should like to find out whether your opinion about Hobbes is the same today; since then, I am sure you have read his *Epistolica dissertatio de principiis iusti et decori* [actually by van Velthuysen], his *Le Corps politique*, translated by Sorbière into French from the English, and Sorbière's own *Lettres et discours*, published in French

---

[225] The key text is his *Ondersoeck of de christelijcke overheydt eenigh quaedt in haer gebiedt mach toe laeten* (Middelburg, 1660): see pp. 14–19, 63–4 (on punishment), 291–6 (on toleration, including Jews). See also his *Het predick-ampt en 't recht der kercke, bepaelt nae de regelen van Godts woordt* (Amsterdam, 1660), and *Apologie voor het tractaet van de afgoderye en superstitie* (Utrecht, 1669).

[226] On the project see Hochstrasser, *Natural Law Theories*, pp. 49–52; on von Boineburg's special interest in Grotius (and role as a would-be coordinator of Grotianism) see E. Ultsch, *Johann Christian von Boineburg: ein Beitrag zur Geistesgeschichte des 17. Jahrhunderts* (Würzburg, 1936), pp. 71–6.

[227] Von Boineburg included *De cive* in a list of recent publications in a letter to Johann Conrad Dietrich, 17 Oct. 1650: see his *Epistolae ad Dietericum*, p. 126. For Conring's response see above, n. 63.

[228] Gruber, *Commercii epistolici tomus prodromus*, I, pp. 141, 15 Dec. 1655 ('*Hobbius* edidit librum, cui titulum fecit *Leuiathan*. Eo ostendere contendit, summarum potestatum authoritatem pendere ab opinione vulgi'; 149, 23 Jan. 1656 ('HOBBII Leuiathan non nisi Anglice prodiit. Eum mihi breui redditurus est quidam Anglus, qui degit Coloniae'). This Englishman may perhaps have been a Catholic Royalist in exile; but I have not been able to identify him.

a year and a half ago, in which you will find Hobbes expressly defended in several places.'[229]

Soon after writing that letter, von Boineburg struck up an epistolary friendship with Sorbière; later in 1661 he learned that Sorbière was preparing an 'apology' for Hobbes, along the lines of the defence made in the editorial materials (described by von Boineburg as 'worth reading') which he added to his translation of *De cive*. It thus seems highly likely that Hobbes was one of the topics discussed in their correspondence—although, unfortunately, the surviving letters from Sorbière to von Boineburg make no mention of him.[230] By September 1662 von Boineburg had summoned up the courage to remark, in a discussion of modern political authors in one of his letters to Conring: 'Bodin is the leader of them all; Hobbes, however, is a wonderful craftsman in the art of politics.'[231] And eight years later, writing to Henry Oldenburg in London and forwarding a letter from his protégé Leibniz to Hobbes, he referred to the elderly English philosopher as 'that most excellent of men'.[232]

Even conservative-minded theorists were capable of seeing that Hobbes's arguments made a strong and distinctive contribution to political theory. An example is the Dutch scholar Maarten Schoock, who is best known to historians of philosophy for his attack on Descartes. Schoock's outlook was essentially Aristotelian, but leavened by a spirited eclecticism that reflected his quirky character. (His publications, covering a huge range of subjects, included dissertations on beer, on herrings, and on the dislike of cheese.[233]) In his *Diatriba de jure naturali* (1659) he quoted approvingly, and at length, from *De cive* II.1, where Hobbes argued that natural law could not be derived from universal human practice, and set out his

[229] Gruber, *Commercii epistolici tomus prodromus*, I, pp. 456–7, 11 Feb. 1661 ('Optem resiscere, an hodieque idem de *Hobbio* arbitreris, postquam haud dubie ex illo tempore legisti dissertationem eius epistolicam de principiis iusti atque decori; tum corpus eius politicum, quod ex Anglico Gallice reddidit *Sorberius*; atque huiusce ipsius discursus et epistolas Gallice ante sesquiannum editas, quibus *Hobbium* ex instituto non semel defensum conspicies'). Conring's reply (p. 473) was, predictably, that he had not changed his mind.

[230] Ibid., I, pp. 557–8, 14 June 1661 ('Eius apologiam *Sorberius* iam parat'; 'Digna . . . lectu'). No further traces of this 'apology' have survived. The four letters from Sorbière to von Boineburg (from 1661–4) are in the Staatsarchiv, Würzburg, Schönborn-Archiv, Korrespondenz Johann Philipp, MS 2952, foliated 90–101. One letter from von Boineburg to Sorbière (1662) is printed in the latter's *Illustrium & eruditorum virorum epistolae*, pp. 591–3.

[231] Gruber, *Commercii epistolici tomus prodromus*, II, p. 931, 21 Sept. 1662 ('Princeps est omnium *Bodinus*. Mirus autem politices faber est *Hobbius*').

[232] H. Oldenburg, *Correspondence*, ed. A. R. Hall and M. B. Hall, 13 vols. (Madison, Wis., and London, 1965–86), XIII, pp. 422–3: 'I earnestly beg you to take charge of this letter for Hobbes, and also to let him [sc. Leibniz] know what that most excellent of men is working upon now, and whether he has published anything since his recent book in quarto' ('epistolam isthanc ad Hobbium ut curandam suspicias, obnixe rogo: simul ut significes ei quid summus ille vir impraesens agitet, et nunquid, post nuperum in 4to librum, ediderit'). The recent book could have been *De principiis et ratiocinatione geometrarum* (1666), the *Opera philosophica* (1668), or *Quadratura circuli* (1669).

[233] On Schoock, see the entry in *Nieuw nederlandsch biografisch woordenboek*, X, cols. 889–891; P. Dibon, *La Philosophie néerlandaise au siècle d'or*, vol. I (Paris, 1954), pp. 180–8; T. Verbeek, ed., *La Querelle d'Utrecht* (Paris, 1988).

own definition of it instead. He also accepted Hobbes's key distinction between 'jus naturale' (the right of nature) and 'lex naturalis' (the law of nature), criticizing a Jesuit author for confusing the two. And when it came to considering the contents of the laws of nature, he cited the entire list of natural laws given in *De cive*, making only two mild criticisms of Hobbes's presentation of the subject.[234]

Another conservative-minded writer with a respectful attitude to Hobbes (though more critical than Schoock) was the Lutheran jurist Erich Mauritius, who was professor of law at Tübingen (1660) and Kiel (1665).[235] In a dissertation delivered at Tübingen in 1662 he discussed Hobbes's definition of 'jus' (right), citing both *De cive* and *Le Corps politique*. Unusually, he also displayed a knowledge of *De homine*, quoting from chapter 10 of that work (where Hobbes argues that we can have certain knowledge of what is just and unjust because we 'make' the material of justice, pacts, ourselves): this showed, he suggested, that Hobbes had now abandoned his earlier belief in the existence of an objective natural law.[236] In other dissertations of the 1660s, Mauritius discussed Hobbes's argument about the relation between natural and international law, dissenting from it but referring to Hobbes as 'ingeniosus'; recommended Hobbes's 'pithy and forceful' treatment of the laws of war and peace in *De cive* and *Le Corps politique*; and referred to Hobbes's denial of the natural sociability of man, dismissing his view as false and dangerous, but noting that it was supported by 'arguments of some weight' in *De cive*.[237] The passage about natural and international law in *De cive* with which Mauritius disagreed was similarly discussed in a later work by his colleague at Kiel, the jurist Samuel Rachelius: again, the treatment of Hobbes was critical, but respectful.[238]

That Hobbes had made some original and significant contributions to these areas of legal and political theory was widely acknowledged. Even a sharp critic such as Conrad Samuel Schurzfleisch, whose pseudonymous remarks about Hobbes (reprinted by Deckherr) have already been mentioned, recognized this: 'I do not think there is anyone so lacking in sense and intelligence as to refuse to give Hobbes some credit,' he wrote. He described *De cive* as 'not inelegant' and Hobbes himself as having 'a very subtle brain', and merely warned that his theories were to be used for contemplation rather than practical application.[239]

---

[234] M. Schoock, *Diatriba de jure naturali* (Groningen, 1659), pp. 18 (*De cive*, II.1), 23 (jus/lex), 36–7 (list of natural laws). The criticisms (p. 37) were that Hobbes had omitted the duty to worship God, which should have been placed first, and that he had mixed together remote derivations of natural law with more immediate ones.

[235] On Mauritius (1631–91) see C. G. Jöcher, *Allgemeines Gelehrten-Lexicon*, 4 vols. (Leipzig, 1750–1), III, cols. 306–07.

[236] E. Mauritius, *Dissertationes et opuscula*, ed. J. N. Hertius (Strasbourg, 1724), pp. 1–2 ('jus'), 50 (*De homine*).

[237] Ibid., pp. 55 ('argumentis non nullius momenti'); 494 ('ingeniosus Hobbeus'), 543 ('succinctè et nervosè').

[238] S. Rachelius, *De jure naturae et gentium dissertationes* (Kiel, 1676), pp. 306–8, 313–14. On Rachelius, see Schneider, *Justitia universalis*, pp. 208–23.

[239] C. S. Schurzfleisch, *Epistolae nunc primum editae* (Wittenberg, 1700), pp. 182, 10 Apr. 1674 ('adeo neminem puto esse sine mente et sensu, ut non aliqvid Hobbesio tribuat'), 304 (27 Mar. 1675), 'nec

Of all the writers on law and politics in this period, however, one stands out for the depth of his engagement with—and indebtedness to—Hobbes's ideas: Samuel Pufendorf. Thanks to Pufendorf's own writings, which were widely studied throughout northern Europe, a significant mass of Hobbesian assumptions, methods, and arguments was incorporated into the mainstream of European natural law theory. In the dedicatory epistle to his first book, *Elementorum jurisprudentiae universalis libri II* (1660), Pufendorf openly acknowledged a debt to Hobbes: 'I have derived many things from that marvellous work by the incomparable Hugo Grotius, *De iure belli ac pacis*; I also declare that I owe not a little to Thomas Hobbes, whose theory in *De cive*, even if it has a certain savour of impiety, is nevertheless for the most part quite penetrating and sound.'[240] The dedicatee of this book, the Elector Palatine Karl Ludwig, was so impressed by it that he appointed Pufendorf to a chair at Heidelberg University; gossip later recorded by Leibniz would have it that Pufendorf had inserted this reference to Hobbes because he knew that the Elector was 'an extreme admirer of Hobbes', and that his professorial appointment was made on the strength of it.[241] (How much truth there is in this story is uncertain, but it is quite likely that the Elector did have an admiration for Hobbes: he was a man of keen philosophical and mathematical interests, and one of the key intellectual figures at the Palatine court in exile during his youth, Dr Samson Johnson, had taken a strong interest in Hobbes's work.[242]) Nevertheless, the tribute to Hobbes was truthful and sincere.

A few years later, having been contacted by von Boineburg—who recognized that Pufendorf's attempt to found a 'universal jurisprudence' chimed closely with his own project—Pufendorf sent him an account of the origins of his book. He explained that he had been imprisoned for eight months in Copenhagen under suspicion of spying for the Swedes (who were besieging the city), and that during that whole time he had been deprived both of books and of 'the conversation of

---

inelegans'); C. S. Schurzfleisch ['Schurtzfleisch'], *Freimuthige singularia von haupt-gelehrten Männern und auserlesenen alten und neuen Schriften* (Leipzig, 1711), p. 324 ('ein sehr subtiler Kopff'). Unfortunately, Schurzfleisch reserved his highest praise for the book *Dux vitae sive statera morum* (London, 1672), which he assumed to be by Hobbes. The author was in fact Hobbes's old sparring-partner Thomas White (see the entry in V. Placcius, *Theatrum anonymorum et pseudonymorum* (Hamburg, 1708), part 2, pp. 588–9).

[240] S. Pufendorf, *Elementorum jurisprudentiae universalis libri II* (The Hague, 1660), sig. π3r ('multa nos desumsisse ex mirando illo opere de Iure belli & pacis Viri incomparabilis *Hugonis Grotii* . . . Nec parum debere nos profitemur *Thomae Hobbes*, cujus hypothesis in libro de Cive etsi nescio quid profani sapiat; pleraque tamen caetera satis arguta ac sana').

[241] Leibniz, *Otium hanoveranum*, p. 181 ('summum Hobbesii admiratorem').

[242] See U. Chevreau, *Chevraeana, ou diverses pensées d'histoire, de critique, d'érudition et de morale*, 2 vols. (Amsterdam, 1700), II, pp. 99–100 (story of Karl Ludwig's interest in Spinoza, whom he also invited to Heidelberg); A. Vlacq, *Trigonometria artificialis* (Gouda, 1633), epistle dedicatory to Karl Ludwig, sig. +3r (on his interest in mathematics); Hobbes, *Correspondence*, I, p. 128 (on Johnson's interest in Hobbes); O. Ogle et al., eds., *Calendar of the Clarendon State Papers preserved in the Bodleian Library*, 5 vols. (Oxford, 1872–1970), II, p. 142 (Hyde recording in 1652 that Johnson expressed 'a great reverence for Mr Hobbs, and it seems is of his faith in all things').

learned men'. To keep up his spirits, he had gone over in his mind 'those things which I had once read in Grotius and Hobbes', adding some modifications of his own; after his release, he wrote out the contents of these solitary meditations.[243] The lack of detailed textual references to Grotius and Hobbes in his book tends to confirm this account; and what the whole story significantly implies is that Pufendorf had already made such a close study of *De cive* that its arguments were fully present in his mind. Certainly his analysis of the nature of law in his book, distinguishing it from 'consilium' (counsel) and from 'jus', as well as his whole list of the laws of nature, beginning with the fundamental law 'That each person should protect his life and limbs so far as he is able, and preserve himself and what is his,' was Hobbesian through and through.[244]

By the time Pufendorf came to publish his very influential treatise on natural and international law, *De iure naturae et gentium*, in 1672, his involvement with Hobbes's theories had become both more intense and more problematic. His reading had now extended to other works, including *De homine* and *Leviathan* (which he knew in the Dutch translation); and his new book was filled with passages which, in the words of the leading modern Pufendorf scholar, 'do not just contain brief allusions to Hobbes's doctrines, but discuss almost every line of *De cive* with such fullness, depth, and philological and philosophical acuity that, if we were to amuse ourselves by extracting from *De iure naturae et gentium* all the passages that deal with Hobbes and placing them as notes to the corresponding passages of his work, we would obtain the most imposing and most important commentary that *De cive* has ever had'.[245] On the other hand, however, Pufendorf's critics (of whom

---

[243] Staatsarchiv, Würzburg, Schönborn-Archiv, Korrespondenz Johann Philipp, MS 2946, fols. 40–3, Pufendorf to von Boineburg, 13 Jan. 1663, here fol. 40v ('eruditorum conversatione'; 'ea, quae quondam apud Grotium et Hobbesium legeram'). Later in the letter Pufendorf commented that 'Hobbes's intellect should not be denied praise, even though he scarcely progresses beyond first principles', and repeated, in a significantly modified form, his remark about impiety: 'and his theory *seems to have for many people* [my emphasis] a certain savour of impiety' (fols. 43r–43v: 'Neque Hobbesij acumen laude sua est privandum; etsi ille vix ultra principia progrediatur, et eiusdem hypothesis plerisque nescio quid profani videatur sapere'). This letter is printed and discussed in F. Palladini, 'Le due lettere di Pufendorf al Barone di Boineburg: quella nota e quella "perduta" ', *Nouvelles de la République des Lettres*, 1 (1984), pp. 119–44 (here pp. 131, 133).

[244] Pufendorf, *Elementa*, pp. 186–8 (nature of law), 304–52 (laws of nature; here p. 308 'Vt quilibet vitam & membra sua quantum potest tueatur, seque ac sua conservet'). The next laws after this are: do not disturb human society; omit those things that weaken your reason or harm your body; forgive others when they seek pardon; when imposing punishments, so do on the basis of deterring future wrongs; conserve social life; in controversies, go to arbitration; be grateful to benefactors; do not use signs that deceive others (pp. 308–46).

[245] F. Palladini, *Samuel Pufendorf discepolo di Hobbes: per una reinterpretazione del giusnaturalismo moderno* (Bologna, 1990), p. 19 ('non contengono solo brevi accenni alle dottrine hobbesiane, ma discutono quasi ogni riga del *De cive* con tale ampiezza, approfondimento, finezza filologica e filosofica che, qualora ci divertissimo a estrarre dal *De iure* tutti i passi riguardanti Hobbes e a metterli in nota ai corrispondenti passi della sua opera, otterremmo il commentario più imponente e importante che il *De cive* abbia mai avuto'). Palladini lists a selection of such passages in Pufendorf's book, with the Hobbes passages (mainly in *De cive*, but also in *De homine* and *Leviathan*) to which they refer or from which they derive: pp. 28–9, nn. 8–14. On his ownership of the Dutch *Leviathan* see above, n. 35.

there were many) had been quick to seize on his use of Hobbesian principles as a stick with which to beat him; a certain defensiveness had now crept into his use of Hobbes, and many of his references to that author's works in this text consisted of attempts to distinguish—often on quite minor points—Hobbes's ideas from his own.[246] His first real praise of Hobbes came in his discussion of the state of nature. '*Hobbes* has been lucky enough in painting the Inconveniences of such a State,' he observed, though his comment on the identification of this as a state of war was more guarded: 'These Notions are, in some measure, tolerable, if propos'd only by way of Hypothesis.'[247]

Pufendorf now insisted that his entire theory of natural law was fundamentally different from Hobbes's: his own theory was founded not on self-preservation, but on 'socialitas' (sociality or sociability). In another defensive work, written two years later, he claimed that he was as much an opponent of Hobbes on this point as Cumberland was.[248] Pufendorf's attempt here to insert himself into a line of argument running from Grotius to Cumberland was somewhat disingenuous: his 'socialitas' was in fact not a natural quality or disposition but a *dictate*, made necessary by the facts of human nature (above all, weakness and self-love), corresponding very closely to Hobbes's dictate, 'seek peace'.[249] If Pufendorf's theory was based on 'sociality', then Hobbes's might just as well have been described as based on 'pacificity'.

A curious episode from the following decade illustrates how awkward the position of a Hobbesian theorist had now become. In 1681 a little-known Dutch scholar, Adriaen Houtuyn, brought out a treatise, *Politica contracta generalis*, which was one of the purest statements of Hobbesian political theory ever published. The primary text was a short sequence of propositions summarizing the theory: state of nature, self-preservation the highest good, right to all things, state of war, reason dictating means to peace, need for 'absolute sovereignty', and so on. (In all of this, Hobbes's name was not mentioned.) This was followed by a lengthy commentary on each proposition in turn, adducing biblical examples, quotations from classical authors, and some references to Roman law. Tacked on at the end, however, was a list of 'Hobbesian errors'—evidently a precautionary measure, designed to give the book some quite spurious anti-Hobbesian credentials.[250]

---

[246] For a valuable guide to the criticisms of Pufendorf, with numerous examples of the accusation of Hobbesianism, see Palladini, *Discussioni seicentesche*.

[247] S. Pufendorf, *The Law of Nature and Nations*, ed. J. Barbeyrac, tr. B. Kennet, 5th edn (London, 1749), pp. 101 (bk 2, ch. 2, sect. 2), 108 (bk 2, ch. 2, sect. 6).

[248] Ibid., p. 136 (bk 2, ch. 3, sect. 16); S. Pufendorf, *Specimen controversiarum circa jus naturale ipsi nuper motarum* (Uppsala, 1678), sigs. A7r–A7v (letter to Johann Adam Scherzer, 17 Sept. 1674).

[249] On this crucial point see Palladini, *Pufendorf discepolo di Hobbes*, pp. 91–7. Palladini's book also demonstrates the closeness of Pufendorf to Hobbes on a number of other topics of central importance, such as the 'command'-theory of law.

[250] Houtuyn, *Politica contracta*, sigs. B6v–C1v (main text; sig. B7r, 'imperium absolutum'); pp. 1–278 (commentary); sigs Z4r–Z7r ('Errores Hobbesiani').

The fiercest critic of this work was none other than Samuel Pufendorf, who later published a 30-page denunciation of it as an appendix to one of his own books, claiming that he wished to protect 'the unsuspecting young people, to whom, we have noticed, that book has in some places been recommended by university lecturers'.[251] Seizing on the claim that the sovereign had the power to order any 'external' religious observance he wished, and that the subject must be content with merely internal faith, he declared: 'So far as I know, a power of that kind was first invented by Thomas Hobbes, the very worst framer of theological opinions.'[252] Yet it is noteworthy that Pufendorf's criticisms were concerned *only* with Houtuyn's comments about religion: the central claims of Houtuyn's political theory were left untouched. And even where religion was concerned, readers might well have noticed that the book by Pufendorf to which this criticism was appended contained many arguments resting on similar Hobbesian assumptions: it constantly emphasized the difference in kind between religion and civil society, insisted the Christ had not come to earth as a ruler, and so on. The criticism of Houtuyn, tacked on to this text, was to some extent fulfilling the same purpose as Houtuyn's own anti-Hobbesian appendix. Thus, a Hobbesian was protecting himself by attacking a Hobbesian, though without criticizing Hobbes's central theory, and the Hobbesian he was attacking had himself presented Hobbes's theory while pretending to attack it.

Eventually—thanks partly to the efforts of his editor–translator Jean Barbeyrac, whose French version of *De iure naturae et gentium* (1706) would become one of the most widely read works of jurisprudence in the eighteenth century—Pufendorf came to be regarded as having a fundamentally critical and negative attitude towards Hobbes.[253] There was, however, one important area in which his debt to Hobbes was undeniable, not least because he so clearly acknowledged it himself: that of method. In his *Dissertatio de statu hominum naturali* (1675) he described the analytical method of modern political theory in terms drawn directly

---

[251] S. Pufendorf, *De habitu religionis christianae ad vitam civilem* (Bremen, 1687), pp. 196–224, 'Animadversiones ad aliqua loca è *Politica contracta* Adriani Houtuyn', here p. 197 ('incauta juventus, cui libellum istum alicubi à Doctoribus publicis commendari percepimus').

[252] Ibid., p. 223 ('Quam quidem potestatem, quantum mihi constat, primus commentus est *Thomas Hobbes*, pessimus sententiarum Theologicarum autor').

[253] Barbeyrac's notes lost no opportunity to snipe at Hobbes; for example, where Pufendorf agreed with Hobbes that life in the state of nature would be poor, Barbeyrac primly admonished him: 'Labour and good Husbandry would easily furnish us with all things necessary for Life. None but Sluggards and Prodigals would fall into Poverty, and this often happens in civil Societies' (Pufendorf, *Law of Nature*, p. 101 (n.) ). On Barbeyrac's attitude see Glaziou, *Hobbes en France*, pp. 57–60 (where, however, some positive comments about Hobbes are attributed to Barbeyrac (p. 58): Glaziou has not noticed that Barbeyrac was merely copying them from Pufendorf, *Specimen*, pp. 11–12). The desire to detach Pufendorf from Hobbes is apparent in many of his modern commentators (such as L. Krieger, *The Politics of Discretion: Pufendorf and the Acceptance of Natural Law* (Chicago, 1965) ); see the comments on this in H. Medick, *Naturzustand und Naturgeschichte der bürgerlichen Gesellschaft* (Göttingen, 1973), pp. 42 (n.), 44–5 (n.), and Palladini, *Pufendorf discepolo di Hobbes*, pp. 22–30.

from Hobbes's account of his own method in the preface to *De cive*: just as scientists took apart physical bodies to analyse them into their components, so too political theorists had analysed the state. 'They have examined its inner structure ... and ... carefully distinguished the parts of which this huge body is made up. They have gone much further, seeing the final aim of their science as transcending all societies and as conceiving of the condition and state of men outside society.'[254] A few years later, Pufendorf set out a brief history of 'the discipline of natural law': he described Grotius as having been the first to distinguish natural law properly from human positive laws, but then credited Hobbes with having applied to moral theory 'that type of precise demonstration which is customary among the mathematicians'.[255] His final judgement on Hobbes was that his work contained many bad things and many 'exquisitely good' things, and that 'even those false things which he teaches have served as a tool for bringing moral and political science to perfection, so that many of the things that contribute to its perfection would hardly have occurred to anyone, were it not for Hobbes'.[256]

Other writers concurred with this judgement. Johann Christian Becmann, professor of history at the University of Frankfurt an der Oder, began his treatise on politics (published in 1674) with a long list of writers on political theory, culminating in 'those incomparable men' Grotius, Hobbes, and Pufendorf. He agreed with Hobbes's theory of law as a declaration of will, defended at length his account of the state of nature, and cited *Leviathan* in defence of the proposition that obedience to sovereignty involves laying down one's judgement and accepting that of the ruler (explaining that this does not mean that one ceases to reason or have judgements, merely that one ceases to act on them).[257] He admitted that Hobbes's writings on religion were not to be relied on, but he defended him from the charge of atheism, arguing that no one who had tried so hard to 'advance towards the first principles of morality' could be an atheist. Like Pufendorf, Becmann paid special tribute to Hobbes's method; unlike Pufendorf, however, he dispensed with even a token acknowledgement of Grotius's priority or primacy. 'In Hobbes's books about the citizen and the state, the general aim is to derive the subject-matter of politics

---

[254] Cited in A. Dufour, 'Pufendorf', in J. H. Burns and M. Goldie, eds., *The Cambridge History of Political Thought, 1450–1700* (Cambridge, 1991), pp. 561–88, here p. 571 (where the work is misdated '1677').

[255] Pufendorf, *Specimen*, pp. 11–12 ('ἀκριβείαν demonstrandi mathematicis usitatam').

[256] Ibid., p. 13 ('exquisitè bona'; '& illa ipsa, quae ab eo falsa traduntur, ansam praebuerunt scientiam moralem & civilem ad fastigium perducendi, sic ut de non paucis, quae ad perfectionem istius faciunt, vix cogitare alicui in mentem venisset, absque *Hobbesio* si fuisset').

[257] J. C. Becmann ['Becmanus'], *Meditationes politicae iisdemque continuandis & illustrandis addita politica parallela*, 3rd edn (Frankfurt an der Oder, 1679), pp. 7 ('Incomparabiles Viri'), 50–1 (state of nature), 85–6 (*Leviathan*), 182 (law). This text, the *Meditationes*, was first published in 1674; this edition included for the first time a new text, the *Politica parallela*, printed here with separate title page but continuous pagination. On Becmann (1641–1717), who became professor of politics at Frankfurt an der Oder in 1687 and professor of theology in 1690, and also published an annotated edition of Grotius's *De iure belli ac pacis*, see Jöcher, *Gelehrten-Lexicon*, I, cols 994–5; Palladini, *Discussioni seicenteschi*, pp. 284–5.

['res Politicas'] from the first principles of rational nature and social life; and on that account he does indeed deserve to be praised above all others, since no political writer before him had dared to do that.'[258]

This idea of a single science of law and politics, drawn from the first principles of human nature and therefore equally applicable to all societies and forms of government, exerted a powerful attraction. In 1682 the influential Frisian jurist Ulric Huber gave an 'oration' at Franeker University (where he occupied the senior chair in law) on the separation of 'jus civitatis' (roughly, political jurisprudence) from 'politica' (politics, or political science). The aim of the former, he said, should be to teach the rights and duties of citizens in any state whatsoever. Previous writers such as Bodin, Althusius, Besoldus, and Arnisaeus had mixed this up with political science—that is, the study of political forms and actions, constitutions, policies, and so on. Huber wanted to get away from the old style of political writing, full of 'consilia & monita' (practical hints about what to do or what to avoid), and to develop instead a pure theory of rights and duties.[259] Grotius, he observed, had been the first to prepare the way for this separation of the two; he did not mention Hobbes, but many listeners, familiar already with Pufendorf's account of the matter, might reasonably have concluded that, if Grotius was the John the Baptist, a mere forerunner, then the Messiah must have been Hobbes.

Perhaps because of this underlying affinity with Hobbes's project, Huber went out of his way to criticize Hobbes. The first edition of his major treatise on politics, *De jure civitatis* (1673) had a special chapter (dropped from later editions) setting out his disagreements with Hobbes: one of these, interestingly, was that Hobbes's arguments in defence of monarchy as a form of government belonged 'not to jurisprudence but to politics'—in effect, an accusation that Hobbes's method here was not Hobbesian enough.[260] Huber did indeed differ from Hobbes on some major points of substance: while agreeing that the state of nature would be a war of all against all, he denied that this would happen by right, and he also denied

---

[258] Becmann, *Meditationes*, pp. 417–18 ('In *Hobbesii* Libris eorum, quae de Cive & Civitate agunt . . . Scopus generalis est è primis Principiis Naturae Rationalis ac vitae Socialis res Politicas eruere: Qvo quidem nomine prae caeteris laudandus est, cum nemo Politicorum ante illum id ausus fuerit'; 'ad prima usque principia moralium progredi conatur'). This is from the first chapter of the *Politica parallela*. Becmann concluded that Hobbes was a 'neutralist' rather than an atheist; his phrasing here was later borrowed (and put to more hostile use) by Georg Pasch: see above, at n. 86.

[259] U. Huber, *De jure civitatis libri tres*, rev. edn (Franeker, 1684), sigs. 2*5r–2*6v. (The dismissive remark about 'consilia & monita' was a swipe at the Lipsian tradition.) The main text of this book was first published in 1673. On Huber see E. H. Kossmann, 'De Dissertationes Politicae van Ulric Huber', in P. K. King and P. F. Vincent, eds., *European Context: Studies in the History and Literature of the Netherlands presented to Theodoor Weevers* (Cambridge, 1971), pp. 164–77; T. J. Veen, *Recht en nut: studiën over en naar aanleiding van Ulrik Huber (1636–1694)* (Zwolle, 1976) (esp. pp. 12–15 on the separation discussed here); F. Lomonaco, *Lex regia: diritto, filologia e fides historica nella cultura politico-filosofica dell'Olanda di fine seicento* (Naples, 1990), pp. 129–86.

[260] The relevant pages (224–32) from the rare 1st edn are given in photo-reproduction in Veen, *Recht en nut*, pp. 176–8 (here p. 225).

that fear was the basic reason why men desired society.[261] But his account of the origins of the State were distinctly Hobbesian: 'Agreement to form an alliance was not sufficient to do away with conflict. A way and method was needed of such a sort that the will of all individuals would become a single will. But that single will is nothing other than the sovereignty ('Imperium') of a state.'[262]

In the circumstances, it is a strange irony that one of the most fervently pro-Hobbesian works published in this period, *De veritate philosophiae Hobbesianae*, by an obscure Frisian lawyer, Mentet Kettwig, should have been framed as an attack on Huber. 'I ask you, distinguished Sir,' blustered Kettwig in Hobbes's defence, 'is demonstrating the rights of the ruler and the nature of the state the same thing as recommending gross abuses of power?'[263] Huber would have been the first to agree that the two things were not the same, and that Hobbes's arguments, even if faulty, were indeed an attempt to demonstrate 'the rights of the ruler and the nature of the state'.[264]

Stimulated by Pufendorf's account of the development of this modern science of natural law and political jurisprudence (which was recapitulated by Barbeyrac in the preface to his influential edition), a whole succession of writers would agree that the science had begun with Grotius.[265] The intellectual and theological

---

[261] Huber, *De jure civitatis*, pp.12–14. Huber tried where possible to align himself with Grotius against Hobbes. Interestingly, he commented: 'Some people say, I gather, that Grotius wished he had seen Hobbes's theory before he published his *De iure belli ac pacis*. I think he could have prepared his reader against those pestiferous—or, to put it as mildly as possible, dangerous—doctrines' (p. 23: 'Audio, qui *Grotium* optasse ferunt, visa ut sibi fuisset Hobbesiana doctrina, antequam suum *jus belli & pacis* edidisset. Credo, ut praemunire suum lectorem adversus pestifera, vel, ut mollissime dicam, periculosa dogmata potuisset').

[262] Ibid., p. 39 ('Nec tamen consensio in foedus, ad tollendam confusionem sufficiebat. Necessaria fuit ejusmodi ratio & modus, per quem omnium voluntas una fieret . . . Voluntas autem una ista nihil aliud est quam *Imperium* Civitatis').

[263] M. Kettwig, *De veritate philosophiae Hobbesianae: contra virum amplissimum Ulricum Huberum* (n.p. [Bremen?], 1695), p. 10 ('Quaeso Amplissime Vir, an jura imperantis, & naturam Civitatis demonstrare, est flagitia dominationum praescribere?'). For what little is known of Kettwig (who proceeded Doctor of Law at Franeker in 1690), see Veen, *Recht en nut*, pp. 164–6.

[264] Wilhelm Hennis notes that the modern science of universal public jurisprudence ('ius publicum universale', 'allgemeines Staatsrecht') was primarily Hobbesian in origin (*Politik und praktische Philosophie: Schriften zur politischen Theorie* (Stuttgart, 1977), p. 47); Stolleis claims that this is true only in so far as Hobbes's method was taken up by Huber, to whom he attributes its true origin (*Geschichte des öffentlichen Rechts*, p. 291 (n.) ). C. Link goes further, attributing the modern science entirely to Huber and describing it as essentially anti-Hobbesian: *Herrschaftsordnung und bürgerliche Freiheit: Grenzen der Staatsgewalt in der älteren deutschen Staatslehre* (Vienna, 1979), pp. 45–50. But the change was under way well before the publication of Huber's book; two years earlier, in 1671, Hermann Conring observed that one of the 'errors which were common roughly thirty years ago' was 'that politics and public jurisprudence were the same thing. If you look at books published more than thirty years ago, almost all of them suffered from this disease' (Annotations to J. Lampadius, *De republica romano-germanica*, in Conring, *Opera*, II, p. 247: 'errores, qui ante 30. annos admodum erant frequentes . . . politicam & jurispubl. scientiam esse eandem. Si quis videat libros ante 30. annos scriptos, hoc morbo laborarunt fere omnes'). As it happens, Conring's 'thirty years' go back to within just one year of the first publication of *De cive*.

[265] See the comments in R. Tuck, 'Grotius, Carneades and Hobbes', *Grotiana*, n.s., vol. 4 (1983), 43–62, esp. p. 61, and the major study of this theme by Hochstrasser, *Natural Law Theories* (with a listing of writers on pp. 38–9).

respectability of Grotius (once his quarrels with his Calvinist critics had been forgotten) was so great that he achieved an almost talismanic status for the practitioners of the science. Hobbes was quietly demoted; and, thanks to this down-playing of his role, what was in fact an essentially Hobbesian *Problematik* could be all the more safely transmitted—via the writings of theorists such as Pufendorf—to posterity. Before the historiography became thus fixed, however, there was one interestingly dissentient account. In 1709 the German jurist Immanuel Proeleus published a 'Short history of natural law', in which he began by agreeing that Grotius had treated natural law as a separate science (though he noted that earlier authors, such as Benedict Winkler and Alberico Gentili, had done something similar). But the key development, he believed, had come after Grotius. 'The present-day naturalists are especially concerned to find one principle, from which they might derive everything quite directly. If one looks at Grotius, one finds that he was really not too concerned with that. He discourses very well about the material that he has to hand: it comes partly from pure reason, partly from divine law, and partly from the customs of nations.' But, Proeleus observed, it was Hobbes who was the first to achieve the essential theoretical breakthrough, that of deriving the entire system of argument from a single principle—the principle of the natural right of self-preservation.[266]

One other German writer of this period had an admiration for Hobbes's method (not only in political science) that would remain undimmed in spite of his mounting disagreements with most of the contents of Hobbes's theories: Gottfried Wilhelm Leibniz. From his student days onwards, Leibniz was an avid reader of Hobbes's works: the dissertation he wrote for his bachelor's degree in 1663 shows a knowledge of *De corpore* (then available only in the London edition), and there are references to that book and to *De cive* in marginal notes written by Leibniz in 1663–4.[267] In the most important philosophical work of his student years, the *Dissertatio de arte combinatoria* (1666), he paid special tribute to Hobbes: 'That profoundest examiner of basic principles in all matters, Thomas Hobbes, correctly proposed that every operation of our minds is a computation.'[268] Two years later,

---

[266] I. Proeleus, *Grund-Sätze des Rechts der Natur nebst einer kurzen Historie und Anmerckungen über die Lehren des Hrn. Barons von Puffendorff* (Leipzig, 1709), pp. 91–122, 'Kurze Historie des Rechts der Natur', here pp. 110 (Grotius, Winkler, Gentili), 111 ('Die heutige Naturalisten bekümmern sich sonderlich am ein *Principium*, daraus sie ohne Weitläuffigkeit alles deduciren könten, wenn man den *Grotium* ansiehet, hat er sich darum nicht eben zu viel bekümmert. Er raisonniret über die vorkommenden *materien* sehr wohl, theils aus der gesunden Vernunfft, theils nach dem Göttlichen Recht, theils nach den Gewohnheiten der Völcker'), 114 (Hobbes). This work is unfortunately omitted from Hochstrasser's list (see above, n. 265), perhaps because of its rarity. I have consulted the copy in the Library of Congress, Washington, DC, pressmark JC181 P7 Pre-1801 Coll.

[267] L. Couturat, *La Logique de Leibniz d'après des documents inédits* (Paris, 1901), p. 467; G. W. Leibniz, *Sämtliche Schriften und Briefe* (Darmstadt, 1925– ), ser. 6, vol. I, pp. 21–41. *De corpore* would be a major influence on Leibniz's early writings about physics: see H. R. Bernstein, '*Conatus*, Hobbes, and the Young Leibniz', *Studies in the History and Philosophy of Science*, 11 (1980), pp. 25–37.

[268] Leibniz, *Sämtliche Schriften*, ser. 6, vol. I, p. 194 ('Profundissimus principiorum in omnibus rebus scrutator Th. Hobbes meritò posuit omne opus mentis nostrae esse computationem').

having come under the patronage of Johann Christian von Boineburg, he began to work on a project close to von Boineburg's heart: taking the whole corpus of Roman law, reducing it to rational principles, and recodifying it. This prompted a further close engagement with *De cive*: in his correspondence in 1670 Leibniz praised Hobbes's 'almost divine subtlety', and described him as the only person to have constructed anything like a demonstrative science of moral philosophy, regretting merely that he had produced unacceptable conclusions on some matters.[269] Writing to Lambert van Velthuysen in 1671, Leibniz explained: 'I am immersed as deeply as anyone in the philosophy of Hobbes's *De cive*. For me, all his points are diligently considered and thoroughly reasoned.'[270]

Leibniz twice wrote (or at least drafted) letters to Hobbes. The first, in 1670, was forwarded, as we have seen, by von Boineburg to Oldenburg in London, but the second (*c*.1674) exists only in draft; unfortunately, it is not known whether Hobbes received either of these letters. They would certainly have made gratifying reading. 'I think I have read most of your works, partly in separate volumes and partly in the collected edition,' Leibniz wrote in 1670, 'and I freely confess that I have profited from few other works of our age as much as I have from yours.' And in the second letter: 'you were the first person to place the correct method of argument and demonstration . . . in the clear light of political philosophy'.[271]

Such praise for Hobbes's method was quite compatible, however, with real disagreement about some of his conclusions or assumptions. Two such disagreements (about the relevance of the afterlife to the Hobbesian calculus of natural law, and about the right of resistance) were delicately raised by Leibniz in his second letter. Elsewhere, as we have already seen, he expressed himself more strongly in correspondence with Jakob Thomasius, whose intense disapproval of Hobbes was well known. Given the enormous gulf that separated Hobbes's fundamental assumptions from the theology and metaphysics of the mature Leibniz—above all, from the latter's belief that the nature of justice could be derived from eternal principles of wisdom and goodness present in the mind of God—it is not surprising that Leibniz's later comments on Hobbes's theories were generally critical and negative. Defending a modified version of the traditional constitutional theory of the Holy Roman Empire in 1677, he complained that Hobbes's theory had set up a false alternative when it offered the choice between unitary sovereignty and anarchy, concluding that the Hobbesian state had never really existed.[272] In his 'Opinion

---

[269] Leibniz, *Sämtliche Schriften*, ser. 1, vol. I, pp. 89 ('subtilitate sua pene divina'), 108.
[270] Christie's (New York) sale catalogue for 16–17 Dec. 1983, lot 495 (unpublished letter, 7 May 1671).
[271] Hobbes, *Correspondence*, II, pp. 713 ('Opera Tua partim sparsim partim junctim edita pleraque me legisse credo, atque ex iis quantum ex aliis nostro seculo non multis profiteor profecisse'), 731 ('TE, qvi primus illam accuratam disputandi ac demonstratandi rationem . . . in civilis scientiae clara luce posuisti'). These letters are strangely misinterpreted as antagonistic by Patrick Riley in his 'Introduction' to G. W. Leibniz, *The Political Writings*, ed. and tr. P. Riley (Cambridge, 1972), p. 1.
[272] Leibniz, *Political Writings*, pp. 118–20.

on the Principles of Pufendorf' (a hostile critique written originally as a letter, in 1706), he observed that Pufendorf's ideas were mostly borrowed from others, and he singled out Hobbes's theory about the relation between justice and law: 'a view to which I am astonished that anyone could have adhered'.[273] And to his *Essais de théodicée* (1710) he added a brief appendix discussing Hobbes's dispute with Bramhall about liberty and necessity, in which, while conceding that Hobbes reasoned here 'with his usual spirit and subtlety', he expressed his thoroughgoing opposition to Hobbes's main theological assumptions.[274] Nevertheless, even in his most hostile comments on Hobbes's theories, he was always prepared to pay some tribute to what he called 'the profound genius of Hobbes'; a serious engagement with those theories, rather than a scandalized rejection of them, was thereby encouraged.[275]

Leibniz thus contributed, at least indirectly, to the significant flowering of interest in Hobbes which took place in central Germany (Saxony and Prussia) at the end of the seventeenth century and the beginning of the eighteenth. The key thinker here was that other dominant figure of the early Enlightenment in Germany, Christian Thomasius (the son of Jakob), who moved from Leipzig to the nearby Prussian town of Halle in 1690 and became the chief organizer of the new university there from 1694 onwards.[276] Although Thomasius's personal relations with Leibniz were distant and somewhat cool—one reason for this being Thomasius's loyalty to his own teacher, Pufendorf—their rationalist intellectual projects, overall, were not dissimilar. Both belonged to that generation of younger Leipzig academics who had succeeded the older, dogmatic Lutherans and embraced modern philosophy instead.[277] Both, nevertheless, still had strong theological and religious concerns. In Thomasius's case there was quite a strong affinity with the Pietist movement (with which Pufendorf had also been connected); the attraction here was not only the moral and spiritual earnestness of the movement, but its implicitly anti-ecclesial nature.[278] The rational state envisaged by Thomasius had (for Pufendorfian, and ultimately Hobbesian, reasons) no room for churches endowed with their own jurisdictional powers. It is not a coincidence that one of the most

---

[273] Ibid., p. 70. On Leibniz's scornful attitude to Pufendorf see Hochstrasser, *Natural Law Theories*, pp. 72–83.

[274] G. W. Leibniz, *Opera philosophica quae exstant latina, gallica, germanica, omnia*, ed. J. E. Erdmann (Berlin, 1840), pp. 629–32 (here p. 629: 'avec son esprit et sa subtilité ordinaire').

[275] Leibniz, *Political Writings*, p. 65.

[276] On Thomasius see M. Fleischmann, ed., *Christian Thomasius: Leben und Lebenswerk* (Halle, 1931); W. Schneiders, ed., *Christian Thomasius, 1655–1728: Interpretationen zu Werk und Wirkung* (Hamburg, 1989); and the valuable account in Hochstrasser, *Natural Law Theories*, pp. 111–49.

[277] On the Leipzig background see Hammerstein, *Jus und Historie*, pp. 267–72.

[278] On Pufendorf's Pietist connections see S. Wollgast, 'Die deutsche Frühaufklärung und Samuel Pufendorf', in F. Palladini and G. Hartung, eds., *Samuel Pufendorf und die europäische Frühaufklärung* (Berlin, 1996), pp. 40–60 (esp. pp. 47–50, emphasizing the role of Pietism as a counterpart to the secular early Enlightenment).

gentle treatments Hobbes ever received at the hands of a theologian was in the massive survey of Christian heterodoxy by the Pietist intellectual Gottfried Arnold, the *Unparteyische Kircher- und Ketzer-Historie* (1699–1700). Hobbes was presented by Arnold as an earnest seeker after truth. He was described as a 'naturalist', but the charge of atheism was specifically rejected; and, drawing on comments in the prose *Vita*, Arnold noted that 'he was called an "atheist" because he would not give his full approval to the common and inadequate theology of the schoolmen, and refused to be a slave to common opinion'.[279] Nor is it coincidental that a reactionary defender of orthodox Lutheranism such as Valentin Ernst Löscher should have denounced Hobbes, fought against Pietism and also mounted a campaign against Thomasius.[280]

Rationalism and Pietist pessimism about man's fallen nature were combined in Thomasius's political theory. Drawn at first to the idea of a natural law grounded in knowledge of God's nature (or, at least, of the evident purpose of God's creation), Thomasius underwent a crisis of confidence in the 1690s, doubting whether man's corrupt nature would be able to lead a virtuous life even if the dictates of virtue were demonstrable. The solution to this crisis was presented by him in an essay of 1700 entitled 'Natura hominis, libertas voluntatis, imputatio in poenam' ('The nature of man, free will, and culpability'). In the words of one modern scholar, 'The argument of this piece is wholly Hobbesian in its insistence that the will may be compelled to obey both reason's dictates and political norms, but only through fear of punishment.'[281] In a manner broadly similar to the French Augustinians, he thus envisaged the State and its positive laws as creating a motivational framework by means of which people would be obliged to perform virtuous actions, but for self-interested reasons. His political theory developed some of the most Hobbesian elements in Pufendorf's position: a complete division between divine authority and the authority of the State (which was purely human), for example, and the concept of the sovereign as a 'persona moralis' into which all the powers and wills of the subjects must be gathered. At the same time, Thomasius's emphasis on the prudential and consequentialist nature of human obligation led to a theory of penal law in which punishments were justified (in true Hobbesian fashion) only by their deterrent effects: this meant that nothing more than the level of punishment sufficient for deterrence was required, and it also implied that certain 'crimes' which themselves lacked real effects (such as witchcraft or heresy) could be decriminalized. The gradual abolition of witch-trials in Brandenburg–Prussia in the

---

[279] G. Arnold, *Unparteyische Kirchen- und Ketzer-Historie von Anfang des Neuen Testaments biss auff das Jahr Christi 1688*, 4 parts in 2 vols. (Frankfurt am Main, 1699–1700), vol. I, part 2, pp. 608–10; here p. 609 ('Naturalist'; 'er deswegen ein *Atheiste* geheissen worden, weil er die gemeine und unzulängliche Lehrart der schulen von Gott nicht alle gut heissen, noch ein Sclave von allen gemeinen meynungen seyn wollen'). This work was published by Thomas Fritsch.
[280] See F. Blanckmeister, *Der Prophet von Kursachsen*, esp. pp. 208–14, and above, n. 90.
[281] Hochstrasser, *Natural Law Theories*, p. 131.

period 1714–28 was largely due to the influence of Thomasius's arguments.[282] In such ways, elements of an essentially Hobbesian heritage of political thought were passed on to the eighteenth-century ideology of 'enlightened absolutism'.

Thomasius's own attitude towards Hobbes was refreshingly positive. Presenting his extensive German summary of the text of Hobbes's *Historia ecclesiastica* in 1715, he emphasized at the start the theme of a self-interested priesthood using metaphysics and theology as instruments for the promotion of its own power, and recommended that the reader compare this with the contents of chapter 45 of *Leviathan*. Then, after summarizing Hobbes's account of the theology of the early Church, he commented: 'If I have to reveal my own opinion about everything Hobbes has written up to this point, then I must say that Hobbes has written many true things here.' At the end of his presentation of the whole text, he remarked that he had to differ from Hobbes on two points: his idea that the subject must obey the sovereign in all religious matters, and his denial of an incorporeal soul. 'Leaving those points aside, I say, this is certainly no trifling work that Hobbes has written; with it, he has thrust his hand, so to speak, into the heart and bowels of the Pope, and has found out his hiding-place better than anyone before him.'[283] Similarly, his German synthesis of Hobbes's *Vitae* and the Aubrey-Blackburne 'Vitae auctarium' was unmistakably pro-Hobbesian. 'Most people,' he announced at the outset, 'are so constituted that when they read the writings of someone whose name is in the black book . . . they are immediately gripped by their prejudices, and try to find the most harmful poison and most dreadful heresies in every word and syllable . . . Now, even though Hobbes has written much that most orthodox people would not be happy to repeat, nevertheless he has also written and discovered much that we should accept from him with thanks.' And he concluded: 'So what should we think of Hobbes? Does he belong to the list of atheists? I do not want to, indeed I cannot, say so.'[284]

As the leading light of the University of Halle, Thomasius was a very influential figure; his comments on Hobbes would no doubt have found many sympathetic

---

[282] On all these points see H. Rüping, 'Thomasius und seine Schüler im brandenburgischen Staat', in H. Thieme, ed., *Humanismus und Naturrecht in Berlin-Brandenburg-Preussen* (Berlin, 1979), pp. 76–89.

[283] Thomasius, *Summarischer Nachrichten*, part 4 (1715), pp. 315–17 (priesthood, *Leviathan*), 325 ('Wenn ich bey allem dem, was *Hobbesius* bishero geschrieben, meine Meinung entdecken soll, so kann ich nicht anders sagen, als dass *Hobbesius* allhier viele wahrheiten geschrieben'), 357 ('Wenn ich, sage ich, diese Puncte bey Seite setze, so ist gewisslich dieses keine geringe Schrifft, die *Hobbes* geschrieben, sondern er hat damit dem Pabste so zu sagen recht ins Hertze und ins Eingeweyde gegriffen, und die Schluppwinckel ehe erhandt, als jemand vor ihm').

[284] Ibid., part 2 (1715), pp. 166 ('Die meisten Menschen sind so beschaffen, wenn sie die Schrifften eines Mannes lesen, dessen Nahme in dem schwartzen Register stehet . . . so sind sie gleich von ihnen Vorurtheilen eingenommen, und suchen in allen Sylben und Worten das schädligste Gifft und greuligste Ketzereyen . . . Wenn nun gleich *Hobbes* vieles geschrieben, was ihm die meisten Rechtgläubigen nicht gerne nachsagen wolten; so hat er doch auch vieles geschrieben und entdecket, welches man von ihm mit Dank annehmen solte'), 182 ('Was nun vom *Hobbesio* zu halten? und ob er in die Atheisten Rolle mit gehöre? will, und kan ich itzo nicht sagen').

readers and listeners. A growth of interest in Hobbes among the students and intellectuals at Halle may well have been one reason why the publisher Thomas Fritsch, in nearby Leipzig, thought he would find willing buyers for a new edition of Hobbes's works.[285] And it must surely have been thanks to such local interest that the Halle publisher Johann Friedrich Zeitler issued, probably in the first decade of the eighteenth century, a new edition of *De cive*: Zeitler had a close relationship with the new university, publishing a work by Thomasius in 1694 and the catalogue of the university library in 1700.[286] Nor, then, is it surprising that the staunchest defender of Hobbes in early eighteenth-century Europe was a protégé and close friend of Thomasius whose academic career took place entirely at Halle: Nicolaus Hieronymus Gundling. Having previously studied theology and been a schoolmaster and Lutheran preacher in Nuremberg, Gundling came to Halle to study law, gaining his doctorate in 1703; he was appointed professor of philosophy in 1705 and professor of natural and international law in 1709, later becoming Rector Magnificus of the university. A quirky polymath with an ironic and amusing manner, he was a very popular teacher—so popular that even after his death (in 1729) many of his lectures were prepared for publication from his notes.[287] Also after his death his entire library was auctioned: the printed catalogue fills 1,060 pages (at roughly twelve books per page), and includes *De cive*, *Le Corps politique*, and the 1670 edition of the Latin *Leviathan*.[288]

Gundling's first published defence of Hobbes was an essay entitled 'Hobbesius ab atheismo liberatus' ('Hobbes freed from atheism'), issued in 1707. Like Thomasius, he used material from the Aubrey-Blackburne 'Vitae auctarium' to defend Hobbes's character and personal morality. As for Hobbes's religious beliefs, he observed, it was true that he was not a supporter of Roman Catholicism, Lutheranism, Calvinism, or any other sect; but it was not true that he was an atheist. *De cive* contained nothing profane or destructive of belief in God: in fact 'no one has demonstrated the attributes of God more lucidly'. Gundling was happy to accept the argument of the appendix to *Leviathan*, in which Hobbes claimed that describing God as 'body' was just a way of saying that God was substantial or real. Robustly, Gundling dismissed the complaints of Cumberland and Parker on this point; and he was particularly scornful about Gijsbert Cocq, whose *Hobbesianismi anatome* he called 'a book worthy of an incompetent theologian'.

---

[285] See above, at n. 13.

[286] P. Poiret, *De eruditione editio nova cui accessit Chr. Thomasii dissertatio de scriptis autoris* (Frankfurt and Leipzig: J. F. Zeitler, 1694); C. Thurmann, *Bibliotheca academica . . . Halae* (Halle: J. F. Zeitler, 1700). The Zeitler edn of *De cive* has no date or place of publication. The prefatory materials to the 1742 (Amsterdam?) edition of *De cive* refer to it as having been printed in Halle in 1704 (sig. †4r).

[287] On Gundling see Jöcher, *Gelehrten-Lexicon*, II, cols. 1279–81; G. Zart, *Einfluss der englischen Philosophen seit Bacon auf die deutsche Philosophie des 18. Jahrhunderts* (Berlin, 1881), pp. 44–9; Hammerstein, *Jus und Historie*, pp. 205–65.

[288] C. B. Michaelis, ed., *Catalogus bibliothecae gundlingianae*, 2 vols. (Halle, 1731), I, p. 183; II, pp. 447, 570.

The overall impression given by Gundling was that, while Hobbes's critics were bigots with ecclesiastical axes to grind, Hobbes stood in the mainstream of modern philosophy: in particular, he noted the similarity between Hobbes's views on the impossibility of forming a proper idea of God and those of Locke in his *Essay concerning Human Understanding*. The only criticism he made was that Hobbes took the power of the prince over religion a little too far; on this point he recommended Pufendorf's *De habitu religionis christianae* as a corrective.[289] Ten years later he returned to the topic of Hobbes's 'atheism', making several of the same points in a stronger form. He ridiculed those continental writers who depended on 'the authority and testimony of some Englishmen', such as Samuel Parker: this was worthless, as the English critics were simply 'biassed', and Hobbes was well known to have been 'no friend of the upper clergy'. Gundling noted, but merely shrugged off, the criticism he had received 'on account of the fact that I, *with other clever people* [my italics], have on the contrary observed much that is good and useful in his writings'.[290]

Gundling also wrote a short treatise specifically on Hobbes's theory of the state of nature. In his preface to this work he commended Pufendorf, again, for correcting Hobbes's views on Church and State; and he also declared, very unspecifically, that there were things in the last part of *Leviathan* that one would have to be mad to approve. But the whole body of the treatise was an unapologetic defence of Hobbes's views on the state of nature and the need for sovereign authority. Gundling played down the differences between Hobbes, Pufendorf, and Grotius, explaining that they all grounded the laws of nature on essentially the same principle: seeking 'peace and tranquillity'. He also cleverly enlisted Ulric Huber on the side of the Hobbesians, noting that he had accepted the essential truth of Hobbes's 'state of nature' argument. Many of the standard criticisms of Hobbes, accusing him of approving conflict or denying the advantages of society, were absurd: Hobbes agreed about the importance of social life, but merely insisted that it could not be assured without sovereignty. And against the accusation that Hobbes's state of nature was a fiction, he had a simple riposte: 'Logicians use fictions; legal theorists use fictions.' Gundling's overall conclusion was one with which any student of Hobbes, then or now, could heartily sympathize: 'Hobbes cries out for a reader who is attentive, acute and deeply thoughtful—not one blinded by prejudices, nor overwhelmed by much reading of useless things.'[291] (In this connection, however,

---

[289] N. H. Gundling, *Observationum selectarum ad rem litterariam spectantium*, vol. I (Frankfurt, 1707), pp. 37–77, esp. pp. 43 ('nemo Dei attributa demonstrauit dilucidius'), 48 ('librum inepto Theologo dignum').

[290] N. H. Gundling, *Gundlingiana*, part 14 (1717) (= vol. III, paginated 303–39); here pp. 305 ('da ich hingegen mit andern klugen Leuten viel gutes und nützliches in seinen Schriffen [*sic*] wahrgenommen'), 305–06 ('die Auctorität und Aussage einiger Engelländer'; 'partheyisch'; 'Hobbes war kein Freund von der hohen Geistlichkeit').

[291] N. H. Gundling, *Commentatio de statu naturali Hobbesii in corpore iuris civilis defenso et defendendo occasione L. 5 de iust. et I.* (Halle, 1735), esp. pp. 22 ('Fingunt Logici . . . Fingunt Jcti'), 32 ('Hobbesius

some disagreement is always possible about which things are useless, and which may turn out to be useful.)

## VII

This somewhat schematic survey of the European reception of Hobbes in the period up to *c.*1750 may serve to indicate both the widespread nature of Hobbes's influence, and the difficulty of assessing it. The relationship between the three categories discussed here—orthodox denunciation, radical celebration, and mainstream use—was sometimes conflictual and sometimes mutually supportive; and the dividing-lines between them were always fairly blurred. Denunciation was a constant presence, at least from the 1670s onwards; it did not prevent some mainstream writers from coming to Hobbes's defence, but it must have ensured that many who were knowingly influenced by Hobbes's ideas took care to avoid the invocation of his name. Many more, in turn, would have been influenced unknowingly. Of the three categories, that of the radicals may perhaps have been the least important in terms of the degree of influence exercised on European thought overall; if any balance could be constructed in which to weigh such things, it might be found that Hobbes's undoubted importance to the underground anti-Christianity of the clandestine manuscripts was of little weight in comparison with his influence on republicanism, Cameralism, enlightened absolutism, toleration theory, the new science of 'universal public jurisprudence' (leading to the Enlightenment tradition of analysing political authority in terms of the origins of society), or the whole moral–psychological theory of 'enlightened self-interest'.

The most recent panoramic study of European intellectual life in this period, Jonathan Israel's dazzlingly impressive work *Radical Enlightenment*, takes a very negative view of Hobbes's influence, which it systematically down-plays in favour of that of Spinoza. Israel is concerned above all with the 'radical' category; his general argument is that only Spinoza had a major (in fact, foundational) influence here, and that Hobbes's own thought was not significantly radical at all. 'All new streams of thought which gained any broad support in Europe between 1650 and 1750', he writes, 'sought to substantiate and defend the truth of revealed religion,' with the sole major exception of Spinoza:

If the great thinkers of the late seventeenth and early eighteenth century uniformly reviled bigotry and 'superstition' . . . all except Spinoza and Bayle sought to accommodate the new advances in science and mathematics to Christian belief . . . They asserted as fundamental features of our cosmos the ceaseless working of divine Providence,

---

Lectorem attentum, acrem, meditabundum flagitat, non excoecatum praeiudiciis, non obrutum multa inutilium rerum lectione'). The preface to the reader is dated 1706; according to Zart, *Einfluss der englischen Philosophen*, p. 45, this text was first published (under the title *Dissertatio de statu naturali*) in Halle in 1709.

the authenticity of biblical prophecy, the reality of miracles, the immortality of the soul. . . .'[292]

Assuming that Hobbes is at least allowed the status of a 'great thinker' here, one must point out that these comments involve taking his arguments more at face value than almost any of his contemporaries were prepared to do. To present Hobbes as a defender of revealed religion and of the authenticity of biblical prophecy would require more argumentation than is offered by Professor Israel—who quotes many early critics who said that Spinoza was more extreme than Hobbes, but tends to leave unquoted very many who observed that Spinoza was merely making fully explicit arguments that were already clearly implicit, or partly explicit, in Hobbes's works.

Israel argues that Hobbes could not have had a major influence on any aspect of radical thinking, because his politics supported the kind of governmental authority to which radicals were opposed: 'Given Hobbes's politics, and his attitude to ecclesiastical power and censorship, as well as his being (by his own admission) philosophically less bold and comprehensive, he simply was not, and could not have been, the source and inspiration for a systematic redefinition of man, cosmology, politics, social hierarchy, sexuality, and ethics in the radical sense Spinoza was.'[293] This is, on one important matter of fact, simply wrong: far from being a supporter of 'ecclesiastical power', Hobbes was one of its most radical critics—a point not missed by other radicals of the time, if they read the second half of *Leviathan* or the *Historia ecclesiastica*. More generally, two questionable assumptions seem to be at work here: the idea that a writer who defends state power is somehow disqualified thereby from influencing, in any other area of his thinking, any people who are opposed to the State or suffer from its attentions; and the idea, neatly betrayed by the phrasing of that sentence, that the historian should look for '*the* source and inspiration' of radical thought, rather than a plurality of sources and inspirations.

But the largest issue of all is, in the end, left unresolved in Israel's account. Having divided, at the outset, the 'radical Enlightenment' from the more moderate mainstream Enlightenment, he seems thereafter to assume that, because the former was the vanguard, moving forward at the cutting edge of new thinking, and because the latter tended, over time, to follow in its steps, it is the motive power of the former that explains the entire long-term shift in European thought during this period. This is to beg the question of whether it was the vanguard that was pulling forward the rest of the army, or whether the main body of troops may have been

---

[292] Israel, *Radical Enlightenment*, p. 15.
[293] Ibid., p. 159; cf. also p. 602, where Israel writes that his 'anti-libertarian politics, High Church sympathies, and support for rigorous political and intellectual censorship' must have 'prevented Hobbes serving as a major stimulus to radical thought'.

operating with a dynamic of its own. A vanguard of a sort had existed, after all, for a very long time: elements of radical anti-Christian naturalism had been available in European culture since at least the sixteenth century. The explanation for the fact that the mainstream did not follow in their steps then, but did move in that direction in this later period, may perhaps be found more in changes that went on within mainstream theology, mainstream metaphysics, mainstream psychological and moral theory, and so on. Professor Israel has made an enormously powerful case for supposing that Spinoza was the greatest single influence on the radical Enlightenment; yet Hobbes, who had not only a significant influence on the radicals but also a rich and multifarious influence on mainstream thinking throughout this period, may still have been the more far-reachingly and deeply influential of the two.[294]

## VIII

This essay has tried to show that the European 'Republic of Letters' in its most general sense—the world of editors, journals, scholars, intellectuals, publicists, and their interested readers—did not exclude Hobbes from its ranks or its considerations, and that his ideas enjoyed a wide circulation in continental Europe. The popular image (mainly nineteenth- and early twentieth-century) of Hobbes as an isolated figure, a freak, a sterile thinker without progeny, is quite unjustified. One reason for this image may be that he has been marginalized by those standard historiographies which have concentrated on the traditions of Cartesianism or Lockeanism. A second reason, obviously, is that he was indeed portrayed as beyond the pale of acceptable debate by quite a few of his early critics. But he was never really isolated or excluded. No matter how ostentatiously his ideas were expelled with a pitchfork, they always crept back in again through the many side-entrances of the edifice of European thought.

However, there is perhaps a third reason why Hobbes has been pictured as something of an outsider to the European Republic of Letters—a reason that contains a

---

[294] It must be borne in mind, however, that this reduction of complex currents in intellectual history to a story of individual 'influences' always runs certain dangers of reductivist simplification (to which Prof. Israel's book, a story of individual influence on the grandest scale, is not immune). When A influences B, there may always be reasons (in principle, separately statable) why B was *apt* to be influenced by A; and at the same time what B gets out of, or sees in, A may well be different from what C, D, or E get out of him—again, because of factors in B's intellectual formation that are both more general, and more specific to B. The nexus of 'influence' is thus a much more complex interaction than any mere transfer of ideas from one person to another. This is true even where the evidential grounds for a direct attribution of 'influence' exist (e.g., where B acknowledges A's work). Some of the writers discussed by Israel are described as Spinozists because they expressed naturalistic ideas; but the fact that Spinoza himself produced the strongest or purest expression of those ideas need not mean that they were influenced by him. I have tried to guard against such a tendency in my account of Hobbes's influence in this essay, but am aware that no exercise in influence-attribution can be entirely free of such problems.

small but interesting kernel of truth. During his own lifetime, he may not have been an outsider to the Republic of Letters, but he was not a very full participant in its most characteristic activities. Here it is necessary to narrow slightly the meaning of the term. In the early and mid-seventeenth century, the phrase 'Republic of Letters' could of course be used in the general sense of the 'orbis literarius', the world of books and publications, but it also had a more specific meaning: the international quasi-society of scholars who not only wrote books but also communicated among themselves, above all through learned correspondence.[295] Hobbes's participation in this sort of activity was less than that of almost any other great thinker of his age (the other main exception being, as it happens, Spinoza).

There are of course some contingent reasons for this that must be taken into account. The period in Hobbes's life when he was taking part most fully in that intellectual world—his years in Paris, when he attended the discussions held by one of the greatest *animateurs* of the Republic of Letters, Marin Mersenne—generated almost no records of such activities: letters did not need to be written to the other participants when he was participating with them in the flesh. And from the subsequent period, after his return to England in 1651, when letters did need to be written, many that were have simply not survived. But there are, perhaps, some more general reasons why Hobbes never involved himself in the sort of intellectual networking, news-gathering and opinion-sharing that so preoccupied Mersenne and many of his friends. Their hunger for the latest information about the latest publications far exceeded that of Hobbes, who, while he certainly read more than he admitted, admitted to reading little indeed. Again, much of the subject-matter of the Republic's learned correspondence (and of the publications about which news was exchanged) was, in the broad sense of the term, philology: arguments about classical and biblical studies, new editions of ancient authors, medieval chronicles or church historians, and so on. Hobbes, though a serious Grecian scholar in his early years, was not much interested in this. And where the natural sciences were concerned, his own interests did not generate the sort of 'research' that might lead to the discussion of a newly recognized phenomenon, the description of a novel experiment or the propounding of a new solution to a problem (the exception being, unfortunately, his various 'solutions' to the squaring of the circle and duplication of the cube). For, at the deepest level of his intellectual character, Hobbes was a system-builder: what was of consuming interest to him was not this

---

[295] On the various meanings of the phrase, see F. Waquet, 'Qu'est-ce que la République des Lettres? Essai de sémantique historique', *Bibliothèque de l'École des Chartes*, 147 (1989), pp. 473–502. On the importance of correspondence see the classic essays by Paul Dibon, 'Communication in the *respublica literaria* of the 17th Century' and 'Communication épistolaire et mouvement des idées au XVIIe siècle', reprinted in his *Regards sur la Hollande du siècle d'or* (Naples, 1990), pp. 153–70, 171–90; F. Waquet, 'Les Éditions de correspondances savantes et les idéaux de la République des Lettres, *XVIIe Siècle*, 45 (1993), pp. 99–118; M. Ultee, 'The Republic of Letters: Learned Correspondence, 1680–1720', *The Seventeenth Century*, 2 (1987), pp. 95–112.

or that new discovery, but the overall theory into which all the phenomena could be fitted.

One other fundamental difference between Hobbes and the seventeenth-century Republic of Letters should also be added to this list. In ways that were occasionally explicit but usually only implicit, the Republic of Letters during Hobbes's lifetime had what might be called an ideology of its own. Both the idea and the practice of this 'Republic' implied, that is, certain assumptions about the relationship between critical understanding and political life—between knowledge and power. And while the ideology of the Republic of Letters resembled, or overlapped with, Hobbes's thinking in some respects, there remained a very important underlying difference between them.

A word of warning is needed when approaching the topic of the ideology of this seventeenth-century 'Republic'. Many of the modern studies of the Republic of Letters tend to read back into the seventeenth century those ideological descriptions of it that they find in the writings of the Republic's spokesmen in the early eighteenth. These are then combined with a curiously teleological version of Jürgen Habermas's argument about the emergence of a 'public space', to create the impression that from an early stage the participants in the Republic were striving to establish a quasi-political entity, a public realm over and against the State.[296] The very use of the term 'Republic', harped on by early eighteenth-century publicists such as Jean Le Clerc and Pierre Desmaizeaux, seems to encourage this: when Desmaizeaux calls the Republic of Letters 'a state that extends throughout all states', it is easy to suppose that he is thinking of something that acts more or less politically, rivalling or even trumping the existing units of political power.[297] Some of the leading modern writers on the Republic of Letters have succumbed to the temptation to read back into the seventeenth century such quasi-political aspirations: thus Hans Bots, for example, emphasizes the desire of the learned world 'to form its own state', and Françoise Waquet argues that the whole phenomenon of the Republic of Letters in the seventeenth century embodied a positive political programme, consisting of ecumenism, irenicism, universalism, or even utopianism.[298]

---

[296] See J. Habermas, *The Structural Transformation of the Public Sphere*, tr. T. Burger and F. Lawrence (Cambridge, 1989). For an eloquent (but, I believe, mistaken) application of this to the 17th-century Republic of Letters, see D. Goodman, *The Republic of Letters: A Cultural History of the French Enlightenment* (Ithaca, NY, 1994), pp. 12–23.

[297] P. Desmaizeaux, 'Préface' to P. Bayle, *Lettres*, ed. P. Desmaizeaux, 3 vols. (Amsterdam, 1729), I, pp. i–xliv, here p. xxiv; cf. J. Le Clerc, *Parrhasiana, ou pensées diverses sur des matières de critique, d'histoire, de morale et de politique*, 2nd edn (Amsterdam, 1701), p. 146, describing the Republic as 'a country of reason and light, not of authority' ('un païs de raison et de lumière, et non d'autorité') and Henri Basnage de Beauval, cited in H. Broekmans, T. Gruntjes and H. Bots, 'Het beeld van de Republiek der Letteren in het tijdschrift van H. Basnage de Beauval', in H. Bots, ed., *Henri Basnage de Beauval en de Histoire des ouvrages des savans, 1687–1709*, 2 vols. (Amsterdam, 1976), pp. 109–305, here p. 113, calling it 'a free country' ('un païs libre').

[298] H. Bots, *Republiek der Letteren: ideaal en werkelijkheid* (Amsterdam, 1977), p. 6; Waquet, 'Qu'est-ce que la République des Lettres?', esp. pp. 495–497.

In fact, as Waquet herself has demonstrated in some detail, the term 'Republic of Letters' was used in many ways, most of which were devoid of political implications. It is true that some writers in the sixteenth and seventeenth centuries did make use of the political connotations of 'respublica' in the phrase 'respublica literaria'; but they usually did so ironically, often self-deprecatingly, to emphasize the *non*-political nature of the world of scholars, its detachment from the political—and confessional—world. As Anne Goldgar has written, summarizing her findings about the intellectual community of the late seventeenth century: 'The "public" my scholars cared about was each other. Their work was not primarily directed at public utility, their ideal society was not intended for general emulation, and the political aspect of their lives was to be divorced absolutely from their scholarship.'[299]

If 'ideology' is a system of justification for politics, then the ideology of the seventeenth-century Republic of Letters was a peculiarly negative one, an ideology of the non-political. It is of course true that any ideology of the non-political is still a political position, as it justifies, or at least inertially defends, the political status quo. Such an ideology is peculiarly well adapted for those who are not inclined to be ideologists; most members of the seventeenth-century Republic of Letters fell into that category, and their adherence to this ideology was simply implicit in their acceptance of the Republic's practices. They accepted that differences of political allegiance and religion between the scholars in their 'Republic' could be set aside for their purposes; that some basic framework of State authority was required, to supply the conditions of security needed for their work; that the rules of action that applied in the public, political world might have to differ from the ones they themselves adhered to in their personal and intellectual dealings with one another; and that some of the things set aside by them as 'indifferent' (such as customary laws, religious practices and social conventions) might be necessary components of authority and stability in the public realm. This ideology rests, therefore, on a distinction between the shared, private world of the scholars and the public world outside them. It draws on the neo-Stoicism of Lipsius; on the private–public dichotomy and the cultural relativism of Montaigne; and on the Machiavellian tradition, especially as developed by Cardano and Charron. Indeed, if this implicit ideology of the seventeenth-century Republic of Letters has any explicit exponents, they are Pierre Charron, Gabriel Naudé, and François de La Mothe le Vayer.[300]

---

[299] A. Goldgar, *Impolite Learning: Conduct and Community in the Republic of Letters, 1680–1750* (New Haven, Conn., 1995), p. 6.

[300] The best accounts of this ideological tradition are R. Pintard, *Le Libertinage érudit dans la première moitié du XVII<sup>e</sup> siècle* (Paris, 1943), pp. 539–64; Procacci, *Studi sulla fortuna di Machiavelli*, pp. 77–106; A. M. Battista, *Alle origini del pensiero politico libertino: Montaigne e Charron* (Milan, 1966); Keohane, *Philosophy and the State*, pp. 119–50; E. Castrucci, *Ordine convenzionale e pensiero decisionista: saggio sui presupposti intellettuali dello stato moderno nel seicento francese* (Milan, 1981); F. Charles-Daubert, 'Le "Libertinage érudit" et

Such an ideology is at least potentially radical in intellectual terms: within the Republic of Letters, critical thinking can dismantle all sorts of publicly accepted beliefs and superstitions. But it is thoroughly non-radical politically: it relies on, and defends, the powers that be. Generally, members of this Republic support the State; their natural political programme is not ecumenist universalism, but a pragmatic Erastianism. In so far as such a Republic of Letters has any political force or charge, it is directed not against the State, but against the common people. The literati know that customs are absurd, that law is not grounded directly in nature, that religion functions as a political device; but they feel the need, at least to some extent, to keep this knowledge to themselves. They obey the law, and show respect for custom and religion, for prudential, functionalist reasons. The 'sotte multitude' does so for reasons drawn from passion (mainly fear), ignorance and superstition; and it is good that it should do so, since, if it were not kept in check by such means, its violence and volatility would make the conditions of life of the wise élite impossible.[301]

A number of recent studies have suggested that this ideology or set of assumptions supplied the basic framework of Hobbes's own political thought.[302] It is certainly true that the Parisian circles in which he moved in the 1640s offered some strong expressions of it: one of the most explicit spokesmen for this ideology, La Mothe le Vayer, became a personal friend. It is also true that there are some important generic similarities between this set of assumptions and Hobbes's ideas: the view of human nature as driven by the passions and therefore possessing an inherent instability; the 'conventionalist' perception that laws are grounded in human will and agreement, not in nature; the idea (a corollary of conventionalism) that the value of the State is purely instrumental, not teleological; and the tendency (derived from all of the above) to make a strong separation between the public, external world of politics and law, and the internal world of private beliefs.

Hobbes did express some low opinions of the common people, who were both passionate ('Ambition, and Covetousness are Passions also that are perpetually incumbent, and pressing; whereas Reason is not perpetually present, to resist them') and ignorant ('For such is the ignorance, and aptitude to error generally of all men, but especially of them that have not much knowledge of naturall

---

le problème du conservatisme politique', in H. Méchoulan, ed., *L'État baroque: regards sur la pensée politique de la France du premier XVIIe siècle* (Paris, 1985), pp. 179–202; Taranto, *Pirronismo ed assolutismo*, pp. 17–129. The version of Habermas's argument presented by Reinhart Koselleck is more convincing precisely because it is more attuned to this tradition: see R. Koselleck, *Critique and Crisis: Enlightenment and the Pathogenesis of Modern Society* (Oxford, 1988), pp. 104–13.

[301] See Charles-Daubert, 'Le "Libertinage érudit" ', esp. pp. 182–6.

[302] See especially Battista, *Alle origini*, pp. 26, 131, 168(n.), 280; Castrucci, *Ordine convenzionale*, pp. 35, 55, 139–42, 165; this argument is implicit in Taranto, *Pirronismo ed assolutismo*, and in parts of G. Borelli, *Ragione di stato e Leviatano: conservazione e scambio alle origini della modernità politica* (Bologna, 1993), esp. the discussion of Charron (pp. 51–61).

causes'.)[303] As the second speaker in his dialogue *Behemoth* put it, 'people always have been, and always will be, ignorant of their duty to the public, as never meditating anything but their particular interest. . . .'[304] However, the greatest danger to the public good came not from passions in themselves (which could be controlled by a mechanism of rewards and punishments), nor from mere ignorance (which was in itself inert), but from the manipulation of those passions and that ignorance by interested parties who inculcated false beliefs. The passage just quoted about men ignorant of natural causes went on to point out that they were 'by innumerable and easie tricks to be abused'; the speaker in *Behemoth* continued: 'in other things following their immediate leaders; which are either the preachers, or the most potent of the gentlemen'. This whole theme became, one might say, the obsession of Hobbes's mature political philosophy: again and again in *Leviathan*, the demonstration of the truth of his own theory is interlarded with passages analysing the origins of misunderstanding and absurdity, and pointing the finger of blame at those interested parties that have inculcated such errors (above all, the clergy with its bogus metaphysics).

Discussing the nature of error in chapter 4 of *Leviathan*, Hobbes observed that people who absorbed the false teachings of the schools were 'as much below the condition of ignorant men, as men endued with true Science are above it. For between true Science, and erroneous Doctrines, Ignorance is in the middle.'[305] A two-fold task thus presented itself: people first had to be disabused of the false doctrines which had corrupted their understanding, and then they could be supplied with at least the rudiments of 'true Science'. The first task involved uprooting a variety of errors: romanticized versions of classical teachings about democracy and tyrannicide; Christianized versions of pagan 'demonology'; and, most pernicious of all, scholastic metaphysics and its progeny (sacerdotalism, papalism, and so on). Had Hobbes been able to speak his mind with complete freedom, he might have added much of traditional Christian theology to this list. Jean-Baptiste Lantin, who knew Hobbes in Paris, later recalled: 'He used to say that he sometimes made openings, but could not reveal his thoughts more than half-way; he said he imitated people who open the window for a few moments, but then close it again immediately for fear of the storm.'[306] Prudence was needed here, not only for fear of popular outrage, but also because his own political theory required outward acceptance of doctrine that was 'publicly allowed' by sovereign authority. But in

---

[303] Hobbes, *Leviathan*, pp. 155, 236.
[304] T. Hobbes, *Behemoth*, ed. F. Tönnies (London, 1889), p. 39.
[305] Hobbes, *Leviathan*, p. 15.
[306] BN, MS f.fr. 23253, 'Lantiniana', fol. 89r ('Il disoit, quil faisoit quelquefois des ouuertures, mais qu'il ne pouuoit decouurir ses pensées quá demi. qu'il imitoit ceux qui ourrent la fenestre pendant quelques momens, mais qui la referment promtement de peur de lorage'). Most of Lantin's notes on Hobbes (including this one) were printed (with minor modifications) in P. Joly, *Remarques critiques sur le Dictionnaire de Bayle*, 2 vols. (Paris, 1752), II, pp. 433–4.

*Leviathan* he did go as far as he could (and further than almost any other radical of the time who dared to publish over his own name): he was profiting from the hiatus in political authority in England, and at the same time, probably, hoping to influence the religious settlement that would eventually emerge there. So, although his comment to Lantin makes him sound like an archetypal *esprit fort* —La Mothe le Vayer, for example—with an esoteric radical doctrine largely withheld from public view, the nature of his enterprise was really quite different. He wanted to disabuse the general public, not just to share his superior insight with the like-minded.

Hobbes's obsession with the pernicious effects of false beliefs takes us right to the heart of his political theory. It is entirely fitting that his chapter on 'Those things that Weaken, or tend to the Dissolution of a Common-wealth' should be concerned mainly with false *doctrines*. For, as he explained in his chapter on the rights of sovereigns, 'the Actions of men proceed from their Opinions; and in the wel governing of Opinions, consisteth the well governing of mens Actions'.[307] Outlining the 'office' (i.e. the duties) of the sovereign, he dealt first with the duty to maintain the sovereign rights entire, and then added: 'Secondly, it is against his Duty, to let the people be ignorant, or mis-informed of the grounds, and reasons of those his essentiall Rights.' The passage that followed is one of the most important in the entire text of *Leviathan*:

And the grounds of these Rights, have the rather need to be diligently, and truly taught; because they cannot be maintained by any Civill Law, or terrour of legall punishment. For a Civill Law, that shall forbid Rebellion, (and such is all resistance to the essentiall Rights of Soveraignty,) is not (as a Civill Law) any obligation, but by vertue onely of the Law of Nature, that forbiddeth the violation of Faith; which naturall obligation if men know not, they cannot know the Right of any Law the Soveraign maketh.[308]

It is thus one of the central paradoxes of Hobbes's political philosophy that his emphasis on the control of doctrines by the sovereign, which strikes modern readers as one of the most 'illiberal' aspects of his theory, should derive directly from his belief that 'the authority of all . . . Princes, must be grounded on the Consent of the People'—the belief that links him so closely to one essential part of the 'liberal' tradition.[309]

Accordingly, Hobbes added to his negative programme of demystification a positive programme of political education: he dismissed the objections of those who 'say . . . that though the Principles be right, yet Common people are not of

---

[307] Hobbes, *Leviathan*, p. 91.
[308] Ibid., pp. 175–6. Cf. the discussion in D. Johnston, *The Rhetoric of Leviathan: Thomas Hobbes and the Politics of Cultural Transformation* (Princeton, NJ, 1986), pp. 77–84, in a section aptly entitled 'The Cultural Foundations of Political Power'.
[309] Ibid., p. 250.

capacity enough to be made to understand them'. On the contrary: 'the Common-peoples minds, unlesse they be tainted with dependance on the Potent, or scribbled over with the opinions of their Doctors, are like clean paper, fit to receive whatsoever by Publique Authority shall be imprinted in them.'[310] He hoped that the principles expounded in *Leviathan* would be taught in the universities, from where they would trickle down to the common people through clerics, teachers, and gentry; and he even set out a list of simple civic doctrines (boldly modelled on the Ten Commandments) which could in any case be preached directly to the general population.[311]

This entire programme, both negative and positive, has been described not unreasonably as a project of 'cultural transformation'. Far-reaching advantages would accrue, Hobbes believed, to any state that eliminated false doctrine and superstition, and put rational principles in their place. Yet it is important to note that this change would be a transformation only of culture; human nature itself would remain the same. It would always be true that human beings were driven by passions, and that those passions were not aligned in any teleologically ordained, naturally harmonious pattern. Laws would still be required, and punishments, inspiring fear, would still need to be attached to them. A rationally justified fear of the sovereign power would be a useful thing; even an image, in popular psychology, of that sovereign power as an entity greater than any human individual. But such fears would serve ends directly justified by reason; they would be quite different from the superstitious fears instilled and manipulated in the past by self-serving priestcraft.

What this implied was, in other words, not utopianism, but enlightenment.[312] Hobbes's programme could even be described as a project of liberation—liberation, that is, from falsehood, and from the power of those groups, elites, and confederacies that manipulate falsehood for their own ends.[313] That special groups possessing cultural power always tend to use it to advance their own economic and political power was for him almost axiomatic; his view of the whole history of organized Christianity could be summed up by his phrase, 'worldly ambition creeping by degrees into the Pastors'.[314] Even in his criticisms of the Royal Society, readers

---

[310] Ibid., p. 176.

[311] Ibid., pp. 177–80; cf. *Behemoth*, pp. 39–40, and see the valuable discussion by Mary Dietz, 'Hobbes's Subject as Citizen', in M. G. Dietz, ed., *Thomas Hobbes and Political Theory* (Lawrence, Kansas, 1990), pp. 91–119.

[312] See the important study by Robert P. Kraynak, *History and Modernity in the Thought of Thomas Hobbes* (Ithaca, NY, 1990), e.g. p. 31: 'This new type of philosophical enterprise is Hobbes's science of enlightenment. It seeks to transform the nature of civil society by abolishing the historical realm of authoritative opinion and replacing it with a universally recognized doctrine of science that stands on its own evident foundations.'

[313] Deborah Baumgold has commented on Hobbes's concern for 'the victimization of common people in the power struggle of political elites': *Hobbes's Political Theory* (Cambridge, 1988), p. 135.

[314] Hobbes, *Leviathan*, p. 364.

might also detect an element of ingrained hostility to a (potentially) self-interested elite group—especially one that claimed a public status but met as a private body.[315] So it is not hard to guess what his underlying feelings would have been about a 'Republic of Letters' which saw itself as a quasi-society, an intellectual elite standing over and apart from the general population, sharing its most critical insights among its own members and keeping them from the common people.

One might almost say—at the risk of a little rhetorical extravagance—that, just as the confederacy of priests had created what he called a 'Kingdom of Darkness', so too this confederacy of mainly secular intellectuals had the potential to become a Republic of Darkness. To make such a direct parallel would be unfair, of course; the critical insights developed within the Republic of Letters were ones with which, to a large extent, Hobbes himself agreed, and in his war against the Kingdom of Darkness this Republic would often function as his strategic ally. Yet, in the end, Hobbes did stand apart from it. Which is not to say that he was peripheral or eccentric—quite the opposite, in fact, if he is looked at from the viewpoint of the thinkers of Enlightenment Europe. For not only did his ideas supply them with some of the materials they needed; his project of enlightenment was, in the end, the Enlightenment's project too.

---

[315] See S. Shapin and S. Schaffer, *Leviathan and the Air-Pump: Hobbes, Boyle and the Experimental Life* (Princeton, 1985), pp. 113–14.

# LIST OF MANUSCRIPTS

This listing is confined to manuscripts cited or referred to in the text and notes. Only summary descriptions of the contents are given; in the case of composite volumes, these descriptions concern only the item or items cited or referred to. Printed items are included here if they contain substantial annotations or tipped-in letters.

ABERYSTWYTH

*National Library of Wales*
5297: notes on draft of Hobbes, *De corpore*

AMSTERDAM

*Amsterdam University Library*
III. E. 8²¹³: Sorbière to Vossius

*Gemeentelijke Archiefdienst*
NA 3206: Blaeu assignment

AUSTIN, TEXAS

*Harry Ransom Humanities Research Center, University of Texas at Austin*
pressmark Pforzheimer 491: Hobbes, *Leviathan*, de Cardonnel annotations

BAKEWELL, DERBYSHIRE

*Chatsworth*
Hardwick 14: Privy Purse accounts
Hardwick 29: first Earl, stewards' accounts
Hardwick 30: Countess, stewards' accounts
Hardwick 33: third Earl, stewards' accounts
Hardwick, drawer 145, item 18: Hobbes on heresy
Hardwick, drawer 145, item 21: Sorbière, medical treatise
Hardwick, drawer 146, item 3: 'Purchas' (Ferrar), on Virginia
Hardwick, unnumbered: library catalogue, late 1650s
Hobbes MSS: see the listing on pp. 140–4.

BERLIN

*Staatsbibliothek*
Lat. 2° 129: Ebert, Latin translation of *Behemoth*

BORDEAUX

*Archives Départementales de la Gironde*
3 E 12995: du Verdus, will

CAEN

*Archives Départementales du Calvados ['ADC']*
1 B 880: de Cardonnel marriage contract

## LIST OF MANUSCRIPTS

F 5377: Carel, genealogical notes
F 6181: Marguerite Le Coq document

*Archives Municipales de Caen*
Gustave Dupont, 'Registres de l'Hôtel de Ville de Caen: inventaire sommaire'

CAMBRIDGE

*Cambridge University Library*
Add. 1: Strype correspondence
Mm. 1. 38: Mason documents

*Magdalene College Library*
Ferrar papers: list of shareholders, Somer Islands Company
Ferrar papers: Hobbes and Ferrar, reply to colonists' petition
Ferrar papers: list of transfers of shares

COPENHAGEN

*Royal Library*
Thott 213 4°: Hobbes, *Historia ecclesiastica*

DERBY

*Derby Central Library*
8470: Cotton, poems

DRESDEN

*Sächsisches Hauptstaatsarchiv*
10753: Elector of Saxony to 'Büchercommissarien'.

HAMBURG

*Staats- und Universitätsbibliothek*
Pe. 1a (= Sup. ep. 97), no. 85: Cavendish to Jungius
Pe. 47b, item 18: Jungius, notes on *De cive*

LEIDEN

*Leiden University Library*
BPL 302: Sorbière to Rivet

LEIPZIG

*Leipzig University Library*
Stadtbibliothek Rep. IV. 47: Guiraud notes on Hobbes, *Anti-White*

LONDON

*British Library ['BL']*
Add. 4278: Pell correspondence
Add. 4279: Warner–Payne correspondence
Add. 4280: Pell correspondence
Add. 4395: Warner, note on optics, draft letter to Cavendish; Hobbes, 'analogy'
Add. 4407: Cavendish to Warner

Add. 4423: Pell notes
Add. 4444: Cavendish to Warner
Add. 4458: Payne to Warner
Add. 6193: Hooke to Boyle
Add. 11309: Micanzio, letters to Cavendish, tr. Hobbes
Add. 27979: abstract of evidences, Ware
Add. 28001: Oxenden correspondence
Add. 32553: Stubbe to Hobbes
Add. 51324: Fox memoirs
Add. 70499: Newcastle correspondence
Birch (= Add.) 4162: Payne to Sheldon
Egerton 1910: Hobbes, *Leviathan*
Egerton 2005: Hobbes, *Elements of Law*
Evelyn Papers, JE A16, items 1340–1348: Waller to Evelyn
Harl. 3360: Hobbes, English Optical MS
Harl. 4235: Hobbes, *Elements of Law*
Harl. 4955: Jonson to Newcastle
Harl. 6002: Roberval proposition
Harl. 6083: extracts from Roberval
Harl. 6320: Webbe, translation of Galileo
Harl. 6460: Magdalen Hall oration
Harl. 6796: Hobbes, Latin Optical MS; Payne, translations of Castelli, Galileo; 'Short Tract'
Harl. 6942: Payne to Sheldon; Payne to Hobbes; Hammond to Sheldon
Harl. 7257: Commons journal
Lansdowne 93: Payne to Sheldon
Lansdowne 841: Payne to Sheldon
Sloane 1466: Webbe, list of works
Sloane 1731B: de Cardonnel notebook
Sloane 3995: Sloane notebook

*French Protestant Church of London, Soho Square ['FPCL']*
5: Consistory Acts, 1615–1680
6: Consistory Acts, 1658–1679
45: Copies of letters, 1652–1695

*Guildhall Library*
7670: registers of St Lawrence, 1538–1740.

*House of Lords Record Office ['HLRO']*
House of Lords papers, 1676/7, item 338: Seymour accusations, Stationers' Company reply

*Huguenot Library, University College, London ['HL']*
MS T 8/1, no. 115: Wagner, notes on de Cardonnel family

*Public Record Office ['PRO']*
C 66/3038: de Cardonnel patent
E 190 44/3: Port Book, London, aliens, Christmas 1639–Christmas 1640
E 190 824/2: Port Book, Southampton, Christmas 1636–Christmas 1637

## LIST OF MANUSCRIPTS

E 190 824/7: Port Book, Southampton, imported wines, Christmas 1637–Christmas 1638
E 190 824/8: Port Book, Southampton, Christmas 1637–Christmas 1638
E 190 824/10: Port Book, Southampton, Easter–Michaelmas 1638
E 190/826/7: Port Book, Portsmouth, Outwards, Christmas 1662–Christmas 1663
E 190/826/10: Port Book, Southampton, Christmas 1665–1666
Map room, pressmark 12/82: Indexes to the Privy Council Registers, 1637–1645
Prob. 11/219 (microfilm): Payne, will
Prob. 11/183 (microfilm): Sir George Fane, will
Prob. 11/311 (microfilm): Lucas, will
Prob. 11/313 (microfilm): Anne Fane, will
RG 4/4600: Walloon Church, Southampton, register, 1567–1779
SP 29/77/32: de Cardonnel petition
SP 29/187/172: accusation against Royston
SP 29/243/181: survey of printers
SP 29/279/95: Redmayne affidavit, Mearne note
SP 44/15: Bennet, Warrant Book
T 51/8: Commissioners of the Treasury, minutes

*Stationers' Hall*
Stationers' Company records ['SC'] (Chadwyck Healey microfilm edition)
Court Book D (reel 56)
Wardens' Accounts (reel 76)
Box A, envelope 3, item vi (reel 97): order for damasking *Leviathan*
Box A, envelope 3, item vii (reel 97): Bailey, receipt for damasking *Leviathan*
Box A, envelope 4, item vii (reel 97): memorandum about damasking *Leviathan*
Box A, envelope 11, item (ii) (reel 97): Mearne memorandum

### MAIDSTONE

*Centre for Kentish Studies, Maidstone*
Papillon papers, C 13 (4): Papillon to Ashe

### NOTTINGHAM

*Nottingham University Library*
Clifton C. 138: Cotton (Sr) to Clifton
Pl E 12/10/1/9/1: Earl of Newcastle, rentals
Pw 1/54–66: Countess of Devonshire letters
Pw 1 181: Mayne to Newcastle
Pw 1 668: list of telescopes

*Nottinghamshire Archives*
DD P6/1/6/5: Cavendish indenture

### OXFORD

*Bodleian Library ['Bodl.']*
Aubrey 6: Aubrey, 'brief life' of Waller
Ballard 14: Aubrey to Wood

Clar. 126: Hyde, notes on Hobbes, *Elements of Law*
Univ. Coll. 47–49: Payne, Roger Bacon transcripts
Wood F 46: Morse to W. de Cardonnel
pressmark Arch. A. e. 62: de Cardonnel dedicatory letter to Charles II
pressmark Savile Q. 9: Cavendish to Payne (tipped in)

*Christ Church*
Christ Church library, 'Donor's Book'

*Merton College Archive*
Reg. 1.3: College register

PARIS

*Archives de l'Académie des Sciences ['AAS']*
Fonds Roberval, carton 6, dossier 47: Roberval, draft treatise on optics
Fonds Roberval, carton 7, dossier 124 (formerly carton 9, chemise 15): Roberval, 'Quelle Creance l'homme doit auoir'

*Archives Nationales*
Minutier Central, ET/XLV/232: Séguier, probate inventory
Minutier Central, ET/LI/435: Séguier's widow, probate inventory

*Bibliothèque de l'Arsenal*
6203: Minim convent, place Royale, library catalogue

*Bibliothèque Mazarine ['BMP']*
1189: 'La Foi annéantie'
1193: Fréret, 'Lettre de Thrasybule à Leucippe'
1194: 'Dissertation et preuves de l'éternité du monde'

*Bibliothèque Nationale ['BN']*
f.fr. 9119: Roberval geometry course
f.fr. 12279: Roberval, 'Dioptrique'
f.fr. 12499: de Cardonnel poem
f.fr. 17375: C. and J.-B. du Lieu to Séguier
f.fr. 17378: C. du Lieu to Séguier
f.fr. 17379: J.-B. du Lieu to Séguier
f.fr. 17384: J.-B. du Lieu to Séguier
f.fr. 17386: J.-B. du Lieu to Séguier
f.fr. 17387: J.-B. du Lieu to Séguier
f.fr. 17388: C. du Lieu to Séguier
f.fr. 18600: de Cardonnel petition, procès-verbal, decree
f.fr. 23253: 'Lantiniana'
f.fr. n.a. 3252: Wallis to Brouncker
f.fr. n.a. 5175: Mersenne, 'Catoptrique', Roberval's copy for printers; Roberval, 'L'Euidence . . .'.
f.l. 10352: Sorbière correspondence
f.l. 10353: Rivet to Sorbière

LIST OF MANUSCRIPTS

*Bibliothèque Sainte-Geneviève*
1060: treatises on geometry, fortification; Roberval broadsheet
2215: 'Abrégé de politique'
2997: 'Abrégé de politique'
3082: 'Abrégé de politique'

*Bibliothèque de la Société de l'Histoire du Protestantisme Français*
397/2: list of students, Montauban

ROME

*Archivio di Stato*
Fondo Cartari-Febei, vol. 64: Ecchellensis memoir

*Pontificia Università Gregoriana*
557: Niceron to Kircher

ROUEN

*Bibliothèque Municipale*
74: 'Notes de Hobbes sur le nouveau testament'

SAN MARINO, CALIFORNIA

*Huntington Library*
Hastings Collection, Irish papers, box 8, MS HA 14117: Ormonde to John Bramhall

SHEFFIELD

*Sheffield University Library*
Hartlib Papers (electronic edition (Ann Arbor, Mich., 1995))
8/27/2A: Worsley letter
8/29/1A–1B: Cavendish to Petty
31/12/14A: Pell, 'Quaeres'
31/20/12A: bookseller's bill
42/1/1A–2B: Worsley letters
62/21/1A: Rand to Worsley

SOUTHAMPTON

*City Archives Office ['CAO']*
D/LY/38: Greenfield, 'Extracts from Journals of the Corporation'
D/LY38/144: notes on Pescod
SC 5/4/89: Petty Customs Book, 1637–1644
SC 9/3/11: Examination Book, 1622–1644

TROWBRIDGE

*Wiltshire Records Office*
Archdeaconry of Wilts, Act Books (Office), vol. 1 (formerly vol. 40)
Bishop's Transcripts, Brokenborough, bundle 1
Bishop's Transcripts, Westport, bundle 1
Episcopal Act Book (Instance), vol. 33a

Episcopal Deposition Book (Instance), vol. 22b
Quarter Sessions, Criminal Business, 1598–1603

VATICAN CITY

*Biblioteca Apostolica Vaticana*
Cod. Barb. Lat. 6471: Naudé to Barberini

VIENNA

*Österreichische Nationalbibliothek*
7050: Wallis to Brouncker
7071: 'Naudéana'

*Stiftung Fürst Liechtenstein*
N-7-6: Hobbes, *Historia ecclesiastica*, with Servetus, *De trinitatis erroribus*

WINCHESTER

*Hampshire Record Office ['HRO']*
'Calendar of Sloane Stanley MSS'
4 M 60/126: indenture between de Cardonnels and executors
4 M 60/165: de Cardonnel indenture
15 M 55/8: judgment of Court of Exchequer
16 M 55/2: de Cardonnel patent
16 M 55/3: grant of manors
46 M 48/38a: Pescod-de Cardonnel indenture
46 M 48/39: Pescod indenture
46 M 48/40: indenture between Pescod and executors
46 M 48/41: Nicholas Pescod, will
46 M 48/42: Pescod children, agreement
46 M 48/73: Exchequer case, paper

WÜRZBURG

*Staatsarchiv*
Schönborn-Archiv, Korrespondenz Johann Philipp, 2946: Pufendorf to von Boineburg
Schönborn-Archiv, Korrespondenz Johann Philipp, 2952: Sorbière to von Boineburg

# BIBLIOGRAPHY

This bibliography is confined to works cited or referred to in the text and notes. Items that appear in the listings of books owned by Payne (above, pp. 144–5) and de Cardonnel (pp. 313–16), but are not otherwise discussed, are not included here. The alphabetical order is of the first element of the name that bears a capital letter.

Abbadie, J., *Traité de la vérité de la religion chrétienne*, 2 vols. (Rotterdam, 1684).
Accolti, P., *Lo inganno de gl'occhi, prospettiva pratica* (Florence, 1625).
Aereboe, R., *Autobiografi (1685–1744)*, ed. G. L. Grove (Copenhagen, 1889).
Agrippa, H. C., *De vanitate scientiarum* (Leiden, 1644).
—— *The Vanity of Arts and Sciences*, tr. anon. (London, 1676).
Aguilon ['Aguilonius'], F., *Opticorum libri sex* (Antwerp, 1613).
Airaksinen, T., and M. A. Bertman, eds., *Hobbes: War among Nations* (Aldershot, 1989).
Åkerman, S., 'Johan Adler Salvius' Questions to Baruch de Castro concerning De tribus impostoribus', in S. Berti, F. Charles-Daubert, and R. Popkin, eds., *Heterodoxy, Spinozism, and Free Thought in Early Eighteenth Century Europe* (Dordrecht, 1996), pp. 397–423.
Allan, D., ' "An Ancient Sage Philosopher": Alexander Ross and the Defence of Philosophy', *The Seventeenth Century*, 16 (2001), pp. 68–94.
Allison, C. F., *The Rise of Moralism: The Proclamation of the Gospel from Hooker to Baxter* (London, 1966).
Almack, E., *A Bibliography of the King's Book or Eikon Basilike* (London, 1896).
Anderson, R. C., *Naval Wars in the Levant 1559–1853* (Liverpool, 1952).
Andrews, C. M., *The Colonial Period of American History*, 4 vols. (New Haven, Conn., 1934).
[Anon.], *Bedenkwürdige Berichtung der Niederländischen Ost–Indien Gesellschaft in dem Kaiserreich Taising oder Sina* (Amsterdam, 1675).
[Anon.], *The Carl H. Pforzheimer Library: English Literature, 1475–1700*, 3 vols. (New York, 1940).
[Anon.] [Joseph Jane?], *ΕΙΚΩΝ ΑΚΛΑΣΤΟΣ: The Image Unbroken. A Perspective of the Impudence, Falshood, Vanitie, and Prophannes, Published in a Libell entitled ΕΙΚΟΝΟΚΛΑΣΤΗΣ* (n.p., 1651).
[Anon.], *Essais de morale et de politique, ou il est traité des devoirs de l'homme, consideré comme particulier, & comme vivant en societé* (Lyon, 1687).
[Anon.], *Fürstellung vier neuer Welt–Weisen, nahmentlich Renati des Cartes, Thomae Hobbes, Benedicti Spinosa, Balthasar Beckers, nach ihrem Leben und führnemsten Irrthümern* (n.p., 1702).
[Anon.], *Historisch verhaal, van den beklaaglyken opstand 't sedert eenige Jaren in de gemeente, toegedaan de onveranderde Confessie van Augsburgh, binnen deser Stede, ontstaan* (Amsterdam, 1690).
[Anon.], *Relation de l'entrée magnifique de Monsieur le Prince de Ligne* (London, 1660).

Apostolidès, J.-M., *Le Roi-Machine: spectacle et politique au temps de Louis XIV* (Paris, 1981).

Archambault, P., 'The Analogy of the "Body" in Renaissance Political Literature', *Bibliothèque d'humanisme et de renaissance*, 29 (1967), pp. 21–53.

Arendt, H., *The Origins of Totalitarianism*, 2nd edn (London, 1958).

Arnold, G., *Unparteyische Kirchen- und Ketzer-Historie von Anfang des Neuen Testaments biss auff das Jahr Christi 1688*, 4 parts in 2 vols. (Frankfurt am Main, 1699–1700).

Ascoli, G., *La Grande-Bretagne devant l'opinion française au XVII$^e$ siècle*, 2 vols. (Paris, 1930).

Ashcraft, R., 'Political Theory and Practical Action: A Reconsideration of Hobbes's State of Nature', *Hobbes Studies*, 1 (1988), pp. 63–88.

Asín Palacios, M., *Abenházam de Córdoba y su historia crítica de las ideas religiosas* (Madrid, 1927).

Astruc, J., *Conjectures sur les mémoires originaux dont il paroit que Moyse s'est servi pour composer le livre de la Genèse* (Brussels, 1753).

Aubert de Vertot d'Aubeuf, R., *Histoire des révolutions de Portugal*, 4th edn (The Hague, 1734).

Aubrey, J., *Letters Written by Eminent Persons . . . to which are added . . . Lives of Eminent Men, by John Aubrey, Esq.*, 3 vols. (London, 1813).

—— *Wiltshire: The Topographical Collections*, ed. J. E. Jackson (Devizes, 1862).

—— *'Brief Lives', chiefly of Contemporaries, set down by John Aubrey, between the years 1669 & 1696*, ed. A. Clark, 2 vols. (Oxford, 1898).

—— *Aubrey on Education: A Hitherto Unpublished Manuscript by the Author of* Brief Lives, ed. J. E. Stephens (London, 1972).

—— and R. Blackburne, 'Vitae Hobbianae auctarium', in T. Hobbes, *Thomae Hobbes angli malmesburiensis philosophi vita* (London, 1681), pp. 21–221.

Auger, L., *Gilles Personne de Roberval (1602–1675): son activité intellectuelle dans les domaines mathématique, physique, mécanique et philosophique* (Paris, 1962).

Auvray, P., 'Jean Morin (1591–1659)', *Revue Biblique*, 66 (1959), pp. 397–414.

d'Auzoles de Lapeyre, J., *Le Mercure charitable, ou contre-touche et souverain remede pour des-empierrer le R. P. Petau jesuite d'Orleans* (Paris, 1638).

B., R., *see* Brome, R.

*Baba Bathra*, tr. M. Simon and I. W. Slotki, 2 vols. (London, 1935) (= vols. V and VI of *Seder Nezikin*, ed. I. Epstein, 6 vols. (London, 1935)).

Bacon, R., *Perspectiva* (Frankfurt, 1614).

—— *Roger Bacon's Philosophy of Nature: A Critical Edition . . . of* De multiplicatione specierum *and* De speculis comburentibus, ed. D. C. Lindberg (Oxford, 1983).

Baillet, A., *Vie de Monsieur Descartes* (Paris, 1946).

Baldi, B., *In mechanica Aristotelis problemata exercitationes* (Mainz, 1621).

Baltrušaitis, J., 'L'Anamorphose à miroir à la lumière de documents nouveaux', *La Revue des arts*, 6 (1956), pp. 85–98.

—— *Anamorphic Art*, tr. W. J. Strachan (Cambridge, 1977).

Bamberger, F., 'The Early Editions of Spinoza's *Tractatus Theologico-Politicus*: a Bibliohistorical Reexamination', *Studies in Bibliography and Booklore*, 5 (1961), pp. 9–33.

Bann, S., *Under the Sign: John Bargrave as Collector, Traveler, and Witness* (Ann Arbor, Mich., 1994).
Bardon, F., *Le Portrait mythologique à la cour de France sous Henri IV et Louis XIII: mythologie et politique* (Paris, 1974).
Bargrave, J., *Pope Alexander the Seventh and the College of Cardinals, with a Catalogue of Dr Bargrave's Museum*, ed. J. C. Robertson (London, 1867).
Barlaeus, C., *Discours oft vertoogh van Caspar Barleus, Onder-regent van 't Collegie der Godtheydt tot Leyden* (Leiden, 1616).
—— *Send-Brief op de naam van Me-Vrouwe de Princesse Amalia* (Leiden, 1630).
Barnouw, J., 'Vico and the Continuity of Science: The Relation of his Epistemology to Bacon and Hobbes', *Isis*, 71 (1980), pp. 609–20.
Bartolocci, G., *Bibliotheca magna rabbinica*, 4 vols. (Rome, 1675–93).
Barwick, P., *The Life of the Reverend Dr John Barwick, D. D.* (London, 1724).
Bastide, C., *The Anglo-French Entente in the Seventeenth Century* (London, 1914).
Bateman, T., 'Notes on a Few of the Old Libraries of Derbyshire, and their Existing Remains', *The Reliquary*, 1 (1860–1), pp. 167–74.
Batten, J. M., *John Dury, Advocate of Christian Reunion* (Chicago, 1944).
Battista, A. M., *Alle origini del pensiero politico libertino: Montaigne e Charron* (Milan, 1966).
—— 'Psicologia e politica nella cultura eterodossa francese del Seicento', in T. Gregory et al., *Ricerche su letteratura libertina e letteratura clandestina nel Seicento* (Florence, 1981), pp. 320–51.
Bauer, A., 'Johann Ludwig Gleditsch: Leichenpredigt mit Lebenslauf 1741', *Archiv für Geschichte des Buchwesens*, 9 (1969), cols. 1597–1612.
Baumgarten, S. J., *Nachrichten von merkwürdigen Bücher*, 12 vols. (Halle, 1752–8).
Baumgold, D., *Hobbes's Political Theory* (Cambridge, 1988).
Bayle, P., *Réponse aux questions d'un provincial*, 5 vols. (Rotterdam, 1704–7).
—— *Oeuvres diverses*, 4 vols. (The Hague, 1727–31).
—— 'Hobbes', in T. Hobbes, *Le Citoyen, ou les fondements de la politique*, tr. S. Sorbière, ed. S. Goyard-Fabre (Paris, 1982), pp. 367–78.
Beal, P., *Index of English Literary Manuscripts*, 5 vols. (London, 1980–).
Beats, L., 'Politics and Government in Derbyshire, 1640–1660', Sheffield University Ph.D. dissertation, 1978.
Beaujour, S., *Essai sur l'histoire de l'église réformée de Caen* (Caen, 1877).
Beaulieu, A., 'Lumière et matière chez Mersenne', *XVII$^e$ siècle*, 34 (1982), pp. 311–16.
—— 'Torricelli et Mersenne', in F. de Gandt, ed., *L'Oeuvre de Torricelli: science galiléenne et nouvelle géométrie* (Nice, 1987), pp. 39–51.
Becmann ['Becmanus'], J. C., *Meditationes politicae iisdemque continuandis & illustrandis addita politica parallela*, 3rd edn (Frankfurt an der Oder, 1679).
Beeman, G., 'Notes on the Sites and History of the French Churches in London', *Proceedings of the Huguenot Society of London*, 8, 1905–08 (London, 1909), pp. 13–59.
Beitz, C., *Political Theory and International Relations* (Princeton, NJ, 1979).
Bekker, B., *De betoverde weereld, zijnde een grondig ondersoek van 't gemeen gevoelen aangaande de geesten*, 4 vols. (Amsterdam, 1691–4).

—— *Kort beright . . . aangaande alle de schriften, welke over sijn boek de Betoverde Wereld . . . verwisseld sijn* (Amsterdam, 1692).
Bellarmine, R., *Opera omnia*, 8 vols. (Naples, 1872).
Benedetti, G. B., *Diversarum speculationum mathematicarum, & physicarum liber* (Turin, 1585).
Benítez, M., 'La Composition de la *Lettre de Thrasybule à Leucippe*: une conjecture raisonnable', in C. Grell and C. Volpilhac-Auger, eds., *Nicolas Fréret, légende et vérité* (Oxford, 1994), pp. 177–92.
—— *La Face cachée des Lumières: recherches sur les manuscrits philosophiques clandestins de l'âge classique* (Oxford, 1996).
—— 'Une Histoire interminable: origine et développement du *Traité des Trois Imposteurs*', in S. Berti, F. Charles-Daubert and R. H. Popkin, eds., *Heterodoxy, Spinozism, and Free Thought in Early Eighteenth-Century Europe: Studies on the* Traité des trois imposteurs (Dordrecht, 1996), pp. 53–74.
Benlowes, E., *Theophila* (London, 1652).
Bentivoglio, Cardinal, *Relatione* (Cologne, 1629).
van den Berg, J., 'Quaker and Chiliast: The "contrary thoughts" of William Ames and Petrus Serrarius', in *Reformation, Conformity and Dissent: Essays in Honour of Geoffrey Nuttall*, ed. R. Buick Knox (London, 1977), pp. 180–98.
Berghman, G., *Supplément à l'ouvrage sur les Elzevier de M. Alphonse Willems* (Stockholm, 1897).
Bergvelt, E., and R. Kistemaker, eds., *De wereld binnen handbereik: nederlandse kunst- en rariteitenverzamelingen 1585–1735* (Zwolle, 1992).
Bérigard ['Berigardus'], C., *Circulus pisanus* (Udine, 1643).
Berkvens-Stevelinck, C., and J. Vercruysse, *Le Métier de journaliste au dix-huitième siècle: correspondance entre Prosper Marchand, Jean Rousset de Missy et Lambert Ignace Douxfils* (Oxford, 1993).
Bernard, A., *Antoine Vitré et les caractères orientaux de la Bible polyglotte de Paris* (Paris, 1857).
Bernhardt, J., 'Hobbes et le mouvement de la lumière', *Revue d'histoire des sciences*, 30 (1977), pp. 3–24.
Berns, M., *Altar der Atheisten, der Heyden und der Christen . . . wider die 3 Ertz-Betrieger Hobbert* [sic], *Hobbes und Spinosa* (Hamburg, 1692).
Bernstein, H. R., '*Conatus*, Hobbes, and the Young Leibniz', *Studies in the History and Philosophy of Science*, 11 (1980), pp. 25–37.
Berriot, F., 'Hétérodoxie religieuse et utopie dans les "erreurs estranges" de Noël Journet (1582)', *Bulletin de la Société de l'Histoire du Protestantisme Français*, 124 (1978), pp. 236–48.
Berti, S., '*L'Esprit de Spinosa*: ses origines et sa première édition dans leur contexte spinozien', in S. Berti, F. Charles-Daubert and R. Popkin, eds., *Heterodoxy, Spinozism, and Free Thought in Early Eighteenth Century Europe. Studies on the* Traité des trois imposteurs (Dordrecht, 1996), pp. 3–51.
Bessire, F., *La Bible dans la correspondance de Voltaire* (Oxford, 1999).
Bettini, M., *Apiaria universae philosophiae mathematicae*, 2 vols. (Bologna, 1646).

## BIBLIOGRAPHY

Beverley, T. ['T. B.'], *The General Inefficacy and Insincerity of a Late, or Death-Bed Repentance* (London, 1670).

*Bibliotheca fratrum polonorum*, 6 vols. (Amsterdam, 1665–8).

*Bibliotheca hohendorfiana, ou catalogue de la bibliotheque de feu Monsieur George Guillaume Baron de Hohendorf*, 3 vols. (The Hague, 1720).

de Bils, L., *Anatomische beschrijvinge van een wanschepsel* (Middelburg, 1659).

Biscardi, S., *Epistola pro augusto Hispaniorum monarcha Philippo V* (Naples, 1703).

Blagden, C., *The Stationers' Company: A History, 1403–1959* (London, 1960).

Blanckmeister, F., *Der Prophet von Kursachsen Valentin Ernst Löscher und seine Zeit* (Dresden, 1920).

Blekastad, M., *Comenius: Versuch eines Umrisses von Leben, Werk und Schicksal des Jan Amos Komenský* (Oslo, 1969).

Bloch, O., *La Philosophie de Gassendi: nominalisme, matérialisme et métaphysique* (The Hague, 1971).

—— 'Hobbes et le matérialisme des Lumières', in A. Napoli and G. Canziani, eds., *Hobbes oggi* (Milan, 1990), pp. 553–76.

Blok, F. F., *Isaac Vossius and His Circle: His Life until his Farewell to Queen Christina of Sweden, 1618–1655* (Groningen, 2000).

Blount, C., *The Oracles of Reason* (London, 1693).

Bochart, S., *Phaleg* [*Geographiae sacrae pars prior Phaleg*, and *Geographiae sacrae pars altera Chanaan*] (Caen, 1646).

—— *Lettre de Monsieur Bochart à Monsieur Morley Chapelain du Roy d'Angleterre* (Paris, 1650).

—— *Hierozoicon, sive bipertitum opus de animalibus Sacrae Scripturae* (London, 1663).

Bodenstein, A., *De canonicis scripturis libellus* (Wittenberg, 1520).

Bodington, E. J., 'The Church Survey of Wiltshire, 1649–50', *Wiltshire Archaeological and Natural History Magazine*, 41 (1920), pp. 1–39.

Bögels, T. S. J. G., *Govert Basson: Printer, Bookseller, Publisher: Leiden 1612–1630* (Nieuwkoop, 1992).

Bøgh, K., *Det Kongelige Bibliotek gennem 300 år* (Copenhagen, 1980).

Böhme, J., *Jakob Böhmens erste Apologia wider Balthasar Tilken* (Amsterdam, 1677).

von Boineburg, J. C., *Epistolae ad virum clarissimum Jo. Conradum Dietericum*, ed. R. M. Meelfuhrer (Nuremberg, 1703).

Bonelli, M. L., 'Una lettera di Evangelista Torricelli a Jean François Niceron', in *Convegno di studi Torricelliani in occasione del 3500 anniversario della nascita di Evangelista Torricelli (19–20 ottobre 1958)* (Faenza, 1959), pp. 37–41.

Bonfrerius, J., *Pentateuchus Moysis commentario illustratus* (Antwerp, 1625).

*Book-Auction Records: A Priced and Annotated Annual Record* (London and Folkestone, 1902–).

Boonin-Vail, D., *Thomas Hobbes and the Science of Moral Virtue* (Cambridge, 1994).

Borch [Borrichius], O., *Olai Borrichii itinerarium 1660–1665*, ed. H. C. Scheperlern, 4 vols. (Copenhagen, London, 1983).

Borelli, G., *Ragione di stato e Leviatano: conservazione e scambio alle origini della modernità politica* (Bologna, 1993).

Bornemann, M., *Der mystische Spiritualist Joachim Betke (1601–1663) und seine Theologie* (Berlin, 1959).
Bossuet, J.-B., *Oeuvres complètes*, ed. F. Lachat, 31 vols. (Paris, 1862–6).
—— *Politique tirée des propres paroles de l'Escriture Sainte*, ed. J. Le Brun (Geneva, 1967).
Bots, J. A. H., ed., *Correspondance de Jacques Dupuy et de Nicolas Heinsius (1646–1656)* (The Hague, 1971).
—— *Republiek der Letteren: ideaal en werkelijkheid* (Amsterdam, 1977).
—— and P. Leroy, eds., *Correspondance intégrale d'André Rivet et de Claude Sarrau*, 3 vols. (Amsterdam, 1978–82).
Boucher, D., *Political Theories of International Relations: From Thucydides to the Present* (Oxford, 1998).
Bouchilloux, H., 'La Pensée politique de Pierre Nicole', *Chroniques de Port-Royal*, 45 (1996), pp. 197–209.
Bouillier, F., *Histoire de la philosophie cartésienne*, 3rd edn, 2 vols. (Paris, 1868).
Boulliau, I., *De natura lucis* (Paris, 1638).
Bousquet, J., *Recherches sur le séjour des peintres français à Rome au XVIIème siècle* (Montpellier, 1980).
Boxhorn, M. Z., *Varii tractatus politici* (Utrecht, 1663).
Boyle, R., *Works*, ed. T. Birch, 5 vols. (London, 1744).
—— *Selected Philosophical Papers*, ed. M. A. Stewart (Manchester, 1979).
Bramhall, J., *The Works of the Most Reverend Father in God, John Bramhall, D. D.*, 5 vols. (Oxford, 1842–5).
Brandt, F., *Den mekaniske naturopfattelse hos Thomas Hobbes* (Copenhagen, 1921).
—— *Thomas Hobbes's Mechanical Conception of Nature*, tr. V. Maxwell and A. I. Fausbøll (Copenhagen, 1928).
Brandt, R., 'Das Titelblatt des Leviathan und Goyas El Gigante', in U. Bermbach and K.-M. Kodalle, eds., *Furcht und Freiheit:* Leviathan-*Diskussion 300 Jahre nach Thomas Hobbes* (Opladen, 1982), pp. 201–31.
Breckling, F., *Religio libera persecutio relegata* ('Freystat' [Amsterdam], 1663).
Bredekamp, H., *The Lure of Antiquity and the Cult of the Machine: The Kunstkammer and the Evolution of Nature, Art and Technology* (Princeton, NJ, 1995).
—— *Thomas Hobbes visuelle Strategien: Der Leviathan, Urbild des modernen Staates* (Berlin, 1999).
Breger, H., 'Der mechanistische Denkstil in der Mathematik des 17. Jahrhunderts', in H. Hecht, ed., *Gottfried Wilhelm Leibniz im philosophischen Diskurs über Geometrie und Erfahrung* (Berlin, 1991), pp. 15–46.
Brennan, M. G., ed., *The Travel Diary (1611–12) of an English Catholic, Sir Charles Somerset*, Proceedings of the Leeds Philosophical and Literary Society, 23 (Leeds, 1993).
Brentius [Brentz], J., *Apologiae confessionis . . . Christophoris Ducis Wirtenbergensis* (Frankfurt, 1559).
Breuer, E., *The Limits of Enlightenment: Jews, Germans, and the Eighteenth-Century Study of Scripture* (Cambridge, Mass., 1996).
du Breuil, J., *La Perspective pratique*, 2nd edn, 3 vols. (Paris, 1663–9).

Briggs, H., *A Treatise of the Northwest Passage to the South Sea*, 1st edn 1622; reprinted in *The English Experience . . . in Facsimile*, 276 (Amsterdam, 1970).

—— *Trigonometria britannica, sive de doctrina, triangulorum, libri duo* (Gouda, 1633).

Brincourt, J.-B., *Jean Jannon, ses fils, leurs oeuvres* (Sedan, 1902).

von Brockdorff, C., *Die Urform der 'Computatio sive logica' des Hobbes*, Veröffentlichungen der Hobbes-Gesellschaft, Ortsgruppe Kiel, 2 (Kiel, 1934).

—— *Des Sir Charles Cavendish Bericht für Joachim Jungius über die Grundzüge der Hobbes'schen Naturphilosophie*, Veröffentlichungen der Hobbes-Gesellschaft, Ortsgruppe Kiel, 3 (Kiel, 1934).

Broekmans, H., Gruntjes, T., and H. Bots, 'Het beeld van de Republiek der Letteren in het tijdschrift van H. Basnage de Beauval', in H. Bots, ed., *Henri Basnage de Beauval en de Histoire des ouvrages des savans, 1687–1709*, 2 vols. (Amsterdam, 1976), pp. 109–305.

Brome, R. ['R. B.'], ed., *Lachrymae musarum* (London, 1649).

Brown, A., *The Genesis of the United States*, 2 vols. (London, 1890).

—— *English Politics in Early Virginia History*, 2nd edn (New York, 1968).

Brown, H., *Scientific Organizations in Seventeenth Century France (1620–1680)* (New York, 1934).

Brown, K., 'The Artist of the *Leviathan* Title-Page', *The British Library Journal*, 4 (1978), pp. 24–36.

Browne, Sir Thomas, *Religio medici* (London, 1642).

Brucker, J., *Historia critica philosophiae*, 6 vols. (Leipzig, 1744–5).

Bruckner, J., *A Bibliographical Catalogue of Seventeenth-Century German Books published in Holland* (The Hague, 1971).

Brummel, L., 'Jacob Boehme en het 17e-eeuwsche Amsterdam', in *Historische opstellen aangebeden aan J. Huizinga* (Haarlem, 1948), pp. 7–28.

Bruys, F., *Mémoires historiques, critiques, et littéraires*, 2 vols. (Paris, 1751).

Brydon, G. M., *Religious Life of Virginia in the Seventeenth Century* (Williamsburg, Va, 1957).

Buddecke, W., *Die Jakob Böhme-Ausgaben: ein beschreibendes Verzeichnis*, 2 vols. (Göttingen, 1937–57).

Bukovszky, A., 'Londoni magyar vonatkozású kiadványok és az 1664. évi Zrínyi-életrajz', *Irodalomtörténeti közlemények*, nos. 1–2 (1987–8), pp. 207–11.

Bull, H., *The Anarchical Society: A Study of Order in World Politics* (London, 1977).

—— 'Hobbes and the International Anarchy,' *Social Research: An International Quarterly of the Social Sciences*, 48 (1981), pp. 717–38.

Burckhard, J., *Historia bibliothecae Augustae quae Wolffenbutteli est*, 2 vols. (Leipzig, 1744–6).

de Bure, G.-F., *Bibliographie instructive: ou traité de la connoissance des livres rares et singuliers*, 7 vols. (Paris, 1763–8).

Burnet, G., *Some Passages of the Life and Death . . . of Rochester* (London, 1680).

—— *The Abridgment of the History of the Reformation of the Church of England* (London, 1682).

Burnett, S. G., *From Christian Hebraism to Jewish Studies: Johannes Buxtorf (1564–1629) and Hebrew Learning in the Seventeenth Century* (Leiden, 1996).

Burns, N. T., *Christian Mortalism from Tyndale to Milton* (Cambridge, Mass., 1972).
Burrows, M., ed., *The Register of the Visitors of the University of Oxford, from A.D. 1647 to A.D. 1658* (London, 1881).
Burton, R., *The Anatomy of Melancholy* (Oxford, 1621).
Bush, D., Letter to *The Times Literary Supplement*, 31 July 1943, p. 367.
—— 'Hobbes, William Cavendish and "Essayes" ', *Notes and Queries*, n.s., 20 (1973), pp. 162–4.
Butler, K. T., 'Louis Machon's "Apologie pour Machiavelle"—1643 and 1668', *Journal of the Warburg and Courtauld Institutes*, 3 (1939–40), pp. 208–27.
Buxton, J., *A Tradition of Poetry* (London, 1967).
Buxtorf, J., ed., *Biblia rabbinica*, 2 vols. (Basel, 1618–19).
—— *Tiberias sive commentarius masorethicus* (Basel, 1620).
*Calendar of State Papers, Domestic, 1611–1618*, ed. M. A. E. Green (London, 1858).
*Calendar of State Papers, Domestic, 1619–1623*, ed. M. A. E. Green (London, 1858).
*Calendar of State Papers, Domestic, 1638–1639*, ed. J. Bruce and W. D. Hamilton (London, 1871).
*Calendar of State Papers, Domestic, 1645–1647*, ed. W. D. Hamilton (London, 1891).
*Calendar of State Papers, Domestic, 1651*, ed. M. A. E. Green (London, 1877).
*Calendar of State Papers, Domestic, February–December 1685*, ed. F. Bickley (London, 1960).
*Calendar of State Papers, Domestic, 1690–1691*, ed. W. J. Hardy (London, 1898).
*Calendar of State Papers, Venetian, 1621–1623*, ed. A. B. Hinds (London, 1911).
Calvin, J., *Institutes of the Christian Religion*, tr. H. Beveridge, 2 vols. (London, 1953).
Cano, M., *De locis theologicis libri duodecim* (Louvain, 1564).
Cantelli, G., *Teologia e ateismo: saggio sul pensiero filosofico e religioso di Pierre Bayle* (Florence, 1969).
Canziani, G., 'Tra Descartes e Hobbes: la morale nel "Système" de Pierre-Sylvain Regis', in A. Napoli and G. Canziani, eds., *Hobbes oggi* (Milan, 1990), pp. 491–552.
—— 'Critica della religione e fonti moderne nel *Cymbalum mundi* o *Symbolum sapientiae*: prime note di lettura', in G. Canziani, ed., *Filosofia e religione nella letteratura clandestina: secoli XVII e XVIII* (Milan, 1994), pp. 35–81.
—— and G. Paganini, eds., *Theophrastus redivivus*, 2 vols. (Florence, 1981).
Cappel, L., *Critica sacra* (Paris, 1650).
de Cardonnel, P. ['P.D.C.'], *The Fortunate Islands* (London, 1661).
—— *Complementum fortunatarum insularum* (London, 1662).
—— *Tagus* (London, 1662).
Carel, P., *Histoire de la ville de Caen depuis Philippe-Auguste jusqu'à Charles IX* (Paris, n.d.).
Caron, E., 'Défense de la chrétienté ou gallicanisme dans la politique de la France à l'égard de l'empire ottoman à la fin du XVII$^e$ siècle', *XVII$^e$ siècle* (no. 199), 50 (1998), pp. 359–72.
Carpzovius, J. B., *Historia critica Veteri Testamenti autore Ricardo Simone . . . edita, oratione inaugurali discussa* (Leipzig, 1684).
Carr, E. H., *The Twenty Years' Crisis 1919–1939: An Introduction to the Study of International Relations* (London, 1939).

## BIBLIOGRAPHY

Carte, T., *The Life of James, Duke of Ormond*, 6 vols. (Oxford, 1851).
Casaubon, M., *A Letter . . . to P. du Moulin . . . concerning Natural Experimental Philosophie, and some Books lately set out about it* (Cambridge, 1669).
Castelli, B., *Della misura dell'acque correnti* (Rome, 1628).
Castrucci, E., *Ordine convenzionale e pensiero decisionista: saggio sui presupposti intellettuali dello stato moderno nel seicento francese* (Milan, 1981).
*Catalogus librorum manuscriptorum Bibliothecae Sloanianae* (n.p., n.d.).
Caton, W., *Den matelijken ondersoeker voldaen* (n.p., 1659).
Cau, C., et al., *Groot placaet-boek, vervattende de placaten, ordonnantien ende edicten van de . . . Staten Generael van de Vereenighde Nederlanden*, 7 vols. (The Hague, Amsterdam, 1658–1797).
Cavalieri, B., *Exercitationes geometricae sex* (Bologna, 1647).
Cavendish, M., Duchess of Newcastle, *The Life of the Duke of Newcastle* (London, 1915).
[Cavendish, W., Earl of Devonshire,] *A Discourse against Flatterie* (London, 1611).
—— *Horae subsecivae* (London, 1620).
Cavendish, W., Marquess of Newcastle, 'Opinion concerning the Ground of Natural Philosophy', in M. Cavendish, Marchioness of Newcastle, *Philosophical and Physical Opinions* (London, 1663), pp. 459–64.
Caws, P., ed., *The Causes of Quarrel: Essays on Peace, War, and Thomas Hobbes* (Boston, Mass., 1989).
Céleste, R., *Louis Machon, apologiste de Machiavel et de la politique du Cardinal de Richelieu: nouvelles recherches sur sa vie et ses oeuvres (1600–1672)* (Bordeaux, 1883).
Ceñal, E., 'Emmanuel Maignan: su vida, su obra, su influencia', *Revista de estudios politicos*, 46 (= year 12, no. 66) (1952), pp. 111–49.
van Ceulen, L., *Fundamenta arithmetica et geometrica cum eorundem usu* (Leiden, 1615).
Chamier, D., *Panstratiae catholicae, sive controversiarum de religione adversus Pontificios corpus*, 4 vols. (Geneva, 1626).
Chaney, E., *The Grand Tour and the Great Rebellion: Richard Lassels and 'The Voyage of Italy' in the Seventeenth Century* (Geneva, 1985).
Chapple, A. J., 'A Critical Bibliography of the Works of Charles Cotton', University of London MA dissertation, 1955.
Charles-Daubert, F., 'Le "Libertinage érudit" et le problème du conservatisme politique', in H. Méchoulan, ed., *L'État baroque: regards sur la pensée politique de la France du premier XVII<sup>e</sup> siècle* (Paris, 1985), pp. 179–202.
—— ed., *Le 'Traité des trois imposteurs' et 'L'Esprit de Spinosa': philosophie clandestine entre 1678 et 1768* (Oxford, 1999).
Charleton, W., *Deliramenta catarrhi: or, the Incongruities, Impossibilities and Absurdities couched under the Vulgar Opinion of Defluxions* (London, 1650).
—— *A Ternary of Paradoxes: The Magnetick Cure of Wounds, The Nativity of Tartar in Wine, The Image of God in Man* (London, 1650).
—— *The Darknes of Atheism Dispelled by the Light of Nature: A Physico-Theological Treatise* (London, 1652).
Chassanion, J., *La Refutation des erreurs estranges & blasphemes horribles contre Dieu & l'Escripture saincte* (Strasbourg, 1583).

Chéruel, M., ed., *Journal d'Olivier Lefèvre d'Ormesson et extraits des mémoires d'André Lefèvre d'Ormesson*, 2 vols. (Paris, 1860–1).

Chester, J. L., ed., *The Marriage, Baptismal, and Burial Registers of the Collegiate Church or Abbey of St Peter, Westminster*, Publications of the Harleian Society, 10, for 1875 (1876).

Chevreau, U., *Chevraeana, ou diverses pensées d'histoire, de critique, d'érudition et de morale*, 2 vols. (Amsterdam, 1700).

Chillingworth, W., *The Religion of Protestants a Safe Way to Salvation* (Oxford, 1638).

Chopius, F.-J., *Philosophia juris vera* (Leipzig, 1650).

Churchill, W. A., *Watermarks in Paper in Holland, England, France, etc., in the XVII and XVIII Centuries and their Interconnection* (Amsterdam, 1935).

Clark, P. A., 'Hobbes and the Enlightenment Rejection of Military Virtue', Catholic University of America Ph.D. dissertation, 1996.

Clarke, W., 'Illustrations of the State of the Church during the Great Rebellion', *The Theologian and Ecclesiastic*, 6 (1848), pp. 165–74, 217–24; 12 (1851), pp. 86–96.

Clay, C., *Public Finance and Private Wealth: The Career of Sir Stephen Fox, 1627–1716* (Oxford, 1978).

Clifford, A., ed., *Tixall Poetry: With Notes and Illustrations* (Edinburgh, 1813).

Cluverius, P., *Germaniae antiquae libri tres* (Leiden, 1631).

Cobbett, W., Howell, T. B., et al., eds., *A Complete Collection of State Trials*, 34 vols. (London, 1809–28).

Cocq, G., *Hobbes ἐλεγκόμενος, sive vindiciae pro lege, imperio, & religione, contra tractatus Thomae Hobbesii, quibus tit. De cive & Leviathan* (Utrecht, 1668).

—— *Hobbesianismi anatome, qua innumeris assertionibus ex tractatibus de homine, cive, Leviathan juxta seriem locorum theologiae christianae philosophi illius à religione christianâ apostasia demonstratur, & refutatur* (Utrecht, 1680).

Cokayne ['Cokain'], Sir Aston, *Poems. With the Obstinate Lady, and Trapolin a suppos'd Prince* (London, 1662).

Cokayne, G. E., *Complete Baronetage*, 5 vols. (Exeter, 1900–6).

—— *The Complete Peerage*, ed. V. Gibbs, G. H. White, and R. S. Lea, 12 vols. (London, 1912–59).

Coleman, D. C., 'The Early British Paper Industry and the Huguenots', *Proceedings of the Huguenot Society of London*, 19 (1956), pp. 210–25.

Coleridge, K. A., 'The Printing and Publishing of Clement Walker's *History of Independency 1647–1661*', *Bulletin of the Bibliographical Society of Australia and New Zealand*, 8 (1984), pp. 22–61.

Colerus, J., *Des menschen roem, is maer een bloem* (Amsterdam, 1683).

—— *La Vie de B. de Spinoza, tirée des ecrits de ce fameux philosophe* (The Hague, 1706).

Colie, R. L., 'Some Paradoxes in the Language of Things', in J. A. Mazzeo, ed., *Reason and the Imagination: Studies in the History of Ideas, 1600–1800* (New York, 1962).

*Collectio, of versamelinge, van eenige van de tractaten, boeken, en brieven, die geschreven sijn door verscheyde vrienden der waerheyt, die van de wereld, spots-gewijse, genoemt worden Quakers* (Amsterdam, 1657–74).

Collins, A., *Discours sur la liberté de penser*, 2 vols. ('London', 1713–14).

Collins, A., *The Peerage of England*, 5th edn, 8 vols. (London, 1779).

Collins, J., 'Christian Ecclesiology and the Composition of *Leviathan*: A Newly Discovered Letter to Thomas Hobbes', *The Historical Journal*, 43 (2000), pp. 217–31.
Colomiès, P., *Gallia orientalis, sive Gallorum qui linguam hebraeam vel alios orientales excoluerunt vitae* (The Hague, 1665).
de Colonia, D., *Histoire littéraire de la ville de Lyon, avec une bibliothèque des auteurs lyonnais*, 2 vols. (Lyon, 1728–30).
Comenius [Komenský], J. A., *Lux in tenebris* (Amsterdam, 1657).
—— *Opera didactica omnia* (Amsterdam, 1657).
—— *Lux e tenebris, novis radiis aucta* (Leiden, 1665; 2nd, enlarged edn '1665' [1667]).
—— *Unum necessarium, scire quid sibi sit necessarium, in vita & morte, & post mortem* (Amsterdam, 1668).
—— *Janua linguarum cum versione anglicana* (London, 1670).
—— *Janua linguarum trilinguis* (London, 1670).
—— *Unbekannte Briefe des Comenius und seiner Freunde 1641–1661*, ed. M. Blekastad (Kastellaun, 1976).
*Confessie, ofte belijdenisse des geloofs* (Amsterdam, 1650).
Conring, H., *De bello contra Turcas prudenter gerendo* (Helmstedt, 1664).
—— *Opera*, ed. J. W. Goebel, 7 vols. (Braunschweig, 1730).
Consett, H., *The Practice of the Spiritual or Ecclesiastical Courts* (London, 1847).
'Constans', *see* 'Lucius'.
Contant, J.-P., *L'Enseignement de la chimie au Jardin royal des plantes de Paris* (Cahors, 1952).
Cooke, P. D., *Hobbes and Christianity: Reassessing the Bible in* Leviathan (Lanham, Md 1996).
Cooper, W., *Catalogus librorum bibliothecae viri cujusdam literati. Quorum auctio habenda est Londini, ad insigne Pelicani in vico vulgò dicto Little-Britain sexto Junii, 1681* ([London, 1681)].
Coote, H. C., *The Practice of Ecclesiastical Courts* (London, 1847).
Cope, E., and W. H. Coates, eds., *Proceedings of the Short Parliament of 1640*, Camden Society, 4th ser., 19 (London, 1977).
Copland, P., *Virginia's God be Thanked* (London, 1622).
Corbett, M., and R. Lightbown, *The Comely Frontispiece: The Emblematic Title-Page in England, 1550–1660* (London, 1979).
Corbett, P. E., *Law and Society in the Relations of States* (New York, 1951).
Cosentino, G., 'Le matematiche nella "Ratio studiorum" della Compagnia di Gesù', *Miscellanea storica Ligure*, 2 (1970), pp. 207–12.
Cosins, R., *An Apologie for Sundrie Proceedings by Jurisdiction Ecclesiasticall* (London, 1593).
Cospi, A. M., *see* J.-F. Niceron.
Costabel, P., 'Gilles Personne de Roberval', *Cahiers d'histoire et de philosophie des sciences*, n.s., no. 14 (1986), pp. 21–31.
Cotton, C., *The Wonders of the Peake* (London, 1681).
—— *Poems*, ed. J. Beresford (London, 1923).
Cottret, B., *The Huguenots in England: Immigration and Settlement c.1550–1700*, tr. P. Stevenson and A. Stevenson (Cambridge, 1991).

de la Court, J., and P. de la Court ['V.H.'], *Consideratien en exempelen van staat, omtrent de fundamenten van allerley regeringe* (Amsterdam, 1660; 2nd edn, entitled *Consideratien van staat, ofte politike wegen-schaal*, Amsterdam, 1661).

de la Court, P. ['V.D.H.'], *Interest van Holland, ofte gronden van Hollands-Welvaren* (Amsterdam, 1662; 2nd edn, entitled *Aanwysing der heilsame politike gronden en maximen van de Republike van Holland en West-Vriesland*, Amsterdam, 1669).

—— ['V.D.H.'], *Naeuwkeurige consideratie van staet* (Amsterdam, 1662).

—— ['D.C.'], *Politike discoursen handelde in ses onderscheide boeken, van steeden, landen, oorlogen, kerken, regeeringen, en zeeden* (Amsterdam, 1662).

—— *'t Welvaren der stad Leiden*, ed. F. Driessen (Leiden, 1911).

—— see also 'Lucius'.

Couturat, L., *La Logique de Leibniz d'après des documents inédits* (Paris, 1901).

Cox, M., *The Story of Abingdon*, 4 vols. (n.p. [Abingdon], 1987–99).

Cozzi, G., 'Sir Edwin Sandys e la *Relazione dello stato della religione*', *Revista storica italiana*, 79 (1967), pp. 1097–1121.

Cranston, M., 'John Locke and John Aubrey', *Notes and Queries*, 197 (1952), pp. 383–4.

Craven, W. F., *The Dissolution of the Virginia Company* (Oxford, 1932).

Crelly, W. R., *The Painting of Simon Vouet* (New Haven, Conn., 1962).

Cumberland, R., *De legibus naturae* (London, 1672).

Curtis, M. H., *Oxford and Cambridge in Transition, 1558–1642* (Oxford, 1959).

Cussans, J. E., *History of Hertfordshire*, 3 vols. (London, 1870–81).

de Dainville, F., 'L'Enseignement des mathématiques dans les Collèges Jésuites de France du XVI$^e$ au XVIII$^e$ siècle', *Revue d'histoire des sciences et de leurs applications*, 7 (1954), pp. 6–21, 109–23.

van Dale, A., *Dissertationes de origine ac progressu idololatriae et superstitionum* (Amsterdam, 1696).

Dannhauer, J. C., *Dissertatio historico-theologica . . . cui adjectus . . . dialogus apologeticus pro mysterio syncretismi* (Strasbourg, 1668).

*Dansk biografisk leksikon*, 3rd edn, 16 vols. (Copenhagen, 1979–84).

Dapper, O., *Naukeurige beschrijvinge der Afrikaensche eylanden* (Amsterdam, 1676).

—— *Naukeurige beschrijvinge der Afrikaensche gewesten*, 2nd edn (Amsterdam, 1676).

—— *Naukeurige beschryving van gantsch Syrie, en Palestyn of Heilige Lant* (Amsterdam, 1677).

—— *Naukeurige beschryving van Asie* (Amsterdam, 1680).

—— *Asia, oder genaue und grundliche Beschreibung* (Amsterdam, 1681).

Darnton, R., *The Literary Underground of the Old Regime* (Cambridge, Mass., 1982).

Davenant, Sir William, *Gondibert*, ed. D. F. Gladish (Oxford, 1971).

Davies, D. W., 'The Geographic Extent of the Dutch Book Trade in the Seventeenth Century', *Het Boek*, n.s., 31 (1952–4), pp. 10–21.

Davies, J. S., *A History of Southampton, partly from the MS of Dr Speed, in the Southampton Archives* (Southampton, 1883).

Davis, R. B., *George Sandys, Poet–Adventurer* (London, 1955).

Debû-Bridel, J., *Anne-Geneviève de Bourbon, duchesse de Longueville* (Paris, 1938).

Debus, A. G., *The English Paracelsians* (London, 1965).

Deckherr ['Deckherrus'], J., *De scriptis adespotis, pseudepigraphis, et supposititiis conjecturae*, 3rd edn (Amsterdam, 1686).
Denter, T., *Die Stellung der Bücher Esdras im Kanon des Alten Testaments: eine kanongeschichtliche Untersuchung* (Freiburg, 1962).
Denzler, G., *Die Propagandakongregation in Rom und die Kirche in Deutschland im ersten Jahrzehnt nach dem Westfälischen Frieden* (Paderborn, 1969).
Desbans, L., *Principes naturels du droit et de la politique* (Paris, 1715; subsequent edns Paris, 1716, 1765, 1768).
Descartes, R., *Meditationes de prima philosophia* (Paris, 1641).
—— *Principia philosophiae* (Amsterdam, 1644; 2nd edn, 1650).
—— *Musicae compendium* (Utrecht, 1650).
—— *Specimina philosophiae, seu dissertatio de methodo* (Amsterdam, 1650).
—— *Lettres de Mr Descartes, où sont traittées les plus belles questions de la morale, de la physique, de la médecine, & des mathématiques*, ed. C. Clerselier, 3 vols. (Paris, 1657–67).
—— *The Philosophical Works*, tr. E. S. Haldane and G. R. T. Ross, 2 vols. (Cambridge, 1931).
—— *Oeuvres*, ed. C. Adam and P. Tannery, rev. edn, 11 vols. (Paris, 1974).
Desgraves, L., 'Les Thèses soutenues à l'Académie protestante de Saumur au XVII$^e$ siècle', *Bulletin de la Société de l'Histoire du Protestantisme Français*, 125 (1979), pp. 76–97.
—— et al., *Répertoire bibliographique des livres imprimés en France au XVII$^e$ siècle*, xiii, *Normandie II*, ed. A. R. Girard (Baden-Baden, 1985).
Desmaizeaux, P., 'Préface' to P. Bayle, *Lettres*, ed. P. Desmaizeaux, 3 vols. (Amsterdam, 1729), I, pp. i–xliv.
Detel, W., *Scientia rerum natura occultarum: methodologische Studien zur Physik Pierre Gassendis* (Berlin, 1978).
D'Ewes, Sir Simonds, *A Compleat Journal of the Votes, Speeches and Debates, both of the House of Lords and House of Commons* (London, 1682).
Dézallier d'Argenville, A. N., *Voyage pittoresque de Paris*, 4th edn (Paris, 1765).
Dibon, P., *La Philosophie néerlandaise au siècle d'or* (Paris, 1954).
—— *Regards sur la Hollande du siècle d'or* (Naples, 1990).
*Dictionnaire de biographie française*, ed. J. Balteau *et al.* (Paris, 1933–).
Diderot, D., 'Hobbisme', in T. Hobbes, *Le Citoyen, ou les fondements de la politique*, tr. S. Sorbière, ed. S. Goyard-Fabre (Paris, 1982), pp. 379–405.
Diderot, D., *et al.*, eds., *Encyclopédie ou dictionnaire raisonné des sciences, des arts et des métiers*, 17 vols. (Paris, 1751–65).
Diecmann, J., *De naturalismo cum aliorum, tum maxime Io. Bodini, ex opere ejus MSCto, & usque adhuc ἀνέκδοτω, de abditis rerum sublimium arcanis* (Kiel, 1683).
Diestel, L., *Geschichte des Alten Testaments in der christlichen Kirche* (Jena, 1869).
Dietz, M. G., 'Hobbes's Subject as Citizen', in M. G. Dietz, ed., *Thomas Hobbes and Political Theory* (Lawrence, Kan., 1990), pp. 91–119.
Dietze, W., *Quirinus Kuhlmann, Ketzer und Poet: Versuch einer monographischen Darstellung von Leben und Werk* (Berlin, 1963).
Digby, J., Earl of Bristol, *An Apologie of John Earl of Bristol Consisting of Two Tracts*, 2nd edn ('Caen' [London?], 1656).

Dimier, L., 'La Perspective des peintres et les amusements d'optique dans l'ancienne école de peinture', *Bulletin de la société de l'histoire de l'art français* (1925), pp. 7–22.
Dissel, K., *Philipp von Zesen und die deutschgesinnte Genossenschaft* (Hamburg, 1890).
Dittrich, E., *Die deutschen und österreichischen Kameralisten* (Darmstadt, 1974).
Dix, B., *Lebensgefährdung und Verpflichtung bei Hobbes* (Würzburg, 1994).
Dodge, G. H., *The Political Theory of the Huguenots of the Dispersion* (New York, 1947).
van der Does, M., *Antoinette Bourignon (1616–1680): la vie et l'oeuvre d'une mystique chrétienne* (Amsterdam, 1974).
Domat, J., *Les Loix civiles dans leur ordre naturel*, 2 vols. (Paris, 1689–94).
de Dominis, M. A., *De radiis visus et lucis* (Venice, 1611).
Donne, J., *A Sermon upon the VIII verse of the I chapter of the Acts of the Apostles preach'd to the Honourable Company of the Virginian Plantation, 13° Nouemb. 1622* (London, 1622).
Dreitzel, H., *Protestantischer Aristotelismus und absoluter Staat: die Politica des H. Arnisaeus* (Wiesbaden, 1970).
—— 'Hermann Conring und die politische Wissenschaft seiner Zeit', in M. Stolleis, ed., *Hermann Conring (1606–1681): Beiträge zu Leben und Werk* (Berlin, 1983), pp. 135–72.
Drummond, H. J. H., 'Hobbes's *Philosophicall Rudiments*, 1651', *The Library*, 5th ser., 28 (1973), pp. 54–6.
Dryden, J., *The Poems of John Dryden*, ed. P. Hammond, (London, 1995–).
Dufour, A., 'Pufendorf', in J. H. Burns and M. Goldie, eds., *The Cambridge History of Political Thought, 1450–1700* (Cambridge, 1991), pp. 561–88.
Dugard, W., *The English Rudiments* (London, 1665).
Duker, A. C., *Gisbertus Voetius*, 4 vols. (Leiden, 1897–1915).
Durel, J., *Theoremata philosophiae rationalis, moralis, naturalis et supernaturalis* (Caen, n.d. [1644]).
—— *The Liturgy of the Church of England Asserted in a Sermon Preached at the Chappel of the Savoy* (London, 1662).
—— *A View of the Government and Publick Worship of God in the Reformed Churches beyond the Seas* (London, 1662).
Dust, A. I., 'The *Seventh and Last Canto of Gondibert* and Two Dedicatory Poems', *Journal of English and Germanic Philology*, 60 (1961), pp. 282–5.
—— 'Charles Cotton: His Books and Autographs', *Notes and Queries*, 217 (1972), pp. 20–3.
Duverdier, G., 'Les Impressions orientales en Europe et le Liban', in C. Aboussouan, ed., *Le Livre et le Liban jusqu'à 1900* (Paris, 1982), pp. 157–279.
Dzelzainis, M., 'Edward Hyde and Thomas Hobbes's *The Elements of Law, Natural and Politic*', *The Historical Journal*, 32 (1989), pp. 303–17.
Ecchellensis, A., *Epistola apologetica prima* (n.p. [Paris], 1647).
Edmond, M., *Sir William Davenant* (Manchester, 1987).
Edwards, W. F., 'Randall on the Development of Scientific Method in the School of Padua—A Continuing Reappraisal', in J. Anton, ed., *Naturalism and Historical Understanding: Essays on the Philosophy of John Herman Randall Jr.* (Buffalo, NY, 1967), pp. 53–68.

# BIBLIOGRAPHY

van Eeghen, I. H., 'De "Uitgever" Henricus Cunrath of Künraht van de polygamist Lyserus en van de Philosoof Spinoza', *Amstelodamum: maandblad voor de kennis van Amsterdam*, 50 (April, 1953), pp. 73–80.

—— *De Amsterdamse boekhandel 1680–1725*, 5 vols. (Amsterdam, 1963–78).

Eller, P., *Kongelige portraetmalere i Danmark 1630–82: en undersøgelse af kilderne til Karel van Manders og Abraham Wuchters' virksomhed* (Copenhagen, 1971).

Ellies du Pin, L., *Nouvelle bibliothèque des auteurs ecclesiastiques*, 3 vols. (Paris, 1688–9).

Episcopius, S., *Opera theologica*, 2 vols. (Amsterdam–Rotterdam, 1650–65).

d'Espagne, J., *Popular Errors in Generall Poynts concerning the Knowledge of Religion* (London, 1648).

—— *Shibboleth, ou reformation de quelques passages és versions françoise & angloise de la Bible* (London, 1653).

—— *Essay des merveilles de Dieu en l'harmonie des temps* (London, 1657).

—— *Examen de XVII maximes judaiques* (London, 1657).

—— *The Joyfull Convert: Represented in a Short, but Elegant Sermon, Preached at the Baptizing of a Turke* (London, 1658).

d'Espagnet, J., *Enchiridion physicae restitutae* (Paris, 1647).

Evans, R. C., *Jonson and the Contexts of his Time* (London, 1994).

Evelyn, J., *Diary and Correspondence*, ed. W. Bray, 4 vols. (London, 1859).

—— *Diary*, ed. E. S. de Beer, 6 vols. (Oxford, 1955).

Everitt, A., *The Community of Kent and the Great Rebellion, 1640–60* (Leicester, 1966).

Faak, M., 'Die Verbreitung der Handschriften des Buches "De impostoribus religionum" im 18. Jahrhundert unter Beteiligung von G. W. Leibniz', *Deutsche Zeitschrift für Philosophie*, 18 (1970), pp. 212–28.

Falck, N., *Dissertationes quatuor, de daemonologia recentiorum autorum falsa* (n.p. [Stettin?], 1694).

Fanshawe, Lady Ann, *The Memoirs of Ann Lady Fanshawe*, ed. H. C. Fanshawe (London, 1907).

Fanshawe, H. C., *The History of the Fanshawe Family* (Newcastle-upon-Tyne, 1927).

Fanshawe, Sir Richard, *A Critical Edition of Sir Richard Fanshawe's 1647 Translation of Giovanni Battista Guarini's Il pastor fido*, ed. W. F. Staton and W. E. Simeone (Oxford, 1964).

—— *The Poems and Translations*, ed. P. Davidson, 2 vols. (Oxford, 1997–).

Feingold, M., *The Mathematicians' Apprenticeship: Science, Universities and Society in England 1560–1640* (Cambridge, 1984).

—— 'A Friend of Hobbes and an Early Translator of Galileo: Robert Payne of Oxford', in J. D. North and J. J. Roche, eds., *The Light of Nature: Essays in the History and Philosophy of Science Presented to A. C. Crombie* (Dordrecht, 1985), pp. 265–80.

—— 'The Mathematical Sciences and New Philosophies', in N. Tyacke, ed., *The History of the University of Oxford, IV, Seventeenth-Century Oxford* (Oxford, 1997), pp. 359–448.

Felbinger, J., *Een christelik bericht* (Amsterdam, 1660).

Felgenhauer, P., *Probatorium theologicum, eller theologischer proberung* (Amsterdam, 1664).

Ferrar, N., *Sir Thomas Smith's Misgovernment of the Virginia Company*, ed. D. R. Ransome (Cambridge, 1990).
Findlen, P., *Possessing Nature: Museums, Collecting, and Scientific Culture in Early Modern Italy* (Berkeley, Calif., 1994).
Firth, C. H., *The Last Years of the Protectorate 1656–1658*, 2 vols. (London, 1909).
Fischer, M., 'Machiavelli's Theory of Foreign Politics', in B. Frankel, ed., *Roots of Realism* (London, 1996), pp. 248–79.
Fisher, P. ['Paganus Piscator'], *Marston-Moor: sive de obsidione praelioque eboracensi carmen; cum quibusdam miscellaneis* (London, 1650).
Fisher, S., *Rusticus ad academicos in exercitationibus explostulatoriis, apologeticis quatuor: The Rustick's Alarm to the Rabbies: Or, the Country Correcting the University, and Clergy* (London, 1660).
Fitzherbert, N., *Oxoniensis in Anglia academiae descriptio* (Rome, 1602).
Fix, A., *Prophecy and Reason: The Dutch Collegiants in the Early Enlightenment* (Princeton, NJ, 1991).
Fleischmann, M., ed., *Christian Thomasius: Leben und Lebenswerk* (Halle, 1931).
Fleitmann, S., *Walter Charleton (1620–1707), 'Virtuoso': Leben und Werk* (Frankfurt am Main, 1986).
Fletcher, J., 'Athanasius Kircher and his Correspondence', in J. Fletcher, ed., *Athanasius Kircher und seine Beziehungen zum gelehrten Europa seiner Zeit* (Wiesbaden, 1988), pp. 139–78.
Focher, F., *Vico e Hobbes* (Naples, 1977).
Foister, S., Roy, A., and M. Wyld, *Making and Meaning in Holbein's Ambassadors* (London, 1997).
de la Fontaine Verwey, H., 'Het werk van Blaeu's', in H. de la Fontaine Verwey and W. G. Hellinga, *In officina Ioannis Blaev* (Amsterdam, 1961), pp. 1–12.
Force, P., ed., *Tracts and Other Papers, Relating Principally to the Origin, Settlement, and Progress of the Colonies in North America*, 4 vols. (Washington, DC, 1836–46; reprinted New York, 1947).
Forest Duchesne, N., *Florilegium universale liberalium artium et scientiarum* (Paris, 1650).
de Formigny de La Londe, A.-R., ed., *Documents inédits pour servir à l'histoire de l'ancienne Académie Royale des Belles Lettres de Caen* (Caen, 1854).
Forset, E., *A Comparative Discourse of the Bodies Natural and Politique* (London, 1606).
Forster, L., 'Philip von Zesen, Johann Heinrich Ott, John Dury, and Others', *The Slavonic and East European Review*, 32 (1953–4), pp. 475–85.
Forstner, H. F., *Antesignanus politicus, sive de studii politici ortu & progressu, dissertatio* (Tübingen, 1662).
Forsyth, M., 'Thomas Hobbes and the External Relations of States', *British Journal of International Studies*, 5 (1979), pp. 196–209.
—— 'Thomas Hobbes and the Constituent Power of the People', *Political Studies*, 29 (1981), pp. 191–203.
Foster, J., *Alumni oxonienses: The Members of the University of Oxford, 1500–1714*, 4 vols. (Oxford, 1891–2).

Fourmont, É., *Lettres à Monsieur \*\* sur le commentaire du Père Calmet sur la Genèse* (Paris, 1709–10).

Fournier, G., *Hydrographie, contenant la théorie et la pratique de toutes les parties de la navigation*, 2nd edn (Paris, 1667).

Francescon, C. M., *Chiesa e stato nei consulti di fra Paolo Sarpi* (Vicenza, 1942).

Frassen, C., *Disquisitiones biblicae quatuor libris comprehensae* (Paris, 1682).

Fréret, N., *Lettre de Thrasybule à Leucippe*, ed. S. Landucci (Florence, 1986).

Freudenthal, J., *Die Lebensgeschichte Spinoza's in Quellenschriften, Urkunden und nichtamtlichen Nachrichten* (Leipzig, 1899).

Fritsch, E., *Islam und Christentum im Mittelalter: Beiträge zur Geschichte der muslimischen Polemik gegen das Christentum in arabischer Sprache* (Breslau, 1930).

Fuller, T., *The Church-History of Britain* (London, 1655).

—— *The Holy State* (1663).

Gabbey, A., 'Huygens et Roberval', in R. Taton, ed., *Huygens et la France* (Paris, 1982), pp. 68–83.

—— 'Mariotte et Roberval, son collaborateur involontaire', in P. Costabel, ed., *Mariotte, savant et philosophe (†1684): analyse d'une renommée* (Paris, 1986), pp. 205–44.

Gabrieli, V., 'Bacone, la riforma e Roma nella versione Hobbesiana d'un carteggio di Fulgenzio Micanzio', *The English Miscellany*, 8 (1957), pp. 195–250.

Gadave, R., *Thomas Hobbes et les théories du contrat et de la souveraineté* (Toulouse, 1907).

Galatinus, P., *Opus de arcanis catholicae veritatis* (Basel, 1550).

Galilei, G., *Il saggiatore* (Rome, 1623).

—— *Dialogo . . . sopra i due massimi sistemi del mondo* (Florence, 1632).

—— *Systema cosmicum* (Strasbourg, 1635).

—— *Discorsi e dimostrazioni matematiche, intorno à due nuove scienze attenenti alla mecanica & i movimenti locali* (Leiden, 1638).

Galland, A., *Essai sur l'histoire du protestantisme à Caen et en Basse-Normandie de l'Édit de Nantes à la Révolution (1598–1791)* (Paris, 1898).

Galluzzi, P., and M. Torrini, eds., *Le opere dei discepoli di Galileo Galilei: carteggio 1642–1648*, I (Florence, 1975).

Garber, D., *Descartes Embodied: Reading Cartesian Philosophy through Cartesian Science* (Cambridge, 2001).

Gardiner, S. R., *History of England from the Accession of James I to the Outbreak of the Civil War*, 10 vols. (London, 1883–4).

de Garencières, T., *Angliae flagellum seu tabes anglica* (n.p., 1647).

Gargani, A., *Hobbes e la scienza* (Turin, 1971).

Garin, E., 'Appunti per una storia della fortuna di Hobbes nel settecento italiano', *Rivista critica di storia della filosofia*, 17 (1962), pp. 514–27.

Gassendi, P., *Animadversiones in decimum librum Diogenis Laertis*, 3 vols. (Lyon, 1649).

—— *Opera omnia*, 6 vols. (Lyon, 1658).

—— *Dissertations en forme de paradoxes contre les Aristotéliciens*, ed. and tr. B. Rochot (Paris, 1959).

—— *Disquisitio metaphysica seu dubitationes et instantiae adversus Renati Cartesii metaphysicam et responsa*, ed. and tr. B. Rochot (Paris, 1962).

Gauthier, D., *The Logic of Leviathan: The Moral and Political Theory of Thomas Hobbes* (Oxford, 1969).
Gelbart, N. R., 'The Intellectual Development of Walter Charleton', *Ambix*, 18 (1971), pp. 149–68.
van Gelder, H. A. E., *Getemperde vrijheid* (Groningen, 1972).
Gelderblom, A.-J., 'The Publisher of Hobbes's Dutch *Leviathan*', in S. Roach, ed., *Across the Narrow Seas: Studies in the History and Bibliiography of Britain and the Low Countries* (London, 1991), pp. 162–6.
Génébrard, G., *Chronographia in duos libros distincta*, 2nd edn (Louvain, 1572).
Gericke, W., 'Die handschriftliche Überlieferung des Buches Von den Drei Betrügern (De Tribus Impostoribus)', *Studien zum Buch- und Bibliothekswesen*, 6 (1988), pp. 5–28; 9 (1995), pp. 37–45.
Gert, B., 'Hobbes, Mechanism and Egoism', *Philosophical Quarterly*, 15 (1965), pp. 341–9.
—— 'Hobbes and Psychological Egoism', *Journal of the History of Ideas*, 28 (1967), pp. 503–20.
Geyl, P., 'Het stadhouderschap in de partij-literatuur onder de Witt', *Mededeelingen der koninklijke Nederlandsche akademie van wetenschapen*, afd. Letterkunde, n.s., 10 (1947), pp. 17–84.
Gibbs, G. C., 'The Role of the Dutch Republic as the intellectual entrepôt of Europe in the seventeenth and eighteenth centuries', *Bijdragen en mededelingen betreffende de geschiedenis der Nederlanden*, 86 (1971), pp. 323–49.
Gibson, S., ed., *Statuta antiqua universitatis oxoniensis* (Oxford, 1931).
Gilbert, W., *De magnete*, tr. P. Fleury Mottelay (London, 1893).
Gilman, E. B., *The Curious Perspective: Literary and Pictorial Wit in the Seventeenth Century* (New Haven, Conn., 1978).
Ginzburg, L., *The Legends of the Jews*, tr. H. Szold, 7 vols. (Philadelphia, 1913–38).
Girard, A. R., *see* Desgraves, L., *et al.*
Girard, G., *The History of the Life of the Duke of Espernon, the Great Favourite of France*, tr. C. Cotton (London, 1670).
Giudice, F., *Luce e visione: Thomas Hobbes e la scienza dell'ottica* (Florence, 1999).
Glanvill, J., *The Vanity of Dogmatizing* (London, 1661).
—— *Scepsis scientifica* (London, 1665).
—— *Philosophia pia: Or, a Discourse of the Religious Temper, and Tendencies of the Experimental Philosophy, which is Profest by the Royal Society* (London, 1671).
Glaziou, Y., *Hobbes en France au XVIII$^e$ siècle* (Paris, 1993).
Godfray, H. M., ed., *Registre des Baptesmes, Mariages & Mortz . . . de l'eglise Wallonne . . . à Southampton*, Publications of the Huguenot Society of London, 4 (Lymington, 1890).
Godfrey, J. T., *Notes on the Churches of Nottinghamshire: Hundred of Bingham* (London, 1907).
Godwin, G. N., *The Civil War in Hampshire (1642–45) and the Story of Basing House* (Southampton, 1904).
Goldgar, A., *Impolite Learning: Conduct and Community in the Republic of Letters, 1680–1750* (New Haven, Conn., 1995).

Goldie, M., 'The Reception of Hobbes', in J. H. Burns and M. Goldie, eds., *The Cambridge History of Political Thought, 1450–1700* (Cambridge, 1991), pp. 589–615.

Goldsmith, M. M., *Hobbes's Science of Politics* (London, 1966).

—— 'Picturing Hobbes's Politics? The Illustrations to *Philosophicall Rudiments*', *Journal of the Warburg and Courtauld Institutes*, 44 (1981), pp. 232–7.

Golius, J., ed., *Proverbia quaedam Alis, imperatoris muslimici, et carmen Togra'ï, poëtae doctis, nec non dissertatio quaedam Aben Sinae* (Leiden, 1629).

Goodman, D., *The Republic of Letters: A Cultural History of the French Enlightenment* (Ithaca, NY, 1994).

Göransson, S., *Ortodoxi och synkretism i Sverige, 1647–1660* (Uppsala, 1950).

Gordon Huntley, J., *A Summary of Controversies, wherein are briefly treated the cheefe Questions of Divinity, now a dayes in dispute betweene Catholickes & Protestants*, tr. by 'I. L.', 2nd edn (n.p., 1618).

Goshen-Gottstein, M., 'The Textual Criticism of the Old Testament: Rise, Decline, Rebirth', *Journal of Biblical Literature*, 102 (1983), pp. 365–99.

Gosselin, A., *Historia Gallorum veterum* (Caen, 1636).

Gouhier, P., 'La Société intellectuelle à Caen aux XVIe et XVIIe siècles', in R. Lebegue, ed., *La Basse-Normandie et ses poètes à l'époque classique* (Caen, 1977), 179–94.

Goyard-Fabre, S., 'Les Silences de Hobbes et de Rousseau devant le droit international', *Archives de philosophie du droit*, 32 (1987), pp. 59–69.

Graf, G., *Geschichte der christlichen arabischen Literatur*, 5 vols. (Vatican City, 1944–53).

Grafton, A., *Defenders of the Text: The Traditions of Scholarship in an Age of Science, 1450–1800* (Cambridge, Mass., 1991).

Graham, J., 'Sir Richard Fanshawe's Work as Public Poetry', University of Maryland PhD dissertation, 1984.

Grapius, Z., *Systema novissimarum controversiarum*, 4 vols. (Rostock, 1738) (first published 1709).

Green, M. A. E., ed., *Calendar of the Proceedings of the Committee for the Advance of Money, 1642–1656*, 3 vols. (London, 1888).

—— ed., *A Calendar of the Proceedings of the Committee for Compounding, &c., 1643–1660*, 5 vols. (London, 1889–92).

Greenslade, B. D., 'The Falkland Circle: A Study in Tradition from Donne to Halifax', University of London MA dissertation, 1955.

Gregory, T., *Scetticismo ed empirismo: studio su Gassendi* (Bari, 1961).

Grivel, M., 'Excudit et privilèges: les éditeurs de Simon Vouet', in S. Loire, ed., *Simon Vouet: actes du colloque international, Galeries nationales du Grand Palais, 5-6-7 février 1991* (Paris, 1992), pp. 307–29.

Groenveld, S., 'The Mecca of Authors? States Assemblies and Censorship in the Seventeenth-Century Dutch Republic', in A. Duke and C. A. Tamse, eds., *Too Mighty to be Free: Censorship and the Press in Britain and the Netherlands* (Zutphen, 1987), pp. 63–86.

Grotius, H., *Mare liberum, sive de iure quod Batavis competit ad Indicana commercia dissertatio* (Leiden, 1609).

—— *De imperio summarum potestatum circa sacra* (Paris, 1647).

—— *Opera theologica* (London, 1679).

—— *Epistolae quotquot reperiri potuerunt* (Amsterdam, 1687).
—— *Opera theologica*, 4 vols. (Basel, 1732).
—— *De jure belli et pacis libri tres*, ed. & tr. W. Whewell, 3 vols. (Cambridge, n.d. [1854]).
Grove, G. L., ed., *Des kgl. Dänischen Envoyé Georg Grund's Bericht über Russland in den Jahren 1705–1710*, Zapiski imperatorskoi akademii nauk, ser. 8, vol. 4, no. 7 (St Petersburg, 1900).
Grover, R. A., 'Hobbes and the Concept of International Law,' in T. Airaksinen and M. A. Bertman, eds., *Hobbes: War among Nations* (Aldershot, 1989), pp. 79–90.
Gruber, J. D., ed., *Commercii epistolici Leibnitiani . . . tomus prodromus, qui totus est boineburgicus*, 2 vols. (Hanover, 1745).
Guarnieri, G. G., *Cavalieri di Santo Stefano: contributo alla storia della marina militare italiana (1562–1859)* (Pisa, 1928).
Guhrauer, G. E., *Kur-Mainz in der Epoche von 1672*, 2 vols. (Hamburg, 1839).
Gullan-Whur, M., *Within Reason: A Life of Spinoza* (London, 1998).
Gundling, N. H., *Observationum selectarum ad rem litterariam spectantium*, vol. I (Frankfurt, 1707).
—— *Gundlingiana, darinnen allerhand zur Jurisprudenz, Philosophie, Historie, Critic, Litteratur, und übrigen Gelehrsamkeit gehörige Sachen abgehandelt werden*, 45 parts (Halle, 1715–32).
—— *Commentatio de statu naturali Hobbesii in corpore iuris civilis defenso et defendendo occasione L. 5 de iust. et I.* (Halle, 1735).
Gunn, J. A. W., *Politics and the Public Interest in the Seventeenth Century* (London, 1969).
Guys, J. A., and C. de Wolf, *Thesaurus 1473–1800: Nederlandse boekdrukkers en boekverkopers met plaatsen en jaren van werkzaamheid* (Nieuwkoop, 1989).
Gwynn, R. D., ed., *A Calendar of the Letter Books of the French Church of London from the Civil War to the Restoration, 1643–1659*, Huguenot Society of London, Quarto series, 54 (London, 1979).
Haag, E., ed., *La France protestante, ou vies des protestants français*, 2nd edn, 6 vols. (Paris, 1877–88).
Habermas, J., *The Structural Transformation of the Public Sphere*, tr. T. Burger and F. Lawrence (Cambridge, 1989).
Hagen, F. C., ed., *Memoriae philosophorum, oratorum, poetarum, historicorum et philologorum nostrae aetatis clarissimorum* (Frankfurt, 1710).
Haitsma Mulier, E. O. G., *The Myth of Venice and Dutch Republican Thought in the Seventeenth Century* (Assen, 1980).
—— 'De *Naeuwkeurige consideratie van staet* van de gebroeders De la Court: een nadere beschouwing', *Bijdragen en mededelingen betreffende de geschiedenis der Nederlanden*, 99 (1984), pp. 396–407.
Hakewill, G., *An Apologie of the Power and Providence of God in the Government of the World* (Oxford, 1627).
Hall, J., *Confusion Confounded* (London, 1654).
—— *Hierocles upon the Golden Verses of Pythagoras* (London, 1657).
Halliwell, J., ed., *A Collection of Letters Illustrative of the Progress of Science in England from the Reign of Queen Elizabeth to that of Charles the Second* (London, 1841).

du Hamel, J., *Reflexions critiques sur le système cartésien de la philosophie de M' Regis* (Paris, 1692).
Hamilton, A., *The Apocryphal Apocalypse: The Reception of the Second Book of Esdras (4 Ezra) from the Renaissance to the Enlightenment* (Oxford, 1999).
Hamilton, J. J., 'Hobbes's Study and the Hardwick Library', *Journal of the History of Philosophy*, 16 (1978), pp. 445–53.
Hamilton, S. G., *Hertford College* (London, 1903).
Hammerstein, N., *Jus und Historie: ein Beitrag zur Geschichte des historischen Denkens an deutschen Universitäten im späten 17. und im 18. Jahrhundert* (Göttingen, 1972).
Hampton, J., *Nicolas-Antoine Boulanger et la science de son temps* (Geneva, 1958).
Hampton, J., 'Hobbesian Reflections on Glory as a Cause of Conflict,' in P. Caws, ed., *The Causes of Quarrel: Essays on Peace, War, and Thomas Hobbes* (Boston, Mass., 1989), pp. 78–96.
Hanke, L., *Aristotle and the American Indians: A Study in Race Prejudice in the Modern World* (London, 1959).
Hanson, D. W., 'Thomas Hobbes's "Highway to Peace" ', *International Organization*, 38 (1984), pp. 329–54.
Hara, K., 'Roberval', in *Dictionary of Scientific Biography*, 18 vols. (New York, 1970–90), XI, pp. 486–91.
Harbage, A., Letter to the *Times Literary Supplement*, no. 1587 (30 June 1932), p. 480.
Hardacre, P., 'A Letter from Edmund Waller to Thomas Hobbes', *Huntington Library Quarterly*, 11 (1948), pp. 431–3.
Harrington, J., *The Political Works*, ed. J. G. A. Pocock (Cambridge, 1977).
Harvey, W., *Exercitationes de generatione animalium* (London, 1651).
Harwood, J. T., ed., *The Rhetorics of Thomas Hobbes and Bernard Lamy* (Carbondale, Ill., 1986).
Hasler, P. W., ed., *The House of Commons, 1558–1603*, 3 vols. (London, 1981).
Hasted, E., *The History and Topographical Survey of the County of Kent*, 13 vols. (Canterbury, 1797–1801).
Hauser, H., 'La Révocation de l'édit de Nantes et la papeterie en Angleterre', *Bulletin de la Société de l'Histoire du Protestantisme Français*, 80 (1931), pp. 230–2.
Havens, G. R., and N. L. Torrey, 'The Private Library of Voltaire at Leningrad', *Publications of the Modern Language Association of America*, 43 (1928), pp. 990–1009.
—— 'Voltaire's Books: A Selected List', *Modern Philology*, 27 (1929), pp. 1–22.
Hayward, J. C., 'The *Mores* of Great Tew: Literary, Philosophical, and Political Idealism in Falkland's Circle', Cambridge University Ph.D. dissertation, 1983.
—— 'New Directions in Studies of the Falkland Circle', *The Seventeenth Century*, 2 (1987), pp. 19–48.
Heawood, E., 'Papers used in England after 1600: I. The Seventeenth Century to *c*.1680', *The Library*, 2nd ser., 11 (1930), pp. 263–93.
—— *Watermarks mainly of the 17th and 18th Centuries* (Hilversum, 1950).
Heberden, C. B., ed., *Brasenose College Register, 1509–1909*, 2 vols. (Oxford, 1909).
Heering, J.-P., *Hugo de Groot als apologeet van de christelijke godsdienst* (The Hague, 1992).

Heidegger, J. H., *Exercitationes Biblicae, Capelli, Simonis, Spinosae & aliorum sive aberrationibus, sive fraudibus oppositae* (Zurich, 1700).

Heijting, W., 'Hendrick Beets (1625?–1708), Publisher to the German Adherents of Jacob Böhme in Amsterdam', *Quaerendo*, 3 (1973), pp. 250–80.

Helvétius, C.-A., *De l'Esprit* (Paris, 1758).

Henke, E. L. T., *Georg Calixtus und seine Zeit*, 2 vols. (Halle, 1853–60).

Hennis, W., *Politik und praktische Philosophie: Schriften zur politischen Theorie* (Stuttgart, 1977).

Henry, C., *Huygens et Roberval: documents nouveaux* (Leiden, 1880).

Hepp, N., 'Moisant de Brieux devant l'antiquité classique', in R. Lebegue, ed., *La Basse-Normandie et ses poètes à l'époque classique* (Caen, 1977), pp. 211–22.

Hetet, J. S. T., 'The Wardens' Accounts of the Stationers' Company, 1663–79', in *Economics of the British Booktrade 1605–1939*, ed. R. Myers and M. Harris (Cambridge, 1985), pp. 32–59.

—— 'A Literary Underground in Restoration England: Printers and Dissenters in the Context of Constraints 1660–1689', Cambridge University Ph.D. dissertation, 1987.

Hill, C., *The World Turned Upside Down* (London, 1972).

Hill, W. S., 'The Evolution of Hooker's *Laws of Ecclesiastical Polity*', in W. S. Hill, ed., *Studies in Richard Hooker* (Cleveland, Ohio, 1972), pp. 117–58.

Hinde, S., *England's Prospective-Glasse* (London, 1663).

Hinnant, C. H., *Thomas Hobbes: A Reference Guide* (Boston, Mass., 1980).

Hippeau, C., 'Jean-François Sarasin', in *Littérateurs normands* (composite volume, n.p., n.d.: BN, pressmark 8-LN9-261).

Historical Manuscripts Commission, *Ninth Report* (London, 1883; modern reference no. 8).

—— *Portland Manuscripts, Welbeck Abbey. Thirteenth Report, Appendix*, II (London, 1893; modern reference no. 29).

—— *Report on the Manuscripts of the Earl of Denbigh*, V (London, 1911; modern reference no. 68).

—— *Supplementary Report on the Manuscripts of the Late Montagu Bertie Twelfth Earl of Lindsey* (London, 1942; modern reference no. 79).

—— *see also*: Royal Commission on Historical Manuscripts.

Hobbes, T., *Elementorum philosophiae sectio tertia de cive* (Paris, 1642; subsequent edns: Amsterdam, 1647; Amsterdam, 1657; Amsterdam, 1669; Amsterdam, 1696; Halle(?), c.1704; Amsterdam(?), 1742; Lausanne, 1760; Basel, 1782).

—— *Elémens philosophiques du citoyen*, tr. S. Sorbière (Amsterdam, 1649; 2nd edn Paris, 1649–51).

—— *Humane Nature: Or, The Fundamental Elements of Policie* (Oxford and London, 1650; 2nd edn London, 1651).

—— *De corpore politico, Or, The Elements of Law* (London, 1650; 2nd edn 1652).

—— *Philosophicall Rudiments concerning Government and Society*, tr. 'C. C.' [Charles Cotton] (London, 1651).

—— *Leviathan* (London, 1651).

—— *Le Corps politique, ou les elemens de la loy morale et civile*, tr. anon. [J. Davies?] (n.p. [Rouen?], 1652; 2nd edn Leiden, 1653).

—— *Of Libertie and Necessitie* (London, 1654).
—— *Elementorum philosophiae sectio prima de corpore* (London, 1655).
—— *Elements of Philosophy, the First Section, Concerning Body*, with *Six Lessons to the Professors of Mathematicks* (London, 1656).
—— *The Questions concerning Liberty, Necessity, and Chance* (London, 1656).
—— ΣΤΙΓΜΑΙ . . . *or Markes of the Absurd Geometry, Rural Language, Scottish Church-Politicks, and Barbarisms of John Wallis Professor of Geometry and Doctor of Divinity* (London, 1657).
—— *Elementorum philosophiae sectio secunda de homine* (London, 1658).
—— *Les Elemens de la politique de Monsieur Hobbes*, tr. F. du Verdus (1st and 2nd edns, Paris, 1660; 3rd edn entitled *Maximes heroïques de la politique moderne au roy*, Paris, 1665).
—— *Examinatio & emendatio mathematicae hodiernae* (London, 1660).
—— *Dialogus physicus, sive de natura aeris conjectura* (London, 1661).
—— *La Duplication du cube par V.A.Q.R.* (n.p., n.d. [Paris, 1661]).
—— *Mr. Hobbes Considered in his Loyalty, Religion, Reputation, and Manners* (London, 1662).
—— *Problemata physica* (London, 1662).
—— *De principiis et ratiocinatione geometrarum* (London, 1666).
—— *Opera philosophica quae latinè scripsit, omnia* (Amsterdam, 1668).
—— *Quadratura circuli* (London, 1669).
—— *Leviathan, sive de materia, forma, & potestate civitatis ecclesiasticae et civilis* (Amsterdam, 1670).
—— *De eerste beginselen van een burger-staat*, tr. anon. (Amsterdam, 1675).
—— *Decameron physiologicum: Or, Ten Dialogues of Natural Philosophy* (London, 1678).
—— *De mirabilibus pecci* (London, 1678).
—— *Thomae Hobbesii malmesburiensis vita* (London, 1679).
—— *Thomae Hobbes angli malmesburiensis philosophi vita* (London, 1681).
—— *Seven Philosophical Problems, and Two Propositions of Geometry* (London, 1682).
—— *Historia ecclesiastica* (London, 1688).
—— *Een tractaatje van vrijwillighe yd en noodsaakelijkheyd daar in alle verschillen aangaande prdistinatie* [sic], *verkiesinge, vrye wil, genade, verdienste, verwerpinge &c. ten volle besligt en verklaart wort*, tr. anon. (Rotterdam, 1698).
—— 'Léviathan', tr. anon., *Le Conservateur* (July–October 1760).
—— *De la Nature humaine*, tr. d'Holbach (London, 1772).
—— *Nachal'nya osnevaniia filosoficheskaia o grazhdaninie*, tr. S. Venitsieev (St Petersburg and Moscow, 1776).
—— *Des Engländers Thomas Hobbes Leviathan, oder der kirchliche und bürgerliche Staat*, tr. anon., 2 vols. (Halle, 1794–5).
—— *The English Works of Thomas Hobbes of Malmesbury*, [*EW*], ed. W. Molesworth, 11 vols. (London, 1839–45).
—— *Thomae Hobbes malmesburiensis opera philosophica quae latine scripsit omnia*, [*OL*], ed. W. Molesworth (London, 1839–45).
—— *Behemoth: Or, the Long Parliament*, ed. F. Tönnies (London, 1889).
—— *The Elements of Law*, ed. F. Tönnies (London, 1889).

—— *Leviathan*, ed. A. R. Waller (Cambridge, 1904).
—— *Leviathan*, ed. W. G. Pogson Smith (Oxford, 1909).
—— *The Elements of Law*, ed. F. Tönnies (Cambridge, 1928).
—— 'Tractatus opticus', ed. F. Alessio, *Rivista critica di storia della filosofia*, 18 (1963), pp. 147–228.
—— *Leviathan*, ed. C. B. Macherson (Harmondsworth, 1968).
—— *A Dialogue between a Philosopher and a Student of the Common Laws of England*, ed. J. Cropsey (Chicago, 1971).
—— *Léviathan*, tr. F. Tricaud (Paris, 1971).
—— *Critique du* De mundo *de Thomas White*, ed. J. Jacquot and H. W. Jones (Paris, 1973).
—— *Thomas White's* De mundo *Examined*, tr. H. W. Jones (London, 1976).
—— *Le Corps politique*, ed. L. Roux (Saint-Étienne, 1977).
—— *Le Citoyen, ou les fondements de la politique*, tr. S. Sorbière, ed. S. Goyard-Fabre (Paris, 1982).
—— *De cive: The English Version*, ed. J. H. Warrender, Clarendon Edition of the Works of Thomas Hobbes, 3 (Oxford, 1983).
—— *De cive: The Latin Version*, ed J. H. Warrender, Clarendon Edition of the Works of Thomas Hobbes, II (Oxford, 1983).
—— (attrib.), *Court Traité des premiers principes: le Short Tract on First Principles de 1630–1631. La naissance de Thomas Hobbes à la pensée moderne*, ed. and tr. J. Bernhardt (Paris, 1988).
—— *Leviathan*, ed. R. Tuck (Cambridge, 1991).
—— *De cive: elementi filosofici sul cittadino*, ed. and tr. T. Magri, 3rd edn (Rome, 1992).
—— *The Correspondence*, ed. N. Malcolm, 2 vols., Clarendon Edition of the Works of Thomas Hobbes, VI, VII (Oxford, 1994).
—— (attrib.), *Three Discourses: A Critical Modern Edition of Newly Identified Work of the Young Hobbes*, ed. N. B. Reynolds and A. W. Saxonhouse (Chicago, 1995).
—— *Elemente der Philosophie: erste Abteilung, Der Körper*, ed. and tr. K. Schuhmann (Hamburg, 1997).
—— *De corpore: elementorum philosophiae sectio prima*, ed. K. Schuhmann (Paris, 1999).
—— *On the Citizen*, ed. and tr. R. Tuck and M. Silverthorne (Cambridge, 1999).
Hochstrasser, T. J., *Natural Law Theories in the Early Enlightenment* (Cambridge, 2000).
Hodgson, N., and Blagden, C., *The Notebook of Thomas Bennet and Henry Clements (1686–1719) with Some Aspects of Book Trade Practice*, Oxford Bibliographical Society Publications, n.s., 6 (Oxford, 1953).
Hoekstra, K., 'The Savage, the Citizen, and the Foole: The Compulsion for Civil Society in the Philosophy of Thomas Hobbes', Oxford University D.Phil. dissertation, 1998.
Hoffmann, S., *The State of War: Essays on the Theory and Practice of International Politics* (London, 1965).
Hoftijzer, P. G., *Engelse boekverkopers bij de Beurs: de geschiedenis van de Amsterdamse boekhandels Bruyning en Swart, 1637–1724* (Amsterdam, 1987).
Hohfeld, W. N., *Fundamental Legal Conceptions*, ed. W. W. Cook (New Haven, Conn., 1946).

Holstenius, L., *see* Porphyrius.

Hombergk zu Vach, J. F., *Pacem et societatem humani generis natura constitutam ex ipsis principiis T. Hobbii probatam* (Marburg, 1722).

Hooker, R., *Works*, 7th edn, 3 vols. ed. J. Keble, R. W. Church, and F. Paget (Oxford, 1888).

Hoüard, D., *Dictionnaire analytique, historique, étymologique, critique et interpretatif de la coutume normande*, 4 vols. (Rouen, 1780–2).

Houtuyn, A., *Politica contracta generalis, notis illustrata* (The Hague, 1681).

Howells, R. J., *Pierre Jurieu: Antinomian Radical* (Durham, 1983).

Huber, U., *De jure civitatis libri tres*, rev. edn (Franeker, 1684).

Huet, P. D., *Demonstratio evangelica ad serenissimum Delphinum* (Paris, 1679).

—— *Commentarius de rebus ad eum pertinentibus* (Amsterdam, 1718).

d'Huisseau, I., *La Reünion du christianisme, ou la maniere de rejoindre tous les Chretiens sous une seule confession de foy* (Saumur, n.d. [1671]).

van Huisstede, P., and J. P. J. Brandhorst, *Dutch Printer's Devices 15th–17th Century: A Catalogue*, 3 vols. (Nieuwkoop, 1999).

Hull, W. I., *The Rise of Quakerism in Amsterdam 1655–1665* (Philadelphia, 1938).

—— *Benjamin Furly and Quakerism in Rotterdam* (Philadelphia, 1941).

Hunter, M., 'The Debate over Science', in J. R. Jones, ed., *The Restored Monarchy 1660–1668* (London, 1979), pp. 176–95.

—— *The Royal Society and its Fellows, 1660–1700*, British Society for the History of Science Monographs, 4 (Chalfont St Giles, 1982).

—— ' "Aikenhead the Atheist": The Context and Consequences of Articulate Irreligion in the Late Seventeenth Century', in M. Hunter and D. Wootton, eds., *Atheism from the Reformation to the Enlightenment* (Oxford, 1992), pp. 221–54.

Hunter, M., Mandelbrote, G., Ovenden, R., and N. Smith, eds., *A Radical's Books: The Library Catalogue of Samuel Jeake of Rye, 1623–90* (Cambridge, 1999).

Hurrell, A., 'Society and Anarchy in the 1990s', in B. A. Roberson, ed., *International Society and the Development of International Relations Theory* (London, 1998), pp. 17–42.

Huygens, C., *Oeuvres complètes*, 22 vols. (The Hague, 1888–1950).

Huygens, L., *The English Journal, 1651–1652*, ed. and tr. A. G. H. Bachrach and R. G. Collmer (Leiden, 1982).

Hyde, E., Earl of Clarendon, *A Brief View and Survey of the Dangerous and Pernicious Errors to Church and State in Mr. Hobbes's Book, entitled Leviathan* (Oxford, 1676).

—— *The History of the Rebellion and Civil Wars in England*, 3 vols. (Oxford, 1807).

—— *The Life of Edward Earl of Clarendon*, 3 vols. (Oxford, 1827).

'Illustrations of the State of the Church during the Great Rebellion': *see* Clarke, W.

Impey, O., and A. MacGregor, eds., *The Origins of Museums: The Cabinet of Curiosities in Sixteenth- and Seventeenth-Century Europe* (Oxford, 1985).

*Index librorum prohibitorum* (Vatican City, 1938).

*Index librorum prohibitorum Alexandri VII. Pontificis maximi iussu editus* (Rome, 1664).

*Index librorum prohibitorum sanctissimi domini nostri Gregorii XVI. Pontificis maximi jussu editus* (Naples, 1853).

van Inghen, F., *Böhme und Böhmisten in den Niederlanden im 17. Jahrhundert* (Bonn, 1984).
Isham, Sir Gyles, ed., *The Correspondence of Bishop Brian Duppa and Sir Justinian Isham, 1650–1660*, Publications of the Northamptonshire Record Society, 17 (Northampton, 1951).
Israel, J. I., *Radical Enlightenment: Philosophy and the Making of Modernity 1650–1750* (Oxford, 2001).
ben Israel, M., *Conciliador* (Frankfurt, Amsterdam, 1632–51).
—— *Vindiciae Judaeorum* (London, 1656).
Jacob, J. R., *Henry Stubbe, Radical Protestantism and the Early Enlightenment* (Cambridge, 1983).
Jacob, M. C., *The Radical Enlightenment: Pantheists, Freemasons and Republicans* (London, 1981).
Jacquot, J., 'Sir Charles Cavendish and his Learned Friends', *Annals of Science*, 8 (1952), pp. 13–27, 175–91.
—— 'Harriot, Hill, Warner and the New Philosophy', in J. W. Shirley, ed., *Thomas Harriot, Renaissance Scientist* (Oxford, 1974), pp. 107–28.
Janssen, F. A., ed., *Abraham Willemsz van Beyerland: Jacob Böhme en het Nederlandse hermetisme in de 17e eeuw* (Amsterdam, 1986).
Jansson, M., ed., *Proceedings in Parliament, 1614 (House of Commons)*, Memoirs of the American Philosophical Society, 172 (Philadelphia, 1988).
Jesseph, D., *Squaring the Circle: The War between Hobbes and Wallis* (Chicago, 1999).
Jöcher, C. G., *Allgemeines Gelehrten-Lexicon*, 4 vols. (Leipzig, 1750–1).
Johnson, F. R., 'Thomas Digges, the Copernican System and the Idea of the Infinity of the Universe in 1576', *Huntington Library Bulletin*, 5 (1934), pp. 69–117.
Johnson, L. M., *Thucydides, Hobbes, and the Interpretation of Realism* (DeKalb, Ill., 1993).
Johnson, P., 'Hobbes's Anglican Doctrine of Salvation', in R. Ross, H. Schneider and T. Waldman, eds., *Thomas Hobbes in his Time* (Minneapolis, 1974), pp. 102–25.
Johnson, T. J., 'The Idea of Power Politics: The Sophistic Foundations of Realism', in B. Frankel, ed., *Roots of Realism* (London, 1996), pp. 194–247.
Johnston, D., *The Rhetoric of* Leviathan: *Thomas Hobbes and the Politics of Cultural Transformation* (Princeton, NJ, 1986).
—— 'Hobbes's Mortalism', *History of Political Thought*, 10 (1989), pp. 647–63.
Joly, P., *Remarques critiques sur le Dictionnaire de Bayle*, 2 vols. (Paris, 1752).
Jongeneelen, G. H., 'An Unknown Pamphlet of Adriaan Koerbagh', *Studia Spinozana*, 3 (1987), pp. 405–15.
Jonson, B., *Works*, ed. C. H. Herford, P. Simpson, and E. Simpson, 11 vols. (Oxford, 1925–52).
Jørgensen, A. D., *Peter Schumacher Griffenfeld*, 2 vols. (Copenhagen, 1893).
*The Journals . . . of the House of Commons* (London, 1742–).
Jouvin, *Solution et esclaircissement de quelques propositions de mathematiqui* (Paris, 1658).
Jusserand, J. J., *A French Ambassador at the Court of Charles the Second: Le Comte de Cominges, from his Unpublished Correspondence* (London, 1892).
Juynboll, W. M. C., *Zeventiende-eeuwsche beoefenaars van het Arabisch in Nederland* (Utrecht, 1931).

## BIBLIOGRAPHY

Kantorowicz, E., *The King's Two Bodies: A Study in Mediaeval Political Theory* (Princeton, NJ, 1957).
Kargon, R. H., *Atomism in England from Hariot to Newton* (Oxford, 1966).
Kearney, H., *Scholars and Gentlemen: Universities and Society in Pre-Industrial Britain, 1500–1700* (London, 1970).
Keith, G., *An Account of the Quakers Politicks* (London, 1700).
Keohane, N. O., *Philosophy and the State in France: The Renaissance and the Enlightenment* (Princeton, NJ, 1980).
Kepler, J., *Gesammelte Werke*, ed. M. Caspar and W. von Dyck (Munich, 1938–).
Kerviler, R., *Le Chancelier Pierre Séguier* (Paris, 1874).
Kettnerus, F. E., *De duobus impostoribus, Benedicto Spinosa et Balthasare Bekkero, dissertatio historica* (Leipzig, 1694).
Kettwig, M., *De veritate philosophiae Hobbesianae: contra virum amplissimum Ulricum Huberum* (n.p. [Bremen?], 1695).
Keynes, G., *The Life of William Harvey* (Oxford, 1978).
Kiessling, N. K., *The Library of Robert Burton*, Oxford Bibliographical Society Publications, n.s., XXII (Oxford, 1988).
Kingsbury, S. M., ed., *Records of the Virginia Company of London*, 4 vols. (Washington, DC, 1906–35).
Kircher, A., *Magnes sive de arte magnetica libri tres* (Rome, 1641; 3rd edn Rome, 1654).
—— *Ars magna lucis et umbrae* (Rome, 1646).
Kitchin, G., *Sir Roger L'Estrange: A Contribution to the History of the Press in the Seventeenth Century* (London, 1913).
Kleerkooper, M. M., 'Daniel Elseviers betrekkingen met Engeland', *Tijdschrift voor boek- en bibliotheekwezen*, 8 (1910), pp. 115–25.
—— and van Stockum, W. P., *De boekhandel te Amsterdam voornamelijk in de 17e eeuw*, 2 vols. (The Hague, 1914–16).
Klein, J., *Greek Mathematical Thought and the Origin of Algebra* (Cambridge, Mass., 1968).
Klever, W. N. A., *Verba et sententiae Spinozae or Lambertus van Velthuysen (1622–1685) on Benedictus de Spinoza* (Amsterdam, 1991).
Klinkenborg, V., ed., *British Literary Manuscripts*, series 1 (New York, 1981).
Knuttel, W. P. C., *Balthasar Bekker: de bestrijder van het bijgeloof* (The Hague, 1906).
—— *Verboden boeken in de Republiek der Vereenigde Nederlanden*, Bijdragen tot de geschiedenis van den Nederlandschen boekhandel, 11 (The Hague, 1914).
Kobuch, A., *Zensur und Aufklärung in Kursachsen: ideologische Strömungen und politische Meinungen zur Zeit der sächsisch-polnischen Union (1697–1763)* (Weimar, 1988).
Koelman, J., *Wederlegging van B. Bekkers betoverde werelt* (Amsterdam, 1692).
—— *Het vergift van de cartesiaansche philosophie grondig ontdekt* (Amsterdam, 1692).
Kolakowski, L., *Świadowość religijna i więź kościelna* (Warsaw, 1965).
Kortholt, C., *De tribus impostoribus magnis*, 2nd [or 3rd?] edn (Hamburg, 1701) [previously published at Kiel, 1680].
Koselleck, R., *Critique and Crisis: Enlightenment and the Pathogenesis of Modern Society* (Oxford, 1988).

Kossmann, E. F., *De boekhandel te 's-Gravenhage tot het einde van de 18e eeuw* (The Hague, 1937).

Kossmann, E. H., 'Politieke theorie in het zeventiende-eeuwse Nederland', *Verhandelingen der Koninklijke Nederlandse Akademie van Wetenschappen, afdeling letterkunde*, n.s., 67: no. 2 (1960), pp. 24–5.

—— 'De Dissertationes Politicae van Ulric Huber', in P. K. King and P. F. Vincent, eds., *European Context: Studies in the History and Literature of the Netherlands presented to Theodoor Weevers* (Cambridge, 1971), pp. 164–77.

Krailsheimer, A. J., *Studies in Self-Interest from Descartes to La Bruyère* (Oxford, 1962).

Kraus, H.-J., *Geschichte der historisch-kritischen Erforschung des Alten Testaments*, 2nd edn (Neukirchen, 1969).

Krause, J. G., ed., *Neue Zeitungen von Gelehrten Sachen*, vol. 2, no. 16 (15 April 1716).

Kraynak, R. P., *History and Modernity in the Thought of Thomas Hobbes* (Ithaca, NY, 1990).

Kretzer, H., *Calvinismus und französische Monarchie im 17. Jahrhundert* (Berlin, 1975).

Krieg, G. A., *Der mystische Kreis: Wesen und Werden der Theologie Pierre Poirets* (Göttingen, 1979).

Krieger, L., *The Politics of Discretion: Pufendorf and the Acceptance of Natural Law* (Chicago, 1965).

Kritzeck, J., *Peter the Venerable and Islam* (Princeton, NJ, 1964).

Krivatsy, P., ed., *A Catalogue of Seventeenth Century Printed Books in the National Library of Medicine* (Bethesda, Md, 1989).

Kuhlmann, Q., *The General London Epistle* (London, 1679).

—— *Quinary of Slingstones* (London and Oxford, 1683).

—— *Der neubegeisterte Böhme*, ed. J. Clark, 2 vols. (Stuttgart, 1995).

Kvačala, J., ed., *Korrespondence Jana Amosa Komenského*, 2 vols. (Prague, 1898–1902).

—— ['Kvacsala'], *Johann Amos Comenius: sein Leben und seine Schriften* (Berlin, 1892).

de La Barre de Beaumarchais, A., *Lettres serieuses et badines sur les ouvrages des savans*, 8 vols. (The Hague, 1729–33).

Lacour-Gayet, G., *L'Éducation politique de Louis XIV* (Paris, 1898).

—— 'Les Traductions françaises de Hobbes sous le règne de Louis XIV', *Archiv für Geschichte der Philosophie*, 12 (= n.s., 5) (1899), pp. 202–7.

Lactantius, *Epitome institutionum divinarum*, ed. and tr. E. H. Blakeney (London, 1950).

de La Forge, L., *Traitté de l'esprit de l'homme, de ses facultez et fonctions, et de son union avec le corps, suivant les principes de René Descartes* (Paris, 1666).

Lagrée, J., 'Christian Kortholt et son *De tribus impostoribus magnis*', in P. Cristofolini, ed., *L'Hérésie spinoziste: la discussion sur le Tractatus Theologico-Politicus, 1670–1677, et la réception immédiate du spinozisme* (Amsterdam, 1995).

—— and P.-F. Moreau, 'La Lecture de la Bible dans le cercle de Spinoza', in J.-R. Armogathe, ed., *Le Grand Siècle et la Bible* (Paris, 1989), pp. 97–115.

Land, J. P. N., 'Over de uitgaven en den text der Ethica van Spinoza', *Verslagen en mededeelingen der Koninklijke Akademie van Wetenschapen, afdeeling letterkunde*, 2nd ser., 11 (1882), pp. 4–24.

# BIBLIOGRAPHY

Lange, K.-P., *Theoretiker des literarischen Manierismus: Tesauros und Pellegrinis Lehre von der 'Acutezza' oder von der Macht der Sprache* (Munich, 1968).

Lankhorst, O. S., *Reinier Leers (1654–1714), uitgever & boekverkoper te Rotterdam: een Europees 'Libraire' en zijn fonds* (Amsterdam, 1983).

Lansberg, P., *Tabulae motuum coelestium perpetuae* (Leiden, 1632).

—— *Ephemerides: The Celestiall Motions, for the yeeres . . . 1633. 1634. 1635. 1636* (London, 1635).

La Peyrère, I., *Du Rappel des Juifs* (Paris, 1643).

—— *Prae-adamitae, sive exercitatio super versibus . . . capitis quinti Epistolae D. Pauli ad Romanos*, with *Systema theologicum ex praeadamitarum hypothesi pars prima* (n.p., 1655).

à Lapide, C., *In Pentateuchum Mosis commentaria* (Paris, 1630).

—— *Commentarius in Esdram, Nehemiam, Tobiam, Judith, Esther, et Machabaeos* (Antwerp, 1734).

Laplanche, F., *L'Écriture, le sacré et l'histoire: érudits et politiques protestants devant la Bible en France au XVII<sup>e</sup> siècle* (Amsterdam, 1986).

Lart, C. E., ed., *The Registers of the Protestant Church at Caen (Normandy)* (Vannes, 1907).

—— 'French Noblesse and Arms', *Proceedings of the Huguenot Society of London*, 15 (1933–7), pp. 476–88.

Lavin, M. A., *Seventeenth-Century Barberini Documents and Inventories of Art* (New York, 1975).

Lawler, J., *Book Auctions in England in the Seventeenth Century (1676–1700)* (London, 1898).

Lazarus-Yafeh, H., *Intertwined Worlds: Medieval Islam and Bible Criticism* (Princeton, NJ, 1992).

Lebram, J. C. H., 'Ein Streit um die hebräische Bibel und die Septuaginta', in T. H. Lunsingh Scheurleer and G. H. M. Posthumus Meyjes, eds., *Leiden University in the Seventeenth Century: An Exchange of Learning* (Leiden, 1975), pp. 21–63.

Le Clerc, J., *Sentimens de quelques théologiens de Hollande sur l'Histoire Critique du Vieux Testament* (Amsterdam, 1685).

—— *Parrhasiana, ou pensées diverses sur des matières de critique, d'histoire, de morale et de politique*, 2nd edn (Amsterdam, 1701).

Ledeboer, A. M., *De boekdrukkers, boekverkoopers en uitgevers in Noord-Nederland* (Deventer, 1872).

—— *Alfabetische lijst der boekdrukkers, boekverkoopers en uitgevers in Noordnederland* (Utrecht, 1876).

Lee, M., ed., *Dudley Carleton to John Chamberlain, 1603–1624* (New Brunswick, NJ, 1972).

Leeman, F., *Anamorphosen: ein Spiel mit der Wahrnehmung, dem Schein und der Wirklichkeit* (Cologne, 1975).

Lefèvre, N., *A Compendious Body of Chymistry* [tr. P. de Cardonnel?] (London, 1664).

Lefranc, A., *Histoire du Collège de France depuis ses origines jusqu'à la fin du premier empire* (Paris, 1893).

Lefroy, J. H., ed., *The Historye of the Bermudaes or Summer Islands* (London, 1882).
Le Gallois, P., *Conversations de l'académie de Monsieur l'abbé Bourdelot* (Paris, 1672).
Le Gendre, P., *La Vie de Pierre du Bosc* (Rotterdam, 1694).
Leibniz, G. W., *Otium hanoveranum, sive miscellanea, ex ore & schedis illustris viri, piae memoriae, Godefr. Guilielmi Leibnitii*, ed. J. F. Feller (Leipzig, 1718).
—— *Opera philosophica quae exstant latina, gallica, germanica, omnia*, ed. J. E. Erdmann (Berlin, 1840).
—— *Sämtliche Schriften und Briefe* (Darmstadt, 1925–).
—— *The Political Writings*, ed. and tr. P. Riley (Cambridge, 1972).
Leijenhorst, C., 'Hobbes and Fracastoro', *Hobbes Studies*, 9 (1996), pp. 98–128.
—— 'Motion, Monks and Golden Mountains: Campanella and Hobbes on Perception and Cognition', *Bruniana & Campanelliana*, 3 (1997), pp. 93–121.
—— *Hobbes and the Aristotelians: The Aristotelian Setting of Thomas Hobbes's Natural Philosophy* (Utrecht, 1998).
Le Maire, C., *Paris ancien et nouveau*, 3 vols. (Paris, 1685).
Lennon, T. M., *The Battle of the Gods and the Giants: The Legacies of Descartes and Gassendi, 1655–1715* (Princeton, NJ, 1993).
Lenoble, R., *Mersenne ou la naissance du mécanisme* (Paris, 1943).
—— 'A propos du tricentenaire de la mort de Mersenne', *Archives internationales d'histoire des sciences*, no. 7 (April 1949), pp. 583–97.
—— 'Histoire et physique: à propos des conseils de Mersenne aux historiens et de l'intervention de Jean de Launoy dans la querelle gassendiste', *Revue d'histoire des sciences et de leurs applications*, 6 (1953), pp. 112–34.
—— 'Roberval "éditeur" de Mersenne et du P. Niceron', *Revue d'histoire des sciences et de leurs applications*, 10 (1957), pp. 235–54.
Lepreux, G., *Gallia typographica, ou répertoire biographique et chronologique de tous les imprimeurs de France*, Série départementale, 4 vols. (Paris, 1909–13).
L'Escalopier, N., *Relation de ce qui s'est passé à l'arrivée de la Reine Christine de Suède, a Essaune en la Maison de Monsieur Hesselin* (Paris, 1656).
Levie, S. H., and F. Mathey, eds., *Anamorfosen: spel met perspectief* (Cologne, 1975).
Levy, D., *Voltaire et son exégèse du Pentateuque: critique et polémique* (Banbury, 1975).
Lewis, J. M., 'Hobbes and the Blackloists: A Study in the Eschatology of the English Revolution', Harvard University Ph.D. dissertation, 1976.
Liceti, F., *De quaesitis per epistolas a claris viris responsa*, 7 vols. (Bologna and Udine, 1640–50).
Lindberg, D. C., *Theories of Vision from Al-Kindi to Kepler* (Chicago, 1976).
van der Linde, A., *Benedictus Spinoza: bibliografie* (The Hague, 1871; reprinted Nieukoop, 1961).
Link, C., *Herrschaftsordnung und bürgerliche Freiheit: Grenzen der Staatsgewalt in der älteren deutschen Staatslehre* (Vienna, 1979).
*La Liturgie, c'est a dire, le formulaire des prieres publiques . . . selon l'usage de l'Eglise Anglicane*, tr. J. Durel (Geneva, 1665).
Lomonaco, F., *Lex regia: diritto, filologia e fides historica nella cultura politico-filosofica dell'Olanda di fine seicento* (Naples, 1990).

Long, W. H., ed., *The Oglander Memoirs* (London, 1888).
Löscher, V. E., *Praenotationes theologicae contra naturalistarum et fanaticorum omne penus atheos, deistas, indifferentistas, antiscripturarios &c.* (Wittenberg, 1708).
Lovelace, R., *Lucasta*, ed. W. C. Hazlitt (London, 1864).
—— *Poems*, ed. C. H. Wilkinson, 2nd edn (Oxford, 1930).
Lucä, F., ed., *Der Chronist Friedrich Lucä: ein Zeit- und Sittenbild aus der zweiten Hälfte des siebenzehnten Jahrhunderts* (Frankfurt, 1854).
Luce, Sir Richard, 'An Old Malmesbury Minute Book', *Wiltshire Archaeological and Natural History Magazine*, 47 (1935–7), pp. 321–6.
Lucchi, B., *Oratio pro studiis primae philosophiae* (Padua, 1737).
'Lucius Antistius Constans' [P. de la Court?], *De jure ecclesiasticorum* ('Alethopolis' [Amsterdam?], 1665).
Lugli, A., *Naturalia et mirabilia: il collezionismo enciclopedico nelle Wunderkammern d'Europa* (Milan, 1983).
Luneschlos, J., *Thesaurus mathematum reseratus per algebram novam tam speciebus quam numeris declaratam et demonstratam* (Padua, 1646).
—— ['à Leuneschlos'], *Tractatus de corpore* (Heidelberg, 1659).
de Lyra, N., *Bibliarum sacrarum cum glossa ordinaria, primum quidem a Strabo Fuldensi collecta*, 6 vols. (Lyon, Paris, 1589–90).
'M., G. V.' [Gerard van der Meulen?], *Dissertationes de origine juris naturalis & societatis civilis* (Utrecht, 1684).
McCusker, J. J., *Money and Exchange in Europe and America, 1600–1775* (Chapel Hill, NC, 1978).
Macdonald, H., and M. Hargreaves, *Thomas Hobbes: A Bibliography* (London, 1952).
McKee, D. R., *Simon Tyssot de Patot and the Seventeenth-Century Background of Critical Deism*, Johns Hopkins Studies in Romance Literatures and Languages, 40, (Baltimore, Md, 1941).
—— 'Isaac de la Peyrère, a Precursor of Eighteenth-Century Critical Deists', *Publications of the Modern Language Association of America*, 59 (1944), pp. 456–65.
McKenzie, D. F., 'Printers of the Mind: Some Notes on Bibliographical Theories and Printing-House Practices', *Studies in Bibliography*, 22 (1969), pp. 1–75.
—— 'Masters, Wardens and Liverymen of the Stationers' Company, 1605–1800', typescript (1974).
McKitterick, D., *Cambridge University Library: A History. The Eighteenth and Nineteenth Centuries* (Cambridge, 1986).
—— *A History of the Cambridge University Press*, 3 vols. (Cambridge, 1992–).
Macleane, D., *History of Pembroke College, Oxford* (Oxford, 1897).
McLeod, M. S. G., et al., *The Cathedral Libraries Catalogue: Books Printed before 1701 in the Libraries of the Anglican Cathedrals of England and Wales*, 3 vols. (London, 1984–98).
McManaway, 'The "Lost" Canto of *Gondibert*', *Modern Language Quarterly*, 1 (1940), pp. 63–78.
McNeilly, F. S., *The Anatomy of Leviathan* (London, 1968).
Machiavelli, N., *Opere letterarie*, ed. A. Borlenghi (Naples, 1969).

Machon, L., 'Apologie pour Machiavelle', in N. Machiavelli, *Oeuvres complètes*, ed. J. A. C. Buchon, 2 vols. (Paris, 1837), I, pp. xxiii–lxiv.

—— 'Discours pour servir de regle ou d'avis aux bibliothecaires', ed. Daspit de Saint-Amand, *Tablettes des bibliophiles de Guienne*, 9 (1882), pp. 41–113.

Madan, F., 'Milton, Salmasius, and Dugard', *The Library*, 4th ser., 4 (1923–4), pp. 119–45.

—— ed., 'Robert Burton and the *Anatomy of Melancholy*', *Proceedings and Papers of the Oxford Bibliographical Society*, 1 (1927), pp. 159–246.

al-Maghribi, *see* Samau'al al-Maghribi.

Mahoney, M., 'Niceron', in *The Dictionary of Scientific Biography*, 18 vols. (New York, 1970–90), X, pp. 103–04.

Maier, W., 'Aben-Ezra's Meinung über den Verfasser des Pentateuchs', *Theologische Studien und Kritiken*, 5 (1832), pp. 634–44.

Maignan, E., *Perspectiva horaria sive de horographia gnomonica* (Rome, 1648).

—— *Philosophia sacra*, 2 vols. (Toulouse and Lyon, 1661–72).

Maimonides, M., *The Guide for the Perplexed*, ed. and tr. M. Friedlander (London, 1904).

—— *Ethical Writings*, ed. and tr. R. L. Weiss and C. Butterworth (New York, 1975).

Malcolm, N., *De Dominis (1560–1624): Venetian, Anglican, Ecumenist and Relapsed Heretic* (London, 1984).

—— 'Citizen Hobbes' (review of Hobbes, *De cive: The English Version* and *De cive: The Latin Version*, ed. J. H. Warrender (Oxford, 1983)), in *London Review of Books*, 6, no. 19 (18 October 1984), p. 22.

—— 'Hobbes, the Latin Optical Manuscript, and the Parisian Scribe', *English Manuscript Studies*, ed. P. Beal and J. Griffith, 13 (2003) (forthcoming).

Malebranche, N., *Oeuvres*, ed. G. Rodis-Lewis, 2 vols. (Paris, 1979–92).

Malnes, R., *The Hobbesian Theory of International Conflict* (Oslo, 1993).

de Malthe, F., *Traité des feux artificiels pour la guerre, et pour la recreation* (Paris, 1632).

Mancosu, P., 'Aristotelian Logic and Euclidean Mathematics: Seventeenth-Century Developments of the *Quaestio de certitudine mathematicarum*', *Studies in the History and Philosophy of Science*, 23 (1992), pp. 241–64.

—— *Philosophy of Mathematics and Mathematical Practice in the Seventeenth Century* (New York, 1996).

Mannarino, L., 'Pietro Giannone e la letteratura "empia" ', *Annali dell'istituto di filosofia dell'Università di Firenze, facoltà di lettere e filosofia*, 2 (1980), pp. 195–241.

de Marolles, M., *Les Memoires de Michel de Marolles, Abbé de Villeloin* (Paris, 1656).

Marquard, E., ed., *Kongelige kammerregnskaber fra Frederik III.s of Christian V.s tid* (Copenhagen, 1918).

Martin, F., *Athenae Normannorum*, ed. V. Bourrienne and T. Genty, 2 vols. (Caen, 1904–05).

Martin, G. H., and J. R. L. Highfield, *A History of Merton College* (Oxford, 1997).

Masius, A., *Iosuae imperatoris historia illustrata atque explicata* (Antwerp, 1574).

Mauritius, E., *Dissertationes et opuscula*, ed. J. N. Hertius (Strasbourg, 1724).

Maurolycus, F., *Photismi de lumine, & umbra* (Naples, 1611).

## BIBLIOGRAPHY

Maycock, A. L., *Nicholas Ferrar of Little Gidding* (London, 1938).
Mayer, J. F., ed., *Dissertationes selectae kilonienses & hamburgenses* (Frankfurt am Main, 1693).
Mazzeo, J. A., *Renaissance and Seventeenth-Century Studies* (New York, 1964).
Medick, L., *Naturzustand und Naturgeschichte der bürgerlichen Gesellschaft* (Göttingen, 1973).
Meinecke, F., *Die Idee der Staatsräson in der neueren Geschichte*, 3rd edn (Munich, 1929).
Meinsma, K. O., *Spinoza en zijn kring, over Hollandse vrijgeesten* (The Hague, 1896).
Melchior, J. ['J.M.V.D.M.'], *Epistola ad amicum, continens censuram libri, cui titulus: Tractatus theologico-politicus* (Utrecht, 1671).
Ménestrier, C. F., *L'Art des emblèmes* (Lyon, 1662).
—— *La Philosophie des images énigmatiques* (Lyon, 1682).
Mennung, A., *Jean-François Sarasin's Leben und Werke, seine Zeit und Gesellschaft*, 2 vols. (Halle, 1902–4).
Merlat, É., *Traité du pouvoir absolu des souverains: pour servir d'instruction, de consolation & d'apologie aux Églises Réformées de France qui sont affligées* (Cologne, 1685).
Mersenne, M., *Quaestiones celeberrimae in Genesim* (Paris, 1623).
—— *La Verité des sciences: contre les septiques ou Pyrrhoniens* (Paris, 1625).
—— *Questions inouyes, ou recreation des scavans* (Paris, 1634).
—— *Harmonicorum libri* (Paris, 1635; later issues 1636, 1641, 1648).
—— *Harmonie universelle* (Paris, 1636).
—— *Cogitata physico-mathematica* (Paris, 1644).
—— *Universae geometriae synopsis* (Paris, 1644).
—— *Novarum observationum . . . tomus III* (Paris, 1647).
—— *L'Optique et la catoptrique*, in *La Perspective curieuse du R. P. Niceron . . . avec l'Optique et la Catoptrique du R. P. Mersenne*, ed. G. P. de Roberval (Paris, 1652).
—— *Correspondance*, ed. C. de Waard *et al.*, 17 vols. (Paris, 1933–88).
—— *Harmonie universelle*, ed. F. Lesure, 3 vols. (Paris, 1963).
Meslier, J., *Oeuvres complètes*, ed. J. Deprun, R. Desné, and A. Soboul, 3 vols. (Paris, 1970).
Messeri, M., *Causa e spiegazione: la fisica di Pierre Gassendi* (Milan, 1985).
Metcalfe, W. C., ed., *The Visitations of Hertfordshire*, Harleian Society Publications, 22 (London, 1886).
Metzger, H., *Les Doctrines chimiques en France du début du XVII$^e$ à la fin du XVIII$^e$ siècle* (Paris, 1969).
Meyer, L., *Philosophia S. Scripturae interpres* ('Eleutheropolis' [Amsterdam], 1666).
Meyer, W., 'De veris et fictis Tractatus theologico-politici editoribus', *Chronicon Spinozanum*, 1 (1921), pp. 264–7.
Michaelis, C. B., ed., *Catalogus bibliothecae gundlingianae*, 2 vols. (Halle, 1731).
Middleton, W. E. K., *The History of the Barometer* (Baltimore, 1964).
Migne, J.-P., ed., *Patrologia latina*, 221 vols. (Paris, 1844–55).
—— ed., *Patrologia graeca*, 161 vols. (Paris, 1857–66).
Mill, J. S., *System of Logic* (London, 1893).

Miller, P., 'The Religious Impulse in the Founding of Virginia: Religion and Society in the Early Literature', *William and Mary Quarterly*, 3rd ser., 5 (1948), pp. 492–522.

Milton, P., 'Did Hobbes Translate *De cive*?' *History of Political Thought*, 11 (1990), pp. 627–38.

—— 'Hobbes, Heresy and Lord Arlington', *History of Political Thought*, 14 (1993), pp. 501–46.

Milward, J., *Diary*, ed. C. Robbins (Cambridge, 1938).

Milward, P., *Religious Controversies of the Jacobean Age: A Survey of Printed Sources* (London, 1978).

Minerbi Belgrado, A., *Paura e ignoranza: studio sulla teoria della religione in d'Holbach* (Florence, 1983).

—— *Linguaggio e mondo in Hobbes* (Rome, 1993).

Mintz, S., *The Hunting of Leviathan: Seventeenth-Century Reactions to the Materialism and Moral Philosophy of Thomas Hobbes* (Cambridge, 1962).

—— 'Hobbes on the Law of Heresy: A New Manuscript', *Journal of the History of Ideas*, 29 (1968), pp. 409–14.

Mochi Onori, L., and R. Vodret Adamo, *La Galleria Nazionale d'Arte Antica: regesto delle didascalie* (Rome, 1989).

Moens, W. J. C., ed., *The Registers of the French Church, Threadneedle Street, London*, Publications of the Huguenot Society of London, 20 (Lymington, 1896).

van Moerkerken, P. H., *Adriaan Koerbagh, 1633–1669: een strijder voor het vrije denken* (Amsterdam, 1948).

Molhuysen, P. C., ed., *Bronnen tot de geschiedenis der Leidsche Universiteit*, 7 vols. (The Hague, 1913–24).

du Molinet, C., *Le Cabinet de la bibliothèque de Sainte Genevieve* (Paris, 1692).

Moller, J., *Cimbria literata, sive scriptorum ducatus utriusque Slesvicensis et Holsatici . . . historia*, 3 vols. (Copenhagen, 1744).

Møller Pedersen, K., 'Roberval's Comparison of the Arclength of a Spiral and a Parabola', *Centaurus*, 15 (1970), pp. 26–43.

Mondolfo, R., *Il 'verum-factum' prima di Vico* (Naples, 1969).

Moniglia, T. V., *Dissertazione contra i materialisti, e altri increduli*, 2 vols. (Padua, 1750).

Montagu, J., 'The Painted Enigma and French Seventeenth-Century Art', *Journal of the Warburg and Courtauld Institutes*, 31 (1968), pp. 307–35.

Moore, G. F., *Judaism in the First Centuries of the Christian Era: The Age of the Tannaim*, 3 vols. (Cambridge, 1927–30).

Moranus, G., *Animadversiones in elementorum philosophiae sectionem I. De corpore, editam a Thoma Hobbes Anglo Malmesburiensi Londini 1655* (Brussels, 1655).

Morgenthau, H. J., *American Foreign Policy: A Critical Examination* (London, 1952).

—— *Politics among Nations: The Struggle for Power and Peace*, 2nd edn (New York, 1955).

Mori, G., *Fra Descartes e Bayle: Poiret e la teodicea* (Bologna, 1990).

—— 'L'ateismo "malebranchiano" di Meslier: fisica e metafisica della materia', in G. Canziani, ed., *Filosofia e religione nella letteratura clandestina: secoli XVII e XVIII* (Milan, 1994), pp. 123–60.

Morin, J., *Exercitationes biblicae* (Paris, 1633).

—— *Exercitationes ecclesiasticae* (Paris, 1635).
—— *Diatribe... contra... de Muys* (Paris, 1639).
Morize, A., 'Th. Hobbes et Samuel Sorbière: notes sur l'introduction de Hobbes en France', *Revue germanique*, 4 (1908), pp. 195–204.
du Moulin, P., *A Vindication of the Sincerity of the Protestant Religion* (London, 1664).
Mousnier, R., ed., *Lettres et mémoires adressés au Chancelier Séguier (1633–1649)* 2 vols. (Paris, 1964).
Moutová, N., and J. Polišenský, *Komenský v Amsterodamu* (Prague, 1970).
Mouy, P., *Le Développement de la physique cartésienne, 1646–1712* (Paris, 1934).
Mühlpfort, J. J., *Exercitatio politica de latrocinio gentis in gentem* (Leipzig, 1672).
Mulder, M. J., 'The Transmission of the Biblical Text', in M. J. Mulder and H. Sysling, eds., *Mikra: Text, Translation, Reading and Interpretation of the Bible in Ancient Judaism and Early Christianity* (Assen, 1988), pp. 87–135.
Müller ['Mullern'], A., *Des verwirrten Europae Continuation* (Amsterdam, 1680).
Müller, J. J., *De imposturis religionum (De tribus impostoribus); Von den Betrügereyen der Religionen*, ed. W. Schröder (Stuttgart, 1999).
Müller, K., *Die Geschichte der Zensur im alten Bern* (Bern, 1904).
M[unby], A. N. L., 'A Catalogue of First and Early Editions of the Works of Thomas Hobbes, Forming Part of the Library Bequeathed by John Maynard, Baron Keynes of Tilton to King's College, Cambridge', typescript (Cambridge, 1949).
Munk, W., et al., *The Roll of the Royal College of Physicians of London* (London, 1861–).
Murr, S., ed., *Bernier et les Gassendistes*, 'Corpus', no. 20/1 (Paris, 1992).
—— ed., *Gassendi et l'Europe, 1592–1792* (Paris, 1997).
de Muys, S., *Assertatio hebraicae veritatis* (1631).
—— *Censura* (1634).
—— *Castigatio Morini* (1639).
Mydorge, C., *Examen du livre des recreations mathematiques* (Paris, 1630).
Myers, J. M., ed., *The Anchor Bible: I and II Esdras* (New York, 1974).
Mysłakowsi, Z., 'O. Waleryan Magni i kontrowersya w sprawie odkrycia prózni (1638–48)', *Rozprawy wydziału matematyczno-przyrodniczego akademii umiejętności*, ser. 3, vol. II, section A (1911), pp. 325–77.
Naudé, G., *The History of Magick, by way of Apology for all the Wise Men who have Unjustly been Reputed Magicians*, tr. J. Davies (London, 1657).
—— see also Wolfe, P.
Navari, C., 'Hobbes and the "Hobbesian Tradition" in International Thought', *Millennium: Journal of International Studies*, 11 (1982), pp. 203–22.
Naville, P., *D'Holbach et la philosophie scientifique au XVIII<sup>e</sup> siècle*, 2nd edn (Paris, 1967).
Neill, E. D., *History of the Virginia Company of London* (Albany, NY, 1869).
—— *The English Colonization of America during the Seventeenth Century* (London, 1871).
Nellen, H. J. M., *Ismaël Boulliau (1605–1694): astronome, épistolier, nouvelliste et intermédiaire scientifique* (Amsterdam, 1994).
Nemoy, L., 'Al-Qirqisani's Account of the Jewish Sects and Christianity', *Hebrew Union College Annual*, 7 (1930), pp. 317–97.
Neumann, J., *Obrazárna pražského hradu* (Prague, 1964).

*Das Newe Testament*, with *Cathechismus, oder kurze Unterricht* (Amsterdam, 1669).
Newton, I., *Mathematical Papers*, ed. D. Whiteside, M. A. Hoskin, and D. Prag, 8 vols. (Cambridge, 1967–81).
Niceron, J.-F., *La Perspective curieuse* (Paris, 1638).
—— ['F.I.F.N.P.M.',] *L'Interpretation des chiffres, ou reigle pour bien entendre & expliquer facilement toutes sortes de chiffres simples, tirée de l'italien du Sr Ant. Maria Cospi* (Paris, 1641).
—— *Thaumaturgus opticus* (Paris, 1646).
—— *La Perspective curieuse du R. P. Niceron . . . avec L'Optique et la catoptrique du R. P. Mersenne*, ed. G. P. de Roberval (Paris, 1652).
Niceron, J.-P., *Mémoires pour servir à l'histoire des hommes illustres dans la République des lettres*, 44 vols. (Paris, 1727–45).
Nickson, M. A. E., 'Books and Manuscripts', in A. MacGregor, ed., *Sir Hans Sloane: Collector, Scientist, Antiquary, Founding Father of the British Museum* (London, 1994), pp. 263–77.
Nicole, P., *Essais de morale, contenus en divers traittez sur plusieurs devoirs importans*, 4 vols. (Paris, 1672–8).
Nicolini, F., 'Di alcuni rapporti ideali tra il Vico e il Hobbes con qualche riferimento al Machiavelli', *English Miscellany: A Symposium of History, Literature, and the Arts*, 1 (1950), pp. 43–70.
Niderst, A., ed., *L'Âme matérielle (ouvrage anonyme)* (Paris, 1973).
Nieuhof ['Neuhof'], J., *Die Gesandtschaft der Ost-Indischen Gesellschaft in den Vereinigten Niederländern an den tartarischen Cham* (Amsterdam, 1669).
—— *Zee en Lant-reize, door verscheide gewesten van Oostindien* (Amsterdam, 1682).
*Nieuw nederlandsch biografisch woordenboek*, 10 vols. (Leiden, 1911–37).
Nightingale, J. E., *The Church Plate of the County of Wiltshire* (Salisbury, 1891).
Noël, E., *Le Plein du vuide* (Paris, 1648), in B. Pascal, *Oeuvres*, ed. C. Bossut, 5 vols. ('The Hague' [Paris], 1779), pp. 108–46.
Noel, N., *Bibliotheca nobilissimi principis Johannis Ducis de Novo-Castro* (London, 1719).
Notestein, W., Relf, F. H., and H. Simpson, *Commons Debates in 1621*, 7 vols. (New Haven, Conn., 1935).
Nussbaum, A., *A Concise History of the Law of Nations*, rev. edn (New York, 1954).
Ogle, O., *et al.*, eds., *Calendar of the Clarendon State Papers preserved in the Bodleian Library*, 5 vols. (Oxford, 1872–1970).
Oldenburg, H., *Correspondence*, ed. A. R. Hall and M. B. Hall, 13 vols. (Madison, Wis., and London, 1965–86).
Olearius, A., *The Voyages and Travells of the Ambassadors sent by Frederick Duke of Holstein, to the Great Duke of Muscovy, and the King of Persia*, tr. J. Davies, 2nd edn, 2 vols. (London, 1669).
Ollard, R., *Clarendon and his Friends* (London, 1987).
Oman, C. C., and J. Hamilton, *Wallpapers: A History and Catalogue of the Collection of the Victoria and Albert Museum* (London, 1982).
Orfali, M., 'Abraham Ibn Ezra, crítico de los exégetas de la Biblia', in F. Díaz Esteban, ed., *Abraham Ibn Ezra y su tiempo: actas del simposio internacional Madrid, Tudela, Toledo 1–8 febrero 1989* (Madrid, 1990), pp. 225–32.

Orr, R., *Reason and Authority: The Thought of William Chillingworth* (Oxford, 1967).
Osborn, J. M., *John Dryden: Some Biographical Facts and Problems* (New York, 1940).
Osgood, H. L., *The American Colonies in the Seventeenth Century*, 3 vols. (New York, 1904–7).
Osier, J. P., 'L'Herméneutique de Hobbes et de Spinoza', *Studia Spinozana*, 3 (1987), pp. 319–47.
Oughtred, W., *Arithmeticae . . . institutio . . . quasi clavis* (London, 1631).
Overend, G. H., 'Notes upon the Earlier History of the Manufacture of Paper in England', *Proceedings of the Huguenot Society of London*, 8, for 1905–8 (1909), pp. 177–220.
Owen, J., *Of the Divine Originall, Authority, Self-evidencing Light, and Power of the Scriptures* (Oxford, '1659' [1658]).
Pacchi, A., *Convenzione e ipotesi nella formazione della filosofia naturale di Thomas Hobbes* (Florence, 1965).
—— 'Ruggero Bacone e Roberto Grossatesta in un inedito hobbesiano del 1634', *Rivista critica di storia della filosofia*, 20 (1965), pp. 499–502.
—— 'Una "biblioteca ideale" di Thomas Hobbes: il MS E2 dell'archivio di Chatsworth', *Acme: annali della facoltà di lettere e filosofia dell'università degli studi di Milano*, 21 (1968), pp. 5–42.
—— *Cartesio in Inghilterra da More a Boyle* (Rome, 1973).
—— 'Hobbes e l'epicureismo', *Rivista critica di storia della filosofia*, 33 (1978), pp. 54–71.
—— *Scritti hobbesiani (1978–1990)*, ed. A. Lupoli (Milan, 1998).
*The Palatine Note-Book: For the Intercommunication of . . . Investigators into the History and Literature of the Counties of Lancaster, Cheshire, etc.*, 5 vols. (Manchester, 1881–5).
Palladini, F., *Discussioni seicentesche su Samuel Pufendorf: scritti latini, 1663–1700* (n.p. [Bologna], 1978).
—— 'Le due lettere di Pufendorf al Barone di Boineburg: quella nota e quella "perduta"', *Nouvelles de la République des Lettres*, 1 (1984), pp. 119–44.
—— *Samuel Pufendorf discepolo di Hobbes: per una reinterpretazione del giusnaturalismo moderno* (Bologna, 1990).
—— ed., *La biblioteca di Samuel Pufendorf: catalogo dell'asta di Berlin del settembre 1697* (Wiesbaden, 1999)
Palmer, R. R., *Catholics and Unbelievers in Eighteenth-Century France* (Princeton, NJ, 1939).
Pangle, T. L., 'A Critique of Hobbes's Critique of Biblical and Natural Religion in *Leviathan*', *Jewish Political Studies Review*, 4: 2 (1992), pp. 25–57.
Pareus, D., *In Genesin Mosis commentarius* (Frankfurt, 1615).
Parker, S., *Disputationes de Deo et providentia divina* (London, 1678).
Parks, S., 'Charles Cotton and the Derby Manuscript', in S. Parks and P. J. Croft, *Literary Autographs* (Los Angeles, 1983).
*Parnassus Heidelbergensis omnium illustrissimae huius academiae professorum icones exhibens* (Heidelberg, 1660).
Parry, G., 'A Troubled Arcadia', in T. Healy and J. Sawday, eds., *Literature and the English Civil War* (Cambridge, 1990), pp. 38–55.

Pasch, G., *De novis inventis, quorum accuratiori cultui facem praetulit antiquitas, tractatus* (Leipzig, 1700).
Patterson, W. B., *King James VI and I and the Reunion of Christendom* (Cambridge, 1997).
Pattison, M., *Essays*, ed. H. Nettleship, 2 vols. (Oxford, 1889).
Paul, Sir James B., *The Scots Peerage*, 9 vols. (Edinburgh, 1904–14).
Pearman, A. J., 'The Kentish Family of Lovelace', *Archaeologia cantiana*, 10 (1876), pp. 184–220.
Pecham, J., *Perspectiva communis*, ed. G. Hartmann (Nuremberg, 1542).
Peck, L. L., 'Hobbes on the Grand Tour: Paris, Venice or London?', *Journal of the History of Ideas*, 57 (1996), pp. 177–82.
Peckard, P., *Memoirs of the Life of Mr Nicholas Ferrar* (Cambridge, 1790).
Pell, J., *Controversiae de vera circuli mensura . . . pars prima* (Amsterdam, 1647).
Pennington, R., *A Descriptive Catalogue of the Etched Work of Wenceslaus Hollar, 1607–1677* (Cambridge, 1982).
Pepys, S., *Diary*, ed. R. Latham and W, Matthews, 11 vols. (London, 1970–83).
Pererius, B., *Commentariorum et disputationum in Genesim, tomi quatuor* (Cologne, 1622).
Peter, R., 'Noel Journet, détracteur de l'Ecriture sainte (1582)', in M. Lienhard, ed., *Croyants et sceptiques au XVI<sup>e</sup> siècle: le dossier des 'Épicuriens'* (Strasbourg, 1981).
Petit, L., *La Fontaine et Saint-Evremond, ou la tentation de l'Angleterre* (Toulouse, 1953).
Petry, M. J., 'Behmenism and Spinozism in the Religious Culture of the Netherlands, 1660–1730', in *Spinoza in der Frühzeit seiner religiösen Wirkung*, ed. K. Gründer and W. Schmidt-Biggemann (Heidelberg, 1984).
Philipot, T., *An Historical Discourse of the First Invention of Navigation* (London, 1661).
Pintard, R., *Le Libertinage érudit dans la première moitié du XVII<sup>e</sup> siècle* (Paris, 1943; 2nd edn, Geneva, 1983).
Placcius, V., *Theatrum anonymorum et pseudonymorum* (Hamburg, 1708).
Pliny the Elder, *Natural History*, ed. and tr. H. Rackham, W. H. S. Jones, and D. E. Eichholz, 10 vols. (London, 1967).
Plomer, H. R., *A Dictionary of the Booksellers and Printers who were at work in England, Scotland and Ireland from 1641 to 1667* (London, 1907).
—— *A Dictionary of the Booksellers and Printers who were at work in England, Scotland and Ireland from 1668 to 1725*, ed. A. Esdaile (Oxford, 1922).
Plutarch, *Tractaet Plutarchi van de op-voedinghe der kinderen* (Middelburg, 1619).
Pocock, J. G. A., *Politics, Language and Time* (New York, 1971).
Poiret, P., *Cogitationes rationales de Deo, anima et malo*, 2nd edn (Amsterdam, 1685).
—— *De eruditione editio nova cui accessit Chr. Thomasii dissertatio de scriptis autoris* (Frankfurt and Leipzig, 1694).
Polin, R., *Politique et philosophie chez Thomas Hobbes* (Paris, 1953).
—— *Hobbes, Dieu et les hommes* (Paris, 1981).
Pomian, K., *Collectors and Curiosities: Paris and Venice, 1500–1800*, tr. E. Wiles-Portier (London, 1990).
Pope, W., *The Life of the Right Reverend Father in God Seth, Lord Bishop of Salisbury* (London, 1697).

## BIBLIOGRAPHY

Popkin, R., 'Spinoza and La Peyrère', in R. W. Shahan and J. I. Biro, eds., *Spinoza, New Perspectives* (Norman, Okla., 1978), pp. 177–95.
—— *The History of Scepticism from Erasmus to Spinoza* (Berkeley, Calif., 1979).
—— *Isaac La Peyrère (1596–1676): His Life, Work and Influence* (Leiden, 1987).
—— 'Spinoza and Bible Scholarship', in J. E. Force and R. Popkin, eds., *The Books of Nature and Scripture: Recent Essays on Natural Philosophy, Theology and Biblical Criticism in the Netherlands of Spinoza's Time and the British Isles of Newton's Time* (Dordrecht, 1994), pp. 1–20.
—— and Signer, M. A., *Spinoza's Earliest Publication? The Hebrew Translation of Margaret Fell's* A Loving Salutation to the Seed of Abraham among the Jews (Assen, 1987).
Porphyrius, *De abstinentia ab animalibus necandis libri quatuor*, ed. L. Holstenius (Cambridge, 1655).
Portal, W. W., *Some Account of the Settlement of Refugees (L'Eglise Wallonne) at Southampton, and of the Chapel of St Julian* (Winchester, 1902).
Porter, H. C., *The Inconstant Savage: England and the North American Indian 1500–1660* (London, 1979).
de Prades, J.-M., *Thèse soutenue en Sorbonne le 18 novembre 1751* (Amsterdam, n.d. [1753] ).
—— *Apologie*, 2 vols. (Amsterdam, 1753).
Préposiet, J., *Bibliographie spinoziste* (Paris, 1973).
Prestwich, E., *Hippolitus Translated out of Seneca* (London, 1651).
Prideaux, H., *Letters to John Ellis, 1674–1722*, ed. E. M. Thompson, Camden Society, n.s., 15 (1875).
Pritchard, A., 'The Last Days of Hobbes: The Evidence of the Wood Manuscripts', *Bodleian Library Record*, 10 (1980), pp. 178–87.
Procacci, G., *Studi sulla fortuna del Machiavelli* (Rome, 1965).
Proeleus, I., *Grund-Sätze des Rechts der Natur nebst einer kurzen Historie und Anmerckungen über die Lehren des Hrn. Barons von Puffendorff* (Leipzig, 1709).
Prokhovnik, R., *Rhetoric and Philosophy in Hobbes's Leviathan* (New York, 1991).
Prost, J., *La Philosophie à l'Académie protestante de Saumur* (Paris, 1907).
Prothero, G. W., ed., *Select Statutes and Other Constitutional Documents . . . 1558–1625*, 4th edn (Oxford, 1913).
Proust, J., *Diderot et l'Encyclopédie*, 3rd edn (Paris, 1982).
Prümer, R., ed., 'Tagebuch Adam Samuel Hartmanns über seine Kollektenreise im Jahre 1657–1659', *Zeitschrift der historischen Gesellschaft für die Provinz Posen*, 14 (1899), 67–140, 241–308; 15 (1900), 95–160, 203–46.
Pufendorf, S., *Elementorum jurisprudentiae universalis libri II* (The Hague, 1660).
—— *De iure naturae et gentium* (Berlin, 1672).
—— *Specimen controversiarum circa jus naturale ipsi nuper motarum* (Uppsala, 1678).
—— *De habitu religionis christianae ad vitam civilem* (Bremen, 1687).
—— *The Law of Nature and Nations*, ed. J. Barbeyrac, tr. B. Kennet, 5th edn (London, 1749).
Purchas, S., *Purchas his Pilgrimage, Or Relations of the World and the Religions Observed in Al Ages and Places Discovered, from the Creation unto this present*, 3rd edn (London, 1617).

Purver, M., *The Royal Society: Concept and Creation* (Cambridge, Mass., 1967).

Putnam, G. H., *The Censorship of the Church of Rome and its Influence upon the Production and Distribution of Literature*, 2 vols. (New York, 1906).

Pye, C., 'The Sovereign, the Theater, and the Kingdome of Darknesse: Hobbes and the Spectacle of Power', in S. Greenblatt, ed., *Representing the English Renaissance* (Berkeley, Calif., 1988), pp. 279–301.

Rabb., T. K., 'The Editions of Sir Edwin Sandys' *Relation of the State of Religion*', *Huntington Library Quarterly*, 26 (1963), pp. 323–36.

—— 'Sir Edwin Sandys and the Parliament of 1604', *American Historical Review*, 69 (1964), pp. 646–70.

—— *Jacobean Gentleman: Sir Edwin Sandys, 1561–1629* (Princeton, NJ, 1998).

Rabinowitz, L., 'Abravanel as Exegete', in J. B. Trend and H. Loewe, eds., *Isaac Abravanel: Six Lectures* (Cambridge, 1937), pp. 75–92.

Rachelius, S., *De jure naturae et gentium dissertationes* (Kiel, 1676).

Rahir, É., *Catalogue d'une collection unique de volumes imprimés par les Elzeviers et divers typographes hollandais du XVII$^e$ siècle* (Paris, 1896).

Raleigh, Sir Walter, *Remains of Sir Walter Raleigh* (London, 1669).

Ramsay, G. D., ed., *Two Sixteenth Century Taxation Lists: 1545 and 1576*, Wiltshire Archaeological and Natural History Society, Records Branch, 10 (Salisbury, 1954).

Rango, C. T., *Brevis de origine & progressu syncretismi à mundo condito historia, das ist, historische Beschreibung der Religions-Mengerey von Anfang der Welt* (Stettin, n. d. [1674] ).

Raphael, P., *Le Rôle du Collège Maronite romain dans l'orientalisme aux XVII$^e$ et XVIII$^e$ siècles* (Beirut, 1950).

[Rapin, R.] *Reflexions sur la philosophie ancienne et moderne, et sur l'usage qu'on en doit faire pour la religion* (Paris, 1676).

Raylor, T., 'Newcastle's Ghosts: Robert Payne, Ben Jonson, and the "Cavendish Circle" ', in C. J. Summers and E.-L. Pebworth, eds., *Literary Circles and Cultural Communities in Renaissance England* (Columbia, Mo., 2000), pp. 92–114.

—— 'Hobbes, Payne, and *A Short Tract on First Principles*', *The Historical Journal*, 44 (2001), pp. 29–58.

—— 'The Date and Script of Hobbes's Latin Optical Manuscript', *English Manuscript Studies*, ed. P. Beal and J. Griffith, 13 (2003) (forthcoming).

Raynaud, T., *Opera omnia*, 20 vols. (Lyon and Cracow, 1665–9).

*Realencyklopädie für protestantische Theologie und Kirche*, 3rd edn, 24 vols. (Leipzig, 1896–1913).

Rechenberg, A., Εὕρημα *compendiarium in religione Christianâ novum* (Leipzig, 1674).

—— *De origine et usu scholarum, contra Thomae Hobbesii Leviathanis cap. XLVI ex historia* (Leipzig, 1684).

Regev, S., ' "Ta'amei ha-mitzvot" in R. Avraham Ibn-Ezra's Commentary: Secrets', in F. Díaz Esteban, ed., *Abraham Ibn Ezra y su tiempo: actas del simposio internacional Madrid, Tudela, Toledo 1–8 febrero 1989* (Madrid, 1990), pp. 233–40.

Regis, P.-S., *Système de philosophie*, 3 vols. (Paris, 1690).

Reik, M., *The Golden Lands of Thomas Hobbes* (Detroit, 1977).

Reiserus, A., *De origine, progressu et incremento antitheismi, seu atheismi* (Augsburg, 1669).

# BIBLIOGRAPHY

Reisner ['Risnerus'], F., *Opticae libri quatuor* (Kassel, 1606).
Revah, I. S., *Spinoza et le Dr Juan de Prado* (Paris, 1959).
Reventlow, H., *The Authority of the Bible and the Rise of the Modern World*, tr. J. Bowden (London, 1984).
Ricuperati, G., *L'Esperienza civile e religiosa di Pietro Giannone* (Milan, 1970).
Rietbergen, P. J. A. N., 'A Maronite Mediator between Seventeenth-Century Mediterranean Cultures: Ibrahim al-Hakilani, or Abraham Ecchellense [*sic*] (1605–1664) between Christendom and Islam', *Lias: Sources and Documents relating to the Early Modern History of Ideas*, 16 (1989), pp. 13–41.
Rivet, A., *Opera theologica*, 3 vols. (Rotterdam, 1651–60).
Robertson, G. C., *Hobbes* (London, 1886).
de Roberval, G. P., *Traité de méchanique* (Paris, 1636).
—— *Aristarchi Samii de mundi systemate, partibus, & motibus eiusdem, libellus* (Paris, 1644).
—— *Ouvrages de mathématique* (The Hague, 1731).
—— 'De vacuo narratio', in B. Pascal, *Oeuvres*, ed. L. Brunschvicg and P. Boutroux, 14 vols. (Paris, 1908–23), II, pp. 21–35.
—— *Éléments de géométrie*, ed. V. Jullien (Paris, 1996).
Röd, W., 'Van den Hoves "Politische Waage" und die Modifikation der hobbesschen Staatsphilosophie bei Spinoza', *Journal of the History of Philosophy*, 8 (1970), pp. 29–48.
Rogow, A., *Thomas Hobbes: Radical in the Service of Reaction* (New York, 1986).
Rood, W., *Comenius and the Low Countries* (Amsterdam, 1970).
Rooke, D. W., *Zadok's Heirs: The Role and Development of the High Priesthood in Ancient Israel* (Oxford, 1999).
de la Roque, J., *Voyage de Syrie et du Mont-Liban*, 2 vols. (Paris, 1722).
Roseveare, H., *Markets and Merchants of the Late Seventeenth Century: The Marescoe-David Letters, 1668–1680* (Oxford, 1987).
Ross, A., *Leviathan Drawn out with a Hook: Or, Animadversions upon Mr Hobbs his Leviathan* (London, 1653).
Rossi, M. M., *Alle fonti del deismo e del materialismo moderno* (Florence, 1942).
Rothkrug, L., *Opposition to Louis XIV: The Political and Social Origins of the French Enlightenment* (Princeton, NJ, 1965).
Rothschild, J.-P., 'Autour du Pentateuque samaritain: voyageurs, enthousiastes et savants', in J.-R. Armogathe, ed., *Le Grand Siècle et la Bible* (Paris, 1989), pp. 61–74.
du Roure, J., *La Philosophie divisée en toutes ses parties, établie sur des principes évidents*, 3 vols. (Paris, 1654).
Rowse, A. L., *Shakespeare's Southampton, Patron of Virginia* (London, 1965).
Roy, P., *Louis XIV et le second siège de Vienne* (Paris, 1999).
Royal Commission on Historical Manuscripts, 'Report on the Miscellaneous Deeds, Letters, Treatises, etc. of the Earls and Dukes of Devonshire from the Muniment Room at Hardwick', typescript (1977).
—— 'Report on the MSS and papers of Thomas Hobbes (1588–1679) Philosopher, c.1591–1684, in the Devonshire Collection, Chatsworth, Bakewell, Derbyshire', typescript (1977).

Rüping, H., 'Thomasius und seine Schüler im brandenburgischen Staat', in H. Thieme, ed., *Humanismus und Naturrecht in Berlin-Brandenburg-Preussen* (Berlin, 1979).
Russell, C. F., *A History of King Edward VI School Southampton* (Cambridge, 1940).
Russell Barker, G. F., and A. H. Stenning, eds., *The Record of Old Westminsters*, 2 vols. (London, 1928).
Ryan, A., *The Philosophy of the Social Sciences* (London, 1970).
Rye, W. B., *England as Seen by Foreigners in the Days of Elizabeth & James the First* (London, 1865).
Sabra, A. I., *Theories of Light from Descartes to Newton* (London, 1967).
Sacksteder, W., 'How Much of Hobbes might Spinoza have Read?' *Southwestern Journal of Philosophy*, 11 (1980), pp. 23–39.
—— 'Mutually Acceptable Glory: Rating among Nations in Hobbes', in P. Caws, ed., *The Causes of Quarrel: Essays on Peace, War, and Thomas Hobbes* (Boston, Mass., 1989), pp. 97–113.
Sadrin, P., *Nicolas-Antoine Boulanger (1722–1759), ou avant nous le déluge* (Oxford, 1986).
Saguens, J., *De vita, moribus, et scriptis R. P. Emanuelis Maignani tolosatis ordinis Minimorum* (n.p., 1703).
Salmon, V., 'Joseph Webbe: Some Seventeenth-Century Views on Language-Teaching and the Nature of Meaning', *Bibliothèque d'humanisme et de renaissance: travaux et documents*, 23 (1961), pp. 324–40.
de Saluste du Bartas, G., *La Sepmaine (texte de 1581)*, ed. Y. Bellenger (Paris, 1981).
Samau'al al-Maghribi, 'Ifham al-Yahud: Silencing the Jews', ed. M. Perlmann, *Proceedings of the American Academy for Jewish Research*, 32 (1964), pp. 1–104.
Samuel, E. R., 'Death in the Glass—A New View of Holbein's "Ambassadors"', *The Burlington Magazine*, 105 (1963), pp. 436–41.
Sandius, C. C., *Bibliotheca anti-trinitariorum* ('Freistadt', 1684).
Sandys, Sir Edwin, *A Relation of the State of Religion* (London, 1605)
—— *Europae speculum* (London, 1629).
Sandys, E. S., *History of the Family of Sandys*, 2 parts (Barrow-in-Furness, 1930).
Sarasin, J.-F., *Oeuvres*, ed. P. Festugière, 2 vols. (Paris, 1926).
Sarrau ['Sarravius'], C., *Claudii Sarravii senatoris parisiensis epistolae, opus posthumum* (Orange, 1654).
Saumaise ['Salmasius'], C., *De annis climactericis et antiqua astrologia diatribae* (Leiden, 1648).
Schader, B., *Johann Jakob Redinger (1619–1688), Sprachwissenschaftler und Pädagoge im Gefolge des Comenius* (Zurich, 1985).
Schaller, K., 'Johann Jakob Redinger in seinem Verhältnis zu Johann Amos Comenius', in M. Bircher, W. Sparn, and E. Weyrauch, eds., *Schweizerisch-deutsch Beziehungen im konfessionellen Zeitalter: Beiträge zur Kulturgeschichte 1580–1650* (Wiesbaden, 1984), pp. 139–66.
Scheiner, C., *Oculus, hoc est: fundamentum opticum* (Innsbruck, 1619).
Schepelern, H. D., *Museum Wormianum: dets forudsaetninger og tilblivelse* (Odense, 1971).
de Schickler, F., *Les Églises du refuge en Angleterre*, 3 vols. (Paris, 1892).

Schino, A. L., 'Tre lettere inedite di Gabriel Naudé', *Rivista di storia della filosofia*, 4 (1987), pp. 697–708.
von Schlosser, J., *Die Kunst- und Wunderkammern der Spätrenaissance: ein Beitrag zur Geschichte des Sammelwesens* (Leipzig, 1908).
Schmitt, C. B., 'Philosophy and Science in Sixteenth-Century Universities: Some Preliminary Comments', in E. Murdoch and D. Sylla, eds., *The Cultural Context of Medieval Learning* (Dordrecht, 1975), pp. 485–530.
—— *John Case and Aristotelianism in Renaissance England* (Montreal, 1983).
Schmittlein, R., *L'Aspect politique du différend Bossuet-Fénelon* (Mainz, 1954).
Schnapper, A., *Curieux du grand siècle: collections et collectionneurs dans la France du XVIIe siècle* (Paris, 1994).
Schneider, H.-P., *Justitia universalis: Quellenstudien zur Geschichte des 'christlichen Naturrechts' bei Gottfried Wilhelm Leibniz* (Frankfurt am Main, 1967).
Schneiders, W., ed., *Christian Thomasius, 1655–1728: Interpretationen zu Werk und Wirkung* (Hamburg, 1989).
Schochet, G., *Patriarchalism in Political Thought* (Oxford, 1975).
Schoeps, H. J., *Philosemitismus im Barock* (Tübingen, 1957).
Scholder, K., *Ursprünge und Probleme der Bibelkritik im 17. Jahrhundert: ein Beitrag zur Entstehung der historisch-kritischen Theologie* (Munich, 1966).
Schoneveld, C. W., 'Some Features of the Seventeenth-Century Editions of Hobbes's *De Cive* Printed in Holland and Elsewhere', in *Thomas Hobbes: His View of Man*, ed. J. G. van der Bend (Amsterdam, 1982), pp. 125–42.
—— *Intertraffic of the Mind: Studies in Seventeenth-Century Anglo–Dutch Translation with a Checklist of Books Translated from English into Dutch, 1600–1700* (Leiden, 1983).
Schoock, M., *Diatriba de jure naturali* (Groningen, 1659).
Schott, G., *Magia universalis naturae et artis*, 4 vols. (Würzburg, 1657–9).
Schreiner, M., 'Zur Geschichte der Polemik zwischen Juden und Muhammedanern', *Zeitschrift der deutschen morgenländischen Gesellschaft*, 42 (1888), pp. 628–30.
Schröder, W., ed., *Traktat über die drei Betrüger* (Hamburg, 1992).
von Schröder ['Schroeter'], W., *Magni monarchae Caroli secundi . . . institutio felix* (Leiden, 1661).
—— ['Schröter'], *Dissertatio academica, cuius prima pars de ratione status, altera de nobilitate, tertia de ministrissimo* (Jena, 1663).
—— ['Schröter'], *Dissertatio de ministrissimo* (n.p., 1671).
—— ['von Schrödern'], *Fürstliche Schatz- und Rent-Kammer* (Leipzig, 1744).
Schuhmann, K., 'Hobbes dans les publications de Mersenne en 1644', *Archives de philosophie*, 58 (1995), no. 2, 'Bulletin hobbesien' (separate pagination), pp. 2–7.
—— 'Le *Short Tract*: première oeuvre philosophique de Hobbes', *Hobbes Studies*, 8 (1995), pp. 3–36.
Schüling, H., *Die Geschichte der axiomatischen Methode im 16. und beginnenden 17. Jahrhundert* (Hildesheim, 1969).
Schurzfleisch, C. S., *Epistolae nunc primum editae* (Wittenberg, 1700).
—— ['Schurtzfleisch',] *Freimuthige singularia von haupt-gelehrten Männern und auserlesenen alten und neuen Schriften* (Leipzig, 1711).

Schüssler, H., *Georg Calixt: Theologie und Kirchenpolitik* (Mainz, 1961).
Schyrlaeus de Rheita, A. M., *Oculus Enoch et Eliae* (Antwerp, 1645).
Scott, W. R., *The Constitution and Finance of English, Scottish and Irish Joint-Stock Companies to 1720*, 2 vols. (Cambridge, 1910–12).
Scouloudi, I., *Returns of Strangers in the Metropolis, 1593, 1627, 1635, 1639: A Study of an Active Minority*, Publications of the Huguenot Society of London, Quarto series, 57 (London, 1985).
von Seckendorff, V. L., *Christen-Staat* (Leipzig, 1693).
'Select Documents XXXIX: A List of the Department of the Lord Chamberlain of the Household, Autumn, 1663', *Bulletin of the Institute for Historical Research*, 19 (1942–3), pp. 13–24.
de Sepi ['de Sepibus'], G., *Romani Collegii Societatis Jesu musaeum celeberrimum* (Amsterdam, 1678).
Sepp, C., *Geschiedkundige nasporingen*, 3 vols. (Leiden, 1872–5).
—— *Het staatstoezicht op de godsdienstige letterkunde in de noordelijke Nederlanden* (Leiden, 1891).
Sepper, D. L., 'Imagination, Phantasms, and the Making of Hobbesian and Cartesian Science', *The Monist*, 71 (1988), pp. 526–42.
Serrarius, P., *Vox clamantis in Babylone* (Amsterdam, 1663).
—— *De Judaeorum universali conversione* (Amsterdam, 1665).
—— *Responsio ad exercitationem paradoxicam* (Amsterdam, 1667).
Sewel, W., *A New Dictionary English and Dutch* (Amsterdam, 1691).
Shapin, S., and S. Schaffer, *Leviathan and the Air-Pump: Hobbes, Boyle and the Experimental Life* (Princeton, NJ, 1985).
Shapiro, A. E., 'Kinematic Optics: A Study of the Wave Theory of Light in the Seventeenth Century', *Archive for the History of the Exact Sciences*, 11 (1973), pp. 134–266.
Shapiro, B., *John Wilkins, 1614–72: An Intellectual Biography* (Berkeley, Calif., 1969).
Sharp, L., 'Walter Charleton's Early Life, 1620–1659, and Relationship to Natural Philosophy in mid-Seventeenth Century England', *Annals of Science*, 30 (1973), pp. 311–40.
Sharpe, K., *The Personal Rule of Charles I* (New Haven, Conn., 1992).
Sharrock, R., Ὑπόθεσις ἠθική, *de officiis secundum naturae jus* (Oxford, 1660; another edn, Gotha, 1667).
Shaw, W. A., ed., *Calendar of Treasury Books, 1667–1668* (London, 1905).
—— ed., *Letters of Denization and Acts of Naturalization for Aliens in England and Ireland, 1603–1700*, Publications of the Huguenot Society of London, 18, (Lymington, 1911).
Shorthouse, J. H., 'Charles Cotton the Angler, and Sir Richard Fanshawe', *Notes and Queries*, 4th ser., 1 (1868), p. 146.
Siebrand, H. J., *Spinoza and the Netherlanders: An Enquiry into the Early Reception of his Philosophy of Religion* (Assen, 1988).
Siegfried, C., *Spinoza als kritiker und Ausleger des Alten Testaments: ein Beitrag zur Geschichte der alttestamentlichen Kritik und Exegese* (Berlin, 1867).
Simeone, W. E., 'Sir Richard Fanshawe: An Account of his Life and Writings', University of Pennsylvania Ph.D. dissertation, 1950.
Simon, R., *Histoire critique du Vieux Testament*, 2nd edn (Rotterdam, 1685).

## BIBLIOGRAPHY

—— *Lettre à Monsieur l'Abbé P., D. & P. en T., touchant l'inspiration des livres sacrés* (Rotterdam, 1687).

—— *Lettres choisies*, 4 vols. (Amsterdam, 1730).

Skinner, Q., 'Thomas Hobbes and his Disciples in France and England', *Comparative Studies in Society and History*, 8 (1965–6), pp. 153–67.

—— 'Thomas Hobbes and the Nature of the Early Royal Society', *The Historical Journal*, 12 (1969), pp. 217–39.

—— *Machiavelli* (Oxford, 1981).

—— *Reason and Rhetoric in the Philosophy of Hobbes* (Cambridge, 1996).

Skippon, P., 'An Account of a Journey made thro' Part of the Low-Countries, Germany, Italy, and France', in J. Churchill, ed., *A Collection of Voyages and Travels*, 8 vols. (London, 1704–52), VI, pp. 359–736.

Smith, E.-H., *Samuel Bochart: recherches sur la vie et les ouvrages de cet auteur illustre* (Caen, 1833).

Smith, L. P., *The Life and Letters of Sir Henry Wotton*, 2 vols. (Oxford, 1907).

Socinus, F., *De sacrae Scripturae auctoritate* ('Seville' [Amsterdam?], 1588).

Sommer, L., *Die österreichischen Kameralisten in dogmengeschichtlicher Darstellung*, 2 vols. (Vienna, 1920–5).

Sommerville, J. P., *Thomas Hobbes: Political Ideas in Historical Context* (London, 1992).

Sommervogel, C., ed., *Bibliothèque de la Compagnie de Jésus: première partie, Bibliographie*, 2nd edn, 10 vols. (Brussels, 1890–1909).

Sorbière, S., 'II. Discours sceptique', in M. de Marolles, *Suitte des memoires de Michel de Marolles, abbé de Villeloin* (Paris, 1657), pp. 80–6.

—— *Lettres et discours . . . sur diverses matieres curieuses* (Paris, 1660).

—— *Relation d'un voyage en Angleterre* (Paris, 1664).

—— *Illustrium et eruditorum epistolae* (n.p., n.d. [Paris, 1669]).

—— *Sorberiana, ou bons mots, rencontres agreables, pensées judicieuses, et observations curieuses, de M. Sorbiere* (Paris, 1694).

—— *A Voyage to England* (London, 1709).

Sorell, T., *Hobbes* (London, 1986).

—— 'Descartes, Hobbes and the Body of Natural Science', *The Monist*, 71 (1988), pp. 515–25.

—— 'Hobbes without Doubt', *History of Philosophy Quarterly*, 10 (1993), pp. 121–35.

Spada, F. A., *Antelucanae vigiliae* (Venice, 1725).

Spanheim, F., *Opera*, 3 vols. (Leiden, 1701–3).

Spedding, J., *The Letters and Life of Francis Bacon*, 7 vols. (London, 1861–74).

Spicer, A., *The French-Speaking Reformed Community and their Church in Southampton, 1567–c.1620*, Huguenot Society, n.s., 3 (London, 1997).

Spink, J. S., *French Free-Thought from Gassendi to Voltaire* (London, 1969).

Spinoza, B., *Opera*, ed. C. Gebhardt, 4 vols. (Heidelberg, 1924).

—— *The Correspondence*, ed. and tr. A. Wolf (London, 1928).

Sprat, T., *The History of the Royal Society* (London, 1667).

Squibb, G. D., ed., *The Visitation of Derbyshire, Begun in 1662 and Finished in 1664*, Harleian Society Publications, n.s., 8 (London, 1989).

von Srbik, H., 'Wilhelm von Schröder: ein Beitrag zur Geschichte der Staatswissenschaften', *Sitzungsberichte der kaiserlichen Akademie der Wissenschaften in Wien, philosophisch-historische Klasse*, 164, part 1 (1910), pp. 1–161.

Staalkopff, J., *Ab impiis detorsionibus Thomae Hobbesii, & Benedicti de Spinoza, oraculum Paulinum Per ipsum vivimus, movemur, & sumus, Act. XVII, 28* (Greifswald, 1707).

Stapleton, T., *Principiorum fidei doctrinalium relectio scholastica & compendiaria* (Antwerp, 1596).

Steinmann, J., *Richard Simon et les origines de l'exégèse biblique* (Paris, 1960).

Stern, M., ed. and tr., *Greek and Latin Authors on Jews and Judaism*, 3 vols. (Jerusalem, 1974–84).

Stevin, S., *La Castrametation*, 1st and 2nd edns (Leiden, 1618).

Stiehler, G., 'Friedrich Wilhelm Stosch', in G. Stiehler, ed., *Beiträge zur Geschichte des vormarxistischen Materialismus* (Berlin, 1961), pp. 139–63.

Stolle, G., *Anleitung zur Historie der Gelahrheit* (Jena, 1724).

Stolleis, M., 'Machiavellismus und Staatsräson: ein Beitrag zu Conrings politischem Denken', in M. Stolleis, ed., *Hermann Conring (1606–1681): Beiträge zu Leben und Werk* (Berlin, 1983), pp. 173–99.

—— *Geschichte des öffentlichen Rechts in Deutschland*, vol. I: *Reichspublizistik und Policeywissenschaft, 1600–1800* (Munich, 1988).

Stosch, F. W., *Concordia rationis et fidei*, ed. W. Schröder (Stuttgart, 1992).

Stoye, J. W., *English Travellers Abroad, 1604–1667* (London, 1952).

Strauss, L., *The Political Philosophy of Hobbes: Its Basis and Genesis*, tr. E. M. Sinclair (Chicago, 1952).

—— *Spinoza's Critique of Religion*, tr. E. M. Sinclair (Chicago, 1997).

Strong, S. A., *A Catalogue of Letters and Other Historical Documents Exhibited in the Library at Welbeck* (London, 1903).

Struve, B. G., *Acta litteraria ex manuscriptis eruta atque collecta*, 2 vols. (Jena, 1703–20).

Struys, J., *Joh. Jansz. Straussens sehr schwere, wiederwertige, und denckwürdige Reysen durch Italien, Griechenland, Lifland, Moscau* (Amsterdam, 1678).

Stummer, F., *Die Bedeutung Richard Simons für die Pentateuchkritik*, Alttestamentliche Abhandlungen, 3, Heft 4 (Münster in Wuppertal, 1912).

Sturdy, D. J., *Science and Social Status: The Members of the Académie des Sciences, 1666–1750* (Woodbridge, 1995).

Suárez, F., *De legibus*, ed. L. Pereña *et al.*, 8 vols. (Madrid, 1971–81).

Suarez, P. L., *Noematica biblico-mesianica de Alfonso Tostado de Madrigal, Obispo de Avila (1400–1455)* (Madrid, 1956).

Sutch, V. D., *Gilbert Sheldon, Architect of Anglican Survival, 1640–1675* (The Hague, 1973).

T., J., *The Old Halls, Manors, and Families of Derbyshire*, 4 vols. (London, Buxton, 1892–1902).

Talaska, R., *The Hardwick Library and Hobbes's Early Philosophical Development* (Bowling Green, Ohio, forthcoming).

Tallemant des Réaux, G., *Les Historiettes*, ed. A. Adam, 2 vols. (Paris, 1960).

Taranto, D., *Pirronismo ed assolutismo nella Francia del '600: studi sul pensiero politico dello scetticismo da Montaigne a Bayle (1580–1697)* (Milan, 1994).

# BIBLIOGRAPHY

Tarde, J., *Borbonia sidera* (Paris, 1620).

Tarlton, C. D., 'The Creation and Maintenance of Government: A Neglected Dimension of Hobbes's Leviathan', *Political Studies*, 26 (1978), pp. 307–27.

Temple-Leader, G., and G. Marcotti, eds., *Un'ambasciata: diario dell'abate G. Fr.ᶜᵒ Rucellai* (Florence, 1884).

Templer, J., *Idea theologiae Leviathanis* (London, 1673).

Terzago, P. M., *Musaeum septalanium Manfredi Septalae patritii mediolanensis industrioso labore constructum* (Tortona, 1664).

Tesauro, E., *Il cannocchiale aristotelico*, facsimile of 1670 Turin edn, ed. A. Buck (Bad Homburg, 1968).

—— *Idea delle perfette imprese*, ed. M. L. Doglio (Florence, 1975).

Thielemann, L. J., 'Diderot and Hobbes', in *Diderot Studies II*, ed. O. E. Fellows and N. L. Torrey (Syracuse, NY, 1952), pp. 221–78.

—— 'Voltaire and Hobbism', *Studies on Voltaire and the Eighteenth Century*, 10 (1959), pp. 237–58.

van Thijn, T., 'Pieter de la Court: zijn leven en zijn economische denkbeelden', *Tijdschrift voor geschiedenis*, 69 (1956), pp. 304–70.

Thomasius, C., *Summarischer Nachrichten von auserlesenen, mehrentheils alten, in der Thomasischen Bibliotheque verhandenen Büchern*, 24 parts (Halle and Leipzig, 1715–18).

Thomson, A., *Materialism and Society in the Mid-Eighteenth Century: La Mettrie's Discours Préliminaire* (Geneva, 1981).

Thomson, S. D., ed., *Southampton in 1620 and the 'Mayflower': An Exhibition of Documents by the Southampton City Record Office* (Southampton, 1970).

—— ed., *The Book of Examinations and Depositions before the Mayor and Justices of Southampton 1648–1663*, Southampton Records Series, 37 (Southampton, 1994).

Thoroton, R., *The Antiquities of Nottinghamshire*, ed. J. Throsby, 3 vols. (Nottingham, 1790–6).

Thuillier, R., *Diarium patrum, fratrum et sororum ordinis minimorum provinciae Franciae*, 2 vols. (Paris, 1709).

Thurmann, C., *Bibliotheca academica ... Halae* (Halle, 1700).

Tocanne, B., *L'Idée de nature en France dans la seconde moitié du XVIIᵉ siècle: contribution à l'histoire de la pensée classique* (Paris, 1978).

Todd, W., 'An Early MS of Hobbes's *Leviathan*', *Notes and Queries*, 218 (1973), p. 181.

Tönnies, F., 'Siebzehn Briefe des Thomas Hobbes an Samuel Sorbière, nebst Briefen Sorbière's, Mersenne's ...', *Archiv für Geschichte der Philosophie*, 3 (1889–90), pp. 58–71, 192–232.

—— 'Hobbes-Analekten I', *Archiv für Geschichte der Philosophie*, n.s., 17 (1904), pp. 291–317.

—— *Thomas Hobbes: Leben und Lehre*, 3rd edn (Stuttgart, 1925).

—— 'Contributions à l'histoire de la pensée de Hobbes', *Archives de philosophie*, 12: 2 (1936), pp. 73–98.

Toomer, G. J., *Eastern Wisedome and Learning: The Study of Arabic in Seventeenth-Century England* (Oxford, 1996).

Torricelli, E., *Opera geometrica* (Florence, 1644).

Tostatus, A., *Opera omnia*, 23 vols. (Venice, 1596).
*A Transcript of the Registers of the Worshipful Company of Stationers from 1640–1708 AD*, 3 vols. (London, 1913–14).
Treadwell, M., 'London Printers and Printing Houses in 1705', *Publishing History*, 7 (1980), pp. 5–44.
—— 'London Trade Publishers 1675–1750', *The Library*, 6th ser., 4 (1982), pp. 99–134.
Trevor-Roper, H. R., *Catholics, Anglicans and Puritans: Seventeenth Century Essays* (London, 1987).
Tuck, R., *Natural Rights Theories: Their Origin and Development* (Cambridge, 1979).
—— 'Grotius, Carneades and Hobbes', *Grotiana*, n.s., 4 (1983), 43–62.
—— Review of Hobbes, *De cive: The English Version* and *De cive: The Latin Version*, ed. J. H. Warrender (Oxford, 1983), in *Political Studies*, 33 (1985), pp. 308–15.
—— 'Hobbes and Descartes', in G. A. J. Rogers and A. Ryan, eds., *Perspectives on Thomas Hobbes* (Oxford, 1988), pp. 11–41.
—— 'Optics and Sceptics: The Philosophical Foundations of Hobbes's Political Thought', in E. Leites, ed., *Conscience and Casuistry in Early Modern Europe* (Cambridge, 1988), pp. 235–63.
—— *Hobbes* (Oxford, 1989).
—— *Philosophy and Government, 1572–1671* (Cambridge, 1993).
Tucker, J., 'John Davies of Kidwelly (1627?–1693), Translator from the French', *Papers of the Bibliographical Society of America*, 44 (1950), pp. 119–51.
Turnbull, G. H., *Hartlib, Dury and Comenius: Gleanings from Hartlib's Papers* (London, 1947).
Turner, E. M., 'The Life and Work of Charles Cotton (1630–1687), with a Bibliographical Account of Cotton's Writings', Oxford University B.Litt. dissertation, 1954.
Turner, J., *The Politics of Landscape: Rural Scenery and Society in English Poetry 1630–1660* (Oxford, 1979).
[Tyssot de Patot, S.,] *Les Voyages et avantures de Jaques Massé* ('Bordeaux', 1710).
Ulianich, B., 'Considerazioni e documenti per una ecclesiologia di Paolo Sarpi', in F. Iserloh and P. Manns, eds., *Festgabe Joseph Lortz*, 2 vols. (Baden-Baden, 1968), II, pp. 363–444.
Ultee, M., 'The Republic of Letters: Learned Correspondence, 1680–1720', *The Seventeenth Century*, 2 (1987), pp. 95–112.
Ultsch, E., *Johann Christian von Boineburg: ein Beitrag zur Geistesgeschichte des 17. Jahrhunderts* (Würzburg, 1936).
Uri, I., *Un Cercle savant au XVIIe siècle: François Guyet (1575–1655), d'après des documents inédits* (Paris, 1886).
den Uyl, D. J., *Power, State and Freedom* (Assen, 1983).
Vaillé, E., *Histoire générale des postes françaises*, 6 vols. (Paris, 1947–53).
du Vair, G., *The Morall Philosophy of the Stoicks*, tr. C. Cotton (London, 1667).
Valckenier ['Valkenier'], P., *Das verwirrte Europa*, vol. I (Amsterdam, 1677).
Vandenbossche, H., *Adriaen Koerbagh en Spinoza* (Leiden, 1978).
Vanel, G., *Une Grande Ville aux XVIIe et XVIIIe siècles*, 2 vols. (Caen, 1910–12).
Várkonyi, A. R., *Europica* [sic] *varietas, Hungarica varietas* (Budapest, 2000).

Varro, M., *De motu tractatus* (Geneva, 1584).

Vartanian, A., *Diderot and Descartes: A Study of Scientific Naturalism in the Enlightenment* (Princeton, NJ, 1953).

—— *La Mettrie's 'Homme machine': A Study in the Origins of an Idea* (Princeton, NJ, 1960).

—— 'Quelques réflexions sur le concept d'âme dans la littérature clandestine', in O. Bloch, ed., *Le Matérialisme du XVIII$^e$ siècle et la littérature clandestine* (Paris, 1982), pp. 149–63.

Vaughan, R., ed., *The Protectorate of Oliver Cromwell*, 2 vols. (London, 1838).

de Vaulezard, J. L., *Perspective cilindrique et conique: ou traicté des apparences veuës par le moyen des miroirs cilindriques & coniques, soient convexes ou concaves* (Paris, 1630).

Vaz Dias, A. M., and W. G. van der Tak, *Spinoza mercator & autodidactus: oorkonden en andere authentike documenten betreffende des wijsgeers jeugd en diens betrekking* (The Hague, 1932).

van Veen, O., *Q. Horatii Flacci emblemata* (Antwerp, 1607).

Veen, T. J., *Recht en nut: studiën over en naar aanleiding van Ulrik Huber (1636–1694)* (Zwolle, 1976).

van Velthuysen, L., *Epistolica dissertatio de principiis iusti et decori, continens apologiam pro tractatu clarissimi Hobbaei, De cive* (Amsterdam, 1651).

—— *Ondersoeck of de christelijcke overheydt eenigh quaedt in haer gebiedt mach toe laeten* (Middelburg, 1660).

—— *Het predick-ampt en 't recht der kercke, bepaelt nae de regelen van Godts woordt* (Amsterdam, 1660).

—— *Apologie voor het tractaet van de afgoderye en superstitie* (Utrecht, 1669).

—— *A Dissertation, wherein the Fundamentals of Natural or Moral Justice and Decorum are Stated, according to the Principles of Mr. Hobbes. By a Learned Pen*, tr. anon. (London, 1706).

—— Unpublished letter to Leibniz, 7 May 1671, Christie's (New York) sale catalogue for 16–17 December 1983, lot 495.

—— *Des Principes du juste et du convenable: une apologie du* De cive *de Hobbes (1651–1680)*, tr. C. Secretan (Caen, 1995).

Venn, J., and J. A. Venn, *Alumni cantabrigienses*, part 1, 4 vols. (Cambridge, 1922–4).

Verbeek, T., *La Querelle d'Utrecht* (Paris, 1988).

Vernière, P., *Spinoza et la pensée française avant la révolution*, 2 vols. (Paris, 1954).

Vico, G., *Opere*, ed. F. Nicolini (Milan, 1953).

*Victoria County History, Bedfordshire*, 3 vols. (London, 1904–12).

*Victoria County History, Hampshire*, 5 vols. (London, 1900–12).

*Victoria County History, Hertfordshire*, 4 vols. (London, 1902–14).

*Victoria County History, Northamptonshire: Genealogical Volume, 'Northamptonshire Families'* (London, 1906).

Vieta [Viète], F., *De aequationum resolutione* (Paris, 1615).

—— *Opera mathematica*, ed. F. van Schooten (Leiden, 1646).

de Villemandy, P., *Manuductio ad philosophiam veterem-novam* (Saumur, 1674).

Viola, F., *Behemoth o Leviathan? Diritto e obbligo nel pensiero di Hobbes* (Milan, 1979).

Vitale, E., 'La lettura diderotiana di Hobbes nell'*Encyclopédie*', *Il pensiero politico: rivista di storia delle idee politiche e sociali*, 28 (1995), pp. 384–406.
Vlacq, A., *Trigonometria artificialis* (Gouda, 1633).
de Vocht, H., 'Andreas Masius (1514–1573)', in *Miscellanea Giovanni Mercati*, 6 vols. (Vatican City, 1946), IV, pp. 425–41.
Voetius, G., *Selectae disputationes theologicae*, 5 vols. (Utrecht, Amsterdam, 1648–69).
—— *Politia ecclesiastica*, 4 vols. (Amsterdam, 1663–76), vol. II, *Politiae ecclesiasticae partis primae libri duo posteriores*, 1666.
Volkelius, J., *De vera religione libri quinque* (n.p., n.d. [Amsterdam, 1642] ).
Voltaire, F.-M. Arouet de, *Mélanges*, ed. J. van den Heuvel (Paris, 1965).
Vonka, R. J., 'Een Cechische boekdrukkerij te Amsterdam in de XVIIe eeuw', in *Cechoslovakije en de internationale tentoonstelling voor oeconomische ontwikkeling te Amsterdam, 1929*, ed. B. Mendl and R. J. Vonka (Prague, n.d. [1929] ), pp. 15–20.
de Waard, C., *L'Expérience barométrique: ses antécédents et ses explications* (Thouars, 1936).
Wächtler, C., *De societatis civilis statu naturali ac legali, dissertatio politica* (Leipzig, 1670).
Wade, I. O., *The Clandestine Organization and Diffusion of Philosophic Ideas in France from 1700 to 1750* (Princeton, NJ, 1938).
Walker, C., *The High Court of Justice: Or, Cromwells New Slaughter House in England* (London, 1660).
Walker, E., *A Study of the Traité des indivisibles of Gilles Persone de Roberval* (New York, 1932).
van der Wall, E. G. E., *De mystieke chiliast Petrus Serrarius (1600–1669) en zijn wereld* (Leiden, 1987).
Wallace, W. M., *Sir Edwin Sandys and the First Parliament of James I* (Philadelphia, 1940).
Waller, E., *Poems* (London, 1645).
Wallis, J., *Elenchus geometriae hobbianae* (Oxford, 1655).
—— *Due Correction for Mr Hobbes: Or, Schoole Discipline, for not Saying his Lessons Right* (Oxford, 1656).
—— *Commercium epistolicum de quaestionibus quibusdam mathematicis* (Oxford, 1658).
—— *Tractatus duo: prior, de cycloide . . . ; posterior, . . . de cissoide* (Oxford, 1659).
—— *Hobbius heauton-timorumenos* (Oxford, 1662).
—— *A Defence of the Royal Society* (London, 1678).
Walton, I., and Cotton, C., *The Complete Angler*, ed. Sir Harris Nicolas (London, 1903).
Walzer, M., *Just and Unjust Wars: A Moral Argument with Historical Illustrations* (Harmondsworth, 1980).
Wansink, H., *Politike wetenschappen aan de Leidse Universiteit, 1575–c.1650* (Utrecht, 1981).
Waquet, F., 'Qu'est-ce que la République des Lettres? Essai de sémantique historique', *Bibliothèque de l'École des Chartes*, 147 (1989), pp. 473–502.
—— 'Les Éditions de correspondances savantes et les idéaux de la République des Lettres, *XVII$^e$ Siècle*, 45 (1993), pp. 99–118.
Ward, S., *In Thomae Hobbii philosophiam exercitatio epistolica* (Oxford, 1656).
—— *Against Resistance of Lawful Powers* (London, n.d.).
Warner, G. F., ed., *The Nicholas Papers: Correspondence of Sir Edward Nicholas, Secretary of State*, 4 vols., Camden Society, n.s., 40, 50, 57; 3rd ser., 31 (London, 1886–1920).

Warrender, J. H., *The Political Philosophy of Hobbes: His Theory of Obligation* (Oxford, 1957).
Warton, T., *The Life and Literary Remains of Ralph Bathurst* (London, 1761).
Warwick, Sir Philip, *A Discourse of Government, as Examined by Reason, Scripture, and Law of the Land* (London, 1694).
—— *Memoires of the Reigne of King Charles I, with a Continuation to the Happy Restoration of King Charles II* (London, 1701).
Waterfield, G., ed., *Mr Cartwright's Pictures: A Seventeenth Century Collection* (London, 1988).
Watkins, J. W. N., *Hobbes's System of Ideas* (London, 1965).
Watt, R., *Bibliotheca Britannica*, 4 vols. (Edinburgh 1824).
Weber, I., *Beurtheilung der atheisterey* (Frankfurt, 1697).
Webster, C., 'The Discovery of Boyle's Law, and the Concept of the Elasticity of the Air in the Seventeenth Century', *Archive for History of Exact Sciences*, 2 (1965), pp. 441–502.
Weekhout, I., *Boekencensuur in de noordelijken Nederlanden: de vrijheid van drukpers in de zeventiende eeuw* (The Hague, 1998).
Weemes ['Weemse'], J., *Exercitations Divine: Containing diverse Questions and Solutions for the Right Understanding of the Scripture* (London, 1632).
Weidhorn, M., *Richard Lovelace* (New York, 1970).
Weigle, T., 'Die deutschen Doktorpromotionen in Philosophie und Medizin an der Universität Padua von 1616–1663', *Quellen und Forschungen aus italienischen Archiven und Bibliotheken*, 45 (1965), pp. 325–84.
Weil, G. E., *Élie Lévita: humaniste et massorète (1469–1549)* (Leiden, 1963).
Welch, E., ed., *The Minute-Book of the French Church at Southampton, 1702–1939* (Southampton, 1979).
Wernham, A. G., 'General Introduction' to B. Spinoza, *Political Works*, ed. A. G. Wernham (Oxford, 1958).
Westlake, H. F., Tanner, L. E., and W. Ward, eds., *The Registers of St Margaret's Westminster*, 3 vols., Publications of the Harleian Society, 64, 88, 89 (1935, 1959, 1977).
Wheldon, J., Letter to A. Barker, *The Gentleman's Magazine*, 54, part 2, no. 4 (October 1784), p. 729.
White, T., *De mundo dialogi tres* (Paris, 1642).
—— *Dux vitae sive statera morum* (London, 1672).
Whitmore, P. J. S., *The Order of Minims in Seventeenth-Century France* (The Hague, 1967).
Wight, M., *International Theory: The Three Traditions*, ed. G. Wight and B. Porter (Leicester, 1991).
Wikelund, P., ' "Thus I passe my time in this place": An Unpublished Letter of Thomas Hobbes', *English Language Notes*, 6 (1969), pp. 263–8.
Wilkins, J. ['N. S.'] and Ward, S., ['H. D.'], *Vindiciae academiarum* (Oxford, 1654).
Wilkinson, H., *Conciones sex ad academicos oxonienses latinè habitae* (Oxford, 1658).
Wilkinson, H., *The Adventurers of Bermuda* (London, 1933).
Willems, A., *Les Elzevier: histoire et annales typographiques* (Brussels, 1880).

William of Ockham, *Philosophical Writings*, ed. and tr. P. Boehner (New York, 1957).
Williams, A., *The Common Expositor: An Account of the Commentaries on Genesis 1527–1633* (Chapel Hill, NC, 1948).
Williams, N. J., ed., *Tradesmen in Early-Stuart Wiltshire: A Miscellany*, Wiltshire Archaeological and Natural History Society, Records Branch, 15 (Salisbury, 1959).
Williams, W. P., 'Was There a 1670 Edition of *Leviathan*?', *The Papers of the Bibliographical Society of America*, 69 (1975), pp. 81–4.
Willman, R., 'Hobbes on the Law of Heresy', *Journal of the History of Ideas*, 31 (1970), pp. 607–13.
Wilson, I. M., *The Influence of Hobbes and Locke in the Shaping of the Concept of Sovereignty in Eighteenth Century France* (Banbury, 1973).
Wing, D., *Short-Title Catalogue . . . 1641–1700*, 2nd edn, revised, 3 vols. (New York, 1982–94).
Witsius, H., *Miscellaneorum sacrorum libri IV* (Utrecht, 1692).
Wokler, R., 'The Manuscript Authority of Political Thoughts', *History of Political Thought*, 20 (1999), pp. 107–23.
Wolf, A., ed. and tr., *The Correspondence of Spinoza* (London, 1928).
Wolf, F., *Die neue Wissenschaft des Thomas Hobbes* (Stuttgart, 1969).
Wolfe, P., ed., *Lettres de Gabriel Naudé à Jacques Dupuy (1632–1652)* (Edmonton, 1982).
Wollgast, S., 'Die deutsche Frühaufklärung und Samuel Pufendorf', in F. Palladini and G. Hartung, eds., *Samuel Pufendorf und die europäische Frühaufklärung* (Berlin, 1996).
Wood, A., *Athenae oxonienses*, ed. P. Bliss, 4 vols. (London, 1813–20).
—— *The Life and Times of Anthony Wood, Antiquary, of Oxford, 1632–1695, Described by Himself*, ed. A. Clark, 5 vols., Oxford Historical Society, 19, 21, 26, 30, 40 (Oxford, 1891–1900).
Woodbridge, J. D., 'Richard Simon's Reaction to Spinoza's "Tractatus Theologico-Politicus"', in K. Gründer and K. W. Schmidt-Biggemann, eds., *Spinoza in der Frühzeit seiner religiösen Wirkung* (Heidelberg, 1984), pp. 201–26.
—— 'German Responses to the Biblical Critic Richard Simon: From Leibniz to J. S. Semler', in H. Reventlow, W. Sparn, and J. Woodbridge, eds., *Historische Kritik und biblischer Kanon in der deutschen Aufklärung*, Wolfenbütteler Forschungen, 41 (Wiesbaden, 1988).
Woodward, B. B., Wilks, T. C., and C. Lockhart, *A General History of Hampshire, or the County of Southampton*, 3 vols. (London, 1863).
Wormald, B. H. G., *Clarendon: Politics, History, and Religion 1640–1660* (Cambridge, 1951).
Wren, C., *Parentalia: Or, Memoirs of the Family of the Wrens* (London, 1750).
Wren, M., *Considerations on Mr. Harrington's Commonwealth of Oceana* (London, 1657).
—— *Monarchy Asserted* (Oxford, 1659).
Yale, D. E. C., 'A View of the Admiralty Jurisdiction: Sir Matthew Hale and the Civilians,' in D. Jenkins, ed., *Legal History Studies 1972: Papers Presented to the Legal History Conference, Aberystwyth, 18–21 July 1972* (Cardiff, 1972), pp. 87–109.
Yeivin, I., *Introduction to the Tiberian Masorah*, tr. E. J. Revell (Missoula, Mont., 1980).
Zagorin, P., 'Thomas Hobbes's Departure from England in 1640: An Unpublished Letter', *The Historical Journal*, 21 (1978), pp. 157–60.

—— 'Hobbes's Early Philosophical Development', *Journal of the History of Ideas*, 54 (1993), pp. 505–18.

—— 'Two Books on Thomas Hobbes', *Journal of the History of Ideas*, 60 (1999), pp. 361–71.

Zart, G., *Einfluss der englischen Philosophen seit Bacon auf die deutsche Philosophie des 18. Jahrhunderts* (Berlin, 1881).

von Zesen, P. ['F'], *Beschreybung der Stadt Amsterdam* (Amsterdam, 1664).

—— *Des geistlichen Standes Urteile wider den Gewissenszwang in Glaubenssachen* (Amsterdam, 1665).

—— *Des weltlichen Standes Handlungen und Urteile wider den Gewissenszwang in Glaubenssachen* (Amsterdam, 1665).

Zielenziger, K., *Die alten deutschen Kameralisten: ein Beitrag zur Geschichte der Nationalökonomie und zum Problem des Merkantilismus* (Jena, 1914).

Zouch ['Zouche'], R., *Juris et judicii fecialis, sive, juris inter gentes, et quaestionum de eodem explicatio* (Oxford, 1650).

# INDEX

Note: 'TH' denotes Thomas Hobbes.

Abbadie, Jacques 388, 430
Abdera 227
Aberdeen University 342
Abingdon 83, 86, 92, 97, 98
'Abrégé de politique' (Anon.) 507
absolutism 14, 15, 28, 291, 484, 507, 514
   enlightened 532
   monarchical 16, 490, 504, 511
   TH's support for 488
absurdity 542
'accidents' 125
Accolti, Pietro 205, 208
Acontius/Acontianism 478, 479
Act of Oblivion (1660) 350
Act of Supremacy (1534/59) 69
actions 49, 114, 126, 443, 543
   causally determined 137
   designed to bring about peace 32
   infinitesimal 30
   intentional 151
   key to all 48
   'objective' 211
   sovereign 446
   voluntary 31
Acton Turville 88
adiaphorism 69
admiration 48
Aesop 345, 354, 383, 420
aesthetic pleasure 206
'agreement' 49
Agrippa, Heinrich Cornelius 295, 296, 297
Aguilon, François 121, 127–8
Aikenhead, Thomas 383, 386, 427
air 111, 194, 196
   successive illumination of 112
   vibrations of 131
   wave-motions of 132
Aix-en-Provence 217
alchemy 87, 301
Alciati, Andrea 224
Alexander the Great, king of Macedonia 441
algebra 89, 205
Alhazen 120

Ali (Prophet Mohammed's son-in-law) 270
Alicante 279
allegiance 238, 512
allegorical description 222, 225, 237
Allen, Thomas 86, 87
alliances 434, 449, 527
   defensive 450
   temporary 451
al-Maghribi, *see* Samau'al
Althusius 526
Amazons 451
ambitions 435
Ambras 207
America, *see* Virginia Company
*amour-propre* 509–10, 517
Amsterdam 46, 280, 306, 482, 487
   Classis decrees 381
   Latin *Leviathan* published 41, 339
   Lutherans 361, 374
   printing/publishing 338, 339, 340, 342, 362, 363, 368, 372–8 *passim*, 380, 459, 461, 463, 465–6
Amsterdam University 160, 361
analogy 120, 150, 151, 189, 224, 434
   political 424
'analysis' 153
anamorphoses 215, 226
   cylindrical 204–5, 207, 208, 212, 217–18, 219
anarchy 7, 15, 332, 506
   fear of 505
Andreas, Samuel 471
angels 487, 488
Anglicanism/Anglicans 18, 22, 40, 64, 287
   bishops 23
   chaplains 275
   liberal 334
   moderate and rational 10
   ordination 65
   Paris 288
   pragmatic 327
Anglo-Dutch war (1652) 453
animal spirits 108, 110, 111, 118, 126

# INDEX

annihilatory hypothesis 18, 124–5, 177, 185
Anthony, Francis 74
anti-Aristotelians 193
anti-Cartesianism 177, 181, 182, 192, 475, 499
anti-Catholicism 40, 67, 71, 271, 291, 483
antichrist 67
anti-Christianity 431, 427, 495, 535
anti-clericalism 40, 45, 46, 50, 326, 329, 493
    radical 21
anti-demonism 486
anti-Judaic polemicists 402
anti-Orange cause 514
'antipathy' 119, 131
anti-religious writing 386
anti-royalists 15, 16, 57
anti-scripturalism 482
anti-spiritualism 486
anti-theological views 493
anti-Trinitarian heresy 10
Antwerp 109, 241, 265, 280
apocrypha 400, 416, 426
Apollo 214
apologetics 387
appearances 118, 186, 187
apriorism 168
Apuleius, Lucius 262
Arabic 268, 271, 282, 401, 402
    scholarship 267, 269, 270
Aramaic 399
Archimedes 165, 325
Arcimboldo, Giuseppe 224, 225
Ardennes 384, 413
Arendt, Hannah 434
Aretino, P. 470
Aristarchus of Samos 167
aristocracy 1, 287
Aristotelianism/Aristotelians 5, 17, 133, 175, 193, 195, 283, 318, 500, 506, 519
    argument 151
    attacked 194
    diehard 290
    dismissed 299
    dogmatic 296
    Gassendi's attack on 186
    logic and physics 4
    Protestant humanist 474
    scholastic 326
Aristotle 5, 9, 31, 441–2
    Aldine edition 312
    Paduan tradition of commentary on 153

arithmetic 171, 173, 175, 178, 179
Arlington, Henry Bennett, 1st Earl of 19, 351–2
Arminians 479, 483
Arminius, Jacobus 41
Arnisaeus, H. 526
Arnold, Gottfried 531
'arrogance' 175
artefacts 149, 150
artificial man 150–1
'artificialia' 207, 208
Ashbourne 243, 247, 251
Ashford 256
Aston, Constantia 255
Aston, Walter Aston, Baron 255–6
astral influence 126
astrolabes 207
astrologers 87
astronomy 5, 9, 73, 93, 158, 166, 174, 320, 321
    Copernican 74, 133, 167–8
Astruc, Jean 408, 431
atheism 23, 310, 330, 384, 388, 475, 477, 481, 482–3, 511, 525, 531, 532, 533, 534
    'direct' 495
    metaphysical theories regarded as leading to 332
    philosophical 478, 480
    rampant 495
Athens 8–9, 400, 441
atmospheric pressure 194
attraction 138
attributes 51
Aubray, Dreux d' 274
Aubrey, John 6, 9, 13, 24, 53, 63, 75, 234–5, 257, 317–18, 321–2, 325, 329, 348, 460, 464, 532, 533
Augsburg 265
Augsburg Confession (1530) 374
Augustine, St 65, 504, 506, 507
Augustinianism/Augustinians 502, 504, 506, 531
Australia, Victoria State Library 341, 343
Austria 491
authoritarianism 327
authority 426
    divine 531
    established 488
    governmental 507, 536
    independent locus of 425
    intellectual 490

personal 52
political 476, 509, 535, 543
pragmatic acceptance of need for 327, 328
religious 476
royal 511
sovereign 443, 444, 512, 514–15, 518, 542
spiritual 66
state 516, 531
authorization 44, 507
Authorized Version 406
automata 150–1, 207
'autonomy thesis' 146
aversion 30, 114, 138
avoidance of death 32, 139
axioms 153, 176, 185, 205
Aylesbury, Sir Thomas 11, 87
Aylesbury, William 241

Backhouse, Sir William 86
Bacon, Francis, Baron Verulam, Viscount St Albans 1, 6–7, 8, 53, 73, 78, 290, 318, 323, 458, 499, 500
Bacon, Roger 86, 87, 112, 115
badness 136, 139
Bagshaw, Edward 380
Bailey, William 354, 355
Baldi, B. 97
Baltic region 466
Barberini, Francesco 393
Barbeyrac, Jean 524–5, 527
Barebones Parliament (1653) 22, 326
Bargrave, Captain John 70, 206, 207, 208
Barham, Thomas 251
Barlaeus, Caspar 478
Barlow, T. 331
Barlow, William 115
barometric experiments 192
Barrowists 68, 69
Barth, Caspar 478
Bartholin, Thomas 324
Basil, St 400
Basson, Govert 366
Bathurst, Ralph 324–5, 327
Baudry, Guillaume 131–2
Bayle, Pierre 462, 484, 488, 503, 510–11, 535
Beal, Peter 140, 249
Beale, John 331
beams 119, 120, 121
Beaugrand, Jean de 123

Beaumont de Péréfixe, Hardouin de, Archbishop of Paris 303, 306, 307, 331
Becmann, Johann Christian 525–7
Bedell, William 66
Bedfordshire, *see* Sharnbrook
Beeckman, Isaac 14
Beets, Hendrick 378
*Behemoth* (TH) 24, 37, 57, 317–18, 461, 542
ill-will of Scots towards English 453
papal threat to Kings and States 454
permission to publish 348–9
safety and well-being of the people 448
Behmenist tradition 377, 378
Beitz, Charles 432, 433, 434, 435, 438, 450, 452, 454
Bekker, Balthasar 481, 485–6
beliefs 179, 180, 478
accepted 485
Christian 535
false 20, 542, 543
laws forbidding 50
orthodox 388, 472
private 541
publicly accepted 541
rational 331, 332
religious 533
Bellarmine, Robert 416–17, 418, 420, 424, 427–8
Benedictines 210, 416
benefactions 88
benevolence 31
Benlowes, Edward 282
Bennett, Sir John 67–8, 69
Beresford Hall 242, 246, 247, 257
Berg, Conrad 478
Berkel, Abraham van 340, 391, 465, 476, 486
Berkshire, *see* Abingdon
Berlin 487
Bermudas 8, 55, 73, 78
Bern 470
Bernard, Francis 313
Bernhardt, Jean 104–5, 113
Berns, Michael 481
Bertie, Charles 210
Besoldus, C. 526
Bethersden 256
Betke, Joachim 376, 377, 378
Bettini, Mario 215
Beverley, Thomas 360

# INDEX

Bible 40, 46–7, 65, 268, 271, 371, 380, 485
  Aikenhead's opinions about 383
  Hebrew 383–431 *passim*
  *Leviathan*'s approach to 488
  Paris Polyglot 269, 418, 419
  Polish 375
binomials 87
Biscardi, Serafino 511
Blackburne, R. 460, 464, 532, 533
Blaeu, Johan 25, 236, 339, 367, 459, 460, 463, 502
blasphemy 285, 310, 383, 475
blind men 170–1, 174, 178
blood 122
Blount, Charles 429
Boccalini, T. 458
Bochart, Samuel 269–73, 276, 277, 281, 282, 287–8, 394
Bodenstein, Andreas 407
bodies 113, 118, 148, 190, 191, 482, 525
  definition of 117
  development of 51
  humid 126
  internal spirits of 123
  invisible parts of 121, 122, 124
  natural 222
  transparent 170
Bodin, J. 458, 519, 526
Bodleian Library (Oxford) 87, 297, 325, 342
  Savile collection 85, 88, 127, 136, 144–5
body politic 224, 225
Bohemia 71
Böhme, Jakob 376, 377, 378
Boineburg, Johann Christian von 305, 474, 478–9, 518–9, 521, 529
Bologna 215
Bolsover 90, 91
Bonfrerius (Jacques Bonfrère) 410, 411, 413
Book of Common Prayer 287
Boom, Dirk 378
Booth, Sir George 246
Borch, Ole 322
Bordeaux 24, 162, 263, 264, 504
Bosc, Charles du 16, 221, 466–7, 497
Bosc, Pierre du 288
Bossuet, Jean-Bénigne 506–7
Boteler family 255
Boteler, Anne, *see* Fane, Anne
Boteler, Joan, Lady 253, 254
Boteler, John 252

Boteler, Sir Oliver 251–2, 254
Boteler, Sir William 252–3, 254, 256
Botero, G. 458
Bots, Hans 539
Boulanger, Nicolas-Antoine 494
Boulliau, Ismaël 133
Bourdelot, Pierre 497
bourgeoisie 261
Bourignon, Antoinette 376
Bowman, Francis 324
Boxhorn, M. Z. 41, 43
Boyle, Robert 187–9, 318, 321, 322, 323, 330, 331, 499, 512
Brahe, Tycho 167
brain 30, 111, 118, 126, 152
  motion in 116
  physiology of 147
Bramhall, John, Bishop of Armagh 18, 23, 365, 530
Branche, Thomas 86
Branche, William 86
Brandenburg-Prussia 531–2
Brandt, Frithiof 110, 113, 116
Brazil 503
Breckling, Friedrich 376, 377–8
Breda 109, 160
Bredekamp, Horst 340, 341
Bremen 265
Brereton, William 328
Breuil, Jean du 214
Brewster, William 70
Briggs, Henry 74, 87
Briot, Nicolas 286
British Library 80, 82, 234, 247, 312
  Harleian papers 104
  Sloane collection 313
Brockdorff, Cay von 99–100
Brokenborough 2, 3, 4, 93
Brotier, Abbé 496
Brown, Alexander 63
Brown, Keith 200, 201
Browne, Sir Richard 287
Browne, Sir Thomas 465, 478, 480
Brownists 68, 69, 70
Bruce, Lord 77
Brucker, Jakob 495
Bruges 254
Bruno, G. 290
Brussels 276, 498
Buckingham, George Villiers, 1st Duke of 72

– 610 –

# INDEX

Buckingham, George Villiers, 2nd Duke of 161–2
Buckinghamshire 92, 289
Bull, Hedley 433, 434
Bunyan, John 331
Burnet, Gilbert 338
Burton, Robert 96
Bush, Douglas 78
Buston/Burston manor 253
Butler, Richard 276
Butler, Thomas, Earl of Ossory 276–7
Buxtorf, Johannes (the elder) 418, 419
by-laws 351, 352

Cadiz 279, 297
Cadlands 266, 280, 300
Caen 261–81 *passim*, 287, 288
'caesaro-papism' 476
Cahaignes, Jacques and Étienne de 281
Calixtus, Georg 478
Calmet, Dom Augustin 431
Calvert, Sir George 59, 60
Calvin, John 4, 290, 420
Calvinism/Calvinists 66, 67, 305, 376, 476, 478, 483, 533, 528
    authorities 470
    Church 41, 42, 45, 288
    diehard 421
    Dutch 471
    French writers 504
    preachers 485
    theologians 389, 417, 473, 479
Cambridge University 1, 66, 246, 312
    Jesus College 252
    Lucasian Chair of Mathematics 255
    Magdalene College 54, 341, 343
    St John's College 5, 72
    Trinity College 313, 342, 343
Cameralism 513, 514, 535
Camoens, Luis de 255
Campanella, Tommaso 90, 129, 500
Canada 503
Cano, Melchior 415–16
canonicity 396
Canterbury, Archbishops of 348
    Prerogative Court 68
    *see also* Laud; Sheldon
Cappel, Louis 272, 419, 420, 431
Capuchins 193
Cardano, G. 386, 540

Cardonnel, Adam de (brother of Pierre) 266, 267, 278–9, 280, 285, 299, 300, 308
Cardonnel, Adam de (nephew of Pierre) 260, 308
Cardonnel, Daniel de 280
Cardonnel, James de 308
Cardonnel, Jean de 267, 283
Cardonnel, John de 308
Cardonnel, Judith de 279
Cardonnel, Katherine de 301, 308
Cardonnel, Peter de 309
Cardonnel, Philippe de 267, 280, 302, 308
Cardonnel, Pierre de 229, 259–316
Cardonnel, Vincent de 261
Cardonnel, William de 266, 309–11
Carleton, Dudley 77–8
Carneades 295
Carpzov, Johann Benedict 388, 483
Carr, E. H. 432, 433–4, 442
Carswell 75
Cartesianism/Cartesians 42, 45, 181–2, 194, 283, 471, 482, 485, 490–1, 501, 509, 537
    anti-Hobbesian 489
    hostility to 498
    invocation of arguments 507
    one of the first publicists of 500
    steady advance of 499
Cartwright, Christopher 240
Cartwright, William 206, 208
Casaubon, Meric 331, 333–4, 478
Case Western Reserve 342, 343
Cassander 478, 480
Castelli, Benedetto 89, 105, 106, 109, 131
Castle, Martha 97, 104
*casus belli* 453
Catalonia 217
Catherine of Braganza, Queen of England 298
Catholic Church 40, 67, 271, 453, 454, 470
    authority and tradition 416
    ferocious attack on 20
    temporal power 67
Catholicism/Catholics 22, 39, 71, 380, 388, 407, 421, 422, 423, 424, 470, 473, 478, 506, 533
    converts 286, 305, 513
    defence against 10
    doctrines 67, 414
    hard-line 415
    Hebraist 419, 430

Catholicism/Catholics (*cont.*)
  heretics 479
  intransigent churchmen 504
  misuse of power by authorities 290
  moral theology 502
  orthodox 210, 387
  pious 498
  post-Tridentine polemicists 415
  relations between Protestants and 271
  respected commentators 409
  scientists 168
  theologians 483
  TH's ferociously sarcastic comments on 466
  writers 416, 418, 420, 483
  *see also* Jesuits
Caton, William 379
catoptrics 172, 204–5, 212, 217, 220
Caumont, Armand de, marquis de Montpouillan 286
Caus, Isaac de 286, 307
causal process 14, 30
causation 135, 136, 189
  mechanical 30, 131
  non-mechanical 110
  physical 154
causes 182, 196
  ignorance of 493
  knowledge of 17, 154, 155, 180, 184, 188, 206
  mechanistic science of 155
  natural 541–2
  of phenomena 153
  physical 29, 154
  real 188
  sufficient and necessary 137
Cavalieri, Bonaventura, 85, 160, 215
Cavendish family 1, 2, 16, 28, 80, 245
  *see individual entries below; also under* Newcastle
Cavendish, Sir Charles 85, 95, 98, 162, 165, 240, 324, 497
  estates 20
  London contact with TH 21
  notes on *De Corpore* 101–3, 154
  Pell and 18, 160–1
  Petty and 194–5
  scientific and mathematical pursuits 10, 11–12, 81, 88, 89, 132
  'Short Tract' and 104, 109, 115, 116, 119–20, 121, 122, 131–2
Cavendish, Margaret, Marchioness of Newcastle 284
Cavendish, William, 1st Earl of Devonshire 5, 6, 53
Cavendish, William, 2nd Earl of Devonshire 41, 53–4, 91, 458
  friendship with TH 5–6
  influence of Bacon's *Essayes* on 7
  Micanzio letters 53, 80
  Virginia Company and 28, 54, 55, 56, 60, 71–2, 73, 74, 76, 77, 78–9
Cavendish, William, 3rd Earl of Devonshire 19, 21, 24, 91, 93, 287, 307, 308, 310, 320–1, 329, 343, 467
  attempts to get TH elected MP 15
  christening present to de Cardonnel 286, 288–9
  Continental tour with TH 11
  estates 20
  majority attained 95
  marriage 245
  poem dedicated to 259–60, 276, 299
  wardship over 28–9
Caylus, Charles-Gabriel de, Bishop of Auxerre 496
censorship 380, 536
central Europe 302, 305, 514
certainty 69, 168, 179, 180, 187, 189
  definitional and causal 166
  problems of 333
Chaldaean chronologies 394
Chamier, Daniel 417
Chancery 57
Channel Islanders 263
chaos 506
Chapelain, Jean 274, 281
charity 31, 509
Charles I, King of Great Britain and Ireland 14–15, 64, 208, 237, 252
  book attributed to 238
  de Cardonnel and 277, 278
  execution 20, 250, 288
  secretary to 254
Charles II, King of Scotland and England 20, 24, 286–7, 306, 321, 348–9
  de Cardonnel and 278, 300, 301
  exile 254
  marriage 259, 298
  Restoration of 512
  TH's gift of *Leviathan* manuscript 200, 228

INDEX

Charles, Prince of Wales (later Charles II) 95, 134
   dedicatory epistles to 202, 275, 277, 278
   mathematical lessons from TH 18, 93, 221
Charles City 64
Charleton, Walter 228, 260, 280, 283, 284, 289, 299, 320
Charron, Pierre 540
Chart 256
Chatsworth 16, 24, 28, 258, 289
   Cavendish Discourses 7, 78
   'Hardwick' manuscript 248
   TH manuscripts 80, 81, 83, 84, 87, 91, 93, 99, 100, 102, 104, 106, 109, 127, 139–44, 154
cheese 519
chemistry 10, 90, 301
Chillingworth, William 10, 40, 67, 69
Chipping Sodbury 88
Chiswell, Richard 338, 342, 356–7, 358, 371, 372, 380
'Christendom' 453, 454
Christian V, King of Denmark 512
Christianity 293–4, 334, 384, 429, 483, 492
   anti-confessional type of 376
   controversies that divided 305
   conversion to 61, 304, 306
   eighteenth-century attacks on 386
   institutional 39–40
   Islamic writers against 401
   manuscript treatises attacking 488
   organized, TH's view of the whole history of 544
   radical critique of 385
   rational 480
   simplified 296
   theology 16, 98
   triumph of 305
Christie's 341
Christina, Queen of Sweden 273
Chronicles 426
Church 3, 5, 68, 331, 333, 454, 532
   authority of 421, 423
   early, history of 281
   government 66, 328, 330, 334
   index of prohibited books 470, 498, 501, 508
   printed works offensive to 350
   rejection of traditional ideas of spiritual authority in 10
   sacerdotalists 327
   State and 8, 39, 45, 46, 66, 70, 71, 475, 534
   *see also* Catholic Church; Church of England
Church of England 65, 67, 71, 284, 424
   bishops 39
   liturgy and discipline 287
Churchill, W. A. 342
civil discord 503
civil law 513
civil society 44
   establishment of 495–6
   religion and 524
civil war 7, 452
   *see also* English Civil War
civilization 75–6
Clare, John Holles, 2nd/Earl of 285
Clarendon, Earl of, *see* Hyde
Clarendon Press 239
Clarke, Samuel 496
classical scholarship 281
Clauberg, Johannes 471
Clavius, Christopher 209
Clayton, Sir Thomas 309
Cleaver (Stationers' Company officer) 346
clericalism 327, 487
Clerselier, Claude 499
Clifton, Gervase (son of below) 9, 91
Clifton, Sir Gervase 9, 244
coalitions 434
Cocq, Gijsbert 471, 476–7, 533
code of honour 453
coercion 48, 503, 505, 515
   justification for 504
cognition 110, 227
coins 89
Cokayne family 255
Cokayne, Sir Aston 243, 245
Coke, Sir Edward 58, 59
Coleridge, K. A. 347
Colerus, Johannes 372, 374
Colladon, Jean 286
collective identity 224, 228
Collège de Maître Gervais (Paris) 156
Collège du Bois (Caen) 262
Collège Royal (Paris) 269, 419
   Ramus chair of mathematics 156–7, 162, 166
Collegiants 376, 379, 487
Collegium Romanum 409, 416

– 613 –

# INDEX

Collins, Anthony 468, 488
Collins, Jeffrey 99
Cologne 265, 518
colonization 57, 441, 442
   justification of 61
Colorado University, Boulder 342
colours 115, 125, 137, 169
   acquaintance with 178
Comenius, Jan Amos 288, 302, 304, 305–6, 363, 375–7
Comenius, Maria 375
Cominges, Comte de 306
Commandinus, F. 93
commercial law 452
Committee for the Advance of Money 278
common culture 453, 455
common good 43
Common Law 7, 57, 58, 59, 78
Commons, House of 23, 252
   Bill against Atheism and Profaneness (1666) 344, 349, 365
   debates on foreign policy 71
Commons Journal 58–9
commonwealth(s) 27, 28, 151, 152, 155, 223, 224, 225, 227, 437–8, 441, 444, 446, 447, 448, 450, 456, 475–6
   'Leagues between' 451
   theory of collective personhood of 443
   well-being of 452
compasses 161
composition 153
comprehension 137–8
compulsion 44
   'absolute' 188
Comte, Auguste 146
'conatus' 30
'conceptual compounding' 153
condemnation 470, 471, 473
Condé, Prince de, Louis II, 4th prince de Bourbon 395
'confederacies' 449, 451, 454, 545
confession 67
conflict 139, 496, 505, 508
   jural 31
   primary state of 31
   rights 44
   state of nature 514
conformity 45, 287
conjectures 155
Conring, Hermann 305, 474, 478, 518, 519

'consensus' 49, 517
Constans, Lucius Antistius, *see* Court, Johan and Pieter de la
constitutions 44, 48
   building 515, 516
'contacts' 73
contract 45, 49–50, 153
   social 46
control 67, 514
Conventicle Act (1670) 350
conventionalism 541
conversion 60, 61, 304, 305, 306, 513
cooperation 451, 452
   international 455
   social 48
Cooper, William 311
Copenhagen 521
Copernicanism 74, 133
Copernicus, Nicolaus 42, 167, 168
Copland, Patrick 61, 65
Coptic 401
corpuscles 113, 170
Cosin, John (later Bishop of Durham) 18–19
cosmology 509, 536
Cotterell, Sir Charles 240–1
Cotton, Cassandra 257
Cotton, Charles 234–58
Cotton, Charles (father of above) 242–5, 248, 254, 255–6, 257
Cotton, Sir Robert 77
Council of State 237–8, 280, 328
Council of Trent (1545–63) 414
Counter-Remonstrants 41
countermarks 101
Courcelles, Étienne de 480
Court, Johan and Pieter de la 42, 43–4, 45, 48, 514–16
Court of Admiralty 452
court wits 11
covenants 44
Cowley, Abraham 299
Cranfield, Sir Lionel 56
Craven, W. F. 64
creation 394
crimes 349, 531
Crisp, Steven 379
Cromwell, Oliver 21, 327, 329
Crooke, Andrew 336, 338, 341, 343, 345, 347–8, 349, 350, 351, 355, 356–7, 363, 364, 369, 370

– 614 –

# INDEX

Crooke, Elizabeth 357, 371
Crooke, William 348, 349
Cropredy Bridge, battle of (1644) 253
Croy, Philippe de 464
cruelty 438
cryptography 215–16
Cudworth, Ralph 1
Culpepper (Colepeper), Sir John 254
cultural relativism 540
'cultural transformation' 544
Cumberland, Richard 523, 533
Cunradus, Christoffel 338, 361–2, 363, 364, 365, 366–7, 368, 369, 370, 372–82
curves 154, 156
Cusanus 290
custom 541
cycloids 156, 157, 158
Czech language/books 306, 375

Dale, Antonie van 429
damasking 355
'Dan' (place-name) 408
d'Angennes, Charles marquis de Rambouillet 27
d'Angennes, Charles marquis du Fargis 274
d'Angennes, Jacques Bishop of Bayeux 274
Daniel, Roger 346, 347, 369
Dannhauer, Johann Conrad 479
Danvers, Henry 352
Danvers, Sir John 56, 57, 73
Danzig 279
Dapper, Olfert 362, 363
Davenant, Sir William 19, 75, 217, 202, 222, 242, 243–4
David, 1st King of the Judean dynasty 430, 431
Davies, John 21, 329, 465
Davila, Enrico C. 241
Davisson (Davidson), William 12, 90, 301
Day, Peter 140
death:
  avoidance of 32, 139
  fear of 510
debauchery 23
deception 175
decision-making 48, 515
*De cive* (TH) 13, 15, 20, 28, 49, 180, 223, 239, 397, 471, 485, 488, 491, 497, 504, 507, 508, 521, 529, 533

arguments in favour of monarchy 44
'artificial man' 150–1
canonicity 396
church and commonwealth 475–6
Cotton and 234–58
dedicatory epistle to 454
defence of 518
Dutch translation 381
duties of instituted sovereigns 447
early responses to 474
first edition 201, 459
frequent reprinting of 25
inexpensive editions 470
Latin version 459, 460, 463, 464
Mersenne and printing/publication of 16, 218, 472
method 516–17
natural justice 146, 519–20
placed on index of prohibited books 470, 501
political theory 500
preface to 525
Pufendorf's close study of 522
Russian translation 463
second edition 33, 40–1, 324, 438; preface 147, 148–9, 514
Sorbière and 458, 465, 473, 494, 502, 510, 519
sovereign power 76
van Velthuysen's 'apologia' for 42
Deckherr, Johannes 511, 520
*De corpore* (TH) 13, 17, 19, 147, 163, 187, 320, 459, 460, 500, 501, 528
argument against Cartesian separation of 'thought'/'extension' 490
botched mathematical demonstrations 498
drafts 17–18, 82, 84, 100, 101, 103, 154
geometrical sections 22, 162
'Logica' 102
magnification (microscopy) 183
mathematical excursions 325–6
method chapter 155
Payne's notes on 99
'Philosophia prima' 102
plenist principles 190, 196
possible generation of effects 179
Rapin's judgement on 499
'ratiocination' process 129
'Short Tract' and 128

– 615 –

*De corpore* (TH) (*cont.*)
  similarities 153
  'space' 191
  two parts of philosophy 148
  du Verdus translation 464
deduction 6, 147
Dee, John 290
defence:
  mutual 450, 451
  of monarchy as a form of government 526
  of religious toleration 516
definitions 6, 31, 130, 153, 154, 205
  knowledge derived from 166
  of power 32
*De homine* (TH) 13, 17, 18, 22, 99, 147, 180, 226, 325, 459, 460, 488, 491, 522
  suppositional basis of physics 182
  du Verdus translation 464
delusions 211
demagogic politicians 9
democracy 28, 48
  Athenian 8–9
  incompetent 9
  romanticized versions of classical teachings about 542
'democratizing' tendencies 63
Democritus 114
demonology/demons 210, 211, 483, 485, 487, 488, 492
  pagan, Christianized versions of 542
demonstrations 180, 525
demonstrative necessity 188
Denmark 491, 512
denunciations 380–1, 477, 486, 537
Derby, James, 7th Earl of 250
Derby manuscript 246, 247, 250
Derbyshire 5, 21, 92, 244
  *see also* Bolsover; Chatsworth; Hardwick; Peak District; Tissington
Dering, Sir Edmund 252
Desbans, Louis 508
Descartes, René 12, 25, 95, 160, 164, 165, 192, 195, 210, 458, 476, 496, 517
  anonymous tract denouncing 481
  anti-vacuist theory 190
  exchange of letters between TH and 14
  Gassendi's objections to 177
  low opinion of TH 499
  opinion of *De cive* 473
  TH's 'Objections' to 14, 176, 178, 218, 460

works: *Dioptrics* 13, 320; *Discours de la méthode* 157–8; *Meditations* 97, 185, 497, 498; Les *Passions de l'âme* 98, 501; *Principia* 97, 290; *Specimina* 290
  *see also* Cartesianism
description 149, 150, 151
  allegorized 222, 225
  hierarchy of levels of 152, 153
desire 15, 30, 51, 114, 138, 139, 147, 508
  fulfilment of 31
  individual 31–2
  object of 32, 436
  pleasures 510
  psychology of 110
  reason simply the servant of 52
  satisfaction of 441
  shared 443
Desmaizeaux, Pierre 539
Desnoyers, Pierre 193, 194
d'Espagne, Jean 285–6, 287, 307
d'Espagnet, Jean 97
despotism 503
  oriental 484, 493
determinism 136
deterrence 449, 531
Deuteronomy 396, 397, 400, 402, 403, 405, 407, 410, 411, 422
  'Book of the Law' 425, 427
  last chapter 409
  opening phrase 406
devils 487
Devonshire, Christian Cavendish, Countess of 9
Devonshire, Elizabeth Cavendish, Countess of 245
  *see also* Cavendish, William (2nd & 3rd Earls)
d'Holbach, Paul Henri Thiry, baron 493, 494, 495
d'Huisseau, Isaac 479
diagnosis 153
*Dictionary of National Biography* 63, 260
Diderot, Denis 494–5, 496, 497
Diecmann, Johannes 482
Dieppe 279
Diestel, Ludwig 426–7
Digby, John, Earl of Bristol 276
Digby, Sir Kenelm 1, 12, 13, 14, 85, 87, 320, 329, 512
Digges, Sir Dudley 56, 57, 71, 74, 75

– 616 –

## INDEX

Digges, Thomas 74
dimension 191
Diodati, Jean 67
Diogenes Laertius 113
dioptrics 204, 212, 216, 218, 220
discourse 7, 130, 179, 227, 503, 528
disobedience 515
dissenters 39, 352, 371, 380, 503
dissimilarity 148
distance 120, 153, 170, 192, 213
   measurement of 161
distortion 205, 212
Dittmers, Gert 208
divine grace 507, 509
divine law 47, 528
divine-right theory 514
divinity 297
Divino, Eustachio 320
dogmatism 168, 185, 186, 332, 333
Domat, Jean 509
Dominis, Marc'Antonio de 8, 458, 478, 479, 480
Doni, Giovanni Battista 215
Donne, John 60, 61–2, 63, 66, 242
Douai University 410, 415
Dover 253, 265, 297
Drabík, Mikuláš 302, 306
dreams 118, 187
Dresden 481
dressage 90
Drummond, H. J. H. 235, 240, 241
drunkenness 438
Drusius, Johannes 281
Dryden, John 260, 298, 299
Dublin 279
Duchesne, Nicolas Forest 214
Duhamel, Abbé 496
Dupin, Nicolas 280
Duppa, Brian, Anglican bishop of Salisbury 21
Dupuy, Pierre and Jacques 394–5, 396
Durand, Giles 84, 101
Durel, Jean 284, 287, 288
Durham 21, 329
Dury, John 288
Dutch language 361, 362, 370, 374, 379, 518
   *Leviathan* 380, 381, 465, 466, 476–7, 522
   *Of Libertie and Necessitie* 469
Dutch Republic 40–52, 485

duties 148, 149, 152, 446, 454, 500, 526
   jural 444, 445, 455
   moral 442, 444, 445, 455, 456
   mutual 444
   natural 445, 455, 517
   religious 475
   sovereign 507

Earles, John 275
Ecchellensis, Abraham (Ibrahim al-Hakilani) 419, 420
ecclesiastical law 3
'ecclesiastics' 22
Ecclesiasticus (apocryphal book) 294–5
ecclesiology 348
economic policy 513
ecumenism 478, 539
Edict of Nantes (1598), Revocation (1685) 280, 504
Edinburgh University 341, 383
Edward VI, King of England 208
effects 196
   beautiful and admirable 212
   knowledge of 188
   observed 184
   optical 209
   possible generations of 179
   psychological 208, 209
   wonderful 206
egoisms 31
Egyptian chronologies 394
*Elements of Law, The* (TH) 9–10, 20, 27, 28, 81, 95, 136, 139, 223, 247, 248, 250
   annihilatory hypothesis 124–5
   circulation 16, 96, 244,
   completed and scribally published 135
   dedication to patron 15
   defence of royal power 238
   *Humane Nature* 323, 324, 464, 465, 494, 495
   importance of 29
   laws of nature 452
   'phantasms' 130
   prime example of vain-glory 175
   sovereign's duty 39
   spectra 118
   'spirits incorporeal' 191
   truth of propositions 178–9
*Elements of philosophy* (TH) 234, 390
   *see also De cive; De corpore; De homine*

Elizabeth, Queen of Bohemia 71
Ellies du Pin, Louis 388–9, 483
Ellis, John 310
Elzevier 16, 131, 324, 366, 390, 459, 464
emanationist theory 113, 120, 121
emotion 51
'endeavour' 30
ends 30, 544
English Civil War (1642–51) 237, 253, 267, 275, 277
 *see also* Behemoth
English Optical Manuscript 189–90, 325
enigmas 211
Enlightenment 384, 485, 530, 535, 545
 French 494, 495
 radical 431, 493, 536, 537
 responses to TH 506
 'underground' literature 484
'Enthusiasts' 476
*entia* 14
entities 5
 conceptual 152
 corporate 223
 jural 148
Épernon, Jean-Louis de La Valette, duc d' 242, 251
Epicureanism/Epicureans 113, 115, 330, 332, 477, 488
 atomism 498
 Christianized 98
 defence of the doctrine 114
 species theory of 'Short Tract' 119, 133
 TH categorized 499, 500
Epicurus 113, 114, 115, 499
episcopacy 99, 135
 condemned 288
Episcopius, Simon 417–18, 478
epistemology 12, 13, 166, 176
 fundamental problems in 29
 implications of optics for 218
equilibrium theory 195, 196
Erasmus, Desiderius 414
Erastianism/Erastians 288, 476, 478
 pragmatic 541
Erpenius, Thomas 270
errors 542
eschatological theory 349
Esdras, Second Book of (apocryphal book) 384, 399–401, 416, 426
*Essais de morale et de politique* (Anon.) 507, 508

'esse existentiae'/'esse essentiae' 29
essences 14, 18, 30, 52, 185, 191
 formal 5
 intelligible 29
 nominal 153
 real 153
Estienne, Robert (III) 269
ethics 5, 135, 136, 153, 536
 law and 518
 theological 517
Euclid 5, 6, 9, 12, 73, 93, 153, 166, 205
Eugene of Savoy, Prince 489, 490, 493
Evelyn, John 222, 284, 329
evidence:
 empirical 194
 experimental 192, 193
evil 43, 138, 490, 514, 515
 'good' and 32
 public determination of what is 45
Exclusion crisis (1679) 81
excommunication 3, 46, 47
exile 19, 275, 289
 Huguenot 284
 political 274
existence 177, 185
 demons 485
 God 178, 383, 482
 rational kind of 52
Exodus 403, 422
experiences 51, 147, 509
explanations 111, 150, 181, 186, 190
 causal 186–7
 mechanistic 183
 mediumistic 119, 193
 scientific 166
extension 51, 499
external world 177
extramission 167
Ezekiel 214, 225
Ezra the Scribe 383–7, 397–410 *passim*, 413–19 *passim*, 421, 426, 427, 429, 431, 486
 importance of 424

facts:
 consequences of 155
 contingent 31
 known 193
 observed 111
 value and 150

# INDEX

faith:
  ambiguous, general and deceptive confession of 479
  article of 480
  'external' profession 505
  internal 524
Falck, Nathanael 482
Falkland, Lucius Cary, Viscount 10, 11, 40, 74, 75, 243, 244
falsehood 544
fanaticism 332
Fane, Anne, Lady 252, 253, 235–6, 239, 240, 243, 246, 250, 251, 254, 255, 256, 257
Fane, Sir Francis, 1st Earl of Westmorland 235, 253, 254
Fane, Sir George 235, 253
Fane, Mildmay, 2nd Earl of Westmorland 243, 251
Fane, Spencer 253
Fanshawe family 256
Fanshawe, Ann 253–4
Fanshawe, Richard 202–3, 217, 218–19, 221–2, 252, 253–4, 255
Fanshawe, Sir Thomas 252
Fawkham 256
Fawley 266
fears 48, 51, 118, 130, 147, 527, 541, 544
  mutual 435, 473
  punishment 531
  shared 443
  unknown powers 493
Feingold, M. 88, 95
Felbinger, Jeremias 379
Felgenhauer, Paul 378
felicity 507
Fell, John 23, 24, 348
Ferdinand, Archduke of Austria 207
Fermat, Pierre de 158, 160, 164
Ferrar, John 54, 55, 56
Ferrar, Nicholas 56, 66, 74
fictions 534
Fiesque, Charles-Léon, comte de 274
Fire of London (1666) 344, 357
Fisher, Ferdinand 282
Fisher, Payne 282, 283
Fisher, Samuel 429–30
fishing/fish 62, 72, 83
Fitzherbert, William 248
Flavigny, Valérian de 419
Flesher (Stationers' Company officer) 346

Fletcher, John 256
Florence, Museo di Storia della Scienza 216
Fludd, Robert 290
Fontaine, François 265, 278
Fontaine, Pierre 265
Fontevrault 210
Ford, W. 247
foreign affairs/policy 8, 71–2
foreshortening 212
form(s) 6, 29, 30, 152, 189
  incorporeal 114
  matter and 151, 155
  visible 167
Forstner, Heinrich Friedrich 474–5
Forterie, Abraham and Jacob de la 265
fortresses 161
Fourmont, Étienne 430–1
Fox, George 379
Foxley 3
France 6, 71, 192, 203, 216, 260, 304, 321, 460, 491
  see also Bordeaux; Marseilles; Montpellier; Normandy; Paris
Francis of Paola, St 215
Franckenberg, Abraham von 377, 378
François I, King of France 224
Franeker University 526
Frankfurt an der Oder, University 525
Frassen, Claude 483
fraud 504
Frederick III, King of Denmark and Norway 208, 512
Frederick V, Elector of the Palatinate 71
free agents 110
free will 531
freedom 46, 47, 48, 50
  rationalist theory of 51
Freiberg 374, 375, 378
French language 89, 241, 275, 298, 299, 384, 462
  *De cive* 458, 460, 465, 473, 494, 502, 510, 519
  *De corpore* 464
  Koran 282
  *Leviathan* 466, 467, 468
  poetry 260, 281
French Reformed Church 288
Fréret, Nicolas 385, 427, 488, 491
friction 149
Friedrich Augustus, Elector of Saxony 461, 470

– 619 –

Fritsch, Caspar  461, 468, 489
Fritsch, Thomas  461, 462, 470, 533
Fuller, Thomas  346, 347, 369
function  149
funeral odes  282
Furly, Benjamin  379

Gabrieli, V.  78
Galatinus, Petrus  416
Galenist tradition  153, 318
Galileo  14, 109, 135, 153, 164, 458, 499, 500
    condemnation of  168
    subjectivity of secondary qualities  29
    works: *Della scienza mecanica* 89; *Dialogo* 11, 96–7; *Discorsi e dimonstrazioni* 131; *Il saggiatore* 123
Gallican argument  40
Garencières, Théophile de  286
Gassendi, Pierre  17, 99, 115, 156, 162, 174–5, 189, 210, 320, 322, 395, 458, 460, 475, 497, 499
    atomism  283, 498
    death of  24
    departure to south of France  20
    illness  163
    mechanistic science  187
    objections to Descartes  177
    praise for  97–8
    scepticism  185–6
    sense perception  183
    works: *Animadversiones* 97; *De apparente magnitudine solis* 114; *Exercitationes paradoxicae adversus Aristoteleos* 186
Gaston d'Orléans  274
Gates, Sir Thomas  64
Geer, Laurentius de  375, 378
Génébrard, Gilbert  416
generations  148, 151
    actual  179
    possible, knowledge of  154
Genesis  292–3, 393, 400, 403, 406, 408
    Mersenne's commentary on  413
Geneva  9, 70, 306
Gentili, Alberico  439, 528
gentry  252
geometry  5, 12, 89, 154, 157, 171, 173, 174–5, 178, 179, 180, 323
    algebraic  165–6
    challenge to demonstrate TH's superiority in  326

defective  498
exercises  84
instruments  161
laws of  206
no place in universities for  4
objects as conceptual entities  152
problems  85, 93–4
proofs  22
propositions  155
TH's first encounter with  9
George I, King of Great Britain and Ireland  312
German language  361, 362, 374, 377, 384, 462, 464
    *Leviathan* 469
    New Testament  379
Germany  41, 78, 466, 468, 491, 514
    first person to take notice of *Leviathan* in  518
    Protestant  471
    *see also* Berlin; Bremen; Cologne; Hamburg; Jena; Karlstadt; Kiel; Rostock; Tübingen
Giannone, P.  484
Gilbert, William  114, 115
Gillingham, Michael  344
Girard, G.  251
Glanvill, Joseph  332–3
Glaziou, Yves  460, 465
'glory'  453
Gloucestershire  75
    *see also* Tormarton
goals  32
God  61, 69, 70, 187, 384, 420, 428, 436, 487, 501, 529, 534
    all reality comprehended in  51
    attributes to  533
    corporeal  482, 493
    determination of the wisdom of  29
    disobedience to  385
    existence of  178, 383, 482
    freedom to create the world  30
    glory of  502
    inducement to greater piety towards  335
    knowledge of  47
    law of  398
    love of  51
    man's duties towards  500
    man's relation to  507
    men can have no idea of  490

– 620 –

# INDEX

nature of 40, 49, 531
power of 49, 399, 475
preservation willed by 517
'railing upon' 383
reasonableness of 10, 331
revelation from 515
'spirit' of 391
will of 182
Word of 396, 391, 399, 414, 422–3, 425
Godolphin, Sidney 75
Goldgar, Anne 540
Goldsmith, Maurice 148, 236, 339
Golius (Jacob Gool) 270, 311
Gondomar, Diego Sarmiento, conde de 57
goodness/good 136, 138, 139, 514, 515, 529
  and evil 32
  highest 523
  of operation 29
  origin of 490
  others 31
  public determination of what is 45
Gordon Huntley, James 415, 417
Gorges, Sir Fernando 62
Goring, George, Earl of Norwich 276
Gosselin, Antoine 262
government 253, 507
  civil, hatred or human animosities as the basis of 474
  coercive 505
  debate about the origins of 495
  democratic 28, 44
  monarchist 327, 514, 526
  Moses' system of 48
  republican 52, 515
  rudimentary forms of 60
  secure 75–6
  sovereign 515
governor concept 149
Graeco-Roman philosophy 453
Grapius, Zacharias 481
Great Massacre (1622) 56, 61
'Great Synagogue' 399
Great Tew circle 10, 11, 40, 63, 66, 69, 74–5, 92, 103, 244, 325, 334
Greece 8
Greek 182, 294–5, 309, 385, 418
  'analysis' and 'synthesis' 153
  Arabic translations from 401
  de Cardonnel's proficiency in 262
  Euclid's *Elements* 93

Lemoine's verse in praise of Bochart 281
New Testament 414
  taught to TH 3
  TH's translation of Thucydides 8–9
Greifswald University 482
Grenoble 220
Gresham College 74, 318
Grosseteste, Robert 87, 112, 115
Grotius, Hugo 62, 431, 439, 458, 475, 478, 506, 518, 522, 523, 526, 534
  'caesaro-papism' 476
  intellectual and theological respectability 528–9
  natural law 525
  objections to *De cive* 472–3
  Scriptures 422, 428
  jurisdiction and dominion 63
  works: *De imperio summarum potestatum circa sacra* 41; *De iure belli ac pacis* 521
Guarini, G. B. 202, 222, 255
Gundling, Nicolaus Hieronymus 533–4
Gunter, Edmund 87

Haberdashers' Company 350
Habermas, Jürgen 539
Habsburg territory 511
Habsburgs 71, 302, 305, 513
hagiography 237
Hague, The 272, 280, 461, 468, 473
  Royal Library 361
Hakewill, George 405
Hall, John 21, 329
Halle 530
Halle University 532–3
Halley, Antoine 262
Hamburg 265, 378, 389, 481, 491
Hamel, Jean du 502
Hammond, Henry 11, 103, 247
Hampshire 279
Hampton Court 298
Hardwick Hall 24, 25, 28, 80, 81, 310
  library 96, 114, 458
'Hardwick' manuscript 248
Hardy, Claude 93
Hargreaves, Mary 338, 339, 356, 361
Hariot, Thomas 10, 60, 87, 88
Harley family 109
harmony 456
Harrington, J. 327, 328
Harrison family 254

– 621 –

# INDEX

Hartlib, Samuel 228, 288, 329, 343, 380
Harvey, William 21, 98, 320, 328, 329
Hastings, Henry, Lord 243, 251
Hault Hucknall 25
heat 125, 126, 169
Heawood, E. 342
Hebraists 281, 419, 430
Hebrew 267, 269, 270, 271, 273, 281, 398, 406, 417
   de Cardonnel's proficiency in 262
   scholarship 286, 311, 404, 407, 414–15, 418–20
   TH's ignorance of 413
Hebrew Bible 383–431 *passim*
Hebron 408, 414
Heidegger, Johann Heinrich 389
Heidelberg University 521
Hell 487
Helmont, Jean Baptiste van 499
Helmontianism 283
Helmstedt University 474
Helvétius, Claude-Adrien 494
Hendricksz, Pieter 379
Henri IV, King of France 212
Henrico 64
Henrietta Maria, Queen consort of Charles I 20, 275
Henry VIII, King of England 454
Herbert, Edward 73, 94, 334, 470, 478, 480, 481
Herbert, Philip, 5th Earl of Pembroke 306–7
Herbert, Captain Richard 73
'Hercules gallicus' 224, 225
heresy/heretics 23, 46, 284, 413, 473, 483, 531, 532
   anti-Trinitarian 10
   Catholic 479
   denunciation of 477
Hermann, Wolfgang 420
Herodotus 113
Hersent, Daniel 264
Hertelius, Laurentius 461–2
Hertfordshire 252
Hesselin, Louis 216, 218
Hetet, John 354
Hicks, Mary 308
hierocracy 68
Hinde, Samuel 360
Hobbes, Edmund, alderman of Malmesbury (probable great-uncle of TH) 2–3

Hobbes, Edmund (relationship to TH unknown) 2–3
Hobbes, Francis, alderman of Malmesbury (uncle of TH) 2, 3, 92
Hobbes, Robert (relationship to TH unknown) 2–3
Hobbes, Thomas:
   birth 2
   Cavendish employment 5–9, 28, 53–4, 80, 91, 95, 96, 245, 320–1
   Continental tours 6, 9, 11, 76, 91, 96, 105, 106, 115, 458–9
   death 25, 310
   earliest surviving work 55
   early years 2–9, 53
   family background 1, 2–3
   friendships/acquaintances 22; *see also* Aubrey; du Bosc; Cavendish; Charleton; Davenant; Evelyn; Gassendi; Herbert (Edward); Hyde; de La Mothe le Vayer; Mersenne; Payne; Pierrepont; du Prat; Roberval; Rooke; Sorbière; Vaughan; Waller
   intellectual development 9–12, 16, 86, 93, 103–4, 156
   interests in science 73
   international relations theory 432–56
   Oxford years 1, 3–5, 11, 28, 53, 119, 325
   Paris years 11, 12, 16, 18, 19, 20–1, 28, 92, 94, 99, 101, 102–3, 106, 115, 134, 154, 156, 158, 165, 200, 289, 325, 411–13, 420, 458, 466, 497, 542
   pension granted by Charles II 24
   philosophical awakening/development 29, 156, 458
   political introduction 7–8, 57, 238
   reputation 24, 325
   sense of humour 25, 325
   'shaking palsy' 24
   works: *Anti-White* 17; *Cogitata physico-mathematica* 17; *Decameron physiologicum* 22–3; *De mirabilibus pecci* 258; *Dialogue of the Common Laws of England* 38, 59, 348, 441, 449, 452, 455–6, 461; *Dialogus physicus* 323, 459; *Examinatio et emendatio* 164; *La Duplication du cube* 165; *Le Corps politique* 465, 475, 518, 520, 533; *Mr Hobbes Considered* 23, 458; 'Objections' to Descartes 14, 176, 178, 218, 460;

– 622 –

## INDEX

*Of Libertie and Necessitie* 18, 329, 462, 464, 465, 469; *Opera philosophica omnia* 390, 459, 460, 461, 462, 469, 489; *Problemata physica* 22, 23, 459; *Seven Philosophical Problems* 187; *Six Lessons* 458; *see also under individual headings:* Behemoth; De cive; De corpore; De homine; Elements of Law; Leviathan
Hobbes, Thomas, vicar of Westport (father of TH) 2, 3, 93
Hobbes, William (cousin of TH) 2
Hoburg, Christian 376, 377, 378
Hoffman, Stanley 433
Hohendorf, Baron 489
Hohfeld, W. N. 444, 445
Holbein, Hans 204
Holbury 266, 300
Holland 56, 272, 273, 282, 371, 383, 419, 429, 491, 512
  Court of 460, 470
  second edition of *De cive* 324
  Synods of South and North 381
  *see also* Amsterdam; Antwerp; Dutch Republic; Elzevier; Hague; Rotterdam
Hollar, Wenceslaus 200, 236, 237, 238
holy orders 88
Holy Roman Empire 302, 512, 529
Holy Spirit 422, 424, 426
Hombergk, Johann Friedrich 471
Homer 24, 348, 386
honour 283
Hooke, Robert 318, 321, 322
Hooker, Richard 29, 66, 68, 69, 70
Horace 237, 250
*Horae subsecivae* 7, 53, 78–9
hostility 31
Hôtel de Rambouillet 275
Houghton, John 330
House of Burgesses 63
Houtuyn, Adriaen 466, 523–4
Huarte, J. 458
Huber, Ulric 534, 571
Huet, Pierre Daniel 271, 388, 483
Huguenots 17, 280, 305, 307, 499
  exiled 284
  exodus (1685) 260
  leading theologian 416
  maverick 392
  prominent 287
  scholars 419

Hull 371
human nature 30–1, 149, 151, 155, 177, 516, 541, 544
  first principles of 526
  malice, brutality, and violence ingrained in 504
  TH's famously low opinion of 455
Hungary 306
Hunter, Michael 317, 319–20
Huntington Library, San Marino, Calif. 342, 343
Hunton 253, 254
Huygens, Christiaan 81, 498
Huygens, Lodewijk 458
Hyde, Sir Edward (later 1st Earl of Clarendon) 10, 11, 19, 20, 75, 238–9, 241, 242–3, 244, 254, 276, 288, 298, 327
Hyde, Sir Lawrence 75
Hyde, Nicholas 75
hypocrisy 175, 227
hypotheses 167, 183, 185, 188, 189, 193, 195, 389
  causal 190
  physical 190
Hythe 252

Ibn Da'ud, (Abraham ben David) 402
Ibn Ezra, Abraham 392, 397, 402–4, 403, 410, 413
Ibn Hazm 401–2
ideas 17, 51, 105, 129, 472, 487, 490
  borrowed 530
  causal dependence of 14
  common stock of, re-worked 488
  pernicious 482
  plagiarized 164
ideology 532, 539, 540–1
Ignatius Loyola, St 214
ignorance 541, 542
Ilam 247
illusions 204, 206, 210, 216, 226–7
images 119, 120, 122, 123, 202, 214, 227
  distorted 203, 204, 208
  iconic 208
  mental 30
  multiple 222
  'normal' 204
  specimen 225
  symbolic 211, 223
  unified 213
  visual 200, 220, 224

– 623 –

# INDEX

imaginations 118, 122, 135, 476
   artistic 213
immortality of soul 47, 349, 536
immunity 291
imperatives 32
imperialism 433, 434
imprisonment 487
Independents 327, 429
Indians 61, 66, 75, 76
   conversion of 60
indifferentism 478, 479, 518
'indivisibles' 165
infant baptism 352
infinitesimals 165
intellect 29
intellectuals 10, 11, 496, 497, 498, 533
   avant-garde 283–4
   elite 545
   Jansenist 508
   Jewish 402
   mainly secular 545
   maverick Catholic 12
intentions 30, 149, 151, 152, 429, 438
   description in terms of 150
international law 439, 520, 522, 533
international relations 432–56
Interregnum 75, 328
intromission 167
introspection 147
intuitions 59
inventions 207–8, 210
Iraq 402
Ireland 263, 280, 308
irenicism 478, 539
irreligion 475, 477
Isidore of Seville, St 400
Islam 401, 402
Israel, Jonathan 485, 535, 536, 537
Israel, Menasseh ben 286
Istanbul 271
Italian language 6, 89, 458
Italy 160, 192, 204, 214, 218, 491
   international mail between France and 220
   *see also* Florence; Livorno; Milan; Naples; Pisa; Rome; Turin; Venice

Jacob, J. R. 326, 327
Jacob, Margaret 490
Jacquot, Jean 100
James I, King of England 56, 57, 59, 62, 72
   foreign policy criticized 71
Jamestown 61, 74
Jannon, Jean 268, 269
Jansenists 506, 508, 509
Jeane, Richard 3
Jena University 512, 513
Jeremiah 181
Jermyn, Henry 275, 276
Jerome, St 400, 415
Jersey 275, 287
Jerusalem 383, 384, 398
Jesseph, Douglas 165
Jesuits 211, 271, 291, 473, 520
   Flemish 409
   Scottish 417
   Spanish 409
   Walloon 410
   *see also* Aguilon; du Breuil; Kircher; du Lieu (Jean-Baptiste); Ménestrier; Noël; Petau; Rapin; Raynaud; Schott
Jesus Christ 307, 491, 501, 524
Jews, *see* Judaism
Job 293
John the Evangelist, St 215, 218
Johnson, Alderman 56
Johnson, Samson 521
Johnson, Thomas 433
Jones, Harold Whitmore 100
Jonson, Ben 11, 90–1, 92, 242, 243
Jordan 402, 403, 406, 414
Joshua 292, 405, 407–8, 409, 410, 426
Josiah 425
Journet, Noël 413
Judaism/Jews 47, 48, 383, 385, 393, 397, 399, 408, 428, 518
   arguments about authorship of Pentateuch 398
   Hebrew allegedly corrupted by 415, 417
   Hellenistic 418
   intellectuals 402
   Islamic writers against 401
   Karaite 401
   liberal 334
   polemics 401
   political history of 426
   religion 47
   scholars 415
   scriptures 486

teachers of 416
tradition 403
judgements 443, 525
    ethical 68
    hostile 511
    private 45, 515
Judges 408, 426
Jungius, Joachim 102, 497
Juniata College, Penn. 342
Jurieu, Pierre 479, 506
jurisprudence 524, 526
    political 527
    universal public 535
'just cause' 449
justice 148, 153, 513
justification 62, 514
    of colonization 61
    of natural law 517

Karl Ludwig, Elector Palatine 521
Karlstadt 407
Keith, George 379
Kennett, White 80
Kent County Committee 254
    see also Ashford; Maidstone; Hythe
'Kentish Petition' (1642) 252
Kepler, Johann 112, 120, 133, 500
Kettner, Friedrich Ernst 481
Kettwig, Mentet 527
Kiel University 480, 482, 520
Killigrew, Sir Robert 74
kinematic approach 120, 121, 165, 180
Kings 408, 426
Kingsbury, Susan 54
Kingsdown 256
kingship theme 237
Kircher, Athanasius 83, 84, 97, 101, 209, 210, 215, 220
Kirjath-Arba 408
knowledge 147, 150, 171, 293
    all-encompassing system of 6
    of causes 154, 155, 180, 184, 188, 206
    certain 155, 168, 175, 520
    derived either directly or indirectly from senses 176
    direct 488, 489
    empirical and practical 333
    ethical 69
    mathematical 168
    natural 330

nature of 166
new, geometry's ability to yield 153, 154
religious 69
scientific 17, 155, 166
sociology of 319
special 75
Koelman, Jacobus 485
Koerbagh, Adriaen 391, 465, 486, 487, 488
Köprülü, Ahmed (Grand Vizier) 306
Kopydanský, Jan Teofil 375
Koran 282, 401, 402
Kortholt, Christian 480
Kotter, Christoph 302
Kuhlmann, Quirinus 377, 378
Kunraht, Heinrich 378
*Kunstkammer* 207
Kuyper, Frans 367

La Barre de Beaumarchais, Antoine de 467, 468, 489
La Bruyère, Jean de 495
Lactantius, L. C. 295
La Flèche 210
La Forge, Louis de 489, 491, 499
La Mettrie, Julien Offray de 494
La Mothe le Vayer, François de 221, 395, 493, 497, 540, 541, 543
Lamy, Guillaume 488
language:
    false entities generated by 6
    normative 32
    universal 457
La Noue, François de 217, 218
Lantin, Jean-Baptiste 395, 542, 543
Lapeyre, Jacques d'Auzoles de 212
La Peyrère, I. 387, 388, 389–90, 392–7, 410, 411, 413, 414, 429, 430, 478, 496
Lapide, Cornelius à 409–11, 413, 422, 428, 431
Lardier, Fr 210
La Rochefoucauld, François de 495, 502
Latimer, Robert 3–4
Latimers (Bucks) 289
Latin 83, 89, 131, 134, 153, 167, 246, 249, 371, 374, 421, 457, 462, 464, 470
    Aristotle's *Rhetoric* 9
    Bacon's *Essayes* 6
    de Cardonnel's proficiency in 262
    Comenius's educational works 375
    *De cive* 149, 236, 237, 459, 460, 463

# INDEX

Latin (*cont.*)
  *De corpore* 17, 460
  *De homine* 460
  geometrical problems in 93
  geometry and 4
  Koran 402
  *Leviathan* 21, 22, 23, 25, 41, 47, 117, 339, 365, 390, 447–8, 460, 466, 468–9, 477, 493, 533
  Niceron's *La Perspective curieuse* 172, 217
  Payne Fisher's epic 282
  poems 262, 259–60, 273, 281, 289, 298, 299
  proverbs 268, 270
  taught to TH 3
Latin Optical MS 13, 14, 109, 183–4, 320
Latin *Vitae* 53
Latitudinarianism 327, 330, 331, 332, 333, 334
Laud, William, Archbishop of Canterbury 66
Laudians 10
Lausanne 459
laws 152, 223, 348, 425, 445, 541, 515
  civil 224
  customary 540
  dietary and ceremonial 47–8
  forbidding beliefs 50
  immutable 47
  natural 227, 501
  positive 531
  rational 52
laws of nature 29, 32, 435–6, 437–9, 447, 452, 455, 500, 520, 522, 534
  unjustified breach of 445
Lawson, George 290
Leak (Master of the Company of Stationers) 345
Lebanon 269, 419
Le Clerc, Jean 430, 539
*Le Conservateur* (journal) 468
Lecoq, Marguerite 261
Leers, Reinier 461
Lefèvre, Nicaise 301
legal claims 279
legal positivism 68
Leibniz, Gottfried Wilhelm 25, 305, 461–2, 462, 471, 513, 519, 521, 528–30
Leiden 366, 367, 368, 464, 465
Leiden University 41, 42, 43, 45, 270, 389, 486, 516

Leijenhorst, Cees 114, 129
Leipzig 379, 461, 530, 533
Leipzig University 74, 388, 471, 479, 481, 483
leisure 75–6
Lemoine, Étienne 281
lenses 204, 214, 222
  polygonal 213, 215
  refracting 212
Leo II, Byzantine Emperor 401
Le Pailleur, Jacques 161
lèse-majesté 271
L'Estrange, Sir Roger 350–1, 352, 353
Letters Patents 299
*Leviathan* (TH) 4, 15, 44, 57, 99, 179, 238–9, 241, 258, 389, 395, 450–1, 457, 464, 471, 483, 485–6, 489, 499, 507, 516, 532, 536, 543, 544
  added to index of prohibited books 470
  attempts to reprint 24
  biblical criticism 40, 397, 488, 490
  blindness from birth 178
  de Cardonnel and 259, 270, 290, 293–4, 296, 297, 307
  colonies 76, 442
  complimentary copies to Bathurst 325
  corporate entity 38
  criticism of the universities 326
  'De tribus impostoribus' treatise and 491
  definition of 'science' 155
  diagram of the sciences 148
  'diseases' of a commonwealth 441
  Dutch 41, 47, 380, 381, 391, 465, 466, 476–7, 522
  first person in Germany to take notice of 518
  French 466, 467, 468
  German translation 469
  good of the Sovereign and People 513
  interpersonal state of nature as state of war 435
  introduction to 150, 151
  Latin 21, 22, 23, 25, 41, 47, 117, 339, 365, 390, 447–8, 460, 466, 468–9, 477, 493, 533
  laws and right 32–3
  Laws of Nature 438–9
  'nasty, brutish, and short' passage 452
  nature and reliability of Scriptures 427
  nature of error 542
  'Nosce Teipsum' maxim 147

– 626 –

office of sovereign 447–8
opening chapter, 'Thoughts of men' 176
origins of religion in human psychology 492
passions 31
points of doctrine 475
printing/publishing of 2, 19, 28
'prophets' and 'visions' 181
psychological origins of religion 491
rational religion 333
refutation of 327
scathing attack on superstition and clerical power 494
second edition 335–82
self-preservation 449
sovereignty 20
special large-paper copies 257
superiority over all other forms of government 514
theological arguments 21–2
theological critiques of 326
title page 200–33, 259, 443
treatise attacking religious ideas of 476
vacuums 191
'vain-glory' 175
Levita, Elias 415, 416
Levite priests 48
Leviticus 422
libellous remarks 23
liberation 544
*libertinage érudit* 502, 503, 504
'Libertines' 476
liberty 51, 461, 462, 530
licences 350
Licensing Act (1662) 348, 358
licensing process 466
Lieu, Charles du 219–20, 221
Lieu, Jean-Baptiste du 214, 220–1
light 112, 113, 116, 120, 126, 137
  cause of 169
  derivative 125
  dynamic conception of the action of 121
  mediumistic theory of 117, 122
  movement of 111
  nature and production of 117
  'primitive' 125
  projection of patterns of 215
  propagation of 132, 133
  reflection of 181

sound and 123
theory of 115, 117, 122, 133, 181
transmission of 117, 119, 132, 181, 192–3, 195
underlying nature of 121
Lincoln, Richard Neale, Bishop of 70
linen-makers 280
lines 154, 159, 166
Lipsius, J. 290, 540
Lisbon 279
literary piracy 43
litigation 279
'Little Chapel of the Savoy' 287
Littleton 88
liturgy 67, 287
Livorno 279
Livy 389, 420, 423, 425
locality 191
Locke, John 1, 153, 495, 447, 455, 468, 481, 495, 534
Lockeanism 537
Lockey, Thomas 244, 248, 249, 324, 325
logic 17, 18, 129, 228
  metaphors used to conceal deficiencies of 227
  primary axioms of 176
  scholastic 5
  writings on 12
London 19, 59, 109, 139, 242, 244, 254, 255, 339, 381, 458, 459–60, 512
  aborted printing of *Leviathan* 338
  Bishop of 287, 348, 352–3, 354
  Blackheath 256
  Bloomsbury Book Auctions 342, 343
  de Cardonnel in 277, 278, 288, 289, 298, 306
  City of 297
  Covent Garden 243, 281–2, 283
  East Greenwich 60
  Falkland's circle 11
  Fleet Street 253
  French Protestant community/Church 265, 284, 286
  Gray's Inn 252
  Guildhall Library 342
  Laurence Pountney Lane 265, 279
  parliamentary stronghold in Civil War 267
  Payne's imprisonment 97
  Port Book 265
  printers 372, 519, 529

# INDEX

London (*cont.*)
  St Lawrence Pountney 285–6
  TH settles in 21, 24, 328
  Threadneedle Street 284, 285, 286–7
  Tower of 243
  Westminster 297, 302; Abbey 302; School 309
  Whitehall 352
  *see also* Royal Society
Long Parliament (1640–60) 16, 252
Longomontanus, Christian Severinus 160
Longueville, Anne-Geneviève de Bourbon, duchesse de 274–5
Longueville, Henri II, duc de 274–5
Lords, House of 349, 352
  Library 342, 343
Lords Commissioners of the Treasury 299
Löscher, Valentin Ernst 481, 531
lotteries 56
Louis XII, King of France 208
Louis XIII, King of France 212, 213, 217, 275
Louis XIV, King of France 209, 214, 216, 222, 275, 302–3, 305, 306, 307
  generosity towards writers 304
Louvain University 409, 415
love 48, 51
Lovelace, Richard 242, 252–3, 256–7
loyalty 530
Lübeck 279
Lucas, Henry 255
Lucas, Jean Maximilien 492
Lucchi, Bonaventura 484
Lucian 224
Lucretius 113, 114
Lucy, W. 290
luminous body 120, 123, 127–8
lunar influence 126
Luneschlos, Johannes 84, 98, 101
Luther, Martin 67, 374
Lutheranism/Lutherans 305, 374, 375, 376, 478, 480, 483
  churches 288
  hard-line 389
  jurists 520
  older, dogmatic 530
  orthodox 479, 531
  pastors 372, 373, 379
  philosophers 475
  pious 471

preachers 481, 533
scholars 474, 482
Lyon 211, 214, 507
  Jesuit College 219
  'Maître des Courriers' 220
Lyser, Johannes 378, 379

Macdonald, Hugh 338, 339, 356, 361
Machiavelli, Niccolò 43, 48, 432, 433, 440–1, 458, 470, 504, 540
Machon, Louis 504
Macpherson, C. B. 339
Madrid 255
magic 210, 211, 212
magnetism 113, 114–15, 126, 131, 189, 215
Magni, Valerian 193
magnification (microscopy) 183
Maidstone 251, 252, 253
Maignan, Emmanuel 209, 210–11, 215
Maimonides, Moses 47
Malachi 399
Malaga 263
Malebranche, Nicolas 496, 498–9
Malmesbury 2, 3, 92
Malthe, François de 90
Marburg 471
Marchand, Prosper 461, 468, 489
Marche, Jean de la 285
Mariotte, Edmé 166
Marlborough, John Churchill, 1st Duke of 308
Maronites 269, 419
Marseille 224, 279
Marsilian argument 40
Marston Moor, battle of (1644) 282
Martel, Thomas de 17, 24, 323, 458, 497
martial law 63, 64
Mary Magdalene, St 215
Masius, Andreas 407–9, 410, 413, 414, 431
Mason, Robert 53–4, 72
Masoretic Bible 399, 414, 415, 417, 418
materialism 190, 191, 482, 490
'materialisti' 484
mathematical instruments 207, 220
mathematical problems 85, 153
mathematics 87, 88, 95, 100, 101, 158–9, 160, 186, 209, 211
  applied 166
  'mixed' 166, 174
  Niceron's intensive studies of 212

– 628 –

# INDEX

polemical exchanges on subjects 22
'resolution' and 'composition' in 96
science of miracles 210
superior certainty of 180
works on 24
*see also* algebra; arithmetic; geometry; trigonometry
matter 126, 152, 195, 196
  'form' and 151, 155
  motion and 154, 185, 187, 189
  'subtle' 182, 194, 195, 196
Matthew, St 420
Mauritius, Erich 520
Mayerne, *see* Turquet de Mayerne
Mayer, Johann Friedrich 389
Mayne, Jasper 95
Mazarin, Cardinal Jules 217, 218, 276, 513
meaning(s) 151, 155, 398, 467
  definitional 17
  symbolic 211
Mearne, Samuel 345, 346, 350, 351, 352–3
mechanics 105, 115, 166
mechanistic theories 52, 111, 126, 152, 181, 183, 187
Medea legend 214, 225
Medici, Cardinal Carlo de' 208
Medici, Cosimo II de' 208
Medici, Ferdinando II de', Grand Duke of Tuscany 208, 216
medicine 301
mediumistic theory 115, 119, 121, 123, 124, 126, 132, 134, 193, 195
memory 30, 226
Ménage, Giles 274
Ménestrier, Claude 211
Mennonites 376
merchants 263, 264–5, 277, 279, 287
  Protestant families 261
mercury 192, 195, 196
Merlat, Élie 504–6, 509
Mersenne, Marin 12, 14, 16–17, 123, 132, 134, 209, 210, 211, 217, 220, 322, 323, 324, 394, 395, 413, 419–20, 458, 459, 460, 472, 473, 499, 538
  death of 20, 24, 162, 172
  Roberval and 156, 158, 159, 162, 163, 166, 167–74, 176, 177, 178, 180, 181, 183, 184, 185–6, 187, 192, 193
  works: *Cogitata physico-mathematica* 159, 163, *Harmonicorum libri* 131;

*Hydraulica* 154; 'La Catoptrique' 168–74; *La Verité des sciences* 186; (ed.), 'Objections' to Descartes's *Meditations* 218, 497
Meslier, Jean 384–5, 427, 489
metals 89
metaphors 226, 227
  literary 227
metaphysics 6, 12–13, 17, 50–1, 52, 119, 125, 158, 168, 190, 193, 326, 459, 499, 500, 517, 529, 532
  attack on 30
  Cartesian 14, 196
  false 195
  fundamental problems in 29
  scholastic 29, 112, 133, 187, 196
  teleological 455
  TH's work on 14
Metz 413
Meurs, Jacob van 362, 365, 374, 377
Meyer, Lodowijk 46
Micanzio, Fulgenzio 8, 53, 66, 71, 73, 77, 80, 458
microscopes 183, 320
Middelburg 367
Milan 207
Mill, J. S. 146, 150
Miller, Perry 65
mind 210, 528
  delusions 211
  deprived of all senses 177
  development of 51
Minims 209
  convents 211, 213, 215, 217, 218, 219, 221, 322, 413, 420
  friars 203, 210, 211, 322, 419
  General of 218
Mintz, Samuel 457
miracles 47, 385, 536
  naturalistic rejection/treatment of 386, 428
  undermining faith in 477–8
mirrors 204, 216
misprints 363–4
misunderstanding 542
Mohammed (Prophet) 491
molecules 150
monarchy 44, 455, 526
  absolute 16, 490, 504, 511
  argument against 515

# INDEX

monarchy (*cont.*)
   covert 48
   defence of 327
   superiority over all other forms of government 514
monastic scientists 210
Moniglia, Tommaso Vincenzio 484
Monmouth, James, Duke of 308
monopolies 62
Montaigne, Michel Eyquem de 250, 458, 540
Montauban 262
Montmor, Henri Louis Habert de 497, 329
Montpellier 220
Moore, John 312
moral philosophy 180, 437, 473, 517, 529
moralism 237, 331
morality 436, 445, 533, 500, 501
   first principles of 525
   no objective principles of 433
   rules of 437
   'science' of 516
   TH a dangerous subverter of 495
   TH's derivation of 444
   true 509
   violations of 437
Moranus, G. 289, 498
Moravian Church 305
More, Henry 1, 330
Morgenthau, Hans 433, 442
Moriah, Mount 403
Morin, Étienne 281
Morin, Jean 418–19, 420
Morley, George, Bishop of Winchester 10, 11, 92, 97, 98, 103, 127, 287–8, 325
Morse, Justinian 310
'mortalism' 349
Moscow 377
Moses 22, 48, 383–431 *passim*, 483, 486, 491
motion 13, 14, 108, 110, 118, 119, 120, 122, 130, 136, 147, 155
   analysis by computation of 165
   beginnings of 30
   brain 116
   causative 184
   even 149
   generative 115
   image-creating 123
   imperceptible 124
   internal 123, 182
   local 111, 117, 121, 126, 134

   matter in 115, 154, 185, 187, 189
   similar 152
   supposed 184, 189
   TH's theory of 497
   tiny jiggling 123
   uneven 149
   variety of 124
motivation 31, 48
Moulin, Peter du 290, 360
Mühlpfort, Johannes Justinus 475
Müller, Johann Joachim 491
Münster 275
Muslim polemicists 402
mutual benefit 50
mutual respect 283
Muys, Siméon de 420
Mydorge, Claude 12, 85, 95, 122, 132
Mylon, Claude 164

names 152, 167
Naomi 406
Naples 76
national boundaries 434, 455
*National Union Catalog* 356
Nationalism 433
natural law 58, 59, 60, 61, 69, 227, 436, 439, 447, 495, 501, 522, 527, 528, 529, 533
   brief history of 525
   Ciceronian and Thomist traditions 35
   could not be derived from universal human practice 519
   derivation of 455, 516
   development of 514
   justification of 517
   objective 520
   obligation 450
   reducing to a new, unified system 518
   state-based 448
   theory 517, 521, 523
   theory of sovereignty 68
   traditional, denial of 475
natural philosophy 148, 174, 182, 497, 499, 500
'natural slaves' 441
'naturalia' 207, 208
naturalism 6, 482
   extreme 477
nature 52, 497
   mechanical conception of 110
   right of 520
   *see also* laws of nature; state of nature

– 630 –

# INDEX

Naudé, Gabriel 215, 217, 290, 329, 393, 493, 504, 540
necessary consent 20
necessity 31, 449, 461, 513, 530
   simple 2
Nehemiah 383, 398, 399, 421
Neill, E. D. 63, 73
neo-Stoicism 250, 540
nervous system 147
Netherlands 466, 486, 514
   *see also* Holland
Nevers 217
New England 62
New Testament 393, 394, 414
   'falsity' of the main facts contained in 490
   German 379
New York Public Library, Berg Collection 341
Newcastle, William Cavendish, Earl of (later Marquess and Duke) 10, 11, 12, 15, 18, 27, 29, 63, 77, 81, 85, 91, 90–2, 95, 98, 105, 115, 117, 123, 240, 245, 248, 249, 276, 282, 287, 320, 371
   active scientific interests 89
   English Optical Manuscript dedicated to 116
   Payne appointed chaplain to 88
   TH's 'mediumistic' letter to 121–2
Newfoundland 263
Niceron, Jean (uncle of below) 211
Niceron, Jean-François 172, 192, 203, 206, 207, 209, 211–19, 221, 222, 225, 228
Nicholas, Sir Edward 276, 278, 351
Nicole, Pierre 508–10, 517
Nigrin, Christian Vladislav 306, 307
Nîmes 262
nobility 117, 261
Noël, Étienne 192
Noenart, Cornelis 367
nominalism 152
non-conformity 287
Normandy 263, 272, 275
   customary law 262
   *see also* Caen; Rouen
norms 531
North West Passage 74
Northumberland, Henry Percy, 9th Earl of 10
Norton (Stationers' Company officer) 345
Norway 263

Nottinghamshire 244
   *see also* Welbeck
Numbers 410, 422
Nuremberg 533

obedience 44, 49
   passionate 228
   political 47
   power to instil 47
   protection and 238
   rational 228
   to sovereignty 525
objects 14, 125, 138, 149
   actions of 114
   artificial 151
   desired 30
   distant 129
   external 130
   geometric 152
   intentional 155
   mental 29
   moving 196
   multiple 222
   natural 153
   physical, plurality of 173
   similar 152
   'strength of action' of 120, 121
   theory of species emanating from 113
obligations 15, 20, 513
   contractual 46
   divine 493
   innate 475
   natural-law 450
   prudential and consequentialist nature of 531
   religious 238
   rights and 155
observances 66
observation 182
occultism 210
'officium' 149
Oklahoma University 344
Old Testament 47, 213, 222, 383, 476
   'falsity' of main facts in 490
   *see also* Pentateuch, Torah
Oldenburg, Henry 329, 519, 529
ontology 115, 147, 153
   'modern' 110
   scholastic 190, 191
Opachankano (American Indian chief) 61

opinion(s) 175, 180, 181, 228, 543, 544
    'science' and 178, 179
optical devices 203, 204, 207, 209–10, 211, 225
    elaborate 211
optics 9–14 *passim*, 16–17, 18, 92, 94, 112, 113, 114, 127, 166, 167, 172, 206, 211, 217, 218, 321, 323, 459
    intensive work on 212, 320
    mainstream tradition 121
    researchers 88
Oratorians 387, 418
oriental matters:
    linguistics 269–70
    manuscripts 273
    studies 281
original sin 393
Ormonde, Elizabeth Butler, Duchess of 287
Ormonde, James Butler, Earl of (later 1st Duke) 276, 287
Osiander, Andreas 168
Osmaston 251
Ossory, Elizabeth Butler, Countess of 287
Ossory, Thomas Butler, Earl of 298
Ottoman Empire 221, 302
    campaign headquarters of army in Hungary 306
    future victory of French arms over 304
    sultans 213, 216, 217
Oudart, Nicolas 278
Oughtred, William 87, 88, 96, 127, 325
Owen, John 429
Oxford (city) 88, 97, 103, 253
*Oxford English Dictionary* 181, 457
Oxford University 19, 21, 22, 23, 25, 74, 92, 93, 96, 242, 248, 249, 287, 326–7
    Brasenose College 246, 247
    Broadgates Hall 88
    Christ Church 86, 87, 95, 97, 98, 244, 309
    expulsion of Royalist Fellows 246
    *Leviathan* publicly burnt by order of Convocation (1683) 356
    Magdalen College 309
    Magdalen Hall 4, 5
    mathematicians 329
    Merton College 309, 310
    Pembroke College 88, 97
    politics of scientists defined 327
    TH at 1, 3–5, 11, 28, 53, 119, 325
    *see also* Bodleian Library

Pacchi, Arrigo 100, 101
'pacificity' 523
Padua, University of 74, 484
paganism 60, 385, 492
Palatinate 71, 72
pamphlets 45
Papacy 453, 454, 542
Papillon, Thomas 287
Papists 67
Pappus of Alexandria 96
parabola 154, 163, 164
Paracelsus 74, 90
parallelograms 159, 226
Pareus, David 421–2
Paris 24, 75, 122, 160, 162, 163, 194, 217, 218–19, 271, 275–9 *passim*, 286, 287, 330, 393, 394, 395, 459, 463, 465, 483, 501, 503
    Académie des Inscriptions et Belles-Lettres 385
    Anglicans 288
    Archbishop of 496
    Bibliothèque Nationale 307
    Bibliothèque Sainte-Geneviève 161
    clergy 466
    Fontainebleau 306
    Jardin royal des plantes 301, 320
    Louvre 18
    Maison de Saint-Victor 467
    Minim convent, Place Royale 211, 213, 215, 322, 413
    most famous literary salon in 274
    Parlement de 496
    policing of 274
    printing-house of Estiennes 268
    St Germain 18, 306
    Versailles 209
    *see also* Hobbes, Thomas (Paris years)
Paris Polyglot Bible 269, 418, 419
Parker, Samuel 39, 477, 533, 534
Parkinson's disease 24
parliament 58, 59–60
    constitutional role of 57
    printed works offensive to 350
Parliamentarians 57, 103, 277
    moderate 286
particles 113, 147, 181
Parvis, Henry 76
Pascal, Blaise 192
Pasch, Georg 480

– 632 –

# INDEX

passions 31, 48, 51, 98, 135, 179, 515, 541, 542
  common 49
  human beings driven by 544
  men governed by 43
  private 44
  satisfaction of 510
  self-regarding 514
Patrizzi, Francesco 133
patronage 1–2, 15, 24, 27, 54, 87, 208, 220, 245, 274, 277, 298, 307, 320, 529
  aristocratic 285
  posthumous 69
  royal 297, 299
Pattison, Mark 331
Paulmier de Grentemesnil, Jean 281
Paul, St 394
Payne, Robert 10, 11, 12, 19, 81–145, 238, 239, 241–2, 244, 248–9, 324, 325, 343, 466
Payne, Robert (father of above) 86, 92
peace 31, 45, 330, 440, 446, 500, 501, 502
  actions designed to bring about 32
  conduciveness to 139
  devotion to 332
  disadvantaged 439
  disturbance of 65
  international 448
  laws of war and 520
  reason dictating means to 523
Peak District 245
Pecham, John 94, 112
Pelagianism 477
Pell, John 18, 97, 98, 102, 109, 157, 160–1, 240, 460
Pembroke, Philip Herbert, 4th Earl of 285
Pennington, Richard 236
Pentateuch 22, 383–431, 483
  defending the entire Mosaicity of 496
  *see also* Torah
Pepys, Samuel 341, 344
perception 13, 153
  sense 29, 30, 124, 130, 152
Percy, Algernon 87
Pererius, Benedictus 409, 410, 411, 413
perfection 29, 183, 525
Pericles 8
Perkins, William 65
Pernambuco 279
persecution 515
'person' theory 151, 223

perspective 205, 226, 228
  'curious' 212
Pescod, Katherine 266, 268, 279
Pescod, Mary 279
Pescod, Nicholas 263–4, 266, 267, 300, 308
Petau, Denis 419
Peter, St 213
Peter the Venerable 402
Petition of Right (1628) 28
Petty, William 194–5, 320, 325
phantasma 107, 118, 130, 138
phenomena 22, 186, 189
  causes of 153, 188
  chance 122
  extraordinary 207, 208
  observed 179
  optical 221
  visual, mysterious 211
Philipot, Thomas 282, 283
philology 538
philosophy 1, 6, 95, 114, 171, 173, 181, 188, 530
  civil 148, 180
  'corpuscularian' 189
  dangerous rationalistic tendencies in 478
  description of 154
  experimental 333
  fundamental problems of 516
  scholastic 14, 29, 318
  single definition of 179
  study of 484
  theology and 47
  *see also* moral philosophy; natural philosophy; political philosophy
physical features 83, 84
physical parts 149, 151
physicalism 6
physics 11, 14, 16–17, 30, 95, 146, 149, 150, 152, 155, 166, 179, 184, 185, 188, 323, 324, 459, 499
  basic principles of 13
  experimental 192
  explanatory theories in 187, 190
  fundamental problems in 29
  major work on 320
  mechanistic 13, 15, 104, 151
  Mersenne circle's preoccupation with 154
  'modern' 110
  physiology must be rooted in 147
  plenist 192, 498
  politics and 148

physics (*cont.*)
  scholastic  29, 119, 193
  suppositional basis of  182
  transmission through a medium  83
  true principles of  180–1
physiology  147
Pierrepont, Henry, Marquis of Dorchester  284
Pietism  531
Pilgrim Fathers  70
Pisa University  484
plagiarism  14, 163, 164, 215
Platonists  68
pleasure  206, 510
plenism  182, 191, 192, 498
  materialist  190
Pliny the Elder  296
plurality  180
Plutarch  423
Plymouth Company  62
Pocock, J. G. A.  327
poetry/poets  11, 222, 243, 293
  complimentary  279
  eulogistic  245
  French, elegant  281
  prefatory  245, 280, 282
  secular  304
  travelogue  258
Poiret, Pierre  482
polemics  28, 387, 477, 479, 506
  against Torah  402
  anti-Hobbesian  476
  anti-Protestant  416
  Jewish or intra-Jewish  401
  post-Tridentine Catholic  415
  Protestant  67
Polish books  375
political philosophy  43, 135, 275, 514, 517, 529
  Cartesian  500
  Catholic absolutist  507
  history of republicanism in  52
  Spinoza's  516
  TH's  9–10, 15, 200, 432; mature, obsession of  543; one of the central paradoxes of  543
politics  14, 57, 443, 481, 501, 504, 507, 519, 536
  attitudes to  334
  church  22, 290

foreign  304
general ban imposed on publication of works  348
harmful practices  20
importance of deception and self-interest in  7
inter-confessional  480
practice of  226
reducing to a new, unified system  518
science of  146–54, 226, 228, 516
subject-matter of  525–6
system of justification for  540
Pollard, A. F.  63
Polybius  389
polygamy  379
Pomponazzi, Pietro  386, 481
Poniatowska, Kristina  302
Pope, Walter  321, 329
popes  222, 419, 453–4, 496, 532
  *see also* Urban VIII
Popkin, Richard  395
Porphyry  400–1
Port, C.  247
Port, I.  247
Port, Robert  247
Portsmouth  298
positivist tradition  440
Potemkin, G. A.  463
Potier, Bernard, marquis de Blérancourt  274
power  443, 455
  absolute  505
  active  111, 112
  clerical  489
  coercive  515
  definition of  32
  desire for  442
  different meanings of the word  60
  ecclesiastical  200, 505, 536
  gross abuse of  527
  impairment of  51
  individual  44
  instruments for the promotion of  532
  judicial  515
  legislative  515
  misuse of  515
  monarchic  58, 513
  natural  50, 516
  papal threat to  454

# INDEX

political 48, 505, 539, 544
princely 473
relatively equal 450
right and 46
royal 238
sovereign 14, 44, 45, 50, 76, 228, 503, 505, 515, 524, 544
state 45–6, 433, 536
temporal 67, 200
transfer of 49
urge to acquire more and more 442
'will' to 442
Prades, Jean-Martin de 495–6, 506
Prague 207
Prat, Abraham du 24, 162, 330, 497, 501
Prat, François du 467
Prayer Book 4
precedents 58
prejudices 532, 534
premises 171
Presbyterianism/Presbyterians 4, 22, 326, 327, 380
ministers/pastors 65, 288
see also Calvinism
Prestwich, Edmund 245, 246–7, 250
Prideaux, Humphrey 310
Prideaux, John 86
printing and publishing 1, 268–70, 336–82
private property 58
privilege 451
Privy Chamber 301–2
Privy Council 56, 277
Proeleus, Immanuel 528
prognosis 153
properties 148, 169, 170, 176, 177, 182
emergent 150
known 154
physical 29
prophecies 47, 385, 417, 536
naturalistic treatment of 386, 428
Prophets 181, 213, 222, 396, 422
revelations of 302
propositions 5, 96, 130, 165, 174, 177
certain 155
functioning of 18
true 152, 178–9
uncertain 155
universal 154
prosecution 349
prosperity 45, 261, 448

Protestantism/Protestants 10, 67, 304, 318, 421, 422, 473
academies/academic world 262, 269, 474
biblical scholarship 271
Catholics and 333
countries banned some of TH's works 470
credal and ceremonial differences between churches 376
doctrinal warfare 414
ecumenism 288, 290
elevation of Hebrew text 415
foreign policy 71
free-thinkers 498
French 261, 263–4, 269, 271, 277, 283, 284–5, 287, 288, 307, 308
German 471
hard-line 418, 419
mainstream theology 290
moral theology 502
old theology/theory 332, 423
orthodox 240, 387
polemics 67
scholars 410, 419
theological attacks on TH from 483
theory of authority of Bible 420
writers 417, 418, 479, 483
see also Calvinism; Lutheranism
proverbs 268, 270
Prujean, Francis 283, 312, 313
Prussia 530
psychology 11, 15, 50, 94, 135, 139, 146, 324, 443
cognition and desire 110
deterministic 104, 136, 494
individual 442
materialistic 494
mechanistic 45, 515
moral, 'egoistic' 31
must be rooted in physiology 147
origins of religion in 492
popular 492, 544
religion a powerful force in 48
scholastic 30
social sciences must be rooted in 147
urge for power 433
writings on 12
Ptolemy 167
Public Record Office 338
Pucci, F. 480

– 635 –

# INDEX

Puccianism 479
Pufendorf, Samuel, Freiherr von 439, 466, 475, 521–8 *passim*, 530, 531, 534
punishment 487
  corporal 3
  eternal 349
  fear of 531
  justified 531
  must be justified by the principle of utility 507
  reward and 151, 542
  temporal 68
  utilitarian theory of 518
Purchas, Samuel 60–1, 75
Puritanism 4, 63, 64, 66
  exaltation of practical activity 333
Puy-de-Dôme 192
Pym, John 16, 27, 71
Pyrrhonism 176, 185, 186, 332

Quakers 379, 429, 476, 487
qualities 13, 111, 112, 125, 151
  hypostatized 14
  inherent 126
  primary 29
  secondary, subjectivity of 29
  sensible, subjectivity of 89, 116, 117, 119, 124, 126
  subjectively experienced 124
  visible 126
'quiddities' 5

Rabbanites 401
rabbinical writings 286
Rachelius, Samuel 520
radicalism/radicals 496, 535, 536
Rainsford, Sir Henry 75
Raleigh, Walter 65, 75
Ramsey, William 77
Ramus, Petrus 500
Rand, William 380
Rango, Conrad 479
Rapin, René 499
rarefaction 195, 196
ratiocination 30, 129
rational beings 52
'rational foresight' 49
rationalism 482, 455, 530
rationality 52, 510, 516
Rawson, Ralph 246–7, 248–9

Raylor, Timothy 82, 91, 105, 127, 131
Raynaud, Théophile 210, 220
rays 120, 167
Realism/Realists 432, 455, 456
reality 14, 150, 182
  objective 124
  ultimate 29
reason 15, 30, 49, 59, 438, 444
  above revelation 482
  conformity with 487
  conscious act of 50
  dictating means to peace 523
  ends directly justified by 544
  'formal' 517
  laws of 29
  prevalence of 48
  pure 516, 528
  reason simply the servant of 52
  Spinoza's theory of 51
reasoning 9, 58, 61, 130, 133, 185, 510
  correct 154
  faulty 322
  instrumental 15
rebellion 455
Rechenberg, Adam 471, 479–80, 483
recusants 68, 71
Redinger, Johann Jakob 306
Redmayne, John 338, 345–8 *passim*, 350, 351, 353–6 *passim*, 354, 355, 356, 360, 362, 363, 364, 369, 370, 372, 380
Reeve, Richard 321
reflection 120, 121, 170, 172, 187
  angle of 169
  explanations of 181
Reformation/Reformers 414, 424
Reformed Church 71, 380, 467
  jurisdictional power 517
refraction 10, 89, 115, 170, 187
  correct dynamic explanation of sine-law of 320
  kinematic approach to 120, 121
regicide 57
Regis, Pierre-Sylvain 501–2, 509
Regius, Henricus 42, 43, 499
Reik, Miriam 53
Reiser, Anton 479
Reisner, Friedrich 114
religion 61, 68, 293, 481, 492
  advancement of 65
  bogus doctrines 454

confessional 379
corruption of doctrine 67
dangerous rationalistic tendencies in 478
epistemological and psychological account
    of origins of 493
essential nature of 505
established, implications for 490
externals 511, 524
fanaticism 332
low-church 64
manipulation of for political purposes
    504
moralizing version of 332
natural 478
orders 209; *see also* Benedictines; Jesuits;
    Minims
organized 20, 487
pagan 492
persecution 379
psychological origins of 491
rational 10, 331, 333, 334
reasonableness of 331
respect 541
revealed 60
revealed, truth of 535
rights over 47
scientists 210
state and 46, 515
Tacitean view of 41–2
TH's approach to 479, 493, 525
toleration of 45, 518
use as an instrument of political power 48
*see also* Catholicism; Protestantism
Remonstrants 376, 417, 430, 476
reparations 452
representation 223, 226–7
    theatrical 227
republicanism 52, 514
repulsion 138
resemblance 150–1, 152
resistance 58
resolutive-compositive method 153
Restoration 24, 39, 331
    libertinism of the court 23
'Returns of Strangers' (1639) 265
revelation 46, 47, 48, 385, 387, 422, 423, 429,
    430, 480, 483, 487, 493, 515
    reason above 482
    undermining faith in 478
reward and punishment 151, 542

Ribera de Madrigal, Alfonso Tostado, Bishop
    of Avila, *see* Tostatus
Rich, Robert, Earl of Warwick 56–7
Rich, Sir Nathanael 55, 70, 71
Richelieu, Armand J. D., Cardinal, duc de
    208, 209, 274, 393, 504, 513
Rieuwertsz, Jan 373, 379
'right and power' 46
righteousness 31
rights 31, 45, 148, 152, 357, 372, 510, 526
    'claim' 444, 445
    conflict of 44
    encroached 350
    fishing 60
    freedom 445, 446
    ideal political entity of 149
    monarchical sovereigns 511
    moral 446, 455, 456
    mutual 444
    natural 49, 50, 58, 60, 445, 455, 528
    obligations and 155
    over religion 47
    private property 15
    property 443
    proprietary, over the sea 62
    sovereign 453, 507, 543
    transfer of 436, 443, 444
    universal 445, 446
rites 66
Rivet, André 272, 394, 416, 422, 473
Robertson, George Croom 53, 457
Roberval, Gilles Personne de 17, 93, 154,
    156–99, 217, 322
Robinson, John 70
Rochester University, NY 341
Rocques, A. 264
Rocques, Peter 264
Rogow, Arnold 339
Roman law 452, 523, 529
Romans (book) 393
Rome 7, 11, 76, 78, 209, 216, 220, 269, 441
    Holy Office 470
    Jesuit college 214
    Minim convent, S. Trinità dei Monti 215
Rooke, Lawrence 325
Roper (Warden, Stationers' Company) 345
Rosicrucianism 210
Ross, Alexander 264, 281–2, 283, 284, 290,
    296
Rostock 481

# INDEX

Rotrou, Jean de 274
Rotterdam 461, 462, 469
Rouen 273, 276, 277, 278, 279, 289, 464
   Parlement 268
roulette 156
Roure, Jacques du 500–1
Rousset de Missy, Jean 468, 489
Roux, Louis 464
Royal College of Physicians 74
royal prerogative 57
Royal Society 22–3, 299, 317–35, 512, 544–5
Royalism/Royalists 8, 15, 27, 97, 135, 238, 239, 246, 255, 256, 267, 275, 277, 285, 286, 287, 288, 290, 291
   amnesty arrangements 254
   besieged enclave 103
   contacts in France 276
   émigrés on the Continent 254
   exiled 19, 289
   expulsion of Fellows from Oxford 246
   leading, secret dealings conducted on behalf of 278
   quasi-religious iconography 237, 238, 250
   staunch 242, 252
   strong sympathies 246
Royston, Richard 234, 237–8, 239, 249, 250, 352, 353, 357
Rucellai (Tuscan envoy) 218
Rudolf II, Holy Roman Emperor 207
Ruggle, George 66
rules 31, 32, 437
Rupert, Prince 275, 299
Russia 491
Ruth 406
Ruvigny, Henri Massue, 1st marquis de 306
Ryan, Alan 146–7
Ryer, André du 282

sacerdotalism 542
Sackville, Sir Edward 56, 71, 73
Sadducism 477
St Lugar 299
St Petersburg 463
Salmasius, see Saumaise, Claude
Saltwood castle 252
'salus populi' theory 448
salvation 505
Samaria 430
Samaritans 418
Samau'al al-Maghribi 402

Samuel 426
Sandwich 253
Sandys, Sir Edwin 8, 56, 57–76
Sandys, George 74, 75
Sandys, Margaret 74
Sandys, Sir Samuel 56, 74
Sarasin, Jean-François 262, 274, 275
Sarpi, Paolo 8, 66, 458
Sarrau, Claude 271–2, 394
satanic possession 485
Saumaise, Claude 290, 394
Saumur 262
savages 76, 503
Savary de Brèves, François 271
Savoy 71
Sawbridge, Thomas 353
Saxon court 512
Saxony 530
   see also Friedrich Augustus
Scaliger, Julius Caesar 270, 290
scandal 352, 393, 480, 513
Scarborough, Charles 21, 329, 330
Scargill, Daniel 331
scepticism 168, 185–6
   Cartesian 14
   modified 333
   Pyrrhonist 332
   radical 14
Schaffer, Simon 185, 187–8, 190, 191, 317, 319
Scheurleer, Hendrick 468
scholasticism 5, 6, 110, 115, 119, 191, 193
scholia 205
Schomberg, Frederick, 1st Duke of 308
Schön, Erhard 204, 208
Schoneveld, Cornelis 340
Schoock, Maarten 519–20
Schott, Gaspar 210, 214
Schröder (Schröter), Wilhelm von 512
Schröder, Winfried 491
Schuhmann, Karl 100, 101, 105, 116, 117, 118, 128
Schurzfleisch, Conrad Samuel 511, 520
science(s) 5, 9, 73–4, 173, 181
   applied 212
   civil 180
   classification of 148
   demonstrative 175, 179
   description of 154
   Galilean 135
   mechanistic 190

natural 12
new 210
non-mathematical 179
'opinion' and 178, 179
physical 1
theory of 146–55
TH's interest in/work on 9, 14, 320–1
*see also* chemistry; optics; physics
scientific instruments 207
Scioppius, G. 478
Scots 417, 453
scribes 248
Seckendorff, Veit Ludwig von 481
Second World War 261
security 50, 434, 448, 449, 451
   state 228
Sedan 262, 269, 274
sedition 50, 503
Segrais, Jean R. de 274
Séguier, Pierre 218–19, 220–1, 268, 273–4, 277, 304
Selden, John 8, 21, 35, 62, 63, 75, 328, 475
self-deception 176
self-defence 32, 61
self-interest 20, 31, 531, 532, 545
   long-term 455
   mutual 510
   short-term 48
   'enlightened' 502, 509, 535
self-love 43, 508, 515, 523
   origin of all actions 514
self-preservation 32, 43, 49, 438, 446, 528, 502, 517, 523
   individual 455
   long-term means to/prospects of 445, 449
   national right of 434
   primacy of 52
selfishness 31, 496
Seneca 237, 245, 246, 250
Senior, William 93
sensations 126, 135, 169
   cause of 124
   strong 130
sense-experiences 168, 177
   primacy of 180
sense-perception 29, 30, 124, 130, 152
senses 126, 136, 169, 173, 182, 183, 212
   deception of 210
   importance of 176

knowledge derived either directly or indirectly from 176
mind deprived of all 177
separatism 68, 70, 71
Septuagint 418
Sepúlveda, Juan G. de 60
Sergius (Sarkis el-Jamari) 268, 269
sermons 45
Serrarius, Petrus 376, 377, 378, 379
Settala, Manfredo 207
Seville 279, 400
Sewel, Willem 341, 363
Sexby, Edward 371
sexuality 536
Seymour, John 352, 353
'shadows' 118
Shaftesbury, Anthony Ashley Cooper, 3rd Earl of 468
shapes 125, 149, 178, 225, 227
Shapin, Steven 185, 187–8, 190, 191, 317, 319
Sharnbrook 251, 252
Sheldon, Gilbert, Archbishop of Canterbury 10, 11, 83, 84, 92, 98, 99, 103, 239, 241–2, 244, 247, 248, 249, 324, 466
*Ship Money* case (1637) 14, 36
Short Parliament (April 1640) 15, 27
'Short Tract' 12, 30, 104–39
sight 212
similarity 148, 149, 166, 167
   essential 152
   real 152–3
Simon, Richard 387, 389, 390, 408, 430, 431, 470, 483
Sionita, Gabriel (Jibrail as-Sahyuni) 268, 269
Skinner, Quentin 319
Sloane, Hans 313
Sluse, René-François de 498
Smidt, Henrik 367
Smith, Francis 352
Smythe, Sir Thomas 56–7, 64–5
socage 60
sociability 520, 523
social cohesion 47
social hierarchy 536
social organization 495
social relations 32
social science 146–7, 150
society 495

## INDEX

Society of Jesus 219
Socinianism/Socinians 10, 367, 379, 477, 479, 481, 482, 483, 487
Socrates 129, 293
Solomon 426
Somer ('Somers', 'Summer') Islands Company 8, 54–5, 56, 62, 73, 74
Someren, Johan van 362
Sorbière, Samuel 17, 19, 24, 25, 320, 321, 322, 324, 329–30, 395, 459, 460, 463, 464–5, 484, 494, 497, 498, 503, 518–19
  translation of *De cive* 458, 460, 465, 473, 494, 502, 510, 519
Sorbonne 466, 495
Sorell, Tom 146, 148–9
Sotheby's 341
soul 110, 135, 190, 487
  immortality of 47, 349, 490, 536
  incorporeality of 490, 532
sound 123, 126, 132, 169
Sourdis, Cardinal, Archbishop of Bordeaux 420
South Langley 266, 300
Southampton, Henry Wriothesley, 3rd Earl of 55, 56, 61, 63, 71
Southampton 262, 266, 279, 281, 299, 302, 308
  parliamentary stronghold in Civil War 267
  Port Books 263, 264, 300
Southern California, University of 341
sovereignty 15, 20, 27, 223, 534
  absolute 28, 507, 523
  civil 39, 293, 425, 428
  conditional 447
  Natural Law theory of 68
  obedience to 525
  popular 506
  rights of 453
  sole exercise of 515
  state 527
  territorial 454
  TH's theory of 506, 514
space 111, 120, 125, 196
  empty 190, 191, 192, 193, 194
Spada, Francesco Antonio 483–4
Spain 470
Spanheim, Friedrich 389
Spanish Holy Office 470
Spanish Netherlands 274

Spanish translations 240
special-interest groups 22
species 108, 118, 128, 137
  action of 135
  constant expansion of 120
  different types of 126
  efflux of 120, 131
  intentional, modification of 220
  multiplication of 112
  'similitude' of 126
  substantial 125
  visible 113, 114
  'weaker' or 'stronger' 120
spectra 118
Spencer, Elizabeth 253
Spink, John 488
Spinoza, Baruch (Benedict) de 25, 40–5, 387, 388, 397, 402, 403, 404, 410–14 *passim*, 426, 429, 430, 431, 465, 470, 480–8 *passim*, 493, 496, 516, 535–8 *passim*
  one of the earliest biographies of 492
  works: *Ethics* 50–2; *Tractatus theologico-politicus* 46, 47, 48, 49–51, 372–4, 379, 381, 389, 390–2, 477
spirals 154, 159, 163, 164
spirits 123, 190, 191, 326, 391, 487, 492
  'incorporeal' 482
Sprat, T. 330, 333–4, 480
Staalkopff, Jakob 482
Staffordshire 242, 246, 248, 255
Stanley, William 279, 308
Stapleton, Thomas 415
state 42
  absolutist 514
  Church and 39, 45, 46, 66, 70, 71, 475, 534
  economic management of 513
  internal workings of 41
  range of things which might be forbidden by 38
  rationality of 52, 516
  religion and 68, 515
  republican and puritan, designs to establish 70
  security of 228
  sovereign 434, 436, 454
  Spinoza's writings on the nature of 46
  subjects and 44, 223
Supreme Power 50

– 640 –

# INDEX

state of nature  44, 45, 444, 445, 446, 450, 451, 452, 474–5, 515, 525, 526, 534
  basic causes of conflict in  453
  conflict in  514
  initial tendency of  510
  international  440, 449, 456
  interpersonal  434, 435
  mutual defence association in  443
  peace through adjudication in  514
  peaceful  503
  perpetual war in  501
statements  152
static electricity  114
Stationers' Company  24, 338, 346, 348, 350–4, 356, 370
  Court of  345, 357, 351, 353
  registers  202, 234, 249, 301
  restrictive practices  371
Steen, Cornelis van den, *see* Lapide
Steten, Christoph van  265
Stewart, Sir Francis  77
Stewart, Richard  275
Stillingfleet, Edward, Bishop of Worcester  39
stimuli  137
Stockholm  273
Stoicism  32, 257, 455
  Horatian  250
  Senecan  236–7, 250
Stolle, Gottlieb  462
Stosch, Friedrich Wilhelm  487, 488
Stoye, J. W.  78
Strafford, Thomas Wentworth, 1st Earl of  28
Strangways, Sir John  27
Strauss, Leo  429
Struys, Johan  362
Strype, John  357
Stubbe, Henry  21, 318, 326, 327, 331
Suárez, Francisco  439
subjectivity  125, 126, 139
  of secondary qualities  29
  of sensible qualities  116, 117, 119
subjects  152
  ill-natured  515
  prince independent of  513
substance  113, 125, 150, 499
  incorporeal  190, 490
suicide  310
'summum bonum' notion  32
superstition  494, 535, 541

supposition  179, 183, 184
Swart, Steven  340–1, 363
Sweden  287, 521
Swift, Jonathan  468
Switzerland  419
syllogisms  5, 18, 179
'sympathy'  119, 131
'syncretism'  479, 480, 483
'synthesis'  153
Syriac  269, 401

Tacitus  7, 41–2, 43, 48
Tacquet, André  498
Talaska, Richard  100
Tallemant des Réaux, G.  219
Talmud  46, 399, 403
Tancarville  280
tangents  158
Targum  399
taxes  8, 240
taxonomy  207
Taylor, Jeremy  97
Taylor, Randall  353, 354
teleology  31, 150
  innate  29
  rejected  52
telescopes  74, 320
Telesio, Bernardino  6
Temple University  342
Templer, John  477
Ten Commandments  423, 544
terms  18, 152–3
territory  59
Tertullian  493
Tesauro, Emanuele  205, 211
Teston  251, 252, 253, 256
Texas, University of, Austin, Pforzheimer Library  341, 343
Thames, River  259, 287
theology  16, 17, 30, 326, 413, 488, 529, 533
  apocalyptic  285, 330, 376
  Augustinian  517
  Christian, subverter of  489
  controversial  318, 416
  doctrinal  331, 332, 333
  dogmatic  331
  general ban imposed on publication of works  348
  liberal  332
  moral  502

theology (cont.)
    natural 60, 178
    orthodox 331, 517
    philosophy and 47, 49
    rationalist, deist 46
    TH's, attacks on 22, 475, 477
    traditional Christian 542
'Theophrastus redivivus' 386
theorems 9, 32, 157, 160
Thomasius, Christian 464, 530, 531–3
Thomasius, Jakob 475, 479, 481, 513, 529
Thomason, George 234
Thompson, Francis 78
Thomson, Nathaniel 353
Thorpe, George 61
thought 51, 128, 499, 537
    Aristotelian and Neoplatonist 29
    feeling of desire a special kind of 30
    political 484, 514, 516, 532, 541
    radical 488–9
    religious 331
    subtractive experiments 178
three-dimensionality 180, 201
Thucydides 8–9, 28, 53, 72, 201, 328, 389, 423, 432
Tideswell 258
Tilbourne 321
time 121
Tissington 248
Tixall 255
Toland, John 468, 481, 484, 488, 493
Toledo 402
tolerationist argument 50
Tönnies, Ferdinand 80, 104, 106, 115–16, 248
Torah 46, 399, 401
    polemic against 402
Tormarton 88, 93
Torricelli, Evangelista 84, 85, 157, 160, 192, 216, 320
Tostatus 404–5, 406, 407, 409, 410, 411, 413, 414
trade 261, 267, 279, 513
    international 448, 452
*Traité des trois imposteurs* 387, 492
transubstantiation 210
triangles 169, 176
    spherical 161
trigonometry 93
Tripoli 269

trochoids 154, 156
truth(s) 150, 509
    analytic 152
    certain 186
    contingent 152
    definitional 15
    general 15, 32, 152
    necessary 152, 155
    primary 179
    theological 380
    universal 152, 152, 154, 155
Tschesch, Johann Theodor von 377
Tübingen University 474, 520
Tuck, Richard 104, 105, 185, 339
Tudely 253
Turquet de Mayerne, Theodore 283, 286
Turin 211
Twyne, Brian 86
Twysden, Sir Roger 255
Tyler (Stationers' Company officer) 346
'Typographia Savariana' 271
typography/typefaces 269, 358–9, 360
tyrannicide 542
tyranny 454
Tyssot de Patot, Simon 384

Umar II, Caliph 401
uncertainty 69, 180
underground literature 491, 495
understanding 136, 227
    defective 48
    inadequate 182
    obedience an inferior substitute for 47
    rational 20, 206
unity 65, 137–8
    collective 225
    religious 67
'universal thing' 176
universalism 539, 541
universals 167
universe 23, 49, 115, 154, 185, 191, 442
    deterministic 138, 139
    physical, mechanistic nature of 334
    plenist 182
Urban VIII, Pope 213
utility 510, 512, 513
    punishments must be justified by the principle of 507
utopianism 539
Utrecht 367

– 642 –

# INDEX

Utrecht, University of 42, 43, 45, 389, 465, 476, 483, 516

vacuums 189–90, 191, 192, 193, 194, 195
  interspersed 115
'vain-glory' 175
Vair, G. du 249, 250, 251
Vale of the White Horse 83
Valla, Laurentius 414
value-judgements 138
values 137
  aesthetic 150
  individual 31
  interpersonal scheme of 455
  moral 23
  quasi-teleological scale of 52
  second-order system of 139
  shared 453
  teleological 30
Vanini, L. 386, 481, 482
Varro, M. 136
Vartanian, Aram 488
Vaughan, John 21, 24, 328–9
Vaulezard, Jean de 205–6
Veen, Otto van 236
velocity 133
Velthuysen, Lambert van 42, 45, 516–18, 529
Venice 6, 8, 71, 76, 77, 78, 279, 414, 484
  Bomberg press 286
verbal communication 116
Verdus, François de Bonneau, sieur du 24, 159, 162, 165, 458, 463–4, 467, 504
Vere, Sir Horace 72
'verisimilitude' 167
Vernon 280
Véron, François 271
Vesalius, Andreas 320
vibration 131, 132
vices 32
Vico, G. 484, 511–12
Vienna 219, 279, 493
Vieta, Franciscus 96, 97, 205
Villemandy, Pierre de 499–500
violence 32, 504, 541
  anarchic 15
  anarchic 449
  fear of 510
Virgin Mary 213
Virginia Company 8, 28, 54–76, 441

virtue(s) 112, 303, 517, 531
  military 283
  moral 47–8, 330, 331, 332
  practice of 294
  theological 509
  vices and 32
vision 110, 123, 167, 226
  physiology and epistemology of 89
'visionnaire' 181
Visscher, Volckard 361, 374
Vitoria, Francisco de 439
Vives, J. L. 290
vocalization 398–9, 417
Voetius, Gijsbert 45, 475–6, 485
Voltaire 385, 400, 462, 494
voluntary agents 29
Vossius, Isaac 478, 502
Vouet, Simon 204–5, 219
Vulgate 406, 414, 415, 419

Wächtler, Christfried 475
Wagenaar, Jacobus 465–6
Walker, Clement 346, 347
Waller, Edmund 10, 11, 19, 75, 103, 234–5, 260, 276, 289, 298, 299, 308, 311, 329
Waller, Elizabeth 308
Wallis, John 22, 144, 162–5, 196, 318–19, 326, 327, 328
  *Elenchus geometriae hobbianae* 498
Walloons 263
Walzer, Michael 432
Waquet, Françoise 539–40
Ward, Seth 22, 96, 127, 321, 324–5, 326, 328, 329
  Latin refutation of TH 499
Ware Park 252
Warner, Walter 10, 11, 85, 88–9, 92, 119, 120, 122, 134–5, 325
warrants 350
Warrender, Howard 236, 238, 239
Warsaw 193, 194
Warton, T. 327
Warwick, Sir Philip 254, 257
Wassenaar, Gerard 42, 43
watches 149–50
watermarks 84, 101, 109, 360
Watkins, John 147
wealth 237, 513
  taxes on 240
Webbe, Joseph 89

# INDEX

Weber, Immanuel 471
Welbeck Abbey/'academy' 10, 11, 12
   Payne and 85, 94, 95, 98, 114, 116, 131, 134, 139
well-being 448, 452, 513
Wenman, Sir Francis 74
West Indies 71
Westmorland, *see* Fane
Westphalia, Treaty of (1648) 275
Westport 2, 3
Wheldon, James 80
Whitaker, Alexander 64
White, Richard 323, 329
White, Robert 346, 352, 353
White, Thomas 17, 21, 30, 73, 130, 179, 190, 218, 329
wickedness 31
Wickham, William 64
Wight, Martin 432
Wight, Isle of 281
Wilkins, John 22, 325, 326, 327, 328
Wilkinson, Henry 62
Wilkinson, John 4, 5
will 44, 50, 51–2, 73, 228, 442, 527
   declaration of 525
   freak of 152
   sovereign's 511
William II, of Orange 42
William III, Prince of Orange (later King William III of Great Britain and Ireland) 42
William of Ockham 129
Williams, John 338, 345, 346, 347, 348, 350, 351, 354, 355, 369, 370, 372, 380
Williams, William 338
Williamson, Joseph 351, 352
wills 68
Wilton 307
Winkler, Benedict 528
Winston, Dr (Gresham College professor) 74

wisdom 29, 490, 529
witchcraft/witch-trials 329, 531–2
Witsius, Hermann 389, 483
Witt, John de 42–3
Wittenberg University 482
Wolf, Friedrich 78
Wolley, Edward 275
Wolvercote 254
Wood, Anthony 25, 256, 309, 310, 338, 339, 342, 458, 460
Worcester, battle of (1651) 20, 250
Worde, Wynkyn de 312
Worm, Ole 208
worship 47, 515
Worsley, Benjamin 320
Wotton, Sir Henry 58, 77
Wren, Matthew 327–8
Wright, John 357, 371, 358, 372, 380
Wulfris, Thomas 299
*Wunderkammer* 207
Wyatt, Sir Francis 74, 75

Xenophon 389

Yafeh, Hava Lazarus 402
*yeshivah* 46
York, Edwin Sandys, Archbishop of 70
York, John Williams, Archbishop of 241
York, James, Duke of 275
York 252
   siege of (1644) 282

Zachariah 399
Zagorin, Perez 105, 108, 116, 127
Zeitler, Johann Friedrich 533
Zesen, Philip von 374, 377
Zrínyi, Miklós 305
Zurich 389, 483
Zwicker, Daniel 480
Zwingli, U. 290

*Index compiled by Frank Pert*